Peterson's Graduate Schools in the U.S. 2006

THOMSON

PETERSON'S

Australia • Canada • Mexico • Singapore • Spain • United Kingdom • United States

About Thomson Peterson's

Thomson Peterson's (www.petersons.com) is a leading provider of education information and advice, with books and online resources focusing on education search, test preparation, and financial aid. Its Web site offers searchable databases and interactive tools for contacting educational institutions, online practice tests and instruction, and planning tools for securing financial aid. Thomson Peterson's serves 110 million education consumers annually.

For more information, contact Thomson Peterson's, 2000 Lenox Drive, Lawrenceville, NJ 08648; 800-338-3282; or find us on the World Wide Web at www.petersons.com/about.

© 2005 Thomson Peterson's, a part of The Thomson Corporation
Thomson Learning™ is a trademark used herein under license.

Previous editions © 2000, 2001, 2002, 2003, 2004

Editor: Fern A. Oram; Production Editor: Susan W. Dilts; Research Project Manager: Peter Delaney; Research Associate: Kristina Moran; Programmer: John Raba; Manufacturing Manager: Ray Golaszewski; Composition Manager: Linda M. Williams.

Thomson Peterson's makes every reasonable effort to obtain accurate, complete, and timely data from reliable sources. Nevertheless, Thomson Peterson's and the third-party data suppliers make no representation or warranty, either expressed or implied, as to the accuracy, timeliness, or completeness of the data or the results to be obtained from using the data, including, but not limited to, its quality, performance, merchantability, or fitness for a particular purpose, non-infringement or otherwise.

Neither Thomson Peterson's nor the third-party data suppliers warrant, guarantee, or make any representations that the results from using the data will be successful or will satisfy users' requirements. The entire risk to the results and performance is assumed by the user.

ALL RIGHTS RESERVED. No part of this work covered by the copyright herein may be reproduced or used in any form or by any means—graphic, electronic, or mechanical, including photocopying, recording, taping, Web distribution, or information storage and retrieval systems—without the prior written permission of the publisher.

For permission to use material from this text or product, submit a request online at www.thomsonrights.com

Any additional questions about permissions can be submitted by e-mail to thomsonrights@thomson.com

ISSN 1528-5901
ISBN 0-7689-1914-2

Printed in Canada

10 9 8 7 6 5 4 3 2 1   07 06 05

Sixth Edition

Contents

A Note from the Peterson's Editors ... 1

THE GRADUATE ADVISER
The Admissions Process ... 5
Financial Support ... 9
Accreditation and Accrediting Agencies ... 15
How to Use This Guide ... 23

DIRECTORY OF GRADUATE AND PROFESSIONAL PROGRAMS BY FIELD
Graduate and Professional Programs by Field ... 27

PROFILES OF INSTITUTIONS OFFERING GRADUATE AND PROFESSIONAL WORK
Profiles ... 182

INDEX
Alphabetical Listing of Schools ... 631

A Note from the Peterson's Editors

If you are a student seeking to continue your education beyond college, *Peterson's Graduate Schools in the U.S.* is just what you need to discover an array of possibilities in a wide variety of academic disciplines available at nearly 1,000 graduate schools across the United States.

Inside you'll find advice on graduate education, including topics such as admission tests, financial aid, and accreditation. **The Graduate Adviser** includes two essays and information about accreditation. The first essay, "The Admissions Process," discusses general admission requirements, admission tests, factors to consider when selecting a graduate school or program, when and how to apply, and how admission decisions are made. Special information for international students and tips for minority students are also included. The second essay, "Financial Support," is an overview of the broad range of support available at the graduate level. Fellowships, scholarships, and grants; assistantships and internships; federal and private loan programs, as well as Federal Work-Study; and the GI bill are detailed. This essay concludes with advice on applying for need-based financial aid. "Accreditation and Accrediting Agencies" gives information on accreditation and its purpose and lists first institutional accrediting agencies and then specialized accrediting agencies relevant to specific fields of study.

If you know the field of study that interests you, turn to the **Directory of Graduate and Professional Programs by Field.** You will find, at a glance, all institutions that offer that field of study.

For geographical or financial reasons, you may already have a specific institution in mind. Turn to the **Profiles of Institutions Offering Graduate and Professional Work,** which contain information on nearly 1,000 graduate schools. **Profiles** detail information from student enrollment and the number of full-time faculty members to tuition and application contacts and are followed by a list of graduate units and the specific programs of study they offer.

Thomson Peterson's publishes a full line of resources to help you with any information you need to guide you through the graduate admissions process. Peterson's graduate publications can be found at your local bookstore or library—or visit us on the Web at www.petersons.com.

Colleges and universities will be pleased to know that Thomson Peterson's helped you in your selection. Admissions staff members are more than happy to answer questions, address specific problems, and help in any way they can. The editors at Peterson's wish you great success in your graduate college search!

The Graduate
Adviser

The Admissions Process

Generalizations about graduate admissions practices are not always helpful because each institution has its own set of guidelines and procedures. Nevertheless, some broad statements can be made about the admissions process that may help you plan your strategy.

General Requirements

Graduate schools and departments have requirements that applicants for admission must meet. Typically, these requirements include undergraduate transcripts (which provide information about undergraduate grade point average and course work applied toward a major), admission test scores, and letters of recommendation. Most graduate programs also ask for an essay or personal statement that describes your personal reasons for seeking graduate study. In some fields, such as art and music, portfolios or auditions may be required in addition to other evidence of talent. Some institutions require that the applicant have an undergraduate degree in the same subject as the intended graduate major.

Most institutions evaluate each applicant on the basis of the applicant's total record, and the weight accorded any given factor varies widely from institution to institution and from program to program.

Admission Tests

The major testing program used in graduate admissions is the Graduate Record Examinations (GRE) testing program, sponsored by the GRE Board and administered by Educational Testing Service, Princeton, New Jersey.

The Graduate Record Examinations testing program consists of a General Test and eight Subject Tests. The General Test measures verbal reasoning, quantitative reasoning, and analytical writing skills. It is offered as a computer-adaptive test (CAT) in the United States, Canada, and many other countries. In the CAT, the computer determines which question to present next by adjusting to your previous responses. Paper-based General Test administrations are offered in some parts of the world.

The computer-adaptive General Test consists of a 30-minute verbal section, a 45-minute quantitative section, and a 75-minute analytical writing section. In addition, an unidentified verbal or quantitative section that doesn't count toward a score may be included and an identified research section that is not scored may also be included.

The paper-based General Test consists of two 30-minute verbal sections, two 30-minute quantitative sections, and a 75-minute analytical writing section. In addition, an unidentified verbal or quantitative section that doesn't count toward a score may be included.

The Subject Tests measure achievement and assume undergraduate majors or extensive background in the following eight disciplines:

- Biochemistry, Cell and Molecular Biology
- Biology
- Chemistry
- Computer Science
- Literature in English
- Mathematics
- Physics
- Psychology

The Subject Tests are available at regularly scheduled paper-based administrations at test centers around the world. Testing time is approximately 2 hours and 50 minutes. You can obtain more information about the GRE tests by visiting the GRE Web site at www.gre.org or

The Admissions Process

consulting the *GRE Information and Registration Bulletin*. The *Bulletin* can be obtained at many undergraduate colleges. You can also download it from the GRE Web site or obtain it by contacting Graduate Record Examinations, Educational Testing Service, PO Box 6000, Princeton, NJ 08541-6000, telephone 1-609-771-7670.

If you expect to apply for admission to a program that requires any of the GRE tests, you should select a test date well in advance of the application deadline. Scores on the computer-adaptive General Test are reported within ten to fifteen days; scores on the paper-based General Test and the Subject Tests are reported within six weeks.

Another testing program, the Miller Analogies Test (MAT), is administered at more than 600 Controlled Testing Centers, licensed by Harcourt Assessment, Inc., in the United States, Canada, and other countries. The MAT computer-based test is now available in select areas. Testing time is 50 minutes. The test consists of 100 partial analogies. You can obtain the *Candidate Information Booklet*, which contains a list of test centers and instructions for taking the test, from http://www.milleranalogies.com or by calling 1-800-622-3231.

Check the specific requirements of the programs to which you are applying.

Factors Involved in Selecting a Graduate School or Program

Selecting a graduate school and a specific program of study is a complex matter. Quality of the faculty; program and course offerings; the nature, size, and location of the institution; admission requirements; cost; and the availability of financial assistance are among the many factors that affect one's choice of institution. Other considerations are job placement and achievements of the program's graduates and the institution's resources, such as libraries, laboratories, and computer facilities. If you are to make the best possible choice, you need to learn as much as you can about the schools and programs you are considering before you apply.

The following steps may help you narrow your choices.

- Talk to alumni of the programs or institutions you are considering to get their impressions of how well they were prepared for work in their fields of study.
- Remember that graduate school requirements change, so be sure to get the most up-to-date information possible.
- Talk to department faculty and the graduate adviser at your undergraduate institution. They often have information about programs of study at other institutions.
- Visit the Web sites of the graduate schools in which you are interested to request a graduate catalog. Contact the department chair in your chosen field of study for additional information about the department and the field.
- Visit as many campuses as possible. Call ahead for an appointment with the graduate adviser in your field of interest and be sure to check out the facilities and talk to students.

When and How to Apply

You should begin the application process at least one year before you expect to begin your graduate study. Find out the application deadline for each institution (many are provided in the profile section of this volume). Go to the institution Web site and find out if you can apply online. If not, request a paper application form. Fill out this form thoroughly and neatly. Assume that the school needs all the information it is requesting and that the admissions officer will be sensitive to the neatness and overall quality of what you submit. Do not supply more information than the school requires.

The institution may ask at least one question that will require a three- or four-paragraph answer. Compose your response on the assumption that the admissions officer is interested in both what you think and how you express yourself. Keep your statement brief and to the point, but, at the same time, include all pertinent information about your past experiences and your educational goals. Individual statements vary greatly in style and content, which helps admissions officers to differentiate among applicants. Many graduate departments give considerable weight to the statement in making their admissions decisions, so be sure to take the time to prepare a thoughtful and concise statement.

If recommendations are a part of the admissions requirements, carefully choose the individuals you ask to write them. It is generally best to ask current or former professors to write the recommendations, provided they are able to attest to your intellectual ability and motivation for doing the work required of a graduate student. It is advisable to provide stamped, preaddressed envelopes to people being asked to submit recommendations on your behalf.

Completed applications, including references and transcripts and admission test scores, should be received at the institution by the specified date.

Be advised that institutions do not usually make admissions decisions until all materials have been received. Enclose a self-addressed postcard with your application, requesting confirmation of receipt. Allow at least 10 days for the return of the postcard before making further inquiries.

If you plan to apply for financial support, it is imperative that you file your application early.

How Admission Decisions Are Made

The program you apply to is directly involved in the admissions process. Although the final decision is usually made by the graduate dean (or an associate) or by the faculty admissions committee, recommendations from faculty members in your intended field are important. At some institutions, an interview is incorporated into the decision process.

A Special Note for International Students

In addition to the steps already described, there are some special considerations for international students who intend to apply for graduate study in the United States. All graduate schools require an indication of competence in English. The purpose of the Test of English as a Foreign Language (TOEFL) is to evaluate the English proficiency of people who are nonnative speakers of English and want to study at colleges and universities where English is the language of instruction. The TOEFL is administered by Educational Testing Service (ETS) under the general direction of a policy board established by the College Board and the Graduate Record Examinations Board.

The TOEFL is administered as a computer-based test throughout most of the world and is available year-round by appointment only. It is not necessary to have previous computer experience to take the test. The test consists of four sections—listening, reading, structure, and writing. Total testing time is approximately 4 hours.

The TOEFL is offered in the paper-based format in areas of the world where computer-based testing is not available. The paper-based TOEFL consists of three sections—listening comprehension, structure and written expression, and reading comprehension. Testing time is approximately 3 hours. The Test of Written English (TWE) is also given. TWE is a 30-minute essay that measures the examinee's ability to compose in English. Examinees receive a TWE score separate from their TOEFL score. The *Information Bulletin* contains information on local fees and registration procedures.

A new TOEFL (the next generation TOEFL) that assesses the four basic language skills, listening, reading, writing, and speaking, will be administered for the first time in September 2005. The new test will be administered via the Internet at secure, official test centers. Testing time will be approximately 4 hours. Because the next generation TOEFL will include a speaking section, the TSE will no longer be needed.

Additional information and registration materials are available from TOEFL Services,

The Admissions Process

Educational Testing Service, P.O. Box 6151, Princeton, New Jersey 08541-6151. Telephone: 1-609-771-7100. E-mail: toefl@ets.org. World Wide Web: http://www.toefl.org.

International students should apply especially early because of the number of steps required to complete the admissions process. Furthermore, many United States graduate schools have a limited number of spaces for international students, and many more students apply than the schools can accommodate.

International students may find financial assistance from institutions very limited. The U.S. government requires international applicants to submit a certification of support, which is a statement attesting to the applicant's financial resources. In addition, international students *must* have health insurance coverage.

Tips for Minority Students

Indicators of a university's values in terms of diversity are found both in its recruitment programs and its resources directed to student success. Important questions: Does the institution vigorously recruit minorities for its graduate programs? Is there funding available to help with the costs associated with visiting the school? Are minorities represented in the institution's brochures or Web site or on their faculty rolls? What campus-based resources or services (including assistance in locating housing or career counseling and placement) are available? Is funding available to members of underrepresented groups?

At the program level, it is particularly important for minority students to investigate the "climate" of a program under consideration. How many minority students are enrolled and how many have graduated? What opportunities are there to work with diverse faculty and mentors whose research interests match yours? How are conflicts resolved or concerns addressed? How interested are faculty in building strong and supportive relations with students? "Climate" concerns should be addressed by posing questions to various individuals, including faculty members, current students, and alumni.

Information is also available through various organizations, such as the Hispanic Association of Colleges and Universities (HACU), and publications, such as *Black Issues in Higher Education* and *Hispanic Outlook* magazine. There are also books devoted to this topic, such as *The Multicultural Student's Guide to Colleges* by Robert Mitchell.

Financial Support

The range of financial support at the graduate level is very broad. The following descriptions will give you a general idea of what you might expect and what will be expected of you as a financial support recipient.

Fellowships, Scholarships, and Grants

These are usually outright awards of a few hundred to many thousands of dollars with no service to the institution required in return. Fellowships and scholarships are usually awarded on the basis of merit and are highly competitive. Grants are made on the basis of financial need or special talent in a field of study. Many grants not only cover tuition, fees, and supplies but also include stipends for living expenses with allowances for dependents. However, the terms of each grant should be examined because some do not permit recipients to supplement their income with outside work. Fellowships, scholarships, and grants may vary in the number of years for which they are awarded.

In addition to the availability of these funds at the university or program level, many excellent fellowship programs are available at the national level and may be applied for before and during enrollment in a graduate program. A listing of many of these programs can be found at the Council of Graduate Schools' Web site: http://www.cgsnet.org/ResourcesForStudents/fellowships.htm.

Assistantships and Internships

Many graduate students receive financial support through assistantships, particularly involving teaching or research duties. It is important to recognize that such appointments should not be simply employment relationships but rather should constitute an integral and important part of a student's graduate education. As such, the appointments should be accompanied by strong faculty mentoring and increasingly responsible apprenticeship experiences (these are often lacking for teaching assistantships). The specific nature of these appointments in a given program should be considered in selecting that graduate program.

Teaching Assistantships

These usually provide a salary and full or partial tuition remission and may also provide health benefits. Unlike fellowships, scholarships, and grants, which require no service to the institution, teaching assistantships require recipients to provide the institution with a specific amount of undergraduate teaching, ideally related to the student's field of study. Some teaching assistants are limited to grading papers, compiling bibliographies, taking notes, or monitoring laboratories. At some graduate schools, teaching assistants must carry lighter course loads than regular full-time students.

Research Assistantships

These are very similar to teaching assistantships in the manner in which financial assistance is provided. The difference is that recipients are given basic research assignments in their disciplines rather than teaching responsibilities. The work required is normally related to the student's field of study; in most instances, the assistantship supports the student's thesis or dissertation research.

Administrative Internships

These are similar to assistantships in application of financial assistance funds, but the student is given an assignment on a part-time basis, usually as a special assistant with one of the university's administrative offices. The assignment may not necessarily be directly related to the recipient's discipline.

Residence Hall and Counseling Assistantships

These assistantships are frequently assigned to graduate students in psychology, counseling, and social work. Duties can vary from being available in a dean's office for a specific number of hours for consultation with undergraduates to living in campus residences and being responsible for both counseling and administrative tasks or advising student activity groups. Residence hall assistantships sometimes include room and board in addition to tuition and stipends.

Health Insurance

The availability and affordability of health insurance is an important issue and one that should be considered in an applicant's choice of institution and program. While often included with assistantships and fellowships, this is not always the case and, even if provided, the benefits may be limited. It is important to note that the U.S. government requires international students to have health insurance.

The GI Bill

This provides financial assistance for students who are veterans of the United States armed forces. If you are a veteran, contact your local Veterans Administration office to determine your eligibility and to get full details about benefits. There are a number of programs that offer educational benefits to current military enlistees. Some states have tuition assistance programs for members of the National Guard. Contact the VA office at the college for more information.

Federal Work-Study Program (FWS)

Employment is another way some students finance their graduate studies. The federally funded Federal Work-Study Program provides eligible students with employment opportunities, usually in public and private nonprofit organizations. Federal funds pay up to 75 percent of the wages, with the remainder paid by the employing agency. FWS is available to graduate students who demonstrate financial need. Not all schools have these funds, and some only award them to undergraduates. Each school sets its application deadline and work-study earnings limits. Wages vary and are related to the type of work done.

Loans

Many graduate students borrow to finance their graduate programs when other sources of assistance (which do not have to be repaid) prove insufficient. You should always read and understand the terms of any loan program before submitting your application.

Federal Loans

Federal Stafford Loans. The Federal Stafford Loan Program offers government-sponsored, low-interest loans to students through a private lender such as a bank, credit union, or savings and loan association.

There are two components of the Federal Stafford Loan program. Under the *subsidized* component of the program, the federal government pays the interest on the loan while you are enrolled in graduate school on at least a half-time basis. Under the *unsubsidized* component of the program, you pay the interest on the loan from the day proceeds are issued. Eligibility for the federal subsidy is based on demonstrated financial need as determined by the financial aid office from the information you provide on the Free Application for Federal Student Aid (FAFSA). A cosigner is not required, since the loan is not based on creditworthiness.

Although *unsubsidized* Federal Stafford Loans may not be as desirable as *subsidized* Federal Stafford Loans from the student's perspective, they are a useful source of support for those who may not qualify for the subsidized loans or who need additional financial assistance.

Graduate students may borrow up to $18,500 per year through the Stafford Loan Program, up to a cumulative maximum of $138,500, including undergraduate borrowing. This may include up to $8500 in Subsidized Stafford Loans annually, depending on eligibility, up to a cumulative maximum of $65,500, including undergraduate borrowing. The amount of the loan borrowed through the *unsubsidized* Stafford Program equals the total amount of the loan (as much $18,500) minus your eligibility for a Subsidized Stafford Loan (as much as $8500). You may borrow up to the cost of the school in which you are enrolled or will attend, minus estimated financial assistance from other federal, state, and private sources, up to a maximum of $18,500.

The interest rate for the Federal Stafford Loans varies annually and is set every July. The rate during in-school, grace, and deferment periods is based on the 91-Day U.S. Treasury Bill rate plus 1.7 percent, capped at 8.25 percent. The rate during repayment is based on the 91-Day U.S. Treasury Bill rate plus 2.3 percent, capped at 8.25 percent. The 2004–05 rate during repayment is 3.37 percent.

Two fees may be deducted from the loan proceeds upon disbursement: a guarantee fee of up to 1 percent, which is deposited in an insurance pool to ensure repayment to the lender if the borrower defaults, and a federally mandated 3 percent origination fee, which is used to offset the administrative cost of the Federal Stafford Loan Program.

Under the *subsidized* Federal Stafford Loan Program, repayment begins six months after your last enrollment on at least a half-time basis. Under the *unsubsidized* program, repayment of interest begins within thirty days from disbursement of the loan proceeds, and repayment of the principal begins six months after your last enrollment on at least a half-time basis. Some borrowers may choose to defer interest payments while they are in school. The accrued interest is added to the loan balance when the borrower begins repayment. There are several repayment options.

Federal Direct Loans. Some schools participate in the Department of Education's William D. Ford Direct Lending Program instead of the Federal Stafford Loan Program. The two programs are essentially the same except that with the Direct Loans, schools themselves provide the loans with funds from the federal government. Terms and interest rates are virtually the same except that there are a few additional repayment options with Federal Direct Loans.

Federal Perkins Loans. The Federal Perkins Loan is available to students demonstrating financial need and is administered directly by the school. Not all schools have these funds, and some may award them to undergraduates only. Eligibility is determined from the information you provide on the FAFSA. The school will notify you of your eligibility.

Eligible graduate students may borrow up to $6000 per year, up to a maximum of $40,000, including undergraduate borrowing (even if your previous Perkins Loans have been repaid). The interest rate for Federal Perkins Loans is 5 percent, and no interest accrues while you remain in school at least half-time. There are no guarantee, loan, or disbursement fees. Repayment begins nine months after your last enrollment on at least a half-time basis and may extend over a maximum of ten years with no prepayment penalty.

Deferring Your Federal Loan Repayments. If you borrowed under the Federal Stafford Loan Program or the Federal Perkins Loan Program for previous undergraduate or graduate study, your repayments may be deferred when you return to graduate school, depending on when you borrowed and under which program.

There are other deferment options available if you are temporarily unable to repay your loan. Information about these deferments is provided at your entrance and exit interviews. If you believe you are eligible for a deferment of your loan repayments, you must contact your lender to

Financial Support

complete a deferment form. The deferment must be filed prior to the time your repayment is due, and it must be refiled when it expires if you remain eligible for deferment at that time.

Supplemental (Private) Loans

Many lending institutions offer supplemental loan programs and other financing plans, such as the ones described here, to students seeking additional assistance in meeting their educational expenses. Some loan programs target all types of graduate students; others are designed specifically for business, law, or medical students. In addition, you can use private loans not specifically designed for education to help finance your graduate degree.

If you are considering borrowing through a supplemental or private loan program, you should carefully consider the terms and be sure to "read the fine print." Check with the program sponsor for the most current terms that will be applicable to the amounts you intend to borrow for graduate study. Most supplemental loan programs for graduate study offer unsubsidized, credit-based loans. In general, a credit-ready borrower is one who has a satisfactory credit history or no credit history at all. A creditworthy borrower generally must pass a credit test to be eligible to borrow or act as a cosigner for the loan funds.

Many supplemental loan programs have a minimum annual loan limit and a maximum annual loan limit. Some offer amounts equal to the cost of attendance minus any other aid you will receive for graduate study. If you are planning to borrow for several years of graduate study, consider whether there is a cumulative or aggregate limit on the amount you may borrow. Often this cumulative or aggregate limit will include any amounts you borrowed and have not repaid for undergraduate or previous graduate study.

The combination of the annual interest rate, loan fees, and the repayment terms you choose will determine how much you will repay over time. Compare these features in combination before you decide which loan program to use. Some loans offer interest rates that are adjusted monthly, some quarterly, some annually. Some offer interest rates that are lower during the in-school, grace, and deferment periods, and then increase when you begin repayment. Most programs include a loan "origination" fee, which is usually deducted from the principal amount you receive when the loan is disbursed, and must be repaid along with the interest and other principal when you graduate, withdraw from school, or drop below half-time study. Sometimes the loan fees are reduced if you borrow with a qualified cosigner. Some programs allow you to defer interest and/or principal payments while you are enrolled in graduate school. Many programs allow you to capitalize your interest payments; the interest due on your loan is added to the outstanding balance of your loan, so you don't have to repay immediately, but this increases the amount you owe. Other programs allow you to pay the interest as you go, which reduces the amount you later have to repay.

Some examples of supplemental programs follow.

CitiAssist Loans. Offered by Citibank, these no-fee loans help graduate students fill the gap between the financial aid they receive and the money they need for school. Visit www.studentloan.com for more loan information from Citibank.

EXCEL Loan. This program, sponsored by Nellie Mae, is designed for students who are not ready to borrow on their own and wish to borrow with a creditworthy cosigner. Visit www.nelliemae.com for more information.

Key Alternative Loan. This loan can bridge the gap between education costs and traditional funding. Visit www.keybank.com for more information.

Graduate Access Loan. Sponsored by the Access Group, this is for graduate students enrolled at least half-time. The Web site is www.accessgroup.com.

Signature Student Loan. A loan program for students who are enrolled at least half-time, this is sponsored by Sallie Mae. Visit www.salliemae.com for more information.

Applying for Need-Based Financial Aid

Schools that award federal and institutional financial assistance based on need will require you to complete the FAFSA and, in some cases, an institutional financial aid application.

If you are applying for federal student assistance, you **must** complete the FAFSA. A service of the U.S. Department of Education, it is free to all applicants. You must send the FAFSA to the address listed in the FAFSA instructions (a self-addressed envelope is provided) or you can apply online at http://www.fafsa.ed.gov.

After your FAFSA information has been processed, you will receive a Student Aid Report (SAR). If you provided an e-mail address on the FAFSA, this will be sent to you electronically; otherwise, it will be mailed to your home address.

Follow the instructions on the SAR if you need to correct information reported on your original application. If your situation changes after you file your FAFSA, contact your financial aid officer to discuss amending your information. You can also appeal your financial aid award if you have extenuating circumstances.

If you would like more information on federal student financial aid, visit the FAFSA Web site or download *The Student Guide 2005–2006* at http://studentaid.ed.gov/students/publications/student_guide/index.html.

The U.S. Department of Education also has a toll-free number for questions concerning federal student aid programs. The number is 1-800-4-FED AID (1-800-433-3243). If you are hearing impaired, call toll-free, 1-800-730-8913.

Summary

Remember that these are generalized statements about financial assistance at the graduate level. Because each institution allots its aid differently, you should communicate directly with the school and the specific department of interest to you. It is not unusual, for example, to find that an endowment vested within a specific department supports one or more fellowships. You may fit its requirements and specifications precisely.

Accreditation and Accrediting Agencies

Colleges and universities in the United States, and their individual academic and professional programs, are accredited by nongovernmental agencies concerned with monitoring the quality of education in this country. Agencies with both regional and national jurisdictions grant accreditation to institutions as a whole, while specialized bodies acting on a nationwide basis—often national professional associations—grant accreditation to departments and programs in specific fields.

Institutional and specialized accrediting agencies share the same basic concerns: the purpose an academic unit—whether university or program—has set for itself and how well it fulfills that purpose, the adequacy of its financial and other resources, the quality of its academic offerings, and the level of services it provides. Agencies that grant institutional accreditation take a broader view, of course, and examine university-wide or college-wide services with which a specialized agency may not concern itself.

Both types of agencies follow the same general procedures when considering an application for accreditation. The academic unit prepares a self-evaluation, focusing on the concerns mentioned above and usually including an assessment of both its strengths and weaknesses; a team of representatives of the accrediting body reviews this evaluation, visits the campus, and makes its own report; and finally, the accrediting body makes a decision on the application. Often, even when accreditation is granted, the agency makes a recommendation regarding how the institution or program can improve. All institutions and programs are also reviewed every few years to determine whether they continue to meet established standards; if they do not, they may lose their accreditation.

Accrediting agencies themselves are reviewed and evaluated periodically by the U.S. Department of Education and the Council for Higher Education Accreditation (CHEA). Recognized agencies adhere to certain standards and practices, and their authority in matters of accreditation is widely accepted in the educational community.

This does not mean, however, that accreditation is a simple matter, either for schools wishing to become accredited or for students deciding where to apply. Indeed, in certain fields the very meaning and methods of accreditation are the subject of a good deal of debate. For their part, those applying to graduate school should be aware of the safeguards provided by regional accreditation, especially in terms of degree acceptance and institutional longevity. (NOTE: Most institutions profiled in this guide are regionally accredited.) Beyond this, applicants should understand the role that specialized accreditation plays in their field, as this varies considerably from one discipline to another. In certain professional fields, it is necessary to have graduated from a program that is accredited in order to be eligible for a license to practice, and in some fields the federal government also makes this a hiring requirement. In other disciplines, however, accreditation is not as essential, and there can be excellent programs that are not accredited. In fact, some programs choose not to seek accreditation, although most do.

Institutions and programs that present themselves for accreditation are sometimes granted the status of candidate for accreditation, or what is known as "preaccreditation." This may happen, for example, when an academic unit is too new to have met all the requirements for accreditation. Such status signifies initial recognition and indicates that the school or program in question is

Accreditation and Accrediting Agencies

working to fulfill all requirements; it does not, however, guarantee that accreditation will be granted.

Institutional Accrediting Agencies—Regional

MIDDLE STATES ASSOCIATION OF COLLEGES AND SCHOOLS

Accredits institutions in Delaware, District of Columbia, Maryland, New Jersey, New York, Pennsylvania, Puerto Rico, and the Virgin Islands.

Jean Avnet Morse, Executive Director
Commission on Higher Education
3624 Market Street
Philadelphia, Pennsylvania 19104
Telephone: 215-662-5606
Fax: 215-662-5501
E-mail: jmorse@msache.org
World Wide Web: http://www.msache.org

NEW ENGLAND ASSOCIATION OF SCHOOLS AND COLLEGES

Accredits institutions in Connecticut, Maine, Massachusetts, New Hampshire, Rhode Island, and Vermont.

Charles M. Cook, Director
Commission on Institutions of Higher Education
209 Burlington Road
Bedford, Massachusetts 01730
Telephone: 781-271-0022
Fax: 781-271-0950
E-mail: ccook@neasc.org
World Wide Web: http://www.neasc.org

NORTH CENTRAL ASSOCIATION OF COLLEGES AND SCHOOLS

Accredits institutions in Arizona, Arkansas, Colorado, Illinois, Indiana, Iowa, Kansas, Michigan, Minnesota, Missouri, Nebraska, New Mexico, North Dakota, Ohio, Oklahoma, South Dakota, West Virginia, Wisconsin, and Wyoming.

Steven D. Crow, Executive Director
The Higher Learning Commission
30 North LaSalle Street, Suite 2400
Chicago, Illinois 60602
Telephone: 312-263-0456
Fax: 312-263-7462
E-mail: scrow@hlcommission.org
World Wide Web: http://www.ncacihe.org

NORTHWEST COMMISSION ON COLLEGES AND UNIVERSITIES

Accredits institutions in Alaska, Idaho, Montana, Nevada, Oregon, Utah, and Washington.

Sandra E. Elman, Executive Director
8060 165th Avenue, NE, Suite 100
Redmond, Washington 98052
Telephone: 425-558-4224
Fax: 425-376-0596
E-mail: selman@nwccu.org
World Wide Web: http://www.nwccu.org

SOUTHERN ASSOCIATION OF COLLEGES AND SCHOOLS

Accredits institutions in Alabama, Florida, Georgia, Kentucky, Louisiana, Mississippi, North Carolina, South Carolina, Tennessee, Texas, and Virginia.

James T. Rogers, Executive Director
Commission on Colleges
1866 Southern Lane
Decatur, Georgia 30033
Telephone: 404-679-4500
Fax: 404-679-4558
E-mail: jrogers@sacscoc.org
World Wide Web: http://www.sacscoc.org

WESTERN ASSOCIATION OF SCHOOLS AND COLLEGES

Accredits institutions in California, Guam, and Hawaii.

Ralph A. Wolff, Executive Director
The Senior College Commission
985 Atlantic Avenue, Suite 100
Alameda, California 94501
Telephone: 510-748-9001
Fax: 510-748-9797
E-mail: rwolff@wascsenior.org
World Wide Web: http://www.wascweb.org/senior

Institutional Accrediting Agencies—Other

ACCREDITING COUNCIL FOR INDEPENDENT COLLEGES AND SCHOOLS

Steven A. Eggland, Executive Director
750 First Street, NE, Suite 980
Washington, DC 20002
Telephone: 202-336-6780
Fax: 202-842-2593
E-mail: steve@acics.org
World Wide Web: http://www.acics.org

DISTANCE EDUCATION AND TRAINING COUNCIL

Accrediting Commission
Michael P. Lambert, Executive Director
1601 18th Street, NW
Washington, DC 20009
Telephone: 202-234-5100
Fax: 202-332-1386
E-mail: mike@detc.org
World Wide Web: http://www.detc.org

Accreditation and Accrediting Agencies

Specialized Accrediting Agencies

ACUPUNCTURE AND ORIENTAL MEDICINE
David M. Sale, Executive Director
Accreditation Commission for Acupuncture and Oriental Medicine
7501 Greenway Center Drive, Suite 820
Greenbelt, Maryland 20770
Telephone: 301-313-0868
Fax: 301-313-0869
E-mail: ccaom1@compuserve.com
World Wide Web: http://www.ccaom.org

ART AND DESIGN
Samuel Hope, Executive Director
National Association of Schools of Art and Design
11250 Roger Bacon Drive, Suite 21
Reston, Virginia 20190
Telephone: 703-437-0700
Fax: 703-437-6312
E-mail: shope@arts-accredit.org
World Wide Web: http://nasad.arts-accredit.org

BUSINESS
Milton R. Blood, Managing Director
AACSB International—The Association to Advance Collegiate Schools of Business
600 Emerson Road, Suite 300
St. Louis, Missouri 63141
Telephone: 314-872-8481
Fax: 314-872-8495
E-mail: milton@aacsb.edu
World Wide Web: http://www.aacsb.edu

Douglas Viehland, Executive Director
Association of Collegiate Business Schools and Programs
7007 College Boulevard, Suite 420
Overland Park, Kansas 66211
Telephone: 913-339-9356
Fax: 913-339-6226
E-mail: dviehland@acbsp.org
World Wide Web: http://www.acbsp.org

CHIROPRACTIC
Martha O'Connor, Executive Vice President
Council on Chiropractic Education
8049 North 85th Way
Scottsdale, Arizona 85258
Telephone: 480-443-8877
Fax: 480-483-7333
E-mail: cce@cce-usa.org
World Wide Web: http://www.cce-usa.org

CLINICAL LABORATORY SCIENCES
Olive M. Kimball, Chief Executive Officer
National Accrediting Agency for Clinical Laboratory Sciences
8410 West Bryn Mawr Avenue, Suite 670
Chicago, Illinois 60631
Telephone: 773-714-8880
Fax: 773-714-8886
E-mail: kimball@naacls.org
World Wide Web: http://www.naacls.org

CLINICAL PASTORAL EDUCATION
Teresa E. Snorton, Executive Director
Accreditation Commission
Association for Clinical Pastoral Education, Inc.
1549 Claremont Road, Suite 103
Decatur, Georgia 30033-4611
Telephone: 404-320-1472
Fax: 404-320-0849
E-mail: teresa@acpe.edu
World Wide Web: http://www.acpe.edu

DANCE
Samuel Hope, Executive Director
National Association of Schools of Dance
11250 Roger Bacon Drive, Suite 21
Reston, Virginia 20190
Telephone: 703-437-0700
Fax: 703-437-6312
E-mail: shope@arts-accredit.org
World Wide Web: http://nasd.arts-accredit.org

DENTISTRY
Karen M. Hart, Director
Commission on Dental Accreditation
American Dental Association
211 East Chicago Avenue
Chicago, Illinois 60611
Telephone: 312-440-4653
Fax: 312-440-7494
E-mail: hartk@ada.org
World Wide Web: http://www.ada.org

EDUCATION
Arthur Wise, President
National Council for Accreditation of Teacher Education
2010 Massachusetts Avenue, NW, Suite 500
Washington, DC 20036
Telephone: 202-466-7496
Fax: 202-296-6620
E-mail: art@ncate.org
World Wide Web: http://www.ncate.org

Frank B. Murray, President
Teacher Education Accreditation Council (TEAC)
One Dupont Circle, Suite 320
Washington, DC 20036
Telephone: 202-466-7236
Fax: 202-466-7238
E-mail: frank@teac.org
World Wide Web: http://www.teac.org

Accreditation and Accrediting Agencies

ENGINEERING
George D. Peterson, Executive Director
Accreditation Board for Engineering and Technology, Inc.
111 Market Place, Suite 1050
Baltimore, Maryland 21202
Telephone: 410-347-7700
Fax: 410-625-2238
E-mail: gpeterson@abet.org
World Wide Web: http://www.abet.org

FORESTRY
Michael T. Goergen Jr.
Executive Vice President and CEO
Society of American Foresters
5400 Grosvenor Lane
Bethesda, Maryland 20814
Telephone: 301-897-8720
Fax: 301-897-3690
E-mail: goergenm@safnet.org
World Wide Web: http://www.safnet.org

HEALTH SERVICES ADMINISTRATION
Accrediting Commission on Education for Health Services Administration
Jeptha Dalston
President and CEO
2000 14th Street North, Suite 780
Arlington, Virginia 22201
Telephone: 703-894-0960
Fax: 703-894-0941
E-mail: jdalston@acehsa.org
World Wide Web: http://acehsa.org

INTERIOR DESIGN
Kayem Dunn, Executive Director
Foundation for Interior Design Education Research
146 Monroe Center, NW, Suite 1318
Grand Rapids, Michigan 49503
Telephone: 616-458-0400
Fax: 616-458-0460
E-mail: kayem@fider.org
World Wide Web: http://www.fider.org

JOURNALISM AND MASS COMMUNICATIONS
Susanne Shaw, Executive Director
Accrediting Council on Education in Journalism and Mass Communications
School of Journalism
Stauffer-Flint Hall
University of Kansas
1435 Jayhawk Boulevard
Lawrence, Kansas 66045-7575
Telephone: 785-864-3973
Fax: 785-864-5225
E-mail: sshaw@ku.edu
World Wide Web: http://www.ukans.edu/~acejmc

LANDSCAPE ARCHITECTURE
Ronald C. Leighton
Director of Education and Academic Affairs
Landscape Architectural Accreditation Board
American Society of Landscape Architects
636 Eye Street, NW
Washington, DC 20001
Telephone: 202-898-2444
Fax: 202-898-1185
E-mail: rleighton@asla.org
World Wide Web: http://www.asla.org

LAW
John A. Sebert, Consultant on Legal Education
American Bar Association
321 North Clark Street, 21st Floor
Chicago, Illinois 60610
Telephone: 312-988-6738
Fax: 312-988-5681
E-mail: legaled@abanet.org
World Wide Web: http://www.abanet.org/legaled/

LIBRARY
Ann L. O'Neill, Director
Office for Accreditation
American Library Association
50 East Huron Street
Chicago, Illinois 60611
Telephone: 312-280-2432
Fax: 312-280-2433
E-mail: aoneill@ala.org
World Wide Web: http://www.ala.org/education

MARRIAGE AND FAMILY THERAPY
Donald B. Kaveny, Director, Accreditation Services
Commission on Accreditation for Marriage and Family Therapy Education
American Association for Marriage and Family Therapy
112 South Alfred Street
Alexandria, Virginia 22314
Telephone: 703-838-9808
Fax: 703-838-9805
E-mail: dkaveny@aamft.org
World Wide Web: http://www.aamft.org

MEDICAL ILLUSTRATION
Commission on Accreditation of Allied Health Education Programs (CAAHEP)
Kathleen Megivern, Executive Director
35 East Wacker Drive, Suite 1970
Chicago, Illinois 60601
Telephone: 312-553-9355
Fax: 312-553-9616
E-mail: megivern@caahep.org
World Wide Web: http://www.caahep.org

Accreditation and Accrediting Agencies

MEDICINE

Liaison Committee on Medical Education (LCME)

In even-numbered years beginning each July 1, contact:

Carol A. Aschenbrener, M.D.
Association of American Medical Colleges Secretary to the LCME and Vice President, AAMC Medical School Standards & Assessment
Association of American Medical Colleges
2450 N Street, NW
Washington, DC 20037
Telephone: 202-828-0596
Fax: 202-828-1125
E-mail: caschenbrener@aamc.org
World Wide Web: http://www.lcme.org

In odd-numbered years beginning each July 1, contact:

Frank Simon, M.D.
Director, Undergraduate and Graduate Medical Education, Policy, and Standards
American Medical Association
515 North State Street
Chicago, Illinois 60610
Telephone: 312-464-4933
Fax: 312-464-5830
E-mail: frank_simon@ama-assn.org
World Wide Web: http://www.lcme.org

MUSIC

Samuel Hope, Executive Director
National Association of Schools of Music
11250 Roger Bacon Drive, Suite 21
Reston, Virginia 20190
Telephone: 703-437-0700
Fax: 703-437-6312
E-mail: shope@arts-accredit.org
World Wide Web: http://nasm.arts-accredit.org

NATUROPATHIC MEDICINE

Diane Melanson, Office Administrator
Council on Naturopathic Medical Education
3535 Peachtree Road, Suite 520-209
Atlanta, Georgia 30326-3287
Telephone: 404-467-0045
Fax: 404-442-8831
E-mail: cnme@bellsouth.net
World Wide Web: http://www.cnme.org

NURSE ANESTHESIA

Jeffery Beutler, Executive Director
Council on Accreditation of Nurse Anesthesia Educational Programs
222 South Prospect Avenue
Park Ridge, Illinois 60068
Telephone: 847-692-7050 Ext. 3154
Fax: 847-692-7137
E-mail: jbeutler@aana.com
World Wide Web: http://www.aana.com

NURSE EDUCATION

Jennifer Butlin, Director
Commission on Collegiate Nursing Education (CCNE)
One Dupont Circle, NW, Suite 530
Washington, DC 20036
Telephone: 202-887-6791
Fax: 202-887-8476
E-mail: jbutlin@aacn.nche.edu
World Wide Web: http://www.aacn.nche.edu/accreditation

NURSE MIDWIFERY

Deanne Williams, Executive Director
Division of Accreditation
American College of Nurse-Midwives
8403 Colesville Road, Suite 1550
Silver Spring, Maryland 20910
Telephone: 240-485-1800
Fax: 240-485-1818
World Wide Web: http://www.midwife.org

Mary Ann Baul, Executive Director
Midwifery Education Accreditation Council
220 West Birch
Flagstaff, Arizona 86001
Telephone: 928-214-0997
Fax: 928-773-9694
E-mail: info@meacschools.org
World Wide Web: http://www.meacschools.org

NURSING

Barbara R. Grumet, Executive Director
National League for Nursing Accrediting Commission
61 Broadway, 33rd Floor
New York, New York 10006
Telephone: 212-363-5555
Fax: 212-812-0390
E-mail: bgrumet@nlnac.org
World Wide Web: http://www.nlnac.org

OCCUPATIONAL THERAPY

Sue Graves, Senior Program Manager
American Occupational Therapy Association
4720 Montgomery Lane
P.O. Box 31220
Bethesda, Maryland 20824
Telephone: 301-652-2682
TDD: 800-377-8555
Fax: 301-652-7711
E-mail: sgraves@aota.org
World Wide Web: http://www.aota.org

Peterson's Graduate Schools in the U.S. 2006

Accreditation and Accrediting Agencies

OPTOMETRY
Joyce Urbeck, Administrative Director
Accreditation Council on Optometric Education
American Optometric Association
243 North Lindbergh Boulevard
St. Louis, Missouri 63141
Telephone: 314-991-4100
Fax: 314-991-4101
E-mail: jlurbeck@aoa.org
World Wide Web: http://www.theaoa.org

OSTEOPATHIC MEDICINE
John Crosby, Executive Director
Bureau of Professional Education
American Osteopathic Association
142 East Ontario Street
Chicago, Illinois 60611
Telephone: 312-202-8000
Fax: 312-202-8200
E-mail: info@osteotech.org
World Wide Web: http://www.do-online.org

PHARMACY
Peter H. Vlasses, Executive Director
Accreditation Council for Pharmacy Education
20 North Clark Street, Suite 2500
Chicago, Illinois 60602-5109
Telephone: 312-664-3575
Fax: 312-664-4652
E-mail: pvlasses@acpe-accredit.org
World Wide Web: http://www.acpe-accredit.org

PHYSICAL THERAPY
Mary Jane Harris, Director
Commission on Accreditation
American Physical Therapy Association
1111 North Fairfax Street
Alexandria, Virginia 22314
Telephone: 703-684-2782
Fax: 703-684-7343
E-mail: maryjaneharris@apta.org
World Wide Web: http://www.apta.org

PHYSICIAN ASSISTANT STUDIES
John McCarty, Executive Director
Accreditation Review Commission on Education for the Physician Assistant
1000 North Oak Avenue
Marshfield, Wisconsin 54449-5788
Telephone: 715-389-3785
Fax: 715-387-5163
E-mail: mccarty.john@marshfieldclinic.org
World Wide Web: http://www.arc-pa.org

PLANNING
Beatrice Clupper, Executive Director
American Institute of Certified Planners/Association of Collegiate Schools of Planning/American Planning Association
Planning Accreditation Board (PAB)
Merle Hay Tower, Suite 302
3800 Merle Hay Road
Des Moines, Iowa 50310
Telephone: 515-252-0729
Fax: 515-252-7404
E-mail: fi_pab@netins.net
World Wide Web: http://www.netins.net/showcase/pab_fi66

PODIATRIC MEDICINE
Alan R. Tinkleman, Director
Council on Podiatric Medical Education
American Podiatric Medical Association
9312 Old Georgetown Road
Bethesda, Maryland 20814
Telephone: 301-581-9290
Fax: 301-571-4903
E-mail: artinkleman@apma.org
World Wide Web: http://www.apma.org

PSYCHOLOGY AND COUNSELING
Susan F. Zlotlow, Director
Office of Program Consultation and Accreditation
American Psychological Association
750 First Street, NE
Washington, DC 20002
Telephone: 202-336-5500
Fax: 202-336-6123
E-mail: szlotlow@apa.org
World Wide Web: http://www.apa.org

Carol L. Bobby, Executive Director
Council for Accreditation of Counseling and Related Educational Programs
American Counseling Association
5999 Stevenson Avenue
Alexandria, Virginia 22304
Telephone: 703-823-9800
Fax: 703-823-1581
E-mail: cacrep@cacrep.org
World Wide Web: http://www.counseling.org/cacrep

PUBLIC AFFAIRS AND ADMINISTRATION
Laurel L. McFarland, Managing Director
Commission on Peer Review and Accreditation
National Association of Schools of Public Affairs and Administration
1120 G Street, NW, Suite 730
Washington, DC 20005
Telephone: 202-628-8965
Fax: 202-626-4978
E-mail: mcfarland@naspaa.org
World Wide Web: http://www.naspaa.org

Accreditation and Accrediting Agencies

PUBLIC HEALTH
Laura Rasar King, Acting Executive Director
Council on Education for Public Health
800 Eye Street, NW, Suite 202
Washington, DC 20001-3710
Telephone: 202-789-1050
Fax: 202-789-1895
E-mail: lking@ceph.org
World Wide Web: http://www.ceph.org

REHABILITATION EDUCATION
Donald C. Linkowski, Executive Director
Council on Rehabilitation Education
Commission on Standards and Accreditation
1835 Rohlwing Road, Suite E
Rolling Meadows, Illinois 60008
Telephone: 847-394-1785
Fax: 847-394-2108
E-mail: dclink@wans.net
World Wide Web: http://www.core-rehab.org

SOCIAL WORK
Julia Watkins, Executive Director
Division of Standards and Accreditation
Council on Social Work Education
1725 Duke Street, Suite 500
Alexandria, Virginia 22314
Telephone: 703-683-8080 Ext. 205
Fax: 703-683-8099
E-mail: jwatkins@cswe.org
World Wide Web: http://www.cswe.org

SPEECH-LANGUAGE PATHOLOGY AND AUDIOLOGY
Patrima Tice, Director of Credentialing
American Speech-Language-Hearing Association
10801 Rockville Pike
Rockville, Maryland 20852
Telephone: 301-897-5700
Fax: 301-571-0481
E-mail: ptice@asha.org
World Wide Web: http://www.asha.org

TECHNOLOGY
Elise Scanlon, Executive Director
Accrediting Commission of Career Schools and Colleges of Technology
2101 Wilson Boulevard, Suite 302
Arlington, Virginia 22201
Telephone: 703-247-4212
Fax: 703-247-4533
E-mail: escanlon@accsct.org
World Wide Web: http://www.accsct.org

THEATER
Samuel Hope, Executive Director
National Association of Schools of Theatre
11250 Roger Bacon Drive, Suite 21
Reston, Virginia 20190
Telephone: 703-437-0700
Fax: 703-437-6312
E-mail: shope@arts-accredit.org
World Wide Web: http://nast.arts-accredit.org

THEOLOGY
Bernard Fryshman, Executive Vice President
Association of Advanced Rabbinical and Talmudic Schools
11 Broadway, Suite 405
New York, New York 10004
Telephone: 212-363-1991
Fax: 212-533-5335

Daniel O. Aleshire, Executive Director
Association of Theological Schools in the United States and Canada
10 Summit Park Drive
Pittsburgh, Pennsylvania 15275
Telephone: 412-788-6505
Fax: 412-788-6510
E-mail: ats@ats.edu
World Wide Web: http://www.ats.edu

Russell Guy Fitzgerald, Executive Director
Transnational Association of Christian Colleges and Schools
Accreditation Commission
P.O. Box 328
Forest, Virginia 24551
Telephone: 434-525-9539
Fax: 434-525-9538
E-mail: info@tracs.org
World Wide Web: http://www.tracs.org

VETERINARY MEDICINE
Donald G. Simmons, Director of Education and Research
American Veterinary Medical Association
1931 North Meacham Road, Suite 100
Schaumburg, Illinois 60173
Telephone: 847-925-8070 Ext. 6674
Fax: 847-925-1329
E-mail: dsimmons@avma.org
World Wide Web: http://www.avma.org

How to Use This Guide

The graduate and professional programs in *Peterson's Graduate Schools in the U.S.* are offered by colleges and universities in the United States and U.S. territories. They are accredited by U.S. accrediting bodies recognized by the Department of Education or the Council on Higher Education Accreditation. Each institution qualifies as a doctorate/research- or master's-level institution according to the *Carnegie Classification of Institutions of Higher Education*, and most are regionally accredited.

Profiles of Institutions Offering Graduate and Professional Work

Information in this guide is presented in profile form. Each profile provides basic information about an institution. The format of the profiles is consistent throughout the guide, making it easier to compare institutions. Any item that does not apply to or was not provided by a graduate unit is omitted. Information about the overall institution comes first. Information about autonomous graduate units follows with lists of the specific graduate degree programs offered. For complex institutions that combine their graduate studies under a unified administrative structure, degrees may be listed under divisional subheadings.

Institution Information. The institution's name, city, and Web address make up the heading. The following paragraph begins with information about the institution's control, gender makeup of the student body, and category of institutional structure. The total figure for graduate, professional, and undergraduate student enrollment precedes specific figures for full-time and part-time graduate students, including number of women. Next comes the number of full-time and part-time graduate faculty members. Information about the institution's computer and library facilities follows. Graduate tuition and fee information for full-time and part-time students follows. (Please be aware that tuition can be different, and frequently higher, in specific graduate programs. You should always check with the particular program if a tuition difference will be a factor in your selection.) A general graduate program application contact and telephone number ends this first paragraph.

Graduate Units. The name of the unit is followed by the name and title of the head of the unit. Institutions have varying levels of discreteness in defining administrative units, and these are presented according to the information that the institution has provided to Thomson Peterson's. Each degree-program field of study offered by the unit is listed with abbreviations for all postbaccalaureate degrees awarded.

For Further Information. For many programs there is more in-depth narrative style information that can be located at www.petersons.com/gradchannel. There is a notation of the availability of this information at the end of the relevant profiles.

Data Collection Procedures

The information published in this book was collected through *Thomson Peterson's Annual Survey of Graduate and Professional Institutions*. Each spring and summer, this survey is sent to accredited institutions in the United States and U.S. territories

How to Use This Guide

that offer postbaccalaureate degree programs. Deans and other administrators provide information on specific programs as well as overall institutional information. Thomson Peterson's staff then goes over each returned survey carefully and verifies or revises responses after further research and discussion with institution administrators.

While every effort is made to ensure the accuracy and completeness of the data, information is sometimes unavailable or changes occur after publication deadlines. The omission of any particular item from a profile signifies either that the item is not applicable to the institution or program or that information was not available.

Directory of Graduate and Professional Programs by Field

Directory of Graduate and Professional Programs by Field

■ ACCOUNTING

Abilene Christian University	M
Adelphi University	M
Alabama State University	M
American University	M
Anderson University	M,D
Angelo State University	M
Appalachian State University	M
Argosy University/Sarasota	M,D
Argosy University/Schaumburg	M,D
Arizona State University	M,D
Arizona State University West	O
Arkansas State University	M
Auburn University	M
Baldwin-Wallace College	M
Ball State University	M
Bayamón Central University	M
Baylor University	M
Bentley College	M,O
Bernard M. Baruch College of the City University of New York	M,D
Boise State University	M
Boston College	M
Boston University	M,D,O
Bowling Green State University	M
Bradley University	M
Brenau University	M
Bridgewater State College	M
Brigham Young University	M
Brooklyn College of the City University of New York	M
California State University, Chico	M
California State University, Fullerton	M
California State University, Hayward	M
California State University, Los Angeles	M
California State University, Sacramento	M
Canisius College	M
Carnegie Mellon University	D
Case Western Reserve University	M,D
The Catholic University of America	M
Central Michigan University	M
Central Missouri State University	M
Central Washington University	M
Charleston Southern University	M
Clark University	M
Clemson University	M
Cleveland State University	M
College of Charleston	M
The College of Saint Rose	M
The College of William and Mary	M
Colorado State University	M
Columbia University	M,D
Cornell University	D
Dallas Baptist University	M
DePaul University	M
Dominican University	M
Drexel University	M,D,O
Eastern Connecticut State University	M
Eastern Michigan University	M
Eastern University	M
East Tennessee State University	M
Emory University	D
Fairfield University	M,O
Fairleigh Dickinson University, College at Florham	M,O
Fairleigh Dickinson University, Metropolitan Campus	M,O
Fitchburg State College	M
Florida Agricultural and Mechanical University	M
Florida Atlantic University	M
Florida Gulf Coast University	M
Florida International University	M
Florida Metropolitan University–South Orlando Campus	M
Florida Metropolitan University–Tampa Campus	M
Florida State University	M,D
Fordham University	M
Fort Hays State University	M
Gannon University	O
The George Washington University	M,D
Georgia College & State University	M
Georgia Institute of Technology	M,D,O
Georgia Southern University	M
Georgia State University	M,D
Gonzaga University	M
Governors State University	M
Grand Valley State University	M
Hawai'i Pacific University	M
Hofstra University	M,O
Howard University	M
Illinois State University	M
Indiana University Bloomington	M,D
Indiana University Northwest	M,O
Indiana University South Bend	M
Indiana University Southeast	M,O
Inter American University of Puerto Rico, Metropolitan Campus	M
Inter American University of Puerto Rico, San Germán Campus	M
Iowa State University of Science and Technology	M
Jackson State University	M
James Madison University	M
John Carroll University	M
Johnson & Wales University	M
Kansas State University	M
Kean University	M
Kennesaw State University	M
Kent State University	M,D
Lamar University	M
Lehigh University	M,D,O
Lehman College of the City University of New York	M
Lincoln University (MO)	M
Lindenwood University	M
Long Island University, Brooklyn Campus	M
Long Island University, C.W. Post Campus	M
Louisiana State University and Agricultural and Mechanical College	M,D
Louisiana Tech University	M,D
Loyola University Chicago	M
Marquette University	M
Maryville University of Saint Louis	M,O
Miami University	M
Michigan State University	M,D
Middle Tennessee State University	M
Mississippi College	M
Mississippi State University	M,D
Monmouth University	M,O
Montana State University–Bozeman	M
Montclair State University	M
Murray State University	M
National University	M
New Jersey City University	M
New Mexico State University	M
New York Institute of Technology	M,O
New York University	M,D
North Carolina State University	M
Northeastern Illinois University	M
Northeastern State University	M
Northeastern University	M,O
Northern Illinois University	M
Northern Kentucky University	M
Northwestern University	D
Northwest Missouri State University	M
Nova Southeastern University	M
Nyack College	M
Oakland University	M,O
The Ohio State University	M,D
Oklahoma City University	M
Oklahoma State University	M,D
Old Dominion University	M
Oral Roberts University	M
Pace University	M
Pace University, White Plains Campus	M
The Pennsylvania State University University Park Campus	M,D
Philadelphia University	M
Pittsburg State University	M
Pontifical Catholic University of Puerto Rico	M,D
Prairie View A&M University	M
Purdue University	M,D
Purdue University Calumet	M
Queens College of the City University of New York	M
Quinnipiac University	M
Regis University	M,O
Rhode Island College	M
Rider University	M
Robert Morris University	M
Rochester Institute of Technology	M
Roosevelt University	M
Rutgers, The State University of New Jersey, Newark	M,D,O
St. Ambrose University	M
St. Bonaventure University	M,O
St. Edward's University	M,O
St. John's University (NY)	M,O
Saint Joseph's University	M
Saint Louis University	M
St. Mary's University of San Antonio	M
Saint Peter's College	M,O
St. Thomas University	M,O
San Diego State University	M
San Jose State University	M
Seattle University	M
Seton Hall University	M,O
Southeastern University	M
Southeast Missouri State University	M
Southern Illinois University Carbondale	M,D
Southern Illinois University Edwardsville	M
Southern Methodist University	M
Southern University and Agricultural and Mechanical College	M
Southern Utah University	M

27

Directory of Graduate and Professional Programs by Field

Accounting

Institution	Degree
Southwest Missouri State University	M
State University of New York at Binghamton	M,D
State University of New York at New Paltz	M
State University of New York Institute of Technology	M
State University of West Georgia	M
Stephen F. Austin State University	M
Stetson University	M
Strayer University	M
Suffolk University	M,O
Syracuse University	M,D
Temple University	M,D
Texas A&M International University	M
Texas A&M University	M,D
Texas A&M University–Corpus Christi	M
Texas A&M University–Texarkana	M
Texas Christian University	M
Texas State University-San Marcos	M
Texas Tech University	M,D
Towson University	M
Trinity University	M
Troy University Dothan	M
Truman State University	M
Universidad del Turabo	M
Universidad Metropolitana	M,O
University at Albany, State University of New York	M
University at Buffalo, The State University of New York	M,D
The University of Akron	M
The University of Alabama	M,D
The University of Alabama in Huntsville	M,O
The University of Arizona	M
University of Arkansas	M
University of Baltimore	M
University of California, Berkeley	D
University of Central Arkansas	M
University of Central Florida	M
University of Cincinnati	M,D
University of Colorado at Boulder	M,D
University of Colorado at Colorado Springs	M
University of Colorado at Denver	M
University of Connecticut	M,D
University of Delaware	M
University of Denver	M
University of Florida	M,D
University of Georgia	M
University of Hartford	M,O
University of Hawaii at Manoa	M,D
University of Houston	M,D
University of Houston–Clear Lake	M
University of Idaho	M
University of Illinois at Chicago	M
University of Illinois at Springfield	M
University of Illinois at Urbana–Champaign	M,D
University of Indianapolis	M
The University of Iowa	M,D
University of Kansas	M,D
University of Kentucky	M
University of La Verne	M
University of Louisville	M
University of Maine	M
University of Maryland University College	M,O
University of Massachusetts Amherst	M,D
University of Massachusetts Dartmouth	M,O
The University of Memphis	M,D
University of Miami	M
University of Michigan–Dearborn	M
University of Minnesota, Twin Cities Campus	M,D
University of Mississippi	M,D
University of Missouri–Columbia	M,D
University of Missouri–Kansas City	M,D
University of Missouri–St. Louis	M,O
The University of Montana–Missoula	M
University of Nebraska at Omaha	M
University of Nebraska–Lincoln	M,D
University of Nevada, Las Vegas	M
University of Nevada, Reno	M
University of New Hampshire	M
University of New Haven	M
University of New Mexico	M
University of New Orleans	M
The University of North Carolina at Chapel Hill	M,D
The University of North Carolina at Charlotte	M
The University of North Carolina at Greensboro	M
The University of North Carolina at Wilmington	M
University of Northern Iowa	M
University of North Florida	M
University of North Texas	M,D
University of Notre Dame	M
University of Oklahoma	M
University of Oregon	M,D
University of Pennsylvania	M,D
University of Rhode Island	M
University of St. Thomas (MN)	M
University of San Diego	M,O
The University of Scranton	M
University of South Alabama	M
University of South Carolina	M
The University of South Dakota	M
University of Southern California	M
University of Southern Indiana	M
University of Southern Maine	M
University of Southern Mississippi	M
University of South Florida	M
The University of Tampa	M
The University of Tennessee	M,D
The University of Tennessee at Chattanooga	M
The University of Tennessee at Martin	M
The University of Texas at Arlington	M,D
The University of Texas at Austin	M,D
The University of Texas at Dallas	M
The University of Texas at El Paso	M
The University of Texas at San Antonio	M,D
The University of Texas of the Permian Basin	M
University of Toledo	M
University of Utah	M,D
University of Virginia	M
University of West Florida	M
University of Wisconsin–Madison	M,D
University of Wisconsin–Whitewater	M
University of Wyoming	M
Utah State University	M
Villanova University	M
Virginia Commonwealth University	M,D
Virginia Polytechnic Institute and State University	M,D
Wagner College	M
Wake Forest University	M
Washington State University	M,D
Weber State University	M
Western Carolina University	M
Western Connecticut State University	M
Western Illinois University	M
Western Michigan University	M
Western New England College	M
West Texas A&M University	M
West Virginia University	M
Wheeling Jesuit University	M
Wichita State University	M
Widener University	M
Wilkes University	M
William Woods University	M
Wright State University	M
Xavier University	M
Yale University	D
Youngstown State University	M

■ ACOUSTICS

Institution	Degree
The Catholic University of America	M,D
The Pennsylvania State University University Park Campus	M,D
Rensselaer Polytechnic Institute	M

■ ACTUARIAL SCIENCE

Institution	Degree
Ball State University	M
Boston University	M
Central Connecticut State University	M
Georgia State University	M
Roosevelt University	M
St. John's University (NY)	M
Temple University	M
University of Central Florida	M
University of Connecticut	M,D
The University of Iowa	M,D
University of Nebraska–Lincoln	M
University of Wisconsin–Madison	M

■ ACUPUNCTURE AND ORIENTAL MEDICINE

Institution	Degree
Mercy College	M
Santa Barbara College of Oriental Medicine	M
University of Bridgeport	M

■ ADDICTIONS/SUBSTANCE ABUSE COUNSELING

Institution	Degree
Antioch New England Graduate School	M
The College of New Jersey	M,O
The College of William and Mary	M,D
Coppin State University	M
East Carolina University	M
Eastern Kentucky University	M
Fitchburg State College	M,O
Georgian Court University	M,O
Governors State University	M
Hofstra University	M,O
The Johns Hopkins University	M,D,O
Kean University	M,O
Loyola College in Maryland	M,O
Marywood University	M
Mercy College	M,O
Monmouth University	M,O
National-Louis University	M,O
Notre Dame de Namur University	M,O
Pace University, White Plains Campus	M
Palm Beach Atlantic University	M
Sage Graduate School	M
St. Mary's University of San Antonio	M,D,O
Springfield College	M,O
Stony Brook University, State University of New York	M
Thomas Edison State College	M
University of Alaska Anchorage	O
University of Detroit Mercy	M,O
University of Great Falls	M
University of Illinois at Springfield	M
University of Louisiana at Monroe	M
University of New England	M,O
University of North Florida	M,O
Wayne State University	O

■ ADULT EDUCATION

Institution	Degree
Armstrong Atlantic State University	M
Auburn University	M,D,O
Ball State University	M,D
Buffalo State College, State University of New York	M,O
Central Missouri State University	M,O
Cheyney University of Pennsylvania	M
Cleveland State University	M,O
Coppin State University	M
Cornell University	M,D
Drake University	M

Directory of Graduate and Professional Programs by Field
Advertising and Public Relations

Institution	Degrees
East Carolina University	M,O
Eastern Washington University	M
Florida Agricultural and Mechanical University	M,D
Florida Atlantic University	M,D,O
Florida International University	M,D
Florida State University	M,D,O
Fordham University	M,D,O
Grand Valley State University	M
Harvard University	M,D
Indiana University of Pennsylvania	M
Kansas State University	M,D
Kean University	M,O
Marshall University	M
Marygrove College	M
Michigan State University	M,D,O
Morehead State University	M,O
National-Louis University	M,D,O
North Carolina Agricultural and Technical State University	M
North Carolina State University	M,D
Northern Illinois University	M,D
Northwestern Oklahoma State University	M
Northwestern State University of Louisiana	M
Nova Southeastern University	D
Oregon State University	M
The Pennsylvania State University Harrisburg Campus of the Capital College	D
The Pennsylvania State University University Park Campus	M,D
Portland State University	M,D
Regis University	M,O
Rutgers, The State University of New Jersey, New Brunswick/Piscataway	M,D
San Francisco State University	M,O
Seattle University	M,O
Suffolk University	M,O
Teachers College Columbia University	M,D
Texas A&M University–Kingsville	M
Texas A&M University–Texarkana	M
Troy University Montgomery	M
Tusculum College	M
University of Alaska Anchorage	M
University of Arkansas	M,D,O
University of Arkansas at Little Rock	M
University of Central Oklahoma	M
University of Connecticut	M,D
University of Denver	M,D,O
University of Georgia	M,D,O
University of Idaho	M,D,O
The University of Memphis	M,D,O
University of Minnesota, Twin Cities Campus	M,D,O
University of Missouri–Columbia	M,D,O
University of Missouri–St. Louis	M,D
University of New Hampshire	M,D,O
University of Oklahoma	M,D
University of Rhode Island	M
University of St. Francis (IL)	M
University of South Carolina	M
University of Southern Maine	M,O
University of Southern Mississippi	M,D
University of South Florida	M,D,O
The University of Tennessee	M
The University of Texas at San Antonio	M
University of the Incarnate Word	M
The University of West Alabama	M
University of Wisconsin–Madison	M,D
University of Wisconsin–Platteville	M
University of Wyoming	M,D,O
Valdosta State University	M,D,O
Virginia Commonwealth University	M
Virginia Polytechnic Institute and State University	M,D,O
Western Washington University	M
Widener University	M,D
Wright State University	O

■ **ADVANCED PRACTICE NURSING**

Institution	Degrees
Barry University	M
Baylor University	M
Bowie State University	M
Brenau University	M
California State University, Fresno	M
Carlow University	M,O
Carson-Newman College	M
Case Western Reserve University	M,D
The Catholic University of America	M,D
College of Mount Saint Vincent	M,O
The College of New Jersey	M,O
Columbia University	M,O
Concordia University Wisconsin	M
Coppin State University	M,O
DePaul University	M
DeSales University	M
Duke University	M,O
Duquesne University	M
Eastern Kentucky University	M
East Tennessee State University	M,D,O
Edinboro University of Pennsylvania	M
Emory University	M
Fairfield University	M,O
Florida State University	M,O
Gannon University	M,O
George Mason University	M,D
The George Washington University	M,O
Georgia Southern University	M,O
Georgia State University	M,D
Grambling State University	M
Grand Valley State University	M
Gwynedd-Mercy College	M
Hardin-Simmons University	M
Hawai'i Pacific University	M
Holy Names University	M
Howard University	M,O
Hunter College of the City University of New York	M,O
Husson College	M
Indiana University–Purdue University Indianapolis	M
The Johns Hopkins University	M,O
Kennesaw State University	M
La Roche College	M
La Salle University	M,O
Long Island University, Brooklyn Campus	M,O
Long Island University, C.W. Post Campus	M,O
Loyola University Chicago	M
Loyola University New Orleans	M
Madonna University	M
Malone College	M
Marquette University	M,D,O
Marymount University	M,O
Mercy College	M
Midwestern State University	M
Minnesota State University Mankato	M
Molloy College	M
Monmouth University	M,O
Mount Saint Mary College	M
New York University	M,O
Northeastern University	M,O
North Georgia College & State University	M
Oakland University	M,O
Pacific Lutheran University	M
Quinnipiac University	M
Rutgers, The State University of New Jersey, Newark	M
Sacred Heart University	M
Sage Graduate School	M
Saginaw Valley State University	M
Saint Joseph College	M,O
Saint Xavier University	M,O
San Francisco State University	M
San Jose State University	M,O
Seattle Pacific University	O
Seattle University	M
Seton Hall University	M
Shenandoah University	M,O
Simmons College	M,O
Sonoma State University	M
Southern Illinois University Edwardsville	M
Southern University and Agricultural and Mechanical College	M,D,O
Spalding University	M
State University of New York Institute of Technology	M,O
Stony Brook University, State University of New York	M,O
Texas Woman's University	M,D
University at Buffalo, The State University of New York	M,D,O
University of Cincinnati	M,D
University of Colorado at Colorado Springs	M
University of Delaware	M,O
University of Detroit Mercy	M,O
University of Hawaii at Manoa	M,D,O
University of Mary	M
University of Miami	M,D
University of Michigan	M
University of Minnesota, Twin Cities Campus	M
University of Missouri–Kansas City	M,D
University of Nevada, Las Vegas	M
The University of North Carolina at Charlotte	M
University of Northern Colorado	M
University of North Florida	M,O
University of Pennsylvania	M
University of Pittsburgh	M
University of Portland	M,O
University of San Diego	M,D,O
University of San Francisco	M
The University of Scranton	M,O
University of South Alabama	M
University of South Carolina	M,O
University of Southern Maine	M,O
University of Southern Mississippi	M,D
The University of Tampa	M
The University of Tennessee at Chattanooga	M
The University of Texas at Arlington	M,D
The University of Texas at El Paso	M
The University of Texas at Tyler	M
The University of Texas–Pan American	M
University of Wisconsin–Oshkosh	M
Vanderbilt University	M,D
Villanova University	M,D,O
Virginia Commonwealth University	M,O
Wagner College	O
Wayne State University	M
Western Connecticut State University	M
Wilmington College (DE)	M
Wright State University	M

■ **ADVERTISING AND PUBLIC RELATIONS**

Institution	Degrees
Austin Peay State University	M
Ball State University	M
Boston University	M
California State University, Fullerton	M
Colorado State University	M
Emerson College	M
Marquette University	M
Michigan State University	M
Monmouth University	M,O
Montclair State University	M
Morehead State University	M
Northwestern University	M
Rowan University	M
San Diego State University	M
Syracuse University	M
Texas Christian University	M

Advertising and Public Relations

Institution	Degree
Towson University	O
The University of Alabama	M
University of Denver	M
University of Florida	M,D
University of Houston	M
University of Illinois at Urbana–Champaign	M
University of Miami	M,D
University of New Haven	M
University of Oklahoma	M
University of Southern California	M
University of Southern Mississippi	M,D
The University of Tennessee	M,D
The University of Texas at Austin	M,D
University of the Sacred Heart	M
University of Wisconsin–Stevens Point	M
Virginia Commonwealth University	M
Wayne State University	M,D

AEROSPACE/AERONAUTICAL ENGINEERING

Institution	Degree
Arizona State University	M,D
Auburn University	M,D
Boston University	M,D
Brown University	M,D
California Institute of Technology	M,D,O
California Polytechnic State University, San Luis Obispo	M
California State University, Long Beach	M
California State University, Northridge	M
Case Western Reserve University	M,D
Cornell University	M,D
Embry-Riddle Aeronautical University (FL)	M
Embry-Riddle Aeronautical University, Extended Campus	M
Florida Institute of Technology	M,D
The George Washington University	M,D,O
Georgia Institute of Technology	M,D
Illinois Institute of Technology	M,D
Iowa State University of Science and Technology	M,D
Massachusetts Institute of Technology	M,D,O
Middle Tennessee State University	M
Mississippi State University	M
North Carolina State University	M,D
The Ohio State University	M,D
Old Dominion University	M,D
The Pennsylvania State University University Park Campus	M,D
Princeton University	M,D
Purdue University	M,D
Rensselaer Polytechnic Institute	M,D
Rutgers, The State University of New Jersey, New Brunswick/Piscataway	M,D
Saint Louis University	M
San Diego State University	M,D
San Jose State University	M
Stanford University	M,D,O
Syracuse University	M
Texas A&M University	M,D
University at Buffalo, The State University of New York	M,D
The University of Alabama	M,D
The University of Alabama in Huntsville	M,D
The University of Arizona	M
University of California, Davis	M,D,O
University of California, Irvine	M,D
University of California, Los Angeles	M,D
University of California, San Diego	M,D
University of Central Florida	M
University of Cincinnati	M,D
University of Colorado at Boulder	M,D
University of Colorado at Colorado Springs	M
University of Connecticut	M,D
University of Dayton	M,D
University of Florida	M,D,O
University of Houston	M,D
University of Illinois at Urbana–Champaign	M,D
University of Kansas	M,D
University of Maryland, College Park	M,D,O
University of Michigan	M,D
University of Minnesota, Twin Cities Campus	M,D
University of Missouri–Columbia	M,D
University of Missouri–Rolla	M,D
University of Notre Dame	M,D
University of Oklahoma	M,D
University of Southern California	M,D,O
The University of Tennessee	M,D
The University of Texas at Arlington	M,D
The University of Texas at Austin	M,D
University of Virginia	M,D
University of Washington	M,D
Utah State University	M,D
Virginia Polytechnic Institute and State University	M,D
Webster University	M,D
West Virginia University	M,D
Wichita State University	M,D

AFRICAN-AMERICAN STUDIES

Institution	Degree
Boston University	M
Clark Atlanta University	M,D
Columbia University	M
Cornell University	M,D
Florida Agricultural and Mechanical University	M
Indiana University Bloomington	M
Michigan State University	M,D
Morgan State University	M,D
North Carolina Agricultural and Technical State University	M
The Ohio State University	M
Temple University	M,D
University at Albany, State University of New York	M
University of California, Berkeley	D
University of California, Los Angeles	M
The University of Iowa	M
University of Massachusetts Amherst	M,D
University of Wisconsin–Madison	M
West Virginia University	M,D
Yale University	M,D

AFRICAN STUDIES

Institution	Degree
Boston University	M,O
Colorado State University	M
Columbia University	O
Cornell University	M,D
Florida International University	M
Howard University	M,D
The Johns Hopkins University	M,D,O
Michigan State University	M,D
New York University	M,O
Northwestern University	O
The Ohio State University	M
Ohio University	M
Rutgers, The State University of New Jersey, New Brunswick/Piscataway	D
St. John's University (NY)	M,O
University at Albany, State University of New York	M
University of California, Los Angeles	M
University of Connecticut	M
University of Florida	O
University of Illinois at Urbana–Champaign	M
University of Louisville	M
University of South Florida	M
University of Wisconsin–Madison	M,D
West Virginia University	M,D
Yale University	M

AGRICULTURAL ECONOMICS AND AGRIBUSINESS

Institution	Degree
Alabama Agricultural and Mechanical University	M
Alcorn State University	M
Auburn University	M,D
California Polytechnic State University, San Luis Obispo	M
Clemson University	M
Colorado State University	M,D
Cornell University	M,D
Florida Agricultural and Mechanical University	M
Illinois State University	M
Iowa State University of Science and Technology	M,D
Kansas State University	M,D
Louisiana State University and Agricultural and Mechanical College	M,D
Michigan State University	M,D
Mississippi State University	M,D
Montana State University–Bozeman	M
New Mexico State University	M
North Carolina Agricultural and Technical State University	M
North Carolina State University	M,D
North Dakota State University	M
Northwest Missouri State University	M
The Ohio State University	M,D
Oklahoma State University	M,D
Oregon State University	M,D
The Pennsylvania State University University Park Campus	M,D
Prairie View A&M University	M
Purdue University	M,D
Rutgers, The State University of New Jersey, New Brunswick/Piscataway	M
Sam Houston State University	M
South Carolina State University	M
Southern Illinois University Carbondale	M
Texas A&M University	M,D
Texas A&M University–Kingsville	M
Texas Tech University	M,D
Tuskegee University	M
The University of Arizona	M
University of Arkansas	M
University of California, Berkeley	D
University of California, Davis	M,D
University of California, Santa Barbara	M,D
University of Colorado at Denver	M,D
University of Connecticut	M,D
University of Delaware	M
University of Florida	M,D
University of Georgia	M,D
University of Idaho	M
University of Illinois at Urbana–Champaign	M,D
University of Kentucky	M,D
University of Maine	M
University of Maryland, College Park	M,D
University of Massachusetts Amherst	M,D
University of Minnesota, Twin Cities Campus	M,D
University of Missouri–Columbia	M,D
University of Nebraska–Lincoln	M,D
University of Nevada, Reno	M
University of Puerto Rico, Mayagüez Campus	M
University of Rhode Island	M,D
The University of Tennessee	M
University of Vermont	M
University of Wisconsin–Madison	M,D
University of Wyoming	M
Virginia Polytechnic Institute and State University	M,D
Washington State University	M,D
West Texas A&M University	M

Directory of Graduate and Professional Programs by Field
Agronomy and Soil Sciences

West Virginia University — M

■ AGRICULTURAL EDUCATION

Alcorn State University — M,O
Arkansas State University — M,O
Clemson University — M
Cornell University — M,D
Eastern Kentucky University — M
Florida Agricultural and Mechanical University — M
Iowa State University of Science and Technology — M,D
Louisiana State University and Agricultural and Mechanical College — M,D
Mississippi State University — M
Montana State University–Bozeman — M
New Mexico State University — M
North Carolina Agricultural and Technical State University — M
North Carolina State University — M,D
North Dakota State University — M
Northwest Missouri State University — M
The Ohio State University — M,D
Oklahoma State University — M,D
Oregon State University — M
The Pennsylvania State University University Park Campus — M,D
Purdue University — M,D,O
Sam Houston State University — M
Stephen F. Austin State University — M
Texas A&M University — M,D
Texas A&M University–Commerce — M
Texas A&M University–Kingsville — M
Texas State University-San Marcos — M
Texas Tech University — M,D
The University of Arizona — M
University of Arkansas — M
University of Florida — M,D
University of Georgia — M
University of Idaho — M
University of Illinois at Urbana–Champaign — M
University of Maryland Eastern Shore — M
University of Minnesota, Twin Cities Campus — M,D
University of Missouri–Columbia — M,D,O
University of Nebraska–Lincoln — M
University of Puerto Rico, Mayagüez Campus — M
The University of Tennessee — M
University of Wisconsin–River Falls — M
Utah State University — M
West Virginia University — M

■ AGRICULTURAL ENGINEERING

Colorado State University — M,D
Cornell University — M,D
Illinois Institute of Technology — M,D
Iowa State University of Science and Technology — M,D
Kansas State University — M,D
Louisiana State University and Agricultural and Mechanical College — M,D
Michigan State University — M,D
North Carolina Agricultural and Technical State University — M
North Carolina State University — M,D
North Dakota State University — M,D
The Ohio State University — M,D
Oklahoma State University — M,D
The Pennsylvania State University University Park Campus — M,D
Purdue University — M,D
Rutgers, The State University of New Jersey, New Brunswick/Piscataway — M
South Dakota State University — M,D
Texas A&M University — M,D
The University of Arizona — M

University of Arkansas — M,D
University of Dayton — M
University of Florida — M,D,O
University of Georgia — M,D
University of Idaho — M,D
University of Illinois at Urbana–Champaign — M,D
University of Kentucky — M,D
University of Maryland, College Park — M,D
University of Minnesota, Twin Cities Campus — M,D
University of Missouri–Columbia — M,D
University of Nebraska–Lincoln — M
The University of Tennessee — M,D
University of Wisconsin–Madison — M,D
Utah State University — M,D
Virginia Polytechnic Institute and State University — M,D

■ AGRICULTURAL SCIENCES—GENERAL

Alabama Agricultural and Mechanical University — M,D
Alcorn State University — M
Angelo State University — M
Arkansas State University — M,O
Auburn University — M,D
Brigham Young University — M,D
California Polytechnic State University, San Luis Obispo — M
California State Polytechnic University, Pomona — M
California State University, Fresno — M
Central Missouri State University — M
Clemson University — M,D
Colorado State University — M,D
Illinois State University — M
Iowa State University of Science and Technology — M,D
Kansas State University — M,D
Louisiana State University and Agricultural and Mechanical College — M,D
Michigan State University — M,D
Mississippi State University — M,D
Montana State University–Bozeman — M,D
Murray State University — M
New Mexico State University — M,D
North Carolina Agricultural and Technical State University — M
North Carolina State University — M,D
North Dakota State University — M,D
Northwest Missouri State University — M
The Ohio State University — M,D
Oklahoma State University — M,D
Oregon State University — M,D
The Pennsylvania State University University Park Campus — M,D
Prairie View A&M University — M
Purdue University — M,D
Sam Houston State University — M
South Dakota State University — M,D
Southern Illinois University Carbondale — M
Southern University and Agricultural and Mechanical College — M
Southwest Missouri State University — M
Tarleton State University — M
Tennessee State University — M,D
Texas A&M University — M,D
Texas A&M University–Commerce — M
Texas A&M University–Kingsville — M,D
Texas Tech University — M,D
Tuskegee University — M
The University of Arizona — M,D
University of Arkansas — M,D
University of California, Davis — M
University of Connecticut — M,D
University of Delaware — M,D
University of Florida — M,D

University of Georgia — M,D
University of Hawaii at Manoa — M,D
University of Idaho — M
University of Illinois at Urbana–Champaign — M,D
University of Kentucky — M,D
University of Maine — M,D
University of Maryland, College Park — P,M,D
University of Maryland Eastern Shore — M
University of Minnesota, Twin Cities Campus — M,D
University of Missouri–Columbia — M,D
University of Nebraska–Lincoln — M,D
University of Nevada, Reno — M,D
University of Puerto Rico, Mayagüez Campus — M
The University of Tennessee — M,D
University of Vermont — M,D
University of Wisconsin–Madison — M,D
University of Wisconsin–River Falls — M
University of Wyoming — M,D
Utah State University — M,D
Virginia Polytechnic Institute and State University — M,D
Washington State University — M,D
Western Kentucky University — M
West Texas A&M University — M,D
West Virginia University — M,D

■ AGRONOMY AND SOIL SCIENCES

Alabama Agricultural and Mechanical University — M,D
Alcorn State University — M
Auburn University — M,D
Brigham Young University — M
Colorado State University — M,D
Cornell University — M,D
Iowa State University of Science and Technology — M,D
Kansas State University — M,D
Louisiana State University and Agricultural and Mechanical College — M,D
Michigan State University — M,D
Mississippi State University — M,D
New Mexico State University — M,D
North Carolina State University — M,D
North Dakota State University — M,D
The Ohio State University — M,D
Oklahoma State University — M,D
Oregon State University — M,D
The Pennsylvania State University University Park Campus — M,D
Prairie View A&M University — M
Purdue University — M,D
South Dakota State University — M,D
Southern Illinois University Carbondale — M
Southwest Missouri State University — M
Texas A&M University — M,D
Texas A&M University–Kingsville — M,D
Texas Tech University — M,D
Tuskegee University — M
The University of Arizona — M,D
University of Arkansas — M,D
University of California, Davis — M,D
University of California, Riverside — M,D
University of Connecticut — M,D
University of Delaware — M,D
University of Florida — M,D
University of Georgia — M,D
University of Idaho — M,D
University of Illinois at Urbana–Champaign — M,D
University of Kentucky — M,D
University of Maine — M,D
University of Maryland, College Park — M,D
University of Massachusetts Amherst — M,D

Directory of Graduate and Professional Programs by Field

Agronomy and Soil Sciences

Institution	Degree
University of Minnesota, Twin Cities Campus	M,D
University of Missouri–Columbia	M,D
University of Nebraska–Lincoln	M,D
University of New Hampshire	M
University of Puerto Rico, Mayagüez Campus	M
University of Vermont	M,D
University of Wisconsin–Madison	M,D
University of Wyoming	M,D
Utah State University	M,D
Virginia Polytechnic Institute and State University	M,D
Washington State University	M,D
West Virginia University	M,D

ALLIED HEALTH—GENERAL

Institution	Degree
Alabama State University	M
Andrews University	M
Arkansas State University	M,O
Baylor University	M,D
Belmont University	M,D
Boston University	M,D
Cleveland State University	M
College of Mount Saint Vincent	M,O
Creighton University	P,M,D
Drexel University	M,D,O
Duquesne University	M,D
East Carolina University	M,D
Eastern Kentucky University	M
East Tennessee State University	M,D,O
Emory University	M,D
Florida Agricultural and Mechanical University	M
Florida Gulf Coast University	M
Georgia Southern University	M,O
Georgia State University	M,D
Grand Valley State University	M,D
Idaho State University	M,D,O
Ithaca College	M
Jackson State University	M
Loma Linda University	M,D
Long Island University, C.W. Post Campus	M,O
Marymount University	M,O
Maryville University of Saint Louis	M
Mercy College	M
Minnesota State University Mankato	M,O
Northeastern University	P,M,D,O
Northern Arizona University	M,D,O
Nova Southeastern University	M,D
Oakland University	M,D,O
The Ohio State University	M
Old Dominion University	M,D
Quinnipiac University	M
Regis University	M,D
Saint Louis University	M,D
Seton Hall University	M,D
Shenandoah University	M,D,O
Temple University	M,D
Tennessee State University	M
Texas Christian University	M
Texas State University-San Marcos	M
Texas Woman's University	M,D
Towson University	M
University at Buffalo, The State University of New York	M,D,O
The University of Alabama at Birmingham	M,D,O
University of Connecticut	M
University of Detroit Mercy	M,O
University of Florida	M,D
University of Illinois at Chicago	M,D
University of Kansas	M,D,O
University of Kentucky	M,D
University of Massachusetts Lowell	M,D
The University of North Carolina at Chapel Hill	M,D
University of North Florida	M,O
University of St. Francis (IL)	M
University of Saint Francis (IN)	M
University of South Alabama	M,D
The University of South Dakota	M
University of Southern California	M,D
The University of Texas at El Paso	M
University of Vermont	M
University of Wisconsin–Eau Claire	M
University of Wisconsin–Milwaukee	M,D
Virginia Commonwealth University	M,D,O
Washington University in St. Louis	M,D,O
Wichita State University	M

ALLOPATHIC MEDICINE

Institution	Degree
Boston University	P
Brown University	P
Case Western Reserve University	P
Columbia University	P
Creighton University	P
Dartmouth College	P
Drexel University	P
Duke University	P
East Carolina University	P
East Tennessee State University	P
Emory University	P
Florida State University	P,D
Georgetown University	P
The George Washington University	P
Harvard University	P
Howard University	P,D
Indiana University–Purdue University Indianapolis	P
The Johns Hopkins University	P
Loma Linda University	P,M,D
Loyola University Chicago	P
Marshall University	P
Mercer University	P,M
Michigan State University	P
New York University	P
Northwestern University	P
The Ohio State University	P
Saint Louis University	P,M,D
Southern Illinois University Carbondale	P
Stanford University	P
Stony Brook University, State University of New York	P
Temple University	P
Tufts University	P
Tulane University	P
University at Buffalo, The State University of New York	P
The University of Alabama at Birmingham	P,M,D
The University of Arizona	P
University of California, Davis	P,M
University of California, Irvine	P
University of California, Los Angeles	P
University of California, San Diego	
University of California, San Francisco	P
University of Chicago	P
University of Cincinnati	P,M
University of Florida	P
University of Hawaii at Manoa	P
University of Illinois at Chicago	P
University of Illinois at Urbana–Champaign	
The University of Iowa	P
University of Kansas	P
University of Kentucky	P
University of Louisville	P
University of Maryland	P
University of Miami	P
University of Michigan	
University of Minnesota, Duluth	P
University of Minnesota, Twin Cities Campus	
University of Missouri–Columbia	P
University of Missouri–Kansas City	P
University of Nevada, Reno	P
University of New Mexico	
The University of North Carolina at Chapel Hill	P
University of North Dakota	P
University of Pennsylvania	P
University of Pittsburgh	P
University of Rochester	P
University of South Alabama	P
University of South Carolina	P
The University of South Dakota	P
University of Southern California	P
University of South Florida	P
University of Utah	P
University of Vermont	P
University of Virginia	P,M,D
University of Washington	P
University of Wisconsin–Madison	P
Vanderbilt University	P,M,D
Virginia Commonwealth University	P
Wake Forest University	P
Washington University in St. Louis	P
Wayne State University	P
West Virginia University	P
Wright State University	P
Yale University	P
Yeshiva University	P

AMERICAN INDIAN/NATIVE AMERICAN STUDIES

Institution	Degree
Montana State University–Bozeman	M
The University of Arizona	M,D
University of California, Davis	M,D
University of California, Los Angeles	M
University of Kansas	M

AMERICAN STUDIES

Institution	Degree
American University	M,D,O
Appalachian State University	M
Baylor University	M
Boston University	D
Bowling Green State University	M,D
Brandeis University	M,D
Brown University	M,D
California State University, Fullerton	M
Claremont Graduate University	M,D
The College of William and Mary	M,D
Columbia University	M
Cornell University	M,D
Drake University	M
East Carolina University	M
Eastern Michigan University	M
Fairfield University	M
Florida State University	M,O
Fordham University	M,D
The George Washington University	M,D
Harvard University	D
Lehigh University	M
Michigan State University	M,D
New Mexico Highlands University	M
New York University	M,D
Northeastern State University	M
The Pennsylvania State University Harrisburg Campus of the Capital College	M
Pepperdine University	M
Purdue University	M,D
Saint Louis University	M,D
State University of New York College at Cortland	O
Stony Brook University, State University of New York	M,O
University at Buffalo, The State University of New York	M,D
The University of Alabama	M
University of Central Oklahoma	M
University of Delaware	M
University of Hawaii at Manoa	M,D
The University of Iowa	M,D
University of Kansas	M,D
University of Louisiana at Lafayette	D

Directory of Graduate and Professional Programs by Field
Anthropology

University of Maryland, College Park — M,D
University of Massachusetts Boston — M
University of Michigan — M,D
University of Michigan–Flint — M
University of Minnesota, Twin Cities Campus — D
University of Mississippi — M
University of New Mexico — M,D
University of Pennsylvania — M,D
University of Southern California — D
University of Southern Maine — M
University of South Florida — M
The University of Texas at Austin — M,D
University of Wyoming — M
Utah State University — M
Washington State University — M,D
Western Carolina University — M
West Virginia University — M,D
Yale University — M,D

■ ANALYTICAL CHEMISTRY

Brigham Young University — M,D
California State University, Fullerton — M
California State University, Los Angeles — M
Case Western Reserve University — M,D
Clarkson University — M,D
Cleveland State University — M,D
Cornell University — D
Florida State University — M,D
Georgetown University — M,D
The George Washington University — M,D
Governors State University — M
Howard University — M,D
Illinois Institute of Technology — M,D
Indiana University Bloomington — M,D
Kansas State University — M,D
Kent State University — M,D
Marquette University — M,D
Miami University — M,D
Northeastern University — M,D
Old Dominion University — M
Oregon State University — M,D
Purdue University — M,D
Rensselaer Polytechnic Institute — M,D
Rutgers, The State University of New Jersey, Newark — M,D
Rutgers, The State University of New Jersey, New Brunswick/Piscataway — M,D
Seton Hall University — M,D
South Dakota State University — M,D
Southern University and Agricultural and Mechanical College — M
State University of New York at Binghamton — M,D
Stevens Institute of Technology — M,D,O
Tufts University — M,D
University of Cincinnati — M,D
University of Georgia — M,D
University of Louisville — M,D
University of Maryland, College Park — M,D
University of Michigan — D
University of Missouri–Columbia — M,D
University of Missouri–Kansas City — M,D
The University of Montana–Missoula — M,D
University of Nebraska–Lincoln — M,D
University of Southern Mississippi — M,D
University of South Florida — M,D
The University of Tennessee — M,D
The University of Texas at Austin — M,D
University of Toledo — M,D
Vanderbilt University — M,D
Wake Forest University — M,D
Washington State University — M,D
West Virginia University — M,D

■ ANATOMY

Auburn University — M,D
Boston University — M,D
Case Western Reserve University — M,D
Columbia University — M,D
Cornell University — M,D
Duke University — D
East Carolina University — D
East Tennessee State University — M,D
Howard University — M,D
Indiana University Bloomington — M,D
Indiana University–Purdue University Indianapolis — M,D
The Johns Hopkins University — D
Kansas State University — M,D
Loma Linda University — M,D
Loyola University Chicago — M,D
Michigan State University — M,D
The Ohio State University — M,D
Purdue University — M,D
Saint Louis University — M,D
Stony Brook University, State University of New York — D
Temple University — D
Texas A&M University — M,D
University at Buffalo, The State University of New York — M,D
The University of Arizona — D
University of California, Irvine — M,D
University of California, Los Angeles — D
University of California, San Francisco — D
University of Chicago — D
University of Florida — D
University of Georgia — M
University of Hawaii at Manoa — M,D
University of Illinois at Chicago — M,D
The University of Iowa — D
University of Kansas — M,D
University of Kentucky — D
University of Louisville — M,D
University of Maryland — M,D
University of Minnesota, Duluth — M,D
University of North Dakota — M,D
University of Rochester — M,D
University of Southern California — M,D
University of South Florida — M,D
The University of Tennessee — M,D
University of Utah — M,D
University of Vermont — D
University of Wisconsin–Madison — M,D
Virginia Commonwealth University — M,D,O
Wake Forest University — D
Wayne State University — M,D
West Virginia University — M,D
Wright State University — M
Yeshiva University — D

■ ANIMAL BEHAVIOR

Arizona State University — M,D
University of California, Davis — M,D
University of Colorado at Boulder — M,D
University of Minnesota, Twin Cities Campus — M,D
University of Missouri–St. Louis — M,D,O
The University of Montana–Missoula — M,D
The University of Tennessee — M,D
The University of Texas at Austin — D

■ ANIMAL SCIENCES

Alabama Agricultural and Mechanical University — M,D
Alcorn State University — M
Angelo State University — M
Auburn University — M,D
Brigham Young University — M
California State Polytechnic University, Pomona — M
California State University, Fresno — M
Colorado State University — M,D
Cornell University — M,D
Florida Agricultural and Mechanical University — M
Fort Valley State University — M
Iowa State University of Science and Technology — M,D
Kansas State University — M,D
Louisiana State University and Agricultural and Mechanical College — M,D
Michigan State University — M,D
Mississippi State University — M
Montana State University–Bozeman — M,D
New Mexico State University — M,D
North Carolina State University — M,D
North Dakota State University — M,D
The Ohio State University — M,D
Oklahoma State University — M,D
Oregon State University — M,D
The Pennsylvania State University University Park Campus — M,D
Prairie View A&M University — M
Purdue University — M,D
Rutgers, The State University of New Jersey, New Brunswick/Piscataway — M,D
South Dakota State University — M,D
Southern Illinois University Carbondale — M
Sul Ross State University — M
Tarleton State University — M
Texas A&M University — M,D
Texas A&M University–Kingsville — M
Texas Tech University — M,D
Tuskegee University — M
The University of Arizona — M,D
University of Arkansas — M,D
University of California, Davis — M
University of Connecticut — M,D
University of Florida — M,D
University of Georgia — M,D
University of Hawaii at Manoa — M
University of Idaho — M,D
University of Illinois at Urbana–Champaign — M,D
University of Kentucky — M,D
University of Maine — M
University of Maryland, College Park — M,D
University of Massachusetts Amherst — M,D
University of Minnesota, Twin Cities Campus — M,D
University of Missouri–Columbia — M,D
University of Nebraska–Lincoln — M,D
University of Nevada, Reno — M
University of New Hampshire — M,D
University of Puerto Rico, Mayagüez Campus — M
University of Rhode Island — M
The University of Tennessee — M,D
University of Vermont — M,D
University of Wisconsin–Madison — M,D
University of Wyoming — M,D
Utah State University — M,D
Virginia Polytechnic Institute and State University — M,D
Washington State University — M,D
West Texas A&M University — M
West Virginia University — M,D

■ ANTHROPOLOGY

American University — M,D,O
Arizona State University — M,D
Ball State University — M
Boston University — M,D
Brandeis University — M,D
Brigham Young University — M
Brown University — M,D
California State University, Bakersfield — M
California State University, Chico — M
California State University, Fullerton — M
California State University, Hayward — M
California State University, Long Beach — M
California State University, Los Angeles — M

Peterson's Graduate Schools in the U.S. 2006   *www.petersons.com*   33

Directory of Graduate and Professional Programs by Field

Anthropology

Institution	Degree
California State University, Northridge	M
California State University, Sacramento	M
Case Western Reserve University	M,D
The Catholic University of America	M,D
City College of the City University of New York	M
Claremont Graduate University	M,D
The College of William and Mary	M,D
Colorado State University	M
Columbia University	M,D
Cornell University	D
Duke University	D
East Carolina University	M
Eastern New Mexico University	M
Emory University	D
Florida Atlantic University	M
Florida State University	M,D
The George Washington University	M,D
Georgia State University	M
Harvard University	M,D
Hunter College of the City University of New York	M
Idaho State University	M
Indiana University Bloomington	M,D
Iowa State University of Science and Technology	M
The Johns Hopkins University	D
Kent State University	M,D
Lehigh University	M
Louisiana State University and Agricultural and Mechanical College	M,D
Marshall University	M
Michigan State University	M,D
Minnesota State University Mankato	M
Mississippi State University	M,D
New Mexico Highlands University	M
New Mexico State University	M
New School University	M,D
New York University	M,D
Northern Arizona University	M
Northern Illinois University	M
Northwestern University	D
The Ohio State University	M,D
Oregon State University	M
The Pennsylvania State University University Park Campus	M,D
Portland State University	M,D,O
Princeton University	D
Purdue University	M,D
Rice University	M,D
Rutgers, The State University of New Jersey, New Brunswick/Piscataway	M,D
San Diego State University	M
San Francisco State University	M
Southern Illinois University Carbondale	M,D
Southern Methodist University	M,D
Stanford University	M,D
State University of New York at Binghamton	M,D
Stony Brook University, State University of New York	M,D
Syracuse University	M,D
Teachers College Columbia University	M,D
Temple University	M,D
Texas A&M University	M,D
Texas Tech University	M
Tulane University	M,D
University at Albany, State University of New York	M,D
University at Buffalo, The State University of New York	M,D
The University of Alabama	D
The University of Alabama at Birmingham	M
University of Alaska Fairbanks	M,D
The University of Arizona	M,D
University of Arkansas	M,D
University of California, Berkeley	D
University of California, Davis	M,D
University of California, Irvine	M,D
University of California, Los Angeles	M,D
University of California, Riverside	M,D
University of California, San Diego	D
University of California, San Francisco	D
University of California, Santa Barbara	M,D
University of California, Santa Cruz	M,D
University of Chicago	M,D
University of Cincinnati	M
University of Colorado at Boulder	M,D
University of Colorado at Denver	M
University of Connecticut	M,D
University of Denver	M
University of Florida	M,D
University of Georgia	M,D
University of Hawaii at Manoa	M,D
University of Houston	M
University of Idaho	M
University of Illinois at Chicago	M,D
University of Illinois at Urbana–Champaign	M,D
The University of Iowa	M,D
University of Kansas	M,D
University of Kentucky	M,D
University of Maryland, College Park	M
University of Massachusetts Amherst	M,D
The University of Memphis	M
University of Michigan	D
University of Minnesota, Duluth	M
University of Minnesota, Twin Cities Campus	M,D
University of Mississippi	M
University of Missouri–Columbia	M,D
The University of Montana–Missoula	M,D
University of Nebraska–Lincoln	M
University of Nevada, Las Vegas	M,D
University of Nevada, Reno	M,D
University of New Mexico	M,D
The University of North Carolina at Chapel Hill	M,D
University of North Texas	M
University of Oklahoma	M,D
University of Oregon	M,D
University of Pennsylvania	M,D
University of Pittsburgh	M,D
University of South Carolina	M
University of Southern California	M,D,O
University of Southern Mississippi	M
University of South Florida	M,D
The University of Tennessee	M,D
The University of Texas at Arlington	M
The University of Texas at Austin	M,D
The University of Texas at San Antonio	M
University of Toledo	M
University of Tulsa	M
University of Utah	M,D
University of Virginia	M,D
University of Washington	M,D
University of West Florida	M
University of Wisconsin–Madison	M,D
University of Wisconsin–Milwaukee	M,D
University of Wyoming	M,D
Vanderbilt University	M,D
Washington State University	M,D
Washington University in St. Louis	M,D
Wayne State University	M,D
West Chester University of Pennsylvania	M,O
Western Michigan University	M
Western Washington University	M
Wichita State University	M
Yale University	M,D

■ APPLIED ARTS AND DESIGN—GENERAL

Institution	Degree
Alfred University	M
Arizona State University	M
Bradley University	M
California State University, Chico	M
California State University, Fresno	M
California State University, Fullerton	M,O
California State University, Los Angeles	M
Cardinal Stritch University	M
Carnegie Mellon University	D
Drexel University	M
Ferris State University	M
Florida Atlantic University	M
The George Washington University	M,D
Howard University	M
Illinois Institute of Technology	M,D
Indiana University Bloomington	M
Iowa State University of Science and Technology	M
Lamar University	M
Louisiana State University and Agricultural and Mechanical College	M
Louisiana Tech University	M
New School University	M
New York University	M
North Carolina State University	M,D
Oklahoma State University	M,D
Pratt Institute	M
Purdue University	M
Rutgers, The State University of New Jersey, New Brunswick/Piscataway	M
San Diego State University	M
San Jose State University	M
Southern Illinois University Carbondale	M
Stephen F. Austin State University	M
Suffolk University	M
Sul Ross State University	M
Syracuse University	M
University of California, Berkeley	M
University of California, Los Angeles	M
University of Central Oklahoma	M
University of Cincinnati	M
University of Illinois at Urbana–Champaign	M,D
University of Kansas	M
University of Massachusetts Dartmouth	M
University of Michigan	M
University of Minnesota, Twin Cities Campus	M,D
University of Notre Dame	M
University of Oklahoma	M
The University of Texas at Austin	M
University of Wisconsin–Madison	M,D
Virginia Commonwealth University	M
Virginia Polytechnic Institute and State University	M
Wayne State University	M
Western Michigan University	M
Yale University	M

■ APPLIED ECONOMICS

Institution	Degree
American University	M,D,O
Buffalo State College, State University of New York	M
Clemson University	M,D
Cornell University	D
Eastern Michigan University	M
The Johns Hopkins University	M
Mississippi State University	M,D
Montana State University–Bozeman	M
New York University	M,D,O
North Carolina Agricultural and Technical State University	M
Northeastern University	M,D
Ohio University	M
Portland State University	M,D
Roosevelt University	M
St. Cloud State University	M
San Jose State University	M
Southern Methodist University	M,D
Texas Tech University	M,D

Directory of Graduate and Professional Programs by Field
Aquaculture

Institution	Degree
University of California, Santa Cruz	M
University of Georgia	M,D
University of Michigan	M
University of Minnesota, Twin Cities Campus	M,D
University of Nevada, Reno	M
The University of North Carolina at Greensboro	M
University of North Texas	M
The University of Texas at Dallas	M,D
University of Vermont	M
University of Wisconsin–Madison	M,D
University of Wyoming	M
Utah State University	M
Virginia Polytechnic Institute and State University	M,D
Western Michigan University	M,D
Wright State University	M

■ APPLIED MATHEMATICS

Institution	Degree
Arizona State University	M,D
Auburn University	M,D
Brown University	M,D
California Institute of Technology	M,D
California State Polytechnic University, Pomona	M
California State University, Fullerton	M
California State University, Long Beach	M,D,O
California State University, Los Angeles	M
Case Western Reserve University	M,D
Central Missouri State University	M
Claremont Graduate University	M,D
Clark Atlanta University	M
Clemson University	M,D
Cleveland State University	M
Columbia University	M,D,O
Cornell University	M,D
East Carolina University	M
Florida Atlantic University	M,D
Florida Institute of Technology	M,D
Florida State University	M,D
The George Washington University	M,D
Georgia Institute of Technology	M,D
Hampton University	M
Harvard University	M,D
Hofstra University	M
Howard University	M,D
Hunter College of the City University of New York	M
Illinois Institute of Technology	M,D
Indiana University Bloomington	M,D
Indiana University of Pennsylvania	M
Indiana University–Purdue University Fort Wayne	M
Indiana University–Purdue University Indianapolis	M,D
Indiana University South Bend	M
Inter American University of Puerto Rico, San Germán Campus	M
Iowa State University of Science and Technology	M,D
The Johns Hopkins University	M,D
Kent State University	M,D
Lehigh University	M,D
Long Island University, C.W. Post Campus	M
Michigan State University	M,D
Montclair State University	M,O
New Jersey Institute of Technology	M
New Mexico Institute of Mining and Technology	M,D
Nicholls State University	M
North Carolina State University	M,D
North Dakota State University	M,D
Northwestern University	M,D
Oakland University	M
Oklahoma State University	M,D
The Pennsylvania State University University Park Campus	M,D
Princeton University	M,D
Rensselaer Polytechnic Institute	M
Rice University	M,D
Rochester Institute of Technology	M
Rutgers, The State University of New Jersey, New Brunswick/Piscataway	M,D
St. John's University (NY)	M
San Diego State University	M
Santa Clara University	M
Southern Methodist University	M,D
Stevens Institute of Technology	M,D
Stony Brook University, State University of New York	M,D
Temple University	M,D
Texas State University-San Marcos	M
Towson University	M
Tulane University	M,D
The University of Akron	M,D
The University of Alabama	M,D
The University of Alabama at Birmingham	M,D
The University of Alabama in Huntsville	M,D
The University of Arizona	M,D
University of Arkansas at Little Rock	M
University of California, Berkeley	D
University of California, Davis	M,D
University of California, San Diego	M,D
University of California, Santa Barbara	M
University of California, Santa Cruz	M,D
University of Central Oklahoma	M
University of Chicago	M,D
University of Cincinnati	M,D
University of Colorado at Boulder	M,D
University of Colorado at Colorado Springs	M
University of Colorado at Denver	M,D
University of Connecticut	M,D
University of Dayton	M
University of Delaware	M,D
University of Denver	M
University of Florida	M,D
University of Georgia	M,D
University of Houston	M,D
University of Illinois at Chicago	M,D
University of Illinois at Urbana–Champaign	M,D
The University of Iowa	D
University of Kansas	M,D
University of Louisville	M,D
University of Maryland, Baltimore County	M,D
University of Maryland, College Park	M,D
University of Massachusetts Amherst	M
University of Massachusetts Lowell	M,D
The University of Memphis	M,D
University of Michigan–Dearborn	M
University of Minnesota, Duluth	M
University of Missouri–Columbia	M
University of Missouri–Rolla	M
University of Missouri–St. Louis	M,D,O
University of Nevada, Las Vegas	M
University of New Hampshire	M,D
The University of North Carolina at Charlotte	M,D
University of Notre Dame	M,D
University of Pittsburgh	M,D
University of Puerto Rico, Mayagüez Campus	M
University of Rhode Island	M
University of Southern California	M,D
University of South Florida	M,D
The University of Tennessee	M,D
The University of Texas at Austin	M,D
The University of Texas at Dallas	M,D
The University of Texas at San Antonio	M
University of Toledo	M,D
University of Washington	M,D
Utah State University	M,D
Virginia Commonwealth University	M
Virginia Polytechnic Institute and State University	M,D
Wayne State University	M,D
Western Michigan University	M
West Virginia University	M,D
Wichita State University	M,D
Worcester Polytechnic Institute	M,D,O
Wright State University	M
Yale University	M,D

■ APPLIED PHYSICS

Institution	Degree
Alabama Agricultural and Mechanical University	M,D
Appalachian State University	M
Brooklyn College of the City University of New York	M,D
California Institute of Technology	M,D
Columbia University	M,D,O
Cornell University	M,D
DePaul University	M
George Mason University	M
Harvard University	M,D
Iowa State University of Science and Technology	M,D
The Johns Hopkins University	M
New Jersey Institute of Technology	M,D
Northern Arizona University	M
Pittsburg State University	M
Princeton University	M,D
Rensselaer Polytechnic Institute	M,D
Rice University	M,D
Rutgers, The State University of New Jersey, Newark	M,D
Stanford University	M,D
State University of New York at Binghamton	M
Texas A&M University	M,D
Texas Tech University	M,D
The University of Arizona	M
University of Arkansas	M
University of California, San Diego	M,D
University of Central Oklahoma	M
University of Maryland, Baltimore County	M,D
University of Massachusetts Boston	M
University of Massachusetts Lowell	M,D
University of Michigan	D
University of Missouri–St. Louis	M,D
The University of North Carolina at Charlotte	M,D
University of Puerto Rico, Río Piedras	M,D
University of Washington	M,D
Virginia Commonwealth University	M
Virginia Polytechnic Institute and State University	M,D
West Virginia University	M,D
Yale University	M,D

■ APPLIED SCIENCE AND TECHNOLOGY

Institution	Degree
The College of William and Mary	M,D
Harvard University	M,O
James Madison University	M
Oklahoma State University	M
Rensselaer Polytechnic Institute	M
Southern Methodist University	M,D
Southwest Missouri State University	M
University of Arkansas at Little Rock	M,D
University of California, Berkeley	D
University of California, Davis	M,D
University of Colorado at Denver	M
University of Mississippi	M,D

■ AQUACULTURE

Institution	Degree
Auburn University	M,D
Clemson University	M,D

Directory of Graduate and Professional Programs by Field

Aquaculture

Kentucky State University	M
Purdue University	M,D
University of Florida	M,D
University of Rhode Island	M

■ ARCHAEOLOGY

Boston University	M,D
Brown University	M,D
Columbia University	M,D
Cornell University	M,D
Florida State University	M,D
George Mason University	M
Harvard University	M,D
Illinois State University	M
Michigan Technological University	M,D
New York University	M,D
Northern Arizona University	M
Princeton University	D
Southern Methodist University	M,D
Tufts University	M
University of California, Berkeley	M,D
University of California, Los Angeles	M,D
University of Chicago	M,D
University of Massachusetts Boston	M
The University of Memphis	M
University of Michigan	D
University of Minnesota, Twin Cities Campus	M,D
University of Missouri–Columbia	M,D
The University of North Carolina at Chapel Hill	M,D
University of Pennsylvania	M,D
The University of Tennessee	M,D
The University of Texas at Austin	M,D
University of Virginia	M,D
Washington University in St. Louis	M,D
Yale University	M

■ ARCHITECTURAL ENGINEERING

Illinois Institute of Technology	M,D
Kansas State University	M
North Carolina Agricultural and Technical State University	M
Oklahoma State University	M
The Pennsylvania State University University Park Campus	M,D
Rensselaer Polytechnic Institute	M
University of Colorado at Boulder	M,D
University of Detroit Mercy	M
University of Kansas	M,D
University of Louisiana at Lafayette	M
University of Miami	M,D
University of Nebraska–Lincoln	M
The University of Texas at Austin	M

■ ARCHITECTURAL HISTORY

Arizona State University	D
Cornell University	M,D
University of California, Berkeley	M,D
University of Pittsburgh	M,D
University of Virginia	M,D

■ ARCHITECTURE

Andrews University	M
Arizona State University	M
Auburn University	M
Ball State University	M
California Polytechnic State University, San Luis Obispo	
California State Polytechnic University, Pomona	M
Carnegie Mellon University	M,D
The Catholic University of America	M
City College of the City University of New York	M
Clemson University	M
Columbia College Chicago	M
Columbia University	M,D
Cornell University	M,D
Drexel University	M
Florida Agricultural and Mechanical University	M
Florida International University	M
Georgia Institute of Technology	M,D
Harvard University	M,D
Illinois Institute of Technology	M,D
Iowa State University of Science and Technology	M
Kansas State University	M
Kent State University	M,O
Lawrence Technological University	M
Louisiana State University and Agricultural and Mechanical College	M
Massachusetts Institute of Technology	M,D
Miami University	M
Mississippi State University	M
Montana State University–Bozeman	M
Morgan State University	M
New Jersey Institute of Technology	M
New School University	M
New York Institute of Technology	M
North Carolina State University	M
Northeastern University	M
The Ohio State University	M
Oklahoma State University	M
The Pennsylvania State University University Park Campus	M
Prairie View A&M University	M
Pratt Institute	M
Princeton University	M,D
Rensselaer Polytechnic Institute	M
Rice University	M,D
Syracuse University	M
Texas A&M University	M,D
Texas Tech University	M
Tulane University	M
University at Buffalo, The State University of New York	M
The University of Arizona	M
University of California, Berkeley	M,D
University of California, Los Angeles	M,D
University of Cincinnati	M
University of Colorado at Denver	M,D
University of Florida	M,D
University of Hartford	M
University of Hawaii at Manoa	D
University of Houston	M
University of Idaho	M
University of Illinois at Chicago	M
University of Illinois at Urbana–Champaign	M
University of Kansas	M
University of Kentucky	M
University of Maryland, College Park	M
University of Miami	M
University of Michigan	M,D
University of Minnesota, Twin Cities Campus	M
University of Missouri–Columbia	M
University of Nebraska–Lincoln	M
University of Nevada, Las Vegas	M
University of New Mexico	M
The University of North Carolina at Charlotte	M
The University of North Carolina at Greensboro	M
University of Notre Dame	M
University of Oklahoma	M
University of Oregon	M
University of Pennsylvania	M,D,O
University of Puerto Rico, Río Piedras	M
University of Southern California	M,O
University of South Florida	M
The University of Tennessee	M
The University of Texas at Arlington	M
The University of Texas at Austin	M,D
The University of Texas at San Antonio	M
University of Utah	M
University of Virginia	M
University of Washington	M,O
University of Wisconsin–Milwaukee	M,D
Virginia Polytechnic Institute and State University	M
Washington State University	M
Washington University in St. Louis	M
Yale University	M

■ ART/FINE ARTS

Adams State College	M
Adelphi University	M
Alfred University	M
American University	M
Arizona State University	M
Arkansas State University	M
Arkansas Tech University	M
Auburn University	M,D
Ball State University	M
Barry University	M
Bloomsburg University of Pennsylvania	M
Boise State University	M
Boston University	M
Bowling Green State University	M
Bradley University	M
Brandeis University	O
Brigham Young University	M
Brooklyn College of the City University of New York	M,D
California State University, Chico	M
California State University, Fresno	M
California State University, Fullerton	M,O
California State University, Long Beach	M
California State University, Los Angeles	M
California State University, Northridge	M
California State University, Sacramento	M
California State University, San Bernardino	M
Carnegie Mellon University	M,D
Central Michigan University	M
Central Washington University	M
City College of the City University of New York	M
Claremont Graduate University	M
Clemson University	M
The College of New Rochelle	M
Colorado State University	M
Columbia University	M
Cornell University	M
Drake University	M
East Carolina University	M
Eastern Illinois University	M
Eastern Michigan University	M
East Tennessee State University	M
Edinboro University of Pennsylvania	M
Ferris State University	M
Florida Atlantic University	M
Florida International University	M
Florida State University	M
Fontbonne University	M
Fort Hays State University	M
Framingham State College	M
The George Washington University	M,D
Georgia Southern University	M
Georgia State University	M
Governors State University	M
Hofstra University	M
Howard University	M
Hunter College of the City University of New York	M
Idaho State University	M
Illinois State University	M
Indiana State University	M
Indiana University Bloomington	M
Indiana University of Pennsylvania	M
Inter American University of Puerto Rico, San Germán Campus	M
James Madison University	M

Art Education

Institution	Degree
John F. Kennedy University	M
Johnson State College	
Kansas State University	M
Kent State University	M
Lamar University	M
Lehman College of the City University of New York	M
Long Island University, C.W. Post Campus	M
Louisiana State University and Agricultural and Mechanical College	M
Louisiana Tech University	M
Marshall University	
Marywood University	M
Massachusetts Institute of Technology	M,D,O
Miami University	M
Michigan State University	M
Minnesota State University Mankato	M
Mississippi College	M
Mississippi State University	M
Montana State University–Bozeman	M
Montclair State University	M
Morehead State University	M
New Jersey City University	M
New Mexico State University	M
New School University	M
New York University	M,D
Norfolk State University	M
Northern Illinois University	M
Northwestern State University of Louisiana	M
Northwestern University	M
The Ohio State University	M
Ohio University	M
Oklahoma City University	M
Old Dominion University	M
The Pennsylvania State University University Park Campus	M
Pittsburg State University	M
Portland State University	M
Pratt Institute	M
Purchase College, State University of New York	M
Purdue University	M
Queens College of the City University of New York	M
Radford University	M
Regis University	M,O
Rensselaer Polytechnic Institute	M
Rhode Island College	M
Rochester Institute of Technology	M
Rutgers, The State University of New Jersey, New Brunswick/Piscataway	M
St. Cloud State University	M
Sam Houston State University	M
San Diego State University	M
San Francisco State University	M
San Jose State University	M
Southern Illinois University Carbondale	M
Southern Illinois University Edwardsville	M
Southern Methodist University	M
Southern Utah University	M
Stanford University	M,D
State University of New York at New Paltz	M
State University of New York at Oswego	M
State University of New York College at Brockport	M
Stephen F. Austin State University	M
Stony Brook University, State University of New York	M
Sul Ross State University	M
Syracuse University	M
Temple University	M
Texas A&M University–Commerce	M
Texas A&M University–Corpus Christi	M
Texas A&M University–Kingsville	M
Texas Christian University	M
Texas Tech University	M,D
Texas Woman's University	M
Towson University	M
Tufts University	M
Tulane University	M
Union Institute & University	M
University at Albany, State University of New York	M
University at Buffalo, The State University of New York	M,O
The University of Alabama	M
University of Alaska Fairbanks	M
The University of Arizona	M
University of Arkansas	M
University of Arkansas at Little Rock	M
University of California, Berkeley	M
University of California, Davis	M
University of California, Irvine	M
University of California, Los Angeles	M
University of California, Riverside	M
University of California, San Diego	M,D
University of California, Santa Barbara	M
University of California, Santa Cruz	M
University of Chicago	M,D
University of Cincinnati	M
University of Colorado at Boulder	M
University of Colorado at Denver	M
University of Connecticut	M
University of Delaware	M
University of Denver	M
University of Florida	M
University of Georgia	M,D
University of Guam	M
University of Hartford	M
University of Hawaii at Manoa	M
University of Houston	M
University of Idaho	M
University of Illinois at Chicago	M
University of Indianapolis	M
The University of Iowa	M
University of Kansas	M
University of Kentucky	M
University of Louisville	M
University of Maryland, Baltimore County	M
University of Maryland, College Park	M
University of Massachusetts Amherst	M
University of Massachusetts Dartmouth	M,O
The University of Memphis	M
University of Miami	M
University of Michigan	M
University of Minnesota, Duluth	M
University of Minnesota, Twin Cities Campus	M
University of Mississippi	M
University of Missouri–Columbia	M
University of Missouri–Kansas City	M,D
The University of Montana–Missoula	M
University of Nebraska–Lincoln	M
University of Nevada, Las Vegas	M
University of New Hampshire	M
University of New Mexico	M
University of New Orleans	M
The University of North Carolina at Chapel Hill	M
The University of North Carolina at Greensboro	M
University of North Dakota	M
University of Northern Colorado	M
University of Northern Iowa	M
University of North Texas	M,D
University of Notre Dame	M
University of Oklahoma	M
University of Oregon	M
University of Pennsylvania	M
University of Rochester	M,D
University of Saint Francis (IN)	M
University of South Carolina	M
The University of South Dakota	M
University of Southern California	M
The University of Tennessee	M
The University of Texas at Austin	M
The University of Texas at El Paso	M
The University of Texas at San Antonio	M
The University of Texas at Tyler	M
The University of Texas–Pan American	M
University of Tulsa	M
University of Utah	M
University of Washington	M
University of Wisconsin–Madison	M
University of Wisconsin–Milwaukee	M
University of Wisconsin–Superior	M
Utah State University	M
Vanderbilt University	M
Virginia Commonwealth University	M
Washington State University	M
Washington University in St. Louis	M
Wayne State University	M
Webster University	M
Western Carolina University	M
Western Connecticut State University	M
West Texas A&M University	M
West Virginia University	M
Wichita State University	M
William Paterson University of New Jersey	M
Winthrop University	M
Yale University	M

■ ART EDUCATION

Institution	Degree
Arcadia University	M,D,O
Averett University	M
Ball State University	M
Boise State University	M
Boston University	M
Bridgewater State College	M
Brigham Young University	M
Brooklyn College of the City University of New York	M,O
Buffalo State College, State University of New York	M
California State University, Long Beach	M
California State University, Los Angeles	M
California State University, Northridge	M
Carlow University	M
Carthage College	M,O
Case Western Reserve University	
Central Connecticut State University	M
College of Mount St. Joseph	M
The College of New Rochelle	M
The College of Saint Rose	M,O
Columbus State University	M
Eastern Kentucky University	M
Eastern Michigan University	M
Eastern Washington University	M
East Tennessee State University	M
Fitchburg State College	M,O
Florida Atlantic University	M
Florida International University	M,D
Florida State University	M,D,O
Georgia Southern University	M,O
Georgia State University	M,D,O
Harvard University	M,D
Hofstra University	M
Indiana University Bloomington	M,D,O
Indiana University–Purdue University Indianapolis	M
Iowa State University of Science and Technology	M
Jacksonville University	M
James Madison University	M
Kean University	M
Kent State University	M
Kutztown University of Pennsylvania	M,O
Lesley University	M,D,O

Directory of Graduate and Professional Programs by Field

Art Education

Institution	Degree
Long Island University, C.W. Post Campus	M
Manhattanville College	M
Mansfield University of Pennsylvania	M
Maryville University of Saint Louis	M
Marywood University	M
Miami University	M
Millersville University of Pennsylvania	M
Minnesota State University Mankato	M
Mississippi College	M
Montclair State University	M
Morehead State University	M
Nazareth College of Rochester	M
New Jersey City University	M
New York University	M,D
North Carolina Agricultural and Technical State University	M
North Georgia College & State University	M,O
The Ohio State University	M,D
Ohio University	M
The Pennsylvania State University University Park Campus	M,D
Pittsburg State University	M
Pratt Institute	M
Purdue University	M,D,O
Queens College of the City University of New York	M,O
Radford University	M
Rhode Island College	M
Rochester Institute of Technology	M
Rockford College	M
Rowan University	M
Saint Michael's College	M,O
Salisbury University	M
Southeast Missouri State University	M
Southern Connecticut State University	M
Southwestern Oklahoma State University	M
Stanford University	M,D
State University of New York at New Paltz	M
State University of New York at Oswego	M
State University of West Georgia	M
Sul Ross State University	M
Syracuse University	M,O
Teachers College Columbia University	M,D
Temple University	M
Texas Tech University	M,D
Towson University	M
The University of Alabama at Birmingham	M
The University of Arizona	M
University of Arkansas at Little Rock	M
University of Central Florida	M
University of Cincinnati	M
University of Dayton	M
University of Florida	M
University of Georgia	M,D,O
University of Houston	M,D
University of Idaho	M
University of Illinois at Urbana–Champaign	M,D
University of Indianapolis	M
The University of Iowa	M,D
University of Kansas	M
University of Kentucky	M
University of Louisville	M
University of Massachusetts Amherst	M
University of Massachusetts Dartmouth	M
University of Minnesota, Twin Cities Campus	M,D,O
University of Mississippi	M
University of Missouri–Columbia	M,D,O
University of Nebraska at Kearney	M
University of New Mexico	M
The University of North Carolina at Greensboro	M
The University of North Carolina at Pembroke	M
University of Northern Iowa	M
University of North Texas	M,D
University of Rio Grande	M
University of South Alabama	M
University of South Carolina	M,D
University of Southern Mississippi	M
The University of Tennessee	M,D,O
The University of Texas at Austin	M
The University of Texas at Tyler	M
University of Wisconsin–Madison	M,D
University of Wisconsin–Milwaukee	M
University of Wisconsin–Superior	M
Virginia Commonwealth University	M
Wayne State University	M,D,O
Western Carolina University	M
Western Kentucky University	M
West Virginia University	M
Wichita State University	M
William Carey College	M,O
Winthrop University	M

■ ART HISTORY

Institution	Degree
American University	M
Bloomsburg University of Pennsylvania	M
Boston University	M,D,O
Bowling Green State University	M
Brigham Young University	M
Brooklyn College of the City University of New York	M,D
Brown University	M,D
California State University, Fullerton	M,O
California State University, Long Beach	M
California State University, Los Angeles	M
California State University, Northridge	M
Case Western Reserve University	M,D
City College of the City University of New York	M
Cleveland State University	M
Columbia University	M,D
Cornell University	D
Duke University	M
East Tennessee State University	M
Emory University	D
Florida State University	M,D,O
The George Washington University	M,D
Georgia State University	M
Harvard University	D
Howard University	M
Hunter College of the City University of New York	M
Illinois State University	M
Indiana University Bloomington	M,D
James Madison University	M
The Johns Hopkins University	M,D
Kent State University	M
Lamar University	M
Louisiana State University and Agricultural and Mechanical College	M
Montclair State University	M
New York University	M,D
Northwestern University	D
The Ohio State University	M,D
Ohio University	M
The Pennsylvania State University University Park Campus	M,D
Pratt Institute	M
Purchase College, State University of New York	M
Queens College of the City University of New York	M
Rutgers, The State University of New Jersey, New Brunswick/Piscataway	M,D
San Diego State University	M
San Francisco State University	M
San Jose State University	M
Southern Methodist University	M
State University of New York at Binghamton	M,D
Stony Brook University, State University of New York	M,D
Sul Ross State University	M
Syracuse University	M
Temple University	M,D
Texas A&M University–Commerce	M
Texas Christian University	M
Tufts University	M
Tulane University	M
University at Buffalo, The State University of New York	M
The University of Alabama	M
The University of Alabama at Birmingham	M
The University of Arizona	M,D
University of Arkansas at Little Rock	M
University of California, Berkeley	D
University of California, Davis	M
University of California, Irvine	M,D
University of California, Los Angeles	M,D
University of California, Riverside	M
University of California, Santa Barbara	D
University of Chicago	M,D
University of Cincinnati	M
University of Colorado at Boulder	M
University of Connecticut	M
University of Delaware	M,D
University of Denver	M
University of Florida	M
University of Georgia	M
University of Hawaii at Manoa	M
University of Illinois at Chicago	M,D
University of Illinois at Urbana–Champaign	M,D
The University of Iowa	M,D
University of Kansas	M,D
University of Kentucky	M
University of Louisville	M,D
University of Maryland, College Park	M,D
University of Massachusetts Amherst	M
The University of Memphis	M
University of Miami	M
University of Michigan	D
University of Minnesota, Twin Cities Campus	M,D
University of Mississippi	M
University of Missouri–Columbia	M,D
University of Missouri–Kansas City	M,D
University of Nebraska–Lincoln	M
University of New Mexico	M,D
The University of North Carolina at Chapel Hill	M,D
University of North Texas	M,D
University of Notre Dame	M
University of Oklahoma	M
University of Oregon	M,D
University of Pennsylvania	M,D
University of Pittsburgh	M,D
University of Rochester	M,D
University of St. Thomas (MN)	M
University of South Carolina	M
University of Southern California	M,D,O
University of South Florida	M
The University of Texas at Austin	M,D
The University of Texas at San Antonio	M
University of Utah	M
University of Virginia	M,D
University of Washington	M,D
University of Wisconsin–Madison	M,D
University of Wisconsin–Milwaukee	M,O
University of Wisconsin–Superior	M
Virginia Commonwealth University	M,D
Washington University in St. Louis	M,D
Wayne State University	M
West Virginia University	M
Yale University	D

ARTIFICIAL INTELLIGENCE/ROBOTICS

Carnegie Mellon University	M,D
The Catholic University of America	M,D
Cornell University	M,D
Indiana University–Purdue University Indianapolis	M,D
Ohio University	D
Portland State University	M,D,O
University of California, San Diego	M,D
University of Georgia	M
University of Southern California	M
The University of Tennessee	M,D

ARTS ADMINISTRATION

American University	M,O
Boston University	M
Carnegie Mellon University	M
Columbia College Chicago	M
Drexel University	M
Eastern Michigan University	M
Florida State University	M,D
Indiana University Bloomington	M
New York University	M
The Ohio State University	M
Oklahoma City University	M
Pratt Institute	M
Rhode Island College	M
Saint Mary's University of Minnesota	M
Seton Hall University	M
Shenandoah University	M,D,O
Southern Methodist University	
Teachers College Columbia University	M
Temple University	M,D
The University of Akron	M
University of Cincinnati	M
University of New Orleans	M
The University of North Carolina at Charlotte	M
University of Oregon	M
University of Southern California	M
University of Wisconsin–Madison	M
Virginia Polytechnic Institute and State University	M
Webster University	M
Winthrop University	M

ART THERAPY

California State University, Los Angeles	M
The College of New Rochelle	M
Drexel University	M
Emporia State University	M
The George Washington University	M,O
Hofstra University	M
Lesley University	M,D,O
Long Island University, C.W. Post Campus	M
Marylhurst University	M,O
Marywood University	M
Mount Mary College	M
Nazareth College of Rochester	M
New York University	M
Notre Dame de Namur University	M
Pratt Institute	M
Sage Graduate School	M
Salve Regina University	M,O
Southern Illinois University Edwardsville	M
Springfield College	M,O
University of Louisville	M
University of Wisconsin–Superior	M
Ursuline College	M

ASIAN-AMERICAN STUDIES

California State University, Long Beach	M,O
University of California, Los Angeles	M

ASIAN LANGUAGES

Columbia University	M,D
Cornell University	M,D
Harvard University	M,D
Indiana University Bloomington	M,D
Kent State University	M
The Ohio State University	M,D
University of California, Berkeley	M,D
University of California, Irvine	M,D
University of California, Los Angeles	M,D
University of Chicago	M,D
University of Hawaii at Manoa	M,D
University of Illinois at Urbana–Champaign	M,D
University of Kansas	M
University of Michigan	M,D
University of Southern California	M,D
The University of Texas at Austin	M,D
University of Washington	M,D
University of Wisconsin–Madison	M,D
Washington University in St. Louis	M,D
Yale University	D

ASIAN STUDIES

California State University, Long Beach	M,O
Columbia University	M,D,O
Cornell University	M,D
Duke University	M,O
Florida State University	M
The George Washington University	M
Harvard University	M,D
Indiana University Bloomington	M,D
The Johns Hopkins University	M,D,O
Maharishi University of Management	M,D
Ohio University	M
Princeton University	D
St. John's University (NY)	M,O
San Diego State University	M
Seton Hall University	M
Stanford University	M
The University of Arizona	M,D
University of California, Berkeley	M,D
University of California, Los Angeles	M,D
University of California, Santa Barbara	M
University of Chicago	M,D
University of Hawaii at Manoa	M
University of Illinois at Urbana–Champaign	M,D
The University of Iowa	M
University of Kansas	M
University of Michigan	M,D
University of Minnesota, Twin Cities Campus	M
University of Oregon	M
University of Pennsylvania	M,D
University of Pittsburgh	M
University of San Francisco	M
University of Southern California	M,D
The University of Texas at Austin	M,D
University of Virginia	M
University of Washington	M
University of Wisconsin–Madison	M,D
Washington University in St. Louis	M,D
West Virginia University	M,D
Yale University	M

ASTRONOMY

Arizona State University	M,D
Boston University	M,D
Bowling Green State University	M
Brigham Young University	M,D
California Institute of Technology	D
Case Western Reserve University	M,D
Clemson University	M
Columbia University	M
Cornell University	D
Dartmouth College	M,D
Georgia State University	D
Harvard University	M,D
Indiana University Bloomington	M,D
Iowa State University of Science and Technology	M,D
The Johns Hopkins University	D
Louisiana State University and Agricultural and Mechanical College	M,D
Michigan State University	M,D
Minnesota State University Mankato	M
New Mexico State University	M,D
Northwestern University	M,D
The Ohio State University	M,D
The Pennsylvania State University University Park Campus	M,D
Rice University	M,D
San Diego State University	M
Texas Christian University	D
The University of Arizona	M,D
University of California, Los Angeles	M,D
University of California, Santa Cruz	D
University of Chicago	M,D
University of Delaware	M,D
University of Florida	M,D
University of Georgia	M,D
University of Hawaii at Manoa	M,D
University of Illinois at Urbana–Champaign	M,D
The University of Iowa	M
University of Kansas	M,D
University of Kentucky	M,D
University of Maryland, College Park	M,D
University of Massachusetts Amherst	M,D
University of Michigan	M,D
University of Minnesota, Twin Cities Campus	M,D
University of Missouri–Columbia	M,D
University of Nebraska–Lincoln	M,D
The University of North Carolina at Chapel Hill	M,D
University of Rochester	M,D
University of South Carolina	M,D
University of Southern Mississippi	M
The University of Texas at Austin	M,D
University of Virginia	M,D
University of Washington	M,D
University of Wisconsin–Madison	D
Vanderbilt University	M,D
West Chester University of Pennsylvania	M
Yale University	M,D

ASTROPHYSICS

Clemson University	M
Cornell University	D
Harvard University	M,D
Indiana University Bloomington	D
Iowa State University of Science and Technology	M,D
Louisiana State University and Agricultural and Mechanical College	M,D
Michigan State University	M,D
New Mexico Institute of Mining and Technology	M,D
Northwestern University	M,D
The Pennsylvania State University University Park Campus	M,D
Princeton University	D
Rensselaer Polytechnic Institute	M,D
San Francisco State University	M
Texas Christian University	D
University of Alaska Fairbanks	M,D
University of California, Berkeley	D
University of California, Los Angeles	M,D
University of California, Santa Cruz	D
University of Chicago	M,D
University of Colorado at Boulder	M,D
University of Minnesota, Twin Cities Campus	M,D

Directory of Graduate and Professional Programs by Field
Astrophysics

University of Missouri–St. Louis	M,D
The University of North Carolina at Chapel Hill	M,D
University of Oklahoma	M,D
University of Pennsylvania	M,D

■ ATHLETIC TRAINING AND SPORTS MEDICINE

Armstrong Atlantic State University	M
Barry University	M
Brigham Young University	M,D
California University of Pennsylvania	M
Georgia State University	M
Humboldt State University	M
Indiana State University	M,D
Indiana University Bloomington	M,D,O
Long Island University, Brooklyn Campus	M
Montana State University–Billings	M
Ohio University	M
Plymouth State University	M
Seton Hall University	M
Shenandoah University	M
Stephen F. Austin State University	M
University of Florida	D
University of Miami	M
The University of North Carolina at Chapel Hill	M
University of North Florida	M
University of Pittsburgh	M
The University of Tennessee at Chattanooga	M
The University of West Alabama	M
University of Wisconsin–La Crosse	M
West Chester University of Pennsylvania	M
Western Michigan University	M
West Virginia University	M,D

■ ATMOSPHERIC SCIENCES

City College of the City University of New York	M,D
Clemson University	M,D
Colorado State University	M,D
Columbia University	M,D
Cornell University	M,D
Creighton University	M
Georgia Institute of Technology	M,D
Howard University	M,D
Massachusetts Institute of Technology	M,D
New Mexico Institute of Mining and Technology	M,D
North Carolina State University	M,D
The Ohio State University	M,D
Oregon State University	M,D
Princeton University	D
Purdue University	M,D
Rutgers, The State University of New Jersey, New Brunswick/Piscataway	M,D
South Dakota State University	D
Stony Brook University, State University of New York	M,D
Texas Tech University	M,D
University at Albany, State University of New York	M,D
The University of Alabama in Huntsville	M,D
University of Alaska Fairbanks	M,D
The University of Arizona	M,D
University of California, Davis	M,D
University of California, Los Angeles	M,D
University of Chicago	M,D
University of Colorado at Boulder	M,D
University of Delaware	D
University of Illinois at Urbana–Champaign	M,D
University of Maryland, Baltimore County	M,D
University of Miami	M,D

University of Michigan	M,D
University of Missouri–Columbia	M,D
University of Nevada, Reno	M,D
The University of North Carolina at Chapel Hill	M,D
University of North Dakota	M
University of Washington	M,D
University of Wisconsin–Madison	M,D
University of Wyoming	M,D

■ AUTOMOTIVE ENGINEERING

Central Michigan University	M,O
Lawrence Technological University	M,D
University of Detroit Mercy	M,D
University of Michigan	M
University of Michigan–Dearborn	M

■ AVIATION

Central Missouri State University	M
Middle Tennessee State University	M
Saint Louis University	M
University of New Haven	M
University of North Dakota	M
The University of Tennessee	M

■ AVIATION MANAGEMENT

Delta State University	M
Dowling College	M,O
Embry-Riddle Aeronautical University (FL)	M
Embry-Riddle Aeronautical University, Extended Campus	M
Lynn University	M,D

■ BACTERIOLOGY

Purdue University	M,D
The University of Iowa	M,D
University of Washington	M,D
University of Wisconsin–Madison	M
West Virginia University	M,D

■ BIOCHEMICAL ENGINEERING

Bethel University	M,O
California Polytechnic State University, San Luis Obispo	M
Cornell University	M,D
Dartmouth College	M,D
Drexel University	M
Rutgers, The State University of New Jersey, New Brunswick/Piscataway	M,D
University of California, Irvine	M,D
The University of Iowa	M,D
University of Maryland, Baltimore County	M,D
University of Massachusetts Dartmouth	D

■ BIOCHEMISTRY

Arizona State University	M,D
Boston College	M,D
Boston University	M,D
Brandeis University	M,D
Brigham Young University	M,D
Brown University	M,D
California Institute of Technology	D
California State University, Fullerton	M
California State University, Hayward	M
California State University, Long Beach	M
California State University, Los Angeles	M
Carnegie Mellon University	M,D
Case Western Reserve University	M,D
City College of the City University of New York	M,D
Clemson University	M,D
Colorado State University	M,D
Columbia University	M,D
Cornell University	D
Dartmouth College	D
DePaul University	M

Drexel University	M,D
Duke University	D,O
Duquesne University	M,D
East Carolina University	D
East Tennessee State University	M,D
Emory University	D
Florida Atlantic University	M,D
Florida State University	M,D
Georgetown University	M,D
The George Washington University	M,D
Georgia Institute of Technology	M,D
Georgia State University	M,D
Harvard University	M,D
Howard University	M,D
Hunter College of the City University of New York	M
Illinois Institute of Technology	M,D
Indiana University Bloomington	M,D
Indiana University–Purdue University Indianapolis	M,D
Iowa State University of Science and Technology	M,D
The Johns Hopkins University	M,D
Kansas State University	M,D
Kent State University	M,D
Lehigh University	D
Loma Linda University	M
Louisiana State University and Agricultural and Mechanical College	M,D
Loyola University Chicago	M,D
Massachusetts Institute of Technology	D
Mayo Graduate School	D
Miami University	M,D
Michigan State University	M,D
Mississippi State University	M,D
Montana State University–Bozeman	M,D
Montclair State University	M
New Mexico Institute of Mining and Technology	M,D
New Mexico State University	M,D
New York University	M,D
North Carolina State University	M,D
North Dakota State University	M,D
Northeastern University	M,D
Northern Illinois University	M,D
Northern Michigan University	M
Northwestern University	D
The Ohio State University	M,D
Ohio University	M,D
Oklahoma State University	M,D
Old Dominion University	M
Oregon State University	M,D
The Pennsylvania State University University Park Campus	M,D
Purdue University	M,D
Queens College of the City University of New York	M
Rensselaer Polytechnic Institute	M,D
Rice University	M,D
Rutgers, The State University of New Jersey, Newark	M,D
Rutgers, The State University of New Jersey, New Brunswick/Piscataway	M,D
Saint Louis University	D
San Francisco State University	M
Seton Hall University	M,D
South Dakota State University	M,D
Southern Illinois University Carbondale	M,D
Southern University and Agricultural and Mechanical College	M
Stanford University	D
State University of New York College of Environmental Science and Forestry	M,D
Stevens Institute of Technology	M,D,O
Stony Brook University, State University of New York	D
Syracuse University	D

Directory of Graduate and Professional Programs by Field
Biological and Biomedical Sciences—General

Temple University	M,D
Texas A&M University	M,D
Texas State University-San Marcos	M
Tufts University	D
Tulane University	M,D
University at Albany, State University of New York	M,D
University at Buffalo, The State University of New York	M,D
The University of Alabama at Birmingham	D
University of Alaska Fairbanks	M,D
The University of Arizona	M,D
University of California, Berkeley	M,D
University of California, Davis	M,D
University of California, Irvine	M,D
University of California, Los Angeles	M,D
University of California, Riverside	M,D
University of California, San Diego	M,D
University of California, San Francisco	D
University of California, Santa Barbara	D
University of Chicago	D
University of Cincinnati	M,D
University of Colorado at Boulder	M,D
University of Connecticut	M,D
University of Delaware	M,D
University of Detroit Mercy	M
University of Florida	M,D
University of Georgia	M,D
University of Hawaii at Manoa	M,D
University of Houston	M,D
University of Idaho	M,D
University of Illinois at Chicago	M,D
University of Illinois at Urbana–Champaign	M,D
The University of Iowa	M,D
University of Kansas	M,D
University of Kentucky	D
University of Louisville	M,D
University of Maine	M,D
University of Maryland	D
University of Maryland, Baltimore County	D
University of Maryland, College Park	M,D
University of Massachusetts Amherst	M,D
University of Massachusetts Lowell	M,D
University of Miami	D
University of Michigan	D
University of Minnesota, Duluth	M,D
University of Minnesota, Twin Cities Campus	D
University of Missouri–Columbia	M,D
University of Missouri–Kansas City	D
University of Missouri–St. Louis	M,D,O
The University of Montana–Missoula	M,D
University of Nebraska–Lincoln	M,D
University of Nevada, Las Vegas	M,D
University of Nevada, Reno	M,D
University of New Hampshire	M,D
University of New Mexico	M,D
The University of North Carolina at Chapel Hill	M,D
University of North Dakota	M,D
University of North Texas	M,D
University of Notre Dame	M,D
University of Oklahoma	M,D
University of Oregon	M,D
University of Pennsylvania	D
University of Pittsburgh	M,D
University of Rhode Island	M,D
University of Rochester	M,D
The University of Scranton	M
University of South Alabama	D
University of South Carolina	M,D
University of Southern California	M,D
University of Southern Mississippi	M,D
University of South Florida	M,D
The University of Tennessee	M,D
The University of Texas at Austin	M,D
University of Toledo	M,D

University of Utah	M,D
University of Vermont	M,D
University of Virginia	D
University of Washington	D
University of Wisconsin–Madison	M,D
Utah State University	M,D
Vanderbilt University	M,D
Virginia Commonwealth University	M,D,O
Virginia Polytechnic Institute and State University	M,D
Wake Forest University	D
Washington State University	M,D
Washington University in St. Louis	D
Wayne State University	M,D
West Virginia University	M,D
Worcester Polytechnic Institute	M,D
Wright State University	M
Yale University	M,D
Yeshiva University	D

■ **BIOENGINEERING**

Alfred University	M,D
Arizona State University	M,D
California Institute of Technology	M,D
California Polytechnic State University, San Luis Obispo	M
Carnegie Mellon University	M,D
Case Western Reserve University	M,D
Clemson University	M,D
Colorado State University	M,D
Cornell University	M,D
Georgia Institute of Technology	M,D,O
The Johns Hopkins University	M,D
Kansas State University	M,D
Louisiana State University and Agricultural and Mechanical College	M,D
Massachusetts Institute of Technology	M,D
Mississippi State University	M,D
North Carolina State University	M,D
The Ohio State University	M,D
Oklahoma State University	M,D
Oregon State University	M,D
The Pennsylvania State University University Park Campus	M,D
Purdue University	M,D
Rice University	M,D
Rutgers, The State University of New Jersey, New Brunswick/Piscataway	M
Stanford University	M,D
Syracuse University	M,D
Texas A&M University	M,D
Tufts University	O
University at Buffalo, The State University of New York	M,D
University of Arkansas	M,D
University of California, Berkeley	D
University of California, Davis	M,D
University of California, San Diego	M,D
University of California, San Francisco	D
University of Florida	M,D,O
University of Georgia	M,D
University of Hawaii at Manoa	M,D
University of Illinois at Chicago	M,D
University of Maine	M
University of Maryland, College Park	M,D
University of Missouri–Columbia	M,D
University of Nebraska–Lincoln	M
University of Notre Dame	M,D
University of Oklahoma	M,D
University of Pennsylvania	M,D
University of Pittsburgh	M,D
University of Toledo	M,D
University of Utah	M,D
University of Washington	M,D
University of Wisconsin–Madison	M,D
Virginia Polytechnic Institute and State University	M,D

■ **BIOETHICS**

Case Western Reserve University	M,D
Cleveland State University	M,O
Duquesne University	M,D,O
Loma Linda University	M
Michigan State University	M
Saint Louis University	D
University of Pennsylvania	M
University of Pittsburgh	M
The University of Tennessee	M,D
University of Virginia	M

■ **BIOINFORMATICS**

Boston University	M,D
Duke University	D
George Mason University	M,D
The George Washington University	M
Georgia Institute of Technology	M,D
Indiana University Bloomington	M
Iowa State University of Science and Technology	M,D
The Johns Hopkins University	M
Marquette University	M
Morgan State University	M
North Carolina State University	M,D
Northeastern University	M
Northwestern University	M
Polytechnic University, Brooklyn Campus	M
Rochester Institute of Technology	M
Texas Tech University	M,D
University of California, Riverside	D
University of California, San Diego	D
University of California, Santa Cruz	M,D
University of Cincinnati	M,D
University of Idaho	M,D
University of Michigan	M
University of Pittsburgh	M,D,O
University of South Florida	M,D
The University of Texas at El Paso	M
University of Washington	M
Vanderbilt University	M,D
Virginia Polytechnic Institute and State University	D
Yale University	D

■ **BIOLOGICAL AND BIOMEDICAL SCIENCES—GENERAL**

Adelphi University	M
Alabama Agricultural and Mechanical University	M
Alabama State University	M,O
Alcorn State University	M
American University	M
Andrews University	M
Angelo State University	M
Appalachian State University	M
Arizona State University	M,D
Arkansas State University	M,O
Auburn University	M,D
Austin Peay State University	M
Ball State University	M,D
Barry University	M
Baylor University	M,D
Bemidji State University	M
Bloomsburg University of Pennsylvania	M
Boise State University	M
Boston College	M,D
Boston University	M,D
Bowling Green State University	M,D,O
Bradley University	M
Brandeis University	M,D,O
Brigham Young University	M,D
Brooklyn College of the City University of New York	M,D
Brown University	M,D
Buffalo State College, State University of New York	M
California Institute of Technology	D

Peterson's Graduate Schools in the U.S. 2006   *www.petersons.com*   **41**

Directory of Graduate and Professional Programs by Field
Biological and Biomedical Sciences—General

Institution	Degree
California Polytechnic State University, San Luis Obispo	M
California State Polytechnic University, Pomona	M
California State University, Chico	M
California State University, Dominguez Hills	M,O
California State University, Fresno	M
California State University, Fullerton	M
California State University, Hayward	M
California State University, Long Beach	M
California State University, Los Angeles	M
California State University, Northridge	M
California State University, Sacramento	M
California State University, San Bernardino	M
California State University, San Marcos	M
California University of Pennsylvania	M
Carnegie Mellon University	M,D
Case Western Reserve University	M,D
The Catholic University of America	M,D
Central Connecticut State University	M,O
Central Michigan University	M
Central Missouri State University	M
Central Washington University	M
Chicago State University	M
City College of the City University of New York	M,D
Clarion University of Pennsylvania	M
Clark Atlanta University	M,D
Clark University	M,D
Clemson University	M,D
Cleveland State University	M,D
College of Staten Island of the City University of New York	M,D
The College of William and Mary	M
Colorado State University	M,D
Columbia University	M,D
Cornell University	M,D
Creighton University	M,D
Dartmouth College	D
Delaware State University	M
Delta State University	M
DePaul University	M
Drexel University	M,D,O
Duke University	D
Duquesne University	M,D
East Carolina University	M,D
Eastern Illinois University	M
Eastern Kentucky University	M
Eastern Michigan University	M
Eastern New Mexico University	M
Eastern Washington University	M
East Stroudsburg University of Pennsylvania	M
East Tennessee State University	M,D
Edinboro University of Pennsylvania	M
Emory University	D
Emporia State University	M
Fairleigh Dickinson University, College at Florham	M
Fairleigh Dickinson University, Metropolitan Campus	M
Fayetteville State University	M
Florida Agricultural and Mechanical University	M
Florida Atlantic University	M
Florida Institute of Technology	M,D
Florida International University	M,D
Florida State University	P,M,D
Fordham University	M,D
Fort Hays State University	M
Frostburg State University	M
George Mason University	M,D
Georgetown University	M,D
The George Washington University	M,D
Georgia College & State University	M
Georgia Institute of Technology	M,D
Georgian Court University	M,O
Georgia Southern University	M
Georgia State University	M,D
Grand Valley State University	M
Hampton University	M
Harvard University	M,D,O
Hofstra University	M
Hood College	M,O
Howard University	M,D
Humboldt State University	M
Hunter College of the City University of New York	M,D
Idaho State University	M,D
Illinois Institute of Technology	M,D
Illinois State University	M,D
Indiana State University	M,D
Indiana University Bloomington	M,D
Indiana University of Pennsylvania	M
Indiana University–Purdue University Fort Wayne	M
Indiana University–Purdue University Indianapolis	M,D
Iowa State University of Science and Technology	M,D
Jackson State University	M,D
Jacksonville State University	M
James Madison University	M
John Carroll University	M
The Johns Hopkins University	M,D
Kansas State University	M,D
Kent State University	M,D
Lamar University	M
Lehigh University	D
Lehman College of the City University of New York	M,D
Loma Linda University	M,D
Long Island University, Brooklyn Campus	M
Long Island University, C.W. Post Campus	M
Louisiana State University and Agricultural and Mechanical College	M,D
Louisiana Tech University	M
Loyola University Chicago	M
Marquette University	M,D
Marshall University	M
Massachusetts Institute of Technology	P,M,D
Mayo Graduate School	P,D
McNeese State University	M
Miami University	M,D
Michigan State University	M,D
Michigan Technological University	M,D
Middle Tennessee State University	M
Midwestern State University	M
Millersville University of Pennsylvania	M
Minnesota State University Mankato	M
Mississippi College	M
Mississippi State University	M,D
Montana State University–Bozeman	M,D
Montclair State University	M,O
Morehead State University	M
Morgan State University	M
Murray State University	M,D
New Jersey Institute of Technology	M,D
New Mexico Highlands University	M
New Mexico Institute of Mining and Technology	M
New Mexico State University	M,D
New York University	M,D
North Carolina Agricultural and Technical State University	M
North Carolina Central University	M
North Carolina State University	M,D
Northeastern Illinois University	M
Northeastern University	M,D
Northern Arizona University	M,D
Northern Illinois University	M,D
Northern Michigan University	M
Northwestern University	D
Northwest Missouri State University	M
Notre Dame de Namur University	O
Nova Southeastern University	M
Oakland University	M
The Ohio State University	M,D
Ohio University	M,D
Old Dominion University	M,D
The Pennsylvania State University University Park Campus	M,D
Pittsburg State University	M
Portland State University	M,D
Prairie View A&M University	M
Princeton University	D
Purdue University	M,D
Purdue University Calumet	M
Queens College of the City University of New York	M
Quinnipiac University	M
Rensselaer Polytechnic Institute	M,D
Rhode Island College	M
Rochester Institute of Technology	M
The Rockefeller University	D
Rutgers, The State University of New Jersey, Camden	M
Rutgers, The State University of New Jersey, Newark	M,D
St. Cloud State University	M
Saint Francis University	M
St. John's University (NY)	M,D
Saint Joseph College	M
Saint Joseph's University	M
Saint Louis University	M,D
Salem International University	M
Sam Houston State University	M
San Diego State University	M
San Francisco State University	M
San Jose State University	M
Seton Hall University	M,D
Shippensburg University of Pennsylvania	M
Sonoma State University	M
South Dakota State University	M,D
Southeastern Louisiana University	M
Southeast Missouri State University	M
Southern Connecticut State University	M
Southern Illinois University Carbondale	M,D
Southern Illinois University Edwardsville	M
Southern Methodist University	M,D
Southern University and Agricultural and Mechanical College	M
Southwest Missouri State University	M
Stanford University	M,D
State University of New York at Binghamton	M,D
State University of New York at New Paltz	M
State University of New York College at Brockport	M
State University of New York College at Fredonia	M
State University of New York College at Oneonta	M
State University of West Georgia	M
Stephen F. Austin State University	M
Stony Brook University, State University of New York	D
Sul Ross State University	M
Syracuse University	M,D
Tarleton State University	M
Temple University	M,D
Tennessee State University	M,D
Tennessee Technological University	M
Texas A&M International University	M
Texas A&M University	M,D
Texas A&M University–Commerce	M
Texas A&M University–Corpus Christi	M
Texas A&M University–Kingsville	M
Texas Christian University	M

Directory of Graduate and Professional Programs by Field
Biomedical Engineering

Institution	Degree
Texas Southern University	M
Texas State University–San Marcos	M
Texas Tech University	M,D
Texas Woman's University	M,D
Touro College	M
Towson University	M
Truman State University	M
Tufts University	M,D,O
Tulane University	M,D,O
Tuskegee University	M
University at Albany, State University of New York	M,D
University at Buffalo, The State University of New York	M,D
The University of Akron	M
The University of Alabama	M,D
The University of Alabama at Birmingham	M,D
The University of Alabama in Huntsville	M
University of Alaska Anchorage	M
University of Alaska Fairbanks	M,D
The University of Arizona	M,D
University of Arkansas	M,D
University of California, Berkeley	D
University of California, Irvine	M,D
University of California, Los Angeles	M,D
University of California, Riverside	M,D
University of California, San Diego	M,D
University of California, San Francisco	D
University of California, Santa Cruz	M,D
University of Central Arkansas	M
University of Central Florida	M,O
University of Central Oklahoma	M
University of Chicago	M,D
University of Cincinnati	M,D
University of Colorado at Denver	M
University of Connecticut	D
University of Dayton	M
University of Delaware	M,D
University of Denver	M,D
University of Florida	M,D
University of Guam	M
University of Hartford	M
University of Hawaii at Manoa	M,D
University of Houston	M,D
University of Houston–Clear Lake	M
University of Idaho	M
University of Illinois at Chicago	M,D
University of Illinois at Springfield	M
University of Illinois at Urbana–Champaign	M,D
University of Indianapolis	M
The University of Iowa	M,D
University of Kansas	M,D
University of Kentucky	M,D
University of Louisiana at Lafayette	M,D
University of Louisiana at Monroe	M
University of Louisville	M
University of Maine	D
University of Maryland	M,D
University of Maryland, Baltimore County	M,D
University of Maryland, College Park	M,D
University of Massachusetts Amherst	M,D
University of Massachusetts Boston	M
University of Massachusetts Dartmouth	M
University of Massachusetts Lowell	M,D
The University of Memphis	M,D
University of Miami	M,D
University of Michigan	M,D
University of Michigan–Flint	M
University of Minnesota, Duluth	M
University of Minnesota, Twin Cities Campus	M,D
University of Mississippi	M,D
University of Missouri–Columbia	M,D
University of Missouri–Kansas City	M,D
University of Missouri–Rolla	M
University of Missouri–St. Louis	M,D,O
The University of Montana–Missoula	M,D
University of Nebraska at Kearney	M
University of Nebraska at Omaha	M
University of Nebraska–Lincoln	M,D
University of Nevada, Las Vegas	M,D
University of Nevada, Reno	M,D
University of New Mexico	M,D
University of New Orleans	M,D
The University of North Carolina at Chapel Hill	M,D
The University of North Carolina at Charlotte	M,D
The University of North Carolina at Greensboro	M
The University of North Carolina at Wilmington	M,D
University of North Dakota	M,D
University of Northern Colorado	M,D
University of Northern Iowa	M
University of North Florida	M
University of North Texas	M,D
University of Notre Dame	M,D
University of Oregon	M,D
University of Pennsylvania	M,D
University of Pittsburgh	M,D
University of Puerto Rico, Mayagüez Campus	M
University of Puerto Rico, Río Piedras	M,D
University of Rhode Island	M,D
University of Richmond	M
University of Rochester	M,D
University of San Francisco	M
University of South Alabama	M,D
University of South Carolina	M,D,O
The University of South Dakota	M,D
University of Southern California	M,D
University of Southern Maine	M
University of Southern Mississippi	M,D
University of South Florida	M,D
The University of Tennessee	M,D
The University of Texas at Arlington	M,D
The University of Texas at Austin	M,D
The University of Texas at Brownsville	M
The University of Texas at El Paso	M,D
The University of Texas at San Antonio	M,D
The University of Texas at Tyler	M
The University of Texas of the Permian Basin	M
The University of Texas–Pan American	M
University of the Incarnate Word	M
University of the Pacific	M
University of Toledo	M,D
University of Tulsa	M
University of Utah	M,D
University of Vermont	M,D
University of Virginia	M,D
University of Washington	M,D
University of West Florida	M
University of Wisconsin–Eau Claire	M
University of Wisconsin–La Crosse	M
University of Wisconsin–Madison	M,D
University of Wisconsin–Milwaukee	M,D
University of Wisconsin–Oshkosh	M
Utah State University	M,D
Vanderbilt University	M,D
Villanova University	M
Virginia Commonwealth University	M,D,O
Virginia Polytechnic Institute and State University	M,D
Virginia State University	M
Wagner College	M
Wake Forest University	M,D
Walla Walla College	M
Washington State University	M,D
Washington University in St. Louis	D
Wayne State University	M,D,O
West Chester University of Pennsylvania	M
Western Carolina University	M
Western Connecticut State University	M
Western Illinois University	M,O
Western Kentucky University	M
Western Michigan University	M,D
Western Washington University	M
West Texas A&M University	M
West Virginia University	M,D
Wichita State University	M
William Paterson University of New Jersey	M
Winthrop University	M
Worcester Polytechnic Institute	M,D
Wright State University	M,D
Yale University	D
Yeshiva University	D
Youngstown State University	M

■ BIOMEDICAL ENGINEERING

Institution	Degree
Arizona State University	M,D
Boston University	M,D
Brown University	M,D
California Polytechnic State University, San Luis Obispo	M
California State University, Northridge	M
Carnegie Mellon University	M,D
Case Western Reserve University	M,D
The Catholic University of America	M,D
City College of the City University of New York	M,D
Clemson University	M,D
Cleveland State University	D
Colorado State University	M,D
Columbia University	M,D
Cornell University	M,D
Dartmouth College	M,D
Drexel University	M,D
Duke University	M,D
Florida Agricultural and Mechanical University	M,D
Florida International University	M
Georgia Institute of Technology	M,D,O
Harvard University	M,D
Illinois Institute of Technology	D
Indiana University–Purdue University Indianapolis	M,D
The Johns Hopkins University	M,D
Louisiana Tech University	M,D
Marquette University	M,D
Massachusetts Institute of Technology	M,D,O
Mayo Graduate School	D
Mercer University	M
Mississippi State University	M,D
New Jersey Institute of Technology	M,D
North Carolina State University	M,D
Northwestern University	M,D
The Ohio State University	M,D
The Pennsylvania State University University Park Campus	M,D
Polytechnic University, Brooklyn Campus	M
Purdue University	M,D
Rensselaer Polytechnic Institute	M,D
Rice University	M,D
Rutgers, The State University of New Jersey, New Brunswick/Piscataway	M,D
Stanford University	M
Stony Brook University, State University of New York	M,D,O
Syracuse University	M,D
Texas A&M University	M,D
Tufts University	M,D
Tulane University	M,D
The University of Akron	M,D
The University of Alabama at Birmingham	M,D
University of California, Berkeley	D
University of California, Davis	M,D
University of California, Irvine	M
University of California, Los Angeles	M,D
University of California, San Diego	M,D

Peterson's Graduate Schools in the U.S. 2006

Directory of Graduate and Professional Programs by Field
Biomedical Engineering

University of California, San Francisco	D
University of Cincinnati	M,D
University of Connecticut	M,D
University of Florida	M,D,O
University of Houston	M,D
University of Illinois at Chicago	M,D
The University of Iowa	M,D
University of Kentucky	M,D
The University of Memphis	M,D
University of Miami	M,D
University of Michigan	M,D
University of Minnesota, Twin Cities Campus	M,D
University of Nevada, Reno	M,D
The University of North Carolina at Chapel Hill	M,D
University of Pennsylvania	M,D
University of Pittsburgh	M,D
University of Rochester	M,D
University of Southern California	M,D
University of South Florida	M
The University of Tennessee	M,D
The University of Texas at Arlington	M,D
The University of Texas at Austin	M,D
The University of Texas at San Antonio	M,D
University of Utah	M,D
University of Vermont	M
University of Virginia	M,D
University of Washington	M,D
University of Wisconsin–Madison	M,D
Vanderbilt University	M,D
Virginia Commonwealth University	M,D
Virginia Polytechnic Institute and State University	M,D
Wake Forest University	D
Washington University in St. Louis	M,D
Wayne State University	M,D
Worcester Polytechnic Institute	M,D,O
Wright State University	M

■ **BIOMETRICS**

Cornell University	M,D
North Carolina State University	M,D
Oregon State University	M,D
San Diego State University	D
University at Albany, State University of New York	M,D
The University of Alabama at Birmingham	M,D
University of California, Los Angeles	M,D
University of Nebraska–Lincoln	M
University of Southern California	M
University of Wisconsin–Madison	M

■ **BIOPHYSICS**

Boston University	M,D
Brandeis University	D
California Institute of Technology	D
Carnegie Mellon University	M,D
Case Western Reserve University	M,D
Clemson University	M,D
Columbia University	M,D
Cornell University	D
Duke University	O
East Carolina University	M,D
East Tennessee State University	M,D
Emory University	D
Florida State University	D
Georgetown University	M,D
Harvard University	D
Howard University	D
Illinois Institute of Technology	M,D
Indiana University–Purdue University Indianapolis	M,D
Iowa State University of Science and Technology	M,D
The Johns Hopkins University	M,D
Massachusetts Institute of Technology	D
Northwestern University	D
The Ohio State University	M,D
Oregon State University	M,D
Princeton University	D
Purdue University	D
Rensselaer Polytechnic Institute	M,D
Stanford University	D
Stony Brook University, State University of New York	D
Syracuse University	D
Texas A&M University	M,D
University at Buffalo, The State University of New York	M,D
The University of Alabama at Birmingham	D
University of California, Berkeley	D
University of California, Davis	M,D
University of California, Irvine	D
University of California, San Diego	M,D
University of California, San Francisco	D
University of Cincinnati	D
University of Connecticut	D
University of Hawaii at Manoa	M,D
University of Illinois at Chicago	M,D
University of Illinois at Urbana–Champaign	D
The University of Iowa	M,D
University of Kansas	M,D
University of Louisville	M,D
University of Maryland, College Park	D
University of Miami	D
University of Michigan	D
University of Minnesota, Twin Cities Campus	M,D
University of Missouri–Kansas City	D
The University of North Carolina at Chapel Hill	M,D
University of Pennsylvania	D
University of Pittsburgh	D
University of Rochester	M,D
University of Southern California	M,D
University of South Florida	M,D
University of Vermont	M,D
University of Virginia	M,D
University of Washington	D
University of Wisconsin–Madison	D
Vanderbilt University	D
Virginia Commonwealth University	M,D,O
Washington State University	M,D
Washington University in St. Louis	D
Wright State University	M
Yale University	M,D
Yeshiva University	D

■ **BIOPSYCHOLOGY**

American University	M
Boston University	M
Carnegie Mellon University	D
Columbia University	M,D
Cornell University	D
Drexel University	M,D
Duke University	D
Emory University	D
Harvard University	M,D
Howard University	M,D
Hunter College of the City University of New York	M
Indiana University–Purdue University Indianapolis	M,D
Louisiana State University and Agricultural and Mechanical College	M,D
Northwestern University	D
The Ohio State University	D
The Pennsylvania State University University Park Campus	M,D
Rutgers, The State University of New Jersey, Newark	D
Rutgers, The State University of New Jersey, New Brunswick/Piscataway	D
State University of New York at Binghamton	M,D
Stony Brook University, State University of New York	D
Texas A&M University	D
University at Albany, State University of New York	M,D
University of Colorado at Boulder	M,D
University of Illinois at Urbana–Champaign	M,D
University of Michigan	D
University of Minnesota, Twin Cities Campus	D
University of Missouri–Columbia	M,D
University of Oregon	M,D
University of Wisconsin–Madison	D

■ **BIOSTATISTICS**

Arizona State University	M,D
Boston University	M,D
Brown University	M,D
Case Western Reserve University	M,D
Columbia University	M,D
Drexel University	M,D
Emory University	M,D
Georgetown University	M
The George Washington University	M,D
Harvard University	M,D
Iowa State University of Science and Technology	M,D
The Johns Hopkins University	M,D
Loma Linda University	M
Northwestern University	M
The Ohio State University	D
Rice University	M,D
Rutgers, The State University of New Jersey, New Brunswick/Piscataway	M,D
Saint Louis University	M
San Diego State University	M,D
Tufts University	M,D
Tulane University	M,D
University at Buffalo, The State University of New York	M,D
The University of Alabama at Birmingham	M,D
University of California, Berkeley	M,D
University of California, Davis	M,D
University of California, Los Angeles	M,D
University of Cincinnati	M,D
University of Illinois at Chicago	M,D
The University of Iowa	M,D
University of Louisville	M,D
University of Michigan	M,D
University of Minnesota, Twin Cities Campus	M,D
The University of North Carolina at Chapel Hill	M,D
University of Pennsylvania	M,D
University of Pittsburgh	M,D
University of Rochester	M,D
University of South Carolina	M,D
University of Southern California	M,D
University of South Florida	M,D
University of Utah	M,D
University of Vermont	M
University of Washington	M,D
Virginia Commonwealth University	M,D
Western Michigan University	M
Yale University	M,D

■ **BIOTECHNOLOGY**

Brown University	M,D
Dartmouth College	M,D
East Carolina University	M
Florida Institute of Technology	M,D
Howard University	M,D
Illinois Institute of Technology	M,D
Illinois State University	M
The Johns Hopkins University	M
Kean University	M

Directory of Graduate and Professional Programs by Field
Business Administration and Management—General

Northeastern University	M,D
Northwestern University	D
The Pennsylvania State University Great Valley Campus	M
The Pennsylvania State University University Park Campus	M
Roosevelt University	M
Salem International University	M
Stephen F. Austin State University	M
Texas A&M University	M
Texas Tech University	M,D
Tufts University	O
University at Albany, State University of New York	M,D
The University of Alabama in Huntsville	M,D
University of California, Irvine	M
University of Connecticut	M,D
University of Delaware	M,D
University of Illinois at Chicago	M,D
University of Maryland University College	M,O
University of Massachusetts Amherst	M,D
University of Massachusetts Boston	M
University of Massachusetts Dartmouth	D
University of Massachusetts Lowell	M,D
University of Minnesota, Twin Cities Campus	M
University of Missouri–St. Louis	M,D,O
University of Pennsylvania	M
The University of Texas at San Antonio	M
University of Washington	D
William Paterson University of New Jersey	M
Worcester Polytechnic Institute	M,D
Worcester State College	M

■ **BOTANY**

Auburn University	M,D
California State University, Chico	M
California State University, Fullerton	M
Claremont Graduate University	M,D
Colorado State University	M,D
Emporia State University	M
Illinois State University	M,D
Kent State University	M
Miami University	M,D
Michigan State University	M,D
North Carolina State University	M,D
North Dakota State University	M,D
Oklahoma State University	M,D
Oregon State University	M,D
Purdue University	M,D
Texas A&M University	M,D
University of Alaska Fairbanks	M,D
University of California, Riverside	M,D
University of Connecticut	M,D
University of Florida	M,D
University of Hawaii at Manoa	M,D
University of Kansas	M,D
University of Maine	M
University of Missouri–St. Louis	M,D,O
The University of North Carolina at Chapel Hill	M,D
University of North Dakota	M,D
University of Oklahoma	M,D
University of South Florida	M,D
The University of Tennessee	M,D
University of Vermont	M,D
University of Washington	M,D
University of Wisconsin–Madison	M,D
University of Wisconsin–Oshkosh	M
University of Wyoming	M,D
Virginia Polytechnic Institute and State University	M,D
Washington State University	M

■ **BUILDING SCIENCE**

Arizona State University	M

Auburn University	M
Carnegie Mellon University	M,D
Colorado State University	M
Cornell University	M,D
Georgia Institute of Technology	M,D
Rensselaer Polytechnic Institute	M
University of California, Berkeley	M,D
University of Florida	M
University of Southern California	M,O

■ **BUSINESS ADMINISTRATION AND MANAGEMENT—GENERAL**

Adelphi University	M,O
Alabama Agricultural and Mechanical University	M
Alabama State University	M
Alaska Pacific University	M
Albany State University	M
Alcorn State University	M
Alfred University	M
American International College	M
American University	M,O
Anderson University	M,D
Andrews University	M
Angelo State University	M
Anna Maria College	M,O
Antioch New England Graduate School	M
Antioch University Los Angeles	M
Antioch University McGregor	M
Antioch University Seattle	M
Appalachian State University	M
Aquinas College	M
Argosy University/Sarasota	M,D
Argosy University/Schaumburg	M,D
Arizona State University	M,D
Arizona State University West	M
Arkansas State University	M,O
Ashland University	M
Assumption College	M,O
Auburn University	M,D
Auburn University Montgomery	M
Augusta State University	M
Aurora University	M
Averett University	M
Avila University	M
Azusa Pacific University	M
Baker University	M
Baldwin-Wallace College	M
Ball State University	M
Barry University	M,O
Bayamón Central University	M
Baylor University	M
Bellarmine University	M
Bellevue University	M
Belmont University	M
Benedictine College	M
Benedictine University	M
Bentley College	M,O
Bernard M. Baruch College of the City University of New York	M,D,O
Biola University	M
Bloomsburg University of Pennsylvania	M
Boise State University	M
Boston College	M
Boston University	M,D,O
Bowie State University	M
Bowling Green State University	M
Bradley University	M
Brandeis University	M
Brenau University	M
Bridgewater State College	M
Brigham Young University	M
Butler University	M
California Baptist University	M
California Lutheran University	M
California Polytechnic State University, San Luis Obispo	M

California State Polytechnic University, Pomona	M
California State University, Bakersfield	M
California State University, Chico	M
California State University, Dominguez Hills	M
California State University, Fresno	M
California State University, Fullerton	M
California State University, Hayward	M
California State University, Long Beach	M
California State University, Los Angeles	M
California State University, Sacramento	M
California State University, San Bernardino	M
California State University, San Marcos	M
California State University, Stanislaus	M
California University of Pennsylvania	M
Cameron University	M
Campbellsville University	M
Campbell University	M
Canisius College	M
Capital University	M
Cardinal Stritch University	M
Carnegie Mellon University	M,D
Case Western Reserve University	M,D,O
The Catholic University of America	M
Centenary College of Louisiana	M
Central Connecticut State University	M
Central Michigan University	M
Central Missouri State University	M
Central Washington University	M
Chadron State College	M
Chaminade University of Honolulu	M
Chapman University	M,O
Charleston Southern University	M
Christian Brothers University	M
The Citadel, The Military College of South Carolina	M
City University	M,O
Claremont Graduate University	M,D,O
Clarion University of Pennsylvania	M
Clark Atlanta University	M
Clarkson University	M
Clark University	M
Clemson University	M,D
Cleveland State University	M,D,O
College of Charleston	M
College of Notre Dame of Maryland	M
College of St. Joseph	M
The College of Saint Rose	M
The College of St. Scholastica	M
College of Santa Fe	M
The College of William and Mary	M
Colorado Christian University	M
Colorado State University	M
Colorado State University-Pueblo	M
Colorado Technical University	M,D
Columbia University	M,D
Columbus State University	M
Concordia University (CA)	M
Concordia University Wisconsin	M
Cornell University	M,D
Creighton University	M
Cumberland University	M
Dallas Baptist University	M
Dartmouth College	M
Delaware State University	M
Delta State University	M
DePaul University	M
DeSales University	M
Doane College	M
Dominican University	M
Dominican University of California	M
Dowling College	M,O
Drake University	M
Drexel University	M,D,O
Drury University	M
Duke University	M,D

Peterson's Graduate Schools in the U.S. 2006 *www.petersons.com* 45

Directory of Graduate and Professional Programs by Field
Business Administration and Management—General

Institution	Degree
Duquesne University	M
East Carolina University	M,D,O
Eastern Illinois University	M,O
Eastern Kentucky University	M
Eastern Michigan University	M
Eastern New Mexico University	M
Eastern University	M
Eastern Washington University	M
East Tennessee State University	M,O
Edgewood College	M
Elon University	M
Embry-Riddle Aeronautical University (FL)	M
Emmanuel College	M
Emory University	M,D
Emporia State University	M
Fairfield University	M,O
Fairleigh Dickinson University, College at Florham	M,O
Fairleigh Dickinson University, Metropolitan Campus	M,O
Fayetteville State University	M
Ferris State University	M
Fitchburg State College	M
Florida Agricultural and Mechanical University	M
Florida Atlantic University	M,D
Florida Gulf Coast University	M
Florida Institute of Technology	M
Florida International University	M,D
Florida Metropolitan University–Brandon Campus	M
Florida Metropolitan University–North Orlando Campus	M
Florida Metropolitan University–Pinellas Campus	M
Florida Metropolitan University–South Orlando Campus	M
Florida Metropolitan University–Tampa Campus	M
Florida State University	M,D
Fontbonne University	M
Fordham University	M
Fort Hays State University	M
Framingham State College	M
Franciscan University of Steubenville	M
Francis Marion University	M
Fresno Pacific University	M
Friends University	M
Frostburg State University	M
Gannon University	M,O
Gardner-Webb University	M
Geneva College	M
George Fox University	M
George Mason University	M
Georgetown University	M
The George Washington University	M,D
Georgia College & State University	M
Georgia Institute of Technology	M,D,O
Georgian Court University	M
Georgia Southern University	M
Georgia Southwestern State University	M
Georgia State University	M,D
Gonzaga University	M
Governors State University	M
Grand Canyon University	M
Grand Valley State University	M
Hamline University	M
Hampton University	M
Harding University	M
Hardin-Simmons University	M
Harvard University	M,D,O
Hawai'i Pacific University	M
Heidelberg College	M
Henderson State University	M
Hofstra University	M,O
Holy Family University	M
Holy Names University	M
Hood College	M
Houston Baptist University	M
Howard University	M
Humboldt State University	M
Husson College	M
Idaho State University	M,O
Illinois Institute of Technology	M,D
Illinois State University	M
Indiana State University	M
Indiana University Bloomington	M,D
Indiana University Northwest	M,O
Indiana University of Pennsylvania	M
Indiana University–Purdue University Fort Wayne	M
Indiana University–Purdue University Indianapolis	M
Indiana University South Bend	M
Indiana University Southeast	M,O
Indiana Wesleyan University	M,D,O
Inter American University of Puerto Rico, San Germán Campus	M,D
Iona College	M,O
Iowa State University of Science and Technology	M
Ithaca College	M
Jackson State University	M,D
Jacksonville State University	M
Jacksonville University	M
James Madison University	M
John Carroll University	M
John F. Kennedy University	M,O
The Johns Hopkins University	M,O
Kansas State University	M
Kean University	M,O
Kennesaw State University	M
Kent State University	M
King's College	M
Kutztown University of Pennsylvania	M
Lake Erie College	M
Lamar University	M
La Salle University	M,O
La Sierra University	M,O
Lawrence Technological University	M,D
Lebanon Valley College	M
Lehigh University	M,D,O
Le Moyne College	M
LeTourneau University	M
Lewis University	M
Liberty University	M
Lincoln Memorial University	M
Lincoln University (MO)	M
Lindenwood University	M
Lipscomb University	M
Long Island University, Brooklyn Campus	M
Long Island University, C.W. Post Campus	M,O
Louisiana State University and Agricultural and Mechanical College	M,D
Louisiana State University in Shreveport	M
Louisiana Tech University	M,D
Loyola College in Maryland	M
Loyola Marymount University	M
Loyola University Chicago	M
Loyola University New Orleans	M
Lynchburg College	M
Lynn University	M,D
Madonna University	M
Maharishi University of Management	M,D
Malone College	M
Marian College of Fond du Lac	M
Marist College	M,O
Marquette University	M
Marshall University	M
Marylhurst University	M
Marymount University	M,O
Maryville University of Saint Louis	M,O
Marywood University	M
Massachusetts Institute of Technology	M,D
McNeese State University	M
Mercer University	M
Mercy College	M
Meredith College	M
Metropolitan State University	M
Miami University	M
Michigan State University	M,D
Michigan Technological University	M
MidAmerica Nazarene University	M
Middle Tennessee State University	M
Midwestern State University	M
Millersville University of Pennsylvania	M
Minot State University	M
Mississippi College	M
Mississippi State University	M,D
Monmouth University	M,O
Montclair State University	M
Monterey Institute of International Studies	M
Morehead State University	M
Morgan State University	M,D
Mount Saint Mary College	M
Mount Saint Mary's University	M
Murray State University	M
National-Louis University	M
National University	M
Nazareth College of Rochester	M
New Jersey Institute of Technology	M
Newman University	M
New Mexico Highlands University	M
New Mexico State University	M,D
New School University	M,D,O
New York Institute of Technology	M,O
New York University	P,M,D,O
Niagara University	M
Nicholls State University	M
North Carolina Central University	M
North Carolina State University	M
North Central College	M
North Dakota State University	M
Northeastern Illinois University	M
Northeastern State University	M
Northeastern University	M,O
Northern Arizona University	M
Northern Illinois University	M
Northern Kentucky University	M
North Park University	M
Northwestern University	M
Northwest Missouri State University	M
Northwest Nazarene University	M
Norwich University	M
Notre Dame de Namur University	M
Nova Southeastern University	M,D
Nyack College	M
Oakland City University	M
Oakland University	M,O
The Ohio State University	M,D
Ohio University	M
Oklahoma City University	M
Oklahoma State University	M,D
Old Dominion University	M,D
Olivet Nazarene University	M
Oral Roberts University	M
Oregon State University	M,O
Our Lady of the Lake University of San Antonio	M
Pace University	M,D,O
Pace University, White Plains Campus	M,O
Pacific Lutheran University	M
Palm Beach Atlantic University	M
Park University	M
The Pennsylvania State University at Erie, The Behrend College	M
The Pennsylvania State University Great Valley Campus	M
The Pennsylvania State University Harrisburg Campus of the Capital College	M
The Pennsylvania State University University Park Campus	M,D
Pepperdine University	M

Directory of Graduate and Professional Programs by Field
Business Administration and Management—General

Institution	Degree
Pfeiffer University	M
Philadelphia University	M
Piedmont College	M
Pittsburg State University	M
Plymouth State University	M
Point Loma Nazarene University	M
Point Park University	M
Polytechnic University, Brooklyn Campus	M
Polytechnic University, Westchester Graduate Center	M
Pontifical Catholic University of Puerto Rico	M,D
Portland State University	M,D,O
Prairie View A&M University	M
Providence College	M
Purdue University	M,D
Purdue University Calumet	M
Queens University of Charlotte	M
Quincy University	M
Quinnipiac University	M
Radford University	M
Regent University	M
Regis College (MA)	M
Regis University	M,O
Rensselaer Polytechnic Institute	M,D
Rice University	M
Rider University	M
Rivier College	M
Robert Morris University	M
Roberts Wesleyan College	M
Rochester Institute of Technology	M
Rockford College	M
Rockhurst University	M
Rollins College	M
Roosevelt University	M
Rowan University	M
Rutgers, The State University of New Jersey, Camden	M
Rutgers, The State University of New Jersey, Newark	M,D,O
Sacred Heart University	M
Sage Graduate School	M
Saginaw Valley State University	M
St. Ambrose University	M,D
St. Bonaventure University	M,O
St. Cloud State University	M
St. Edward's University	M,O
Saint Francis University	M
St. John Fisher College	M
St. John's University (NY)	M,O
Saint Joseph's College of Maine	M
Saint Joseph's University	M,O
Saint Leo University	M
Saint Louis University	M,D
Saint Martin's College	M
Saint Mary's College of California	M
Saint Mary's University of Minnesota	M,O
St. Mary's University of San Antonio	M
Saint Michael's College	M,O
Saint Peter's College	M
St. Thomas Aquinas College	M
St. Thomas University	M,O
Saint Xavier University	M,O
Salem International University	M
Salem State College	M
Salisbury University	M
Salve Regina University	M,O
Samford University	M
Sam Houston State University	M
San Diego State University	M
San Francisco State University	M
San Jose State University	M
Santa Clara University	M
School for International Training	M,O
Seattle Pacific University	M
Seattle University	M,O
Seton Hall University	M,O
Shenandoah University	M,O
Shippensburg University of Pennsylvania	M
Silver Lake College	M
Simmons College	M
Slippery Rock University of Pennsylvania	M
Sonoma State University	M
Southeastern Louisiana University	M
Southeastern Oklahoma State University	M
Southeastern University	M
Southeast Missouri State University	M
Southern Connecticut State University	M
Southern Illinois University Carbondale	M,D
Southern Illinois University Edwardsville	M
Southern Methodist University	M
Southern Nazarene University	M
Southern Oregon University	M
Southern University and Agricultural and Mechanical College	M
Southern Utah University	M
Southern Wesleyan University	M
Southwest Baptist University	M
Southwestern Oklahoma State University	M
Southwest Missouri State University	M
Spalding University	M
Spring Arbor University	M
Spring Hill College	M
Stanford University	M,D
State University of New York at Binghamton	M,D
State University of New York at New Paltz	M
State University of New York at Oswego	M
State University of New York Empire State College	M
State University of New York Institute of Technology	M
State University of West Georgia	M
Stephen F. Austin State University	M
Stetson University	M
Stevens Institute of Technology	M,D,O
Stony Brook University, State University of New York	M,O
Strayer University	M
Suffolk University	M,O
Sul Ross State University	M
Syracuse University	M,D
Tarleton State University	M
Temple University	M,D
Tennessee State University	M
Tennessee Technological University	M
Texas A&M International University	M
Texas A&M University	M,D
Texas A&M University–Commerce	M
Texas A&M University–Corpus Christi	M
Texas A&M University–Kingsville	M
Texas A&M University–Texarkana	M
Texas Christian University	M,D
Texas Southern University	M
Texas State University-San Marcos	M
Texas Tech University	M,D,O
Texas Wesleyan University	M
Texas Woman's University	M
Thomas Edison State College	M
Trevecca Nazarene University	M
Trinity College (DC)	M
Trinity University	M
Troy University	M
Troy University Dothan	M
Troy University Montgomery	M
Tulane University	M,D
Union University	M
Universidad del Turabo	M
Universidad Metropolitana	M,O
University at Albany, State University of New York	M,D
University at Buffalo, The State University of New York	M,D
The University of Akron	M
The University of Alabama	M,D
The University of Alabama at Birmingham	M,D
The University of Alabama in Huntsville	M,O
University of Alaska Anchorage	M
University of Alaska Fairbanks	M
The University of Arizona	M,D
University of Arkansas	M,D
University of Arkansas at Little Rock	M
University of Baltimore	M
University of Bridgeport	M
University of California, Berkeley	M,D
University of California, Davis	M
University of California, Irvine	M,D
University of California, Los Angeles	M,D
University of California, Riverside	M
University of Central Arkansas	M
University of Central Florida	M,D
University of Central Oklahoma	M
University of Chicago	M,D
University of Cincinnati	M,D
University of Colorado at Boulder	M,D
University of Colorado at Colorado Springs	M
University of Colorado at Denver	M
University of Connecticut	M,D
University of Dayton	M
University of Delaware	M,D
University of Denver	M,O
University of Detroit Mercy	M
University of Dubuque	M
The University of Findlay	M
University of Florida	M
University of Georgia	M,D
University of Guam	M
University of Hartford	M
University of Hawaii at Manoa	M
University of Houston	M,D
University of Houston–Clear Lake	M
University of Houston–Victoria	M
University of Idaho	M
University of Illinois at Chicago	M,D
University of Illinois at Springfield	M
University of Illinois at Urbana–Champaign	M,D
University of Indianapolis	M
The University of Iowa	M,D
University of Kansas	M,D
University of Kentucky	M,D
University of La Verne	M
University of Louisiana at Lafayette	M
University of Louisiana at Monroe	M
University of Louisville	M
University of Maine	M
University of Mary	M
University of Mary Hardin-Baylor	M
University of Maryland, College Park	M,D
University of Maryland University College	M,D,O
University of Massachusetts Amherst	M,D
University of Massachusetts Boston	M
University of Massachusetts Dartmouth	M,O
University of Massachusetts Lowell	M
The University of Memphis	M,D
University of Miami	M,D
University of Michigan	D
University of Michigan–Dearborn	M
University of Michigan–Flint	M
University of Minnesota, Duluth	M
University of Minnesota, Twin Cities Campus	M,D
University of Mississippi	M,D
University of Missouri–Columbia	M,D
University of Missouri–Kansas City	M,D

Business Administration and Management—General

Institution	Degrees
University of Missouri–St. Louis	M,O
University of Mobile	M
The University of Montana–Missoula	M
University of Nebraska at Kearney	M
University of Nebraska at Omaha	M
University of Nebraska–Lincoln	M,D
University of Nevada, Las Vegas	M
University of Nevada, Reno	M
University of New Hampshire	M
University of New Haven	M
University of New Mexico	M
University of New Orleans	M
University of North Alabama	M
The University of North Carolina at Chapel Hill	M,D
The University of North Carolina at Charlotte	M
The University of North Carolina at Greensboro	M,O
The University of North Carolina at Pembroke	M
The University of North Carolina at Wilmington	M
University of North Dakota	M
University of Northern Iowa	M
University of North Florida	M
University of North Texas	M,D
University of Notre Dame	M
University of Oklahoma	M,D
University of Oregon	M,D
University of Pennsylvania	M,D
University of Pittsburgh	M,D
University of Portland	M
University of Puerto Rico, Mayagüez Campus	M
University of Puerto Rico, Río Piedras	M,D
University of Redlands	M
University of Rhode Island	M,D
University of Richmond	M
University of Rochester	M,D
University of St. Francis (IL)	M
University of Saint Francis (IN)	M
University of Saint Mary	M
University of St. Thomas (MN)	M
University of St. Thomas (TX)	M
University of San Diego	M,O
University of San Francisco	M
The University of Scranton	M
University of Sioux Falls	M
University of South Alabama	M
University of South Carolina	M,D
The University of South Dakota	M
University of Southern California	M,D
University of Southern Indiana	M
University of Southern Maine	M
University of Southern Mississippi	M
University of South Florida	M
The University of Tampa	M
The University of Tennessee	M,D
The University of Tennessee at Chattanooga	M
The University of Tennessee at Martin	M
The University of Texas at Arlington	M,D
The University of Texas at Austin	M,D
The University of Texas at Brownsville	M
The University of Texas at Dallas	M,D
The University of Texas at El Paso	M
The University of Texas at San Antonio	M,D
The University of Texas at Tyler	M
The University of Texas of the Permian Basin	M
The University of Texas–Pan American	M,D
University of the District of Columbia	M
University of the Incarnate Word	M
University of the Pacific	M
University of the Sacred Heart	M
University of the Virgin Islands	M
University of Toledo	M,D
University of Tulsa	M
University of Utah	M,D
University of Vermont	M
University of Virginia	M,D
University of Washington	M,D
University of West Florida	M
University of Wisconsin–Eau Claire	M
University of Wisconsin–Green Bay	M
University of Wisconsin–La Crosse	M
University of Wisconsin–Madison	M,D
University of Wisconsin–Milwaukee	M,D
University of Wisconsin–Oshkosh	M
University of Wisconsin–Parkside	M
University of Wisconsin–River Falls	M
University of Wisconsin–Stevens Point	M
University of Wisconsin–Whitewater	M
University of Wyoming	M
Ursuline College	M
Utah State University	M
Valdosta State University	M
Valparaiso University	M
Vanderbilt University	M,D
Villanova University	M
Virginia Commonwealth University	M,D,O
Virginia Polytechnic Institute and State University	M,D
Virginia State University	M
Wagner College	M
Wake Forest University	M
Walden University	M,D
Walsh University	M
Washburn University	M
Washington State University	M,D
Washington University in St. Louis	M,D
Wayland Baptist University	M
Waynesburg College	M
Wayne State College	M
Wayne State University	M
Weber State University	M
Webster University	M,D
West Chester University of Pennsylvania	M
Western Carolina University	M
Western Connecticut State University	M
Western Illinois University	M
Western International University	M
Western Kentucky University	M
Western Michigan University	M
Western New England College	M
Western New Mexico University	M
Western Washington University	M
Westminster College (UT)	M,O
West Texas A&M University	M
West Virginia University	M
Wheeling Jesuit University	M
Whitworth College	M
Wichita State University	M
Widener University	M
Wilkes University	M
William Carey College	M
William Paterson University of New Jersey	M
William Woods University	M
Wilmington College (DE)	M
Winthrop University	M
Woodbury University	M
Worcester Polytechnic Institute	M,O
Wright State University	M
Xavier University	M
Yale University	M,D
York College of Pennsylvania	M
Youngstown State University	M

■ BUSINESS EDUCATION

Institution	Degrees
Albany State University	M
Arkansas State University	M,O
Armstrong Atlantic State University	M
Ashland University	M
Auburn University	M,D,O
Ball State University	M
Bloomsburg University of Pennsylvania	M
Bowling Green State University	M
Buffalo State College, State University of New York	M
Central Connecticut State University	M
Central Michigan University	M
Central Washington University	M
Chadron State College	M,O
The College of Saint Rose	M,O
Drake University	M
Eastern Kentucky University	M
Eastern Michigan University	M
Emporia State University	M
Florida Agricultural and Mechanical University	M
Georgia Southern University	M
Georgia Southwestern State University	M,O
Hofstra University	M
Inter American University of Puerto Rico, Metropolitan Campus	M
Inter American University of Puerto Rico, San Germán Campus	M
Iona College	M
Jackson State University	M
Johnson & Wales University	M
Lehman College of the City University of New York	M
Louisiana State University and Agricultural and Mechanical College	M,D
Louisiana Tech University	M,D
Maryville University of Saint Louis	M,O
McNeese State University	M
Middle Tennessee State University	M
Mississippi College	M
Nazareth College of Rochester	M
New York University	M,D,O
Northwestern State University of Louisiana	M,O
Old Dominion University	M
Rider University	O
Robert Morris University	M
Salisbury University	M
South Carolina State University	M
Southeast Missouri State University	M
State University of West Georgia	M,O
Texas Southern University	M
Troy University Dothan	M
University of Delaware	M,D
University of Idaho	M,D,O
University of Minnesota, Twin Cities Campus	M,D
University of Missouri–Columbia	M,D,O
University of South Alabama	M
University of South Carolina	M,D
University of Toledo	M,D,O
University of Wisconsin–Whitewater	M
Utah State University	M,D
Valdosta State University	M,D,O
Western Kentucky University	M
Wright State University	M

■ CANADIAN STUDIES

Institution	Degrees
The Johns Hopkins University	M,D,O

■ CANCER BIOLOGY/ONCOLOGY

Institution	Degrees
Brown University	M,D
Drexel University	M,D
Duke University	D
Emory University	M,D
The George Washington University	D
Harvard University	D
Kansas State University	M,D
Mayo Graduate School	P,D
New York University	D
Northwestern University	D
Stanford University	D
University at Buffalo, The State University of New York	D
The University of Arizona	D
University of California, San Diego	D

Directory of Graduate and Professional Programs by Field
Chemical Engineering

University of Chicago	D
University of Pennsylvania	D
University of South Florida	D
University of Utah	M,D
University of Wisconsin–Madison	D
Vanderbilt University	M,D
Wake Forest University	D
Wayne State University	M,D
West Virginia University	M,D

■ CARDIOVASCULAR SCIENCES

Long Island University, C.W. Post Campus	M,O
Northeastern University	M
University of California, San Diego	D
The University of South Dakota	M,D

■ CELL BIOLOGY

Arizona State University	M,D
Boston University	M,D
Brandeis University	M,D
Brown University	M,D
California Institute of Technology	D
Carnegie Mellon University	M,D
Case Western Reserve University	M,D
The Catholic University of America	D
Central Connecticut State University	M,O
Colorado State University	M,D
Columbia University	M,D
Cornell University	M,D
Drexel University	M,D
Duke University	D,O
East Carolina University	D
Emory University	D
Emporia State University	M
Florida Institute of Technology	D
Florida State University	M,D
Fordham University	M,D
George Mason University	M,D
Georgetown University	D
Georgia State University	M,D
Harvard University	D
Illinois Institute of Technology	M,D
Indiana University Bloomington	M,D
Indiana University–Purdue University Indianapolis	M,D
Iowa State University of Science and Technology	M,D
The Johns Hopkins University	D
Kansas State University	M,D
Kent State University	M,D
Loyola University Chicago	M,D
Marquette University	M,D
Massachusetts Institute of Technology	D
Mayo Graduate School	D
Michigan State University	M,D
New York University	M,D
North Carolina State University	M,D
North Dakota State University	M,D
Northwestern University	D
Oakland University	M
The Ohio State University	M,D
Ohio University	M,D
Oregon State University	M,D
The Pennsylvania State University University Park Campus	M,D
Purdue University	D
Quinnipiac University	M
Rensselaer Polytechnic Institute	M,D
Rice University	M,D
Rutgers, The State University of New Jersey, New Brunswick/Piscataway	M,D
Saint Joseph College	M
San Diego State University	M,D
San Francisco State University	M
Southwest Missouri State University	M
Stony Brook University, State University of New York	M,D
Temple University	D
Texas A&M University	D
Tufts University	D
Tulane University	M,D
University at Albany, State University of New York	M,D
University at Buffalo, The State University of New York	D
The University of Alabama at Birmingham	D
The University of Arizona	M,D
University of Arkansas	M,D
University of California, Berkeley	D
University of California, Davis	M,D
University of California, Irvine	M,D
University of California, Los Angeles	M,D
University of California, Riverside	M,D
University of California, San Diego	D
University of California, San Francisco	D
University of California, Santa Barbara	M,D
University of California, Santa Cruz	M,D
University of Chicago	D
University of Cincinnati	M,D
University of Colorado at Boulder	M,D
University of Connecticut	M,D
University of Delaware	M,D
University of Florida	M,D
University of Georgia	M,D
University of Hawaii at Manoa	M,D
University of Illinois at Chicago	M,D
University of Illinois at Urbana–Champaign	D
The University of Iowa	D
University of Kansas	M,D
University of Maryland	D
University of Maryland, Baltimore County	D
University of Maryland, College Park	M,D
University of Massachusetts Amherst	D
University of Massachusetts Boston	M,D
The University of Memphis	M,D
University of Miami	D
University of Michigan	M,D
University of Minnesota, Duluth	M,D
University of Minnesota, Twin Cities Campus	M,D
University of Missouri–Columbia	M,D
University of Missouri–Kansas City	D
University of Missouri–St. Louis	M,D,O
University of Nevada, Reno	M,D
University of New Haven	M
University of New Mexico	M,D
The University of North Carolina at Chapel Hill	D
University of Notre Dame	M,D
University of Pennsylvania	D
University of Pittsburgh	M,D
University of Rhode Island	M,D
University of South Alabama	D
University of South Carolina	M,D
The University of South Dakota	M,D
University of Southern California	M,D
The University of Texas at Austin	D
The University of Texas at Dallas	M,D
The University of Texas at San Antonio	D
University of Vermont	M,D
University of Virginia	D
University of Washington	D
University of Wisconsin–La Crosse	M
University of Wisconsin–Madison	M,D
Vanderbilt University	M,D
Washington State University	M,D
Washington University in St. Louis	D
Wayne State University	M,D
West Virginia University	M,D
Yale University	D
Yeshiva University	D

■ CELTIC LANGUAGES

Harvard University	M,D

■ CERAMIC SCIENCES AND ENGINEERING

Alfred University	M,D
Case Western Reserve University	M,D
Clemson University	M,D
The Pennsylvania State University University Park Campus	M,D
Rensselaer Polytechnic Institute	M,D
Rutgers, The State University of New Jersey, New Brunswick/Piscataway	M,D
University of California, Berkeley	M,D
University of California, Los Angeles	M,D
University of Cincinnati	M,D
University of Missouri–Rolla	M,D

■ CHEMICAL ENGINEERING

Arizona State University	M,D
Auburn University	M,D
Brigham Young University	M,D
Brown University	M,D
California Institute of Technology	M,D
Carnegie Mellon University	M,D
Case Western Reserve University	M,D
City College of the City University of New York	M,D
Clarkson University	M,D
Clemson University	M,D
Cleveland State University	M,D
Colorado State University	M,D
Columbia University	M,D,O
Cornell University	M,D
Drexel University	M,D
Fairleigh Dickinson University, College at Florham	M,O
Florida Agricultural and Mechanical University	M,D
Florida Institute of Technology	M,D
Florida State University	M,D
Georgia Institute of Technology	M,D
Howard University	M
Illinois Institute of Technology	M,D
Iowa State University of Science and Technology	M,D
The Johns Hopkins University	M,D
Kansas State University	M,D
Lamar University	M,D
Lehigh University	M,D
Louisiana State University and Agricultural and Mechanical College	M,D
Louisiana Tech University	M,D
Manhattan College	M
Massachusetts Institute of Technology	M,D
McNeese State University	M
Michigan State University	M,D
Michigan Technological University	M,D
Mississippi State University	M,D
Montana State University–Bozeman	M,D
New Jersey Institute of Technology	M,D
New Mexico State University	M,D
North Carolina Agricultural and Technical State University	M
North Carolina State University	M,D
Northeastern University	M,D
Northwestern University	M,D
The Ohio State University	M,D
Ohio University	M,D
Oklahoma State University	M,D
Oregon State University	M,D
The Pennsylvania State University University Park Campus	M,D
Polytechnic University, Brooklyn Campus	M,D
Polytechnic University, Westchester Graduate Center	M
Princeton University	M,D
Purdue University	M,D
Rensselaer Polytechnic Institute	M,D
Rice University	M,D

Directory of Graduate and Professional Programs by Field
Chemical Engineering

Institution	Degree
Rutgers, The State University of New Jersey, New Brunswick/Piscataway	M,D
San Jose State University	M
Stanford University	M,D,O
Stevens Institute of Technology	M,D,O
Syracuse University	M,D
Tennessee Technological University	M,D
Texas A&M University	M,D
Texas A&M University–Kingsville	M
Texas Tech University	M,D
Tufts University	M,D
Tulane University	M,D
University at Buffalo, The State University of New York	M,D
The University of Akron	M,D
The University of Alabama	M,D
The University of Alabama in Huntsville	M,D
The University of Arizona	M,D
University of Arkansas	M,D
University of California, Berkeley	M,D
University of California, Davis	M,D
University of California, Irvine	M,D
University of California, Los Angeles	M,D
University of California, Riverside	M,D
University of California, San Diego	M,D
University of California, Santa Barbara	M,D
University of Cincinnati	M,D
University of Colorado at Boulder	M,D
University of Connecticut	M,D
University of Dayton	M
University of Delaware	M,D
University of Detroit Mercy	M,D
University of Florida	M,D,O
University of Houston	M,D
University of Idaho	M,D
University of Illinois at Chicago	M,D
University of Illinois at Urbana–Champaign	M,D
The University of Iowa	M,D
University of Kansas	M,D
University of Kentucky	M,D
University of Louisiana at Lafayette	M
University of Louisville	M,D
University of Maine	M,D
University of Maryland, Baltimore County	M,D
University of Maryland, College Park	M,D,O
University of Massachusetts Amherst	M,D
University of Massachusetts Lowell	M
University of Michigan	M,D,O
University of Minnesota, Twin Cities Campus	M,D
University of Missouri–Columbia	M,D
University of Missouri–Rolla	M,D
University of Nebraska–Lincoln	M,D
University of Nevada, Reno	M,D
University of New Hampshire	M,D
University of New Mexico	M,D
University of North Dakota	M
University of Notre Dame	M,D
University of Oklahoma	M,D
University of Pennsylvania	M,D
University of Pittsburgh	M,D
University of Puerto Rico, Mayagüez Campus	M
University of Rhode Island	M,D
University of Rochester	M,D
University of South Alabama	M
University of South Carolina	M,D
University of Southern California	M,D,O
University of South Florida	M,D
The University of Tennessee	M,D
The University of Texas at Austin	M,D
University of Toledo	M,D
University of Tulsa	M,D
University of Utah	M,D
University of Virginia	M,D
University of Washington	M,D
University of Wisconsin–Madison	M,D
University of Wyoming	M,D
Vanderbilt University	M,D
Villanova University	M
Virginia Polytechnic Institute and State University	M,D
Washington State University	M,D
Washington University in St. Louis	M,D
Wayne State University	M,D
Western Michigan University	M,D
West Virginia University	M,D
Widener University	M
Worcester Polytechnic Institute	M,D
Yale University	M,D
Youngstown State University	M

■ CHEMISTRY

Institution	Degree
American University	M
Arizona State University	M,D
Arkansas State University	M,O
Auburn University	M,D
Ball State University	M
Baylor University	M,D
Boston College	M,D
Boston University	M,D
Bowling Green State University	M,D
Bradley University	M
Brandeis University	M,D
Brigham Young University	M,D
Brooklyn College of the City University of New York	M,D
Brown University	M,D
Buffalo State College, State University of New York	M
California Institute of Technology	M,D
California State Polytechnic University, Pomona	M
California State University, Fresno	M
California State University, Fullerton	M
California State University, Hayward	M
California State University, Long Beach	M
California State University, Los Angeles	M
California State University, Northridge	M
California State University, Sacramento	M
Carnegie Mellon University	M,D
Case Western Reserve University	M,D
The Catholic University of America	M
Central Connecticut State University	M
Central Michigan University	M
Central Washington University	M
City College of the City University of New York	M,D
Clark Atlanta University	M,D
Clarkson University	M,D
Clark University	M,D
Clemson University	M,D
Cleveland State University	M,D
College of Staten Island of the City University of New York	D
The College of William and Mary	M
Colorado State University	M,D
Columbia University	M,D
Converse College	M,O
Cornell University	D
Dartmouth College	D
Delaware State University	M
DePaul University	M
Drexel University	M,D
Duke University	D
Duquesne University	M,D
East Carolina University	M
Eastern Illinois University	M
Eastern Kentucky University	M
Eastern Michigan University	M
Eastern New Mexico University	M
East Tennessee State University	M
Emory University	D
Emporia State University	M
Fairleigh Dickinson University, College at Florham	M
Florida Agricultural and Mechanical University	M
Florida Atlantic University	M,D
Florida Institute of Technology	M,D
Florida International University	M,D
Florida State University	M,D
George Mason University	M
Georgetown University	M,D
The George Washington University	M,D
Georgia Institute of Technology	M,D
Georgia State University	M,D
Hampton University	M
Harvard University	M,D
Howard University	M,D
Idaho State University	M
Illinois Institute of Technology	M,D
Illinois State University	M
Indiana University Bloomington	M,D
Indiana University of Pennsylvania	M
Indiana University–Purdue University Indianapolis	M,D
Iowa State University of Science and Technology	M,D
Jackson State University	M,D
John Carroll University	M
The Johns Hopkins University	M,D
Kansas State University	M,D
Kent State University	M,D
Lamar University	M
Lehigh University	M,D
Long Island University, Brooklyn Campus	M
Louisiana State University and Agricultural and Mechanical College	M,D
Louisiana Tech University	M
Loyola University Chicago	M,D
Marquette University	M,D
Marshall University	M
Massachusetts Institute of Technology	D
McNeese State University	M,D
Miami University	M,D
Michigan State University	M,D
Michigan Technological University	M,D
Middle Tennessee State University	M,D
Minnesota State University Mankato	M
Mississippi College	M
Mississippi State University	M,D
Montana State University–Bozeman	M,D
Montclair State University	M
Morgan State University	M
Murray State University	M
New Jersey Institute of Technology	M,D
New Mexico Highlands University	M
New Mexico Institute of Mining and Technology	M,D
New Mexico State University	M,D
New York University	M,D
North Carolina Agricultural and Technical State University	M
North Carolina Central University	M
North Carolina State University	M,D
North Dakota State University	M,D
Northeastern Illinois University	M
Northeastern University	M
Northern Arizona University	M
Northern Illinois University	M,D
Northern Michigan University	M
Northwestern University	D
Oakland University	M,D
The Ohio State University	M,D
Oklahoma State University	M,D
Old Dominion University	M
Oregon State University	M,D
The Pennsylvania State University University Park Campus	M,D
Pittsburg State University	M

Directory of Graduate and Professional Programs by Field
Child and Family Studies

Institution	Degree
Polytechnic University, Brooklyn Campus	M,D
Polytechnic University, Westchester Graduate Center	M
Pontifical Catholic University of Puerto Rico	M
Portland State University	M,D
Prairie View A&M University	M
Princeton University	M,D
Purdue University	M,D
Queens College of the City University of New York	M
Rensselaer Polytechnic Institute	M,D
Rice University	M,D
Rochester Institute of Technology	M
Roosevelt University	M
Rutgers, The State University of New Jersey, Camden	M
Rutgers, The State University of New Jersey, Newark	M,D
Rutgers, The State University of New Jersey, New Brunswick/Piscataway	M,D
Sacred Heart University	M
St. John's University (NY)	M
Saint Joseph College	M
Saint Louis University	M
Sam Houston State University	M
San Diego State University	M,D
San Francisco State University	M
San Jose State University	M
Seton Hall University	M,D
South Dakota State University	M,D
Southeast Missouri State University	M
Southern Connecticut State University	M
Southern Illinois University Carbondale	M,D
Southern Illinois University Edwardsville	M
Southern Methodist University	M
Southern University and Agricultural and Mechanical College	M
Southwest Missouri State University	M
Stanford University	D
State University of New York at Binghamton	M,D
State University of New York at New Paltz	M
State University of New York at Oswego	M
State University of New York College at Fredonia	M
State University of New York College of Environmental Science and Forestry	M,D
Stephen F. Austin State University	M
Stevens Institute of Technology	M,D,O
Stony Brook University, State University of New York	M,D
Sul Ross State University	M
Syracuse University	M,D
Temple University	M,D
Tennessee State University	M
Tennessee Technological University	M
Texas A&M University	M,D
Texas A&M University–Commerce	M
Texas A&M University–Kingsville	M
Texas Christian University	M,D
Texas Southern University	M
Texas State University-San Marcos	M
Texas Tech University	M,D
Texas Woman's University	M
Tufts University	M,D
Tulane University	M,D
Tuskegee University	M
University at Albany, State University of New York	M,D
University at Buffalo, The State University of New York	M,D
The University of Akron	M,D
The University of Alabama	M,D
The University of Alabama at Birmingham	M,D
The University of Alabama in Huntsville	M
University of Alaska Fairbanks	M,D
The University of Arizona	M,D
University of Arkansas	M,D
University of Arkansas at Little Rock	M
University of California, Berkeley	M,D
University of California, Davis	M,D
University of California, Irvine	M,D
University of California, Los Angeles	M,D
University of California, Riverside	M,D
University of California, San Diego	M,D
University of California, San Francisco	M,D
University of California, Santa Barbara	M,D
University of California, Santa Cruz	M,D
University of Central Florida	M
University of Central Oklahoma	M
University of Chicago	D
University of Cincinnati	M,D
University of Colorado at Boulder	M,D
University of Colorado at Denver	M
University of Connecticut	M,D
University of Dayton	M
University of Delaware	M,D
University of Denver	M,D
University of Detroit Mercy	M
University of Florida	M,D
University of Georgia	M,D
University of Hawaii at Manoa	M,D
University of Houston	M,D
University of Houston–Clear Lake	M
University of Idaho	M,D
University of Illinois at Chicago	M,D
University of Illinois at Urbana–Champaign	M,D
The University of Iowa	M,D
University of Kansas	M,D
University of Kentucky	M,D
University of Louisiana at Monroe	M
University of Louisville	M,D
University of Maine	M,D
University of Maryland, Baltimore County	M,D
University of Maryland, College Park	M,D
University of Massachusetts Amherst	M,D
University of Massachusetts Boston	M
University of Massachusetts Dartmouth	M
University of Massachusetts Lowell	M,D
The University of Memphis	M,D
University of Miami	M,D
University of Michigan	D
University of Minnesota, Duluth	M
University of Minnesota, Twin Cities Campus	M,D
University of Mississippi	M,D
University of Missouri–Columbia	M,D
University of Missouri–Kansas City	M,D
University of Missouri–Rolla	M,D
University of Missouri–St. Louis	M,D
The University of Montana–Missoula	M,D
University of Nebraska–Lincoln	M,D
University of Nevada, Las Vegas	M
University of Nevada, Reno	M,D
University of New Hampshire	M,D
University of New Mexico	M,D
University of New Orleans	M,D
The University of North Carolina at Chapel Hill	M,D
The University of North Carolina at Charlotte	M
The University of North Carolina at Greensboro	M
The University of North Carolina at Wilmington	M
University of North Dakota	M,D
University of Northern Colorado	M,D
University of Northern Iowa	M
University of North Texas	M,D
University of Notre Dame	M,D
University of Oklahoma	M,D
University of Oregon	M,D
University of Pennsylvania	M,D
University of Pittsburgh	M,D
University of Puerto Rico, Mayagüez Campus	M
University of Puerto Rico, Río Piedras	M,D
University of Rhode Island	M
University of Rochester	M,D
University of San Francisco	M
The University of Scranton	M
University of South Carolina	M,D
The University of South Dakota	M
University of Southern California	M,D
University of Southern Mississippi	M,D
University of South Florida	M,D
The University of Tennessee	M,D
The University of Texas at Arlington	M,D
The University of Texas at Austin	M,D
The University of Texas at Dallas	M,D
The University of Texas at El Paso	M
The University of Texas at San Antonio	M
The University of Texas at Tyler	M
University of Toledo	M,D
University of Tulsa	M
University of Utah	M,D
University of Vermont	M,D
University of Virginia	M,D
University of Washington	M,D
University of Wisconsin–Madison	M,D
University of Wisconsin–Milwaukee	M,D
University of Wyoming	M,D
Utah State University	M,D
Vanderbilt University	M,D
Villanova University	M
Virginia Commonwealth University	M,D
Virginia Polytechnic Institute and State University	M,D
Wake Forest University	M,D
Washington State University	M,D
Washington University in St. Louis	M,D
Wayne State University	M,D
West Chester University of Pennsylvania	M
Western Carolina University	M
Western Illinois University	M
Western Kentucky University	M
Western Michigan University	M,D
Western Washington University	M
West Texas A&M University	M
West Virginia University	M,D
Wichita State University	M,D
Worcester Polytechnic Institute	M,D
Wright State University	M
Yale University	D
Youngstown State University	M

■ CHILD AND FAMILY STUDIES

Institution	Degree
Arizona State University	D
Auburn University	M,D
Bowling Green State University	M,D
Brandeis University	M
Brigham Young University	M,D
California State University, Los Angeles	M
Central Michigan University	M
Central Washington University	M
Colorado State University	M
Concordia University Wisconsin	M
Cornell University	D
East Carolina University	M
Fitchburg State College	M,O
Florida State University	M,D
Indiana State University	M
Iowa State University of Science and Technology	M,D
Kansas State University	M,D
Loma Linda University	M,O

Directory of Graduate and Professional Programs by Field

Child and Family Studies

Miami University	M
Michigan State University	M,D
Middle Tennessee State University	M
Montclair State University	M
North Dakota State University	M,D
Northern Illinois University	M
Nova Southeastern University	M,D
The Ohio State University	M,D
Ohio University	M
Oklahoma State University	M,D
Oregon State University	M,D
The Pennsylvania State University University Park Campus	M,D
Purdue University	M,D
Roberts Wesleyan College	M
Sage Graduate School	M
St. Cloud State University	M
Saint Joseph College	M,O
San Diego State University	M
San Jose State University	M
South Carolina State University	M
Spring Arbor University	P,M
Springfield College	M,O
Stanford University	D
Syracuse University	M,D
Tennessee State University	M,D
Texas State University-San Marcos	M
Texas Tech University	M,D
Texas Woman's University	M,D
Tufts University	M,D,O
The University of Akron	M
The University of Alabama	M
The University of Arizona	M,D
University of California, Davis	M
University of Connecticut	M,D
University of Delaware	M
University of Denver	M,D,O
University of Georgia	M,D
University of Great Falls	M
University of Illinois at Springfield	M
University of Kentucky	M,D
University of La Verne	M
University of Maryland, College Park	M,D
University of Minnesota, Twin Cities Campus	M,D
University of Missouri–Columbia	M,D
University of Nebraska–Lincoln	M,D
University of Nevada, Reno	M
University of New Hampshire	M
University of New Mexico	M,D
The University of North Carolina at Charlotte	M,D
The University of North Carolina at Greensboro	M,D
University of North Texas	M,D
University of Rhode Island	M
University of Southern Mississippi	M
The University of Tennessee	M,D
The University of Tennessee at Martin	M
The University of Texas at Austin	M,D
The University of Texas at Dallas	M
University of Utah	M
University of Vermont	M
University of Wisconsin–Madison	M,D
Utah State University	M,D
Vanderbilt University	M,D
Virginia Polytechnic Institute and State University	M,D
Wayne State University	O
West Virginia University	M
Wheelock College	M

■ CHINESE

Brigham Young University	M
Cornell University	M,D
Harvard University	M,D
Indiana University Bloomington	M,D
San Francisco State University	M
Stanford University	M,D
University of California, Berkeley	

University of California, Irvine	M,D
University of Colorado at Boulder	M
University of Kansas	M
University of Massachusetts Amherst	M
University of Oregon	M,D
University of Washington	M,D
University of Wisconsin–Madison	M,D
Washington University in St. Louis	M,D

■ CHIROPRACTIC

University of Bridgeport	P

■ CIVIL ENGINEERING

Arizona State University	M,D
Auburn University	M,D
Boise State University	M
Bradley University	M
Brigham Young University	M,D
California Institute of Technology	M,D
California Polytechnic State University, San Luis Obispo	M
California State University, Fresno	M
California State University, Fullerton	M
California State University, Long Beach	M,D,O
California State University, Los Angeles	M
California State University, Northridge	M
California State University, Sacramento	M
Carnegie Mellon University	M,D
Case Western Reserve University	M,D
The Catholic University of America	M,D
Central Connecticut State University	M
City College of the City University of New York	M,D
Clarkson University	M,D
Clemson University	M,D
Cleveland State University	M,D
Colorado State University	M,D
Columbia University	M,D,O
Cornell University	M,D
Drexel University	M,D
Duke University	M,D
Florida Agricultural and Mechanical University	M,D
Florida Atlantic University	M
Florida Institute of Technology	M,D
Florida International University	M,D
Florida State University	M
George Mason University	M
The George Washington University	M,D,O
Georgia Institute of Technology	M,D
Howard University	M
Illinois Institute of Technology	M,D
Iowa State University of Science and Technology	M,D
The Johns Hopkins University	M,D
Kansas State University	M,D
Lamar University	M,D
Lawrence Technological University	M,D
Lehigh University	M,D
Louisiana State University and Agricultural and Mechanical College	M,D
Louisiana Tech University	M,D
Loyola Marymount University	M
Manhattan College	M
Marquette University	M,D
Massachusetts Institute of Technology	M,D,O
McNeese State University	M
Michigan State University	M,D
Michigan Technological University	M,D
Mississippi State University	M,D
Montana State University–Bozeman	M,D
New Jersey Institute of Technology	M,D
New Mexico State University	M,D
North Carolina Agricultural and Technical State University	M
North Carolina State University	M,D
North Dakota State University	M,D

Northeastern University	M,D
Northwestern University	M,D
The Ohio State University	M,D
Ohio University	M,D
Oklahoma State University	M,D
Old Dominion University	M,D
Oregon State University	M,D
The Pennsylvania State University University Park Campus	M,D
Polytechnic University, Brooklyn Campus	M,D
Portland State University	M,D,O
Princeton University	M,D
Purdue University	M,D
Rensselaer Polytechnic Institute	M,D
Rice University	M,D
Rutgers, The State University of New Jersey, New Brunswick/Piscataway	M,D
Saint Martin's College	M
San Diego State University	M
San Jose State University	M
Santa Clara University	M
South Dakota State University	M
Southern Illinois University Carbondale	M
Southern Illinois University Edwardsville	M
Southern Methodist University	M,D
Stanford University	M,D,O
Stevens Institute of Technology	M,D,O
Syracuse University	M,D
Temple University	M
Tennessee Technological University	M,D
Texas A&M University	M,D
Texas A&M University–Kingsville	M
Texas Tech University	M,D
Tufts University	M,D
Tulane University	M,D
University at Buffalo, The State University of New York	M,D
The University of Akron	M,D
The University of Alabama	M,D
The University of Alabama at Birmingham	M,D
The University of Alabama in Huntsville	M,D
University of Alaska Anchorage	M
University of Alaska Fairbanks	M,D
The University of Arizona	M,D
University of Arkansas	M,D
University of California, Berkeley	M,D
University of California, Davis	M,D,O
University of California, Irvine	M,D
University of California, Los Angeles	M,D
University of Central Florida	M,D,O
University of Cincinnati	M,D
University of Colorado at Boulder	M,D
University of Colorado at Denver	M,D
University of Connecticut	M,D
University of Dayton	M
University of Delaware	M,D
University of Detroit Mercy	M
University of Florida	M,D,O
University of Hawaii at Manoa	M,D
University of Houston	M,D
University of Idaho	M,D
University of Illinois at Chicago	M,D
University of Illinois at Urbana–Champaign	M,D
The University of Iowa	M,D
University of Kansas	M,D
University of Kentucky	M,D
University of Louisiana at Lafayette	M
University of Louisville	M,D
University of Maine	M,D
University of Maryland, College Park	M,D,O
University of Massachusetts Amherst	M,D
University of Massachusetts Lowell	M
The University of Memphis	M,D
University of Miami	M,D

Directory of Graduate and Professional Programs by Field
Clinical Psychology

Institution	Degree
University of Michigan	M,D,O
University of Minnesota, Twin Cities Campus	M,D
University of Missouri–Columbia	M,D
University of Missouri–Kansas City	M,D
University of Missouri–Rolla	M,D
University of Nebraska–Lincoln	M,D
University of Nevada, Las Vegas	M,D
University of Nevada, Reno	M,D
University of New Hampshire	M,D
University of New Mexico	M,D
The University of North Carolina at Charlotte	M
University of North Dakota	M
University of Notre Dame	M,D
University of Oklahoma	M,D
University of Pittsburgh	M,D
University of Puerto Rico, Mayagüez Campus	M
University of Rhode Island	M,D
University of South Carolina	M,D
University of Southern California	M,D,O
University of South Florida	M,D
The University of Tennessee	M,D
The University of Texas at Arlington	M,D
The University of Texas at Austin	M,D
The University of Texas at El Paso	M,D
The University of Texas at San Antonio	M
University of Toledo	M,D
University of Utah	M,D
University of Vermont	M,D
University of Virginia	M,D
University of Washington	M,D
University of Wisconsin–Madison	M,D
University of Wyoming	M,D
Utah State University	M,D,O
Vanderbilt University	M,D
Villanova University	M
Virginia Polytechnic Institute and State University	M,D
Washington State University	M,D
Washington University in St. Louis	M,D
Wayne State University	M,D
West Virginia University	M,D
Widener University	M
Worcester Polytechnic Institute	M,D,O
Youngstown State University	M

■ **CLASSICS**

Institution	Degree
Boston College	M
Boston University	M,D
Brown University	M,D
The Catholic University of America	M,D
Columbia University	M,D
Cornell University	D
Duke University	D
Florida State University	M,D
Fordham University	M,D
Harvard University	M,D
Hunter College of the City University of New York	M
Indiana University Bloomington	M,D
The Johns Hopkins University	M,D
Kent State University	M
New York University	M,D,O
The Ohio State University	M,D
Princeton University	D
Rutgers, The State University of New Jersey, New Brunswick/Piscataway	M,D
San Francisco State University	M
Stanford University	M,D
Texas Tech University	M
Tufts University	M
Tulane University	M
University at Buffalo, The State University of New York	M,D
The University of Arizona	M
University of California, Berkeley	M,D
University of California, Irvine	M,D

Institution	Degree
University of California, Los Angeles	M,D
University of California, Riverside	M,D
University of California, Santa Barbara	M,D
University of Chicago	M,D
University of Cincinnati	M,D
University of Colorado at Boulder	M,D
University of Florida	M,D
University of Georgia	M
University of Hawaii at Manoa	M
University of Illinois at Urbana–Champaign	M,D
The University of Iowa	M,D
University of Kansas	M
University of Kentucky	M
University of Maryland, College Park	M
University of Massachusetts Amherst	M
University of Michigan	M,D,O
University of Minnesota, Twin Cities Campus	M,D
University of Mississippi	M
University of Missouri–Columbia	M,D
University of Nebraska–Lincoln	M
The University of North Carolina at Chapel Hill	M,D
The University of North Carolina at Greensboro	M
University of Oregon	M
University of Pennsylvania	M,D
University of Pittsburgh	M,D
University of Southern California	M,D
The University of Texas at Austin	M,D
University of Vermont	M
University of Virginia	M,D
University of Washington	M,D
University of Wisconsin–Madison	M,D
University of Wisconsin–Milwaukee	M
Vanderbilt University	M,D
Villanova University	M
Washington University in St. Louis	M
Wayne State University	M
West Chester University of Pennsylvania	M
Yale University	D

■ **CLINICAL LABORATORY SCIENCES/MEDICAL TECHNOLOGY**

Institution	Degree
California State University, Dominguez Hills	M,O
California State University, Long Beach	M
Case Western Reserve University	M
The Catholic University of America	M,D
Duke University	M
Fairleigh Dickinson University, Metropolitan Campus	M
Inter American University of Puerto Rico, Metropolitan Campus	M
Long Island University, C.W. Post Campus	M
Michigan State University	M
Northeastern University	M,D
Quinnipiac University	M
Rochester Institute of Technology	M
St. John's University (NY)	M
San Francisco State University	M
University at Buffalo, The State University of New York	M
The University of Alabama at Birmingham	M
The University of Iowa	M,D
University of Kentucky	M,D
University of Maryland	M
University of Massachusetts Lowell	M
University of Minnesota, Twin Cities Campus	M
University of North Dakota	M
University of Rhode Island	M
University of Southern Mississippi	M
University of the Sacred Heart	O
University of Utah	M

Institution	Degree
University of Vermont	M
University of Washington	M
University of Wisconsin–Milwaukee	M
Virginia Commonwealth University	M
Wayne State University	M,O

■ **CLINICAL PSYCHOLOGY**

Institution	Degree
Abilene Christian University	M
Adelphi University	D,O
Alabama Agricultural and Mechanical University	M,O
American International College	M
American University	D
Antioch New England Graduate School	D
Antioch University Los Angeles	M
Appalachian State University	M
Argosy University/Sarasota	M,D,O
Argosy University/Schaumburg	M,D
Arizona State University	D
Austin Peay State University	M
Azusa Pacific University	M,D
Ball State University	M
Barry University	M,O
Baylor University	M,D
Bowling Green State University	M,D
Brigham Young University	M,D
California Lutheran University	M
California State University, Dominguez Hills	M
California State University, Fullerton	M
California State University, San Bernardino	M
Cardinal Stritch University	M
Case Western Reserve University	D
The Catholic University of America	D
Central Michigan University	D
Chapman University	M
Chestnut Hill College	D
City College of the City University of New York	M,D
Clark University	D
Cleveland State University	M,O
College of St. Joseph	M
The College of William and Mary	D
DePaul University	M,D
Drexel University	D
Duke University	D
Duquesne University	D
East Carolina University	M
Eastern Illinois University	M,O
Eastern Kentucky University	M,O
Eastern Michigan University	M,D
East Tennessee State University	M
Edinboro University of Pennsylvania	M
Emory University	D
Emporia State University	M
Fairleigh Dickinson University, College at Florham	M
Fairleigh Dickinson University, Metropolitan Campus	M,D
Florida Institute of Technology	M,D
Florida State University	D
Fordham University	D
Francis Marion University	M
Gallaudet University	D
George Fox University	M,D
George Mason University	M,D
The George Washington University	D
Hofstra University	D,O
Howard University	M,D
Idaho State University	D
Illinois Institute of Technology	M,D
Illinois State University	M,D,O
Immaculata University	M,D,O
Indiana State University	M,D
Indiana University of Pennsylvania	D
Indiana University–Purdue University Indianapolis	M,D
Jackson State University	D

Peterson's Graduate Schools in the U.S. 2006

Directory of Graduate and Professional Programs by Field

Clinical Psychology

Institution	Degree
Kent State University	M,D
Lamar University	M
La Salle University	M,D
Lesley University	M,D,O
Loma Linda University	D
Long Island University, Brooklyn Campus	D
Long Island University, C.W. Post Campus	D
Loras College	M
Louisiana State University and Agricultural and Mechanical College	M,D
Loyola College in Maryland	M,D,O
Loyola University Chicago	M,D
Madonna University	M
Marquette University	M,D
Marshall University	M,D
Marywood University	M,D
Miami University	D
Millersville University of Pennsylvania	M
Minnesota State University Mankato	M
Mississippi State University	M,D
Montclair State University	M
Morehead State University	M
Murray State University	M
New College of California	M
New School University	M,D
New York University	M,D,O
Norfolk State University	
North Dakota State University	M,D
Northwestern State University of Louisiana	M
Northwestern University	D
Nova Southeastern University	D,O
The Ohio State University	D
Ohio University	D
Oklahoma State University	M,D
Old Dominion University	D
Pace University	M,D
The Pennsylvania State University Harrisburg Campus of the Capital College	M
The Pennsylvania State University University Park Campus	M,D
Pontifical Catholic University of Puerto Rico	M,D
Queens College of the City University of New York	M
Radford University	M,O
Roosevelt University	M,D
Rutgers, The State University of New Jersey, New Brunswick/Piscataway	M,D
St. John's University (NY)	M,D
Saint Louis University	M,D
St. Mary's University of San Antonio	M
Saint Michael's College	M
Sam Houston State University	M,D
San Diego State University	M,D
San Jose State University	M
Seattle Pacific University	D
Southern Illinois University Carbondale	M,D
Southern Illinois University Edwardsville	M
Southern Methodist University	M,D
Spalding University	M,D
State University of New York at Binghamton	M,D
Stony Brook University, State University of New York	D
Suffolk University	D
Syracuse University	D
Teachers College Columbia University	M,D
Temple University	D
Texas A&M University	M,D
Texas Tech University	M,D
Towson University	M
University at Albany, State University of New York	M,D
University at Buffalo, The State University of New York	M,D
The University of Alabama	D
The University of Alabama at Birmingham	M,D
University of Alaska Anchorage	M
University of California, San Diego	D
University of California, Santa Barbara	M,D
University of Central Florida	M,D
University of Cincinnati	D
University of Connecticut	M,D
University of Dayton	M
University of Delaware	D
University of Denver	M,D
University of Detroit Mercy	M,D
University of Florida	D
University of Hartford	M,D
University of Hawaii at Manoa	M,D
University of Houston	D
University of Houston–Clear Lake	M
University of Illinois at Urbana–Champaign	M,D
University of Kansas	M,D
University of La Verne	D
University of Louisville	D
University of Maine	D
University of Maryland, College Park	M,D
University of Massachusetts Amherst	M,D
University of Massachusetts Boston	D
University of Massachusetts Dartmouth	M
The University of Memphis	M,D
University of Miami	M,D
University of Michigan	D
University of Minnesota, Twin Cities Campus	D
University of Mississippi	M,D
University of Missouri–St. Louis	M,D,O
The University of Montana–Missoula	M,D,O
University of Nevada, Las Vegas	M,D
University of New Mexico	M,D
The University of North Carolina at Chapel Hill	D
The University of North Carolina at Charlotte	M
The University of North Carolina at Greensboro	M,D
University of North Dakota	M,D
University of North Texas	M,D
University of Oregon	D
University of Pennsylvania	D
University of Rhode Island	D
University of Rochester	M,D
University of South Carolina	D
The University of South Dakota	M,D
University of Southern California	M,D
University of South Florida	M,D
The University of Tennessee	M,D
The University of Texas at El Paso	M,D
The University of Texas at Tyler	M
The University of Texas of the Permian Basin	M
The University of Texas–Pan American	M
University of the District of Columbia	M
University of Toledo	M,D
University of Tulsa	M,D
University of Vermont	D
University of Virginia	M,D,O
University of Washington	M,D
University of Wisconsin–Madison	D
University of Wisconsin–Milwaukee	M,D
Utah State University	M,D
Valdosta State University	M,O
Valparaiso University	M
Virginia Commonwealth University	D
Virginia Polytechnic Institute and State University	M,D
Washburn University	M
Washington State University	M,D
Washington University in St. Louis	M,D
Wayne State University	M,D
West Chester University of Pennsylvania	M
Western Carolina University	M
Western Illinois University	M,O
Western Michigan University	M,D,O
Westfield State College	M
West Virginia University	M,D
Wichita State University	M,D
Widener University	D
William Paterson University of New Jersey	
Wright State University	D
Xavier University	M,D
Yeshiva University	D

■ CLINICAL RESEARCH

Institution	Degree
Boston University	M
Case Western Reserve University	M
Duke University	M
Emory University	M
The Johns Hopkins University	M,D,O
New York University	M
Northwestern University	M,O
Tufts University	M,D
University of California, Los Angeles	M
University of California, San Diego	M
University of Florida	M
The University of Iowa	O
University of Louisville	O
University of Michigan	M
University of Minnesota, Twin Cities Campus	M
University of Pittsburgh	M,O
University of Virginia	M
Vanderbilt University	M

■ CLOTHING AND TEXTILES

Institution	Degree
Auburn University	M
Cornell University	M,D
Florida State University	M,D
Indiana State University	M
Indiana University Bloomington	M
Iowa State University of Science and Technology	M,D
Kansas State University	M,D
The Ohio State University	M,D
Oklahoma State University	M,D
Oregon State University	M,D
Philadelphia University	M
Purdue University	M
Syracuse University	M
The University of Akron	M
The University of Alabama	M
University of California, Davis	M
University of Georgia	M,D
University of Kentucky	M
University of Missouri–Columbia	M
University of Nebraska–Lincoln	M
University of North Texas	M
University of Rhode Island	M
The University of Tennessee	M,D
Virginia Polytechnic Institute and State University	M,D
Washington State University	M

■ COGNITIVE SCIENCES

Institution	Degree
Arizona State University	D
Ball State University	M
Boston University	M,D
Brandeis University	M,D
Brown University	M,D
Carnegie Mellon University	D
Claremont Graduate University	M,D
Colorado State University	M,D
Dartmouth College	D
Duke University	D
Emory University	D
Florida State University	D
The George Washington University	D
Harvard University	M,D

54   www.petersons.com   Peterson's Graduate Schools in the U.S. 2006

Institution	Degrees
Hunter College of the City University of New York	M
Indiana University Bloomington	D
Iowa State University of Science and Technology	M,D
The Johns Hopkins University	D
Louisiana State University and Agricultural and Mechanical College	M,D
Massachusetts Institute of Technology	D
Mississippi State University	M,D
New Mexico Highlands University	M
New York University	M,D,O
Northwestern University	D
The Ohio State University	D
The Pennsylvania State University University Park Campus	M,D
Rensselaer Polytechnic Institute	D
Rice University	M,D
Rutgers, The State University of New Jersey, Newark	D
Rutgers, The State University of New Jersey, New Brunswick/Piscataway	D
State University of New York at Binghamton	M,D
Temple University	D
Texas A&M University	M,D
University at Buffalo, The State University of New York	M,D
The University of Akron	M,D
The University of Alabama	D
University of California, San Diego	D
University of Colorado at Colorado Springs	M,D
University of Connecticut	M,D
University of Delaware	D
University of Illinois at Urbana–Champaign	M,D
University of Louisiana at Lafayette	D
University of Maryland	M,D
University of Maryland, Baltimore County	M,D
University of Maryland, College Park	D
University of Minnesota, Twin Cities Campus	D
The University of North Carolina at Chapel Hill	D
The University of North Carolina at Greensboro	M,D
University of Notre Dame	D
University of Oregon	M,D
University of Pittsburgh	D
University of Rochester	M,D
The University of Texas at Austin	M,D
The University of Texas at Dallas	M
University of Wisconsin–Madison	D
Wayne State University	M,D

■ COMMUNICATION—GENERAL

Institution	Degrees
Abilene Christian University	M
American University	M
Andrews University	M
Angelo State University	M
Arizona State University	M,D
Arizona State University West	M,O
Arkansas State University	M,O
Arkansas Tech University	M
Auburn University	M
Austin Peay State University	M
Ball State University	M
Barry University	M,O
Baylor University	M
Bethel University	M
Boise State University	M
Boston University	M
Bowling Green State University	M,D
Brigham Young University	M
California State University, Chico	M
California State University, Fullerton	M
California State University, Hayward	M
California State University, Long Beach	M
California State University, Los Angeles	M
California State University, Northridge	M
California State University, Sacramento	M
California State University, San Bernardino	M
California University of Pennsylvania	M
Carnegie Mellon University	M
Central Connecticut State University	M
Central Michigan University	M
Central Missouri State University	M
Clarion University of Pennsylvania	M
Clark University	M
Clemson University	M
Cleveland State University	M
The College of New Rochelle	M,O
College of Notre Dame of Maryland	M
Colorado State University	M
Columbia University	M,D
Cornell University	M,D
DePaul University	M
Drexel University	M
Drury University	M
Duquesne University	M,D
Eastern Michigan University	M
Eastern New Mexico University	M
Eastern Washington University	M
East Tennessee State University	M
Edinboro University of Pennsylvania	M
Emerson College	M
Fairleigh Dickinson University, Metropolitan Campus	M
Fitchburg State College	M,O
Florida Atlantic University	M
Florida Institute of Technology	M
Florida State University	M,D
Fordham University	M
Fort Hays State University	M
George Mason University	M
Georgetown University	M
Georgia State University	M,D
Governors State University	M
Grand Valley State University	M
Harvard University	M,O
Hawai'i Pacific University	M
Howard University	M,D
Hunter College of the City University of New York	M
Illinois Institute of Technology	M,D
Illinois State University	M
Indiana State University	M
Indiana University Bloomington	M,D
Indiana University–Purdue University Fort Wayne	M
Iona College	M,O
Ithaca College	M
The Johns Hopkins University	M
Kean University	M,O
Kent State University	M,D
Louisiana State University and Agricultural and Mechanical College	M,D
Loyola Marymount University	M
Loyola University New Orleans	M
Marquette University	M
Marshall University	M
Marywood University	M
Miami University	M
Michigan State University	M,D
Mississippi College	M
Monmouth University	M,O
Montana State University–Billings	M
Montclair State University	M
Morehead State University	M
National University	M
New Jersey Institute of Technology	M
New Mexico State University	M
New School University	M
New York Institute of Technology	M
New York University	M,D,O
Norfolk State University	M
North Carolina State University	M
North Dakota State University	M,D
Northeastern State University	M
Northern Illinois University	M
Northwestern University	M,D
The Ohio State University	M,D
Ohio University	M,D
The Pennsylvania State University University Park Campus	M,D
Pepperdine University	M
Pittsburg State University	M
Point Park University	M
Polytechnic University, Brooklyn Campus	M
Purdue University	M,D
Purdue University Calumet	M
Quinnipiac University	M
Regis University	M,O
Rensselaer Polytechnic Institute	M,D
Rochester Institute of Technology	M
Roosevelt University	M
Rutgers, The State University of New Jersey, New Brunswick/Piscataway	M,D
Sage Graduate School	M
Saginaw Valley State University	M
Saint Louis University	M
St. Mary's University of San Antonio	M
St. Thomas University	M,O
San Diego State University	M
San Jose State University	M
Seton Hall University	M
Shippensburg University of Pennsylvania	M
South Dakota State University	M
Southeastern Louisiana University	M
Southern Illinois University Carbondale	M,D
Southwest Missouri State University	M
Spalding University	M
Stanford University	M,D
State University of New York College at Brockport	M
State University of New York College of Environmental Science and Forestry	M,D
Stephen F. Austin State University	M
Suffolk University	M
Syracuse University	M,D
Teachers College Columbia University	M,D
Temple University	M,D
Texas A&M University	M,D
Texas Southern University	M
Texas State University-San Marcos	M
Texas Tech University	M
Towson University	M,O
Trinity College (DC)	M
University at Albany, State University of New York	M,D
University at Buffalo, The State University of New York	M,D
The University of Akron	M
The University of Alabama	M,D
The University of Alabama at Birmingham	M
University of Alaska Fairbanks	M
The University of Arizona	M,D
University of Arkansas	M
University of Baltimore	M,D
University of California, San Diego	M,D
University of California, Santa Barbara	D
University of California, Santa Cruz	O
University of Central Florida	M
University of Cincinnati	M
University of Colorado at Boulder	M,D
University of Colorado at Colorado Springs	M
University of Colorado at Denver	M

Directory of Graduate and Professional Programs by Field
Communication—General

Institution	Degree
University of Connecticut	M,D
University of Dayton	M
University of Delaware	M
University of Denver	M,D,O
University of Dubuque	M
University of Florida	M,D
University of Georgia	M,D
University of Hartford	M
University of Hawaii at Manoa	M
University of Houston	M
University of Illinois at Chicago	M
University of Illinois at Springfield	M
University of Illinois at Urbana–Champaign	D
The University of Iowa	M,D
University of Kansas	M,D
University of Kentucky	M,D
University of Louisiana at Lafayette	M
University of Louisiana at Monroe	M
University of Louisville	M
University of Maine	M
University of Maryland, Baltimore County	M
University of Maryland, College Park	M,D
University of Massachusetts Amherst	M,D
The University of Memphis	M,D
University of Miami	M,D
University of Minnesota, Twin Cities Campus	M,D
University of Missouri–Columbia	M,D
University of Missouri–St. Louis	M
The University of Montana–Missoula	M
University of Nebraska at Omaha	M
University of Nebraska–Lincoln	M,D
University of Nevada, Las Vegas	M
University of New Mexico	M,D
The University of North Carolina at Chapel Hill	M,D
The University of North Carolina at Charlotte	M
The University of North Carolina at Greensboro	M
University of North Dakota	M,D
University of Northern Colorado	M
University of Northern Iowa	M
University of North Texas	M
University of Oklahoma	M,D
University of Oregon	M,D
University of Pennsylvania	M,D
University of Pittsburgh	M,D
University of Portland	M
University of South Alabama	M
University of Southern California	M,D
University of South Florida	M,D
The University of Tennessee	M,D
The University of Texas at Austin	M,D
The University of Texas at Dallas	D
The University of Texas at El Paso	M
The University of Texas at Tyler	M
The University of Texas–Pan American	M
University of the Incarnate Word	M
University of the Pacific	M
University of the Sacred Heart	M
University of Utah	M,D
University of Vermont	M
University of Washington	M,D
University of West Florida	M
University of Wisconsin–Madison	M,D
University of Wisconsin–Milwaukee	M
University of Wisconsin–Stevens Point	M
University of Wisconsin–Superior	M
University of Wisconsin–Whitewater	M
University of Wyoming	M
Utah State University	M
Wake Forest University	M
Washington State University	M,D
Wayne State College	M
Wayne State University	M,D
Webster University	M
West Chester University of Pennsylvania	M
Western Illinois University	M
Western Kentucky University	M
Western Michigan University	M
Westminster College (UT)	M
West Texas A&M University	M
West Virginia University	M
Wichita State University	M
William Paterson University of New Jersey	M

■ COMMUNICATION DISORDERS

Institution	Degree
Abilene Christian University	M
Adelphi University	M,D
Alabama Agricultural and Mechanical University	M
Appalachian State University	M
Arizona State University	M,D
Arkansas State University	M
Armstrong Atlantic State University	M
Auburn University	M
Ball State University	M,D
Baylor University	M
Bloomsburg University of Pennsylvania	M,D
Boston University	M,D,O
Bowling Green State University	M,D
Brigham Young University	M
Brooklyn College of the City University of New York	M,D
Buffalo State College, State University of New York	M
California State University, Chico	M
California State University, Fresno	M
California State University, Fullerton	M
California State University, Hayward	M
California State University, Long Beach	M
California State University, Los Angeles	M
California State University, Northridge	M
California State University, Sacramento	M
California University of Pennsylvania	M
Case Western Reserve University	M,D,O
Central Michigan University	M,D
Central Missouri State University	M
Clarion University of Pennsylvania	M
Cleveland State University	M
College Misericordia	M
The College of New Jersey	M
The College of New Rochelle	M
The College of Saint Rose	M
Duquesne University	M,D
East Carolina University	M,D
Eastern Illinois University	M
Eastern Kentucky University	M
Eastern Michigan University	M
Eastern New Mexico University	M
Eastern Washington University	M
East Stroudsburg University of Pennsylvania	M
East Tennessee State University	M,D
Edinboro University of Pennsylvania	M
Emerson College	M
Florida Atlantic University	M
Florida International University	M
Florida State University	M,D
Fontbonne University	M
Fort Hays State University	M
Gallaudet University	M,D
The George Washington University	M
Georgia State University	M
Governors State University	M
Hampton University	M
Harvard University	D
Hofstra University	M,O
Howard University	M,D
Hunter College of the City University of New York	M
Idaho State University	M,D
Illinois State University	M
Indiana State University	M
Indiana University Bloomington	M,D
Indiana University of Pennsylvania	M
Ithaca College	M
Jackson State University	M
James Madison University	M,D
Kean University	M
Kent State University	M,D
Lamar University	M,D
La Salle University	M
Lehman College of the City University of New York	M
Loma Linda University	M
Long Island University, Brooklyn Campus	M
Long Island University, C.W. Post Campus	M
Louisiana State University and Agricultural and Mechanical College	M,D
Louisiana Tech University	M
Loyola College in Maryland	M,O
Marquette University	M
Marshall University	M
Marywood University	M
Massachusetts Institute of Technology	D
Mercy College	M
Miami University	M
Michigan State University	M,D
Minnesota State University Mankato	M
Minnesota State University Moorhead	M
Minot State University	M
Mississippi University for Women	M
Montclair State University	M
Murray State University	M
Nazareth College of Rochester	M
New Mexico State University	M
New York University	M,D
North Carolina Central University	M
Northeastern Illinois University	M
Northeastern University	M
Northern Arizona University	M
Northern Illinois University	M,D
Northern Michigan University	M
Northwestern University	M,D
Nova Southeastern University	M,D
The Ohio State University	M,D
Ohio University	M,D
Oklahoma State University	M
Old Dominion University	M
Our Lady of the Lake University of San Antonio	M
The Pennsylvania State University University Park Campus	M,D
Portland State University	M
Purdue University	M,D
Queens College of the City University of New York	M
Radford University	M
Rockhurst University	M
St. Cloud State University	M
St. John's University (NY)	M
Saint Louis University	M
Saint Xavier University	M
San Diego State University	M,D
San Francisco State University	M
San Jose State University	M
Seton Hall University	M,D
South Carolina State University	M
Southeastern Louisiana University	M
Southeast Missouri State University	M
Southern Connecticut State University	M
Southern Illinois University Carbondale	M
Southern Illinois University Edwardsville	M
Southwest Missouri State University	D
State University of New York at New Paltz	M

Directory of Graduate and Professional Programs by Field
Comparative Literature

State University of New York at Plattsburgh	M
State University of New York College at Fredonia	M
State University of New York College at Geneseo	M
State University of West Georgia	M
Stephen F. Austin State University	M
Syracuse University	M,D
Teachers College Columbia University	M,D
Temple University	M
Texas A&M University–Kingsville	M
Texas Christian University	M
Texas State University-San Marcos	M
Texas Woman's University	M
Towson University	M,D
Truman State University	M
University at Buffalo, The State University of New York	M,D
The University of Akron	M,D
The University of Alabama	M
The University of Arizona	M,D
University of Arkansas	M
University of California, San Diego	D
University of Central Arkansas	M
University of Central Florida	M
University of Central Oklahoma	M
University of Cincinnati	M,D
University of Colorado at Boulder	M,D
University of Connecticut	M,D
University of Florida	M,D
University of Georgia	M,D,O
University of Hawaii at Manoa	M
University of Houston	M
University of Illinois at Urbana–Champaign	M,D
The University of Iowa	M,D
University of Kansas	M,D
University of Kentucky	M
University of Louisiana at Lafayette	M,D
University of Louisiana at Monroe	M
University of Louisville	M,D
University of Maine	M
University of Maryland, College Park	M,D
University of Massachusetts Amherst	M,D
The University of Memphis	M,D
University of Minnesota, Duluth	M
University of Minnesota, Twin Cities Campus	M,D
University of Mississippi	M
University of Missouri–Columbia	M
University of Montevallo	M
University of Nebraska at Kearney	M
University of Nebraska at Omaha	M
University of Nebraska–Lincoln	M
University of Nevada, Reno	M,D
University of New Hampshire	M
University of New Mexico	M
The University of North Carolina at Chapel Hill	M,D
The University of North Carolina at Greensboro	M
University of North Dakota	M,D
University of Northern Colorado	M
University of Northern Iowa	M
University of North Texas	M,D
University of Pittsburgh	M,D
University of Redlands	M
University of Rhode Island	M
University of South Alabama	M,D
University of South Carolina	M,D
The University of South Dakota	M
University of Southern Mississippi	M,D
University of South Florida	M
The University of Tennessee	M,D,O
The University of Texas at Austin	M,D
The University of Texas at Dallas	M,D
The University of Texas at El Paso	M
The University of Texas–Pan American	M
University of the District of Columbia	M
University of the Pacific	M
University of Toledo	M
University of Tulsa	M
University of Utah	M,D
University of Virginia	M
University of Washington	M,D
University of Wisconsin–Eau Claire	M
University of Wisconsin–Madison	M,D
University of Wisconsin–Milwaukee	M
University of Wisconsin–River Falls	M
University of Wisconsin–Stevens Point	M
University of Wisconsin–Whitewater	M
University of Wyoming	M
Utah State University	M,D,O
Valdosta State University	M,O
Vanderbilt University	D
Washington University in St. Louis	M,D
Wayne State University	M,D
West Chester University of Pennsylvania	M
Western Carolina University	M
Western Illinois University	M
Western Kentucky University	M
Western Michigan University	M
Western Washington University	M
West Texas A&M University	M
West Virginia University	M
Wichita State University	M,D
William Paterson University of New Jersey	M
Worcester State College	M

■ COMMUNITY COLLEGE EDUCATION

Clemson University	M,D
Eastern Washington University	M
George Mason University	D,O
Morgan State University	D
North Carolina State University	M,D
Northern Arizona University	M,D
Old Dominion University	M,D
Pittsburg State University	O
Princeton University	D
University of South Florida	M,D,O
Western Carolina University	M

■ COMMUNITY HEALTH

Arcadia University	M
Brooklyn College of the City University of New York	M
Brown University	M,D
Columbia University	M,D
Eastern Kentucky University	M
East Tennessee State University	M,O
Emory University	M
The George Washington University	M,O
Harvard University	M
Idaho State University	O
Indiana State University	M
The Johns Hopkins University	M,D
Long Island University, Brooklyn Campus	M
Minnesota State University Mankato	M
New Jersey City University	M
New York University	M,D
Old Dominion University	M
Sage Graduate School	M
Saint Louis University	M
Stony Brook University, State University of New York	M,D,O
Temple University	M
University at Buffalo, The State University of New York	M,D
University of California, Los Angeles	M,D
University of Florida	M,D
University of Illinois at Chicago	M,D
University of Illinois at Urbana–Champaign	M,D
The University of Iowa	M,D
University of Miami	M,D
University of Minnesota, Twin Cities Campus	M
University of Missouri–Columbia	M
University of New Orleans	M,O
The University of North Carolina at Greensboro	M
University of Northern Colorado	M
University of North Florida	M,O
University of North Texas	M
University of Pittsburgh	M,O
University of South Florida	M,D
The University of Tennessee	M,D
University of Wisconsin–La Crosse	M
University of Wisconsin–Madison	M,D
Wayne State University	M,O
West Virginia University	M

■ COMMUNITY HEALTH NURSING

Augsburg College	M
Bellarmine University	M
Boston College	M,D
Capital University	M
Case Western Reserve University	M,D
Cleveland State University	M
Georgia Southern University	M,O
Hawai'i Pacific University	M
Holy Names University	M
Hunter College of the City University of New York	M
Indiana Wesleyan University	M,O
The Johns Hopkins University	M
Kean University	M
La Roche College	M
La Salle University	M,O
Northeastern University	M,O
Rutgers, The State University of New Jersey, Newark	M
Sage Graduate School	M
Saint Joseph's College of Maine	M,O
Saint Xavier University	M,O
Seattle University	M
Southern Illinois University Edwardsville	M
University of Cincinnati	M,D
University of Colorado at Colorado Springs	M
University of Hartford	M
University of Hawaii at Manoa	M,D,O
University of Illinois at Chicago	M
University of Maryland	M,D
University of Massachusetts Lowell	M
University of Michigan	M
University of Minnesota, Twin Cities Campus	M
The University of North Carolina at Chapel Hill	M
The University of North Carolina at Charlotte	M
University of South Alabama	M
University of South Carolina	M
University of Southern Mississippi	M,D
The University of Texas at Brownsville	M
The University of Texas at El Paso	M
Valdosta State University	M
Wayne State University	M
Worcester State College	M
Wright State University	M

■ COMPARATIVE AND INTERDISCIPLINARY ARTS

Bradley University	M
Columbia College Chicago	M
Florida Atlantic University	D
Goddard College	M
John F. Kennedy University	M
Ohio University	D

■ COMPARATIVE LITERATURE

American University	M

Comparative Literature

Antioch University McGregor	M
Arizona State University	M,D
Brigham Young University	M
Brown University	M,D
California State University, Fullerton	M
Carnegie Mellon University	M,D
Case Western Reserve University	M,D
The Catholic University of America	M,D
Claremont Graduate University	M,D
Columbia University	M,D
Cornell University	D
Dartmouth College	M
Duke University	D
Emory University	D,O
Fairleigh Dickinson University, Metropolitan Campus	M
Florida Atlantic University	M
Harvard University	D
Indiana University Bloomington	M,D
The Johns Hopkins University	D
Kent State University	M,D
Long Island University, Brooklyn Campus	M
Louisiana State University and Agricultural and Mechanical College	M,D
New York University	M,D
Northwestern University	M,D,O
Ohio University	M
Oklahoma City University	M
The Pennsylvania State University University Park Campus	M,D
Princeton University	D
Purdue University	M,D
Rutgers, The State University of New Jersey, New Brunswick/Piscataway	M,D
San Francisco State University	M
San Jose State University	M,O
Stanford University	D
State University of New York at Binghamton	M,D
Stony Brook University, State University of New York	M,D
University at Buffalo, The State University of New York	M,D
The University of Arizona	M,D
University of Arkansas	M,D
University of California, Berkeley	D
University of California, Davis	D
University of California, Irvine	M,D
University of California, Los Angeles	M,D
University of California, Riverside	M,D
University of California, San Diego	M,D
University of California, Santa Barbara	D
University of California, Santa Cruz	M,D
University of Chicago	M,D
University of Colorado at Boulder	M,D
University of Connecticut	M,D
University of Georgia	M
University of Illinois at Urbana–Champaign	M,D
The University of Iowa	M,D
University of Maryland, College Park	M,D
University of Massachusetts Amherst	M,D
University of Michigan	D
University of Minnesota, Twin Cities Campus	D
University of Missouri–Columbia	M,D
University of New Hampshire	M,D
University of New Mexico	M,D
The University of North Carolina at Chapel Hill	D
University of Notre Dame	M,D
University of Oregon	M,D
University of Pennsylvania	M,D
University of Puerto Rico, Río Piedras	M
University of Southern California	M,D
The University of Texas at Austin	M,D
The University of Texas at Dallas	M,D
University of Utah	M
University of Washington	M,D
University of Wisconsin–Madison	M,D
University of Wisconsin–Milwaukee	M,D
Vanderbilt University	M,D
Washington University in St. Louis	M,D
Wayne State University	M
Western Kentucky University	M
West Virginia University	M
Yale University	D

■ COMPUTATIONAL SCIENCES

Arizona State University	M,D
California Institute of Technology	M,D
Carnegie Mellon University	M,D
Claremont Graduate University	M,D
Clemson University	M
The College of William and Mary	M
Cornell University	M,D
George Mason University	M,D,O
Iowa State University of Science and Technology	M,D
Kean University	M
Louisiana Tech University	M,D
Massachusetts Institute of Technology	D
Michigan Technological University	D
New Jersey Institute of Technology	M
Princeton University	D
Rice University	M,D
Rutgers, The State University of New Jersey, Newark	M
Sam Houston State University	M
San Diego State University	M,D
Southern Methodist University	M,D
Stanford University	M,D
State University of New York College at Brockport	M
Temple University	M,D
University of California, Santa Barbara	D
University of Colorado at Denver	D
University of Idaho	M,D
The University of Iowa	D
University of Massachusetts Lowell	M,D
University of Michigan–Dearborn	M
University of Minnesota, Duluth	M
University of Minnesota, Twin Cities Campus	M,D
University of Mississippi	M,D
University of Puerto Rico, Mayagüez Campus	M
University of South Florida	M,D
The University of Texas at Austin	M,D
Virginia Polytechnic Institute and State University	D
Washington University in St. Louis	D
Western Michigan University	M
Yale University	D

■ COMPUTER ART AND DESIGN

Alfred University	M
Carnegie Mellon University	M
Claremont Graduate University	M
Clemson University	M
Columbia University	M
Cornell University	M,D
DePaul University	M
Florida Atlantic University	M
Indiana University Bloomington	M
Long Island University, Brooklyn Campus	M
Long Island University, C.W. Post Campus	M
Mississippi State University	M
New Mexico Highlands University	M
New School University	M
New York University	M
Philadelphia University	M
Rensselaer Polytechnic Institute	M
Rochester Institute of Technology	M
State University of New York at New Paltz	M
Syracuse University	M
University at Buffalo, The State University of New York	M,O
University of Baltimore	M,D
University of California, Santa Cruz	M
University of Missouri–Columbia	M

■ COMPUTER EDUCATION

Arcadia University	M,D,O
Ashland University	M
California State University, Dominguez Hills	M,O
California State University, Los Angeles	M
California University of Pennsylvania	M
Cardinal Stritch University	M
DeSales University	M,O
Eastern Washington University	M
Florida Institute of Technology	M,D,O
Fontbonne University	M
Jacksonville University	M
Lesley University	M,D,O
Long Island University, C.W. Post Campus	M
Mississippi College	M
Nazareth College of Rochester	M
Nova Southeastern University	M,D,O
Ohio University	M,D
Providence College	M
Saint Martin's College	M
Shenandoah University	M,D,O
Stanford University	M,D
Stony Brook University, State University of New York	M,O
Teachers College Columbia University	M
University of Bridgeport	M,O
University of Central Oklahoma	M
University of Maryland, Baltimore County	M,D,O
University of Michigan	M,D
The University of North Carolina at Wilmington	M
University of North Texas	M,D
Wilkes University	M
Wright State University	M

■ COMPUTER ENGINEERING

Auburn University	M,D
Boise State University	M
Boston University	M,D
California State University, Chico	M
California State University, Long Beach	M
California State University, Northridge	M
Carnegie Mellon University	M,D
Case Western Reserve University	M,D
Clarkson University	M,D
Clemson University	M,D
Cleveland State University	M,D
Colorado State University	M,D
Colorado Technical University	M
Cornell University	M,D
Dartmouth College	M,D
Drexel University	M
Duke University	M,D
Fairfield University	M
Fairleigh Dickinson University, Metropolitan Campus	M
Florida Atlantic University	M,D
Florida Institute of Technology	M,D
Florida International University	M
George Mason University	M,D
The George Washington University	M,D,O
Georgia Institute of Technology	M,D
Grand Valley State University	M
Illinois Institute of Technology	M,D
Indiana State University	M
Indiana University–Purdue University Indianapolis	M,D

Directory of Graduate and Professional Programs by Field
Computer Science

Institution	Degrees
Iowa State University of Science and Technology	M,D
The Johns Hopkins University	M,D
Kansas State University	M,D
Lawrence Technological University	M,D
Lehigh University	M,D
Louisiana State University and Agricultural and Mechanical College	M,D
Manhattan College	M
Marquette University	M,D
Massachusetts Institute of Technology	M,D,O
Mercer University	M
Michigan Technological University	D
Mississippi State University	M,D
New Jersey Institute of Technology	M,D
New Mexico State University	M,D
New York Institute of Technology	M
Norfolk State University	M
North Carolina State University	M,D
Northeastern University	M,D
Northwestern University	M,D,O
Oakland University	M
Oklahoma State University	M,D
Old Dominion University	M,D
The Pennsylvania State University University Park Campus	M,D
Polytechnic University, Brooklyn Campus	M
Polytechnic University, Westchester Graduate Center	M
Portland State University	M,D
Purdue University	M,D
Rensselaer Polytechnic Institute	M,D
Rice University	M,D
Rochester Institute of Technology	M
Rutgers, The State University of New Jersey, New Brunswick/Piscataway	M,D
St. Mary's University of San Antonio	M
San Jose State University	M
Santa Clara University	M,D,O
Southern Methodist University	M,D
State University of New York at New Paltz	M
Stevens Institute of Technology	M,D,O
Stony Brook University, State University of New York	M,D
Syracuse University	M,D,O
Temple University	M
Texas A&M University	M,D
The University of Alabama at Birmingham	M,D
The University of Alabama in Huntsville	M,D
University of Alaska Fairbanks	M,D
The University of Arizona	M,D
University of Arkansas	M,D
University of Bridgeport	M
University of California, Davis	M,D
University of California, Irvine	M,D
University of California, San Diego	M,D
University of California, Santa Barbara	M,D
University of California, Santa Cruz	M,D
University of Central Florida	M,D,O
University of Cincinnati	M,D
University of Colorado at Boulder	M,D
University of Colorado at Colorado Springs	M,D
University of Colorado at Denver	M,D
University of Dayton	M,D
University of Denver	M
University of Florida	M,D,O
University of Houston	M,D
University of Houston–Clear Lake	M
University of Idaho	M
University of Illinois at Chicago	M,D
University of Illinois at Urbana–Champaign	M,D
The University of Iowa	M,D
University of Kansas	M
University of Louisiana at Lafayette	M,D
University of Louisville	M,D
University of Maine	M,D
University of Maryland, Baltimore County	M,D
University of Maryland, College Park	M,D
University of Massachusetts Amherst	M,D
University of Massachusetts Dartmouth	M,D,O
University of Massachusetts Lowell	M
The University of Memphis	M,D
University of Miami	M,D
University of Michigan	M,D
University of Michigan–Dearborn	M
University of Minnesota, Duluth	M
University of Minnesota, Twin Cities Campus	M,D
University of Missouri–Rolla	M,D
University of Nebraska–Lincoln	M,D
University of Nevada, Las Vegas	M,D
University of Nevada, Reno	M,D
University of New Mexico	M,D
The University of North Carolina at Charlotte	M,D
University of Notre Dame	M,D
University of Oklahoma	M,D
University of Puerto Rico, Mayagüez Campus	M
University of Rhode Island	M,D
University of Rochester	M,D
University of South Carolina	M,D
University of Southern California	M,D
University of South Florida	M,D
The University of Texas at Arlington	M,D
The University of Texas at Austin	M,D
The University of Texas at Dallas	M,D
The University of Texas at El Paso	M,D
University of Utah	M,D
University of Virginia	M,D
Villanova University	M,O
Virginia Polytechnic Institute and State University	M,D
Washington University in St. Louis	M,D
Wayne State University	M,D
Western Michigan University	M,D
Western New England College	M
West Virginia University	D
Widener University	M
Worcester Polytechnic Institute	M,D,O
Wright State University	M,D

■ COMPUTER SCIENCE

Institution	Degrees
Alabama Agricultural and Mechanical University	M
Alcorn State University	M
American University	M
Appalachian State University	M
Arizona State University	M,D
Arkansas State University	M
Armstrong Atlantic State University	M
Auburn University	M,D
Averett University	M
Azusa Pacific University	M,O
Ball State University	M
Baylor University	M
Boise State University	M
Boston University	M,D
Bowie State University	M
Bowling Green State University	M
Bradley University	M
Brandeis University	M,D,O
Bridgewater State College	M
Brigham Young University	M,D
Brooklyn College of the City University of New York	M,D
Brown University	M,D
California Institute of Technology	M,D
California Polytechnic State University, San Luis Obispo	M
California State Polytechnic University, Pomona	M
California State University, Chico	M
California State University, Fresno	M
California State University, Fullerton	M
California State University, Hayward	M
California State University, Long Beach	M
California State University, Northridge	M
California State University, Sacramento	M
California State University, San Bernardino	M
California State University, San Marcos	M
Carnegie Mellon University	M,D
Case Western Reserve University	M,D
The Catholic University of America	M,D
Central Connecticut State University	M
Central Michigan University	M
Chicago State University	M
The Citadel, The Military College of South Carolina	M
City College of the City University of New York	M,D
City University	M,O
Clark Atlanta University	M
Clarkson University	M,D
Clemson University	M,D
College of Charleston	M
The College of Saint Rose	M
College of Staten Island of the City University of New York	M,D
The College of William and Mary	M,D
Colorado State University	M,D
Colorado Technical University	M,D
Columbia University	M,D,O
Columbus State University	M
Cornell University	M,D
Creighton University	M
Dartmouth College	M,D
DePaul University	M,D
Drexel University	M,D
Duke University	M,D
East Carolina University	M,D,O
Eastern Illinois University	M,O
Eastern Michigan University	M
Eastern Washington University	M
East Stroudsburg University of Pennsylvania	M
East Tennessee State University	M
Emory University	M,D
Emporia State University	M
Fairleigh Dickinson University, Metropolitan Campus	M,O
Ferris State University	M
Fitchburg State College	M
Florida Atlantic University	M,D
Florida Gulf Coast University	M
Florida Institute of Technology	M,D
Florida International University	M,D
Florida State University	M,D
Fordham University	M
Frostburg State University	M
George Mason University	M,D
The George Washington University	M,D,O
Georgia Institute of Technology	M,D
Georgia Southwestern State University	M
Georgia State University	M,D
Governors State University	M
Hampton University	M
Harvard University	M,D
Hofstra University	M
Hood College	M
Howard University	M
Illinois Institute of Technology	M,D
Indiana State University	M
Indiana University Bloomington	M,D
Indiana University–Purdue University Fort Wayne	M
Indiana University–Purdue University Indianapolis	M

Peterson's Graduate Schools in the U.S. 2006   www.petersons.com   **59**

Directory of Graduate and Professional Programs by Field
Computer Science

Institution	Degree
Indiana University South Bend	M
Inter American University of Puerto Rico, Metropolitan Campus	M
Iona College	M
Iowa State University of Science and Technology	M,D
Jackson State University	M
Jacksonville State University	M
James Madison University	M
The Johns Hopkins University	M,D
Kansas State University	M,D
Kennesaw State University	M
Kent State University	M,D
Kutztown University of Pennsylvania	M
Lamar University	M
La Salle University	M
Lawrence Technological University	M
Lehigh University	M,D
Lehman College of the City University of New York	M
Long Island University, Brooklyn Campus	M
Long Island University, C.W. Post Campus	M
Louisiana State University and Agricultural and Mechanical College	M,D
Louisiana Tech University	M
Loyola Marymount University	M
Loyola University Chicago	M
Maharishi University of Management	M
Marist College	M
Marquette University	M,D
Marymount University	M,O
Massachusetts Institute of Technology	M,D,O
McNeese State University	M
Michigan State University	M,D
Michigan Technological University	M,D
Middle Tennessee State University	M
Midwestern State University	M
Minnesota State University Mankato	M
Mississippi College	M
Mississippi State University	M,D
Monmouth University	M
Montana State University–Bozeman	M,D
Montclair State University	M,O
National University	M
New Jersey Institute of Technology	M,D
New Mexico Highlands University	M
New Mexico Institute of Mining and Technology	M,D
New Mexico State University	M,D
New York Institute of Technology	M
New York University	M,D
Norfolk State University	M
North Carolina Agricultural and Technical State University	M
North Carolina State University	M,D
North Central College	M
North Dakota State University	M,D,O
Northeastern Illinois University	M
Northeastern University	M,D
Northern Illinois University	M
Northern Kentucky University	M
Northwestern University	M,D
Northwest Missouri State University	M
Nova Southeastern University	M,D
Oakland University	M
The Ohio State University	M,D
Ohio University	M,D
Oklahoma City University	M
Oklahoma State University	M,D
Old Dominion University	M,D
Oregon State University	M,D
Pace University	M,D,O
Pace University, White Plains Campus	M,D,O
The Pennsylvania State University Harrisburg Campus of the Capital College	M
The Pennsylvania State University University Park Campus	M,D
Polytechnic University, Brooklyn Campus	M,D
Polytechnic University, Westchester Graduate Center	M,D
Portland State University	M,D
Prairie View A&M University	M,D
Princeton University	M,D
Purdue University	M,D
Queens College of the City University of New York	M
Regis University	M,O
Rensselaer Polytechnic Institute	M,D
Rice University	M,D
Rivier College	M
Rochester Institute of Technology	M
Roosevelt University	M
Rutgers, The State University of New Jersey, New Brunswick/Piscataway	M,D
Sacred Heart University	M,O
St. Cloud State University	M
St. John's University (NY)	M
Saint Joseph's University	M
St. Mary's University of San Antonio	M
Saint Xavier University	M
San Diego State University	M
San Francisco State University	M
San Jose State University	M,O
Santa Clara University	M,D,O
Shippensburg University of Pennsylvania	M
South Dakota State University	M
Southeastern University	M
Southern Connecticut State University	M
Southern Illinois University Carbondale	M
Southern Illinois University Edwardsville	M
Southern Methodist University	M,D
Southern Oregon University	M
Southern University and Agricultural and Mechanical College	M
Stanford University	M,D
State University of New York at Binghamton	M,D
State University of New York at New Paltz	M
State University of New York Institute of Technology	M
State University of West Georgia	M
Stephen F. Austin State University	M
Stevens Institute of Technology	M,D,O
Stony Brook University, State University of New York	M,D,O
Suffolk University	M
Syracuse University	M,D
Tarleton State University	M
Temple University	M,D
Tennessee Technological University	M
Texas A&M University	M,D
Texas A&M University–Commerce	M
Texas A&M University–Corpus Christi	M
Texas A&M University–Kingsville	M
Texas State University-San Marcos	M
Texas Tech University	M,D
Towson University	M
Tufts University	M,D,O
Tulane University	M,D
University at Albany, State University of New York	M,D
University at Buffalo, The State University of New York	M,D
The University of Akron	M
The University of Alabama	M,D
The University of Alabama at Birmingham	M
The University of Alabama in Huntsville	M,D,O
University of Alaska Fairbanks	M,D
The University of Arizona	M,D
University of Arkansas	M,D
University of Arkansas at Little Rock	M
University of Bridgeport	M
University of California, Berkeley	M,D
University of California, Davis	M,D
University of California, Irvine	M,D
University of California, Los Angeles	M,D
University of California, Riverside	M,D
University of California, San Diego	M,D
University of California, Santa Barbara	D
University of California, Santa Cruz	M,D
University of Central Florida	M,D
University of Central Oklahoma	M
University of Chicago	M
University of Cincinnati	M,D
University of Colorado at Boulder	M,D
University of Colorado at Colorado Springs	M,D
University of Colorado at Denver	M,D
University of Connecticut	M,D
University of Dayton	M
University of Delaware	M,D
University of Denver	M,D,O
University of Detroit Mercy	M
University of Florida	M,D
University of Georgia	M,D
University of Hawaii at Manoa	M,D,O
University of Houston	M,D
University of Houston–Clear Lake	M
University of Idaho	M,D
University of Illinois at Chicago	M,D
University of Illinois at Springfield	M
University of Illinois at Urbana–Champaign	M,D
The University of Iowa	M,D
University of Kansas	M,D
University of Kentucky	M,D
University of Louisiana at Lafayette	M,D
University of Louisville	M,D
University of Maine	M,D
University of Maryland, Baltimore County	M,D
University of Maryland, College Park	M,D
University of Maryland Eastern Shore	M
University of Massachusetts Amherst	M,D
University of Massachusetts Boston	M
University of Massachusetts Dartmouth	M,O
University of Massachusetts Lowell	M,D
The University of Memphis	M,D
University of Miami	M
University of Michigan	M,D
University of Michigan–Dearborn	M
University of Minnesota, Duluth	M
University of Minnesota, Twin Cities Campus	M,D
University of Missouri–Columbia	M,D
University of Missouri–Kansas City	M,D
University of Missouri–Rolla	M,D
University of Missouri–St. Louis	M,D,O
The University of Montana–Missoula	M
University of Nebraska at Omaha	M
University of Nebraska–Lincoln	M,D
University of Nevada, Las Vegas	M,D
University of Nevada, Reno	M,D
University of New Hampshire	M,D
University of New Haven	M
University of New Mexico	M,D
University of New Orleans	M
The University of North Carolina at Chapel Hill	M,D
The University of North Carolina at Charlotte	M
The University of North Carolina at Greensboro	M
University of North Dakota	M
University of Northern Iowa	M
University of North Florida	M
University of North Texas	M,D
University of Notre Dame	M,D

University of Oklahoma	M,D
University of Oregon	M,D
University of Pennsylvania	M,D
University of Pittsburgh	M,D
University of Rhode Island	M,D
University of Rochester	M,D
University of San Francisco	M
University of South Alabama	M
University of South Carolina	M,D
The University of South Dakota	M
University of Southern California	M,D
University of Southern Maine	M
University of Southern Mississippi	M,D
University of South Florida	M,D
The University of Tennessee	M,D
The University of Tennessee at Chattanooga	M
The University of Texas at Arlington	M,D
The University of Texas at Austin	M,D
The University of Texas at Dallas	M,D
The University of Texas at El Paso	M
The University of Texas at San Antonio	M,D
The University of Texas at Tyler	M
The University of Texas–Pan American	M
University of Toledo	M,D
University of Tulsa	M,D
University of Utah	M,D
University of Vermont	M,D
University of Virginia	M,D
University of Washington	M,D
University of West Florida	M
University of Wisconsin–Madison	M,D
University of Wisconsin–Milwaukee	M,D
University of Wisconsin–Parkside	M
University of Wyoming	M,D
Utah State University	M,D
Vanderbilt University	M
Villanova University	M
Virginia Commonwealth University	M
Virginia Polytechnic Institute and State University	M,D
Wake Forest University	M
Washington State University	M,D
Washington University in St. Louis	M,D
Wayne State University	M,D,O
Webster University	M,O
West Chester University of Pennsylvania	M,O
Western Carolina University	M
Western Connecticut State University	M
Western Illinois University	M
Western Kentucky University	M
Western Michigan University	M,D
Western Washington University	M
West Virginia University	M,D
Wichita State University	M
Worcester Polytechnic Institute	M,D,O
Wright State University	M,D
Yale University	D

■ CONDENSED MATTER PHYSICS

Cleveland State University	M
Iowa State University of Science and Technology	M,D
Rutgers, The State University of New Jersey, New Brunswick/Piscataway	M,D
West Virginia University	M,D

■ CONFLICT RESOLUTION AND MEDIATION/PEACE STUDIES

Abilene Christian University	O
American University	M,D,O
Antioch University McGregor	M
Arcadia University	M
Brandeis University	M
Brenau University	O
California State University, Dominguez Hills	M,O
Chaminade University of Honolulu	M
Cornell University	M,D
Dallas Baptist University	M
Duquesne University	M
Fresno Pacific University	M
George Mason University	M,D
John F. Kennedy University	O
The Johns Hopkins University	M,D,O
Kennesaw State University	M
Lesley University	M,O
Montclair State University	M,O
Nova Southeastern University	M,D
Pepperdine University	M
Portland State University	M
Regis University	M,O
St. Edward's University	M,O
School for International Training	M
Tufts University	M,D
University of Baltimore	M
University of Denver	M,O
University of Massachusetts Boston	M,O
University of Missouri–Columbia	M
University of Missouri–St. Louis	M
University of Notre Dame	M
University of San Diego	M
Wayne State University	M,O

■ CONSERVATION BIOLOGY

Arizona State University	M,D
Central Michigan University	M
Columbia University	M,D,O
Frostburg State University	M
North Dakota State University	M,D
San Francisco State University	M
State University of New York College of Environmental Science and Forestry	M,D
University at Albany, State University of New York	M
University of Arkansas	D
University of Central Florida	M,O
University of Hawaii at Manoa	M,D
University of Maryland, College Park	M
University of Minnesota, Twin Cities Campus	M,D
University of Missouri–St. Louis	M,D,O
University of Nevada, Reno	D
University of Wisconsin–Madison	M

■ CONSTRUCTION ENGINEERING AND MANAGEMENT

Arizona State University	M
Auburn University	M,D
Bradley University	M
Brigham Young University	M
Carnegie Mellon University	M,D
The Catholic University of America	M,D
Central Connecticut State University	M
Clemson University	M
Colorado State University	M
Florida International University	M
Georgia Institute of Technology	M,D
Illinois Institute of Technology	M,D
Iowa State University of Science and Technology	M,D
Lawrence Technological University	M,D
Marquette University	M
Massachusetts Institute of Technology	M,D,O
Michigan State University	M
Montana State University–Bozeman	M,D
New York University	M,O
Oregon State University	M,D
State University of New York College of Environmental Science and Forestry	M,D
Stevens Institute of Technology	M
Texas A&M University	M,D
University of Cincinnati	M,D
University of Colorado at Boulder	M,D
University of Denver	M
University of Florida	M
University of Houston	M
University of Kansas	M,D
University of Michigan	M,D,O
University of Missouri–Rolla	M,D
University of Southern California	M
University of Washington	M,D
Washington State University	M
Washington University in St. Louis	M
Western Michigan University	M

■ CONSUMER ECONOMICS

Colorado State University	M
Cornell University	M,D
Eastern Illinois University	M
Florida State University	M,D
Indiana State University	M
Iowa State University of Science and Technology	M,D
Michigan State University	M,D
Minnesota State University Mankato	M
Montclair State University	M
The Ohio State University	M,D
Purdue University	M,D
Texas Tech University	D
The University of Alabama	M
The University of Arizona	M,D
University of Georgia	M,D
University of Illinois at Urbana–Champaign	M,D
The University of Memphis	M
University of Missouri–Columbia	M
University of Nebraska–Lincoln	M,D
The University of Tennessee	M,D
University of Utah	M
University of Vermont	M
University of Wisconsin–Madison	M,D
University of Wyoming	M
Utah State University	M
Virginia Polytechnic Institute and State University	M,D

■ CORPORATE AND ORGANIZATIONAL COMMUNICATION

Austin Peay State University	M
Barry University	M,O
Bentley College	M,O
Bernard M. Baruch College of the City University of New York	M
Bowie State University	M,O
Canisius College	M
Central Connecticut State University	M
Central Michigan University	M
Columbia University	M
Concordia University Wisconsin	M
DePaul University	M
Emerson College	M
Fairleigh Dickinson University, College at Florham	M
Florida State University	M,D
Fordham University	M
Howard University	M,D
Illinois Institute of Technology	M
Iowa State University of Science and Technology	M,D
John Carroll University	M
La Salle University	M
Lindenwood University	M
Loyola University Chicago	M
Manhattanville College	M
Marist College	M
Marylhurst University	M
Monmouth University	M,O
Montclair State University	M
Murray State University	M
North Carolina State University	M
Northwestern University	M

Directory of Graduate and Professional Programs by Field
Corporate and Organizational Communication

Institution	Degree
Oklahoma City University	M
Queens University of Charlotte	M
Radford University	M
Regis College (MA)	M
Rollins College	M
Roosevelt University	M
Sage Graduate School	M
Seton Hall University	M
Simmons College	M
Spalding University	M
Syracuse University	M
Towson University	M
University of Alaska Fairbanks	M
University of Arkansas at Little Rock	M
University of Colorado at Boulder	M,D
University of Connecticut	M,D
University of Portland	M
University of St. Thomas (MN)	M
University of Southern California	D
University of Wisconsin–Stevens Point	M
University of Wisconsin–Whitewater	M
Wayne State University	M,D
Western Kentucky University	M
Western Michigan University	M
West Virginia University	M

■ COUNSELING PSYCHOLOGY

Institution	Degree
Abilene Christian University	M
Alabama Agricultural and Mechanical University	M,O
Alaska Pacific University	M
Andrews University	D
Angelo State University	M
Anna Maria College	M,O
Antioch New England Graduate School	M
Antioch University McGregor	M
Arcadia University	M
Argosy University/Sarasota	M,D,O
Argosy University/Schaumburg	M,D
Arizona State University	D
Assumption College	M,O
Auburn University	M,D,O
Avila University	M
Ball State University	M,D
Benedictine University	M
Bethel University	M,O
Boston College	M,D
Boston University	M,D
Bowie State University	M
Brigham Young University	M,D
California Baptist University	M
California State University, Bakersfield	M
California State University, Sacramento	M
California State University, San Bernardino	M
California State University, Stanislaus	M
Carlow University	M
Central Washington University	M
Chaminade University of Honolulu	M
Chestnut Hill College	M,O
City University	M
Cleveland State University	M,O
College of Mount Saint Vincent	M,O
The College of New Rochelle	M
College of St. Joseph	M
Colorado Christian University	M
Colorado State University	M,D
Columbus State University	M,O
Concordia University (IL)	M
Dallas Baptist University	M
Dominican University of California	M
Eastern Nazarene College	M
Eastern University	M
Eastern Washington University	M
Fitchburg State College	M,O
Florida Atlantic University	M,O
Florida State University	D
Fordham University	M,D,O
Fort Valley State University	M
Framingham State College	M
Franciscan University of Steubenville	M
Frostburg State University	M
Gallaudet University	M
Gannon University	M,D
Gardner-Webb University	M
Geneva College	M
George Fox University	M
Georgian Court University	M,O
Georgia State University	M,D,O
Goddard College	M
Gonzaga University	M
Governors State University	M
Gwynedd-Mercy College	M
Heidelberg College	M
Holy Family University	M
Holy Names University	M,O
Hope International University	M
Houston Baptist University	M
Howard University	M,D
Idaho State University	M,O
Illinois State University	M,D
Immaculata University	M,D,O
Indiana State University	M,D
Indiana Wesleyan University	M
Inter American University of Puerto Rico, San Germán Campus	M,D
Iowa State University of Science and Technology	M,D
James Madison University	M,O
John Carroll University	M,O
John F. Kennedy University	M
Kean University	M,O
Kent State University	M
Kutztown University of Pennsylvania	M
La Salle University	M
Lehigh University	M,D,O
Lesley University	M,D,O
Lewis University	M
Liberty University	P,M,D
Lindenwood University	M
Louisiana State University in Shreveport	M,O
Louisiana Tech University	M,D
Loyola College in Maryland	M,O
Loyola University Chicago	D
Marist College	M,O
Marylhurst University	M,O
Marymount University	M,O
Marywood University	M
MidAmerica Nazarene University	M
Mississippi College	M
Monmouth University	M,O
Morehead State University	M
Mount St. Mary's College	M
National University	M
New Jersey City University	M
New Mexico State University	M,D,O
New York Institute of Technology	M
New York University	M,D,O
Nicholls State University	M,O
Northeastern State University	M
Northeastern University	M,D,O
Northern Arizona University	D
Northwestern Oklahoma State University	M
Northwestern University	M
Northwest Missouri State University	M
Notre Dame de Namur University	M,O
Nova Southeastern University	M
The Ohio State University	D
Our Lady of the Lake University of San Antonio	M,D
Palm Beach Atlantic University	M
The Pennsylvania State University University Park Campus	D
Prescott College	M
Radford University	M,O
Regent University	M,D,O
Regis University	M
Rivier College	M,O
Rowan University	M
Rutgers, The State University of New Jersey, New Brunswick/Piscataway	M
St. Edward's University	M
Saint Joseph College	M,O
Saint Leo University	M
Saint Martin's College	M
Saint Mary's University of Minnesota	M,O
St. Mary's University of San Antonio	M,D,O
St. Thomas University	M
Saint Xavier University	M,O
Salve Regina University	M,O
San Francisco State University	M
San Jose State University	M
Santa Clara University	M
Seton Hall University	D
Southern Illinois University Carbondale	M,D
Southern Methodist University	M
Southern Nazarene University	M
Spring Arbor University	P,M
Springfield College	M,O
Stanford University	D
State University of New York at Oswego	M,O
Tarleton State University	M
Teachers College Columbia University	M,D
Temple University	M,D
Tennessee State University	M,D
Texas A&M International University	M
Texas A&M University	D
Texas A&M University–Commerce	M,D
Texas A&M University–Texarkana	M
Texas Tech University	D
Texas Woman's University	M,D
Trevecca Nazarene University	M
University at Albany, State University of New York	M,D,O
The University of Akron	M,D
University of Baltimore	M
University of California, Santa Barbara	M,D
University of Central Arkansas	M
University of Central Oklahoma	M
University of Colorado at Denver	M
University of Connecticut	M,D
University of Denver	M,D,O
University of Georgia	M,D
University of Great Falls	M
University of Houston	D
The University of Iowa	M,D,O
University of Kansas	M,D
University of Kentucky	M,D
University of La Verne	M
University of Louisville	M,D
University of Mary Hardin-Baylor	M
University of Maryland, College Park	M,D,O
University of Massachusetts Boston	M,O
The University of Memphis	M,D
University of Miami	D
University of Minnesota, Twin Cities Campus	D
University of Missouri–Columbia	M,D
University of Missouri–Kansas City	M,D,O
University of Nevada, Las Vegas	M
The University of North Carolina at Greensboro	M,D,O
University of North Dakota	M,D
University of Northern Colorado	M,D
University of North Florida	M
University of North Texas	M,D
University of Notre Dame	D
University of Oklahoma	D
University of Pennsylvania	M
University of Rhode Island	M
University of Saint Francis (IN)	M
University of St. Thomas (MN)	M,D,O
University of San Francisco	M,D
The University of Scranton	M,O
University of Southern California	M,D,O

The University of Tennessee	M,D,O
The University of Texas at Austin	M,D
The University of Texas at Tyler	M
University of the District of Columbia	M
University of Vermont	M
University of Wisconsin–Madison	D
University of Wisconsin–Stout	M
Utah State University	M,D
Valdosta State University	M,O
Valparaiso University	M
Virginia Commonwealth University	M,D,O
Walla Walla College	M
Walsh University	M
Washington State University	M,D
Webster University	M
Western Michigan University	M,D
Western Washington University	M
Westfield State College	M
West Virginia University	M,D
William Carey College	M

■ COUNSELOR EDUCATION

Abilene Christian University	M
Adams State College	M
Alabama Agricultural and Mechanical University	M,O
Alabama State University	M,O
Albany State University	M
Alcorn State University	M
Alfred University	M
Angelo State University	M
Appalachian State University	M,O
Argosy University/Sarasota	M,D,O
Arizona State University	M
Arkansas State University	M,O
Arkansas Tech University	M
Auburn University	M,D,O
Auburn University Montgomery	M,O
Augusta State University	M,O
Austin Peay State University	M,O
Azusa Pacific University	M
Barry University	M,D,O
Bayamón Central University	M
Boise State University	M
Boston University	M,O
Bowie State University	M
Bowling Green State University	M
Bradley University	M
Bridgewater State College	M,O
Brigham Young University	M,D
Brooklyn College of the City University of New York	M,O
Butler University	M
California Lutheran University	M
California Polytechnic State University, San Luis Obispo	M
California State University, Bakersfield	M
California State University, Dominguez Hills	M
California State University, Fresno	M
California State University, Fullerton	M
California State University, Hayward	M
California State University, Long Beach	M,O
California State University, Los Angeles	M
California State University, Northridge	M,O
California State University, Sacramento	M
California State University, San Bernardino	M
California State University, Stanislaus	M
California University of Pennsylvania	M
Campbell University	M
Canisius College	M,O
Carson-Newman College	M
Carthage College	M,O
The Catholic University of America	M,D
Central Connecticut State University	M
Central Michigan University	M
Central Washington University	M
Chadron State College	M,O
Chapman University	M
Chicago State University	M
The Citadel, The Military College of South Carolina	M
Clark Atlanta University	M,D
Clemson University	M
Cleveland State University	M,D,O
The College of New Jersey	M
College of St. Joseph	M
The College of Saint Rose	M
College of Santa Fe	M
College of the Southwest	M
The College of William and Mary	M,D
Columbus State University	M,O
Concordia University (IL)	M,O
Concordia University Wisconsin	M
Creighton University	M
Dallas Baptist University	M
Delta State University	M
DePaul University	M
Doane College	M
Drake University	M
Duquesne University	M,D
East Carolina University	M,O
East Central University	M
Eastern Illinois University	M
Eastern Kentucky University	M
Eastern Michigan University	M,O
Eastern New Mexico University	M
Eastern University	M
Eastern Washington University	M
East Tennessee State University	M
Edinboro University of Pennsylvania	M,O
Emporia State University	M
Fairfield University	M,O
Fitchburg State College	M,O
Florida Agricultural and Mechanical University	M,D
Florida Atlantic University	M,O
Florida Gulf Coast University	M
Florida International University	M
Florida State University	M,O
Fordham University	M,D,O
Fort Hays State University	M
Fort Valley State University	M,O
Freed-Hardeman University	M
Fresno Pacific University	M
Frostburg State University	M
Gallaudet University	M
Geneva College	M
George Mason University	M
The George Washington University	M,D,O
Georgia Southern University	M,O
Georgia State University	M,D,O
Gwynedd-Mercy College	M
Hampton University	M
Harding University	M
Hardin-Simmons University	M
Henderson State University	M
Heritage College	M
Hofstra University	M,O
Houston Baptist University	M
Howard University	M,O
Hunter College of the City University of New York	M
Idaho State University	M,D,O
Illinois State University	M,D
Immaculata University	M,D,O
Indiana State University	M
Indiana University Bloomington	M,D,O
Indiana University of Pennsylvania	M
Indiana University–Purdue University Fort Wayne	M
Indiana University–Purdue University Indianapolis	M
Indiana University South Bend	M
Indiana University Southeast	M
Indiana Wesleyan University	M
Inter American University of Puerto Rico, Metropolitan Campus	M
Inter American University of Puerto Rico, San Germán Campus	M
Iona College	M
Iowa State University of Science and Technology	M,D
Jackson State University	M,D
Jacksonville State University	M
John Carroll University	M,O
The Johns Hopkins University	M,D,O
Johnson State College	M
Kansas State University	M,D
Kean University	M,O
Keene State College	M
Kent State University	M,D,O
Kutztown University of Pennsylvania	M
Lamar University	M
La Sierra University	M,O
Lehigh University	M,D,O
Lehman College of the City University of New York	M
Lewis University	M
Liberty University	M,D
Lincoln Memorial University	M,O
Lincoln University (MO)	M,O
Long Island University, Brooklyn Campus	M,O
Long Island University, C.W. Post Campus	M
Longwood University	M
Louisiana State University and Agricultural and Mechanical College	M,D,O
Louisiana Tech University	M,D
Loyola College in Maryland	M,O
Loyola Marymount University	M
Loyola University Chicago	M
Loyola University New Orleans	M
Lynchburg College	M
Malone College	M
Manhattan College	M,O
Marshall University	M,O
Marymount University	M
Marywood University	M
McNeese State University	M
Mercy College	M
Michigan State University	M,D,O
Middle Tennessee State University	M,O
Midwestern State University	M
Millersville University of Pennsylvania	M
Minnesota State University Mankato	M
Minnesota State University Moorhead	M
Mississippi College	M,O
Mississippi State University	M,D,O
Montana State University–Billings	M
Montana State University–Northern	M
Montclair State University	M
Morehead State University	M,O
Murray State University	M,O
National University	M
New Mexico Highlands University	M
New Mexico State University	M,D,O
New York Institute of Technology	M
New York University	M,D,O
Niagara University	M,O
Nicholls State University	M,O
North Carolina Agricultural and Technical State University	M
North Carolina Central University	M
North Carolina State University	M,D
North Dakota State University	M
Northeastern Illinois University	M
Northeastern State University	M
Northeastern University	M
Northern Arizona University	M
Northern Illinois University	M,D
Northern State University	M
Northwestern Oklahoma State University	M

Directory of Graduate and Professional Programs by Field
Counselor Education

Institution	Degrees
Northwestern State University of Louisiana	M,O
Northwest Missouri State University	M
Northwest Nazarene University	M
Oakland University	M,O
Ohio University	M,D
Oklahoma State University	M,D
Old Dominion University	M,O
Oregon State University	M,D
Our Lady of the Lake University of San Antonio	M
Palm Beach Atlantic University	M
The Pennsylvania State University University Park Campus	M,D
Pittsburg State University	M
Plymouth State University	M
Portland State University	M
Prairie View A&M University	M,D
Providence College	M
Purdue University	M,D,O
Purdue University Calumet	M
Queens College of the City University of New York	M
Radford University	M
Regent University	M,D,O
Rhode Island College	M,O
Rider University	M,O
Rivier College	M,O
Rollins College	M
Roosevelt University	M
Sage Graduate School	M,O
St. Bonaventure University	M,O
St. Cloud State University	M
St. John's University (NY)	M,O
Saint Joseph College	M,O
Saint Louis University	M,D,O
Saint Martin's College	M
Saint Mary's College of California	M
St. Mary's University of San Antonio	M,D,O
St. Thomas University	M,O
Saint Xavier University	M
Salem State College	M
Sam Houston State University	M,D
San Diego State University	M
San Jose State University	M
Santa Clara University	M
Seattle Pacific University	M
Seattle University	M,O
Seton Hall University	M
Shippensburg University of Pennsylvania	M,O
Siena Heights University	M,O
Slippery Rock University of Pennsylvania	M
Sonoma State University	M
South Carolina State University	M,D,O
South Dakota State University	M
Southeastern Louisiana University	M
Southeastern Oklahoma State University	M
Southeast Missouri State University	M,D,O
Southern Arkansas University–Magnolia	M
Southern Connecticut State University	M,O
Southern Illinois University Carbondale	M,D
Southern Oregon University	M
Southern University and Agricultural and Mechanical College	M
Southwestern Oklahoma State University	M
Southwest Missouri State University	M
Spalding University	M
Springfield College	M,O
State University of New York at Plattsburgh	M,O
State University of New York College at Brockport	M,O
State University of New York College at Oneonta	M,O
State University of West Georgia	M,O
Stephen F. Austin State University	M
Stetson University	M
Suffolk University	M,O
Sul Ross State University	M
Syracuse University	M,D,O
Tarleton State University	M
Tennessee State University	M,D
Texas A&M University	M,D
Texas A&M University–Commerce	M,D
Texas A&M University–Corpus Christi	M
Texas A&M University–Kingsville	M
Texas Christian University	M,O
Texas Southern University	M,D
Texas State University-San Marcos	M
Texas Tech University	M,D,O
Texas Woman's University	M,D
Trevecca Nazarene University	M
Trinity College (DC)	M
Troy University	M
Troy University Dothan	M,O
Troy University Montgomery	M,O
Truman State University	M
University at Albany, State University of New York	M,D,O
University at Buffalo, The State University of New York	M,D,O
The University of Akron	M
The University of Alabama	M,D,O
The University of Alabama at Birmingham	M
University of Alaska Anchorage	M
University of Alaska Fairbanks	M
University of Arkansas	M,D,O
University of Arkansas at Little Rock	M
University of Central Arkansas	M
University of Central Florida	M,D
University of Central Oklahoma	M
University of Cincinnati	M,D,O
University of Colorado at Colorado Springs	M
University of Colorado at Denver	M
University of Dayton	M
University of Delaware	M,D
University of Detroit Mercy	M
University of Florida	M,D,O
University of Georgia	M,D
University of Great Falls	M
University of Guam	M
University of Hartford	M,O
University of Hawaii at Manoa	M
University of Houston–Clear Lake	M
University of Idaho	M,D,O
University of Illinois at Urbana–Champaign	M,D,O
The University of Iowa	M,D
University of La Verne	M,O
University of Louisiana at Lafayette	M
University of Louisiana at Monroe	M
University of Louisville	M,D
University of Maine	M,D
University of Maryland, College Park	M,D,O
University of Maryland Eastern Shore	M
University of Massachusetts Amherst	M,D,O
University of Massachusetts Boston	M,O
The University of Memphis	M,D
University of Miami	M,O
University of Minnesota, Twin Cities Campus	M,D,O
University of Mississippi	M,D,O
University of Missouri–St. Louis	M,D
The University of Montana–Missoula	M,D,O
University of Montevallo	M
University of Nebraska at Kearney	M,O
University of Nebraska at Omaha	M
University of Nevada, Reno	M,D,O
University of New Hampshire	M
University of New Mexico	M,D
University of New Orleans	M,D,O
University of North Alabama	M
The University of North Carolina at Chapel Hill	M
The University of North Carolina at Charlotte	M,D
The University of North Carolina at Greensboro	M,D,O
The University of North Carolina at Pembroke	M
University of Northern Colorado	M,D
University of Northern Iowa	M,D
University of North Florida	M
University of North Texas	M,D
University of Puerto Rico, Río Piedras	M,D
University of Saint Francis (IN)	M
University of San Diego	M
University of San Francisco	M,D
The University of Scranton	M
University of South Alabama	M,O
University of South Carolina	D,O
The University of South Dakota	M,D,O
University of Southern Maine	M,O
University of South Florida	M,D,O
The University of Tennessee	M,D,O
The University of Tennessee at Chattanooga	M,O
The University of Tennessee at Martin	M
The University of Texas at Austin	M,D
The University of Texas at Brownsville	M
The University of Texas at San Antonio	M
The University of Texas of the Permian Basin	M
The University of Texas–Pan American	M
University of the District of Columbia	M
University of Toledo	M,D,O
University of Vermont	M
University of Virginia	M,D,O
University of Washington	M,D
The University of West Alabama	M
University of West Florida	M
University of Wisconsin–Madison	M
University of Wisconsin–Oshkosh	M
University of Wisconsin–Platteville	M
University of Wisconsin–River Falls	M,O
University of Wisconsin–Stevens Point	M
University of Wisconsin–Superior	M
University of Wisconsin–Whitewater	M
University of Wyoming	M,D
Utah State University	M,D
Valdosta State University	M,O
Vanderbilt University	M
Villanova University	M
Virginia Commonwealth University	M
Virginia Polytechnic Institute and State University	M,D,O
Virginia State University	M
Walsh University	M
Wayne State College	M
Wayne State University	M,D,O
West Chester University of Pennsylvania	M
Western Carolina University	M
Western Connecticut State University	M
Western Illinois University	M,O
Western Kentucky University	M,O
Western Michigan University	M,D
Western New Mexico University	M
Western Washington University	M
West Texas A&M University	M
Whitworth College	M
Wichita State University	M,D,O
Widener University	M,D
William Paterson University of New Jersey	M
Wilmington College (DE)	M
Winona State University	M
Winthrop University	M
Wright State University	M
Xavier University	M
Xavier University of Louisiana	M

Directory of Graduate and Professional Programs by Field
Cultural Studies

Youngstown State University — M

■ CRIMINAL JUSTICE AND CRIMINOLOGY

Institution	Degree
Albany State University	M
American International College	M
American University	M,D
Anna Maria College	M
Arizona State University West	M
Armstrong Atlantic State University	M
Auburn University Montgomery	M
Boise State University	M
Boston University	M
Bowling Green State University	M,D
Bridgewater State College	M
Buffalo State College, State University of New York	M
California State University, Fresno	M
California State University, Long Beach	M
California State University, Los Angeles	M
California State University, Sacramento	M
California State University, San Bernardino	M
California State University, Stanislaus	M
Central Connecticut State University	M
Central Michigan University	M
Central Missouri State University	M,O
Chaminade University of Honolulu	M
Charleston Southern University	M
Chicago State University	M
Clark Atlanta University	M
Coppin State University	M
Delta State University	M
Drury University	M
East Carolina University	M
East Central University	M
Eastern Kentucky University	M
Eastern Michigan University	M
East Tennessee State University	M
Ferris State University	M
Fitchburg State College	M
Florida Agricultural and Mechanical University	M
Florida Atlantic University	M
Florida Gulf Coast University	M
Florida International University	M
Florida Metropolitan University–Brandon Campus	M
Florida Metropolitan University–Pinellas Campus	M
Florida State University	M,D
Fordham University	M,D
The George Washington University	M,O
Georgia College & State University	M
Georgia State University	M
Grambling State University	M
Grand Valley State University	M
Illinois State University	M
Indiana State University	M
Indiana University Bloomington	M,D
Indiana University Northwest	M,O
Indiana University of Pennsylvania	M,D
Inter American University of Puerto Rico, Metropolitan Campus	M
Iona College	M
Jackson State University	M
Jacksonville State University	M
The Johns Hopkins University	M
Kent State University	M
Lamar University	M
Lewis University	M
Lincoln University (MO)	M
Lindenwood University	M
Long Island University, C.W. Post Campus	M
Longwood University	M
Loyola University Chicago	M
Loyola University New Orleans	M
Lynn University	M,O
Madonna University	M
Marshall University	M
Marywood University	M
Metropolitan State University	M
Michigan State University	M,D
Middle Tennessee State University	M
Midwestern State University	M
Minot State University	M
Mississippi College	M
Monmouth University	M,O
Morehead State University	M
New Jersey City University	M
New Mexico State University	M
Niagara University	M
Norfolk State University	M
North Carolina Central University	M
North Dakota State University	M,D
Northeastern State University	M
Northeastern University	M
Northern Arizona University	M,O
Northern Michigan University	M
Norwich University	M
Nova Southeastern University	M
Oklahoma City University	M
Oklahoma State University	M,D
The Pennsylvania State University Harrisburg Campus of the Capital College	M
The Pennsylvania State University University Park Campus	M,D
Point Park University	M
Pontifical Catholic University of Puerto Rico	M,D
Portland State University	M,D
Radford University	M
Rutgers, The State University of New Jersey, Camden	M
Rutgers, The State University of New Jersey, Newark	M,D
St. Ambrose University	M
St. Cloud State University	M
St. John's University (NY)	M
Saint Joseph's University	M
Saint Louis University	M
Saint Mary's University of Minnesota	M,O
St. Thomas University	M,O
Salve Regina University	M,O
Sam Houston State University	M,D
San Diego State University	M
San Jose State University	M
Shippensburg University of Pennsylvania	M
Southeast Missouri State University	M
Southern Illinois University Carbondale	M
Suffolk University	M
Sul Ross State University	M
Tarleton State University	M
Temple University	M,D
Tennessee State University	M
Texas A&M International University	M
Texas State University–San Marcos	M
Troy University	M
Universidad del Turabo	M
University at Albany, State University of New York	M,D
The University of Alabama	M
The University of Alabama at Birmingham	M
University of Alaska Fairbanks	M
University of Arkansas at Little Rock	M
University of Baltimore	M
University of California, Irvine	M,D
University of Central Florida	M,O
University of Central Oklahoma	M
University of Cincinnati	M,D
University of Colorado at Colorado Springs	M
University of Colorado at Denver	M
University of Delaware	M,D
University of Denver	M,O
University of Detroit Mercy	M
University of Great Falls	M
University of Houston–Clear Lake	M
University of Illinois at Chicago	M
University of Louisiana at Monroe	M
University of Louisville	M
University of Maryland, College Park	M,D
University of Massachusetts Lowell	M
The University of Memphis	M
University of Missouri–Kansas City	M,D
University of Missouri–St. Louis	M,D
The University of Montana–Missoula	M
University of Nebraska at Omaha	M,D
University of Nevada, Las Vegas	M
University of New Haven	M
University of North Alabama	M
The University of North Carolina at Charlotte	M
University of North Dakota	D
University of North Florida	M
University of North Texas	M
University of Pennsylvania	M,D
University of Pittsburgh	M,D
University of South Carolina	M
University of Southern Mississippi	M,D
University of South Florida	M,D
The University of Tennessee	M,D
The University of Tennessee at Chattanooga	M
The University of Texas at Arlington	M
The University of Texas at San Antonio	M
The University of Texas at Tyler	M
The University of Texas of the Permian Basin	M
The University of Texas–Pan American	M
University of Toledo	M
University of Wisconsin–Milwaukee	M
University of Wisconsin–Platteville	M
Valdosta State University	M
Villanova University	M
Virginia Commonwealth University	M,O
Washburn University	M
Washington State University	M
Wayne State University	M
Webster University	M,D
West Chester University of Pennsylvania	M
Western Connecticut State University	M
Western Illinois University	M,O
Western New England College	M
Western Oregon University	M
Westfield State College	M
West Texas A&M University	M
Wichita State University	M
Widener University	M
Wilmington College (DE)	M
Wright State University	M
Xavier University	M
Youngstown State University	M

■ CULTURAL STUDIES

Institution	Degree
Biola University	M,D,O
Claremont Graduate University	M,D
Cornell University	M,D
Cornerstone University	P,M
George Mason University	D
Simmons College	M
Southern Illinois University Carbondale	M
Stony Brook University, State University of New York	M,O
Union University	M
University of California, Davis	M,D
University of Chicago	M,D
University of Houston–Clear Lake	M
University of Minnesota, Twin Cities Campus	D

Peterson's Graduate Schools in the U.S. 2006 — www.petersons.com — 65

Directory of Graduate and Professional Programs by Field
Cultural Studies

Institution	Degree
University of Pittsburgh	M,D
The University of Texas at San Antonio	M,D
University of the Sacred Heart	M
Valparaiso University	M

■ CURRICULUM AND INSTRUCTION

Institution	Degree
Andrews University	M,D,O
Angelo State University	M
Appalachian State University	M
Argosy University/Sarasota	M,D,O
Argosy University/Schaumburg	M,D,O
Arizona State University	M,D
Arkansas State University	M,D,O
Arkansas Tech University	M
Ashland University	M
Auburn University	M,D,O
Aurora University	M,D
Austin Peay State University	M,O
Averett University	M
Azusa Pacific University	M
Ball State University	M,O
Baylor University	M,D,O
Benedictine University	M
Bloomsburg University of Pennsylvania	M
Boise State University	M,D
Boston College	M,D,O
Boston University	M,D,O
Bowling Green State University	M
Bradley University	M
California Baptist University	M
California Polytechnic State University, San Luis Obispo	M
California State University, Bakersfield	M
California State University, Chico	M
California State University, Dominguez Hills	M
California State University, Fresno	M
California State University, Sacramento	M
California State University, San Bernardino	M
California State University, Stanislaus	M
Campbellsville University	M
Carson-Newman College	M
Castleton State College	M
The Catholic University of America	M,D
Centenary College of Louisiana	M
Central Missouri State University	M,O
Central Washington University	M
Chapman University	M
City University	M,O
Clark Atlanta University	M,O
Clemson University	D
Cleveland State University	M
College Misericordia	M
The College of St. Scholastica	M
College of Santa Fe	M
College of the Southwest	M
The College of William and Mary	M,D
Colorado Christian University	M
Concordia University (CA)	M
Concordia University (IL)	M
Concordia University (NE)	M
Concordia University (OR)	M
Concordia University Wisconsin	M
Converse College	O
Coppin State University	M
Cornell University	M,D
Delaware State University	M
Delta State University	D
DePaul University	M,D
Doane College	M
Dominican University	M
Dominican University of California	M
Drexel University	M
Duquesne University	D
East Carolina University	M
Eastern Kentucky University	M
Eastern Michigan University	M
Eastern Washington University	M
East Tennessee State University	M
Emporia State University	M
Fairleigh Dickinson University, Metropolitan Campus	M
Ferris State University	M
Florida Atlantic University	M,D,O
Florida Gulf Coast University	M
Florida International University	M,D,O
Fordham University	M,D,O
Framingham State College	M
Franciscan University of Steubenville	M
Freed-Hardeman University	M
Fresno Pacific University	M
Frostburg State University	M
Gannon University	M
The George Washington University	M,D,O
Georgia Southern University	D
Gonzaga University	M
Grambling State University	M,D
Harvard University	M,D
Henderson State University	M
Holy Names University	M,O
Hood College	M
Houston Baptist University	M
Idaho State University	M,O
Illinois State University	M,D
Indiana State University	M,D
Indiana University Bloomington	M,D,O
Indiana University of Pennsylvania	M,D
Indiana Wesleyan University	M,D,O
Iowa State University of Science and Technology	M,D
The Johns Hopkins University	M
Johnson State College	M
Kansas State University	M,D
Kean University	M,O
Keene State College	M
Kent State University	M,D,O
Kutztown University of Pennsylvania	M,O
Lander University	M
La Sierra University	M,D,O
Lesley University	M,D,O
Lewis University	M
Lincoln Memorial University	M,O
Lock Haven University of Pennsylvania	M
Loras College	M
Louisiana State University and Agricultural and Mechanical College	M,D,O
Louisiana Tech University	M,D
Loyola College in Maryland	M,O
Loyola University Chicago	M,D
Lynchburg College	M
Malone College	M
Miami University	M
Michigan State University	M,D,O
MidAmerica Nazarene University	M
Middle Tennessee State University	M,O
Midwestern State University	M
Minnesota State University Mankato	M,O
Minnesota State University Moorhead	M
Mississippi State University	M,D,O
Montana State University–Billings	M
Montclair State University	M
Morehead State University	O
National-Louis University	M,D,O
Newman University	M
New Mexico Highlands University	M
New Mexico State University	M,D,O
Nicholls State University	M
North Carolina State University	M,D,O
Northern Arizona University	D
Northern Illinois University	M,D
Northwest Nazarene University	M
Notre Dame de Namur University	M
Oakland University	M,D,O
Ohio University	M,D
Oklahoma City University	M
Oklahoma State University	M,D,O
Olivet Nazarene University	M
Oral Roberts University	M,D
Our Lady of the Lake University of San Antonio	M,D
Pace University	M,O
Pace University, White Plains Campus	M,O
Pacific Lutheran University	M
The Pennsylvania State University Great Valley Campus	M
The Pennsylvania State University Harrisburg Campus of the Capital College	M
The Pennsylvania State University University Park Campus	M,D
Piedmont College	M,O
Point Park University	M
Pontifical Catholic University of Puerto Rico	M,D
Portland State University	M,D
Prairie View A&M University	M
Purdue University	M,D,O
Purdue University Calumet	M
Radford University	M
Rhode Island College	O
Rider University	M
Rivier College	M,O
Rowan University	M
St. Cloud State University	M
Saint Louis University	M,D
Saint Martin's College	M
Saint Mary's University of Minnesota	M,O
Saint Michael's College	M,O
Saint Peter's College	M,O
Saint Xavier University	M,O
San Diego State University	M
Seattle University	M,O
Shippensburg University of Pennsylvania	M
Siena Heights University	M
Sonoma State University	M
South Dakota State University	M
Southeastern Louisiana University	M
Southern Illinois University Carbondale	M,D
Southwest Missouri State University	M
Stanford University	M,D
State University of New York at Plattsburgh	M
Suffolk University	M,O
Syracuse University	M,D,O
Tarleton State University	M
Teachers College Columbia University	M,D
Tennessee State University	D
Tennessee Technological University	M,O
Texas A&M International University	M
Texas A&M University	M,D
Texas A&M University–Commerce	M,D
Texas A&M University–Corpus Christi	M
Texas Southern University	M,D
Texas Tech University	M,D,O
Trevecca Nazarene University	M
Troy University Dothan	M,O
Tuskegee University	M
Universidad Metropolitana	M
University at Albany, State University of New York	M,D,O
The University of Alabama	M,D,O
University of Alaska Fairbanks	M
University of Arkansas	D
University of California, Davis	M,D
University of Central Florida	M,D
University of Cincinnati	M,D
University of Colorado at Boulder	M,D
University of Colorado at Colorado Springs	M
University of Colorado at Denver	M
University of Connecticut	M,D
University of Delaware	M,D
University of Denver	M,D,O
University of Detroit Mercy	M
University of Florida	M,D,O

University of Great Falls	M
University of Hawaii at Manoa	M,D
University of Houston	M,D
University of Houston–Clear Lake	M
University of Illinois at Chicago	M,D
University of Illinois at Urbana–Champaign	M,D
The University of Iowa	M,D
University of Kansas	M,D
University of Kentucky	M,D
University of Louisiana at Lafayette	M
University of Louisiana at Monroe	D
University of Louisville	D
University of Maryland, College Park	M,D,O
University of Massachusetts Amherst	M,D,O
University of Massachusetts Boston	M
University of Massachusetts Lowell	M,D,O
The University of Memphis	M,D
University of Michigan	M,D
University of Michigan–Dearborn	M,O
University of Minnesota, Twin Cities Campus	M,D,O
University of Mississippi	M,D,O
University of Missouri–Columbia	M,D,O
University of Missouri–Kansas City	M,D,O
University of Missouri–St. Louis	M,D
The University of Montana–Missoula	M,D
University of Nebraska at Kearney	M
University of Nebraska–Lincoln	M,D,O
University of Nevada, Las Vegas	M,D,O
University of Nevada, Reno	M,D,O
University of New Orleans	M,D,O
The University of North Carolina at Chapel Hill	M,D
The University of North Carolina at Charlotte	M,D,O
The University of North Carolina at Greensboro	D
The University of North Carolina at Wilmington	M
University of Northern Iowa	M,D
University of North Texas	D
University of Oklahoma	M,D,O
University of Puerto Rico, Río Piedras	M,D
University of Redlands	M
University of Saint Mary	M
University of St. Thomas (MN)	M,D,O
University of San Diego	M,D
University of San Francisco	M,D
The University of Scranton	M
University of South Carolina	M,D,O
The University of South Dakota	M,D,O
University of Southern California	M,D
University of Southern Mississippi	M,D,O
The University of Tennessee	M,D,O
The University of Tennessee at Martin	M
The University of Texas at Arlington	M
The University of Texas at Austin	M,D
The University of Texas at Brownsville	M
The University of Texas at San Antonio	M
The University of Texas at Tyler	M
University of the Pacific	M,D
University of Toledo	M,D,O
University of Vermont	M
University of Virginia	M,D,O
University of Washington	M,D
University of West Florida	M,D,O
University of Wisconsin–Madison	M,D
University of Wisconsin–Milwaukee	M
University of Wisconsin–Oshkosh	M
University of Wisconsin–Superior	M
University of Wisconsin–Whitewater	M
University of Wyoming	M,D
Utah State University	D
Valparaiso University	M
Vanderbilt University	M
Virginia Commonwealth University	M,O
Virginia Polytechnic Institute and State University	M,D,O
Walla Walla College	M
Washburn University	M
Washington State University	M,D
Wayne State College	M,O
Wayne State University	M,D,O
Weber State University	M
Western Connecticut State University	M
Western Illinois University	M,O
West Texas A&M University	M
West Virginia University	M,D
Wichita State University	M
William Woods University	M
Wright State University	M,O
Xavier University of Louisiana	M

■ DANCE

American University	M,O
Arizona State University	M
California State University, Fullerton	M
California State University, Long Beach	M
California State University, Sacramento	M
Case Western Reserve University	M
Florida State University	M
George Mason University	M
New York University	M,D
Northern Illinois University	M
The Ohio State University	M
Purchase College, State University of New York	M
Sam Houston State University	M
San Diego State University	M
Shenandoah University	M,D,O
Southern Methodist University	M
State University of New York College at Brockport	M
Teachers College Columbia University	M
Temple University	M,D
Texas Tech University	M
Texas Woman's University	M,D
Tufts University	M,D
University of California, Irvine	M
University of California, Los Angeles	M,D
University of California, Riverside	M,D
University of Colorado at Boulder	M,D
University of Hawaii at Manoa	M,D
University of Illinois at Urbana–Champaign	M
The University of Iowa	M
University of Maryland, College Park	M
University of Michigan	M
University of Minnesota, Twin Cities Campus	M,D
University of Nevada, Las Vegas	M,D
University of New Mexico	M
The University of North Carolina at Greensboro	M
University of Oklahoma	M
University of Oregon	M
University of Utah	M
University of Washington	M
University of Wisconsin–Milwaukee	M

■ DECORATIVE ARTS

New School University	M

■ DEMOGRAPHY AND POPULATION STUDIES

Arizona State University	M,D
Bowling Green State University	M,D
Brown University	D
Cornell University	M,D
Duke University	D
Florida State University	M,O
Fordham University	M,D
Georgetown University	M
Harvard University	M,D
Princeton University	D,O
University at Albany, State University of New York	M,D,O
University of California, Berkeley	M,D
University of California, Irvine	M
University of Illinois at Urbana–Champaign	M,D
University of Pennsylvania	M,D

■ DENTAL HYGIENE

Boston University	P,M,D,O
Old Dominion University	M
University of Maryland	M
University of Missouri–Kansas City	P,M,D,O

■ DENTISTRY

Boston University	P,M,D,O
Case Western Reserve University	P
Columbia University	P
Creighton University	P
Harvard University	P,M,D,O
Howard University	P,O
Idaho State University	O
Indiana University–Purdue University Indianapolis	P
Loma Linda University	P,M,O
Marquette University	P
New York University	P
Nova Southeastern University	P,M
The Ohio State University	P
Southern Illinois University Edwardsville	P
Stony Brook University, State University of New York	P,O
Temple University	P
Tufts University	P
University at Buffalo, The State University of New York	P
The University of Alabama at Birmingham	P
University of California, Los Angeles	P,O
University of California, San Francisco	P
University of Detroit Mercy	P
University of Florida	P,O
University of Illinois at Chicago	P
The University of Iowa	P,M,D,O
University of Kentucky	P,M
University of Louisville	P
University of Maryland	P,M,O
University of Michigan	P
University of Minnesota, Twin Cities Campus	P
University of Missouri–Kansas City	P,M,D,O
The University of North Carolina at Chapel Hill	P
University of Pennsylvania	P
University of Pittsburgh	P,O
University of Southern California	P,O
University of the Pacific	P,M,O
University of Washington	P
Virginia Commonwealth University	P
West Virginia University	P

■ DEVELOPMENTAL BIOLOGY

Arizona State University	M,D
Brigham Young University	M,D
Brown University	M,D
California Institute of Technology	D
Carnegie Mellon University	M,D
Case Western Reserve University	M,D
Columbia University	M,D
Cornell University	M,D
Duke University	D,O
Emory University	D
Florida State University	M,D
Indiana University Bloomington	D
Iowa State University of Science and Technology	M,D
The Johns Hopkins University	D
Kansas State University	M,D
Marquette University	M,D
Massachusetts Institute of Technology	D
Northwestern University	D

Directory of Graduate and Professional Programs by Field
Developmental Biology

Institution	Degree
The Ohio State University	M,D
The Pennsylvania State University University Park Campus	M,D
Purdue University	D
Rensselaer Polytechnic Institute	M,D
Rutgers, The State University of New Jersey, New Brunswick/Piscataway	M,D
Stanford University	D
Stony Brook University, State University of New York	M,D
Tufts University	D
University at Albany, State University of New York	M,D
University of California, Davis	M,D
University of California, Irvine	M,D
University of California, Los Angeles	M,D
University of California, Riverside	M,D
University of California, San Diego	D
University of California, San Francisco	D
University of California, Santa Barbara	M,D
University of Chicago	D
University of Cincinnati	M,D
University of Colorado at Boulder	M,D
University of Connecticut	M,D
University of Illinois at Chicago	M,D
University of Kansas	M,D
University of Massachusetts Amherst	D
University of Miami	D
University of Michigan	M,D
University of Minnesota, Twin Cities Campus	M,D
University of Missouri–St. Louis	M,D,O
The University of North Carolina at Chapel Hill	M,D
University of Pennsylvania	D
University of Pittsburgh	D
University of South Carolina	M,D
The University of Texas at Austin	D
Virginia Polytechnic Institute and State University	M,D
Washington University in St. Louis	D
West Virginia University	M,D
Yale University	D
Yeshiva University	D

■ **DEVELOPMENTAL EDUCATION**

Institution	Degree
Edinboro University of Pennsylvania	O
Ferris State University	M
Grambling State University	M,D
National-Louis University	M,O
North Carolina State University	M
Rutgers, The State University of New Jersey, New Brunswick/Piscataway	M
Texas State University-San Marcos	M
University of California, Berkeley	M
The University of Iowa	M,D

■ **DEVELOPMENTAL PSYCHOLOGY**

Institution	Degree
Andrews University	M,D
Arizona State University	D
Boston College	M,D
Bowling Green State University	M,D
Brandeis University	M,D
California State University, San Bernardino	M
Carnegie Mellon University	D
Claremont Graduate University	M,D
Clark University	D
Cornell University	D
Duke University	D
Duquesne University	D
Eastern Washington University	M
Emory University	D
Florida International University	M,D
Fordham University	D
Gallaudet University	M,O
George Mason University	M,D
Harvard University	M,D
Howard University	M,D
Illinois State University	M,D,O

Institution	Degree
Indiana University Bloomington	D
Louisiana State University and Agricultural and Mechanical College	M,D
Loyola University Chicago	D
New York University	M,D,O
The Ohio State University	D
The Pennsylvania State University University Park Campus	M,D
Rutgers, The State University of New Jersey, New Brunswick/Piscataway	D
Stanford University	D
Suffolk University	D
Teachers College Columbia University	M,D
Temple University	D
Texas A&M University	M,D
Tufts University	M,D,O
The University of Alabama at Birmingham	M,D
University of California, Santa Cruz	D
University of Connecticut	M,D
University of Illinois at Urbana–Champaign	M,D
University of Kansas	M,D
University of Maine	M,D
University of Maryland, Baltimore County	D
University of Maryland, College Park	M,D
University of Miami	M,D
University of Michigan	D
The University of Montana–Missoula	M,D,O
University of Nebraska at Omaha	M,D,O
The University of North Carolina at Chapel Hill	D
The University of North Carolina at Greensboro	M,D
University of Notre Dame	D
University of Oregon	M,D
University of Pittsburgh	M,D
University of Rochester	M,D
University of Wisconsin–Madison	D
Virginia Polytechnic Institute and State University	M,D
Wayne State University	M,D
West Virginia University	M,D
Yeshiva University	D

■ **DISABILITY STUDIES**

Institution	Degree
The Johns Hopkins University	M,D,O
Suffolk University	M,O
Syracuse University	O
University of Illinois at Chicago	M,D

■ **DISTANCE EDUCATION DEVELOPMENT**

Institution	Degree
Florida State University	M,D,O
New York Institute of Technology	M,O
New York University	M
Nova Southeastern University	M,D
University of La Verne	M
University of Maryland, Baltimore County	M,D,O
University of Maryland University College	M,O
University of Wyoming	M,D,O
Western Illinois University	M,O

■ **EARLY CHILDHOOD EDUCATION**

Institution	Degree
Alabama Agricultural and Mechanical University	M,O
Alabama State University	M,O
Albany State University	M
Anna Maria College	M
Appalachian State University	M
Arcadia University	M,D,O
Arkansas State University	M,O
Armstrong Atlantic State University	M
Ashland University	M
Auburn University	M,D,O

Institution	Degree
Auburn University Montgomery	M,O
Augusta State University	M,O
Barry University	M
Bayamón Central University	M
Bellarmine University	M
Belmont University	M
Bloomsburg University of Pennsylvania	M
Boise State University	M
Boston College	M
Boston University	M,D,O
Brenau University	M,O
Bridgewater State College	M
Brooklyn College of the City University of New York	M
Buffalo State College, State University of New York	M
California State University, Fresno	M
California State University, Sacramento	M
Carlow University	M
Central Connecticut State University	M
Central Michigan University	M
Chestnut Hill College	M
Cheyney University of Pennsylvania	O
Chicago State University	M
City College of the City University of New York	M
Cleveland State University	M
College of Charleston	M
College of Mount St. Joseph	M
The College of New Jersey	M
The College of New Rochelle	M
The College of Saint Rose	M
Columbus State University	M,O
Concordia University (IL)	M,D
Concordia University (NE)	M
Concordia University Wisconsin	M,O
Converse College	M
Cumberland College	M
Dallas Baptist University	M
Dominican University	M
Duquesne University	M
Eastern Connecticut State University	M
Eastern Illinois University	M
Eastern Michigan University	M
Eastern Nazarene College	M,O
Eastern Washington University	M
East Tennessee State University	M
Edinboro University of Pennsylvania	M
Elms College	M,O
Emporia State University	M
Fitchburg State College	M
Florida Agricultural and Mechanical University	M
Florida International University	M
Florida State University	M,D,O
Fordham University	M,D,O
Fort Valley State University	M
Francis Marion University	M
Gallaudet University	M,D,O
Gannon University	M,O
George Mason University	M
The George Washington University	M
Georgia College & State University	M,O
Georgia Southern University	M
Georgia Southwestern State University	M,O
Georgia State University	M,D,O
Golden Gate Baptist Theological Seminary	P,M,D,O
Governors State University	M
Grambling State University	M
Grand Valley State University	M
Harding University	M
Henderson State University	M
Heritage College	M
Hofstra University	M,O
Hood College	M
Howard University	M,O
Hunter College of the City University of New York	M,O
Idaho State University	M,O

Directory of Graduate and Professional Programs by Field
Ecology

Institution	Degrees
Indiana State University	M
Indiana University of Pennsylvania	M
Indiana University–Purdue University Indianapolis	M
Jackson State University	M,D,O
Jacksonville State University	M
Jacksonville University	M,O
James Madison University	M
John Carroll University	M
Kean University	M,O
Kennesaw State University	M
Kent State University	M
Kutztown University of Pennsylvania	M,O
Lehman College of the City University of New York	M
Lesley University	M,D,O
Liberty University	M,D
Long Island University, C.W. Post Campus	M
Loyola College in Maryland	M,O
Lynchburg College	M
Manhattan College	M,O
Manhattanville College	M
Marshall University	M
Maryville University of Saint Louis	M
Marywood University	M
McNeese State University	M
Mercer University	M,O
Miami University	M
Middle Tennessee State University	M,O
Millersville University of Pennsylvania	M
Minnesota State University Mankato	M
Minot State University	M
Montana State University–Billings	M
Montclair State University	M
Mount Saint Mary College	M
Murray State University	M
National-Louis University	M,O
Nazareth College of Rochester	M
New Jersey City University	M
New York University	M,D,O
Norfolk State University	M
North Carolina Agricultural and Technical State University	M
Northeastern State University	M
Northern Arizona University	M
Northern Illinois University	M,D
North Georgia College & State University	M,O
Northwestern State University of Louisiana	M
Northwest Missouri State University	M
Nova Southeastern University	M,D,O
Oakland University	M,D,O
Oklahoma City University	M
Old Dominion University	M
Oral Roberts University	M,D
Pacific University	M
The Pennsylvania State University University Park Campus	M,D
Piedmont College	M,O
Pittsburg State University	M
Portland State University	M,D
Queens College of the City University of New York	M,O
Regis University	M,O
Rhode Island College	M
Rivier College	M,O
Roosevelt University	M
Rutgers, The State University of New Jersey, New Brunswick/Piscataway	M,D
Saginaw Valley State University	M
St. John's University (NY)	M
Saint Joseph College	M
Saint Mary's College of California	M
Saint Xavier University	M,O
Salem State College	M
Salisbury University	M
Samford University	M,D,O
Sam Houston State University	M
San Francisco State University	M
Siena Heights University	M
Slippery Rock University of Pennsylvania	M
South Carolina State University	M
Southern Oregon University	M
Southwestern Oklahoma State University	M
Southwest Missouri State University	M
Spring Hill College	M
State University of New York at Binghamton	M
State University of New York at New Paltz	M
State University of New York College at Cortland	M
State University of West Georgia	M,O
Stephen F. Austin State University	M
Syracuse University	M
Teachers College Columbia University	M,D
Temple University	M,D
Tennessee Technological University	M,O
Texas A&M International University	M
Texas A&M University–Commerce	M
Texas A&M University–Corpus Christi	M,D
Texas A&M University–Kingsville	M
Texas Southern University	M,D
Texas State University-San Marcos	M
Texas Woman's University	M,D
Towson University	M
Trinity College (DC)	M
Troy University	M,O
Tufts University	M,D,O
Universidad Metropolitana	M
University at Buffalo, The State University of New York	M,D,O
The University of Alabama at Birmingham	M,D
University of Alaska Southeast	M
University of Arkansas	M
University of Arkansas at Little Rock	M,O
University of Bridgeport	M,O
University of Central Arkansas	M
University of Central Florida	M
University of Central Oklahoma	M
University of Cincinnati	M
University of Colorado at Denver	M
University of Dayton	M
University of Detroit Mercy	M
The University of Findlay	M
University of Florida	M,D,O
University of Georgia	M,D,O
University of Hartford	M
University of Houston	M,D
University of Houston–Clear Lake	M
The University of Iowa	M,D
University of Louisville	M
University of Mary	M
University of Maryland, Baltimore County	M,D,O
University of Maryland, College Park	M,D
University of Massachusetts Amherst	M,D,O
The University of Memphis	M,D
University of Miami	M,O
University of Michigan	M,D
University of Michigan–Flint	M
University of Minnesota, Twin Cities Campus	M,D,O
University of Missouri–Columbia	M,D,O
University of Montevallo	M
University of New Hampshire	M
The University of North Carolina at Chapel Hill	M,D
The University of North Carolina at Greensboro	M
University of North Dakota	M
University of Northern Colorado	M
University of Northern Iowa	M
University of North Texas	M,D
University of Oklahoma	M,D,O
University of Pennsylvania	M
University of Pittsburgh	M
University of Portland	M
University of Puerto Rico, Río Piedras	M
The University of Scranton	M
University of South Alabama	M,O
University of South Carolina	M,D
University of Southern Mississippi	M,D,O
University of South Florida	M,D,O
The University of Tennessee	M,D,O
The University of Texas at Brownsville	M
The University of Texas at San Antonio	M
The University of Texas at Tyler	M
The University of Texas of the Permian Basin	M
The University of Texas–Pan American	M
University of the District of Columbia	M
University of the Incarnate Word	M
University of Toledo	M,D,O
The University of West Alabama	M
University of West Florida	M
University of Wisconsin–Milwaukee	M
University of Wisconsin–Oshkosh	M
Valdosta State University	M,O
Vanderbilt University	M
Virginia Commonwealth University	M,O
Wagner College	M
Wayne State University	M,D,O
Webster University	M
Western Illinois University	M,O
Western Kentucky University	M
Western Michigan University	M
Western Oregon University	M
Westfield State College	M
Wheelock College	M
Widener University	M,D
Worcester State College	M
Wright State University	M
Xavier University	M
Youngstown State University	M

■ EAST EUROPEAN AND RUSSIAN STUDIES

Institution	Degrees
Boston College	M
Columbia University	M,O
Cornell University	M,D
Florida State University	M
Georgetown University	M
Harvard University	M
Indiana University Bloomington	M,O
The Johns Hopkins University	M,D,O
La Salle University	M
The Ohio State University	M,D,O
Stanford University	M
University of Illinois at Chicago	M,D
University of Illinois at Urbana–Champaign	M
University of Kansas	M
University of Michigan	M,O
University of Minnesota, Twin Cities Campus	M
The University of North Carolina at Chapel Hill	M
The University of Texas at Austin	M
University of Washington	M
Yale University	M

■ ECOLOGY

Institution	Degrees
Arizona State University	M,D
Brown University	D
Colorado State University	M,D
Columbia University	D,O
Cornell University	M,D
Duke University	M,D,O
Eastern Kentucky University	M
Emory University	D
Florida Institute of Technology	M
Florida State University	M,D

Peterson's Graduate Schools in the U.S. 2006

Directory of Graduate and Professional Programs by Field

Ecology

Fordham University	M,D
Frostburg State University	M
George Mason University	M,D
Goddard College	M
Illinois State University	M,D
Indiana State University	M,D
Indiana University Bloomington	M,D
Iowa State University of Science and Technology	M,D
Kansas State University	M,D
Kent State University	M,D
Lesley University	M,D,O
Marquette University	M,D
Michigan Technological University	M
Minnesota State University Mankato	M
Montana State University–Bozeman	M,D
North Carolina State University	M,D
Northern Arizona University	M,O
The Ohio State University	M,D
Oklahoma State University	M,D
Old Dominion University	D
The Pennsylvania State University University Park Campus	M,D
Prescott College	M
Princeton University	D
Purdue University	M,D
Rice University	M,D
Rutgers, The State University of New Jersey, New Brunswick/Piscataway	M,D
San Diego State University	M,D
San Francisco State University	M
State University of New York College of Environmental Science and Forestry	M,D
Stony Brook University, State University of New York	D
Texas Christian University	M
University at Albany, State University of New York	M,D
The University of Arizona	M,D
University of California, Davis	M,D
University of California, Irvine	M,D
University of California, San Diego	D
University of California, Santa Barbara	M,D
University of California, Santa Cruz	M,D
University of Chicago	D
University of Colorado at Boulder	M,D
University of Connecticut	M,D
University of Delaware	M,D
University of Florida	M,D
University of Georgia	M,D
University of Hawaii at Manoa	M,D
University of Illinois at Chicago	M,D
University of Illinois at Urbana–Champaign	D
University of Kansas	M,D
University of Maine	M,D
University of Maryland, College Park	M,D
University of Miami	M,D
University of Michigan	M,D
University of Minnesota, Twin Cities Campus	M,D
University of Missouri–Columbia	M,D
University of Missouri–St. Louis	M,D,O
The University of Montana–Missoula	M,D
University of Nevada, Reno	D
The University of North Carolina at Chapel Hill	M,D
University of North Dakota	M,D
University of Notre Dame	M,D
University of Oregon	M,D
University of Pennsylvania	D
University of Pittsburgh	M,D
University of South Carolina	M,D
University of South Florida	M,D
The University of Tennessee	D
The University of Texas at Austin	M,D
University of Toledo	M,D
University of Utah	M,D
University of Wisconsin–Madison	M,D
Utah State University	M,D
Virginia Polytechnic Institute and State University	M,D
Washington University in St. Louis	D
William Paterson University of New Jersey	M
Yale University	D

■ ECONOMICS

Alabama Agricultural and Mechanical University	M
Albany State University	M
American University	M,D,O
Arizona State University	M,D
Auburn University	M,D
Baylor University	M
Bentley College	M,O
Bernard M. Baruch College of the City University of New York	M
Boston College	D
Boston University	M,D
Bowling Green State University	M
Brandeis University	M,D
Brooklyn College of the City University of New York	M
Brown University	M,D
Buffalo State College, State University of New York	M
California Institute of Technology	D
California State Polytechnic University, Pomona	M
California State University, Fullerton	M
California State University, Hayward	M
California State University, Long Beach	M
California State University, Los Angeles	M
Carnegie Mellon University	M,D
Case Western Reserve University	M
The Catholic University of America	M
Central Michigan University	M
Central Missouri State University	M
City College of the City University of New York	M
Claremont Graduate University	M,D
Clark Atlanta University	M
Clark University	D
Clemson University	M,D
Cleveland State University	M,O
Colorado State University	M,D
Columbia University	M,D
Cornell University	M
DePaul University	M
Drexel University	M,D,O
Duke University	M,D
East Carolina University	M
Eastern Illinois University	M
Eastern Michigan University	M
Eastern University	M
East Tennessee State University	M
Emory University	D
Florida Agricultural and Mechanical University	M
Florida Atlantic University	M
Florida International University	M,D
Florida State University	M,D
Fordham University	M,D,O
George Mason University	M,D
Georgetown University	D
The George Washington University	M,D
Georgia Institute of Technology	M
Georgia State University	M,D
Harvard University	M,D
Hawai'i Pacific University	M
Howard University	M,D
Hunter College of the City University of New York	M
Illinois State University	M
Indiana University Bloomington	M,D
Indiana University–Purdue University Indianapolis	M
Indiana University Southeast	M,O
Iowa State University of Science and Technology	M,D
The Johns Hopkins University	D
Kansas State University	M,D
Kent State University	M
Lehigh University	M,D
Long Island University, Brooklyn Campus	M
Louisiana State University and Agricultural and Mechanical College	M,D
Louisiana Tech University	M,D
Loyola College in Maryland	M
Marquette University	M
Massachusetts Institute of Technology	M,D
Miami University	M
Michigan State University	M,D
Middle Tennessee State University	M,D
Mississippi State University	M,D
Montclair State University	M
Morgan State University	M
Murray State University	M
New Mexico State University	M
New School University	M,D
New York Institute of Technology	M
New York University	M,D,O
North Carolina State University	M,D
Northeastern University	M,D
Northern Illinois University	M,D
Northwestern University	M,D
The Ohio State University	M,D
Ohio University	M
Oklahoma State University	M,D
Old Dominion University	M
Oregon State University	M,D
Pace University	M
Pace University, White Plains Campus	M
The Pennsylvania State University University Park Campus	M,D
Portland State University	M,D,O
Princeton University	D,O
Purdue University	M,D
Quinnipiac University	M
Rensselaer Polytechnic Institute	M
Rice University	M,D
Roosevelt University	M
Rutgers, The State University of New Jersey, Newark	M
Rutgers, The State University of New Jersey, New Brunswick/Piscataway	M,D
St. Cloud State University	M
St. John's University (NY)	M,O
Saint Louis University	M
St. Mary's University of San Antonio	M
San Diego State University	M
San Francisco State University	M
San Jose State University	M
Seattle Pacific University	M
South Dakota State University	M
Southern Illinois University Carbondale	M,D
Southern Illinois University Edwardsville	M
Southern Methodist University	M,D
Stanford University	D
State University of New York at Binghamton	M,D
Stony Brook University, State University of New York	M,D
Suffolk University	M,D
Syracuse University	M,D
Teachers College Columbia University	M,D
Temple University	M,D
Texas A&M University	M,D
Texas A&M University–Commerce	M
Texas Tech University	M,D
Tufts University	M

Directory of Graduate and Professional Programs by Field
Education—General

Institution	Degrees
Tulane University	M,D
University at Albany, State University of New York	M,D,O
University at Buffalo, The State University of New York	M,D,O
The University of Akron	M
The University of Alabama	M,D
University of Alaska Fairbanks	M
The University of Arizona	M,D
University of Arkansas	M,D
University of California, Berkeley	D
University of California, Davis	M,D
University of California, Irvine	M,D
University of California, Los Angeles	M,D
University of California, Riverside	M,D
University of California, San Diego	M,D
University of California, Santa Barbara	M,D
University of California, Santa Cruz	M,D
University of Central Arkansas	M
University of Central Florida	M
University of Chicago	D
University of Cincinnati	M
University of Colorado at Boulder	M,D
University of Colorado at Denver	M
University of Connecticut	M,D
University of Delaware	M,D
University of Denver	M
University of Florida	M,D
University of Georgia	M,D
University of Hawaii at Manoa	M,D
University of Houston	M,D
University of Idaho	M
University of Illinois at Chicago	M,D
University of Illinois at Urbana–Champaign	M,D
The University of Iowa	D
University of Kansas	M,D
University of Kentucky	M,D
University of Maine	M
University of Maryland, Baltimore County	M
University of Maryland, College Park	M,D
University of Massachusetts Amherst	M,D
University of Massachusetts Lowell	M
The University of Memphis	M,D
University of Miami	M,D
University of Michigan	M,D
University of Minnesota, Twin Cities Campus	D
University of Mississippi	M,D
University of Missouri–Columbia	M,D
University of Missouri–Kansas City	M,D
University of Missouri–St. Louis	M,O
The University of Montana–Missoula	M
University of Nebraska at Omaha	M
University of Nebraska–Lincoln	M,D
University of Nevada, Las Vegas	M
University of Nevada, Reno	M
University of New Hampshire	M,D
University of New Mexico	M,D
University of New Orleans	D
The University of North Carolina at Chapel Hill	M,D
The University of North Carolina at Charlotte	M
The University of North Carolina at Greensboro	M
University of North Texas	M
University of Oklahoma	M,D
University of Oregon	M,D
University of Pennsylvania	M,D
University of Pittsburgh	M,D
University of Puerto Rico, Río Piedras	M
University of Rhode Island	M,D
University of Rochester	M,D
University of San Francisco	M
University of South Carolina	M,D
University of Southern California	M,D
University of Southern Mississippi	M,D
University of South Florida	M,D
The University of Tennessee	M,D
The University of Tennessee at Chattanooga	M
The University of Texas at Arlington	M,D
The University of Texas at Austin	M,D
The University of Texas at Dallas	M,D
The University of Texas at El Paso	M
The University of Texas at San Antonio	M
University of Toledo	M,D,O
University of Utah	M,D
University of Virginia	M,D
University of Washington	M,D
University of Wisconsin–Madison	D
University of Wisconsin–Milwaukee	M,D
University of Wyoming	M,D
Utah State University	M,D
Vanderbilt University	M,D
Virginia Commonwealth University	M
Virginia Polytechnic Institute and State University	M,D
Virginia State University	M
Washington State University	M,D,O
Washington University in St. Louis	M
Wayne State University	M,D,O
West Chester University of Pennsylvania	M
Western Illinois University	M
Western Michigan University	M,D
West Texas A&M University	M
West Virginia University	M,D
Wichita State University	M
Wright State University	M
Yale University	M,D
Youngstown State University	M

■ EDUCATION—GENERAL

Institution	Degrees
Abilene Christian University	M
Adams State College	M
Adelphi University	M,D,O
Alabama Agricultural and Mechanical University	M,O
Alabama State University	M,D,O
Alaska Pacific University	M
Albany State University	M,O
Alcorn State University	M,O
Alfred University	M
American International College	M,D,O
American University	M,D,O
Andrews University	M,D,O
Angelo State University	M
Anna Maria College	M
Antioch New England Graduate School	M
Antioch University Los Angeles	M
Antioch University McGregor	M
Antioch University Seattle	M
Appalachian State University	M,D,O
Aquinas College	M
Arcadia University	M,D,O
Argosy University/Sarasota	M,D,O
Argosy University/Schaumburg	M,D,O
Arizona State University	M,D
Arizona State University West	M,O
Arkansas State University	M,D,O
Arkansas Tech University	M
Armstrong Atlantic State University	M
Ashland University	M,D
Auburn University	M,D
Auburn University Montgomery	M,O
Augsburg College	M
Augusta State University	M,O
Aurora University	M,D
Austin Peay State University	M,O
Averett University	M
Avila University	M
Azusa Pacific University	M,D
Baker University	M
Baldwin-Wallace College	M
Ball State University	M,D,O
Barry University	M,D,O
Bayamón Central University	M
Baylor University	M,D,O
Bellarmine University	M
Belmont University	M
Bemidji State University	M
Benedictine University	M
Bethel University	M,O
Biola University	M
Bloomsburg University of Pennsylvania	M
Boise State University	M,D
Boston College	M,D,O
Boston University	M,D,O
Bowie State University	M,D
Bowling Green State University	M,D,O
Bradley University	M
Brenau University	M,O
Bridgewater State College	M,O
Brigham Young University	M,D
Brooklyn College of the City University of New York	M,O
Brown University	M
Butler University	M
Cabrini College	M,O
California Baptist University	M
California Lutheran University	M,O
California Polytechnic State University, San Luis Obispo	M
California State Polytechnic University, Pomona	M
California State University, Bakersfield	M
California State University, Chico	M
California State University, Dominguez Hills	M,O
California State University, Fresno	M,D
California State University, Fullerton	M
California State University, Hayward	M
California State University, Long Beach	M,D,O
California State University, Los Angeles	M,D
California State University, Northridge	M,O
California State University, Sacramento	M
California State University, San Bernardino	M
California State University, San Marcos	M
California State University, Stanislaus	M
California University of Pennsylvania	M
Cameron University	M
Campbellsville University	M
Campbell University	M
Canisius College	M,O
Cardinal Stritch University	M,D
Carlow University	M
Carnegie Mellon University	M,D
Carson-Newman College	M
Carthage College	M,O
Castleton State College	M,O
The Catholic University of America	M,D
Centenary College of Louisiana	M
Central Connecticut State University	M,D,O
Central Michigan University	M,D,O
Central Missouri State University	M,O
Central Washington University	M
Chadron State College	M,O
Chaminade University of Honolulu	M
Chapman University	M,O
Charleston Southern University	M
Chestnut Hill College	M
Cheyney University of Pennsylvania	M,O
Chicago State University	M
The Citadel, The Military College of South Carolina	M,O
City College of the City University of New York	M,O
City University	M,O
Claremont Graduate University	M,D
Clarion University of Pennsylvania	M,O
Clark Atlanta University	M,D,O
Clark University	M

Peterson's Graduate Schools in the U.S. 2006
www.petersons.com 71

Directory of Graduate and Professional Programs by Field
Education—General

Institution	Degrees
Clemson University	M,D,O
Cleveland State University	M,D,O
College Misericordia	M
College of Charleston	M
College of Mount St. Joseph	M
College of Mount Saint Vincent	M,O
The College of New Jersey	M,O
The College of New Rochelle	M,O
College of Notre Dame of Maryland	M
College of St. Catherine	M
College of St. Joseph	M
The College of Saint Rose	M,O
The College of St. Scholastica	M
College of Santa Fe	M
College of Staten Island of the City University of New York	M,O
College of the Southwest	M
The College of William and Mary	M,D,O
Colorado Christian University	M
Columbia College Chicago	M
Columbus State University	M,O
Concordia University (CA)	M
Concordia University (IL)	M
Concordia University (NE)	M
Concordia University (OR)	M
Concordia University Wisconsin	M
Converse College	M,O
Coppin State University	M
Cornell University	M,D
Creighton University	M
Cumberland College	M,O
Cumberland University	M
Dallas Baptist University	M
Delaware State University	M
Delta State University	M,D,O
DePaul University	M
DeSales University	M,O
Doane College	M
Dominican University	M
Dominican University of California	M
Dowling College	M,D,O
Drake University	M,D,O
Drexel University	M,D
Drury University	M
Duke University	M
Duquesne University	M,D,O
East Carolina University	M,D,O
East Central University	M
Eastern Connecticut State University	M
Eastern Illinois University	M,O
Eastern Kentucky University	M
Eastern Michigan University	M,D,O
Eastern Nazarene College	M,O
Eastern New Mexico University	M
Eastern Oregon University	M
Eastern University	M,O
Eastern Washington University	M
East Stroudsburg University of Pennsylvania	M
East Tennessee State University	M,D,O
Edgewood College	M,O
Edinboro University of Pennsylvania	M,O
Elms College	M,O
Elon University	M
Emmanuel College	M,O
Emory University	M,D,O
Emporia State University	M,O
Fairfield University	M,O
Fairleigh Dickinson University, College at Florham	M,O
Fairleigh Dickinson University, Metropolitan Campus	M,O
Ferris State University	M
Fitchburg State College	M,O
Florida Agricultural and Mechanical University	M,D
Florida Atlantic University	M,D,O
Florida Gulf Coast University	M
Florida International University	M,D,O
Florida State University	M,D,O
Fontbonne University	M
Fordham University	M,D,O
Fort Hays State University	M,O
Franciscan University of Steubenville	M
Francis Marion University	M
Freed-Hardeman University	M
Fresno Pacific University	M
Friends University	M
Frostburg State University	M
Gallaudet University	M,D,O
Gannon University	M,D,O
Gardner-Webb University	M
Geneva College	M
George Fox University	M,D
George Mason University	M,D
The George Washington University	M,D,O
Georgia College & State University	M,O
Georgian Court University	M,O
Georgia Southern University	M,D,O
Georgia Southwestern State University	M,O
Georgia State University	M,D,O
Goddard College	M
Gonzaga University	M,D
Grambling State University	M,D
Grand Canyon University	M
Grand Valley State University	M
Gratz College	M
Gwynedd-Mercy College	M
Hamline University	M,D
Hampton University	M
Harding University	M
Hardin-Simmons University	M
Harvard University	M,D
Heidelberg College	M
Henderson State University	M,O
Heritage College	M
Hofstra University	M,D,O
Holy Family University	M
Holy Names University	M,O
Hood College	M
Hope International University	M
Houston Baptist University	M
Howard University	M,D,O
Hunter College of the City University of New York	M,O
Idaho State University	M,D,O
Illinois State University	M,D
Indiana State University	M,D,O
Indiana University Bloomington	M,D,O
Indiana University Northwest	M
Indiana University of Pennsylvania	M,D,O
Indiana University–Purdue University Fort Wayne	M
Indiana University–Purdue University Indianapolis	M
Indiana University South Bend	M
Indiana University Southeast	M
Indiana Wesleyan University	M
Inter American University of Puerto Rico, Metropolitan Campus	M,D
Iowa State University of Science and Technology	M,D
Jackson State University	M,D,O
Jacksonville State University	M,O
Jacksonville University	M,O
James Madison University	M
John Carroll University	M
John F. Kennedy University	M
The Johns Hopkins University	M,D,O
Johnson & Wales University	M
Johnson State College	M
Kansas State University	M,D
Kean University	M,O
Keene State College	M,O
Kennesaw State University	M
Kent State University	M,D,O
Kutztown University of Pennsylvania	M,O
Lake Erie College	M
Lamar University	M,O
Lander University	M
La Salle University	M
La Sierra University	M,D,O
Lawrence Technological University	M
Lehigh University	M,D,O
Lehman College of the City University of New York	M
Le Moyne College	M
Lesley University	M,D,O
Lewis University	M,O
Liberty University	M,D
Lincoln Memorial University	M,O
Lincoln University (MO)	M,O
Lindenwood University	M,O
Lipscomb University	M
Lock Haven University of Pennsylvania	M
Long Island University, Brooklyn Campus	M,O
Long Island University, C.W. Post Campus	M,O
Longwood University	M
Louisiana State University and Agricultural and Mechanical College	M,D,O
Louisiana State University in Shreveport	M,O
Louisiana Tech University	M,D
Loyola College in Maryland	M,O
Loyola Marymount University	M,D
Loyola University Chicago	M,D,O
Loyola University New Orleans	M
Lynchburg College	M
Madonna University	M
Maharishi University of Management	M
Malone College	M
Manhattan College	M,O
Manhattanville College	M
Mansfield University of Pennsylvania	M
Marian College of Fond du Lac	M
Marquette University	M,D,O
Marshall University	M,D,O
Mary Baldwin College	M
Marygrove College	M
Marymount University	M,O
Maryville University of Saint Louis	M
Marywood University	M
McNeese State University	M
Mercer University	M,O
Mercy College	M,O
Meredith College	M
Miami University	M,D,O
Michigan State University	M,D,O
MidAmerica Nazarene University	M
Middle Tennessee State University	M,D,O
Midwestern State University	M
Millersville University of Pennsylvania	M
Milligan College	M
Minnesota State University Mankato	M,O
Minnesota State University Moorhead	M,O
Mississippi College	M,O
Mississippi State University	M,D,O
Mississippi University for Women	M
Monmouth University	M,O
Montana State University–Billings	M,O
Montana State University–Bozeman	M,D,O
Montana State University–Northern	M
Montclair State University	M,D,O
Morehead State University	M,O
Morgan State University	M,D
Mount Mary College	M
Mount Saint Mary College	M
Mount St. Mary's College	M
Mount Saint Mary's University	M
Murray State University	M,D,O
National-Louis University	M,D,O
National University	M
Nazareth College of Rochester	M
New Jersey City University	M
Newman University	M
New Mexico Highlands University	M
New Mexico State University	M,D,O

Directory of Graduate and Professional Programs by Field
Education—General

Institution	Degrees
New York Institute of Technology	M,O
New York University	M,D,O
Niagara University	M,O
Nicholls State University	M
Norfolk State University	M
North Carolina Agricultural and Technical State University	M
North Carolina Central University	M
North Carolina State University	M,D,O
North Central College	M
North Dakota State University	M,D,O
Northeastern Illinois University	M
Northeastern State University	M
Northeastern University	M
Northern Arizona University	M,D,O
Northern Illinois University	M,D,O
Northern Kentucky University	M
Northern Michigan University	M,O
Northern State University	M
North Georgia College & State University	M,O
North Park University	M
Northwestern Oklahoma State University	M
Northwestern State University of Louisiana	M,O
Northwestern University	M,D
Northwest Missouri State University	M,O
Northwest Nazarene University	M
Notre Dame de Namur University	M
Nova Southeastern University	M,D,O
Nyack College	M
Oakland City University	M,D
Oakland University	M,D,O
The Ohio State University	M,D,O
Ohio University	M,D
Oklahoma City University	M
Oklahoma State University	M,D,O
Old Dominion University	M,D,O
Olivet Nazarene University	M
Oral Roberts University	M,D
Oregon State University	M,D
Our Lady of the Lake University of San Antonio	M,D
Pace University	M,O
Pace University, White Plains Campus	M,O
Pacific Lutheran University	M
Pacific University	M
Palm Beach Atlantic University	M
Park University	M
The Pennsylvania State University Great Valley Campus	M
The Pennsylvania State University Harrisburg Campus of the Capital College	M,D
The Pennsylvania State University University Park Campus	M,D
Peru State College	M
Pfeiffer University	M
Piedmont College	M,O
Pittsburg State University	M,O
Plymouth State University	M,O
Point Loma Nazarene University	M,O
Point Park University	M
Pontifical Catholic University of Puerto Rico	M,D
Portland State University	M,D
Prairie View A&M University	M,D
Prescott College	M
Providence College	M
Purdue University	M,D,O
Purdue University Calumet	M
Queens College of the City University of New York	M,O
Queens University of Charlotte	M
Quincy University	M
Quinnipiac University	M
Radford University	M
Regent University	M,D,O
Regis College (MA)	M
Regis University	M,O
Rhode Island College	D
Rice University	M
Rider University	M,O
Rivier College	M,O
Robert Morris University	M
Roberts Wesleyan College	M,O
Rockford College	M
Rockhurst University	M
Rollins College	M
Roosevelt University	M,D
Rowan University	M,D,O
Rutgers, The State University of New Jersey, New Brunswick/Piscataway	M,D
Sacred Heart University	M,O
Sage Graduate School	M,O
Saginaw Valley State University	M,O
St. Bonaventure University	M,O
St. Cloud State University	M,O
Saint Francis University	M
St. John's University (NY)	M,D,O
Saint Joseph College	M
Saint Joseph's College of Maine	M
Saint Joseph's University	M,D,O
Saint Leo University	M
Saint Louis University	M,D
Saint Martin's College	M
Saint Mary's College of California	M
Saint Mary's University of Minnesota	M
St. Mary's University of San Antonio	M,O
Saint Michael's College	M,O
Saint Peter's College	M,O
St. Thomas Aquinas College	M,O
St. Thomas University	M,O
Saint Xavier University	M,O
Salem International University	M
Salem State College	M,O
Salisbury University	M
Samford University	M,D,O
San Diego State University	M,D
San Francisco State University	M,D,O
San Jose State University	M,O
Santa Clara University	M,O
School for International Training	M
Seattle Pacific University	M,D,O
Seattle University	M,D,O
Seton Hall University	M,D,O
Shenandoah University	M,D,O
Shippensburg University of Pennsylvania	M,O
Siena Heights University	M
Silver Lake College	M
Simmons College	M,O
Simpson University	M
Slippery Rock University of Pennsylvania	M
Sonoma State University	M
South Carolina State University	M,D,O
South Dakota State University	M
Southeastern Louisiana University	M
Southeastern Oklahoma State University	M
Southern Arkansas University–Magnolia	M
Southern Connecticut State University	M,D,O
Southern Illinois University Carbondale	M,D
Southern Illinois University Edwardsville	M,O
Southern Methodist University	M
Southern Nazarene University	M
Southern Oregon University	M
Southern University and Agricultural and Mechanical College	M
Southern Utah University	M
Southern Wesleyan University	M
Southwest Baptist University	M,O
Southwestern Oklahoma State University	M
Southwest Missouri State University	M
Spalding University	M,D
Spring Arbor University	M
Springfield College	M
Spring Hill College	M
Stanford University	M,D
State University of New York at Binghamton	M,D
State University of New York at New Paltz	M,O
State University of New York at Oswego	M,O
State University of New York College at Brockport	M
State University of New York College at Cortland	M,O
State University of New York College at Fredonia	M,O
State University of New York College at Geneseo	M
State University of New York College at Oneonta	M,O
State University of New York College at Potsdam	M
State University of New York Empire State College	M
State University of West Georgia	M,D,O
Stephen F. Austin State University	M,D
Stetson University	M,O
Suffolk University	M,O
Sul Ross State University	M
Syracuse University	M,D,O
Tarleton State University	M
Teachers College Columbia University	M,D
Temple University	M,D
Tennessee State University	M
Tennessee Technological University	M,D,O
Texas A&M International University	M
Texas A&M University	M,D
Texas A&M University–Commerce	M,D
Texas A&M University–Corpus Christi	M,D
Texas A&M University–Kingsville	M,D
Texas A&M University–Texarkana	M
Texas Christian University	M,O
Texas Southern University	M,D
Texas State University-San Marcos	M
Texas Tech University	M,D,O
Texas Wesleyan University	M
Texas Woman's University	M,D
Towson University	M
Trevecca Nazarene University	M,D
Trinity College (DC)	M
Trinity University	M
Troy University	M,O
Troy University Dothan	M,O
Troy University Montgomery	M,O
Truman State University	M
Tufts University	M,O
Tusculum College	M
Tuskegee University	M
Union Institute & University	M,O
Union University	M,D,O
Universidad del Turabo	M
Universidad Metropolitana	M
University at Albany, State University of New York	M,D,O
University at Buffalo, The State University of New York	M,D,O
The University of Akron	M,D
The University of Alabama at Birmingham	M,D,O
University of Alaska Anchorage	M
University of Alaska Fairbanks	M
University of Alaska Southeast	M
The University of Arizona	M,D,O
University of Arkansas	M,D,O
University of Arkansas at Little Rock	M,D,O
University of Bridgeport	M,D,O
University of California, Berkeley	M,D,O
University of California, Davis	M,D

Directory of Graduate and Professional Programs by Field
Education—General

Institution	Degree
University of California, Irvine	M,D
University of California, Los Angeles	M,D
University of California, Riverside	M,D
University of California, San Diego	M,D
University of California, Santa Barbara	M,D
University of California, Santa Cruz	M,O
University of Central Arkansas	M
University of Central Florida	M,D,O
University of Central Oklahoma	M
University of Cincinnati	M,D,O
University of Colorado at Boulder	M,D
University of Colorado at Colorado Springs	M
University of Colorado at Denver	M,D
University of Connecticut	M,D
University of Dayton	M,D,O
University of Delaware	M,D
University of Denver	M,D,O
University of Detroit Mercy	M
University of Evansville	M
The University of Findlay	M
University of Florida	M,D,O
University of Georgia	M,D
University of Great Falls	M
University of Guam	M
University of Hartford	M,D,O
University of Hawaii at Manoa	M,D
University of Houston	M,D
University of Houston–Clear Lake	M
University of Houston–Victoria	M,D,O
University of Idaho	M,D
University of Illinois at Chicago	M,D
University of Illinois at Urbana–Champaign	M,D,O
University of Indianapolis	M
The University of Iowa	M,D,O
University of Kansas	M,D,O
University of Kentucky	M,D,O
University of La Verne	M,O
University of Louisiana at Lafayette	M
University of Louisiana at Monroe	M,D,O
University of Louisville	M,D,O
University of Maine	M,D,O
University of Mary	M
University of Mary Hardin-Baylor	M
University of Maryland, Baltimore County	M,D,O
University of Maryland, College Park	M,D,O
University of Maryland Eastern Shore	M
University of Maryland University College	M
University of Massachusetts Amherst	M,D,O
University of Massachusetts Boston	M,D,O
University of Massachusetts Dartmouth	M,O
University of Massachusetts Lowell	M,D,O
The University of Memphis	M,D,O
University of Miami	M,D,O
University of Michigan	M,D
University of Michigan–Dearborn	M
University of Michigan–Flint	M
University of Minnesota, Twin Cities Campus	M,D,O
University of Mississippi	M,D,O
University of Missouri–Columbia	M,D,O
University of Missouri–Kansas City	M,D,O
University of Missouri–St. Louis	M,D,O
University of Mobile	M
The University of Montana–Missoula	M,D,O
University of Montevallo	M,O
University of Nebraska at Kearney	M,O
University of Nebraska at Omaha	M,D,O
University of Nebraska–Lincoln	M,D,O
University of Nevada, Las Vegas	M,D,O
University of Nevada, Reno	M,D,O
University of New England	M
University of New Hampshire	M,D,O
University of New Haven	M
University of New Mexico	M,D,O
University of New Orleans	M,D,O
University of North Alabama	M,O
The University of North Carolina at Chapel Hill	M,D
The University of North Carolina at Charlotte	M
The University of North Carolina at Greensboro	M,D,O
The University of North Carolina at Pembroke	M
The University of North Carolina at Wilmington	M
University of North Dakota	M,D,O
University of Northern Colorado	M,D,O
University of Northern Iowa	M,D,O
University of North Florida	M,D
University of North Texas	M,D,O
University of Notre Dame	M
University of Oklahoma	M,D,O
University of Oregon	M,D
University of Pennsylvania	M,D
University of Pittsburgh	M,D
University of Portland	M
University of Puerto Rico, Río Piedras	M,D
University of Redlands	M
University of Rhode Island	M
University of Rio Grande	M
University of Rochester	M,D
University of St. Francis (IL)	M
University of Saint Francis (IN)	M
University of Saint Mary	M
University of St. Thomas (MN)	M
University of St. Thomas (TX)	M
University of San Diego	M,D,O
University of San Francisco	M,D
The University of Scranton	M
University of Sioux Falls	M
University of South Alabama	M,D,O
University of South Carolina	M,D,O
The University of South Dakota	M,D,O
University of Southern California	M,D,O
University of Southern Indiana	M
University of Southern Maine	M,D,O
University of Southern Mississippi	M,D,O
University of South Florida	M,D,O
The University of Tennessee	M,D,O
The University of Tennessee at Chattanooga	M,O
The University of Tennessee at Martin	M
The University of Texas at Arlington	M
The University of Texas at Austin	M,D
The University of Texas at Brownsville	M
The University of Texas at El Paso	M,D
The University of Texas at San Antonio	M
The University of Texas at Tyler	M
The University of Texas of the Permian Basin	M
The University of Texas–Pan American	M,D
University of the District of Columbia	M
University of the Incarnate Word	M
University of the Pacific	M,D,O
University of the Sacred Heart	M
University of the Virgin Islands	M,O
University of Toledo	M,D,O
University of Tulsa	M
University of Utah	M,D
University of Vermont	M,D
University of Virginia	M,D,O
University of Washington	M,D,O
The University of West Alabama	M
University of Wisconsin–Eau Claire	M
University of Wisconsin–Green Bay	M
University of Wisconsin–La Crosse	M
University of Wisconsin–Madison	M,D,O
University of Wisconsin–Milwaukee	M,D
University of Wisconsin–Oshkosh	M
University of Wisconsin–Platteville	M
University of Wisconsin–River Falls	M
University of Wisconsin–Stevens Point	M
University of Wisconsin–Stout	M
University of Wisconsin–Superior	M
University of Wisconsin–Whitewater	M
University of Wyoming	M,D,O
Ursuline College	M
Utah State University	M,D,O
Valdosta State University	M,D,O
Valparaiso University	M
Vanderbilt University	M,D
Villanova University	M
Virginia Commonwealth University	M,D,O
Virginia State University	M,O
Viterbo University	M
Wagner College	M
Wake Forest University	M
Walden University	M,D
Walla Walla College	M
Walsh University	M
Washburn University	M
Washington State University	M,D
Washington University in St. Louis	M,D
Wayland Baptist University	M
Wayne State College	M,O
Wayne State University	M,D,O
Weber State University	M
Webster University	M,O
West Chester University of Pennsylvania	M,O
Western Carolina University	M,D,O
Western Connecticut State University	M
Western Illinois University	M,O
Western Kentucky University	M,O
Western Michigan University	M,D,O
Western New Mexico University	M
Western Oregon University	M
Western Washington University	M,O
Westfield State College	M
Westminster College (UT)	M
West Texas A&M University	M
West Virginia University	M,D
Wheelock College	M
Whitworth College	M
Wichita State University	M,D,O
Widener University	M,D
Wilkes University	M
William Carey College	M
William Paterson University of New Jersey	M
William Woods University	M,O
Wilmington College (DE)	M
Winona State University	M
Winthrop University	M
Worcester State College	M
Wright State University	M,O
Xavier University	M
Xavier University of Louisiana	M
York College of Pennsylvania	M
Youngstown State University	M,D

■ **EDUCATIONAL ADMINISTRATION**

Institution	Degree
Abilene Christian University	M
Adelphi University	M,O
Alabama Agricultural and Mechanical University	M,O
Alabama State University	M,D,O
Albany State University	M,O
American International College	M,D,O
American University	M,D
Andrews University	M,D,O
Angelo State University	M
Antioch New England Graduate School	M
Appalachian State University	M,D
Arcadia University	M,D,O
Argosy University/Sarasota	M,D,O
Argosy University/Schaumburg	M,D,O
Arizona State University	M,D
Arizona State University West	M,O
Arkansas State University	M,D,O
Arkansas Tech University	M
Ashland University	M,D
Auburn University	M,D,O

Directory of Graduate and Professional Programs by Field
Educational Administration

Institution	Degrees
Auburn University Montgomery	M,O
Augusta State University	M,O
Aurora University	M,D
Austin Peay State University	M,O
Azusa Pacific University	M,D
Baldwin-Wallace College	M
Ball State University	M,D,O
Barry University	M,D,O
Bayamón Central University	M
Baylor University	M,D,O
Benedictine College	M
Benedictine University	M
Bernard M. Baruch College of the City University of New York	M,O
Boston College	M,D,O
Boston University	M,O
Bowie State University	M,D
Bowling Green State University	M,D,O
Bradley University	M
Bridgewater State College	M,O
Brigham Young University	M,D
Brooklyn College of the City University of New York	O
Buffalo State College, State University of New York	O
Butler University	M
Cabrini College	M,O
California Baptist University	M
California Lutheran University	M
California Polytechnic State University, San Luis Obispo	M
California State University, Bakersfield	M
California State University, Chico	M
California State University, Dominguez Hills	M
California State University, Fresno	M,D
California State University, Fullerton	M
California State University, Hayward	M
California State University, Long Beach	M
California State University, Los Angeles	M
California State University, Northridge	M
California State University, Sacramento	M
California State University, San Bernardino	M
California State University, Stanislaus	M
California University of Pennsylvania	M
Cameron University	M
Campbell University	M
Canisius College	M,O
Cardinal Stritch University	M,D
Carlow University	M
Carthage College	M,O
Castleton State College	M,O
The Catholic University of America	M,D
Centenary College of Louisiana	M
Central Connecticut State University	M,D,O
Central Michigan University	M,D,O
Central Missouri State University	M,O
Central Washington University	M
Chadron State College	M,O
Chapman University	M
Charleston Southern University	M
Chestnut Hill College	M
Cheyney University of Pennsylvania	M,O
Chicago State University	M
The Citadel, The Military College of South Carolina	M,O
City College of the City University of New York	M,O
City University	M,O
Claremont Graduate University	M,D
Clark Atlanta University	M,D,O
Clemson University	M,D,O
Cleveland State University	M,D,O
College of Mount St. Joseph	M
The College of New Jersey	M
The College of New Rochelle	M,O
College of Notre Dame of Maryland	M
The College of Saint Rose	M,O
College of Santa Fe	M
College of Staten Island of the City University of New York	O
College of the Southwest	M
The College of William and Mary	M,D
Columbus State University	M,O
Concordia University (CA)	M
Concordia University (IL)	M,D,O
Concordia University (NE)	M
Concordia University (OR)	M
Concordia University Wisconsin	M
Converse College	M,O
Creighton University	M
Cumberland College	O
Dallas Baptist University	M
Delta State University	M,D,O
DePaul University	M,D
Doane College	M
Dominican University	M
Dowling College	D,O
Drake University	M,D,O
Drexel University	D
Duquesne University	M,D
East Carolina University	M,D,O
Eastern Illinois University	M,O
Eastern Kentucky University	M
Eastern Michigan University	M,D,O
Eastern Nazarene College	M,O
Eastern Washington University	M
East Tennessee State University	M,D,O
Edgewood College	M,O
Edinboro University of Pennsylvania	M,O
Emmanuel College	M,O
Emporia State University	M
Fairleigh Dickinson University, College at Florham	M
Fairleigh Dickinson University, Metropolitan Campus	M
Fayetteville State University	M,D
Ferris State University	M
Fitchburg State College	M,O
Florida Agricultural and Mechanical University	M,D
Florida Atlantic University	M,D,O
Florida Gulf Coast University	M
Florida International University	M,D,O
Florida State University	M,D,O
Fordham University	M,D,O
Fort Hays State University	M,O
Framingham State College	M
Franciscan University of Steubenville	M
Fresno Pacific University	M
Friends University	M
Frostburg State University	M
Gallaudet University	M,D,O
Gardner-Webb University	M
Geneva College	M
George Mason University	M
The George Washington University	M,D,O
Georgia College & State University	M,O
Georgian Court University	M,O
Georgia Southern University	M,D,O
Georgia State University	M,D,O
Gonzaga University	M,D
Governors State University	M
Grambling State University	M,D
Grand Valley State University	M
Gwynedd-Mercy College	M
Harding University	M
Harvard University	M,D
Henderson State University	M
Heritage College	M
Hofstra University	M,D,O
Hood College	M
Houston Baptist University	M
Howard University	M,D,O
Hunter College of the City University of New York	O
Idaho State University	M,D,O
Illinois State University	M,D
Immaculata University	M,D,O
Indiana State University	M,D,O
Indiana University Bloomington	M,D,O
Indiana University of Pennsylvania	M,D,O
Indiana University–Purdue University Fort Wayne	M
Indiana University–Purdue University Indianapolis	M
Inter American University of Puerto Rico, Metropolitan Campus	M
Inter American University of Puerto Rico, San Germán Campus	M
Iona College	M
Iowa State University of Science and Technology	M,D
Jackson State University	M,D,O
Jacksonville State University	M,O
James Madison University	M
John Carroll University	M
The Johns Hopkins University	M,D,O
Johnson & Wales University	D
Kansas State University	M,D
Kean University	M,O
Keene State College	M,O
Kent State University	M,D,O
Kutztown University of Pennsylvania	M
Lamar University	M
La Sierra University	M,D,O
Lehigh University	M,D,O
Lesley University	M,D,O
Lewis University	M
Liberty University	M,D
Lincoln Memorial University	M,O
Lincoln University (MO)	M,O
Lindenwood University	M,O
Long Island University, Brooklyn Campus	M
Long Island University, C.W. Post Campus	M,O
Longwood University	M
Loras College	M
Louisiana State University and Agricultural and Mechanical College	M,D,O
Louisiana Tech University	M,D
Loyola College in Maryland	M,O
Loyola Marymount University	M,D
Loyola University Chicago	M,D
Lynchburg College	M
Lynn University	M,D
Madonna University	M
Manhattan College	M,O
Manhattanville College	M
Marian College of Fond du Lac	M
Marshall University	M,D,O
Marygrove College	M
Marymount University	M,O
Maryville University of Saint Louis	M
Marywood University	M
McNeese State University	M,O
Mercy College	M
Miami University	M
Michigan State University	M,D,O
Middle Tennessee State University	M,O
Midwestern State University	M
Minnesota State University Mankato	M,O
Minnesota State University Moorhead	M,O
Mississippi College	M
Mississippi State University	M,D,O
Monmouth University	M,O
Montclair State University	M
Morehead State University	M,O
Morgan State University	M,D
Mount St. Mary's College	M
Murray State University	M,O
National-Louis University	M,D,O
National University	M
New Jersey City University	M
Newman University	M

Peterson's Graduate Schools in the U.S. 2006

Directory of Graduate and Professional Programs by Field
Educational Administration

Institution	Degrees
New Mexico Highlands University	M
New Mexico State University	M,D
New York Institute of Technology	O
New York University	M,D,O
Niagara University	M,O
Nicholls State University	M
Norfolk State University	M
North Carolina Agricultural and Technical State University	M
North Carolina Central University	M
North Carolina State University	M,D
North Central College	M
North Dakota State University	M,O
Northeastern Illinois University	M
Northeastern State University	M
Northern Arizona University	M,D
Northern Illinois University	M,D,O
Northern Kentucky University	M
Northern Michigan University	M,O
Northern State University	M
North Georgia College & State University	M,O
Northwestern State University of Louisiana	M,O
Northwest Missouri State University	M,O
Northwest Nazarene University	M
Notre Dame de Namur University	M,O
Nova Southeastern University	M,D,O
Oakland City University	M,D
Oakland University	M,D,O
The Ohio State University	M,D,O
Ohio University	M,D
Oklahoma State University	M,D,O
Old Dominion University	M,O
Oral Roberts University	M,D
Our Lady of the Lake University of San Antonio	M,D
Pace University	M,O
Pace University, White Plains Campus	M,O
Pacific Lutheran University	M
Park University	M
The Pennsylvania State University University Park Campus	M,D
Pittsburg State University	M
Plymouth State University	M
Point Park University	M
Portland State University	M,D
Prairie View A&M University	M,D
Providence College	M
Purdue University	M,D,O
Purdue University Calumet	M
Queens College of the City University of New York	O
Radford University	M
Rhode Island College	M,O
Rider University	M
Rivier College	M,O
Robert Morris University	M
Roosevelt University	M,D
Rowan University	M,D
Rutgers, The State University of New Jersey, New Brunswick/Piscataway	M,D
Sacred Heart University	M,O
Saginaw Valley State University	M,O
St. Bonaventure University	M,O
St. Cloud State University	M,O
Saint Francis University	M
St. John Fisher College	M
St. John's University (NY)	M,D,O
Saint Joseph's University	D
Saint Louis University	M,D,O
Saint Mary's College of California	M
Saint Mary's University of Minnesota	M,D,O
St. Mary's University of San Antonio	M,O
Saint Michael's College	M,O
Saint Peter's College	M,O
St. Thomas University	M,O
Saint Xavier University	M,O
Salem State College	M
Salisbury University	M
Samford University	M,D,O
Sam Houston State University	M,D
San Diego State University	M
San Francisco State University	M,O
San Jose State University	M,O
Santa Clara University	M
Seattle Pacific University	M,D
Seattle University	M,D,O
Seton Hall University	M,D,O
Shenandoah University	M,D,O
Shippensburg University of Pennsylvania	M
Silver Lake College	M
Simmons College	M,O
Simpson University	M
Slippery Rock University of Pennsylvania	M
Sonoma State University	M
South Carolina State University	M,D,O
South Dakota State University	M
Southeastern Louisiana University	M
Southeastern Oklahoma State University	M
Southeast Missouri State University	M,D,O
Southern Arkansas University–Magnolia	M
Southern Connecticut State University	D,O
Southern Illinois University Carbondale	M,D
Southern Illinois University Edwardsville	M,O
Southern Oregon University	M
Southern University and Agricultural and Mechanical College	M
Southwest Baptist University	M,O
Southwestern Oklahoma State University	M
Southwest Missouri State University	M,O
Spalding University	M,D
Stanford University	M,D
State University of New York at New Paltz	M,O
State University of New York at Oswego	M,O
State University of New York at Plattsburgh	O
State University of New York College at Brockport	M,O
State University of New York College at Cortland	O
State University of New York College at Fredonia	O
State University of West Georgia	M,O
Stephen F. Austin State University	M,D
Stetson University	M,O
Stony Brook University, State University of New York	M,O
Suffolk University	M,O
Sul Ross State University	M
Syracuse University	M,D,O
Tarleton State University	M,O
Teachers College Columbia University	M,D
Temple University	M,D
Tennessee State University	M,D
Tennessee Technological University	M,O
Texas A&M International University	M
Texas A&M University	M,D
Texas A&M University–Commerce	M,D
Texas A&M University–Corpus Christi	M,D
Texas A&M University–Kingsville	M,D
Texas A&M University–Texarkana	M
Texas Christian University	M
Texas Southern University	M,D
Texas State University-San Marcos	M,D,O
Texas Tech University	M,D
Texas Woman's University	M,D
Towson University	M,O
Trevecca Nazarene University	M
Trinity College (DC)	M
Trinity University	M
Troy University	M
Troy University Dothan	M,O
Troy University Montgomery	O
Union University	M,D,O
Universidad del Turabo	M
Universidad Metropolitana	M
University at Albany, State University of New York	M,D,O
University at Buffalo, The State University of New York	M,D,O
The University of Akron	M,D
The University of Alabama	M,D
The University of Alabama at Birmingham	M,D,O
University of Alaska Anchorage	M
University of Alaska Fairbanks	M
The University of Arizona	D
University of Arkansas	M,D,O
University of Arkansas at Little Rock	M,O
University of Bridgeport	D,O
University of California, Berkeley	M,D
University of California, Irvine	M,D
University of Central Arkansas	M,O
University of Central Florida	M,D,O
University of Central Oklahoma	M
University of Cincinnati	M,D,O
University of Colorado at Colorado Springs	M
University of Colorado at Denver	M,D,O
University of Connecticut	M,D
University of Dayton	M,D
University of Delaware	M,D
University of Denver	M,D,O
University of Detroit Mercy	M
The University of Findlay	M
University of Florida	M,D,O
University of Georgia	M,O
University of Great Falls	M
University of Guam	M
University of Hartford	M,D,O
University of Hawaii at Manoa	M,D
University of Houston	M,D
University of Houston–Clear Lake	M
University of Idaho	M,D,O
University of Illinois at Chicago	M,D
University of Illinois at Springfield	M
University of Illinois at Urbana–Champaign	M,D,O
The University of Iowa	M,D,O
University of Kansas	M,D
University of Kentucky	M,D,O
University of La Verne	M,D,O
University of Louisiana at Lafayette	M
University of Louisiana at Monroe	M,D
University of Louisville	M,D,O
University of Maine	M,D,O
University of Mary	M
University of Mary Hardin-Baylor	M
University of Maryland, College Park	M,D,O
University of Massachusetts Amherst	M,D,O
University of Massachusetts Boston	M,D,O
University of Massachusetts Lowell	M,D,O
The University of Memphis	M,D,O
University of Miami	M
University of Michigan	M,D
University of Michigan–Dearborn	M,O
University of Minnesota, Twin Cities Campus	M,D,O
University of Mississippi	M,D,O
University of Missouri–Columbia	M,D,O
University of Missouri–St. Louis	M,D
The University of Montana–Missoula	M,D,O
University of Montevallo	M,O
University of Nebraska at Kearney	M
University of Nebraska at Omaha	M,D,O
University of Nebraska–Lincoln	M,D,O
University of Nevada, Las Vegas	M,D,O
University of Nevada, Reno	M,D,O
University of New England	O
University of New Hampshire	M,O

Directory of Graduate and Professional Programs by Field
Educational Media/Instructional Technology

Institution	Degree
University of New Mexico	M,D,O
University of New Orleans	M,D,O
University of North Alabama	M,O
The University of North Carolina at Chapel Hill	M,D
The University of North Carolina at Charlotte	M,D,O
The University of North Carolina at Greensboro	M,D,O
The University of North Carolina at Pembroke	M
The University of North Carolina at Wilmington	M
University of North Dakota	M,D,O
University of Northern Colorado	M,D,O
University of Northern Iowa	M,D
University of North Florida	M,D
University of North Texas	M,D
University of Oklahoma	M,D
University of Pennsylvania	M,D
University of Pittsburgh	M,D
University of Puerto Rico, Río Piedras	M,D
University of Redlands	M
University of St. Francis (IL)	M
University of St. Thomas (MN)	M,D,O
University of San Diego	M,D,O
University of San Francisco	M,D
The University of Scranton	M
University of Sioux Falls	M
University of South Alabama	M,O
University of South Carolina	M,D,O
University of South Dakota	M,D,O
University of Southern California	M,D,O
University of Southern Maine	M,O
University of Southern Mississippi	M,D,O
University of South Florida	M,D,O
The University of Tennessee	M,D,O
The University of Tennessee at Chattanooga	M,O
The University of Tennessee at Martin	M
The University of Texas at Arlington	M
The University of Texas at Austin	M,D
The University of Texas at Brownsville	M
The University of Texas at El Paso	M,D
The University of Texas at San Antonio	M,D
The University of Texas at Tyler	M
The University of Texas of the Permian Basin	M
The University of Texas–Pan American	M
University of the Pacific	M,D
University of Toledo	M,D,O
University of Utah	M,D
University of Vermont	M,D
University of Virginia	M,D,O
University of Washington	M,D,O
The University of West Alabama	M
University of West Florida	M,O
University of Wisconsin–Madison	M,D,O
University of Wisconsin–Milwaukee	M
University of Wisconsin–Oshkosh	M
University of Wisconsin–Stevens Point	M
University of Wisconsin–Superior	M,O
University of Wisconsin–Whitewater	M
University of Wyoming	M,D,O
Ursuline College	M
Valdosta State University	M,D,O
Vanderbilt University	M,D
Villanova University	M
Virginia Commonwealth University	M,O
Virginia Polytechnic Institute and State University	D,O
Virginia State University	M
Walla Walla College	M
Washburn University	M
Washington State University	M,D
Wayne State College	M,O
Wayne State University	M,D,O
Webster University	M,O
Western Carolina University	M,D,O
Western Connecticut State University	D
Western Illinois University	M,O
Western Kentucky University	M,O
Western Michigan University	M,D,O
Western New Mexico University	M
Western Washington University	M
Westfield State College	M,O
West Texas A&M University	M
West Virginia University	M,D
Wheelock College	M
Whitworth College	M
Wichita State University	M,D,O
Widener University	M,D
Wilkes University	M
William Paterson University of New Jersey	M
William Woods University	M
Wilmington College (DE)	M,D
Winona State University	M,O
Winthrop University	M
Worcester State College	M
Wright State University	M,O
Xavier University	M
Xavier University of Louisiana	M
Yeshiva University	M,D,O
Youngstown State University	M,D

■ **EDUCATIONAL MEASUREMENT AND EVALUATION**

Institution	Degree
Abilene Christian University	M
Angelo State University	M
Arkansas State University	M,O
Boston College	M,D,O
Claremont Graduate University	M,D
College of the Southwest	M
Florida State University	M,D
Gallaudet University	O
George Mason University	M
Georgia State University	M,D
Houston Baptist University	M
Iowa State University of Science and Technology	M,D
Kent State University	M,D
Louisiana State University and Agricultural and Mechanical College	M,D,O
Loyola University Chicago	M,D
Michigan State University	M,D,O
Mississippi College	M
New York University	M,D,O
North Carolina State University	D
Ohio University	M,D
Rutgers, The State University of New Jersey, New Brunswick/Piscataway	M
Seattle University	O
Southern Connecticut State University	M
Southern Illinois University Carbondale	M,D
Southwestern Oklahoma State University	M
Stanford University	M,D
State University of West Georgia	D
Sul Ross State University	M
Syracuse University	M,D,O
Teachers College Columbia University	M,D
Texas A&M University	M,D
Texas Christian University	M
Texas Southern University	M,D
University at Albany, State University of New York	M,D,O
University of California, Berkeley	M,D
University of Colorado at Boulder	D
University of Connecticut	M,D
University of Denver	M,D,O
University of Florida	M,D,O
The University of Iowa	M,D,O
University of Kansas	M,D
University of Kentucky	M,D
University of Louisville	M
University of Maryland, College Park	M,D
University of Massachusetts Amherst	M,D,O
The University of Memphis	M,D
University of Miami	M
University of Michigan	M,D
University of Minnesota, Twin Cities Campus	M,D
University of Missouri–St. Louis	M,D
University of Nevada, Las Vegas	M,D,O
The University of North Carolina at Chapel Hill	M,D
The University of North Carolina at Greensboro	M,D
University of North Dakota	D
University of Northern Colorado	M,D
University of North Texas	D
University of Pennsylvania	M,D
University of Pittsburgh	M,D
University of Puerto Rico, Río Piedras	M
University of South Carolina	M,D
University of South Florida	M,D,O
The University of Tennessee	M,D,O
The University of Texas–Pan American	M
University of Toledo	M,D,O
University of Virginia	M,D
University of Washington	M,D
Utah State University	M,D
Vanderbilt University	M,D
Virginia Polytechnic Institute and State University	D
Washington University in St. Louis	D
Wayne State University	M,D,O
West Chester University of Pennsylvania	M
Western Michigan University	M,D
West Texas A&M University	M
Wilkes University	M

■ **EDUCATIONAL MEDIA/ INSTRUCTIONAL TECHNOLOGY**

Institution	Degree
Adelphi University	M,O
Alabama State University	M,O
American University	M
Appalachian State University	M,O
Arcadia University	M,D,O
Arizona State University	M,D
Arkansas Tech University	M
Auburn University	M,D,O
Azusa Pacific University	M
Baldwin-Wallace College	M
Barry University	M,D,O
Belmont University	M
Bloomsburg University of Pennsylvania	M
Boise State University	M
Boston University	M,D,O
Bowling Green State University	M
Bridgewater State College	M
Brigham Young University	M,D
Buffalo State College, State University of New York	M
Cabrini College	M,O
California State University, Chico	M
California State University, Fullerton	M
California State University, Los Angeles	M
California State University, San Bernardino	M
California State University, Stanislaus	M
Central Connecticut State University	M
Central Michigan University	M
Central Missouri State University	M
Chestnut Hill College	M,O
Chicago State University	M
City University	M,O
College of Mount Saint Vincent	M,O
The College of New Jersey	M,O
The College of Saint Rose	M,O
The College of St. Scholastica	M
The College of William and Mary	M,D
Concordia University (CA)	M
DePaul University	M,D

Directory of Graduate and Professional Programs by Field
Educational Media/Instructional Technology

Institution	Degree
DeSales University	M,O
Dowling College	D,O
Drexel University	D
Duquesne University	M,D
East Carolina University	M,O
Eastern Connecticut State University	M
Eastern Washington University	M
East Stroudsburg University of Pennsylvania	M
East Tennessee State University	M
Emporia State University	M
Fairfield University	M,O
Fairleigh Dickinson University, Metropolitan Campus	M,O
Ferris State University	M
Florida Atlantic University	M
Florida Gulf Coast University	M
Florida State University	M,D,O
Fort Hays State University	M
Framingham State College	M
Fresno Pacific University	M
Frostburg State University	M
Gallaudet University	O
Gannon University	M
George Mason University	M
The George Washington University	M
Georgia College & State University	M,O
Georgian Court University	M,O
Georgia Southern University	M
Georgia State University	M,D,O
Governors State University	M
Grand Valley State University	M
Harvard University	M,D
Hofstra University	M
Idaho State University	M,D,O
Indiana State University	M,D
Indiana University Bloomington	M,D,O
Indiana University of Pennsylvania	M
Indiana University–Purdue University Indianapolis	M
Inter American University of Puerto Rico, Metropolitan Campus	M
Iona College	M,O
Iowa State University of Science and Technology	M,D
Jackson State University	M,D,O
Jacksonville State University	M
Jacksonville University	M
The Johns Hopkins University	M,D,O
Kean University	M,O
Kent State University	M
Kutztown University of Pennsylvania	M,O
Lamar University	M
Lehigh University	M,D
Lindenwood University	M,O
Long Island University, Brooklyn Campus	M
Long Island University, C.W. Post Campus	M,D,O
Longwood University	M
Louisiana State University and Agricultural and Mechanical College	M,D,O
Loyola College in Maryland	M
Malone College	M
Marist College	M,O
Marywood University	M
McNeese State University	M
Mercy College	M,O
Michigan State University	M,D,O
MidAmerica Nazarene University	M
Minnesota State University Mankato	M,O
Mississippi State University	M,D,O
Mississippi University for Women	M
Montana State University–Billings	M
National-Louis University	M,O
National University	M
Nazareth College of Rochester	M
New Jersey City University	M
New York Institute of Technology	M,O
New York University	M,D,O
North Carolina Agricultural and Technical State University	M
North Carolina Central University	M
North Carolina State University	M,D
Northern Arizona University	M,O
Northern Illinois University	M,D
Northern State University	M
Northwestern State University of Louisiana	M,O
Northwestern University	M,D
Northwest Missouri State University	M
Notre Dame de Namur University	M,O
Nova Southeastern University	M,D,O
Oakland University	O
Ohio University	M,D
Old Dominion University	M
Our Lady of the Lake University of San Antonio	M
Pacific Lutheran University	M
The Pennsylvania State University Great Valley Campus	M
The Pennsylvania State University University Park Campus	M,D
Philadelphia University	M
Pittsburg State University	M
Pontifical Catholic University of Puerto Rico	M,D
Portland State University	M,D
Purdue University	M,D,O
Purdue University Calumet	M
Radford University	M
Regis University	M,O
Rochester Institute of Technology	M
Rowan University	M
St. Cloud State University	M
Saint Joseph's University	M
Saint Michael's College	M,O
Salem State College	M
Salisbury University	M
San Diego State University	M,D
San Francisco State University	M,O
San Jose State University	M,O
Seton Hall University	M,O
Simmons College	M
Southeastern Oklahoma State University	M
Southern Connecticut State University	M,O
Southern Illinois University Edwardsville	M
Southern University and Agricultural and Mechanical College	M
Southwest Missouri State University	M
Spalding University	M
State University of New York College at Potsdam	M
State University of West Georgia	M,O
Stony Brook University, State University of New York	M,O
Syracuse University	M,O
Teachers College Columbia University	M,D
Texas A&M University	M
Texas A&M University–Commerce	M,D
Texas A&M University–Corpus Christi	M,D
Texas Southern University	M
Texas Tech University	M,D,O
Towson University	M,D
Troy University Dothan	M,O
University at Albany, State University of New York	M,D,O
University at Buffalo, The State University of New York	M,D,O
The University of Akron	M
The University of Alabama	M,D
University of Alaska Southeast	M
University of Arkansas	M
University of Arkansas at Little Rock	M
University of Central Arkansas	M
University of Central Florida	M,D
University of Central Oklahoma	M
University of Colorado at Denver	M
University of Connecticut	M,D
University of Dayton	M
The University of Findlay	M
University of Florida	M,D,O
University of Georgia	M,D,O
University of Hartford	M
University of Hawaii at Manoa	M
University of Houston–Clear Lake	M
University of Louisville	M
University of Maine	M
University of Maryland, Baltimore County	M,D,O
University of Maryland, College Park	M,D,O
University of Massachusetts Amherst	M,D,O
The University of Memphis	M,D
University of Michigan	M,D
University of Minnesota, Twin Cities Campus	M,D,O
University of Missouri–Columbia	M,D,O
University of Nebraska at Kearney	M,O
University of Nebraska at Omaha	M,O
University of Nevada, Las Vegas	M,D,O
University of New Mexico	M,D,O
The University of North Carolina at Charlotte	M,D,O
The University of North Carolina at Wilmington	M
University of North Dakota	M
University of Northern Colorado	M,D
University of Northern Iowa	M
University of San Francisco	M,D
University of Sioux Falls	M
University of South Alabama	M,D
University of South Carolina	M
The University of South Dakota	M,O
University of Southern California	M,D
University of South Florida	M,D,O
The University of Tennessee	M,D,O
The University of Tennessee at Chattanooga	O
The University of Texas at Brownsville	M
The University of Texas at San Antonio	M
University of the Incarnate Word	M
University of the Sacred Heart	M
University of Toledo	M,D,O
University of Washington	M,D
The University of West Alabama	M
University of West Florida	M
University of Wyoming	M,D,O
Utah State University	M,D,O
Vanderbilt University	M
Virginia Polytechnic Institute and State University	M,D,O
Wayne State College	M
Wayne State University	M,D,O
Webster University	M,O
West Chester University of Pennsylvania	M,O
Western Connecticut State University	M
Western Illinois University	M,O
Western Kentucky University	M
Western Oregon University	M
Westfield State College	M
West Texas A&M University	M
Widener University	M,D
Wilkes University	M
Wilmington College (DE)	M

■ EDUCATIONAL POLICY

Institution	Degree
Alabama State University	M,D,O
The College of William and Mary	M,D
Georgia State University	M,D,O
Illinois State University	M,D
Indiana University Bloomington	M,D,O
Loyola University Chicago	M,D
Michigan State University	D
The Ohio State University	M,D,O
Portland State University	M,D

Rutgers, The State University of New Jersey, New Brunswick/Piscataway	D
University of Hawaii at Manoa	D
University of Illinois at Chicago	M,D
University of Illinois at Urbana–Champaign	M,D,O
The University of Iowa	M,D,O
University of Kansas	D
University of Kentucky	M,D
University of Minnesota, Twin Cities Campus	M,D
University of Pennsylvania	M,D
University of Virginia	M,D
University of Washington	M,D
University of Wisconsin–Madison	M,D,O
University of Wisconsin–Milwaukee	M
Vanderbilt University	M,D
Wayne State University	M,D

■ EDUCATIONAL PSYCHOLOGY

American International College	M,D,O
Andrews University	M,D
Arcadia University	M
Arizona State University	M,D
Auburn University	M,D,O
Austin Peay State University	M,O
Ball State University	M,D,O
Baylor University	M,D,O
Boston College	M,D
Brigham Young University	M,D
California State University, Long Beach	M
California State University, Northridge	M,O
California State University, San Bernardino	M
The Catholic University of America	M,D
Chapman University	M,O
Clark Atlanta University	M,D
The College of Saint Rose	M
Eastern Michigan University	M
Eastern University	M
Edinboro University of Pennsylvania	M
Florida Atlantic University	M,D,O
Florida State University	M,D
Fordham University	M,D,O
Georgian Court University	M,O
Georgia State University	M,D
Harvard University	M,D
Holy Names University	M,O
Howard University	M,D,O
Illinois State University	M,D,O
Indiana State University	M,D,O
Indiana University Bloomington	M,D,O
Indiana University of Pennsylvania	M,O
John Carroll University	M
Johnson State College	M
Kansas State University	M,D
Kean University	M
Kent State University	M,D
La Sierra University	M,O
Loyola Marymount University	M
Loyola University Chicago	M,D
Marist College	M,O
Miami University	M
Mississippi State University	M,D,O
Montclair State University	M
National-Louis University	M,D,O
New Jersey City University	M,O
New York University	M,D,O
Northeastern University	M
Northern Arizona University	D
Northern Illinois University	M,D,O
Oklahoma State University	M,D
The Pennsylvania State University University Park Campus	M,D
Purdue University	M,D,O
Rhode Island College	M
Rutgers, The State University of New Jersey, New Brunswick/Piscataway	M,D
Southern Illinois University Carbondale	M,D
Southern Illinois University Edwardsville	M
Stanford University	D
State University of New York College at Oneonta	M,O
Teachers College Columbia University	M,D
Temple University	M,D
Tennessee Technological University	M,O
Texas A&M University	M,D
Texas A&M University–Commerce	M,D
Texas Christian University	M,O
Texas Tech University	M,D,O
University at Albany, State University of New York	M,D,O
University at Buffalo, The State University of New York	M,D,O
The University of Arizona	M,D
University of California, Berkeley	M,D
University of California, Davis	M,D
University of Colorado at Boulder	M,D
University of Colorado at Denver	M
University of Connecticut	M
University of Denver	M,D,O
University of Florida	M,D,O
University of Georgia	M,D,O
University of Hawaii at Manoa	M,D
University of Houston	M,D
University of Illinois at Chicago	M,D
University of Illinois at Urbana–Champaign	M,D,O
The University of Iowa	M,D,O
University of Kansas	M,D
University of Kentucky	M,D,O
University of Louisville	M,D
University of Mary Hardin-Baylor	M
University of Maryland, College Park	M,D
The University of Memphis	M,D
University of Minnesota, Twin Cities Campus	M,D,O
University of Missouri–Columbia	M,D,O
University of Missouri–Kansas City	M,D,O
University of Missouri–St. Louis	M,D
University of Nebraska at Omaha	M,D,O
University of Nebraska–Lincoln	M,O
University of Nevada, Las Vegas	M,D
University of Nevada, Reno	M,D,O
University of New Mexico	M,D
The University of North Carolina at Chapel Hill	M,D
University of Northern Colorado	M,D
University of Northern Iowa	M,O
University of Oklahoma	M,D
University of Pennsylvania	M,D
University of South Carolina	M,D
The University of South Dakota	M,D,O
University of Southern California	M,D,O
The University of Tennessee	M,D,O
The University of Texas at Austin	M,D
The University of Texas at El Paso	M
The University of Texas at San Antonio	M
The University of Texas–Pan American	M
University of the Pacific	M,D,O
University of Toledo	M,D,O
University of Utah	M,D
University of Virginia	M,D
University of Washington	M,D
University of Wisconsin–Madison	M,D
University of Wisconsin–Milwaukee	M,D
Wayne State University	M,D,O
West Virginia University	M,D
Wichita State University	M,D,O
Widener University	M,D

■ EDUCATION OF THE GIFTED

Arkansas State University	M,D,O
Arkansas Tech University	M
Ashland University	M
Barry University	M,D,O
Belmont University	M
California State University, Los Angeles	M,D
California State University, Northridge	M
Carthage College	M,O
Clark Atlanta University	M,O
The College of New Rochelle	M,O
The College of William and Mary	M
Converse College	M
Drury University	M
Emporia State University	M
Grand Valley State University	M
Hardin-Simmons University	M
Hofstra University	M,O
Jacksonville University	M,O
The Johns Hopkins University	M,D,O
Johnson State College	M
Kent State University	M,D,O
Liberty University	M,D
Lynn University	M,D
Maryville University of Saint Louis	M
Minnesota State University Mankato	M
Mississippi University for Women	M
Northeastern Illinois University	M
Nova Southeastern University	M,O
Purdue University	M,D,O
Teachers College Columbia University	M,D
Tennessee Technological University	D
Texas A&M University	M,D
University of Arkansas at Little Rock	M
University of Central Arkansas	M
University of Connecticut	M,D
University of Georgia	M,D,O
University of Houston	M,D
University of Louisiana at Lafayette	M
University of Minnesota, Twin Cities Campus	M,D,O
University of Missouri–Columbia	M,D
University of Northern Colorado	M
University of Northern Iowa	M
University of South Alabama	M
University of Southern Mississippi	M,D,O
University of South Florida	M,D,O
The University of Texas–Pan American	M
Western Washington University	M
West Virginia University	M,D
Whitworth College	M
Wright State University	M
Youngstown State University	M

■ EDUCATION OF THE MULTIPLY HANDICAPPED

Boston College	M,O
Cleveland State University	M
Fresno Pacific University	M
Gallaudet University	M,D,O
Georgia State University	M
Hunter College of the City University of New York	M
Minnesota State University Mankato	M
Minot State University	M
Montclair State University	M
Norfolk State University	M
University of Arkansas at Little Rock	M
University of Illinois at Urbana–Champaign	M,D,O
University of South Alabama	M
Western Oregon University	M
West Virginia University	M,D

■ ELECTRICAL ENGINEERING

Alfred University	M
Arizona State University	M,D
Auburn University	M,D
Boise State University	M
Boston University	M,D
Bradley University	M
Brigham Young University	M,D

Directory of Graduate and Professional Programs by Field
Electrical Engineering

Institution	Degrees
Brown University	M,D
California Institute of Technology	M,D
California Polytechnic State University, San Luis Obispo	M
California State Polytechnic University, Pomona	M
California State University, Chico	M
California State University, Fresno	M
California State University, Fullerton	M
California State University, Long Beach	M
California State University, Los Angeles	M
California State University, Northridge	M
California State University, Sacramento	M
Carnegie Mellon University	M,D
Case Western Reserve University	M,D
The Catholic University of America	M,D
City College of the City University of New York	M,D
Clarkson University	M,D
Clemson University	M,D
Cleveland State University	M,D
Colorado State University	M,D
Colorado Technical University	M
Columbia University	M,D,O
Cornell University	M,D
Dartmouth College	M,D
Drexel University	M,D
Duke University	M,D
Fairfield University	M
Fairleigh Dickinson University, Metropolitan Campus	M
Florida Agricultural and Mechanical University	M,D
Florida Atlantic University	M,D
Florida Institute of Technology	M,D
Florida International University	M,D
Florida State University	M,D
Gannon University	M
George Mason University	M,D
The George Washington University	M,D,O
Georgia Institute of Technology	M,D
Grand Valley State University	M
Howard University	M,D
Illinois Institute of Technology	M,D
Indiana University–Purdue University Indianapolis	M,D
Iowa State University of Science and Technology	M,D
The Johns Hopkins University	M,D
Kansas State University	M,D
Lamar University	M,D
Lawrence Technological University	M,D
Lehigh University	M,D
Louisiana State University and Agricultural and Mechanical College	M,D
Louisiana Tech University	M,D
Loyola Marymount University	M
Manhattan College	M
Marquette University	M
Massachusetts Institute of Technology	M,D,O
McNeese State University	M
Mercer University	M
Michigan State University	M,D
Michigan Technological University	M,D
Minnesota State University Mankato	M
Mississippi State University	M,D
Montana State University–Bozeman	M,D
New Jersey Institute of Technology	M,D
New Mexico Institute of Mining and Technology	M
New Mexico State University	M,D
New York Institute of Technology	M
Norfolk State University	M
North Carolina Agricultural and Technical State University	M,D
North Carolina State University	M,D
North Dakota State University	M,D
Northeastern University	M,D
Northern Illinois University	M
Northwestern University	M,D,O
Oakland University	M
The Ohio State University	M,D
Ohio University	M,D
Oklahoma State University	M,D
Old Dominion University	M,D
Oregon State University	M,D
The Pennsylvania State University Harrisburg Campus of the Capital College	M
The Pennsylvania State University University Park Campus	M,D
Polytechnic University, Brooklyn Campus	M,D
Polytechnic University, Westchester Graduate Center	M,D
Portland State University	M,D
Prairie View A&M University	M,D
Princeton University	M,D
Purdue University	M,D
Rensselaer Polytechnic Institute	M,D
Rice University	M,D
Rochester Institute of Technology	M
Rutgers, The State University of New Jersey, New Brunswick/Piscataway	M,D
St. Cloud State University	M
St. Mary's University of San Antonio	M
San Diego State University	M
San Jose State University	M
Santa Clara University	M,D,O
South Dakota State University	M
Southern Illinois University Carbondale	M,D
Southern Illinois University Edwardsville	M
Southern Methodist University	M,D
Stanford University	M,D,O
State University of New York at Binghamton	M,D
State University of New York at New Paltz	M
Stevens Institute of Technology	M,D,O
Stony Brook University, State University of New York	M,D
Syracuse University	M,D,O
Temple University	M
Tennessee Technological University	M,D
Texas A&M University	M,D
Texas A&M University–Kingsville	M
Texas Tech University	M,D
Tufts University	M,D,O
Tulane University	M,D
Tuskegee University	M
University at Buffalo, The State University of New York	M,D
The University of Akron	M,D
The University of Alabama	M,D
The University of Alabama at Birmingham	M,D
The University of Alabama in Huntsville	M,D
University of Alaska Fairbanks	M,D
The University of Arizona	M,D
University of Arkansas	M,D
University of Bridgeport	M
University of California, Berkeley	M,D
University of California, Davis	M,D
University of California, Irvine	M,D
University of California, Los Angeles	M,D
University of California, Riverside	M,D
University of California, San Diego	M,D
University of California, Santa Barbara	M,D
University of California, Santa Cruz	M,D
University of Central Florida	M,D,O
University of Cincinnati	M,D
University of Colorado at Boulder	M,D
University of Colorado at Colorado Springs	M,D
University of Colorado at Denver	M
University of Connecticut	M,D
University of Dayton	M,D
University of Delaware	M,D
University of Denver	M,D
University of Detroit Mercy	M,D
University of Florida	M,D,O
University of Hawaii at Manoa	M,D
University of Houston	M,D
University of Idaho	M,D
University of Illinois at Chicago	M,D
University of Illinois at Urbana–Champaign	M,D
The University of Iowa	M,D
University of Kansas	M,D
University of Kentucky	M,D
University of Louisville	M
University of Maine	M,D
University of Maryland, Baltimore County	M,D
University of Maryland, College Park	M,D,O
University of Massachusetts Amherst	M,D
University of Massachusetts Dartmouth	M,D,O
University of Massachusetts Lowell	M,D
The University of Memphis	M,D
University of Miami	M,D
University of Michigan	M,D
University of Michigan–Dearborn	M
University of Minnesota, Duluth	M
University of Minnesota, Twin Cities Campus	M,D
University of Missouri–Columbia	M,D
University of Missouri–Kansas City	M,D
University of Missouri–Rolla	M,D
University of Nebraska–Lincoln	M,D
University of Nevada, Las Vegas	M,D
University of Nevada, Reno	M,D
University of New Hampshire	M,D
University of New Haven	M
University of New Mexico	M,D
The University of North Carolina at Charlotte	M,D
University of North Dakota	M
University of Notre Dame	M,D
University of Oklahoma	M,D
University of Pennsylvania	M,D
University of Pittsburgh	M,D
University of Puerto Rico, Mayagüez Campus	M
University of Rhode Island	M,D
University of Rochester	M,D
University of South Alabama	M
University of South Carolina	M,D
University of Southern California	M,D,O
University of South Florida	M,D
The University of Tennessee	M,D
The University of Texas at Arlington	M,D
The University of Texas at Austin	M,D
The University of Texas at Dallas	M,D
The University of Texas at El Paso	M,D
The University of Texas at San Antonio	M,D
University of Toledo	M,D
University of Tulsa	M
University of Utah	M,D,O
University of Vermont	M,D
University of Virginia	M,D
University of Washington	M,D
University of Wisconsin–Madison	M,D
University of Wyoming	M
Utah State University	M,D,O
Vanderbilt University	M,D
Villanova University	M
Virginia Polytechnic Institute and State University	M,D
Washington State University	M,D
Washington University in St. Louis	M,D
Wayne State University	M,D
Western Michigan University	M,D

Directory of Graduate and Professional Programs by Field
Elementary Education

Institution	Degree
Western New England College	M
West Virginia University	M,D
Wichita State University	M,D
Wilkes University	M
Worcester Polytechnic Institute	M,D,O
Wright State University	M
Yale University	M,D
Youngstown State University	M

■ ELECTRONIC COMMERCE

Institution	Degree
Adelphi University	M
American University	M
Arkansas State University	M
Bentley College	M,O
Boston University	M
California State University, Hayward	M
Carnegie Mellon University	M
City University	M,O
Claremont Graduate University	M,D
Clemson University	M
Creighton University	M
Dallas Baptist University	M
DePaul University	M
Fairleigh Dickinson University, Metropolitan Campus	M,O
Ferris State University	M
Florida Atlantic University	M
Florida Institute of Technology	M
Georgia Institute of Technology	M,O
Hawai'i Pacific University	M
Illinois Institute of Technology	M
The Johns Hopkins University	M,O
Lynn University	M,D
Maryville University of Saint Louis	M,O
Marywood University	M
Mercy College	M
Morehead State University	M
National University	M
New York Institute of Technology	M
Northwestern University	M
Regis University	M,O
Rensselaer Polytechnic Institute	M,D
Sacred Heart University	M,O
St. Edward's University	M,O
Southern Illinois University Edwardsville	M
Stevens Institute of Technology	M,O
Temple University	M
Texas Tech University	M
University at Buffalo, The State University of New York	M,D
The University of Akron	M
University of Cincinnati	M
University of Denver	M,O
University of Maryland University College	M,O
University of Missouri–St. Louis	M,D,O
University of St. Thomas (MN)	M
University of San Francisco	M
West Chester University of Pennsylvania	M
Xavier University	M

■ ELECTRONIC MATERIALS

Institution	Degree
Massachusetts Institute of Technology	M,D,O
Northwestern University	M,D,O
University of Arkansas	M,D

■ ELEMENTARY EDUCATION

Institution	Degree
Abilene Christian University	M
Adams State College	M
Adelphi University	M,O
Alabama Agricultural and Mechanical University	M,O
Alabama State University	M,O
Alaska Pacific University	M
Alcorn State University	M,O
American International College	M,D,O
American University	M
Andrews University	M,D,O
Anna Maria College	M
Appalachian State University	M
Arcadia University	M,D,O
Arizona State University West	M,O
Arkansas State University	M,O
Armstrong Atlantic State University	M
Auburn University	M,D,O
Auburn University Montgomery	M,O
Austin Peay State University	M,O
Averett University	M
Ball State University	M,D
Barry University	M,O
Bayamón Central University	M
Bellarmine University	M
Belmont University	M
Benedictine University	M
Bloomsburg University of Pennsylvania	M
Boston College	M
Boston University	M
Bowie State University	M
Bridgewater State College	M
Brigham Young University	M,D
Brooklyn College of the City University of New York	M
Brown University	M
Buffalo State College, State University of New York	M
Butler University	M
California State University, Fullerton	M
California State University, Long Beach	M
California State University, Los Angeles	M
California State University, Northridge	M
California State University, San Bernardino	M
California State University, Stanislaus	M
California University of Pennsylvania	M
Campbell University	M
Carson-Newman College	M
Centenary College of Louisiana	M
Central Connecticut State University	M
Central Michigan University	M
Central Missouri State University	M,O
Central Washington University	M
Chadron State College	M,O
Chapman University	M
Charleston Southern University	M
Chestnut Hill College	M
Cheyney University of Pennsylvania	M
Chicago State University	M
City College of the City University of New York	M
Clarion University of Pennsylvania	M
Clemson University	M
Cleveland State University	M
College of Charleston	M
The College of New Jersey	M
The College of New Rochelle	M
College of St. Joseph	M
The College of Saint Rose	M
College of Staten Island of the City University of New York	M
The College of William and Mary	M
Columbia College Chicago	M
Concordia University (CA)	M
Concordia University (OR)	M
Converse College	M
Cumberland College	M,O
Dallas Baptist University	M
Delta State University	M,O
DePaul University	M
Drake University	M
Drury University	M
Duquesne University	M
East Carolina University	M
Eastern Connecticut State University	M
Eastern Illinois University	M
Eastern Kentucky University	M
Eastern Michigan University	M
Eastern Nazarene College	M,O
Eastern Oregon University	M
Eastern Washington University	M
East Stroudsburg University of Pennsylvania	M
East Tennessee State University	M
Edinboro University of Pennsylvania	M
Elms College	M,O
Elon University	M
Emmanuel College	M,O
Emporia State University	M
Fairfield University	M,O
Fayetteville State University	M
Ferris State University	M
Fitchburg State College	M
Florida Agricultural and Mechanical University	M
Florida Atlantic University	M
Florida Gulf Coast University	M
Florida International University	M
Florida State University	M,D,O
Fordham University	M,D,O
Fort Hays State University	M
Francis Marion University	M
Friends University	M
Frostburg State University	M
Gallaudet University	M,D,O
Gardner-Webb University	M
The George Washington University	M
Grambling State University	M
Grand Canyon University	M
Grand Valley State University	M
Hampton University	M
Harding University	M
Harvard University	M,D
Hofstra University	M,O
Holy Family University	M
Hood College	M
Howard University	M
Hunter College of the City University of New York	M
Immaculata University	M,D,O
Indiana State University	M
Indiana University Bloomington	M,D,O
Indiana University Northwest	M
Indiana University–Purdue University Fort Wayne	M
Indiana University–Purdue University Indianapolis	M
Indiana University South Bend	M
Indiana University Southeast	M
Inter American University of Puerto Rico, Metropolitan Campus	M
Iona College	M
Iowa State University of Science and Technology	M,D
Jackson State University	M,D,O
Jacksonville State University	M
Jacksonville University	M
The Johns Hopkins University	M
Kean University	M,O
Kutztown University of Pennsylvania	M,O
Lander University	M
Lehigh University	M,O
Lehman College of the City University of New York	M
Lesley University	M,D,O
Liberty University	M,D
Lincoln University (MO)	M,O
Long Island University, Brooklyn Campus	M
Longwood University	M
Louisiana State University and Agricultural and Mechanical College	M,D,O
Loyola Marymount University	M
Loyola University New Orleans	M
Maharishi University of Management	M
Manhattanville College	M
Mansfield University of Pennsylvania	M

Peterson's Graduate Schools in the U.S. 2006

Directory of Graduate and Professional Programs by Field
Elementary Education

Institution	Degree
Marshall University	M
Mary Baldwin College	M
Marygrove College	M
Marymount University	M,O
Maryville University of Saint Louis	M
Marywood University	M
McNeese State University	M
Mercy College	M,O
Miami University	M
Middle Tennessee State University	M,O
Millersville University of Pennsylvania	M
Minnesota State University Mankato	M,O
Minot State University	M
Mississippi College	M
Mississippi State University	M,D,O
Monmouth University	M,O
Montana State University–Northern	M
Montclair State University	M
Morehead State University	M
Morgan State University	M
Mount Saint Mary College	M
Mount St. Mary's College	M
Murray State University	M,O
National-Louis University	M
Nazareth College of Rochester	M
New Jersey City University	M
Newman University	M
New York Institute of Technology	M,O
New York University	M,D,O
Niagara University	M
North Carolina Agricultural and Technical State University	M
North Carolina Central University	M
Northeastern University	M
Northern Arizona University	M
Northern Illinois University	M,D
Northern Kentucky University	M
Northern Michigan University	M
Northern State University	M
Northwestern Oklahoma State University	M
Northwestern State University of Louisiana	M,O
Northwestern University	M
Northwest Missouri State University	M,O
Nova Southeastern University	M,O
Oklahoma City University	M
Old Dominion University	M
Olivet Nazarene University	M
Oregon State University	M
Pacific Lutheran University	M
Pacific University	M
Palm Beach Atlantic University	M
The Pennsylvania State University University Park Campus	M,D
Pfeiffer University	M
Pittsburg State University	M
Plymouth State University	M
Portland State University	M,D
Purdue University	M,D,O
Purdue University Calumet	M
Queens College of the City University of New York	M,O
Queens University of Charlotte	M
Quinnipiac University	M
Regis University	M,O
Rhode Island College	M
Rider University	O
Rivier College	M,O
Rockford College	M
Rollins College	M
Roosevelt University	M
Rowan University	M
Rutgers, The State University of New Jersey, New Brunswick/Piscataway	M,D
Sacred Heart University	M,O
Sage Graduate School	M
Saginaw Valley State University	M
St. John Fisher College	M
St. John's University (NY)	M
Saint Joseph's University	M
Saint Peter's College	M,O
St. Thomas Aquinas College	M,O
Saint Xavier University	M,O
Salem International University	M
Salem State College	M
Salisbury University	M
Samford University	M,D,O
Sam Houston State University	M
San Diego State University	M
San Francisco State University	M
San Jose State University	M,O
Seton Hall University	M
Shenandoah University	M,D,O
Siena Heights University	M
Simmons College	M,O
Slippery Rock University of Pennsylvania	M
Sonoma State University	M
South Carolina State University	M
Southeastern Louisiana University	M
Southeastern Oklahoma State University	M
Southeast Missouri State University	M
Southern Arkansas University–Magnolia	M
Southern Connecticut State University	M,O
Southern Illinois University Edwardsville	M
Southern Oregon University	M
Southern University and Agricultural and Mechanical College	M
Southwestern Oklahoma State University	M
Southwest Missouri State University	M,O
Spalding University	M
Spring Hill College	M
State University of New York at Binghamton	M
State University of New York at New Paltz	M
State University of New York at Oswego	M
State University of New York at Plattsburgh	M
State University of New York College at Brockport	M
State University of New York College at Fredonia	M
State University of New York College at Geneseo	M
State University of New York College at Oneonta	M
State University of New York College at Potsdam	M
Stephen F. Austin State University	M
Stetson University	M
Sul Ross State University	M
Syracuse University	M,O
Teachers College Columbia University	M
Temple University	M,D
Tennessee State University	M,D
Tennessee Technological University	M,O
Texas A&M University–Commerce	M,D
Texas A&M University–Corpus Christi	M
Texas A&M University–Kingsville	M
Texas A&M University–Texarkana	M
Texas Christian University	M,O
Texas Southern University	M,D
Texas State University-San Marcos	M
Texas Tech University	M,D,O
Texas Woman's University	M,D
Towson University	M
Trinity College (DC)	M
Troy University	M,O
Troy University Montgomery	M
Tufts University	M
University at Buffalo, The State University of New York	M,D,O
The University of Akron	M,D
The University of Alabama	M,D,O
The University of Alabama at Birmingham	M
University of Alaska Southeast	M
The University of Arizona	M,D
University of Arkansas	M,O
University of Bridgeport	M,O
University of California, Irvine	M,D
University of Central Arkansas	M,O
University of Central Florida	M,D
University of Central Oklahoma	M
University of Cincinnati	M
University of Connecticut	M,D
The University of Findlay	M
University of Florida	M,D,O
University of Georgia	M,D,O
University of Great Falls	M
University of Hartford	M
University of Hawaii at Manoa	M
University of Houston	M,D
University of Idaho	M,D,O
University of Illinois at Chicago	M,D
University of Indianapolis	M
The University of Iowa	M,D
University of Louisiana at Monroe	M
University of Louisville	M
University of Maine	M,O
University of Mary	M
University of Maryland, Baltimore County	M,D,O
University of Massachusetts Amherst	M,D,O
University of Massachusetts Boston	M,D,O
The University of Memphis	M,D
University of Miami	M,O
University of Michigan	M,D
University of Michigan–Flint	M
University of Minnesota, Twin Cities Campus	M,D,O
University of Missouri–Columbia	M,D,O
University of Missouri–St. Louis	M,D
University of Montevallo	M
University of Nebraska at Omaha	M
University of Nevada, Las Vegas	M,D,O
University of Nevada, Reno	M,O
University of New Hampshire	M
University of New Mexico	M
University of North Alabama	M,O
The University of North Carolina at Charlotte	M
The University of North Carolina at Pembroke	M
The University of North Carolina at Wilmington	M
University of North Dakota	M,D
University of Northern Colorado	M,D
University of Northern Iowa	M
University of North Florida	M
University of North Texas	M
University of Oklahoma	M,D,O
University of Pennsylvania	M
University of Pittsburgh	M
University of Rhode Island	M
University of St. Francis (IL)	M
The University of Scranton	M
University of South Alabama	M,O
University of South Carolina	M,D
The University of South Dakota	M
University of Southern Indiana	M
University of Southern Mississippi	M,D,O
University of South Florida	M,D,O
The University of Tennessee	M,D,O
The University of Tennessee at Chattanooga	M,O
The University of Tennessee at Martin	M
The University of Texas at Brownsville	M
The University of Texas at San Antonio	M
The University of Texas–Pan American	M
University of the Incarnate Word	M
University of Toledo	M,D,O

Directory of Graduate and Professional Programs by Field
Engineering and Applied Sciences—General

Institution	Degree
The University of West Alabama	M
University of West Florida	M
University of Wisconsin–Eau Claire	M
University of Wisconsin–La Crosse	M
University of Wisconsin–Milwaukee	M
University of Wisconsin–Platteville	M
University of Wisconsin–River Falls	M
University of Wisconsin–Stevens Point	M
Utah State University	M
Vanderbilt University	M
Villanova University	M
Wagner College	M
Washington State University	M,D
Washington University in St. Louis	M
Wayne State College	M
Wayne State University	M,D,O
West Chester University of Pennsylvania	M
Western Carolina University	M
Western Illinois University	M,O
Western Kentucky University	M,O
Western Michigan University	M
Western New England College	M
Western New Mexico University	M
Western Washington University	M
Westfield State College	M
West Virginia University	M
Wheelock College	M
Widener University	M,D
Wilkes University	M
William Carey College	M,O
William Paterson University of New Jersey	M
Wilmington College (DE)	M
Winthrop University	M
Worcester State College	M
Wright State University	M
Xavier University	M
Xavier University of Louisiana	M
Youngstown State University	M

■ EMERGENCY MEDICAL SERVICES

Institution	Degree
California State University, Long Beach	M
Drexel University	M
The George Washington University	M,O
Lynn University	M,O
Oklahoma State University	M

■ ENERGY AND POWER ENGINEERING

Institution	Degree
New York Institute of Technology	M,O
Rensselaer Polytechnic Institute	M,D
Southern Illinois University Carbondale	D
University of Massachusetts Lowell	M,D
The University of Memphis	M,D
University of Wisconsin–Madison	M,D
Worcester Polytechnic Institute	M,D,O

■ ENERGY MANAGEMENT AND POLICY

Institution	Degree
Boston University	M
New York Institute of Technology	M,O
University of California, Berkeley	M,D

■ ENGINEERING AND APPLIED SCIENCES—GENERAL

Institution	Degree
Alabama Agricultural and Mechanical University	M
Andrews University	M
Arizona State University	M,D
Auburn University	M,D
Boston University	M,D
Bradley University	M
Brigham Young University	M,D
Brown University	M,D
California Institute of Technology	M,D,O
California Polytechnic State University, San Luis Obispo	M
California State Polytechnic University, Pomona	M
California State University, Chico	M
California State University, Fresno	M
California State University, Fullerton	M
California State University, Long Beach	M,D,O
California State University, Los Angeles	M
California State University, Northridge	M
California State University, Sacramento	M
Carnegie Mellon University	M,D
Case Western Reserve University	M
The Catholic University of America	M,D
Central Connecticut State University	M
Central Missouri State University	M,O
Central Washington University	M
Christian Brothers University	M
City College of the City University of New York	M,D
Clarkson University	M,D
Clemson University	M,D
Cleveland State University	M,D
Colorado State University	M,D
Colorado State University–Pueblo	M
Columbia University	M,D,O
Cornell University	M,D
Dartmouth College	M,D
Drexel University	M,D
Duke University	M,D
Eastern Illinois University	M,O
Fairfield University	M
Fairleigh Dickinson University, Metropolitan Campus	M,O
Florida Agricultural and Mechanical University	M,D
Florida Atlantic University	M,D
Florida Institute of Technology	M,D
Florida International University	M,D
Florida State University	M,D
Gannon University	M
George Mason University	M,D,O
The George Washington University	M,D,O
Georgia Institute of Technology	M,D,O
Georgia Southern University	M
Grand Valley State University	M
Harvard University	M,D
Howard University	M,D
Idaho State University	M,D,O
Illinois Institute of Technology	M,D
Indiana State University	M,D
Indiana University–Purdue University Fort Wayne	M
Indiana University–Purdue University Indianapolis	M
Iowa State University of Science and Technology	M,D
The Johns Hopkins University	M,D
Kansas State University	M,D
Kent State University	M
Lamar University	M,D
Lawrence Technological University	M,D
Lehigh University	M,D
Louisiana State University and Agricultural and Mechanical College	M,D
Louisiana Tech University	M,D
Loyola College in Maryland	M
Loyola Marymount University	M
Manhattan College	M
Marquette University	M,D
Marshall University	M
Massachusetts Institute of Technology	M,D,O
McNeese State University	M
Mercer University	M
Miami University	M,O
Michigan State University	M,D
Michigan Technological University	M,D
Mississippi State University	M,D
Montana State University–Bozeman	M,D
Morgan State University	M,D
National University	M
New Jersey Institute of Technology	M,D,O
New Mexico State University	M,D
New York Institute of Technology	M,O
North Carolina Agricultural and Technical State University	M,D
North Carolina State University	M,D,O
North Dakota State University	M,D
Northeastern University	M,D
Northern Arizona University	M
Northern Illinois University	M
Northwestern University	M,D,O
Oakland University	M,D
The Ohio State University	M,D
Ohio University	M,D
Oklahoma State University	M,D
Old Dominion University	M,D
Oregon State University	M,D
The Pennsylvania State University at Erie, The Behrend College	M
The Pennsylvania State University Harrisburg Campus of the Capital College	M
The Pennsylvania State University University Park Campus	M,D
Pittsburg State University	M
Portland State University	M,D,O
Prairie View A&M University	M,D
Purdue University	M,D
Purdue University Calumet	M
Rensselaer Polytechnic Institute	M,D
Rice University	M,D
Rochester Institute of Technology	M,D,O
Rowan University	M
Rutgers, The State University of New Jersey, New Brunswick/Piscataway	M,D
Saginaw Valley State University	M
St. Cloud State University	M
St. Mary's University of San Antonio	M
San Diego State University	M,D
San Francisco State University	M
San Jose State University	M
Santa Clara University	M,D,O
Seattle University	M
South Dakota State University	M,D
Southern Illinois University Carbondale	M,D
Southern Illinois University Edwardsville	M
Southern Methodist University	M,D
Stanford University	M,D,O
State University of New York at Binghamton	M,D
State University of New York Institute of Technology	M
Stevens Institute of Technology	M,D,O
Stony Brook University, State University of New York	M,D,O
Syracuse University	M,D,O
Temple University	M,D
Tennessee State University	M,D
Tennessee Technological University	M,D
Texas A&M University	M,D
Texas A&M University–Kingsville	M,D
Texas Tech University	M,D
Tufts University	M,D
Tulane University	M,D
Tuskegee University	M,D
University at Buffalo, The State University of New York	M,D
The University of Akron	M,D
The University of Alabama	M,D
The University of Alabama at Birmingham	M,D
The University of Alabama in Huntsville	M,D
University of Alaska Anchorage	M

Directory of Graduate and Professional Programs by Field
Engineering and Applied Sciences—General

Institution	Degrees
University of Alaska Fairbanks	M,D
The University of Arizona	M,D
University of Arkansas	M,D
University of Bridgeport	M
University of California, Berkeley	M,D
University of California, Davis	M,D,O
University of California, Irvine	M,D
University of California, Los Angeles	M,D
University of California, Santa Barbara	M,D
University of California, Santa Cruz	M,D
University of Central Florida	M,D,O
University of Cincinnati	M,D
University of Colorado at Boulder	M,D
University of Colorado at Colorado Springs	M,D
University of Colorado at Denver	M
University of Connecticut	M,D
University of Dayton	M,D
University of Delaware	M,D
University of Denver	M,D
University of Detroit Mercy	M,D
University of Florida	M,D,O
University of Hartford	M
University of Hawaii at Manoa	M,D
University of Houston	M,D
University of Idaho	M,D
University of Illinois at Chicago	M,D
University of Illinois at Urbana–Champaign	M,D
The University of Iowa	M,D
University of Kansas	M,D
University of Kentucky	M,D
University of Louisiana at Lafayette	M,D
University of Louisville	M,D
University of Maine	M,D
University of Maryland, Baltimore County	M,D
University of Maryland, College Park	M,D,O
University of Massachusetts Amherst	M,D
University of Massachusetts Dartmouth	M,D,O
University of Massachusetts Lowell	M,D,O
The University of Memphis	M,D
University of Miami	M,D
University of Michigan	M,D,O
University of Michigan–Dearborn	M,D
University of Minnesota, Twin Cities Campus	M,D
University of Mississippi	M,D
University of Missouri–Columbia	M,D
University of Missouri–Rolla	M,D
University of Nebraska–Lincoln	M,D
University of Nevada, Las Vegas	M,D
University of Nevada, Reno	M,D,O
University of New Haven	M,O
University of New Mexico	M,D
University of New Orleans	M,D,O
The University of North Carolina at Charlotte	M,D
University of North Dakota	D
University of North Texas	M
University of Notre Dame	M,D
University of Oklahoma	M,D
University of Pennsylvania	M,D,O
University of Pittsburgh	M,D,O
University of Portland	M
University of Puerto Rico, Mayagüez Campus	M,D
University of Rhode Island	M,D
University of Rochester	M,D
University of St. Thomas (MN)	M,O
University of South Alabama	M
University of South Carolina	M,D
University of Southern California	M,D,O
University of Southern Indiana	M
University of Southern Mississippi	M
University of South Florida	M,D
The University of Tennessee	M,D
The University of Tennessee at Chattanooga	M
The University of Texas at Arlington	M,D
The University of Texas at Austin	M,D
The University of Texas at Dallas	M,D
The University of Texas at El Paso	M,D
The University of Texas at San Antonio	M,D
The University of Texas at Tyler	M
University of Toledo	M,D
University of Tulsa	M,D
University of Utah	M,D,O
University of Vermont	M,D
University of Virginia	M,D
University of Washington	M,D
University of Wisconsin–Madison	M,D,O
University of Wisconsin–Milwaukee	M,D
University of Wisconsin–Platteville	M
University of Wyoming	M,D
Utah State University	M,D,O
Vanderbilt University	M,D
Villanova University	M,D,O
Virginia Commonwealth University	M,D
Virginia Polytechnic Institute and State University	M,D
Washington State University	M,D
Washington University in St. Louis	M,D
Wayne State University	M,D,O
Western Michigan University	M,D
Western New England College	M
West Texas A&M University	M
West Virginia University	M,D
Wichita State University	M,D
Widener University	M
Worcester Polytechnic Institute	M,D,O
Wright State University	M,D
Yale University	M,D
Youngstown State University	M

■ **ENGINEERING DESIGN**

Institution	Degrees
The Catholic University of America	M,D
Rochester Institute of Technology	M
San Diego State University	M,D
Stanford University	M
University of Central Florida	M,D,O
University of Illinois at Urbana–Champaign	M
University of New Haven	M,O

■ **ENGINEERING MANAGEMENT**

Institution	Degrees
California State University, Long Beach	M,D
California State University, Northridge	M
Case Western Reserve University	M
The Catholic University of America	M
Clarkson University	M
Colorado State University	M,D
Cornell University	M,D
Dallas Baptist University	M
Dartmouth College	M
Drexel University	M,D
Duke University	M
Florida Institute of Technology	M
The George Washington University	M,D,O
Hofstra University	M
Kansas State University	M,D
Lamar University	M,D
Long Island University, C.W. Post Campus	M
Loyola Marymount University	M
Marquette University	M,D
Massachusetts Institute of Technology	M
McNeese State University	M
Mercer University	M
Michigan State University	M,D
Montana State University–Bozeman	M,D
New Jersey Institute of Technology	M
New Mexico Institute of Mining and Technology	M
Northeastern University	M,D
Northwestern University	M
Oakland University	M
Old Dominion University	M,D
The Pennsylvania State University University Park Campus	M
Point Park University	M
Portland State University	M,D,O
Rensselaer Polytechnic Institute	M,D
Robert Morris University	M
Rochester Institute of Technology	M
St. Cloud State University	M
Saint Martin's College	M
St. Mary's University of San Antonio	M
Santa Clara University	M
Southern Methodist University	M,D
Stanford University	M,D
Syracuse University	M
Texas Tech University	M,D
Tufts University	M
The University of Akron	M
University of Alaska Anchorage	M
University of Alaska Fairbanks	M
University of California, Berkeley	M,D
University of Central Florida	M,D,O
University of Colorado at Boulder	M
University of Colorado at Colorado Springs	M
University of Dayton	M
University of Detroit Mercy	M
University of Kansas	M
University of Louisiana at Lafayette	M
University of Louisville	M
University of Maryland, Baltimore County	M
University of Massachusetts Amherst	M
University of Michigan–Dearborn	M
University of Minnesota, Duluth	M
University of Missouri–Rolla	M,D
University of New Haven	M
University of New Orleans	M,O
The University of North Carolina at Charlotte	M
University of St. Thomas (MN)	M,O
University of Southern California	M
University of South Florida	M,D
The University of Tennessee	M
The University of Tennessee at Chattanooga	M
University of Tulsa	M
Virginia Polytechnic Institute and State University	M,D
Wayne State University	M
Western Michigan University	M
Widener University	M

■ **ENGINEERING PHYSICS**

Institution	Degrees
Cornell University	M,D
Dartmouth College	M,D
George Mason University	M
Michigan Technological University	D
Mississippi State University	M,D
Polytechnic University, Brooklyn Campus	M
Rensselaer Polytechnic Institute	M,D
Stevens Institute of Technology	M,D,O
University of California, San Diego	M,D
University of Maine	M
University of Oklahoma	M,D
University of Virginia	M,D
University of Wisconsin–Madison	M,D
Yale University	M,D

■ **ENGLISH**

Institution	Degrees
Abilene Christian University	M
Adelphi University	M
Andrews University	M
Angelo State University	M
Appalachian State University	M
Arcadia University	M
Arizona State University	M,D
Arkansas State University	M,O
Arkansas Tech University	M

English

Institution	Degree
Auburn University	M,D
Austin Peay State University	M
Ball State University	M,D
Baylor University	M,D
Belmont University	M
Bemidji State University	M
Boise State University	M
Boston College	M,D,O
Boston University	M,D
Bowling Green State University	M,D
Bradley University	M
Brandeis University	M,D
Bridgewater State College	M
Brigham Young University	M
Brooklyn College of the City University of New York	M,D
Brown University	M,D
Buffalo State College, State University of New York	M
Butler University	M
California Baptist University	M
California Polytechnic State University, San Luis Obispo	M
California State Polytechnic University, Pomona	M
California State University, Bakersfield	M
California State University, Chico	M
California State University, Dominguez Hills	M,O
California State University, Fresno	M
California State University, Fullerton	M
California State University, Hayward	M
California State University, Long Beach	M
California State University, Los Angeles	M
California State University, Northridge	M
California State University, Sacramento	M
California State University, San Bernardino	M
California State University, San Marcos	M
California State University, Stanislaus	M
Carnegie Mellon University	M,D
Case Western Reserve University	M,D
The Catholic University of America	M,D
Central Connecticut State University	M
Central Michigan University	M
Central Missouri State University	M
Central Washington University	M
Chapman University	M
Chicago State University	M
The Citadel, The Military College of South Carolina	M
City College of the City University of New York	M
Claremont Graduate University	M,D
Clarion University of Pennsylvania	M
Clark Atlanta University	M
Clark University	M
Clemson University	M
Cleveland State University	M
College of Charleston	M
The College of New Jersey	M
The College of Saint Rose	M
College of Staten Island of the City University of New York	M
Colorado State University	M
Columbia University	M,D
Converse College	M
Cornell University	M,D
DePaul University	M
Duke University	D
Duquesne University	M,D
East Carolina University	M
Eastern Illinois University	M
Eastern Kentucky University	M
Eastern Michigan University	M
Eastern New Mexico University	M
Eastern Washington University	M
East Tennessee State University	M
Emory University	D
Emporia State University	M
Fairleigh Dickinson University, Metropolitan Campus	M
Fayetteville State University	M
Florida Atlantic University	M
Florida International University	M
Florida State University	M,D
Fordham University	M,D
Fort Hays State University	M
Gannon University	M
Gardner-Webb University	M
George Mason University	M
Georgetown University	M
The George Washington University	M,D
Georgia College & State University	M
Georgia Southern University	M
Georgia State University	M,D
Governors State University	M
Hardin-Simmons University	M
Harvard University	M,D,O
Hofstra University	M
Howard University	M,D
Humboldt State University	M
Hunter College of the City University of New York	M
Idaho State University	M,D
Illinois State University	M,D
Indiana State University	M,O
Indiana University Bloomington	M,D
Indiana University of Pennsylvania	M,D
Indiana University–Purdue University Fort Wayne	M
Indiana University–Purdue University Indianapolis	M
Iona College	M
Iowa State University of Science and Technology	M,D
Jackson State University	M
Jacksonville State University	M
James Madison University	M
John Carroll University	M
The Johns Hopkins University	D
Kansas State University	M
Kent State University	M,D
Kutztown University of Pennsylvania	M
Lamar University	M
La Sierra University	M
Lehigh University	M,D
Lehman College of the City University of New York	M
Long Island University, Brooklyn Campus	M
Long Island University, C.W. Post Campus	M
Longwood University	M
Loras College	M
Louisiana State University and Agricultural and Mechanical College	M,D
Louisiana Tech University	M
Loyola Marymount University	M
Loyola University Chicago	M,D
Marquette University	M,D
Marshall University	M
Marymount University	M
McNeese State University	M
Mercy College	M
Miami University	M,D
Michigan State University	M,D
Middle Tennessee State University	M,D
Midwestern State University	M
Millersville University of Pennsylvania	M
Minnesota State University Mankato	M
Mississippi College	M
Mississippi State University	M
Montana State University–Bozeman	M
Montclair State University	M
Morehead State University	M
Morgan State University	M,D
Murray State University	M
National University	M
New Mexico Highlands University	M
New Mexico State University	M,D
New York University	M,D
North Carolina Agricultural and Technical State University	M
North Carolina Central University	M
North Carolina State University	M
North Dakota State University	M
Northeastern Illinois University	M
Northeastern State University	M
Northeastern University	M,D,O
Northern Arizona University	M
Northern Illinois University	M,D
Northern Michigan University	M
Northwestern State University of Louisiana	M
Northwestern University	M,D
Northwest Missouri State University	M
Notre Dame de Namur University	M
Oakland University	M
The Ohio State University	M,D
Ohio University	M,D
Oklahoma State University	M,D
Old Dominion University	M
Oregon State University	M
Our Lady of the Lake University of San Antonio	M
The Pennsylvania State University University Park Campus	M,D
Pittsburg State University	M
Portland State University	M
Prairie View A&M University	M
Princeton University	D
Purdue University	M,D
Purdue University Calumet	M
Queens College of the City University of New York	M
Radford University	M
Rhode Island College	M
Rice University	M,D
Rivier College	M
Roosevelt University	M
Rutgers, The State University of New Jersey, Camden	M
Rutgers, The State University of New Jersey, Newark	M
Rutgers, The State University of New Jersey, New Brunswick/Piscataway	D
St. Bonaventure University	M
St. Cloud State University	M
St. John's University (NY)	M,D
Saint Louis University	M,D
St. Mary's University of San Antonio	M
Saint Xavier University	M,O
Salem State College	M
Salisbury University	M
Sam Houston State University	M
San Diego State University	M
San Francisco State University	M,O
San Jose State University	M,O
Seton Hall University	M
Simmons College	M
Slippery Rock University of Pennsylvania	M
Sonoma State University	M
South Dakota State University	M
Southeastern Louisiana University	M
Southeast Missouri State University	M
Southern Connecticut State University	M
Southern Illinois University Carbondale	M,D
Southern Illinois University Edwardsville	M
Southern Methodist University	M
Southwest Missouri State University	M
Stanford University	M,D
State University of New York at Binghamton	M,D

Directory of Graduate and Professional Programs by Field
English

Institution	Degree
State University of New York at New Paltz	M
State University of New York at Oswego	M
State University of New York College at Brockport	M
State University of New York College at Cortland	M
State University of New York College at Fredonia	M
State University of New York College at Potsdam	M
State University of West Georgia	M
Stephen F. Austin State University	M
Stetson University	M
Stony Brook University, State University of New York	M,D
Sul Ross State University	M
Syracuse University	M,D
Tarleton State University	M
Temple University	M,D
Tennessee State University	M
Tennessee Technological University	M
Texas A&M International University	M
Texas A&M University	M,D
Texas A&M University–Commerce	M,D
Texas A&M University–Corpus Christi	M
Texas A&M University–Kingsville	M
Texas Christian University	M,D
Texas Southern University	M
Texas State University-San Marcos	M
Texas Tech University	M,D
Texas Woman's University	M,D
Truman State University	M
Tufts University	M,D
Tulane University	M,D
University at Albany, State University of New York	M,D
University at Buffalo, The State University of New York	M,D
The University of Akron	M
The University of Alabama	M,D
The University of Alabama at Birmingham	M
The University of Alabama in Huntsville	M,O
University of Alaska Anchorage	M
University of Alaska Fairbanks	M
The University of Arizona	M,D
University of Arkansas	M,D
University of California, Berkeley	D
University of California, Davis	M,D
University of California, Irvine	M,D
University of California, Los Angeles	M,D
University of California, Riverside	M,D
University of California, San Diego	M
University of California, Santa Barbara	D
University of Central Arkansas	M
University of Central Florida	M,D,O
University of Central Oklahoma	M
University of Chicago	M,D
University of Cincinnati	M,D
University of Colorado at Boulder	M,D
University of Colorado at Denver	M
University of Connecticut	M,D
University of Dayton	M
University of Delaware	M,D
University of Denver	M,D
University of Florida	M,D
University of Georgia	M,D
University of Hawaii at Manoa	M,D
University of Houston	M,D
University of Houston–Clear Lake	M
University of Idaho	M
University of Illinois at Chicago	M,D
University of Illinois at Springfield	M
University of Illinois at Urbana–Champaign	M,D
University of Indianapolis	M
The University of Iowa	M,D
University of Kansas	M,D
University of Kentucky	M,D
University of Louisiana at Lafayette	M,D
University of Louisiana at Monroe	M
University of Louisville	M,D
University of Maine	M
University of Maryland, College Park	M,D
University of Massachusetts Amherst	M,D
University of Massachusetts Boston	M
The University of Memphis	M,D
University of Miami	M,D
University of Michigan	M,D,O
University of Minnesota, Duluth	M
University of Minnesota, Twin Cities Campus	M,D
University of Mississippi	M,D
University of Missouri–Columbia	M,D
University of Missouri–Kansas City	M,D
University of Missouri–St. Louis	M
The University of Montana–Missoula	M
University of Montevallo	M
University of Nebraska at Kearney	M
University of Nebraska at Omaha	M,O
University of Nebraska–Lincoln	M,D
University of Nevada, Las Vegas	M,D
University of Nevada, Reno	M,D
University of New Hampshire	M,D
University of New Mexico	M,D
University of New Orleans	M
University of North Alabama	M
The University of North Carolina at Chapel Hill	M,D
The University of North Carolina at Charlotte	M
The University of North Carolina at Greensboro	M,D,O
The University of North Carolina at Wilmington	M
University of North Dakota	M,D
University of Northern Colorado	M
University of Northern Iowa	M
University of North Florida	M
University of North Texas	M,D
University of Notre Dame	M,D
University of Oklahoma	M,D
University of Oregon	M,D
University of Pennsylvania	M,D
University of Pittsburgh	M,D
University of Puerto Rico, Mayagüez Campus	M
University of Puerto Rico, Río Piedras	M,D
University of Rhode Island	M,D
University of Richmond	M
University of Rochester	M,D
University of St. Thomas (MN)	M
University of South Alabama	M
University of South Carolina	M,D
The University of South Dakota	M,D
University of Southern Mississippi	M,D
University of South Florida	M,D
The University of Tennessee	M,D
The University of Tennessee at Chattanooga	M
The University of Texas at Arlington	M,D
The University of Texas at Austin	M,D
The University of Texas at Brownsville	M
The University of Texas at El Paso	M
The University of Texas at San Antonio	M,D
The University of Texas at Tyler	M
The University of Texas of the Permian Basin	M
The University of Texas–Pan American	M
University of the District of Columbia	M
University of the Incarnate Word	M
University of Toledo	M
University of Tulsa	M,D
University of Utah	M,D
University of Vermont	M
University of Virginia	M,D
University of Washington	M,D
University of West Florida	M
University of Wisconsin–Eau Claire	M
University of Wisconsin–Madison	M,D
University of Wisconsin–Milwaukee	M,D
University of Wisconsin–Oshkosh	M
University of Wisconsin–Stevens Point	M
University of Wyoming	M
Utah State University	M
Valdosta State University	M
Valparaiso University	M
Vanderbilt University	M,D
Villanova University	M
Virginia Commonwealth University	M
Virginia Polytechnic Institute and State University	M
Virginia State University	M
Wake Forest University	M
Washington State University	M,D
Washington University in St. Louis	M,D
Wayne State University	M,D
West Chester University of Pennsylvania	M
Western Carolina University	M
Western Connecticut State University	M
Western Illinois University	M
Western Kentucky University	M
Western Michigan University	M,D
Western Washington University	M
Westfield State College	M
West Texas A&M University	M
West Virginia University	M,D
Wichita State University	M
William Paterson University of New Jersey	M
Winona State University	M
Winthrop University	M
Wright State University	M
Xavier University	M
Yale University	M,D
Youngstown State University	M

■ ENGLISH AS A SECOND LANGUAGE

Institution	Degree
Adelphi University	M,O
American University	M,O
Andrews University	M,D,O
Arizona State University	M
Arkansas Tech University	M
Azusa Pacific University	M
Ball State University	M,D
Biola University	M,D,O
Boston University	M,O
Bowling Green State University	M,D
Brigham Young University	M,O
California State University, Dominguez Hills	M,O
California State University, Fresno	M
California State University, Fullerton	M
California State University, Los Angeles	M
California State University, Sacramento	M
California State University, San Bernardino	M
California State University, Stanislaus	M
Carson-Newman College	M
The Catholic University of America	M,D
Central Connecticut State University	M
Central Michigan University	M
Central Missouri State University	M
Central Washington University	M
Cleveland State University	M
The College of New Jersey	M,O
The College of New Rochelle	M,O
College of Notre Dame of Maryland	M
DeSales University	M,O
Eastern Michigan University	M
Eastern Nazarene College	M,O
Eastern University	O
Elms College	M,O

Institution	Degree
Emporia State University	M
Fairfield University	M,O
Florida International University	M
Fordham University	M,D,O
Framingham State College	M
Fresno Pacific University	M
George Mason University	M
Georgetown University	M,D,O
Georgia State University	M,O
Gonzaga University	M
Grand Canyon University	M
Grand Valley State University	M
Hawai'i Pacific University	M
Henderson State University	M
Heritage College	M
Hofstra University	M,O
Holy Names University	M,O
Houston Baptist University	M
Hunter College of the City University of New York	M
Indiana State University	M,O
Indiana University Bloomington	M,D,O
Indiana University of Pennsylvania	M,D
Inter American University of Puerto Rico, Metropolitan Campus	M
Inter American University of Puerto Rico, San Germán Campus	M
Kean University	M,O
Kent State University	M,D
Lehman College of the City University of New York	M
Long Island University, Brooklyn Campus	M
Madonna University	M
Manhattanville College	M
Marymount University	M,O
Mercy College	M,O
Michigan State University	M,D
Montclair State University	M
Monterey Institute of International Studies	M
Murray State University	M
Nazareth College of Rochester	M
New Jersey City University	M
Newman University	M
New York University	M,D,O
Northern Arizona University	M,D,O
Nova Southeastern University	M,O
Ohio University	M
Oklahoma City University	M
Oral Roberts University	M,D
The Pennsylvania State University University Park Campus	M
Pontifical Catholic University of Puerto Rico	M,D
Portland State University	M
Prescott College	M
Queens College of the City University of New York	M
Regis University	M,O
Rhode Island College	M
Rutgers, The State University of New Jersey, New Brunswick/Piscataway	M,D
St. Cloud State University	M
St. John's University (NY)	M
Saint Michael's College	M,O
Salem State College	M
Salisbury University	M
San Diego State University	M,O
San Francisco State University	M
San Jose State University	M,O
School for International Training	M
Seattle Pacific University	M
Seattle University	M,O
Seton Hall University	M,O
Shenandoah University	M,D,O
Simmons College	M
Southeast Missouri State University	M
Southern Connecticut State University	M
Southern Illinois University Carbondale	M
Southern Illinois University Edwardsville	M
State University of New York at New Paltz	M
State University of New York College at Cortland	M
Stony Brook University, State University of New York	M,D
Teachers College Columbia University	M,D
Texas A&M University	M,D
Texas A&M University–Kingsville	M
Trinity College (DC)	M
Universidad del Turabo	M
University at Buffalo, The State University of New York	M,D,O
The University of Alabama	M,D
The University of Alabama in Huntsville	M,O
The University of Arizona	M,D
University of California, Los Angeles	M
University of Central Florida	M,O
University of Central Oklahoma	M
University of Colorado at Denver	M
University of Delaware	M,D
The University of Findlay	M
University of Florida	M,D,O
University of Guam	M
University of Hawaii at Manoa	M,D
University of Houston	M,D
University of Idaho	M
University of Illinois at Chicago	M
University of Illinois at Urbana–Champaign	M
University of Maryland, Baltimore County	M
University of Maryland, College Park	M,D,O
University of Massachusetts Boston	M
University of Miami	M,D,O
University of Minnesota, Twin Cities Campus	M
University of Nebraska at Omaha	M,O
University of Nevada, Las Vegas	M,O
University of Northern Iowa	M
University of Pennsylvania	M,D
University of Pittsburgh	O
University of Puerto Rico, Río Piedras	M
University of San Francisco	M,D
University of South Carolina	M,D,O
University of Southern California	M,D
University of Southern Maine	M,O
University of South Florida	M
The University of Tennessee	M,D,O
The University of Texas at Arlington	M
The University of Texas at Brownsville	M
The University of Texas at San Antonio	M,D
The University of Texas of the Permian Basin	M
The University of Texas–Pan American	M
University of Toledo	M,D,O
University of Washington	M,D
Wayne State College	M
West Chester University of Pennsylvania	M
Western Kentucky University	M
West Virginia University	M
Whitworth College	M
Wright State University	M

■ ENGLISH EDUCATION

Institution	Degree
Alabama State University	M,O
Albany State University	M
Andrews University	M,D,O
Appalachian State University	M
Arcadia University	M,D,O
Arkansas State University	M,O
Arkansas Tech University	M
Armstrong Atlantic State University	M
Auburn University	M,D,O
Austin Peay State University	M
Averett University	M
Belmont University	M
Boston College	M
Boston University	M,D,O
Brooklyn College of the City University of New York	M
Brown University	M
Buffalo State College, State University of New York	M
California State University, San Bernardino	M
Campbell University	M
Carthage College	M,O
Central Missouri State University	M
Chadron State College	M,O
Charleston Southern University	M
City College of the City University of New York	M,O
Clemson University	M
College of St. Joseph	M
The College of Saint Rose	M,O
The College of William and Mary	M
Colorado State University	M
Columbia College Chicago	M
Columbus State University	M,O
Converse College	M
Delta State University	M
DeSales University	M,O
Drake University	M
East Carolina University	M
Eastern Kentucky University	M
Edinboro University of Pennsylvania	M
Elms College	M,O
Fitchburg State College	M
Florida Agricultural and Mechanical University	M
Florida Gulf Coast University	M
Florida International University	M,D
Florida State University	M,D,O
Framingham State College	M
Gardner-Webb University	M
Georgia College & State University	M,O
Georgia Southern University	M
Georgia State University	M,D,O
Henderson State University	M
Hofstra University	M
Hunter College of the City University of New York	M
Indiana University Bloomington	M,D
Indiana University of Pennsylvania	M,D
Indiana University–Purdue University Fort Wayne	M
Indiana University–Purdue University Indianapolis	M
Iona College	M
Jackson State University	M
Jacksonville University	M
Kent State University	M,D
Kutztown University of Pennsylvania	M,O
Lehman College of the City University of New York	M
Long Island University, Brooklyn Campus	M
Long Island University, C.W. Post Campus	M
Longwood University	M
Louisiana Tech University	M,D
Lynchburg College	M
Manhattanville College	M
Maryville University of Saint Louis	M
McNeese State University	M
Miami University	M,D
Michigan State University	M,D
Millersville University of Pennsylvania	M
Minnesota State University Mankato	M
Montclair State University	M
National-Louis University	M,O
New York University	M,D,O

Directory of Graduate and Professional Programs by Field
English Education

Institution	Degree
North Carolina Agricultural and Technical State University	M
Northeastern Illinois University	M
Northern State University	M
North Georgia College & State University	M,O
Northwest Missouri State University	M
Nova Southeastern University	M,O
Plymouth State University	M
Purdue University	M,D,O
Queens College of the City University of New York	M,O
Quinnipiac University	M
Rider University	O
Rockford College	M
Rollins College	M
Rutgers, The State University of New Jersey, New Brunswick/Piscataway	M
Sage Graduate School	M
Salem State College	M,O
Salisbury University	M
San Francisco State University	M,O
South Carolina State University	M
Southern Illinois University Edwardsville	M
Stanford University	M,D
State University of New York at Binghamton	M
State University of New York at Plattsburgh	M
State University of New York College at Brockport	M
State University of New York College at Cortland	M
State University of West Georgia	M,O
Stony Brook University, State University of New York	M,O
Syracuse University	D,O
Teachers College Columbia University	M
Texas A&M University	M,D
Texas A&M University–Commerce	M,D
Texas Tech University	M,D,O
University at Buffalo, The State University of New York	M,D,O
University of Alaska Fairbanks	M
The University of Arizona	M,D
University of Central Florida	M
University of Colorado at Denver	M
University of Connecticut	M,D
University of Florida	M,D,O
University of Georgia	M,D,O
University of Idaho	M
University of Illinois at Chicago	M,D
University of Indianapolis	M
The University of Iowa	M,D
University of Michigan	M,D
University of Minnesota, Twin Cities Campus	M
University of Missouri–Columbia	M,D,O
The University of Montana–Missoula	M
University of Nevada, Las Vegas	M,D,O
University of New Hampshire	M,D
The University of North Carolina at Chapel Hill	M
The University of North Carolina at Charlotte	M
The University of North Carolina at Greensboro	M,D,O
The University of North Carolina at Pembroke	M
University of Oklahoma	M,D,O
University of Pittsburgh	M,D
University of Puerto Rico, Río Piedras	M,D
University of St. Francis (IL)	M
University of South Carolina	M,D
University of South Florida	M,D,O
The University of Tennessee	M,D,O
The University of Texas at El Paso	M
The University of Texas at Tyler	M
University of Toledo	M,D,O
University of Vermont	M
University of Washington	M,D
The University of West Alabama	M
University of Wisconsin–Eau Claire	M
University of Wisconsin–Madison	M,D
University of Wisconsin–River Falls	M
Vanderbilt University	M
Washington State University	M,D
Wayne State College	M
Wayne State University	M,D,O
Western Carolina University	M
Western Connecticut State University	M
Western Kentucky University	M
Western New England College	M
Widener University	M,D
Wilkes University	M
William Carey College	M,O
Worcester State College	M

■ ENTOMOLOGY

Institution	Degree
Auburn University	M,D
Clemson University	M,D
Colorado State University	M,D
Cornell University	M,D
Florida Agricultural and Mechanical University	M
Iowa State University of Science and Technology	M,D
Kansas State University	M,D
Louisiana State University and Agricultural and Mechanical College	M,D
Michigan State University	M,D
Mississippi State University	M,D
Montana State University–Bozeman	M
New Mexico State University	M
North Carolina State University	M,D
North Dakota State University	M,D
The Ohio State University	M,D
Oklahoma State University	M,D
The Pennsylvania State University University Park Campus	M,D
Purdue University	M,D
Rutgers, The State University of New Jersey, New Brunswick/Piscataway	M,D
South Dakota State University	M
State University of New York College of Environmental Science and Forestry	M,D
Texas A&M University	M,D
Texas Tech University	M,D
The University of Arizona	M,D
University of Arkansas	M,D
University of California, Davis	M,D
University of California, Riverside	M,D
University of Connecticut	M,D
University of Delaware	M,D
University of Florida	M,D
University of Georgia	M,D
University of Hawaii at Manoa	M,D
University of Idaho	M,D
University of Illinois at Urbana–Champaign	M,D
University of Kansas	M,D
University of Kentucky	M,D
University of Maine	M
University of Maryland, College Park	M,D
University of Massachusetts Amherst	M,D
University of Minnesota, Twin Cities Campus	M,D
University of Missouri–Columbia	M,D
University of Nebraska–Lincoln	M,D
University of North Dakota	M,D
University of Rhode Island	M,D
The University of Tennessee	M,D
University of Wisconsin–Madison	M,D
University of Wyoming	M,D
Virginia Polytechnic Institute and State University	M,D
Washington State University	M,D
West Virginia University	M

■ ENTREPRENEURSHIP

Institution	Degree
American University	M
Baldwin-Wallace College	M
Bentley College	M,O
Bernard M. Baruch College of the City University of New York	M,D
California Lutheran University	M
California State University, Hayward	M
Columbia University	M
DePaul University	M
Fairleigh Dickinson University, College at Florham	M,O
Fairleigh Dickinson University, Metropolitan Campus	M,O
Florida Atlantic University	M
Georgia Institute of Technology	M,O
Georgia State University	M,D
Illinois Institute of Technology	M
Indiana University Bloomington	M
Inter American University of Puerto Rico, San Germán Campus	D
Kennesaw State University	M
Newman University	M
Park University	M
Rensselaer Polytechnic Institute	M,D
St. Edward's University	M,O
San Diego State University	M
Texas Tech University	M
The University of Akron	M
University of Colorado at Boulder	M,D
University of Delaware	M,D
University of Hawaii at Manoa	M
University of Houston	D
The University of Iowa	M
University of Minnesota, Twin Cities Campus	M
The University of Tampa	M
University of the Incarnate Word	D
University of Wisconsin–Madison	M
Western Carolina University	M
Xavier University	M

■ ENVIRONMENTAL AND OCCUPATIONAL HEALTH

Institution	Degree
Anna Maria College	M
Boston University	M,D
California State University, Fresno	M
California State University, Northridge	M
Central Missouri State University	M,O
Colorado State University	M,D
Columbia University	M,D
Duke University	M,D
East Carolina University	M
Eastern Kentucky University	M
East Tennessee State University	M
Emory University	M
Fort Valley State University	M
The George Washington University	M,D
Harvard University	M,D
Hunter College of the City University of New York	M
Illinois State University	M
Indiana University of Pennsylvania	M
The Johns Hopkins University	D
Loma Linda University	M
Montclair State University	M,D,O
Murray State University	M
New Jersey Institute of Technology	M
New York University	M,D
Old Dominion University	M
Oregon State University	M
The Pennsylvania State University University Park Campus	M
Polytechnic University, Brooklyn Campus	M
Purdue University	M,D
Saint Joseph's University	M,O

Directory of Graduate and Professional Programs by Field
Environmental Engineering

Institution	Degree
Saint Louis University	M
San Diego State University	M,D
Stony Brook University, State University of New York	M,O
Temple University	M,D
Towson University	D
Tufts University	M,D
Tulane University	M,D
University at Albany, State University of New York	M,D
The University of Alabama at Birmingham	D
University of California, Berkeley	M,D
University of California, Los Angeles	M,D
University of Cincinnati	M,D
University of Georgia	M,D
University of Illinois at Chicago	M,D
The University of Iowa	M,D
University of Miami	M
University of Michigan	M,D
University of Minnesota, Twin Cities Campus	M,D,O
University of Nevada, Reno	M,D
University of New Haven	M
The University of North Carolina at Chapel Hill	M,D
University of Oklahoma	M,D
University of Pittsburgh	M,D
University of South Carolina	M,D
University of Southern Mississippi	M
University of South Florida	M,D
University of the Sacred Heart	M
University of Washington	M,D
University of Wisconsin–Eau Claire	M
University of Wisconsin–Whitewater	M
Virginia Commonwealth University	M
Wayne State University	M,O
West Chester University of Pennsylvania	M
Western Kentucky University	M
West Virginia University	M,D
Yale University	M,D

■ ENVIRONMENTAL BIOLOGY

Institution	Degree
Antioch New England Graduate School	M
Baylor University	M,D
Emporia State University	M
Georgia State University	M,D
Governors State University	M
Hood College	M
Massachusetts Institute of Technology	M,D,O
Montana State University–Bozeman	M,D
Morgan State University	D
New York University	M,D
Nicholls State University	M
Ohio University	M,D
Rutgers, The State University of New Jersey, New Brunswick/Piscataway	M,D
Sonoma State University	M
State University of New York College of Environmental Science and Forestry	M,D
Tennessee Technological University	M
University of California, Santa Cruz	M,D
University of Louisiana at Lafayette	M,D
University of Louisville	D
University of Massachusetts Amherst	M,D
University of Massachusetts Boston	D
University of Missouri–Rolla	M
University of North Dakota	M,D
University of Southern Mississippi	M,D
University of Wisconsin–Madison	M,D
Washington University in St. Louis	D
West Virginia University	M,D

■ ENVIRONMENTAL DESIGN

Institution	Degree
Arizona State University	D
Cornell University	M
Michigan State University	M,D
San Diego State University	M
Texas Tech University	D
University of California, Berkeley	M
University of California, Irvine	M,D
University of Missouri–Columbia	M
Virginia Polytechnic Institute and State University	D
Yale University	M

■ ENVIRONMENTAL EDUCATION

Institution	Degree
Antioch New England Graduate School	M
Arcadia University	M,D,O
Brooklyn College of the City University of New York	M
California State University, Fullerton	M
California State University, San Bernardino	M
Florida Institute of Technology	M,D,O
Gannon University	M,O
Indiana University Bloomington	M,D,O
Lesley University	M,D,O
Maryville University of Saint Louis	M
New York University	M
Prescott College	M
Rowan University	M
Slippery Rock University of Pennsylvania	M
Southern Connecticut State University	M,O
Southern Oregon University	M
State University of New York at New Paltz	M
Universidad Metropolitana	M
University of Minnesota, Twin Cities Campus	M,D,O
University of New Hampshire	M
West Virginia University	M

■ ENVIRONMENTAL ENGINEERING

Institution	Degree
Auburn University	M,D
California Institute of Technology	M,D
California Polytechnic State University, San Luis Obispo	M
Carnegie Mellon University	M,D
The Catholic University of America	M,D
Clarkson University	M,D
Clemson University	M,D
Cleveland State University	M,D
Colorado State University	M,D
Columbia University	M,D
Cornell University	M,D
Drexel University	M,D
Duke University	M,D
Florida Agricultural and Mechanical University	M,D
Florida International University	M
Florida State University	M,D
The George Washington University	M,D,O
Georgia Institute of Technology	M,D
Harvard University	M,D
Idaho State University	M,D,O
Illinois Institute of Technology	M,D
Iowa State University of Science and Technology	M,D
The Johns Hopkins University	M,D
Lamar University	M,D
Lehigh University	M,D
Louisiana State University and Agricultural and Mechanical College	M,D
Manhattan College	M
Marquette University	M,D
Massachusetts Institute of Technology	M,D,O
Michigan State University	M,D
Michigan Technological University	M,D
Montana State University–Bozeman	M,D
National University	M
New Jersey Institute of Technology	M,D
New Mexico Institute of Mining and Technology	M
New Mexico State University	M,D
New York Institute of Technology	M
North Carolina Agricultural and Technical State University	M
North Dakota State University	M,D
Northeastern University	M,D
Northwestern University	M,D
Ohio University	M,D
Oklahoma State University	M,D
Old Dominion University	M,D
Oregon State University	M,D
The Pennsylvania State University Harrisburg Campus of the Capital College	M
The Pennsylvania State University University Park Campus	M,D
Polytechnic University, Brooklyn Campus	M
Portland State University	M,D
Princeton University	M,D
Rensselaer Polytechnic Institute	M,D
Rice University	M,D
Rutgers, The State University of New Jersey, New Brunswick/Piscataway	M,D
San Jose State University	M
South Dakota State University	M
Southern Methodist University	M
Stanford University	M,D,O
State University of New York College of Environmental Science and Forestry	M,D
Stevens Institute of Technology	M,D,O
Syracuse University	M,D
Temple University	M
Texas A&M University	M,D
Texas A&M University–Kingsville	M,D
Texas Tech University	M,D
Tufts University	M,D
Tulane University	M,D
University at Buffalo, The State University of New York	M,D
The University of Alabama	M,D
The University of Alabama at Birmingham	M,D
The University of Alabama in Huntsville	M,D
University of Alaska Fairbanks	M,D
The University of Arizona	M,D
University of Arkansas	M
University of California, Berkeley	M,D
University of California, Davis	M,D,O
University of California, Irvine	M,D
University of California, Los Angeles	M,D
University of California, Riverside	M,D
University of California, Santa Barbara	D
University of Central Florida	M,D,O
University of Cincinnati	M,D
University of Colorado at Boulder	M,D
University of Connecticut	M,D
University of Dayton	M
University of Delaware	M,D
University of Detroit Mercy	M
University of Florida	M,D,O
University of Hawaii at Manoa	M,D
University of Houston	M,D
University of Idaho	M,D
University of Illinois at Urbana–Champaign	M,D
The University of Iowa	M,D
University of Kansas	M,D
University of Louisville	M,D
University of Maine	M
University of Maryland, College Park	M,D
University of Massachusetts Amherst	M
University of Massachusetts Lowell	M
The University of Memphis	M,D
University of Michigan	M,D,O
University of Missouri–Columbia	M,D
University of Missouri–Rolla	M,D
University of Nebraska–Lincoln	M,D

Peterson's Graduate Schools in the U.S. 2006

Directory of Graduate and Professional Programs by Field

Environmental Engineering

University of Nevada, Las Vegas	M,D
University of New Haven	M,O
The University of North Carolina at Chapel Hill	M,D
University of North Dakota	M
University of Notre Dame	M,D
University of Oklahoma	M,D
University of Pittsburgh	M,D
University of Rhode Island	M,D
University of Southern California	M,D
University of South Florida	M,D
The University of Tennessee	M
The University of Texas at Arlington	M,D
The University of Texas at Austin	M
The University of Texas at El Paso	M,D
The University of Texas at San Antonio	M,D
University of Utah	M,D
University of Vermont	M,D
University of Washington	M,D
University of Wisconsin–Madison	M,D
University of Wyoming	M
Utah State University	M,D,O
Vanderbilt University	M,D
Villanova University	M
Virginia Polytechnic Institute and State University	M,D
Washington State University	M
Wayne State University	M,D
West Virginia University	M,D
Worcester Polytechnic Institute	M,D,O
Youngstown State University	M

■ ENVIRONMENTAL MANAGEMENT AND POLICY

Adelphi University	M
American University	M,D,O
Antioch New England Graduate School	M,D
Antioch University Seattle	M
Baylor University	M
Bemidji State University	M
Boise State University	M
Boston University	M,O
Brown University	M
California State University, Fullerton	M
Central Washington University	M
Clark University	M
Clemson University	M,D
Cleveland State University	M
Colorado State University	M,D
Columbia University	M
Cornell University	M,D
Drexel University	M
Duke University	M,D
Duquesne University	M,O
East Carolina University	D
Florida Gulf Coast University	M
Florida Institute of Technology	M,D
Florida International University	M
Friends University	M
George Mason University	M,D
The George Washington University	M,D
Georgia Institute of Technology	M,D
Hardin-Simmons University	M
Harvard University	M,O
Illinois Institute of Technology	M,D
Iowa State University of Science and Technology	M,D
The Johns Hopkins University	M
Kansas State University	M
Kean University	M
Lamar University	M,D
Long Island University, C.W. Post Campus	M
Louisiana State University and Agricultural and Mechanical College	M
Michigan State University	M,D
Michigan Technological University	M

Montana State University–Bozeman	M,D
Montclair State University	M,D
Monterey Institute of International Studies	M
New Jersey Institute of Technology	M,D
New Mexico Highlands University	M
New York Institute of Technology	M,O
North Dakota State University	M,D
Northeastern Illinois University	M
Northern Arizona University	M,O
Ohio University	M
Oregon State University	M,D
The Pennsylvania State University University Park Campus	M
Portland State University	M,D
Prescott College	M
Princeton University	M,D
Purdue University	M
Rensselaer Polytechnic Institute	M,D
Rice University	M
Rochester Institute of Technology	M
St. Cloud State University	M
Saint Joseph's University	M
Saint Mary's University of Minnesota	M,O
San Francisco State University	M
San Jose State University	M
Shippensburg University of Pennsylvania	M
Slippery Rock University of Pennsylvania	M
Southeast Missouri State University	M
Southwest Missouri State University	M
Stanford University	M
State University of New York College of Environmental Science and Forestry	M,D
Stony Brook University, State University of New York	M,O
Texas State University-San Marcos	M
Texas Tech University	D
Towson University	M
Troy University	M
Tufts University	M,D,O
Universidad del Turabo	M
Universidad Metropolitana	M
University at Albany, State University of New York	M
University of Alaska Fairbanks	M
The University of Arizona	M
University of California, Berkeley	M,D
University of California, Irvine	M,D
University of California, Santa Barbara	M,D
University of California, Santa Cruz	D
University of Chicago	M,D
University of Colorado at Boulder	M,D
University of Connecticut	M,D
University of Delaware	M
University of Denver	M,O
The University of Findlay	M
University of Hawaii at Manoa	M,D
University of Houston–Clear Lake	M
University of Idaho	M,D
University of Illinois at Springfield	M
University of Maine	M,D
University of Maryland University College	M,O
University of Massachusetts Lowell	M,D,O
University of Miami	M,D
University of Michigan	M,D
University of Minnesota, Twin Cities Campus	M,D
University of Missouri–St. Louis	M,D,O
The University of Montana–Missoula	M,D
University of Nevada, Reno	M
University of New Hampshire	M
The University of North Carolina at Chapel Hill	M,D
University of Oregon	M,D
University of Pennsylvania	M
University of Pittsburgh	M

University of Rhode Island	M,D
University of St. Thomas (MN)	M
University of San Francisco	M
University of South Carolina	M
University of South Florida	M,D
The University of Tennessee	M,D
The University of Texas at Austin	M
University of Vermont	M,D
University of Washington	M,D
University of Wisconsin–Green Bay	M
University of Wisconsin–Madison	M,D
Utah State University	M,D
Vanderbilt University	M,D
Virginia Commonwealth University	M
Webster University	M,D
West Virginia University	M,D
Wright State University	M
Yale University	M,D
Youngstown State University	M,O

■ ENVIRONMENTAL SCIENCES

Alabama Agricultural and Mechanical University	M,D
Alaska Pacific University	M
American University	M
Antioch New England Graduate School	M,D
Arkansas State University	D
California State University, Chico	M
California State University, Fullerton	M
City College of the City University of New York	M,D
Clarkson University	M,D
Clemson University	M,D
Cleveland State University	M,D
College of Charleston	M
College of Staten Island of the City University of New York	M
Columbus State University	M
Cornell University	M,D
Drexel University	M,D
Duke University	M,D
Duquesne University	M,O
Florida Agricultural and Mechanical University	M,D
Florida Atlantic University	M
Florida Gulf Coast University	M
Florida Institute of Technology	M,D
Florida International University	M
George Mason University	M,D
Georgia Institute of Technology	M,D
Harvard University	M,D
Howard University	M,D
Humboldt State University	M
Hunter College of the City University of New York	M,O
Idaho State University	M
Indiana University Bloomington	M,D
Inter American University of Puerto Rico, San Germán Campus	M
Jackson State University	M,D
Lehigh University	M,D
Louisiana State University and Agricultural and Mechanical College	M,D
Loyola Marymount University	M
Marshall University	M
Massachusetts Institute of Technology	M,D,O
McNeese State University	M,D
Miami University	M
Michigan State University	M,D
Minnesota State University Mankato	M
Montana State University–Bozeman	M
Montclair State University	M,D,O
New Jersey Institute of Technology	M,D
New Mexico Institute of Mining and Technology	M,D
North Carolina Agricultural and Technical State University	M
North Dakota State University	M,D

90   *www.petersons.com*   *Peterson's Graduate Schools in the U.S. 2006*

Evolutionary Biology

Northern Arizona University	M,O
Nova Southeastern University	M
Oakland University	M,D
The Ohio State University	M,D
Ohio University	M
Oklahoma State University	M,D
Oregon State University	M,D
Pace University, White Plains Campus	M
The Pennsylvania State University Harrisburg Campus of the Capital College	M
The Pennsylvania State University University Park Campus	M
Polytechnic University, Brooklyn Campus	M
Portland State University	M,D
Queens College of the City University of New York	M
Rensselaer Polytechnic Institute	M,D
Rice University	M,D
Rutgers, The State University of New Jersey, Newark	M,D
Rutgers, The State University of New Jersey, New Brunswick/Piscataway	M,D
South Dakota State University	D
Southern Illinois University Carbondale	D
Southern Illinois University Edwardsville	M
Southern Methodist University	M,D
Southern University and Agricultural and Mechanical College	M
Stanford University	M,D,O
State University of New York College of Environmental Science and Forestry	M,D
Stephen F. Austin State University	M
Tarleton State University	M
Tennessee Technological University	D
Texas A&M University–Corpus Christi	M
Texas Christian University	M
Texas Tech University	M,D
Towson University	M,O
Tufts University	M,D
Tuskegee University	M
University at Albany, State University of New York	M
The University of Alabama in Huntsville	M,D
University of Alaska Anchorage	M
University of Alaska Fairbanks	M,D
The University of Arizona	M,D
University of California, Berkeley	M,D
University of California, Davis	M,D
University of California, Los Angeles	D
University of California, Riverside	M,D
University of California, Santa Barbara	M,D
University of Chicago	M,D
University of Cincinnati	M,D
University of Colorado at Colorado Springs	M
University of Colorado at Denver	M
University of Guam	M
University of Houston–Clear Lake	M
University of Idaho	M
University of Illinois at Urbana–Champaign	M,D
University of Kansas	M,D
University of Maine	M
University of Maryland	M,D
University of Maryland, Baltimore County	M,D
University of Maryland, College Park	M,D
University of Maryland Eastern Shore	M,D
University of Massachusetts Boston	M,D
University of Massachusetts Lowell	M,D,O
University of Michigan–Dearborn	M
The University of Montana–Missoula	M
University of Nevada, Las Vegas	M,D
University of Nevada, Reno	M,D
University of New Haven	M
The University of North Carolina at Chapel Hill	M,D
University of Northern Iowa	M
University of North Texas	M,D
University of Oklahoma	M,D
University of South Carolina	M,D
University of South Florida	M,D
The University of Tennessee at Chattanooga	M
The University of Texas at Arlington	M,D
The University of Texas at El Paso	M,D
The University of Texas at San Antonio	M,D
University of Toledo	D
University of Virginia	M,D
University of Wisconsin–Green Bay	M
University of Wisconsin–Madison	M,D
Virginia Commonwealth University	M
Virginia Polytechnic Institute and State University	M,D
Washington State University	M,D
Western Connecticut State University	M
Western Washington University	M
West Texas A&M University	M
Wichita State University	M
Wright State University	M,D
Yale University	M,D

■ EPIDEMIOLOGY

Boston University	M,D
Brown University	M,D
California State University, Long Beach	M
Case Western Reserve University	M,D
Columbia University	M,D
Cornell University	M,D
Emory University	M,D
Georgetown University	M
The George Washington University	M,D
Georgia State University	M,D
Harvard University	M,D
The Johns Hopkins University	M,D
Loma Linda University	M,D
Michigan State University	M,D
North Carolina State University	M,D
Purdue University	M,D
Saint Louis University	M
San Diego State University	M,D
Stanford University	M,D
Texas A&M University	M,D
Tufts University	M,D,O
Tulane University	M,D
University at Albany, State University of New York	M,D
University at Buffalo, The State University of New York	M,D
The University of Alabama at Birmingham	D
The University of Arizona	M,D
University of California, Berkeley	M,D
University of California, Davis	M,D
University of California, Los Angeles	M,D
University of California, San Diego	D
University of Cincinnati	M,D
University of Hawaii at Manoa	M,D
University of Illinois at Chicago	M,D
The University of Iowa	M,D
University of Louisville	M,D
University of Maryland	M,D
University of Maryland, Baltimore County	M
University of Massachusetts Lowell	M,D,O
University of Miami	D
University of Michigan	M
University of Minnesota, Twin Cities Campus	M,D
The University of North Carolina at Chapel Hill	M,D
University of Pennsylvania	M,D
University of Pittsburgh	M,D
University of Rochester	M,D
University of South Carolina	M,D
University of Southern California	M,D
University of South Florida	M,D
University of Washington	M,D
Virginia Commonwealth University	D
Yale University	M,D

■ ERGONOMICS AND HUMAN FACTORS

Bentley College	M
The Catholic University of America	M
Clemson University	M,D
Cornell University	M
Embry-Riddle Aeronautical University (FL)	M
Florida Institute of Technology	M
New York University	M,D
Purdue University	M,D
San Jose State University	M
Tufts University	M,D
University of Central Florida	M,D,O
University of Cincinnati	M,D
The University of Iowa	M,D
University of Massachusetts Lowell	M,D,O
University of Miami	M,D
University of Washington	M,D
Wright State University	M,D

■ ETHICS

American University	M,D,O
Azusa Pacific University	M
Biola University	P,M,D
Claremont Graduate University	M,D
Marquette University	M,D
St. Edward's University	M
University of Baltimore	M
University of Maryland, Baltimore County	M,O
University of Nevada, Las Vegas	M
University of North Florida	M
Valparaiso University	M

■ ETHNIC STUDIES

Cornell University	M,D
San Francisco State University	M
University of California, Berkeley	D
University of California, San Diego	M,D

■ EVOLUTIONARY BIOLOGY

Arizona State University	M,D
Brown University	D
Columbia University	D,O
Cornell University	D
Emory University	D
Florida State University	M,D
George Mason University	M,D
Harvard University	D
Indiana University Bloomington	M,D
Iowa State University of Science and Technology	M,D
The Johns Hopkins University	D
Marquette University	M,D
Northwestern University	D
The Ohio State University	M,D
The Pennsylvania State University University Park Campus	M,D
Princeton University	D
Purdue University	M,D
Rice University	M,D
Rutgers, The State University of New Jersey, New Brunswick/Piscataway	M,D
Stony Brook University, State University of New York	D
University at Albany, State University of New York	M,D
The University of Arizona	M,D
University of California, Davis	D

Peterson's Graduate Schools in the U.S. 2006

Directory of Graduate and Professional Programs by Field

Evolutionary Biology

Institution	Degree
University of California, Irvine	M,D
University of California, Riverside	M,D
University of California, San Diego	D
University of California, Santa Barbara	M,D
University of California, Santa Cruz	M,D
University of Chicago	D
University of Colorado at Boulder	M,D
University of Delaware	M,D
University of Hawaii at Manoa	M,D
University of Illinois at Chicago	M,D
University of Illinois at Urbana–Champaign	D
University of Kansas	M,D
University of Louisiana at Lafayette	M,D
University of Maryland, College Park	M,D
University of Massachusetts Amherst	M,D
University of Miami	M,D
University of Michigan	M,D
University of Minnesota, Twin Cities Campus	M,D
University of Missouri–Columbia	M,D
University of Missouri–St. Louis	M,D,O
University of Nevada, Reno	D
The University of North Carolina at Chapel Hill	M,D
University of Notre Dame	M,D
University of Oregon	M,D
University of Pennsylvania	D
University of Pittsburgh	M,D
University of South Carolina	M,D
The University of Tennessee	M,D
The University of Texas at Austin	D
University of Utah	M,D
Virginia Polytechnic Institute and State University	M,D
Washington University in St. Louis	D
West Virginia University	M,D
Yale University	D

Exercise and Sports Science

Institution	Degree
American University	M
Appalachian State University	M
Arizona State University	M,D
Arkansas State University	M,O
Armstrong Atlantic State University	M
Ashland University	M
Austin Peay State University	M
Ball State University	D
Barry University	M
Benedictine University	M
Bloomsburg University of Pennsylvania	M
Boise State University	M
Brigham Young University	M,D
Brooklyn College of the City University of New York	M
California State University, Fresno	M
California University of Pennsylvania	M
Case Western Reserve University	M,D
Central Connecticut State University	M
Central Michigan University	M
Central Missouri State University	M
Cleveland State University	M
The College of St. Scholastica	M
Colorado State University	M
East Carolina University	M,D
East Stroudsburg University of Pennsylvania	M
East Tennessee State University	M
Florida Atlantic University	M
Florida State University	M,D
Gardner-Webb University	M
George Mason University	M
The George Washington University	M
Georgia State University	M,D
Howard University	M
Humboldt State University	M
Indiana State University	M
Indiana University Bloomington	M,D,O
Indiana University of Pennsylvania	M
Iowa State University of Science and Technology	M,D
Ithaca College	M
Kean University	M
Kent State University	M,D
Long Island University, Brooklyn Campus	M
Louisiana Tech University	M
Marshall University	M
Miami University	M
Mississippi State University	M
Montclair State University	M
Morehead State University	M
New Mexico Highlands University	M
North Dakota State University	M
Northeastern University	M
Northern Arizona University	M
Northern Michigan University	M
Oakland University	M,O
Ohio University	M
Oregon State University	M,D
Purdue University	M,D
Queens College of the City University of New York	M
St. Cloud State University	M
San Diego State University	M
Slippery Rock University of Pennsylvania	M
Southeast Missouri State University	M
Southern Connecticut State University	M
Southern Illinois University Edwardsville	M,O
Springfield College	M,D,O
State University of New York College at Cortland	M
Syracuse University	M,D
Tennessee State University	M
Texas Tech University	M
Texas Woman's University	M
University at Buffalo, The State University of New York	M,D
The University of Akron	M
University of California, Davis	M
University of Central Florida	M,D
University of Connecticut	M,D
University of Dayton	M
University of Delaware	M
University of Florida	M,D
University of Georgia	M,D,O
University of Houston	M,D
University of Houston–Clear Lake	M
The University of Iowa	M,D
University of Kentucky	M,D
University of Louisiana at Monroe	M
University of Louisville	M
University of Massachusetts Amherst	M,D
The University of Memphis	M
University of Miami	M,D
University of Minnesota, Twin Cities Campus	M,D,O
University of Mississippi	M,D
University of Missouri–Columbia	M,D
The University of Montana–Missoula	M
University of Nebraska at Kearney	M
University of Nevada, Las Vegas	M
University of New Orleans	M,O
The University of North Carolina at Chapel Hill	M
The University of North Carolina at Greensboro	M,D
University of Northern Colorado	M,D
University of North Florida	M,O
University of Oklahoma	M
University of Oregon	M,D
University of Pittsburgh	M,D
University of South Alabama	M
University of South Carolina	M,D
The University of Tennessee	M,D,O
The University of Texas at Arlington	M
The University of Texas at El Paso	M
The University of Texas at Tyler	M
University of the Pacific	M
University of Toledo	M,D
University of Utah	M,D
University of West Florida	M
University of Wisconsin–La Crosse	M
Wake Forest University	M
Wayne State College	M
West Chester University of Pennsylvania	M,O
Western Michigan University	M
West Texas A&M University	M
West Virginia University	M,D
Wichita State University	M

Experimental Psychology

Institution	Degree
American University	M
Appalachian State University	M
Bowling Green State University	M,D
Brooklyn College of the City University of New York	M,D
California State University, San Bernardino	M
Case Western Reserve University	D
The Catholic University of America	M,D
Central Michigan University	M,D
Central Washington University	M
City College of the City University of New York	M,D
Cleveland State University	M,O
The College of William and Mary	M
Columbia University	M,D
Cornell University	D
DePaul University	M,D
Duke University	D
Fairleigh Dickinson University, Metropolitan Campus	M,O
George Mason University	M,D
Harvard University	M,D
Howard University	M,D
Illinois State University	M,D,O
The Johns Hopkins University	D
Kent State University	M,D
Lehigh University	M,D
Long Island University, C.W. Post Campus	M,O
Miami University	D
Mississippi State University	M,D
Morehead State University	M
Northeastern University	M,D
The Ohio State University	D
Ohio University	D
Oklahoma State University	M,D
St. John's University (NY)	M
Saint Louis University	M,D
Seton Hall University	M
Southern Illinois University Carbondale	M,D
Stony Brook University, State University of New York	D
Syracuse University	D
Temple University	D
Texas Tech University	M,D
Towson University	M
University at Albany, State University of New York	M,D
University of California, Santa Cruz	D
University of Central Florida	D
University of Cincinnati	D
University of Connecticut	M,D
University of Dayton	M
University of Hartford	M
University of Louisville	M
University of Maine	M,D
University of Maryland, College Park	M,D
The University of Memphis	D
University of Michigan	D
University of Mississippi	M,D
University of Missouri–St. Louis	M,D,O
The University of Montana–Missoula	M,D,O

Directory of Graduate and Professional Programs by Field
Finance and Banking

Institution	Degree
University of Nebraska at Omaha	M,D,O
University of Nevada, Las Vegas	M,D
The University of North Carolina at Chapel Hill	D
University of North Dakota	M,D
University of North Texas	M,D
University of Rhode Island	D
University of South Carolina	M,D
University of South Florida	M,D
The University of Tennessee	M,D
The University of Tennessee at Chattanooga	M
The University of Texas at Arlington	M,D
The University of Texas at El Paso	M,D
The University of Texas–Pan American	M
University of Toledo	M,D
University of Wisconsin–Oshkosh	M
Washington University in St. Louis	M,D
Western Michigan University	M,D,O

■ FACILITIES MANAGEMENT

Institution	Degree
Cornell University	M
Indiana University of Pennsylvania	M
Michigan State University	M,D
Pratt Institute	M
Southern Methodist University	M,D
University of North Texas	M,O

■ FAMILY AND CONSUMER SCIENCES-GENERAL

Institution	Degree
Alabama Agricultural and Mechanical University	M,D
Appalachian State University	M
Ball State University	M
Bowling Green State University	M
California State University, Fresno	M
California State University, Long Beach	M
California State University, Northridge	M
Central Michigan University	M
Central Washington University	M
Cornell University	M,D
Eastern Illinois University	M
Eastern Michigan University	M
Florida State University	M,D
Fontbonne University	M
Illinois State University	M
Indiana State University	M
Iowa State University of Science and Technology	M,D
Kansas State University	M,D
Kent State University	M,O
Lamar University	M,O
Louisiana State University and Agricultural and Mechanical College	M,D
Louisiana Tech University	M
Marshall University	M
Michigan State University	M,D
Montclair State University	M
New Mexico State University	M
North Carolina Central University	M
North Dakota State University	M
The Ohio State University	M,D
Ohio University	M
Oklahoma State University	M,D
Oregon State University	M
Prairie View A&M University	M
Purdue University	M,D
Queens College of the City University of New York	M
Sam Houston State University	M
San Francisco State University	M
South Carolina State University	M
South Dakota State University	M
Southeast Missouri State University	M
State University of New York College at Oneonta	M
Stephen F. Austin State University	M

Institution	Degree
Texas A&M University–Kingsville	M
Texas Southern University	M
Texas Tech University	M,D
The University of Akron	M
The University of Alabama	M,D
The University of Arizona	M,D
University of Arkansas	M
University of Central Arkansas	M
University of Central Oklahoma	M
University of Georgia	M,D
University of Idaho	M
University of Kentucky	M,D
University of Louisiana at Lafayette	M
University of Minnesota, Twin Cities Campus	M,D
University of Missouri–Columbia	M,D
University of Nebraska–Lincoln	M,D
The University of North Carolina at Greensboro	M,D
University of North Florida	M,O
University of Puerto Rico, Río Piedras	M
The University of Tennessee	D
The University of Tennessee at Martin	M
The University of Texas at Austin	M,D
University of Wisconsin–Madison	M,D
University of Wisconsin–Stevens Point	M
University of Wisconsin–Stout	M
Utah State University	M,D
Western Michigan University	M

■ FILM, TELEVISION, AND VIDEO PRODUCTION

Institution	Degree
American University	M
Antioch University McGregor	M
Boston University	M
Brigham Young University	M,D
Brooklyn College of the City University of New York	M
California State University, Fullerton	M
Carnegie Mellon University	M
Central Michigan University	M
Chapman University	M
Chestnut Hill College	M,O
Columbia College Chicago	M
Columbia University	M
Emerson College	M
Florida State University	M
George Mason University	M
Howard University	M
Loyola Marymount University	M
Marywood University	M
Montana State University–Bozeman	M
New Mexico Highlands University	M
New York University	M
Northwestern University	M,D
Ohio University	M
Rochester Institute of Technology	M
San Diego State University	M
San Francisco State University	M
San Jose State University	M
Southern Methodist University	M
Stanford University	M,D
Syracuse University	M
Temple University	M
The University of Alabama	M
University of California, Los Angeles	M,D
University of Denver	M
The University of Iowa	M
The University of Memphis	M,D
University of Miami	M,D
University of Michigan	O
The University of Montana–Missoula	M
University of Nevada, Las Vegas	M
University of New Orleans	M
The University of North Carolina at Greensboro	M
University of North Texas	M
University of Oklahoma	M
University of Southern California	M
The University of Texas at Austin	M,D

Institution	Degree
University of Utah	M
University of Wisconsin–Milwaukee	M

■ FILM, TELEVISION, AND VIDEO THEORY AND CRITICISM

Institution	Degree
Boston University	M
Chapman University	M
Claremont Graduate University	M,D
College of Staten Island of the City University of New York	M
Emory University	M,D,O
National University	M
New York University	M,D
Ohio University	M
San Francisco State University	M
University of Chicago	M
The University of Iowa	M,D
University of Kansas	M,D
University of Miami	M,D
University of Southern California	M,D

■ FINANCE AND BANKING

Institution	Degree
Adelphi University	M
Alabama Agricultural and Mechanical University	M
American University	M,D,O
Argosy University/Sarasota	M,D
Argosy University/Schaumburg	M,D
Arizona State University	M,D
Auburn University	M
Bentley College	M,O
Bernard M. Baruch College of the City University of New York	M,D
Boston College	M,D
Boston University	P,M,D
Brandeis University	M,D
Bridgewater State College	M
California Lutheran University	M
California State University, Fullerton	M
California State University, Hayward	M
California State University, Los Angeles	M
Cardinal Stritch University	M
Carnegie Mellon University	D
Case Western Reserve University	M,D
The Catholic University of America	M
Central Michigan University	M
Charleston Southern University	M
City University	M,O
Claremont Graduate University	M
Clark Atlanta University	M
Clark University	M
Cleveland State University	M,O
Columbia University	M,D
Concordia University Wisconsin	M
Cornell University	D
Dallas Baptist University	M
DePaul University	M,O
Dowling College	M,O
Drexel University	M,D,O
Eastern Michigan University	M
Eastern University	M
East Tennessee State University	M
Emory University	D
Fairfield University	M
Fairleigh Dickinson University, College at Florham	M,O
Fairleigh Dickinson University, Metropolitan Campus	M,O
Florida Agricultural and Mechanical University	M
Florida Atlantic University	M
Florida International University	M
Florida State University	M,D
Fordham University	M
Gannon University	O
The George Washington University	M,D
Georgia Institute of Technology	M,D,O
Georgia State University	M,D

Peterson's Graduate Schools in the U.S. 2006 www.petersons.com 93

Directory of Graduate and Professional Programs by Field

Finance and Banking

Institution	Degree
Hawai'i Pacific University	M
Hofstra University	M,O
Howard University	M
Illinois Institute of Technology	P,M
Indiana University Bloomington	M,D
Indiana University Southeast	M,O
Inter American University of Puerto Rico, Metropolitan Campus	M
Inter American University of Puerto Rico, San Germán Campus	M
Iona College	M,O
The Johns Hopkins University	M,O
Johnson & Wales University	M
Kennesaw State University	M
Kent State University	D
Lehigh University	M,D
Lindenwood University	M
Long Island University, C.W. Post Campus	M,O
Louisiana State University and Agricultural and Mechanical College	M,D
Louisiana Tech University	M,D
Loyola College in Maryland	M
Marywood University	M
Mercy College	M
Metropolitan State University	M
Miami University	M
Michigan State University	M,D
Middle Tennessee State University	M,D
Mississippi State University	M,D
Montclair State University	M
Mount Saint Mary College	M
National University	M
New School University	M
New York Institute of Technology	M,O
New York University	M,D,O
Northeastern Illinois University	M
Northeastern State University	M
Northeastern University	M
Northwestern University	D
Ohio University	M
Oklahoma City University	M
Oklahoma State University	M,D
Oral Roberts University	M
Our Lady of the Lake University of San Antonio	M
Pace University	M
Pace University, White Plains Campus	M
The Pennsylvania State University University Park Campus	D
Philadelphia University	M
Polytechnic University, Westchester Graduate Center	M,O
Pontifical Catholic University of Puerto Rico	M,D
Portland State University	M
Princeton University	M
Purdue University	M,D
Quinnipiac University	M
Regis University	M,O
Rensselaer Polytechnic Institute	M,D
Robert Morris University	M
Rochester Institute of Technology	M
Rutgers, The State University of New Jersey, Newark	M,D,O
Sage Graduate School	M
St. Bonaventure University	M,O
St. Cloud State University	M
St. Edward's University	M,O
St. John's University (NY)	M,O
Saint Joseph's University	M
Saint Louis University	M
St. Mary's University of San Antonio	M
Saint Peter's College	M
St. Thomas Aquinas College	M
Saint Xavier University	M,O
Sam Houston State University	M
San Diego State University	M
Seattle University	M,O
Seton Hall University	M,O
Southeastern University	M
Southeast Missouri State University	M
Southern Illinois University Edwardsville	M
State University of New York at Binghamton	M,D
State University of New York at New Paltz	M
Suffolk University	M,O
Syracuse University	D
Temple University	M,D
Texas A&M International University	M
Texas A&M University	M,D
Texas Tech University	M,D
University at Albany, State University of New York	M
The University of Akron	M
The University of Alabama	M,D
University of Alaska Fairbanks	M
The University of Arizona	M,D
University of Baltimore	M
University of California, Berkeley	D
University of Central Florida	M,D
University of Cincinnati	M,D
University of Colorado at Boulder	M,D
University of Colorado at Colorado Springs	M
University of Colorado at Denver	M
University of Connecticut	M,D
University of Denver	M
The University of Findlay	M
University of Florida	M,D
University of Hawaii at Manoa	M,D
University of Houston	M,D
University of Houston–Clear Lake	M
University of Illinois at Urbana–Champaign	M,D
The University of Iowa	M,D
University of La Verne	M
University of Maryland University College	M,O
The University of Memphis	M,D
University of Miami	M
University of Michigan–Dearborn	M
University of Minnesota, Twin Cities Campus	M,D
University of Missouri–St. Louis	M,O
University of Nebraska–Lincoln	M,D
University of New Haven	M
University of New Mexico	M
The University of North Carolina at Chapel Hill	D
University of North Texas	M,D
University of Oregon	D
University of Pennsylvania	M,D
University of Rhode Island	M,D
University of St. Thomas (MN)	M
University of San Diego	M,O
University of San Francisco	M
The University of Scranton	M
University of Southern California	M
University of Southern Mississippi	M,D
University of South Florida	D
The University of Tennessee	M,D
The University of Tennessee at Chattanooga	M
The University of Texas at Arlington	M,D
The University of Texas at Austin	D
The University of Texas at San Antonio	M,D
University of Toledo	M
University of Tulsa	M
University of Utah	M,D
University of Wisconsin–Madison	M,D
University of Wisconsin–Whitewater	M
University of Wyoming	M
Vanderbilt University	D
Virginia Commonwealth University	M
Virginia Polytechnic Institute and State University	M,D
Virginia State University	M
Wagner College	M
Webster University	M
West Chester University of Pennsylvania	M
Western International University	M
Western New England College	M
West Texas A&M University	M
Wilkes University	M
Wright State University	M
Xavier University	M
Yale University	D
Youngstown State University	M

■ FINANCIAL ENGINEERING

Institution	Degree
Claremont Graduate University	M,D
Columbia University	M,D,O
Kent State University	M
Polytechnic University, Brooklyn Campus	M
Polytechnic University, Westchester Graduate Center	M,O
Princeton University	M,D
University of California, Berkeley	M
University of Michigan	M
University of Tulsa	M

■ FIRE PROTECTION ENGINEERING

Institution	Degree
Anna Maria College	M
Oklahoma State University	M
University of Maryland, College Park	M,O
University of New Haven	M
Worcester Polytechnic Institute	M,D,O

■ FISH, GAME, AND WILDLIFE MANAGEMENT

Institution	Degree
Arkansas Tech University	M
Auburn University	M,D
Brigham Young University	M,D
Clemson University	M,D
Colorado State University	M,D
Cornell University	M,D
Frostburg State University	M
Iowa State University of Science and Technology	M,D
Louisiana State University and Agricultural and Mechanical College	M,D
Michigan State University	M,D
Mississippi State University	M
Montana State University–Bozeman	M,D
New Mexico State University	M
North Carolina State University	M
Oregon State University	M,D
The Pennsylvania State University University Park Campus	M,D
Purdue University	M,D
South Dakota State University	M,D
State University of New York College of Environmental Science and Forestry	M,D
Sul Ross State University	M
Tennessee Technological University	M
Texas A&M University	M,D
Texas A&M University–Kingsville	M,D
Texas State University-San Marcos	M
Texas Tech University	M,D
University of Alaska Fairbanks	M,D
The University of Arizona	M,D
University of Florida	M,D
University of Idaho	M,D
University of Maine	M,D
University of Massachusetts Amherst	M,D
University of Miami	M,D
University of Minnesota, Twin Cities Campus	M,D
University of Missouri–Columbia	M,D

Forensic Sciences

The University of Montana–Missoula M,D
University of New Hampshire M
University of North Dakota M,D
University of Rhode Island M,D
The University of Tennessee M
University of Vermont M
University of Washington M,D
Utah State University M,D
Virginia Polytechnic Institute and State University M,D
West Virginia University M

■ FOLKLORE

The George Washington University M
Indiana University Bloomington M,D
University of California, Berkeley M
University of Louisiana at Lafayette M,D
The University of North Carolina at Chapel Hill M
University of Oregon M
University of Pennsylvania M,D
The University of Texas at Austin M,D
Utah State University M
Western Kentucky University M

■ FOOD SCIENCE AND TECHNOLOGY

Alabama Agricultural and Mechanical University M,D
Auburn University M,D
Brigham Young University M
California State Polytechnic University, Pomona M
California State University, Fresno M
Chapman University M
Clemson University M,D
Colorado State University M,D
Cornell University M,D
Drexel University M,D
Florida Agricultural and Mechanical University M
Florida State University M,D
Framingham State College M
Illinois Institute of Technology M
Iowa State University of Science and Technology M,D
Kansas State University M,D
Louisiana State University and Agricultural and Mechanical College M,D
Marywood University M
Michigan State University M,D
Mississippi State University M,D
North Carolina State University M,D
North Dakota State University M,D
The Ohio State University M,D
Oklahoma State University M,D
Oregon State University M,D
The Pennsylvania State University University Park Campus M,D
Purdue University M,D
Rutgers, The State University of New Jersey, New Brunswick/Piscataway M,D
Texas A&M University M,D
Texas Tech University M,D
Texas Woman's University M,D
Tuskegee University M
The University of Akron M
University of Arkansas M,D
University of California, Davis M,D
University of Delaware M,D
University of Florida M,D
University of Georgia M,D
University of Hawaii at Manoa M
University of Idaho M
University of Illinois at Urbana–Champaign M,D
University of Maine M,D
University of Maryland, College Park M,D
University of Maryland Eastern Shore M
University of Massachusetts Amherst M,D
University of Minnesota, Twin Cities Campus M,D
University of Missouri–Columbia M,D
University of Nebraska–Lincoln M,D
University of Puerto Rico, Mayagüez Campus M
University of Rhode Island M,D
University of Southern Mississippi M,D
The University of Tennessee M,D
The University of Tennessee at Martin M
University of Wisconsin–Madison M,D
University of Wisconsin–Stout M
University of Wyoming M
Utah State University M,D
Virginia Polytechnic Institute and State University M,D
Washington State University M,D
Wayne State University M,D,O
West Virginia University M,D

■ FOREIGN LANGUAGES EDUCATION

Andrews University M,D,O
Auburn University M,D,O
Boston College M
Boston University M
Bowling Green State University M
Brigham Young University M
Brooklyn College of the City University of New York M
California State University, Chico M
Central Connecticut State University M
College of Charleston M
The College of New Jersey M
The College of Saint Rose M,O
The College of William and Mary M
Cornell University M,D
Eastern Washington University M
Elms College M,O
Fairfield University M,O
Florida Atlantic University M
Florida International University M,D
Framingham State College M
George Mason University M
Georgia Southern University M
Georgia State University M,D,O
Hofstra University M
Hunter College of the City University of New York M
Indiana University Bloomington M,D
Iona College M
Long Island University, C.W. Post Campus M
Louisiana Tech University M,D
Manhattanville College M
Marquette University M
Middle Tennessee State University M
Mississippi State University M
Monterey Institute of International Studies M
New York University M,D,O
Northern Arizona University M
North Georgia College & State University M,O
Portland State University M
Purdue University M,D,O
Queens College of the City University of New York M,O
Quinnipiac University M
Rhode Island College M
Rider University O
Rivier College M
Rutgers, The State University of New Jersey, New Brunswick/Piscataway M,D
Salisbury University M
School for International Training M
Stanford University M
State University of New York at Binghamton M
State University of New York College at Cortland M
State University of West Georgia M
Stony Brook University, State University of New York M,O
Teachers College Columbia University M,D
Texas A&M University–Kingsville M
University at Buffalo, The State University of New York M,D,O
The University of Arizona M,D
University of California, Irvine M,D
University of Central Arkansas M
University of Connecticut M,D
University of Delaware M
University of Florida M,D,O
University of Georgia M,D,O
University of Hawaii at Manoa M,D
University of Idaho M
University of Illinois at Urbana–Champaign M,D
University of Indianapolis M
The University of Iowa M,D
University of Louisville M,D
University of Maine M
University of Massachusetts Amherst M
University of Massachusetts Boston M
University of Michigan M,D
University of Minnesota, Twin Cities Campus M
University of Missouri–Columbia M,D,O
University of Nebraska at Kearney M
University of Nevada, Reno M
The University of North Carolina at Chapel Hill M
University of Pittsburgh M,D
University of Puerto Rico, Río Piedras M,D
University of South Carolina M,D
University of Southern Mississippi M
University of South Florida M,D,O
The University of Tennessee M,D,O
The University of Texas at Austin M,D
University of Toledo M,D,O
University of Utah M,D
University of Vermont M
University of Wisconsin–Madison M,D
Vanderbilt University M,D
West Chester University of Pennsylvania M

■ FORENSIC NURSING

Cleveland State University M
Fitchburg State College M,O
Quinnipiac University M
University of Colorado at Colorado Springs M

■ FORENSIC PSYCHOLOGY

American International College M
Castleton State College M
Drexel University M,D
Marymount University M
Prairie View A&M University M,D
Sage Graduate School M
Sam Houston State University M,D
University of Massachusetts Boston M,O

■ FORENSIC SCIENCES

Florida Atlantic University M
Florida International University M,D
The George Washington University M,O
Marshall University M
Michigan State University M,D
National University M
Pace University M
Sam Houston State University M,D
University at Albany, State University of New York M,D

Directory of Graduate and Professional Programs by Field

Forensic Sciences

The University of Alabama at Birmingham	M
University of Central Florida	M,O
University of Illinois at Chicago	M
University of New Haven	M
Virginia Commonwealth University	M,O

■ FORESTRY

Auburn University	M,D
California Polytechnic State University, San Luis Obispo	M
Clemson University	M,D
Colorado State University	M,D
Cornell University	M,D
Duke University	M,D
Harvard University	M
Iowa State University of Science and Technology	M,D
Louisiana State University and Agricultural and Mechanical College	M,D
Michigan State University	M,D
Michigan Technological University	M,D
Mississippi State University	M
North Carolina State University	M,D
Northern Arizona University	M,D
Oklahoma State University	M
Oregon State University	M,D
The Pennsylvania State University University Park Campus	M,D
Purdue University	M,D
Southern Illinois University Carbondale	M
Southern University and Agricultural and Mechanical College	M
State University of New York College of Environmental Science and Forestry	M,D
Stephen F. Austin State University	M,D
Texas A&M University	M,D
The University of Arizona	M,D
University of California, Berkeley	M,D
University of Florida	M,D
University of Georgia	M,D
University of Idaho	M,D
University of Kentucky	M
University of Maine	M,D
University of Massachusetts Amherst	M,D,O
University of Michigan	M,D,O
University of Minnesota, Twin Cities Campus	M,D
University of Missouri–Columbia	M,D
The University of Montana–Missoula	M,D
University of New Hampshire	M
The University of Tennessee	M
University of Vermont	M
University of Washington	M,D
University of Wisconsin–Madison	M,D
Utah State University	M,D
Virginia Polytechnic Institute and State University	M,D
West Virginia University	M,D
Yale University	M,D

■ FOUNDATIONS AND PHILOSOPHY OF EDUCATION

Antioch New England Graduate School	M
Arizona State University	M
Ashland University	M
Brigham Young University	M,D
California State University, Long Beach	M
California State University, Los Angeles	M
California State University, Northridge	M
Central Connecticut State University	M
College of Mount St. Joseph	M
DePaul University	M
Duquesne University	M
Eastern Michigan University	M
Eastern Washington University	M
Fairfield University	M,O
Florida Atlantic University	M,D,O
Florida State University	M,D,O
The George Washington University	M
Georgia State University	M,D
Harvard University	M,D,O
Hofstra University	M,O
Indiana University Bloomington	M,D,O
Iowa State University of Science and Technology	M,D
Kansas State University	M,D
Kent State University	M,D
Loyola College in Maryland	M,O
Loyola University Chicago	M,D
Millersville University of Pennsylvania	M
New York University	M,D
Niagara University	M
Northern Illinois University	M,D,O
The Pennsylvania State University University Park Campus	M,D
Purdue University	M,D,O
Rutgers, The State University of New Jersey, New Brunswick/Piscataway	M,D
Saint Louis University	M,D
Southeast Missouri State University	M
Southern Connecticut State University	O
Stanford University	M,D
State University of New York at Binghamton	D
Suffolk University	M,O
Syracuse University	M,D,O
Teachers College Columbia University	M,D
Texas A&M University	M,D
Troy University	M
Troy University Dothan	M,O
University of California, Berkeley	M,D
University of Cincinnati	M,D
University of Connecticut	M,D
University of Florida	M,D,O
University of Georgia	M,D,O
University of Hawaii at Manoa	M,D
University of Houston	M,D
University of Houston–Clear Lake	M
The University of Iowa	M,D,O
University of Kansas	D
University of Maryland, College Park	M,D,O
University of Michigan	M,D
University of Minnesota, Twin Cities Campus	M,D,O
University of New Mexico	M,D
University of New Orleans	M,D,O
University of Oklahoma	M,D
University of Pennsylvania	M,D
University of Pittsburgh	M,D
University of South Carolina	D
The University of Tennessee	M,D,O
The University of Texas at El Paso	M,D
The University of Texas of the Permian Basin	M
University of Toledo	M,D,O
University of Utah	M,D
University of Washington	M,D
The University of West Alabama	M
University of Wisconsin–Milwaukee	M
Western Illinois University	M
Widener University	M,D
Youngstown State University	M,D

■ FRENCH

American University	M,O
Arizona State University	M
Auburn University	M
Boston College	M,D
Boston University	M,D
Bowling Green State University	M
Brigham Young University	M
Brooklyn College of the City University of New York	M,D
Brown University	M,D
California State University, Fullerton	M
California State University, Long Beach	M
California State University, Los Angeles	M
California State University, Sacramento	M
Case Western Reserve University	M,D
The Catholic University of America	M,D
Central Connecticut State University	M
Colorado State University	M
Columbia University	M,D
Cornell University	D
Duke University	D
Eastern Michigan University	M
Emory University	D
Florida Atlantic University	M
Florida State University	M,D
Georgia State University	M
Harvard University	M,D
Hofstra University	M
Howard University	M
Hunter College of the City University of New York	M
Illinois State University	M
Indiana State University	M,O
Indiana University Bloomington	M,D
The Johns Hopkins University	D
Kansas State University	M
Kent State University	M
Louisiana State University and Agricultural and Mechanical College	M,D
Miami University	M
Michigan State University	M,D
Millersville University of Pennsylvania	M
Minnesota State University Mankato	M
Mississippi State University	M
Montclair State University	M
New York University	M,D,O
North Carolina State University	M
Northern Illinois University	M
Northwestern University	D,O
The Ohio State University	M,D
Ohio University	M
The Pennsylvania State University University Park Campus	M,D
Portland State University	M
Princeton University	D
Purdue University	M,D
Queens College of the City University of New York	M
Rhode Island College	M
Rice University	M,D
Rutgers, The State University of New Jersey, New Brunswick/Piscataway	M,D
Saint Louis University	M
San Diego State University	M
San Francisco State University	M
San Jose State University	M
Southern Connecticut State University	M
Stanford University	M,D
State University of New York at Binghamton	M
Stony Brook University, State University of New York	M,D
Syracuse University	M
Texas Tech University	M
Tufts University	M
Tulane University	M,D
University at Albany, State University of New York	M,D
The University of Alabama	M,D
The University of Arizona	M,D
University of Arkansas	M
University of California, Berkeley	D
University of California, Davis	D
University of California, Irvine	M,D

University of California, Los Angeles M,D
University of California, San Diego M
University of California, Santa Barbara M,D
University of Chicago M,D
University of Cincinnati M,D
University of Colorado at Boulder M,D
University of Connecticut M,D
University of Delaware M
University of Denver M
University of Florida M,D
University of Georgia M
University of Hawaii at Manoa M
University of Houston M,D
University of Idaho M
University of Illinois at Chicago M
University of Illinois at Urbana–Champaign M,D
The University of Iowa M,D
University of Kansas M,D
University of Kentucky M
University of Louisiana at Lafayette M,D
University of Louisville M
University of Maine M
University of Maryland, Baltimore County M
University of Maryland, College Park M,D
University of Massachusetts Amherst M
The University of Memphis M
University of Miami D
University of Michigan D
University of Minnesota, Twin Cities Campus M,D
University of Mississippi M
University of Missouri–Columbia M,D
The University of Montana–Missoula M
University of Nebraska–Lincoln M,D
University of Nevada, Las Vegas M
University of Nevada, Reno M
University of New Mexico M,D
The University of North Carolina at Chapel Hill M,D
The University of North Carolina at Greensboro M
University of Northern Iowa M
University of North Texas M
University of Notre Dame M
University of Oklahoma M,D
University of Oregon M
University of Pennsylvania M,D
University of Pittsburgh M,D
University of Rhode Island M
University of Southern California M,D
University of South Florida M
The University of Tennessee M,D
The University of Texas at Arlington M
The University of Texas at Austin M,D
University of Toledo M
University of Utah M,D
University of Vermont M
University of Virginia M,D
University of Washington M
University of Wisconsin–Madison M,D,O
University of Wisconsin–Milwaukee M
University of Wyoming M
Vanderbilt University M,D
Washington University in St. Louis M,D
Wayne State University M
West Chester University of Pennsylvania M
West Virginia University M
Yale University M,D

■ GENDER STUDIES

Cornell University M,D
Harvard University M,D
Northwestern University
Roosevelt University M
Rutgers, The State University of New Jersey, New Brunswick/Piscataway M,D
Simmons College M

University of Central Florida M,O
University of Missouri–St. Louis O

■ GENETIC COUNSELING

Arcadia University M
Brandeis University M
California State University, Northridge M,O
Case Western Reserve University M
The Johns Hopkins University M,D
Northwestern University M
University of California, Berkeley M
University of California, Irvine M
University of Cincinnati M
University of Minnesota, Twin Cities Campus M,D
University of Pittsburgh M
University of South Carolina M
Virginia Commonwealth University M,D,O

■ GENETICS

Arizona State University M,D
Brandeis University M,D
California Institute of Technology D
Carnegie Mellon University M,D
Case Western Reserve University D
Clemson University M,D
Colorado State University M,D
Columbia University M,D
Cornell University D
Dartmouth College D
Drexel University M,D
Duke University D
Emory University D
Florida State University M,D
The George Washington University M,D
Georgia State University M,D
Harvard University D
Howard University M
Illinois State University M,D
Indiana University Bloomington D
Indiana University–Purdue University Indianapolis M,D
Iowa State University of Science and Technology M,D
The Johns Hopkins University M,D
Kansas State University M,D
Marquette University M
Massachusetts Institute of Technology D
Mayo Graduate School D
Michigan State University M,D
New York University M,D
North Carolina State University M,D
Northwestern University D
The Ohio State University M,D
Oklahoma State University M,D
Oregon State University M,D
The Pennsylvania State University University Park Campus M,D
Purdue University M,D
Rutgers, The State University of New Jersey, New Brunswick/Piscataway M,D
Stanford University D
Stony Brook University, State University of New York D
Temple University D
Texas A&M University M,D
Tufts University D
University at Albany, State University of New York M,D
The University of Alabama at Birmingham D
The University of Arizona M,D
University of California, Davis M,D
University of California, Irvine M,D
University of California, Los Angeles M,D
University of California, Riverside D
University of California, San Diego D
University of California, San Francisco D
University of Chicago D
University of Cincinnati M,D

University of Colorado at Boulder M,D
University of Connecticut M,D
University of Delaware M,D
University of Florida M,D
University of Georgia M,D
University of Hawaii at Manoa M,D
University of Illinois at Chicago M,D
The University of Iowa M,D,O
University of Kansas D
University of Maryland, College Park M,D
University of Miami M,D
University of Minnesota, Twin Cities Campus M,D
University of Missouri–Columbia M,D
University of Missouri–St. Louis M,D,O
University of New Hampshire M,D
University of New Mexico M,D
The University of North Carolina at Chapel Hill M,D
University of North Dakota M,D
University of Notre Dame M,D
University of Oregon M,D
University of Pennsylvania D
University of Pittsburgh M,D
University of Rochester M,D
University of Southern California M,D
The University of Tennessee M,D
The University of Texas at Austin D
University of Utah M,D
University of Vermont M,D
University of Virginia D
University of Washington M,D
University of Wisconsin–Madison M,D
Virginia Commonwealth University M,D,O
Virginia Polytechnic Institute and State University M,D
Wake Forest University D
Washington State University M
Washington University in St. Louis M,D,O
Wayne State University M,D
West Virginia University M,D
Yale University D
Yeshiva University D

■ GENOMIC SCIENCES

Case Western Reserve University D
Duke University D
The George Washington University M
Harvard University D
North Carolina State University M,D
North Dakota State University M,D
Texas A&M University D
University of California, Riverside D
University of California, San Francisco D
University of Connecticut M
University of Florida D
The University of Tennessee M,D
University of Washington D
Wake Forest University D

■ GEOCHEMISTRY

California Institute of Technology M,D
California State University, Fullerton M
Columbia University M,D
Cornell University M,D
Georgia Institute of Technology M,D
Indiana University Bloomington M,D
The Johns Hopkins University M,D
Massachusetts Institute of Technology M,D
New Mexico Institute of Mining and Technology M,D
Ohio University M
The Pennsylvania State University University Park Campus M,D
Rensselaer Polytechnic Institute M,D
University of California, Los Angeles M,D
University of Hawaii at Manoa M,D
University of Illinois at Chicago M,D
University of Illinois at Urbana–Champaign M,D

Directory of Graduate and Professional Programs by Field

Geochemistry

University of Michigan	M,D
University of Missouri–Rolla	M,D
University of Nevada, Reno	M,D,O
University of New Hampshire	M
Washington University in St. Louis	M,D
Wright State University	M
Yale University	D

■ GEODETIC SCIENCES

Columbia University	M,D
The Ohio State University	M,D

■ GEOGRAPHIC INFORMATION SYSTEMS

Boston University	M
Clark University	M
George Mason University	M
Georgia Institute of Technology	M,D
Hunter College of the City University of New York	M,O
North Carolina State University	M,D
Northern Arizona University	M,O
Northwest Missouri State University	M
Saint Mary's University of Minnesota	M,O
Texas State University-San Marcos	M,D
University at Albany, State University of New York	M,O
University at Buffalo, The State University of New York	M,D,O
University of Central Arkansas	O
University of Denver	M,O
University of Minnesota, Twin Cities Campus	M
The University of Montana–Missoula	M
University of Pittsburgh	M,D
The University of Texas at Dallas	M
University of Wisconsin–Madison	M,D,O
West Virginia University	M,D

■ GEOGRAPHY

Appalachian State University	M
Arizona State University	M,D
Auburn University	M
Boston University	M,D
Brigham Young University	M
California State University, Chico	M
California State University, Fullerton	M
California State University, Hayward	M
California State University, Long Beach	M
California State University, Los Angeles	M
California State University, Northridge	M
California University of Pennsylvania	M
Central Connecticut State University	M
Chicago State University	M
Clark University	D
East Carolina University	M
Eastern Michigan University	M
Florida Atlantic University	M
Florida State University	M,D
George Mason University	M
The George Washington University	M
Georgia State University	M
Hunter College of the City University of New York	M,O
Indiana State University	M,D
Indiana University Bloomington	M,D
Indiana University of Pennsylvania	M
The Johns Hopkins University	M,D
Kansas State University	M,D
Kent State University	M,D
Louisiana State University and Agricultural and Mechanical College	M,D
Marshall University	M
Miami University	M
Michigan State University	M,D
Minnesota State University Mankato	M

New Mexico State University	M
Northeastern Illinois University	M
Northern Arizona University	M,O
Northern Illinois University	M
Northwest Missouri State University	M
The Ohio State University	M,D
Ohio University	M
Oklahoma State University	M
Oregon State University	M,D
The Pennsylvania State University University Park Campus	M,D
Portland State University	M,D
Rutgers, The State University of New Jersey, New Brunswick/Piscataway	M,D
St. Cloud State University	M
Salem State College	M
San Diego State University	M
San Francisco State University	M
San Jose State University	M,O
South Dakota State University	M
Southern Illinois University Carbondale	M,D
Southern Illinois University Edwardsville	M
Southwest Missouri State University	M
State University of New York at Binghamton	M
Syracuse University	M,D
Temple University	M
Texas A&M University	M,D
Texas State University-San Marcos	M,D
Towson University	M
University at Albany, State University of New York	M,O
University at Buffalo, The State University of New York	M,D,O
The University of Akron	M
The University of Alabama	M
The University of Arizona	M,D
University of Arkansas	M,D
University of California, Berkeley	D
University of California, Davis	M,D
University of California, Los Angeles	M,D
University of California, Santa Barbara	M,D
University of Cincinnati	M,D
University of Colorado at Boulder	M,D
University of Colorado at Colorado Springs	M
University of Connecticut	M,D
University of Delaware	M,D
University of Denver	M,D
University of Florida	M,D
University of Georgia	M,D
University of Hawaii at Manoa	M,D
University of Idaho	M,D
University of Illinois at Chicago	M
University of Illinois at Urbana–Champaign	M,D
The University of Iowa	M,D
University of Kansas	M,D
University of Kentucky	M,D
University of Louisiana at Lafayette	M
University of Maryland, College Park	M,D
University of Massachusetts Amherst	M
The University of Memphis	M
University of Minnesota, Twin Cities Campus	M,D
University of Missouri–Columbia	M
The University of Montana–Missoula	M
University of Nebraska at Omaha	M,O
University of Nebraska–Lincoln	M,D
University of Nevada, Reno	M
University of New Mexico	M
University of New Orleans	M
The University of North Carolina at Chapel Hill	M,D
The University of North Carolina at Charlotte	M
The University of North Carolina at Greensboro	M

University of North Dakota	M
University of Northern Iowa	M
University of North Texas	M
University of Oklahoma	M,D
University of Oregon	M,D
University of South Carolina	M,D
University of Southern California	M,D
University of Southern Mississippi	M
University of South Florida	M
The University of Tennessee	M,D
The University of Texas at Austin	M,D
University of Toledo	M
University of Utah	M,D
University of Washington	M,D
University of Wisconsin–Madison	M,D,O
University of Wisconsin–Milwaukee	M,D
University of Wyoming	M
Utah State University	M,D
Virginia Polytechnic Institute and State University	M
Wayne State University	M
West Chester University of Pennsylvania	M
Western Illinois University	M,O
Western Kentucky University	M
Western Michigan University	M
Western Washington University	M
West Virginia University	M,D

■ GEOLOGICAL ENGINEERING

Arizona State University	M,D
Columbia University	M,D
Drexel University	M
Michigan Technological University	M,D
University of Alaska Fairbanks	M,O
University of California, Berkeley	M,D
University of Connecticut	M,D
University of Idaho	M
University of Minnesota, Twin Cities Campus	M,D
University of Missouri–Rolla	M,D
University of Nevada, Reno	M,D,O
University of North Dakota	M
University of Oklahoma	M
University of Utah	M,D
University of Wisconsin–Madison	M,D

■ GEOLOGY

Auburn University	M
Ball State University	M
Baylor University	M,D
Boise State University	M
Boston College	M
Bowling Green State University	M
Brigham Young University	M
Brooklyn College of the City University of New York	M,D
California Institute of Technology	M,D
California State University, Bakersfield	M
California State University, Chico	M
California State University, Fresno	M
California State University, Fullerton	M
California State University, Hayward	M
California State University, Long Beach	M
California State University, Los Angeles	M
California State University, Northridge	M
Case Western Reserve University	M,D
Central Washington University	M
Cleveland State University	M,D
Colorado State University	M,D
Cornell University	M,D
Duke University	M,D
East Carolina University	M
Eastern Kentucky University	M,D
Eastern Washington University	M
Florida Atlantic University	M
Florida State University	M,D
Fort Hays State University	M

Geosciences

The George Washington University	M,D
Georgia State University	M
Idaho State University	M,O
Indiana University Bloomington	M,D
Indiana University–Purdue University Indianapolis	M
Iowa State University of Science and Technology	M,D
The Johns Hopkins University	M,D
Kansas State University	M
Kent State University	M,D
Lehigh University	M,D
Loma Linda University	M
Louisiana State University and Agricultural and Mechanical College	M,D
Massachusetts Institute of Technology	M,D
Miami University	M,D
Michigan State University	M,D
Michigan Technological University	M,D
New Mexico Institute of Mining and Technology	M,D
New Mexico State University	M
Northern Arizona University	M
Northern Illinois University	M,D
Northwestern University	M,D
The Ohio State University	M,D
Ohio University	M
Oklahoma State University	M
Oregon State University	M,D
The Pennsylvania State University University Park Campus	M,D
Portland State University	M,D
Princeton University	D
Queens College of the City University of New York	M
Rensselaer Polytechnic Institute	M,D
Rutgers, The State University of New Jersey, Newark	M
Rutgers, The State University of New Jersey, New Brunswick/Piscataway	M,D
San Diego State University	M
San Jose State University	M
Southern Illinois University Carbondale	M,D
Southern Methodist University	M,D
Southwest Missouri State University	M
State University of New York at Binghamton	M,D
State University of New York at New Paltz	M
Stephen F. Austin State University	M
Sul Ross State University	M
Syracuse University	M,D
Temple University	M
Texas A&M University	M,D
Texas A&M University–Kingsville	M
Texas Christian University	M
Tulane University	M,D
University at Albany, State University of New York	M,D
University at Buffalo, The State University of New York	M,D
The University of Akron	M
The University of Alabama	M,D
University of Alaska Fairbanks	M,D
University of Arkansas	M
University of California, Berkeley	M,D
University of California, Davis	M,D
University of California, Los Angeles	M,D
University of California, Riverside	M,D
University of California, San Diego	M,D
University of California, Santa Barbara	M,D
University of Chicago	M,D
University of Cincinnati	M,D
University of Colorado at Boulder	M,D
University of Connecticut	M,D
University of Delaware	M,D
University of Florida	M,D
University of Georgia	M,D
University of Hawaii at Manoa	M,D
University of Houston	M,D
University of Idaho	M,D
University of Illinois at Chicago	M,D
University of Illinois at Urbana–Champaign	M,D
University of Kansas	M,D
University of Kentucky	M,D
University of Louisiana at Lafayette	M
University of Maine	M,D
University of Maryland, College Park	M,D
The University of Memphis	M,D
University of Miami	M,D
University of Michigan	M,D
University of Minnesota, Duluth	M
University of Minnesota, Twin Cities Campus	M,D
University of Missouri–Columbia	M,D
University of Missouri–Kansas City	M,D
University of Missouri–Rolla	M,D
The University of Montana–Missoula	M,D
University of Nevada, Reno	M,D,O
University of New Hampshire	M
University of New Orleans	M
The University of North Carolina at Chapel Hill	M,D
The University of North Carolina at Wilmington	M
University of North Dakota	M,D
University of Oklahoma	M,D
University of Oregon	M,D
University of Pennsylvania	M,D
University of Pittsburgh	M,D
University of Puerto Rico, Mayagüez Campus	M
University of Rochester	M,D
University of South Carolina	M,D
University of Southern Mississippi	M
University of South Florida	M,D
The University of Tennessee	M,D
The University of Texas at Arlington	M,D
The University of Texas at Austin	M,D
The University of Texas at El Paso	M,D
The University of Texas at San Antonio	M,D
The University of Texas of the Permian Basin	M
University of Toledo	M,D
University of Tulsa	M
University of Utah	M,D
University of Vermont	M
University of Washington	M,D
University of Wisconsin–Madison	M,D
University of Wisconsin–Milwaukee	M,D
University of Wyoming	M,D
Utah State University	M
Vanderbilt University	M
Virginia Polytechnic Institute and State University	M,D
Washington State University	M,D
Washington University in St. Louis	M,D
Wayne State University	M
West Chester University of Pennsylvania	M
Western Kentucky University	M
Western Michigan University	M,D
Western Washington University	M
West Virginia University	M,D
Wichita State University	M
Wright State University	M
Yale University	D

■ GEOPHYSICS

Boise State University	M,D
Boston College	M
California Institute of Technology	M,D
Columbia University	M,D
Cornell University	M,D
Florida State University	D
Georgia Institute of Technology	M,D
Idaho State University	M,O
Indiana University Bloomington	M,D
The Johns Hopkins University	M,D
Louisiana State University and Agricultural and Mechanical College	M,D
Massachusetts Institute of Technology	M,D
Michigan Technological University	M
New Mexico Institute of Mining and Technology	M,D
Ohio University	M
Oregon State University	M,D
The Pennsylvania State University University Park Campus	M,D
Princeton University	D
Rensselaer Polytechnic Institute	M,D
Rice University	M
Saint Louis University	M,D
Southern Methodist University	M,D
Stanford University	M,D
Texas A&M University	M,D
The University of Akron	M
University of Alaska Fairbanks	M,D
University of California, Berkeley	M,D
University of California, Los Angeles	M,D
University of California, Santa Barbara	M,D
University of Chicago	M,D
University of Colorado at Boulder	M,D
University of Hawaii at Manoa	M,D
University of Houston	M,D
University of Idaho	M
University of Illinois at Chicago	M,D
University of Illinois at Urbana–Champaign	M,D
The University of Memphis	M,D
University of Miami	M,D
University of Minnesota, Twin Cities Campus	M,D
University of Missouri–Rolla	M,D
University of Nevada, Reno	M,D,O
University of New Orleans	M
University of Oklahoma	M
The University of Texas at El Paso	M
University of Utah	M,D
University of Washington	M,D
University of Wisconsin–Madison	M,D
University of Wyoming	M,D
Virginia Polytechnic Institute and State University	M,D
Washington University in St. Louis	M,D
West Virginia University	M,D
Wright State University	M
Yale University	D

■ GEOSCIENCES

Ball State University	M
Baylor University	M,D
Boise State University	M
Boston University	M,D
Brown University	M,D
California State University, Chico	M
California University of Pennsylvania	M
Case Western Reserve University	M,D
Central Connecticut State University	M
City College of the City University of New York	M,D
Colorado State University	M,D
Columbia University	M,D
Cornell University	M,D
Dartmouth College	M,D
Emporia State University	M
Florida International University	M,D
The George Washington University	M,D
Georgia Institute of Technology	M,D
Georgia State University	M
Harvard University	M,D
Hunter College of the City University of New York	M,O
Idaho State University	M,O
Indiana State University	M,D

Peterson's Graduate Schools in the U.S. 2006

Directory of Graduate and Professional Programs by Field
Geosciences

Indiana University Bloomington	M,D
Iowa State University of Science and Technology	M,D
Lehigh University	M,D
Massachusetts Institute of Technology	M,D
Michigan State University	M,D
Mississippi State University	M
Montana State University–Bozeman	M,D
Montclair State University	M,O
Murray State University	M
New Mexico Institute of Mining and Technology	M,D
North Carolina Central University	M
North Carolina State University	M,D
Northeastern Illinois University	M
Northern Arizona University	M
Northwestern University	M,D
Oregon State University	M,D
The Pennsylvania State University University Park Campus	M,D
Princeton University	D
Purdue University	M,D
Radford University	M
Rensselaer Polytechnic Institute	M,D
Rice University	M,D
Saint Louis University	M,D
San Francisco State University	M
Southeast Missouri State University	M
Southwest Missouri State University	M
Stanford University	M,D,O
State University of New York College at Oneonta	M
Stony Brook University, State University of New York	M,D
Texas A&M University–Commerce	M
Texas Christian University	M
Texas Tech University	M,D
University at Albany, State University of New York	M,D
The University of Akron	M
The University of Arizona	M,D
University of California, Irvine	M,D
University of California, Los Angeles	M,D
University of California, Santa Cruz	M,D
University of Chicago	M,D
University of Florida	M,D
University of Illinois at Chicago	M,D
University of Illinois at Urbana–Champaign	M,D
The University of Iowa	M,D
University of Louisiana at Monroe	M
University of Maine	M,D
University of Massachusetts Amherst	M,D
The University of Memphis	M,D
University of Missouri–Kansas City	M,D
University of Nebraska–Lincoln	M,D
University of Nevada, Las Vegas	M,D
University of New Hampshire	M
University of New Mexico	M,D
The University of North Carolina at Charlotte	M
The University of North Carolina at Wilmington	M
University of North Dakota	M,D
University of Northern Colorado	M
University of Notre Dame	M,D
University of Rhode Island	M
University of Rochester	M,D
University of San Diego	M,D,O
University of South Carolina	M,D
University of Southern California	M,D
The University of Texas at Arlington	M,D
The University of Texas at Austin	M,D
The University of Texas at Dallas	M,D
University of Toledo	M,D
University of Tulsa	M,D
Washington University in St. Louis	M,D
Western Connecticut State University	M
Western Michigan University	M
Yale University	D

■ **GEOTECHNICAL ENGINEERING**

Auburn University	M,D
The Catholic University of America	M,D
Colorado State University	M,D
Cornell University	M,D
Illinois Institute of Technology	M,D
Iowa State University of Science and Technology	M,D
Louisiana State University and Agricultural and Mechanical College	M,D
Marquette University	M
Massachusetts Institute of Technology	M,D,O
Northwestern University	M,D
Ohio University	M,D
The Pennsylvania State University University Park Campus	M,D
Rensselaer Polytechnic Institute	M,D
Texas A&M University	M,D
Tufts University	M,D
University of California, Berkeley	M,D
University of California, Los Angeles	M,D
University of Central Florida	M,D,O
University of Colorado at Boulder	M,D
University of Delaware	M,D
University of Illinois at Chicago	D
University of Maine	M
University of Missouri–Columbia	M,D
University of Missouri–Rolla	M,D
University of Oklahoma	M
University of Rhode Island	M,D
University of Southern California	M
The University of Texas at Austin	M,D
University of Washington	M,D

■ **GERMAN**

Arizona State University	M
Bowling Green State University	M
Brigham Young University	M
Brown University	M,D
California State University, Fullerton	M
California State University, Long Beach	M
California State University, Sacramento	M
Colorado State University	M
Columbia University	M,D
Cornell University	M,D
Duke University	D
Eastern Michigan University	M
Florida Atlantic University	M
Florida State University	M
Georgetown University	M,D
Georgia State University	M
Harvard University	M,D
Hofstra University	M
Illinois State University	M
Indiana University Bloomington	M,D
The Johns Hopkins University	D
Kansas State University	M
Kent State University	M
Michigan State University	M,D
Millersville University of Pennsylvania	M
Minnesota State University Mankato	M
Mississippi State University	M
New York University	M,D
Northwestern University	D
The Ohio State University	M,D
The Pennsylvania State University University Park Campus	M,D
Portland State University	M
Princeton University	D
Purdue University	M,D
Rutgers, The State University of New Jersey, New Brunswick/Piscataway	M,D
San Francisco State University	M
Stanford University	M,D
Stony Brook University, State University of New York	M,D
Texas Tech University	M

Tufts University	M
The University of Alabama	M,D
The University of Arizona	M
University of Arkansas	M
University of California, Berkeley	M,D
University of California, Davis	M,D
University of California, Irvine	M,D
University of California, Los Angeles	M,D
University of California, San Diego	M
University of California, Santa Barbara	M,D
University of Chicago	M,D
University of Cincinnati	M,D
University of Colorado at Boulder	M
University of Connecticut	M,D
University of Delaware	M
University of Denver	M
University of Florida	M,D
University of Georgia	M
University of Hawaii at Manoa	M
University of Illinois at Chicago	M,D
University of Illinois at Urbana–Champaign	M,D
The University of Iowa	M,D
University of Kansas	M,D
University of Kentucky	M
University of Maryland, Baltimore County	M
University of Maryland, College Park	M,D
University of Massachusetts Amherst	M,D
University of Michigan	M,D
University of Minnesota, Twin Cities Campus	M,D
University of Mississippi	M
University of Missouri–Columbia	M
The University of Montana–Missoula	M
University of Nebraska–Lincoln	M,D
University of Nevada, Reno	M
University of New Mexico	M,D
The University of North Carolina at Chapel Hill	M,D
University of Northern Iowa	M
University of Notre Dame	M
University of Oklahoma	M
University of Oregon	M,D
University of Pennsylvania	M,D
University of Pittsburgh	M,D
University of South Carolina	M
The University of Tennessee	M,D
The University of Texas at Austin	M,D
University of Toledo	M
University of Utah	M,D
University of Vermont	M
University of Virginia	M,D
University of Washington	M,D
University of Wisconsin–Madison	M,D
University of Wisconsin–Milwaukee	M
University of Wyoming	M
Vanderbilt University	M,D
Washington University in St. Louis	M,D
Wayne State University	M,D
West Chester University of Pennsylvania	M
West Virginia University	M
Yale University	M,D

■ **GERONTOLOGICAL NURSING**

Abilene Christian University	O
Arkansas State University	M,O
Boston College	M,D
Case Western Reserve University	M,D
The Catholic University of America	M,D
College of Mount Saint Vincent	M,O
College of Staten Island of the City University of New York	M
Columbia University	M,O
Concordia University Wisconsin	M
Duke University	M,O
Gannon University	M,O
Gwynedd-Mercy College	M

Directory of Graduate and Professional Programs by Field
Health Education

Institution	Degree
Hunter College of the City University of New York	M
Lehman College of the City University of New York	M
Loma Linda University	M
Marquette University	M,D,O
Nazareth College of Rochester	M
New York University	M,O
Rutgers, The State University of New Jersey, Newark	M
San Jose State University	M,O
Seton Hall University	M
State University of New York at New Paltz	M
Stony Brook University, State University of New York	M
Texas Wesleyan University	M
University at Buffalo, The State University of New York	M,D,O
University of Colorado at Colorado Springs	M
University of Delaware	M,O
University of Maryland	M,D
University of Massachusetts Lowell	M
University of Michigan	M
University of Minnesota, Twin Cities Campus	M
University of Nevada, Las Vegas	M
The University of North Carolina at Greensboro	M,O
University of South Alabama	M
University of Utah	M,O
Vanderbilt University	M,D
Villanova University	M,D,O

■ GERONTOLOGY

Institution	Degree
Abilene Christian University	M,O
Appalachian State University	M
Arizona State University	O
Arizona State University West	O
Ball State University	M
Bethel University	M
California State University, Dominguez Hills	M,O
California State University, Fullerton	M
California State University, Long Beach	M
Case Western Reserve University	M,D,O
Central Missouri State University	M
Chestnut Hill College	M,O
The College of New Rochelle	M,O
College of Notre Dame of Maryland	M
Concordia University (IL)	M
Eastern Illinois University	M
East Tennessee State University	M,O
Emory University	M
Florida State University	M
Gannon University	O
George Mason University	M
Hofstra University	M,O
Kent State University	M,O
Lindenwood University	M
Long Island University, C.W. Post Campus	M,O
Marylhurst University	M
Miami University	M
Minnesota State University Mankato	M
Morehead State University	M
Mount Mary College	M
National-Louis University	M,O
North Dakota State University	M,D
Northeastern Illinois University	M
Notre Dame de Namur University	M,O
Oregon State University	M
Portland State University	O
Rochester Institute of Technology	O
Roosevelt University	M
Sacred Heart University	M
Sage Graduate School	M
St. Cloud State University	M
Saint Joseph College	O
Saint Joseph's University	M
San Diego State University	M
San Francisco State University	M
San Jose State University	M,O
Shippensburg University of Pennsylvania	M,O
State University of West Georgia	M
Texas A&M University–Kingsville	M
Towson University	M
The University of Arizona	M,O
University of Arkansas at Little Rock	M,O
University of Central Florida	M,O
University of Central Oklahoma	M
University of Illinois at Springfield	M
University of Indianapolis	M
University of Kansas	M,D
University of Kentucky	D
University of La Verne	M
University of Louisiana at Monroe	M,O
University of Maryland	D
University of Maryland, Baltimore County	M,D,O
University of Massachusetts Boston	M,D,O
University of Missouri–St. Louis	M,O
University of Nebraska at Omaha	M,O
University of New England	M,O
University of New Orleans	M,O
The University of North Carolina at Charlotte	M
University of Northern Colorado	M
University of North Florida	M,O
University of North Texas	M,O
University of Pittsburgh	M,D,O
University of South Alabama	O
University of South Carolina	O
University of Southern California	M,D,O
University of South Florida	M,D
The University of Tennessee	M
University of Utah	M,O
Virginia Commonwealth University	M,O
Virginia Polytechnic Institute and State University	M,D
Wayne State University	M
Webster University	M
West Chester University of Pennsylvania	M,O
Western Kentucky University	M
Wichita State University	M
Wilmington College (DE)	M

■ GRAPHIC DESIGN

Institution	Degree
Boston University	M
California State University, Los Angeles	M
Cardinal Stritch University	M
City College of the City University of New York	M
The College of New Rochelle	M
Colorado State University	M
Florida Atlantic University	M
George Mason University	M
Illinois Institute of Technology	M,D
Illinois State University	M
Indiana State University	M
Indiana University Bloomington	M
Iowa State University of Science and Technology	M
Kean University	M
Kent State University	M
Louisiana State University and Agricultural and Mechanical College	M
Louisiana Tech University	M
Marywood University	M
North Carolina State University	M
The Pennsylvania State University University Park Campus	M
Pittsburg State University	M
Pratt Institute	M
Rochester Institute of Technology	M
San Diego State University	M
Syracuse University	M
Temple University	M
University of Baltimore	M
University of Cincinnati	M
University of Guam	M
University of Houston	M
University of Illinois at Chicago	M
University of Illinois at Urbana–Champaign	M
The University of Memphis	M
University of Miami	M
University of Minnesota, Duluth	M
University of North Texas	M,D
University of Notre Dame	M
The University of Tennessee	M
University of Utah	M
Western Illinois University	M,O
Western Michigan University	M
West Virginia University	M
Yale University	M

■ HAZARDOUS MATERIALS MANAGEMENT

Institution	Degree
California State University, Long Beach	M,D,O
Idaho State University	M
New Mexico Institute of Mining and Technology	M
Rutgers, The State University of New Jersey, New Brunswick/Piscataway	M,D
Southern Methodist University	M,D
Stony Brook University, State University of New York	M,O
Tufts University	M,D
University of Central Florida	M,D,O
University of Idaho	M
University of Oklahoma	M,D
University of South Carolina	M,D
Wayne State University	M,O

■ HEALTH EDUCATION

Institution	Degree
Adams State College	M
Adelphi University	M,O
Alabama State University	M
Albany State University	M
Alcorn State University	M,O
Arcadia University	M
Auburn University	M,D,O
Austin Peay State University	M
Ball State University	M
Baylor University	M
Boston University	M,O
Brigham Young University	M
Brooklyn College of the City University of New York	M,O
California State University, Long Beach	M
California State University, Los Angeles	M
California State University, Northridge	M
California State University, San Bernardino	M
Central Washington University	M
The Citadel, The Military College of South Carolina	M
Cleveland State University	M
The College of New Jersey	M
East Carolina University	M
Eastern Kentucky University	M
Eastern University	M
East Stroudsburg University of Pennsylvania	M
Florida Agricultural and Mechanical University	M
Florida International University	M
Florida State University	M,D
Fort Hays State University	M

Peterson's Graduate Schools in the U.S. 2006

www.petersons.com   101

Directory of Graduate and Professional Programs by Field

Health Education

Georgia College & State University	M,O
Georgia Southern University	M
Georgia Southwestern State University	M,O
Hofstra University	M
Howard University	M
Idaho State University	M
Illinois State University	M
Indiana State University	M
Indiana University of Pennsylvania	M
Indiana University–Purdue University Indianapolis	M
Inter American University of Puerto Rico, Metropolitan Campus	M
Iowa State University of Science and Technology	M,D
Jackson State University	M
Jacksonville State University	M
James Madison University	M
John F. Kennedy University	M
The Johns Hopkins University	M,D
Kent State University	M,D
Lehman College of the City University of New York	M
Lesley University	M,O
Loma Linda University	M,D
Long Island University, Brooklyn Campus	M
Louisiana Tech University	M,D
Marshall University	M
McNeese State University	M
Middle Tennessee State University	M,D
Minnesota State University Mankato	M
Mississippi State University	M
Mississippi University for Women	M
Montana State University–Bozeman	M
Montclair State University	M,O
Morehead State University	M
Mount Mary College	M
New Jersey City University	M
New York University	M,D
North Carolina Agricultural and Technical State University	M
Northeastern State University	M
Northern Arizona University	M
Northern State University	M
Northwestern State University of Louisiana	M
Northwest Missouri State University	M
Nova Southeastern University	D
Oklahoma State University	M,D
Oregon State University	M
The Pennsylvania State University Harrisburg Campus of the Capital College	M
Plymouth State University	M
Portland State University	M,O
Prairie View A&M University	M
Rhode Island College	M
Sage Graduate School	M
Saint Joseph's University	M
Saint Louis University	M
South Dakota State University	M
Southeastern Louisiana University	M
Southern Connecticut State University	M
Southern Illinois University Carbondale	M,D
Southern Illinois University Edwardsville	M,O
Southwestern Oklahoma State University	M
Springfield College	M,D,O
State University of New York College at Brockport	M
State University of New York College at Cortland	M
Tarleton State University	M,O
Teachers College Columbia University	M,D
Temple University	M,D
Tennessee Technological University	M
Texas A&M University	M,D

Texas A&M University–Commerce	M,D
Texas A&M University–Kingsville	M
Texas Southern University	M
Texas State University-San Marcos	M
Texas Woman's University	M,D
Tulane University	M
The University of Alabama	M,D
The University of Alabama at Birmingham	M,D
University of Arkansas	M,D
University of California, Berkeley	M
University of Central Arkansas	M
University of Central Oklahoma	M
University of Cincinnati	M
University of Colorado at Denver	D
University of Florida	M,D
University of Georgia	M,D,O
University of Houston	M,D
University of Illinois at Chicago	M
University of Maryland, Baltimore County	M
University of Maryland, College Park	M,D
University of Michigan–Flint	M
University of Missouri–Columbia	M,D,O
The University of Montana–Missoula	M
University of Nebraska at Omaha	M
University of Nebraska–Lincoln	M
University of New Mexico	M
University of New Orleans	M,O
The University of North Carolina at Chapel Hill	M,D
University of Northern Iowa	M
University of Pennsylvania	M,D
University of Pittsburgh	M,O
University of Rhode Island	M
University of South Alabama	M
University of South Carolina	M,D,O
The University of South Dakota	M
University of Southern Mississippi	M
The University of Tennessee	M
The University of Texas at Austin	M,D
The University of Texas at El Paso	M
The University of Texas at Tyler	M
University of Toledo	D
University of Utah	M,D
University of Virginia	M,D
University of West Florida	M
University of Wisconsin–La Crosse	M
University of Wyoming	M
Utah State University	M
Valdosta State University	M
Virginia Polytechnic Institute and State University	M,D,O
Wayne State College	M
Wayne State University	M
West Chester University of Pennsylvania	M
Western Illinois University	M,O
Western Oregon University	M
West Virginia University	M,D
Widener University	M
Worcester State College	M
Wright State University	M

■ HEALTH INFORMATICS

Case Western Reserve University	M
The College of St. Scholastica	M
Duke University	M,O
Emory University	M,D
The George Washington University	M,O
La Salle University	M,O
Loma Linda University	M
Molloy College	M,O
New York University	M,O
Touro College	M
The University of Alabama at Birmingham	M
University of Central Florida	M,O
University of La Verne	M

University of Minnesota, Twin Cities Campus	M,D
University of Missouri–Columbia	M
University of Pittsburgh	M
University of the Incarnate Word	M
University of Virginia	M
University of Washington	M
University of Wisconsin–Milwaukee	M

■ HEALTH PHYSICS/ RADIOLOGICAL HEALTH

Drexel University	M,D
Emory University	M,D
Georgetown University	M
Georgia Institute of Technology	M,D
Illinois Institute of Technology	M,D
The Johns Hopkins University	M,D
Midwestern State University	M
Oregon State University	M,D
Purdue University	M,D
San Diego State University	M
Texas A&M University	M
University of Cincinnati	M
University of Illinois at Urbana–Champaign	M,D
University of Kentucky	M
University of Massachusetts Lowell	M,D
University of Michigan	M,D,O
University of Missouri–Columbia	M,D
University of Nevada, Las Vegas	M
Virginia Commonwealth University	D
Wayne State University	M,D

■ HEALTH PROMOTION

Ball State University	M
Boston University	M,D
Bridgewater State College	M
Brigham Young University	M,D
California State University, Fresno	M
Canisius College	M
Central Michigan University	M
Emerson College	M
Emory University	M
Georgetown University	M,D
The George Washington University	M,O
Georgia State University	M,D
Goddard College	M
Harvard University	M,D
Indiana State University	M
Lehman College of the City University of New York	M
Loma Linda University	M,D
Marymount University	M
Marywood University	M,D
Northern Arizona University	M
Northwestern State University of Louisiana	M
Old Dominion University	M
Portland State University	M,O
Purdue University	M,D
San Diego State University	M,D
Simmons College	M,O
Southwest Missouri State University	M
The University of Alabama	M,D
The University of Alabama at Birmingham	D
University of Chicago	M
University of Delaware	M
University of Florida	M,D
University of Georgia	M,D,O
University of Kentucky	M,D
University of Massachusetts Lowell	D
The University of Memphis	M
University of Michigan	M,D
The University of Montana–Missoula	M
University of Nevada, Las Vegas	M
The University of North Carolina at Chapel Hill	M
The University of North Carolina at Charlotte	M

Directory of Graduate and Professional Programs by Field
Health Services Management and Hospital Administration

University of North Texas	M
University of South Carolina	M,D,O
University of Southern California	M
The University of Tennessee	M
University of Utah	M,D
University of Wisconsin–Stevens Point	M
Western Illinois University	M,O
West Virginia University	M
Wright State University	M

■ HEALTH PSYCHOLOGY

Appalachian State University	M
Central Connecticut State University	M
Drexel University	M,D
Duke University	D
Emporia State University	M
The George Washington University	D
National-Louis University	M,O
Northern Arizona University	M
Rutgers, The State University of New Jersey, New Brunswick/Piscataway	D
San Diego State University	M,D
Santa Clara University	M
Shenandoah University	M,O
Stony Brook University, State University of New York	D
Texas State University-San Marcos	M
University of Florida	M,D
University of Michigan–Dearborn	M
The University of Montana–Missoula	M
University of North Texas	M,D
Yeshiva University	D

■ HEALTH SERVICES MANAGEMENT AND HOSPITAL ADMINISTRATION

Albany State University	M
Antioch New England Graduate School	M,O
Argosy University/Sarasota	M,D
Argosy University/Schaumburg	M,D
Arizona State University	M
Armstrong Atlantic State University	M
Baldwin-Wallace College	M
Barry University	M
Baylor University	M
Bellevue University	M
Bernard M. Baruch College of the City University of New York	M
Boston University	M,D,O
Brandeis University	M
Brenau University	M
Brooklyn College of the City University of New York	M
California Lutheran University	M
California State University, Bakersfield	M
California State University, Chico	M
California State University, Fresno	M
California State University, Long Beach	M,O
California State University, Los Angeles	M
California State University, Northridge	M
California State University, San Bernardino	M
Cardinal Stritch University	M
Carlow University	M
Carnegie Mellon University	M
Central Michigan University	M,D,O
Charleston Southern University	M
Clark University	M
Clemson University	M
Cleveland State University	M,D,O
College of Mount Saint Vincent	M,O
Columbia University	M
Concordia University (IL)	M
Concordia University Wisconsin	M
Cornell University	M,D
Dallas Baptist University	M
DePaul University	M
Duke University	M
Duquesne University	M,D
Eastern Kentucky University	M
East Tennessee State University	M,D,O
Emory University	M
Fairleigh Dickinson University, College at Florham	M
Florida International University	M
Framingham State College	M
Francis Marion University	M
The George Washington University	M,D,O
Georgia Institute of Technology	M
Georgia Southern University	M
Georgia State University	M,D
Governors State University	M
Grand Valley State University	M
Harvard University	M,D
Hofstra University	M,O
Houston Baptist University	M
Indiana State University	M
Indiana University Northwest	M,O
Indiana University–Purdue University Indianapolis	M,D
Indiana University South Bend	M,O
Iona College	M,O
The Johns Hopkins University	M,D,O
Kean University	M
King's College	M
Lake Erie College	M
LeTourneau University	M
Lindenwood University	M
Loma Linda University	M
Long Island University, Brooklyn Campus	M
Long Island University, C.W. Post Campus	M,O
Louisiana State University in Shreveport	M
Loyola University Chicago	M
Loyola University New Orleans	M
Lynn University	M,D
Madonna University	M
Marshall University	M
Marymount University	M
Maryville University of Saint Louis	M
Marywood University	M
Mercy College	M,O
Midwestern State University	M
Mississippi College	M
Monmouth University	M,O
Montana State University–Billings	M
National University	M
New Jersey City University	M
New School University	M,O
New York Institute of Technology	M
New York University	M,O
Northeastern University	M
Northwest Missouri State University	M
Norwich University	M
Nova Southeastern University	M
The Ohio State University	M,D
Ohio University	M
Oklahoma City University	M
Oklahoma State University	M
Old Dominion University	M,D
Oregon State University	M
Our Lady of the Lake University of San Antonio	M
Pace University	M
Pace University, White Plains Campus	M
Park University	M
The Pennsylvania State University Great Valley Campus	M
The Pennsylvania State University Harrisburg Campus of the Capital College	M
The Pennsylvania State University University Park Campus	M,D
Philadelphia University	M
Portland State University	M
Quinnipiac University	M
Regis University	M,D
Rochester Institute of Technology	M,O
Rutgers, The State University of New Jersey, Camden	M
Rutgers, The State University of New Jersey, Newark	M,D
Sage Graduate School	M
St. Ambrose University	M
St. Edward's University	M,O
Saint Joseph's College of Maine	M,O
Saint Joseph's University	M
Saint Louis University	M,D
Saint Mary's University of Minnesota	M
St. Thomas University	M,O
Saint Xavier University	M,O
Salve Regina University	M,O
San Diego State University	M,D
Seton Hall University	M
Shenandoah University	M
Simmons College	M,O
Southeastern University	M
Southwest Missouri State University	M
Springfield College	M
State University of New York at Binghamton	M,D
State University of New York Institute of Technology	M
Stony Brook University, State University of New York	M,D,O
Suffolk University	M,O
Syracuse University	O
Temple University	M,D
Texas State University-San Marcos	M
Texas Tech University	M,O
Texas Wesleyan University	M
Texas Woman's University	M
Touro College	O
Towson University	O
Trinity University	M
Tulane University	M,D
University at Albany, State University of New York	M
The University of Alabama at Birmingham	M,D
University of Arkansas at Little Rock	M
University of Baltimore	M
University of California, Berkeley	M,D
University of California, Los Angeles	M,D
University of California, San Diego	M
University of California, San Francisco	D
University of Central Florida	M,O
University of Colorado at Colorado Springs	M
University of Colorado at Denver	M
University of Connecticut	M,D
University of Detroit Mercy	M
University of Florida	M,D
University of Houston–Clear Lake	M
University of Illinois at Chicago	M,D
The University of Iowa	M,D
University of Kansas	M
University of Kentucky	M
University of La Verne	M
University of Louisiana at Lafayette	M
University of Mary Hardin-Baylor	M
University of Maryland, Baltimore County	M
University of Maryland University College	M,O
University of Massachusetts Boston	M,D,O
University of Massachusetts Lowell	M
The University of Memphis	M
University of Michigan	M,D
University of Minnesota, Twin Cities Campus	M,D
University of Missouri–Columbia	M
University of Missouri–St. Louis	M,O
University of New Hampshire	M

Directory of Graduate and Professional Programs by Field
Health Services Management and Hospital Administration

Institution	Degree
University of New Haven	M
University of New Orleans	M
The University of North Carolina at Chapel Hill	M,D
The University of North Carolina at Charlotte	M
University of North Florida	M,O
University of North Texas	M,O
University of Pennsylvania	M,D
University of Pittsburgh	M,D
University of St. Francis (IL)	M
University of St. Thomas (MN)	M
University of San Francisco	M
The University of Scranton	M
University of South Carolina	M,D
University of Southern California	M
University of Southern Indiana	M
University of Southern Maine	M,O
University of Southern Mississippi	M
University of South Florida	M,D
The University of Texas at Arlington	M
The University of Texas at Dallas	M
The University of Texas at Tyler	M
University of Virginia	M
University of Washington	M
University of Wisconsin–Oshkosh	M
University of Wisconsin–Whitewater	M
Villanova University	M,D,O
Virginia Commonwealth University	M,D
Wagner College	M
Walden University	D
Washington University in St. Louis	M
Wayland Baptist University	M
Webster University	M,D
West Chester University of Pennsylvania	M
Western Carolina University	M
Western Connecticut State University	M
Western Illinois University	M,O
Western Kentucky University	M
Widener University	M
Wilkes University	M
William Woods University	M
Wilmington College (DE)	M
Worcester State College	M
Wright State University	M
Xavier University	M
Yale University	M
Youngstown State University	M

■ HEALTH SERVICES RESEARCH

Institution	Degree
Arizona State University	M,D
Brown University	M,D
Clarkson University	M
Dartmouth College	M,D
Florida State University	M
Indiana University–Purdue University Indianapolis	M
The Johns Hopkins University	M,D
Lehigh University	M
Stanford University	M
Texas State University-San Marcos	M
University of Florida	M,D
University of Maryland	D
University of Minnesota, Twin Cities Campus	M,D
University of Rochester	D
University of Southern California	M,D
University of Virginia	M
University of Washington	M,D
Virginia Commonwealth University	D
Wake Forest University	M

■ HIGHER EDUCATION

Institution	Degree
Appalachian State University	M,O
Arizona State University	M,D
Auburn University	M,D,O
Azusa Pacific University	M
Ball State University	M,D
Barry University	M,D
Bernard M. Baruch College of the City University of New York	M
Boston College	M,D
Bowling Green State University	D
Claremont Graduate University	M,D
Dallas Baptist University	M
DePaul University	M
Eastern Kentucky University	M
Eastern Washington University	M
Florida Atlantic University	M,D,O
Florida International University	M,D,O
Florida State University	M,D,O
Geneva College	M
The George Washington University	M,D,O
Georgia Southern University	M
Georgia State University	D
Grand Valley State University	M
Harvard University	M,D
Illinois State University	M,D
Indiana University Bloomington	M,D,O
Indiana University of Pennsylvania	M
Indiana University–Purdue University Indianapolis	M
Inter American University of Puerto Rico, Metropolitan Campus	M
Iowa State University of Science and Technology	M,D
Kent State University	M,D,O
Louisiana State University and Agricultural and Mechanical College	M,D,O
Loyola University Chicago	M,D
Michigan State University	M,D,O
Minnesota State University Mankato	M,O
Morehead State University	M,O
Morgan State University	D
New York University	M,D
North Carolina State University	M,D
Northeastern State University	M
Northern Illinois University	M,D
Northwestern University	M
Nova Southeastern University	D
Ohio University	M,D
Oklahoma State University	M,D,O
Old Dominion University	M,D,O
The Pennsylvania State University University Park Campus	M,D
Pittsburg State University	M,O
Portland State University	M,D
Purdue University	M,D,O
Rowan University	M
St. John's University (NY)	M,O
Saint Louis University	M,D,O
San Jose State University	M,O
Seton Hall University	D
Southern Illinois University Carbondale	M
Stanford University	M,D
Syracuse University	M,D,O
Teachers College Columbia University	M,D
Texas A&M University–Commerce	M,D
Texas A&M University–Kingsville	D
Texas Southern University	M,D
Texas Tech University	M,D,O
University at Buffalo, The State University of New York	M,D
The University of Akron	M
The University of Arizona	M,D
University of Arkansas	M,D,O
University of Arkansas at Little Rock	D
University of Central Oklahoma	M
University of Connecticut	M,D
University of Delaware	M
University of Denver	M,D,O
University of Florida	M,D,O
University of Georgia	D
University of Houston	M,D
University of Illinois at Urbana–Champaign	M,D,O
The University of Iowa	M,D,O
University of Kansas	M,D
University of Kentucky	M,D
University of Louisville	M,D,O
University of Maine	M,D,O
University of Mary	M
University of Maryland, Baltimore County	M,D,O
University of Massachusetts Amherst	M,D,O
University of Massachusetts Boston	M,D,O
The University of Memphis	M,D,O
University of Miami	M
University of Michigan	M,D
University of Minnesota, Twin Cities Campus	M,D
University of Mississippi	M,D,O
University of Missouri–Columbia	M,D,O
University of Missouri–St. Louis	M,D,O
University of Nevada, Las Vegas	M,D,O
University of New Hampshire	M
The University of North Carolina at Greensboro	M,D,O
University of Northern Colorado	D
University of Northern Iowa	M
University of North Texas	D
University of Oklahoma	M,D
University of Pennsylvania	M,D
University of Pittsburgh	M,D
University of South Carolina	M
University of South Florida	M,D,O
The University of Texas at San Antonio	M
University of Toledo	M,D,O
University of Virginia	D,O
University of Washington	M,D
University of Wisconsin–Whitewater	M
Vanderbilt University	M,D
Wayne State University	M,D,O
West Virginia University	M,D
Wright State University	M,O

■ HISPANIC STUDIES

Institution	Degree
Brown University	M,D
California State University, Los Angeles	M
California State University, Northridge	M
Michigan State University	M,D
New Mexico Highlands University	M
Pontifical Catholic University of Puerto Rico	M
St. Thomas University	M,O
San Jose State University	M
Stony Brook University, State University of New York	M,D
University of California, Berkeley	M,D
University of California, Los Angeles	D
University of California, Riverside	M
University of California, Santa Barbara	M,D
University of Illinois at Chicago	M,D
University of Pittsburgh	M,D
University of Puerto Rico, Mayagüez Campus	M
University of Puerto Rico, Río Piedras	M,D
University of Washington	M

■ HISTORIC PRESERVATION

Institution	Degree
Ball State University	M
Boston University	M
Buffalo State College, State University of New York	M,O
Clemson University	M
Colorado State University	M
Columbia University	M
Cornell University	M,D
Eastern Michigan University	M
The George Washington University	M
Georgia State University	M
Michigan Technological University	D
Middle Tennessee State University	M,D
New York University	M
Rensselaer Polytechnic Institute	M

Rutgers, The State University of New Jersey, New Brunswick/Piscataway	M,D
Texas Tech University	M
University of California, Riverside	M,D
University of Delaware	M,D
University of Georgia	M
University of Kentucky	M
University of Maryland, College Park	M,O
University of Oregon	M
University of Pennsylvania	M,O
University of South Carolina	M,O
University of Southern California	O
University of Vermont	M
University of Washington	O
Western Kentucky University	M

■ HISTORY

American University	M,D
Andrews University	M
Angelo State University	M
Appalachian State University	M
Arizona State University	M,D
Arkansas State University	M,D,O
Arkansas Tech University	M
Armstrong Atlantic State University	M
Auburn University	M,D
Ball State University	M
Baylor University	M
Boise State University	M
Boston College	M,D
Boston University	M,D
Bowling Green State University	M,D
Brandeis University	M,D
Brigham Young University	M
Brooklyn College of the City University of New York	M,D
Brown University	M,D
Buffalo State College, State University of New York	M
Butler University	M
California State Polytechnic University, Pomona	M
California State University, Bakersfield	M
California State University, Chico	M
California State University, Fresno	M
California State University, Fullerton	M
California State University, Hayward	M
California State University, Long Beach	M
California State University, Los Angeles	M
California State University, Northridge	M
California State University, Stanislaus	M
Carnegie Mellon University	M,D
Case Western Reserve University	M,D
The Catholic University of America	M,D
Central Connecticut State University	M
Central Michigan University	M,D
Central Missouri State University	M
Central Washington University	M
Chicago State University	M
The Citadel, The Military College of South Carolina	M
City College of the City University of New York	M
Claremont Graduate University	M,D
Clark Atlanta University	M
Clark University	M,D,O
Clemson University	M
Cleveland State University	M
College of Charleston	M
The College of Saint Rose	M
College of Staten Island of the City University of New York	M
The College of William and Mary	M,D
Colorado State University	M
Columbia University	M,D
Converse College	M
Cornell University	M,D
DePaul University	M

Drake University	M
Duke University	M,D
Duquesne University	M
East Carolina University	M
Eastern Illinois University	M
Eastern Kentucky University	M
Eastern Michigan University	M
Eastern Washington University	M
East Stroudsburg University of Pennsylvania	M
East Tennessee State University	M
Emory University	D
Emporia State University	M
Fairleigh Dickinson University, Metropolitan Campus	M
Fayetteville State University	M
Florida Agricultural and Mechanical University	M
Florida Atlantic University	M
Florida International University	M,D
Florida State University	M,D
Fordham University	M,D
Fort Hays State University	M
George Mason University	M,D
Georgetown University	M,D
The George Washington University	M,D
Georgia College & State University	M
Georgia Southern University	M
Georgia State University	M,D
Hardin-Simmons University	M
Harvard University	D
Howard University	M,D
Hunter College of the City University of New York	M
Illinois State University	M
Indiana State University	M
Indiana University Bloomington	M,D
Indiana University of Pennsylvania	M
Indiana University–Purdue University Indianapolis	M
Iona College	M
Iowa State University of Science and Technology	M,D
Jackson State University	M
Jacksonville State University	M
James Madison University	M
John Carroll University	M
The Johns Hopkins University	D
Kansas State University	M,D
Kent State University	M,D
Lamar University	M
Lehigh University	M,D
Lehman College of the City University of New York	M
Lincoln University (MO)	M
Long Island University, Brooklyn Campus	M,O
Long Island University, C.W. Post Campus	M
Louisiana State University and Agricultural and Mechanical College	M,D
Louisiana Tech University	M
Loyola University Chicago	M,D
Marquette University	M,D
Marshall University	M
Miami University	M,D
Michigan State University	M,D
Middle Tennessee State University	M,D
Midwestern State University	M
Millersville University of Pennsylvania	M
Minnesota State University Mankato	M
Mississippi College	M
Mississippi State University	M,D
Monmouth University	M
Montana State University–Bozeman	M
Montclair State University	M
Morgan State University	M,D
Murray State University	M
New Jersey Institute of Technology	M

New Mexico Highlands University	M
New Mexico State University	M
New School University	M,D
New York University	M,D,O
North Carolina Central University	M
North Carolina State University	M
North Dakota State University	M,D
Northeastern Illinois University	M
Northeastern University	M,D
Northern Arizona University	M,D
Northern Illinois University	M,D
Northwestern University	D
Northwest Missouri State University	M
Oakland University	M
The Ohio State University	M,D,O
Ohio University	M,D
Oklahoma State University	M,D
Old Dominion University	M
Oregon State University	M,D
The Pennsylvania State University University Park Campus	M,D
Pepperdine University	M
Pittsburg State University	M
Pontifical Catholic University of Puerto Rico	M
Portland State University	M
Prescott College	M
Princeton University	D
Providence College	M
Purdue University	M,D
Purdue University Calumet	M
Queens College of the City University of New York	M
Rhode Island College	M
Rice University	M,D
Roosevelt University	M
Rutgers, The State University of New Jersey, Camden	M
Rutgers, The State University of New Jersey, Newark	M
Rutgers, The State University of New Jersey, New Brunswick/Piscataway	D
St. Cloud State University	M
St. John's University (NY)	M,D
Saint Louis University	M,D
St. Mary's University of San Antonio	M
Salem State College	M
Salisbury University	M
Sam Houston State University	M
San Diego State University	M
San Francisco State University	M
San Jose State University	M
Shippensburg University of Pennsylvania	M
Slippery Rock University of Pennsylvania	M
Sonoma State University	M
Southeastern Louisiana University	M
Southeast Missouri State University	M
Southern Connecticut State University	M
Southern Illinois University Carbondale	M,D
Southern Illinois University Edwardsville	M
Southern Methodist University	M,D
Southern University and Agricultural and Mechanical College	M
Southwest Missouri State University	M
Stanford University	M,D
State University of New York at Binghamton	M,D
State University of New York at Oswego	M
State University of New York College at Brockport	M
State University of New York College at Cortland	M
State University of West Georgia	M
Stephen F. Austin State University	M

Directory of Graduate and Professional Programs by Field

History

Institution	Degree
Stony Brook University, State University of New York	M,D
Sul Ross State University	M
Syracuse University	M,D
Tarleton State University	M
Temple University	M,D
Texas A&M International University	M
Texas A&M University	M,D
Texas A&M University–Commerce	M
Texas A&M University–Corpus Christi	M
Texas A&M University–Kingsville	M
Texas Christian University	M,D
Texas Southern University	M
Texas State University-San Marcos	M
Texas Tech University	M,D
Texas Woman's University	M
Troy University Dothan	M
Truman State University	M
Tufts University	M,D
Tulane University	M,D
University at Albany, State University of New York	M,D,O
University at Buffalo, The State University of New York	M,D
The University of Akron	M,D
The University of Alabama	M,D
The University of Alabama at Birmingham	M
The University of Alabama in Huntsville	M
The University of Arizona	M,D
University of Arkansas	M,D
University of California, Berkeley	M,D
University of California, Davis	M,D
University of California, Irvine	M,D
University of California, Los Angeles	M,D
University of California, Riverside	M,D
University of California, San Diego	M,D
University of California, Santa Barbara	M,D
University of California, Santa Cruz	D
University of Central Arkansas	M
University of Central Florida	M
University of Central Oklahoma	M
University of Chicago	M,D
University of Cincinnati	M,D
University of Colorado at Boulder	M,D
University of Colorado at Colorado Springs	M
University of Colorado at Denver	M
University of Connecticut	M,D
University of Delaware	M,D
University of Denver	M
University of Florida	M,D
University of Georgia	M,D
University of Hawaii at Manoa	M,D
University of Houston	M,D
University of Houston–Clear Lake	M
University of Idaho	M,D
University of Illinois at Chicago	M,D
University of Illinois at Urbana–Champaign	M,D
University of Indianapolis	M
The University of Iowa	M,D
University of Kansas	M,D
University of Kentucky	M,D
University of Louisiana at Lafayette	M
University of Louisiana at Monroe	M
University of Louisville	M
University of Maine	M,D
University of Maryland, Baltimore County	M
University of Maryland, College Park	M,D
University of Massachusetts Amherst	M,D
University of Massachusetts Boston	M
The University of Memphis	M,D
University of Miami	M,D
University of Michigan	D,O
University of Minnesota, Twin Cities Campus	M,D
University of Mississippi	M
University of Missouri–Columbia	M,D
University of Missouri–Kansas City	M,D
University of Missouri–St. Louis	M,O
The University of Montana–Missoula	M,D
University of Nebraska at Kearney	M
University of Nebraska at Omaha	M
University of Nebraska–Lincoln	M,D
University of Nevada, Las Vegas	M,D
University of Nevada, Reno	M,D
University of New Hampshire	M,D
University of New Mexico	M,D
University of New Orleans	M
The University of North Carolina at Chapel Hill	M,D
The University of North Carolina at Charlotte	M
The University of North Carolina at Greensboro	M,O
The University of North Carolina at Wilmington	M
University of North Dakota	M,D
University of Northern Colorado	M
University of Northern Iowa	M
University of North Florida	M
University of North Texas	M,D
University of Notre Dame	M,D
University of Oklahoma	M,D
University of Oregon	M,D
University of Pennsylvania	M,D
University of Pittsburgh	M,D
University of Puerto Rico, Río Piedras	M,D
University of Rhode Island	M
University of Richmond	M
University of Rochester	M,D
University of San Diego	M
The University of Scranton	M
University of South Alabama	M
University of South Carolina	M,D,O
The University of South Dakota	M
University of Southern California	M,D
University of Southern Mississippi	M,D
University of South Florida	M
The University of Tennessee	M,D
The University of Texas at Arlington	M,D
The University of Texas at Austin	M,D
The University of Texas at Brownsville	M
The University of Texas at El Paso	M,D
The University of Texas at San Antonio	M
The University of Texas at Tyler	M
The University of Texas of the Permian Basin	M
The University of Texas–Pan American	M
University of Toledo	M,D
University of Tulsa	M
University of Utah	M,D
University of Vermont	M
University of Virginia	M,D
University of Washington	M,D
University of West Florida	M
University of Wisconsin–Eau Claire	M
University of Wisconsin–Madison	M,D
University of Wisconsin–Milwaukee	M,D
University of Wisconsin–Stevens Point	M
University of Wyoming	M
Utah State University	M
Valdosta State University	M
Valparaiso University	M
Vanderbilt University	M,D
Villanova University	M
Virginia Commonwealth University	M
Virginia Polytechnic Institute and State University	M
Virginia State University	M
Washington State University	M,D
Washington University in St. Louis	M,D
Wayne State University	M,D,O
West Chester University of Pennsylvania	M
Western Carolina University	M
Western Connecticut State University	M
Western Illinois University	M
Western Kentucky University	M
Western Michigan University	M,D
Western Washington University	M
Westfield State College	M
West Texas A&M University	M
West Virginia University	M,D
Wichita State University	M
William Paterson University of New Jersey	M
Winthrop University	M
Wright State University	M
Yale University	M,D
Youngstown State University	M

■ HISTORY OF MEDICINE

Institution	Degree
Duke University	
New Jersey Institute of Technology	M
Rutgers, The State University of New Jersey, New Brunswick/Piscataway	D
University of Minnesota, Twin Cities Campus	M,D
Yale University	M,D

■ HISTORY OF SCIENCE AND TECHNOLOGY

Institution	Degree
Arizona State University	M,D
Brown University	M,D
Cornell University	M,D
Drexel University	M
Georgia Institute of Technology	M,D
Harvard University	M,D
Indiana University Bloomington	M,D
Iowa State University of Science and Technology	M,D
The Johns Hopkins University	D
Massachusetts Institute of Technology	D
New Jersey Institute of Technology	M
Polytechnic University, Brooklyn Campus	M
Princeton University	D
Rensselaer Polytechnic Institute	M,D
Rutgers, The State University of New Jersey, New Brunswick/Piscataway	D
University of California, Berkeley	D
University of California, San Diego	M,D
University of California, San Francisco	M,D
University of Chicago	M,D
University of Massachusetts Amherst	M,D
University of Minnesota, Twin Cities Campus	M,D
University of Notre Dame	M,D
University of Oklahoma	M,D
University of Pennsylvania	M,D
University of Pittsburgh	M,D
University of Wisconsin–Madison	M,D
Virginia Polytechnic Institute and State University	M,D
West Virginia University	M,D
Yale University	M,D

■ HIV/AIDS NURSING

Institution	Degree
Columbia University	M,O
Duke University	M,O
University of Delaware	M,O

■ HOLOCAUST STUDIES

Institution	Degree
Clark University	D

■ HOME ECONOMICS EDUCATION

Institution	Degree
Brooklyn College of the City University of New York	M
Central Washington University	M
Eastern Kentucky University	M
Florida International University	M
Indiana State University	M
Iowa State University of Science and Technology	M,D

Humanities

Louisiana State University and Agricultural and Mechanical College — M,D
Montclair State University — M
Northwestern State University of Louisiana — M
The Ohio State University — M,D
Purdue University — M,D,O
Queens College of the City University of New York — M
South Carolina State University — M
State University of New York College at Oneonta — M
Texas Tech University — M,D
University of Central Oklahoma — M
University of Rhode Island — M
Utah State University — M
Wayne State College — M
Western Carolina University — M

■ HORTICULTURE
Auburn University — M,D
Brigham Young University — M
Colorado State University — M,D
Cornell University — M,D
Iowa State University of Science and Technology — M,D
Kansas State University — M,D
Louisiana State University and Agricultural and Mechanical College — M,D
Michigan State University — M,D
New Mexico State University — M,D
North Carolina State University — M,D
The Ohio State University — M,D
Oklahoma State University — M,D
Oregon State University — M,D
The Pennsylvania State University University Park Campus — M,D
Purdue University — M,D
Rutgers, The State University of New Jersey, New Brunswick/Piscataway — M,D
Southern Illinois University Carbondale — M
Texas A&M University — M,D
Texas Tech University — M,D
University of Arkansas — M
University of California, Davis — M
University of Delaware — M
University of Florida — M,D
University of Georgia — M,D
University of Hawaii at Manoa — M,D
University of Maine — M
University of Maryland, College Park — D
University of Missouri–Columbia — M,D
University of Nebraska–Lincoln — M,D
University of Puerto Rico, Mayagüez Campus — M
The University of Tennessee — M
University of Washington — M,D
University of Wisconsin–Madison — M,D
Virginia Polytechnic Institute and State University — M,D
Washington State University — M,D
West Virginia University — M

■ HOSPICE NURSING
Madonna University — M

■ HOSPITALITY MANAGEMENT
Central Michigan University — M,O
Cornell University — M,D
Fairleigh Dickinson University, College at Florham — M
Fairleigh Dickinson University, Metropolitan Campus — M
Florida International University — M
The George Washington University — M
Iowa State University of Science and Technology — M,D

Johnson & Wales University — M
Kansas State University — M,D
Lynn University — M,D
Michigan State University — M
New York University — M,D,O
The Ohio State University — M,D
Oklahoma State University — M
The Pennsylvania State University University Park Campus — M,D
Purdue University — M,D
Rochester Institute of Technology — M
Roosevelt University — M
Saint Joseph's College of Maine — M
Temple University — M
Texas Tech University — M,D
Texas Woman's University — M,D
The University of Alabama — M
University of Central Florida — M
University of Delaware — M
University of Denver — M
University of Hawaii at Manoa — M,O
University of Houston — M
University of Kentucky — M
University of Massachusetts Amherst — M
University of Nevada, Las Vegas — M,D
University of New Haven — M
University of New Orleans — M
University of North Texas — M
University of South Carolina — M
The University of Tennessee — M
University of Wisconsin–Stout — M
Virginia Polytechnic Institute and State University — M,D

■ HUMAN-COMPUTER INTERACTION
Carnegie Mellon University — M,D
DePaul University — M
Georgia Institute of Technology — M
Indiana University Bloomington — M
Iowa State University of Science and Technology — M,D
Tufts University — O
University of Baltimore — M,D
University of Michigan — M,D

■ HUMAN DEVELOPMENT
Appalachian State University — M
Arizona State University — M,D
Auburn University — M,D
Boston University — M,D,O
Bowling Green State University — M
Bradley University — M
Brigham Young University — M,D
The Catholic University of America — D
Central Michigan University — M
Claremont Graduate University — M,D
Colorado State University — M
Cornell University — D
Dowling College — M
Duke University — D
East Tennessee State University — M
The George Washington University — M,D
Harvard University — M,D
Howard University — M
Iowa State University of Science and Technology — M,D
Kent State University — D
Marywood University — M,D
Montana State University–Bozeman — M
National-Louis University — M,D,O
New York Institute of Technology — M
North Dakota State University — D
Northwestern University — D
The Ohio State University — M,D
Oregon State University — M,D
Our Lady of the Lake University of San Antonio — M
The Pennsylvania State University University Park Campus — M,D

Purdue University — M,D
Saint Joseph College — O
Saint Louis University — M,D,O
Saint Mary's University of Minnesota — M
Salve Regina University — M,O
Southern Illinois University Carbondale — M,D
Texas A&M University — M,D
Texas Southern University — M
Texas Tech University — M,D
Troy University — M
Troy University Montgomery — M,O
The University of Alabama — M
The University of Arizona — M,D
University of California, Berkeley — M,D
University of California, Davis — D
University of Central Arkansas — M
University of Central Oklahoma — M
University of Chicago — D
University of Connecticut — M,D
University of Dayton — M
University of Delaware — M,D
University of Illinois at Chicago — M,D
University of Illinois at Springfield — M
University of Illinois at Urbana–Champaign — M,D
University of Kansas — M,D
University of Maine — M
University of Maryland, College Park — M,D
University of Missouri–Columbia — M,D
University of Nevada, Reno — M
The University of North Carolina at Greensboro — M,D
University of North Texas — M,D
University of Pennsylvania — M,D
University of St. Thomas (MN) — M,D,O
The University of Texas at Austin — M
University of Washington — M,D
University of Wisconsin–Madison — M,D
University of Wisconsin–Stevens Point — M
Utah State University — M,D
Vanderbilt University — M,D
Virginia Polytechnic Institute and State University — M,D
Washington State University — M
Wayne State University — M
Wheelock College — M

■ HUMAN GENETICS
Case Western Reserve University — D
Drexel University — M,D
Hofstra University — M
Howard University — M,D
The Johns Hopkins University — D
Tulane University — M,D
University of California, Los Angeles — M,D
University of Chicago — D
University of Maryland — M,D
University of Michigan — M,D
University of Pittsburgh — M,D
University of Utah — M,D
Virginia Commonwealth University — M,D,O
Wake Forest University — D
West Virginia University — D

■ HUMANITIES
Arcadia University — M
Arizona State University — M
Brigham Young University — M
California State University, Dominguez Hills — M
Central Michigan University — M
Claremont Graduate University — M,D
Clark Atlanta University — D
Dominican University of California — M
Duke University — M
Florida State University — M,D
Grambling State University — M
Hofstra University — M
Hood College — M

Directory of Graduate and Professional Programs by Field
Humanities

John Carroll University	M
Marshall University	M
Marymount University	M
Massachusetts Institute of Technology	M
Michigan State University	M
New College of California	M
New York University	M,O
Nova Southeastern University	M
Old Dominion University	M
The Pennsylvania State University Harrisburg Campus of the Capital College	M
Pepperdine University	M
Point Park University	M
Polytechnic University, Brooklyn Campus	M
Prescott College	M
Salve Regina University	M,D,O
San Francisco State University	M
Stanford University	M
Texas Tech University	M,D
Towson University	M
University at Buffalo, The State University of New York	M
University of California, Santa Cruz	D
University of Chicago	M
University of Colorado at Denver	M
University of Houston–Clear Lake	M
University of Louisville	M,D
The University of Texas at Arlington	M
The University of Texas at Dallas	M,D
University of West Florida	M
Wright State University	M
Xavier University	M

■ HUMAN RESOURCES DEVELOPMENT

Abilene Christian University	M
American International College	M,O
Antioch University Los Angeles	M
Azusa Pacific University	M
Barry University	M,D
Bowie State University	M
California State University, Sacramento	M
Carlow University	M
Clemson University	M
The College of New Rochelle	M,O
Florida International University	M
Friends University	M
The George Washington University	M,D,O
Heritage College	M
Illinois Institute of Technology	M,D
Indiana State University	M
Indiana University Bloomington	M
Indiana University of Pennsylvania	M
Inter American University of Puerto Rico, Metropolitan Campus	M
Inter American University of Puerto Rico, San Germán Campus	M
Iowa State University of Science and Technology	M,D
John F. Kennedy University	M,O
The Johns Hopkins University	M,O
Kennesaw State University	M
Manhattanville College	M
Marquette University	M
Midwestern State University	M
Mississippi State University	M,D,O
National-Louis University	M
North Carolina Agricultural and Technical State University	M
Northeastern Illinois University	M
Oakland University	M
Palm Beach Atlantic University	M
The Pennsylvania State University University Park Campus	M
Pittsburg State University	M,O
Rochester Institute of Technology	M
Rollins College	M
St. John Fisher College	M
Salve Regina University	M,O
Siena Heights University	M
Suffolk University	M,O
Syracuse University	D
Texas A&M University	M,D
Towson University	M,O
Universidad del Turabo	M
University of Bridgeport	M
University of Connecticut	M
University of Georgia	M,D,O
University of Illinois at Urbana–Champaign	M,D,O
University of Louisville	M
University of Minnesota, Twin Cities Campus	M,D,O
University of Pittsburgh	M
University of San Francisco	M
The University of Scranton	M
University of Southern Mississippi	M
The University of Tennessee	M,D
The University of Texas at Austin	M
University of Wisconsin–Milwaukee	M
University of Wisconsin–Stout	M
Vanderbilt University	M,D
Villanova University	M
Virginia Polytechnic Institute and State University	M,D
Webster University	M,D
Western Carolina University	M
Western Michigan University	M,D,O
Western New England College	M
William Woods University	M
Xavier University	M

■ HUMAN RESOURCES MANAGEMENT

Adelphi University	M,O
Alabama Agricultural and Mechanical University	M,O
Albany State University	M
American University	M
Argosy University/Sarasota	M,D
Argosy University/Schaumburg	M,D
Auburn University	M,D
Baldwin-Wallace College	M
Bernard M. Baruch College of the City University of New York	M,D
Boston University	M,O
Buffalo State College, State University of New York	M,O
California State University, Hayward	M
California State University, Sacramento	M
Case Western Reserve University	M,D
The Catholic University of America	M
Central Michigan University	M,O
Chapman University	M,O
City University	M,O
Claremont Graduate University	M
Clarkson University	M
Cleveland State University	M
Colorado Technical University	M,D
Columbia University	M
Concordia University Wisconsin	M
Cornell University	M,D
Cumberland University	M
Dallas Baptist University	M
DePaul University	M
East Central University	M
Eastern Michigan University	M
Emmanuel College	M,O
Fairfield University	M,O
Fairleigh Dickinson University, College at Florham	M
Fairleigh Dickinson University, Metropolitan Campus	M,O
Fitchburg State College	M
Florida Institute of Technology	M
Florida Metropolitan University–South Orlando Campus	M
Florida Metropolitan University–Tampa Campus	M
Fordham University	M,D,O
Framingham State College	M
Gannon University	O
George Mason University	M
The George Washington University	M,D,O
Georgia State University	M,D
Hawai'i Pacific University	M
Hofstra University	M,O
Holy Family University	M
Houston Baptist University	M
Indiana University Bloomington	M
Inter American University of Puerto Rico, Metropolitan Campus	M
Inter American University of Puerto Rico, San Germán Campus	M,D
Iona College	M,O
Kennesaw State University	M
La Roche College	M
Lesley University	M,O
Lindenwood University	M
Long Island University, Brooklyn Campus	M
Loyola University Chicago	M
Lynchburg College	M
Manhattanville College	M
Marquette University	M
Marshall University	M
Marygrove College	M
Marymount University	M,O
Mercy College	M
Metropolitan State University	M
Michigan State University	M,D
National-Louis University	M
National University	M
New School University	M,O
New York Institute of Technology	M,O
New York University	M,D,O
North Carolina Agricultural and Technical State University	M
Nova Southeastern University	M
The Ohio State University	M,D
Oral Roberts University	M
Pontifical Catholic University of Puerto Rico	M,D
Purdue University	M,D
Regis University	M,O
Rivier College	M
Rollins College	M
Roosevelt University	M
Rutgers, The State University of New Jersey, Newark	M,D
Rutgers, The State University of New Jersey, New Brunswick/Piscataway	M,D
Sage Graduate School	M
St. Edward's University	M,O
Saint Francis University	M
Saint Joseph's University	M
Saint Mary's University of Minnesota	M
St. Thomas University	M,O
Salve Regina University	M,O
San Diego State University	M
Stony Brook University, State University of New York	M,O
Suffolk University	M,O
Tarleton State University	M
Temple University	M,D
Texas A&M University	M,D
Thomas Edison State College	M
Troy University	M
Troy University Dothan	M
Troy University Montgomery	M
Universidad del Turabo	M
Universidad Metropolitana	M
University at Albany, State University of New York	M
University at Buffalo, The State University of New York	M,D,O
The University of Akron	M

Directory of Graduate and Professional Programs by Field
Industrial/Management Engineering

The University of Alabama in Huntsville	M,O
University of Connecticut	M,D
University of Denver	M,O
The University of Findlay	M
University of Hawaii at Manoa	M
University of Houston–Clear Lake	M
University of Illinois at Urbana–Champaign	M,D
University of Minnesota, Twin Cities Campus	M,D
University of Missouri–St. Louis	M,O
University of New Haven	M
University of New Mexico	M
University of North Florida	M
University of Pittsburgh	O
University of Redlands	M
University of St. Thomas (MN)	M
The University of Scranton	M
University of South Carolina	M
The University of Texas at Arlington	M,D
University of the Sacred Heart	M
University of Wisconsin–Madison	M,D
University of Wisconsin–Whitewater	M
Utah State University	M
Valdosta State University	M
Virginia Commonwealth University	M
Wayland Baptist University	M
Webster University	M,D
Western New England College	M
Widener University	M
Wilkes University	M
Wilmington College (DE)	M

■ **HUMAN SERVICES**

Abilene Christian University	M,O
Andrews University	M
Antioch New England Graduate School	M
Bellevue University	M
Brandeis University	M
Brooklyn College of the City University of New York	M
California State University, Sacramento	M
Chestnut Hill College	M,O
Concordia University (IL)	M
Coppin State University	M
DePaul University	M
Drury University	M
Ferris State University	M
Georgia State University	M
Indiana University Northwest	M,O
Kansas State University	M,D
Lehigh University	M,D,O
Lesley University	M,O
Lincoln University (PA)	M
Lindenwood University	M
Louisiana State University in Shreveport	M
Minnesota State University Mankato	M
Minnesota State University Moorhead	M,O
Montclair State University	M
Murray State University	M
National-Louis University	M,O
Pontifical Catholic University of Puerto Rico	M,D
Rider University	M
Roberts Wesleyan College	M
Sage Graduate School	M
St. Edward's University	M,O
St. John Fisher College	M
Saint Joseph's University	M
St. Mary's University of San Antonio	M,D,O
Southern Oregon University	M
Springfield College	M
State University of New York at Oswego	M
Texas Southern University	M
Universidad del Turabo	M
University of Baltimore	M
University of Bridgeport	M
University of Colorado at Colorado Springs	M
University of Great Falls	M
University of Illinois at Springfield	M
University of Maryland, Baltimore County	M,D
University of Massachusetts Boston	M
University of Oklahoma	M
University of Toledo	M,D,O
Walden University	D
Wayne State University	O
West Virginia University	M
Wichita State University	M
Youngstown State University	M

■ **HYDRAULICS**

Auburn University	M,D
Colorado State University	M,D
Massachusetts Institute of Technology	M,D,O
Texas A&M University	M,D
University of Missouri–Rolla	M,D
University of Washington	M,D

■ **HYDROLOGY**

Auburn University	M,D
California State University, Bakersfield	M
California State University, Chico	M
Clemson University	M
Colorado State University	M,D
Cornell University	M,D
Georgia Institute of Technology	M,D
Idaho State University	M,O
Illinois State University	M
Massachusetts Institute of Technology	M,D,O
New Mexico Institute of Mining and Technology	M,D
Ohio University	M
State University of New York College of Environmental Science and Forestry	M,D
Texas A&M University	M,D
The University of Arizona	M,D
University of California, Davis	M,D
University of Hawaii at Manoa	M,D
University of Idaho	M
University of Illinois at Chicago	M,D
University of Missouri–Rolla	M,D
University of Nevada, Reno	M,D
University of New Hampshire	M
University of Southern Mississippi	M,D
University of South Florida	M,D
University of Washington	M,D
West Virginia University	M,D
Wright State University	M

■ **ILLUSTRATION**

Bradley University	M
California State University, Long Beach	M
Kent State University	M
Syracuse University	M
University of Utah	M
Western Connecticut State University	M

■ **IMMUNOLOGY**

Boston University	D
Brown University	M,D
California Institute of Technology	D
Case Western Reserve University	M,D
Colorado State University	M,D
Cornell University	M,D
Creighton University	M,D
Drexel University	M,D
Duke University	D
East Carolina University	D
Emory University	D
Florida State University	M,D
Georgetown University	M,D
The George Washington University	D
Harvard University	D
Indiana University–Purdue University Indianapolis	M,D
Iowa State University of Science and Technology	M,D
The Johns Hopkins University	M,D
Kansas State University	M,D
Long Island University, C.W. Post Campus	M
Loyola University Chicago	M,D
Massachusetts Institute of Technology	D
Mayo Graduate School	D
New York University	D
North Carolina State University	M,D
Northwestern University	D
The Ohio State University	M
Purdue University	M,D
Rutgers, The State University of New Jersey, New Brunswick/Piscataway	M,D
Saint Louis University	D
Stanford University	D
Stony Brook University, State University of New York	M,D
Temple University	M,D
Tufts University	D
Tulane University	M,D
University at Albany, State University of New York	M,D
University at Buffalo, The State University of New York	M,D
The University of Arizona	M,D
University of California, Berkeley	D
University of California, Davis	D
University of California, Los Angeles	M,D
University of California, San Diego	D
University of California, San Francisco	D
University of Chicago	D
University of Cincinnati	M,D
University of Florida	M,D
University of Illinois at Chicago	D
The University of Iowa	M,D
University of Kansas	D
University of Kentucky	D
University of Louisville	M,D
University of Maryland	M,D
University of Miami	D
University of Michigan	D
University of Minnesota, Duluth	M,D
University of Missouri–Columbia	M,D
The University of North Carolina at Chapel Hill	M,D
University of North Dakota	M,D
University of Pennsylvania	D
University of Pittsburgh	M,D
University of Rochester	M,D
University of South Alabama	D
The University of South Dakota	M,D
University of Southern California	M,D
University of Southern Maine	M
University of South Florida	M,D
The University of Texas at Austin	D
University of Virginia	D
University of Washington	D
Vanderbilt University	M,D
Virginia Commonwealth University	M,D,O
Wake Forest University	D
Washington University in St. Louis	D
Wayne State University	M,D
West Virginia University	M,D
Wright State University	M
Yale University	D
Yeshiva University	D

■ **INDUSTRIAL/MANAGEMENT ENGINEERING**

Arizona State University	M,D
Auburn University	M,D
Bradley University	M
Buffalo State College, State University of New York	M

Peterson's Graduate Schools in the U.S. 2006

Directory of Graduate and Professional Programs by Field
Industrial/Management Engineering

Institution	Degrees
California Polytechnic State University, San Luis Obispo	M
California State University, Fresno	M
California State University, Northridge	M
Central Missouri State University	M,O
Central Washington University	M
Clemson University	M,D
Cleveland State University	M,D
Colorado State University	M,D
Colorado State University–Pueblo	M
Columbia University	M,D,O
Cornell University	M,D
East Carolina University	M,D,O
Eastern Kentucky University	M
Eastern Michigan University	M
Florida Agricultural and Mechanical University	M,D
Florida International University	M
Florida State University	M,D
Georgia Institute of Technology	M,D
Illinois State University	M
Indiana State University	M
Iowa State University of Science and Technology	M,D
Kansas State University	M,D
Lamar University	M,D
Lehigh University	M,D
Louisiana State University and Agricultural and Mechanical College	M,D
Louisiana Tech University	M,D
Loyola Marymount University	M
Mississippi State University	M,D
Montana State University–Bozeman	M
New Jersey Institute of Technology	M,D
New Mexico State University	M,D
North Carolina Agricultural and Technical State University	M,D
North Carolina State University	M,D
North Dakota State University	M,D
Northeastern University	M,D
Northern Illinois University	M
Northwestern University	M,D
The Ohio State University	M,D
Ohio University	M
Oklahoma State University	M,D
Oregon State University	M,D
The Pennsylvania State University University Park Campus	M,D
Polytechnic University, Brooklyn Campus	M
Purdue University	M,D
Rensselaer Polytechnic Institute	M
Rochester Institute of Technology	M
Rutgers, The State University of New Jersey, New Brunswick/Piscataway	M,D
St. Mary's University of San Antonio	M
Sam Houston State University	M
San Jose State University	M
South Dakota State University	M
Stanford University	M,D
State University of New York at Binghamton	M,D
Stony Brook University, State University of New York	M,O
Tennessee Technological University	M,D
Texas A&M University	M,D
Texas A&M University–Commerce	M
Texas A&M University–Kingsville	M
Texas State University-San Marcos	M
Texas Tech University	M,D
University at Buffalo, The State University of New York	M,D
The University of Alabama	M
The University of Alabama in Huntsville	M,D
The University of Arizona	M,D
University of Arkansas	M,D
University of California, Berkeley	M,D
University of Central Florida	M,D,O
University of Cincinnati	M,D
University of Dayton	M
University of Florida	M,D,O
University of Houston	M,D
University of Illinois at Chicago	M,D
University of Illinois at Urbana–Champaign	M,D
The University of Iowa	M,D
University of Louisville	M,D
University of Massachusetts Amherst	M,D
University of Massachusetts Lowell	M,D,O
The University of Memphis	M,D
University of Miami	M,D
University of Michigan	M,D
University of Michigan–Dearborn	M
University of Minnesota, Twin Cities Campus	M,D
University of Missouri–Columbia	M,D
University of Nebraska–Lincoln	M,D
University of New Haven	M,O
University of Oklahoma	M,D
University of Pittsburgh	M,D
University of Puerto Rico, Mayagüez Campus	M
University of Rhode Island	M
University of Southern California	M,D,O
University of South Florida	M,D
The University of Tennessee	M,D
The University of Texas at Arlington	M
The University of Texas at Austin	M,D
The University of Texas at El Paso	M
University of Toledo	M,D
University of Washington	M,D
University of Wisconsin–Madison	M,D
Virginia Polytechnic Institute and State University	M,D
Wayne State University	M,D
Western Carolina University	M
Western Michigan University	M,D
Western New England College	M
West Virginia University	M,D
Wichita State University	M,D
Youngstown State University	M

■ INDUSTRIAL AND LABOR RELATIONS

Institution	Degrees
Bernard M. Baruch College of the City University of New York	M
Case Western Reserve University	M,D
Cleveland State University	M
Cornell University	M,D
Georgia State University	M,D
Indiana University of Pennsylvania	M
Inter American University of Puerto Rico, Metropolitan Campus	M
Inter American University of Puerto Rico, San Germán Campus	M,D
Iowa State University of Science and Technology	M
Loyola University Chicago	M
Michigan State University	M,D
Middle Tennessee State University	M,D
New York Institute of Technology	M,O
The Ohio State University	M,D
The Pennsylvania State University University Park Campus	M
Rutgers, The State University of New Jersey, New Brunswick/Piscataway	M,D
State University of New York Empire State College	M
Stony Brook University, State University of New York	M,O
The University of Akron	M
University of California, Berkeley	D
University of Cincinnati	M
University of Illinois at Urbana–Champaign	M,D
University of Louisville	M
University of Massachusetts Amherst	M
University of Minnesota, Twin Cities Campus	M,D
University of New Haven	M
University of North Texas	M,D
University of Rhode Island	M
University of Wisconsin–Madison	M,D
University of Wisconsin–Milwaukee	M
Virginia Commonwealth University	M
Wayne State University	M
West Virginia University	M

■ INDUSTRIAL AND MANUFACTURING MANAGEMENT

Institution	Degrees
Bentley College	M,O
Boston University	D
California Polytechnic State University, San Luis Obispo	M
Carnegie Mellon University	M,D
Case Western Reserve University	M,D
Central Michigan University	M
Central Missouri State University	M
Clarkson University	M
Clemson University	M,D
DePaul University	M
Eastern Michigan University	M
Florida Institute of Technology	M
The George Washington University	M
Georgia State University	M,D
Illinois Institute of Technology	M
Indiana University Southeast	M,O
Inter American University of Puerto Rico, Metropolitan Campus	M
Lawrence Technological University	M,D
Lynchburg College	M
Massachusetts Institute of Technology	
New York University	M
Northeastern State University	M
Northern Illinois University	M
Northwestern University	M
Oklahoma State University	M,D
The Pennsylvania State University University Park Campus	M
Polytechnic University, Brooklyn Campus	M
Purdue University	M,D
Regis University	M,O
Rensselaer Polytechnic Institute	M,D
Rochester Institute of Technology	M
San Diego State University	M
San Jose State University	M
Southeastern Oklahoma State University	M
Southeast Missouri State University	M
Stevens Institute of Technology	M,O
Stony Brook University, State University of New York	M,O
Syracuse University	D
Texas A&M University	M,D
Texas Tech University	M,D
The University of Alabama	M,D
University of Arkansas	M
University of Cincinnati	M,D
University of Colorado at Boulder	M,D
The University of Iowa	M
University of Massachusetts Lowell	M
University of Minnesota, Twin Cities Campus	M,D
University of North Dakota	M
University of North Texas	M,D
University of Rhode Island	M,D
University of St. Thomas (MN)	M,O
University of Southern Indiana	M
The University of Tennessee	M,D
The University of Tennessee at Chattanooga	M
University of Toledo	D
University of Wisconsin–Madison	M,D
University of Wisconsin–Platteville	M

INDUSTRIAL AND ORGANIZATIONAL PSYCHOLOGY

Angelo State University	M
Antioch University Seattle	M
Appalachian State University	M
Bernard M. Baruch College of the City University of New York	M,D,O
Bowling Green State University	M,D
Brooklyn College of the City University of New York	M,D
California State University, San Bernardino	M
Central Michigan University	M,D
Central Washington University	M
Claremont Graduate University	M,D
Clemson University	D
Cleveland State University	M,O
Colorado State University	M,D
DePaul University	M,D
Eastern Kentucky University	M,O
Emporia State University	M
Fairleigh Dickinson University, College at Florham	M
Florida Institute of Technology	M,D
George Mason University	M,D
The George Washington University	D
Goddard College	M
Hofstra University	M,D
Illinois Institute of Technology	M,D
Illinois State University	M,D,O
Indiana University–Purdue University Indianapolis	M,D
John F. Kennedy University	M,O
Kean University	M,O
Lamar University	M
Louisiana State University and Agricultural and Mechanical College	M,D
Louisiana Tech University	M,D
Marshall University	M,D
Middle Tennessee State University	M,O
Minnesota State University Mankato	M
Montclair State University	M
National-Louis University	M,O
New York University	M,D,O
Ohio University	D
Old Dominion University	D
The Pennsylvania State University University Park Campus	M,D
Pontifical Catholic University of Puerto Rico	M,D
Radford University	M,O
Rice University	M,D
Roosevelt University	M
Rutgers, The State University of New Jersey, New Brunswick/Piscataway	M,D
St. Cloud State University	M
St. Mary's University of San Antonio	M
San Diego State University	M,D
San Jose State University	M
Southern Illinois University Edwardsville	M
Springfield College	M,O
Teachers College Columbia University	M,D
Temple University	M,D
Texas A&M University	M,D
University at Albany, State University of New York	M,D
The University of Akron	M,D
University of Baltimore	M
University of Central Florida	M,D
University of Connecticut	M,D
University of Detroit Mercy	M
University of Houston	D
University of Illinois at Urbana–Champaign	M,D
University of Maryland, College Park	M,D
University of Michigan	D
University of Minnesota, Twin Cities Campus	D
University of Missouri–St. Louis	M,D
University of Nebraska at Omaha	M,D,O
University of New Haven	M,O
The University of North Carolina at Charlotte	M
University of North Texas	M,D
University of South Florida	M,D
The University of Tennessee	D
The University of Tennessee at Chattanooga	M
University of Tulsa	M,D
University of Wisconsin–Oshkosh	M
Valdosta State University	M,O
Virginia Polytechnic Institute and State University	M,D
Wayne State University	M,D
West Chester University of Pennsylvania	M
Western Michigan University	M,D,O
William Carey College	M
Wright State University	M,D

INDUSTRIAL DESIGN

Auburn University	M
Illinois Institute of Technology	M,D
North Carolina State University	M
The Ohio State University	M
Pratt Institute	M
Rochester Institute of Technology	M
San Francisco State University	M
University of Cincinnati	M
University of Illinois at Chicago	M
University of Illinois at Urbana–Champaign	M
University of Notre Dame	M

INDUSTRIAL HYGIENE

Central Missouri State University	M,O
New Jersey Institute of Technology	M
Purdue University	M,D
San Diego State University	M,D
Texas A&M University	M,D
The University of Alabama at Birmingham	D
University of Cincinnati	M
University of Massachusetts Lowell	M,D,O
University of Michigan	M,D
University of Minnesota, Twin Cities Campus	M,D
University of New Haven	M
The University of North Carolina at Chapel Hill	M,D
University of South Carolina	M,D
University of Washington	M,D
Wayne State University	M,O
West Virginia University	M

INFECTIOUS DISEASES

Case Western Reserve University	M
Cornell University	M,D
Georgetown University	M,D
The George Washington University	M
Harvard University	D
The Johns Hopkins University	M,D
Purdue University	M,D
University of California, Berkeley	M,D
University of Minnesota, Twin Cities Campus	M,D
University of Pittsburgh	M,D

INFORMATION SCIENCE

Alcorn State University	M
Arkansas Tech University	M
Ball State University	M
Barry University	M
Bellevue University	M
Bentley College	M
Bradley University	M
Brooklyn College of the City University of New York	M,D
California State University, Fullerton	M
Carnegie Mellon University	M,D
Case Western Reserve University	M,D
Central Washington University	M
The Citadel, The Military College of South Carolina	M
Claremont Graduate University	M,D
Clark Atlanta University	M
Clarkson University	M
Clark University	M
The College of Saint Rose	M
Colorado Technical University	M,D
DePaul University	M
DeSales University	M
Drexel University	D
East Carolina University	M
East Tennessee State University	M
Florida Gulf Coast University	M
Florida Institute of Technology	M,D
George Mason University	M,D,O
Georgia Southwestern State University	M
Grand Valley State University	M
Harvard University	M,O
Hood College	M
Indiana University Bloomington	M,D,O
Iowa State University of Science and Technology	M
Kansas State University	M,D
Kennesaw State University	M
Lamar University	M
Lehigh University	M,D,O
Long Island University, C.W. Post Campus	M
Marshall University	M
Marywood University	M
Massachusetts Institute of Technology	M,D,O
Montclair State University	M,O
New Jersey Institute of Technology	M,D
Northeastern University	M
Northern Kentucky University	M
Northwestern University	M
Nova Southeastern University	M,D
Oakland University	M,O
The Ohio State University	M,D
Pace University	M,D,O
Pace University, White Plains Campus	M,D,O
The Pennsylvania State University Great Valley Campus	M
The Pennsylvania State University University Park Campus	M,D
Polytechnic University, Westchester Graduate Center	M
Regis University	M,O
Rensselaer Polytechnic Institute	M
Robert Morris University	M,D
Rochester Institute of Technology	M
Sacred Heart University	M,O
St. Mary's University of San Antonio	M
Saint Xavier University	M
Sam Houston State University	M
Shippensburg University of Pennsylvania	M
Southern Methodist University	M,D
State University of New York Institute of Technology	M
Stevens Institute of Technology	M,O
Strayer University	M
Syracuse University	M,D
Tarleton State University	M
Temple University	M,D
Towson University	O
Trevecca Nazarene University	M
University at Albany, State University of New York	M,D,O
The University of Alabama at Birmingham	M,D
University of Baltimore	M,D

Directory of Graduate and Professional Programs by Field

Information Science

University of California, Irvine	M,D
University of Colorado at Colorado Springs	M
University of Colorado at Denver	D
University of Delaware	M,D
University of Florida	M,D
University of Great Falls	M
University of Hawaii at Manoa	M,D
University of Houston	M,D
University of Houston–Clear Lake	M
University of Maryland, Baltimore County	M,D,O
University of Maryland University College	M,O
University of Michigan	M,D
University of Michigan–Dearborn	M
University of Minnesota, Twin Cities Campus	M,D
University of Missouri–Rolla	M
University of Nebraska at Omaha	M,D
University of New Haven	M
The University of North Carolina at Charlotte	M,D
University of North Florida	M
University of Oregon	M,D
University of Pennsylvania	M,D
University of Pittsburgh	M,D,O
University of South Alabama	M
The University of Tennessee	M,D
The University of Texas at El Paso	M
The University of Texas at San Antonio	M,D
University of Washington	M,D
University of Wisconsin–Parkside	M
Virginia Polytechnic Institute and State University	M

■ INFORMATION STUDIES

California State University, Chico	M
The Catholic University of America	M
Central Connecticut State University	M
Central Missouri State University	M,O
Claremont Graduate University	M,D
Clark Atlanta University	M,O
College of St. Catherine	M
Dominican University	M,O
Drexel University	M,D,O
Emporia State University	M,D
Florida State University	M,D,O
Indiana University Bloomington	M,D,O
Indiana University–Purdue University Indianapolis	M
Long Island University, C.W. Post Campus	M,D,O
Louisiana State University and Agricultural and Mechanical College	M,O
Mansfield University of Pennsylvania	M
Metropolitan State University	M
North Carolina Central University	M
Pratt Institute	M,O
Queens College of the City University of New York	M,O
Rutgers, The State University of New Jersey, New Brunswick/Piscataway	M,D
St. John's University (NY)	M,O
San Jose State University	M
Simmons College	M,D,O
Southern Connecticut State University	M,O
Syracuse University	M,D,O
University at Buffalo, The State University of New York	M,D,O
The University of Alabama	M,D
The University of Arizona	M,D
University of California, Berkeley	M,D
University of California, Los Angeles	M,D,O
University of Denver	M,O
University of Hawaii at Manoa	M,D,O
University of Illinois at Urbana–Champaign	M,D,O

The University of Iowa	M
University of Maryland, College Park	M,D
University of Michigan	M,D
University of Missouri–Columbia	M,D,O
The University of North Carolina at Chapel Hill	M,D,O
The University of North Carolina at Greensboro	M
University of North Texas	M,D
University of Oklahoma	M,O
University of Pittsburgh	M,D,O
University of Puerto Rico, Río Piedras	M,O
University of Rhode Island	M
University of South Carolina	M,O
University of South Florida	M
The University of Tennessee	M
The University of Texas at Austin	M,D
University of Wisconsin–Madison	M,D,O
University of Wisconsin–Milwaukee	M,O
Valdosta State University	M
Wayne State University	M,O

■ INORGANIC CHEMISTRY

Boston College	M,D
Brandeis University	M,D
Brigham Young University	M,D
California State University, Fullerton	M
California State University, Los Angeles	M
Case Western Reserve University	M,D
Clark Atlanta University	M,D
Clarkson University	M,D
Cleveland State University	M,D
Columbia University	D
Cornell University	D
Florida State University	M,D
Georgetown University	M,D
The George Washington University	M,D
Harvard University	M,D
Howard University	M,D
Illinois Institute of Technology	M,D
Indiana University Bloomington	M,D
Kansas State University	M,D
Kent State University	M,D
Marquette University	M,D
Massachusetts Institute of Technology	D
Miami University	M,D
Northeastern University	M,D
Oregon State University	M,D
Purdue University	M,D
Rensselaer Polytechnic Institute	M,D
Rice University	M,D
Rutgers, The State University of New Jersey, Newark	M,D
Rutgers, The State University of New Jersey, New Brunswick/Piscataway	M,D
Seton Hall University	M,D
South Dakota State University	M,D
Southern University and Agricultural and Mechanical College	M
State University of New York at Binghamton	M,D
Tufts University	M,D
University of Cincinnati	M,D
University of Georgia	M,D
University of Louisville	M,D
University of Maryland, College Park	M,D
University of Miami	M,D
University of Michigan	D
University of Missouri–Columbia	M,D
University of Missouri–Kansas City	M,D
University of Missouri–St. Louis	M,D
The University of Montana–Missoula	M,D
University of Nebraska–Lincoln	M,D
University of Notre Dame	M,D
University of Southern Mississippi	M,D
University of South Florida	M,D
The University of Tennessee	M,D
The University of Texas at Austin	M,D
University of Toledo	M,D

Vanderbilt University	M,D
Wake Forest University	M,D
Washington State University	M,D
West Virginia University	M,D
Yale University	D

■ INSURANCE

Florida State University	M,D
Georgia State University	M,D
St. John's University (NY)	M
Temple University	M,D
Thomas Edison State College	M
University of North Texas	M,D
University of Pennsylvania	M,D
University of St. Thomas (MN)	M
University of Wisconsin–Madison	M,D
Virginia Commonwealth University	M

■ INTERDISCIPLINARY STUDIES

Alaska Pacific University	M
American University	M,O
Angelo State University	M
Antioch New England Graduate School	M
Arizona State University West	M
Baylor University	M,D
Boise State University	M
Boston University	M,D
Bowling Green State University	M,D
Buffalo State College, State University of New York	M
California State University, Bakersfield	M
California State University, Chico	M
California State University, Hayward	M,O
California State University, Long Beach	M
California State University, Northridge	M
California State University, Sacramento	M
California State University, San Bernardino	M
California State University, Stanislaus	M
Campbell University	M
Central Washington University	M
Clarkson University	M,D
Columbia University	M
Cornerstone University	P,M
Dallas Baptist University	M
DePaul University	M
Eastern Washington University	M
Emory University	D
Fitchburg State College	O
Fresno Pacific University	M
Frostburg State University	M
George Mason University	M
Goddard College	M
Hofstra University	M
Idaho State University	M
Iowa State University of Science and Technology	M
John F. Kennedy University	M,O
Kent State University	M
Lesley University	M,D,O
Long Island University, C.W. Post Campus	M
Loras College	M
Loyola College in Maryland	M
Marquette University	D
Marylhurst University	M
Marywood University	M
Minnesota State University Mankato	M
Montana State University–Billings	M
New Mexico State University	M,D
New York University	M
The Ohio State University	M,D
Ohio University	D
Oregon State University	M
Rochester Institute of Technology	M
Roosevelt University	M
Rutgers, The State University of New Jersey, New Brunswick/Piscataway	D

Directory of Graduate and Professional Programs by Field
International Business

San Diego State University	M
San Jose State University	M
Sonoma State University	M
Southern Methodist University	M
Stanford University	M,D
Stephen F. Austin State University	M
Teachers College Columbia University	M,D
Texas A&M International University	M
Texas A&M University–Texarkana	M
Texas State University-San Marcos	M
Texas Tech University	M,D
Union Institute & University	M,D
University of Alaska Anchorage	M
University of Alaska Fairbanks	M,D,O
The University of Arizona	M,D,O
University of Cincinnati	D
University of Houston–Victoria	M
University of Idaho	M
University of Illinois at Springfield	M
University of Kansas	M,D
University of Louisville	M
University of Maine	D
University of Minnesota, Twin Cities Campus	D
University of Missouri–Kansas City	D
The University of Montana–Missoula	M,D
University of Northern Colorado	M,D,O
University of North Texas	M
University of Oklahoma	M,D
University of Oregon	M
The University of South Dakota	M
The University of Texas at Arlington	M
The University of Texas at Brownsville	M
The University of Texas at Dallas	M
The University of Texas at El Paso	M
The University of Texas at San Antonio	M
The University of Texas at Tyler	M
The University of Texas–Pan American	M
University of the Incarnate Word	M
University of Wisconsin–Milwaukee	D
Villanova University	D
Virginia Commonwealth University	M
Virginia State University	M
Wayland Baptist University	M
Wayne State College	M
Wayne State University	M,D
Western New Mexico University	M
West Texas A&M University	M
Worcester Polytechnic Institute	M,D
Wright State University	M

■ **INTERIOR DESIGN**

Columbia College Chicago	M
Cornell University	M
Drexel University	M
Florida State University	M
The George Washington University	M,D
Indiana University Bloomington	M
Iowa State University of Science and Technology	M
Louisiana Tech University	M
Marymount University	M
Michigan State University	M,D
New School University	M
The Ohio State University	M
Pratt Institute	M
San Diego State University	M
Suffolk University	M
The University of Alabama	M
University of Central Oklahoma	M
University of Cincinnati	M
University of Florida	M
University of Georgia	M,D
University of Houston	M
University of Kentucky	M
University of Massachusetts Amherst	M
The University of Memphis	M
University of Minnesota, Twin Cities Campus	M,D

The University of North Carolina at Greensboro	M
University of North Texas	M,D
University of Oregon	M
Utah State University	M
Virginia Commonwealth University	M
Virginia Polytechnic Institute and State University	M,D
Washington State University	M

■ **INTERNATIONAL AFFAIRS**

American University	M,D,O
Baylor University	M
Boston University	M,O
Brandeis University	M,D
Brigham Young University	M
California State University, Fresno	M
California State University, Sacramento	M
California State University, Stanislaus	M
The Catholic University of America	M
Central Connecticut State University	M
Central Michigan University	M,O
City College of the City University of New York	M
Claremont Graduate University	M,D
Clark Atlanta University	M,D
Columbia University	M
Cornell University	D
Creighton University	M
DePaul University	M
East Carolina University	M
Fairleigh Dickinson University, Metropolitan Campus	M
Florida Agricultural and Mechanical University	M
Florida International University	M,D
Florida State University	M
George Mason University	M
Georgetown University	M,D
The George Washington University	M
Georgia Institute of Technology	M
Harvard University	M,D
The Johns Hopkins University	M,D,O
Kansas State University	M
Lesley University	M,O
Long Island University, Brooklyn Campus	M,O
Long Island University, C.W. Post Campus	M
Loyola University Chicago	M,D
Marquette University	M
Michigan State University	M
Monterey Institute of International Studies	M
Morgan State University	M
New School University	M
New York University	M,D,O
North Carolina State University	M
Northeastern University	M,D
Northwestern University	O
Norwich University	M
Ohio University	M
Oklahoma City University	M
Oklahoma State University	M
Old Dominion University	M,D
Princeton University	M,D
Rutgers, The State University of New Jersey, Camden	M
Rutgers, The State University of New Jersey, Newark	M,D
Rutgers, The State University of New Jersey, New Brunswick/Piscataway	D
St. John Fisher College	M
St. Mary's University of San Antonio	M
Salve Regina University	M,O
San Francisco State University	M
School for International Training	M,O
Seton Hall University	M
Southwest Missouri State University	M
Stanford University	M

Syracuse University	M
Texas A&M University	M
Texas State University-San Marcos	M
Troy University	M
Tufts University	M,D
University of California, Berkeley	M
University of California, San Diego	M,D
University of California, Santa Cruz	M,D
University of Central Oklahoma	M
University of Chicago	M
University of Colorado at Boulder	M,D
University of Connecticut	M
University of Delaware	M,D
University of Denver	M,D
University of Florida	M,D
University of Kansas	M
University of Kentucky	M
University of Miami	M,D
University of Nebraska at Omaha	M
University of Oklahoma	M
University of Oregon	M
University of Pennsylvania	M
University of Pittsburgh	M,D
University of Rhode Island	M,O
University of San Diego	M
University of South Carolina	M,D
University of Southern California	M,D
University of South Florida	M
University of the Pacific	P,M,D
University of Virginia	M,D
University of Washington	M
University of Wyoming	M
Virginia Polytechnic Institute and State University	M
Webster University	M
West Virginia University	M,D
Yale University	M

■ **INTERNATIONAL AND COMPARATIVE EDUCATION**

American University	M
Boston University	M
Claremont Graduate University	M,D
The College of New Jersey	M
Concordia University (CA)	M
Florida International University	M,D,O
Florida State University	M,D,O
The George Washington University	M
Harvard University	M,D
Indiana University Bloomington	M,D,O
Lesley University	M,O
Louisiana State University and Agricultural and Mechanical College	M,D
Loyola University Chicago	M,D
Lynn University	M,D
Morehead State University	M
New York University	M,D,O
School for International Training	M,O
Stanford University	M,D
Teachers College Columbia University	M,D
Tufts University	M,D
University of Bridgeport	M,O
University of Massachusetts Amherst	M,D,O
University of Minnesota, Twin Cities Campus	M,D
University of Pittsburgh	M,D
University of San Francisco	M,D
University of Southern California	M,D
University of the Incarnate Word	M,D
Vanderbilt University	M,D
Wright State University	M

■ **INTERNATIONAL BUSINESS**

American University	M
Argosy University/Sarasota	M,D
Argosy University/Schaumburg	M,D
Azusa Pacific University	M
Baldwin-Wallace College	M

Peterson's Graduate Schools in the U.S. 2006

Directory of Graduate and Professional Programs by Field

International Business

Institution	Degree
Baylor University	M
Bentley College	M,O
Bernard M. Baruch College of the City University of New York	M
Boston University	M
Brandeis University	M,D
California Lutheran University	M
California State University, Fullerton	M
California State University, Hayward	M
California State University, Long Beach	M
California State University, Los Angeles	M
Central Connecticut State University	M
Central Michigan University	M
City University	M,O
Claremont Graduate University	M
Clark Atlanta University	M,D
Clark University	M
Columbia University	M
Concordia University Wisconsin	M
Dallas Baptist University	M
DePaul University	M
Dominican University of California	M
Drury University	M
Eastern Michigan University	M
Emerson College	M
Fairfield University	M,O
Fairleigh Dickinson University, College at Florham	M,O
Fairleigh Dickinson University, Metropolitan Campus	M
Florida Atlantic University	M
Florida International University	M
Florida Metropolitan University–South Orlando Campus	M
Florida Metropolitan University–Tampa Campus	M
The George Washington University	M,D
Georgia Institute of Technology	M,O
Georgia State University	M
Hawai'i Pacific University	M
Hofstra University	M,O
Hope International University	M
Howard University	M
Illinois Institute of Technology	M
Indiana University Bloomington	M
Inter American University of Puerto Rico, Metropolitan Campus	M
Inter American University of Puerto Rico, San Germán Campus	D
Iona College	M,O
The Johns Hopkins University	M,O
Johnson & Wales University	M
Lindenwood University	M
Long Island University, C.W. Post Campus	M,O
Loyola College in Maryland	M
Lynn University	M,D
Madonna University	M
Marymount University	M,O
Maryville University of Saint Louis	M,O
Mercy College	M
Metropolitan State University	M
Montclair State University	M
Monterey Institute of International Studies	M
National University	M
Newman University	M
New School University	M
New York Institute of Technology	M,O
New York University	M,D
Norwich University	M
Nova Southeastern University	M,D
Oklahoma City University	M
Our Lady of the Lake University of San Antonio	M
Pace University	M
Pace University, White Plains Campus	M
Park University	M
Pepperdine University	M
Philadelphia University	M
Portland State University	M
Quinnipiac University	M
Regis University	M,O
Rochester Institute of Technology	M
Roosevelt University	M
Rutgers, The State University of New Jersey, Newark	M,D
St. Edward's University	M,O
St. John's University (NY)	M
Saint Joseph's University	M
Saint Louis University	M,D
Saint Mary's University of Minnesota	M
St. Mary's University of San Antonio	M
Saint Peter's College	M
St. Thomas University	M,O
San Diego State University	M
School for International Training	M,O
Seattle University	M,O
Seton Hall University	M,O
Southeastern University	M
Southeast Missouri State University	M
State University of New York at New Paltz	M
Suffolk University	M,D
Sul Ross State University	M
Temple University	M,D
Texas A&M International University	M
Texas Christian University	M
Texas Tech University	M
Tufts University	M,D
The University of Akron	M
University of Central Arkansas	M
University of Chicago	M
University of Cincinnati	M
University of Colorado at Colorado Springs	M
University of Colorado at Denver	M
University of Denver	M
The University of Findlay	M
University of Florida	M
University of Hawaii at Manoa	M,D
University of Kentucky	M
University of La Verne	M
University of Maryland University College	M,O
The University of Memphis	M
University of Miami	M
University of Minnesota, Twin Cities Campus	M
University of New Haven	M
University of New Mexico	M
The University of North Carolina at Greensboro	M,O
University of Oklahoma	M
University of Pennsylvania	M
University of Pittsburgh	M
University of Rhode Island	M,D
University of San Francisco	M
The University of Scranton	M
University of South Carolina	M
University of Southern California	M
University of Southern Mississippi	M,D
The University of Tampa	M
The University of Texas at Dallas	M,D
University of the Incarnate Word	M
University of Tulsa	M
University of Washington	O
University of Wisconsin–Madison	M
University of Wisconsin–Whitewater	M
Valparaiso University	M
Wagner College	M
Washington State University	M,D,O
Wayland Baptist University	M
Webster University	M
Western International University	M
Whitworth College	M
Wilkes University	M
Wright State University	M
Xavier University	M

■ INTERNATIONAL DEVELOPMENT

Institution	Degree
American University	M,D,O
Andrews University	M
Brandeis University	M
Clark Atlanta University	M,D
Clark University	M
Cornell University	M
Duke University	M,O
Fordham University	M,O
The George Washington University	M
Harvard University	M
Hope International University	M
The Johns Hopkins University	M,D,O
New School University	M
Ohio University	M
Old Dominion University	M
Rutgers, The State University of New Jersey, Camden	M
Tufts University	M,D
Tulane University	M,D
University of Florida	M,D,O
The University of Iowa	M
University of Pittsburgh	M
University of Rhode Island	M,O

■ INTERNATIONAL HEALTH

Institution	Degree
Boston University	M,D,O
Brandeis University	M
Emory University	M
The George Washington University	M,D
Harvard University	M,D
The Johns Hopkins University	M,D
Loma Linda University	M
New York University	M,D
Tufts University	M,D
Tulane University	M,D
University of Michigan	M,D
University of Washington	M,D
Yale University	M

■ INTERNET AND INTERACTIVE MULTIMEDIA

Institution	Degree
Alfred University	M
American University	M
Chestnut Hill College	M,O
City University	M,O
DePaul University	M
Duquesne University	M,O
Florida State University	M,D
Georgetown University	M
Georgia Institute of Technology	M
Georgia State University	M,D
Indiana University–Purdue University Indianapolis	M
Long Island University, C.W. Post Campus	M
New Mexico Highlands University	M
New York University	M
Pratt Institute	M
Quinnipiac University	M
Regis University	M,O
Robert Morris University	M
Rochester Institute of Technology	O
Sacred Heart University	M,O
San Diego State University	M
Syracuse University	M
Towson University	M,D,O
University of Miami	M
University of Southern California	M,D
Virginia Commonwealth University	M
Western Illinois University	M,O

■ INVESTMENT MANAGEMENT

Institution	Degree
Boston University	M
The George Washington University	M,D
The Johns Hopkins University	M,O
Lindenwood University	M

Marywood University — M
Pace University — M
Pace University, White Plains Campus — M
University of Tulsa — M
University of Wisconsin–Madison — M,D

■ ITALIAN

Boston College — M,D
Brown University — M,D
The Catholic University of America — M
Columbia University — M,D
Cornell University — D
Florida State University — M
Harvard University — M,D
Hunter College of the City University of New York — M
Indiana University Bloomington — M,D
The Johns Hopkins University — D
New York University — M,D
Northwestern University — D,O
The Ohio State University — M,D
Princeton University — D
Queens College of the City University of New York — M
Rutgers, The State University of New Jersey, New Brunswick/Piscataway — M,D
San Francisco State University — M
Stanford University — M,D
State University of New York at Binghamton — M
Stony Brook University, State University of New York — M,D
University at Albany, State University of New York — M
University of California, Berkeley — D
University of California, Los Angeles — M,D
University of Chicago — M,D
University of Connecticut — M,D
University of Illinois at Urbana–Champaign — M,D
University of Massachusetts Amherst — M
University of Minnesota, Twin Cities Campus — M,D
The University of North Carolina at Chapel Hill — M,D
University of Notre Dame — M
University of Oregon — M
University of Pennsylvania — M,D
University of Pittsburgh — M
The University of Tennessee — D
University of Virginia — M
University of Washington — M,D
University of Wisconsin–Madison — M,D
University of Wisconsin–Milwaukee — M
Wayne State University — M
Yale University — D

■ JAPANESE

Brigham Young University — M
Cornell University — M,D
Harvard University — M,D
Indiana University Bloomington — M,D
San Francisco State University — M
Stanford University — M,D
University at Buffalo, The State University of New York — M,D,O
University of California, Berkeley — M,D
University of California, Irvine — M,D
University of Colorado at Boulder — M
University of Kansas — M
University of Massachusetts Amherst — M
University of Oregon — M,D
University of Washington — M,D
University of Wisconsin–Madison — M,D
Washington University in St. Louis — M,D

■ JEWISH STUDIES

Brandeis University — M,D
Brooklyn College of the City University of New York

Brown University — M,D
Columbia University — M,D
Cornell University — M,D
Emory University — M
Gratz College — M
Harvard University — M,D
New York University — M,D,O
Seton Hall University — M
Touro College — M
University of California, Berkeley — D
University of California, San Diego — M,D
University of Chicago — M,D
University of Denver — M
The University of Montana–Missoula — M
University of Wisconsin–Madison — M,D
University of Wisconsin–Milwaukee — M
Washington University in St. Louis — M
Yeshiva University — M,D

■ JOURNALISM

American University — M
Angelo State University — M
Arizona State University — M
Arkansas State University — M
Arkansas Tech University — M
Auburn University — M
Austin Peay State University — M
Ball State University — M
Baylor University — M
Bernard M. Baruch College of the City University of New York — M
Boston University — M
California State University, Fullerton — M
California State University, Northridge — M
Columbia College Chicago — M
Columbia University — M,D
Drake University — M
Emerson College — M
Florida Agricultural and Mechanical University — M
Indiana University Bloomington — M,D
Iona College — M,O
Iowa State University of Science and Technology — M
Kent State University — M
Marquette University — M
Marshall University — M
Michigan State University — M
Morehead State University — M
New York University — M,D,O
Northeastern University — M
Northwestern University — M
The Ohio State University — M
Ohio University — M,D
Point Park University — M
Polytechnic University, Brooklyn Campus — M
Quinnipiac University — M
Roosevelt University — M
South Dakota State University — M
Stanford University — M,D
Syracuse University — M
Temple University — M
Texas A&M University — M
Texas Christian University — M
Texas Southern University — M
The University of Alabama — M
University of Alaska Fairbanks — M
The University of Arizona — M
University of Arkansas — M
University of Arkansas at Little Rock — M
University of California, Berkeley — M
University of Colorado at Boulder — M,D
University of Florida — M,D
University of Georgia — M,D
University of Illinois at Springfield — M
University of Illinois at Urbana–Champaign — M
The University of Iowa — M
University of Kansas — M

University of Maryland, College Park — M,D
The University of Memphis — M
University of Miami — M,D
University of Mississippi — M
University of Missouri–Columbia — M,D
The University of Montana–Missoula — M
University of Nebraska–Lincoln — M
University of Nevada, Reno — M
University of North Texas — M
University of Oregon — M,D
University of South Carolina — M,D
University of Southern California — M
The University of Tennessee — M,D
The University of Texas at Austin — M,D
The University of Texas at Tyler — M
University of the Sacred Heart — M
University of Wisconsin–Madison — M,D
University of Wisconsin–Milwaukee — M
West Virginia University — M

■ KINESIOLOGY AND MOVEMENT STUDIES

Angelo State University — M
Barry University — M
Boston University — M,D,O
Bowling Green State University — M
California Baptist University — M
California Polytechnic State University, San Luis Obispo — M
California State Polytechnic University, Pomona — M
California State University, Fresno — M
California State University, Long Beach — M
California State University, Los Angeles — M
California State University, Northridge — M
Florida State University — M,D
Georgia Southern University — M
Humboldt State University — M
Indiana University Bloomington — M,D,O
Inter American University of Puerto Rico, San Germán Campus — M
James Madison University — M
Kansas State University — M
Lamar University — M
Louisiana State University and Agricultural and Mechanical College — M,D
Michigan State University — M,D
Midwestern State University — M
New York University — M,D
Oregon State University — M
The Pennsylvania State University University Park Campus — M,D
Saint Mary's College of California — M
Sam Houston State University — M
San Jose State University — M
Sonoma State University — M
Southeastern Louisiana University — M
Southern Arkansas University–Magnolia — M
Southern Illinois University Edwardsville — M,O
Springfield College — M,D
Teachers College Columbia University — M,D
Temple University — M,D
Texas A&M University — M,D
Texas A&M University–Commerce — M,D
Texas A&M University–Kingsville — M
Texas Christian University — M
Texas Woman's University — M,D
The University of Alabama — M,D
University of Arkansas — M,D
University of Central Arkansas — M
University of Colorado at Boulder — M,D
University of Connecticut — M,D
University of Delaware — M,D
University of Florida — D
University of Hawaii at Manoa — M

Directory of Graduate and Professional Programs by Field
Kinesiology and Movement Studies

Institution	Degree
University of Illinois at Chicago	M
University of Illinois at Urbana–Champaign	M,D
University of Kentucky	M,D
University of Maine	M
University of Maryland, College Park	M,D
University of Michigan	M,D
University of Minnesota, Twin Cities Campus	M,D
University of Nevada, Las Vegas	M
University of New Hampshire	M
The University of North Carolina at Chapel Hill	M,D
The University of North Carolina at Charlotte	M
University of North Dakota	M
University of North Texas	M
University of Oregon	M,D
University of Pittsburgh	M,D
University of Southern California	M,D
The University of Texas at Austin	M,D
The University of Texas at El Paso	M
The University of Texas at San Antonio	M
The University of Texas at Tyler	M
The University of Texas of the Permian Basin	M
The University of Texas–Pan American	M
University of Toledo	M,D
University of Virginia	M,D
University of Wisconsin–Madison	M,D
University of Wisconsin–Milwaukee	M
Washington University in St. Louis	D
West Chester University of Pennsylvania	M,O
Western Washington University	M

■ LANDSCAPE ARCHITECTURE

Institution	Degree
Auburn University	M
Ball State University	M
California State Polytechnic University, Pomona	M
Colorado State University	M,D
Cornell University	M
Florida Agricultural and Mechanical University	M
Florida International University	M
Harvard University	M,D
Iowa State University of Science and Technology	M
Kansas State University	M
Louisiana State University and Agricultural and Mechanical College	M
Mississippi State University	M
Morgan State University	M
North Carolina State University	M
The Ohio State University	M
Oklahoma State University	M,D
The Pennsylvania State University University Park Campus	M
State University of New York College of Environmental Science and Forestry	M
Texas A&M University	M,D
Texas Tech University	M
The University of Arizona	M
University of California, Berkeley	M
University of Colorado at Denver	M
University of Florida	M
University of Georgia	M
University of Idaho	M
University of Illinois at Urbana–Champaign	M
University of Massachusetts Amherst	M
University of Michigan	M,D
University of Minnesota, Twin Cities Campus	M
University of New Mexico	M
University of Oklahoma	M
University of Oregon	M
University of Pennsylvania	M,O
University of Southern California	M,O
The University of Texas at Arlington	M
University of Virginia	M
University of Washington	M
University of Wisconsin–Madison	M
Utah State University	M
Virginia Polytechnic Institute and State University	M
Washington State University	M,D

■ LATIN AMERICAN STUDIES

Institution	Degree
American University	M,O
Arizona State University	M,D
Brown University	M,D
California State University, Los Angeles	M
Columbia University	O
Cornell University	M,D
Duke University	M,D,O
Florida International University	M
Georgetown University	M
The George Washington University	M
Indiana University Bloomington	M
The Johns Hopkins University	M,D,O
La Salle University	M
New York University	M,O
The Ohio State University	M,D,O
Ohio University	M
San Diego State University	M
Tulane University	M,D
University at Albany, State University of New York	M,O
The University of Alabama	M,O
The University of Arizona	M
University of California, Berkeley	M,D
University of California, Los Angeles	M
University of California, San Diego	M
University of California, Santa Barbara	M,D
University of Central Florida	M,O
University of Chicago	M
University of Connecticut	M
University of Florida	M
University of Illinois at Urbana–Champaign	M
University of Kansas	M,O
University of New Mexico	M,D
The University of North Carolina at Chapel Hill	M,D,O
University of Notre Dame	M
University of Pittsburgh	O
The University of Texas at Austin	M,D
University of Wisconsin–Madison	M
Vanderbilt University	M
West Virginia University	M,D

■ LAW

Institution	Degree
American University	P,M
Arizona State University	P
Barry University	P
Baylor University	P
Boston College	P
Boston University	P,M
Brigham Young University	P,M
Campbell University	P
Capital University	P,M
Case Western Reserve University	P,M
The Catholic University of America	P
Chapman University	P,M
City University of New York School of Law at Queens College	P
Cleveland State University	P,M
The College of William and Mary	P
Columbia University	P,M,D
Cornell University	P,M,D
Creighton University	P
DePaul University	P,M
Drake University	P
Duke University	P,M,D
Duquesne University	P
Emory University	P,M,O
Florida Agricultural and Mechanical University	P
Florida International University	P
Florida State University	P
Fordham University	P,M
Friends University	M
George Mason University	P,M
Georgetown University	P,M,D
The George Washington University	P,M,D
Georgia State University	P
Gonzaga University	P
Hamline University	P,M
Harvard University	P,M,D
Hofstra University	P,M
Howard University	P,M
Illinois Institute of Technology	P,M
Indiana University Bloomington	P,M,D
Inter American University of Puerto Rico, Metropolitan Campus	P
John F. Kennedy University	P
The Johns Hopkins University	M,D,O
Louisiana State University and Agricultural and Mechanical College	P,M
Loyola Marymount University	P,M
Loyola University Chicago	P,M,D
Loyola University New Orleans	P
Marquette University	P
Mercer University	P
Minnesota State University Mankato	
Mississippi College	P
New College of California	P
New York University	P,M,D,O
North Carolina Central University	P
Northeastern University	P
Northern Illinois University	P
Northern Kentucky University	P
Northwestern University	P,M,O
Nova Southeastern University	P,M
The Ohio State University	P
Oklahoma City University	P
Pace University, White Plains Campus	P,M,D
Park University	M
Pepperdine University	P
Pontifical Catholic University of Puerto Rico	P
Quinnipiac University	P
Regent University	P
Rutgers, The State University of New Jersey, Camden	P
Rutgers, The State University of New Jersey, Newark	P
St. John's University (NY)	P,M
Saint Louis University	P,M
St. Mary's University of San Antonio	P
St. Thomas University	P,M
Samford University	P,M
Santa Clara University	P,M,O
Seattle University	P
Seton Hall University	P,M
Southern Illinois University Carbondale	P
Southern Methodist University	P,M,D
Southern University and Agricultural and Mechanical College	P
Stanford University	P,M,D
Stetson University	P,M
Suffolk University	P
Syracuse University	P
Temple University	P,M
Texas Southern University	P
Texas Tech University	P
Texas Wesleyan University	P
Touro College	P,M
Tulane University	P,M,D
University at Buffalo, The State University of New York	P,M
The University of Akron	P

Directory of Graduate and Professional Programs by Field
Liberal Studies

Institution	Degree
The University of Alabama	P,M
The University of Arizona	P,M
University of Arkansas	P,M
University of Arkansas at Little Rock	P
University of Baltimore	P,M
University of California, Berkeley	P,M,D
University of California, Davis	P,M
University of California, Los Angeles	P,M
University of Chicago	P,M,D
University of Cincinnati	P
University of Colorado at Boulder	P
University of Connecticut	P
University of Dayton	P
University of Denver	P,M
University of Detroit Mercy	P
University of Florida	P,M,D
University of Georgia	P,M
University of Hawaii at Manoa	P
University of Houston	P,M
University of Idaho	P
University of Illinois at Urbana–Champaign	P,M,D
The University of Iowa	P,M
University of Kansas	P
University of Kentucky	P
University of La Verne	P
University of Louisville	P
University of Maryland	P
University of Maryland, College Park	P
The University of Memphis	P
University of Miami	P,M
University of Michigan	P,M,D
University of Minnesota, Twin Cities Campus	P,M
University of Mississippi	P
University of Missouri–Columbia	P,M
University of Missouri–Kansas City	P,M
The University of Montana–Missoula	P
University of Nebraska–Lincoln	P,M
University of Nevada, Las Vegas	P
University of New Mexico	P
The University of North Carolina at Chapel Hill	P
University of North Dakota	P
University of Notre Dame	P,M,D
University of Oklahoma	P
University of Oregon	P
University of Pennsylvania	P,M,D
University of Pittsburgh	P,M,O
University of Puerto Rico, Río Piedras	P,M
University of Richmond	P
University of St. Thomas (MN)	P
University of San Diego	P,M,O
University of San Francisco	P,M
University of South Carolina	P
The University of South Dakota	P
University of Southern California	P,M
University of Southern Maine	P
The University of Tennessee	P
The University of Texas at Austin	P,M
University of the District of Columbia	P
University of the Pacific	P,M,D
University of Toledo	P
University of Tulsa	P,M
University of Utah	P,M
University of Virginia	P,M,D
University of Washington	P,M,D
University of Wisconsin–Madison	M,D
University of Wyoming	P
Valparaiso University	P,M
Vanderbilt University	P,M
Villanova University	P
Wake Forest University	P,M
Washburn University	P
Washington University in St. Louis	P,M,D
Wayne State University	P,M
Western New England College	P
West Virginia University	P
Widener University	P,M,D
Yale University	P,M,D
Yeshiva University	P,M

■ LEGAL AND JUSTICE STUDIES

Institution	Degree
American University	M,D,O
Arizona State University	M,D
Boston University	M
Capital University	M
Case Western Reserve University	P,M
The Catholic University of America	D,O
College of Charleston	M
DePaul University	M
Governors State University	M
Hofstra University	P,M
Indiana University Bloomington	P,M,D
Marymount University	M,O
Montclair State University	M,O
New York University	M,D
Northeastern University	M,D
Nova Southeastern University	M
Pace University, White Plains Campus	P,M,D
Prairie View A&M University	M,D
Regis University	M,O
Rutgers, The State University of New Jersey, New Brunswick/Piscataway	D
St. John's University (NY)	M
San Francisco State University	M,O
Texas State University-San Marcos	M
University of Baltimore	M
University of California, Berkeley	D
University of Denver	M
University of Illinois at Springfield	M
University of Nebraska–Lincoln	M
University of Nevada, Reno	M
University of Pittsburgh	M,O
University of San Diego	P,M,O
University of the Pacific	P,M,D
University of Washington	P,M,D
University of Wisconsin–Madison	M
Weber State University	M
Webster University	M,O
West Virginia University	M

■ LEISURE STUDIES

Institution	Degree
Aurora University	M
Boston University	M
Bowling Green State University	M
California State University, Long Beach	M
California State University, Northridge	M
Central Michigan University	M
East Carolina University	M
Gallaudet University	M
Howard University	M
Indiana University Bloomington	M,D,O
Murray State University	M
New Mexico Highlands University	M
Oklahoma State University	M,D
The Pennsylvania State University University Park Campus	M,D
Prescott College	M
San Francisco State University	M
Southeast Missouri State University	M
Southern Connecticut State University	M
State University of New York College at Brockport	M
Temple University	M
Texas State University-San Marcos	M
Universidad Metropolitana	M
University of Connecticut	M,D
University of Georgia	M,D
University of Hawaii at Manoa	M
University of Illinois at Urbana–Champaign	M,D
The University of Iowa	M
The University of Memphis	M
University of Minnesota, Twin Cities Campus	M,D
University of Mississippi	M,D
University of Nevada, Las Vegas	M
The University of North Carolina at Chapel Hill	M
University of Northern Iowa	M,D
University of North Texas	M,O
University of South Alabama	M
University of Toledo	M
University of Utah	M,D
University of West Florida	M

■ LIBERAL STUDIES

Institution	Degree
Abilene Christian University	M
Antioch University McGregor	M
Arkansas Tech University	M
Auburn University Montgomery	M
Baker University	M
Boston University	M
Bradley University	M
Brooklyn College of the City University of New York	M
California State University, Sacramento	M
Christian Brothers University	M
Clark University	M
College of Notre Dame of Maryland	M
College of Staten Island of the City University of New York	M
Columbia University	M
Concordia University (IL)	M
Converse College	M
Creighton University	M
Dallas Baptist University	M
Dartmouth College	M
DePaul University	M
Dowling College	M
Duke University	M
Duquesne University	M
East Tennessee State University	M
Elms College	M
Florida Atlantic University	M
Fordham University	M
Fort Hays State University	M
George Mason University	M
Georgetown University	M
Hamline University	M,O
Harvard University	M,O
Henderson State University	M
Houston Baptist University	M
Indiana University–Purdue University Fort Wayne	M
Indiana University South Bend	M
Indiana University Southeast	M
The Johns Hopkins University	M
Kean University	M
Kent State University	M
Lock Haven University of Pennsylvania	M
Louisiana State University and Agricultural and Mechanical College	M
Louisiana State University in Shreveport	M
Manhattanville College	M
Marylhurst University	M
Minnesota State University Moorhead	M
Mississippi College	M
Monmouth University	M
Nazareth College of Rochester	M
New School University	M
North Carolina State University	M
North Central College	M
Northern Arizona University	M
Northwestern University	M
Oakland University	M
Oklahoma City University	M
Queens College of the City University of New York	M
Regis University	M,O
Rollins College	M
Roosevelt University	M
Rutgers, The State University of New Jersey, Camden	M

Directory of Graduate and Professional Programs by Field
Liberal Studies

Institution	Degree
Rutgers, The State University of New Jersey, Newark	M
Sacred Heart University	M
St. Edward's University	M,O
Saint Mary's College of California	M
San Diego State University	M
Spring Hill College	M
State University of New York at Plattsburgh	M
State University of New York College at Brockport	M
State University of New York Empire State College	M
Stony Brook University, State University of New York	M,O
Temple University	M
Texas Christian University	M
Thomas Edison State College	M
Towson University	M
Tulane University	M
University at Albany, State University of New York	M
University of Arkansas at Little Rock	M
University of Central Florida	M
University of Delaware	M
University of Denver	M,O
University of Detroit Mercy	M
The University of Findlay	M
University of Maine	M
The University of Memphis	M
University of Miami	M
University of Michigan–Dearborn	M
University of New Hampshire	M
The University of North Carolina at Charlotte	M
The University of North Carolina at Greensboro	M
The University of North Carolina at Wilmington	M
University of Oklahoma	M
University of Pennsylvania	M
University of Richmond	M
University of St. Thomas (TX)	M
University of Southern Indiana	M
University of South Florida	M
University of Toledo	M
University of Wisconsin–Milwaukee	M
Ursuline College	M
Valparaiso University	M
Vanderbilt University	M
Villanova University	M
Wake Forest University	M
Washburn University	M
West Virginia University	M
Wichita State University	M
Widener University	M
Winthrop University	M

■ LIBRARY SCIENCE

Institution	Degree
Appalachian State University	M,O
Azusa Pacific University	M
The Catholic University of America	M
Central Missouri State University	M,O
Chicago State University	M
Clarion University of Pennsylvania	M,O
Clark Atlanta University	M,O
College of St. Catherine	M
Dominican University	M
Drexel University	M,D,O
East Carolina University	M,O
Emporia State University	M,D
Florida State University	M,D,O
Gratz College	O
Indiana University Bloomington	M,D,O
Indiana University–Purdue University Indianapolis	M
Inter American University of Puerto Rico, San Germán Campus	M
Kent State University	M
Kutztown University of Pennsylvania	M,O
Long Island University, C.W. Post Campus	M,D,O
Louisiana State University and Agricultural and Mechanical College	M,O
Mansfield University of Pennsylvania	M
Marywood University	M
North Carolina Central University	M
Old Dominion University	M,O
Pratt Institute	M
Queens College of the City University of New York	M,O
Rutgers, The State University of New Jersey, New Brunswick/Piscataway	M
St. John's University (NY)	M,O
Sam Houston State University	M
San Jose State University	M
Simmons College	M,D,O
Southern Arkansas University–Magnolia	M
Southern Connecticut State University	M,O
Spalding University	M
Syracuse University	M,O
Tennessee Technological University	M
Texas Woman's University	M,D
Trevecca Nazarene University	M
University at Albany, State University of New York	M,D,O
University at Buffalo, The State University of New York	M,D,O
The University of Alabama	M,D
The University of Arizona	M,D
University of California, Los Angeles	M,D,O
University of Central Arkansas	M
University of Denver	M,D,O
University of Hawaii at Manoa	M,D,O
University of Houston–Clear Lake	M
University of Illinois at Urbana–Champaign	M,D,O
The University of Iowa	M
University of Kentucky	M
University of Maryland, College Park	M
University of Michigan	M,D
University of Missouri–Columbia	M,D,O
The University of North Carolina at Chapel Hill	M,D,O
The University of North Carolina at Greensboro	M
University of North Texas	M,D
University of Oklahoma	M,O
University of Pittsburgh	M,D,O
University of Puerto Rico, Río Piedras	M,O
University of Rhode Island	M
University of South Carolina	M,O
University of Southern Mississippi	M,O
University of South Florida	M
The University of Tennessee	M
The University of Texas at Austin	M,D
University of Washington	M,D
University of Wisconsin–Madison	M,D,O
University of Wisconsin–Milwaukee	M,O
Valdosta State University	M
Wayne State University	M,O
Wright State University	M

■ LIMNOLOGY

Institution	Degree
Baylor University	M,D
Cornell University	D
University of Alaska Fairbanks	M,D
University of Florida	M,D
University of Wisconsin–Madison	M,D
William Paterson University of New Jersey	M

■ LINGUISTICS

Institution	Degree
Arizona State University	M,D
Ball State University	D
Biola University	M,D,O
Boston College	M
Boston University	M,D
Brigham Young University	M,O
Brown University	M,D
California State University, Fresno	M
California State University, Fullerton	M
California State University, Long Beach	M
California State University, Northridge	M
Carnegie Mellon University	M,D
Claremont Graduate University	M,D
Cornell University	M,D
Eastern Michigan University	M
Florida International University	M
Gallaudet University	M
George Mason University	M
Georgetown University	M,D,O
Georgia State University	M
Harvard University	M,D
Hofstra University	M
Indiana State University	M,O
Indiana University Bloomington	M,D,O
Indiana University of Pennsylvania	M,D
Louisiana State University and Agricultural and Mechanical College	M,D
Massachusetts Institute of Technology	D
Michigan State University	M,D
Montclair State University	M
New York University	M,D
Northeastern Illinois University	M
Northern Arizona University	M,D,O
Northwestern University	M,D
Oakland University	M
The Ohio State University	M,D
Ohio University	M
Old Dominion University	M
The Pennsylvania State University University Park Campus	D
Purdue University	M,D
Queens College of the City University of New York	M
Rice University	M,D
Rutgers, The State University of New Jersey, New Brunswick/Piscataway	D
San Diego State University	M,O
San Francisco State University	M
San Jose State University	M,O
Southern Illinois University Carbondale	M
Stanford University	M,D
Stony Brook University, State University of New York	M,D
Syracuse University	M
Teachers College Columbia University	M,D
Temple University	M
Texas Tech University	M
University at Buffalo, The State University of New York	M,D
The University of Alabama	M,D
The University of Arizona	M,D
University of California, Berkeley	M,D
University of California, Davis	M
University of California, Los Angeles	M,D
University of California, San Diego	D
University of California, Santa Barbara	D
University of California, Santa Cruz	M,D
University of Chicago	M,D
University of Colorado at Boulder	M,D
University of Connecticut	M,D
University of Delaware	M,D
University of Florida	M,D,O
University of Georgia	M,D
University of Hawaii at Manoa	M,D
University of Houston	M,D
University of Illinois at Chicago	M
University of Illinois at Urbana–Champaign	M,D
The University of Iowa	M,D
University of Kansas	M,D
University of Maryland, Baltimore County	M

Directory of Graduate and Professional Programs by Field
Management Information Systems

University of Maryland, College Park	M,D
University of Massachusetts Amherst	M,D
University of Massachusetts Boston	M
University of Michigan	M,D
University of Minnesota, Twin Cities Campus	M,D
University of Missouri–St. Louis	M
The University of Montana–Missoula	M,D
University of New Hampshire	M,D
University of New Mexico	M,D
The University of North Carolina at Chapel Hill	M,D
University of North Dakota	M
University of Oregon	M,D
University of Pennsylvania	M,D
University of Pittsburgh	M,D
University of Puerto Rico, Río Piedras	
University of South Carolina	M,D,O
University of Southern California	M,D
University of South Florida	M
The University of Tennessee	D
The University of Texas at Arlington	M,D
The University of Texas at Austin	M,D
The University of Texas at El Paso	M
University of Utah	M
University of Virginia	M
University of Washington	M,D
University of Wisconsin–Madison	M,D
Wayne State University	M
West Virginia University	M
Yale University	D

■ **LOGISTICS**

Arizona State University	M,D
California State University, Hayward	M
Case Western Reserve University	M,D
Colorado Technical University	M,D
East Carolina University	M,D,O
Florida Institute of Technology	M
George Mason University	M
The George Washington University	M
Georgia College & State University	M
Long Island University, C.W. Post Campus	M,O
Massachusetts Institute of Technology	M
Michigan State University	M,D
North Dakota State University	M,D
The Pennsylvania State University University Park Campus	M,D
Rutgers, The State University of New Jersey, Newark	D
Syracuse University	D
Universidad del Turabo	M
University at Buffalo, The State University of New York	M,D
University of Arkansas	M
University of Minnesota, Twin Cities Campus	M,D
University of New Hampshire	M,D
University of New Haven	M,O
The University of Tennessee	M,D
The University of Texas at Arlington	M
University of Washington	O
University of Wisconsin–Madison	M
Virginia Polytechnic Institute and State University	M,D
Wilmington College (DE)	M
Wright State University	M

■ **MANAGEMENT INFORMATION SYSTEMS**

Adelphi University	M
American University	M,O
Appalachian State University	O
Argosy University/Sarasota	M,D
Argosy University/Schaumburg	M,D
Arizona State University	M,D
Arkansas State University	M
Auburn University	M,D
Barry University	M,O
Baylor University	M
Bellevue University	M
Benedictine University	M
Bentley College	M,O
Bernard M. Baruch College of the City University of New York	M,D
Boise State University	M
Boston University	D
Bowie State University	M,O
Brigham Young University	M
California Lutheran University	M
California State University, Dominguez Hills	M
California State University, Fullerton	M
California State University, Hayward	M
California State University, Los Angeles	M
California State University, Northridge	M
California State University, Sacramento	M
Carnegie Mellon University	M,D
Case Western Reserve University	M,D
Central Michigan University	M,O
Central Missouri State University	M
Charleston Southern University	M
City University	M,O
Claremont Graduate University	M,D
Clarkson University	M
Clark University	M
Cleveland State University	M
Colorado State University	M
Colorado Technical University	M,D
Concordia University Wisconsin	M
Cornell University	D
Creighton University	M
Dallas Baptist University	M
DePaul University	M
Dominican University	M
Duquesne University	M
East Carolina University	M,D,O
Eastern Michigan University	M
Edinboro University of Pennsylvania	M,O
Emory University	D
Fairfield University	M,O
Fairleigh Dickinson University, Metropolitan Campus	M,O
Ferris State University	M
Florida Agricultural and Mechanical University	M
Florida Institute of Technology	M
Florida International University	D
Florida State University	M,D
Fordham University	M
Friends University	M
The George Washington University	M
Georgia College & State University	M
Georgia Institute of Technology	M,D,O
Georgia Southwestern State University	M
Georgia State University	M,D
Governors State University	M
Harvard University	D
Hawai'i Pacific University	M
Hofstra University	M,O
Holy Family University	M
Houston Baptist University	M
Howard University	M
Idaho State University	M,O
Illinois Institute of Technology	M,D
Illinois State University	M
Indiana University Bloomington	M,D
Indiana University South Bend	M
Indiana University Southeast	M,O
Inter American University of Puerto Rico, San Germán Campus	M
Iowa State University of Science and Technology	M
Jackson State University	M
The Johns Hopkins University	M,O
Kean University	M
Kennesaw State University	M
Kent State University	D
Lawrence Technological University	M,D
Lindenwood University	M
Long Island University, C.W. Post Campus	M,O
Louisiana State University and Agricultural and Mechanical College	M,D
Loyola University Chicago	M
Marist College	M
Marymount University	M,O
Maryville University of Saint Louis	M,O
Marywood University	M
Metropolitan State University	M
Miami University	M
Michigan State University	M,D
Middle Tennessee State University	M
Mississippi State University	M
Montclair State University	M
National University	M
Newman University	M
New York Institute of Technology	M,O
New York University	M,D,O
North Central College	M
Northeastern University	M
Northern Arizona University	M
Northern Illinois University	M
Northwestern University	M
Northwest Missouri State University	M
Norwich University	M
Nova Southeastern University	M
Oakland University	M,O
The Ohio State University	M,D
Oklahoma City University	M
Oklahoma State University	M,D
Pace University	M
Pace University, White Plains Campus	M
Park University	M
The Pennsylvania State University Harrisburg Campus of the Capital College	M
The Pennsylvania State University University Park Campus	M,D
Philadelphia University	M
Polytechnic University, Westchester Graduate Center	M,O
Prairie View A&M University	M,D
Purdue University	M,D
Quinnipiac University	M
Regis University	M,O
Rensselaer Polytechnic Institute	M,D
Rivier College	M
Robert Morris University	M,D
Rochester Institute of Technology	O
Roosevelt University	M
Rutgers, The State University of New Jersey, Newark	M,D
Sacred Heart University	M,O
St. Edward's University	M,O
St. John's University (NY)	M,O
Saint Joseph's University	M
Saint Peter's College	M
Salve Regina University	M,O
San Diego State University	M
San Jose State University	M
Seattle Pacific University	M
Seton Hall University	M,O
Shenandoah University	M,O
Southeastern University	M
Southern Illinois University Edwardsville	M
Southwest Missouri State University	M
Stevens Institute of Technology	M,D,O
Stony Brook University, State University of New York	M,O
Strayer University	M
Syracuse University	M,D,O
Temple University	M,D
Texas A&M International University	M
Texas A&M University	M,D

Peterson's Graduate Schools in the U.S. 2006

Directory of Graduate and Professional Programs by Field
Management Information Systems

Institution	Degree
Texas Tech University	M,D,O
Towson University	M,D,O
Troy University Dothan	M
Troy University Montgomery	M
University at Albany, State University of New York	M
University at Buffalo, The State University of New York	M,D
The University of Akron	M
The University of Alabama in Huntsville	M
The University of Arizona	M,D
University of Arkansas	M
University of Baltimore	M
University of Central Florida	M
University of Cincinnati	M
University of Colorado at Colorado Springs	M
University of Colorado at Denver	M,D
University of Delaware	M
University of Denver	M
University of Detroit Mercy	M
University of Florida	M,D
University of Hawaii at Manoa	M,D
University of Houston–Clear Lake	M
University of Illinois at Chicago	M,D
University of Illinois at Springfield	M
The University of Iowa	M
University of Kansas	M,D
University of La Verne	M
University of Maine	M
University of Mary Hardin-Baylor	M
University of Maryland, Baltimore County	M,D,O
University of Maryland University College	M,O
The University of Memphis	M,D
University of Miami	M
University of Minnesota, Twin Cities Campus	M,D
University of Mississippi	M,D
University of Missouri–St. Louis	M,D,O
University of Nebraska at Omaha	M,D
University of Nebraska–Lincoln	M
University of Nevada, Las Vegas	M
University of New Haven	M
University of New Mexico	M
The University of North Carolina at Chapel Hill	D
The University of North Carolina at Greensboro	M
University of North Texas	M,D
University of Oklahoma	M
University of Oregon	M
University of Pennsylvania	M,D
University of Pittsburgh	M
University of Rhode Island	M,D
University of St. Thomas (MN)	M
University of San Francisco	M
The University of Scranton	M
University of Southern California	M
University of Southern Mississippi	M
University of South Florida	M,D
The University of Tampa	M
The University of Texas at Arlington	M,D
The University of Texas at Austin	D
The University of Texas at Dallas	M
The University of Texas at San Antonio	M
The University of Texas–Pan American	M,D
University of the Sacred Heart	M
University of Toledo	M,D
University of Virginia	M
University of Wisconsin–Madison	M,D
University of Wisconsin–Oshkosh	M
University of Wisconsin–Whitewater	M
Utah State University	M,D
Virginia Commonwealth University	M,D
Virginia Polytechnic Institute and State University	M,D,O
Washington State University	M
Wayland Baptist University	M
Webster University	M,D,O
Western International University	M
Western New England College	M
Wilmington College (DE)	M
Worcester Polytechnic Institute	M,O
Wright State University	M
Xavier University	M

■ MANAGEMENT OF TECHNOLOGY

Institution	Degree
Bentley College	M,O
Boston University	M
California Polytechnic State University, San Luis Obispo	M
California University of Pennsylvania	M
Carlow University	M
Carnegie Mellon University	M,D
Central Connecticut State University	M
Dallas Baptist University	M
East Carolina University	M,D,O
Embry-Riddle Aeronautical University, Extended Campus	M
Fairfield University	M
Fairleigh Dickinson University, College at Florham	M,O
George Mason University	M,D
The George Washington University	M,D
Georgia Institute of Technology	M,O
Idaho State University	M
Illinois State University	D
Indiana State University	M
Iona College	M,O
The Johns Hopkins University	M
Kean University	M
La Salle University	M
Lawrence Technological University	M,D
Marquette University	M
Marshall University	M
Mercer University	M
Murray State University	M
National University	M
New Jersey Institute of Technology	M,D
New York Institute of Technology	M
New York University	M,D,O
North Carolina Agricultural and Technical State University	M
North Carolina State University	D
Northern Kentucky University	M
Ohio University	M
Oklahoma State University	M
Pacific Lutheran University	M
Polytechnic University, Brooklyn Campus	M
Portland State University	M,O
Regis University	M
Rensselaer Polytechnic Institute	M,D
Saginaw Valley State University	M
St. Ambrose University	M
State University of New York Institute of Technology	M
Stevens Institute of Technology	M,D,O
Stony Brook University, State University of New York	M,O
Texas A&M University–Commerce	M
Texas State University-San Marcos	M
The University of Akron	M
University of Bridgeport	M
University of Cincinnati	M,D
University of Colorado at Boulder	M,D
University of Colorado at Colorado Springs	M
University of Delaware	M
University of Denver	M,O
University of Illinois at Urbana–Champaign	M
University of Maryland University College	M,O
University of Miami	M,D
University of Minnesota, Twin Cities Campus	M
University of New Hampshire	M
University of New Haven	M
University of New Mexico	M
University of Pennsylvania	M
University of St. Thomas (MN)	M,O
The University of Scranton	M
The University of Tampa	M
The University of Texas at San Antonio	M
University of Tulsa	M
University of Wisconsin–Stout	M
Vanderbilt University	M,D
Washington State University	M,D

■ MANAGEMENT STRATEGY AND POLICY

Institution	Degree
Azusa Pacific University	M
Bernard M. Baruch College of the City University of New York	M,D
Brenau University	M
Case Western Reserve University	M,D
Claremont Graduate University	M,D,O
DePaul University	M
Dominican University of California	M
Drexel University	M,D,O
The George Washington University	M,D
Georgia Institute of Technology	M,D,O
Illinois Institute of Technology	M
Lamar University	M
Manhattanville College	M
Marymount University	M,O
Michigan State University	D
New York Institute of Technology	M
Northwestern University	D
Pace University	M
Purdue University	M,D
Regent University	M,D,O
Rutgers, The State University of New Jersey, Newark	M
Stevens Institute of Technology	M
Syracuse University	D
Temple University	M,D
Tufts University	O
The University of Arizona	M
University of Houston–Clear Lake	M
The University of Iowa	M
University of Minnesota, Twin Cities Campus	M,D
University of New Haven	M
University of New Mexico	M
The University of North Carolina at Chapel Hill	D
University of North Texas	M,D

■ MANUFACTURING ENGINEERING

Institution	Degree
Boston University	M,D
Bowling Green State University	M
Bradley University	M
Brigham Young University	M
California Polytechnic State University, San Luis Obispo	M
Central Connecticut State University	M
Colorado State University	M,D
Cornell University	M,D
Dartmouth College	M,D
Drexel University	M,D
East Carolina University	M,D,O
Eastern Kentucky University	M
East Tennessee State University	M
Grand Valley State University	M
Illinois Institute of Technology	M,D
Kansas State University	M,D
Lawrence Technological University	M,D
Lehigh University	M
Louisiana Tech University	M,D
Marquette University	M,D
Massachusetts Institute of Technology	

Michigan State University	M,D
Minnesota State University Mankato	M
New Jersey Institute of Technology	M
North Carolina State University	M
North Dakota State University	M,D
Northeastern University	M,D
Northwestern University	M
Ohio University	M,D
Oklahoma State University	M
Old Dominion University	M,D
Oregon State University	M,D
The Pennsylvania State University University Park Campus	M
Polytechnic University, Brooklyn Campus	M
Portland State University	M
Purdue University	M,D
Rensselaer Polytechnic Institute	M
Rochester Institute of Technology	M
Southern Illinois University Carbondale	M
Southern Methodist University	M,D
Syracuse University	M
Texas Tech University	M,D
Tufts University	O
University of California, Los Angeles	M
University of Central Florida	M,D,O
University of Colorado at Colorado Springs	M
University of Detroit Mercy	M,D
University of Houston	M
The University of Iowa	M,D
University of Kentucky	M
University of Maryland, College Park	M,D
University of Massachusetts Amherst	M
University of Massachusetts Lowell	M,D,O
The University of Memphis	M
University of Michigan	M,D
University of Michigan–Dearborn	M,D
University of Missouri–Columbia	M,D
University of Missouri–Rolla	M
University of Nebraska–Lincoln	M,D
University of New Mexico	M
University of Rhode Island	M
University of St. Thomas (MN)	M,O
University of Southern California	M
University of Southern Maine	M
The University of Tennessee	M,D
The University of Texas at Austin	M,D
The University of Texas at El Paso	M
University of Wisconsin–Madison	M
Villanova University	M,O
Wayne State University	M
Western Michigan University	M
Western New England College	M
Wichita State University	M
Worcester Polytechnic Institute	M,D,O

■ MARINE AFFAIRS

Duke University	M,D
East Carolina University	D
Florida Institute of Technology	M,D
Louisiana State University and Agricultural and Mechanical College	M,D
Nova Southeastern University	M
Oregon State University	M
Stevens Institute of Technology	M
University of Delaware	M,D
University of Maine	M
University of Miami	M
University of Rhode Island	M,D
University of San Diego	M
University of Washington	M
University of West Florida	M

■ MARINE BIOLOGY

California State University, Stanislaus	M
College of Charleston	M
Florida Institute of Technology	M
Florida State University	M,D
Murray State University	M
Nicholls State University	M
Nova Southeastern University	M,D
Rutgers, The State University of New Jersey, New Brunswick/Piscataway	M,D
San Francisco State University	M
Texas State University–San Marcos	M
University of Alaska Fairbanks	M,D
University of California, San Diego	M,D
University of California, Santa Barbara	M,D
University of Colorado at Boulder	M,D
University of Guam	M
University of Hawaii at Manoa	M,D
University of Maine	M,D
University of Massachusetts Dartmouth	M
University of Miami	M,D
The University of North Carolina at Wilmington	M,D
University of Oregon	M,D
University of Southern California	D
University of Southern Mississippi	M,D
Western Illinois University	M,O

■ MARINE SCIENCES

California State University, Fresno	M
California State University, Hayward	M
California State University, Sacramento	M
The College of William and Mary	M,D
Cornell University	M,D
Duke University	M,D
Florida Institute of Technology	M,D
Murray State University	M
North Carolina State University	M,D
Nova Southeastern University	M
Oregon State University	M
San Jose State University	M
Savannah State University	M
Stony Brook University, State University of New York	M,D
University of Alaska Fairbanks	M,D
University of California, San Diego	M,D
University of California, Santa Barbara	M,D
University of California, Santa Cruz	M,D
University of Connecticut	M,D
University of Delaware	M,D
University of Florida	M,D
University of Georgia	M,D
University of Maine	M,D
University of Maryland	M,D
University of Maryland, Baltimore County	M,D
University of Maryland, College Park	M,D
University of Maryland Eastern Shore	M,D
University of Massachusetts Boston	D
University of Massachusetts Dartmouth	M,D
University of Miami	M,D
The University of North Carolina at Chapel Hill	M,D
The University of North Carolina at Wilmington	M
University of Puerto Rico, Mayagüez Campus	M,D
University of San Diego	M
University of South Alabama	M,D
University of South Carolina	M,D
University of Southern California	D
University of Southern Mississippi	M,D
University of South Florida	M,D
The University of Texas at Austin	M,D
University of Wisconsin–La Crosse	M
University of Wisconsin–Madison	M,D

■ MARKETING

Adelphi University	M
Alabama Agricultural and Mechanical University	M
American University	M
Andrews University	M
Argosy University/Sarasota	M,D
Argosy University/Schaumburg	M,D
Arizona State University	M,D
Bayamón Central University	M
Bentley College	M,O
Bernard M. Baruch College of the City University of New York	M,D
Boston University	D
California Lutheran University	M
California State University, Fullerton	M
California State University, Hayward	M
California State University, Los Angeles	M
Carnegie Mellon University	D
Case Western Reserve University	M,D
Central Michigan University	M
City University	M,O
Claremont Graduate University	M
Clark Atlanta University	M
Clark University	M
Columbia University	M,D
Concordia University Wisconsin	M
Cornell University	D
Dallas Baptist University	M
Delta State University	M
DePaul University	M
Drexel University	M,D,O
Eastern Michigan University	M
Eastern University	M
Emerson College	M
Emory University	D
Fairfield University	M,O
Fairleigh Dickinson University, College at Florham	M
Fairleigh Dickinson University, Metropolitan Campus	M,O
Florida Agricultural and Mechanical University	M
Florida Atlantic University	M
Florida State University	M,D
Fordham University	M
The George Washington University	M,D
Georgia Institute of Technology	M,D,O
Georgia State University	M,D
Hawai'i Pacific University	M
Hofstra University	M,O
Howard University	M
Illinois Institute of Technology	M
Indiana University Bloomington	M,D
Indiana University Southeast	M,O
Inter American University of Puerto Rico, Metropolitan Campus	M
Inter American University of Puerto Rico, San Germán Campus	M
Iona College	M,O
The Johns Hopkins University	M,O
Johnson & Wales University	M
Kennesaw State University	M
Kent State University	D
Lindenwood University	M
Long Island University, C.W. Post Campus	M,O
Louisiana State University and Agricultural and Mechanical College	M,D
Louisiana Tech University	M,D
Loyola College in Maryland	M
Loyola University Chicago	M
Lynn University	M,D
Maryville University of Saint Louis	M,O
Mercy College	M
Metropolitan State University	M
Miami University	M
Michigan State University	M,D
Middle Tennessee State University	M
Mississippi State University	M,D
Montclair State University	M
National University	M
New York Institute of Technology	M,O
New York University	M,D
Northeastern Illinois University	M

Directory of Graduate and Professional Programs by Field
Marketing

Northwestern University	M,D
Oklahoma City University	M
Oklahoma State University	M,D
Oral Roberts University	M
Pace University	M
Pace University, White Plains Campus	M
The Pennsylvania State University University Park Campus	D
Philadelphia University	M
Pontifical Catholic University of Puerto Rico	M,D
Purdue University	M,D
Quinnipiac University	M
Regis University	M,O
Rensselaer Polytechnic Institute	M,D
Rutgers, The State University of New Jersey, Newark	M,D
Sage Graduate School	M
St. Bonaventure University	M,O
St. Cloud State University	M
St. Edward's University	M,O
St. John's University (NY)	M,O
Saint Joseph's University	M,O
Saint Peter's College	M
St. Thomas Aquinas College	M
Saint Xavier University	M,O
San Diego State University	M
Seton Hall University	M,O
Southeastern University	M
State University of New York at New Paltz	M
Stephen F. Austin State University	M
Syracuse University	D
Temple University	M,D
Texas A&M University	M,D
Texas Tech University	M,D
Troy University Dothan	M
Universidad del Turabo	M
Universidad Metropolitana	M
University at Albany, State University of New York	M
The University of Akron	M
The University of Alabama	M,D
The University of Arizona	D
University of Baltimore	M
University of California, Berkeley	D
University of Central Florida	D
University of Cincinnati	M,D
University of Colorado at Boulder	M,D
University of Colorado at Colorado Springs	M
University of Colorado at Denver	M
University of Connecticut	M,D
University of Denver	M
The University of Findlay	M
University of Florida	M,D
University of Hawaii at Manoa	M,D
University of Houston	D
The University of Iowa	M,D
University of La Verne	M
The University of Memphis	M,D
University of Miami	M
University of Minnesota, Twin Cities Campus	M,D
University of Missouri–St. Louis	M,O
University of Nebraska–Lincoln	M,D
University of New Haven	M
University of New Mexico	M
The University of North Carolina at Chapel Hill	D
The University of North Carolina at Greensboro	M,D
University of North Texas	M,D
University of Oregon	D
University of Pennsylvania	M,D
University of Rhode Island	M,D
University of St. Thomas (MN)	M
University of San Francisco	M
The University of Scranton	M
University of South Florida	M,D
The University of Tampa	M
The University of Tennessee	M,D
The University of Tennessee at Chattanooga	M
The University of Texas at Arlington	M,D
The University of Texas at Austin	D
The University of Texas at San Antonio	M
University of the Sacred Heart	M
University of Toledo	M
University of Wisconsin–Whitewater	M
Vanderbilt University	D
Virginia Commonwealth University	M
Virginia Polytechnic Institute and State University	M,D
Wagner College	M
Webster University	M,D
Western International University	M
Western New England College	M
West Virginia University	M
Wilkes University	M
Worcester Polytechnic Institute	M,O
Wright State University	M
Xavier University	M
Yale University	D
Youngstown State University	M

■ **MARKETING RESEARCH**

Hofstra University	M,O
Pace University	M
Pace University, White Plains Campus	M
Southern Illinois University Edwardsville	M
University of Georgia	M
The University of Texas at Arlington	M
University of Wisconsin–Madison	M,D

■ **MARRIAGE AND FAMILY THERAPY**

Abilene Christian University	M
Antioch New England Graduate School	M
Appalachian State University	M
Azusa Pacific University	M,D
Barry University	M,O
Brigham Young University	M,D
California Baptist University	M
California Lutheran University	M
California State University, Bakersfield	M,O
California State University, Chico	M
California State University, Dominguez Hills	M
California State University, Fresno	M
California State University, Northridge	M,O
Central Connecticut State University	M
Chapman University	M
The College of New Jersey	O
The College of William and Mary	M,D
Converse College	O
Drexel University	M,D
East Carolina University	M
Eastern Nazarene College	M
East Tennessee State University	M
Edgewood College	M
Fairfield University	M
Fitchburg State College	M,O
Florida Atlantic University	M,O
Florida State University	M,D
Friends University	M
Geneva College	M
George Fox University	M
Harding University	M
Hardin-Simmons University	M
Hofstra University	M,O
Hope International University	M,O
Idaho State University	M,D
Indiana State University	M
Indiana Wesleyan University	M
Iona College	M,O
Iowa State University of Science and Technology	M,D
Kean University	M,O
Kutztown University of Pennsylvania	M
La Salle University	D
Loma Linda University	M,D
Loyola Marymount University	M
Mercy College	M,O
Michigan State University	M,D
Montclair State University	M
Northwestern University	M
Notre Dame de Namur University	M
Nova Southeastern University	M,D,O
Our Lady of the Lake University of San Antonio	M,D
Pacific Lutheran University	M
Palm Beach Atlantic University	M
Prairie View A&M University	M
Purdue University	M,D
Purdue University Calumet	M
Saint Joseph College	M,O
Saint Louis University	M,D,O
Saint Mary's College of California	M
Saint Mary's University of Minnesota	M,O
St. Mary's University of San Antonio	M,D,O
St. Thomas University	M,O
San Francisco State University	M
Santa Clara University	M
Seattle Pacific University	M
Seton Hall University	M,D,O
Sonoma State University	M
Southern Connecticut State University	M
Southern Nazarene University	M
Springfield College	M,O
Stetson University	M
Syracuse University	M,D
Texas Tech University	M,D
Texas Woman's University	M,D
Trevecca Nazarene University	M
The University of Akron	M
The University of Alabama at Birmingham	M
University of Florida	M,D,O
University of Great Falls	M
University of Houston–Clear Lake	M
University of La Verne	M
University of Louisiana at Monroe	M,D
University of Maryland, College Park	M,D
University of Massachusetts Boston	M,O
University of Miami	M,O
University of Mobile	M
University of Nevada, Las Vegas	M
University of New Hampshire	M
The University of North Carolina at Greensboro	M,D,O
University of Pittsburgh	O
University of Rochester	M
University of St. Thomas (MN)	M,D,O
University of San Diego	M
University of San Francisco	M,D
University of Southern California	M,D,O
University of Southern Mississippi	M
University of Wisconsin–Stout	M
Utah State University	M,D
Valdosta State University	M
Virginia Polytechnic Institute and State University	M
Western Illinois University	M,O
Western Michigan University	M,D

■ **MASS COMMUNICATION**

American University	M
Auburn University	M
Boston University	M
Brigham Young University	M
California State University, Fresno	M
California State University, Northridge	M
Central Michigan University	M
Central Missouri State University	M
The College of Saint Rose	M

Directory of Graduate and Professional Programs by Field
Materials Sciences

Institution	Degree
Florida International University	M
Florida State University	M,D
Fordham University	M
The George Washington University	M
Grambling State University	M
Howard University	M,D
Indiana University Bloomington	M,D
Iowa State University of Science and Technology	M
Jackson State University	M
Kansas State University	M
Kent State University	M
Lindenwood University	M
Louisiana State University and Agricultural and Mechanical College	M,D
Loyola University New Orleans	M
Lynn University	M,D
Marquette University	M
Marshall University	M
Miami University	M
Middle Tennessee State University	M
Murray State University	M
New School University	M
North Dakota State University	M,D
Oklahoma State University	M,D
The Pennsylvania State University University Park Campus	M,D
Point Park University	M
St. Cloud State University	M
San Diego State University	M
San Jose State University	M
Seton Hall University	M
Southern Illinois University Edwardsville	M
Southern University and Agricultural and Mechanical College	M
Stephen F. Austin State University	M
Syracuse University	D
Temple University	D
Texas State University–San Marcos	M
Texas Tech University	M
University of Colorado at Boulder	M,D
University of Denver	M
University of Florida	M,D
University of Georgia	M,D
University of Houston	M
University of Illinois at Chicago	M
The University of Iowa	M,D
University of Louisiana at Lafayette	M
University of Maryland, College Park	D
University of Michigan	D
University of Minnesota, Twin Cities Campus	M,D
University of Nebraska–Lincoln	M
University of Nevada, Las Vegas	M
The University of North Carolina at Chapel Hill	M,D
University of Oklahoma	M
University of Puerto Rico, Río Piedras	M
The University of South Dakota	M
University of Southern California	D
University of Southern Mississippi	M,D
University of South Florida	M
University of the Sacred Heart	M
University of Wisconsin–Madison	M,D
University of Wisconsin–Milwaukee	M
University of Wisconsin–Stevens Point	M
University of Wisconsin–Superior	M
University of Wisconsin–Whitewater	M
Virginia Commonwealth University	M

■ MATERIALS ENGINEERING

Institution	Degree
Arizona State University	M,D
Auburn University	M,D
Boise State University	M
California State University, Northridge	M
Carnegie Mellon University	M,D
Case Western Reserve University	M,D
Clemson University	M,D
Colorado State University	M,D
Columbia University	M,D
Cornell University	M,D
Dartmouth College	M,D
Drexel University	M,D
Georgia Institute of Technology	M,D
Illinois Institute of Technology	M,D
Iowa State University of Science and Technology	M,D
The Johns Hopkins University	M,D
Lehigh University	M,D
Massachusetts Institute of Technology	M,D,O
Michigan State University	M,D
Michigan Technological University	M,D
New Jersey Institute of Technology	M,D
New Mexico Institute of Mining and Technology	M,D
North Carolina State University	M,D
Northwestern University	M,D,O
The Ohio State University	M,D
Old Dominion University	M
The Pennsylvania State University University Park Campus	M,D
Purdue University	M,D
Rensselaer Polytechnic Institute	M,D
Rochester Institute of Technology	M
Rutgers, The State University of New Jersey, New Brunswick/Piscataway	M,D
San Jose State University	M
Stanford University	M,D,O
Stevens Institute of Technology	M,D,O
Stony Brook University, State University of New York	M,D
Texas A&M University	M,D
Tuskegee University	D
The University of Alabama	M,D
The University of Alabama at Birmingham	M,D
The University of Arizona	M,D
University of California, Berkeley	M,D
University of California, Davis	M,D
University of California, Irvine	M,D
University of California, Los Angeles	M,D
University of California, Santa Barbara	M,D
University of Central Florida	M,D
University of Cincinnati	M,D
University of Connecticut	M,D
University of Dayton	M
University of Delaware	M,D
University of Florida	M,D,O
University of Houston	M,D
University of Illinois at Chicago	M,D
University of Illinois at Urbana–Champaign	M,D
University of Maryland, College Park	M,D,O
University of Massachusetts Lowell	M,D
University of Michigan	M,D
University of Minnesota, Twin Cities Campus	M,D
University of Nebraska–Lincoln	M,D
University of Pennsylvania	M,D
University of Pittsburgh	M,D
University of Southern California	M
The University of Tennessee	M,D
The University of Texas at Arlington	M,D
The University of Texas at Austin	M,D
The University of Texas at El Paso	D
University of Utah	M,D
University of Washington	M,D
Virginia Polytechnic Institute and State University	M,D
Washington State University	M,D
Wayne State University	M,D,O
Western Michigan University	M
Worcester Polytechnic Institute	M,D,O
Wright State University	M

■ MATERIALS SCIENCES

Institution	Degree
Alabama Agricultural and Mechanical University	M,D
Alfred University	M,D
Arizona State University	M,D
Brown University	M,D
California Institute of Technology	M,D
California Polytechnic State University, San Luis Obispo	M
Carnegie Mellon University	M,D
Case Western Reserve University	M,D
Clemson University	M,D
Columbia University	M,D,O
Cornell University	M,D
Dartmouth College	M,D
Duke University	M,D
The George Washington University	M,D
Illinois Institute of Technology	M,D
Iowa State University of Science and Technology	M,D
Jackson State University	M
The Johns Hopkins University	M,D
Lehigh University	M,D
Massachusetts Institute of Technology	M,D,O
Michigan State University	M,D
New Jersey Institute of Technology	M,D
Norfolk State University	M
North Carolina State University	M,D
Northwestern University	M,D,O
The Ohio State University	M,D
Ohio University	D
Old Dominion University	M
Oregon State University	M
The Pennsylvania State University University Park Campus	M,D
Polytechnic University, Brooklyn Campus	M
Rensselaer Polytechnic Institute	M,D
Rice University	M,D
Rochester Institute of Technology	M
Rutgers, The State University of New Jersey, New Brunswick/Piscataway	M,D
Southwest Missouri State University	M
Stanford University	M,D,O
Stevens Institute of Technology	M,D,O
Stony Brook University, State University of New York	M,D
University at Albany, State University of New York	M,D
University at Buffalo, The State University of New York	M,O
The University of Alabama	D
The University of Alabama at Birmingham	D
The University of Alabama in Huntsville	M,D
The University of Arizona	M,D
University of California, Berkeley	M,D
University of California, Davis	M,D
University of California, Irvine	M,D
University of California, Los Angeles	M,D
University of California, San Diego	M,D
University of California, Santa Barbara	M,D
University of Central Florida	M,D
University of Cincinnati	M,D
University of Connecticut	M,D
University of Delaware	M,D
University of Denver	M,D
University of Florida	M,D,O
University of Illinois at Urbana–Champaign	M,D
University of Kentucky	M,D
University of Maryland, College Park	M,D,O
University of Michigan	M,D
University of Minnesota, Twin Cities Campus	M,D
University of New Hampshire	M,D
The University of North Carolina at Chapel Hill	M,D
University of North Texas	M,D
University of Pennsylvania	M,D
University of Pittsburgh	M,D
University of Rochester	M,D

Peterson's Graduate Schools in the U.S. 2006

Directory of Graduate and Professional Programs by Field
Materials Sciences

Institution	Degree
University of Southern California	M,D,O
The University of Tennessee	M,D
The University of Texas at Arlington	M,D
The University of Texas at Austin	M,D
The University of Texas at El Paso	D
University of Utah	M,D
University of Vermont	M,D
University of Virginia	M,D
University of Washington	M,D
University of Wisconsin–Madison	M,D
Vanderbilt University	M,D
Virginia Polytechnic Institute and State University	M,D
Washington State University	M,D
Wayne State University	M,D,O
Western Michigan University	M
Worcester Polytechnic Institute	M,D,O
Wright State University	M

■ MATERNAL/CHILD NURSING

Institution	Degree
Baylor University	M
Boston College	M,D
Columbia University	M,O
Duke University	M,O
Hardin-Simmons University	M
Hunter College of the City University of New York	M
Indiana University–Purdue University Indianapolis	M
Lehman College of the City University of New York	M
Marquette University	M,D,O
Pontifical Catholic University of Puerto Rico	M
Rutgers, The State University of New Jersey, Newark	M
Saint Joseph College	M,O
Stony Brook University, State University of New York	M,O
University at Buffalo, The State University of New York	M,D,O
The University of Alabama in Huntsville	M,O
University of Cincinnati	M,D
University of Colorado at Colorado Springs	M
University of Delaware	M,O
University of Illinois at Chicago	M
University of Maryland	M,D
University of Missouri–Kansas City	M,D
University of Pennsylvania	M,O
University of South Alabama	M
University of Southern Mississippi	M,D
Vanderbilt University	M,D
Wayne State University	M
Wichita State University	M

■ MATERNAL AND CHILD HEALTH

Institution	Degree
Boston University	M,O
Columbia University	M
Emory University	M
The George Washington University	M,O
Harvard University	M,D,O
Oakland University	M,D,O
Tulane University	M,D
The University of Alabama at Birmingham	M
University of California, Berkeley	M
University of Minnesota, Twin Cities Campus	M
The University of North Carolina at Chapel Hill	M,D
University of Washington	M,D

■ MATHEMATICAL AND COMPUTATIONAL FINANCE

Institution	Degree
Bernard M. Baruch College of the City University of New York	M
Boston University	M,D
Carnegie Mellon University	M,D
Florida State University	M,D
Georgia Institute of Technology	M,D
New York University	M,D
North Carolina State University	M
Polytechnic University, Westchester Graduate Center	M,O
Purdue University	M,D
Rice University	M,D
Stanford University	M,D
University of Chicago	M
University of Connecticut	M,D
The University of North Carolina at Charlotte	M
University of Pittsburgh	M,D

■ MATHEMATICAL PHYSICS

Institution	Degree
New Mexico Institute of Mining and Technology	M,D
Princeton University	D
University of Colorado at Boulder	M,D
Virginia Polytechnic Institute and State University	M,D

■ MATHEMATICS

Institution	Degree
Alabama State University	M,O
American University	M
Andrews University	M
Appalachian State University	M
Arizona State University	M,D
Arkansas State University	M
Auburn University	M,D
Ball State University	M
Baylor University	M,D
Boston College	M
Boston University	M,D
Bowling Green State University	M,D,O
Brandeis University	M,D
Brigham Young University	M,D
Brooklyn College of the City University of New York	M,D
Brown University	M,D
California Institute of Technology	D
California Polytechnic State University, San Luis Obispo	M
California State Polytechnic University, Pomona	M
California State University, Fresno	M
California State University, Fullerton	M
California State University, Hayward	M
California State University, Long Beach	M
California State University, Los Angeles	M
California State University, Northridge	M
California State University, Sacramento	M
California State University, San Bernardino	M
California State University, San Marcos	M
Carnegie Mellon University	M,D
Case Western Reserve University	M,D
Central Connecticut State University	M
Central Michigan University	M,D
Central Missouri State University	M
Central Washington University	M
Chicago State University	M
City College of the City University of New York	M
Claremont Graduate University	M,D
Clarkson University	M,D
Clemson University	M,D
Cleveland State University	M
College of Charleston	M
Colorado State University	M,D
Columbia University	M,D
Cornell University	D
Dartmouth College	D
Delaware State University	M
DePaul University	M
Dowling College	M
Drexel University	M,D
Duke University	D
Duquesne University	M
East Carolina University	M
Eastern Illinois University	M
Eastern Kentucky University	M
Eastern Michigan University	M
Eastern New Mexico University	M
Eastern Washington University	M
East Tennessee State University	M
Emory University	M,D
Emporia State University	M
Fairfield University	M
Fayetteville State University	M
Florida Atlantic University	M,D
Florida International University	M
Florida State University	M,D
George Mason University	M
The George Washington University	M,D
Georgia Institute of Technology	M,D
Georgian Court University	M,O
Georgia Southern University	M
Georgia State University	M
Harvard University	M,D
Hofstra University	M
Howard University	M,D
Hunter College of the City University of New York	M
Idaho State University	M
Illinois State University	M
Indiana State University	M
Indiana University Bloomington	M,D
Indiana University of Pennsylvania	M
Indiana University–Purdue University Fort Wayne	M
Indiana University–Purdue University Indianapolis	M,D
Iowa State University of Science and Technology	M,D
Jackson State University	M
Jacksonville State University	M
John Carroll University	M
The Johns Hopkins University	M,D
Kansas State University	M,D
Kean University	M
Kent State University	M,D
Kutztown University of Pennsylvania	M
Lamar University	M
Lehigh University	M,D
Lehman College of the City University of New York	M
Long Island University, C.W. Post Campus	M
Louisiana State University and Agricultural and Mechanical College	M,D
Louisiana Tech University	M
Loyola University Chicago	M
Marquette University	M,D
Marshall University	M
Massachusetts Institute of Technology	D
McNeese State University	M
Miami University	M
Michigan State University	M,D
Michigan Technological University	M,D
Middle Tennessee State University	M
Minnesota State University Mankato	M
Mississippi College	M
Mississippi State University	M,D
Montana State University–Bozeman	M,D
Montclair State University	M
Morgan State University	M
Murray State University	M
New Jersey Institute of Technology	D
New Mexico Institute of Mining and Technology	M,D
New Mexico State University	M,D
New York University	M,D
Nicholls State University	M
North Carolina Central University	M

Peterson's Graduate Schools in the U.S. 2006

Institution	Degree
North Carolina State University	M,D
North Dakota State University	M,D
Northeastern Illinois University	M
Northeastern University	M,D
Northern Arizona University	M
Northern Illinois University	M,D
Northwestern University	D
Oakland University	M
The Ohio State University	M,D
Ohio University	M,D
Oklahoma State University	M,D
Old Dominion University	M,D
Oregon State University	M,D
The Pennsylvania State University University Park Campus	M,D
Pittsburg State University	M
Polytechnic University, Brooklyn Campus	M,D
Portland State University	M,D,O
Prairie View A&M University	M
Princeton University	D
Purdue University	M,D
Purdue University Calumet	M
Queens College of the City University of New York	M
Rensselaer Polytechnic Institute	M,D
Rhode Island College	M,O
Rice University	M,D
Rivier College	M
Roosevelt University	M
Rowan University	M
Rutgers, The State University of New Jersey, Camden	M
Rutgers, The State University of New Jersey, Newark	D
Rutgers, The State University of New Jersey, New Brunswick/Piscataway	M,D
St. Cloud State University	M
St. John's University (NY)	M
Saint Louis University	M,D
Saint Xavier University	M
Salem State College	M
Sam Houston State University	M
San Diego State University	M,D
San Francisco State University	M
San Jose State University	M
South Dakota State University	M
Southeast Missouri State University	M
Southern Connecticut State University	M
Southern Illinois University Carbondale	M,D
Southern Illinois University Edwardsville	M
Southern Methodist University	M,D
Southern Oregon University	M
Southern University and Agricultural and Mechanical College	M
Southwest Missouri State University	M
Stanford University	M,D
State University of New York at Binghamton	M,D
State University of New York at New Paltz	M
State University of New York College at Brockport	M
State University of New York College at Cortland	M
State University of New York College at Potsdam	M
Stephen F. Austin State University	M
Stevens Institute of Technology	M,D
Stony Brook University, State University of New York	M,D
Syracuse University	M,D
Tarleton State University	M
Temple University	M,D
Tennessee State University	M
Tennessee Technological University	M
Texas A&M International University	M
Texas A&M University	M,D
Texas A&M University–Commerce	M
Texas A&M University–Kingsville	M
Texas Christian University	M
Texas Southern University	M
Texas State University-San Marcos	M
Texas Tech University	M,D
Texas Woman's University	M,D
Tufts University	M,D
Tulane University	M,D
University at Albany, State University of New York	M,D
University at Buffalo, The State University of New York	M,D
The University of Akron	M
The University of Alabama	M,D
The University of Alabama at Birmingham	M,D
The University of Alabama in Huntsville	M,D
University of Alaska Fairbanks	M,D
The University of Arizona	M,D
University of Arkansas	M,D
University of California, Berkeley	M,D
University of California, Davis	M,D
University of California, Irvine	M,D
University of California, Los Angeles	M,D
University of California, Riverside	M,D
University of California, San Diego	M,D
University of California, Santa Barbara	M,D
University of California, Santa Cruz	M,D
University of Central Arkansas	M
University of Central Florida	M,D
University of Central Oklahoma	M
University of Chicago	M,D
University of Cincinnati	M,D
University of Colorado at Boulder	M,D
University of Colorado at Denver	M
University of Connecticut	M,D
University of Delaware	M,D
University of Denver	M
University of Detroit Mercy	M
University of Florida	M,D
University of Georgia	M,D
University of Hawaii at Manoa	M,D
University of Houston	M,D
University of Houston–Clear Lake	M
University of Idaho	M,D
University of Illinois at Chicago	M,D
University of Illinois at Urbana–Champaign	M,D
The University of Iowa	M,D
University of Kansas	M,D
University of Kentucky	M,D
University of Louisiana at Lafayette	M,D
University of Louisville	M,D
University of Maine	M
University of Maryland, College Park	M,D
University of Massachusetts Amherst	M,D
University of Massachusetts Lowell	M,D
The University of Memphis	M,D
University of Miami	M,D
University of Michigan	M,D
University of Minnesota, Twin Cities Campus	M,D
University of Mississippi	M,D
University of Missouri–Columbia	M,D
University of Missouri–Kansas City	M,D
University of Missouri–Rolla	M,D
University of Missouri–St. Louis	M,D,O
The University of Montana–Missoula	M,D
University of Nebraska at Omaha	M
University of Nebraska–Lincoln	M,D
University of Nevada, Las Vegas	M
University of Nevada, Reno	M
University of New Hampshire	M,D
University of New Mexico	M,D
University of New Orleans	M
The University of North Carolina at Chapel Hill	M,D
The University of North Carolina at Charlotte	M,D
The University of North Carolina at Greensboro	M
The University of North Carolina at Wilmington	M
University of North Dakota	M
University of Northern Colorado	M,D
University of Northern Iowa	M
University of North Florida	M
University of North Texas	M,D
University of Notre Dame	M,D
University of Oklahoma	M,D
University of Oregon	M,D
University of Pennsylvania	M,D
University of Pittsburgh	M,D
University of Puerto Rico, Mayagüez Campus	M
University of Puerto Rico, Río Piedras	M,D
University of Rhode Island	M,D
University of Rochester	M,D
University of South Alabama	M
University of South Carolina	M,D
The University of South Dakota	M
University of Southern California	M,D
University of Southern Mississippi	M
University of South Florida	M,D
The University of Tennessee	M,D
The University of Texas at Arlington	M,D
The University of Texas at Austin	M,D
The University of Texas at Dallas	M,D
The University of Texas at El Paso	M
The University of Texas at Tyler	M
The University of Texas–Pan American	M
University of the District of Columbia	M
University of the Incarnate Word	M
University of Toledo	M,D
University of Tulsa	M
University of Utah	M,D
University of Vermont	M,D
University of Virginia	M,D
University of Washington	M,D
University of West Florida	M
University of Wisconsin–Madison	M,D
University of Wisconsin–Milwaukee	M,D
University of Wyoming	M,D
Utah State University	M,D
Vanderbilt University	M,D
Villanova University	M
Virginia Commonwealth University	M,O
Virginia Polytechnic Institute and State University	M,D
Virginia State University	M
Wake Forest University	M
Washington State University	M,D
Washington University in St. Louis	M,D
Wayne State University	M,D
West Chester University of Pennsylvania	M
Western Carolina University	M
Western Connecticut State University	M
Western Illinois University	M
Western Kentucky University	M
Western Michigan University	M,D
Western Washington University	M
West Texas A&M University	M
West Virginia University	M,D
Wichita State University	M,D
Wilkes University	M
Winthrop University	M
Worcester Polytechnic Institute	M,D,O
Wright State University	M
Yale University	M,D
Youngstown State University	M

■ **MATHEMATICS EDUCATION**

Institution	Degree
Alabama State University	M,O
Albany State University	M
Appalachian State University	M
Arcadia University	M,D,O

Mathematics Education

Institution	Degree
Arkansas Tech University	M
Armstrong Atlantic State University	M
Auburn University	M,D,O
Averett University	M
Ball State University	M
Belmont University	M
Bemidji State University	M
Boise State University	M
Boston College	M
Boston University	M,D,O
Bowling Green State University	M,D,O
Bridgewater State College	
Brigham Young University	M
Brooklyn College of the City University of New York	M,D
Buffalo State College, State University of New York	M
California State University, Bakersfield	M
California State University, Dominguez Hills	M
California State University, Fresno	M
California State University, Fullerton	M
California University of Pennsylvania	M
Campbell University	M
Cheyney University of Pennsylvania	O
The Citadel, The Military College of South Carolina	M
City College of the City University of New York	M,O
Clemson University	M
College of Charleston	M
The College of Saint Rose	M,O
The College of William and Mary	M
Columbus State University	M,O
Converse College	M
Cornell University	M,D
Delta State University	M
DePaul University	M
DeSales University	M,O
Drake University	M
East Carolina University	M
Eastern Illinois University	M
Eastern Kentucky University	M
Eastern Michigan University	M
Eastern Washington University	M
Edinboro University of Pennsylvania	M
Fitchburg State College	M
Florida Agricultural and Mechanical University	M
Florida Gulf Coast University	M
Florida Institute of Technology	M,D,O
Florida International University	M
Florida State University	M,D,O
Framingham State College	M
Fresno Pacific University	M
Georgia College & State University	M,O
Georgia Southern University	M
Georgia State University	M,D,O
Harvard University	M,D
Henderson State University	M
Hofstra University	M
Hood College	M
Hunter College of the City University of New York	M
Illinois Institute of Technology	M,D
Illinois State University	D
Indiana University Bloomington	M,D
Indiana University of Pennsylvania	M
Indiana University–Purdue University Indianapolis	M
Iona College	M
Iowa State University of Science and Technology	M,D
Jackson State University	M
Jacksonville University	M
Kean University	M,O
Kutztown University of Pennsylvania	M,O
Lehman College of the City University of New York	M
Long Island University, Brooklyn Campus	M
Long Island University, C.W. Post Campus	M
Louisiana Tech University	M,D
Manhattanville College	M
Marquette University	M,D
McNeese State University	M
Miami University	M
Michigan State University	M,D
Middle Tennessee State University	M
Millersville University of Pennsylvania	M
Minnesota State University Mankato	M
Minot State University	M
Mississippi College	M
Montclair State University	M,D
Morgan State University	M,D
National-Louis University	M,O
New Jersey City University	M
New York University	M,D
North Carolina Agricultural and Technical State University	M
North Carolina State University	M,D
Northeastern Illinois University	M
Northern Arizona University	M
Northern Michigan University	M
North Georgia College & State University	M,O
Northwestern State University of Louisiana	M,O
Northwest Missouri State University	M
Nova Southeastern University	M,O
Ohio University	M,D
Oregon State University	M,D
Plymouth State University	M
Portland State University	M,D
Providence College	M
Purdue University	M,D,O
Purdue University Calumet	M
Queens College of the City University of New York	M,O
Quinnipiac University	M
Rider University	O
Rollins College	M
Rowan University	M
Rutgers, The State University of New Jersey, New Brunswick/Piscataway	M,D
Sage Graduate School	M
St. John Fisher College	M
Saint Joseph's University	M
Salem State College	M,O
Salisbury University	M
San Diego State University	M
San Francisco State University	M
San Jose State University	M
Slippery Rock University of Pennsylvania	M
South Carolina State University	M
Southern University and Agricultural and Mechanical College	D
Southwestern Oklahoma State University	M
Stanford University	M,D
State University of New York at Binghamton	M
State University of New York at New Paltz	M
State University of New York at Plattsburgh	M
State University of New York College at Brockport	M
State University of New York College at Cortland	M
State University of New York College at Fredonia	M
State University of West Georgia	M,O
Stephen F. Austin State University	M
Syracuse University	M,D
Teachers College Columbia University	M,D
Temple University	M,D
Texas A&M University	M,D
Texas State University-San Marcos	M
Texas Woman's University	M
Towson University	M
Trinity College (DC)	M
University at Albany, State University of New York	M,D
University at Buffalo, The State University of New York	M,D,O
University of Arkansas	M
University of California, Berkeley	M,D
University of California, San Diego	D
University of Central Florida	M,D
University of Central Oklahoma	M
University of Cincinnati	M,D
University of Connecticut	M,D
University of Detroit Mercy	M
University of Florida	M,D,O
University of Georgia	M,D,O
University of Houston	M,D
University of Idaho	M,D
University of Illinois at Chicago	M
University of Illinois at Urbana–Champaign	M,D
University of Indianapolis	M
The University of Iowa	M,D
University of Massachusetts Lowell	M,D,O
University of Miami	M,O
University of Michigan	M,D
University of Minnesota, Twin Cities Campus	M
University of Missouri–Columbia	M,D,O
University of Missouri–Rolla	M,D
The University of Montana–Missoula	M,D
University of Nevada, Las Vegas	M,D,O
University of Nevada, Reno	M
University of New Hampshire	M,D
The University of North Carolina at Chapel Hill	M
The University of North Carolina at Charlotte	M
The University of North Carolina at Greensboro	M
The University of North Carolina at Pembroke	M
University of Northern Colorado	M,D
University of Northern Iowa	M
University of North Florida	M
University of Oklahoma	M,D,O
University of Pittsburgh	M
University of Puerto Rico, Río Piedras	M,D
University of Rio Grande	M
University of St. Francis (IL)	M
University of South Carolina	M,D
University of South Florida	M,D,O
The University of Tennessee	M,D,O
The University of Texas at Austin	M,D
The University of Texas at Dallas	M
The University of Texas at San Antonio	M
The University of Texas at Tyler	M
University of the Incarnate Word	D
University of Toledo	M,D,O
University of Tulsa	M
University of Vermont	M,D
University of Washington	M,D
The University of West Alabama	M
University of West Florida	M
University of Wisconsin–Eau Claire	M
University of Wisconsin–Madison	M
University of Wisconsin–Oshkosh	M
University of Wisconsin–River Falls	M
University of Wyoming	M,D
Vanderbilt University	M
Virginia State University	M
Washington State University	M,D
Washington University in St. Louis	M,D
Wayne State College	M
Wayne State University	M,D,O
Webster University	M,O

Western Carolina University — M
Western Connecticut State University — M
Western Illinois University — M,O
Western Michigan University — M,D
Western New England College — M
Western Oregon University — M
West Virginia University — M,D
Wheeling Jesuit University — M
Widener University — M,D
Wilkes University — M
Wright State University — M

■ MECHANICAL ENGINEERING

Alfred University — M
Arizona State University — M,D
Auburn University — M,D
Boise State University — M
Boston University — M,D
Bradley University — M
Brigham Young University — M,D
Brown University — M,D
California Institute of Technology — M,D,O
California State Polytechnic University, Pomona — M
California State University, Chico — M
California State University, Fresno — M
California State University, Fullerton — M
California State University, Long Beach — M,D
California State University, Los Angeles — M
California State University, Northridge — M
California State University, Sacramento — M
Carnegie Mellon University — M,D
Case Western Reserve University — M,D
The Catholic University of America — M,D
Central Connecticut State University — M
City College of the City University of New York — M,D
Clarkson University — M,D
Clemson University — M,D
Cleveland State University — M,D
Colorado State University — M,D
Columbia University — M,D
Cornell University — M,D
Dartmouth College — M,D
Drexel University — M,D
Duke University — M,D
Florida Agricultural and Mechanical University — M,D
Florida Atlantic University — M,D
Florida Institute of Technology — M,D
Florida International University — M,D
Florida State University — M,D
Gannon University — M
The George Washington University — M,D,O
Georgia Institute of Technology — M,D
Grand Valley State University — M
Howard University — M,D
Illinois Institute of Technology — M,D
Indiana University–Purdue University Indianapolis — M
Iowa State University of Science and Technology — M,D
The Johns Hopkins University — M,D
Kansas State University — M,D
Lamar University — M,D
Lawrence Technological University — M,D
Lehigh University — M,D
Louisiana State University and Agricultural and Mechanical College — M,D
Louisiana Tech University — M,D
Loyola Marymount University — M
Manhattan College — M
Marquette University — M,D
Massachusetts Institute of Technology — M,D,O
McNeese State University — M
Mercer University — M
Michigan State University — M,D
Michigan Technological University — M,D
Minnesota State University Mankato — M
Mississippi State University — M,D
Montana State University–Bozeman — M,D
New Jersey Institute of Technology — M,D,O
New Mexico State University — M,D
North Carolina Agricultural and Technical State University — M,D
North Carolina State University — M,D
North Dakota State University — M,D
Northeastern University — M,D
Northern Illinois University — M
Northwestern University — M,D
Oakland University — M,D
The Ohio State University — M,D
Ohio University — M,D
Oklahoma State University — M,D
Old Dominion University — M,D
Oregon State University — M,D
The Pennsylvania State University University Park Campus — M,D
Polytechnic University, Brooklyn Campus — M,D
Portland State University — M,D,O
Princeton University — M,D
Purdue University — M,D
Rensselaer Polytechnic Institute — M,D
Rice University — M,D
Rochester Institute of Technology — M
Rutgers, The State University of New Jersey, New Brunswick/Piscataway — M,D
St. Cloud State University — M
Saint Louis University — M
San Diego State University — M,D
San Jose State University — M
Santa Clara University — M,D,O
South Dakota State University — M
Southern Illinois University Carbondale — M
Southern Illinois University Edwardsville — M
Southern Methodist University — M,D
Stanford University — M,D,O
State University of New York at Binghamton — M,D
Stevens Institute of Technology — M,D,O
Stony Brook University, State University of New York — M,D,O
Syracuse University — M,D
Temple University — M
Tennessee Technological University — M,D
Texas A&M University — M,D
Texas A&M University–Kingsville — M
Texas Tech University — M,D
Tufts University — M,D
Tulane University — M,D
Tuskegee University — M
University at Buffalo, The State University of New York — M,D
The University of Akron — M,D
The University of Alabama — M,D
The University of Alabama at Birmingham — M,D
The University of Alabama in Huntsville — M,D
University of Alaska Fairbanks — M,D
The University of Arizona — M,D
University of Arkansas — M,D
University of Bridgeport — M
University of California, Berkeley — M,D
University of California, Davis — M,D,O
University of California, Irvine — M,D
University of California, Los Angeles — M,D
University of California, Riverside — M,D
University of California, San Diego — M,D
University of California, Santa Barbara — M,D
University of Central Florida — M,D,O
University of Cincinnati — M,D
University of Colorado at Boulder — M,D
University of Colorado at Colorado Springs — M
University of Colorado at Denver — M
University of Connecticut — M,D
University of Dayton — M,D
University of Delaware — M,D
University of Denver — M,D
University of Detroit Mercy — M,D
University of Florida — M,D,O
University of Hawaii at Manoa — M,D
University of Houston — M,D
University of Idaho — M,D
University of Illinois at Chicago — M,D
University of Illinois at Urbana–Champaign — M,D
The University of Iowa — M,D
University of Kansas — M,D
University of Kentucky — M,D
University of Louisiana at Lafayette — M
University of Louisville — M
University of Maine — M,D
University of Maryland, Baltimore County — M,D
University of Maryland, College Park — M,D,O
University of Massachusetts Amherst — M,D
University of Massachusetts Dartmouth — M
University of Massachusetts Lowell — M,D,O
The University of Memphis — M,D
University of Miami — M,D
University of Michigan–Dearborn — M
University of Minnesota, Twin Cities Campus — M,D
University of Missouri–Columbia — M,D
University of Missouri–Kansas City — M,D
University of Missouri–Rolla — M,D
University of Nebraska–Lincoln — M,D
University of Nevada, Las Vegas — M,D
University of Nevada, Reno — M,D
University of New Hampshire — M,D
University of New Haven — M
University of New Mexico — M,D
University of New Orleans — M
The University of North Carolina at Charlotte — M,D
University of North Dakota — M
University of Notre Dame — M,D
University of Oklahoma — M,D
University of Pennsylvania — M,D
University of Pittsburgh — M,D
University of Puerto Rico, Mayagüez Campus — M
University of Rhode Island — M,D
University of Rochester — M,D
University of South Alabama — M
University of South Carolina — M,D
University of Southern California — M,D,O
University of South Florida — M,D
The University of Tennessee — M,D
The University of Texas at Arlington — M,D
The University of Texas at Austin — M,D
The University of Texas at El Paso — M
The University of Texas at San Antonio — M
University of Toledo — M,D
University of Tulsa — M,D
University of Utah — M,D
University of Vermont — M,D
University of Virginia — M,D
University of Washington — M,D
University of Wisconsin–Madison — M,D
University of Wyoming — M,D
Utah State University — M,D
Vanderbilt University — M,D
Villanova University — M,O
Virginia Polytechnic Institute and State University — M,D
Washington State University — M,D
Washington University in St. Louis — M,D
Wayne State University — M,D
Western Michigan University — M,D

Directory of Graduate and Professional Programs by Field
Mechanical Engineering

Western New England College	M
West Virginia University	M,D
Wichita State University	M,D
Widener University	M
Worcester Polytechnic Institute	M,D,O
Wright State University	M
Yale University	M,D
Youngstown State University	M

■ MECHANICS

Brown University	M,D
California Institute of Technology	M,D
California State University, Fullerton	M
California State University, Northridge	M
Case Western Reserve University	M,D
The Catholic University of America	M,D
Colorado State University	M,D
Columbia University	M,D,O
Cornell University	M,D
Drexel University	M,D
Georgia Institute of Technology	M,D
Idaho State University	M,D,O
Iowa State University of Science and Technology	M,D
The Johns Hopkins University	M,D
Lehigh University	M,D
Louisiana State University and Agricultural and Mechanical College	M,D
Massachusetts Institute of Technology	M,D,O
Michigan Technological University	M
Mississippi State University	M
New Mexico Institute of Mining and Technology	M
North Dakota State University	M,D
Northwestern University	M,D
The Ohio State University	M,D
Old Dominion University	M,D
The Pennsylvania State University University Park Campus	M,D
Rensselaer Polytechnic Institute	M,D
Rutgers, The State University of New Jersey, New Brunswick/Piscataway	M,D
San Diego State University	M,D
Southern Illinois University Carbondale	M,D
The University of Alabama	M,D
The University of Arizona	M,D
University of California, Berkeley	M,D
University of California, San Diego	M,D
University of Dayton	M
University of Florida	M,D,O
University of Illinois at Urbana–Champaign	M,D
University of Maryland, College Park	M,D
University of Massachusetts Lowell	M,D
University of Minnesota, Twin Cities Campus	M,D
University of Missouri–Rolla	M,D
University of Nebraska–Lincoln	M,D
University of Pennsylvania	M,D
University of Rhode Island	M,D
University of Southern California	M
The University of Tennessee	M,D
The University of Texas at Austin	M,D
University of Virginia	M
University of Wisconsin–Madison	M,D
Virginia Polytechnic Institute and State University	M,D
Yale University	M,D

■ MEDIA STUDIES

American University	M
Arkansas State University	M
Austin Peay State University	M
Boston University	M
Brooklyn College of the City University of New York	O
California State University, Fullerton	M
Carnegie Mellon University	M
Central Michigan University	M
City College of the City University of New York	M
College of Staten Island of the City University of New York	M
Columbia College Chicago	M
Emerson College	M
Fordham University	M
Governors State University	M
Hunter College of the City University of New York	M
Indiana State University	M
Kutztown University of Pennsylvania	M
Lesley University	M,O
Louisiana State University and Agricultural and Mechanical College	M,D
Lynn University	M,D
Marquette University	M
Marywood University	M
Massachusetts Institute of Technology	M,D
Michigan State University	M,D
Monmouth University	M,O
New College of California	M
New School University	M
New York University	M,D
Norfolk State University	M
Northwestern University	M,D
Ohio University	M,D
The Pennsylvania State University University Park Campus	M
Queens College of the City University of New York	M
Rochester Institute of Technology	M
Saginaw Valley State University	M
San Diego State University	M
San Francisco State University	M
Syracuse University	M
Temple University	M,D
Texas Southern University	M
University at Buffalo, The State University of New York	M
The University of Alabama	M
The University of Arizona	M
University of Chicago	M,D
University of Colorado at Boulder	D
University of Denver	M
University of Florida	M,D
University of Maryland, College Park	M,D
University of Michigan	M
University of Oklahoma	M
University of South Carolina	M
University of Southern California	M
The University of Tennessee	M,D
The University of Texas at Austin	M,D
Wayne State University	M,D
Webster University	M
William Paterson University of New Jersey	M

■ MEDICAL/SURGICAL NURSING

Angelo State University	M
Brigham Young University	M
Case Western Reserve University	M,D
The Catholic University of America	M,D
College of Mount Saint Vincent	M,O
College of Staten Island of the City University of New York	M
Columbia University	M,O
Duke University	M,O
Emory University	M
Gannon University	M,O
George Mason University	M,D
The George Washington University	M,O
Georgia State University	M,D
Gwynedd-Mercy College	M
Hunter College of the City University of New York	M
Indiana University–Purdue University Indianapolis	M,D
The Johns Hopkins University	M,O
Kent State University	M,D
La Salle University	M,O
Lehman College of the City University of New York	M
Loyola University Chicago	M
Madonna University	M
Marian College of Fond du Lac	M
Marquette University	M,D,O
Marymount University	M,O
Molloy College	M,O
Mount Saint Mary College	M
New York University	M,O
Oakland University	M
Pontifical Catholic University of Puerto Rico	M
Quinnipiac University	M
Rutgers, The State University of New Jersey, Newark	M
Sage Graduate School	M
Saint Xavier University	M,O
Seton Hall University	M
Southern Illinois University Edwardsville	M
Spalding University	M
State University of New York Institute of Technology	M,O
Stony Brook University, State University of New York	M,O
Texas Christian University	M
University at Buffalo, The State University of New York	M,D,O
University of Central Florida	M,O
University of Cincinnati	M,D
University of Colorado at Colorado Springs	M
University of Delaware	M,O
University of Hawaii at Manoa	M,D,O
University of Illinois at Chicago	M
University of Maryland	M,D
University of Miami	M,D
University of Michigan	M
University of Minnesota, Twin Cities Campus	M
University of Missouri–Kansas City	M,D
The University of North Carolina at Charlotte	M
University of Pennsylvania	M
University of San Diego	M,D,O
University of San Francisco	M
The University of Scranton	M,O
University of South Alabama	M
University of South Carolina	M
University of Southern Maine	M,O
University of Southern Mississippi	M,D
The University of Tampa	M
The University of Tennessee at Chattanooga	M
The University of Texas–Pan American	M
Vanderbilt University	M,D
Villanova University	M,D,O
Virginia Commonwealth University	M,D,O
Wayne State University	M
Western Connecticut State University	M
Wichita State University	M
Wright State University	M

■ MEDICAL ILLUSTRATION

The Johns Hopkins University	M
Rochester Institute of Technology	M
University of Illinois at Chicago	M
University of Michigan	M

■ MEDICAL INFORMATICS

Columbia University	M,D
Emory University	M
Harvard University	M
Massachusetts Institute of Technology	M
Stanford University	M,D
University of California, Davis	M

University of California, San Francisco M,D
University of Utah M,D
University of Washington M

■ MEDICAL MICROBIOLOGY

Creighton University M,D
Idaho State University M,D
The Ohio State University M
Rutgers, The State University of New Jersey, New Brunswick/Piscataway M,D
University of Georgia M,D
University of Hawaii at Manoa M,D
University of Minnesota, Duluth M,D
University of South Florida M,D
University of Wisconsin–La Crosse M
University of Wisconsin–Madison D

■ MEDICAL PHYSICS

Cleveland State University M
Columbia University M,D,O
Drexel University M,D
East Carolina University M,D
Georgia Institute of Technology M,D
Harvard University M,D
Massachusetts Institute of Technology D
Oakland University M,D
Purdue University M,D
Stony Brook University, State University of New York D
University of California, Los Angeles M,D
University of Central Arkansas M
University of Chicago D
University of Cincinnati M
University of Colorado at Boulder M,D
University of Kentucky M
University of Minnesota, Twin Cities Campus M,D
University of Missouri–Columbia M,D
University of Pennsylvania D
University of Wisconsin–Madison M,D
Vanderbilt University M
Wayne State University M,D
Wright State University M

■ MEDICINAL AND PHARMACEUTICAL CHEMISTRY

Duquesne University M,D
Florida Agricultural and Mechanical University M,D
Idaho State University M,D
Long Island University, Brooklyn Campus M
Long Island University, C.W. Post Campus M
The Ohio State University M,D
Purdue University M,D
Rutgers, The State University of New Jersey, New Brunswick/Piscataway M,D
St. John's University (NY) M,D
Temple University M,D
University at Buffalo, The State University of New York M,D
University of California, San Francisco D
University of Connecticut M,D
University of Florida M,D
University of Georgia M,D
University of Kansas M,D
University of Michigan D
University of Minnesota, Twin Cities Campus M,D
University of Mississippi M,D
University of Rhode Island M,D
University of Toledo M,D
University of Utah M,D
University of Washington D
West Virginia University M,D

■ MEDIEVAL AND RENAISSANCE STUDIES

Arizona State University O

The Catholic University of America M,D,O
Columbia University M
Cornell University M,D
Duke University O
Fordham University M,D
Harvard University M,D
Indiana University Bloomington M,D
Marquette University M,D
Rutgers, The State University of New Jersey, New Brunswick/Piscataway D
Southern Methodist University M
University of Colorado at Boulder M,D
University of Connecticut M,D
University of Minnesota, Twin Cities Campus M,D
University of Notre Dame M,D
Western Michigan University M
Yale University M,D

■ METALLURGICAL ENGINEERING AND METALLURGY

Massachusetts Institute of Technology M,D,O
Michigan Technological University M,D
The Ohio State University M,D
The Pennsylvania State University University Park Campus M,D
Rensselaer Polytechnic Institute M,D
Rutgers, The State University of New Jersey, New Brunswick/Piscataway M,D
The University of Alabama M,D
The University of Alabama at Birmingham M,D
University of California, Berkeley M,D
University of California, Los Angeles M,D
University of Cincinnati M,D
University of Connecticut M,D
University of Idaho M,D
University of Missouri–Rolla M,D
University of Nevada, Reno M,D,O
University of Pittsburgh M,D
The University of Texas at El Paso M
University of Utah M,D
University of Wisconsin–Madison M,D

■ METEOROLOGY

Columbia University M
Florida Institute of Technology M,D
Florida State University M,D
Iowa State University of Science and Technology M,D
North Carolina State University M,D
The Pennsylvania State University University Park Campus M,D
Saint Louis University M,D
San Jose State University M
Texas A&M University M,D
University of Hawaii at Manoa M,D
University of Maryland, College Park M,D
University of Miami M,D
University of Oklahoma M,D
University of Utah M,D
Utah State University M,D
Yale University D

■ MICROBIOLOGY

Arizona State University M,D
Auburn University M,D
Boston University M,D
Brandeis University M,D
Brigham Young University M,D
Brown University M,D
California State University, Fullerton M
California State University, Long Beach M
Case Western Reserve University D
The Catholic University of America M,D
Clemson University M,D
Colorado State University M,D
Columbia University M,D

Cornell University D
Drexel University M,D
Duke University D
East Carolina University D
East Tennessee State University M,D
Emory University D
Emporia State University M
Florida State University D
George Mason University M,D
Georgetown University M,D
The George Washington University M
Georgia State University M,D
Harvard University D
Howard University D
Idaho State University M,D
Illinois Institute of Technology M,D
Illinois State University M,D
Indiana University M,D
Indiana University Bloomington M,D
Indiana University–Purdue University Indianapolis M,D
Iowa State University of Science and Technology M,D
The Johns Hopkins University M,D
Kansas State University M,D
Loma Linda University M,D
Long Island University, C.W. Post Campus M
Loyola University Chicago M,D
Marquette University M,D
Massachusetts Institute of Technology D
Miami University M,D
Michigan State University D
Montana State University–Bozeman M,D
New York University M,D
North Carolina State University M,D
North Dakota State University M
Northwestern University D
The Ohio State University M,D
Ohio University M,D
Oklahoma State University M,D
Oregon State University M,D
The Pennsylvania State University University Park Campus M,D
Purdue University M,D
Quinnipiac University M
Rensselaer Polytechnic Institute M,D
Rutgers, The State University of New Jersey, New Brunswick/Piscataway M,D
Saint Louis University D
San Diego State University M
San Francisco State University M
San Jose State University M
Seton Hall University M,D
South Dakota State University M
Southern Illinois University Carbondale M,D
Stanford University D
Stony Brook University, State University of New York D
Temple University M,D
Texas A&M University M,D
Texas Tech University M,D
Tufts University D
Tulane University M,D
University at Buffalo, The State University of New York M,D
The University of Alabama at Birmingham D
The University of Arizona M,D
University of California, Berkeley D
University of California, Davis M,D
University of California, Irvine M,D
University of California, Los Angeles M,D
University of California, Riverside M,D
University of California, San Diego D
University of California, San Francisco D
University of Central Florida M
University of Chicago D
University of Cincinnati M,D

Microbiology

University of Colorado at Boulder	M,D
University of Connecticut	M,D
University of Delaware	M,D
University of Florida	M,D
University of Georgia	M,D
University of Hawaii at Manoa	M,D
University of Idaho	M,D
University of Illinois at Chicago	D
University of Illinois at Urbana–Champaign	M,D
The University of Iowa	M,D
University of Kansas	M,D
University of Kentucky	D
University of Louisville	M,D
University of Maine	M,D
University of Maryland	M,D
University of Maryland, College Park	M,D
University of Massachusetts Amherst	M,D
The University of Memphis	M,D
University of Miami	D
University of Michigan	D
University of Minnesota, Twin Cities Campus	D
University of Missouri–Columbia	M,D
The University of Montana–Missoula	M,D
University of New Hampshire	M,D
University of New Mexico	M,D
The University of North Carolina at Chapel Hill	M,D
University of North Dakota	M,D
University of Oklahoma	M,D
University of Pennsylvania	D
University of Pittsburgh	M,D
University of Rhode Island	M,D
University of Rochester	M,D
University of South Alabama	D
The University of South Dakota	M,D
University of Southern California	M,D
University of Southern Mississippi	M,D
University of South Florida	M,D
The University of Tennessee	M,D
The University of Texas at Austin	M,D
University of Vermont	M,D
University of Virginia	D
University of Washington	D
University of Wisconsin–La Crosse	M
University of Wisconsin–Madison	D
University of Wisconsin–Oshkosh	M
Utah State University	M,D
Vanderbilt University	M,D
Virginia Commonwealth University	M,D,O
Virginia Polytechnic Institute and State University	M,D
Wagner College	M
Wake Forest University	D
Washington State University	M,D
Washington University in St. Louis	D
Wayne State University	M,D
West Virginia University	M,D
Wright State University	M
Yale University	D
Yeshiva University	D

■ MIDDLE SCHOOL EDUCATION

Alaska Pacific University	M
Albany State University	M
Armstrong Atlantic State University	M
Ashland University	M
Augusta State University	M,O
Ball State University	M
Bellarmine University	M
Belmont University	M
Brenau University	M,O
Brooklyn College of the City University of New York	M
California State University, Fullerton	M
Campbell University	M
Central Michigan University	M
City College of the City University of New York	M,O
Clemson University	M,D,O
College of Mount Saint Vincent	M,O
Columbus State University	M,O
Cumberland College	M
Drury University	M
East Carolina University	M
Eastern Illinois University	M
Eastern Michigan University	M
Eastern Nazarene College	M,O
Emory University	M,D,O
Fayetteville State University	M
Fitchburg State College	M
Fort Valley State University	M
Gardner-Webb University	M
George Mason University	M
Georgia College & State University	M,O
Georgia Southern University	M
Georgia Southwestern State University	M,O
Georgia State University	M,D,O
Grand Valley State University	M
Henderson State University	M
Hofstra University	M,O
James Madison University	M
John Carroll University	M
Kennesaw State University	M
Kent State University	M
Lesley University	M,D,O
Lynchburg College	M
Manhattanville College	M
Mary Baldwin College	M
Maryville University of Saint Louis	M
Mercer University	M,O
Middle Tennessee State University	M,O
Morehead State University	M
Morgan State University	M
Mount Saint Mary College	M
Murray State University	M,O
Nazareth College of Rochester	M
Newman University	M
North Carolina Agricultural and Technical State University	M
North Carolina State University	M
Northern Kentucky University	M
North Georgia College & State University	M,O
Northwest Missouri State University	M
Ohio University	M,D
Old Dominion University	M
Pacific University	M
Park University	M
Plymouth State University	M
Quinnipiac University	M
Saginaw Valley State University	M
St. John Fisher College	M
St. Thomas Aquinas College	M,O
Salem State College	M
Shenandoah University	M,D,O
Siena Heights University	M
Southeast Missouri State University	M
Southwest Missouri State University	M
Spalding University	M
State University of New York College at Oneonta	M
State University of West Georgia	M,O
Tufts University	M
University at Buffalo, The State University of New York	M,D,O
University of Arkansas	M,D,O
University of Arkansas at Little Rock	M,O
University of Dayton	M
University of Georgia	M,D,O
University of Louisville	M
University of Nevada, Las Vegas	M,D,O
The University of North Carolina at Charlotte	M
The University of North Carolina at Pembroke	M
The University of North Carolina at Wilmington	M
University of Northern Iowa	M
University of South Florida	M,D,O
University of West Florida	M
University of Wisconsin–Milwaukee	M
University of Wisconsin–Platteville	M
Valdosta State University	M,O
Virginia Commonwealth University	M,O
Wagner College	M
Western Carolina University	M
Western Kentucky University	M
Western Michigan University	M
Westfield State College	M
Widener University	M,D
Winthrop University	M
Worcester State College	M
Wright State University	M
Youngstown State University	M

■ MILITARY AND DEFENSE STUDIES

California State University, San Bernardino	M
Florida State University	M,D,O
Georgetown University	M
The George Washington University	M
Hawai'i Pacific University	M
Southwest Missouri State University	M
University of Pittsburgh	M

■ MINERAL/MINING ENGINEERING

Columbia University	M,D,O
Michigan Technological University	M,D
New Mexico Institute of Mining and Technology	M
The Pennsylvania State University University Park Campus	M,D
Southern Illinois University Carbondale	M
University of Alaska Fairbanks	M
The University of Arizona	M,D
University of California, Berkeley	M,D
University of Idaho	M,D
University of Kentucky	M
University of Missouri–Rolla	M,D
University of Nevada, Reno	M,O
University of North Dakota	M
The University of Texas at Austin	M
University of Utah	M,D
Virginia Polytechnic Institute and State University	M,D
West Virginia University	M,D

■ MINERAL ECONOMICS

Michigan Technological University	M
The University of Texas at Austin	M

■ MINERALOGY

Cornell University	M,D
Indiana University Bloomington	M,D
University of Illinois at Chicago	M,D
University of Michigan	M,D
Yale University	D

■ MISSIONS AND MISSIOLOGY

Abilene Christian University	M
Anderson University	P,M,D
Biola University	M,D,O
Concordia University (CA)	M
Gardner-Webb University	P,D
Grand Rapids Theological Seminary of Cornerstone University	P,M
Oral Roberts University	P,M,D
Regent University	P,M,D
Simpson University	M

■ MOLECULAR BIOLOGY

Arizona State University	M,D
Boston University	M,D
Brandeis University	M,D
Brigham Young University	M,D

Directory of Graduate and Professional Programs by Field
Multilingual and Multicultural Education

Brown University	M,D
California Institute of Technology	D
Carnegie Mellon University	M,D
Case Western Reserve University	M,D
Central Connecticut State University	M,O
Colorado State University	M,D
Columbia University	M,D
Cornell University	D
Drexel University	M,D
Duke University	D,O
East Carolina University	M
Emory University	D
Florida Institute of Technology	D
Florida State University	M,D
Fordham University	M,D
George Mason University	M,D
Georgetown University	D
The George Washington University	M,D
Harvard University	D
Howard University	M,D
Illinois Institute of Technology	M,D
Indiana University Bloomington	M,D
Indiana University–Purdue University Indianapolis	M,D
Iowa State University of Science and Technology	M,D
The Johns Hopkins University	M,D
Kansas State University	M,D
Kent State University	M,D
Lehigh University	D
Loyola University Chicago	D
Marquette University	M,D
Massachusetts Institute of Technology	D
Mayo Graduate School	D
Michigan State University	M,D
Mississippi State University	M,D
Montana State University–Bozeman	M,D
Montclair State University	M,O
New Mexico State University	M,D
New York University	D
North Dakota State University	M,D
Northwestern University	D
The Ohio State University	M,D
Ohio University	M,D
Oklahoma State University	M,D
Oregon State University	M,D
The Pennsylvania State University University Park Campus	M,D
Princeton University	D
Purdue University	M,D
Quinnipiac University	M
Rensselaer Polytechnic Institute	M,D
Rutgers, The State University of New Jersey, New Brunswick/Piscataway	M,D
Saint Joseph College	M
Saint Louis University	D
Salem International University	M
San Diego State University	M,D
San Francisco State University	M
San Jose State University	M
Seton Hall University	D
Southern Illinois University Carbondale	M,D
Southwest Missouri State University	M
Stony Brook University, State University of New York	M,D
Temple University	D
Texas A&M University	D
Texas Woman's University	M,D
Tufts University	D
Tulane University	M,D
University at Albany, State University of New York	M,D
University at Buffalo, The State University of New York	D
The University of Arizona	M,D
University of Arkansas	M,D
University of California, Berkeley	D
University of California, Davis	M,D
University of California, Irvine	M,D
University of California, Los Angeles	M,D
University of California, Riverside	M,D
University of California, San Diego	D
University of California, San Francisco	D
University of California, Santa Barbara	M,D
University of California, Santa Cruz	M,D
University of Central Florida	M,D
University of Chicago	D
University of Cincinnati	M,D
University of Colorado at Boulder	M,D
University of Connecticut	M,D
University of Delaware	M,D
University of Florida	M,D
University of Georgia	M,D
University of Hawaii at Manoa	M,D
University of Idaho	M,D
University of Illinois at Chicago	M,D
The University of Iowa	D
University of Kansas	M,D
University of Louisville	M,D
University of Maine	M,D
University of Maryland	D
University of Maryland, Baltimore County	M,D
University of Maryland, College Park	D
University of Massachusetts Amherst	D
University of Massachusetts Boston	D
The University of Memphis	M,D
University of Miami	D
University of Michigan	M,D
University of Minnesota, Duluth	M,D
University of Minnesota, Twin Cities Campus	M,D
University of Missouri–Columbia	M,D
University of Missouri–Kansas City	D
University of Missouri–St. Louis	M,D,O
University of Nevada, Reno	M,D
University of New Hampshire	M,D
University of New Haven	M
University of New Mexico	M,D
The University of North Carolina at Chapel Hill	M,D
University of North Texas	M,D
University of Notre Dame	M,D
University of Oregon	M,D
University of Pennsylvania	D
University of Pittsburgh	D
University of Rhode Island	M,D
University of South Alabama	D
University of South Carolina	M,D
The University of South Dakota	M,D
University of Southern California	M,D
University of Southern Maine	M
University of Southern Mississippi	M,D
University of South Florida	M,D
The University of Texas at Austin	D
The University of Texas at Dallas	M,D
The University of Texas at San Antonio	D
University of Vermont	M,D
University of Washington	D
University of Wisconsin–La Crosse	M
University of Wisconsin–Madison	M,D
University of Wisconsin–Parkside	M
University of Wyoming	M,D
Utah State University	M,D
Vanderbilt University	D
Virginia Commonwealth University	M,D,O
Wake Forest University	D
Washington State University	M,D
Washington University in St. Louis	D
Wayne State University	M,D
West Virginia University	M,D
William Paterson University of New Jersey	M
Wright State University	M
Yale University	D
Yeshiva University	D

■ **MOLECULAR MEDICINE**

Boston University	D
Cornell University	M,D
The Johns Hopkins University	D
The Pennsylvania State University University Park Campus	M,D
University of Cincinnati	D
University of Washington	M,D
Wake Forest University	M,D
Yale University	D

■ **MULTILINGUAL AND MULTICULTURAL EDUCATION**

Adelphi University	M
Azusa Pacific University	M
Boston University	M,O
Brooklyn College of the City University of New York	M
Brown University	M,D
Buffalo State College, State University of New York	M
California Baptist University	M
California State University, Bakersfield	M
California State University, Chico	M
California State University, Dominguez Hills	M
California State University, Fullerton	M
California State University, Los Angeles	M,D
California State University, Sacramento	M
California State University, San Bernardino	M
California State University, Stanislaus	M
Chicago State University	M
City College of the City University of New York	M
College of Mount Saint Vincent	M,O
The College of New Rochelle	M,O
The College of Saint Rose	M,O
College of Santa Fe	M
Columbia College Chicago	M
DeSales University	M,O
Eastern Michigan University	M
Eastern University	M
Emmanuel College	M,O
Fairfield University	M,O
Fairleigh Dickinson University, Metropolitan Campus	M
Florida Atlantic University	M,D,O
Florida State University	M,D,O
Fordham University	M,D,O
Fresno Pacific University	M
George Mason University	M
Georgetown University	M,D,O
Heritage College	M
Hofstra University	M,O
Hunter College of the City University of New York	M
Immaculata University	M
Indiana State University	M,O
Iona College	M
Kean University	M,O
Lehman College of the City University of New York	M
Lesley University	M,O
Long Island University, Brooklyn Campus	M
Long Island University, C.W. Post Campus	M
Loyola Marymount University	M
Mercy College	M,O
National University	M
New Jersey City University	M
New York University	M,D,O
Northeastern Illinois University	M
Northern Arizona University	M,O
Ohio University	M,D
Park University	M

Peterson's Graduate Schools in the U.S. 2006

Directory of Graduate and Professional Programs by Field

Multilingual and Multicultural Education

Institution	Degree
The Pennsylvania State University University Park Campus	M,D
Prescott College	M
Queens College of the City University of New York	M,O
Rhode Island College	M
Rutgers, The State University of New Jersey, New Brunswick/Piscataway	M,D
St. John's University (NY)	M
Salem State College	M
San Diego State University	M,D
Seton Hall University	M,O
Southern Connecticut State University	M
Southern Methodist University	M
State University of New York at New Paltz	M
State University of New York College at Brockport	M
Sul Ross State University	M
Teachers College Columbia University	M
Texas A&M International University	M
Texas A&M University	M,D
Texas A&M University–Kingsville	M,D
Texas Southern University	M,D
Texas State University-San Marcos	M
Texas Tech University	M,D,O
Universidad del Turabo	M
University at Buffalo, The State University of New York	M,D,O
University of Alaska Fairbanks	M
The University of Arizona	M,D,O
University of California, Berkeley	M,D
University of Colorado at Boulder	M,D
University of Connecticut	M,D
University of Delaware	M,D
The University of Findlay	M
University of Houston	M,D
University of Houston–Clear Lake	M
University of La Verne	O
University of Maryland, Baltimore County	M,D,O
University of Massachusetts Amherst	M,D,O
University of Massachusetts Boston	M
University of Michigan	M,D
University of Minnesota, Twin Cities Campus	M
University of New Mexico	D,O
University of Pennsylvania	M,D
University of San Francisco	M,D
The University of Tennessee	M,D,O
The University of Texas at Brownsville	M
The University of Texas at San Antonio	M,D
The University of Texas–Pan American	M
University of Washington	M,D
Utah State University	M
Washington State University	M,D
Wayne State University	M,D,O
Western Oregon University	M
Xavier University	M

MUSEUM EDUCATION

Institution	Degree
The College of New Rochelle	O
The George Washington University	M

MUSEUM STUDIES

Institution	Degree
Baylor University	M
Boston University	M,D,O
California State University, Chico	M
California State University, Fullerton	M,O
Case Western Reserve University	M,D
City College of the City University of New York	M
Colorado State University	M
Duquesne University	M
Florida State University	M,D,O
The George Washington University	M,D,O
Hampton University	M
Harvard University	M,O
John F. Kennedy University	M

Institution	Degree
New York University	M,D,O
Rutgers, The State University of New Jersey, New Brunswick/Piscataway	M,D
San Francisco State University	M
Seton Hall University	M
State University of New York College at Oneonta	M
Syracuse University	M
Texas Tech University	M
Tufts University	O
University of California, Riverside	M,D
University of Central Oklahoma	M
University of Colorado at Boulder	M
University of Delaware	O
University of Denver	M
University of Florida	M
University of Kansas	M
University of Missouri–St. Louis	M,O
University of Nebraska–Lincoln	M
University of New Hampshire	M,D
The University of North Carolina at Greensboro	M,O
University of South Carolina	M,O
University of Washington	M
University of Wisconsin–Milwaukee	M,O

■ MUSIC

Institution	Degree
Alabama Agricultural and Mechanical University	M
Alabama State University	M
Andrews University	M
Appalachian State University	M
Arizona State University	M,D
Arkansas State University	M,O
Auburn University	M
Austin Peay State University	M
Azusa Pacific University	M
Baylor University	M
Belmont University	M
Bethel University	M,O
Boise State University	M
Boston University	M,D,O
Bowling Green State University	M
Brandeis University	M,D
Brigham Young University	M
Brooklyn College of the City University of New York	M,D,O
Brown University	M,D
Butler University	M
California State University, Chico	M
California State University, Fresno	M
California State University, Fullerton	M
California State University, Hayward	M
California State University, Long Beach	M
California State University, Los Angeles	M
California State University, Northridge	M
California State University, Sacramento	M
Campbellsville University	M
Capital University	M
Carnegie Mellon University	M
Case Western Reserve University	M,D
The Catholic University of America	M,D
Central Michigan University	M
Central Missouri State University	M
Central Washington University	M
City College of the City University of New York	M
Claremont Graduate University	M,D
Cleveland State University	M
The College of Saint Rose	M
Colorado State University	M
Columbia University	M,D
Concordia University (IL)	M
Concordia University Wisconsin	M
Converse College	M
Cornell University	M,D
Dartmouth College	M
DePaul University	M,O

Institution	Degree
Duke University	M,D
Duquesne University	M,O
East Carolina University	M
Eastern Illinois University	M
Eastern Kentucky University	M
Eastern Michigan University	M
Eastern Washington University	M
Emory University	M
Emporia State University	M
Florida Atlantic University	M
Florida International University	M
Florida State University	M,D
Gardner-Webb University	P,D
George Mason University	M
Georgia Southern University	M
Georgia State University	M,D,O
Golden Gate Baptist Theological Seminary	P,M,D,O
Gratz College	M,O
Hardin-Simmons University	M
Harvard University	M,D
Hofstra University	M
Holy Names University	M,O
Hope International University	M
Howard University	M
Hunter College of the City University of New York	M
Illinois State University	M
Indiana State University	M
Indiana University Bloomington	M,D
Indiana University of Pennsylvania	M
Indiana University–Purdue University Indianapolis	M
Indiana University South Bend	M
Ithaca College	M
Jacksonville State University	M
James Madison University	M
The Johns Hopkins University	M,D,O
Kansas State University	M
Kent State University	M,D
Lamar University	M
Long Island University, C.W. Post Campus	M
Louisiana State University and Agricultural and Mechanical College	M,D
Loyola University New Orleans	M
Lynn University	O
Mansfield University of Pennsylvania	M
Marshall University	M
Marywood University	M
Meredith College	M
Miami University	M
Michigan State University	M,D
Middle Tennessee State University	M
Minnesota State University Mankato	M
Minnesota State University Moorhead	M
Mississippi College	M
Montclair State University	M
Morehead State University	M
Morgan State University	M
Murray State University	M
New Jersey City University	M
New Mexico State University	M
New School University	M,O
New York University	M,D,O
Norfolk State University	M
Northeastern Illinois University	M
Northern Arizona University	M
Northern Illinois University	M,O
Northwestern State University of Louisiana	M
Northwestern University	M,D,O
Notre Dame de Namur University	M
Oakland University	M
The Ohio State University	M,D
Ohio University	M
Oklahoma City University	M
Oklahoma State University	M

The Pennsylvania State University
  University Park Campus   M
Pittsburg State University   M
Point Park University   M
Portland State University   M
Princeton University   D
Purchase College, State University of
  New York   M
Queens College of the City University
  of New York   M
Radford University   M
Regis University   M,O
Rhode Island College   M
Rice University   M,D
Rider University   M
Roosevelt University   M,O
Rowan University   M
Rutgers, The State University of New
  Jersey, Newark   M
Rutgers, The State University of New
  Jersey, New Brunswick/Piscataway M,D,O
St. Cloud State University   M
Samford University   M
Sam Houston State University   M
San Diego State University   M
San Francisco State University   M
San Jose State University   M
Santa Clara University   M
Shenandoah University   M,D,O
Southeastern Louisiana University   M
Southern Illinois University
  Carbondale   M
Southern Illinois University
  Edwardsville   M
Southern Methodist University   M,O
Southern Oregon University   M
Southern Utah University   M
Southwestern Oklahoma State
  University   M
Southwest Missouri State University   M
Stanford University   M,D
State University of New York at
  Binghamton   M
State University of New York College
  at Fredonia   M
State University of New York College
  at Potsdam   M
State University of West Georgia   M
Stephen F. Austin State University   M
Stony Brook University, State
  University of New York   M,D
Syracuse University   M
Temple University   M,D
Texas A&M University–Commerce   M
Texas Christian University   M,O
Texas Southern University   M
Texas State University-San Marcos   M
Texas Tech University   M,D
Texas Woman's University   M
Towson University   M
Truman State University   M
Tufts University   M
Tulane University   M
University at Buffalo, The State
  University of New York   M,D
The University of Akron   M
The University of Alabama   M,D,O
University of Alaska Fairbanks   M
The University of Arizona   M,D
University of Arkansas   M
University of California, Berkeley   M,D
University of California, Davis   M,D
University of California, Irvine   M
University of California, Los Angeles M,D
University of California, Riverside   M
University of California, San Diego   M,D
University of California, Santa Barbara M,D
University of California, Santa Cruz   M
University of Central Arkansas   M
University of Central Oklahoma   M

University of Chicago   M,D
University of Cincinnati   M,D,O
University of Colorado at Boulder   M,D
University of Colorado at Denver   M
University of Connecticut   M,D
University of Delaware   M
University of Denver   M
University of Florida   M,D
University of Georgia   M
University of Hartford   M,D,O
University of Hawaii at Manoa   M,D
University of Houston   M,D
University of Idaho   M
University of Illinois at Urbana–
  Champaign   M,D
The University of Iowa   M,D
University of Kansas   M,D
University of Kentucky   M,D
University of Louisiana at Lafayette   M
University of Louisiana at Monroe   M
University of Louisville   M,D
University of Maine   M
University of Maryland, College Park   M,D
University of Massachusetts Amherst   M,D
University of Massachusetts Lowell   M
The University of Memphis   M,D
University of Miami   M,D
University of Michigan   M,D,O
University of Minnesota, Duluth   M
University of Minnesota, Twin Cities
  Campus   M,D
University of Mississippi   M,D
University of Missouri–Columbia   M
University of Missouri–Kansas City   M,D
The University of Montana–Missoula   M
University of Montevallo   M
University of Nebraska at Omaha   M
University of Nebraska–Lincoln   M,D
University of Nevada, Las Vegas   M,D
University of Nevada, Reno   M
University of New Hampshire   M
University of New Mexico   M
University of New Orleans   M
The University of North Carolina at
  Chapel Hill   M,D
The University of North Carolina at
  Greensboro   M,D
University of North Dakota   M
University of Northern Colorado   M,D
University of Northern Iowa   M
University of North Texas   M,D
University of Notre Dame   M
University of Oklahoma   M,D
University of Oregon   M,D
University of Pennsylvania   M,D
University of Pittsburgh   M,D
University of Portland   M
University of Redlands   M
University of Rhode Island   M
University of Rochester   M,D
University of South Carolina   M,D,O
The University of South Dakota   M
University of Southern California   M,D
University of Southern Mississippi   M,D
University of South Florida   M
The University of Tennessee   M
The University of Tennessee at
  Chattanooga   M
The University of Texas at Arlington   M
The University of Texas at Austin   M,D
The University of Texas at El Paso   M
The University of Texas at San
  Antonio   M
The University of Texas at Tyler   M
The University of Texas–Pan American   M
University of the Pacific   M
University of Toledo   M
University of Utah   M,D
University of Virginia   M,D
University of Washington   M,D

Directory of Graduate and Professional Programs by Field
Music Education

University of Wisconsin–Madison   M,D
University of Wisconsin–Milwaukee   M
University of Wyoming   M
Virginia Commonwealth University   M
Washington State University   M
Washington University in St. Louis   M,D
Wayne State University   M,O
Webster University   M
West Chester University of
  Pennsylvania   M
Western Carolina University   M
Western Illinois University   M
Western Michigan University   M
Western Washington University   M
West Texas A&M University   M
West Virginia University   M,D
Wichita State University   M
William Paterson University of New
  Jersey   M
Winthrop University   M
Wright State University   M
Yale University   M,D,O
Youngstown State University   M

■ MUSIC EDUCATION

Alabama Agricultural and Mechanical
  University   M
Alabama State University   M
Albany State University   M
Appalachian State University   M
Arcadia University   M,D,O
Arkansas State University   M,O
Auburn University   M,D,O
Austin Peay State University   M
Azusa Pacific University   M
Ball State University   M,D
Baylor University   M
Belmont University   M
Boise State University   M
Boston University   M,D
Bowling Green State University   M
Brigham Young University   M
Brooklyn College of the City
  University of New York   M,D,O
Butler University   M
California State University, Fresno   M
California State University, Fullerton M
California State University, Los
  Angeles   M
California State University, Northridge M
Campbellsville University   M
Capital University   M
Carnegie Mellon University   M
Case Western Reserve University   M,D
The Catholic University of America   M,D
Central Connecticut State University   M
Central Michigan University   M
Cleveland State University   M
The College of Saint Rose   M,O
Colorado State University   M
Columbus State University   M
Converse College   M
Delta State University   M
DePaul University   M
Duquesne University   M,O
East Carolina University   M
Eastern Kentucky University   M
Eastern Washington University   M
East Tennessee State University   M
Emporia State University   M
Florida International University   M
Florida State University   M,D
George Mason University   M
Georgia Southern University   M
Georgia State University   M,D,O
Hardin-Simmons University   M
Hofstra University   M
Holy Names University   M,O
Howard University   M

Peterson's Graduate Schools in the U.S. 2006   www.petersons.com   133

Music Education

Hunter College of the City University of New York	M
Indiana State University	M
Indiana University Bloomington	M,D,O
Indiana University of Pennsylvania	M
Ithaca College	M
Jackson State University	M
Jacksonville University	M
James Madison University	M
Kansas State University	M
Kent State University	M,D
Lamar University	M
Lebanon Valley College	M
Lehman College of the City University of New York	M
Long Island University, C.W. Post Campus	M
Louisiana State University and Agricultural and Mechanical College	M,D
Manhattanville College	M
Marywood University	M
McNeese State University	M
Miami University	M
Michigan State University	M,D
Minnesota State University Moorhead	M
Minot State University	M
Mississippi College	M
Montclair State University	M
Morehead State University	M
Murray State University	M
Nazareth College of Rochester	M
New Jersey City University	M
New York University	M,D,O
Norfolk State University	M
Northern Arizona University	M
Northwestern University	M,D
Northwest Missouri State University	M
Notre Dame de Namur University	M
Ohio University	M
Oregon State University	M
The Pennsylvania State University University Park Campus	M,D
Pittsburg State University	M
Portland State University	M
Queens College of the City University of New York	M,O
Radford University	M
Rhode Island College	M
Rider University	M
Rollins College	M
Roosevelt University	M,O
Rowan University	M
St. Cloud State University	M
Salisbury University	M
Samford University	M
Sam Houston State University	M
San Francisco State University	M
Shenandoah University	M,D,O
Silver Lake College	M
Southeast Missouri State University	M
Southern Illinois University Carbondale	M
Southern Illinois University Edwardsville	M
Southern Methodist University	M,O
State University of New York College at Fredonia	M
State University of New York College at Potsdam	M
State University of West Georgia	M
Syracuse University	M
Teachers College Columbia University	M,D
Temple University	M,D
Tennessee State University	M
Texas A&M University–Commerce	M
Texas A&M University–Kingsville	M
Texas Christian University	M,O
Texas State University-San Marcos	M
Texas Tech University	M,D
Towson University	M,O
University at Buffalo, The State University of New York	M,D,O
The University of Akron	M
The University of Alabama	M,D,O
University of Alaska Fairbanks	M
The University of Arizona	M,D
University of Central Arkansas	M
University of Central Florida	M
University of Central Oklahoma	M
University of Cincinnati	M
University of Colorado at Boulder	M,D
University of Connecticut	M,D
University of Delaware	M
University of Denver	M
University of Florida	M,D
University of Georgia	M,D,O
University of Hartford	M,D,O
University of Houston	M,D
The University of Iowa	M,D
University of Kansas	M,D
University of Louisiana at Lafayette	M
University of Louisville	M
University of Maryland, College Park	M,D
University of Massachusetts Lowell	M
The University of Memphis	M,D
University of Miami	M,D
University of Michigan	M,D,O
University of Minnesota, Duluth	M
University of Missouri–Columbia	M,D
University of Missouri–Kansas City	M,D
University of Missouri–St. Louis	M
The University of Montana–Missoula	M
University of Nebraska at Kearney	M
University of Nevada, Las Vegas	M,D
University of New Hampshire	M
The University of North Carolina at Chapel Hill	M
The University of North Carolina at Greensboro	M,D
University of North Dakota	M
University of Northern Colorado	M,D
University of Northern Iowa	M
University of North Florida	M
University of North Texas	M,D
University of Oklahoma	M,D
University of Oregon	M,D
University of Rochester	M,D
University of St. Thomas (MN)	M
University of South Alabama	M
University of South Carolina	M,D,O
University of Southern California	M,D
University of Southern Mississippi	M,D
University of South Florida	M,D
The University of Tennessee	M
The University of Texas at El Paso	M
The University of Texas at Tyler	M
University of the Pacific	M
University of Toledo	M
University of Washington	M,D
University of Wisconsin–Madison	M,D
University of Wisconsin–Stevens Point	M
University of Wyoming	M
Valdosta State University	M
Virginia Commonwealth University	M
Wayne State College	M
Wayne State University	M,O
Webster University	M
West Chester University of Pennsylvania	M
Western Carolina University	M
Western Connecticut State University	M
Western Kentucky University	M
West Virginia University	M,D
Wichita State University	M
Winthrop University	M
Wright State University	M
Youngstown State University	M

■ NATURAL RESOURCES

Ball State University	M
Colorado State University	M,D
Cornell University	M,D
Duke University	M,D
Georgia Institute of Technology	M,D
Humboldt State University	M
Iowa State University of Science and Technology	M,D
Louisiana State University and Agricultural and Mechanical College	M,D
Montana State University–Bozeman	M,D
North Carolina State University	M
The Ohio State University	M,D
Oklahoma State University	M,D
Purdue University	M,D
State University of New York College of Environmental Science and Forestry	M,D
Texas A&M University	M,D
The University of Arizona	M,D
University of Connecticut	M,D
University of Florida	M,D
University of Georgia	M,D
University of Hawaii at Manoa	M,D
University of Illinois at Urbana–Champaign	M,D
University of Maine	M,D
University of Maryland, College Park	M,D
University of Michigan	M,D,O
The University of Montana–Missoula	M,D
University of Nebraska–Lincoln	M,D
University of New Hampshire	D
University of Oklahoma	M
University of Rhode Island	M,D
University of Wisconsin–Stevens Point	M
University of Wyoming	M,D
Utah State University	M
Virginia Polytechnic Institute and State University	M,D
Washington State University	M,D
West Virginia University	D

■ NATUROPATHIC MEDICINE

University of Bridgeport	M,D

■ NEAR AND MIDDLE EASTERN LANGUAGES

Brandeis University	M,D
Brigham Young University	M
The Catholic University of America	M,D
Columbia University	M,D
Georgetown University	M,D
Harvard University	M,D
Indiana University Bloomington	M,D
The Ohio State University	M
University of California, Los Angeles	M,D
University of Chicago	M,D
University of Michigan	M,D
The University of Texas at Austin	M,D
University of Utah	M,D
University of Wisconsin–Madison	M,D
Yale University	M,D

■ NEAR AND MIDDLE EASTERN STUDIES

Brandeis University	M,D
Columbia University	M,D,O
Cornell University	M,D
Georgetown University	M,O
Gratz College	O
Harvard University	M,D
The Johns Hopkins University	M,D,O
New York University	M,D,O
Princeton University	D
The University of Arizona	M,D
University of California, Berkeley	M,D
University of California, Los Angeles	M,D

Directory of Graduate and Professional Programs by Field
Nuclear Engineering

University of Chicago	M,D
University of Michigan	M,D
University of Pennsylvania	M,D
The University of Texas at Austin	M,D
University of Utah	M,D
University of Washington	M,D
Washington University in St. Louis	M
Wayne State University	M

■ **NEUROBIOLOGY**

Boston University	M,D
Brandeis University	M,D
California Institute of Technology	D
Carnegie Mellon University	M,D
Case Western Reserve University	D
Columbia University	M,D
Cornell University	M,D
Duke University	D
Georgia State University	M,D
Harvard University	D
Indiana University–Purdue University Indianapolis	M,D
Loyola University Chicago	M,D
Marquette University	M,D
Massachusetts Institute of Technology	D
Northwestern University	M,D
Purdue University	M,D
Rutgers, The State University of New Jersey, New Brunswick/Piscataway	D
Saint Louis University	M,D
University at Albany, State University of New York	M,D
The University of Alabama at Birmingham	D
University of California, Irvine	M,D
University of California, Los Angeles	D
University of California, San Diego	D
University of Chicago	D
University of Colorado at Boulder	M,D
University of Connecticut	M,D
University of Illinois at Chicago	M,D
The University of Iowa	M,D
University of Kentucky	D
University of Louisville	M,D
University of Maryland	M,D
University of Missouri–Columbia	M,D
The University of North Carolina at Chapel Hill	D
University of Pennsylvania	D
University of Pittsburgh	M,D
University of Rochester	M,D
University of Southern California	M,D
The University of Texas at San Antonio	D
University of Utah	M,D
University of Vermont	D
University of Washington	D
University of Wisconsin–Madison	D
Wake Forest University	D
Wayne State University	D
West Virginia University	M,D
Yale University	D
Yeshiva University	D

■ **NEUROSCIENCE**

American University	D
Arizona State University	M,D
Baylor University	M,D
Boston University	M,D
Brandeis University	M,D
Brigham Young University	M,D
Brown University	D
California Institute of Technology	M,D
Case Western Reserve University	D
College of Staten Island of the City University of New York	M,D
Colorado State University	M,D
Dartmouth College	D
Drexel University	D
Emory University	D
Florida Atlantic University	D
Florida State University	D
Georgetown University	D
The George Washington University	D
Harvard University	D
Indiana University Bloomington	D
Iowa State University of Science and Technology	M,D
The Johns Hopkins University	D
Kent State University	M,D
Loyola University Chicago	M,D
Massachusetts Institute of Technology	D
Mayo Graduate School	D
Michigan State University	M,D
New York University	M,D
Northwestern University	D
The Ohio State University	D
Ohio University	M,D
The Pennsylvania State University University Park Campus	M,D
Princeton University	D
Purdue University	D
Rutgers, The State University of New Jersey, Newark	D
Rutgers, The State University of New Jersey, New Brunswick/Piscataway	D
Seton Hall University	M
Stanford University	D
Stony Brook University, State University of New York	D
Syracuse University	M,D
Teachers College Columbia University	M,D
Texas A&M University	M,D
Tufts University	D
Tulane University	M,D
University at Albany, State University of New York	M,D
University at Buffalo, The State University of New York	M,D
The University of Alabama at Birmingham	M,D
The University of Arizona	D
University of California, Berkeley	D
University of California, Davis	D
University of California, Los Angeles	D
University of California, Riverside	D
University of California, San Diego	D
University of California, San Francisco	D
University of Cincinnati	D
University of Connecticut	M,D
University of Delaware	D
University of Florida	M,D
University of Hartford	M
University of Hawaii at Manoa	M,D
University of Illinois at Urbana–Champaign	D
The University of Iowa	D
University of Kansas	M,D
University of Maryland	M,D
University of Maryland, Baltimore County	M,D
University of Maryland, College Park	M,D
University of Massachusetts Amherst	M,D
University of Miami	M,D
University of Michigan	D
University of Minnesota, Twin Cities Campus	M,D
University of New Mexico	M,D
University of Oregon	M,D
University of Pennsylvania	D
University of Pittsburgh	D
University of Rochester	M,D
University of South Alabama	D
The University of South Dakota	D
University of Southern California	D
The University of Texas at Austin	M,D
The University of Texas at Dallas	M
University of Utah	D
University of Vermont	D
University of Virginia	D
University of Washington	D
University of Wisconsin–Madison	M,D
Vanderbilt University	D
Virginia Commonwealth University	M,D,O
Wake Forest University	D
Washington State University	M,D
Washington University in St. Louis	D
Yale University	D

■ **NONPROFIT MANAGEMENT**

Azusa Pacific University	M
Boston University	M,O
Carlow University	M
Case Western Reserve University	M,O
Cleveland State University	M,D,O
College of Notre Dame of Maryland	M
The College of Saint Rose	O
DePaul University	M,O
Eastern University	M
Fairleigh Dickinson University, Metropolitan Campus	M,O
Florida Atlantic University	M
The George Washington University	M
Hamline University	M
Hope International University	M
Indiana University Northwest	M,O
Indiana University–Purdue University Indianapolis	M
Indiana University South Bend	M,O
Long Island University, C.W. Post Campus	M,O
Metropolitan State University	M
New School University	M
New York University	M,D,O
North Central College	M
Oral Roberts University	M
Pace University, White Plains Campus	M
Park University	M
Regis University	M,O
Robert Morris University	M
St. Cloud State University	M
San Francisco State University	M
Seattle University	M
Seton Hall University	M
Suffolk University	M,O
Tufts University	O
University of Central Florida	M,O
University of Delaware	M,D
University of Georgia	M,D
The University of Memphis	M
University of Michigan–Dearborn	M,O
University of Missouri–St. Louis	M,O
The University of North Carolina at Greensboro	M,O
University of Pittsburgh	M
University of St. Thomas (MN)	M
University of San Diego	M,D,O
University of San Francisco	M
University of Southern Maine	M,O
University of the Sacred Heart	M
Worcester State College	M

■ **NORTHERN STUDIES**

University of Alaska Fairbanks	M

■ **NUCLEAR ENGINEERING**

Cornell University	M,D
Georgia Institute of Technology	M,D
Idaho State University	M,D,O
Kansas State University	M,D
Massachusetts Institute of Technology	M,D,O
North Carolina State University	M,D
The Ohio State University	M,D
Oregon State University	M,D
The Pennsylvania State University University Park Campus	M,D
Purdue University	M,D
Rensselaer Polytechnic Institute	M,D
Texas A&M University	M,D
The University of Arizona	M,D

Peterson's Graduate Schools in the U.S. 2006

www.petersons.com

Directory of Graduate and Professional Programs by Field

Nuclear Engineering

University of California, Berkeley	M,D
University of Cincinnati	M,D
University of Florida	M,D,O
University of Idaho	M,D
University of Illinois at Urbana–Champaign	M,D
University of Maryland, College Park	M,D
University of Massachusetts Lowell	M
University of Michigan	M,D,O
University of Missouri–Columbia	M,D
University of Missouri–Rolla	M,D
University of New Mexico	M,D
The University of Tennessee	M,D
University of Utah	M,D
University of Wisconsin–Madison	M,D

■ NURSE ANESTHESIA

Arkansas State University	M,O
Barry University	M
Boston College	M,D
California State University, Long Beach	M
Case Western Reserve University	M
Columbia University	M,O
DePaul University	M
Drexel University	M
Duke University	M,O
Emory University	M
Gannon University	M,O
Gonzaga University	M
La Roche College	M
Mount Marty College	M
Newman University	M
Northeastern University	M
Oakland University	M,O
Saint Joseph's University	M
Saint Mary's University of Minnesota	M
Southern Illinois University Edwardsville	M
Southwest Missouri State University	M
Texas Christian University	M
Texas Wesleyan University	M
University at Buffalo, The State University of New York	M,D,O
The University of Alabama at Birmingham	M
University of Cincinnati	M,D
University of Detroit Mercy	M
University of Kansas	M
University of Michigan–Flint	M
University of Minnesota, Twin Cities Campus	M
University of New England	M
The University of North Carolina at Charlotte	M
The University of North Carolina at Greensboro	M,O
University of Pittsburgh	M
The University of Scranton	M,O
University of South Carolina	M
The University of Tennessee at Chattanooga	M
University of Wisconsin–La Crosse	M
Villanova University	M,D,O
Virginia Commonwealth University	M
Wayne State University	M
Webster University	M

■ NURSE MIDWIFERY

Boston University	M,O
Case Western Reserve University	M,D
Columbia University	M
Emory University	M
Illinois State University	M,O
Loyola University Chicago	M
Marquette University	M,D,O
New York University	M,O
Philadelphia University	M
Shenandoah University	M,O

Stony Brook University, State University of New York	M,O
University of Cincinnati	M,D
University of Illinois at Chicago	M
University of Kansas	M,D,O
University of Miami	M,D
University of Michigan	M
University of Minnesota, Twin Cities Campus	M
University of Pennsylvania	M
The University of Texas at El Paso	M
Vanderbilt University	M,D

■ NURSING—GENERAL

Abilene Christian University	M
Adelphi University	M,O
Albany State University	M
Alcorn State University	M
American International College	M
Andrews University	M
Arizona State University	M
Arkansas State University	M,O
Armstrong Atlantic State University	M
Augsburg College	M
Azusa Pacific University	M
Ball State University	M
Barry University	M,D
Baylor University	M
Bellarmine University	M
Belmont University	M
Bethel University	M,O
Bloomsburg University of Pennsylvania	M
Boston College	M,D
Bowie State University	M
Bradley University	M
Brigham Young University	M
California State University, Bakersfield	M
California State University, Chico	M
California State University, Dominguez Hills	M
California State University, Fresno	M
California State University, Fullerton	M
California State University, Long Beach	M
California State University, Los Angeles	M
California State University, Sacramento	M
California State University, San Bernardino	M
Capital University	M
Cardinal Stritch University	M
Carlow University	M,O
Carson-Newman College	M
Case Western Reserve University	M,D
The Catholic University of America	M,D
Central Missouri State University	M
Clarion University of Pennsylvania	M
Clemson University	M
Cleveland State University	M
College Misericordia	M
College of Mount Saint Vincent	M,O
The College of New Jersey	M,O
The College of New Rochelle	M,O
College of St. Catherine	M
The College of St. Scholastica	M
College of Staten Island of the City University of New York	M
Columbia University	M,D,O
Concordia University Wisconsin	M
Coppin State University	M,O
Creighton University	M
Delta State University	M
DePaul University	M
DeSales University	M
Dominican University of California	M
Drexel University	M
Duke University	M,O
Duquesne University	M,D
East Carolina University	M,D
Eastern Kentucky University	M

Eastern Washington University	M
East Tennessee State University	M,D,O
Edgewood College	M
Edinboro University of Pennsylvania	M
Emory University	M,D
Fairfield University	M,O
Fairleigh Dickinson University, Metropolitan Campus	M,O
Florida Agricultural and Mechanical University	M
Florida Atlantic University	M,D,O
Florida Gulf Coast University	M
Florida International University	M,D
Florida State University	M,O
Fort Hays State University	M
Franciscan University of Steubenville	M
Gannon University	M,O
George Mason University	M,D
Georgetown University	M
Georgia College & State University	M
Georgia Southern University	M,O
Georgia State University	M,D
Gonzaga University	M
Governors State University	M
Grambling State University	M
Grand Valley State University	M
Gwynedd-Mercy College	M
Hampton University	M
Hardin-Simmons University	M
Hawai'i Pacific University	M
Holy Family University	M
Holy Names University	M
Howard University	M,O
Hunter College of the City University of New York	M,O
Husson College	M
Idaho State University	M,O
Illinois State University	M,O
Immaculata University	M
Indiana State University	M
Indiana University of Pennsylvania	M
Indiana University–Purdue University Fort Wayne	M
Indiana University–Purdue University Indianapolis	M,D
Indiana Wesleyan University	M,O
Jacksonville State University	M
Jacksonville University	M
The Johns Hopkins University	M,D,O
Kean University	M
Kennesaw State University	M
Kent State University	M,D
Lamar University	M
La Roche College	M
La Salle University	M,O
Lehman College of the City University of New York	M
Lewis University	M
Liberty University	M,D
Loma Linda University	M,O
Long Island University, Brooklyn Campus	M,O
Long Island University, C.W. Post Campus	M,O
Loyola University Chicago	M,D
Loyola University New Orleans	M
Madonna University	M
Malone College	M
Marian College of Fond du Lac	M
Marquette University	M,D,O
Marshall University	M
Maryville University of Saint Louis	M
McNeese State University	M
Mercer University	M
Mercy College	M
Metropolitan State University	M
Michigan State University	M,D
Midwestern State University	M
Millersville University of Pennsylvania	M
Minnesota State University Mankato	M

Directory of Graduate and Professional Programs by Field
Nursing and Healthcare Administration

Institution	Degree
Minnesota State University Moorhead	M,O
Mississippi University for Women	M,O
Molloy College	M,O
Monmouth University	M,O
Montana State University–Bozeman	M
Mount Marty College	M
Mount Saint Mary College	M
Mount St. Mary's College	M
Murray State University	M
National University	M
Nazareth College of Rochester	M
New Jersey City University	M
New Mexico State University	M
New York University	M,D,O
North Dakota State University	M
Northeastern University	M,O
Northern Arizona University	M,O
Northern Illinois University	M
Northern Kentucky University	M,O
Northern Michigan University	M
North Georgia College & State University	M
North Park University	M
Northwestern State University of Louisiana	M
Oakland University	M,O
The Ohio State University	M,D
Old Dominion University	M
Pace University	M,O
Pace University, Pleasantville/Briarcliff Campus	M,O
Pacific Lutheran University	M
The Pennsylvania State University University Park Campus	M,D
Pittsburg State University	M
Point Loma Nazarene University	M
Pontifical Catholic University of Puerto Rico	M
Prairie View A&M University	M
Purdue University Calumet	M
Queens University of Charlotte	M
Quinnipiac University	M
Radford University	M
Regis College (MA)	M,O
Regis University	M
Rivier College	M
Robert Morris University	M
Rutgers, The State University of New Jersey, Newark	M
Sacred Heart University	M
Sage Graduate School	M,O
Saginaw Valley State University	M
St. John Fisher College	M,O
Saint Joseph College	M,O
Saint Joseph's College of Maine	M,O
Saint Louis University	M,D,O
Saint Peter's College	M
Saint Xavier University	M,O
Salem State College	M
Salisbury University	M
Samford University	M
San Diego State University	M
San Francisco State University	M
San Jose State University	M,O
Seattle Pacific University	M,O
Seattle University	M
Seton Hall University	M
Shenandoah University	M,O
Simmons College	M,O
Slippery Rock University of Pennsylvania	M
South Dakota State University	M
Southeastern Louisiana University	M
Southeast Missouri State University	M
Southern Connecticut State University	M
Southern Illinois University Edwardsville	M
Southern Nazarene University	M
Southern University and Agricultural and Mechanical College	M,D,O
Southwest Missouri State University	M
Spalding University	M
State University of New York at Binghamton	M,D,O
State University of New York at New Paltz	M
State University of New York Institute of Technology	M,O
State University of West Georgia	M
Stony Brook University, State University of New York	M,O
Temple University	M
Tennessee State University	M,D
Texas A&M University–Corpus Christi	M
Texas Christian University	M
Texas Woman's University	M,D
Towson University	M,O
Troy University	M
Union University	M,O
University at Buffalo, The State University of New York	M,D,O
The University of Akron	M,D
The University of Alabama	M
The University of Alabama at Birmingham	M,D
The University of Alabama in Huntsville	M,O
University of Alaska Anchorage	M
The University of Arizona	M
University of California, Los Angeles	M,D
University of California, San Francisco	M,D
University of Central Arkansas	M
University of Central Florida	M,O
University of Cincinnati	M,D
University of Colorado at Colorado Springs	M
University of Connecticut	M,D
University of Delaware	M,O
University of Evansville	M
University of Florida	M,D
University of Hartford	M
University of Hawaii at Manoa	M,D,O
University of Illinois at Chicago	M,D
University of Indianapolis	M
The University of Iowa	M,D
University of Kansas	M,D,O
University of Kentucky	M,D
University of Louisiana at Lafayette	M
University of Louisville	M
University of Maine	M,O
University of Mary	M
University of Maryland	M,D
University of Massachusetts Amherst	M,D
University of Massachusetts Boston	M,D
University of Massachusetts Dartmouth	M,O
University of Massachusetts Lowell	M,O
University of Miami	M,D
University of Michigan	M,D
University of Michigan–Flint	M
University of Minnesota, Twin Cities Campus	M,D
University of Missouri–Columbia	M,D
University of Missouri–Kansas City	M,D
University of Missouri–St. Louis	M,D
University of Mobile	M
University of Nevada, Las Vegas	M
University of Nevada, Reno	M
University of New Hampshire	M
University of New Mexico	M,O
The University of North Carolina at Chapel Hill	M,D
The University of North Carolina at Charlotte	M
The University of North Carolina at Greensboro	M,O
The University of North Carolina at Wilmington	M
University of North Dakota	M,D
University of Northern Colorado	M
University of North Florida	M,O
University of Pennsylvania	M,D,O
University of Pittsburgh	M,D
University of Portland	M,O
University of Rhode Island	M,D
University of Rochester	M,D,O
University of St. Francis (IL)	M
University of Saint Francis (IN)	M
University of San Diego	M,D,O
University of San Francisco	M
The University of Scranton	M,O
University of South Alabama	M
University of South Carolina	M,D,O
University of Southern Indiana	M
University of Southern Maine	M,O
University of Southern Mississippi	M,D
University of South Florida	M,D
The University of Tampa	M
The University of Tennessee	M,D
The University of Tennessee at Chattanooga	M
The University of Texas at Arlington	M,D
The University of Texas at Austin	M,D
The University of Texas at El Paso	M
The University of Texas at Tyler	M
The University of Texas–Pan American	M
University of the Incarnate Word	M
University of Utah	M,D
University of Vermont	M
University of Virginia	M,D
University of Washington	M,D
University of Wisconsin–Eau Claire	M
University of Wisconsin–Madison	M,D
University of Wisconsin–Milwaukee	M,D
University of Wisconsin–Oshkosh	M
University of Wyoming	M
Ursuline College	M
Valdosta State University	M
Valparaiso University	M,O
Vanderbilt University	M,D
Villanova University	M,D,O
Virginia Commonwealth University	M,D,O
Viterbo University	M
Wagner College	M
Washington State University	M
Wayne State University	M,D,O
Webster University	M
West Chester University of Pennsylvania	M
Western Carolina University	M
Western Connecticut State University	M
Western Kentucky University	M
Westminster College (UT)	M
West Texas A&M University	M
West Virginia University	M,D,O
Wheeling Jesuit University	M
Wichita State University	M
Widener University	M,D,O
Wilkes University	M
William Carey College	M
William Paterson University of New Jersey	M
Wilmington College (DE)	M
Winona State University	M
Wright State University	M
Xavier University	M
Yale University	M,D,O
York College of Pennsylvania	M
Youngstown State University	M

■ NURSING AND HEALTHCARE ADMINISTRATION

Institution	Degree
Barry University	M,D
Baylor University	M
Bellarmine University	M
Bowie State University	M
Capital University	M
Carlow University	M,O
The Catholic University of America	M,D
College of Mount Saint Vincent	M,O
The College of New Rochelle	M,O

Directory of Graduate and Professional Programs by Field
Nursing and Healthcare Administration

Duke University	M,O
Duquesne University	M
Emory University	M
Florida Agricultural and Mechanical University	M
Florida Atlantic University	M
Gannon University	M,O
George Mason University	M,D
Grand Valley State University	M
Indiana University–Purdue University Fort Wayne	M
The Johns Hopkins University	M
Kean University	M
Kent State University	M,D
Lamar University	M
La Roche College	M
La Salle University	M,O
Lewis University	M
Loma Linda University	M,O
Long Island University, Brooklyn Campus	M
Loyola University Chicago	M
Madonna University	M
Marymount University	M,O
Marywood University	M
Minnesota State University Mankato	M,O
Molloy College	M
Mount Saint Mary College	M
Northeastern University	M
Pacific Lutheran University	M
Queens University of Charlotte	M
Rivier College	M
Sacred Heart University	M
Saginaw Valley State University	M
Saint Joseph's College of Maine	M,O
Saint Xavier University	M,O
San Francisco State University	M
San Jose State University	M,O
Seattle Pacific University	M
Seattle University	M
Seton Hall University	M
Southern Connecticut State University	M
Southern University and Agricultural and Mechanical College	M,D,O
Spalding University	M
State University of New York Institute of Technology	M,O
Texas A&M University–Corpus Christi	M
Texas Woman's University	M,D
Union University	M,O
University of Cincinnati	M,D
University of Colorado at Colorado Springs	M
University of Delaware	M,O
University of Hawaii at Manoa	M,D,O
University of Illinois at Chicago	M
University of Mary	M
University of Maryland	M,D
University of Massachusetts Lowell	D
University of Michigan	M
University of Minnesota, Twin Cities Campus	M
University of Missouri–Kansas City	M,D
The University of North Carolina at Greensboro	M,O
University of Pennsylvania	M,D
University of Pittsburgh	M
University of Portland	M,O
University of Rhode Island	M,D
University of San Diego	M,D,O
University of San Francisco	M
University of South Alabama	M
University of South Carolina	M
University of Southern Maine	M,O
University of Southern Mississippi	M,D
The University of Tampa	M
The University of Tennessee at Chattanooga	M
The University of Texas at Arlington	M,D
The University of Texas at El Paso	M
The University of Texas at Tyler	M
Valdosta State University	M
Vanderbilt University	M,D
Villanova University	M,D,O
Virginia Commonwealth University	M,D,O
Wichita State University	M
Wright State University	M
Xavier University	M

■ NURSING EDUCATION

Barry University	M
Bellarmine University	M
Bethel University	M,O
Bowie State University	M
The Catholic University of America	M,D
The College of New Rochelle	M,O
Concordia University Wisconsin	M
Duke University	M,O
Duquesne University	M
Eastern Michigan University	M
Eastern Washington University	M
Florida State University	M,O
Grand Valley State University	M
Kent State University	M,D
La Salle University	M,O
Lewis University	M
Marian College of Fond du Lac	M
Midwestern State University	M
Minnesota State University Mankato	M
Minnesota State University Moorhead	M
Molloy College	M,O
Mount Saint Mary College	M
New York University	M,O
Rivier College	M
Saginaw Valley State University	M
Saint Joseph's College of Maine	M,O
San Francisco State University	M
San Jose State University	M,O
Seton Hall University	M
Southern Connecticut State University	M
Southern University and Agricultural and Mechanical College	M,D,O
Teachers College Columbia University	M,D
Texas Woman's University	M,D
Union University	M,O
University of Central Florida	M,O
University of Hartford	M
University of Kansas	M,D,O
University of Mary	M
University of Maryland	M,D
University of Minnesota, Twin Cities Campus	M
University of Missouri–Kansas City	M,D
University of Northern Colorado	M
University of Pittsburgh	M
University of Portland	M,O
University of Rhode Island	M,D
University of South Alabama	M
The University of Tampa	M
The University of Tennessee at Chattanooga	M
The University of Texas at Arlington	M,D
The University of Texas at Tyler	M
Villanova University	M,D,O
Wayne State University	O
West Chester University of Pennsylvania	M
Wichita State University	M

■ NUTRITION

Andrews University	M
Auburn University	M,D
Boston University	M,D
Bowling Green State University	M
Brigham Young University	M
Brooklyn College of the City University of New York	M
California State Polytechnic University, Pomona	M
California State University, Chico	M
California State University, Long Beach	M
California State University, Los Angeles	M
Case Western Reserve University	M,D
Central Michigan University	M
Central Washington University	M
Chapman University	M
Clemson University	M
Colorado State University	M,D
Columbia University	M,D
Cornell University	M,D
Drexel University	M,D
East Carolina University	M
Eastern Illinois University	M
Eastern Kentucky University	M
East Tennessee State University	M
Emory University	M,D
Florida International University	M,D
Florida State University	M,D
Framingham State College	M
Georgia State University	M
Harvard University	D
Howard University	M,D
Idaho State University	M,O
Immaculata University	M
Indiana State University	M
Indiana University of Pennsylvania	M
Indiana University–Purdue University Indianapolis	M
Iowa State University of Science and Technology	M,D
The Johns Hopkins University	M,D
Kansas State University	M,D
Kent State University	M,O
Lehman College of the City University of New York	M
Loma Linda University	M,D
Long Island University, C.W. Post Campus	M,O
Louisiana Tech University	M
Marywood University	M,D
Meredith College	M
Michigan State University	M,D
Middle Tennessee State University	M
Montclair State University	M,O
Mount Mary College	M
New York Institute of Technology	M
New York University	M,D
North Carolina Agricultural and Technical State University	M
North Carolina State University	M,D
North Dakota State University	M
Northern Illinois University	M
The Ohio State University	M,D
Ohio University	M
Oklahoma State University	M,D
Oregon State University	M,D
The Pennsylvania State University University Park Campus	M,D
Purdue University	M,D
Rutgers, The State University of New Jersey, New Brunswick/Piscataway	M,D
Sage Graduate School	M
Saint Louis University	M
San Diego State University	M
San Jose State University	M
Simmons College	M,O
South Carolina State University	M
Southeast Missouri State University	M
Southern Illinois University Carbondale	M
Syracuse University	M
Teachers College Columbia University	M,D
Texas A&M University	M,D
Texas Southern University	M
Texas Tech University	M,D
Texas Woman's University	M,D
Tufts University	M,D
Tulane University	M

Directory of Graduate and Professional Programs by Field
Operations Research

Tuskegee University	M
University at Buffalo, The State University of New York	M,D
The University of Akron	M
The University of Alabama	M
The University of Alabama at Birmingham	M,D,O
The University of Arizona	M,D
University of Bridgeport	M
University of California, Berkeley	M,D
University of California, Davis	M,D
University of Central Oklahoma	M
University of Chicago	D
University of Cincinnati	M
University of Connecticut	M,D
University of Delaware	M
University of Florida	M,D
University of Georgia	M,D
University of Hawaii at Manoa	M
University of Illinois at Chicago	M,D
University of Illinois at Urbana–Champaign	M,D
University of Kansas	M,O
University of Kentucky	M,D
University of Maine	M,D
University of Maryland, College Park	M,D
University of Massachusetts Amherst	M
The University of Memphis	M
University of Michigan	M
University of Minnesota, Twin Cities Campus	M,D
University of Missouri–Columbia	M,D
University of Nebraska–Lincoln	M,D
University of Nevada, Reno	M
University of New Hampshire	M,D
University of New Haven	M
University of New Mexico	M
The University of North Carolina at Chapel Hill	M,D
The University of North Carolina at Greensboro	M,D
University of North Florida	M,O
University of Pittsburgh	M
University of Puerto Rico, Río Piedras	M
University of Rhode Island	M,D
University of Southern California	M
University of Southern Mississippi	M,D
The University of Tennessee	M
The University of Tennessee at Martin	M
The University of Texas at Austin	M,D
University of the Incarnate Word	M
University of Utah	M
University of Vermont	M
University of Washington	M,D
University of Wisconsin–Madison	M,D
University of Wisconsin–Stevens Point	M
University of Wisconsin–Stout	M
University of Wyoming	M
Utah State University	M,D
Virginia Polytechnic Institute and State University	M,D
Washington State University	M,D
Wayne State University	M,D,O
West Virginia University	M
Winthrop University	M

■ OCCUPATIONAL HEALTH NURSING

University of Cincinnati	M,D
University of Massachusetts Lowell	M
University of Michigan	M
University of Minnesota, Twin Cities Campus	M,D
The University of North Carolina at Chapel Hill	M
University of Pennsylvania	M
Vanderbilt University	M,D

■ OCCUPATIONAL THERAPY

American International College	M
Barry University	M
Belmont University	M,D
Boston University	M,D
Brenau University	M
Cleveland State University	M
College Misericordia	M
College of St. Catherine	M
The College of St. Scholastica	M
Colorado State University	M
Columbia University	M
Concordia University Wisconsin	M
Creighton University	D
Dominican University of California	M
Duquesne University	M,D
East Carolina University	M
Eastern Kentucky University	M
Eastern Michigan University	M
Florida International University	M
Gannon University	M
Governors State University	M
Grand Valley State University	M
Idaho State University	M
Ithaca College	M
Kean University	M
Maryville University of Saint Louis	M
Mercy College	M
Milligan College	M
Mount Mary College	M
New York Institute of Technology	M
New York University	M,D
Nova Southeastern University	M,D
The Ohio State University	M
Pacific University	M
Philadelphia University	M
Quinnipiac University	M
Rockhurst University	M
Sacred Heart University	M
St. Ambrose University	M
Saint Francis University	M
Saint Louis University	M
San Jose State University	M
Seton Hall University	M
Shenandoah University	M
Spalding University	M
Springfield College	M,O
Stony Brook University, State University of New York	M,D,O
Temple University	M
Texas Woman's University	M,D
Touro College	M
Towson University	M
Tufts University	M,O
University at Buffalo, The State University of New York	M
The University of Alabama at Birmingham	M
University of Central Arkansas	M
The University of Findlay	M
University of Florida	M
University of Illinois at Chicago	M
University of Indianapolis	M,D
University of Kansas	M,D
University of Mary	M
University of New England	M
University of New Hampshire	M
University of New Mexico	M
The University of North Carolina at Chapel Hill	M,D
University of North Dakota	M
University of Pittsburgh	M
The University of Scranton	M
The University of South Dakota	M
University of Southern California	M,D
University of Southern Indiana	M
University of Southern Maine	M
The University of Texas–Pan American	M
University of Utah	M
University of Washington	M
University of Wisconsin–Milwaukee	M
Virginia Commonwealth University	M
Washington University in St. Louis	M,D
Wayne State University	M
Western Michigan University	M
West Virginia University	M
Worcester State College	M

■ OCEAN ENGINEERING

Florida Atlantic University	M,D
Florida Institute of Technology	M,D
Georgia Institute of Technology	M,D
Massachusetts Institute of Technology	M,D,O
Oregon State University	M
Stevens Institute of Technology	M,D
Texas A&M University	M,D
University of California, Berkeley	M,D
University of California, San Diego	M,D
University of Delaware	M,D
University of Florida	M,D,O
University of Hawaii at Manoa	M,D
University of Miami	M,D
University of Michigan	M,D,O
University of New Hampshire	M,D
University of Rhode Island	M,D
University of Southern California	M
Virginia Polytechnic Institute and State University	M,D

■ OCEANOGRAPHY

Columbia University	M,D
Cornell University	D
Florida Institute of Technology	M,D
Florida State University	M,D
The Johns Hopkins University	M,D
Louisiana State University and Agricultural and Mechanical College	M,D
Massachusetts Institute of Technology	M,D,O
North Carolina State University	M,D
Nova Southeastern University	D
Old Dominion University	M,D
Oregon State University	M,D
Princeton University	D
Rutgers, The State University of New Jersey, New Brunswick/Piscataway	M,D
Texas A&M University	M,D
University of Alaska Fairbanks	M,D
University of California, San Diego	M,D
University of Colorado at Boulder	M,D
University of Connecticut	M,D
University of Delaware	M,D
University of Georgia	M,D
University of Hawaii at Manoa	M,D
University of Maine	M,D
University of Miami	M,D
University of Michigan	M,D
University of New Hampshire	M,D
University of Puerto Rico, Mayagüez Campus	M,D
University of Rhode Island	M,D
University of Southern California	D
University of South Florida	M,D
University of Washington	M,D
University of Wisconsin–Madison	M,D
Yale University	D

■ ONCOLOGY NURSING

Columbia University	M,O
Duke University	M,O
Emory University	M
Gwynedd-Mercy College	M
Loyola University Chicago	M
University of Delaware	M,O
University of Pennsylvania	M

■ OPERATIONS RESEARCH

Bernard M. Baruch College of the City University of New York	M
California State University, Fullerton	M
California State University, Hayward	M
Carnegie Mellon University	D

Directory of Graduate and Professional Programs by Field
Operations Research

Case Western Reserve University	M,D
Claremont Graduate University	M,D
Clemson University	M,D
The College of William and Mary	M
Columbia University	M,D,O
Cornell University	M,D
Florida Institute of Technology	M,D
George Mason University	M
Georgia Institute of Technology	M
Georgia State University	M,D
Idaho State University	M,D,O
Indiana University–Purdue University Fort Wayne	M
Iowa State University of Science and Technology	M,D
The Johns Hopkins University	M,D
Kansas State University	M,D
Louisiana Tech University	M,D
Loyola University Chicago	M
Massachusetts Institute of Technology	M,D
Miami University	M
New Mexico Institute of Mining and Technology	M,D
North Carolina State University	M,D
North Dakota State University	M,D,O
Northeastern University	M,D
Northwestern University	M,D
Oklahoma State University	M,D
Oregon State University	M,D
Pace University, White Plains Campus	M
Princeton University	M,D
Purdue University	M,D
Rensselaer Polytechnic Institute	M,D
Rutgers, The State University of New Jersey, New Brunswick/Piscataway	D
St. Mary's University of San Antonio	M
Southern Methodist University	M,D
Temple University	D
The University of Alabama in Huntsville	M
University of Arkansas	M
University of California, Berkeley	M,D
University of California, Los Angeles	M,D
University of Central Florida	M,D,O
University of Colorado at Boulder	M
University of Delaware	M,D
University of Illinois at Chicago	D
The University of Iowa	M,D
University of Massachusetts Amherst	M,D
University of Miami	M,D
University of Michigan	M,D
University of New Haven	M
The University of North Carolina at Chapel Hill	M,D
University of Southern California	M
The University of Texas at Austin	M,D
Virginia Commonwealth University	M
Virginia Polytechnic Institute and State University	M,D
Wayne State University	M,D
Western Michigan University	M

■ OPTICAL SCIENCES

Alabama Agricultural and Mechanical University	M,D
Cleveland State University	M
Columbia University	M,D,O
Indiana University Bloomington	M,D
Norfolk State University	M
The Ohio State University	M,D
Rochester Institute of Technology	M,D
The University of Alabama in Huntsville	D
The University of Arizona	M,D
University of Central Florida	M,D,O
University of Colorado at Boulder	M,D
University of Dayton	M,D
University of Maryland, Baltimore County	M,D
University of Massachusetts Lowell	M,D
University of New Mexico	M,D
The University of North Carolina at Charlotte	M,D
University of Rochester	M,D

■ OPTOMETRY

Ferris State University	P
Indiana University Bloomington	P
Northeastern State University	P
Nova Southeastern University	P,M
The Ohio State University	P
Pacific University	P
The University of Alabama at Birmingham	P
University of California, Berkeley	P,O
University of Houston	P
University of Missouri–St. Louis	P

■ ORAL AND DENTAL SCIENCES

Boston University	P,M,D,O
Case Western Reserve University	M,O
Columbia University	M
The George Washington University	M
Harvard University	M,D,O
Howard University	P,O
Idaho State University	O
Indiana University–Purdue University Indianapolis	M,D
Jacksonville University	O
Loma Linda University	M,O
Marquette University	M
New York University	M,D,O
Nova Southeastern University	P,M
The Ohio State University	M,D
Saint Louis University	M
Stony Brook University, State University of New York	P,D,O
Temple University	M,O
Tufts University	M,O
University at Buffalo, The State University of New York	M,D,O
The University of Alabama at Birmingham	M
University of California, Los Angeles	M,D
University of California, San Francisco	M,D
University of Connecticut	M
University of Detroit Mercy	M,O
University of Florida	M,D,O
University of Illinois at Chicago	M
The University of Iowa	M,D,O
University of Kentucky	M
University of Louisville	M
University of Maryland	P,M,D,O
University of Michigan	M,D,O
University of Minnesota, Twin Cities Campus	M,D
University of Missouri–Kansas City	P,M,D,O
The University of North Carolina at Chapel Hill	M,D
University of Pittsburgh	O
University of Rochester	M
University of Southern California	M,D
University of the Pacific	M,O
University of Washington	M,D
West Virginia University	M

■ ORGANIC CHEMISTRY

Boston College	M,D
Brandeis University	M,D
Brigham Young University	M,D
California State University, Fullerton	M
California State University, Los Angeles	M
Case Western Reserve University	M,D
Clark Atlanta University	M,D
Clarkson University	M,D
Cleveland State University	M,D
Columbia University	M,D
Cornell University	D
Florida State University	M,D
Georgetown University	M,D
The George Washington University	M,D
Harvard University	D
Howard University	M,D
Illinois Institute of Technology	M,D
Kansas State University	M,D
Kent State University	M,D
Marquette University	M,D
Massachusetts Institute of Technology	M,D,O
Miami University	M,D
Northeastern University	M,D
Old Dominion University	M
Oregon State University	M,D
Purdue University	M,D
Rensselaer Polytechnic Institute	M,D
Rice University	M,D
Rutgers, The State University of New Jersey, Newark	M,D
Rutgers, The State University of New Jersey, New Brunswick/Piscataway	M,D
Seton Hall University	M,D
South Dakota State University	M,D
Southern University and Agricultural and Mechanical College	M
State University of New York at Binghamton	M,D
State University of New York College of Environmental Science and Forestry	M,D
Stevens Institute of Technology	M,D,O
Tufts University	M,D
University of Cincinnati	M,D
University of Georgia	M,D
University of Louisville	M,D
University of Maryland, College Park	M,D
University of Miami	M,D
University of Michigan	D
University of Missouri–Columbia	M,D
University of Missouri–Kansas City	M,D
University of Missouri–St. Louis	M,D
The University of Montana–Missoula	M,D
University of Nebraska–Lincoln	M,D
University of Notre Dame	M,D
University of Southern Mississippi	M,D
University of South Florida	M,D
The University of Tennessee	M,D
The University of Texas at Austin	M,D
University of Toledo	M,D
Vanderbilt University	M,D
Wake Forest University	M,D
Washington State University	M,D
West Virginia University	M,D
Yale University	D

■ ORGANIZATIONAL BEHAVIOR

Benedictine University	M
Bernard M. Baruch College of the City University of New York	M,D
Boston College	D
Boston University	M
California Lutheran University	M
Carnegie Mellon University	D
Case Western Reserve University	M,D
Cornell University	M,D
Drexel University	M,D,O
Fairleigh Dickinson University, College at Florham	M,O
The George Washington University	M,D
Georgia Institute of Technology	M,D,O
Harvard University	D
Indiana University Bloomington	D
Lindenwood University	M
Northwestern University	M,D
Polytechnic University, Brooklyn Campus	M
Purdue University	M,D
Silver Lake College	M
Syracuse University	D
Towson University	O
University of California, Berkeley	D

Pathology

University of Hartford M
University of Hawaii at Manoa M
The University of North Carolina at
 Chapel Hill D
University of Pennsylvania M

■ ORGANIZATIONAL MANAGEMENT

American International College M
American University M
Antioch University Los Angeles M
Antioch University Seattle M
Augsburg College M
Azusa Pacific University M
Benedictine University D
Bernard M. Baruch College of the City
 University of New York M,D
Bethel University M
Biola University M
Boston College D
Bowling Green State University M
Brenau University M
Cabrini College M,O
Carnegie Mellon University D
Charleston Southern University M
City University M,O
College Misericordia M
College of Mount St. Joseph M
College of St. Catherine M
Colorado Technical University M,D
Dallas Baptist University M
Dominican University M
Eastern Connecticut State University M
Eastern Michigan University M
Emory University D
Fairleigh Dickinson University, College
 at Florham M,O
Geneva College M
George Fox University M
George Mason University M
The George Washington University M,O
Gonzaga University M
Hawai'i Pacific University M
Immaculata University M
Indiana Wesleyan University M,D,O
John F. Kennedy University M,O
Johnson & Wales University M
Lehigh University M,D,O
Lewis University M
Loyola University Chicago M
Manhattanville College M
Marian College of Fond du Lac M
Marymount University M,O
Mercy College M
Metropolitan State University M
Michigan State University M,D
Newman University M
New School University M
New York University M,D,O
Northwestern University M,D
Nova Southeastern University D
Palm Beach Atlantic University M
Pfeiffer University M
Regent University M,D,O
Regis College (MA) M
Regis University M,O
Roosevelt University M,D
Rutgers, The State University of New
 Jersey, Newark D
Sage Graduate School M
St. Ambrose University M
St. Edward's University M
Saint Joseph's University M
School for International Training M
Shippensburg University of
 Pennsylvania M
Spring Arbor University P,M
Trevecca Nazarene University M
Trinity College (DC) M
Tusculum College M

University at Albany, State University
 of New York D
University at Buffalo, The State
 University of New York M,D
University of Colorado at Boulder M,D
University of Connecticut M
University of Denver M,O
University of Hawaii at Manoa M,D
University of La Verne M,D,O
University of New Mexico M
University of North Texas M,D
University of Pennsylvania M
University of St. Thomas (MN) M,D,O
University of San Francisco M
The University of Scranton M
The University of Tennessee at
 Chattanooga M
The University of Texas at San
 Antonio D
University of the Incarnate Word M,D
Vanderbilt University M,D
Wayland Baptist University M

■ OSTEOPATHIC MEDICINE

Michigan State University P
New York Institute of Technology P
Nova Southeastern University P,M
Ohio University P
University of New England P

■ PAPER AND PULP ENGINEERING

Miami University M
North Carolina State University M,D
Oregon State University M,D
State University of New York College
 of Environmental Science and
 Forestry M,D
University of Washington M,D
Western Michigan University M,D

■ PARASITOLOGY

New York University M,D
Purdue University M,D
Texas A&M University M,D
Tulane University M,D,O
University of Georgia M
University of Notre Dame M,D
University of Pennsylvania D
University of Washington M,D
West Virginia University M,D
Yale University D

■ PASTORAL MINISTRY AND COUNSELING

Abilene Christian University M,D
Andrews University P,M,D,O
Anna Maria College M
Argosy University/Sarasota M,D,O
Azusa Pacific University P,M
Barry University M,D
Bayamón Central University P,M
Boston College M,D
Chaminade University of Honolulu M
Chestnut Hill College M,O
College of Mount St. Joseph M
Concordia University (NE) M
Cornerstone University P,M
Dallas Baptist University M
Fordham University M,D,O
Freed-Hardeman University M
Gannon University M,O
Gardner-Webb University P,D
George Fox University P,M,D
Golden Gate Baptist Theological
 Seminary P,M,D,O
Gonzaga University P,M
Grand Rapids Theological Seminary of
 Cornerstone University P,M
Harding University M

Hardin-Simmons University M
Holy Names University M,O
Hope International University M
Houston Baptist University M
Iona College M,O
The Johns Hopkins University M,D,O
La Salle University M
Lewis University M
Loma Linda University M,O
Loras College M
Loyola College in Maryland M,D,O
Loyola Marymount University M
Loyola University Chicago M
Malone College M
Marygrove College M
Marymount University M,O
Olivet Nazarene University M
Oral Roberts University P,M,D
Providence College M
St. Ambrose University M
Saint Joseph College M,O
Saint Joseph's College of Maine M,O
Saint Mary's University of Minnesota M,O
St. Mary's University of San Antonio M
St. Thomas University M,O
Santa Clara University M
Seattle University M
Seton Hall University P,M,O
Southern Wesleyan University M
Texas Christian University P,M,D,O
University of Dayton M,D
University of Portland M
University of St. Thomas (MN) M,D
University of San Diego M,O
University of San Francisco M
Wake Forest University M
Wayland Baptist University M
Xavier University of Louisiana M

■ PATHOBIOLOGY

Auburn University M,D
Brown University M,D
Columbia University M,D
Drexel University D
The Johns Hopkins University D
Kansas State University M,D
Michigan State University M,D
The Ohio State University M,D
The Pennsylvania State University
 University Park Campus M,D
Purdue University M,D
Texas A&M University M,D
The University of Arizona M,D
University of Cincinnati D
University of Connecticut M,D
University of Illinois at Urbana–
 Champaign M,D
University of Missouri–Columbia M,D
University of Southern California M,D
University of Washington M,D
University of Wyoming M
Wake Forest University M,D

■ PATHOLOGY

Boston University D
Brown University M,D
Case Western Reserve University M,D
Colorado State University M,D
Columbia University M,D
Duke University M,D
East Carolina University D
Georgetown University M,D
Harvard University D
Indiana University–Purdue University
 Indianapolis M,D
Iowa State University of Science and
 Technology M,D
The Johns Hopkins University D
Michigan State University M,D
New York University M,D

Directory of Graduate and Professional Programs by Field
Pathology

North Carolina State University	M,D
The Ohio State University	M
Oregon State University	M
Purdue University	M,D
Quinnipiac University	M
Saint Louis University	D
Stony Brook University, State University of New York	M,D
Temple University	D
Texas A&M University	M,D
University at Albany, State University of New York	M,D
University at Buffalo, The State University of New York	M,D
The University of Alabama at Birmingham	D
University of California, Davis	M,D
University of California, Los Angeles	M,D
University of California, San Diego	D
University of California, San Francisco	D
University of Chicago	D
University of Cincinnati	D
University of Florida	M,D
University of Georgia	M,D
The University of Iowa	M
University of Kansas	M,D
University of Maryland	M,D
University of Michigan	D
University of New Mexico	M,D
The University of North Carolina at Chapel Hill	D
University of Pittsburgh	M,D
University of Rochester	M,D
University of Southern California	M,D
University of South Florida	M,D
University of Utah	M,D
University of Vermont	M
University of Washington	M,D
University of Wisconsin–Madison	D
Vanderbilt University	D
Virginia Commonwealth University	M,D
Washington State University	M,D
Wayne State University	D
Yale University	D
Yeshiva University	D

■ PEDIATRIC NURSING

Baylor University	M
Case Western Reserve University	M,D
The Catholic University of America	M,D
Columbia University	M,O
Duke University	M,O
Emory University	M
Georgia State University	M,D
Gwynedd-Mercy College	M
Hunter College of the City University of New York	M,O
Indiana University–Purdue University Indianapolis	M
The Johns Hopkins University	M,O
Kent State University	M,D
Lehman College of the City University of New York	M
Loma Linda University	M
Loyola University Chicago	M
Marquette University	M,D,O
Molloy College	M
New York University	M,O
Northeastern University	M,O
Seton Hall University	M
Spalding University	M
Stony Brook University, State University of New York	M,O
University at Buffalo, The State University of New York	M,D,O
University of Central Florida	M,O
University of Cincinnati	M,D
University of Delaware	M,O
University of Illinois at Chicago	M
University of Maryland	M,D

University of Michigan	M
University of Minnesota, Twin Cities Campus	M
University of Missouri–Kansas City	M,D
University of Nevada, Las Vegas	M
University of Pennsylvania	M
University of Pittsburgh	M
University of San Diego	M,D,O
University of South Alabama	M
University of South Carolina	M
The University of Texas–Pan American	M
Vanderbilt University	M,D
Villanova University	M,D,O
Virginia Commonwealth University	M,D,O
Wayne State University	M
Wright State University	M

■ PETROLEUM ENGINEERING

Louisiana State University and Agricultural and Mechanical College	M,D
New Mexico Institute of Mining and Technology	M,D
The Pennsylvania State University University Park Campus	M,D
Stanford University	M,D,O
Texas A&M University	M,D
Texas A&M University–Kingsville	M
Texas Tech University	M,D
University of Alaska Fairbanks	M
University of California, Berkeley	M,D
University of Houston	M,D
University of Kansas	M,D
University of Louisiana at Lafayette	M
University of Missouri–Rolla	M,D
University of Oklahoma	M
University of Pittsburgh	M,D
University of Southern California	M,D,O
The University of Texas at Austin	M,D
University of Tulsa	M,D
University of Utah	M,D
University of Wyoming	M,D
West Virginia University	M,D

■ PHARMACEUTICAL ADMINISTRATION

Duquesne University	M
Fairleigh Dickinson University, Metropolitan Campus	M,O
Florida Agricultural and Mechanical University	M,D
Idaho State University	P,M,D
Long Island University, Brooklyn Campus	M
The Ohio State University	M,D
St. John's University (NY)	M
San Diego State University	M
Seton Hall University	M
University of Florida	M,D
University of Georgia	M,D
University of Houston	P,M,D
University of Illinois at Chicago	M,D
University of Maryland	D
University of Michigan	D
University of Minnesota, Twin Cities Campus	M,D
University of Mississippi	M,D
University of Rhode Island	M,D
University of Toledo	M
University of Wisconsin–Madison	M,D
West Virginia University	M,D

■ PHARMACEUTICAL ENGINEERING

New Jersey Institute of Technology	M
University of Michigan	M

■ PHARMACEUTICAL SCIENCES

Auburn University	M,D

Butler University	P,M
Campbell University	P,M
Creighton University	M,D
Duquesne University	M,D
Florida Agricultural and Mechanical University	M,D
Idaho State University	M,D
Loma Linda University	M,D
Long Island University, Brooklyn Campus	M,D
Mercer University	P,D
North Dakota State University	M,D
Northeastern University	P,M,D
The Ohio State University	M,D
Oregon State University	P,M,D
Purdue University	M,D
Rutgers, The State University of New Jersey, New Brunswick/Piscataway	M,D
St. John's University (NY)	M,D
South Dakota State University	M
Temple University	M,D
University at Buffalo, The State University of New York	M,D
The University of Arizona	D
University of California, San Francisco	D
University of Cincinnati	M,D
University of Connecticut	M,D
University of Georgia	M,D
University of Houston	P,M,D
University of Illinois at Chicago	M,D
The University of Iowa	M,D
University of Kansas	M
University of Kentucky	M,D
University of Louisiana at Monroe	M
University of Maryland	D
University of Michigan	D
University of Minnesota, Twin Cities Campus	M,D
University of Mississippi	M,D
University of Missouri–Kansas City	P,M,D
The University of Montana–Missoula	M,D
University of New Mexico	M,D
The University of North Carolina at Chapel Hill	M,D
University of Rhode Island	M,D
University of South Carolina	M,D
University of Southern California	M,D
The University of Texas at Austin	M,D
University of the Pacific	M,D
University of Toledo	M
University of Washington	M,D
University of Wisconsin–Madison	M,D
Virginia Commonwealth University	P,M,D
Wayne State University	M,D
West Virginia University	M,D

■ PHARMACOLOGY

Auburn University	M,D
Boston University	M,D
Brown University	M,D
Case Western Reserve University	M,D
Columbia University	M,D
Cornell University	M,D
Creighton University	D
Dartmouth College	D
Drexel University	M,D
Duke University	D
Duquesne University	M,D
East Carolina University	D
East Tennessee State University	M,D
Emory University	D
Fairleigh Dickinson University, College at Florham	M,O
Florida Agricultural and Mechanical University	M,D
Georgetown University	D
The George Washington University	D
Harvard University	D
Howard University	M,D
Idaho State University	M,D

Indiana University Bloomington	M,D
Indiana University–Purdue University Indianapolis	M,D
The Johns Hopkins University	D
Kent State University	M,D
Long Island University, Brooklyn Campus	M
Loyola University Chicago	M,D
Mayo Graduate School	D
Michigan State University	M,D
New York University	M,D
North Carolina State University	M,D
Northeastern University	M,D
Northwestern University	D
Nova Southeastern University	M
The Ohio State University	M,D
Purdue University	M,D
Rutgers, The State University of New Jersey, New Brunswick/Piscataway	D
St. John's University (NY)	
Saint Louis University	D
Southern Illinois University Carbondale	M,D
Stanford University	D
Stony Brook University, State University of New York	D
Temple University	M,D
Tufts University	D
Tulane University	M,D
University at Buffalo, The State University of New York	M,D
The University of Alabama at Birmingham	D
The University of Arizona	M,D,O
University of California, Davis	M,D
University of California, Irvine	M,D
University of California, Los Angeles	D
University of California, San Diego	D
University of California, San Francisco	D
University of Chicago	D
University of Cincinnati	D
University of Connecticut	M,D
University of Florida	M,D
University of Georgia	M,D
University of Hawaii at Manoa	M,D
University of Houston	P,M,D
University of Illinois at Chicago	D
The University of Iowa	M,D
University of Kansas	M,D
University of Kentucky	D
University of Louisville	M,D
University of Maryland	M,D
University of Miami	D
University of Michigan	D
University of Minnesota, Duluth	M,D
University of Minnesota, Twin Cities Campus	M,D
University of Mississippi	M,D
University of Missouri–Columbia	M,D
The University of Montana–Missoula	M,D
University of Nevada, Reno	M,D
The University of North Carolina at Chapel Hill	D
University of North Dakota	M,D
University of Pennsylvania	D
University of Pittsburgh	D
University of Rhode Island	M,D
University of Rochester	M,D
University of South Alabama	D
The University of South Dakota	M,D
University of Southern California	M,D
University of South Florida	M,D
University of Toledo	M
University of Utah	D
University of Vermont	M,D
University of Virginia	D
University of Washington	M,D
University of Wisconsin–Madison	M,D
Vanderbilt University	D
Virginia Commonwealth University	M,D,O
Wake Forest University	D
Washington State University	M,D
Wayne State University	M,D
West Virginia University	M,D
Wright State University	M
Yale University	D
Yeshiva University	D

■ **PHARMACY**

Auburn University	P
Butler University	P,M
Campbell University	P,M
Creighton University	P
Drake University	P
Duquesne University	P
Ferris State University	P
Florida Agricultural and Mechanical University	P,D
Howard University	P
Idaho State University	P,M,D
Mercer University	P,D
Nova Southeastern University	P
The Ohio State University	P
Oregon State University	P,M,D
Palm Beach Atlantic University	P
Purdue University	P
Rutgers, The State University of New Jersey, New Brunswick/Piscataway	P
St. John's University (NY)	P
Samford University	P
Shenandoah University	P
South Dakota State University	P
Southwestern Oklahoma State University	P
Temple University	P
Texas Southern University	P,M
University at Buffalo, The State University of New York	P
The University of Arizona	P,M,D
University of California, San Diego	P
University of California, San Francisco	P
University of Cincinnati	P
University of Florida	P
University of Georgia	P
University of Houston	P,M,D
University of Illinois at Chicago	P,M,D
The University of Iowa	P
University of Kentucky	P
University of Louisiana at Monroe	P,D
University of Maryland	P,D
University of Michigan	P
University of Minnesota, Twin Cities Campus	P
University of Mississippi	P,D
University of Missouri–Kansas City	P,M,D
University of New Mexico	P
University of Pittsburgh	P
University of Rhode Island	P
University of South Carolina	P
University of Southern California	P
The University of Texas at Austin	P
University of the Pacific	P
University of Toledo	P
University of Utah	P,M
University of Washington	P
University of Wisconsin–Madison	P
University of Wyoming	P
Virginia Commonwealth University	P
Washington State University	P
Wayne State University	P,M
West Virginia University	P,M,D
Wilkes University	P,M
Xavier University of Louisiana	P

■ **PHILANTHROPIC STUDIES**

Indiana University–Purdue University Indianapolis	M
Saint Mary's University of Minnesota	M

■ **PHILOSOPHY**

American University	M
Arizona State University	M
Baylor University	M,D
Boston College	M,D
Boston University	M,D
Bowling Green State University	M,D
Brown University	M,D
California State University, Long Beach	M
California State University, Los Angeles	M
Carnegie Mellon University	M,D
The Catholic University of America	M,D,O
Claremont Graduate University	M,D
Cleveland State University	M,O
Colorado State University	M
Columbia University	M,D
Cornell University	D
DePaul University	M,D
Duke University	M,D
Duquesne University	M,D
Emory University	D
Florida State University	M,D
Fordham University	M,D
Franciscan University of Steubenville	M
Georgetown University	M,D
The George Washington University	M,D
Georgia State University	M
Gonzaga University	M
Harvard University	M,D
Howard University	M
Indiana University Bloomington	M,D
The Johns Hopkins University	M,D
Kent State University	M
Louisiana State University and Agricultural and Mechanical College	M
Loyola Marymount University	M
Loyola University Chicago	M,D
Marquette University	M,D
Massachusetts Institute of Technology	D
Miami University	M
Michigan State University	M,D
Montclair State University	M,D
New School University	M,D
New York University	M,D
Northern Illinois University	M
Northwestern University	D
The Ohio State University	M,D
Ohio University	M
Oklahoma City University	M
Oklahoma State University	M
The Pennsylvania State University University Park Campus	M,D
Princeton University	D
Purdue University	M,D
Purdue University Calumet	M
Rice University	M,D
Rutgers, The State University of New Jersey, New Brunswick/Piscataway	D
Saint Louis University	M,D
San Diego State University	M
San Francisco State University	M,O
San Jose State University	M,O
Southern Illinois University Carbondale	M,D
Stanford University	M,D
State University of New York at Binghamton	M,D
Stony Brook University, State University of New York	M,D
Syracuse University	M,D
Temple University	M,D
Texas A&M University	M,D
Texas Tech University	M
Tufts University	M
Tulane University	M,D

Directory of Graduate and Professional Programs by Field
Philosophy

Institution	Degree
University at Albany, State University of New York	M,D
University at Buffalo, The State University of New York	M,D
The University of Arizona	M,D
University of Arkansas	M,D
University of California, Berkeley	D
University of California, Davis	M,D
University of California, Irvine	M,D
University of California, Los Angeles	M,D
University of California, Riverside	M,D
University of California, San Diego	D
University of California, Santa Barbara	D
University of California, Santa Cruz	M,D
University of Chicago	M,D
University of Cincinnati	M,D
University of Colorado at Boulder	M,D
University of Connecticut	M,D
University of Denver	M
University of Florida	M,D
University of Georgia	M,D
University of Hawaii at Manoa	M,D
University of Houston	M
University of Illinois at Chicago	M,D
University of Illinois at Urbana–Champaign	M,D
The University of Iowa	M,D
University of Kansas	M,D
University of Kentucky	M,D
University of Louisville	M
University of Maryland, Baltimore County	M,O
University of Maryland, College Park	M,D
University of Massachusetts Amherst	M,D
The University of Memphis	M,D
University of Miami	M,D
University of Michigan	M,D
University of Minnesota, Twin Cities Campus	M,D
University of Mississippi	M
University of Missouri–Columbia	M,D
University of Missouri–St. Louis	M
The University of Montana–Missoula	M
University of Nebraska–Lincoln	M,D
University of Nevada, Reno	M
University of New Mexico	M,D
The University of North Carolina at Chapel Hill	M,D
University of North Florida	M
University of North Texas	M
University of Notre Dame	D
University of Oklahoma	M,D
University of Oregon	M,D
University of Pennsylvania	M,D
University of Pittsburgh	M,D
University of Puerto Rico, Río Piedras	M
University of Rhode Island	M
University of Rochester	M,D
University of St. Thomas (TX)	M,D
University of South Carolina	M,D
University of Southern California	M,D
University of Southern Mississippi	M
University of South Florida	M,D
The University of Tennessee	M,D
The University of Texas at Austin	M,D
University of Toledo	M
University of Utah	M,D
University of Virginia	M,D
University of Washington	M,D
University of Wisconsin–Madison	M,D
University of Wisconsin–Milwaukee	M
University of Wyoming	M
Vanderbilt University	M,D
Villanova University	M,D
Virginia Polytechnic Institute and State University	M
Washington University in St. Louis	M,D
Wayne State University	M,D
West Chester University of Pennsylvania	M
Western Michigan University	M
Yale University	D

■ PHOTOGRAPHY

Institution	Degree
Barry University	M
Bradley University	M
Brooklyn College of the City University of New York	M,D
California State University, Fullerton	M,O
California State University, Los Angeles	M
Claremont Graduate University	M
Columbia College Chicago	M
Columbia University	M
Cornell University	M
The George Washington University	M,D
Howard University	M
Illinois State University	M
Indiana State University	M
Indiana University Bloomington	M
Inter American University of Puerto Rico, San Germán Campus	M
James Madison University	M
Lamar University	M
Louisiana State University and Agricultural and Mechanical College	M
Louisiana Tech University	M
Marywood University	M
New School University	M
Ohio University	M
The Pennsylvania State University University Park Campus	M
Pratt Institute	M
Rochester Institute of Technology	M
San Jose State University	M
Southern Methodist University	M
Syracuse University	M
Temple University	M
The University of Alabama	M
University of Colorado at Boulder	M
University of Houston	M
University of Illinois at Chicago	M
The University of Memphis	M
University of Miami	M
The University of Montana–Missoula	M
University of North Texas	M,D
University of Notre Dame	M
University of Oklahoma	M
The University of Tennessee	M
University of Utah	M
Virginia Commonwealth University	M
Washington State University	M
Washington University in St. Louis	M
Yale University	M

■ PHOTONICS

Institution	Degree
Boston University	M,D
Lehigh University	M,D
Oklahoma State University	M,D
University of Arkansas	M,D
University of California, San Diego	M,D

■ PHYSICAL CHEMISTRY

Institution	Degree
Boston College	M,D
Brandeis University	M,D
Brigham Young University	M,D
California State University, Fullerton	M
California State University, Los Angeles	M
Case Western Reserve University	M,D
Clark Atlanta University	M,D
Clarkson University	M,D
Cleveland State University	M,D
Columbia University	M,D
Cornell University	D
Florida State University	M,D
Georgetown University	M,D
The George Washington University	M,D
Harvard University	D
Howard University	M,D
Illinois Institute of Technology	M,D
Indiana University Bloomington	M,D
Kansas State University	M,D
Kent State University	M,D
Marquette University	M,D
Massachusetts Institute of Technology	D
Miami University	M,D
Michigan State University	M,D
Northeastern University	M
The Ohio State University	M,D
Old Dominion University	M
Oregon State University	M,D
Princeton University	M,D
Purdue University	M,D
Rensselaer Polytechnic Institute	M,D
Rice University	M,D
Rutgers, The State University of New Jersey, Newark	M,D
Rutgers, The State University of New Jersey, New Brunswick/Piscataway	M,D
Seton Hall University	M,D
South Dakota State University	M,D
Southern University and Agricultural and Mechanical College	M
State University of New York at Binghamton	M,D
Stevens Institute of Technology	M,D,O
Tufts University	M,D
University of Cincinnati	M,D
University of Colorado at Boulder	M,D
University of Georgia	M,D
University of Louisville	M,D
University of Maryland, College Park	M,D
University of Miami	M,D
University of Michigan	D
University of Missouri–Columbia	M,D
University of Missouri–Kansas City	M,D
University of Missouri–St. Louis	M,D
The University of Montana–Missoula	M,D
University of Nebraska–Lincoln	M,D
University of Nevada, Reno	D
University of Notre Dame	M,D
University of Puerto Rico, Río Piedras	M,D
University of Southern California	D
University of Southern Mississippi	M,D
University of South Florida	M,D
The University of Tennessee	M,D
The University of Texas at Austin	M,D
University of Toledo	M,D
University of Utah	M,D
Vanderbilt University	M,D
Wake Forest University	M
Washington State University	M,D
West Virginia University	M,D
Yale University	D

■ PHYSICAL EDUCATION

Institution	Degree
Adams State College	M
Adelphi University	M,O
Alabama Agricultural and Mechanical University	M
Alabama State University	M,O
Albany State University	M
Alcorn State University	M,O
Appalachian State University	M
Arizona State University	M
Arkansas State University	M,O
Arkansas Tech University	M
Ashland University	M
Auburn University	M,D,O
Auburn University Montgomery	M,O
Averett University	M
Azusa Pacific University	M
Ball State University	M,D
Baylor University	M
Bemidji State University	M
Boston University	M,D,O
Bridgewater State College	M
Brigham Young University	M,D

Directory of Graduate and Professional Programs by Field
Physical Therapy

Institution	Degree
Brooklyn College of the City University of New York	M,O
California Polytechnic State University, San Luis Obispo	M
California State University, Chico	M
California State University, Dominguez Hills	M
California State University, Fullerton	M
California State University, Hayward	M
California State University, Long Beach	M
California State University, Los Angeles	M
California State University, Sacramento	M
California State University, Stanislaus	M
Campbell University	M
Canisius College	M
Central Connecticut State University	M
Central Michigan University	M
Central Missouri State University	M
Central Washington University	M
Chicago State University	M
The Citadel, The Military College of South Carolina	M
Cleveland State University	M
The College of New Jersey	M
Columbus State University	M,O
Delta State University	M
DePaul University	M
Drury University	M
Eastern Illinois University	M
Eastern Kentucky University	M
Eastern Michigan University	M
Eastern New Mexico University	M
Eastern Washington University	M
East Stroudsburg University of Pennsylvania	M
East Tennessee State University	M
Emporia State University	M
Florida Agricultural and Mechanical University	M
Florida International University	M
Florida State University	M,D,O
Fort Hays State University	M
Frostburg State University	M
Gardner-Webb University	M
Georgia College & State University	M,O
Georgia Southern University	M
Georgia Southwestern State University	M,O
Georgia State University	M
Hardin-Simmons University	M
Henderson State University	M
Hofstra University	M,O
Humboldt State University	M
Idaho State University	M
Illinois State University	M
Indiana State University	M
Indiana University Bloomington	M,D,O
Indiana University of Pennsylvania	M
Inter American University of Puerto Rico, Metropolitan Campus	M
Inter American University of Puerto Rico, San Germán Campus	M
Iowa State University of Science and Technology	M,D
Jackson State University	M
Jacksonville State University	M
Kent State University	M,D
Long Island University, Brooklyn Campus	M
Loras College	M
Louisiana Tech University	M,D
Marshall University	M
McNeese State University	M
Middle Tennessee State University	M,D
Minnesota State University Mankato	M,O
Mississippi State University	M
Montclair State University	M
Morehead State University	M
Murray State University	M
New Mexico Highlands University	M
North Carolina Agricultural and Technical State University	M
North Carolina Central University	M
North Dakota State University	M
Northern Arizona University	M
Northern Illinois University	M
Northern State University	M
North Georgia College & State University	M,O
Northwestern State University of Louisiana	M
Northwest Missouri State University	M
The Ohio State University	M,D
Ohio University	M
Oklahoma State University	M,D
Old Dominion University	M
Oregon State University	M
Pittsburg State University	M
Prairie View A&M University	M
Purdue University	M,D
Queens College of the City University of New York	M
St. Cloud State University	M
San Diego State University	M
San Francisco State University	M
Seattle Pacific University	M
South Dakota State University	M
Southern Connecticut State University	M
Southern Illinois University Carbondale	M
Southwestern Oklahoma State University	M
Southwest Missouri State University	M
Springfield College	M,D,O
State University of New York College at Brockport	M
State University of New York College at Cortland	M
State University of West Georgia	M,O
Stephen F. Austin State University	M
Stony Brook University, State University of New York	M,O
Sul Ross State University	M
Tarleton State University	M,O
Teachers College Columbia University	M,D
Temple University	M,D
Tennessee State University	M
Tennessee Technological University	M
Texas A&M University	M,D
Texas A&M University–Commerce	M,D
Texas Southern University	M
Texas State University-San Marcos	M
Universidad Metropolitana	M
The University of Akron	M
The University of Alabama at Birmingham	M
University of Arkansas	M
University of Central Florida	M
University of Colorado at Boulder	M,D
University of Dayton	M
University of Florida	M,D
University of Georgia	M,D,O
University of Houston	M,D
University of Idaho	M,D
University of Indianapolis	M
The University of Iowa	M,D
University of Kansas	M,D
University of Louisville	M
University of Maine	M
University of Massachusetts Amherst	M,D,O
The University of Memphis	M
University of Minnesota, Twin Cities Campus	M,D,O
The University of Montana–Missoula	M
University of Nebraska at Kearney	M
University of Nebraska at Omaha	M
University of Nebraska–Lincoln	M
University of New Mexico	M,D
University of New Orleans	M,O
The University of North Carolina at Chapel Hill	M
The University of North Carolina at Pembroke	M
University of Northern Iowa	M
University of Rhode Island	M
University of South Alabama	M,O
University of South Carolina	M,D
The University of South Dakota	M
University of Southern Mississippi	M,D
University of South Florida	M
The University of Tennessee at Chattanooga	M
The University of Texas at Arlington	M,D
The University of Texas at El Paso	M
University of the Incarnate Word	M,O
University of Toledo	M,D
University of Virginia	M,D
The University of West Alabama	M
University of West Florida	M
University of Wisconsin–La Crosse	M
University of Wyoming	M
Utah State University	M
Valdosta State University	M
Valparaiso University	M
Virginia Commonwealth University	M
Virginia Polytechnic Institute and State University	M,D,O
Wayne State College	M
Wayne State University	M
West Chester University of Pennsylvania	M,O
Western Carolina University	M
Western Illinois University	M
Western Kentucky University	M
Western Michigan University	M
Western Washington University	M
Westfield State College	M
West Virginia University	M,D
Whitworth College	M
Wichita State University	M
Winthrop University	M
Wright State University	M

■ **PHYSICAL THERAPY**

Institution	Degree
Alabama State University	M
American International College	M
Andrews University	D
Angelo State University	M
Arcadia University	D
Arkansas State University	M
Armstrong Atlantic State University	M
Azusa Pacific University	D
Baylor University	M,D
Belmont University	D
Boston University	M,D
Bradley University	M
California State University, Fresno	M
California State University, Long Beach	M
California State University, Northridge	M
Central Michigan University	M,D
Chapman University	D
Clarkson University	M
Cleveland State University	M
College Misericordia	M
College of Mount St. Joseph	M
College of St. Catherine	M,D
The College of St. Scholastica	M
College of Staten Island of the City University of New York	M
Columbia University	M
Concordia University Wisconsin	M,D
Creighton University	D
Drexel University	M,D,O
Duke University	D
Duquesne University	M,D
East Carolina University	M
Eastern Washington University	D
East Tennessee State University	M

Directory of Graduate and Professional Programs by Field

Physical Therapy

Institution	Degree
Elon University	D
Emory University	D
Florida Agricultural and Mechanical University	M
Florida Gulf Coast University	M
Florida International University	M
Gannon University	M
The George Washington University	M
Georgia State University	M
Governors State University	M
Grand Valley State University	M,D
Hampton University	D
Hardin-Simmons University	D
Humboldt State University	M
Hunter College of the City University of New York	M
Husson College	M
Idaho State University	D
Indiana University–Purdue University Indianapolis	M
Ithaca College	M
Loma Linda University	M,D
Long Island University, Brooklyn Campus	D
Marquette University	M
Marymount University	M
Maryville University of Saint Louis	M
Mercy College	M
Mount St. Mary's College	D
New York Institute of Technology	M,D
New York University	M,D
Northern Arizona University	D
Northern Illinois University	M
North Georgia College & State University	M
Northwestern University	D
Nova Southeastern University	D
Oakland University	M,D,O
The Ohio State University	M
Ohio University	D
Old Dominion University	D
Pacific University	D
Quinnipiac University	M
Regis University	D
Rockhurst University	M,D
Rutgers, The State University of New Jersey, Camden	M
Sacred Heart University	M,D
Sage Graduate School	D
St. Ambrose University	D
Saint Francis University	M
Saint Louis University	M,D
San Francisco State University	M,D
Seton Hall University	D
Shenandoah University	D
Simmons College	D
Slippery Rock University of Pennsylvania	D
Southwest Baptist University	M
Southwest Missouri State University	M
Springfield College	M
Stony Brook University, State University of New York	M,D,O
Temple University	M,D
Texas State University-San Marcos	M
Texas Woman's University	M,D
Touro College	M
University at Buffalo, The State University of New York	D
The University of Alabama at Birmingham	M,D
University of California, San Francisco	M
University of Central Arkansas	M,D
University of Central Florida	M
University of Connecticut	M
University of Delaware	M,D
University of Evansville	M
The University of Findlay	M
University of Florida	M
University of Hartford	M
University of Illinois at Chicago	M
University of Indianapolis	M,D
The University of Iowa	M,D
University of Kansas	M,D
University of Kentucky	M
University of Mary	M
University of Maryland	D
University of Maryland Eastern Shore	M
University of Massachusetts Lowell	M
University of Miami	D
University of Michigan–Flint	D
University of Minnesota, Twin Cities Campus	M,D
University of Missouri–Columbia	M
The University of Montana–Missoula	D
University of Nevada, Las Vegas	M
University of New England	M,D
University of New Mexico	M
The University of North Carolina at Chapel Hill	M,D
University of North Dakota	M,D
University of North Florida	M
University of Pittsburgh	M,D
University of Rhode Island	M
The University of Scranton	M
The University of South Dakota	M
University of Southern California	M,D
University of South Florida	M
The University of Tennessee at Chattanooga	M,D
The University of Texas at El Paso	M
University of the Pacific	M,D
University of Utah	M
University of Vermont	M
University of Washington	D
University of Wisconsin–La Crosse	M
Virginia Commonwealth University	M,D,O
Walsh University	M
Washington University in St. Louis	D,O
Wayne State University	M
Western Carolina University	M
West Virginia University	M
Wheeling Jesuit University	M,D
Wichita State University	M
Widener University	M,D
Youngstown State University	M

■ PHYSICIAN ASSISTANT STUDIES

Institution	Degree
Augsburg College	M
Barry University	M
Central Michigan University	M,D
DeSales University	M
Drexel University	M
Duke University	M
Duquesne University	M,D
East Carolina University	M
Emory University	M
Gannon University	M
The George Washington University	M
Grand Valley State University	M
Idaho State University	M
King's College	M
Lock Haven University of Pennsylvania	M
Loma Linda University	M
Marquette University	M
Marywood University	M
Mercy College	M
Northeastern University	M
Nova Southeastern University	M
Pacific University	M
Philadelphia University	M
Quinnipiac University	M
Regis University	M,D
Saint Francis University	M
Saint Louis University	M
Seton Hall University	M
Shenandoah University	M
Southwest Missouri State University	M
Springfield College	M
Towson University	M
Trevecca Nazarene University	M
University of Detroit Mercy	M
University of Florida	M
The University of Iowa	M
University of Kentucky	M
University of New England	M
University of North Dakota	M
University of St. Francis (IL)	M
University of Saint Francis (IN)	M
University of South Alabama	M
The University of South Dakota	M
University of Utah	M
University of Wisconsin–La Crosse	M
Wagner College	M
Wayne State University	M
Western Michigan University	M
Yale University	M

■ PHYSICS

Institution	Degree
Alabama Agricultural and Mechanical University	M,D
American University	O
Arizona State University	M,D
Auburn University	M,D
Ball State University	M
Baylor University	M,D
Boston College	M,D
Boston University	M,D
Bowling Green State University	M
Brandeis University	M,D
Brigham Young University	M,D
Brooklyn College of the City University of New York	M,D
Brown University	M,D
California Institute of Technology	D
California State University, Fresno	M
California State University, Fullerton	M
California State University, Long Beach	M
California State University, Los Angeles	M
California State University, Northridge	M
Carnegie Mellon University	D
Case Western Reserve University	M,D
The Catholic University of America	M,D
Central Connecticut State University	M
Central Michigan University	M
City College of the City University of New York	M,D
Clark Atlanta University	M
Clarkson University	M,D
Clark University	M
Clemson University	M,D
Cleveland State University	M
The College of William and Mary	M,D
Colorado State University	M,D
Columbia University	M,D
Cornell University	M,D
Creighton University	M
Dartmouth College	M,D
Delaware State University	M
DePaul University	M
Drexel University	M,D
Duke University	D
East Carolina University	M,D
Eastern Michigan University	M
Emory University	D
Emporia State University	M
Florida Agricultural and Mechanical University	M,D
Florida Atlantic University	M,D
Florida Institute of Technology	M,D
Florida International University	M,D
Florida State University	M,D
George Mason University	M
The George Washington University	M,D
Georgia Institute of Technology	M,D
Georgia State University	M,D
Hampton University	M,D
Harvard University	M,D

Directory of Graduate and Professional Programs by Field
Physiology

Institution	Degree
Howard University	M,D
Hunter College of the City University of New York	M,D
Idaho State University	M
Illinois Institute of Technology	M,D
Indiana University Bloomington	M,D
Indiana University of Pennsylvania	M
Indiana University–Purdue University Indianapolis	M,D
Iowa State University of Science and Technology	M,D
John Carroll University	M
The Johns Hopkins University	D
Kansas State University	M,D
Kent State University	M,D
Lehigh University	M,D
Louisiana State University and Agricultural and Mechanical College	M,D
Louisiana Tech University	M,D
Marshall University	M
Massachusetts Institute of Technology	M,D
Miami University	M
Michigan State University	M,D
Michigan Technological University	M,D
Minnesota State University Mankato	M
Mississippi State University	M,D
Montana State University–Bozeman	M,D
Morgan State University	M
New Mexico Institute of Mining and Technology	M,D
New Mexico State University	M,D
New York University	M,D
North Carolina State University	M,D
North Dakota State University	M,D
Northeastern University	M,D
Northern Illinois University	M,D
Northwestern University	M,D
Oakland University	M,D
The Ohio State University	M,D
Ohio University	M,D
Oklahoma State University	M,D
Old Dominion University	M,D
Oregon State University	M,D
The Pennsylvania State University University Park Campus	M,D
Pittsburg State University	M
Polytechnic University, Brooklyn Campus	M,D
Portland State University	M,D
Princeton University	D
Purdue University	M,D
Queens College of the City University of New York	M
Rensselaer Polytechnic Institute	M,D
Rice University	M,D
Rutgers, The State University of New Jersey, New Brunswick/Piscataway	M,D
Sam Houston State University	M
San Diego State University	M
San Francisco State University	M
San Jose State University	M
South Dakota State University	M
Southern Illinois University Carbondale	M
Southern Illinois University Edwardsville	M
Southern Methodist University	M,D
Southern University and Agricultural and Mechanical College	M
Stanford University	D
State University of New York at Binghamton	M
Stephen F. Austin State University	M
Stevens Institute of Technology	M,D,O
Stony Brook University, State University of New York	M,D
Syracuse University	M,D
Temple University	M,D
Texas A&M International University	M
Texas A&M University	M,D
Texas A&M University–Commerce	M
Texas Christian University	D
Texas State University-San Marcos	M
Texas Tech University	M,D
Tufts University	M
Tulane University	M,D
University at Albany, State University of New York	M,D
University at Buffalo, The State University of New York	M,D
The University of Akron	M
The University of Alabama	M,D
The University of Alabama at Birmingham	M,D
The University of Alabama in Huntsville	M,D
University of Alaska Fairbanks	M,D
The University of Arizona	M,D
University of Arkansas	M,D
University of California, Berkeley	D
University of California, Davis	M,D
University of California, Irvine	M,D
University of California, Los Angeles	M,D
University of California, Riverside	M,D
University of California, San Diego	M,D
University of California, Santa Barbara	D
University of California, Santa Cruz	M,D
University of Central Florida	M,D
University of Chicago	M,D
University of Cincinnati	M,D
University of Colorado at Boulder	M,D
University of Connecticut	M,D
University of Dayton	M
University of Delaware	M,D
University of Denver	M,D
University of Florida	M,D
University of Georgia	M,D
University of Hawaii at Manoa	M,D
University of Houston	M,D
University of Idaho	M,D
University of Illinois at Chicago	M,D
University of Illinois at Urbana–Champaign	M,D
The University of Iowa	M,D
University of Kansas	M,D
University of Kentucky	M,D
University of Louisiana at Lafayette	M
University of Louisville	M
University of Maine	M,D
University of Maryland, Baltimore County	M,D
University of Maryland, College Park	M,D
University of Massachusetts Amherst	M,D
University of Massachusetts Dartmouth	M
University of Massachusetts Lowell	M,D
The University of Memphis	M
University of Miami	M,D
University of Michigan	M,D
University of Minnesota, Duluth	M
University of Minnesota, Twin Cities Campus	M,D
University of Mississippi	M,D
University of Missouri–Columbia	M,D
University of Missouri–Kansas City	M,D
University of Missouri–Rolla	M,D
University of Missouri–St. Louis	M,D
University of Nebraska–Lincoln	M,D
University of Nevada, Las Vegas	M,D
University of Nevada, Reno	M,D
University of New Hampshire	M,D
University of New Mexico	M,D
University of New Orleans	M,D
The University of North Carolina at Chapel Hill	M,D
University of North Dakota	M,D
University of North Texas	M,D
University of Notre Dame	D
University of Oklahoma	M,D
University of Oregon	M,D
University of Pennsylvania	M,D
University of Pittsburgh	M,D
University of Puerto Rico, Mayagüez Campus	M
University of Puerto Rico, Río Piedras	M,D
University of Rhode Island	M,D
University of Rochester	M,D
University of South Carolina	M,D
University of Southern California	M,D
University of Southern Mississippi	M
University of South Florida	M,D
The University of Tennessee	M,D
The University of Texas at Arlington	M,D
The University of Texas at Austin	M,D
The University of Texas at Dallas	M,D
The University of Texas at El Paso	M
University of Toledo	M,D
University of Utah	M,D
University of Vermont	M
University of Virginia	M,D
University of Washington	M,D
University of Wisconsin–Madison	M,D
University of Wisconsin–Milwaukee	M,D
University of Wisconsin–Oshkosh	M
Utah State University	M,D
Vanderbilt University	M,D
Virginia Commonwealth University	M
Virginia Polytechnic Institute and State University	M,D
Virginia State University	M
Wake Forest University	M,D
Washington State University	M,D
Washington University in St. Louis	M,D
Wayne State University	M,D
Western Illinois University	M
Western Michigan University	M,D
West Virginia University	M,D
Wichita State University	M
Worcester Polytechnic Institute	M,D
Wright State University	M
Yale University	D

■ PHYSIOLOGY

Institution	Degree
Arizona State University	M,D
Auburn University	M,D
Ball State University	M
Boston University	M,D
Brigham Young University	M,D
Brown University	M,D
Case Western Reserve University	M,D
Clemson University	M,D
Columbia University	M,D
Cornell University	M,D
Dartmouth College	D
East Carolina University	D
East Tennessee State University	M,D
Florida State University	M,D
Georgetown University	M,D
Georgia Institute of Technology	M
Georgia State University	M,D
Harvard University	M,D
Howard University	D
Illinois State University	M,D
Indiana State University	M,D
Indiana University Bloomington	M,D
Indiana University–Purdue University Indianapolis	M,D
The Johns Hopkins University	M,D
Kansas State University	M,D
Kent State University	M,D
Loma Linda University	M,D
Loyola University Chicago	M,D
Maharishi University of Management	M,D
Marquette University	M,D
Michigan State University	M,D
New York University	M,D
North Carolina State University	M,D
Northwestern University	M
The Ohio State University	M,D

Peterson's Graduate Schools in the U.S. 2006

Physiology

Institution	Degree
The Pennsylvania State University University Park Campus	M,D
Purdue University	M,D
Rutgers, The State University of New Jersey, New Brunswick/Piscataway	D
Saint Louis University	D
Salisbury University	M
San Francisco State University	M
San Jose State University	M
Southern Illinois University Carbondale	M,D
Southern Illinois University Edwardsville	M,O
Stanford University	D
Stony Brook University, State University of New York	D
Teachers College Columbia University	M,D
Temple University	M,D
Texas A&M University	M,D
Tufts University	D
Tulane University	M,D
University at Buffalo, The State University of New York	M,D
The University of Alabama at Birmingham	D
The University of Arizona	D
University of California, Berkeley	M,D
University of California, Davis	M,D
University of California, Irvine	D
University of California, Los Angeles	M,D
University of California, Riverside	M,D
University of California, San Diego	D
University of California, San Francisco	D
University of Chicago	D
University of Cincinnati	D
University of Colorado at Boulder	M,D
University of Connecticut	M,D
University of Delaware	M,D
University of Florida	D
University of Georgia	M,D
University of Hawaii at Manoa	M,D
University of Illinois at Chicago	M,D
University of Illinois at Urbana–Champaign	M,D
The University of Iowa	M,D
University of Kansas	M,D
University of Kentucky	D
University of Louisville	M,D
University of Maryland	M,D
University of Miami	D
University of Michigan	D
University of Minnesota, Duluth	M,D
University of Minnesota, Twin Cities Campus	M,D
University of Missouri–Columbia	M,D
University of Missouri–St. Louis	M,D,O
University of Nevada, Reno	M,D
University of New Mexico	M,D
The University of North Carolina at Chapel Hill	D
University of North Dakota	M,D
University of Notre Dame	M,D
University of Pennsylvania	D
University of Pittsburgh	M,D
University of Rochester	M,D
University of South Alabama	D
The University of South Dakota	M,D
University of Southern California	M,D
University of South Florida	M,D
The University of Tennessee	M,D
University of Utah	D
University of Vermont	M,D
University of Virginia	D
University of Washington	D
University of Wisconsin–La Crosse	M
University of Wisconsin–Madison	M,D
University of Wyoming	M,D
Vanderbilt University	D
Virginia Commonwealth University	M,D,O
Wake Forest University	D
Wayne State University	M,D
West Virginia University	M,D
William Paterson University of New Jersey	M
Wright State University	M
Yale University	D
Yeshiva University	D

■ PLANETARY AND SPACE SCIENCES

Institution	Degree
California Institute of Technology	M,D
Columbia University	D
Cornell University	D
Florida Institute of Technology	M,D
Harvard University	M,D
The Johns Hopkins University	M,D
Massachusetts Institute of Technology	M,D
Stony Brook University, State University of New York	M,D
The University of Arizona	M,D
University of California, Los Angeles	M,D
University of Chicago	M,D
University of Hawaii at Manoa	M,D
University of Michigan	M,D
University of New Mexico	M,D
University of North Dakota	M
University of Pittsburgh	M,D
Washington University in St. Louis	M,D
Western Connecticut State University	M

■ PLANT BIOLOGY

Institution	Degree
Arizona State University	M,D
Clemson University	M,D
Cornell University	M,D
Florida State University	M,D
Indiana University Bloomington	M,D
Michigan State University	M,D
The Ohio State University	M,D
Ohio University	D
Purdue University	M,D
Rutgers, The State University of New Jersey, New Brunswick/Piscataway	M,D
Southern Illinois University Carbondale	M,D
Texas A&M University	M,D
University of California, Berkeley	D
University of California, Davis	M,D
University of California, Riverside	M,D
University of Colorado at Boulder	M,D
University of Delaware	M,D
University of Florida	M,D
University of Georgia	M,D
University of Hawaii at Manoa	M,D
University of Illinois at Chicago	M,D
University of Illinois at Urbana–Champaign	M,D
University of Maine	M,D
University of Maryland, College Park	M,D
University of Massachusetts Amherst	M,D
University of Minnesota, Twin Cities Campus	M,D
University of Missouri–Columbia	M,D
University of New Hampshire	M,D
University of Pennsylvania	D
The University of Texas at Austin	M,D
Washington University in St. Louis	D
Yale University	D

■ PLANT MOLECULAR BIOLOGY

Institution	Degree
Cornell University	M,D
Michigan Technological University	D
Rutgers, The State University of New Jersey, New Brunswick/Piscataway	M,D
University of California, Los Angeles	M,D
University of California, San Diego	D
University of Florida	M,D
University of Massachusetts Amherst	M,D

■ PLANT PATHOLOGY

Institution	Degree
Auburn University	M,D
Colorado State University	M,D
Cornell University	M,D
Iowa State University of Science and Technology	M,D
Kansas State University	M,D
Louisiana State University and Agricultural and Mechanical College	M,D
Michigan State University	M,D
Mississippi State University	M,D
Montana State University–Bozeman	M,D
New Mexico State University	M
North Carolina State University	M,D
North Dakota State University	M,D
The Ohio State University	M,D
Oklahoma State University	M,D
Oregon State University	M,D
The Pennsylvania State University University Park Campus	M,D
Purdue University	M,D
Rutgers, The State University of New Jersey, New Brunswick/Piscataway	M,D
South Dakota State University	M
State University of New York College of Environmental Science and Forestry	M,D
Texas A&M University	M,D
The University of Arizona	M,D
University of Arkansas	M
University of California, Davis	M,D
University of California, Riverside	M,D
University of Florida	M,D
University of Georgia	M,D
University of Hawaii at Manoa	M,D
University of Idaho	M,D
University of Kentucky	M,D
University of Maine	M
University of Minnesota, Twin Cities Campus	M,D
University of Missouri–Columbia	M,D
University of Rhode Island	M,D
The University of Tennessee	M,D
University of Wisconsin–Madison	M,D
Virginia Polytechnic Institute and State University	M,D
Washington State University	M,D
West Virginia University	M

■ PLANT PHYSIOLOGY

Institution	Degree
Colorado State University	M,D
Cornell University	M,D
Iowa State University of Science and Technology	M,D
Oregon State University	M,D
The Pennsylvania State University University Park Campus	M,D
Purdue University	D
Rutgers, The State University of New Jersey, New Brunswick/Piscataway	M,D
University of Colorado at Boulder	M,D
University of Kentucky	D
University of Massachusetts Amherst	M,D
The University of Tennessee	M,D
Virginia Polytechnic Institute and State University	M,D
Washington State University	M,D

■ PLANT SCIENCES

Institution	Degree
Alabama Agricultural and Mechanical University	M,D
Brigham Young University	M
California State University, Fresno	M
Colorado State University	M,D
Cornell University	M,D
Florida Agricultural and Mechanical University	M
Lehman College of the City University of New York	D
Michigan State University	M,D
Mississippi State University	M,D

Directory of Graduate and Professional Programs by Field
Political Science

Institution	Degree
Montana State University–Bozeman	M,D
New Mexico State University	M
North Carolina Agricultural and Technical State University	M
North Dakota State University	M,D
Oklahoma State University	D
Rutgers, The State University of New Jersey, New Brunswick/Piscataway	M,D
South Dakota State University	M,D
Southern Illinois University Carbondale	M
Southwest Missouri State University	M
State University of New York College of Environmental Science and Forestry	M,D
Texas A&M University	M,D
Texas A&M University–Kingsville	M,D
Texas Tech University	M,D
Tuskegee University	M
The University of Arizona	M,D
University of Arkansas	D
University of California, Riverside	M,D
University of Connecticut	M,D
University of Delaware	M,D
University of Florida	D
University of Hawaii at Manoa	M,D
University of Idaho	M,D
University of Kentucky	M
University of Maine	M,D
University of Massachusetts Amherst	M,D
University of Minnesota, Twin Cities Campus	M,D
University of Rhode Island	M,D
University of Vermont	M,D
University of Wisconsin–Madison	M,D
Utah State University	M,D
West Texas A&M University	M
West Virginia University	M,D

■ PLASMA PHYSICS

Institution	Degree
Columbia University	M,D,O
Massachusetts Institute of Technology	M,D,O
Princeton University	D
University of Colorado at Boulder	M,D
West Virginia University	M,D

■ PODIATRIC MEDICINE

Institution	Degree
Barry University	P
Temple University	P

■ POLITICAL SCIENCE

Institution	Degree
American University	M,D
Appalachian State University	M
Arizona State University	M,D
Arkansas State University	M,O
Auburn University	M,D
Auburn University Montgomery	M
Augusta State University	M
Ball State University	M
Baylor University	M,D
Boston College	M,D
Boston University	M,D
Bowling Green State University	
Brandeis University	M,D
Brooklyn College of the City University of New York	M,D
Brown University	M,D
California Institute of Technology	D
California State University, Chico	M
California State University, Fullerton	M
California State University, Long Beach	M
California State University, Los Angeles	M
California State University, Northridge	M
California State University, Sacramento	M
Case Western Reserve University	M,D
The Catholic University of America	M,D
Central Michigan University	M
Claremont Graduate University	M,D
Clark Atlanta University	M,D
The College of Saint Rose	M
Colorado State University	M,D
Columbia University	M,D
Converse College	M
Cornell University	D
Duke University	M,D
East Carolina University	M
Eastern Illinois University	M
Eastern Kentucky University	M
East Stroudsburg University of Pennsylvania	M
Emory University	D
Fairleigh Dickinson University, Metropolitan Campus	M
Fayetteville State University	M
Florida Agricultural and Mechanical University	M
Florida Atlantic University	M
Florida International University	M,D
Florida State University	M,D
Fordham University	M
Georgetown University	M,D
The George Washington University	M,D,O
Georgia Southern University	M
Georgia State University	M,D
Governors State University	M
Harvard University	M,D
Hawai'i Pacific University	M
Howard University	M,D
Idaho State University	M,D
Illinois State University	M
Indiana State University	M
Indiana University Bloomington	M,D
Indiana University of Pennsylvania	M
Iowa State University of Science and Technology	M
Jackson State University	M
Jacksonville State University	M
The Johns Hopkins University	M,D
Kansas State University	M
Kent State University	M,D
Lamar University	M
Lehigh University	M
Long Island University, Brooklyn Campus	M
Long Island University, C.W. Post Campus	M
Louisiana State University and Agricultural and Mechanical College	M,D
Loyola University Chicago	M,D
Marquette University	M
Marshall University	M
Massachusetts Institute of Technology	M,D
Miami University	M,D
Michigan State University	M,D
Midwestern State University	M
Minnesota State University Mankato	M
Mississippi College	M
Mississippi State University	M,D
New Mexico Highlands University	M
New Mexico State University	M
New School University	M,D
New York University	M,D
North Dakota State University	M,D
Northeastern Illinois University	M
Northeastern University	M,D
Northern Arizona University	M,D,O
Northern Illinois University	M,D
Northwestern University	M,D
The Ohio State University	M,D,O
Ohio University	M
Oklahoma State University	M
The Pennsylvania State University University Park Campus	M,D
Portland State University	M,D
Princeton University	D
Purdue University	M,D
Purdue University Calumet	M
Rice University	M,D
Roosevelt University	M
Rutgers, The State University of New Jersey, Newark	M
Rutgers, The State University of New Jersey, New Brunswick/Piscataway	M,D
St. John's University (NY)	M
St. Mary's University of San Antonio	M
Sam Houston State University	M
San Diego State University	M
San Francisco State University	M
Sonoma State University	M
Southern Connecticut State University	M
Southern Illinois University Carbondale	M,D
Southern University and Agricultural and Mechanical College	M
Southwest Missouri State University	M
Stanford University	M,D
State University of New York at Binghamton	M,D
Stony Brook University, State University of New York	M,D
Suffolk University	M
Sul Ross State University	M
Syracuse University	M,D
Tarleton State University	M
Teachers College Columbia University	M,D
Temple University	M,D
Texas A&M International University	M
Texas A&M University	M,D
Texas A&M University–Kingsville	M
Texas State University-San Marcos	M
Texas Tech University	M,D
Texas Woman's University	M
Troy University Dothan	M
Tulane University	M,D
University at Albany, State University of New York	M,D
University at Buffalo, The State University of New York	M,D
The University of Akron	M
The University of Alabama	M,D
The University of Arizona	M,D
University of Arkansas	M
University of California, Berkeley	D
University of California, Davis	M,D
University of California, Irvine	D
University of California, Los Angeles	M,D
University of California, Riverside	M,D
University of California, San Diego	D
University of California, Santa Barbara	M,D
University of California, Santa Cruz	D
University of Central Florida	M
University of Central Oklahoma	M
University of Chicago	D
University of Cincinnati	M,D
University of Colorado at Boulder	M,D
University of Colorado at Denver	M
University of Connecticut	M,D
University of Dayton	M
University of Delaware	M,D
University of Denver	M,D,O
University of Florida	M,D,O
University of Georgia	M,D
University of Hawaii at Manoa	M,D
University of Houston	M,D
University of Idaho	M,D
University of Illinois at Chicago	M,D
University of Illinois at Springfield	M
University of Illinois at Urbana–Champaign	M,D
The University of Iowa	M,D
University of Kansas	M,D
University of Kentucky	M,D
University of Louisville	M
University of Maryland, College Park	D
University of Massachusetts Amherst	
University of Massachusetts Boston	M,D,O
The University of Memphis	M

Peterson's Graduate Schools in the U.S. 2006

Directory of Graduate and Professional Programs by Field

Political Science

Institution	Degree
University of Miami	M
University of Michigan	M,D
University of Minnesota, Twin Cities Campus	M,D
University of Mississippi	M,D
University of Missouri–Columbia	M,D
University of Missouri–Kansas City	M,D
University of Missouri–St. Louis	M,D
The University of Montana–Missoula	M
University of Nebraska at Omaha	M
University of Nebraska–Lincoln	M,D
University of Nevada, Las Vegas	M
University of Nevada, Reno	M,D
University of New Hampshire	M
University of New Mexico	M,D
University of New Orleans	M,D
The University of North Carolina at Chapel Hill	M,D
The University of North Carolina at Greensboro	M,O
University of Northern Iowa	M
University of North Texas	M,D
University of Notre Dame	D
University of Oklahoma	M,D
University of Oregon	M,D
University of Pennsylvania	M,D
University of Pittsburgh	M,D
University of Rhode Island	M,O
University of Rochester	M,D
University of South Carolina	M,D
The University of South Dakota	M
University of Southern California	M,D
University of Southern Mississippi	M
University of South Florida	M
The University of Tennessee	M,D
The University of Texas at Arlington	M
The University of Texas at Austin	M,D
The University of Texas at Brownsville	M
The University of Texas at Dallas	D
The University of Texas at El Paso	M
The University of Texas at San Antonio	M
The University of Texas at Tyler	M
University of Toledo	M
University of Utah	M,D
University of Virginia	M,D
University of Washington	M,D
University of West Florida	M
University of Wisconsin–Madison	M,D
University of Wisconsin–Milwaukee	M,D
University of Wisconsin–Oshkosh	M
University of Wyoming	M
Utah State University	M
Vanderbilt University	M,D
Villanova University	M
Virginia Polytechnic Institute and State University	M
Washington State University	M,D
Washington University in St. Louis	M,D
Wayne State University	M
Western Illinois University	M
Western Michigan University	M,D
Western Washington University	M
West Texas A&M University	M
West Virginia University	M,D
Wichita State University	M
Yale University	D

■ POLYMER SCIENCE AND ENGINEERING

Institution	Degree
Carnegie Mellon University	M,D
Case Western Reserve University	M,D
Clemson University	M,D
Cornell University	M,D
DePaul University	M
Eastern Michigan University	M
Georgia Institute of Technology	M,D
Lehigh University	M,D
Massachusetts Institute of Technology	M,D,O
North Dakota State University	M,D

Institution	Degree
The Pennsylvania State University University Park Campus	M,D
Polytechnic University, Brooklyn Campus	M
Princeton University	M,D
Rensselaer Polytechnic Institute	M,D
Rutgers, The State University of New Jersey, New Brunswick/Piscataway	M,D
The University of Akron	M,D
University of Cincinnati	M,D
University of Connecticut	M,D
University of Detroit Mercy	M,D
University of Massachusetts Amherst	M,D
University of Massachusetts Lowell	M,D
University of Michigan	M
University of Missouri–Kansas City	M,D
University of Southern Mississippi	M,D
The University of Tennessee	M,D
University of Wisconsin–Madison	M,D
Wayne State University	M,D,O

■ PORTUGUESE

Institution	Degree
Brigham Young University	M
Emory University	D,O
Harvard University	M,D
Indiana University Bloomington	M,D
Michigan State University	M,D
New York University	M,D
The Ohio State University	M,D
Princeton University	D
Tulane University	M,D
University of California, Los Angeles	M
University of California, Santa Barbara	M,D
University of Minnesota, Twin Cities Campus	M,D
University of New Mexico	M,D
The University of North Carolina at Chapel Hill	M,D
The University of Tennessee	D
The University of Texas at Austin	M,D
University of Washington	M
University of Wisconsin–Madison	M,D
Vanderbilt University	M,D
Yale University	M,D

■ PROJECT MANAGEMENT

Institution	Degree
American University	O
Cabrini College	M,O
Carnegie Mellon University	M,D
City University	M,O
Colorado Technical University	M,D
The George Washington University	M,D
Lehigh University	M,D,O
Lesley University	M,O
Mississippi State University	M,D
New York Institute of Technology	M
Northwestern University	M
The Pennsylvania State University at Erie, The Behrend College	M
Regis University	M,O
Saint Mary's University of Minnesota	M
Stevens Institute of Technology	M,O
Texas A&M University	M,D
Thomas Edison State College	M
University of Denver	M,O
University of Wisconsin–Platteville	M
Western Carolina University	M
Winthrop University	M
Wright State University	M

■ PSYCHIATRIC NURSING

Institution	Degree
Boston College	M,D
Case Western Reserve University	M,D
The Catholic University of America	M,D
Columbia University	M,O
Fairfield University	M,O
Georgia State University	M,D
Hunter College of the City University of New York	M
Husson College	M

Institution	Degree
Kent State University	M,D
Molloy College	M,O
New York University	M,O
Northeastern University	M,O
Pontifical Catholic University of Puerto Rico	M
Rutgers, The State University of New Jersey, Newark	M
Sage Graduate School	M
Saint Joseph College	M
Saint Xavier University	M,O
Seattle University	M
Southern Illinois University Edwardsville	M
Stony Brook University, State University of New York	M,O
University at Buffalo, The State University of New York	M,D,O
University of Cincinnati	M,D
University of Delaware	M,O
University of Illinois at Chicago	M
University of Kansas	M,D,O
University of Maryland	M,D
University of Massachusetts Lowell	M
University of Miami	M,D
University of Michigan	M
University of Minnesota, Twin Cities Campus	M
University of Pennsylvania	M
University of Pittsburgh	M
University of South Alabama	M
University of South Carolina	M,O
University of Southern Maine	M,O
University of Southern Mississippi	M,D
Vanderbilt University	M
Virginia Commonwealth University	M,D,O
Wayne State University	M
Wichita State University	M

■ PSYCHOANALYSIS AND PSYCHOTHERAPY

Institution	Degree
New York University	M,D,O
Rivier College	M,O

■ PSYCHOLOGY—GENERAL

Institution	Degree
Abilene Christian University	M
Adelphi University	M,D,O
Alabama Agricultural and Mechanical University	M,O
American International College	M,D
American University	M,D
Andrews University	M,D,O
Angelo State University	M
Anna Maria College	M,O
Antioch New England Graduate School	M
Antioch University Los Angeles	M
Antioch University McGregor	M
Antioch University Seattle	M
Appalachian State University	M,O
Arcadia University	M,D,O
Argosy University/Sarasota	M,D,O
Argosy University/Schaumburg	M,D
Arizona State University	D
Auburn University	M,D
Auburn University Montgomery	M
Augusta State University	M
Austin Peay State University	M
Azusa Pacific University	M,D
Ball State University	M
Barry University	M,O
Bayamón Central University	M
Baylor University	M,D
Biola University	M,D
Boston College	D
Boston University	M,D
Bowling Green State University	M,D
Brandeis University	M,D
Brenau University	M

Psychology—General

Institution	Degrees
Bridgewater State College	M
Brigham Young University	M,D
Brooklyn College of the City University of New York	M,D
Brown University	M,D
California Lutheran University	M
California Polytechnic State University, San Luis Obispo	M
California State Polytechnic University, Pomona	M
California State University, Bakersfield	M,O
California State University, Chico	M
California State University, Dominguez Hills	M
California State University, Fresno	M
California State University, Fullerton	M
California State University, Long Beach	M
California State University, Los Angeles	M
California State University, Northridge	M
California State University, Sacramento	M
California State University, San Bernardino	M
California State University, San Marcos	M
California State University, Stanislaus	M
Cameron University	M
Cardinal Stritch University	M
Carnegie Mellon University	D
Case Western Reserve University	D
Castleton State College	M
The Catholic University of America	M,D
Central Connecticut State University	M
Central Michigan University	M,D,O
Central Missouri State University	M
Central Washington University	M
Chapman University	M
Chestnut Hill College	M,D,O
The Citadel, The Military College of South Carolina	M
City College of the City University of New York	M,D
Claremont Graduate University	M,D
Clark University	D
Clemson University	M,D
Cleveland State University	M,O
College of St. Joseph	M
College of Staten Island of the City University of New York	D
The College of William and Mary	M,D
Colorado State University	M,D
Columbia University	M,D
Concordia University (IL)	M
Cornell University	D
Dartmouth College	D
DePaul University	M,D
Drexel University	M,D
Duke University	D
Duquesne University	D
East Carolina University	M
East Central University	M
Eastern Illinois University	M,O
Eastern Kentucky University	M,O
Eastern Michigan University	M,D
Eastern New Mexico University	M
Eastern Washington University	M
East Tennessee State University	M
Edinboro University of Pennsylvania	M
Emory University	D
Emporia State University	M
Fairfield University	M,O
Fairleigh Dickinson University, College at Florham	M,O
Fairleigh Dickinson University, Metropolitan Campus	M,D,O
Fayetteville State University	M
Florida Agricultural and Mechanical University	M
Florida Atlantic University	M,D
Florida Institute of Technology	M,D
Florida International University	M,D
Florida State University	M,D
Fordham University	D
Fort Hays State University	M,O
Framingham State College	M
Francis Marion University	M
Frostburg State University	M
Gallaudet University	M,D,O
Gardner-Webb University	M
Geneva College	M
George Fox University	M,D
George Mason University	M,D
Georgetown University	D
The George Washington University	D
Georgia Institute of Technology	M,D
Georgia Southern University	M
Georgia State University	D
Governors State University	M
Hardin-Simmons University	M
Harvard University	M,D
Hofstra University	M,D,O
Hood College	M,O
Hope International University	M
Houston Baptist University	M
Howard University	M,D
Humboldt State University	M
Hunter College of the City University of New York	M
Idaho State University	M,D
Illinois Institute of Technology	M,D
Illinois State University	M,D,O
Immaculata University	M,D,O
Indiana State University	M,D
Indiana University Bloomington	D
Indiana University of Pennsylvania	M,D
Indiana University–Purdue University Indianapolis	M,D
Indiana University South Bend	M
Inter American University of Puerto Rico, Metropolitan Campus	M
Inter American University of Puerto Rico, San Germán Campus	M,D
Iona College	M
Iowa State University of Science and Technology	M,D
Jackson State University	D
Jacksonville State University	M
James Madison University	M,D,O
John F. Kennedy University	M,D,O
The Johns Hopkins University	D
Kansas State University	M,D
Kean University	M,O
Kent State University	M,D
Lamar University	M
La Salle University	D
Lehigh University	M,D
Lesley University	M,D,O
Long Island University, Brooklyn Campus	M,D
Long Island University, C.W. Post Campus	M,D,O
Loras College	M
Louisiana State University and Agricultural and Mechanical College	M,D
Louisiana Tech University	M,D
Loyola College in Maryland	M,D,O
Loyola University Chicago	M,D
Madonna University	M
Marist College	M,O
Marquette University	M,D
Marshall University	M,D
Marywood University	M
Massachusetts Institute of Technology	D
McNeese State University	M
Mercy College	M,O
Miami University	D
Michigan State University	M,D
Middle Tennessee State University	M,O
Midwestern State University	M
Millersville University of Pennsylvania	M
Minnesota State University Mankato	M
Mississippi College	M
Mississippi State University	M,D
Monmouth University	M,O
Montana State University–Billings	M
Montana State University–Bozeman	M
Montclair State University	M
Morehead State University	M
Murray State University	M
National-Louis University	M,O
National University	M
New College of California	M
New Jersey City University	M,O
New Mexico Highlands University	M
New Mexico State University	M,D
New School University	M,D
New York University	M,D,O
Norfolk State University	M,D
North Carolina Central University	M
North Carolina State University	M,D
North Dakota State University	M,D
Northeastern Illinois University	M
Northeastern State University	M
Northeastern University	M,D,O
Northern Arizona University	M
Northern Illinois University	M,D
Northern Michigan University	M
Northwestern State University of Louisiana	M
Northwestern University	D
Northwest Missouri State University	M
Notre Dame de Namur University	M,O
Nova Southeastern University	M,D,O
The Ohio State University	D
Ohio University	D
Oklahoma State University	M,D
Old Dominion University	M
Our Lady of the Lake University of San Antonio	M,D
Pace University	M,D
Pace University, White Plains Campus	M
Pacific University	M,D
The Pennsylvania State University Harrisburg Campus of the Capital College	M
The Pennsylvania State University University Park Campus	M,D
Pittsburg State University	M
Pontifical Catholic University of Puerto Rico	M,D
Portland State University	M,D,O
Princeton University	D
Purdue University	D
Queens College of the City University of New York	M
Radford University	M,O
Regis University	M,O
Rhode Island College	M
Rice University	M,D
Roosevelt University	M
Rowan University	M
Rutgers, The State University of New Jersey, Newark	D
Rutgers, The State University of New Jersey, New Brunswick/Piscataway	M,D
Sage Graduate School	M
St. Cloud State University	M
St. John's University (NY)	M,D
Saint Joseph's University	M
Saint Louis University	M,D
St. Mary's University of San Antonio	M
Saint Xavier University	M,O
Salem State College	M
Sam Houston State University	M,D
San Diego State University	M,D
San Francisco State University	M
San Jose State University	M
Seattle University	M
Seton Hall University	M,D,O

Directory of Graduate and Professional Programs by Field

Psychology—General

Institution	Degree
Shippensburg University of Pennsylvania	M
Southeastern Louisiana University	M
Southern Connecticut State University	M
Southern Illinois University Carbondale	M,D
Southern Illinois University Edwardsville	M
Southern Methodist University	M,D
Southern Nazarene University	M
Southern Oregon University	M
Southern University and Agricultural and Mechanical College	M
Southwest Missouri State University	M
Spalding University	M,D
Stanford University	D
State University of New York at Binghamton	M,D
State University of New York at New Paltz	M
State University of New York at Plattsburgh	M,O
State University of New York College at Brockport	M
State University of West Georgia	M
Stephen F. Austin State University	M
Stony Brook University, State University of New York	D
Suffolk University	M
Sul Ross State University	M
Syracuse University	D
Temple University	D
Tennessee State University	M,D
Texas A&M International University	M
Texas A&M University	M,D
Texas A&M University–Commerce	M,D
Texas A&M University–Corpus Christi	M
Texas A&M University–Kingsville	M
Texas A&M University–Texarkana	M
Texas Christian University	M,D
Texas Southern University	M
Texas State University-San Marcos	M
Texas Tech University	M,D
Texas Woman's University	M,D
Tufts University	M,D
Tulane University	M,D
Union Institute & University	D
University at Albany, State University of New York	M,D
University at Buffalo, The State University of New York	M,D
The University of Akron	M,D
The University of Alabama	D
The University of Alabama at Birmingham	M,D
The University of Alabama in Huntsville	M
University of Alaska Anchorage	M
University of Alaska Fairbanks	M
The University of Arizona	D
University of Arkansas	M,D
University of Arkansas at Little Rock	M
University of Baltimore	M
University of California, Berkeley	D
University of California, Davis	D
University of California, Irvine	D
University of California, Los Angeles	M,D
University of California, Riverside	D
University of California, San Diego	D
University of California, Santa Barbara	M,D
University of California, Santa Cruz	D
University of Central Arkansas	M,D
University of Central Florida	M,D
University of Central Oklahoma	M
University of Chicago	D
University of Cincinnati	D
University of Colorado at Boulder	M,D
University of Colorado at Colorado Springs	M,D
University of Colorado at Denver	M
University of Connecticut	M,D
University of Dayton	M
University of Delaware	D
University of Denver	M,D
University of Detroit Mercy	M,D,O
University of Florida	M,D
University of Georgia	M,D
University of Hartford	M,D
University of Hawaii at Manoa	M,D
University of Houston	D
University of Houston–Clear Lake	M
University of Houston–Victoria	M
University of Idaho	M
University of Illinois at Chicago	D
University of Illinois at Urbana–Champaign	M,D
University of Indianapolis	M,D
The University of Iowa	M,D,O
University of Kansas	M,D
University of Kentucky	M,D
University of La Verne	M,D
University of Louisiana at Lafayette	M
University of Louisiana at Monroe	M,O
University of Louisville	M,D
University of Maine	M,D
University of Mary Hardin-Baylor	M
University of Maryland, Baltimore County	M,D
University of Maryland, College Park	M,D
University of Massachusetts Amherst	M,D
University of Massachusetts Dartmouth	M
University of Massachusetts Lowell	M
The University of Memphis	M,D
University of Miami	M,D
University of Michigan	D,O
University of Minnesota, Twin Cities Campus	M,D
University of Mississippi	M,D
University of Missouri–Columbia	M,D
University of Missouri–St. Louis	M,D,O
The University of Montana–Missoula	M,D,O
University of Nebraska at Omaha	M,D
University of Nebraska–Lincoln	M,D
University of Nevada, Las Vegas	M,D
University of Nevada, Reno	M,D
University of New Hampshire	D
University of New Mexico	M,D
University of New Orleans	M,D
The University of North Carolina at Chapel Hill	D
The University of North Carolina at Charlotte	M
The University of North Carolina at Greensboro	M,D
The University of North Carolina at Wilmington	M
University of North Dakota	M,D
University of Northern Colorado	M,D
University of Northern Iowa	M
University of North Florida	M
University of North Texas	M,D
University of Notre Dame	D
University of Oklahoma	M,D
University of Oregon	M,D
University of Pennsylvania	D
University of Pittsburgh	M,D
University of Puerto Rico, Río Piedras	M,D
University of Rhode Island	M,D
University of Richmond	M
University of Rochester	M,D
University of Saint Francis (IN)	M
University of Saint Mary	M
University of St. Thomas (MN)	M,D,O
University of South Alabama	M
University of South Carolina	M,D
The University of South Dakota	M,D
University of Southern California	M,D
University of Southern Mississippi	M,D,O
University of South Florida	M,D
The University of Tennessee	M,D
The University of Tennessee at Chattanooga	M
The University of Texas at Arlington	M,D
The University of Texas at Austin	D
The University of Texas at Brownsville	M
The University of Texas at El Paso	M,D
The University of Texas at San Antonio	M
The University of Texas at Tyler	M
The University of Texas of the Permian Basin	M
The University of Texas–Pan American	M
University of the Pacific	M
University of Toledo	M,D
University of Tulsa	M,D
University of Utah	M,D
University of Vermont	D
University of Virginia	M,D
University of Washington	D
University of West Florida	M
University of Wisconsin–Eau Claire	M,O
University of Wisconsin–La Crosse	M,O
University of Wisconsin–Madison	D
University of Wisconsin–Milwaukee	M,D
University of Wisconsin–Oshkosh	M
University of Wisconsin–Stout	M
University of Wisconsin–Whitewater	M,O
University of Wyoming	M,D
Utah State University	M,D
Valdosta State University	M,O
Valparaiso University	M
Vanderbilt University	M,D
Villanova University	M
Virginia Commonwealth University	D
Virginia Polytechnic Institute and State University	M,D
Virginia State University	M
Wake Forest University	M
Walden University	M,D
Washburn University	M
Washington State University	M,D
Washington University in St. Louis	M,D
Wayne State University	M,D
West Chester University of Pennsylvania	M
Western Carolina University	M
Western Illinois University	M,O
Western Kentucky University	M,O
Western Michigan University	M,D,O
Western Washington University	M
West Texas A&M University	M
West Virginia University	M,D
Wichita State University	M,D
Widener University	
William Carey College	M
Wilmington College (DE)	M
Winthrop University	M,O
Wright State University	M,D
Xavier University	M
Yale University	D
Yeshiva University	M,D

■ PUBLIC HEALTH—GENERAL

Institution	Degree
Armstrong Atlantic State University	M
Benedictine University	M
Boise State University	M
Boston University	P,M,D,O
Bowling Green State University	M
Brooklyn College of the City University of New York	M
Brown University	M
California State University, Fresno	M
California State University, Northridge	M
Case Western Reserve University	M
Cleveland State University	M,D,O
College of St. Catherine	M
Columbia University	M,D
Dartmouth College	M
Drexel University	M
East Carolina University	M

Directory of Graduate and Professional Programs by Field
Public Policy and Administration

East Stroudsburg University of Pennsylvania	M
East Tennessee State University	M,O
Emerson College	M
Emory University	M,D
Florida Agricultural and Mechanical University	M
Florida International University	M
Florida State University	M,O
Fort Valley State University	M
Georgetown University	M,D
The George Washington University	M,D,O
Georgia Southern University	M
Georgia State University	M,D
Harvard University	M,D,O
Hunter College of the City University of New York	M
Idaho State University	M,O
Indiana University Bloomington	M,D,O
The Johns Hopkins University	M,D,O
Kansas State University	M
Kent State University	M
Loma Linda University	M,D
Marywood University	M
Michigan State University	M
Morgan State University	M,D
New Jersey Institute of Technology	M
New Mexico State University	M
New York University	M,D
Northern Arizona University	M
Northern Illinois University	M
Northwestern University	M
Nova Southeastern University	M
The Ohio State University	M,D
Old Dominion University	M
Oregon State University	M
Portland State University	M,O
Purdue University	M,D
Regis College (MA)	M
Rutgers, The State University of New Jersey, New Brunswick/Piscataway	M,D
Saint Louis University	M,D
Saint Xavier University	M,O
San Diego State University	M,D
San Francisco State University	M
San Jose State University	M,O
Southern Connecticut State University	M
Southwest Missouri State University	M
Stony Brook University, State University of New York	M
Temple University	M
Texas A&M University	M,D
Texas Wesleyan University	M
Tufts University	M
Tulane University	M,D,O
University at Albany, State University of New York	M,D
University at Buffalo, The State University of New York	M,D
The University of Akron	M,D
The University of Alabama at Birmingham	M,D
The University of Arizona	M
University of California, Berkeley	M,D
University of California, Los Angeles	M,D
University of California, San Diego	D
University of Connecticut	M
University of Florida	M,D
University of Hawaii at Manoa	M,D
University of Illinois at Chicago	M,D
University of Illinois at Springfield	M
The University of Iowa	M,D,O
University of Kansas	M
University of Kentucky	M,D
University of Maryland, College Park	M,D
University of Massachusetts Amherst	M,D
University of Miami	M
University of Michigan	M,D
University of Minnesota, Twin Cities Campus	M,D,O
University of Nebraska at Omaha	M
University of Nevada, Reno	M
University of New England	O
University of New Hampshire	M
University of New Mexico	M
The University of North Carolina at Chapel Hill	M,D
University of Northern Colorado	M
University of North Florida	M,O
University of Pittsburgh	M,D,O
University of Rochester	M
University of South Carolina	M
University of Southern California	M
University of Southern Mississippi	M
University of South Florida	M,D
The University of Tennessee	M
University of Toledo	M
University of Utah	M,D
University of Virginia	M
University of Washington	M,D
University of Wisconsin–Eau Claire	M
University of Wisconsin–La Crosse	M
Virginia Commonwealth University	M,D
Walden University	M,D
West Chester University of Pennsylvania	M
Western Kentucky University	M
West Virginia University	M
Wichita State University	M
Wright State University	M
Yale University	M,D

■ **PUBLIC HISTORY**

Appalachian State University	M
Arizona State University	M,D
California State University, Sacramento	M
Eastern Illinois University	M
Florida State University	M,D
Indiana University–Purdue University Indianapolis	M
New York University	M,D,O
North Carolina State University	M
Northeastern University	M,D
Rutgers, The State University of New Jersey, Camden	M
Shippensburg University of Pennsylvania	M
Simmons College	M
Sonoma State University	M
University at Albany, State University of New York	M,D,O
University of Arkansas at Little Rock	M
University of Houston	M,D
University of Illinois at Springfield	M
University of Massachusetts Amherst	M,D
University of Massachusetts Boston	M
University of South Carolina	M,O
The University of Texas at Austin	M
Wayne State University	M,D,O

■ **PUBLIC POLICY AND ADMINISTRATION**

Albany State University	M
Alfred University	M
American International College	M
American University	M
Angelo State University	M
Anna Maria College	M
Appalachian State University	M
Arizona State University	M,D
Arkansas State University	M,O
Auburn University	M,D
Auburn University Montgomery	M,D
Ball State University	M
Baylor University	M
Bernard M. Baruch College of the City University of New York	M
Boise State University	M
Boston University	M,O
Bowie State University	M
Bowling Green State University	M
Brandeis University	D
Bridgewater State College	M
Brigham Young University	M
Brooklyn College of the City University of New York	M,D
Brown University	M
California Lutheran University	M
California State Polytechnic University, Pomona	M
California State University, Bakersfield	M
California State University, Chico	M
California State University, Dominguez Hills	M
California State University, Fresno	M
California State University, Fullerton	M
California State University, Hayward	M
California State University, Long Beach	M,O
California State University, Los Angeles	M
California State University, Northridge	M
California State University, Sacramento	M
California State University, San Bernardino	M
California State University, Stanislaus	M
Carnegie Mellon University	M,D
Central Michigan University	M,O
City University	M,O
Claremont Graduate University	M,D
Clark Atlanta University	M
Clark University	M,O
Clemson University	M,D,O
Cleveland State University	M,D,O
College of Charleston	M
The College of William and Mary	M
Columbia University	M
Columbus State University	M
Concordia University Wisconsin	M
Cornell University	M,D
Cumberland University	M
DePaul University	M
Drake University	M
Duke University	M
Duquesne University	M,O
East Carolina University	M
Eastern Kentucky University	M
Eastern Michigan University	M
Eastern Washington University	M
Fairleigh Dickinson University, College at Florham	M
Fairleigh Dickinson University, Metropolitan Campus	M,O
Florida Agricultural and Mechanical University	M
Florida Atlantic University	M,D
Florida Gulf Coast University	M
Florida Institute of Technology	M
Florida International University	M,D
Florida State University	M,D,O
Framingham State College	M
Gannon University	M,O
George Mason University	M,D
Georgetown University	M
The George Washington University	M,D
Georgia College & State University	M
Georgia Institute of Technology	M,D
Georgia Southern University	M
Georgia State University	M,D
Governors State University	M
Grambling State University	M
Grand Valley State University	M
Hamline University	M
Harvard University	M,D
Howard University	M
Idaho State University	M
Illinois Institute of Technology	M
Indiana State University	M
Indiana University Bloomington	M,D

Peterson's Graduate Schools in the U.S. 2006

Directory of Graduate and Professional Programs by Field
Public Policy and Administration

Institution	Degree
Indiana University Northwest	M,O
Indiana University of Pennsylvania	M
Indiana University–Purdue University Fort Wayne	M,O
Indiana University–Purdue University Indianapolis	M,O
Indiana University South Bend	M,O
Iowa State University of Science and Technology	M
Jackson State University	M,D
Jacksonville State University	M
James Madison University	M
The Johns Hopkins University	M
Kansas State University	M
Kean University	M
Kennesaw State University	M
Kent State University	M
Kentucky State University	M
Kutztown University of Pennsylvania	M
Lamar University	M
Lewis University	M
Lindenwood University	M
Long Island University, Brooklyn Campus	M
Long Island University, C.W. Post Campus	M,O
Louisiana State University and Agricultural and Mechanical College	M,D
Marist College	M,O
Marywood University	M
Metropolitan State University	M
Michigan State University	M,D
Midwestern State University	M
Minnesota State University Mankato	M
Minnesota State University Moorhead	M
Mississippi State University	M,D
Montana State University–Bozeman	M
Monterey Institute of International Studies	M
Murray State University	M
National University	M
New Mexico Highlands University	M
New School University	M,D,O
New York University	M
North Carolina Central University	M,D
North Carolina State University	M,D
Northeastern University	M,D,O
Northern Arizona University	M
Northern Illinois University	M,O
Northern Kentucky University	M
Northern Michigan University	
North Georgia College & State University	M
Northwestern University	D
Notre Dame de Namur University	M
Nova Southeastern University	M,D
Oakland University	M
The Ohio State University	M,D
Ohio University	M
Oklahoma City University	M
Old Dominion University	M
Pace University, White Plains Campus	M
Park University	M
The Pennsylvania State University Harrisburg Campus of the Capital College	M,D
Pepperdine University	M
Pontifical Catholic University of Puerto Rico	M,D
Portland State University	M,D
Princeton University	M,D
Regent University	M
Rochester Institute of Technology	M
Roosevelt University	M
Rutgers, The State University of New Jersey, Camden	M
Rutgers, The State University of New Jersey, Newark	M,D
Rutgers, The State University of New Jersey, New Brunswick/Piscataway	M
Sage Graduate School	M
Saginaw Valley State University	M
St. Edward's University	M
Saint Louis University	M,D
Saint Mary's University of Minnesota	M,O
St. Mary's University of San Antonio	M
St. Thomas University	M,O
San Diego State University	M
San Francisco State University	M
San Jose State University	M
Savannah State University	M
Seattle University	M
Seton Hall University	M
Shenandoah University	M,D,O
Shippensburg University of Pennsylvania	M
Sonoma State University	M
Southeastern University	M
Southeast Missouri State University	M
Southern Illinois University Carbondale	M
Southern Illinois University Edwardsville	M
Southern University and Agricultural and Mechanical College	M,D
Southwest Missouri State University	M
State University of New York at Binghamton	M,D
State University of New York College at Brockport	M
State University of New York Empire State College	M
State University of West Georgia	M
Stephen F. Austin State University	M
Stony Brook University, State University of New York	M,D,O
Suffolk University	M,O
Sul Ross State University	M
Syracuse University	M,D,O
Tennessee State University	M,D
Texas A&M International University	M
Texas A&M University	M
Texas A&M University–Corpus Christi	M
Texas Southern University	M
Texas State University-San Marcos	M
Texas Tech University	M,D
Troy University	M
Troy University Montgomery	M
Tufts University	M,O
Tulane University	M
University at Albany, State University of New York	M,D,O
The University of Akron	M
The University of Alabama	M,D
The University of Alabama at Birmingham	M
The University of Alabama in Huntsville	M
University of Alaska Anchorage	M
University of Alaska Southeast	M
The University of Arizona	M,D
University of Arkansas	M,D
University of Arkansas at Little Rock	M
University of Baltimore	M,D
University of California, Berkeley	M,D
University of California, Los Angeles	M
University of Central Florida	M,D,O
University of Chicago	M,D
University of Colorado at Boulder	M,D
University of Colorado at Colorado Springs	M
University of Colorado at Denver	M,D
University of Connecticut	M
University of Dayton	M
University of Delaware	M,D
University of Denver	M
University of Evansville	M
The University of Findlay	M
University of Florida	M,D,O
University of Georgia	M,D
University of Guam	M
University of Hawaii at Manoa	M,O
University of Houston–Clear Lake	M
University of Idaho	M
University of Illinois at Chicago	M,D
University of Illinois at Springfield	M,D
University of Kansas	M
University of Kentucky	M,D
University of La Verne	M,D
University of Louisville	M
University of Maine	M,D
University of Maryland, Baltimore County	M,D
University of Maryland, College Park	M,D
University of Massachusetts Amherst	M
University of Massachusetts Boston	M,D,O
The University of Memphis	M
University of Michigan	M,D
University of Michigan–Dearborn	M,O
University of Michigan–Flint	M
University of Minnesota, Twin Cities Campus	M
University of Missouri–Columbia	M
University of Missouri–Kansas City	M,D
University of Missouri–St. Louis	M,D,O
The University of Montana–Missoula	M
University of Nebraska at Omaha	M,D
University of Nevada, Las Vegas	M
University of Nevada, Reno	M
University of New Hampshire	M
University of New Haven	M
University of New Mexico	M
University of New Orleans	M
The University of North Carolina at Chapel Hill	M,D
The University of North Carolina at Charlotte	M,D
The University of North Carolina at Greensboro	M,O
The University of North Carolina at Pembroke	M
The University of North Carolina at Wilmington	
University of North Dakota	M
University of Northern Iowa	M
University of North Florida	M
University of North Texas	M
University of Oklahoma	M
University of Oregon	M
University of Pennsylvania	M,D
University of Pittsburgh	M,D
University of Puerto Rico, Río Piedras	M
University of Rhode Island	M
University of San Francisco	M
University of South Alabama	M
University of South Carolina	M
The University of South Dakota	M
University of Southern California	M,D,O
University of Southern Indiana	M
University of Southern Maine	M,D,O
University of South Florida	M
The University of Tennessee	M
The University of Tennessee at Chattanooga	M
The University of Texas at Arlington	M,D
The University of Texas at Austin	M,D
The University of Texas at Dallas	M
The University of Texas at San Antonio	M
The University of Texas at Tyler	M
The University of Texas–Pan American	M
University of the District of Columbia	M
University of the Pacific	P,M,D
University of the Virgin Islands	M
University of Toledo	M
University of Utah	M,O
University of Vermont	M
University of Washington	M

University of West Florida	M
University of Wisconsin–Madison	M
University of Wisconsin–Milwaukee	M
University of Wisconsin–Whitewater	M
University of Wyoming	M
Valdosta State University	M
Villanova University	M
Virginia Commonwealth University	M,D,O
Virginia Polytechnic Institute and State University	M,D,O
Walden University	M,D
Washington University in St. Louis	M
Wayne State University	M
Webster University	M,D
West Chester University of Pennsylvania	M
Western Carolina University	M
Western International University	M
Western Kentucky University	M
Western Michigan University	M,D
West Virginia University	M,D
Wichita State University	M
Widener University	M
Wilmington College (DE)	M
Wright State University	M

■ PUBLISHING

Drexel University	M
Emerson College	M
New York University	M
Northwestern University	M
Pace University	M
Rochester Institute of Technology	M
University of Baltimore	M

■ QUALITY MANAGEMENT

California State University, Dominguez Hills	M
Case Western Reserve University	M,D
Dowling College	M,O
Eastern Michigan University	M
Ferris State University	M
Madonna University	M
Marian College of Fond du Lac	M
The Pennsylvania State University University Park Campus	M
Rutgers, The State University of New Jersey, New Brunswick/Piscataway	M,D
Saint Joseph's College of Maine	M
San Jose State University	M
The University of Akron	M
University of Central Florida	M,O

■ QUANTITATIVE ANALYSIS

California State University, Hayward	M
Clark Atlanta University	M
Drexel University	M,D,O
Hofstra University	M,O
Lehigh University	M
Loyola College in Maryland	M
New York University	M,D,O
Purdue University	M,D
St. John's University (NY)	M,O
Syracuse University	D
Texas Tech University	M,D
University of Cincinnati	M,D
University of Missouri–St. Louis	M,O
University of Oregon	M
University of Rhode Island	M,D
The University of Texas at Arlington	M,D
Virginia Commonwealth University	M

■ RADIATION BIOLOGY

Auburn University	M,D
Colorado State University	M,D
Georgetown University	M
The University of Iowa	M,D

■ RANGE SCIENCE

| Colorado State University | M,D |

Kansas State University	M,D
Montana State University–Bozeman	M,D
New Mexico State University	M,D
North Dakota State University	M,D
Oregon State University	M,D
Sul Ross State University	M
Texas A&M University	M,D
Texas A&M University–Kingsville	M
Texas Tech University	M,D
The University of Arizona	M,D
University of California, Berkeley	M
University of Idaho	M,D
University of Wyoming	M,D
Utah State University	M,D

■ READING EDUCATION

Abilene Christian University	M
Adelphi University	M,O
Albany State University	M
Alfred University	M
American International College	M,D,O
Andrews University	M
Angelo State University	M
Anna Maria College	M
Appalachian State University	M
Arcadia University	M,D,O
Arkansas State University	M,O
Ashland University	M
Auburn University	M,D,O
Auburn University Montgomery	M,O
Austin Peay State University	M,O
Averett University	M
Baldwin-Wallace College	M
Barry University	M,O
Benedictine University	M
Bethel University	M,O
Bloomsburg University of Pennsylvania	M
Boise State University	M
Boston College	M,O
Boston University	M,D,O
Bowie State University	M
Bowling Green State University	M,O
Bridgewater State College	M,O
Brigham Young University	M,D
Brooklyn College of the City University of New York	M
Buffalo State College, State University of New York	M
Butler University	M
California Baptist University	M
California Lutheran University	M
California Polytechnic State University, San Luis Obispo	M
California State University, Bakersfield	M
California State University, Chico	M
California State University, Fresno	M
California State University, Fullerton	M
California State University, Los Angeles	M
California State University, Sacramento	M
California State University, San Bernardino	M
California State University, Stanislaus	M
California University of Pennsylvania	M
Canisius College	M
Cardinal Stritch University	M
Carthage College	M,O
Castleton State College	M,O
Central Connecticut State University	M,O
Central Michigan University	M
Central Missouri State University	M,O
Central Washington University	M
Chapman University	M
Chicago State University	M
The Citadel, The Military College of South Carolina	M
City College of the City University of New York	M
City University	M,O
Claremont Graduate University	M,D

Clarion University of Pennsylvania	M
Clemson University	M
Cleveland State University	M
College of Mount St. Joseph	M
The College of New Jersey	M,O
The College of New Rochelle	M
College of St. Joseph	M
The College of Saint Rose	M,O
The College of William and Mary	M
Concordia University (CA)	M
Concordia University (IL)	M
Concordia University (NE)	M
Concordia University Wisconsin	M
Coppin State University	M
Cumberland College	M
Dallas Baptist University	M
DePaul University	M
Dowling College	M
Duquesne University	M
East Carolina University	M
Eastern Connecticut State University	M
Eastern Kentucky University	M
Eastern Michigan University	M
Eastern Nazarene College	M,O
Eastern Washington University	M
East Stroudsburg University of Pennsylvania	M
East Tennessee State University	M
Edinboro University of Pennsylvania	M,O
Elms College	M,O
Emporia State University	M
Fairleigh Dickinson University, Metropolitan Campus	M,O
Ferris State University	M
Florida Atlantic University	M
Florida Gulf Coast University	M
Florida International University	M
Florida State University	M,D,O
Fordham University	M,D,O
Framingham State College	M
Fresno Pacific University	M
Frostburg State University	M
Gannon University	M,O
George Mason University	M
Georgia Southern University	M
Georgia Southwestern State University	M,O
Georgia State University	M,O
Governors State University	M
Grand Canyon University	M
Grand Valley State University	M
Gwynedd-Mercy College	M
Harding University	M
Hardin-Simmons University	M
Harvard University	M,D
Henderson State University	M
Hofstra University	M,D,O
Holy Family University	M
Hood College	M
Houston Baptist University	M
Howard University	M,O
Hunter College of the City University of New York	M,O
Idaho State University	M,O
Illinois State University	M
Indiana State University	M
Indiana University Bloomington	M,D,O
Indiana University of Pennsylvania	M
Indiana University–Purdue University Indianapolis	M
Jacksonville State University	M
Jacksonville University	M
James Madison University	M
The Johns Hopkins University	M,D,O
Johnson State College	M
Kean University	M,O
Kent State University	M
King's College	M
Kutztown University of Pennsylvania	M
Lake Erie College	M

Peterson's Graduate Schools in the U.S. 2006 — www.petersons.com — 155

Directory of Graduate and Professional Programs by Field
Reading Education

Institution	Degree
Lehman College of the City University of New York	M
Lesley University	M,D,O
Liberty University	M,D
Long Island University, Brooklyn Campus	M
Long Island University, C.W. Post Campus	M
Longwood University	M
Loyola College in Maryland	M,O
Loyola Marymount University	M
Loyola University New Orleans	M
Lynchburg College	M
Madonna University	M
Malone College	M
Manhattanville College	M
Marshall University	M,O
Marygrove College	M
Maryville University of Saint Louis	M
Marywood University	M
Mercer University	M,O
Mercy College	M,O
Miami University	M
Michigan State University	M
Middle Tennessee State University	M
Midwestern State University	M
Millersville University of Pennsylvania	M
Minnesota State University Mankato	M
Minnesota State University Moorhead	M
Monmouth University	M,O
Montana State University–Billings	M
Montclair State University	M
Morehead State University	M
Mount Saint Mary College	M
Murray State University	M
National-Louis University	M,D,O
Nazareth College of Rochester	M
New Jersey City University	M
New Mexico State University	M,D,O
New York University	M
Niagara University	M
North Carolina Agricultural and Technical State University	M
Northeastern Illinois University	M
Northeastern State University	M
Northern State University	M
Northwestern Oklahoma State University	M
Northwestern State University of Louisiana	M,O
Northwest Missouri State University	M
Northwest Nazarene University	M
Notre Dame de Namur University	M,O
Nova Southeastern University	M,O
Oakland University	M,D,O
Ohio University	M,D
Old Dominion University	M
Pacific Lutheran University	M
The Pennsylvania State University University Park Campus	M,D
Pittsburg State University	M
Plymouth State University	M
Portland State University	M,D
Providence College	M
Purdue University	M,D,O
Queens College of the City University of New York	M
Radford University	M
Rhode Island College	M,O
Rider University	M
Rivier College	M,O
Rockford College	M
Rowan University	M
Rutgers, The State University of New Jersey, New Brunswick/Piscataway	M,D
Sage Graduate School	M
Saginaw Valley State University	M
St. Bonaventure University	M
St. John Fisher College	M
St. John's University (NY)	M,O
Saint Joseph's University	M
Saint Martin's College	M
Saint Mary's College of California	M
St. Mary's University of San Antonio	M
Saint Michael's College	M
Saint Peter's College	M
St. Thomas Aquinas College	M,O
Saint Xavier University	M,O
Salem State College	M
Salisbury University	M
Sam Houston State University	M
San Diego State University	M
San Francisco State University	M,O
Seattle Pacific University	M
Seattle University	M,O
Shippensburg University of Pennsylvania	M
Siena Heights University	M
Slippery Rock University of Pennsylvania	M
Southern Connecticut State University	M,O
Southern Oregon University	M
Southwest Missouri State University	M
State University of New York at Binghamton	M
State University of New York at New Paltz	M
State University of New York at Oswego	M
State University of New York at Plattsburgh	M
State University of New York College at Brockport	M
State University of New York College at Cortland	M
State University of New York College at Fredonia	M
State University of New York College at Geneseo	M
State University of New York College at Oneonta	M
State University of New York College at Potsdam	M
State University of West Georgia	M
Stetson University	M
Sul Ross State University	M
Syracuse University	M,D,O
Tarleton State University	M,O
Teachers College Columbia University	M
Temple University	M,D
Tennessee Technological University	M,O
Texas A&M International University	M
Texas A&M University	M,D
Texas A&M University–Commerce	M,D
Texas A&M University–Corpus Christi	M,D
Texas A&M University–Kingsville	M
Texas Southern University	M,D
Texas State University-San Marcos	M
Texas Tech University	M,D,O
Texas Woman's University	M,D
Towson University	M,O
Trinity College (DC)	M
University at Albany, State University of New York	M,D,O
University at Buffalo, The State University of New York	M,D,O
The University of Arizona	M,D,O
University of Arkansas at Little Rock	M,O
University of Bridgeport	M,O
University of California, Berkeley	M,D
University of Central Arkansas	M
University of Central Florida	M
University of Central Oklahoma	M
University of Cincinnati	M,D
University of Connecticut	M,D
University of Dayton	M
University of Florida	M,D,O
University of Georgia	M,D,O
University of Guam	M
University of Houston	M
University of Houston–Clear Lake	M
University of Illinois at Chicago	M,D
University of La Verne	M,O
University of Louisiana at Monroe	M
University of Louisville	M
University of Maine	M,D,O
University of Mary	M
University of Mary Hardin-Baylor	M
University of Maryland, College Park	M,D,O
University of Massachusetts Amherst	M,D,O
University of Massachusetts Lowell	M,D,O
The University of Memphis	M,D
University of Miami	M,D,O
University of Michigan	M,D
University of Michigan–Flint	M
University of Minnesota, Twin Cities Campus	M,D,O
University of Missouri–Columbia	M,D,O
University of Missouri–Kansas City	M,D,O
University of Missouri–St. Louis	M,D
University of Nebraska at Kearney	M
University of Nebraska at Omaha	M
University of New Hampshire	M,D
The University of North Carolina at Chapel Hill	M,D
The University of North Carolina at Charlotte	M
The University of North Carolina at Pembroke	M
The University of North Carolina at Wilmington	M
University of North Dakota	M
University of Northern Colorado	M,D
University of Northern Iowa	M
University of North Texas	M,D
University of Oklahoma	M,D,O
University of Pennsylvania	M,D
University of Pittsburgh	M,D
University of Rhode Island	M
University of Rio Grande	M
University of St. Thomas (MN)	M,D,O
The University of Scranton	M
University of Sioux Falls	M
University of South Alabama	M
University of South Carolina	M,D
University of Southern California	M,D
University of Southern Maine	M,O
University of Southern Mississippi	M,D,O
University of South Florida	M,D,O
The University of Tennessee	M,D,O
The University of Texas at Brownsville	M
The University of Texas at San Antonio	M
The University of Texas at Tyler	M
The University of Texas of the Permian Basin	M
The University of Texas–Pan American	M
University of the Incarnate Word	M
University of Vermont	M
University of Washington	M,D
University of West Florida	M
University of Wisconsin–Eau Claire	M
University of Wisconsin–La Crosse	M
University of Wisconsin–Milwaukee	M
University of Wisconsin–Oshkosh	M
University of Wisconsin–River Falls	M
University of Wisconsin–Stevens Point	M
University of Wisconsin–Superior	M
University of Wisconsin–Whitewater	M
Valdosta State University	M,O
Vanderbilt University	M
Virginia Commonwealth University	M
Wagner College	M
Walla Walla College	M
Washburn University	M
Washington State University	M,D
Wayne State University	M,D,O
West Chester University of Pennsylvania	M
Western Carolina University	M

Rehabilitation Counseling

Western Connecticut State University	M
Western Illinois University	M,O
Western Kentucky University	M
Western Michigan University	M
Western New Mexico University	M
Westfield State College	M
West Texas A&M University	M
West Virginia University	M
Wheelock College	M
Whitworth College	M
Widener University	M,D
William Paterson University of New Jersey	M
Wilmington College (DE)	M
Winthrop University	M
Worcester State College	M
Xavier University	M
Youngstown State University	M

■ REAL ESTATE

American University	M
California State University, Sacramento	M
Cleveland State University	M,O
Columbia University	M
Cornell University	M
Florida Atlantic University	M
The George Washington University	M
Georgia State University	M,D
The Johns Hopkins University	M,O
Massachusetts Institute of Technology	M
New York University	M,O
The Pennsylvania State University University Park Campus	D
Texas A&M University	M
University of California, Berkeley	D
University of Cincinnati	M
University of Colorado at Boulder	M,D
University of Denver	M
University of Florida	M,D
University of Hawaii at Manoa	M
The University of Memphis	M,D
University of Michigan	M,D,O
University of North Texas	M,D
University of Pennsylvania	M,D
University of St. Thomas (MN)	M
University of Southern California	M
The University of Texas at Arlington	M,D
University of Wisconsin–Madison	M,D
Virginia Commonwealth University	M,O
Webster University	M

■ RECREATION AND PARK MANAGEMENT

Adams State College	M
Arizona State University	M
Aurora University	M
Bowling Green State University	M
Brigham Young University	M
California State University, Chico	M
California State University, Long Beach	M
California State University, Northridge	M
California State University, Sacramento	M
Central Michigan University	M
Central Washington University	M
Clemson University	M,D
Cleveland State University	M
Colorado State University	M,D
Delta State University	M
East Carolina University	M
Eastern Kentucky University	M
Florida Agricultural and Mechanical University	M
Florida International University	M
Florida State University	M,D,O
Frostburg State University	M
Georgia Southern University	M
Hardin-Simmons University	M
Howard University	M
Indiana University Bloomington	M,D,O
Lehman College of the City University of New York	M
Michigan State University	M,D
Middle Tennessee State University	M,D
Morehead State University	M
Murray State University	M
North Carolina Central University	M
North Carolina State University	M,D
Ohio University	M
Old Dominion University	M
San Francisco State University	M
San Jose State University	M
South Dakota State University	M
Southern Connecticut State University	M
Southern Illinois University Carbondale	M
Southern University and Agricultural and Mechanical College	M
Southwestern Oklahoma State University	M
Southwest Missouri State University	M
Springfield College	M
State University of New York College at Brockport	M
State University of New York College at Cortland	M
State University of New York College of Environmental Science and Forestry	M,D
Temple University	M
Texas A&M University	M,D
Texas State University–San Marcos	M
Universidad Metropolitana	M
University of Arkansas	M,D
University of Florida	M,D
University of Georgia	M,D
University of Idaho	M,D
The University of Iowa	M
University of Minnesota, Twin Cities Campus	M,D
University of Mississippi	M,D
University of Missouri–Columbia	M
The University of Montana–Missoula	M,D
University of Nebraska at Omaha	M
University of Nebraska–Lincoln	M
University of New Hampshire	M
University of New Mexico	M,O
The University of North Carolina at Chapel Hill	M
The University of North Carolina at Greensboro	M
University of North Texas	M,O
University of Rhode Island	M
University of South Alabama	M
University of Southern Mississippi	M,D
The University of Tennessee	M
University of Toledo	M
University of Utah	M,D
University of Wisconsin–La Crosse	M
Utah State University	M,D
Virginia Commonwealth University	M
Virginia Polytechnic Institute and State University	M,D
Wayne State University	M
Western Illinois University	M
Western Kentucky University	M
West Virginia University	M
Wright State University	M

■ REHABILITATION COUNSELING

Arkansas State University	M,O
Assumption College	M,O
Barry University	M,O
Boston University	M,D,O
Bowling Green State University	M
California State University, Fresno	M
California State University, Los Angeles	M
California State University, San Bernardino	M
Central Connecticut State University	M
Coppin State University	M
Drake University	M
East Carolina University	M
East Central University	M
Edinboro University of Pennsylvania	M,O
Emporia State University	M
Florida Atlantic University	M,O
Florida State University	M,D,O
Fort Valley State University	M
The George Washington University	M
Georgia State University	M,O
Hofstra University	M,O
Hunter College of the City University of New York	M
Illinois Institute of Technology	M,D
Indiana University–Purdue University Indianapolis	M,D
Jackson State University	M,O
Kent State University	M,O
La Salle University	D
Maryville University of Saint Louis	M
Michigan State University	M,D,O
Minnesota State University Mankato	M
Montana State University–Billings	M
Northeastern University	M
Ohio University	M,D
St. Cloud State University	M
St. John's University (NY)	M,O
San Diego State University	M
San Francisco State University	M
South Carolina State University	M
Southern Illinois University Carbondale	M,D
Southern University and Agricultural and Mechanical College	M
Springfield College	M,O
Syracuse University	M
University at Albany, State University of New York	M
University at Buffalo, The State University of New York	M,D,O
The University of Alabama at Birmingham	M
The University of Arizona	M,D,O
University of Arkansas	M,D
University of Florida	M
University of Illinois at Urbana–Champaign	M
The University of Iowa	M,D
University of Kentucky	M
University of Louisiana at Lafayette	M
University of Maryland, College Park	M,D,O
University of Massachusetts Boston	M,O
The University of Memphis	M,D
University of Nebraska at Omaha	M
University of Nevada, Las Vegas	M
The University of North Carolina at Chapel Hill	M,D
University of Northern Colorado	M,D
University of North Florida	M,O
University of North Texas	M
University of Pittsburgh	M
University of Puerto Rico, Río Piedras	M
The University of Scranton	M
University of South Carolina	M,O
University of South Florida	M
The University of Tennessee	M
The University of Texas–Pan American	M
University of Wisconsin–Madison	M,D
University of Wisconsin–Stout	M
Utah State University	M
Virginia Commonwealth University	M,O
Wayne State University	M,D,O
Western Michigan University	M
Western Oregon University	M
Western Washington University	M
West Virginia University	M

Directory of Graduate and Professional Programs by Field
Rehabilitation Counseling

Wright State University	M

■ REHABILITATION SCIENCES

Boston University	M,D
Canisius College	M
Central Michigan University	M,D
Clarion University of Pennsylvania	M
Duquesne University	M,D
East Carolina University	M
East Stroudsburg University of Pennsylvania	M
Indiana University–Purdue University Indianapolis	M
Slippery Rock University of Pennsylvania	M
University at Buffalo, The State University of New York	M,D
University of Cincinnati	M
University of Florida	D
University of Illinois at Urbana–Champaign	M
The University of Iowa	M,D
University of Kansas	M,D
University of Kentucky	D
University of Maryland	D
University of Minnesota, Twin Cities Campus	M,D
University of North Texas	M
University of Pittsburgh	M,D,O
University of South Carolina	M,O
University of Toledo	M
University of Wisconsin–La Crosse	M
University of Wisconsin–Madison	M
Wayne State University	M

■ RELIABILITY ENGINEERING

The University of Arizona	M
University of Maryland, College Park	M,D,O

■ RELIGION

Arizona State University	M
Azusa Pacific University	M
Bayamón Central University	P,M
Baylor University	M,D
Biola University	P,M,D
Boston University	M,D
Brown University	M,D
California State University, Long Beach	M
Cardinal Stritch University	M
The Catholic University of America	M,D,O
Chestnut Hill College	M,O
Claremont Graduate University	M,D
Columbia University	M,D
Concordia University (IL)	M
Cornell University	D
Duke University	M,D
Edgewood College	M
Elms College	M
Emory University	D
Florida International University	M
Florida State University	M,D
Fordham University	M,D,O
George Fox University	P,M,D
The George Washington University	M
Gonzaga University	P,M
Grand Rapids Theological Seminary of Cornerstone University	P,M
Hardin-Simmons University	M
Harvard University	M,D
Holy Names University	M,O
Indiana University Bloomington	M,D
John Carroll University	M
La Salle University	M
La Sierra University	M
Liberty University	P,M,D
Lipscomb University	P,M
Loma Linda University	M
Loras College	M
Loyola University New Orleans	M
Miami University	M
Mount St. Mary's College	M
New York University	M,O
Northwest Nazarene University	M
Oklahoma City University	M
Olivet Nazarene University	M
Pepperdine University	P,M
Point Loma Nazarene University	M
Princeton University	D
Providence College	M
Rice University	D
Sacred Heart University	M
Santa Clara University	M
Seton Hall University	M
Southern Methodist University	M,D
Southern Nazarene University	M
Southwest Missouri State University	M
Spring Arbor University	P,M
Stanford University	M,D
Syracuse University	M,D
Temple University	M,D
Trevecca Nazarene University	M
University of California, Berkeley	D
University of California, Santa Barbara	M,D
University of Chicago	P,M,D
University of Colorado at Boulder	M
University of Denver	M
University of Detroit Mercy	M
University of Florida	M,D
University of Georgia	M
University of Hawaii at Manoa	M
The University of Iowa	M,D
University of Kansas	M
University of Mary Hardin-Baylor	M
University of Missouri–Columbia	M
University of Mobile	M
The University of North Carolina at Chapel Hill	M,D
The University of North Carolina at Charlotte	M
University of North Texas	M
University of Notre Dame	M
University of Pennsylvania	D
University of Pittsburgh	M,D
University of St. Thomas (MN)	M
University of South Carolina	M
University of Southern California	M,D
University of South Florida	M
The University of Tennessee	M,D
University of the Incarnate Word	M
University of Virginia	M,D
University of Washington	M
Vanderbilt University	M,D
Wake Forest University	M
Washington University in St. Louis	M
Wayland Baptist University	M
Western Michigan University	M,D
Yale University	D

■ RELIGIOUS EDUCATION

Andrews University	M,D,O
Azusa Pacific University	M
Biola University	P,M,D
Boston College	M,D,O
Campbell University	P,M,D
The Catholic University of America	M,D
Concordia University (IL)	M
Concordia University (NE)	M
Cornerstone University	P,M
Dallas Baptist University	M
Fordham University	M,D,O
Gardner-Webb University	P,D
George Fox University	P,M,D
Golden Gate Baptist Theological Seminary	P,M,D,O
Grand Rapids Theological Seminary of Cornerstone University	P,M
Gratz College	M,O
La Sierra University	M
Loyola Marymount University	M
North Park Theological Seminary	M
Nova Southeastern University	M,O
Oklahoma City University	M
Oral Roberts University	P,M,D
Pfeiffer University	M
Pontifical Catholic University of Puerto Rico	M,D
Teachers College Columbia University	M,D
University of Portland	M
University of St. Thomas (MN)	M,D
University of San Francisco	M,D
Yeshiva University	M,D,O

■ REPRODUCTIVE BIOLOGY

Cornell University	M,D
The Johns Hopkins University	M,D
Northwestern University	D
Texas A&M University	M,D
University of Hawaii at Manoa	M,D
University of Wyoming	M,D
West Virginia University	M,D

■ RHETORIC

Abilene Christian University	M
Ball State University	M
California State University, Dominguez Hills	M,O
Carnegie Mellon University	M
The Catholic University of America	M,D
Colorado State University	M
Duquesne University	M
Florida State University	M,D
Georgia State University	M
Indiana University of Pennsylvania	M,D
Iowa State University of Science and Technology	M,D
Kent State University	M,D
Miami University	M,D
Michigan State University	M,D
Michigan Technological University	M,D
New Mexico Highlands University	M
Northern Arizona University	M
Rensselaer Polytechnic Institute	M,D
San Diego State University	M
Southern Illinois University Carbondale	M,D
Syracuse University	D
Texas Tech University	M,D
Texas Woman's University	M,D
The University of Alabama	M,D
The University of Arizona	M,D
University of Arkansas at Little Rock	M
University of California, Berkeley	D
University of Illinois at Chicago	M,D
The University of Iowa	M,D
University of Louisiana at Lafayette	M,D
University of Louisville	D
University of Minnesota, Twin Cities Campus	M,D
The University of Texas at Arlington	M,D
The University of Texas at El Paso	M
Virginia Commonwealth University	M
Wright State University	M

■ ROMANCE LANGUAGES

Appalachian State University	M
Boston University	M,D
The Catholic University of America	M,D
Clark Atlanta University	M
Columbia University	M,D
Cornell University	M,D
Hunter College of the City University of New York	M
The Johns Hopkins University	D
Michigan State University	M,D
New York University	M,D
Northern Illinois University	M
Queens College of the City University of New York	M
Southern Connecticut State University	M

Stony Brook University, State University of New York — M,D
Texas Tech University — M,D
University at Buffalo, The State University of New York — M,D
The University of Alabama — M,D
University of California, Berkeley — D
University of California, Los Angeles — M,D
University of Chicago — M,D
University of Cincinnati — M,D
University of Georgia — M,D
University of Michigan — D
University of Missouri–Columbia — M,D
University of Missouri–Kansas City — M
University of New Orleans — M
The University of North Carolina at Chapel Hill — M,D
University of Notre Dame — M
University of Oregon — M,D
University of Pennsylvania — M,D
The University of Texas at Austin — M,D
University of Virginia — M,D
University of Washington — M,D
Washington University in St. Louis — M,D

■ RURAL PLANNING AND STUDIES
California State University, Chico — M
Cornell University — M
Iowa State University of Science and Technology — M,D
State University of West Georgia — M
University of Alaska Fairbanks — M
The University of Montana–Missoula — M
University of Wyoming — M

■ RURAL SOCIOLOGY
Auburn University — M,D
Cornell University — M,D
Iowa State University of Science and Technology — M,D
North Carolina State University — M,D
The Ohio State University — M,D
The Pennsylvania State University University Park Campus — M,D
South Dakota State University — M,D
University of Idaho — M
University of Missouri–Columbia — M,D
The University of Montana–Missoula — M
The University of Tennessee — M
University of Wisconsin–Madison — M,D

■ RUSSIAN
American University — M,O
Boston College — M
Brigham Young University — M
Brown University — M,D
Columbia University — M,D
DePaul University — M
Harvard University — M,D
Hofstra University — M
Kent State University — M
New York University — M
The Pennsylvania State University University Park Campus — M
San Francisco State University — M
Stanford University — M,D
Stony Brook University, State University of New York — M,D
University at Albany, State University of New York — M,O
The University of Arizona — M
University of California, Berkeley — M,D
University of Illinois at Urbana–Champaign — M,D
The University of Iowa — M
University of Maryland, Baltimore County — M
University of Maryland, College Park — M
University of Michigan — M,D

The University of North Carolina at Chapel Hill — M,D
University of Oregon — M
The University of Tennessee — D
University of Washington — M,D

■ SAFETY ENGINEERING
Central Missouri State University — M,O
Embry-Riddle Aeronautical University (AZ) — M
Murray State University — M
New Jersey Institute of Technology — M
Texas A&M University — M,D
University of Minnesota, Duluth — M
University of Wisconsin–Stout — M
West Virginia University — M

■ SCANDINAVIAN LANGUAGES
Cornell University — M,D
Harvard University — M,D
University of California, Berkeley — M,D
University of California, Los Angeles — M,D
University of Minnesota, Twin Cities Campus — M,D
University of Washington — M,D
University of Wisconsin–Madison — M,D

■ SCHOOL NURSING
Capital University — M
The College of New Jersey — O
Kutztown University of Pennsylvania — O
La Salle University — M,O
Monmouth University — M,O
Seton Hall University — M
Wright State University — M

■ SCHOOL PSYCHOLOGY
Abilene Christian University — M
Alabama Agricultural and Mechanical University — M,O
Alfred University — M,D,O
Andrews University — M,O
Appalachian State University — M,O
Arcadia University — M
Argosy University/Sarasota — M,D,O
Auburn University — M,D,O
Austin Peay State University — M
Azusa Pacific University — M
Ball State University — M,D,O
Barry University — M,O
Bowling Green State University — M,O
Brigham Young University — M,D
Brooklyn College of the City University of New York — M,O
California State University, Los Angeles — M
California State University, Sacramento — M
California University of Pennsylvania — M
Central Connecticut State University — M
Central Michigan University — D,O
Central Washington University — M
Chapman University — M,O
The Citadel, The Military College of South Carolina — M,O
City University — M,O
Cleveland State University — M,O
The College of New Rochelle — M
College of St. Joseph — M
The College of Saint Rose — M,O
The College of William and Mary — M,O
Duquesne University — M,D,O
East Carolina University — M
Eastern Illinois University — M,O
Eastern Kentucky University — M,O
Eastern Washington University — M
Edinboro University of Pennsylvania — O
Emporia State University — M,O
Fairfield University — M,O
Fairleigh Dickinson University, Metropolitan Campus — M,D

Florida Agricultural and Mechanical University — M
Florida International University — O
Florida State University — M,O
Fordham University — M,D,O
Fort Hays State University — O
Francis Marion University — M
Fresno Pacific University — M
Gallaudet University — M,O
Gardner-Webb University — M
George Mason University — M
Georgia Southern University — M,O
Georgia State University — M,D,O
Grand Valley State University — M
Hofstra University — D,O
Howard University — M,D,O
Idaho State University — M,O
Illinois State University — D,O
Immaculata University — M,D,O
Indiana State University — M,D,O
Indiana University Bloomington — M,D,O
Indiana University of Pennsylvania — D,O
Inter American University of Puerto Rico, San Germán Campus — M,D
Iona College — M
James Madison University — M,O
Kean University — M,O
Kent State University — M,D,O
La Sierra University — M,O
Lehigh University — D,O
Lesley University — M,D,O
Long Island University, Brooklyn Campus — M
Louisiana State University and Agricultural and Mechanical College — M,D
Louisiana State University in Shreveport — M,O
Loyola Marymount University — M
Loyola University Chicago — D,O
Marist College — M,O
Marshall University — O
Maryville University of Saint Louis — M
Marywood University — M
McNeese State University — M
Mercy College — M,O
Miami University — M,O
Michigan State University — M,D,O
Middle Tennessee State University — M,O
Millersville University of Pennsylvania — M
Minnesota State University Moorhead — M,O
Minot State University — O
National-Louis University — M,D,O
National University — M
New Jersey City University — O
New York University — M,D,O
Niagara University — M
Nicholls State University — M,O
Northeastern University — M,D,O
Northern Arizona University — M,D
Nova Southeastern University — M,D,O
Our Lady of the Lake University of San Antonio — M,D
Pace University — M,D
Pacific University — M
The Pennsylvania State University University Park Campus — M,D
Pittsburg State University — O
Pontifical Catholic University of Puerto Rico — M,D
Queens College of the City University of New York — M,O
Radford University — O
Regent University — M,D,O
Rhode Island College — O
Rider University — O
Rochester Institute of Technology — M,O
Rowan University — M,O
Rutgers, The State University of New Jersey, New Brunswick/Piscataway — M,D

School Psychology

Institution	Degree
St. John's University (NY)	M,D
St. Mary's University of San Antonio	M
Sam Houston State University	M,D
San Diego State University	M
Seattle Pacific University	O
Seattle University	O
Seton Hall University	O
Southeast Missouri State University	M
Southern Connecticut State University	M,O
Southern Illinois University Edwardsville	O
State University of New York at Oswego	M,O
State University of New York at Plattsburgh	M,O
Stephen F. Austin State University	M
Syracuse University	D
Tarleton State University	M
Teachers College Columbia University	M,D
Temple University	M,D
Tennessee State University	M,D
Texas A&M University	M,D
Texas State University–San Marcos	M
Texas Woman's University	M,D
Towson University	M,O
Trinity University	M
Tufts University	M,O
University at Albany, State University of New York	M,D,O
University at Buffalo, The State University of New York	M,D,O
The University of Akron	M,D
The University of Alabama at Birmingham	M
University of California, Berkeley	D
University of California, Santa Barbara	M,D
University of Central Arkansas	M,D
University of Central Florida	O
University of Cincinnati	M,D
University of Connecticut	M,D
University of Dayton	M
University of Delaware	M,D
University of Denver	M,D,O
University of Detroit Mercy	O
University of Florida	M,D,O
University of Georgia	M,D,O
University of Great Falls	M
University of Hartford	M
University of Houston–Clear Lake	M
University of Idaho	M,D,O
The University of Iowa	M,D,O
University of Kansas	D,O
University of Louisiana at Monroe	O
University of Maryland, College Park	M,D
University of Massachusetts Amherst	D
University of Massachusetts Boston	M,O
The University of Memphis	M,D
University of Minnesota, Twin Cities Campus	M,D,O
University of Missouri–Columbia	M,D,O
University of Missouri–St. Louis	M,D,O
The University of Montana–Missoula	M,O
University of Nebraska at Kearney	M,O
University of Nebraska at Omaha	M,D,O
University of Nevada, Las Vegas	M,D,O
The University of North Carolina at Chapel Hill	M,D
The University of North Carolina at Greensboro	M,D,O
University of Northern Colorado	D,O
University of Northern Iowa	M,O
University of North Texas	M,D
University of Oklahoma	M,D
University of Pennsylvania	D
University of Rhode Island	M,D
University of South Carolina	D
University of Southern Maine	M,D
University of South Florida	M,D,O
The University of Tennessee	M,D,O
The University of Tennessee at Chattanooga	O
The University of Texas at Austin	M,D
The University of Texas at Tyler	M
The University of Texas–Pan American	M
University of the Pacific	M,D,O
University of the Virgin Islands	O
University of Toledo	M,D,O
University of Virginia	M,D,O
University of Washington	M,D
University of Wisconsin–Eau Claire	M,O
University of Wisconsin–La Crosse	M,O
University of Wisconsin–River Falls	M,O
University of Wisconsin–Stout	M,O
University of Wisconsin–Whitewater	M,O
Utah State University	M,D
Valdosta State University	M,O
Valparaiso University	
Wayne State University	M,D,O
Western Carolina University	M
Western Illinois University	M,O
Western Kentucky University	M,O
Western Michigan University	M,D,O
Wichita State University	M,D,O
Wilmington College (DE)	M
Yeshiva University	D

■ SCIENCE EDUCATION

Institution	Degree
Alabama State University	M,O
Albany State University	M
Andrews University	M,D,O
Antioch New England Graduate School	M
Arcadia University	M,D,O
Arizona State University	M,D
Arkansas State University	M,O
Armstrong Atlantic State University	M
Auburn University	M,D,O
Averett University	M
Ball State University	M,D
Belmont University	M
Bemidji State University	M
Bloomsburg University of Pennsylvania	M
Boise State University	M,D
Boston College	M,D
Boston University	M,D,O
Bowling Green State University	M,D,O
Bridgewater State College	M
Brigham Young University	M,D
Brooklyn College of the City University of New York	M
Brown University	M
Buffalo State College, State University of New York	M
California State University, Fullerton	M
California State University, San Bernardino	M
California University of Pennsylvania	M
Carthage College	M,O
Central Michigan University	M
Charleston Southern University	M
The Citadel, The Military College of South Carolina	M
City College of the City University of New York	M
Clarion University of Pennsylvania	M
Clark Atlanta University	M,D
Clemson University	M
College of Charleston	M
The College of Saint Rose	M,O
The College of William and Mary	M
Columbus State University	M,O
Converse College	M
Cornell University	M,D
Delaware State University	M
DeSales University	M,O
Drake University	M
East Carolina University	M
Eastern Connecticut State University	M
Eastern Kentucky University	M
Eastern Michigan University	M
Eastern Washington University	M
East Stroudsburg University of Pennsylvania	M
Edinboro University of Pennsylvania	M
Elms College	M,O
Fitchburg State College	M
Florida Agricultural and Mechanical University	M
Florida Atlantic University	M
Florida Gulf Coast University	M
Florida Institute of Technology	M,D
Florida International University	M,D
Florida State University	M,D,O
Fresno Pacific University	M
Gannon University	M,O
Georgia College & State University	M,O
Georgia Southern University	M
Georgia State University	M,D,O
Grambling State University	M
Harvard University	M,D
Hofstra University	M
Hood College	M
Hunter College of the City University of New York	M,O
Illinois Institute of Technology	M,D
Indiana State University	M,D
Indiana University Bloomington	M,D,O
Indiana University–Purdue University Indianapolis	M
Inter American University of Puerto Rico, Metropolitan Campus	M
Inter American University of Puerto Rico, San Germán Campus	M
Iona College	M
Jackson State University	M,D
The Johns Hopkins University	M,D,O
Kean University	M,O
Kutztown University of Pennsylvania	M,O
Lawrence Technological University	M
Lebanon Valley College	M
Lehman College of the City University of New York	M
Lesley University	M,D,O
Long Island University, C.W. Post Campus	M
Louisiana State University and Agricultural and Mechanical College	M
Louisiana Tech University	M,D
Manhattanville College	M
McNeese State University	M
Michigan State University	M
Michigan Technological University	M
Middle Tennessee State University	M
Minot State University	M
Mississippi College	M
Montana State University–Northern	M
Montclair State University	M,D,O
Morgan State University	M,D
National-Louis University	M,O
New Mexico Institute of Mining and Technology	M
New York University	M
Niagara University	M,O
North Carolina Agricultural and Technical State University	M
North Carolina State University	M,D
Northern Arizona University	M,D
Northern Michigan University	M
North Georgia College & State University	M,O
Northwestern State University of Louisiana	M,O
Northwest Missouri State University	M
Nova Southeastern University	M,O
Ohio University	M
Oregon State University	M,D
The Pennsylvania State University University Park Campus	M,D

Institution	Degree
Portland State University	M,D
Purdue University	M,D,O
Purdue University Calumet	M
Queens College of the City University of New York	M,O
Quinnipiac University	M
Rhode Island College	M
Rider University	O
Rowan University	M
Rutgers, The State University of New Jersey, New Brunswick/Piscataway	M,D
Sage Graduate School	M
Saginaw Valley State University	M
St. John Fisher College	M
Salem State College	M,O
Salisbury University	M
San Diego State University	M,D
Slippery Rock University of Pennsylvania	M
South Carolina State University	M
Southeast Missouri State University	M
Southern Connecticut State University	M,O
Southern University and Agricultural and Mechanical College	D
Southwestern Oklahoma State University	M
Southwest Missouri State University	M
Stanford University	M,D
State University of New York at Binghamton	M
State University of New York at New Paltz	M
State University of New York at Plattsburgh	M
State University of New York College at Brockport	M
State University of New York College at Cortland	M
State University of West Georgia	M,O
Stevens Institute of Technology	O
Stony Brook University, State University of New York	M,O
Syracuse University	M,D,O
Teachers College Columbia University	M,D
Temple University	M,D
Texas A&M University	M,D
Texas State University-San Marcos	M
Texas Woman's University	M,D
Towson University	M
Trinity College (DC)	M
Tuskegee University	M
University at Albany, State University of New York	M,D
University at Buffalo, The State University of New York	M,D,O
University of Alaska Fairbanks	M,D
University of California, Berkeley	M,D
University of California, Los Angeles	M,D
University of California, San Diego	D
University of Central Florida	M
University of Connecticut	M,D
University of Florida	M,D,O
University of Georgia	M,D,O
University of Houston	M,D
University of Idaho	M,D
University of Indianapolis	M
The University of Iowa	M,D
University of Maine	M,O
University of Massachusetts Amherst	D
University of Massachusetts Lowell	M
University of Michigan	M,D
University of Minnesota, Twin Cities Campus	M
University of Missouri–Columbia	M,D,O
University of Missouri–Rolla	M
The University of Montana–Missoula	M,D
University of Nebraska at Kearney	M
University of New Orleans	M
The University of North Carolina at Chapel Hill	M
The University of North Carolina at Pembroke	M
University of Northern Colorado	M,D
University of Northern Iowa	M,O
University of North Florida	M
University of Oklahoma	M,D,O
University of Pittsburgh	M
University of Puerto Rico, Río Piedras	M,D
University of St. Francis (IL)	M
University of South Alabama	M
University of South Carolina	M,D
University of Southern Mississippi	M,D
University of South Florida	M,D,O
The University of Tennessee	M,D,O
The University of Texas at Austin	M,D
The University of Texas at Dallas	M
The University of Texas at Tyler	M
University of Toledo	M,D
University of Tulsa	M
University of Utah	M,D
University of Vermont	M,D
University of Virginia	M,D
University of Washington	M,D
The University of West Alabama	M
University of West Florida	M
University of Wisconsin–Eau Claire	M
University of Wisconsin–Madison	M
University of Wisconsin–Oshkosh	M
University of Wisconsin–River Falls	M
University of Wisconsin–Stevens Point	M
University of Wyoming	M
Vanderbilt University	M,D
Wayne State College	M
Wayne State University	M,D,O
Webster University	M,O
West Chester University of Pennsylvania	M
Western Carolina University	M
Western Illinois University	M,O
Western Kentucky University	M
Western Michigan University	M,D
Western Oregon University	M
Western Washington University	M
Wheeling Jesuit University	M
Widener University	M,D
Wilkes University	M
Wright State University	M

■ SECONDARY EDUCATION

Institution	Degree
Abilene Christian University	M
Adams State College	M
Adelphi University	M
Alabama Agricultural and Mechanical University	M,O
Alabama State University	M,O
Alcorn State University	M,O
American International College	M,D,O
American University	M,O
Andrews University	M,D,O
Appalachian State University	M
Arcadia University	M,D,O
Arizona State University West	M,O
Armstrong Atlantic State University	M
Auburn University	M,D,O
Auburn University Montgomery	M,O
Augusta State University	M,O
Austin Peay State University	M,O
Ball State University	M
Bellarmine University	M
Belmont University	M
Benedictine University	M
Bethel University	M,O
Boston College	M
Bowie State University	M
Bridgewater State College	M
Brooklyn College of the City University of New York	M
Brown University	M
Butler University	M
California State University, Bakersfield	M
California State University, Fullerton	M
California State University, Long Beach	M
California State University, Los Angeles	M
California State University, Northridge	M
California State University, San Bernardino	M
California State University, Stanislaus	M
Campbell University	M
Canisius College	M
Carson-Newman College	M
Centenary College of Louisiana	M
Central Connecticut State University	M
Central Michigan University	M
Central Missouri State University	M,O
Chadron State College	M,O
Chapman University	M
Charleston Southern University	M
Chicago State University	M
The Citadel, The Military College of South Carolina	M
City College of the City University of New York	M,O
Clemson University	M
Cleveland State University	M
The College of New Jersey	M
College of St. Joseph	M
The College of Saint Rose	M,O
College of Staten Island of the City University of New York	M
The College of William and Mary	M
Columbus State University	M,O
Concordia University (CA)	M
Concordia University (OR)	M
Converse College	M
Cumberland College	M,O
DePaul University	M
Dowling College	M
Drake University	M
Drury University	M
Duquesne University	M
Eastern Connecticut State University	M
Eastern Kentucky University	M
Eastern Michigan University	M
Eastern Nazarene College	M,O
Eastern Oregon University	M
East Stroudsburg University of Pennsylvania	M
East Tennessee State University	M
Edinboro University of Pennsylvania	M
Elms College	M,O
Emmanuel College	M,O
Emory University	M,D,O
Fayetteville State University	M
Fitchburg State College	M
Florida Agricultural and Mechanical University	M
Florida Gulf Coast University	M
Fordham University	M,D,O
Fort Hays State University	M
Francis Marion University	M
Friends University	M
Frostburg State University	M
Gallaudet University	M,D,O
Gannon University	M
George Mason University	M
The George Washington University	M
Georgia College & State University	M,O
Georgia Southwestern State University	M,O
Grand Canyon University	M
Harding University	M
Harvard University	M,D
Hofstra University	M,O
Holy Family University	M
Hood College	M
Howard University	M,O
Hunter College of the City University of New York	M
Immaculata University	M,D,O

Directory of Graduate and Professional Programs by Field
Secondary Education

Institution	Degree
Indiana University Bloomington	M,D,O
Indiana University Northwest	M
Indiana University–Purdue University Fort Wayne	M
Indiana University–Purdue University Indianapolis	M
Indiana University South Bend	M
Indiana University Southeast	M
Iona College	M
Jackson State University	M,D,O
Jacksonville State University	M
James Madison University	M
John Carroll University	M
The Johns Hopkins University	M
Kent State University	M
Kutztown University of Pennsylvania	M,O
Lehigh University	M,O
Liberty University	M,D
Lincoln University (MO)	M,O
Long Island University, C.W. Post Campus	M
Longwood University	M
Louisiana State University and Agricultural and Mechanical College	M,D,O
Louisiana Tech University	M,D
Loyola Marymount University	M
Loyola University New Orleans	M
Lynchburg College	M
Maharishi University of Management	M
Manhattanville College	M
Mansfield University of Pennsylvania	M
Marshall University	M
Marygrove College	M
Marymount University	M,O
Maryville University of Saint Louis	M
McNeese State University	M
Mercer University	M,O
Mercy College	M,O
Miami University	M
Middle Tennessee State University	M,O
Minnesota State University Mankato	M,O
Mississippi College	M
Mississippi State University	M,D,O
Montana State University–Billings	M
Morehead State University	M
Morgan State University	M
Mount Saint Mary College	M
Mount St. Mary's College	M
Murray State University	M,O
National-Louis University	M
Nazareth College of Rochester	M
New Jersey City University	M
Niagara University	M
Norfolk State University	M
Northeastern University	M
Northern Arizona University	M
Northern Illinois University	M,D
Northern Kentucky University	M
Northern Michigan University	M
Northern State University	M
North Georgia College & State University	M,O
Northwestern Oklahoma State University	M
Northwestern State University of Louisiana	M,O
Northwestern University	M
Northwest Missouri State University	M,O
Ohio University	M,D
Old Dominion University	M
Olivet Nazarene University	M
Pacific Lutheran University	M
Pacific University	M
Park University	M
Piedmont College	M,O
Pittsburg State University	M
Plymouth State University	M
Portland State University	M,D
Purdue University Calumet	M
Queens College of the City University of New York	M,O
Quinnipiac University	M
Regis University	M,O
Rhode Island College	M
Rivier College	M,O
Rochester Institute of Technology	M
Rockford College	M
Rollins College	M
Roosevelt University	M
Rowan University	M
Sacred Heart University	M,O
Sage Graduate School	M
Saginaw Valley State University	M
St. John's University (NY)	M,O
Saint Joseph's University	M
St. Thomas Aquinas College	M,O
Saint Xavier University	M,O
Salem International University	M
Salem State College	M
Salisbury University	M
Sam Houston State University	M
San Diego State University	M
San Francisco State University	M,O
San Jose State University	M
Seattle Pacific University	M
Seton Hall University	M
Shenandoah University	M,D,O
Siena Heights University	M
Simmons College	M,O
Slippery Rock University of Pennsylvania	M
South Carolina State University	M
Southeastern Louisiana University	M
Southeastern Oklahoma State University	M
Southeast Missouri State University	M
Southern Arkansas University–Magnolia	M
Southern Illinois University Edwardsville	M
Southern Oregon University	M
Southern University and Agricultural and Mechanical College	M
Southwestern Oklahoma State University	M
Southwest Missouri State University	M,O
Spalding University	M
Springfield College	M
Spring Hill College	M
State University of New York at Binghamton	M
State University of New York at New Paltz	M
State University of New York at Oswego	M
State University of New York at Plattsburgh	M
State University of New York College at Brockport	M
State University of New York College at Cortland	M
State University of New York College at Fredonia	M
State University of New York College at Geneseo	M
State University of New York College at Oneonta	M
State University of New York College at Potsdam	M
State University of West Georgia	M,O
Stephen F. Austin State University	M,D
Suffolk University	M
Sul Ross State University	M
Tarleton State University	M,O
Temple University	M,D
Tennessee Technological University	M,O
Texas A&M University–Commerce	M,D
Texas A&M University–Corpus Christi	M
Texas A&M University–Kingsville	M
Texas A&M University–Texarkana	M
Texas Christian University	M,O
Texas Southern University	M,D
Texas State University-San Marcos	M
Texas Tech University	M,D,O
Towson University	M
Trinity College (DC)	M
Troy University	M,O
Troy University Dothan	M,O
Tufts University	M
The University of Akron	M,D
The University of Alabama	M,D,O
The University of Alabama at Birmingham	M
University of Alaska Southeast	M
The University of Arizona	M,D
University of Arkansas	M,O
University of Arkansas at Little Rock	M
University of Bridgeport	M,O
University of California, Irvine	M,D
University of Central Arkansas	M,O
University of Central Oklahoma	M
University of Cincinnati	M
University of Connecticut	M,D
University of Dayton	M
University of Georgia	M,D,O
University of Great Falls	M
University of Guam	M
University of Hawaii at Manoa	M
University of Houston	M,D
University of Idaho	M,D,O
University of Illinois at Chicago	M,D
University of Indianapolis	M
The University of Iowa	M,D
University of Louisiana at Monroe	M
University of Louisville	M
University of Maine	M,O
University of Mary	M
University of Maryland, Baltimore County	M,D,O
University of Maryland, College Park	M,D,O
University of Massachusetts Amherst	M,D,O
University of Massachusetts Boston	M,D,O
The University of Memphis	M,D
University of Michigan	M,D
University of Mississippi	M,D,O
University of Missouri–St. Louis	M,D
University of Montevallo	M
University of Nebraska at Omaha	M
University of Nevada, Las Vegas	M,D,O
University of Nevada, Reno	M,O
University of New Hampshire	M
University of North Alabama	M
The University of North Carolina at Chapel Hill	M
The University of North Carolina at Charlotte	M
The University of North Carolina at Wilmington	M
University of North Dakota	D
University of North Florida	M
University of North Texas	M
University of Oklahoma	M,D,O
University of Pennsylvania	M
University of Pittsburgh	M,D
University of Portland	M
University of Puerto Rico, Río Piedras	M,D
University of Rhode Island	M
University of St. Francis (IL)	M
The University of Scranton	M
University of South Alabama	M,O
University of South Carolina	M,D
The University of South Dakota	M
University of Southern Indiana	M
University of Southern Mississippi	M,D,O
University of South Florida	M,D,O
The University of Tennessee	M,D,O
The University of Tennessee at Chattanooga	M,O
The University of Tennessee at Martin	M

Directory of Graduate and Professional Programs by Field
Social Sciences

The University of Texas at Tyler	M
The University of Texas–Pan American	M
University of the Incarnate Word	M
University of Toledo	M,D,O
University of Utah	M
University of West Florida	M
University of Wisconsin–Eau Claire	M
University of Wisconsin–La Crosse	M
University of Wisconsin–Milwaukee	M
University of Wisconsin–Platteville	M
University of Wisconsin–Whitewater	M
Utah State University	M
Valdosta State University	M,O
Vanderbilt University	M
Villanova University	M
Virginia Commonwealth University	M,O
Wagner College	M
Wake Forest University	M
Washington State University	M,D
Washington University in St. Louis	M
Wayne State University	M,D,O
West Chester University of Pennsylvania	M
Western Carolina University	M
Western Illinois University	M
Western Kentucky University	M,O
Western New Mexico University	M
Western Oregon University	M
Western Washington University	M
Westfield State College	M
West Virginia University	M,D
Wilkes University	M
Winthrop University	M
Worcester State College	M
Wright State University	M
Xavier University	M
Xavier University of Louisiana	M
Youngstown State University	M

■ SLAVIC LANGUAGES

Boston College	M
Brown University	M,D
Columbia University	M,D
Cornell University	M,D
Duke University	M
Florida State University	M
Harvard University	M,D
Indiana University Bloomington	M,D
New York University	M
Northwestern University	D
The Ohio State University	M,D,O
Princeton University	D
Stanford University	M,D
Stony Brook University, State University of New York	M
University of California, Berkeley	M,D
University of California, Los Angeles	M,D
University of Chicago	M,D
University of Illinois at Chicago	M,D
University of Illinois at Urbana–Champaign	M,D
University of Kansas	M,D
University of Michigan	M,D
The University of North Carolina at Chapel Hill	M,D
University of Pittsburgh	M
University of Southern California	M,D
The University of Texas at Austin	M,D
University of Virginia	M
University of Washington	M,D
University of Wisconsin–Madison	M,D
University of Wisconsin–Milwaukee	M
Yale University	D

■ SOCIAL PSYCHOLOGY

American University	M
Andrews University	M
Appalachian State University	M
Arcadia University	M
Arizona State University	D
Auburn University	M,D,O
Azusa Pacific University	P,M,D
Ball State University	M
Bowling Green State University	M,D
Brandeis University	M,D
Brigham Young University	M,D
Brooklyn College of the City University of New York	M,D
California State University, Fullerton	M
Carnegie Mellon University	D
Central Connecticut State University	M
Claremont Graduate University	M,D
Clark University	D
The College of New Rochelle	M
College of St. Joseph	M
Colorado State University	M,D
Columbia University	M,D
Cornell University	M,D
DePaul University	M,D
Eastern Illinois University	M
Florida Agricultural and Mechanical University	M
Florida State University	D
Francis Marion University	M
The George Washington University	D
Harvard University	M,D
Henderson State University	M
Hofstra University	D
Howard University	M,D
Hunter College of the City University of New York	M
Indiana University Bloomington	D
Indiana Wesleyan University	M
Iowa State University of Science and Technology	M,D
Lamar University	M
Lesley University	M,D,O
Loyola University Chicago	M,D
Malone College	M
Miami University	D
Montclair State University	M
New College of California	M
New York University	M,D,O
Norfolk State University	M
North Carolina State University	M
North Georgia College & State University	M
Northwestern University	D
The Ohio State University	D
Pace University	M,D
The Pennsylvania State University Harrisburg Campus of the Capital College	M
The Pennsylvania State University University Park Campus	M,D
Prescott College	M
Regent University	M,D,O
Rutgers, The State University of New Jersey, Newark	D
Rutgers, The State University of New Jersey, New Brunswick/Piscataway	D
Sage Graduate School	M
St. Cloud State University	M
Saint Joseph College	M,O
Saint Martin's College	M
Southeast Missouri State University	M
Southern Illinois University Edwardsville	M
Stony Brook University, State University of New York	D
Syracuse University	D
Teachers College Columbia University	M,D
Temple University	D
Texas A&M University	M,D
University at Albany, State University of New York	M,D
University at Buffalo, The State University of New York	M,D
University of Alaska Fairbanks	M
University of California, Santa Cruz	D
University of Central Arkansas	M
University of Connecticut	M,D
University of Dayton	M
University of Delaware	D
University of Houston	D
University of Illinois at Urbana–Champaign	M,D
University of La Verne	D
University of Maine	M,D
University of Maryland, College Park	M,D
University of Massachusetts Lowell	M
University of Michigan	D
University of Minnesota, Twin Cities Campus	D
University of Missouri–Kansas City	M,D
University of Nevada, Reno	D
University of New Haven	M,O
The University of North Carolina at Chapel Hill	D
The University of North Carolina at Charlotte	M
The University of North Carolina at Greensboro	M,D
University of Oklahoma	M
University of Oregon	M,D
University of Pennsylvania	D
University of Rochester	M,D
The University of Scranton	M
University of South Carolina	D
University of Toledo	M,D,O
University of Wisconsin–Madison	D
University of Wisconsin–Superior	M
University of Wisconsin–Whitewater	M
Valparaiso University	M
Washington University in St. Louis	M,D
Wayne State University	M,D
Western Carolina University	M
Western Connecticut State University	M
Western Illinois University	M,O
Wichita State University	M,D
Wilmington College (DE)	M

■ SOCIAL SCIENCES

Appalachian State University	M
Arkansas Tech University	M
Ball State University	M
California Institute of Technology	M,D
California State University, Chico	M
California State University, San Bernardino	M
California University of Pennsylvania	M
Campbellsville University	M
Carnegie Mellon University	D
Cleveland State University	M
Columbia University	M
Eastern Michigan University	M
Edinboro University of Pennsylvania	M
Florida Agricultural and Mechanical University	M
Florida State University	M
Humboldt State University	M
Indiana University Bloomington	P,M,D
The Johns Hopkins University	M,D
Kean University	M,O
Lincoln University (MO)	M
Long Island University, Brooklyn Campus	M,O
Long Island University, C.W. Post Campus	M
Massachusetts Institute of Technology	D
Michigan State University	M,D
Mississippi College	M
Montclair State University	M
New School University	M,D
North Dakota State University	M,D
Northwestern University	M,O
Nova Southeastern University	M
Ohio University	M
Old Dominion University	M
Pittsburg State University	M

Peterson's Graduate Schools in the U.S. 2006

Directory of Graduate and Professional Programs by Field
Social Sciences

Institution	Degree
Polytechnic University, Brooklyn Campus	M
Queens College of the City University of New York	M
Regis University	M,O
San Francisco State University	M
San Jose State University	M
Southern Oregon University	M
State University of New York at Binghamton	M
State University of New York College at Fredonia	M
Stony Brook University, State University of New York	M,O
Syracuse University	M,D
Texas A&M International University	M
Texas A&M University–Commerce	M
Towson University	M
University at Buffalo, The State University of New York	M
University of California, Irvine	M,D
University of California, Santa Cruz	D
University of Chicago	M,D
University of Colorado at Denver	M
University of Illinois at Springfield	M
University of Kansas	M,D
University of Michigan	D
The University of Texas at Tyler	M
Yale University	M,D

■ SOCIAL SCIENCES EDUCATION

Institution	Degree
Alabama State University	M,O
Albany State University	M
Andrews University	M,D,O
Arcadia University	M,D,O
Arkansas State University	M,O
Arkansas Tech University	M
Armstrong Atlantic State University	M
Auburn University	M,D,O
Averett University	M
Belmont University	M
Boston College	M
Boston University	M,D,O
Bridgewater State College	M
Brooklyn College of the City University of New York	M
Brown University	M
Buffalo State College, State University of New York	M
California State University, San Bernardino	M
Campbell University	M
Carthage College	M,O
Chadron State College	M,O
Chaminade University of Honolulu	M
Charleston Southern University	M
The Citadel, The Military College of South Carolina	M
City College of the City University of New York	M,O
Clemson University	M
College of St. Joseph	M
The College of Saint Rose	M,O
The College of William and Mary	M
Columbus State University	M,O
Converse College	M
Delta State University	M
Drake University	M
East Carolina University	M
Eastern Kentucky University	M
Eastern Washington University	M
East Stroudsburg University of Pennsylvania	M
Edinboro University of Pennsylvania	M
Emporia State University	M
Fayetteville State University	M
Fitchburg State College	M
Florida Agricultural and Mechanical University	M
Florida Gulf Coast University	M
Florida International University	M
Florida State University	M,D,O
Framingham State College	M
Georgia College & State University	M,O
Georgia Southern University	M
Georgia State University	M,D,O
Grambling State University	M
Henderson State University	M
Hofstra University	M
Hunter College of the City University of New York	M
Indiana University Bloomington	M,D,O
Iona College	M
Kutztown University of Pennsylvania	M,O
Lehman College of the City University of New York	M
Louisiana Tech University	M,D
Manhattanville College	M
McNeese State University	M
Miami University	M
Michigan State University	M,D
Minnesota State University Mankato	M
New Jersey Institute of Technology	M
New York University	M,D
North Carolina Agricultural and Technical State University	M
North Georgia College & State University	M,O
Northwestern State University of Louisiana	M,O
Northwest Missouri State University	M
Nova Southeastern University	M,O
Ohio University	M,D
The Pennsylvania State University University Park Campus	M,D
Portland State University	M
Princeton University	D
Purdue University	M,D,O
Queens College of the City University of New York	M,O
Quinnipiac University	M
Rider University	O
Rivier College	M
Rockford College	M
Rutgers, The State University of New Jersey, New Brunswick/Piscataway	M,D
Sage Graduate School	M
Salem State College	M,O
Salisbury University	M
South Carolina State University	M
Southeast Missouri State University	M
Southwestern Oklahoma State University	M
Stanford University	M,D
State University of New York at Binghamton	M
State University of New York at Plattsburgh	M
State University of New York College at Brockport	M
State University of New York College at Cortland	M
State University of West Georgia	M,O
Stony Brook University, State University of New York	M,O
Syracuse University	M,O
Teachers College Columbia University	M,D
Texas A&M University	M,D
Texas A&M University–Commerce	M
Texas State University–San Marcos	D
Trinity College (DC)	M
University at Buffalo, The State University of New York	M,D,O
University of Central Florida	M
University of Cincinnati	M,D
University of Connecticut	M,D
University of Florida	M,D,O
University of Georgia	M,D,O
University of Houston	M,D
University of Idaho	M
University of Indianapolis	M
The University of Iowa	M,D
University of Maine	M,O
University of Michigan	M,D
University of Minnesota, Twin Cities Campus	M
University of Missouri–Columbia	M,D,O
The University of North Carolina at Chapel Hill	M
The University of North Carolina at Pembroke	M
University of Oklahoma	M,D,O
University of Pittsburgh	M,D
University of Puerto Rico, Río Piedras	M,D
University of St. Francis (IL)	M
University of South Carolina	M,D,O
University of Southern Mississippi	M,D,O
University of South Florida	M,D,O
The University of Tennessee	M,D,O
The University of Texas at Tyler	M
University of Toledo	M,D,O
University of Vermont	M
University of Washington	M,D
The University of West Alabama	M
University of Wisconsin–Eau Claire	M
University of Wisconsin–Madison	M,D
University of Wisconsin–River Falls	M
Virginia Commonwealth University	M,O
Wayne State College	M
Wayne State University	M,D,O
Webster University	M,O
Western Carolina University	M
Western Illinois University	M
Western Oregon University	M
Widener University	M,D
Wilkes University	M
Worcester State College	M

■ SOCIAL WORK

Institution	Degree
Adelphi University	M,D
Alabama Agricultural and Mechanical University	M
Andrews University	M
Arizona State University	M,D
Arizona State University West	M
Augsburg College	M
Aurora University	M
Barry University	M,D
Baylor University	M
Boise State University	M
Boston College	M,D
Boston University	M,D
Bridgewater State College	M
Brigham Young University	M
California State University, Bakersfield	M
California State University, Chico	M
California State University, Fresno	M
California State University, Long Beach	M
California State University, Los Angeles	M
California State University, Sacramento	M
California State University, San Bernardino	M
California State University, Stanislaus	M
California University of Pennsylvania	M
Case Western Reserve University	M,D,O
The Catholic University of America	M,D
Chicago State University	M
Clark Atlanta University	M,D
Cleveland State University	M
College of St. Catherine	M
Colorado State University	M
Columbia University	M,D
Cornell University	M,D
Delaware State University	M
Delta State University	M
Dominican University	M
East Carolina University	M
Eastern Michigan University	M

Directory of Graduate and Professional Programs by Field
Sociology

Eastern Washington University	M
East Tennessee State University	M
Edinboro University of Pennsylvania	M
Florida Agricultural and Mechanical University	M
Florida Atlantic University	M
Florida Gulf Coast University	M
Florida International University	M,D
Florida State University	M,D
Fordham University	M,D
Gallaudet University	M
George Mason University	M
Georgia State University	M
Governors State University	M
Grambling State University	M
Grand Valley State University	M
Gratz College	M,O
Howard University	M,D
Hunter College of the City University of New York	M,D
Illinois State University	M
Indiana University Northwest	M
Indiana University–Purdue University Indianapolis	M,D
Indiana University South Bend	M
Inter American University of Puerto Rico, Metropolitan Campus	M
Jackson State University	M,D
Kean University	M
Kutztown University of Pennsylvania	M
Loma Linda University	M,D
Louisiana State University and Agricultural and Mechanical College	M,D
Loyola University Chicago	M,D
Marywood University	M,D
Miami University	M
Michigan State University	M,D
Monmouth University	M
Nazareth College of Rochester	M
Newman University	M
New Mexico Highlands University	M
New Mexico State University	M
New York University	M,D
Norfolk State University	M,D
North Carolina Agricultural and Technical State University	M
Northwest Nazarene University	M
The Ohio State University	M,D
Ohio University	M
Our Lady of the Lake University of San Antonio	M
Pontifical Catholic University of Puerto Rico	M,D
Portland State University	M,D
Radford University	M
Rhode Island College	M
Roberts Wesleyan College	M
Rutgers, The State University of New Jersey, New Brunswick/Piscataway	M,D
St. Ambrose University	M
Saint Louis University	M
Salem State College	M
Salisbury University	M
San Diego State University	M,D
San Francisco State University	M
San Jose State University	M,O
Savannah State University	M
Simmons College	M,D
Southern Connecticut State University	M
Southern Illinois University Carbondale	M
Southern Illinois University Edwardsville	M
Southern University at New Orleans	M
Southwest Missouri State University	M
Spalding University	M
Springfield College	M,O
State University of New York College at Brockport	M
Stephen F. Austin State University	M
Stony Brook University, State University of New York	M,D
Syracuse University	M
Temple University	M
Texas A&M University–Commerce	M
Texas State University-San Marcos	M
Tulane University	M,D
University at Albany, State University of New York	M,D
University at Buffalo, The State University of New York	M,D
The University of Akron	M
The University of Alabama	M,D
University of Alaska Anchorage	M
University of Arkansas at Little Rock	M
University of California, Berkeley	M,D
University of California, Los Angeles	M,D
University of Central Florida	M,O
University of Chicago	M,D
University of Cincinnati	M
University of Connecticut	M,D
University of Denver	M,D
University of Georgia	M,D
University of Hawaii at Manoa	M,D
University of Houston	M,D
University of Illinois at Chicago	M,D
University of Illinois at Urbana–Champaign	M,D
The University of Iowa	M,D
University of Kentucky	M,D
University of Louisville	M,D
University of Maine	M
University of Maryland	M,D
University of Michigan	M,D
University of Minnesota, Duluth	M
University of Minnesota, Twin Cities Campus	M,D
University of Missouri–Columbia	M
University of Missouri–Kansas City	M
University of Missouri–St. Louis	M,O
University of Nebraska at Omaha	M
University of Nevada, Las Vegas	M
University of Nevada, Reno	M
University of New England	M,O
University of New Hampshire	M
The University of North Carolina at Chapel Hill	M,D
The University of North Carolina at Charlotte	M
The University of North Carolina at Greensboro	M
University of North Dakota	M
University of Northern Iowa	M
University of Oklahoma	M
University of Pennsylvania	M,D
University of Pittsburgh	M,D,O
University of Puerto Rico, Río Piedras	M,D
University of St. Thomas (MN)	M
University of South Carolina	M,D
University of Southern California	M,D
University of Southern Indiana	M
University of Southern Maine	M
University of Southern Mississippi	M
University of South Florida	M
The University of Tennessee	M,D
The University of Texas at Arlington	M,D
The University of Texas at Austin	M,D
The University of Texas–Pan American	M
University of Utah	M,D
University of Vermont	M
University of Washington	M,D
University of Wisconsin–Green Bay	M
University of Wisconsin–Madison	M,D
University of Wisconsin–Milwaukee	M
University of Wisconsin–Oshkosh	M
University of Wyoming	M
Valdosta State University	M
Virginia Commonwealth University	M,D
Walla Walla College	M
Washburn University	M
Washington University in St. Louis	M,D
Wayne State University	M,O
West Chester University of Pennsylvania	M
Western Michigan University	M
West Virginia University	M
Wheelock College	M
Wichita State University	M
Widener University	M
Yeshiva University	M,D

■ **SOCIOLOGY**

American University	M,O
Arizona State University	M,D
Arkansas State University	M,O
Auburn University	M
Ball State University	M
Baylor University	M,D
Boston College	M,D
Boston University	M,D
Bowling Green State University	M,D
Brandeis University	M,D
Brigham Young University	M,D
Brooklyn College of the City University of New York	M,D
Brown University	M,D
California State University, Bakersfield	M
California State University, Dominguez Hills	M,O
California State University, Fullerton	M
California State University, Hayward	M
California State University, Los Angeles	M
California State University, Northridge	M
California State University, Sacramento	M
California State University, San Marcos	M
Case Western Reserve University	D
The Catholic University of America	M,D
Central Michigan University	M
Central Missouri State University	M
City College of the City University of New York	M
Clark Atlanta University	M
Clemson University	M
Cleveland State University	M
Colorado State University	M,D
Columbia University	M,D
Cornell University	M,D
DePaul University	M
Drake University	M
Duke University	M,D
East Carolina University	M
Eastern Michigan University	M
East Tennessee State University	M
Emory University	M,D
Fayetteville State University	M
Florida Agricultural and Mechanical University	M
Florida Atlantic University	M
Florida International University	M,D
Florida State University	M,D
Fordham University	M,D
George Mason University	M
The George Washington University	M
Georgia Southern University	M
Georgia State University	M,D
Harvard University	M,D
Howard University	M,D
Humboldt State University	M
Hunter College of the City University of New York	M
Idaho State University	M
Illinois State University	M
Indiana University Bloomington	M,D
Indiana University of Pennsylvania	M
Indiana University–Purdue University Fort Wayne	M
Iowa State University of Science and Technology	M,D

Peterson's Graduate Schools in the U.S. 2006   *www.petersons.com*   **165**

Directory of Graduate and Professional Programs by Field

Sociology

Institution	Degree
Jackson State University	M
The Johns Hopkins University	D
Kansas State University	M,D
Kent State University	M,D
Lehigh University	M
Lincoln University (MO)	M
Louisiana State University and Agricultural and Mechanical College	M,D
Loyola University Chicago	M,D
Marshall University	M
Michigan State University	M,D
Middle Tennessee State University	M
Minnesota State University Mankato	M
Mississippi College	M
Mississippi State University	M,D
Montclair State University	M
Morehead State University	M
Morgan State University	M
New Mexico Highlands University	M
New Mexico State University	M
New School University	M,D
New York University	M,D
Norfolk State University	M
North Carolina Central University	M
North Carolina State University	M,D
Northeastern University	M,D
Northern Arizona University	M
Northern Illinois University	M
Northwestern University	D
The Ohio State University	M,D
Ohio University	M
Oklahoma State University	M,D
Old Dominion University	M
Our Lady of the Lake University of San Antonio	M
The Pennsylvania State University University Park Campus	M,D
Portland State University	M,D,O
Prairie View A&M University	M
Princeton University	D,O
Purdue University	M,D
Queens College of the City University of New York	M
Roosevelt University	M
Rutgers, The State University of New Jersey, New Brunswick/Piscataway	M,D
St. John's University (NY)	M
Saint Louis University	M
Sam Houston State University	M
San Diego State University	M
San Jose State University	M
Shippensburg University of Pennsylvania	M
Southern Connecticut State University	M
Southern Illinois University Carbondale	M,D
Southern Illinois University Edwardsville	M
Southern University and Agricultural and Mechanical College	M
Stanford University	D
State University of New York at Binghamton	M,D
State University of New York at New Paltz	M
State University of New York Institute of Technology	M
The State University of West Georgia	M
Stony Brook University, State University of New York	M,D
Syracuse University	M,D
Teachers College Columbia University	M,D
Temple University	M,D
Texas A&M International University	M
Texas A&M University	M,D
Texas A&M University–Commerce	M
Texas A&M University–Kingsville	M
Texas Southern University	M
Texas State University-San Marcos	M
Texas Tech University	M
Texas Woman's University	M,D
Tulane University	M,D
University at Albany, State University of New York	M,D,O
University at Buffalo, The State University of New York	M,D
The University of Akron	M,D
The University of Alabama at Birmingham	M,D
The University of Arizona	M,D
University of Arkansas	M
University of California, Berkeley	D
University of California, Davis	M,D
University of California, Irvine	M,D
University of California, Los Angeles	M,D
University of California, Riverside	D
University of California, San Diego	D
University of California, San Francisco	D
University of California, Santa Barbara	M,D
University of California, Santa Cruz	D
University of Central Florida	M,O
University of Chicago	D
University of Cincinnati	M,D
University of Colorado at Boulder	M,D
University of Colorado at Colorado Springs	M
University of Colorado at Denver	M
University of Connecticut	M,D
University of Delaware	M,D
University of Denver	M
University of Florida	M,D
University of Georgia	M,D
University of Hawaii at Manoa	M,D
University of Houston	M
University of Houston–Clear Lake	M
University of Illinois at Chicago	M,D
University of Illinois at Urbana–Champaign	M,D
University of Indianapolis	M
The University of Iowa	M,D
University of Kansas	M,D
University of Kentucky	M,D
University of Louisville	M
University of Maryland, Baltimore County	M,O
University of Maryland, College Park	M,D
University of Massachusetts Amherst	M,D
University of Massachusetts Boston	M
University of Massachusetts Lowell	M
The University of Memphis	M
University of Miami	M,D
University of Michigan	D
University of Minnesota, Duluth	M
University of Minnesota, Twin Cities Campus	M,D
University of Mississippi	M
University of Missouri–Columbia	M,D
University of Missouri–Kansas City	M,D
University of Missouri–St. Louis	M
The University of Montana–Missoula	M
University of Nebraska at Omaha	M
University of Nebraska–Lincoln	M,D
University of Nevada, Las Vegas	M,D
University of Nevada, Reno	M
University of New Hampshire	M,D
University of New Mexico	M,D
University of New Orleans	M
The University of North Carolina at Chapel Hill	M,D
The University of North Carolina at Charlotte	M
The University of North Carolina at Greensboro	M
University of North Dakota	M
University of Northern Colorado	M
University of Northern Iowa	M
University of North Florida	M
University of North Texas	M,D
University of Notre Dame	D
University of Oklahoma	M,D
University of Oregon	M,D
University of Pennsylvania	M,D
University of Pittsburgh	M,D
University of Puerto Rico, Río Piedras	M
University of South Alabama	M
University of South Carolina	M,D
The University of South Dakota	M
University of Southern California	M,D
University of South Florida	M
The University of Tennessee	M,D
The University of Texas at Arlington	M
The University of Texas at Austin	M,D
The University of Texas at Dallas	M
The University of Texas at El Paso	M
The University of Texas at San Antonio	M
The University of Texas at Tyler	M
The University of Texas–Pan American	M
University of Toledo	M
University of Utah	M,D
University of Virginia	M,D
University of Washington	M,D
University of Wisconsin–Madison	M,D
University of Wisconsin–Milwaukee	M
University of Wyoming	M
Utah State University	M,D
Valdosta State University	M
Vanderbilt University	M,D
Virginia Commonwealth University	M,O
Virginia Polytechnic Institute and State University	M,D
Washington State University	M,D
Wayne State University	M,D
West Chester University of Pennsylvania	M,O
Western Illinois University	M
Western Kentucky University	M
Western Michigan University	M,D
West Virginia University	M
Wichita State University	M
William Paterson University of New Jersey	M
Yale University	D

■ SOFTWARE ENGINEERING

Institution	Degree
American University	O
Andrews University	M
Auburn University	M,D
California State University, Sacramento	M
Carnegie Mellon University	M,D
Central Michigan University	M,O
Colorado Technical University	M,D
DePaul University	M
Drexel University	M
East Tennessee State University	M
Embry-Riddle Aeronautical University (FL)	M
Fairfield University	M
Florida Agricultural and Mechanical University	M
Florida Institute of Technology	M,D
Florida State University	M,D
Gannon University	M
George Mason University	M
Grand Valley State University	M
Illinois Institute of Technology	M,D
Jacksonville State University	M
Kansas State University	M,D
Marist College	M
Mercer University	M
Miami University	M,O
Monmouth University	M,O
National University	M
North Dakota State University	M,D,O
Oakland University	M
The Pennsylvania State University Great Valley Campus	M
Rochester Institute of Technology	M
St. Mary's University of San Antonio	M

Directory of Graduate and Professional Programs by Field
Special Education

Institution	Degree
Santa Clara University	M,D,O
Seattle University	M
Southern Methodist University	M,D
Stevens Institute of Technology	O
Stony Brook University, State University of New York	M,D,O
Texas State University–San Marcos	M
Texas Tech University	M,D
Towson University	M,D,O
The University of Alabama in Huntsville	M,D,O
University of Alaska Fairbanks	M,D
University of Colorado at Colorado Springs	M
University of Connecticut	M,D
University of Houston–Clear Lake	M
University of Maryland, College Park	M
University of Maryland University College	M,O
University of Michigan–Dearborn	M
University of Minnesota, Twin Cities Campus	M
University of Missouri–Kansas City	M,D
University of New Haven	M
University of St. Thomas (MN)	M,O
The University of Scranton	M
University of South Carolina	M,D
University of Southern California	M
The University of Texas at Arlington	M,D
The University of Texas at Dallas	M,D
University of Wisconsin–La Crosse	M
Wayne State University	M,D,O
West Virginia University	M
Widener University	M
Winthrop University	M,O

■ SPANISH

Institution	Degree
American University	M,O
Arizona State University	M,D
Arkansas Tech University	M
Auburn University	M
Baylor University	M
Boston College	M,D
Boston University	M,D
Bowling Green State University	M
Brigham Young University	M
Brooklyn College of the City University of New York	M,D
California State University, Bakersfield	M
California State University, Fresno	M
California State University, Fullerton	M
California State University, Long Beach	M
California State University, Los Angeles	M
California State University, Northridge	M
California State University, Sacramento	M
California State University, San Marcos	M
The Catholic University of America	M,D
Central Connecticut State University	M
Central Michigan University	M
City College of the City University of New York	M
Cleveland State University	M
The College of New Jersey	M
Colorado State University	M
Columbia University	M,D
Cornell University	D
Duke University	D
Eastern Michigan University	M
Emory University	D,O
Florida Atlantic University	M
Florida International University	M,D
Florida State University	M,D
Framingham State College	M
Georgetown University	M,D
Georgia State University	M
Harvard University	M,D
Hofstra University	M
Howard University	M
Hunter College of the City University of New York	M
Illinois State University	M
Indiana State University	M,O
Indiana University Bloomington	M,D
Inter American University of Puerto Rico, Metropolitan Campus	M
Iona College	M
The Johns Hopkins University	D
Kansas State University	M
Kent State University	M
Lehman College of the City University of New York	M
Long Island University, C.W. Post Campus	M
Louisiana State University and Agricultural and Mechanical College	M
Loyola University Chicago	M
Marquette University	M
Miami University	M
Michigan State University	M,D
Millersville University of Pennsylvania	M
Minnesota State University Mankato	M
Mississippi State University	M
Montclair State University	M
New Mexico Highlands University	M
New Mexico State University	M
New York University	M,D
North Carolina State University	M
Northern Illinois University	M
Nova Southeastern University	M,O
The Ohio State University	M,D
Ohio University	M
The Pennsylvania State University University Park Campus	M,D
Portland State University	M
Princeton University	D
Purdue University	M,D
Queens College of the City University of New York	M
Rice University	M
Roosevelt University	M
Rutgers, The State University of New Jersey, New Brunswick/Piscataway	M,D
St. John's University (NY)	M
Saint Louis University	M
San Diego State University	M
San Francisco State University	M
San Jose State University	M
Simmons College	M
Southern Connecticut State University	M
Stanford University	M,D
State University of New York at Binghamton	M,O
Syracuse University	M
Temple University	M,D
Texas A&M International University	M
Texas A&M University	M
Texas A&M University–Commerce	M,D
Texas A&M University–Kingsville	M
Texas State University–San Marcos	M
Texas Tech University	M,D
Tulane University	M,D
University at Albany, State University of New York	M,D
The University of Akron	M
The University of Alabama	M,D
The University of Arizona	M,D
University of Arkansas	M
University of California, Berkeley	M,D
University of California, Davis	M,D
University of California, Irvine	M,D
University of California, Los Angeles	M
University of California, Riverside	M,D
University of California, San Diego	M
University of California, Santa Barbara	M,D
University of Central Florida	M
University of Chicago	M,D
University of Cincinnati	M,D
University of Colorado at Boulder	M,D
University of Connecticut	M,D
University of Delaware	M
University of Denver	M
University of Florida	M,D
University of Georgia	M
University of Hawaii at Manoa	M
University of Houston	M,D
University of Idaho	M
The University of Iowa	M,D
University of Kansas	M,D
University of Kentucky	M,D
University of Louisville	M
University of Maryland, Baltimore County	M
University of Maryland, College Park	M,D
University of Massachusetts Amherst	M,D
The University of Memphis	M
University of Miami	M,D
University of Michigan	D
University of Minnesota, Twin Cities Campus	M,D
University of Mississippi	M
University of Missouri–Columbia	M,D
The University of Montana–Missoula	M
University of Nebraska–Lincoln	M,D
University of Nevada, Las Vegas	M
University of Nevada, Reno	M
University of New Hampshire	M
University of New Mexico	M,D
The University of North Carolina at Chapel Hill	M,D
The University of North Carolina at Charlotte	M
The University of North Carolina at Greensboro	M
University of Northern Colorado	M
University of Northern Iowa	M
University of North Texas	M
University of Notre Dame	M
University of Oklahoma	M,D
University of Oregon	M
University of Pennsylvania	M,D
University of Pittsburgh	M,D
University of Rhode Island	M
University of South Florida	M
The University of Tennessee	M,D
The University of Texas at Arlington	M
The University of Texas at Austin	M,D
The University of Texas at Brownsville	M
The University of Texas at El Paso	M
The University of Texas at San Antonio	M
The University of Texas–Pan American	M
University of Toledo	M
University of Utah	M,D
University of Virginia	M
University of Washington	M
University of Wisconsin–Madison	M,D
University of Wisconsin–Milwaukee	M
University of Wyoming	M
Vanderbilt University	M,D
Villanova University	M
Washington State University	M
Washington University in St. Louis	M,D
Wayne State University	M
West Chester University of Pennsylvania	M
Western Michigan University	M
West Virginia University	M
Wichita State University	M
Winthrop University	M
Yale University	M,D

■ SPECIAL EDUCATION

Institution	Degree
Adams State College	M
Adelphi University	M,O
Alabama Agricultural and Mechanical University	M,O
Alabama State University	M

Directory of Graduate and Professional Programs by Field
Special Education

Institution	Degrees
Albany State University	M
Alcorn State University	M,O
American International College	M,D,O
American University	M
Andrews University	M,D,O
Appalachian State University	M
Arcadia University	M,D,O
Arizona State University	M
Arizona State University West	M,O
Arkansas State University	M,D,O
Armstrong Atlantic State University	M
Ashland University	M
Assumption College	M
Auburn University	M,D,O
Auburn University Montgomery	M,O
Augusta State University	M,O
Austin Peay State University	M,O
Averett University	M
Azusa Pacific University	M
Baldwin-Wallace College	M
Ball State University	M,D,O
Barry University	M,D,O
Bayamón Central University	M
Bellarmine University	M
Bemidji State University	M
Benedictine University	M
Bloomsburg University of Pennsylvania	M
Boise State University	M
Boston College	M,O
Boston University	M,D,O
Bowie State University	M
Bowling Green State University	M
Brenau University	M,O
Bridgewater State College	M
Brigham Young University	M,D
Brooklyn College of the City University of New York	M
Buffalo State College, State University of New York	M
Butler University	M
California Baptist University	M
California Lutheran University	M
California Polytechnic State University, San Luis Obispo	M
California State University, Bakersfield	M
California State University, Dominguez Hills	M
California State University, Fresno	M
California State University, Fullerton	M
California State University, Hayward	M
California State University, Long Beach	M
California State University, Los Angeles	M,D
California State University, Northridge	M
California State University, Sacramento	M
California State University, San Bernardino	M
California State University, Stanislaus	M
California University of Pennsylvania	M
Campbellsville University	M
Canisius College	M
Cardinal Stritch University	M
Castleton State College	M,O
Central Connecticut State University	M
Central Michigan University	M
Central Missouri State University	M,O
Central Washington University	M
Chapman University	M
Cheyney University of Pennsylvania	M
Chicago State University	M
City College of the City University of New York	M
Clarion University of Pennsylvania	M
Clemson University	M
Cleveland State University	M
College of Charleston	M
College of Mount St. Joseph	M
The College of New Jersey	M
The College of New Rochelle	M
College of St. Joseph	M
The College of Saint Rose	M
College of Santa Fe	M
College of Staten Island of the City University of New York	M,D
The College of William and Mary	M
Columbus State University	M,O
Converse College	M
Coppin State University	M
Cumberland College	M
Delaware State University	M
Delta State University	M
DePaul University	M
DeSales University	M,O
Dominican University	M
Dominican University of California	O
Dowling College	M
Drake University	M
Duquesne University	M
East Carolina University	M
Eastern Illinois University	M
Eastern Kentucky University	M
Eastern Michigan University	M,O
Eastern Nazarene College	M,O
Eastern New Mexico University	M
Eastern Washington University	M
East Stroudsburg University of Pennsylvania	M
East Tennessee State University	M,D
Edgewood College	M,O
Edinboro University of Pennsylvania	M
Elms College	M
Elon University	M
Emporia State University	M
Fairfield University	M,O
Fairleigh Dickinson University, College at Florham	M
Fairleigh Dickinson University, Metropolitan Campus	M
Ferris State University	M
Fitchburg State College	M
Florida Atlantic University	M,D
Florida Gulf Coast University	M
Florida International University	M,D
Florida State University	M,D,O
Fontbonne University	M
Fordham University	M,D,O
Fort Hays State University	M
Framingham State College	M
Francis Marion University	M
Fresno Pacific University	M
Frostburg State University	M
Gallaudet University	M,D,O
Geneva College	M
George Mason University	M
The George Washington University	M,D,O
Georgia College & State University	M
Georgian Court University	M,O
Georgia Southern University	M
Georgia State University	M,D,O
Gonzaga University	M
Governors State University	M
Grand Valley State University	M
Gwynedd-Mercy College	M
Hampton University	M
Harding University	M
Heritage College	M
Hofstra University	M,O
Holy Names University	M,O
Hood College	M
Howard University	M,O
Hunter College of the City University of New York	M
Idaho State University	M,D,O
Illinois State University	M,D
Immaculata University	M,D,O
Indiana State University	M
Indiana University Bloomington	M,D,O
Indiana University of Pennsylvania	M
Indiana University–Purdue University Indianapolis	M
Indiana University South Bend	M
Inter American University of Puerto Rico, Metropolitan Campus	M
Inter American University of Puerto Rico, San Germán Campus	M
Iowa State University of Science and Technology	M,D
Jackson State University	M,O
Jacksonville State University	M
Jacksonville University	M,O
James Madison University	M
The Johns Hopkins University	M,D,O
Johnson State College	M
Kansas State University	M
Kean University	M
Keene State College	M,O
Kennesaw State University	M
Kent State University	M,D,O
Kutztown University of Pennsylvania	M,O
Lamar University	M,D
La Sierra University	M,D,O
Lehigh University	M,D,O
Lehman College of the City University of New York	M
Lesley University	M,D,O
Lewis University	M
Liberty University	M,D
Lincoln University (MO)	M,O
Long Island University, Brooklyn Campus	M
Long Island University, C.W. Post Campus	M
Longwood University	M
Loras College	M
Louisiana Tech University	M,D
Loyola College in Maryland	M,O
Loyola Marymount University	M
Loyola University Chicago	M
Lynchburg College	M
Lynn University	M,D
Madonna University	M
Malone College	M
Manhattan College	M,O
Manhattanville College	M
Marshall University	M
Marymount University	M
Marywood University	M
McNeese State University	M
Mercy College	M,O
Miami University	M
Michigan State University	M,D,O
MidAmerica Nazarene University	M
Middle Tennessee State University	M
Midwestern State University	M
Millersville University of Pennsylvania	M
Minnesota State University Mankato	M
Minnesota State University Moorhead	M
Minot State University	M
Mississippi State University	M,D,O
Monmouth University	M,O
Montana State University–Billings	M
Montclair State University	M
Morehead State University	M
Mount Saint Mary College	M
Mount St. Mary's College	M
Murray State University	M
National-Louis University	M,O
National University	M
Nazareth College of Rochester	M
New Jersey City University	M
New Mexico Highlands University	M
New Mexico State University	M
New York University	M,O
Norfolk State University	M
North Carolina Central University	M
North Carolina State University	M
Northeastern Illinois University	M
Northeastern State University	M

Directory of Graduate and Professional Programs by Field
Special Education

Institution	Degree
Northeastern University	M,D,O
Northern Arizona University	M
Northern Illinois University	M,D
Northern Michigan University	M
Northern State University	M
North Georgia College & State University	M,O
Northwestern State University of Louisiana	M,O
Northwestern University	M,D
Northwest Missouri State University	M
Northwest Nazarene University	M
Notre Dame de Namur University	M,O
Oakland University	M
Ohio University	M,D
Old Dominion University	M
Our Lady of the Lake University of San Antonio	M
Pacific Lutheran University	M
Pacific University	M
Park University	M
The Pennsylvania State University Great Valley Campus	M
The Pennsylvania State University University Park Campus	M,D
Pittsburg State University	M
Plymouth State University	M,O
Portland State University	M
Prairie View A&M University	M
Pratt Institute	M
Providence College	M
Purdue University	M,D,O
Queens College of the City University of New York	M
Radford University	M
Regis University	M,O
Rhode Island College	M,O
Rider University	M
Rivier College	M,O
Rochester Institute of Technology	M,O
Rockford College	M
Roosevelt University	M
Rowan University	M
Rutgers, The State University of New Jersey, New Brunswick/Piscataway	M,D
Sage Graduate School	M
Saginaw Valley State University	M
St. Ambrose University	M
St. Cloud State University	M
St. John Fisher College	M
St. John's University (NY)	M,O
Saint Joseph College	M
Saint Joseph's University	M
Saint Louis University	M,D
Saint Martin's College	M
Saint Mary's College of California	M
Saint Mary's University of Minnesota	M
Saint Michael's College	M,O
St. Thomas Aquinas College	M,O
St. Thomas University	M,O
Saint Xavier University	M,O
Salem State College	M
Sam Houston State University	M,D
San Diego State University	M
San Francisco State University	M,D,O
San Jose State University	M,O
Santa Clara University	M
Seattle University	M,O
Shippensburg University of Pennsylvania	M
Simmons College	M,O
Slippery Rock University of Pennsylvania	M
Sonoma State University	M
South Carolina State University	M
Southeastern Louisiana University	M
Southeast Missouri State University	M
Southern Connecticut State University	M,O
Southern Illinois University Carbondale	M
Southern Illinois University Edwardsville	M
Southern Oregon University	M
Southern University and Agricultural and Mechanical College	M,D
Southwestern Oklahoma State University	M
Southwest Missouri State University	M,O
Spalding University	M
State University of New York at Binghamton	M
State University of New York at New Paltz	M
State University of New York at Oswego	M
State University of New York at Plattsburgh	M
State University of New York College at Brockport	M
State University of New York College at Cortland	M
State University of New York College at Geneseo	M
State University of New York College at Potsdam	M
State University of West Georgia	M,O
Stephen F. Austin State University	M
Stetson University	M
Syracuse University	M,D
Tarleton State University	M,O
Teachers College Columbia University	M,D
Temple University	M,D
Tennessee State University	M,D
Tennessee Technological University	M,O
Texas A&M International University	M
Texas A&M University	M,D
Texas A&M University–Commerce	M,D
Texas A&M University–Corpus Christi	M
Texas A&M University–Kingsville	M
Texas A&M University–Texarkana	M
Texas Christian University	M
Texas Southern University	M,D
Texas State University-San Marcos	M
Texas Tech University	M,D,O
Texas Woman's University	M,D
Towson University	M
Trinity College (DC)	M
Troy University	M,O
Universidad del Turabo	M
Universidad Metropolitana	M
University at Albany, State University of New York	M
University at Buffalo, The State University of New York	M,D,O
The University of Akron	M
The University of Alabama at Birmingham	M
University of Alaska Anchorage	M
The University of Arizona	M,D,O
University of Arkansas	M
University of Arkansas at Little Rock	M
University of California, Berkeley	D
University of California, Los Angeles	D
University of Central Arkansas	M
University of Central Florida	M,D
University of Central Oklahoma	M
University of Cincinnati	M,D
University of Colorado at Colorado Springs	M
University of Connecticut	M,D
University of Dayton	M
University of Delaware	M,D
University of Detroit Mercy	M
The University of Findlay	M
University of Florida	M,D,O
University of Georgia	M,D,O
University of Guam	M
University of Hawaii at Manoa	M,D
University of Houston	M,D
University of Idaho	M
University of Illinois at Chicago	M,D
University of Illinois at Urbana–Champaign	M,D,O
The University of Iowa	M,D
University of Kansas	M,D
University of Kentucky	M,D,O
University of La Verne	M
University of Louisiana at Monroe	M
University of Louisville	M,D
University of Maine	M,O
University of Mary	M
University of Maryland, College Park	M,D,O
University of Maryland Eastern Shore	M
University of Massachusetts Amherst	M,D,O
University of Massachusetts Boston	M
The University of Memphis	M,D
University of Miami	M,D,O
University of Michigan	M,D
University of Michigan–Dearborn	M
University of Minnesota, Twin Cities Campus	M,D,O
University of Missouri–Columbia	M,D
University of Missouri–Kansas City	M,D,O
University of Missouri–St. Louis	M
University of Nebraska at Kearney	M
University of Nebraska at Omaha	M
University of Nebraska–Lincoln	M
University of Nevada, Las Vegas	M,D,O
University of Nevada, Reno	M,O
University of New Hampshire	M
University of New Mexico	M,D,O
University of New Orleans	M,D,O
University of North Alabama	M
The University of North Carolina at Charlotte	M,D
The University of North Carolina at Greensboro	M
The University of North Carolina at Wilmington	M
University of North Dakota	M,D
University of Northern Colorado	M,D
University of Northern Iowa	M,D
University of North Florida	M
University of North Texas	M,D
University of Oklahoma	M,D
University of Pittsburgh	M,D
University of Portland	M
University of Puerto Rico, Río Piedras	M
University of Rio Grande	M
University of Saint Francis (IN)	M
University of St. Thomas (MN)	M,O
The University of Scranton	M
University of South Alabama	M,O
University of South Carolina	M,D
The University of South Dakota	M
University of Southern California	M,D
University of Southern Maine	M
University of Southern Mississippi	M,D,O
University of South Florida	M,D,O
The University of Tennessee	M,D,O
The University of Tennessee at Chattanooga	M,O
The University of Texas at Austin	M,D
The University of Texas at Brownsville	M
The University of Texas at San Antonio	M
The University of Texas at Tyler	M
The University of Texas of the Permian Basin	M
The University of Texas–Pan American	M
University of the District of Columbia	M
University of the Incarnate Word	M
University of the Pacific	M,D
University of Toledo	M,D,O
University of Utah	M,D
University of Vermont	M
University of Virginia	M,D,O
University of Washington	M,D
The University of West Alabama	M
University of West Florida	M

Special Education

Institution	Degree
University of Wisconsin–Eau Claire	M
University of Wisconsin–La Crosse	M
University of Wisconsin–Madison	M,D
University of Wisconsin–Milwaukee	M
University of Wisconsin–Oshkosh	M
University of Wisconsin–Stevens Point	M
University of Wisconsin–Superior	M
University of Wisconsin–Whitewater	M
University of Wyoming	M,O
Utah State University	M,D,O
Valdosta State University	M,O
Valparaiso University	M
Vanderbilt University	M,D
Virginia Commonwealth University	M
Virginia Polytechnic Institute and State University	D,O
Walla Walla College	M
Washburn University	M
Washington University in St. Louis	M,D
Wayne State College	M
Wayne State University	M,D,O
Webster University	M,O
West Chester University of Pennsylvania	M
Western Carolina University	M
Western Connecticut State University	M
Western Illinois University	M
Western Kentucky University	M
Western Michigan University	M,D
Western New Mexico University	M
Western Oregon University	M
Western Washington University	M
Westfield State College	M
West Texas A&M University	M
West Virginia University	M,D
Wheelock College	M
Whitworth College	M
Wichita State University	M
Widener University	M,D
Wilkes University	M
William Carey College	M,O
William Paterson University of New Jersey	M
Wilmington College (DE)	M
Winona State University	M
Winthrop University	M
Wright State University	M
Xavier University	M
Xavier University of Louisiana	M
Youngstown State University	M

■ SPEECH AND INTERPERSONAL COMMUNICATION

Institution	Degree
Abilene Christian University	M
Arizona State University	M,D
Arkansas State University	M,O
Austin Peay State University	M
Ball State University	M
Bowling Green State University	M,D
Brooklyn College of the City University of New York	M,D
California State University, Fresno	M
California State University, Fullerton	M
California State University, Los Angeles	M
California State University, Northridge	M
Central Michigan University	M
Central Missouri State University	M
Colorado State University	M
Drake University	M
Eastern Illinois University	M
Eastern Michigan University	M
Florida State University	M,D
Hofstra University	M
Idaho State University	M
Indiana University Bloomington	M,D
Kansas State University	M
Kean University	M
Louisiana Tech University	M
Marquette University	M
Miami University	M
Minnesota State University Mankato	M
Montclair State University	M
Morehead State University	M
New York University	M,O
Norfolk State University	M
North Dakota State University	M,D
Northeastern Illinois University	M
Northwestern University	M,D
Ohio University	M,D
Portland State University	M
Rensselaer Polytechnic Institute	M,D
San Francisco State University	M
San Jose State University	M
Southern Illinois University Carbondale	M,D
Southern Illinois University Edwardsville	M
Syracuse University	M
Temple University	M
Texas A&M University–Commerce	M
Texas Christian University	M
Texas Southern University	M
The University of Alabama	M
University of Arkansas at Little Rock	M
University of Denver	M,D
University of Georgia	M,D
University of Hawaii at Manoa	M
University of Houston	M
University of Illinois at Urbana–Champaign	M,D
University of Maryland, College Park	M,D
University of Nevada, Reno	M
The University of North Carolina at Greensboro	M
University of South Carolina	M,D
The University of South Dakota	M
University of Southern California	D
University of Southern Mississippi	M,D
The University of Tennessee	M,D
The University of Texas at Tyler	M
The University of Texas–Pan American	M
University of Wisconsin–Stevens Point	M
University of Wisconsin–Superior	M
Wake Forest University	M
Washington University in St. Louis	D
Wayne State University	M,D
Western Kentucky University	M

■ SPORT PSYCHOLOGY

Institution	Degree
Cleveland State University	M
Florida State University	M,D
John F. Kennedy University	M
Purdue University	M,D
Southern Connecticut State University	M
Springfield College	M,D,O
University of Florida	D
The University of Iowa	M,D
West Virginia University	M,D

■ SPORTS MANAGEMENT

Institution	Degree
Appalachian State University	M
Barry University	M
Belmont University	M
Boise State University	M
Bowling Green State University	M
Brooklyn College of the City University of New York	M
Canisius College	M
Central Michigan University	M
Cleveland State University	M
Eastern Kentucky University	M
East Stroudsburg University of Pennsylvania	M
East Tennessee State University	M
Florida Atlantic University	M
Florida State University	M,D,O
The George Washington University	M
Georgia Southern University	M
Georgia State University	M
Gonzaga University	M
Grambling State University	M
Hardin-Simmons University	M
Henderson State University	M
Indiana State University	M
Indiana University Bloomington	M,D,O
Indiana University of Pennsylvania	M
Lindenwood University	M
Loras College	M
Lynn University	M,D
Millersville University of Pennsylvania	M
Mississippi State University	M
Montana State University–Billings	M
Montclair State University	M
Morehead State University	M
New York University	M,O
North Carolina State University	M,D
North Dakota State University	M
Northern Illinois University	M
Northwestern State University of Louisiana	M
Ohio University	M
Old Dominion University	M
Robert Morris University	M
St. Cloud State University	M
St. Edward's University	M,O
St. Thomas University	M,O
Seton Hall University	M,O
Slippery Rock University of Pennsylvania	M
Springfield College	M,D,O
Temple University	M
University of Central Florida	M
The University of Iowa	M
University of Louisville	M
University of Massachusetts Amherst	M,D
University of Miami	M
University of Michigan	M,D
University of Minnesota, Twin Cities Campus	M,D,O
University of New Haven	M
University of New Orleans	M,O
The University of North Carolina at Chapel Hill	M
University of Northern Iowa	M,D
University of Oklahoma	M
University of Rhode Island	M,D
University of St. Thomas (MN)	M
University of San Francisco	M
University of Southern Mississippi	M,D
The University of Tennessee	M
University of the Incarnate Word	M,O
University of Wisconsin–La Crosse	M
Valparaiso University	M
Wayne State College	M
Wayne State University	M
West Chester University of Pennsylvania	M,O
Western Illinois University	M
Western Michigan University	M
West Virginia University	M,D
Whitworth College	M
Wichita State University	M
Xavier University	M

■ STATISTICS

Institution	Degree
American University	M,O
Arizona State University	M,D
Auburn University	M,D
Ball State University	M
Baylor University	M,D
Bernard M. Baruch College of the City University of New York	M
Bowling Green State University	M,D,O
Brigham Young University	M
California State University, Fullerton	M
California State University, Hayward	M
California State University, Sacramento	M
Carnegie Mellon University	M,D
Case Western Reserve University	M,D

Directory of Graduate and Professional Programs by Field
Student Personnel Services

Central Connecticut State University	M
Claremont Graduate University	M,D
Clemson University	M,D
Colorado State University	M,D
Columbia University	M,D
Cornell University	M,D
DePaul University	M
Duke University	D
Eastern Michigan University	M
Florida International University	M
Florida State University	M,D
George Mason University	M
The George Washington University	M,D
Georgia Institute of Technology	M,D
Harvard University	M,D
Indiana University Bloomington	M,D
Indiana University–Purdue University Indianapolis	M,D
Iowa State University of Science and Technology	M,D
The Johns Hopkins University	M,D
Kansas State University	M,D
Kean University	M
Lehigh University	M
Louisiana State University and Agricultural and Mechanical College	M
Louisiana Tech University	M
Loyola University Chicago	M
Marquette University	M,D
McNeese State University	M
Miami University	M
Michigan State University	M,D
Minnesota State University Mankato	M
Mississippi State University	M,D
Montana State University–Bozeman	M
Montclair State University	M,O
New Jersey Institute of Technology	M
New Mexico State University	M
New York University	M,D
North Carolina State University	M,D
North Dakota State University	M,D
Northern Arizona University	M
Northern Illinois University	M
Northwestern University	M,D
Oakland University	M,D,O
The Ohio State University	M,D
Oklahoma State University	M,D
Oregon State University	M,D
The Pennsylvania State University University Park Campus	M,D
Princeton University	M,D
Purdue University	M,D
Rensselaer Polytechnic Institute	M
Rice University	M,D
Rochester Institute of Technology	M,O
Rutgers, The State University of New Jersey, New Brunswick/Piscataway	M,D
St. John's University (NY)	M
Sam Houston State University	M
San Diego State University	M
Southern Illinois University Carbondale	M,D
Southern Illinois University Edwardsville	M
Southern Methodist University	M,D
Stanford University	M,D
State University of New York at Binghamton	M,D
Stephen F. Austin State University	M
Stevens Institute of Technology	M,O
Stony Brook University, State University of New York	M,D
Syracuse University	M
Temple University	M,D
Texas A&M University	M,D
Tulane University	M,D
University at Albany, State University of New York	M,D,O
The University of Akron	M
The University of Alabama	M,D
University of Alaska Fairbanks	M,D
University of Arkansas	M
University of Arkansas at Little Rock	M
University of California, Berkeley	M,D
University of California, Davis	M,D
University of California, Los Angeles	M,D
University of California, Riverside	M,D
University of California, San Diego	M,D
University of California, Santa Barbara	M,D
University of Central Florida	M
University of Central Oklahoma	M
University of Chicago	M,D
University of Cincinnati	M,D
University of Connecticut	M,D
University of Delaware	M
University of Florida	M,D
University of Georgia	M,D
University of Houston–Clear Lake	M
University of Idaho	M
University of Illinois at Chicago	M,D
University of Illinois at Urbana–Champaign	M,D
The University of Iowa	M,D,O
University of Kansas	M,D
University of Kentucky	M,D
University of Maryland, Baltimore County	M,D
University of Maryland, College Park	M,D
University of Massachusetts Amherst	M,D
The University of Memphis	M,D
University of Miami	M,D
University of Michigan	M,D
University of Minnesota, Twin Cities Campus	M,D
University of Missouri–Columbia	M,D
University of Missouri–Kansas City	M,D
University of Nebraska–Lincoln	M,D
University of Nevada, Las Vegas	M
University of New Hampshire	M,D
University of New Mexico	M,D
The University of North Carolina at Chapel Hill	M,D
University of North Florida	M
University of Pennsylvania	M,D
University of Pittsburgh	M,D
University of Puerto Rico, Mayagüez Campus	M
University of Rhode Island	M,D
University of Rochester	M,D
University of South Carolina	M,D,O
University of Southern California	M,D
University of Southern Maine	M
The University of Tennessee	M,D
The University of Texas at Austin	M
The University of Texas at Dallas	M,D
The University of Texas at El Paso	M
The University of Texas at San Antonio	M
University of Toledo	M,D
University of Utah	M
University of Vermont	M
University of Virginia	M,D
University of Washington	M,D
University of West Florida	M
University of Wisconsin–Madison	M,D
University of Wyoming	M,D
Utah State University	M,D
Villanova University	M
Virginia Commonwealth University	M,O
Virginia Polytechnic Institute and State University	M,D
Washington University in St. Louis	M,D
Wayne State University	M,D
Western Michigan University	M,D
West Virginia University	M,D
Wichita State University	M,D
Worcester Polytechnic Institute	M,D,O
Wright State University	M
Yale University	M,D

■ STRUCTURAL BIOLOGY

Brandeis University	D
Cornell University	M,D
Duke University	O
Harvard University	D
Iowa State University of Science and Technology	M,D
Mayo Graduate School	D
New York University	D
Northwestern University	D
Stanford University	D
Stony Brook University, State University of New York	D
Syracuse University	D
Tulane University	M,D
University at Albany, State University of New York	M,D
University of California, San Diego	D
University of Connecticut	M,D
University of Illinois at Urbana–Champaign	D
University of Pennsylvania	D
University of Washington	D

■ STRUCTURAL ENGINEERING

Auburn University	M,D
California State Polytechnic University, Pomona	M
California State University, Northridge	M
The Catholic University of America	M,D
Cleveland State University	M,D
Colorado State University	M,D
Cornell University	M,D
Illinois Institute of Technology	M,D
Iowa State University of Science and Technology	M,D
Louisiana State University and Agricultural and Mechanical College	M,D
Marquette University	M,D
Massachusetts Institute of Technology	M,D,O
Michigan Technological University	D
Northwestern University	M,D
Ohio University	M,D
The Pennsylvania State University University Park Campus	M,D
Princeton University	M,D
Rensselaer Polytechnic Institute	M,D
Texas A&M University	M,D
Tufts University	M,D
University at Buffalo, The State University of New York	M,D
University of California, Berkeley	M,D
University of California, Los Angeles	M,D
University of California, San Diego	M,D
University of Central Florida	M,D,O
University of Colorado at Boulder	M,D
University of Dayton	M
University of Delaware	M,D
University of Maine	M,D
The University of Memphis	M,D
University of Missouri–Columbia	M,D
University of Missouri–Rolla	M,D
University of North Dakota	M
University of Oklahoma	M,D
University of Rhode Island	M,D
University of Southern California	M
University of Washington	M,D
Washington University in St. Louis	M,D

■ STUDENT PERSONNEL SERVICES

Arkansas State University	M,O
Arkansas Tech University	M
Ashland University	M
Azusa Pacific University	M
Bowling Green State University	M
Buffalo State College, State University of New York	M

Directory of Graduate and Professional Programs by Field

Student Personnel Services

Canisius College	M
The College of Saint Rose	M,O
Concordia University Wisconsin	M
Eastern Illinois University	M
Emporia State University	M
Fresno Pacific University	M
Hampton University	M
Kansas State University	M,D
Kent State University	M,D,O
Lewis University	M
Miami University	M
Minnesota State University Mankato	M
New York University	M,D
Northeastern University	M
Northwestern State University of Louisiana	M,O
Ohio University	M,D
Oklahoma State University	M,D
Oregon State University	M
Rowan University	M
Saint Louis University	M,D,O
San Jose State University	M
Slippery Rock University of Pennsylvania	M
Springfield College	M,O
Teachers College Columbia University	M,D
Tennessee Technological University	M,O
University of Central Arkansas	M
University of Dayton	M
University of Florida	M,D,O
University of Georgia	M,D
The University of Iowa	M,D
University of Louisville	M,D
University of Maryland, College Park	M,D,O
University of Minnesota, Twin Cities Campus	M,D,O
University of Mississippi	M,D,O
University of Northern Colorado	D
University of Northern Iowa	M
University of South Carolina	M
University of Southern California	M,D,O
University of South Florida	M,D,O
The University of Tennessee	M
University of Wisconsin–La Crosse	M
Western Illinois University	M
Western Washington University	M

SURVEYING SCIENCE AND ENGINEERING

The Ohio State University	M,D

SURVEY METHODOLOGY

University of Maryland, College Park	M,D
University of Michigan	M,D,O
University of Nebraska–Lincoln	M

SUSTAINABLE DEVELOPMENT

Brandeis University	M
Carnegie Mellon University	M
Clark University	M
Columbia University	D
Illinois Institute of Technology	M
New College of California	M
Prescott College	M
School for International Training	M,O
Slippery Rock University of Pennsylvania	M
University of Connecticut	M
University of Georgia	M,D
University of Maryland, College Park	M
University of Washington	P,M,D
University of Wisconsin–Madison	M
Western Illinois University	M,O

SYSTEMS ENGINEERING

Auburn University	M,D
Boston University	M,D
California Institute of Technology	M,D
California State University, Fullerton	M
Case Western Reserve University	M,D
Colorado State University–Pueblo	M
Cornell University	M
Embry-Riddle Aeronautical University (FL)	M
Florida Institute of Technology	M
George Mason University	M
The George Washington University	M,D,O
Georgia Institute of Technology	M,D
Iowa State University of Science and Technology	M
The Johns Hopkins University	M
Lehigh University	M,D
Louisiana State University in Shreveport	M
Loyola Marymount University	M
Massachusetts Institute of Technology	M
North Carolina Agricultural and Technical State University	M,D
Northeastern University	M
Oakland University	M,D
The Ohio State University	M,D
Ohio University	M
Oklahoma State University	M
The Pennsylvania State University Great Valley Campus	M
Polytechnic University, Brooklyn Campus	M
Portland State University	M,O
Purdue University	M,D
Rensselaer Polytechnic Institute	M,D
Rochester Institute of Technology	M,D
Rutgers, The State University of New Jersey, New Brunswick/Piscataway	M,D
San Jose State University	M
Southeastern Louisiana University	M
Southern Methodist University	M,D
Stony Brook University, State University of New York	M
Texas Tech University	M,D
The University of Arizona	M,D
University of Central Florida	M,D,O
University of Connecticut	M,D
University of Florida	M,D,O
University of Houston	M,D
University of Houston–Clear Lake	M
University of Idaho	M
University of Illinois at Urbana–Champaign	M
University of Maryland, College Park	M,O
University of Michigan	M,D
University of Michigan–Dearborn	M
University of Minnesota, Twin Cities Campus	M
University of Missouri–Rolla	M
University of Pennsylvania	M,D
University of Rhode Island	M,D
University of St. Thomas (MN)	M,O
University of Southern California	M,D,O
The University of Texas at Arlington	M,D
University of Virginia	M,D
University of West Florida	M
Washington University in St. Louis	D

SYSTEMS SCIENCE

Claremont Graduate University	M,D
Colorado Technical University	M,D
Eastern Illinois University	M,O
Fairleigh Dickinson University, Metropolitan Campus	M
Florida Institute of Technology	M
Hood College	M
Louisiana State University and Agricultural and Mechanical College	M,D
Louisiana State University in Shreveport	M
Miami University	M
Northern Kentucky University	M
Oakland University	M
Old Dominion University	M
Portland State University	M,D,O
Southern Methodist University	M,D
State University of New York at Binghamton	M,D
Syracuse University	M
University of Colorado at Denver	M,D
University of Michigan–Dearborn	M
Washington University in St. Louis	M,D

TAXATION

American University	M
Arizona State University	M
Bentley College	M,O
Bernard M. Baruch College of the City University of New York	M
Boston University	P,M
California State University, Fullerton	M
California State University, Hayward	M
California State University, Los Angeles	M
Capital University	M
Chapman University	P,M
Cleveland State University	M
DePaul University	M
Drexel University	M
Duquesne University	M
Fairfield University	M,O
Fairleigh Dickinson University, College at Florham	M,O
Florida Atlantic University	M
Florida Gulf Coast University	M
Florida International University	M
Florida State University	M,D
Fontbonne University	M
Fordham University	M
Georgetown University	P,M,D
Georgia State University	M
Grand Valley State University	M
Hofstra University	M,O
Illinois Institute of Technology	P,M
Long Island University, Brooklyn Campus	M
Long Island University, C.W. Post Campus	M
Loyola Marymount University	P,M
Mississippi State University	M
National University	M
New York University	P,M,D,O
Northeastern University	M,O
Northern Illinois University	M
Nova Southeastern University	M
Pace University	M
Pace University, White Plains Campus	M
Philadelphia University	M
Robert Morris University	M
Rutgers, The State University of New Jersey, Newark	M
St. John Fisher College	M
St. John's University (NY)	M,O
St. Mary's University of San Antonio	M
St. Thomas University	P,M
Saint Xavier University	M,O
San Jose State University	M
Seton Hall University	M,O
Southeastern University	M
Southern Methodist University	P,M,D
Suffolk University	M,O
Temple University	P,M
Texas Tech University	M,D
University at Albany, State University of New York	M
The University of Akron	M
The University of Alabama	M,D
University of Baltimore	P,M
University of Central Florida	M
University of Cincinnati	M
University of Colorado at Boulder	M
University of Denver	M
University of Florida	M

Directory of Graduate and Professional Programs by Field
Theater

University of Hartford	M,O
University of Hawaii at Manoa	M
The University of Memphis	M
University of Miami	M
University of Minnesota, Twin Cities Campus	M
University of Mississippi	M,D
University of Missouri–Kansas City	P,M
University of Missouri–St. Louis	M,O
University of New Haven	M
University of New Mexico	M
University of New Orleans	M
University of San Diego	P,M,O
University of Southern California	M
The University of Texas at Arlington	M,D
The University of Texas at San Antonio	M
University of the Sacred Heart	M
University of Tulsa	M
University of Washington	P,M,D
Villanova University	M
Virginia Commonwealth University	M,D
Washington State University	M
Wayne State University	M
Widener University	M

■ **TECHNICAL WRITING**

Boise State University	M
Carnegie Mellon University	M
Colorado State University	M
Drexel University	M
Fitchburg State College	M,O
Georgia State University	M,D
Illinois Institute of Technology	M,D
James Madison University	M
The Johns Hopkins University	M
Metropolitan State University	M
Miami University	M
Michigan Technological University	M,D
New Jersey Institute of Technology	M
North Carolina State University	M
Northeastern University	M
Oklahoma State University	M,D
Polytechnic University, Brooklyn Campus	M
Regis University	M,O
Rensselaer Polytechnic Institute	M
Texas State University-San Marcos	M
Texas Tech University	M,D
The University of Alabama in Huntsville	M,O
University of Arkansas at Little Rock	M
University of Central Florida	M,D,O
University of Colorado at Denver	M
University of Minnesota, Twin Cities Campus	M,D
The University of North Carolina at Greensboro	M,D,O
University of Washington	M,D

■ **TECHNOLOGY AND PUBLIC POLICY**

California State University, Los Angeles	M
Carnegie Mellon University	M,D
Eastern Michigan University	M
George Mason University	M
The George Washington University	M
Massachusetts Institute of Technology	M,D
Rensselaer Polytechnic Institute	M,D
Rochester Institute of Technology	M
St. Cloud State University	M
University of Minnesota, Twin Cities Campus	M
The University of Texas at Austin	M
Western Illinois University	M

■ **TELECOMMUNICATIONS**

Azusa Pacific University	M,O
Ball State University	M
Boston University	M
Claremont Graduate University	M,D
Columbia University	M,D,O
DePaul University	M
Drexel University	M
Florida International University	M
George Mason University	M
The George Washington University	M,O
Illinois Institute of Technology	M,D
Iona College	M,O
Michigan State University	M
New Jersey Institute of Technology	M,D
Pace University	M,D,O
Pace University, White Plains Campus	M,D,O
The Pennsylvania State University University Park Campus	M
Polytechnic University, Brooklyn Campus	M
Polytechnic University, Westchester Graduate Center	M
Regis University	M,O
Rochester Institute of Technology	M
Roosevelt University	M
Saint Mary's University of Minnesota	M
Southern Methodist University	M,D
State University of New York Institute of Technology	M
Syracuse University	M
Texas Tech University	M,D
University of Arkansas	M
University of California, San Diego	M,D
University of Colorado at Boulder	M
University of Denver	M,O
University of Louisiana at Lafayette	M
University of Maryland, College Park	M
University of Missouri–Kansas City	M,D
University of Oklahoma	M,D
University of Pennsylvania	M
University of Pittsburgh	M,D,O
The University of Texas at Dallas	M,D
Western Illinois University	M,O
Widener University	M

■ **TELECOMMUNICATIONS MANAGEMENT**

Alaska Pacific University	M
Canisius College	M
Morgan State University	M
Murray State University	M
National University	M
Northeastern University	M
Oklahoma State University	M,D
Polytechnic University, Brooklyn Campus	M
Regis University	M,O
San Diego State University	M
Stevens Institute of Technology	M,D,O
Syracuse University	M,O
University of Colorado at Boulder	M
University of Maryland University College	M,O
University of Miami	M
University of Missouri–St. Louis	M,D,O
University of Pennsylvania	M
University of San Francisco	M
Webster University	M,D

■ **TEXTILE DESIGN**

California State University, Los Angeles	M
Central Washington University	M
Colorado State University	M
Cornell University	M,D
Drexel University	M
Illinois State University	M
Indiana University Bloomington	M
James Madison University	M
Kent State University	M
Marywood University	M
New School University	M
Philadelphia University	M
Southern Illinois University Edwardsville	M
Sul Ross State University	M
Syracuse University	M
Temple University	M
University of California, Davis	M
University of Cincinnati	M
University of Minnesota, Twin Cities Campus	M,D
The University of North Carolina at Greensboro	M,D
University of North Texas	M,D
Western Michigan University	M

■ **TEXTILE SCIENCES AND ENGINEERING**

Auburn University	M,D
Clemson University	M,D
Cornell University	M,D
Georgia Institute of Technology	M,D
North Carolina State University	M,D
Philadelphia University	M
University of Massachusetts Dartmouth	M

■ **THANATOLOGY**

Brooklyn College of the City University of New York	M
The College of New Rochelle	O
Hood College	M,O

■ **THEATER**

Antioch University McGregor	M
Arcadia University	M,D,O
Arizona State University	M,D
Arkansas State University	M,O
Austin Peay State University	M
Averett University	M
Baylor University	M
Boston University	M,O
Bowling Green State University	M,D
Brandeis University	M
Brigham Young University	M,D
Brooklyn College of the City University of New York	M,D
Brown University	M
California State University, Fullerton	M
California State University, Long Beach	M
California State University, Los Angeles	M
California State University, Northridge	M
California State University, Sacramento	M
Carnegie Mellon University	M
Case Western Reserve University	M
The Catholic University of America	M
Central Michigan University	M
Central Missouri State University	M
Central Washington University	M
Columbia University	M,D
Cornell University	D
DePaul University	M,O
Drake University	M
Eastern Kentucky University	M
Eastern Michigan University	M
Emerson College	M
Florida Atlantic University	M
Florida State University	M,D
The George Washington University	M
Humboldt State University	M
Hunter College of the City University of New York	M
Idaho State University	M
Illinois State University	M
Indiana State University	M
Indiana University Bloomington	M,D

Peterson's Graduate Schools in the U.S. 2006 www.petersons.com 173

Directory of Graduate and Professional Programs by Field

Theater

Institution	Degrees
Kent State University	M
Lamar University	M
Lindenwood University	M
Long Island University, C.W. Post Campus	M
Louisiana State University and Agricultural and Mechanical College	M,D
Miami University	M
Michigan State University	M
Minnesota State University Mankato	M
Montana State University–Billings	M
Montclair State University	M
Morehead State University	M
New School University	M
New York University	M,D,O
Northern Illinois University	M
Northwestern University	M,D
The Ohio State University	M,D
Ohio University	M
Oklahoma City University	M
Oklahoma State University	M
The Pennsylvania State University University Park Campus	M
Pittsburg State University	M
Point Park University	M
Portland State University	M
Purchase College, State University of New York	M
Purdue University	M
Rhode Island College	M
Roosevelt University	M
Rowan University	M
Rutgers, The State University of New Jersey, New Brunswick/Piscataway	M
San Diego State University	M
San Francisco State University	M
San Jose State University	M
South Dakota State University	M
Southern Illinois University Carbondale	M,D
Southern Methodist University	M
Southwest Missouri State University	M
Stanford University	D
State University of New York at Binghamton	M
Stony Brook University, State University of New York	M
Temple University	M
Texas A&M University–Commerce	M
Texas State University-San Marcos	M
Texas Tech University	M,D
Texas Woman's University	M
Towson University	M
Tufts University	M,D
Tulane University	M
University at Albany, State University of New York	M
The University of Akron	M
The University of Alabama	M
The University of Arizona	M
University of Arkansas	M
University of California, Berkeley	D
University of California, Davis	M,D
University of California, Irvine	M,D
University of California, Los Angeles	M,D
University of California, San Diego	M,D
University of California, Santa Barbara	M,D
University of California, Santa Cruz	O
University of Central Florida	M
University of Cincinnati	M
University of Colorado at Boulder	M,D
University of Colorado at Denver	M
University of Connecticut	M
University of Delaware	M
University of Florida	M
University of Georgia	M,D
University of Hawaii at Manoa	M,D
University of Houston	M
University of Idaho	M
University of Illinois at Urbana–Champaign	M,D
The University of Iowa	M
University of Kansas	M,D
University of Kentucky	M
University of Louisville	M
University of Maine	M
University of Maryland, College Park	M,D
University of Massachusetts Amherst	M
The University of Memphis	M
University of Michigan	M,D
University of Minnesota, Twin Cities Campus	M,D
University of Mississippi	M
University of Missouri–Columbia	M,D
University of Missouri–Kansas City	M
The University of Montana–Missoula	M
University of Nebraska at Omaha	M
University of Nebraska–Lincoln	M,D
University of Nevada, Las Vegas	M
University of New Mexico	M
University of New Orleans	M
The University of North Carolina at Chapel Hill	M
The University of North Carolina at Greensboro	M
University of North Dakota	M
University of Northern Iowa	M
University of North Texas	M
University of Oklahoma	M
University of Oregon	M,D
University of Pittsburgh	M,D
University of Portland	M
University of San Diego	M
University of South Carolina	M,D
The University of South Dakota	M
University of Southern California	M
University of Southern Mississippi	M
The University of Tennessee	M
The University of Texas at Austin	M,D
The University of Texas at El Paso	M
The University of Texas at Tyler	M
The University of Texas–Pan American	M
University of Utah	M,D
University of Virginia	M
University of Washington	M,D
University of Wisconsin–Madison	M,D
University of Wisconsin–Milwaukee	M
University of Wisconsin–Superior	M
Utah State University	M
Villanova University	M
Virginia Commonwealth University	M
Virginia Polytechnic Institute and State University	M
Washington University in St. Louis	M
Wayne State University	M,D
Western Illinois University	M
Western Washington University	M
West Virginia University	M
Yale University	M,D,O

■ THEOLOGY

Institution	Degrees
Abilene Christian University	P,M
Anderson University	P,M,D
Andrews University	P,M,D,O
Azusa Pacific University	M,D
Barry University	M,D
Bayamón Central University	P,M
Baylor University	P,D
Biola University	P,M,D
Boston College	M,D
Boston University	P,M,D
Campbellsville University	M
Campbell University	M
The Catholic University of America	P,M,D,O
Chaminade University of Honolulu	M
Claremont Graduate University	M,D
College of Mount St. Joseph	M
College of St. Catherine	M
Concordia University (CA)	M
Cornerstone University	P,M
Creighton University	M
Duke University	P,M
Duquesne University	M,D
Emory University	P,M,D
Fordham University	M,D
Franciscan University of Steubenville	M
Freed-Hardeman University	M
Friends University	M
Gardner-Webb University	P,D
George Fox University	P,M,D
Georgian Court University	M,O
Golden Gate Baptist Theological Seminary	P,M,D,O
Gonzaga University	P,M
Grand Rapids Theological Seminary of Cornerstone University	P,M
Hardin-Simmons University	P
Harvard University	P,M,D
Houston Baptist University	M
Howard University	P,M,D
Indiana Wesleyan University	M
Inter American University of Puerto Rico, Metropolitan Campus	D
La Salle University	M
Liberty University	P,M,D
Lipscomb University	P,M
Loyola Marymount University	M
Loyola University Chicago	P,M,D
Loyola University New Orleans	M,O
Malone College	M
Marquette University	M,D
Marylhurst University	M
Mercer University	P,D
Mount Saint Mary's University	P,M
North Park Theological Seminary	P,M,D,O
Oakland City University	P,D
Olivet Nazarene University	M
Oral Roberts University	P,M,D
Palm Beach Atlantic University	M
Pontifical Catholic University of Puerto Rico	M
Providence College	M
Regent University	P,M,D
St. Bonaventure University	M,O
St. John's University (NY)	P,M
Saint Louis University	M,D
St. Mary's University of San Antonio	M
Saint Michael's College	M,O
Samford University	P,M,D
Seattle University	P,M,O
Seton Hall University	P,M,O
Simpson University	M
Southern Methodist University	P,M,D
Southern Nazarene University	M
Spring Hill College	M
Texas Christian University	P,M,D,O
University of Chicago	P,M,D
University of Dayton	M,D
University of Dubuque	P,M,D
University of Mobile	M
University of Notre Dame	P,M,D
University of St. Thomas (MN)	P,M,D
University of St. Thomas (TX)	P,M
University of San Diego	M
University of San Francisco	M
The University of Scranton	M
Ursuline College	M
Valparaiso University	M
Vanderbilt University	P,M
Villanova University	M
Wheeling Jesuit University	M
Xavier University	M
Xavier University of Louisiana	M
Yale University	P,M

■ THEORETICAL CHEMISTRY

Institution	Degrees
Cornell University	D
Georgetown University	M,D
The University of Tennessee	M,D

Directory of Graduate and Professional Programs by Field
Urban and Regional Planning

Vanderbilt University	M,D
West Virginia University	M,D

■ THEORETICAL PHYSICS

Cornell University	M,D
Harvard University	M,D
Rutgers, The State University of New Jersey, New Brunswick/Piscataway	M,D
St. John's University (NY)	M,O
West Virginia University	M,D

■ THERAPIES—DANCE, DRAMA, AND MUSIC

Antioch New England Graduate School	M
Colorado State University	M
Columbia College Chicago	M,O
Drexel University	M
East Carolina University	M
Florida State University	M,D
Georgia College & State University	M,O
Immaculata University	M
Lesley University	M,D,O
Maryville University of Saint Louis	M
Michigan State University	M,D
Montclair State University	M
New York University	M,D
Pratt Institute	M
Shenandoah University	M,D,O
Southern Methodist University	M,O
Temple University	M,D
University of Kansas	M
University of Miami	M,D,O
University of the Pacific	M

■ TOXICOLOGY

American University	M,O
Brown University	M,D
Case Western Reserve University	M,D
Columbia University	M,D
Cornell University	M,D
Dartmouth College	D
Duke University	D,O
Duquesne University	M,D
Florida Agricultural and Mechanical University	M,D
Indiana University–Purdue University Indianapolis	M,D
Iowa State University of Science and Technology	M,D
The Johns Hopkins University	D
Long Island University, Brooklyn Campus	M
Louisiana State University and Agricultural and Mechanical College	M
Massachusetts Institute of Technology	M,D
Michigan State University	M,D
North Carolina State University	M,D
Northeastern University	M,D
Northwestern University	D
The Ohio State University	M,D
Oregon State University	M,D
Purdue University	M,D
Rutgers, The State University of New Jersey, New Brunswick/Piscataway	M,D
St. John's University (NY)	M,D
San Diego State University	M,D
Texas A&M University	M,D
Texas Southern University	M,D
Texas Tech University	M,D
University at Albany, State University of New York	M,D
University at Buffalo, The State University of New York	M,D
The University of Alabama at Birmingham	D
The University of Arizona	M,D,O
University of California, Berkeley	D
University of California, Davis	M,D
University of California, Irvine	M,D
University of California, Los Angeles	D
University of California, Riverside	M,D
University of California, Santa Cruz	M,D
University of Cincinnati	M,D
University of Connecticut	M,D
University of Florida	M,D,O
University of Georgia	M,D
University of Kansas	M,D
University of Kentucky	M,D
University of Louisville	M,D
University of Maryland	M,D
University of Maryland, College Park	M,D
University of Maryland Eastern Shore	M,D
University of Michigan	M,D
University of Minnesota, Duluth	M,D
University of Minnesota, Twin Cities Campus	M,D
University of Mississippi	M,D
The University of Montana–Missoula	M,D
University of Nebraska–Lincoln	M,D
University of New Mexico	M,D
The University of North Carolina at Chapel Hill	M,D
University of Rhode Island	M,D
University of Rochester	M,D
University of Southern California	M,D
University of Utah	M,D
University of Washington	M,D
University of Wisconsin–Madison	M,D
Utah State University	M,D
Virginia Commonwealth University	M,D,O
Washington State University	M,D
Wayne State University	M,D,O
West Virginia University	M,D
Wright State University	M

■ TRANSCULTURAL NURSING

Augsburg College	M
New Jersey City University	M

■ TRANSLATION AND INTERPRETATION

American University	M,O
Gallaudet University	M
Georgia State University	O
Kent State University	M
Monterey Institute of International Studies	M
Rutgers, The State University of New Jersey, New Brunswick/Piscataway	M,D
State University of New York at Binghamton	M,O
University at Albany, State University of New York	M,O
University of Arkansas	M
The University of Iowa	M
University of Puerto Rico, Río Piedras	M,O

■ TRANSPERSONAL AND HUMANISTIC PSYCHOLOGY

John F. Kennedy University	M
Seattle University	M

■ TRANSPORTATION AND HIGHWAY ENGINEERING

Auburn University	M,D
Cornell University	M,D
Illinois Institute of Technology	M,D
Iowa State University of Science and Technology	M,D
Louisiana State University and Agricultural and Mechanical College	M,D
Marquette University	M,D
Massachusetts Institute of Technology	M,D,O
Morgan State University	M,D
New Jersey Institute of Technology	M,D
Northwestern University	M,D
Ohio University	M,D
The Pennsylvania State University University Park Campus	M,D
Polytechnic University, Brooklyn Campus	M
Princeton University	M,D
Rensselaer Polytechnic Institute	M,D
Texas A&M University	M,D
Texas Southern University	M
University of Arkansas	M
University of California, Berkeley	M,D
University of California, Davis	M,D
University of California, Irvine	M,D
University of Central Florida	M,D,O
University of Dayton	M
University of Delaware	M,D
The University of Memphis	M,D
University of Missouri–Columbia	M,D
University of Oklahoma	M,D
University of Rhode Island	M,D
University of Southern California	M
University of Washington	M,D
Villanova University	M
Washington University in St. Louis	D

■ TRANSPORTATION MANAGEMENT

Arizona State University	O
Central Missouri State University	M,O
Florida Institute of Technology	M
George Mason University	M
Iowa State University of Science and Technology	M
Massachusetts Institute of Technology	M
Middle Tennessee State University	M
Morgan State University	M
New Jersey Institute of Technology	M,D
North Dakota State University	M,D
Polytechnic University, Brooklyn Campus	M
San Jose State University	M
University at Buffalo, The State University of New York	M,D,O
University of Arkansas	M
University of California, Davis	M,D
University of Denver	M
The University of Tennessee	M,D
University of Washington	O

■ TRAVEL AND TOURISM

Boston University	M
Central Michigan University	M,O
Clemson University	M,D
The George Washington University	M
New York University	M,O
North Carolina State University	M,D
Purdue University	M,D
Rochester Institute of Technology	M
Temple University	M,D
University of Central Florida	M
University of Denver	M
University of Hawaii at Manoa	M,O
University of Massachusetts Amherst	M
University of New Haven	M
University of New Orleans	M
University of South Carolina	M
The University of Tennessee	M
University of Wisconsin–Stout	M
Virginia Polytechnic Institute and State University	M,D
Western Illinois University	M

■ URBAN AND REGIONAL PLANNING

Alabama Agricultural and Mechanical University	M
Arizona State University	M
Auburn University	M

Peterson's Graduate Schools in the U.S. 2006

Directory of Graduate and Professional Programs by Field
Urban and Regional Planning

Institution	Degree
Ball State University	M
Boston University	M
California Polytechnic State University, San Luis Obispo	M
California State Polytechnic University, Pomona	M
California State University, Chico	M
The Catholic University of America	M
Clark University	M
Clemson University	M
Cleveland State University	M,O
Columbia University	M,D
Cornell University	M,D
Delta State University	M
DePaul University	M,O
Eastern Kentucky University	M
Eastern Washington University	M
East Tennessee State University	M
Florida Atlantic University	M
Florida State University	M,D
Georgia Institute of Technology	M,D
Harvard University	M,D
Hunter College of the City University of New York	M
Indiana University–Purdue University Indianapolis	M
Iowa State University of Science and Technology	M
Jackson State University	M
Kansas State University	M
Massachusetts Institute of Technology	M,D
Michigan State University	M,D
Morgan State University	M
New York University	M,O
North Park University	M
The Ohio State University	M,D
Old Dominion University	M
The Pennsylvania State University University Park Campus	M
Portland State University	M,D
Pratt Institute	M
Rutgers, The State University of New Jersey, New Brunswick/Piscataway	M,D
San Diego State University	M
San Jose State University	M,O
Southwest Missouri State University	M
State University of New York College of Environmental Science and Forestry	M,D
Temple University	M
Texas A&M University	M,D
Texas Southern University	M
Tufts University	M
University at Albany, State University of New York	M
University at Buffalo, The State University of New York	M
The University of Akron	M
The University of Arizona	M
University of California, Berkeley	M,D
University of California, Davis	M
University of California, Irvine	M,D
University of California, Los Angeles	M,D
University of Cincinnati	M
University of Colorado at Denver	M
University of Florida	M
University of Hawaii at Manoa	M
University of Illinois at Chicago	M,D
University of Illinois at Urbana–Champaign	M,D
The University of Iowa	M
University of Kansas	M
University of Louisville	M
University of Maryland, College Park	M,D
University of Massachusetts Amherst	M,D
The University of Memphis	M
University of Michigan	M,D,O
University of Minnesota, Twin Cities Campus	M
University of Nebraska–Lincoln	M
University of New Mexico	M
University of New Orleans	M
The University of North Carolina at Chapel Hill	M,D
The University of North Carolina at Charlotte	M
University of Oklahoma	M
University of Oregon	M
University of Pennsylvania	M,D,O
University of Pittsburgh	M
University of Puerto Rico, Río Piedras	M
University of Rhode Island	M
University of Southern California	M,D
University of Southern Maine	M,O
The University of Tennessee	M
The University of Texas at Arlington	M
The University of Texas at Austin	M,D
University of Toledo	M
University of Virginia	M
University of Washington	M,D
University of Wisconsin–Madison	M,D
University of Wisconsin–Milwaukee	M
Utah State University	M,D
Valdosta State University	M
Virginia Commonwealth University	M,O
Virginia Polytechnic Institute and State University	M
Washington State University	M
Wayne State University	M
West Chester University of Pennsylvania	M
West Virginia University	M,D

■ URBAN DESIGN

Institution	Degree
City College of the City University of New York	M
Cleveland State University	M,O
Columbia University	M
Cornell University	M,D
Georgia Institute of Technology	M,D
Harvard University	M
New York Institute of Technology	M
Prairie View A&M University	M
Pratt Institute	M
Rice University	M,D
State University of New York College of Environmental Science and Forestry	M
University at Buffalo, The State University of New York	M
University of California, Berkeley	M,D
University of California, Los Angeles	M,D
University of Colorado at Denver	M
University of Miami	M
University of Michigan	M
University of Washington	M,D,O
Washington University in St. Louis	M

■ URBAN EDUCATION

Institution	Degree
Claremont Graduate University	M,D
Cleveland State University	D
College of Mount Saint Vincent	M,O
Columbia College Chicago	M
Concordia University (IL)	M
DePaul University	M
Florida International University	M
Georgia State University	M
Harvard University	M,D
Holy Names University	M,O
Marygrove College	M
Mercy College	M,O
Morgan State University	M,D
New Jersey City University	M
Norfolk State University	M
Northeastern Illinois University	M
Old Dominion University	D
Saint Peter's College	M
Simmons College	M,O
Temple University	M,D
Texas A&M University	M,D
Texas Southern University	M,D
University of Illinois at Chicago	M,D
University of Massachusetts Boston	M,D,O
University of Nebraska at Omaha	M,O
University of Wisconsin–Milwaukee	M,D
Virginia Commonwealth University	D

■ URBAN STUDIES

Institution	Degree
Boston University	M
Brooklyn College of the City University of New York	M,D
Cleveland State University	M,D
East Tennessee State University	M
Georgia State University	M
Hunter College of the City University of New York	M
Long Island University, Brooklyn Campus	M
Massachusetts Institute of Technology	M,D
Minnesota State University Mankato	M
New Jersey City University	M
New Jersey Institute of Technology	D
New School University	M
Norfolk State University	M
Old Dominion University	M,D
Portland State University	M,D
Queens College of the City University of New York	M
Rutgers, The State University of New Jersey, Newark	M,D
Saint Louis University	M,D
Savannah State University	M
Southern Connecticut State University	M
Temple University	M
Tufts University	M
University at Albany, State University of New York	M,D,O
The University of Akron	M,D
University of Central Oklahoma	M
University of Delaware	M,D
University of Louisville	D
University of New Orleans	M,D
University of the Incarnate Word	M
University of Wisconsin–Milwaukee	M,D
Wright State University	M

■ VETERINARY MEDICINE

Institution	Degree
Auburn University	P
Colorado State University	P
Cornell University	P
Iowa State University of Science and Technology	P,M
Kansas State University	P
Louisiana State University and Agricultural and Mechanical College	P
Michigan State University	P
Mississippi State University	P
North Carolina State University	P,M
The Ohio State University	P
Oklahoma State University	P
Oregon State University	P
Purdue University	P
Texas A&M University	P,M,D
Tufts University	P
Tuskegee University	P
University of California, Davis	P
University of Florida	P
University of Georgia	P
University of Illinois at Urbana–Champaign	P
University of Maryland, College Park	P
University of Minnesota, Twin Cities Campus	P
University of Missouri–Columbia	P
University of Pennsylvania	P
The University of Tennessee	P
University of Wisconsin–Madison	P
Virginia Polytechnic Institute and State University	P

Directory of Graduate and Professional Programs by Field
Water Resources Engineering

Washington State University	P

■ **VETERINARY SCIENCES**

Auburn University	M,D
Colorado State University	M,D
Drexel University	M
Iowa State University of Science and Technology	M,D
Kansas State University	M
Louisiana State University and Agricultural and Mechanical College	M,D
Michigan State University	M,D
Mississippi State University	M,D
Montana State University–Bozeman	M,D
North Carolina State University	M,D
North Dakota State University	M
The Ohio State University	M,D
Oklahoma State University	M,D
Oregon State University	M,D
The Pennsylvania State University University Park Campus	M,D
Purdue University	M,D
Texas A&M University	M,D
Tufts University	M,D
Tuskegee University	M
University of California, Davis	M,O
University of Florida	M,D,O
University of Georgia	M,D
University of Idaho	M,D
University of Illinois at Urbana–Champaign	M,D
University of Kentucky	M,D
University of Maryland, College Park	M,D
University of Minnesota, Twin Cities Campus	M,D
University of Missouri–Columbia	M,D
University of Nebraska–Lincoln	M,D
University of Washington	M
University of Wisconsin–Madison	M,D
Utah State University	M,D
Virginia Polytechnic Institute and State University	M,D
Washington State University	M,D
West Virginia University	M

■ **VIROLOGY**

Harvard University	D
Kansas State University	M,D
Loyola University Chicago	M,D
Mayo Graduate School	D
Purdue University	M,D
Rutgers, The State University of New Jersey, New Brunswick/Piscataway	M,D
University of California, San Diego	D
The University of Iowa	M,D
University of Pennsylvania	D
University of Pittsburgh	M,D
West Virginia University	M,D

■ **VISION SCIENCES**

Emory University	M
Indiana University Bloomington	M,D
Nova Southeastern University	P,M
Pacific University	M
The University of Alabama at Birmingham	M,D
The University of Alabama in Huntsville	M,D
University of California, Berkeley	M,D
University of Chicago	D
University of Houston	M,D
University of Louisville	M
University of Missouri–St. Louis	M,D

■ **VOCATIONAL AND TECHNICAL EDUCATION**

Alabama Agricultural and Mechanical University	M

Alcorn State University	M,O
Appalachian State University	M
Ball State University	M
Bemidji State University	M
Bowling Green State University	M
Buffalo State College, State University of New York	M
California Baptist University	M
California State University, Long Beach	M
California State University, Sacramento	M
California State University, San Bernardino	M
California University of Pennsylvania	M
Central Connecticut State University	M
Central Michigan University	M
Central Missouri State University	M,O
Chicago State University	M
Clemson University	M,D
Colorado State University	M,D
Drake University	M
East Carolina University	M
Eastern Kentucky University	M
Eastern Michigan University	M
East Tennessee State University	M
Fitchburg State College	M
Florida Agricultural and Mechanical University	M
Florida International University	M
Florida State University	D,O
Georgia Southern University	M
Georgia State University	M,D,O
Idaho State University	M
Indiana State University	M
Inter American University of Puerto Rico, Metropolitan Campus	M
Iowa State University of Science and Technology	M,D
Jackson State University	M
James Madison University	M
Kent State University	M,O
Louisiana State University and Agricultural and Mechanical College	M,D
Marshall University	M
Middle Tennessee State University	M
Millersville University of Pennsylvania	M
Mississippi State University	M,D,O
Morehead State University	M
Murray State University	M
North Carolina Agricultural and Technical State University	M
North Carolina State University	M,D
Northern Arizona University	M
Nova Southeastern University	M
The Ohio State University	D
Oklahoma State University	M,D,O
Old Dominion University	M
Oregon State University	M
The Pennsylvania State University University Park Campus	M,D
Pittsburg State University	M,O
Purdue University	M,D,O
Rhode Island College	M
Sam Houston State University	M
South Carolina State University	M
Southern Illinois University Carbondale	M,D
Southwestern Oklahoma State University	M
Southwest Missouri State University	M,O
State University of New York at Oswego	M
Sul Ross State University	M
Temple University	M,D
Texas A&M University–Corpus Christi	M
Texas State University–San Marcos	M
The University of Akron	M
University of Alaska Anchorage	M
University of Arkansas	M,D,O

University of Central Florida	M
University of Georgia	M,D,O
University of Idaho	M,D,O
University of Illinois at Urbana–Champaign	M,D,O
University of Kentucky	M,D,O
University of Louisville	M
University of Maryland Eastern Shore	M
University of Minnesota, Twin Cities Campus	M,D,O
University of Missouri–Columbia	M,D,O
University of Nevada, Las Vegas	M,D,O
University of New Hampshire	M
University of North Dakota	M
University of Northern Iowa	M,D
University of North Texas	M,D
University of South Carolina	M
University of Southern Maine	M
University of Southern Mississippi	M
University of South Florida	M,D,O
The University of Texas at Tyler	M
University of Toledo	M,D,O
University of West Florida	M
University of Wisconsin–Madison	M,D
University of Wisconsin–Platteville	M
University of Wisconsin–Stout	M,O
Utah State University	M
Valdosta State University	M,D,O
Virginia Polytechnic Institute and State University	M,D,O
Virginia State University	M,O
Wayne State College	M
Wayne State University	M,D,O
Western Michigan University	M
Western Washington University	M
Westfield State College	M
West Virginia University	M,D
Wright State University	M

■ **WATER RESOURCES**

Albany State University	M
Colorado State University	M,D
Duke University	M,D
Iowa State University of Science and Technology	M,D
The Johns Hopkins University	M,D
Montclair State University	M,O
Rutgers, The State University of New Jersey, New Brunswick/Piscataway	M,D
South Dakota State University	D
State University of New York College of Environmental Science and Forestry	M,D
The University of Arizona	M,D
University of Florida	M,D
University of Illinois at Chicago	M,D
University of Kansas	M,D
University of Minnesota, Twin Cities Campus	M,D
University of Missouri–Rolla	M,D
University of Nevada, Las Vegas	M
University of New Hampshire	M
University of New Mexico	M
University of Oklahoma	M,D
University of Vermont	M
University of Wisconsin–Madison	M
University of Wyoming	M,D

■ **WATER RESOURCES ENGINEERING**

California Polytechnic State University, San Luis Obispo	M
Cornell University	M,D
Louisiana State University and Agricultural and Mechanical College	M,D
Marquette University	M,D
New Mexico Institute of Mining and Technology	M

Peterson's Graduate Schools in the U.S. 2006

Directory of Graduate and Professional Programs by Field
Water Resources Engineering

Ohio University	M,D
Oregon State University	M,D
The Pennsylvania State University University Park Campus	M,D
Princeton University	M,D
Texas A&M University	M,D
Tufts University	M,D
The University of Arizona	M,D
University of California, Berkeley	M,D
University of California, Los Angeles	M,D
University of Central Florida	M,D,O
University of Colorado at Boulder	M,D
University of Delaware	M,D
University of Maryland, College Park	M,D
The University of Memphis	M,D
University of Missouri–Columbia	M,D
University of Southern California	M
The University of Texas at Austin	M
Utah State University	M,D
Villanova University	M

WESTERN EUROPEAN STUDIES

Boston College	M,D
Brown University	M,D
The Catholic University of America	M
Claremont Graduate University	M,D
Columbia University	M,O
Cornell University	M,D
East Carolina University	M
Georgetown University	M
The George Washington University	M
Indiana University Bloomington	M,D,O
The Johns Hopkins University	M,D,O
New York University	M
University of California, Santa Barbara	M
University of Connecticut	M
University of Nevada, Reno	D

WOMEN'S HEALTH NURSING

Case Western Reserve University	M,D
Columbia University	M,O
Emory University	M
Georgia Southern University	M,O
Georgia State University	M,D
Indiana University–Purdue University Indianapolis	M
Loyola University Chicago	M
Seton Hall University	M
Stony Brook University, State University of New York	M,O
University at Buffalo, The State University of New York	M,D,O
University of Cincinnati	M,D
University of Colorado at Colorado Springs	M
University of Delaware	M,O
University of Minnesota, Twin Cities Campus	M
University of Missouri–Kansas City	M,D
University of Pennsylvania	M
University of South Alabama	M
University of South Carolina	M,O
The University of Texas at El Paso	M
Vanderbilt University	M,D
Virginia Commonwealth University	M,D,O

WOMEN'S STUDIES

Brandeis University	M
Claremont Graduate University	M,D
Clark Atlanta University	M,D
Clark University	D
Cornell University	M,D
DePaul University	O
Duke University	O
Eastern Michigan University	M
Emory University	D,O
Fairleigh Dickinson University, College at Florham	M
Florida Atlantic University	M,O
The George Washington University	M,D,O
Georgia State University	M
Minnesota State University Mankato	M
New College of California	M
The Ohio State University	M,D
Roosevelt University	M
Rutgers, The State University of New Jersey, New Brunswick/Piscataway	M,D
San Diego State University	M
San Francisco State University	M
Shenandoah University	M,D,O
Southern Connecticut State University	M
Stony Brook University, State University of New York	M,O
Syracuse University	O
Texas Woman's University	M
Towson University	M
University at Albany, State University of New York	M
The University of Alabama	M,D
The University of Arizona	M
University of California, Los Angeles	M,D
University of Cincinnati	M,O
The University of Iowa	D
University of Maryland, College Park	M,D
University of Massachusetts Boston	M,D,O
University of Michigan	D,O
University of Missouri–St. Louis	O
The University of North Carolina at Greensboro	M,D,O
University of Northern Iowa	M
University of Pittsburgh	O
University of South Carolina	O
University of South Florida	M
University of Washington	M,D

WRITING

Abilene Christian University	M
American University	M
Antioch University Los Angeles	M,O
Antioch University McGregor	M
Arizona State University	M
Ball State University	M,D
Belmont University	M
Boise State University	M
Boston University	M,D
Bowling Green State University	M
Brooklyn College of the City University of New York	M
Brown University	M
California State University, Chico	M
California State University, Fresno	M
California State University, Long Beach	M
California State University, Sacramento	M
California State University, San Marcos	M
Carnegie Mellon University	M
Central Michigan University	M
Chapman University	M
City College of the City University of New York	M
Claremont Graduate University	M,D
Clemson University	M
Colorado State University	M
Columbia College Chicago	M
Columbia University	M
Cornell University	M,D
DePaul University	M
Eastern Michigan University	M
Eastern Washington University	M
Emerson College	M
Fairleigh Dickinson University, College at Florham	M
Florida International University	M
Florida State University	M,D
George Mason University	M
Georgia College & State University	M
Georgia State University	M,D
Goddard College	M
Hofstra University	M
Hunter College of the City University of New York	M
Illinois State University	M
Indiana University Bloomington	M,D
Indiana University of Pennsylvania	M,D
The Johns Hopkins University	M
Kennesaw State University	M
Kent State University	M,D
Lesley University	M
Lindenwood University	M
Long Island University, Brooklyn Campus	M
Longwood University	M
Louisiana State University and Agricultural and Mechanical College	M,D
Loyola Marymount University	M
Manhattanville College	M
Massachusetts Institute of Technology	M
McNeese State University	M
Miami University	M,D
Michigan State University	M,D
Minnesota State University Mankato	M
Minnesota State University Moorhead	M
National-Louis University	M
National University	M
New College of California	M
New Mexico Highlands University	M
New Mexico State University	M,D
New School University	M
New York University	M
North Carolina State University	M
Northeastern Illinois University	M
Northeastern University	M,D,O
Northern Arizona University	M
Northern Michigan University	M
Northwestern University	M
Oklahoma City University	M
Oklahoma State University	M,D
Old Dominion University	M
The Pennsylvania State University University Park Campus	M,D
Purdue University	M,D
Queens College of the City University of New York	M
Queens University of Charlotte	M
Rivier College	M
Roosevelt University	M
Rowan University	M
Rutgers, The State University of New Jersey, New Brunswick/Piscataway	M
Saint Joseph's University	M
Saint Mary's College of California	M
Saint Xavier University	M,O
Salisbury University	M
San Diego State University	M
San Francisco State University	M
San Jose State University	M,O
Sonoma State University	M
Southern Illinois University Carbondale	M
Spalding University	M
Syracuse University	M,D
Temple University	M
Texas State University-San Marcos	M
Towson University	M
Union Institute & University	M
The University of Akron	M
The University of Alabama	M,D
University of Alaska Anchorage	M
University of Alaska Fairbanks	M
The University of Arizona	M
University of Arkansas	M
University of Arkansas at Little Rock	M
University of Baltimore	M
University of California, Davis	M,D
University of California, Irvine	M
University of California, Riverside	M
University of Central Florida	M,D,O
University of Central Oklahoma	M

Directory of Graduate and Professional Programs by Field
Zoology

Institution	Degree
University of Colorado at Boulder	M,D
University of Houston	M,D
University of Idaho	M
University of Illinois at Chicago	M,D
The University of Iowa	M,D
University of Louisiana at Lafayette	M,D
University of Maryland, College Park	M,D
University of Massachusetts Amherst	M,D
University of Massachusetts Dartmouth	M
The University of Memphis	M,D
University of Michigan	M
University of Mississippi	M
University of Missouri–St. Louis	M
The University of Montana–Missoula	M
University of Nebraska at Kearney	M
University of Nebraska at Omaha	M,O
University of Nevada, Las Vegas	M,D
University of New Hampshire	M,D
University of New Mexico	M
The University of North Carolina at Greensboro	M
The University of North Carolina at Wilmington	M
University of North Florida	M
University of Notre Dame	M
University of Oklahoma	M
University of Oregon	M
University of Pennsylvania	M,D
University of Pittsburgh	M,D
University of San Francisco	M
University of South Carolina	M,D
University of Southern California	M
University of Southern Maine	M
The University of Texas at Austin	M
The University of Texas at El Paso	M
University of Utah	M,D
University of Virginia	M
Utah State University	M
Virginia Commonwealth University	M
Warren Wilson College	M
Washington University in St. Louis	M
Wayne State University	M,D
Western Illinois University	M
Western Kentucky University	M
Western Michigan University	M,D
Westminster College (UT)	M
West Virginia University	M
Wichita State University	M
Wright State University	M

■ ZOOLOGY

Institution	Degree
Auburn University	M,D
Clemson University	M,D
Colorado State University	M,D
Cornell University	M,D
Emporia State University	M
Illinois State University	M,D
Indiana University Bloomington	M,D
Miami University	M,D
Michigan State University	M,D
Montana State University–Bozeman	M,D
North Carolina State University	M,D
North Dakota State University	M,D
Ohio University	M,D
Oklahoma State University	M,D
Oregon State University	M,D
Southern Illinois University Carbondale	M,D
Texas A&M University	M,D
Texas Tech University	M,D
University of Alaska Fairbanks	M,D
University of California, Davis	M
University of Chicago	D
University of Colorado at Boulder	M,D
University of Connecticut	M,D
University of Florida	M,D
University of Hawaii at Manoa	M,D
University of Illinois at Urbana–Champaign	D
University of Maine	M,D
The University of Montana–Missoula	M,D
University of New Hampshire	M,D
University of North Dakota	M,D
University of Oklahoma	M,D
University of South Florida	M,D
University of Washington	D
University of Wisconsin–Madison	M,D
University of Wisconsin–Oshkosh	M
University of Wyoming	M,D
Virginia Polytechnic Institute and State University	M,D
Washington State University	M,D
Western Illinois University	M,O

Profiles of Institutions Offering Graduate and Professional Work

Alabama

■ ALABAMA AGRICULTURAL AND MECHANICAL UNIVERSITY
Huntsville, AL 35811
http://www.aamu.edu/

State-supported, coed, university. CGS member. *Enrollment:* 6,588 graduate, professional, and undergraduate students; 509 full-time matriculated graduate/professional students (378 women), 753 part-time matriculated graduate/professional students (541 women). *Graduate faculty:* 183. *Computer facilities:* 1,000 computers available on campus for general student use. A campuswide network can be accessed from student residence rooms and from off campus. Internet access is available. *Library facilities:* J. F. Drake Learning Resources Center. *Graduate expenses:* Tuition, state resident: full-time $3,250; part-time $370 per credit hour. Tuition, nonresident: full-time $6,490; part-time $740 per credit hour. *General application contact:* Dr. Chandra Reddy, Dean, School of Graduate Studies, 256-372-5266.

School of Graduate Studies
Dr. Chandra Reddy, Dean, School of Graduate Studies

School of Agricultural and Environmental Sciences
Dr. James W. Shuford, Dean
Programs in:
  agribusiness • MS
  agricultural and environmental sciences • MS, MURP, PhD
  animal sciences • MS
  environmental science • MS
  family and consumer sciences • MS
  food science • MS, PhD
  plant and soil science • PhD
  urban and regional planning • MURP

School of Arts and Sciences
Dr. Jerry Shipman, Dean
Programs in:
  arts and sciences • MS, MSW, PhD
  biology • MS
  computer science • MS
  physics • MS, PhD
  social work • MSW

School of Business
Dr. Barbara A. P. Jones, Dean
Programs in:
  business • MBA, MS
  economics and finance • MS
  management and marketing • MBA

School of Education
Dr. John Vickers, Interim Dean
Programs in:
  communicative disorders • M Ed, MS
  early childhood education • M Ed, MS, Ed S
  education • M Ed, Ed S
  elementary and early childhood education • M Ed, MS, Ed S
  elementary education • M Ed, MS, Ed S
  health and physical education • M Ed, MS
  higher administration • MS
  music • MS
  music education • M Ed, MS
  physical education • M Ed, MS
  psychology and counseling • MS, Ed S
  secondary education • M Ed, MS, Ed S
  special education • M Ed, MS

School of Engineering and Technology
Dr. Arthur Bond, Dean
Programs in:
  engineering and technology • M Ed, MS
  industry and education • MS
  trade and industrial education • M Ed

■ ALABAMA STATE UNIVERSITY
Montgomery, AL 36101-0271
http://www.alasu.edu/

State-supported, coed, comprehensive institution. *Enrollment:* 6,024 graduate, professional, and undergraduate students; 217 full-time matriculated graduate/professional students (158 women), 787 part-time matriculated graduate/professional students (612 women). *Graduate faculty:* 72 full-time (31 women), 29 part-time/adjunct (18 women). *Computer facilities:* Computer purchase and lease plans are available. 380 computers available on campus for general student use. A campuswide network can be accessed from off campus. Internet access and online class registration, e-mail are available. *Library facilities:* Levi Watkins Learning Center. *Graduate expenses:* Tuition, state resident: full-time $2,064; part-time $172 per credit. Tuition, nonresident: full-time $4,128; part-time $344 per credit. *General application contact:* Dr. Allen Stewart, Dean of Graduate Studies, 334-229-4275.

School of Graduate Studies
Dr. Allen Stewart, Dean of Graduate Studies

College of Arts and Sciences
Dr. Thelma Ivery, Acting Dean
Programs in:
  arts and sciences • M Ed, MS, Ed S
  biology • M Ed, MS
  biology education • Ed S
  mathematics • M Ed, MS, Ed S

College of Business Administration
Dr. Percy Vaughn, Dean
Programs in:
  accountancy • M Acc
  business administration • M Acc

College of Education
Dr. Pete Macchia, Acting Dean
Programs in:
  biology education • M Ed
  early childhood education • M Ed, Ed S
  education • M Ed, MS, Ed D, Ed S
  educational administration • M Ed, Ed D, Ed S
  educational leadership, policy and law • Ed D
  elementary education • M Ed, Ed S
  English education/language arts • M Ed
  general counseling • MS, Ed S
  guidance and counseling • M Ed, MS, Ed S
  health and physical education • M Ed
  health education • M Ed
  history education • M Ed
  library educational media • M Ed, Ed S
  mathematics education • M Ed
  physical education • M Ed, Ed S
  school counseling • M Ed, Ed S
  secondary education • M Ed, Ed S
  social sciences • Ed S
  special education • M Ed

College of Health Sciences
Dr. Denise Chapman, Dean
Programs in:
  health sciences • MS
  physical therapy • MS

School of Music
Dr. Horace Lamar, Head
Programs in:
  music • MME
  music education • MME

■ AUBURN UNIVERSITY
Auburn University, AL 36849
http://www.auburn.edu/

State-supported, coed, university. CGS member. *Enrollment:* 23,152 graduate, professional, and undergraduate students; 2,210 full-time matriculated graduate/professional students (1,165 women), 1,463 part-time matriculated graduate/professional students (664 women). *Graduate faculty:* 875 full-time (201 women), 6 part-time/adjunct (1 woman).

Alabama

Computer facilities: 600 computers available on campus for general student use. A campuswide network can be accessed from student residence rooms and from off campus. Online class registration is available. *Library facilities:* R. B. Draughon Library plus 2 others. *Graduate expenses:* Tuition, state resident: part-time $175 per credit hour. Tuition, nonresident: part-time $525 per credit hour. *General application contact:* Dr. Stephen L. McFarland, Interim Dean of the Graduate School, 334-844-4700.

Find an in-depth description at www.petersons.com/gradchannel.

College of Veterinary Medicine
Dr. Timothy R. Boosinger, Dean
Program in:
veterinary medicine • DVM, MS, PhD

Graduate Programs in Veterinary Medicine
Programs in:
anatomy, physiology and pharmacology • MS
biomedical sciences • MS, PhD
clinical sciences • MS
large animal surgery and medicine • MS
pathobiology • MS
radiology • MS
small animal surgery and medicine • MS

Graduate School
Dr. Stephen McFarland, Interim Dean
Programs in:
integrated textile and apparel sciences • MS, PhD
sociology • MA, MS
textile science • MS

College of Agriculture
Dr. John W. Jensen, Interim Dean
Programs in:
agricultural economics and rural sociology • M Ag, MS, PhD
agriculture • M Ag, M Aq, MS, PhD
agronomy and soils • M Ag, MS, PhD
animal sciences • M Ag, MS, PhD
entomology • M Ag, MS, PhD
fisheries and allied aquacultures • M Aq, MS, PhD
horticulture • M Ag, MS, PhD
plant pathology • M Ag, MS, PhD
poultry science • M Ag, MS, PhD

College of Architecture, Design, and Construction
Dan D. Bennett, Dean
Programs in:
architecture, design, and construction • MBS, MCP, MID, MLA
building science • MBS
community planning • MCP
construction management • MBS
industrial design • MID
landscape architecture • MLA

College of Business
Dr. John S. Jahera, Interim Dean
Programs in:
accountancy • M Acc
business • M Acc, MBA, MMIS, MS, PhD
business administration • MBA
economics • MS, PhD
finance • MS
human relations management • PhD
management • MS
management information systems • MMIS, PhD

College of Education
Dr. Frances Kochan, Interim Dean
Programs in:
adult education • M Ed, MS, Ed D
business education • M Ed, MS, PhD
community agency counseling • M Ed, MS, Ed D, PhD, Ed S
counseling psychology • PhD
counselor education • Ed D, PhD
curriculum and instruction • M Ed, MS, Ed D, Ed S
curriculum supervision • M Ed, MS, Ed D, Ed S
early childhood education • M Ed, MS, PhD, Ed S
education • M Ed, MS, Ed D, PhD, Ed S
educational psychology • PhD
elementary education • M Ed, MS, PhD, Ed S
foreign languages • M Ed, MS
health and human performance • M Ed, MS, Ed D, PhD, Ed S
higher education administration • M Ed, MS, Ed D, Ed S
media instructional design • MS
media specialist • M Ed
music education • M Ed, MS, PhD, Ed S
postsecondary education • PhD
reading education • PhD, Ed S
rehabilitation and special education • M Ed, MS, PhD, Ed S
school administration • M Ed, MS, Ed D, Ed S
school counseling • M Ed, MS, Ed D, PhD, Ed S
school psychometry • M Ed, MS, Ed D, PhD, Ed S
secondary education • M Ed, MS, PhD, Ed S

College of Engineering
Dr. Larry Benefield, Dean
Programs in:
aerospace engineering • MAE, MS, PhD
chemical engineering • M Ch E, MS, PhD
computer science and software engineering • MS, MSWE, PhD
construction engineering and management • MCE, MS, PhD
electrical and computer engineering • MEE, MS, PhD
engineering • M Ch E, M Mtl E, MAE, MCE, MEE, MIE, MME, MS, MSWE, PhD
environmental engineering • MCE, MS, PhD
geotechnical/materials engineering • MCE, MS, PhD
hydraulics/hydrology • MCE, MS, PhD
industrial and systems engineering • MIE, MS, PhD
materials engineering • M Mtl E, MS, PhD
mechanical engineering • MME, MS, PhD
structural engineering • MCE, MS, PhD
transportation engineering • MCE, MS, PhD

College of Human Sciences
Dr. June Henton, Dean
Programs in:
apparel and textiles • MS
human development and family studies • MS, PhD
human sciences • MS, PhD
nutrition and food science • MS, PhD

College of Liberal Arts
Dr. Rebekah Pindzola, Interim Dean
Programs in:
art • MFA, PhD
audiology • MCD, MS
communication • MA, MSC
English • MA, PhD
French • MA, MFS
history • MA, PhD
liberal arts • MA, MCD, MFA, MFS, MHS, MM, MPA, MS, MSC, PhD
mass communications • MA, MSC
music • MM
psychology • MS, PhD
public administration • MPA, PhD
Spanish • MA, MHS
speech pathology • MCD, MS

College of Sciences and Mathematics
Dr. Stewart W. Schneller, Dean
Programs in:
botany • MS, PhD
chemistry • MS, PhD
discrete and statistical sciences • M Prob S, MAM, MS, PhD
geology and geography • MS
mathematics • MAM, MS, PhD
microbiology • MS, PhD
physics • MS, PhD
sciences and mathematics • M Prob S, MAM, MS, PhD
zoology • MS, PhD

Alabama

Auburn University (continued)
School of Forestry and Wildlife Sciences
Richard W. Brinker, Dean
Program in:
forestry and wildlife sciences • MF, MS, PhD

School of Pharmacy
Dr. R. Lee Evans, Dean
Program in:
pharmacy • Pharm D, MS, PhD

■ AUBURN UNIVERSITY MONTGOMERY
Montgomery, AL 36124-4023
http://www.aum.edu/

State-supported, coed, comprehensive institution. *Enrollment:* 5,298 graduate, professional, and undergraduate students; 198 full-time matriculated graduate/professional students (134 women), 608 part-time matriculated graduate/professional students (442 women). *Graduate faculty:* 135 full-time (48 women), 32 part-time/adjunct (15 women). *Computer facilities:* 285 computers available on campus for general student use. A campuswide network can be accessed from student residence rooms and from off campus. Internet access and online class registration are available. *Library facilities:* Auburn University Montgomery Library. *Graduate expenses:* Tuition, state resident: full-time $3,744; part-time $156 per credit hour. Tuition, nonresident: full-time $11,232; part-time $468 per credit hour. *General application contact:* Michele M. Moore, Associate Director of Enrollment Services, 334-244-3614.

School of Business
Dr. Jane Goodson, Dean
Program in:
business • MBA

School of Education
Dr. Janet S. Warren, Dean
Programs in:
counseling • M Ed, Ed S
early childhood education • M Ed, Ed S
education • M Ed, Ed S
education administration • M Ed, Ed S
elementary education • M Ed, Ed S
physical education • M Ed
reading education • M Ed, Ed S
secondary education • M Ed, Ed S
special education • M Ed, Ed S

School of Liberal Arts
Dr. Larry C. Mullins, Dean
Program in:
liberal arts • MLA

School of Sciences
Dr. Bradley Moody, Interim Dean
Programs in:
justice and public safety • MSJPS
political science • MPS
psychology • MSPG
public administration • MPA, PhD
sciences • MPA, MPS, MSJPS, MSPG, PhD

■ JACKSONVILLE STATE UNIVERSITY
Jacksonville, AL 36265-1602
http://www.jsu.edu/

State-supported, coed, comprehensive institution. *Enrollment:* 9,031 graduate, professional, and undergraduate students; 484 full-time matriculated graduate/professional students (312 women), 1,258 part-time matriculated graduate/professional students (846 women). *Graduate faculty:* 157 full-time (48 women). *Computer facilities:* 330 computers available on campus for general student use. A campuswide network can be accessed from student residence rooms and from off campus. *Library facilities:* Houston Cole Library. *Graduate expenses:* Tuition, state resident: full-time $4,040; part-time $202 per credit hour. Tuition, nonresident: full-time $8,080; part-time $404 per credit hour. One-time fee: $20 part-time. *General application contact:* Dr. William D. Carr, Dean of the College of Graduate Studies and Continuing Education, 256-782-5329.

College of Graduate Studies and Continuing Education
Dr. William D. Carr, Dean

College of Arts and Sciences
Dr. Earl Wade, Dean
Programs in:
arts and sciences • MA, MPA, MS
biology • MS
computer systems and software design • MS
criminal justice • MS
emergency management • MS
English • MA
history • MA
mathematics • MS
music • MA
political science • MPA
psychology • MS

College of Commerce and Business Administration
Dr. William Fielding, Dean
Programs in:
commerce and business administration • MBA, MPA
public administration • MPA

College of Education
Dr. Cynthia Harper, Dean
Programs in:
early childhood education • MS Ed
education • MS, MS Ed, Ed S
educational administration • MS Ed, Ed S
elementary education • MS Ed
guidance and counseling • MS
health and physical education • MS Ed
instructional media • MS Ed
reading specialist • MS Ed
secondary education • MS Ed
special education • MS Ed

College of Nursing
Prof. Beth Hembree, Director of Graduate Studies
Program in:
nursing • MSN

■ SAMFORD UNIVERSITY
Birmingham, AL 35229-0002

Independent-religious, coed, university. *Enrollment:* 4,440 graduate, professional, and undergraduate students; 1,223 full-time matriculated graduate/professional students (607 women), 313 part-time matriculated graduate/professional students (196 women). *Graduate faculty:* 119 full-time (41 women), 38 part-time/adjunct (12 women). *Computer facilities:* Computer purchase and lease plans are available. 350 computers available on campus for general student use. A campuswide network can be accessed from student residence rooms. Internet access is available. *Library facilities:* Samford University Library plus 3 others. *Graduate expenses:* Tuition: part-time $762 per credit. *General application contact:* Dr. Phil Kimrey, Dean of Admissions and Financial Aid, 205-726-2871.

Beeson School of Divinity
Dr. Timothy George, Dean
Program in:
divinity • M Div, MTS, D Min

Cumberland School of Law
John L. Carroll, Dean
Program in:
law • JD, MCL

Howard College of Arts and Sciences
Dr. David W. Chapman, Dean
Program in:
arts and sciences • MSEM

Ida V. Moffett School of Nursing
Dr. Nena F. Sanders, Dean
Program in:
nursing • MSN

Alabama

McWhorter School of Pharmacy
Dr. Joe Dean, Dean
Program in:
  pharmacy • Pharm D

School of Business
Dr. Marlene M. Reed, Acting Dean
Program in:
  business • M Acc, MBA

School of Education
Dr. Ruth Ash, Dean
Programs in:
  early childhood education • MS Ed, Ed S
  early childhood/elementary education • MS Ed
  education • MS Ed, Ed D, Ed S
  educational administration • MS Ed, Ed D, Ed S
  elementary education • MS Ed, Ed S

School of Performing Arts
Dr. Milburn Price, Dean
Programs in:
  church music • MM
  music education • MME

■ **SPRING HILL COLLEGE**
Mobile, AL 36608-1791
http://www.shc.edu/

Independent-religious, coed, comprehensive institution. *Enrollment:* 1,479 graduate, professional, and undergraduate students; 19 full-time matriculated graduate/professional students (10 women), 201 part-time matriculated graduate/professional students (129 women). *Graduate faculty:* 18 full-time (5 women), 11 part-time/adjunct (4 women). *Computer facilities:* 141 computers available on campus for general student use. A campuswide network can be accessed from student residence rooms and from off campus. Internet access is available. *Library facilities:* Thomas Byrne Memorial Library. *Graduate expenses:* Tuition: part-time $215 per credit hour. Part-time tuition and fees vary according to program. *General application contact:* Joyce Genz, Dean of Life Long Learning and Director of Graduate Programs, 251-380-3094.

Graduate Programs
Joyce Genz, Dean of Life Long Learning and Director of Graduate Programs
Programs in:
  business administration • MBA
  early childhood education • MAT, MS Ed
  elementary education • MAT, MS Ed
  liberal arts • MLA
  secondary education • MAT, MS Ed
  theology • MA, MPS, MTS

■ **TROY UNIVERSITY**
Troy, AL 36082
http://www.troy.edu/

State-supported, coed, comprehensive institution. *Computer facilities:* 487 computers available on campus for general student use. A campuswide network can be accessed from student residence rooms and from off campus. Internet access is available. *Library facilities:* Wallace Library. *General application contact:* Director of Graduate Admissions, 334-670-3178.

Graduate School

College of Arts and Sciences
Programs in:
  administration of criminal justice • MS
  arts and sciences • MS
  corrections • MS
  environmental analysis and management • MS
  international relations • MS
  police administration • MS
  public administration • MS

College of Health and Human Services
Programs in:
  health and human services • MS
  nursing • MS

School of Education
Programs in:
  counseling and human development • MS
  counselor education • MS
  early childhood education • MS, Ed S
  education • MS, Ed S
  educational leadership/administration • MS
  elementary education • MS, Ed S
  emotional conflict • MS
  foundations of education • MS
  guidance services • MS
  learning disabilities • MS
  mental retardation • MS
  mild learning handicapped • MS, Ed S
  N–12 education • MS, Ed S
  secondary education • MS, Ed S

University College
Programs in:
  business administration • MBA
  management • MS
  personnel management • MS

■ **TROY UNIVERSITY DOTHAN**
Dothan, AL 36303
http://www.tsud.edu/

State-supported, coed, comprehensive institution. *Enrollment:* 1,899 graduate, professional, and undergraduate students; 72 full-time matriculated graduate/professional students (61 women), 246 part-time matriculated graduate/professional students (191 women) *Graduate faculty:* 59 full-time (19 women), 12 part-time/adjunct (6 women). *Computer facilities:* 120 computers available on campus for general student use. A campuswide network can be accessed. Internet access is available. *Library facilities:* Troy University Dothan Library. *Graduate expenses:* Tuition, state resident: part-time $161 per credit hour. Tuition, nonresident: part-time $322 per credit hour. *General application contact:* Reta Cordell, Director of Admissions and Records, 334-983-6556 Ext. 228.

Graduate School
Dr. Barbara Alford, Executive Vice President

College of Arts and Sciences
Dr. Alan Belsches, Dean
Programs in:
  arts and sciences • MS
  history and political sciences • MS

College of Business Administration
Dr. Adair Gilbert, Dean
Programs in:
  accounting • MBA, MS
  business administration • MBA, MS
  business education • MS
  business law • MS
  computer information systems • MS
  general business • MBA
  human resource management • MBA, MS

College of Education
Dr. Sandra L. Jones, Dean
Programs in:
  counseling and psychology • MS, Ed S
  curriculum and instruction • MS, Ed S
  leadership, foundations, and technology • MS, Ed S
  secondary education • MS Ed

■ **TROY UNIVERSITY MONTGOMERY**
Montgomery, AL 36103-4419
http://www.tsum.edu/

State-supported, coed, comprehensive institution. *Enrollment:* 3,758 graduate, professional, and undergraduate students; 285 full-time matriculated graduate/professional students (184 women), 294 part-time matriculated graduate/professional students (216 women). *Computer facilities:* 248 computers available on campus for general student use. A campuswide network can be accessed from off campus. Internet access and online class registration are available. *Library facilities:* Rosa L. Parks Library

Peterson's Graduate Schools in the U.S. 2006

Alabama

Troy University Montgomery (continued) and Museum. *Graduate expenses:* Tuition, state resident: part-time $161 per semester hour. Tuition, nonresident: part-time $322 per semester hour. Required fees: $35 per semester. *General application contact:* Dr. Ester Lee, Dean of Graduate Division, 334-241-9581.

Graduate Programs
Dr. Ester Lee, Dean of Graduate Division

College of Business
Dr. Anthony Rhee, Dean
Programs in:
  business administration • MBA
  computer and information science • MS
  human resources management • MS
  management • MS
  public administration • MS

College of Education
Dr. Helen Kitchens, Interim Dean
Programs in:
  adult education • MS
  agency counseling • Ed S
  community and agency counseling • MS
  counseling • MS, Certificate, Ed S
  counseling and human development • MS, Ed S
  elementary education • MS
  general education administration • Ed S
  personnel and human services counseling • MS
  school counseling • MS, Ed S
  school psychometry • Certificate
  teaching • MA

■ TUSKEGEE UNIVERSITY
Tuskegee, AL 36088
http://www.tuskegee.edu/

Independent, coed, comprehensive institution. *Enrollment:* 3,176 graduate, professional, and undergraduate students; 335 full-time matriculated graduate/professional students (207 women), 37 part-time matriculated graduate/professional students (14 women). *Graduate faculty:* 112 full-time (17 women), 11 part-time/adjunct (5 women). *Computer facilities:* 1,000 computers available on campus for general student use. A campuswide network can be accessed from student residence rooms and from off campus. Internet access and online class registration are available. *Library facilities:* Hollis B. Frissell Library plus 3 others. *Graduate expenses:* Tuition: full-time $11,060; part-time $655 per credit hour. Required fees: $250. Tuition and fees vary according to course load. *General application contact:* William E. Mathis, Director of Admissions, 334-727-8580.

Graduate Programs
Dr. William L. Lester, Provost

College of Agricultural, Environmental and Natural Sciences
Dr. Walter A. Hill, Dean
Programs in:
  agricultural and resource economics • MS
  agricultural, environmental and natural sciences • MS
  animal and poultry sciences • MS
  biology • MS
  chemistry • MS
  environmental sciences • MS
  food and nutritional sciences • MS
  plant and soil sciences • MS

College of Engineering, Architecture and Physical Sciences
Dr. Legand L. Burge, Acting Dean
Programs in:
  electrical engineering • MSEE
  engineering, architecture and physical sciences • MSEE, MSME, PhD
  material science engineering • PhD
  mechanical engineering • MSME

College of Liberal Arts and Education
Dr. Benjamin Benford, Interim Dean
Programs in:
  general science education • M Ed
  liberal arts and education • M Ed

College of Veterinary Medicine and Allied Health
Dr. Alfonza Atkinson, Dean
Programs in:
  veterinary medicine • DVM, MS
  veterinary medicine and allied health • DVM, MS

■ THE UNIVERSITY OF ALABAMA
Tuscaloosa, AL 35487
http://www.ua.edu/

State-supported, coed, university. CGS member. *Enrollment:* 20,291 graduate, professional, and undergraduate students; 2,745 full-time matriculated graduate/professional students (1,390 women), 1,330 part-time matriculated graduate/professional students (824 women). *Graduate faculty:* 638 full-time (185 women), 11 part-time/adjunct (5 women). *Computer facilities:* 2,000 computers available on campus for general student use. A campuswide network can be accessed from student residence rooms and from off campus. Internet access is available. *Library facilities:* Amelia Gayle Gorgas Library plus 8 others. *Graduate expenses:* Tuition, state resident: full-time $4,134; part-time $230 per credit hour. Tuition, nonresident: full-time $11,294; part-time $627 per credit hour. Part-time tuition and fees vary according to course load. *General application contact:* Louise F. Labosier, Admissions Officer, 205-348-5921.

Find an in-depth description at www.petersons.com/gradchannel.

Graduate School
Dr. Ronald W. Rogers, Dean

Capstone College of Nursing
Dr. Sara E. Barger, Dean
Program in:
  nursing • MSN

College of Arts and Sciences
Dr. Robert F. Olin, Dean
Programs in:
  acting • MFA
  administration • DMA
  American studies • MA
  anthropology • PhD
  applied linguistics • PhD
  applied mathematics • PhD
  art history • MA
  arts and sciences • MA, MATESOL, MFA, MM, MPA, MS, DMA, Ed D, PhD, Certificate, Ed S
  audiology • MS
  biological sciences • MS, PhD
  chemistry • MS, PhD
  clinical psychology • PhD
  cognitive psychology • PhD
  composition • DMA
  composition, rhetoric and English studies • PhD
  costume design • MFA
  creative writing • MFA
  criminal justice • MS
  directing • MFA
  English • MA, PhD
  French • MA, PhD
  French and Spanish • PhD
  geography • MS
  geological sciences • MS, PhD
  German • MA
  history • MA, PhD
  Latin American studies • MA, Certificate
  literature • MA
  mathematics • MA
  music education • Ed D, Ed S
  musicology • MM
  performance • MM, DMA
  physics • MS, PhD
  political science • MA, MPA, PhD
  public administration • MPA
  pure mathematics • PhD
  Renaissance studies • MA
  Romance languages • MA, PhD
  scene design/technical production • MFA
  Spanish • MA, PhD
  speech-language pathology • MS

Alabama

stage management • MFA
studio art • MA, MFA
teaching English as a second language • MATESOL
theatre • MFA
theatre management/administration • MFA
theory and criticism • MA
women's studies • MA, PhD

College of Communication and Information Sciences
Dr. Yorgo Pasadeos, Acting Associate Dean for Graduate Studies and Research
Programs in:
advertising and public relations • MA
book arts • MFA
communication and information sciences • MA, MFA, MLIS, PhD
communication studies • MA
journalism • MA
library and information studies • MLIS, PhD
telecommunication and film • MA

College of Education
Ross Palmer, Dean
Programs in:
education • MA, Ed D, PhD, Ed S
educational leadership, policy, and technology studies • MA, Ed D
educational studies in psychology, research methodology, and counseling • MA, Ed D, PhD, Ed S
elementary education • MA, Ed D, PhD, Ed S
kinesiology • MA, PhD
music education • MA, Ed D, PhD, Ed S
secondary curriculum, teaching and learning • MA, Ed D, PhD, Ed S
teacher education • MA, Ed D, PhD, Ed S

College of Engineering
Dr. Timothy J. Greene, Dean
Programs in:
aerospace engineering • MAE
chemical engineering • MS Ch E, PhD
civil engineering • MSCE, PhD
computer science • MSCS, PhD
electrical engineering • MSEE, PhD
engineering • MAE, MES, MS, MS Ch E, MS Met E, MSCE, MSCS, MSE, MSEE, MSIE, MSME, PhD
engineering science and mechanics • MES
engineering science and mechanics • PhD
environmental engineering • MS
industrial engineering • MSE, MSIE
materials science • PhD
mechanical engineering • MSME, PhD
metallurgical and materials engineering • MS Met E, PhD

College of Human Environmental Sciences
Dr. Milla D. Boschung, Interim Dean
Programs in:
clothing, textiles, and interior design • MSHES
consumer sciences • MSHES
health education and promotion • PhD
health studies • MA
human development and family studies • MSHES
human environmental sciences • MA, MSHES, PhD
human nutrition and hospitality management • MSHES

Culverhouse College of Commerce and Business Administration
Dr. Joseph Barry Mason, Dean
Programs in:
accounting • M Acc, PhD
applied statistics • MS, PhD
banking and finance • MA, MSC, PhD
business • Exec MBA, M Acc, MA, MBA, MS, MSC, MTA, PhD
economics • MA, MSC, PhD
management science • MA, MBA, MSC, PhD
marketing • MA, PhD
marketing and management • MSC
tax accounting • MTA

School of Social Work
Dr. James P. Adams, Dean
Program in:
social work • MSW, PhD

School of Law
Kenneth C. Randall, Dean
Program in:
law • JD, LL M, LL M in Tax

■ THE UNIVERSITY OF ALABAMA AT BIRMINGHAM
Birmingham, AL 35294

State-supported, coed, university. CGS member. *Enrollment:* 16,357 graduate, professional, and undergraduate students; 3,103 full-time matriculated graduate/professional students (1,606 women), 1,509 part-time matriculated graduate/professional students (986 women). *Graduate faculty:* 1,155. *Computer facilities:* 400 computers available on campus for general student use. A campuswide network can be accessed from off campus. Internet access and online class registration are available. *Library facilities:* Mervyn Sterne Library plus 1 other. *Graduate expenses:* Tuition, state resident: full-time $4,142; part-time $141 per credit hour. Tuition, nonresident: full-time $9,230; part-time $353 per credit hour. Required fees: $4 per credit hour. *General application contact:* Julie Bryant, Director of Graduate Admissions, 205-934-8227.

Find an in-depth description at www.petersons.com/gradchannel.

Graduate Programs in Joint Health Sciences
Dr. William B. Deal, Vice President/Dean, School of Medicine
Programs in:
basic medical sciences • MSBMS
biochemistry • PhD
biochemistry and molecular genetics • PhD
biophysical sciences • PhD
cell biology • PhD
cellular and molecular biology • PhD
genetics • PhD
integrative biomedical sciences • PhD
microbiology • PhD
neurobiology • PhD
neuroscience • PhD
pathology • PhD
pharmacology • PhD
pharmacology and toxicology • PhD
physiology and biophysics • PhD
toxicology • PhD

School of Arts and Humanities
Bert Brouwer, Dean
Programs in:
art history • MA
arts and humanities • MA
communication studies • MA
English • MA

School of Business
Dr. Robert E. Holmes, Dean
Program in:
business • M Acct, MBA, PhD

School of Dentistry
Dr. Huw F. Thomas, Dean
Programs in:
dentistry • DMD, MS, MSBMS, PhD
dentistry and oral biology • MS

School of Education
Dr. Michael J. Froning, Dean
Programs in:
agency counseling • MA
arts education • MA Ed
counseling • MA, MA Ed
early childhood education • MA Ed, PhD
education • Ed S
educational leadership • MA Ed, Ed D, PhD, Ed S
elementary education • MA Ed
health education • MA Ed
health education/health promotion • PhD
high school education • MA Ed
marriage and family counseling • MA
physical education • MA Ed
rehabilitation counseling • MA

Alabama

The University of Alabama at Birmingham (continued)
  school counseling • MA
  school psychology • MA Ed
  special education • MA Ed

School of Engineering
Dr. Linda C. Lucas, Dean
Programs in:
  biomedical engineering • MSBME, PhD
  civil and environmental engineering • MSCE, PhD
  electrical and computer engineering • MSEE, PhD
  engineering • MS Mt E, MSBME, MSCE, MSEE, MSME, PhD
  materials engineering • MS Mt E, PhD
  materials science • PhD
  mechanical engineering • MSME, PhD

School of Health Related Professions
Dr. Harold P. Jones, Dean
Programs in:
  administration-health services • PhD
  clinical laboratory science • MS
  clinical nutrition • MS
  clinical nutrition and dietetics • MS, Certificate
  dietetic internship • Certificate
  health administration • MSHA
  health informatics • MS
  health related professions • MNA, MS, MSHA, DPT, Dr Sc PT, PhD, Certificate
  nurse anesthesia • MNA
  nutrition sciences • PhD
  occupational therapy • MS
  physical therapy • MS, DPT, Dr Sc PT

School of Medicine
Dr. William B. Deal, Vice President/Dean, School of Medicine
Program in:
  medicine • MD, MSBMS, PhD

School of Natural Sciences and Mathematics
Dr. Lowell E. Wenger, Dean
Programs in:
  applied mathematics • PhD
  biology • MS, PhD
  chemistry • MS, PhD
  computer and information sciences • MS, PhD
  mathematics • MS
  natural sciences and mathematics • MS, PhD
  physics • MS, PhD

School of Nursing
Dr. Rachel Z. Booth, Dean
Program in:
  nursing • MSN, PhD

School of Optometry
Dr. John F. Amos, Dean
Programs in:
  optometry • OD, MS, PhD
  vision science • MS, PhD

School of Public Health
Dr. Max Michael, Dean
Programs in:
  biomathematics • MS, PhD
  biostatistics • MS, PhD
  environmental health • PhD
  environmental toxicology • PhD
  epidemiology • PhD
  health care organization and policy • MPH, MSPH
  health education promotion • PhD
  industrial hygiene • PhD
  maternal and child health • MSPH
  public health • MPH, MS, MSPH, PhD

School of Social and Behavioral Sciences
Dr. Tennant S. McWilliams, Dean
Programs in:
  anthropology • MA
  behavioral neuroscience • PhD
  clinical psychology • PhD
  criminal justice • MSCJ
  developmental psychology • PhD
  forensic science • MSFS
  history • MA
  medical psychology • PhD
  medical sociology • PhD
  psychology • MA, PhD
  public administration • MPA
  social and behavioral sciences • MA, MPA, MSCJ, MSFS, PhD
  sociology • MA

■ THE UNIVERSITY OF ALABAMA IN HUNTSVILLE
Huntsville, AL 35899
http://www.uah.edu/

State-supported, coed, university. CGS member. *Enrollment:* 7,051 graduate, professional, and undergraduate students; 628 full-time matriculated graduate/professional students (274 women), 813 part-time matriculated graduate/professional students (323 women). *Graduate faculty:* 204 full-time (56 women), 43 part-time/adjunct (10 women). *Computer facilities:* 960 computers available on campus for general student use. A campuswide network can be accessed from student residence rooms and from off campus. Internet access and online class registration are available. *Library facilities:* University of Alabama in Huntsville Library. *Graduate expenses:* Tuition, state resident: full-time $5,168; part-time $211 per hour. Tuition, nonresident: full-time $10,620; part-time $447 per hour. Tuition and fees vary according to course load. *General application contact:* Dr. Gordon Emslie, Chair, 256-824-6002.

School of Graduate Studies
Dr. Gordon Emslie, Chair
Program in:
  optical science and engineering • PhD

College of Administrative Science
Dr. C. David Billings, Dean
Programs in:
  accounting • M Acc, Certificate
  administrative science • M Acc, MS, MSM, MSMIS, Certificate
  human resource management • Certificate
  management • MS, MSM
  management information systems • MSMIS

College of Engineering
Dr. Jorge Aunon, Dean
Programs in:
  aerospace engineering • MSE
  biotechnology science and engineering • PhD
  chemical engineering • MSE
  civil and environmental engineering • MSE, PhD
  computer engineering • PhD
  electrical and computer engineering • MSE
  electrical engineering • PhD
  engineering • MSE, MSOR, PhD
  industrial engineering • MSE, PhD
  mechanical engineering • MSE, PhD
  operations research • MSOR
  optical science and engineering • PhD
  software engineering • MSE

College of Liberal Arts
Dr. Sue Kirkpatrick, Dean
Programs in:
  English • MA
  history • MA
  liberal arts • MA, Certificate
  psychology • MA
  public affairs • MA
  teaching of English to speakers of other languages • Certificate
  technical communications • Certificate

College of Nursing
Dr. Fay Raines, Dean
Programs in:
  family nurse practitioner • Certificate
  nursing • MSN

College of Science
Dr. Jack Fix, Dean
Programs in:
  applied mathematics • PhD
  atmospheric and environmental science • MS, PhD
  biological sciences • MS

Alabama

chemistry • MS
computer science • MS, PhD
materials science • MS, PhD
mathematics • MA, MS
physics • MS, PhD
science • MA, MS, PhD, Certificate
software engineering • Certificate

■ UNIVERSITY OF MOBILE
Mobile, AL 36663-0220
http://www.umobile.edu/

Independent-religious, coed, comprehensive institution. *Enrollment:* 1,854 graduate, professional, and undergraduate students; 53 full-time matriculated graduate/professional students (39 women), 137 part-time matriculated graduate/professional students (110 women). *Graduate faculty:* 28 full-time (15 women), 36 part-time/adjunct (17 women). *Computer facilities:* 110 computers available on campus for general student use. A campuswide network can be accessed from off campus. Internet access is available. *Library facilities:* J. L. Bedsole Library plus 2 others. *Graduate expenses:* Tuition: full-time $4,086; part-time $27 per semester hour. Required fees: $130; $65 per semester. *General application contact:* Dr. Kaye F. Brown, Dean, Graduate Programs and Director of Institutional Effectiveness, 251-442-2289.

Graduate Programs
Dr. Kaye F. Brown, Dean
Programs in:
   biblical/theological studies • MA
   business administration • MBA
   marriage and family counseling • MA
   nursing • MSN
   religious studies • MA
   teacher education • MA

■ UNIVERSITY OF MONTEVALLO
Montevallo, AL 35115
http://www.montevallo.edu/

State-supported, coed, comprehensive institution. *Computer facilities:* 250 computers available on campus for general student use. A campuswide network can be accessed from student residence rooms and from off campus. Internet access and online class registration are available. *Library facilities:* Carmichael Library. *General application contact:* Coordinator for Graduate Studies, 205-665-6350.

College of Arts and Sciences
Programs in:
   arts and sciences • MA, MS
   English • MA
   speech pathology and audiology • MS

College of Education
Programs in:
   early childhood education • M Ed
   education • M Ed, Ed S
   educational administration • M Ed, Ed S
   elementary education • M Ed
   guidance and counseling • M Ed
   secondary education • M Ed
   teacher leader • Ed S

College of Fine Arts
Programs in:
   fine arts • MM
   music • MM

■ UNIVERSITY OF NORTH ALABAMA
Florence, AL 35632-0001
http://www.una.edu/

State-supported, coed, comprehensive institution. *Enrollment:* 5,630 graduate, professional, and undergraduate students; 99 full-time matriculated graduate/professional students (55 women), 437 part-time matriculated graduate/professional students (303 women). *Graduate faculty:* 58 part-time/adjunct (22 women). *Computer facilities:* 750 computers available on campus for general student use. A campuswide network can be accessed from student residence rooms and from off campus. Internet access and online class registration are available. *Library facilities:* Collier Library. *Graduate expenses:* Tuition, state resident: full-time $2,664; part-time $148 per credit hour. Tuition, nonresident: full-time $5,328; part-time $296 per credit hour. Required fees: $442. *General application contact:* Kim Mauldin, Director of Admissions, 256-765-4608.

College of Arts and Sciences
Dr. Michael Moeller, Dean
Programs in:
   arts and sciences • MAEN, MSCJ
   criminal justice • MSCJ
   English • MAEN

College of Business
Dr. Kerry Gatlin, Dean
Program in:
   business • MBA

College of Education
Dr. John Wakefield, Interim Dean
Programs in:
   counseling • MA, MA Ed
   education • MA, MA Ed, Ed S
   education leadership • Ed S
   elementary education • MA Ed, Ed S
   learning disabilities • MA Ed
   mentally retarded • MA Ed
   mild learning handicapped • MA Ed
   non-school-based counseling • MA
   non-school-based teaching • MA
   principalship • MA Ed
   principalship, superintendency, and supervision of instruction • MA Ed
   secondary education • MA Ed
   special education • MA Ed
   superintendency • MA Ed
   supervision of instruction • MA Ed

■ UNIVERSITY OF SOUTH ALABAMA
Mobile, AL 36688-0002

State-supported, coed, university. CGS member. *Computer facilities:* 500 computers available on campus for general student use. A campuswide network can be accessed from student residence rooms and from off campus. Internet access and online class registration are available. *Library facilities:* University Library plus 1 other. *General application contact:* Associate Vice President for Research and Dean of the Graduate School, 334-460-6310.

Find an in-depth description at www.petersons.com/gradchannel.

College of Medicine
Programs in:
   biochemistry and molecular biology • PhD
   cellular biology and neuroscience • PhD
   medicine • MD, PhD
   microbiology and immunology • PhD
   pharmacology • PhD
   physiology • PhD

Graduate School

College of Allied Health Professions
Programs in:
   allied health professions • MHS, MPT, MS, PhD
   communication sciences and disorders • PhD
   physical therapy • MPT
   physician assistant studies • MHS
   speech and hearing sciences • MS

College of Arts and Sciences
Programs in:
   arts and sciences • MA, MPA, MS, PhD, Certificate
   biological sciences • MS
   communication arts • MA
   English • MA
   gerontology • Certificate
   history • MA
   marine sciences • MS, PhD
   mathematics • MS
   psychology • MS
   public administration • MPA
   sociology • MA

Peterson's Graduate Schools in the U.S. 2006

Alabama

University of South Alabama (continued)
College of Education
Programs in:
art/music education • M Ed
business education • M Ed
counseling • M Ed, MS, Ed S
early childhood education • M Ed, Ed S
education • M Ed, MS, PhD, Ed S
education of the emotionally disturbed • M Ed
education of the gifted • M Ed
educational administration • M Ed, Ed S
educational media • M Ed, MS
elementary education • M Ed, Ed S
exercise technology • MS
health education • M Ed
instructional design • MS
instructional design and development • PhD
learning disability • M Ed
leisure services • MS
mentally retarded • M Ed
multihandicapped education • M Ed
natural science education • M Ed
physical education • M Ed, Ed S
reading • M Ed
science education • M Ed
secondary education • M Ed, Ed S
special education • M Ed, Ed S
therapeutic recreation • MS

College of Engineering
Programs in:
chemical engineering • MS Ch E
computer and electrical engineering • MSEE
engineering • MS Ch E, MSEE, MSME
mechanical engineering • MSME

College of Nursing
Programs in:
advanced adult acute nursing • MSN
advanced child health nursing • MSN
advanced community/public health nursing • MSN
advanced family nursing • MSN
advanced gerontological nursing • MSN
advanced infant/neonatal nursing • MSN
advanced psychiatric/mental health nursing • MSN
advanced women's health nursing • MSN
executive nursing administration • MSN
nurse practitioner/clinical nursing specialist • MSN
nursing education • MSN

Mitchell College of Business
Programs in:
accounting • M Acct
business • M Acct, MBA
general management • MBA

School of Computer and Information Sciences
Programs in:
computer science • MS
information science • MS

■ THE UNIVERSITY OF WEST ALABAMA
Livingston, AL 35470
http://www.uwa.edu/

State-supported, coed, comprehensive institution. *Computer facilities:* 400 computers available on campus for general student use. A campuswide network can be accessed from student residence rooms and from off campus. Internet access is available. *Library facilities:* Julia Tutwiler Library. *General application contact:* Dean of Graduate Studies, 205-652-3647 Ext. 421.

School of Graduate Studies
College of Education
Programs in:
continuing education • MSCE
early childhood education • M Ed
education • M Ed, MAT, MSCE
elementary education • M Ed
guidance and counseling • M Ed, MSCE
library media • M Ed
physical education • M Ed, MAT
school administration • M Ed
special education • M Ed

College of Liberal Arts
Programs in:
history • MAT
language arts • MAT
liberal arts • MAT
social science • MAT

College of Natural Sciences and Mathematics
Programs in:
biological sciences • MAT
mathematics • MAT
natural sciences and mathematics • MAT

Alaska

■ ALASKA PACIFIC UNIVERSITY
Anchorage, AK 99508-4672
http://www.alaskapacific.edu/

Independent, coed, comprehensive institution. *Enrollment:* 673 graduate, professional, and undergraduate students; 86 full-time matriculated graduate/professional students (58 women), 76 part-time matriculated graduate/professional students (43 women). *Graduate faculty:* 17 full-time (6 women), 8 part-time/adjunct (5 women). *Computer facilities:* 40 computers available on campus for general student use. A campuswide network can be accessed from student residence rooms. Internet access is available. *Library facilities:* Consortium Library. *Graduate expenses:* Tuition: full-time $11,400; part-time $475 per semester hour. Required fees: $110. *General application contact:* Jessica Carr, Co-Director of Admissions, 907-564-8248.

Graduate Programs
Dr. Marilyn Barry, Academic Dean
Programs in:
business administration • MBA
environmental science • MSES
psychology • MSCP
self designed programs • MA
teaching (K–8) • MAT
telecommunication management • MBATM

■ UNIVERSITY OF ALASKA ANCHORAGE
Anchorage, AK 99508-8060
http://www.uaa.alaska.edu/

State-supported, coed, comprehensive institution. CGS member. *Computer facilities:* 500 computers available on campus for general student use. A campuswide network can be accessed from student residence rooms and from off campus. Internet access is available. *Library facilities:* Consortium Library. *General application contact:* Director for Enrollment Services, 907-786-1558.

College of Arts and Sciences
Programs in:
arts and sciences • MA, MFA, MS
biological sciences • MS
clinical psychology • MS
creative writing and literary arts • MFA
English • MA
interdisciplinary studies • MA, MS

College of Business and Public Policy
Programs in:
business administration • MBA
business and public policy • MBA, MPA
public administration • MPA

College of Health, Education, and Social Welfare
Programs in:
health, education, and social welfare • M Ed, MAT, MS, MSW, Certificate
substance abuse disorders • Certificate

School of Education
Programs in:
- adult education • M Ed
- counseling and guidance • M Ed
- education • M Ed, MAT
- educational leadership • M Ed
- master teacher • M Ed
- special education • M Ed
- teaching • MAT

School of Nursing
Program in:
- nursing and health science • MS

School of Social Work
Program in:
- social work • MSW

Community and Technical College
Program in:
- vocational education • MS

School of Engineering
Programs in:
- arctic engineering • MS
- civil engineering • MCE, MS
- engineering • MCE, MS
- engineering management • MS
- environmental quality engineering • MS
- environmental quality science • MS
- science management • MS

■ UNIVERSITY OF ALASKA FAIRBANKS
Fairbanks, AK 99775-7520

State-supported, coed, university. CGS member. *Enrollment:* 8,724 graduate, professional, and undergraduate students; 652 full-time matriculated graduate/professional students (320 women), 364 part-time matriculated graduate/professional students (200 women). *Graduate faculty:* 579 full-time (196 women), 256 part-time/adjunct (133 women). *Computer facilities:* Computer purchase and lease plans are available. 199 computers available on campus for general student use. A campuswide network can be accessed from student residence rooms and from off campus. Internet access and online class registration are available. *Library facilities:* Rasmuson Library plus 8 others. *Graduate expenses:* Tuition, state resident: full-time $3,636; part-time $202 per credit. Tuition, nonresident: full-time $7,074; part-time $393 per credit. Required fees: $970; $5 per credit. $30 per term. Tuition and fees vary according to course level and course load. *General application contact:* Nancy Dix, Director of Admissions, 907-474-7500.

College of Liberal Arts
Phyliss Morrow, Dean
Programs in:
- administration of justice • MA
- Alaskan ethnomusicology • MA
- anthropology • MA, PhD
- applied linguistics • MA
- art • MFA
- community psychology • MA
- creative writing • MFA
- English • MA
- journalism • MA
- liberal arts • MA, MFA, PhD
- music education • MA
- music history • MA
- music theory • MA
- northern studies • MA
- performance • MA
- professional communications • MA

College of Rural Alaska
Dr. Bernice Joseph, Executive Dean
Programs in:
- Alaska native and rural development • MA
- rural Alaska • MA

College of Natural Sciences and Mathematics
Dr. Joan Braddock, Interim Dean
Programs in:
- atmospheric science • MS, PhD
- biochemistry • MS, PhD
- biological sciences • MS, PhD
- chemistry • MA, MS
- computer science • MS
- geology • MS, PhD
- geophysics • MS, PhD
- geoscience • MAT
- mathematics • MS, PhD
- natural sciences and mathematics • MA, MAT, MS, MSE, PhD
- physics • MS, PhD
- software engineering • MSE
- space physics • MS, PhD
- statistics • MS
- wildlife biology and management • MS, PhD

Graduate School for Interdisciplinary Studies
Dr. Susan M. Henricha, Dean
Program in:
- interdisciplinary studies • MA, MS, PhD, EM

School of Education
Dr. Eric C. Madsen, Dean
Programs in:
- cross-cultural education • M Ed
- curriculum and instruction • M Ed
- educational administration • M Ed
- guidance and counseling • M Ed
- language and literature • M Ed

School of Fisheries and Ocean Sciences
Dr. Denis Wiesenberg, Dean
Programs in:
- fisheries • MS, PhD
- fisheries and ocean sciences • MS, PhD
- marine biology • MS
- oceanography • MS, PhD

School of Management
Dr. Wayne Marr, Dean
Programs in:
- capital markets • MBA
- general management • MBA
- management • MBA, MS
- resource economics • MS

School of Natural Resources and Agricultural Sciences
Dr. Carol Lewis, Dean
Programs in:
- natural resources and agricultural sciences • MS
- resources management • MS

■ UNIVERSITY OF ALASKA SOUTHEAST
Juneau, AK 99801
http://www.uas.alaska.edu/

State-supported, coed, comprehensive institution. *Computer facilities:* 75 computers available on campus for general student use. A campuswide network can be accessed from student residence rooms and from off campus. Internet access is available. *Library facilities:* Egan Memorial Library. *General application contact:* Recruiter, 907-465-6239.

Graduate Programs
Programs in:
- early childhood education • M Ed
- educational technology • M Ed
- elementary education • M Ed, MAT
- public administration • MPA
- secondary education • M Ed, MAT

Arizona

■ ARIZONA STATE UNIVERSITY
Tempe, AZ 85287
http://www.asu.edu/

State-supported, coed, university. CGS member. *Enrollment:* 48,901 graduate, professional, and undergraduate students; 6,166 full-time matriculated graduate/professional students (2,930 women), 3,344 part-time matriculated graduate/professional students (1,911 women).

Arizona

Arizona State University (continued)
Graduate faculty: 2,165 full-time (851 women), 188 part-time/adjunct (94 women). *Computer facilities:* Computer purchase and lease plans are available. A campuswide network can be accessed from student residence rooms and from off campus. Internet access and online class registration are available. *Library facilities:* Hayden Library plus 4 others. *Graduate expenses:* Tuition, state resident: full-time $3,708; part-time $194 per credit hour. Tuition, nonresident: full-time $12,228; part-time $510 per credit hour. Required fees: $87; $22 per semester. Part-time tuition and fees vary according to program. *General application contact:* Graduate Admissions, 480-965-6113.

College of Law
Patricia D. White, Dean
Program in:
  law • JD

Graduate College
Programs in:
  aerospace engineering • MS, MSE, PhD
  bioengineering • MS, PhD
  chemical engineering • MS, MSE, PhD
  civil engineering • MS, MSE, PhD
  computer science • MCS, MS, PhD
  construction • MS
  creative writing • MFA
  curriculum and instruction • PhD
  electrical engineering • MS, MSE, PhD
  engineering • M Eng, MCS, MS, MSE, PhD
  engineering science • MS, MSE, PhD
  exercise science • PhD
  gerontology • Certificate
  industrial engineering • MS, MSE, PhD
  justice studies • PhD
  materials science and engineering • MS, MSE, PhD
  mechanical engineering • MS, MSE, PhD
  public administration • DPA
  science and engineering of materials • PhD
  speech and hearing science • PhD
  statistics • MS
  transportation systems • Certificate

College of Architecture and Environmental Design
Programs in:
  architecture • M Arch
  architecture and environmental design • M Arch, MEP, MS, MSD, PhD
  building design • MS
  design • MSD, PhD
  history, theory, and criticism • PhD
  planning • MEP, PhD

College of Education
Programs in:
  counseling • M Ed, MC
  counseling psychology • PhD
  curriculum and instruction • M Ed, MA, Ed D
  education • M Ed, MA, MC, Ed D, PhD
  educational administration and supervision • M Ed, Ed D
  educational leadership and policy studies • M Ed, MA, Ed D, PhD
  educational psychology • M Ed, MA, PhD
  higher and post-secondary education • M Ed, Ed D
  learning and instructional technology • M Ed, MA, PhD
  psychology in education • M Ed, MA, MC, PhD
  social and philosophical foundations of education • MA
  special education • M Ed, MA

College of Fine Arts
Programs in:
  art • MA, MFA
  dance • MFA
  fine arts • MA, MFA, MM, DMA, PhD
  music • MA, MM, DMA
  theater • MA, MFA, PhD

College of Liberal Arts and Sciences
Programs in:
  anthropology • MA, PhD
  applied mathematics • MA, PhD
  Asian history • MA, PhD
  behavior • MS, PhD
  behavioral neuroscience • PhD
  biology • MNS
  biology education • MS, PhD
  British history • MA, PhD
  cell and developmental biology • MS, PhD
  chemistry and biochemistry • MNS, MS, PhD
  clinical psychology • PhD
  cognitive/behavioral systems • PhD
  communication disorders • MS
  computational, statistical, and mathematical biology • MS, PhD
  conservation • MS, PhD
  demography and population studies • MA, PhD
  developmental psychology • PhD
  ecology • MS, PhD
  English • MA, PhD
  environmental psychology • PhD
  European history • MA, PhD
  evolution • MS, PhD
  exercise science and physical education • MPE, MS
  family resources and human development • MS
  family science • PhD
  French • MA
  genetics • MS, PhD
  geography • MA, PhD
  geological engineering • MS, PhD
  German • MA
  history and philosophy of biology • MS, PhD
  humanities • MA
  Latin American studies • MA, PhD
  liberal arts and sciences • MA, MNS, MPE, MS, MTESL, PhD, Certificate
  mathematics • MA, MNS, PhD
  medieval studies • Certificate
  microbiology • MNS, MS, PhD
  molecular and cellular biology • MS, PhD
  natural science • MNS
  neuroscience • MS, PhD
  philosophy • MA
  physics and astronomy • MNS, MS, PhD
  physiology • MS, PhD
  plant biology • MNS, MS, PhD
  political science • MA, PhD
  public history • MA
  quantitative research methods • PhD
  religious studies • MA
  Renaissance studies • Certificate
  social psychology • PhD
  sociology • MA, PhD
  Spanish • MA, PhD
  statistics • MA, PhD
  teaching English as a second language • MTESL
  U.S. history • PhD
  U.S. western history • MA

College of Nursing
Program in:
  nursing • MS

College of Public Programs
Programs in:
  communication • PhD
  journalism and telecommunication • MMC
  justice studies • MS
  public affairs • MPA, DPA
  public programs • MA, MMC, MPA, MS, MSW, DPA, PhD
  recreation • MS
  social work • MSW, PhD
  speech and interpersonal communication • MA

W.P. Carey School of Business
Programs in:
  accountancy • M Accy, PhD
  business • M Accy, M Tax, MBA, MHSA, MS, PhD
  business administration • MBA
  economics • MS, PhD
  finance • PhD
  health administration and policy • MHSA
  health services research • PhD
  information management • MS, PhD
  management • PhD
  marketing • PhD
  supply chain management • PhD
  taxation • M Tax

ARIZONA STATE UNIVERSITY WEST
Phoenix, AZ 85069-7100
http://www.west.asu.edu/

State-supported, coed, comprehensive institution. *Enrollment:* 7,105 graduate, professional, and undergraduate students; 363 full-time matriculated graduate/professional students (241 women), 698 part-time matriculated graduate/professional students (421 women). *Graduate faculty:* 77 full-time (36 women), 29 part-time/adjunct (19 women). *Computer facilities:* 400 computers available on campus for general student use. A campuswide network can be accessed from off campus. Internet access and online class registration are available. *Library facilities:* ASU West Library. *Graduate expenses:* Tuition, state resident: part-time $264 per credit hour. Tuition, nonresident: part-time $565 per credit hour. *General application contact:* Marge A. Williams, Student Support Coordinator, 602-543-4567.

College of Arts and Sciences
Dr. Candice Bredbenner, Associate Dean
Program in:
 interdisciplinary studies • MA

College of Education
Dr. Michael Awender, Dean
Programs in:
 educational administration and supervision • M Ed
 elementary education • M Ed, Certificate
 secondary education • M Ed, Certificate
 special education • M Ed

College of Human Services
Dr. Lesley Di Mare, Head
Programs in:
 communication • MA
 communication/human relations • Certificate
 criminal justice • MA
 gerontology • Certificate
 human services • MA, MSW, Certificate
 social work • MSW

School of Management
Dr. Bruce Forster, Dean
Programs in:
 accountancy • Certificate
 business administration • MBA
 management • MBA, Certificate

EMBRY-RIDDLE AERONAUTICAL UNIVERSITY
Prescott, AZ 86301-3720
http://www.embryriddle.edu/

Independent, coed, primarily men, comprehensive institution. *Enrollment:* 1,669 graduate, professional, and undergraduate students; 16 full-time matriculated graduate/professional students (4 women), 20 part-time matriculated graduate/professional students (5 women). *Graduate faculty:* 4 full-time (0 women), 2 part-time/adjunct (0 women). *Computer facilities:* 200 computers available on campus for general student use. A campuswide network can be accessed from student residence rooms and from off campus. Internet access and online class registration are available. *Library facilities:* ERAU—Prescott Campus Library. *Graduate expenses:* Tuition: full-time $16,740; part-time $930 per credit. Required fees: $660. *General application contact:* Dr. Terry Stobbe, Chair, Safety Science Department, 928-777-6948.

Program in Safety Science
Dr. Terry Stobbe, Chair, Safety Science Department
Program in:
 safety science • MSSS

GRAND CANYON UNIVERSITY
Phoenix, AZ 85017-1097
http://www.grand-canyon.edu/

Independent-religious, coed, comprehensive institution. *Computer facilities:* 119 computers available on campus for general student use. Internet access is available. *Library facilities:* Fleming Library. *General application contact:* Director of Admissions, 602-589-2855 Ext. 2811.

College of Business
Program in:
 business • MBA

College of Education
Programs in:
 elementary education • M Ed, MA
 reading education • MA
 secondary education • M Ed
 teaching • MAT
 teaching English as a second language • MA

NORTHERN ARIZONA UNIVERSITY
Flagstaff, AZ 86011
http://www.nau.edu/

State-supported, coed, university. CGS member. *Enrollment:* 18,824 graduate, professional, and undergraduate students; 1,897 full-time matriculated graduate/professional students (1,261 women), 3,912 part-time matriculated graduate/professional students (2,864 women). *Graduate faculty:* 553 full-time (207 women), 327 part-time/adjunct (151 women). *Computer facilities:* Computer purchase and lease plans are available. 903 computers available on campus for general student use. A campuswide network can be accessed from student residence rooms and from off campus. Internet access and online class registration, e-mail are available. *Library facilities:* Cline Library plus 1 other. *Graduate expenses:* Tuition, state resident: full-time $5,103. Tuition, nonresident: full-time $12,623. *General application contact:* Dr. Patricia Baron, Director of Graduate Admissions, 928-523-4348.

Find an in-depth description at www.petersons.com/gradchannel.

Graduate College
Dr. Carl Fox, Vice Provost for Research and Graduate Studies
Program in:
 liberal studies • MLS

College of Arts and Sciences
Dr. Susan Fitzmaurice, Interim Associate Dean
Programs in:
 applied linguistics • PhD
 applied physics • MS
 arts and sciences • MA, MAT, MS, PhD, Certificate
 biology • MS, PhD
 biology education • MAT
 chemistry • MS
 conservation ecology • Certificate
 creative writing • MA
 earth science • MAT, MS
 English • MA
 environmental sciences and policy • MS
 general English • MA
 geographic information systems • Certificate
 geology • MS
 history • MA, PhD
 literature • MA
 mathematics • MAT, MS
 modern languages • MAT
 physical science • MAT
 quaternary sciences • MS
 rhetoric • MA

Peterson's Graduate Schools in the U.S. 2006

Arizona

Northern Arizona University (continued)
  rural geography • MA
  statistics • MS
  teaching English as a second language • MA
  teaching English as a second language/applied linguistics • MA, PhD, Certificate
  teaching English as a second language/English as a second language • Certificate

College of Business Administration
Dr. Joseph Anderson, Coordinator
Programs in:
  general management • MBA
  management • MSM
  management information systems • MBA

College of Education
Dr. Daniel Kain, Dean
Programs in:
  administration • M Ed
  bilingual multicultural education • M Ed
  community college • M Ed
  counseling • M Ed, MA
  counseling psychology • Ed D
  curriculum and instruction • Ed D
  early childhood education • M Ed
  education • M Ed, MA, Ed D, Certificate
  educational leadership • Ed D
  educational technology • M Ed
  elementary education • M Ed
  English as a Second Language/Teaching English as a second language • Certificate
  learning and instruction • Ed D
  school leadership • M Ed
  school psychology • Ed D
  secondary education • M Ed
  special education • M Ed
  teaching • M Ed

College of Engineering
Ernesto Penado, Director
Program in:
  engineering • M Eng

College of Fine Arts
Dr. Louise Scott, Director
Programs in:
  choral conducting • MM
  instrumental conducting • MM
  instrumental performance • MM
  music education • MM
  music history • MM
  theory and composition • MM
  vocal performance • MM

College of Health Professions
Dr. James Blagg, Dean
Programs in:
  case management • Certificate
  communications sciences and disorders • MS
  exercise science • MS
  health education and health promotion • MPH
  health professions • MPH, MS, MSN, DPT, Certificate
  nursing • MSN
  physical education • MS
  physical therapy • DPT

College of Social and Behavioral Sciences
Kathryn Cruz-Uribe, Dean
Programs in:
  anthropology • MA
  applied health psychology • MA
  applied sociology • MA
  archaeology • MA
  criminal justice • MS
  criminal justice policy and planning • Certificate
  general • MA
  political science • MA, PhD, Certificate
  public administration • MPA
  public management • Certificate
  public policy • PhD
  social and behavioral sciences • MA, MPA, MS, PhD, Certificate

School of Forestry
Dr. Thomas Kolb, Coordinator
Program in:
  forestry • MSF, PhD

■ PRESCOTT COLLEGE
Prescott, AZ 86301
http://www.prescott.edu/

Independent, coed, comprehensive institution. *Enrollment:* 995 graduate, professional, and undergraduate students; 133 full-time matriculated graduate/professional students (93 women), 82 part-time matriculated graduate/professional students (48 women). *Graduate faculty:* 6 full-time (4 women), 160 part-time/adjunct (88 women). *Computer facilities:* 30 computers available on campus for general student use. A campuswide network can be accessed. *Library facilities:* Prescott College Library. *Graduate expenses:* Tuition: full-time $10,980; part-time $308 per credit hour. One-time fee: $193 full-time. *General application contact:* Lisa Mauldin, Admissions Counselor, 800-628-6364.

Find an in-depth description at www.petersons.com/gradchannel.

Graduate Programs
Dr. Steve Walters, Dean
Programs in:
  adventure education/wilderness leadership • MA
  agroecology • MA
  bilingual education • MA
  counseling and psychology • MA
  ecopsychology • MA
  education • MA
  environmental education • MA
  environmental studies • MA
  humanities • MA
  multicultural education • MA
  Southwestern regional history • MA
  sustainability • MA

■ THE UNIVERSITY OF ARIZONA
Tucson, AZ 85721
http://www.arizona.edu/

State-supported, coed, university. CGS member. *Enrollment:* 37,083 graduate, professional, and undergraduate students; 6,768 full-time matriculated graduate/professional students (3,344 women), 1,707 part-time matriculated graduate/professional students (938 women). *Graduate faculty:* 1,392 full-time (362 women), 103 part-time/adjunct (32 women). *Computer facilities:* 1,950 computers available on campus for general student use. A campuswide network can be accessed from student residence rooms and from off campus. Internet access is available. *Library facilities:* University of Arizona Main Library plus 5 others. *Graduate expenses:* Tuition, state resident: part-time $196 per unit. Tuition, nonresident: part-time $326 per unit. *General application contact:* Graduate Admissions Office, 520-621-3132.

College of Medicine
Dr. Kenneth J. Ryan, Dean
Programs in:
  biochemistry • MS, PhD
  cell biology and anatomy • PhD
  medicine • MD, MPH, MS, PhD
  microbiology and immunology • MS, PhD
  public health • MPH

Graduate College
Dr. Thomas J. Hixon, Dean
Programs in:
  American Indian studies • MA, PhD
  applied mathematics • MS, PMS, PhD
  arid land resource sciences • PhD
  cancer biology • PhD
  comparative cultural and literary studies • MA, PhD
  dietetics • MS
  epidemiology • MS, PhD
  epidermalogical nutrition/public health nutrition • PhD
  genetics • MS, PhD
  gerontological studies • MS, Certificate
  human/clinical nutrition • PhD
  insect science • PhD

Arizona

mathematical sciences • PMS
molecular nutrition • PhD
neuroscience • PhD
nutritional biochemistry • MS, PhD
nutritional sciences • MS, PhD
pharmacology and toxicology • PhD
physiological sciences • PhD
planning • MS
second language acquisition and teaching • PhD

Arizona Graduate Program in Public Health
Program in:
public health • MPH

College of Agriculture and Life Sciences
Dr. Eugene G. Sander, Dean
Programs in:
agricultural and biosystems engineering • MS, PhD
agricultural and resource economics • MS
agricultural education • M Ag Ed, MS
agriculture and life sciences • M Ag Ed, MHE Ed, MS, PhD
animal sciences • MS, PhD
entomology • MS, PhD
family and consumer sciences • MS
family studies and human development • PhD
natural resources • MS, PhD
pathobiology • MS, PhD
plant pathology • MS, PhD
plant sciences • MS, PhD
rangeland ecology and management • MS, PhD
retailing and consumer sciences • MS, PhD
soil, water and environmental science • MS, PhD
watershed resources • MS, PhD
wildlife, fisheries, conservation, and management • MS, PhD

College of Architecture, Planning and Landscape Architecture
Programs in:
architecture • M Arch
landscape architecture • ML Arch
planning • MS

College of Business and Public Administration
Programs in:
accounting • M Ac
business administration • MBA
business and public administration • M Ac, MA, MBA, MPA, MS, PhD
economics • MA, PhD
finance • MS, PhD
management • PhD
management and policy • MS
management information systems • MS
marketing • MS, PhD
public administration • MPA
public administration and policy • PhD

College of Education
Dr. Ronald Marx, Dean
Programs in:
bilingual education • M Ed
bilingual/multicultural education • MA
education • M Ed, MA, MS, Ed D, PhD, Ed S
educational leadership • Ed D
educational psychology • MA, PhD
elementary education • M Ed, Ed D
higher education • MA, PhD
language, reading and culture • MA, Ed D, PhD, Ed S
school counseling and guidance • M Ed
secondary education • M Ed, Ed D
special education, rehabilitation and school psychology • M Ed, MA, MS, Ed D, PhD, Ed S
teaching and teacher education • MA, PhD

College of Engineering
Dr. Thomas W. Peterson, Dean
Programs in:
aerospace engineering • MS, PhD
chemical engineering • MS, PhD
civil engineering • MS, PhD
electrical and computer engineering • M Eng, MS, PhD
engineering • M Eng, ME, MS, PhD
engineering mechanics • MS, PhD
environmental engineering • MS, PhD
hydrology • MS, PhD
industrial engineering • MS
materials science and engineering • ME, MS, PhD
mechanical engineering • MS, PhD
mining engineering • MS, PhD
nuclear engineering • MS, PhD
reliability and quality engineering • MS
systems and industrial engineering • PhD
systems engineering • MS
water resources engineering • M Eng

College of Fine Arts
Dr. Maurice Sevigny, Dean
Programs in:
art (studio) • MFA
art education • MA
art history • MA, PhD
composition • MM, A Mus D
conducting • MM, A Mus D
fine arts • MA, MFA, MM, A Mus D, PhD
history and theory of art • PhD
media arts • MA
music education • MM, PhD
music theory • MM, PhD
musicology • MM
performance • MM, A Mus D
theatre arts • MA, MFA

College of Humanities
Programs in:
classics • MA
creative writing • MFA
East Asian studies • MA, PhD
English • MA, PhD
English language/linguistics • MA
ESL • MA
French • M Ed, MA, PhD
German • MA
humanities • M Ed, MA, MFA, PhD
literature • MA, PhD
rhetoric, composition and teaching of English • PhD
rhetoric, composition, and the teaching of English • MA
Russian • M Ed, MA
Spanish • M Ed, MA, PhD

College of Nursing
Dr. Marjorie A. Isenberg, Dean
Program in:
nursing • MS, PhD

College of Pharmacy
Programs in:
medical pharmacology • MS, PhD
medicinal and natural products chemistry • MS, PhD
pharmaceutical economics • MS, PhD
pharmaceutics and pharmacokinetics • MS
pharmaceutics and pharmokinetics • PhD
pharmacy • Pharm D, MS, PhD

College of Science
Programs in:
applied and industrial physics • MS
applied biosciences • MS
astronomy • MS, PhD
atmospheric sciences • MS, PhD
chemistry • MA, MS, PhD
computer science • MS, PhD
ecology and evolutionary biology • MS, PhD
geosciences • MS, PhD
mathematical sciences • PMS
mathematics • M Ed, MA, MS, PMS, PhD
molecular and cellular biology • MS, PhD
physics • M Ed, MS, PhD
planetary sciences/lunar and planetary laboratory • MS, PhD
science • M Ed, MA, MS, PMS, PhD
speech and hearing sciences • MS, PhD

College of Social and Behavioral Sciences
Programs in:
anthropology • MA, PhD
communication • MA, PhD
geography • MA, PhD
history • MA, PhD
journalism • MA
Latin American studies • MA
library science • MA, PhD

Arizona

The University of Arizona (continued)
    linguistics and anthropology • PhD
    Native American linguistics • MA
    Near Eastern studies • MA, PhD
    philosophy • MA, PhD
    political science • MA, PhD
    psychology • PhD
    social and behavioral sciences • MA, PhD
    sociology • MA, PhD
    theoretical linguistics • PhD
    women's studies • MA

James E. Rogers College of Law
Toni M. Massaro, Dean
Programs in:
    international indigenous peoples' rights and policy • LL M
    international trade law • LL M
    law • JD

Optical Sciences Center
Program in:
    optical sciences • MS, PhD

■ WESTERN INTERNATIONAL UNIVERSITY
Phoenix, AZ 85021-2718
http://www.wintu.edu/

Proprietary, coed, comprehensive institution. *Computer facilities:* 30 computers available on campus for general student use. A campuswide network can be accessed. Internet access is available. *Library facilities:* Learning Resource Center. *General application contact:* Director of Enrollment, 602-943-2311 Ext. 1063.

Graduate Programs in Business
Programs in:
    business • MBA, MPA, MS
    finance • MBA
    information technology • MBA, MS
    international business • MBA
    management • MBA
    marketing • MBA
    public administration • MPA

Arkansas

■ ARKANSAS STATE UNIVERSITY
Jonesboro, State University, AR 72467
http://www.astate.edu/

State-supported, coed, comprehensive institution. CGS member. *Enrollment:* 10,573 graduate, professional, and undergraduate students; 325 full-time matriculated graduate/professional students (213 women), 835 part-time matriculated graduate/professional students (534 women). *Graduate faculty:* 207 full-time (63 women), 6 part-time/adjunct (4 women). *Computer facilities:* 508 computers available on campus for general student use. A campuswide network can be accessed from student residence rooms and from off campus. Internet access and online class registration are available. *Library facilities:* Dean B. Ellis Library. *Graduate expenses:* Tuition, state resident: full-time $2,844; part-time $158 per hour. Tuition, nonresident: full-time $7,200; part-time $400 per hour. Required fees: $644; $33 per hour. $25 per semester. Tuition and fees vary according to course load. *General application contact:* Dr. Thomas G. Wheeler, Dean of the Graduate School, 870-972-3029.

Graduate School
Dr. Thomas G. Wheeler, Dean of the Graduate School
Programs in:
    biology • MS
    biology education • MSE, SCCT
    chemistry • MS
    chemistry education • MSE, SCCT
    computer science • MS
    environmental sciences • PhD
    mathematics • MS, MSE
    sciences and mathematics • MS, MSE, PhD, SCCT

College of Agriculture
Dr. Gregory Phillips, Dean
Programs in:
    agricultural education • MSA, SCCT
    agriculture • MSA
    vocational-technical administration • MS, SCCT

College of Business
Dr. Jan Duggar, Dean
Programs in:
    accountancy • M Acc
    business • EMBA, M Acc, MBA, MS, MSE, SCCT
    business administration • EMBA, MBA, SCCT
    business education • MSE, SCCT
    information systems and e-commerce • MS

College of Communications
Dr. Russell Shain, Dean
Programs in:
    communications • MA, MSMC, SCCT
    journalism • MSMC
    radio-television • MSMC
    speech communications and theater • MA, SCCT

College of Education
Dr. John Beineke, Dean
Programs in:
    college student personnel services • MS
    counselor education • MSE, Ed S
    early childhood education • MSE
    early childhood services • MS
    education • MRC, MS, MSE, Ed D, Ed S, SCCT
    educational administration • MSE
    educational leadership • Ed D, Ed S
    elementary education • MSE
    exercise science • MS
    physical education • MS, MSE, SCCT
    reading • MSE, SCCT
    rehabilitation counseling • MRC
    special education • MSE
    special education program administration • Ed S

College of Fine Arts
Dr. Daniel Reeves, Dean
Programs in:
    art • MA
    fine arts • MA, MM, MME, SCCT
    music education • MME, SCCT
    performance • MM
    speech communication and theater • MA, SCCT

College of Humanities and Social Sciences
Dr. Andrew Sustich, Interim Dean
Programs in:
    English • MA
    English education • MSE, SCCT
    heritage studies • PhD
    history • MA, SCCT
    humanities and social sciences • MA, MPA, MSE, PhD, SCCT
    political science • MA, SCCT
    public administration • MPA
    social science • MSE
    sociology • MA, SCCT

College of Nursing and Health Professions
Dr. Susan Hanrahan, Dean
Programs in:
    aging studies • Certificate
    communication disorders • MCD
    health sciences • MS, Certificate
    nurse anesthesia • MSN
    nursing • MSN, Certificate
    physical therapy • MPT

■ ARKANSAS TECH UNIVERSITY
Russellville, AR 72801
http://www.atu.edu/

State-supported, coed, comprehensive institution. *Enrollment:* 6,249 graduate, professional, and undergraduate students; 347 full-time matriculated graduate/professional students (226 women), 34 part-time matriculated graduate/

Arkansas

professional students (29 women). *Graduate faculty:* 99 full-time (33 women), 26 part-time/adjunct (11 women). *Computer facilities:* 600 computers available on campus for general student use. A campuswide network can be accessed from student residence rooms and from off campus. Internet access and online class registration are available. *Library facilities:* Ross Pendergraft Library and Technology Center. *Graduate expenses:* Tuition, state resident: full-time $2,628; part-time $146 per credit hour. Tuition, nonresident: full-time $5,256; part-time $242 per credit hour. International tuition: $9,936 full-time. Required fees: $3 per hour. $95 per term. *General application contact:* Dr. Eldon G. Clary, Dean of Graduate Studies, 479-968-0398.

Graduate Studies
Dr. Eldon G. Clary, Dean

School of Education
Dr. C. Glenn Sheets, Dean
Programs in:
  college student personnel • MSE
  education • M Ed, MSE
  educational leadership • M Ed
  English • M Ed
  gifted education • MSE
  instructional improvement • M Ed
  instructional technology • M Ed
  mathematics • M Ed
  physical education • M Ed
  school counseling and leadership • M Ed
  social studies • M Ed
  teaching, learning and leadership • M Ed

School of Liberal Arts
Dr. Georgena Duncan, Dean
Programs in:
  communications • MLA
  English • MA
  fine arts • MLA
  history • MA
  multi-media journalism • MA
  social sciences • MLA
  Spanish • MLA
  teaching English as a second language • MLA

School of Physical and Life Sciences
Dr. Richard Cohoon, Dean
Programs in:
  fisheries and wildlife biology • MS
  physical and life sciences • MS

School of System Science
Dr. John Watson, Dean
Programs in:
  information technology • MS
  system science • MS

■ HARDING UNIVERSITY
Searcy, AR 72149-0001
http://www.harding.edu/

Independent-religious, coed, comprehensive institution. *Enrollment:* 5,110 graduate, professional, and undergraduate students; 197 full-time matriculated graduate/professional students (124 women), 877 part-time matriculated graduate/professional students (717 women). *Graduate faculty:* 10 full-time (4 women), 38 part-time/adjunct (21 women). *Computer facilities:* 192 computers available on campus for general student use. A campuswide network can be accessed from student residence rooms and from off campus. Internet access and online class registration are available. *Library facilities:* Brackett Library plus 1 other. *Graduate expenses:* Tuition: part-time $388 per credit hour. Required fees: $20 per credit hour. *General application contact:* Dr. Larry Long, Vice President, Academic Affairs, 501-279-4335.

College of Bible and Religion
Dr. Tom Alexander, Dean
Programs in:
  Christian counseling • MA
  marriage and family therapy • MFT

School of Business
Bryan Burks, Dean
Program in:
  business • MBA

School of Education
Pat Bashaw, Chair
Programs in:
  counseling • MS
  early childhood education • M Ed
  early childhood special education • M Ed, MSE
  educational leadership • M Ed
  elementary education • M Ed
  reading • M Ed
  secondary education • M Ed
  special education licensure • M Ed
  teaching • MA

■ HENDERSON STATE UNIVERSITY
Arkadelphia, AR 71999-0001
http://www.hsu.edu/

State-supported, coed, comprehensive institution. *Enrollment:* 3,479 graduate, professional, and undergraduate students; 103 full-time matriculated graduate/professional students (65 women), 250 part-time matriculated graduate/professional students (176 women). *Graduate faculty:* 47 full-time (17 women), 6 part-time/adjunct (3 women). *Computer facilities:* 125 computers available on campus for general student use. A campuswide network can be accessed from student residence rooms and from off campus. *Library facilities:* Huie Library. *Graduate expenses:* Tuition, state resident: full-time $1,458; part-time $162 per credit hour. Tuition, nonresident: full-time $2,916; part-time $324 per credit hour. Tuition and fees vary according to class time, course load and campus/location. *General application contact:* Dr. Marck L. Beggs, Graduate Dean, 870-230-5126.

Graduate Studies
Dr. Marck L. Beggs, Graduate Dean
Program in:
  arts and sciences • MLA

School of Business Administration
Dr. Gary Linn, Dean
Program in:
  business administration • MBA

School of Education
Dr. Kenneth Moore, Dean
Programs in:
  community counseling • MS
  early childhood (P–4) • MSE
  education • MAT
  educational leadership • Ed S
  elementary school counseling • MSE
  English • MSE
  English as a second language • MSE
  math • MSE
  middle school • MSE
  reading • MSE
  recreation • MS
  school administration • MSE
  secondary school counseling • MSE
  social science • MSE
  sports administration • MS

■ SOUTHERN ARKANSAS UNIVERSITY–MAGNOLIA
Magnolia, AR 71753
http://www.saumag.edu/

State-supported, coed, comprehensive institution. *Enrollment:* 3,008 graduate, professional, and undergraduate students; 20 full-time matriculated graduate/professional students (12 women), 184 part-time matriculated graduate/professional students (153 women). *Graduate faculty:* 16 full-time (7 women), 9 part-time/adjunct (5 women). *Computer facilities:* 175 computers available on campus for general student use. A campuswide network can be accessed from off campus. Internet access is available. *Library facilities:* Magale Library. *Graduate expenses:* Tuition, state resident: full-time $2,790; part-time $155 per credit hour. Tuition, nonresident: full-time $3,960; part-time $220 per credit hour. Required fees: $182; $9 per credit hour.

Arkansas

Southern Arkansas University–Magnolia (continued)
$10 per term. *General application contact:* Dr. John R. Jones, Associate Dean, Graduate Studies, 870-235-4055.

Graduate Programs
Dr. John R. Jones, Associate Dean, Graduate Studies
Programs in:
  agency counseling • M Ed
  education • M Ed
  library media and information specialist • M Ed
  teaching • MAT

■ UNIVERSITY OF ARKANSAS
Fayetteville, AR 72701-1201
http://www.uark.edu/

State-supported, coed, university. CGS member. *Enrollment:* 16,405 graduate, professional, and undergraduate students; 3,127 full-time matriculated graduate/professional students (1,482 women). *Graduate faculty:* 655 full-time (169 women), 13 part-time/adjunct (2 women). *Computer facilities:* 1,275 computers available on campus for general student use. A campuswide network can be accessed from student residence rooms and from off campus. Internet access is available. *Library facilities:* David W. Mullins Library plus 5 others. *Graduate expenses:* Tuition, state resident: full-time $4,032; part-time $224 per credit hour. Tuition, nonresident: full-time $9,540; part-time $530 per credit hour. Tuition and fees vary according to course load and program. *General application contact:* Benita Wolff, Information Contact, 479-575-4401.

Find an in-depth description at www.petersons.com/gradchannel.

Graduate School
Dr. Patricia R. Koski, Associate Dean
Programs in:
  cell and molecular biology • MS, PhD
  microelectronics and photonics • MS, PhD
  public policy • PhD

College of Education and Health Professions
M. Reed Greenwood, Associate Dean
Programs in:
  adult education • M Ed, Ed D, Ed S
  childhood education • MAT
  communication disorders • MS
  counseling education • MS, PhD, Ed S
  curriculum and instruction • PhD
  education • M Ed, Ed D, Ed S
  education and health professions • M Ed, MAT, MS, Ed D, PhD, Ed S
  educational administration • M Ed, Ed D, Ed S
  educational technology • M Ed
  elementary education • M Ed, Ed S
  health science • MS, PhD
  higher education • M Ed, Ed D, Ed S
  kinesiology • MS, PhD
  middle-level education • MAT
  physical education • M Ed, MAT
  recreation • M Ed, Ed D
  rehabilitation • MS, PhD
  secondary education • M Ed, MAT, Ed S
  special education • M Ed, MAT
  vocational education • M Ed, MAT, Ed D, Ed S

College of Engineering
Neil Schmidt, Head
Programs in:
  biological and agricultural engineering • MSBAE, MSE, PhD
  chemical engineering • MS Ch E, MSE, PhD
  civil engineering • MSCE, MSE, PhD
  computer systems engineering • MSCSE, MSE, PhD
  electrical engineering • MSEE, PhD
  engineering • MS, MS Ch E, MS En E, MS Tc E, MSBAE, MSCE, MSCSE, MSE, MSEE, MSIE, MSME, MSOR, MSTE, PhD
  environmental engineering • MS En E, MSE
  industrial engineering • MSE, MSIE, PhD
  mechanical engineering • MSE, MSME, PhD
  operations management • MS
  operations research • MSE, MSOR
  telecommunications engineering • MS Tc E
  transportation engineering • MSE, MSTE

Dale Bumpers College of Agricultural, Food and Life Sciences
Dr. Greg Weideman, Dean
Programs in:
  agricultural and extension education • MS
  agricultural economics • MS
  agricultural education • MAT
  agricultural, food and life sciences • MAT, MS, PhD
  agronomy • MS, PhD
  animal science • MS, PhD
  entomology • MS, PhD
  food science • MS, PhD
  general agriculture • MS
  horticulture • MS
  human environmental sciences • MS
  plant pathology • MS
  plant science • PhD
  poultry science • MS, PhD

J. William Fulbright College of Arts and Sciences
Don Bobbitt, Dean
Programs in:
  anthropology • MA
  applied physics • MS
  art • MFA
  arts and sciences • MA, MFA, MM, MPA, MS, PhD
  biology • MA, MS, PhD
  chemistry • MS, PhD
  communication • MA
  comparative literature • MA, PhD
  computer science • MS, PhD
  creative writing • MFA
  drama • MA, MFA
  English • MA, PhD
  environmental dynamics • PhD
  French • MA
  geography • MA
  geology • MS
  German • MA
  history • MA, PhD
  journalism • MA
  mathematics • MS, PhD
  music • MM
  philosophy • MA, PhD
  physics • MS, PhD
  physics education • MA
  political science • MA
  psychology • MA, PhD
  public administration • MPA
  secondary mathematics • MA
  sociology • MA
  Spanish • MA
  statistics • MS
  translation • MFA

Sam M. Walton College of Business Administration
Dr. Doyle Williams, Dean
Programs in:
  accounting • M Acc
  business administration • M Acc, MA, MBA, MIS, MTLM, PhD
  economics • MA, PhD
  information systems • MIS
  transportation and logistics management • MTLM

School of Law
Richard Atkinson, Dean
Programs in:
  agricultural law • LL M
  law • JD

■ UNIVERSITY OF ARKANSAS AT LITTLE ROCK
Little Rock, AR 72204-1099
http://www.ualr.edu/

State-supported, coed, university. CGS member. *Enrollment:* 11,757 graduate, professional, and undergraduate students; 881 full-time matriculated graduate/professional students (513 women), 1,253 part-time matriculated graduate/

Arkansas

professional students (915 women). *Graduate faculty:* 345 full-time (196 women). *Computer facilities:* 500 computers available on campus for general student use. A campuswide network can be accessed from off campus. Internet access is available. *Library facilities:* Ottenheimer Library plus 1 other. *Graduate expenses:* Tuition, nonresident: part-time $177 per credit hour. *General application contact:* Dr. Richard Hanson, Dean of the Graduate School, 501-569-3206.

Graduate School
Dr. Richard Hanson, Dean of the Graduate School

College of Arts, Humanities, and Social Science
Dr. Deborah Baldwin, Dean
Programs in:
  applied psychology • MAP
  art education • MA
  art history • MA
  arts, humanities, and social science • MA, MALS, MAP
  expository writing • MA
  liberal studies • MALS
  public history • MA
  studio art • MA
  technical writing • MA

College of Business Administration
Dr. William C. Goolsby, Dean
Program in:
  business administration • MBA

College of Education
Dr. Angela Sewall, Dean
Programs in:
  adult education • M Ed
  counselor education • M Ed
  early childhood education • M Ed, Ed S
  early childhood special education • M Ed
  education • M Ed, MA, Ed D, Ed S
  education of hearing impaired children • M Ed
  educational administration • M Ed, Ed D, Ed S
  educational administration and supervision • M Ed, Ed D, Ed S
  higher education administration • Ed D
  instructional resources • M Ed
  middle childhood education • M Ed, Ed S
  reading • M Ed, Ed S
  rehabilitation for the blind • MA
  school counseling • M Ed
  secondary education • M Ed
  special education • M Ed
  teaching of the mildly disabled student • M Ed
  teaching persons with severe disabilities • M Ed

teaching the gifted and talented • M Ed
teaching the visually impaired child • M Ed

College of Information Science and Systems Engineering
Dr. Bill Wiggins, Dean
Programs in:
  computer science • MS
  information science and systems engineering • MA, MS, PhD
  instrumental sciences • MS, PhD

College of Professional Studies
Dr. John Gray, Dean
Programs in:
  applied gerontology • CG
  clinical social work • MSW
  criminal justice • MA
  gerontology • MA
  health services administration • MHSA
  interpersonal communications • MA
  journalism • MA
  organizational communications • MA
  professional studies • MA, MHSA, MPA, MSW, CG
  public administration • MPA
  social program administration • MSW
  social work • MA, MSW, CG

College of Science and Mathematics
Dr. Bill Wiggins, Dean
Programs in:
  applied mathematics • MS
  chemistry • MA, MS
  science and mathematics • MA, MS

William H. Bowen School of Law
Charles W. Goldner, Dean
Program in:
  law • JD

■ UNIVERSITY OF CENTRAL ARKANSAS
Conway, AR 72035-0001
http://www.uca.edu/

State-supported, coed, comprehensive institution. CGS member. *Enrollment:* 9,516 graduate, professional, and undergraduate students; 441 full-time matriculated graduate/professional students (314 women), 511 part-time matriculated graduate/professional students (406 women). *Graduate faculty:* 186 full-time (78 women), 12 part-time/adjunct (5 women). *Computer facilities:* 1,500 computers available on campus for general student use. A campuswide network can be accessed from student residence rooms and from off campus. Internet access and online class registration are available. *Library facilities:* Torreyson Library. *Graduate expenses:* Tuition, state resident: full-time $3,677; part-time $204 per hour. Tuition, nonresident: full-time $6,455; part-time $362 per hour. Required fees: $130; $52 per semester. *General application contact:* Dr. Elaine M. McNiece, Associate Provost and Dean of the Graduate School, 501-450-3124.

Graduate School
Dr. Elaine M. McNiece, Associate Provost and Dean of the Graduate School

College of Business Administration
Dr. Pat Cantrell, Dean
Programs in:
  accounting • M Acc
  business administration • IMBA, M Acc, MBA
  international business administration • IMBA

College of Education
Dr. Jane McHaney, Dean
Programs in:
  community service counseling • MS
  counseling psychology • MS
  early childhood education • MSE
  early childhood special education • MSE
  education • MS, MSE, PhD
  education media and library science • MS
  elementary education • MSE
  elementary education for the gifted • MSE
  elementary school counseling • MS
  mildly handicapped • MSE
  moderately/profoundly handicapped • MSE
  reading education • MSE
  school counseling • MS
  school psychology • MS, PhD
  secondary school counseling • MS
  seriously emotionally disturbed • MSE
  special education • MSE
  training systems • MSE

College of Fine Arts and Communication
Dr. Jonathan Glen, Interim Dean
Programs in:
  choral conducting • MM
  fine arts and communication • MM
  instrumental conducting • MM
  music education • MM
  music theory • MM
  performance • MM

College of Health and Applied Sciences
Dr. Neil Hattlestad, Dean
Programs in:
  family and consumer sciences • MS
  health and applied sciences • MS, MSN, DPT, PhD
  health education • MS
  health systems • MS

Arkansas

University of Central Arkansas (continued)
- kinesiology • MS
- nursing • MSN
- occupational therapy • MS
- physical therapy • MS, DPT, PhD
- speech-language pathology • MS

College of Liberal Arts
Maurice Lee, Dean
Programs in:
- English • MA
- foreign languages • MSE
- geographic information systems • Certificate
- history • MA
- liberal arts • MA, MSE, Certificate

College of Natural Sciences and Math
Dr. Ron Toll, Dean
Programs in:
- biological science • MS
- mathematics • MA
- natural sciences and math • MA, MS

Graduate School of Management, Leadership, and Administration
Associate Dean
Programs in:
- college student personnel • MS
- community and economic development • MS
- educational leadership—district level • Ed S
- elementary school leadership • MSE
- management, leadership, and administration • MS, MSE, Ed S
- secondary school leadership • MSE

California

■ **ANTIOCH UNIVERSITY LOS ANGELES**
Culver City, CA 90230
http://www.antiochla.edu/

Independent, coed, upper-level institution. *Computer facilities:* 12 computers available on campus for general student use. A campuswide network can be accessed from off campus. Internet access is available. *Library facilities:* Ohiolink. *General application contact:* Information Contact, 310-578-1080 Ext. 103.

Graduate Programs
Programs in:
- clinical psychology • MA
- creative writing • MFA
- education • MA
- human resource development • MA
- leadership • MA
- organizational development • MA
- pedagogy of creative writing • Certificate
- psychology • MA

■ **AZUSA PACIFIC UNIVERSITY**
Azusa, CA 91702-7000
http://online.apu.edu/

Independent-religious, coed, comprehensive institution. CGS member. *Enrollment:* 8,191 graduate, professional, and undergraduate students; 2,021 full-time matriculated graduate/professional students (1,339 women), 2,043 part-time matriculated graduate/professional students (1,269 women). *Graduate faculty:* 50 full-time (25 women). *Computer facilities:* Computer purchase and lease plans are available. 300 computers available on campus for general student use. A campuswide network can be accessed from off campus. Internet access and online class registration are available. *Library facilities:* Marshburn Memorial Library plus 2 others. *Graduate expenses:* Tuition: part-time $398 per unit. Required fees: $195 per semester. *General application contact:* Rebecca Knippelmeyer, Graduate Admissions Office, 626-812-3016.

College of Liberal Arts and Sciences
Dr. David Weeks, Dean
Programs in:
- applied computer science and technology • MS
- client/server technology • Certificate
- computer information systems • Certificate
- computer science • Certificate
- end-user training and support • Certificate
- liberal arts and sciences • MA, MS, DPT, Certificate
- physical therapy • DPT
- teaching English to speakers of other languages • MA
- technical programming • Certificate
- telecommunications • Certificate

Haggard School of Theology
Dr. Kevin W. Mannoia, Dean
Programs in:
- Christian education • MA, MAR
- Christian education in youth ministry • MA
- Christian non-profit leadership • MA
- divinity • M Div
- ministry • D Min
- ministry management • MAMM
- non-profit leadership and theology • MA
- pastoral studies • MAPS
- religion: biblical studies • MAR
- religion: theology and ethics • MAR
- worship leadership • MAWL

School of Business and Management
Dr. Ilene Bezjian, Dean
Programs in:
- business administration • MBA
- human and organizational development • MA
- international business • MBA
- organizational management • MAOM
- strategic management • MBA

School of Education and Behavioral Studies
Dr. Terrence Cannings, Dean
Programs in:
- clinical psychology • MA, Psy D
- college student affairs • M Ed
- curriculum and instruction in a multicultural setting • MA
- education and behavioral studies • M Ed, MA, MFT, Ed D, Psy D
- educational counseling • MA
- educational leadership and administration • Ed D
- educational technology • M Ed
- family therapy • MFT
- language development • MA
- leadership studies • MA
- physical education • M Ed
- pupil personnel services • MA
- school administration • MA
- school librarianship • MA
- school psychology • MA
- special education • MA
- teaching • MA

School of Music
Dr. Duane Funderburk, Dean
Programs in:
- education • M Mus
- performance • M Mus
- worship leadership • MA

School of Nursing
Dr. Rose Liegler, Dean
Program in:
- nursing • MSN

■ **BIOLA UNIVERSITY**
La Mirada, CA 90639-0001
http://www.biola.edu/

Independent-religious, coed, university. *Computer facilities:* Computer purchase and lease plans are available. 150 computers available on campus for general student use. A campuswide network can be accessed from student residence rooms and from off campus. Internet access and online class registration are available. *Library facilities:* The Biola University Library. *General application contact:* Director of Graduate Admissions, 562-903-4752.

Rosemead School of Psychology
Program in:
- psychology • MA, PhD, Psy D

School of Arts and Sciences
Program in:
arts and sciences • MA Ed

School of Business
Program in:
business • MBA

School of Intercultural Studies
Programs in:
applied linguistics • MA
intercultural education • PhD
intercultural studies • MAICS
missiology • D Miss
missions • MA
teaching English to speakers of other languages • MA, Certificate

School of Professional Studies
Programs in:
Christian apologetics • MA
organizational leadership • MA

Talbot School of Theology
Programs in:
Bible exposition • MA
biblical and theological studies • MA
Christian education • MACE
Christian ministry and leadership • MA
divinity • M Div
education • PhD
ministry • MA Min
New Testament • MA
Old Testament • MA
philosophy of religion and ethics • MA
spiritual formation and soul care • MA
theology • Th M, D Min

■ CALIFORNIA BAPTIST UNIVERSITY
Riverside, CA 92504-3206
http://www.calbaptist.edu/

Independent-religious, coed, comprehensive institution. *Enrollment:* 2,359 graduate, professional, and undergraduate students; 190 full-time matriculated graduate/professional students (135 women), 416 part-time matriculated graduate/professional students (320 women). *Graduate faculty:* 26 full-time (14 women), 15 part-time/adjunct (8 women). *Computer facilities:* 130 computers available on campus for general student use. A campuswide network can be accessed from student residence rooms and from off campus. Internet access, intranet are available. *Library facilities:* Annie Gabriel Library. *Graduate expenses:* Tuition: full-time $7,506; part-time $417 per semester hour. Required fees: $30 per semester. Tuition and fees vary according to program. *General application contact:* Gail Ronveaux, Associate Dean, Enrollment Services, 909-343-5045.

Program in Business Administration
Dr. Andrew Herrity, Director
Program in:
business administration • MBA

Program in Education
Dr. Mary Crist, Dean, School of Education
Programs in:
cross-cultural language academic development • MA Ed
educational leadership • MS Ed
educational technology • MS Ed
reading • MS Ed
special education • MS Ed
teaching and curriculum • MS Ed

Program in English
Dr. Dawn Ellen Jacobs, Director
Program in:
English • MA

Program in Marriage and Family Therapy
Dr. Gary Collins, Director
Program in:
counseling psychology • MS

■ CALIFORNIA INSTITUTE OF TECHNOLOGY
Pasadena, CA 91125-0001
http://www.caltech.edu/

Independent, coed, university. CGS member. *Computer facilities:* Computer purchase and lease plans are available. 600 computers available on campus for general student use. A campuswide network can be accessed from student residence rooms and from off campus. Internet access is available. *Library facilities:* Millikan Library plus 10 others. *General application contact:* Graduate Office, 626-395-3812.

Division of Biology
Elliot Meyerowitz, Chairman
Programs in:
biochemistry and molecular biophysics • PhD
cell biology and biophysics • PhD
developmental biology • PhD
genetics • PhD
immunology • PhD
molecular biology • PhD
neurobiology • PhD

Division of Chemistry and Chemical Engineering
Dr. David A. Tirrell, Chairman
Programs in:
chemical engineering • MS, PhD
chemistry • MS, PhD

Division of Engineering and Applied Science
Dr. Tania Davis, Assistant to Division of Engineering and Applied Science
Programs in:
aeronautics • MS, PhD, Engr
applied and computational mathematics • MS, PhD
applied mechanics • MS, PhD
applied physics • MS, PhD
bioengineering • MS, PhD
civil engineering • MS, PhD
computation and neural systems • MS, PhD
computer science • MS, PhD
control and dynamical systems • MS, PhD
electrical engineering • MS, PhD
engineering science • PhD
environmental science and engineering • MS, PhD
materials science • MS, PhD
mechanical engineering • MS, PhD, Engr

Division of Geological and Planetary Sciences
Dr. Edward M. Stolper, Chairman
Programs in:
cosmochemistry • PhD
geobiology • PhD
geochemistry • MS, PhD
geology • MS, PhD
geophysics • MS, PhD
planetary science • MS, PhD

Division of Physics, Mathematics and Astronomy
Programs in:
astronomy • PhD
mathematics • PhD
physics • PhD

Division of the Humanities and Social Sciences
Jean Ensminger, Chair
Programs in:
economics • PhD
humanities and social sciences • MS, PhD
political science • PhD
social science • MS

■ CALIFORNIA LUTHERAN UNIVERSITY
Thousand Oaks, CA 91360-2787
http://www.clunet.edu/

Independent-religious, coed, comprehensive institution. *Computer facilities:* 262 computers available on campus for general student use. A campuswide network can be accessed from student residence rooms and from off campus. Internet access is available. *Library facilities:* Pearson Library. *General application contact:* 805-493-3127.

California

California Lutheran University (continued)
Graduate Studies
Programs in:
  clinical psychology • MS
  marital and family therapy • MS
  public policy and administration • MPPA

School of Business
Programs in:
  finance • MBA
  healthcare management • MBA
  international business • MBA
  management information systems • MBA
  marketing • MBA
  organizational behavior • MBA
  small business/entrepreneurship • MBA

School of Education
Programs in:
  counseling and guidance • MS
  curriculum and instruction • MA
  education • M Ed
  educational administration • MA
  reading education • MA
  special education • MS
  teacher preparation • Certificate

■ CALIFORNIA POLYTECHNIC STATE UNIVERSITY, SAN LUIS OBISPO
San Luis Obispo, CA 93407
http://www.calpoly.edu/

State-supported, coed, comprehensive institution. *Enrollment:* 18,303 graduate, professional, and undergraduate students; 680 full-time matriculated graduate/professional students (332 women), 366 part-time matriculated graduate/professional students (210 women). *Graduate faculty:* 344 full-time, 291 part-time/adjunct. *Computer facilities:* 1,880 computers available on campus for general student use. A campuswide network can be accessed from student residence rooms and from off campus. *Library facilities:* Kennedy Library. *Graduate expenses:* Tuition, nonresident: part-time $188 per unit. Required fees: $3,732. *General application contact:* Jim Maraviglia, Admissions Office, 805-756-2311.

College of Agriculture
Dr. David J. Wehner, Dean
Programs in:
  agriculture • MS
  forestry sciences • MS

College of Architecture and Environmental Design
R. Thomas Jones, Dean
Programs in:
  architecture • MS Arch
  architecture and environmental design • MCRP, MS Arch
  city and regional planning • MCRP

College of Engineering
Dr. Peter Y. Lee, Dean
Programs in:
  aerospace engineering • MSAE
  biochemical engineering • MS
  civil and environmental engineering • MS
  computer science • MSCS
  electrical engineering • MS
  engineering • MS, MSAE, MSCS
  industrial engineering • MS
  integrated technology management • MS
  materials engineering • MS
  water engineering • MS

College of Liberal Arts
Harold Hellenbrand, Dean
Programs in:
  English • MA
  liberal arts • MA, MS
  psychology • MS

College of Science and Mathematics
Dr. Philip S. Bailey, Dean
Programs in:
  biological sciences • MS
  kinesiology • MS
  mathematics • MS
  science and mathematics • MS

Orfalea College of Business
Dr. Terri Swartz, Dean
Programs in:
  agribusiness management • MBA
  architectural management • MBA
  industrial and technical studies • MA
  industrial technology • MA

University Center for Teacher Education
Dr. Bonnie Konopak, Dean
Programs in:
  counseling • MA
  curriculum and instruction • MA
  education • MA
  educational administration • MA
  reading • MA
  special education • MA

■ CALIFORNIA STATE POLYTECHNIC UNIVERSITY, POMONA
Pomona, CA 91768-2557
http://www.csupomona.edu/

State-supported, coed, comprehensive institution. CGS member. *Enrollment:* 19,804 graduate, professional, and undergraduate students; 681 full-time matriculated graduate/professional students (327 women), 550 part-time matriculated graduate/professional students (267 women). *Graduate faculty:* 672 full-time (236 women), 552 part-time/adjunct (242 women). *Computer facilities:* 1,864 computers available on campus for general student use. A campuswide network can be accessed from student residence rooms and from off campus. Internet access is available. *Library facilities:* University Library. *Graduate expenses:* Tuition, nonresident: full-time $6,016; part-time $188 per unit. Required fees: $2,256. *General application contact:* Dan Aseltine, Coordinator, Graduate and International Programs, 909-869-3252.

Academic Affairs
Dr. Tomas D. Morales, Interim Provost/Vice President for Academic Affairs

College of Agriculture
Dr. Wayne R. Bidlack, Dean
Programs in:
  agricultural science • MS
  animal science • MS
  foods and nutrition • MS

College of Business Administration
Dr. Lynn H. Turner, Interim Dean
Program in:
  business administration • MBA, MSBA

College of Education and Integrative Studies
Dr. Joan S. Bissell, Dean
Program in:
  education and integrative studies • MA

College of Engineering
Dr. Edward Hohmann, Dean
Programs in:
  electrical engineering • MSEE
  engineering • MSE
  mechanical engineering • MS
  structural engineering • MS

College of Environmental Design
Karen C. Hanna, Dean
Programs in:
  architecture • M Arch
  environmental design • M Arch, M Land Arch, MURP
  landscape architecture • M Land Arch
  urban and regional planning • MURP

College of Letters, Arts, and Social Sciences
Dr. Barbara J. Way, Dean
Programs in:
  economics • MS

California

English • MA
history • MA
kinesiology • MS
letters, arts, and social sciences • MA, MPA, MS
psychology • MS
public administration • MPA

College of Science
Dr. Donald O. Straney, Dean
Programs in:
applied mathematics • MS
biological sciences • MS
chemistry • MS
computer science • MS
pure mathematics • MS
science • MS

■ CALIFORNIA STATE UNIVERSITY, BAKERSFIELD
Bakersfield, CA 93311-1099
http://www.csubak.edu/

State-supported, coed, comprehensive institution. CGS member. *Computer facilities:* 600 computers available on campus for general student use. A campuswide network can be accessed from student residence rooms and from off campus. Internet access and online class registration are available. *Library facilities:* Walter W. Stiern Library. *General application contact:* Dean of Students, 661-664-2161.

Division of Graduate Studies and Research
Programs in:
administration • MS
counseling psychology • MS
interdisciplinary studies • MA

School of Business and Public Administration
Programs in:
business administration • MBA
business and public administration • MBA, MPA, MSA
health care management • MSA
public administration • MPA

School of Education
Programs in:
bilingual/bicultural education • MA
counseling • MS
counseling and personnel services • MA
curriculum and instruction • MA
education administration • MA
elementary curriculum and instruction • MA
reading education • MA
secondary curriculum and instruction • MA
special education • MA

School of Humanities and Social Sciences
Programs in:
anthropology • MA
English • MA
family and child counseling • MFCC
history • MA
humanities and social sciences • MA, MS, MSW, MFCC
psychology • MS
social work • MSW
sociology • MA
Spanish • MA

School of Natural Sciences, Mathematics, and Engineering
Programs in:
geology • MS
hydrology • MS
natural sciences, mathematics, and engineering • MA, MS
nursing • MS
secondary school mathematics teaching • MA

■ CALIFORNIA STATE UNIVERSITY, CHICO
Chico, CA 95929-0722
http://www.csuchico.edu/

State-supported, coed, comprehensive institution. CGS member. *Enrollment:* 15,516 graduate, professional, and undergraduate students; 556 full-time matriculated graduate/professional students (327 women), 376 part-time matriculated graduate/professional students (202 women). *Graduate faculty:* 883. *Computer facilities:* 840 computers available on campus for general student use. A campuswide network can be accessed from student residence rooms and from off campus. Internet access and online class registration, student account information, email, calendar, transcripts are available. *Library facilities:* Meriam Library. *Graduate expenses:* Tuition, nonresident: part-time $282 per semester hour. Required fees: $1,029 per semester. *General application contact:* Dr. Robert M. Jackson, Dean, Graduate and International Programs, 530-898-6880.

Graduate School
Dr. Robert M. Jackson, Dean, Graduate and International Programs
Programs in:
applied mechanical engineering • MS
interdisciplinary studies • MA, MS
simulation science • MS
teaching international languages • MA

College of Behavioral and Social Sciences
Byron Jackson, Interim Dean
Programs in:
applied psychology • MA
behavioral and social sciences • MA, MPA, MS, MSW
geography • MA
health administration • MPA
marriage and family therapy • MS
museum studies • MA
political science • MA
psychological science • MA
psychology • MA, MS
public administration • MPA
rural and town planning • MA
social science • MA
social work • MSW

College of Business
Steve Adams, Interim Dean
Programs in:
accountancy • MSA
business • MBA, MSA
business administration • MBA

College of Communication and Education
Dr. Stephen King, Dean
Programs in:
communication and education • MA, MS
communication science and disorders • MA
communication studies/design • MA
curriculum and instruction • MA
education • MA
educational administration • MA
information and communication studies • MA
instructional technology • MS
linguistically and culturally diverse learners • MA
physical education • MA
reading/language arts • MA
recreation administration • MA

College of Engineering, Computer Science, and Technology
Dr. Kenneth Derucher, Dean
Programs in:
computer engineering • MS
computer science • MS
electrical engineering • MS
engineering, computer science, and technology • MS

College of Humanities and Fine Arts
Dr. Sarah Blackstone, Acting Dean
Programs in:
art • MA
creative writing • MFA
English • MA
fine arts • MFA
history • MA
humanities and fine arts • MA, MFA
music • MA

Peterson's Graduate Schools in the U.S. 2006

California

California State University, Chico (continued)

College of Natural Sciences
Dr. James Houpis, Dean
Programs in:
  biological sciences • MS
  botany • MS
  earth sciences • MS
  environmental science • MS
  geosciences • MS
  hydrology/hydrogeology • MS
  natural sciences • MS
  nursing • MS
  nutrition education • MS
  nutritional and food science • MS

■ CALIFORNIA STATE UNIVERSITY, DOMINGUEZ HILLS
Carson, CA 90747-0001
http://www.csudh.edu/

State-supported, coed, comprehensive institution. CGS member. *Computer facilities:* 200 computers available on campus for general student use. *Library facilities:* Leo F. Cain Educational Resource Center. *General application contact:* Associate Director, 310-243-3613.

Find an in-depth description at www.petersons.com/gradchannel.

College of Arts and Sciences
Programs in:
  applied behavioral science • MA
  arts and sciences • MA, MS, Certificate
  biology • MA
  clinical psychology • MA
  English • MA
  general psychology • MA
  gerontology • MA
  human cytogenic technology • Certificate
  humanities • MA
  marriage, family, and child counseling • MS
  negotiation and conflict resolution • MA, Certificate
  quality assurance • MS
  rhetoric and composition • Certificate
  social research • Certificate
  sociology • MA
  teaching English as a second language • Certificate

School of Business and Public Administration
Programs in:
  business and public administration • MBA, MPA
  computer information systems • MBA
  public administration • MPA

School of Education
Programs in:
  computer-based education • MA, Certificate
  counseling • MA
  education • MA, Certificate
  educational administration • MA
  individualized education • MA
  learning handicapped • MA
  multicultural education • MA
  physical education and recreation • MA
  severely handicapped • MA
  special education • MA
  teaching mathematics • MA
  teaching/curriculum • MA

School of Health
Programs in:
  health • MS, MSN, Certificate
  nursing • MSN

Division of Clinical Sciences
Program in:
  clinical sciences • MS, Certificate

■ CALIFORNIA STATE UNIVERSITY, FRESNO
Fresno, CA 93740-8027
http://www.csufresno.edu/

State-supported, coed, comprehensive institution. CGS member. *Computer facilities:* 853 computers available on campus for general student use. A campuswide network can be accessed from off campus. Internet access, common applications are available. *Library facilities:* Henry Madden Library. *General application contact:* Administrative Analyst/Specialist, 559-278-2448.

College of Agricultural Sciences and Technology
Programs in:
  agricultural sciences and technology • MS
  family and consumer sciences • MS
  food science and nutritional sciences • MS
  industrial technology • MS
  plant science • MS

College of Arts and Humanities
Programs in:
  art • MA
  arts and humanities • MA, MFA
  communication • MA
  composition theory • MA
  creative writing • MFA
  linguistics • MA
  literature • MA
  mass communication • MA
  music • MA
  music education • MA
  nonfiction prose • MA
  performance • MA
  Spanish • MA

College of Engineering and Computer Science
Programs in:
  civil engineering • MS
  computer science • MS
  electrical engineering • MS
  engineering and computer science • MS
  mechanical engineering • MS

College of Health and Human Services
Programs in:
  communicative disorders • MA
  environmental/occupational health • MPH
  exercise science • MA
  health administration • MPH
  health and human services • MA, MPH, MPT, MS, MSW
  health promotion • MPH
  nursing • MS
  physical therapy • MPT
  social work education • MSW

College of Science and Mathematics
Programs in:
  biology • MA
  chemistry • MS
  geology • MS
  marine sciences • MS
  mathematics • MA
  physics • MS
  psychology • MA, MS
  science and mathematics • MA, MS
  teaching • MA

College of Social Sciences
Programs in:
  criminology • MS
  history • MA
  international relations • MA
  public administration • MPA
  social sciences • MA, MPA, MS

School of Education and Human Development
Programs in:
  counseling and student services • MS
  education • MA
  education and human development • MA, MS, Ed D
  educational leadership • Ed D
  marriage and family therapy • MS
  rehabilitation counseling • MS
  special education • MA

Sid Craig School of Business
Programs in:
  business • MBA
  business administration • MBA

■ CALIFORNIA STATE UNIVERSITY, FULLERTON
Fullerton, CA 92834-9480
http://www.fullerton.edu/

State-supported, coed, comprehensive institution. CGS member. *Enrollment:*

California

32,592 graduate, professional, and undergraduate students; 1,427 full-time matriculated graduate/professional students (825 women), 2,817 part-time matriculated graduate/professional students (1,769 women). *Graduate faculty:* 769 full-time (316 women), 1,087 part-time/adjunct. *Computer facilities:* 1,993 computers available on campus for general student use. A campuswide network can be accessed from student residence rooms and from off campus. Internet access is available. *Library facilities:* California State University, Fullerton Pollak Library. *Graduate expenses:* Tuition, nonresident: part-time $282 per unit. Required fees: $889 per semester. *General application contact:* Gladys M. Fleckles, Director, Graduate Studies, 714-278-2618.

Graduate Studies
Dr. Keith Boyum, Associate Vice President, Academic Programs

College of Business and Economics
Dr. Anil Puri, Dean
Programs in:
  accounting • MBA, MS
  business administration • MBA
  business and economics • MA, MBA, MS
  business economics • MBA
  economics • MA
  finance • MBA
  international business • MBA
  management • MBA
  management information systems • MS
  management science • MBA, MS
  marketing • MBA
  operations research • MS
  statistics • MS
  taxation • MS

College of Communications
Dr. Rick Pullen, Dean
Programs in:
  advertising • MA
  communications • MA
  communicative disorders • MA
  journalism education • MA
  news editorial • MA
  photo communication • MA
  public relations • MA
  radio, television and film • MA
  radio, tv, film • MA
  speech communication • MA
  technical communication • MA
  theory and process • MA

College of Engineering and Computer Science
Dr. Raman Unnikrishnan, Dean
Programs in:
  applications administrative information systems • MS
  applications mathematical methods • MS
  civil engineering and engineering mechanics • MS
  computer science • MS
  electrical engineering • MS
  engineering and computer science • MS
  engineering science • MS
  information processing systems • MS
  mechanical engineering • MS
  systems engineering • MS

College of Human Development and Community Service
Dr. Roberta Rikli, Dean
Programs in:
  bilingual/bicultural education • MS
  counseling • MS
  educational leadership • MS
  elementary curriculum and instruction • MS
  human development and community service • MS
  instructional design and technology • MS
  middle school mathematics • MS
  nursing • MS
  physical education • MS
  reading • MS
  secondary education • MS
  special education • MS
  teacher induction • MS

College of Humanities and Social Sciences
Dr. Thomas Klammer, Dean
Programs in:
  American studies • MA
  analysis of specific language structures • MA
  anthropological linguistics • MA
  anthropology • MA
  applied linguistics • MA
  clinical/community psychology • MS
  communication and semantics • MA
  comparative literature • MA
  disorders of communication • MA
  English • MA
  environmental education and communication • MS
  environmental policy and planning • MS
  environmental sciences • MS
  experimental phonetics • MA
  French • MA
  geography • MA
  German • MA
  gerontology • MS
  history • MA
  humanities and social sciences • MA, MPA, MS
  political science • MA
  psychology • MA
  public administration • MPA
  sociology • MA
  Spanish • MA
  teaching English to speakers of other languages • MS
  technological studies • MS

College of Natural Science and Mathematics
Dr. Kolf Jayaweera, Dean
Programs in:
  analytical chemistry • MS
  applied mathematics • MA
  biochemistry • MS
  biological science • MA
  botany • MA
  geochemistry • MS
  geological sciences • MS
  inorganic chemistry • MS
  mathematics • MA
  mathematics for secondary school teachers • MA
  microbiology • MA
  natural science and mathematics • MA, MS
  organic chemistry • MS
  physical chemistry • MS
  physics • MA
  teaching science • MA

College of the Arts
Jerry Samuelson, Dean
Programs in:
  acting • MFA
  acting and directing • MA
  art • MA, MFA
  art history • MA
  arts • MA, MFA, MM, Certificate
  dance • MA
  design • MA
  directing • MFA
  dramatic literature/criticism • MA
  museum studies • Certificate
  music education • MA
  music history and literature • MA
  oral interpretation • MA
  performance • MM
  playwriting • MA
  technical theater • MA
  technical theater and design • MFA
  television • MA
  theatre for children • MA
  theatre history • MA
  theory-composition • MM

■ **CALIFORNIA STATE UNIVERSITY, HAYWARD**
Hayward, CA 94542-3000
http://www.csuhayward.edu/

State-supported, coed, comprehensive institution. CGS member. *Enrollment:* 13,455 graduate, professional, and undergraduate students; 2,609 full-time matriculated graduate/professional students (1,696 women), 1,161 part-time matriculated graduate/professional students (726 women). *Graduate faculty:* 368. *Computer facilities:* 700 computers available on campus for general student use. A campuswide network can be accessed from student residence rooms and from off campus. Internet access and online class registration are available. *Library facilities:* California State

Peterson's Graduate Schools in the U.S. 2006

California

California State University, Hayward (continued)
University, Hayward Library plus 1 other. *Graduate expenses:* Tuition, nonresident: part-time $188 per unit. Required fees: $560 per quarter hour. *General application contact:* Jennifer Cason, Graduate Program Coordinator/Operations Analyst, 510-885-3286.

Academic Programs and Graduate Studies
Dr. Carl Bellone, Associate Vice President
Program in:
   interdisciplinary studies • MA, MS, Certificate

College of Arts, Letters, and Social Sciences
Dr. Alden Reimonenq, Dean
Programs in:
   anthropology • MA
   arts, letters, and social sciences • MA, MPA, MS
   communication • MA
   English • MA
   geography • MA
   history • MA
   music • MA
   public administration • MPA
   sociology • MA
   speech pathology • MS

College of Business and Economics
Dr. Sam Basu, Interim Dean
Programs in:
   accounting • MBA
   business and economics • MA, MBA, MS
   computer information systems • MBA
   e-business • MBA
   economics • MA, MBA
   finance • MBA
   human resources management • MBA
   international business • MBA
   management sciences • MBA
   marketing management • MBA
   new ventures/small business management • MBA
   operations research • MBA
   quantitative business methods • MS
   supply chain management • MBA
   taxation • MBA, MS

College of Education
Dr. Arthurlene Towner, Dean
Programs in:
   counseling • MS
   education • MS
   educational leadership • MS
   physical education • MS
   special education • MS
   teacher education • MS

College of Science
Dr. Michael Leung, Dean
Programs in:
   biochemistry • MS
   biological sciences • MS
   chemistry • MS
   computer science • MS
   geology • MS
   marine sciences • MS
   mathematics • MS
   science • MS
   statistics • MS

■ CALIFORNIA STATE UNIVERSITY, LONG BEACH
Long Beach, CA 90840
http://www.csulb.edu/

State-supported, coed, comprehensive institution. CGS member. *Enrollment:* 34,715 graduate, professional, and undergraduate students; 4,217 matriculated graduate/professional students. *Graduate faculty:* 903 full-time, 625 part-time/adjunct. *Computer facilities:* 2,000 computers available on campus for general student use. A campuswide network can be accessed from off campus. Internet access is available. *Library facilities:* University Library. *Graduate expenses:* Tuition, nonresident: part-time $282 per unit. Required fees: $504 per semester. *General application contact:* Rachel Brophy, Students Programs Coordinator, 562-985-4546.

Graduate Studies
Dr. Cecile Lindsay, Associate Vice President for Academic Affairs
Program in:
   interdisciplinary studies • MA, MS

College of Business Administration
Dr. Luis Ma. R. Calingo, Dean
Program in:
   business administration • MBA

College of Education
Dr. Jean Houck, Dean
Programs in:
   counseling • MS, Certificate
   education • MA, MS, Ed D, Certificate
   educational administration • MA
   educational administration and leadership • Ed D
   educational psychology • MA
   elementary education • MA
   secondary education • MA
   social and multicultural foundations of education • MA
   special education • MS

College of Engineering
Dr. Michael Mahoney, Interim Dean
Programs in:
   aerospace engineering • MSAE
   civil engineering • MSCE, CE
   computer engineering • MS
   computer science • MS
   electrical engineering • MSE, MSEE
   engineering • MSE
   engineering and industrial applied mathematics • PhD
   interdisciplinary engineering • MSE
   management engineering • MSE
   mechanical engineering • MSME
   waste engineering and management • Graduate Certificate

College of Health and Human Services
Dr. Ronald Vogel, Chair
Programs in:
   audiology • MA
   community health education • MPH
   criminal justice • MS
   emergency services administration • MS
   gerontology • MS
   health and human services • MA, MPA, MPH, MPT, MS, MSW, Certificate
   health care administration • MS, Certificate
   health science • MS
   home economics • MA
   kinesiology and physical education • MA
   nurse anesthesiology • MS
   nursing • MS
   nutritional sciences • MS
   occupational studies • MA
   physical therapy • MPT
   public policy and administration • MPA, Certificate
   recreation and leisure studies • MS
   social work • MSW
   speech pathology • MA

College of Liberal Arts
Dr. Dorothy Abrahamse, Dean
Programs in:
   anthropology • MA
   Asian American studies • Certificate
   Asian studies • MA
   communication studies • MA
   creative writing • MFA
   economics • MA
   English • MA
   French • MA
   geography • MA
   German • MA
   global logistics • MA
   history • MA
   liberal arts • MA, MFA, MS, Certificate
   linguistics • MA
   philosophy • MA
   political science • MA
   psychology • MA, MS
   religious studies • MA
   Spanish • MA

College of Natural Sciences
Dr. Laura Kingsford, Dean
Programs in:

applied mathematics • MA
biochemistry • MS
biological sciences • MS
chemistry • MS
geological sciences • MS
mathematics • MA
medical technology • MPH
metals physics • MS
microbiology • MPH, MS
natural sciences • MA, MPH, MS
nurse epidemiology • MPH
physics • MS

College of the Arts
Dr. Donald Para, Dean
Programs in:
art education • MA
art history • MA
arts • MA, MFA, MM
crafts • MA, MFA
dance • MFA
dance education • MA
illustration • MA, MFA
music • MA, MM
pictorial arts • MA, MFA
theatre arts • MA, MFA

■ CALIFORNIA STATE UNIVERSITY, LOS ANGELES
Los Angeles, CA 90032-8530
http://www.calstatela.edu/

State-supported, coed, comprehensive institution. CGS member. *Enrollment:* 20,637 graduate, professional, and undergraduate students; 1,578 full-time matriculated graduate/professional students (1,059 women), 2,682 part-time matriculated graduate/professional students (1,696 women). *Graduate faculty:* 612 full-time (276 women), 450 part-time/adjunct (220 women). *Computer facilities:* 1,500 computers available on campus for general student use. A campuswide network can be accessed from off campus. Internet access is available. *Library facilities:* John F. Kennedy Memorial Library. *Graduate expenses:* Tuition, nonresident: part-time $188 per unit. Required fees: $2,477. *General application contact:* Dr. Theodore Crovello, Dean of Graduate Studies, 323-343-3820.

Graduate Studies
Dr. Theodore Crovello, Dean

Charter College of Education
Dr. Carol Bartell, Dean
Programs in:
applied behavior analysis • MS
community college counseling • MS
computer education • MA
counseling • MS
early childhood education for the handicapped • MA
education • MA, MS, PhD
education of handicapped adolescents and young adults • MA
education of the communication handicapped • MA
education of the learning handicapped • MA
education of the physically handicapped • MA
education of the severely handicapped • MA
education of the visually handicapped • MA
educational administration • MA
educational foundations and interdivisional studies • MA
elementary teaching • MA
gifted education • MA
instructional technology • MA
multicultural and multilingual special education • MA
orientation and mobility specialist for the blind • MA
psychological foundations • MA
reading • MA
rehabilitation counseling • MS
resource specialist • MA
school counseling and school psychology • MS
secondary teaching • MA
social foundations • MA
special education • PhD
special interests • MA
teaching English to speakers of other languages • MA

College of Arts and Letters
Dr. Carl M. Selkin, Dean
Programs in:
art • MA
arts and letters • MA, MFA, MM
English • MA
fine arts • MFA
French • MA
music composition • MM
music education • MA
musicology • MA
performance • MM
philosophy • MA
Spanish • MA
speech communication • MA
theater arts • MA

College of Business and Economics
Dr. Timothy Haight, Dean
Programs in:
accountancy • MS
accounting • MBA
analytical quantitative economics • MA
business and economics • MA, MBA, MS
business economics • MA, MBA, MS
business information systems • MBA
economics • MA
finance and banking • MBA, MS
finance and law • MBA, MS
health care management • MS
information systems • MBA, MS
international business • MBA, MS
management • MBA, MS
management information systems • MS
marketing • MBA, MS
office management • MBA

College of Engineering, Computer Science, and Technology
Dr. Kuei-wu Tsai, Dean
Programs in:
civil engineering • MS
electrical engineering • MS
engineering, computer science, and technology • MA, MS
industrial and technical studies • MA
mechanical engineering • MS

College of Health and Human Services
Dr. Mitchell Maki, Acting Dean
Programs in:
child development • MA
communicative disorders • MA
criminal justice • MS
criminalistics • MS
health and human services • MA, MS, MSW
health science • MA
hearing • MA
kinesiology • MA
nursing • MS
nutritional science • MS
physical education • MA
physical education and kinesiology • MA
social work • MSW
speech • MA

College of Natural and Social Sciences
Dr. Desdemona Cardoza, Dean
Programs in:
analytical chemistry • MS
anthropology • MA
biochemistry • MS
biology • MS
chemistry • MS
geography • MA
geological sciences • MS
history • MA
inorganic chemistry • MS
Latin American studies • MA
mathematics • MS
Mexican-American studies • MA
natural and social sciences • MA, MS
organic chemistry • MS
physical chemistry • MS
physics • MS
political science • MA
psychology • MA, MS
public administration • MS
sociology • MA

California

■ CALIFORNIA STATE UNIVERSITY, NORTHRIDGE
Northridge, CA 91330
http://www.csun.edu/

State-supported, coed, comprehensive institution. CGS member. *Enrollment:* 1,643 full-time matriculated graduate/professional students (1,106 women), 2,504 part-time matriculated graduate/professional students (1,539 women). *Graduate faculty:* 750 full-time, 1,068 part-time/adjunct. *Computer facilities:* A campuswide network can be accessed from off campus. Internet access and online class registration are available. *Library facilities:* Oviatt Library. *General application contact:* Dr. Mack Johnson, Associate Vice President, 818-677-2138.

Graduate Studies
Dr. Mack Johnson, Associate Vice President
Program in:
  interdisciplinary studies • MA, MS

College of Arts, Media, and Communications
William P. Toutant, Interim Dean
Programs in:
  art education • MA
  art history • MA
  arts • MA, MFA
  arts, media, and communications • MA, MFA, MM
  communication studies • MA
  composition • MM
  mass communication • MA
  music education • MA
  music theory • MA
  musicology • MA
  news communication • MA
  performance • MM
  studio arts • MFA
  theater • MA

College of Business Administration and Economics
Dr. William Hosek, Dean
Programs in:
  business administration and economics • MBA
  management of information systems • MBA

College of Education
Dr. Philip J. Rusche, Head
Programs in:
  administration and supervision • MA
  counseling • MS
  counseling and guidance • MS, MFCC
  early childhood special education • MA
  education • MA, MS, MFCC
  education of the deaf and hard of hearing • MA
  education of the gifted • MA
  education of the learning handicapped • MA
  education of the severely handicapped • MA
  educational psychology and counseling • MA
  educational therapy • MA
  elementary education • MA
  foundations • MA
  genetic counseling • MS
  marriage, family and child counseling • MFCC
  secondary education • MA

College of Engineering and Computer Science
Dr. Laurence Caretto, Interim Dean
Programs in:
  aerospace engineering • MS
  applied engineering • MS
  applied mechanics • MSE
  biomedical engineering • MS
  civil engineering • MS
  communications/radar engineering • MS
  computer science • MS
  control engineering • MS
  digital/computer engineering • MS
  electronics engineering • MS
  engineering and computer science • MS
  engineering management • MS
  industrial engineering • MS
  machine design • MS
  materials engineering • MS
  mechanical engineering • MS
  mechanics • MS
  microwave/antenna engineering • MS
  structural engineering • MS
  thermofluids • MS

College of Health and Human Development
Dr. Ann Stutts, Dean
Programs in:
  communicative disorders and sciences • MS
  environmental and occupational health • MS
  family environmental sciences • MS
  health administration • MSHA
  health and human development • MPH, MPT, MS, MSHA
  health science • MS
  kinesiology • MS
  leisure studies and recreation • MS
  physical therapy • MPT
  public health • MPH

College of Humanities
Dr. Jorge Garcia, Dean
Programs in:
  Chicano studies • MA
  English • MA
  humanities • MA
  linguistics • MA
  Spanish • MA

College of Science and Mathematics
Dr. Edward J. Carroll, Interim Dean
Programs in:
  biology • MS
  chemistry • MS
  genetic counseling • MS
  geological sciences • MS
  mathematics • MS
  physics • MS
  science and mathematics • MS

College of Social and Behavioral Sciences
Dr. Stella Z. Theodoulou, Interim Dean
Programs in:
  anthropology • MA
  geography • MA
  history • MA
  political science • MA
  psychology • MA
  public administration • MPA
  social and behavioral sciences • MA, MPA
  sociology • MA

■ CALIFORNIA STATE UNIVERSITY, SACRAMENTO
Sacramento, CA 95819-6048
http://www.csus.edu/

State-supported, coed, comprehensive institution. CGS member. *Enrollment:* 28,375 graduate, professional, and undergraduate students; 1,821 full-time matriculated graduate/professional students (1,177 women), 2,074 part-time matriculated graduate/professional students (1,309 women). *Graduate faculty:* 359 full-time (152 women), 162 part-time/adjunct (92 women). *Computer facilities:* 700 computers available on campus for general student use. A campuswide network can be accessed from student residence rooms and from off campus. Internet access and online class registration are available. *Library facilities:* California State University, Sacramento Library. *Graduate expenses:* Tuition, state resident: full-time $2,256. Tuition, nonresident: full-time $10,716. *General application contact:* Darleen M. Entrican, Graduate Admissions Supervisor, 916-278-6470.

Graduate Studies
Dr. Miki Vohryzek-Bolden, Associate Dean
Program in:
  special majors • MA, MS

College of Arts and Letters
Dr. William J. Sullivan, Dean
Programs in:

California

arts and letters • MA, MM
communication studies • MA
creative writing • MA
foreign languages • MA
French • MA
German • MA
music • MM
public history • MA
Spanish • MA
studio art • MA
teaching English to speakers of other languages • MA
theater arts • MA
theatre and dance • MA

College of Business Administration
Programs in:
accountancy • MS
business administration • MBA
human resources • MBA
management information science • MS
urban land development • MBA

College of Education
Dr. Michael Lewis, Dean
Programs in:
bilingual/cross-cultural education • MA
career counseling • MS
curriculum and instruction • MA
early childhood education • MA
education • MA, MS
educational administration • MA
generic counseling • MS
guidance • MA
reading education • MA
school counseling • MS
school psychology • MS
special education • MA
vocational rehabilitation • MS

College of Engineering and Computer Science
Dr. Braja Das, Dean
Programs in:
civil engineering • MS
computer systems • MS
electrical engineering • MS
engineering and computer science • MS
mechanical engineering • MS
software engineering • MS

College of Health and Human Services
Dr. Marilyn Hopkins, Dean
Programs in:
audiology • MS
criminal justice • MS
family and children's services • MSW
health and human services • MS, MSW
health care • MSW
mental health • MSW
nursing • MS
physical education • MS
recreation administration • MS
social justice and corrections • MSW
speech pathology • MS

College of Natural Sciences and Mathematics
Marion O'Leary, Dean
Programs in:
biological sciences • MA, MS
chemistry • MS
immunohematology • MS
marine science • MS
mathematics and statistics • MA
natural sciences and mathematics • MA, MS

College of Social Sciences and Interdisciplinary Studies
Joseph F. Sheley, Dean
Programs in:
anthropology • MA
counseling psychology • MA
government • MA
international affairs • MA
public policy and administration • MPPA
social sciences and interdisciplinary studies • MA, MPPA
sociology • MA

■ CALIFORNIA STATE UNIVERSITY, SAN BERNARDINO
San Bernardino, CA 92407-2397
http://www.csusb.edu/

State-supported, coed, comprehensive institution. CGS member. *Enrollment:* 16,927 graduate, professional, and undergraduate students; 1,437 full-time matriculated graduate/professional students (949 women), 883 part-time matriculated graduate/professional students (531 women). *Graduate faculty:* 458 full-time, 496 part-time/adjunct. *Computer facilities:* 1,300 computers available on campus for general student use. A campuswide network can be accessed from student residence rooms and from off campus. Internet access and online class registration are available. *Library facilities:* Pfau Library. *Graduate expenses:* Tuition, nonresident: part-time $188 per unit. Required fees: $657 per quarter. *General application contact:* Olivia Rosas, Director of Admissions, 909-880-5188.

Graduate Studies
Dr. Sandra Kamusikiri, Chair
Program in:
interdisciplinary studies • MA

College of Arts and Letters
Dr. Eri F. Yasuhara, Dean
Programs in:
art • MA
arts and letters • MA
communication studies • MA
English composition • MA
interdisciplinary studies • MA

College of Business and Public Administration
Dr. Norton Marks, Dean
Programs in:
business administration • MBA
business and public administration • MBA, MPA
public administration • MPA

College of Education
Dr. Patricia Arlin, Dean
Programs in:
bilingual/cross-cultural education • MA
curriculum and instruction • MA
educational administration • MA
educational psychology and counseling • MA, MS
elementary education • MA
English as a second language • MA
environmental education • MA
history and English for secondary teachers • MA
instructional technology • MA
reading • MA
rehabilitation counseling • MA
secondary education • MA
special education • MA
special education and rehabilitation counseling • MA
vocational and career education • MA

College of Natural Sciences
Dr. B. Robert Carlson, Dean
Programs in:
biology • MS
computer science • MS
health science • MS
health services administration • MS
mathematics • MA
natural sciences • MA, MAT, MS
nursing • MS
teaching of science • MAT

College of Social and Behavioral Sciences
Dr. John Conley, Chair
Programs in:
child development • MA
clinical/counseling psychology • MS
criminal justice • MA
general/experimental psychology • MA
industrial organizational psychology • MS
national security studies • MA
social and behavioral sciences • MA, MS, MSW
social sciences • MA
social work • MSW

■ CALIFORNIA STATE UNIVERSITY, SAN MARCOS
San Marcos, CA 92096-0001
http://ww2.csusm.edu/

State-supported, coed, comprehensive institution. CGS member. *Enrollment:* 7,723 graduate, professional, and

California

California State University, San Marcos (continued)
undergraduate students; 176 full-time matriculated graduate/professional students (100 women), 370 part-time matriculated graduate/professional students (260 women). *Graduate faculty:* 181 full-time, 262 part-time/adjunct. *Computer facilities:* 487 computers available on campus for general student use. A campuswide network can be accessed from student residence rooms and from off campus. Internet access and online class registration are available. *Library facilities:* Library and Information Services. *Graduate expenses:* Tuition, nonresident: part-time $282 per unit. Required fees: $838 per semester. *General application contact:* Admissions, 760-750-4848.

College of Arts and Sciences
Dr. Vicki Golich, Interim Dean
Programs in:
 arts and sciences • MA, MS
 biological sciences • MS
 computer science • MS
 literature and writing studies • MA
 mathematics • MS
 psychology • MA
 sociological practice • MA
 Spanish • MA

College of Business Administration
Dennis Guseman, Dean
Programs in:
 business management • MBA
 government management • MBA

College of Education
Dr. Steve Lilly, Dean
Program in:
 education • MA

■ CALIFORNIA STATE UNIVERSITY, STANISLAUS
Turlock, CA 95382
http://www.csustan.edu/

State-supported, coed, comprehensive institution. CGS member. *Enrollment:* 8,072 graduate, professional, and undergraduate students; 480 full-time matriculated graduate/professional students (371 women), 604 part-time matriculated graduate/professional students (403 women). *Graduate faculty:* 78. *Computer facilities:* 150 computers available on campus for general student use. A campuswide network can be accessed from student residence rooms and from off campus. Internet access is available. *Library facilities:* Vasche Library. *Graduate expenses:* Tuition, state resident: part-time $282 per unit. Tuition, nonresident: full-time $5,922. Required fees: $2,634. Tuition and fees vary according to course load. *General application contact:* Dr. James Burns, Director, The Graduate School, 209-667-3129.

Graduate Programs
Dr. Diana Demetrulias, Dean, The Graduate School
Program in:
 interdisciplinary studies • MA, MS

College of Arts, Letters, and Sciences
Dr. James Klein, Interim Dean
Programs in:
 arts, letters, and sciences • MA, MPA, MS, MSW
 behavior analysis psychology • MS
 counseling psychology • MS
 criminal justice • MA
 English • MA
 general psychology • MA
 history • MA
 marine sciences • MS
 public administration • MPA
 social work • MSW

College of Business Administration
Dr. Amin Elmallah, Dean
Program in:
 business administration • MBA

College of Education
Dr. Irma Wagner, Dean
Programs in:
 curriculum and instruction • MA Ed
 education • MA Ed
 educational administration • MA Ed
 educational technology • MA Ed
 elementary education • MA Ed
 multilingual education • MA Ed
 physical education • MA Ed
 reading education • MA Ed
 school counseling • MA Ed
 secondary education • MA Ed
 special education • MA Ed

■ CHAPMAN UNIVERSITY
Orange, CA 92866
http://www.chapman.edu/

Independent-religious, coed, comprehensive institution. *Enrollment:* 5,138 graduate, professional, and undergraduate students; 945 full-time matriculated graduate/professional students (545 women), 555 part-time matriculated graduate/professional students (358 women). *Graduate faculty:* 117 full-time (44 women), 158 part-time/adjunct (65 women). *Computer facilities:* Computer purchase and lease plans are available. 278 computers available on campus for general student use. A campuswide network can be accessed from off campus. Internet access is available. *Library facilities:* Thurmond Clarke Memorial Library plus 1 other. *Graduate expenses:* Tuition: full-time $16,320; part-time $680 per credit. Tuition and fees vary according to program. *General application contact:* Saundra Hoover, Director of Graduate Admissions, 714-997-6786.

Find an in-depth description at www.petersons.com/gradchannel.

Graduate Studies
Dr. Raymond Sfeir, Associate Provost
Program in:
 food science and nutrition • MS

Department of Physical Therapy
Dr. Venita Lovelace-Chandler, Chair
Program in:
 physical therapy • DPT

Division of Psychology
Dr. Georg Eifert, Chair
Programs in:
 clinical psychology • MA
 marriage and family therapy • MA
 psychology • MA

The George L. Argyros School of Business and Economics
Dr. Doug Tuggle, Dean
Programs in:
 business and economics • Exec MBA, MBA, MSHRM, Certificate
 human resources and management • MSHRM
 human resources management • Certificate

School of Communication Arts
Dr. Myron Yeager, Dean
Programs in:
 communication arts • MA, MFA
 creative writing • MFA
 literature • MA

School of Education
Dr. Donald Cardinal, Dean
Programs in:
 curriculum and instruction • MA
 education • MA, Ed S
 educational leadership and administration • MA
 educational psychology • MA
 reading education • MA
 school counseling • MA
 school psychology • Ed S
 special education • MA
 teaching: elementary education • MA
 teaching: secondary education • MA

School of Film and Television
Robert Bassett, Dean
Programs in:
 film and television • MA, MFA
 film and television producing • MFA
 film production • MFA
 film studies • MA
 screenwriting • MFA

School of Law
Dr. Parham Williams, Dean
Programs in:
 law • JD
 taxation • LL M

CLAREMONT GRADUATE UNIVERSITY
Claremont, CA 91711-6160
http://www.cgu.edu/

Independent, coed, graduate-only institution. CGS member. *Graduate faculty:* 62 full-time (21 women), 78 part-time/adjunct (23 women). *Computer facilities:* 90 computers available on campus for general student use. A campuswide network can be accessed from student residence rooms and from off campus. Internet access is available. *Library facilities:* Honnold Library plus 3 others. *Graduate expenses:* Tuition: full-time $25,250; part-time $1,099 per semester. *General application contact:* Brenda Wright, Admissions Counselor, 909-627-0434.

Graduate Programs
Dr. Philip H. Dreyer, Vice President for Academic Affairs/Provost
Programs in:
  applied women's studies • MA
  botany • MS, PhD

Centers for the Arts and Humanities
Patricia Easton, Dean
Programs in:
  American studies • MA, PhD
  ancient philosophy • MA, PhD
  archival studies • MA, PhD
  arts • M Phil, MA, MFA, DCM, DMA, PhD
  church music • MA, DCM
  composition • MA, DMA
  contemporary philosophy • MA, PhD
  cultural studies • MA, PhD
  digital media • MA, MFA
  drawing • MA, MFA
  early modern studies • MA, PhD
  English • M Phil, MA, PhD
  European studies • MA, PhD
  literary theory • PhD
  literature • MA, PhD
  literature and creative writing • MA
  literature and film • MA
  modern philosophy • MA, PhD
  musicology • MA, PhD
  new genre • MA, MFA
  oral history • MA, PhD
  painting • MA, MFA
  performance • MA, DMA
  performance/installation • MA, MFA
  photography • MA, MFA
  sculpture • MA, MFA

Peter F. Drucker and Masatoshi Ito Graduate School of Management
Cornelis de Kluyver, Dean
Programs in:
  advanced management • MS
  business administration • MBA
  executive management • EMBA, MA, MS, PhD, Certificate
  finance • MBA
  financial engineering • MS, MSFE, PhD
  international business • MBA
  leadership • MBA, Certificate
  management • MA, MBA, PhD, Certificate
  marketing • MBA
  strategic management • MBA
  strategy • Certificate

School of Behavioral and Organizational Sciences
Stewart Donaldson, Dean
Programs in:
  behavioral and organizational sciences • MA, MS, PhD
  cognitive psychology • MA, PhD
  developmental psychology • MA, PhD
  evaluation and applied methods • MA, PhD
  human resources design • MS
  organizational behavior • MA, PhD
  social psychology • MA, PhD

School of Educational Studies
Mary Poplin, Dean
Programs in:
  comparative educational studies • MA, PhD
  education policy issues • MA, PhD
  higher education • PhD
  higher education administration • MA
  human development • MA, PhD
  linguistics and anthropology • MA, PhD
  organization and administration • PhD
  public school administration • MA, PhD
  reading and language development • MA, PhD
  teacher education • MA, PhD
  teaching and learning • MA, PhD
  teaching/learning process • PhD
  urban education administration • MA, PhD

School of Information Science
Lorne Olfman, Dean
Programs in:
  electronic commerce • MS
  knowledge management • MS
  management of information systems • MS, PhD
  systems development • MS
  telecommunications and networking • MS

School of Mathematical Sciences
John Angus, Chair
Programs in:
  computational science • PhD
  engineering mathematics • PhD
  financial engineering • MS
  operations research and statistics • MA, MS
  physical applied mathematics • MA, MS
  pure mathematics • MA, MS, PhD
  scientific computing • MA, MS
  systems and control theory • MA, MS

School of Politics and Economics
Yi Feng, Dean
Programs in:
  American politics • MA
  business and financial economics • MA, PhD
  economics • PhD
  international economic policy and management • MA, PhD
  international political economy • MA
  international studies • MA
  political economy and public policy • MA, PhD
  political science • PhD
  politics and economics • MA, PhD
  politics, economics and business • MA
  public policy • MA

School of Religion
Karen Jo Torjesen, Dean
Programs in:
  Hebrew Bible • MA, PhD
  history of Christianity and religion in North America • MA, PhD
  New Testament • MA, PhD
  philosophy of religion and theology • MA, PhD
  theology, ethics and culture • MA, PhD
  women's studies in religion • MA, PhD

CONCORDIA UNIVERSITY
Irvine, CA 92612-3299
http://www.cui.edu/

Independent-religious, coed, comprehensive institution. *Enrollment:* 1,747 graduate, professional, and undergraduate students; 267 full-time matriculated graduate/professional students (178 women), 140 part-time matriculated graduate/professional students (97 women). *Graduate faculty:* 31 full-time (9 women), 40 part-time/adjunct (16 women). *Computer facilities:* 42 computers available on campus for general student use. A campuswide network can be accessed from student residence rooms and from off campus. Internet access is available. *Library facilities:* Concordia University Library. *Graduate expenses:* Tuition: part-time $390 per unit. *General application contact:* Information Contact, 800-229-1200.

School of Business Administration
Dr. Richard Harms, Director
Program in:
  entrepreneurial • MBA

California

Concordia University (continued)
School of Education
Dr. Barbara Morton, Dean
Programs in:
curriculum and instruction • MA
education • M Ed
educational administration • MA
k-12 education • MA
professional goals/individual students • MA

School of Theology
Rev. Dr. James V. Bachman, Dean
Programs in:
Christian leadership • MA
family life • MA
mission planting • MA
Reformation theology • MA
research and theology • MA
theology and culture • MA

■ DOMINICAN UNIVERSITY OF CALIFORNIA
San Rafael, CA 94901-2298
http://www.dominican.edu/

Independent-religious, coed, comprehensive institution. *Enrollment:* 1,742 graduate, professional, and undergraduate students; 335 full-time matriculated graduate/professional students (252 women), 285 part-time matriculated graduate/professional students (209 women). *Graduate faculty:* 42 full-time (30 women), 102 part-time/adjunct (70 women). *Computer facilities:* 52 computers available on campus for general student use. A campuswide network can be accessed from student residence rooms and from off campus. Internet access is available. *Library facilities:* Archbishop Alemany Library plus 1 other. *Graduate expenses:* Tuition: full-time $11,610; part-time $645 per unit. Required fees: $400; $200 per term. *General application contact:* Lorrie Crivello, Director of Graduate and Pathways Admissions, 415-458-3754.

Graduate Programs
Dr. Kenneth Porada, Provost and Vice President for Academic Affairs

School of Arts and Sciences
Dr. Martha Nelson, Dean
Programs in:
arts and sciences • MA, MS
counseling psychology • MS
humanities • MA
nursing • MS
occupational therapy • MS

School of Business, Education and Leadership
Dr. Ed Kujawa, Dean
Programs in:
business • MBA
business, education and leadership • MBA, MS, Credential
curriculum and instruction • MS
education • MS, Credential
global strategic management • MBA
multiple subject credential • Credential
single subject credential • Credential
special education credential • Credential
strategic leadership • MBA

■ FRESNO PACIFIC UNIVERSITY
Fresno, CA 93702-4709
http://www.fresno.edu/

Independent-religious, coed, comprehensive institution. *Enrollment:* 2,243 graduate, professional, and undergraduate students; 62 full-time matriculated graduate/professional students (54 women), 515 part-time matriculated graduate/professional students (347 women). *Graduate faculty:* 30 full-time (12 women), 51 part-time/adjunct (27 women). *Computer facilities:* 68 computers available on campus for general student use. A campuswide network can be accessed from student residence rooms and from off campus. *Library facilities:* Hiebert Library. *Graduate expenses:* Tuition: full-time $6,930; part-time $385 per unit. *General application contact:* Shirley N. MacNeil, Admissions Coordinator, 559-453-3667.

Graduate School
Dr. Wendy Wakman, Dean
Programs in:
individualized study • MA
leadership and organizational studies • MA
peacemaking and conflict studies • MA
teaching English to speakers of other languages • MA

Programs in Education
Programs in:
administration • MA Ed
administrative services • MA Ed
bilingual/cross-cultural education • MA Ed
curriculum and teaching • MA Ed
educational technology • MA Ed
foundations, curriculum and teaching • MA Ed
integrated mathematics/science education • MA Ed
language development • MA Ed
language, literacy, and culture • MA Ed
mathematics education • MA Ed
mathematics/science/computer education • MA Ed
middle school mathematics • MA Ed
mild/moderate • MA Ed
moderate/severe • MA Ed
multilingual contexts • MA Ed
physical and health impairments • MA Ed
pupil personnel services • MA Ed
reading • MA Ed
reading/English as a second language • MA Ed
reading/language arts • MA Ed
school counseling • MA Ed
school library and information technology • MA Ed
school psychology • MA Ed
secondary school mathematics • MA Ed
special education • MA Ed

■ GOLDEN GATE BAPTIST THEOLOGICAL SEMINARY
Mill Valley, CA 94941-3197
http://www.ggbts.edu/

Independent-religious, coed, graduate-only institution. *Graduate faculty:* 25 full-time (2 women), 18 part-time/adjunct (8 women). *Computer facilities:* 15 computers available on campus for general student use. A campuswide network can be accessed from off campus. Internet access and online class registration are available. *Graduate expenses:* Tuition: part-time $1,600 per semester. Tuition and fees vary according to degree level, program and student's religious affiliation. *General application contact:* Karen Robinson, Director of Admissions and International Student Advancement, 415-380-1600.

Graduate and Professional Programs
Programs in:
Christian education • MACE, Dip CS
church music • MACM, MMCM
divinity • M Div
early childhood education • Certificate
intercultural ministries • MAIM
ministry • D Min
theological studies • MATS
theology • Th M, Dip CS
worship leadership • MA

■ HOLY NAMES UNIVERSITY
Oakland, CA 94619-1699
http://www.hnc.edu/

Independent-religious, coed, primarily women, comprehensive institution. *Enrollment:* 943 graduate, professional, and undergraduate students; 112 full-time matriculated graduate/professional

California

students (92 women), 238 part-time matriculated graduate/professional students (201 women). *Graduate faculty:* 11 full-time (9 women), 68 part-time/adjunct (45 women). *Computer facilities:* 69 computers available on campus for general student use. A campuswide network can be accessed from student residence rooms and from off campus. Internet access is available. *Library facilities:* Cushing Library. *Graduate expenses:* Tuition: full-time $9,720; part-time $540 per unit. Required fees: $210; $210 per year. *General application contact:* 510-436-1317.

Graduate Division
Dr. David Fike, Vice President for Academic Affairs
Programs in:
  advanced curriculum studies • M Ed
  community health nursing/case manager • MS
  counseling psychology with emphasis in pastoral counseling • MA
  educational therapy • M Ed
  family nurse practitioner • MS
  Kodály music education • Certificate
  management • MBA
  mild/moderate disabilities • Ed S
  multiple subject credential program • M Ed
  music education with a Kodály emphasis • MM
  pastoral counseling • MA, Certificate
  pastoral ministry • MA
  performance • MM
  piano pedagogy • MM
  piano pedagogy with Suzuki emphasis • Certificate
  single subject credential program • M Ed
  special education • M Ed
  teaching English as a second language • M Ed, Certificate
  urban education • M Ed

Sophia Center: Spirituality for the New Millennium
Dr. James Conlon, Program Director
Programs in:
  creation spirituality • Certificate
  culture and creation spirituality • MA

■ **HOPE INTERNATIONAL UNIVERSITY**
Fullerton, CA 92831-3138
http://www.hiu.edu/

Independent-religious, coed, comprehensive institution. *Computer facilities:* 32 computers available on campus for general student use. A campuswide network can be accessed from off campus. Internet access is available. *Library facilities:* Hurst Memorial Library. *General application contact:* Admissions Director, 800-762-1294 Ext. 2604.

School of Graduate Studies
Programs in:
  church music • MA, MCM
  congregational leadership • MA
  counseling • MA
  education • ME
  intercultural studies/urban ministries • MA
  international development • MBA, MSM
  marriage and family therapy • MFT
  marriage, family, and child counseling • MA
  nonprofit management • MBA
  psychology • MA

■ **HUMBOLDT STATE UNIVERSITY**
Arcata, CA 95521-8299
http://www.humboldt.edu/

State-supported, coed, comprehensive institution. CGS member. *Enrollment:* 7,725 graduate, professional, and undergraduate students; 351 full-time matriculated graduate/professional students (203 women), 189 part-time matriculated graduate/professional students (103 women). *Graduate faculty:* 290 full-time (93 women), 199 part-time/adjunct (118 women). *Computer facilities:* 778 computers available on campus for general student use. A campuswide network can be accessed from student residence rooms and from off campus. Internet access and online class registration are available. *Graduate expenses:* Tuition, state resident: full-time $2,539. *General application contact:* Carla Douglas, Research and Graduate Studies, 707-826-3949.

Graduate Studies
Dr. Donna Schafer, Dean

College of Arts, Humanities, and Social Sciences
Dr. Karen Carlton, Dean
Programs in:
  arts, humanities, and social sciences • MA, MFA
  English • MA
  environment and community • MA
  sociology • MA
  theatre arts • MA, MFA

College of Natural Resources and Sciences
Dr. Jim Howard, Dean
Programs in:
  biological sciences • MA
  environmental systems • MS
  natural resources • MS
  natural resources and sciences • MA, MS
  psychology • MA

College of Professional Studies
Dr. Susan Higgins, Dean
Programs in:
  athletic training education • MS
  business • MBA
  exercise science/wellness management • MS
  pre-physical therapy • MS
  professional studies • MBA, MS
  teaching/coaching • MS

■ **JOHN F. KENNEDY UNIVERSITY**
Pleasant Hill, CA 94523-4817
http://www.jfku.edu/

Independent, coed, comprehensive institution. *Enrollment:* 1,606 graduate, professional, and undergraduate students; 535 full-time matriculated graduate/professional students (388 women), 834 part-time matriculated graduate/professional students (654 women). *Graduate faculty:* 29 full-time (16 women), 780 part-time/adjunct (464 women). *Computer facilities:* 50 computers available on campus for general student use. *Library facilities:* Robert M. Fisher Library. *Graduate expenses:* Tuition: part-time $391 per unit. Required fees: $44 per quarter. *General application contact:* Ellena Bloedorn, Director of Admissions, 925-969-3330.

Graduate School for Holistic Studies
K. Sue Duncan, Dean
Programs in:
  consciousness studies • MA, Certificate
  holistic health education • MA
  holistic studies • MA, MFA, Certificate
  integral psychology • MA
  studio arts • MFA
  transformative arts • MA
  transpersonal counseling psychology • MA

Graduate School of Professional Psychology
Dr. H. Keith McConnell, Dean
Programs in:
  counseling psychology • MA
  organizational conflict management • Certificate
  organizational psychology • MA, Certificate

California

John F. Kennedy University (continued)
  professional psychology • MA, Psy D, Certificate
  psychology • Psy D
  sport psychology • MA

School of Law
Therese Cannon, Dean
Program in:
  law • JD

School of Liberal Arts
Jeremiah Hallisey, Dean
Programs in:
  liberal arts • MA, MAT, Certificate
  museum studies • MA, Certificate
  teaching • MAT

School of Management
Michael Lee, Dean
Programs in:
  business administration • MBA
  career development • MA, Certificate
  management • MA, MBA, Certificate
  organizational leadership • Certificate

■ LA SIERRA UNIVERSITY
Riverside, CA 92515-8247
http://www.lasierra.edu/

Independent-religious, coed, comprehensive institution. CGS member. *Computer facilities:* 125 computers available on campus for general student use. A campuswide network can be accessed from student residence rooms and from off campus. Internet access and online class registration are available. *Library facilities:* University Library plus 1 other. *General application contact:* Director of Admissions, 909-785-2176.

College of Arts and Sciences
Programs in:
  arts and sciences • MA
  English • MA

School of Business and Management
Programs in:
  business administration and management • MBA
  executive business administration • EMBA
  leadership, values, and ethics for business and management • Certificate

School of Education
Programs in:
  administration and leadership • MA, Ed D, Ed S
  counseling • MA
  curriculum and instruction • MA, Ed D, Ed S
  education • MA, Ed D, Ed S
  educational psychology • Ed S
  school psychology • Ed S
  special education • MA

School of Religion
Programs in:
  religion • MA
  religious education • MA
  religious studies • MA

■ LOMA LINDA UNIVERSITY
Loma Linda, CA 92350
http://www.llu.edu/

Independent-religious, coed, upper-level institution. CGS member. *Computer facilities:* A campuswide network can be accessed from student residence rooms and from off campus. Internet access and online class registration, on-line courses are available. *Library facilities:* Del E. Webb Memorial Library. *General application contact:* Dean of the Graduate School, 909-824-4528.

Graduate School
Programs in:
  adult and aging family nursing • MS
  biology • MS, PhD
  biomedical and clinical ethics • MA
  clinical ministry • MA, Certificate
  clinical nutrition • MS
  clinical psychology • PhD, Psy D
  counseling and family science • MA, MS, DMFT, PhD, Certificate
  family studies • MA, Certificate
  geology • MS
  growing family nursing • MS
  marriage and family therapy • MS, DMFT, PhD
  natural sciences • MS, PhD
  nursing administration • MS, Certificate
  nutrition care management • MS
  nutritional sciences • MS
  religion and science • MA
  social policy and research • PhD
  social work • MSW

School of Allied Health Professions
Programs in:
  allied health professions • MHIS, MPT, MS, DPT
  health information systems • MHIS
  physical therapy • MPT, DPT
  physician assistant • MS
  speech-language pathology and audiology • MS

School of Dentistry
Programs in:
  dentistry • DDS, MS, Certificate
  endodontics • MS, Certificate
  implant dentistry • MS, Certificate
  oral and maxillofacial surgery • MS, Certificate
  orthodontics • MS, Certificate
  periodontics • MS

School of Medicine
Program in:
  medicine • MD, MS, PhD

Graduate Programs in Biological Science
Programs in:
  anatomy • MS, PhD
  biochemistry • MS, PhD
  biomedical science • MS, PhD
  microbiology • MS, PhD
  pharmaceutical sciences • MS, PhD
  physiology • MS, PhD

School of Public Health
Programs in:
  biostatistics • MPH, MSPH
  environmental and occupational health • MPH, MSPH
  epidemiology • MPH, Dr PH
  health administration • MHA, MPH
  health promotion and education • MPH, Dr PH
  international health • MPH
  public health • MHA, MPH, MSPH, Dr PH
  public health nutrition • MPH, Dr PH

■ LOYOLA MARYMOUNT UNIVERSITY
Los Angeles, CA 90045-2659
http://www.lmu.edu/

Independent-religious, coed, comprehensive institution. CGS member. *Enrollment:* 8,880 graduate, professional, and undergraduate students; 2,165 full-time matriculated graduate/professional students (1,244 women), 742 part-time matriculated graduate/professional students (386 women). *Graduate faculty:* 419 full-time (145 women), 446 part-time/adjunct (202 women). *Computer facilities:* Computer purchase and lease plans are available. 300 computers available on campus for general student use. A campuswide network can be accessed from student residence rooms and from off campus. Internet access is available. *Library facilities:* Charles von der Ahe Library plus 1 other. *Graduate expenses:* Tuition: part-time $664 per unit. Tuition and fees vary according to course load, degree level and program. *General application contact:* Chake Kouyoumjian, Director, Graduate Admissions, 310-338-2721.

Find an in-depth description at www.petersons.com/gradchannel.

Graduate Division
Dr. Joseph G. Jabbra, Academic Vice President and Chair of Graduate Council

College of Business Administration
Dr. John T. Wholihan, Dean
Program in:
  business administration • MBA

College of Liberal Arts
Dr. Michael Engh, Acting Dean
Programs in:
- creative writing • MA
- liberal arts • MA
- literature • MA
- marital and family therapy • MA
- pastoral studies • MA
- philosophy • MA
- theology • MA

College of Science and Engineering
Dr. Gerald S. Jakubowski, Dean
Programs in:
- civil engineering • MS, MSE
- computer science • MS
- electrical engineering • MSE
- engineering and production management • MS
- environmental science • MS
- mechanical engineering • MSE
- science and engineering • MS, MSE
- system engineering and leadership • MS

School of Education
Dr. Albert P. Koppes, Dean
Programs in:
- bilingual and bicultural education • MA
- Catholic inclusive education • MA
- Catholic school administration • MA
- child/adolescent literacy • MA
- counseling • MA
- education • M Ed, MA, Ed D
- educational leadership in social justice • Ed D
- elementary education • MA
- general education • M Ed
- reading/language arts • M Ed
- school administration • M Ed
- school psychology • MA
- secondary education • MA
- special education • MA
- special education specialist in mild and moderate disabilities • MA

School of Film and Television
Teri Schwartz, Dean
Programs in:
- film and television • MA
- film production • MA
- screen writing • MA
- television production • MA

Loyola Law School
David W. Burcham, Dean
Programs in:
- law • JD
- taxation • LL M

■ MONTEREY INSTITUTE OF INTERNATIONAL STUDIES
Monterey, CA 93940-2691
http://www.miis.edu/

Independent, coed, graduate-only institution. *Enrollment:* 642 full-time matriculated graduate/professional students (410 women), 83 part-time matriculated graduate/professional students (49 women). *Graduate faculty:* 47 full-time (21 women), 54 part-time/adjunct (25 women). *Computer facilities:* 140 computers available on campus for general student use. A campuswide network can be accessed from off campus. Internet access is available. *Library facilities:* William Tell Coleman Library. *Graduate expenses:* Tuition: full-time $22,180; part-time $990 per credit. Required fees: $200. *General application contact:* Admissions Office, 831-647-4123.

Fisher Graduate School of International Business
Dr. Ernest J. Scalberg, Dean
Program in:
- international business • MBA

Graduate School of International Policy Studies
Dr. Amy Sands, Dean
Programs in:
- international environmental policy • MA
- international management • MPA
- international policy studies • MA, MPA
- international trade policy • MA

Graduate School of Language and Educational Linguistics
Dr. Ruth Larimer, Dean
Programs in:
- language and educational linguistics • MATESOL, MATFL
- peace corps master's internationalist in TESOL • MATESOL
- teaching English to speakers of other languages • MATESOL
- teaching foreign language • MATFL

Graduate School of Translation and Interpretation
Dr. Chuanyun Bao, Dean
Programs in:
- conference interpretation • MA
- translation • MA
- translation and interpretation • MA

■ MOUNT ST. MARY'S COLLEGE
Los Angeles, CA 90049-1599
http://www.msmc.la.edu/

Independent-religious, coed, primarily women, comprehensive institution. *Enrollment:* 2,127 graduate, professional, and undergraduate students; 253 full-time matriculated graduate/professional students (217 women), 155 part-time matriculated graduate/professional students (116 women). *Graduate faculty:* 16 full-time (all women), 23 part-time/adjunct (19 women). *Computer facilities:* 85 computers available on campus for general student use. A campuswide network can be accessed from student residence rooms and from off campus. *Library facilities:* Charles Williard Coe Memorial Library. *Graduate expenses:* Tuition: part-time $530 per unit. Tuition and fees vary according to degree level. *General application contact:* Tom Hoener, Director, Graduate Recruitment, 213-477-2800.

Graduate Division
Dr. Larry Ryan, Associate Academic Vice President
Programs in:
- administrative studies • MS
- counseling psychology • MS
- elementary education • MS
- nursing • MS
- physical therapy • DPT
- religious studies • MA
- secondary education • MS
- special education • MS

■ NATIONAL UNIVERSITY
La Jolla, CA 92037-1011
http://www.nu.edu/

Independent, coed, comprehensive institution. CGS member. *Computer facilities:* 2,253 computers available on campus for general student use. A campuswide network can be accessed from off campus. Internet access and online class registration are available. *Library facilities:* Central Library. *General application contact:* Associate Regional Dean, 858-541-7701.

Find an in-depth description at www.petersons.com/gradchannel.

Academic Affairs

School of Arts and Sciences
Programs in:
- arts and sciences • MA, MFA, MS
- counseling psychology • MA
- English • MS
- film art studies • MFA
- human behavior • MA
- instructional technology • MS
- nursing • MS

School of Business and Information Management
Programs in:
- accounting • MBA
- business and information management • GMBA, MA, MBA, MFS, MHCA, MPA, MS
- e-business • MBA
- financial management • MBA
- forensic science • MFS

California

National University (continued)
  general business administration • MBA
  global business administration • GMBA
  health care administration • MBA, MHCA
  human resource management • MA
  human resources administration • MBA
  information systems • MS
  international business • MBA
  management • MA
  marketing • MBA
  public administration • MBA, MPA
  taxation • MS
  technology management • MBA, MS
  telecommunication systems management • MS

School of Education
Programs in:
  cross-cultural teaching • M Ed
  education • M Ed, MA, MAT, MS
  educational administration • MS
  school counseling • MS
  school psychology • MS
  special education • MS
  teaching • MA, MAT

School of Engineering and Technology
Programs in:
  computer science • MS
  engineering and technology • MS
  environmental engineering • MS
  software engineering • MS

■ **NEW COLLEGE OF CALIFORNIA**
San Francisco, CA 94102-5206
http://www.newcollege.edu/

Independent, coed, comprehensive institution. *Computer facilities:* 10 computers available on campus for general student use. *Library facilities:* New College Library. *General application contact:* 415-437-3460.

Find an in-depth description at www.petersons.com/gradchannel.

School of Humanities
Program in:
  humanities • MA, MFA

Division of Humanities
Programs in:
  culture, ecology, and sustainable community • MA
  humanities and leadership • MA
  media studies • MA
  poetics • MA, MFA
  poetics and writing • MFA
  psychology • MA
  women's spirituality • MA
  writing and consciousness • MA

School of Law
Program in:
  law • JD

School of Psychology
Programs in:
  feminist clinical psychology • MA
  social-clinical psychology • MA

■ **NOTRE DAME DE NAMUR UNIVERSITY**
Belmont, CA 94002-1908
http://www.ndnu.edu

Independent-religious, coed, comprehensive institution. *Enrollment:* 1,798 graduate, professional, and undergraduate students; 266 full-time matriculated graduate/professional students (202 women), 544 part-time matriculated graduate/professional students (400 women). *Graduate faculty:* 25 full-time (14 women). *Computer facilities:* 50 computers available on campus for general student use. A campuswide network can be accessed from off campus. Internet access is available. *Library facilities:* College of Notre Dame Library. *Graduate expenses:* Tuition: full-time $11,640; part-time $485 per unit. Tuition and fees vary according to course level and course load. *General application contact:* Barbara Sterner, Assistant Director of Graduate Admissions, 650-508-3427.

Division of Academic Affairs
Dr. Lucille H. Sansing, Provost

School of Arts and Humanities
Dr. Christine Bennett, Dean
Programs in:
  arts and humanities • MA, MM
  English • MA
  music • MM
  pedagogy • MM
  performance • MM

School of Business and Management
Henry Roth, Dean
Programs in:
  business administration • MBA
  business and management • MBA, MPA, MSM
  management • MSM
  public administration • MPA

School of Education and Leadership
Dr. Judith Greig, Dean
Programs in:
  curriculum and instruction • M Ed
  education • MA
  education and leadership • M Ed, MA, MAT, MSETA, Certificate
  educational technology administration • MSETA, Certificate
  reading • MA, Certificate
  special education • MA, Certificate
  teaching • MAT

School of Sciences
Dr. Lizbeth Martin, Dean
Programs in:
  art therapy psychology • MAAT, MAMFT
  chemical dependency • MACP
  counseling psychology • MACP
  gerontology • MA, Certificate
  marital and family therapy • MACP, MAMFT
  premedical studies • Certificate
  sciences • MA, MAAT, MACP, MAMFT, Certificate

■ **PEPPERDINE UNIVERSITY**
Malibu, CA 90263
http://www.pepperdine.edu/

Independent-religious, coed, university. CGS member. *Enrollment:* 8,021 graduate, professional, and undergraduate students; 1,071 full-time matriculated graduate/professional students (503 women), 162 part-time matriculated graduate/professional students (86 women). *Graduate faculty:* 82 full-time (19 women), 40 part-time/adjunct (15 women). *Computer facilities:* Computer purchase and lease plans are available. 292 computers available on campus for general student use. A campuswide network can be accessed from student residence rooms. Internet access and online class registration are available. *Library facilities:* Payson Library plus 2 others. *Graduate expenses:* Tuition: full-time $17,100; part-time $855 per unit. Tuition and fees vary according to degree level and program. *General application contact:* Paul Long, Dean of Enrollment Management, 310-506-4392.

Malibu Graduate Business Programs
Dr. John Robert McQuaid, Director
Programs in:
  business administration • MBA
  international business • MIB

School of Law
Dr. Charles I. Nelson, Interim Dean
Programs in:
  dispute resolution • LL M, MDR
  law • JD, LL M, MDR

School of Public Policy
Dr. James Wilburn, Dean
Program in:
  public policy • MPP

Seaver College
Dr. David Baird, Dean
Programs in:
  American studies • MA
  communication • MA

history • MA
ministry • MS
religion • M Div, MA

■ POINT LOMA NAZARENE UNIVERSITY
San Diego, CA 92106-2899
http://www.ptloma.edu/

Independent-religious, coed, comprehensive institution. *Enrollment:* 3,170 graduate, professional, and undergraduate students; 280 full-time matriculated graduate/professional students (194 women), 515 part-time matriculated graduate/professional students (296 women). *Graduate faculty:* 44 full-time (21 women), 47 part-time/adjunct (20 women). *Computer facilities:* Computer purchase and lease plans are available. 125 computers available on campus for general student use. A campuswide network can be accessed from student residence rooms and from off campus. Internet access and online class registration are available. *Library facilities:* Ryan Library. *Graduate expenses:* Tuition: full-time $5,460; part-time $455 per unit. Tuition and fees vary according to campus/location and program. *General application contact:* John Burlison, Director of Graduate Administrative Services, 619-849-2274.

Graduate Programs
Programs in:
business administration • MBA
education • MA, Ed S
nursing • MSN
religion • M Min, MA

■ SAINT MARY'S COLLEGE OF CALIFORNIA
Moraga, CA 94575
http://www.stmarys-ca.edu/

Independent-religious, coed, comprehensive institution. *Enrollment:* 4,486 graduate, professional, and undergraduate students; 463 full-time matriculated graduate/professional students (281 women), 686 part-time matriculated graduate/professional students (516 women). *Graduate faculty:* 42 full-time (24 women), 454 part-time/adjunct (302 women). *Computer facilities:* 250 computers available on campus for general student use. A campuswide network can be accessed from student residence rooms and from off campus. Internet access and online class registration are available. *Library facilities:* St. Albert Hall plus 1 other. *Graduate expenses:* Tuition: part-time $620 per unit. *General application contact:* Michael Beseda, Vice Provost for Enrollment, 925-631-4277.

Graduate Business Programs
Nelson Shelton, Director
Programs in:
business • MBA
business administration • MBA
executive business administration • MBA

School of Education
Dr. Nancy L. Sorenson, Dean
Programs in:
early childhood education and Montessori teacher training • M Ed, MA
education • M Ed, MA
educational leadership • MA
general counseling • MA
marital and family therapy • MA
reading leadership • MA
school counseling • MA
special education • M Ed, MA

School of Extended Education
Dr. Dean Elias, Dean
Programs in:
extended education • MA
leadership • MA

School of Liberal Arts
Stephen Woolpert, Dean
Programs in:
creative writing • MFA
kinesiology • MA
liberal arts • MA, MFA
liberal studies • MA

■ SAN DIEGO STATE UNIVERSITY
San Diego, CA 92182
http://www.sdsu.edu/

State-supported, coed, university. CGS member. *Enrollment:* 33,676 graduate, professional, and undergraduate students; 3,073 full-time matriculated graduate/professional students (2,029 women), 2,956 part-time matriculated graduate/professional students (1,701 women). *Graduate faculty:* 790 full-time (312 women), 158 part-time/adjunct (29 women). *Computer facilities:* 400 computers available on campus for general student use. A campuswide network can be accessed from student residence rooms and from off campus. Internet access and online class registration are available. *Library facilities:* Malcolm A. Love Library. *Graduate expenses:* Tuition, nonresident: part-time $282 per unit. Required fees: $1,349; $875 per year.

Graduate and Research Affairs
Jan Andersen, Interim Graduate Dean

College of Arts and Letters
Paul Wong, Dean
Programs in:
anthropology • MA
applied linguistics and English as a second language • CAL
arts and letters • MA, MFA, PhD, CAL
Asian studies • MA
computational linguistics • MA
creative writing • MFA
economics • MA
English • MA
English as a second language/applied linguistics • MA
French • MA
general linguistics • MA
geography • MA, PhD
history • MA
Latin American studies • MA
liberal arts and sciences • MA
philosophy • MA
political science • MA
rhetoric and writing • MA
sociology • MA
Spanish • MA
women's studies • MA

College of Business Administration
Dr. Gail K. Naughton, Dean
Programs in:
accountancy • MS
business administration • MBA, MS
entrepreneurship • MS
finance • MS
human resources management • MS
information and decision systems • MS
international business • MS
management science • MS
marketing • MS
production and operations management • MS

College of Education
Lionel R. Meno, Dean
Programs in:
counseling and school psychology • MS
education • MA, MS, Ed D, PhD
educational leadership • MA
educational technology • MA
educational technology and teaching and learning • Ed D
elementary curriculum and instruction • MA
multi-cultural emphasis • PhD
policy studies in language and cross cultural education • MA
reading education • MA
rehabilitation counseling • MS
secondary curriculum and instruction • MA
special education • MA

College of Engineering
David A. Hayhurst, Dean
Programs in:

California

San Diego State University (continued)
aerospace engineering • MS
civil engineering • MS
electrical engineering • MS
engineering • MS, PhD
engineering mechanics • MS
engineering sciences and applied mechanics • PhD
flight dynamics • MS
fluid dynamics • MS
manufacture and design • MS
mechanical engineering • MS

College of Health and Human Services
Dolores A. Wozniak, Dean
Programs in:
audiology • Au D
communicative disorders • MA
environmental health • MPH
epidemiology • MPH, PhD
gerontology • MS
health and human services • MA, MPH, MS, MSW, Au D, PhD
health behavior • PhD
health promotion • MPH
health services administration • MPH
industrial hygiene • MS
language and communicative disorders • PhD
nursing • MS
social work • MSW, PhD
toxicology • MS

College of Professional Studies and Fine Arts
Joyce M. Gattas, Dean
Programs in:
advertising and public relations • MA
art history • MA
child development • MS
city planning • MCP
communication • MA
criminal justice administration • MPA
criminal justice and criminology • MS
critical-cultural studies • MA
drama • MA, MFA
exercise physiology • MA
interaction studies • MA
intercultural and international studies • MA
music and dance • MA, MM
new media studies • MA
news and information studies • MA
nutritional science • MS
physical education • MS
professional studies and fine arts • MA, MCP, MFA, MM, MPA, MS
public administration • MPA
studio arts • MA, MFA
telecommunications and media management • MA
television, film, and new media production • MA

College of Sciences
Thomas R. Scott, Dean
Programs in:
applied mathematics • MS
astronomy • MS
biology • MA, MS
biostatistics and biometry • PhD
cell and molecular biology • PhD
chemistry • MA, MS, PhD
clinical psychology • MS, PhD
computational science • MS, PhD
computer science • MS
ecology • MS, PhD
geological sciences • MS
industrial and organizational psychology • MS
mathematics • MA
mathematics and science education • PhD
microbiology • MS
molecular biology • MA, MS
physics • MA, MS
program evaluation • MS
psychology • MA
radiological physics • MS
regulatory affairs • MS
sciences • MA, MS, PhD
statistics • MS

Interdisciplinary Studies
Program in:
interdisciplinary studies • MA, MS

■ SAN FRANCISCO STATE UNIVERSITY
San Francisco, CA 94132-1722
http://www.sfsu.edu/

State-supported, coed, comprehensive institution. CGS member. *Enrollment:* 29,686 graduate, professional, and undergraduate students; 4,642 matriculated graduate/professional students. *Graduate faculty:* 795 full-time (285 women). *Computer facilities:* 1,474 computers available on campus for general student use. A campuswide network can be accessed from student residence rooms and from off campus. *Library facilities:* J. Paul Leonard Library plus 2 others. *Graduate expenses:* Tuition, state resident: part-time $871 per unit. Tuition, nonresident: part-time $1,093 per unit. *General application contact:* John Pliska, Director of Admissions, Division of Graduate Studies, 415-338-2234.

Division of Graduate Studies
Dr. Ann Hallum, Acting Dean

College of Behavioral and Social Sciences
Joel Kassiola, Dean
Programs in:
anthropology • MA
behavioral and social sciences • MA, MPA, MS
economics • MA
geography • MA
history • MA
international relations • MA
nonprofit administration • MPA
policy analysis • MPA
political science • MA
psychology • MA, MS
public management • MPA
social science • MA
urban administration • MPA

College of Business
Dr. Jerry Platt, Dean
Programs in:
business • MBA
business administration • MBA

College of Creative Arts
Keith Morrison, Dean
Programs in:
art • MFA
art history • MA
broadcast and electronic communication arts • MA
chamber music • MM
cinema • MFA
cinema studies • MA
classical performance • MM
composition • MA
conducting • MM
creative arts • MA, MFA, MM
industrial arts • MA
music education • MA
music history • MA
theatre arts • MA, MFA

College of Education
Dr. Jacob Perea, Dean
Programs in:
adult education • MA, AC
communicative disorders • MS
early childhood education • MA
education • MA, MS, Ed D, PhD, AC
educational administration • MA, AC
educational technology • MA
elementary education • MA
equity and social justice • AC
language and literacy education • MA
mathematics education • MA
secondary education • MA, AC
special education • MA, Ed D, PhD, AC
special interest • MA
training systems development • AC

College of Ethnic Studies
Dr. D. Phillip McGee, Dean
Program in:
ethnic studies • MA

College of Health and Human Services
Dr. Donald Zingale, Dean
Programs in:
case management • MS
counseling • MS
ethnogerontology • MA
health and human services • MA, MPH, MS, MSW, Dr Sc PT

California

health education • MPH
healthy aging • MA
home economics • MA
life-long learning • MA
long-term care administration • MA
marriage and family counseling • MS
marriage, family, and child counseling • MS
nursing administration • MS
nursing education • MS
physical education • MA
physical therapy • MS, Dr Sc PT
recreation and leisure studies • MS
rehabilitation counseling • MS
social work education • MSW

College of Humanities
Dr. Paul Sherwin, Dean
Programs in:
Chinese • MA
classics • MA
comparative and world literature • MA
composition • MA, Certificate
creative writing • MA, MFA
French • MA
German • MA
humanities • MA, MFA, Certificate
Italian • MA
Japanese • MA
linguistics • MA
literature • MA
museum studies • MA
philosophy • MA
Russian • MA
Spanish • MA
speech and communication studies • MA
teaching composition • Certificate
teaching critical thinking • Certificate
teaching English to speakers of other languages • MA
teaching post-secondary reading • Certificate
women studies • MA

College of Science and Engineering
Dr. Sheldon Axler, Dean
Programs in:
applied geosciences • MS
biomedical laboratory science • MS
cell and molecular biology • MA
chemistry • MS
computer science • MS
conservation biology • MA
ecology and systematic biology • MA
engineering • MS
marine biology • MA
mathematics • MA
microbiology • MA
physics • MS
physiology and behavioral biology • MA
science and engineering • MA, MS

■ SAN JOSE STATE UNIVERSITY
San Jose, CA 95192-0001
http://www.sjsu.edu/

State-supported, coed, comprehensive institution. CGS member. *Enrollment:* 28,932 graduate, professional, and undergraduate students; 3,259 full-time matriculated graduate/professional students (2,296 women), 4,277 part-time matriculated graduate/professional students (2,602 women). *Computer facilities:* A campuswide network can be accessed from student residence rooms and from off campus. Internet access and online class registration are available. *Library facilities:* Robert D. Clark Library plus 1 other. *Graduate expenses:* Tuition, nonresident: part-time $282 per unit. Required fees: $654 per semester. *General application contact:* Susan Hoagland, Program Coordinator, 408-924-2480.

Graduate Studies and Research
Dr. Pam Stacks, Interim Associate Vice President
Programs in:
human factors/ergonomics • MS
interdisciplinary studies • MA, MS
library and information science • MLS

College of Applied Sciences and Arts
Dr. Michael Ego, Dean
Programs in:
applied arts and sciences • MA, MPH, MS, Certificate
criminal justice administration • MS
gerontology • Certificate
gerontology nurse practitioner • MS
kinesiology • MA
mass communication • MS
nursing • Certificate
nursing administration • MS
nursing education • MS
nutrition and food science • MS
occupational therapy • MS
public health • MPH
recreation • MS

College of Business
Dr. David Conrath, Dean
Programs in:
accountancy • MS
business • MBA, MS
business administration, information management, and manufacturing management • MBA
taxation • MS
transportation management • MS

College of Education
Dr. Susan Myers, Dean
Programs in:
child and adolescent development • MA
education • MA, Certificate
education (counseling and student personnel) • MA
education (higher education) • MA
educational administration and supervision • MA
elementary education • MA, Certificate
instructional technology • MA, Certificate
school business management • Certificate
secondary education • MA
special education • MA, Certificate
speech pathology • MA

College of Engineering
Dr. Belle Wei, Dean
Programs in:
aerospace engineering • MS
chemical engineering • MS
civil and environmental engineering • MS
computer engineering • MS
electrical engineering • MS
engineering • MS
general engineering • MS
industrial and systems engineering • MS
materials engineering • MS
mechanical engineering • MS
quality assurance • MS

College of Humanities and the Arts
Dr. Carmen Sigler, Dean
Programs in:
art • MA, MFA
art history • MA
creative writing • MFA
digital media arts • MFA
English and comparative literature • Certificate
French • MA
humanities and the arts • MA, MFA, Certificate
linguistics • MA, Certificate
literature • MA
music • MA
music performance • MA
philosophy • MA, Certificate
photography • MFA
Spanish • MA
spatial arts • MFA
teaching English to speakers of other languages • MA
theatre arts • MA

College of Science
Dr. Gerry Selter, Dean
Programs in:
biological science • MA, MS
chemistry • MA, MS
computational physics • MS
computer science • MS, Certificate
geology • MS

Peterson's Graduate Schools in the U.S. 2006

California

San Jose State University (continued)
  marine science • MS
  mathematics • MA, MS
  mathematics education • MA
  meteorology • MS
  molecular biology and microbiology • MS
  natural science • MA
  organismal biology and conservation and ecology • MS
  physics • MS
  physiology • MS
  science • MA, MS, Certificate

College of Social Sciences
Dr. Albert Agresti, Dean
Programs in:
  applied economics • MA
  clinical psychology • MS
  counseling • MS
  criminology • MA
  economics • MA
  environmental studies • MS
  geography • MA, Certificate
  history • MA
  history education • MA
  industrial/organizational psychology • MS
  psychology • MA
  public administration • MPA
  research psychology • MA
  social sciences • MA, MPA, MS, Certificate
  sociology • MA
  speech communication • MA

College of Social Work
Dr. Sylvia Andrew, Dean
Programs in:
  Mexican-American studies • MA
  social work • MA, MSW, MUP, Certificate
  urban and regional planning • MUP, Certificate

■ **SANTA BARBARA COLLEGE OF ORIENTAL MEDICINE**
Santa Barbara, CA 93101
http://www.sbcom.edu/

Proprietary, coed, primarily women, graduate-only institution. *Graduate faculty:* 2 full-time (1 woman), 15 part-time/adjunct (9 women). *Computer facilities:* 1 computer available on campus for general student use. Internet access and online class registration are available. *Library facilities:* Santa Barbara College of Oriental Medicine. *Graduate expenses:* Tuition: full-time $12,727. Required fees: $110. *General application contact:* Laura Schlieske, Admissions Officer, 805-898-1180 Ext. 24.

Program in Acupuncture and Oriental Medicine
JoAnn Tall, President
Program in:
  acupuncture and Oriental medicine • M Ac OM

■ **SANTA CLARA UNIVERSITY**
Santa Clara, CA 95053
http://www.scu.edu/

Independent-religious, coed, university. CGS member. *Enrollment:* 7,794 graduate, professional, and undergraduate students; 1,542 full-time matriculated graduate/professional students (747 women), 1,687 part-time matriculated graduate/professional students (713 women). *Graduate faculty:* 201 full-time (66 women), 134 part-time/adjunct (40 women). *Computer facilities:* Computer purchase and lease plans are available. 682 computers available on campus for general student use. A campuswide network can be accessed from student residence rooms and from off campus. Internet access and online class registration are available. *Library facilities:* Orradre Library plus 1 other. *Graduate expenses:* Tuition: part-time $618 per unit. *General application contact:* Richard J. Toomey, Dean, Enrollment Management, 408-554-4505.

College of Arts and Sciences
Dr. Atom Yee, Acting Dean
Programs in:
  arts and sciences • MA
  catechetics • MA
  liturgical music • MA
  pastoral liturgy • MA
  spirituality • MA

Division of Counseling Psychology and Education
Fr. Gerdenio Manuel, S.J., Dean
Programs in:
  counseling psychology • MA
  counseling psychology and education • MA, Certificate
  education • MA
  educational administration • MA
  health psychology • MA
  marriage, family, and child counseling • MA
  multiple subject teaching • Certificate
  pastoral counseling • MA
  single subject teaching • Certificate
  special education • MA

Leavey School of Business
Dr. Barry Posner, Dean
Programs in:
  business • EMBA, MBA
  business administration • EMBA, MBA

School of Engineering
Daniel Pitt, Dean
Programs in:
  applied mathematics • MSAM
  ASIC design and test • Certificate
  civil engineering • MSCE
  computer science and engineering • MSCSE, PhD
  data storage technologies • Certificate
  electrical engineering • MSEE, PhD, Engineer
  engineering • MS, MSAM, MSCE, MSCSE, MSE, MSE Mgt, MSEE, MSME, PhD, Certificate, Engineer
  engineering management • MSE Mgt
  high performance computing • Certificate
  mechanical engineering • MSME, PhD, Engineer
  software engineering • MS, Certificate

School of Law
Donald Polden, Dean
Program in:
  law • JD, LL M, Certificate

■ **SIMPSON COLLEGE AND GRADUATE SCHOOL**
Redding, CA 96003-8606
http://www.simpsonca.edu/

Independent-religious, coed, comprehensive institution. *Enrollment:* 1,175 graduate, professional, and undergraduate students; 98 full-time matriculated graduate/professional students (64 women), 108 part-time matriculated graduate/professional students (70 women). *Graduate faculty:* 12 full-time (3 women), 9 part-time/adjunct (4 women). *Computer facilities:* 58 computers available on campus for general student use. A campuswide network can be accessed from student residence rooms and from off campus. Internet access and online class registration are available. *Library facilities:* Start-Kilgour Memorial Library. *Graduate expenses:* Tuition: full-time $13,800; part-time $580 per credit. *General application contact:* Christy L. Meadows, Director of Enrollment Development, 530-226-4606.

Division of Education
Dr. Judith Fortune, Vice President for Academic Affairs
Programs in:
  education • MA
  education and preliminary administrative services • MA
  education and preliminary teaching • MA
  teaching • MA

California

Simpson Graduate School of Ministry
Dr. Judith Fortune, Vice President for Academic Affairs
Programs in:
Christian ministry • MA
ministry • MA
missiology • MA

■ SONOMA STATE UNIVERSITY
Rohnert Park, CA 94928-3609
http://www.sonoma.edu/

State-supported, coed, comprehensive institution. *Enrollment:* 8,371 graduate, professional, and undergraduate students; 205 full-time matriculated graduate/professional students (154 women), 322 part-time matriculated graduate/professional students (227 women). *Graduate faculty:* 246 full-time (104 women), 344 part-time/adjunct (188 women). *Computer facilities:* 300 computers available on campus for general student use. A campuswide network can be accessed from student residence rooms and from off campus. Internet access is available. *Library facilities:* Jean and Charles Schultz Information Center. *Graduate expenses:* Tuition, nonresident: part-time $282 per unit. Required fees: $1,136 per semester. *General application contact:* Elaine Sundberg, Associate Vice Provost, Academic Programs/Graduate Studies, 707-664-2215.

Institute of Interdisciplinary Studies/Special Major
Dr. Ellen Carlton, Contact
Program in:
special major • MA, MS

School of Arts and Humanities
Dr. William Babula, Dean
Programs in:
American literature • MA
arts and humanities • MA
creative writing • MA
English literature • MA
world literature • MA

School of Business and Economics
T. K. Clarke, Dean
Programs in:
business administration • MBA
business and economics • MBA

School of Education
Dr. Phyllis Fernlund, Dean
Programs in:
curriculum and secondary education • MA
education • MA
educational leadership • MA
literacy studies and elementary education • MA
special education • MA

School of Science and Technology
Dr. Saeid Rahimi, Dean
Programs in:
environmental biology • MA
family nurse practitioner • MS
general biology • MA
kinesiology • MA
natural sciences • MA, MS

School of Social Sciences
Dr. Elaine Leeder, Dean
Programs in:
counseling • MA
cultural resources management • MA
history • MA
marriage, family, and child counseling • MA
political science • MA
public administration • MPA
pupil personnel services • MA
social sciences • MA, MPA

■ STANFORD UNIVERSITY
Stanford, CA 94305-9991
http://www.stanford.edu/

Independent, coed, university. CGS member. *Enrollment:* 17,823 graduate, professional, and undergraduate students; 6,106 full-time matriculated graduate/professional students (2,198 women), 1,694 part-time matriculated graduate/professional students (595 women). *Graduate faculty:* 1,746 full-time (394 women). *Computer facilities:* 1,000 computers available on campus for general student use. A campuswide network can be accessed from student residence rooms and from off campus. Internet access and online class registration are available. *Library facilities:* Green Library plus 18 others. *Graduate expenses:* Tuition: full-time $28,563. *General application contact:* Graduate Admissions, 650-723-4291.

Graduate School of Business
Robert L. Joss, Dean
Program in:
business • MBA, PhD

Law School
Kathleen M. Sullivan, Dean
Program in:
law • JD, JSM, MLS, JSD

School of Earth Sciences
Franklin M. Orr, Dean
Programs in:
earth sciences • MS, PhD, Eng
earth systems • MS
geological and environmental sciences • MS, PhD, Eng
geophysics • MS, PhD
petroleum engineering • MS, PhD, Eng

School of Education
Deborah J. Stipek, Dean
Programs in:
administration and policy analysis • Ed D, PhD
anthropology of education • PhD
art education • MA, PhD
child and adolescent development • PhD
counseling psychology • PhD
dance education • MA
economics of education • PhD
education • MA, Ed D, PhD
educational linguistics • PhD
educational psychology • PhD
English education • MA, PhD
evaluation • MA
general curriculum studies • MA, PhD
higher education • PhD
history of education • PhD
interdisciplinary studies • PhD
international comparative education • MA, PhD
international education administration and policy analysis • MA
languages education • MA
learning, design, and technology • MA, PhD
mathematics education • MA, PhD
philosophy of education • PhD
policy analysis • MA
prospective principal's program • MA
science education • MA, PhD
social studies education • MA, PhD
sociology of education • PhD
symbolic systems in education • PhD
teacher education • MA, PhD

School of Engineering
James D. Plummer, Dean
Programs in:
aeronautics and astronautics • MS, PhD, Eng
biomechanical engineering • MS
chemical engineering • MS, PhD, Eng
civil and environmental engineering • MS, PhD, Eng
computer science • MS, PhD
electrical engineering • MS, PhD, Eng
engineering • MS, PhD, Eng
management science and engineering • MS, PhD
materials science and engineering • MS, PhD, Eng
mechanical engineering • MS, PhD, Eng
product design • MS
scientific computing and computational mathematics • MS, PhD

Stanford University (continued)
School of Humanities and Sciences
Malcolm R. Beasley, Dean
Programs in:
  anthropological sciences • MA, MS, PhD
  applied physics • MS, PhD
  art history • PhD
  art practice • MFA
  biological sciences • MS, PhD
  biophysics • PhD
  chemistry • PhD
  Chinese • MA, PhD
  classics • MA, PhD
  communication theory and research • PhD
  comparative literature • PhD
  computer-based music theory and acoustics • MA, PhD
  cultural and social anthropology • MA, PhD
  documentary film and video • MA
  drama • PhD
  economics • PhD
  English • MA, PhD
  financial mathematics • MS
  French • MA, PhD
  German studies • MA, PhD
  history • MA, PhD
  humanities • MA
  humanities and sciences • MA, MFA, MS, DMA, PhD
  international policy studies • MA
  Italian • MA, PhD
  Japanese • MA, PhD
  journalism • MA
  linguistics • MA, PhD
  mathematics • MS, PhD
  modern thought and literature • PhD
  music composition • MA, DMA
  music history • MA
  music, science, and technology • MA
  musicology • PhD
  philosophy • MA, PhD
  physics • PhD
  political science • MA, PhD
  psychology • PhD
  religious studies • MA, PhD
  Russian • MA
  Slavic languages and literatures • PhD
  sociology • PhD
  Spanish • MA, PhD
  statistics • MS, PhD

Center for East Asian Studies
Jean Oi, Director
Program in:
  East Asian studies • MA

Center for Russian and East European Studies
Nancy Kollman, Director
Program in:
  Russian and East European studies • MA

School of Medicine
Philip A. Pizzo, Dean
Programs in:
  bioengineering • MS, PhD
  medicine • MD, MS, PhD

Graduate Programs in Medicine
Programs in:
  biochemistry • PhD
  biomedical informatics • MS, PhD
  cancer biology • PhD
  developmental biology • PhD
  epidemiology • MS, PhD
  genetics • PhD
  health services research • MS
  immunology • PhD
  medicine • MS, PhD
  microbiology and immunology • PhD
  molecular and cellular physiology • PhD
  molecular pharmacology • PhD
  neurosciences • PhD
  structural biology • PhD

■ UNIVERSITY OF CALIFORNIA, BERKELEY
Berkeley, CA 94720-1500
http://www.berkeley.edu/

State-supported, coed, university. CGS member. *Enrollment:* 33,076 graduate, professional, and undergraduate students; 9,887 matriculated graduate/professional students. *Graduate faculty:* 1,500. *Computer facilities:* Computer purchase and lease plans are available. 600 computers available on campus for general student use. A campuswide network can be accessed from student residence rooms and from off campus. Internet access and online class registration are available. *Library facilities:* Doe Library plus 30 others. *Graduate expenses:* International tuition: $12,491 full-time. Required fees: $5,484. *General application contact:* 510-642-7405.

Graduate Division
Dr. Joseph Cerny, Vice Chancellor for Research and Dean
Programs in:
  ancient history and Mediterranean archaeology • MA, PhD
  Asian studies • PhD
  bioengineering • PhD
  biophysics • PhD
  Buddhist studies • PhD
  comparative biochemistry • MA, PhD
  demography • MA, PhD
  East Asian studies • MA
  endocrinology • MA, PhD
  energy and resources • MA, MS, PhD
  ethnic studies • PhD
  folklore • MA
  French • PhD
  international and area studies • MA
  Italian • PhD
  Jewish studies • PhD
  Latin American studies • MA, PhD
  microbiology • PhD
  molecular and biochemical nutrition • PhD
  molecular toxicology • PhD
  neuroscience • PhD
  Northeast Asian studies • MA
  performance studies • PhD
  range management • MS
  sociology and demography • PhD
  South Asian studies • MA
  Southeast Asian studies • MA
  Spanish • PhD
  vision science • MS, PhD
  wood science and technology • MS, PhD

College of Chemistry
Dr. Clayton H. Heathcock, Dean
Programs in:
  chemical engineering • MS, PhD
  chemistry • MS, PhD

College of Engineering
Dr. Paul R. Gray, Dean
Programs in:
  applied science and technology • PhD
  ceramic sciences and engineering • M Eng, MS, D Eng, PhD
  computer science • MS, PhD
  electrical engineering • MS, PhD
  engineering • M Eng, MS, D Eng, PhD
  engineering and project management • M Eng, MS, D Eng, PhD
  engineering geoscience • M Eng, MS, D Eng, PhD
  environmental engineering • M Eng, MS, D Eng, PhD
  geoengineering • M Eng, MS, D Eng, PhD
  industrial engineering and operations research • M Eng, MS, D Eng, PhD
  materials engineering • M Eng, MS, D Eng, PhD
  mechanical engineering • M Eng, MS, D Eng, PhD
  mineral engineering • M Eng, MS, D Eng, PhD
  nuclear engineering • M Eng, MS, D Eng, PhD
  ocean engineering • M Eng, MS, D Eng, PhD
  petroleum engineering • M Eng, MS, D Eng, PhD
  physical metallurgy • M Eng, MS, D Eng, PhD
  structural engineering, mechanics and materials • M Eng, MS, D Eng, PhD
  transportation engineering • M Eng, MS, D Eng, PhD

College of Environmental Design
Harrison Fraker, Dean
Programs in:

architecture • M Arch
building science • MS, PhD
city and regional planning • MCP, PhD
design • MA
design theories and methods • MS, PhD
environmental design • M Arch, MA, MCP, MLA, MS, MUD, PhD
environmental design in developing countries • MS, PhD
environmental planning • MLA
history of architecture and urban design • MS, PhD
landscape architecture • MLA
landscape architecture and environmental planning • PhD
landscape design and site planning • MLA
social basis of architecture and urban design • MS, PhD
structures and construction • MS, PhD
urban and community design • MLA
urban design • MUD

College of Letters and Science
Dr. Paul Licht, Director
Programs in:
African American studies • PhD
anthropology • PhD
applied mathematics • PhD
art practice • MFA
astrophysics • PhD
Chinese language • MA, PhD
classical archaeology • MA, PhD
classics • MA, PhD
comparative literature • PhD
composition • MA, PhD
Czech • MA, PhD
economics • PhD
English • PhD
ethnomusicology • MA, PhD
French • PhD
geography • PhD
geology • MA, MS, PhD
geophysics • MA, MS, PhD
German • MA, PhD
Greek • MA
Hindi • MA, PhD
Hispanic languages and literature • MA, PhD
history • PhD
history of art • PhD
Indonesian • MA, PhD
integrative biology • PhD
Italian studies • PhD
Japanese language • MA, PhD
Latin • MA
letters and science • MA, MFA, MS, PhD, C Phil
linguistics • MA, PhD
logic and the methodology of science • PhD
mathematics • MA, PhD
medical anthropology • PhD
molecular and cell biology • PhD
musicology • MA, PhD

Near Eastern religions • PhD
Near Eastern studies • MA, PhD
philosophy • PhD
physics • PhD
Polish • MA, PhD
political science • PhD
psychology • PhD
rhetoric • PhD
Russian • MA, PhD
Sanskrit • MA, PhD
Scandinavian languages and literatures • MA, PhD
Serbo-Croatian • MA, PhD
sociology • PhD
statistics • MA, PhD
Tamil • MA, PhD

College of Natural Resources
Dr. Gordon Rausser, Dean
Programs in:
agricultural and environmental chemistry • MS, PhD
agricultural and resource economics • PhD
environmental science, policy, and management • MS, PhD
forestry • MF
natural resources • MF, MS, PhD
plant biology • PhD

Graduate School of Journalism
Orville Schell, Dean
Program in:
journalism • MJ

Graduate School of Public Policy
Michael Nacht, Dean
Program in:
public policy • MPP, PhD

Haas School of Business
Tom Campbell, Dean
Programs in:
accounting • PhD
business • MBA, MFE, PhD
business administration • MBA
business and public policy • PhD
finance • PhD
financial engineering • MFE
marketing • PhD
organizational behavior and industrial relations • PhD
real estate • PhD

School of Education
Dr. P. David Pearson, Dean
Programs in:
developmental teacher education • MA
education • MA, Ed D, PhD, Certificate
education and single subject credential: English • MA
education in mathematics, science, and technology • MA, PhD
education with a multiple subject credential • MA
education/single subject teaching: mathematics • MA

education/single subject teaching: science • MA
educational leadership • Ed D
educational psychology • PhD
human development and education • MA, PhD
language, literacy, and culture • MA, Ed D, PhD
policy • MA
policy research • PhD
program evaluation and assessment • Ed D
quantitative methods in education • PhD
school psychology • PhD
science and mathematics education • MA, PhD
social and cultural analysis and social theory • MA, PhD
social and cultural studies in education • MA, PhD
special education • PhD

School of Information Management and Systems
Dr. Hal R. Varian, Dean
Program in:
information management and systems • MIMS, PhD

School of Public Health
Dr. Edward E. Penhoet, Dean
Programs in:
biostatistics • MA, PhD
community health education • MPH
environmental health sciences • MPH, MS, PhD
epidemiology • MPH, MS, PhD
epidemiology and biostatistics • MPH
epidemiology/biostatistics • MPH
health and medical sciences • MS
health and social behavior • MPH
health policy and management • MPH
health services and policy analysis • PhD
infectious diseases • MPH, PhD
infectious diseases and immunity • PhD
interdisciplinary • MPH
maternal and child health • MPH
public health • MA, MPH, MS, Dr PH, PhD
public health nutrition • MPH

School of Social Welfare
Dr. James Midgley, Dean
Program in:
social welfare • MSW, PhD

School of Law
Christopher J. Edley, Dean
Programs in:
jurisprudence and social policy • PhD
law • JD, LL M, JSD

School of Optometry
Dr. Dennis M. Levi, Dean
Program in:
optometry • OD, Certificate

California

UNIVERSITY OF CALIFORNIA, DAVIS
Davis, CA 95616
http://www.ucdavis.edu/

State-supported, coed, university. CGS member. *Enrollment:* 30,229 graduate, professional, and undergraduate students; 5,540 full-time matriculated graduate/professional students (3,027 women). *Graduate faculty:* 1,371 full-time, 231 part-time/adjunct. *Computer facilities:* 600 computers available on campus for general student use. A campuswide network can be accessed from student residence rooms and from off campus. Internet access, software packages are available. *Library facilities:* Peter J. Shields Library plus 5 others. *Graduate expenses:* Tuition, nonresident: full-time $12,245. Required fees: $7,062. *General application contact:* 530-752-2772.

Find an in-depth description at www.petersons.com/gradchannel.

Graduate School of Management
Nicole W. Biggart, Dean
Programs in:
 management • MBA
 working professional MBA • MBA

Graduate Studies
Jeffery C. Gibeling, Graduate Group Chair
Programs in:
 acting • MFA
 agricultural and environmental chemistry • MS, PhD
 agricultural and resource economics • MS, PhD
 animal behavior • MS, PhD
 animal science • MAM, MS
 anthropology • MA, PhD
 applied linguistics • MA
 applied mathematics • MS, PhD
 art • MFA
 art history • MA
 atmospheric sciences • MS, PhD
 avian sciences • MS
 biochemistry and molecular biology • MS, PhD
 biophysics • MS, PhD
 biostatistics • MS, PhD
 cell and developmental biology • MS, PhD
 chemistry • MS, PhD
 child development • MS
 community development • MS
 comparative literature • PhD
 comparative pathology • MS, PhD
 composition • MA, PhD
 conducting • MA, PhD
 creative writing • MA
 cultural studies • MA, PhD
 dramatic art • PhD
 ecology • MS, PhD
 economics • MA, PhD
 education • MA, Ed D
 English • MA, PhD
 entomology • MS, PhD
 epidemiology • MS, PhD
 exercise science • MS
 food science • MS, PhD
 French • PhD
 genetics • MS, PhD
 geography • MA, PhD
 geology • MS, PhD
 German • MA, PhD
 history • MA, PhD
 horticulture and agronomy • MS
 human development • PhD
 hydrologic sciences • MS, PhD
 immunology • MS, PhD
 instructional studies • PhD
 integrated pest management • MS
 international agricultural development • MS
 linguistics • MA
 mathematics • MA, MAT, PhD
 medical informatics • MS
 microbiology • MS, PhD
 molecular, cellular and integrative physiology • MS, PhD
 musicology • MA, PhD
 Native American studies • MA, PhD
 neuroscience • PhD
 nutrition • MS, PhD
 pharmacology/toxicology • MS, PhD
 philosophy • MA, PhD
 physics • MS, PhD
 plant biology • MS, PhD
 plant pathology • MS, PhD
 political science • MA, PhD
 population biology • PhD
 psychological studies • PhD
 psychology • PhD
 sociocultural studies • PhD
 sociology • MA, PhD
 soil science • MS, PhD
 Spanish • MA, PhD
 statistics • MS, PhD
 textile arts and costume design • MFA
 textiles • MS
 viticulture and enology • MS, PhD

College of Engineering
Dr. Enrique Lavernia, Dean
Programs in:
 aeronautical engineering • M Engr, MS, D Engr, PhD, Certificate
 applied science • MS, PhD
 biological systems engineering • M Engr, MS, D Engr, PhD
 biomedical engineering • MS, PhD
 chemical engineering • MS, PhD
 civil and environmental engineering • M Engr, MS, D Engr, PhD, Certificate
 computer science • MS, PhD
 electrical and computer engineering • MS, PhD
 engineering • M Engr, MS, D Engr, PhD, Certificate
 materials science and engineering • MS, PhD
 mechanical engineering • M Engr, MS, D Engr, PhD, Certificate
 transportation, technology and policy • MS, PhD

School of Law
Rex R. Perschbacher, Dean
Program in:
 law • JD, LL M

School of Medicine
Dr. Joseph Silva, Dean
Program in:
 medicine • MD, MA

School of Veterinary Medicine
Dr. Bennie I. Osburn, Dean
Programs in:
 preventive veterinary medicine • MPVM
 veterinary medicine • DVM, MPVM, Certificate

UNIVERSITY OF CALIFORNIA, IRVINE
Irvine, CA 92697
http://www.uci.edu/

State-supported, coed, university. CGS member. *Enrollment:* 24,874 graduate, professional, and undergraduate students; 4,140 matriculated graduate/professional students. *Graduate faculty:* 1,144. *Computer facilities:* 500 computers available on campus for general student use. A campuswide network can be accessed from student residence rooms and from off campus. Internet access and online class registration are available. *Library facilities:* Main Library plus 1 other. *Graduate expenses:* Tuition, nonresident: full-time $12,245. Required fees: $5,219. Tuition and fees vary according to degree level and program. *General application contact:* Lisa M. Gauf, Office of Graduate Studies, 949-824-4611.

College of Medicine
Dr. Thomas Cesario, Dean
Programs in:
 biological sciences • MS, PhD
 genetic counseling • MS
 medicine • MD, MS, PhD
 pharmacology and toxicology • MS, PhD

Office of Graduate Studies
Dr. William H. Parker, Vice Chancellor for Research and Dean of Graduate Studies
Programs in:

California

educational administration • Ed D
educational administration and
  leadership • Ed D
elementary and secondary education •
  MAT

Claire Trevor School of the Arts
Nohema Fernandez, Dean
Programs in:
  accompanying • MFA
  acting • MFA
  arts • MFA, PhD
  choral conducting • MFA
  composition and technology • MFA
  dance • MFA
  design and stage management • MFA
  directing • MFA
  drama • MFA
  drama and theatre • PhD
  guitar/lute performance • MFA
  instrumental performance • MFA
  jazz instrumental/composition • MFA
  piano performance • MFA
  studio art • MFA
  vocal performance • MFA

Graduate School of Management
Jone Pearce, Dean
Programs in:
  business administration • MBA
  management • PhD

School of Biological Sciences
Dr. Susan V. Bryant, Dean
Programs in:
  biological science • MS
  biological sciences • MS, PhD
  biotechnology • MS

School of Engineering
Dr. Nicolaos G. Alexopoulos, Dean
Programs in:
  biomedical engineering • MS, PhD
  chemical and biochemical engineering
    • MS, PhD
  civil engineering • MS, PhD
  computer engineering • PhD
  computer graphics and visualization •
    MS
  computer networks and distributed
    computing • MS
  computer systems and software • MS
  electrical engineering • MS, PhD
  engineering • MS, PhD
  materials science and engineering •
    MS, PhD
  mechanical and aerospace engineering
    • MS, PhD
  networked systems • MS, PhD

School of Humanities
Karen Lawrence, Dean
Programs in:
  Chinese • MA, PhD
  classics • MA, PhD
  comparative literature • MA, PhD
  creative writing • MFA
  East Asian languages and literatures •
    MA, PhD

  English • MA, PhD
  English (summer program) • MA
  English and American literature •
    PhD
  French • MA, PhD
  German • MA, PhD
  history • MA, PhD
  humanities • MA, MAT, MFA, PhD
  Japanese • MA, PhD
  philosophy • MA, PhD
  Spanish • MA, MAT, PhD
  visual studies • MA, PhD
  writing • MFA

School of Information and Computer Science
Debra J. Richardson, Interim Dean
Programs in:
  information and computer science •
    MS, PhD
  networked systems • MS, PhD

School of Physical Sciences
Ronald Stern, Dean
Programs in:
  chemical and material physics • PhD
  chemical and materials physics • MS
  chemistry • MS, PhD
  earth system science • MS, PhD
  mathematics • MS, PhD
  physical sciences • MS, PhD
  physics • MS, PhD

School of Social Ecology
C. Ronald Huff, Dean
Programs in:
  criminology, law and society • MAS,
    PhD
  environmental health science and
    policy • MS, PhD
  planning, policy and design • PhD
  psychology and social behavior • PhD
  social ecology • PhD
  urban and regional planning • MURP

School of Social Sciences
Barbara Anne Dosher, Dean
Programs in:
  anthropology • MA, PhD
  demographic and social analysis • MA
  economics • MA, PhD
  philosophy • PhD
  political psychology • PhD
  political sciences • PhD
  psychology • PhD
  public choice • MA, PhD
  social networks • PhD
  social networks-social science • MA
  social science • MA, PhD
  social sciences • MA, PhD
  sociology and social relations-social
    science • MA, PhD
  transportation economics • MA, PhD
  transportation science • MA, PhD

■ UNIVERSITY OF CALIFORNIA, LOS ANGELES
Los Angeles, CA 90095
http://www.ucla.edu/

State-supported, coed, university. CGS member. *Enrollment:* 38,598 graduate, professional, and undergraduate students; 11,340 full-time matriculated graduate/professional students (5,411 women). *Computer facilities:* Computer purchase and lease plans are available. A campuswide network can be accessed from student residence rooms and from off campus. Internet access and online class registration are available. *Library facilities:* University Research Library plus 13 others. *Graduate expenses:* Tuition, nonresident: full-time $12,245. Required fees: $6,318. *General application contact:* Graduate Admissions, 310-825-1711.

Graduate Division
Program in:
  East Asian studies • MA

College of Letters and Science
Programs in:
  African studies • MA
  Afro-American studies • MA
  American Indian studies • MA
  anthropology • MA, PhD
  applied linguistics • PhD
  applied linguistics and teaching
    English as a second language • MA
  archaeology • MA, PhD
  art history • MA, PhD
  Asian-American studies • MA
  astronomy • MAT, MS, PhD
  atmospheric sciences • MS, PhD
  biochemistry and molecular biology •
    MS, PhD
  biology • MA, PhD
  chemistry • MS, PhD
  classics • MA, PhD
  comparative literature • MA, PhD
  East Asian languages and cultures •
    MA, PhD
  economics • MA, PhD
  English • MA, PhD
  French and Francophone studies •
    MA, PhD
  geochemistry • MS, PhD
  geography • MA, PhD
  geology • MS, PhD
  geophysics and space physics • MS,
    PhD
  German • MA
  Germanic languages • MA, PhD
  Greek • MA
  Hispanic languages and literature •
    PhD
  history • MA, PhD
  Indo-European studies • PhD
  Islamic studies • MA, PhD

California

University of California, Los Angeles (continued)
  Italian • MA, PhD
  Latin • MA
  Latin American studies • MA
  letters and science • MA, MAT, MS, PhD, Certificate
  linguistics • MA, PhD
  mathematics • MA, MAT, PhD
  molecular and cellular life sciences • PhD
  molecular biology • PhD
  molecular, cellular and integrative physiology • PhD
  musicology • MA, PhD
  Near Eastern languages and cultures • MA, PhD
  philosophy • MA, PhD
  physics • MAT, MS, PhD
  physics education • MAT
  physiological science • MS, PhD
  plant molecular biology • PhD
  political science • MA, PhD
  Portuguese • MA
  psychology • MA, PhD
  Romance linguistics and literature • MA, PhD
  Scandinavian • MA, PhD
  Slavic languages and literatures • MA, PhD
  sociology • MA, PhD
  Spanish • MA
  statistics • MS, PhD
  women's studies • MS, PhD

Graduate School of Education and Information Studies
Programs in:
  archival studies • MLIS
  education • M Ed, MA, Ed D, PhD
  education and information studies • M Ed, MA, MLIS, Ed D, PhD, Certificate
  informatics • MLIS
  library and information science • PhD, Certificate
  library studies • MLIS
  special education • PhD

Henry Samueli School of Engineering and Applied Science
Programs in:
  aerospace engineering • MS, PhD
  biomedical engineering • MS, PhD
  ceramics engineering • MS, PhD
  chemical engineering • MS, PhD
  computer science • MS, PhD
  electrical engineering • MS, PhD
  engineering and applied science • MS, PhD
  engineering optimization/operations research • MS, PhD
  environmental engineering • MS, PhD
  geotechnical engineering • MS, PhD
  manufacturing engineering • MS
  mechanical engineering • MS, PhD
  metallurgy • MS, PhD
  structures • MS, PhD
  water resource systems engineering • MS, PhD

John E. Anderson Graduate School of Management
Program in:
  management • MBA, MS, PhD

School of Nursing
Program in:
  nursing • MSN, PhD

School of Public Health
Programs in:
  biostatistics • MS, PhD
  environmental health sciences • MS, PhD
  environmental science and engineering • D Env
  epidemiology • MS, PhD
  health services • MS, PhD
  molecular toxicology • PhD
  public health • MS, PhD
  public health for health professionals • MPH

School of Public Policy and Social Research
Programs in:
  public policy • MPP
  public policy and social research • MA, MPP, MSW, PhD
  social welfare • MSW, PhD
  urban planning • MA, PhD

School of the Arts and Architecture
Christopher Waterman, Dean
Programs in:
  architecture and urban design • M Arch, MA, PhD
  art • MA, MFA
  arts and architecture • M Arch, MA, MFA, MM, DMA, PhD
  composition • MA, PhD
  culture and performance • MA, PhD
  dance • MA, MFA
  design/media arts • MFA
  ethnomusicology • MA, PhD
  performance • MM, DMA

School of Theater, Film and Television
Programs in:
  film and television • MA, MFA, PhD
  film, television, and digital media • MA, MFA, PhD
  theater • MFA, PhD

School of Dentistry
Programs in:
  dentistry • DDS, MS, PhD, Certificate
  oral biology • MS, PhD

School of Law
Norman Abrams, Interim Dean
Program in:
  law • JD, LL M

School of Medicine
Program in:
  medicine • MD, MA, MS, PhD

Graduate Programs in Medicine
Programs in:
  anatomy and cell biology • PhD
  biological chemistry • MS, PhD
  biomathematics • MS, PhD
  biomedical physics • MS, PhD
  clinical research • MS
  experimental pathology • MS, PhD
  human genetics • MS, PhD
  medicine • MA, MS, PhD
  microbiology, immunology and molecular genetics • MS, PhD
  molecular and medical pharmacology • PhD
  molecular, cell and developmental biology • MA, MS, PhD
  neuroscience • PhD
  physiology • MS, PhD

■ **UNIVERSITY OF CALIFORNIA, RIVERSIDE**
Riverside, CA 92521-0102
http://www.ucr.edu/

State-supported, coed, university. CGS member. *Enrollment:* 17,302 graduate, professional, and undergraduate students; 1,812 full-time matriculated graduate/professional students (876 women), 36 part-time matriculated graduate/professional students (12 women). *Graduate faculty:* 540 full-time (142 women). *Computer facilities:* 600 computers available on campus for general student use. A campuswide network can be accessed from student residence rooms and from off campus. Internet access and online class registration are available. *Library facilities:* Tomas Rivera Library plus 6 others. *Graduate expenses:* Tuition, nonresident: part-time $4,082 per quarter. *General application contact:* Graduate Admissions, 951-827-3313.

Graduate Division
Dr. Dallas Rubenstein, Dean
Programs in:
  anthropology • MA, MS, PhD
  applied mathematics • MS
  applied statistics • PhD
  archival management • MA
  art history • MA
  biochemistry and molecular biology • MS, PhD
  biomedical sciences • PhD
  cell, molecular, and developmental biology • MS, PhD
  chemical and environmental engineering • MS, PhD
  chemistry • MS, PhD
  classics • MA, PhD
  comparative literature • MA, PhD

California

computer science and engineering • MS, PhD
creative writing and writing for the performing arts • MFA
dance • MFA, PhD
dance history and theory • PhD
economics • MA, PhD
electrical engineering • MS, PhD
English • MA, PhD
entomology • MS, PhD
environmental sciences • MS, PhD
environmental toxicology • MS, PhD
evolutionary biology • MS, PhD
genomics and bioinformatics • PhD
geological sciences • MS, PhD
historic preservation • MA
history • MA, PhD
mathematics • MA, MS, PhD
mechanical engineering • MS, PhD
microbiology • MS, PhD
molecular genetics, evolutionary and population genetics • PhD
museum curatorship • MA
music • MA
neuroscience • PhD
philosophy • MA, PhD
physics • MS, PhD
physiology • MS, PhD
plant biology • MS, PhD
plant biology (plant genetics) • PhD
plant pathology • MS, PhD
political science • MA, PhD
psychology • PhD
sociology • PhD
soil and water sciences • MS, PhD
Spanish • MA, PhD
statistics • MS
visual arts • MFA

A. Gary Anderson Graduate School of Management
Rajiv Banker, Dean
Program in:
  management • MBA

Graduate School of Education
Dr. Sharon Duffy, Dean
Program in:
  education • M Ed, MA, PhD

■ **UNIVERSITY OF CALIFORNIA, SAN DIEGO**
La Jolla, CA 92093
http://www.ucsd.edu/

State-supported, coed, university. CGS member. *Enrollment:* 24,707 graduate, professional, and undergraduate students; 4,278 matriculated graduate/professional students (1,793 women). *Graduate faculty:* 2,062. *Computer facilities:* Computer purchase and lease plans are available. 1,020 computers available on campus for general student use. A campuswide network can be accessed from student residence rooms and from off campus. Internet access and online class registration, e-mail are available. *Library facilities:* Geisel Library plus 7 others. *Graduate expenses:* Tuition, nonresident: full-time $12,245. Required fees: $6,959. *General application contact:* Graduate Admissions Office, 858-534-1193.

Graduate Studies and Research
Richard Attiyeh, Dean
Programs in:
  acting • MFA
  aerospace engineering • MS, PhD
  anthropology • PhD
  applied mathematics • MA
  applied mechanics • MS, PhD
  applied ocean science • MS, PhD
  applied physics • MS, PhD
  bilingual education • MA
  bioengineering • M Eng, MS, PhD
  bioinformatics • PhD
  biological oceanography • MS, PhD
  biophysics • MS, PhD
  chemical engineering • MS, PhD
  chemistry • MS, PhD
  clinical psychology • PhD
  cognitive science • PhD
  cognitive science/anthropology • PhD
  cognitive science/communication • PhD
  cognitive science/computer science and engineering • PhD
  cognitive science/linguistics • PhD
  cognitive science/neuroscience • PhD
  cognitive science/philosophy • PhD
  cognitive science/psychology • PhD
  cognitive science/sociology • PhD
  communication • MA, PhD
  communication theory and systems • MS, PhD
  comparative literature • MA, PhD
  computer engineering • MS, PhD
  computer science • MS, PhD
  curriculum design • MA
  design • MFA
  directing • MFA
  drama and theatre • PhD
  economics • PhD
  economics and international affairs • PhD
  electrical engineering • M Eng
  electronic circuits and systems • MS, PhD
  engineering physics • MS, PhD
  ethnic studies • MA, PhD
  French literature • MA
  geochemistry and marine chemistry • MS, PhD
  German literature • MA
  history • MA, PhD
  intelligent systems, robotics and control • MS, PhD
  Judaic studies • MA
  language and communicative disorders • PhD
  Latin American studies • MA
  linguistics • PhD
  literature • PhD
  literatures in English • MA
  marine biology • MS, PhD
  materials science • MS, PhD
  mathematics • MA, PhD
  mathematics and science education • PhD
  mechanical engineering • MS, PhD
  music • MA, DMA, PhD
  philosophy • PhD
  photonics • MS, PhD
  physical oceanography and geological sciences • MS, PhD
  physics • MS, PhD
  physics/materials physics • MS
  playwriting • MFA
  political science • PhD
  political science and international affairs • PhD
  psychology • PhD
  public health and epidemiology • PhD
  science studies • PhD
  signal and image processing • MS, PhD
  sociology • PhD
  Spanish literature • MA
  stage management • MFA
  statistics • MS
  structural engineering • MS, PhD
  teacher education • M Ed
  teaching and learning • Ed D
  theatre • PhD
  visual arts • MFA, PhD

Division of Biology
Dr. Eduardo Macagno, Dean
Programs in:
  biochemistry • PhD
  biology • MS
  cell and developmental biology • PhD
  computational neurobiology • PhD
  ecology, behavior, and evolution • PhD
  genetics and molecular biology • PhD
  immunology, virology, and cancer biology • PhD
  molecular and cellular biology • PhD
  neurobiology • PhD
  plant molecular biology • PhD
  signal transduction • PhD

Graduate School of International Relations and Pacific Studies
Peter Cowhey, Dean
Programs in:
  economics and international affairs • PhD
  Pacific international affairs • MPIA
  political science and international affairs • PhD

School of Medicine
Programs in:
  bioinformatics • PhD
  cancer biology/oncology • PhD
  cardiovascular sciences and disease • PhD
  clinical research • MAS

California

University of California, San Diego (continued)
    leadership in healthcare organizations • MAS
    medicine • MD, MAS, PhD
    microbiology • PhD
    molecular pathology • PhD
    neurologic disease • PhD
    neurosciences • PhD
    stem cell and developmental biology • PhD
    structural biology/drug design • PhD

Graduate Studies in Biomedical Sciences
Jeff Esko, Chair
Programs in:
    cell and molecular biology • PhD
    pharmacology • PhD
    physiology • PhD
    regulatory biology • PhD

■ UNIVERSITY OF CALIFORNIA, SAN FRANCISCO
San Francisco, CA 94143
http://www.ucsf.edu/

State-supported, coed, graduate-only institution. CGS member. *General application contact:* Supervisor, 415-476-2110.

Graduate Division
Programs in:
    anatomy • PhD
    biochemistry and molecular biology • PhD
    bioengineering • PhD
    cell biology • PhD
    developmental biology • PhD
    endocrinology • PhD
    experimental pathology • PhD
    genetics • PhD
    history of health sciences • MA, PhD
    medical anthropology • PhD
    microbiology and immunology • PhD
    neuroscience • PhD
    oral biology • MS, PhD
    physical therapy • MPT
    physiology • PhD

School of Nursing
Programs in:
    health policy • PhD
    nursing • MS, PhD
    sociology • PhD

School of Dentistry
Program in:
    dentistry • DDS

School of Medicine
Dr. David A. Kessler, Dean
Program in:
    medicine • MD

School of Pharmacy
Mary Anne Koda Kimble, Dean
Programs in:
    biological and medical informatics • MS, PhD
    biophysics • PhD
    chemistry and chemical biology • PhD
    pharmaceutical sciences and pharmacogenomics • PhD
    pharmacy • Pharm D, MS, PhD

■ UNIVERSITY OF CALIFORNIA, SANTA BARBARA
Santa Barbara, CA 93106
http://www.ucsb.edu/

State-supported, coed, university. CGS member. *Enrollment:* 20,847 graduate, professional, and undergraduate students; 3,003 matriculated graduate/professional students (1,296 women). *Graduate faculty:* 684 full-time, 165 part-time/adjunct. *Computer facilities:* 3,000 computers available on campus for general student use. A campuswide network can be accessed from off campus. *Library facilities:* Davidson Library. *Graduate expenses:* Tuition, state resident: full-time $7,188. Tuition, nonresident: full-time $19,608. *General application contact:* Sarah Dillingham, Director of Graduate Outreach and Admissions, 805-893-4656.

Graduate Division
Dr. Charles Li, Dean

College of Engineering
Matthew Tirrell, Dean
Programs in:
    chemical engineering • MS, PhD
    computational science and engineering • PhD
    computer science • MS, PhD
    electrical and computer engineering • PhD
    engineering • MS, PhD
    materials science and engineering • MS, PhD
    mathematics • PhD
    mechanical and environmental engineering • PhD
    mechanical engineering • MS, PhD

College of Letters and Sciences
Dr. Everett Zimmerman, Provost
Programs in:
    anthropology • MA, PhD
    applied mathematics • MA
    art studio • MFA
    biochemistry and molecular biology • PhD
    chemistry and biochemistry • MA, MS, PhD
    classics • MA, PhD
    communication • PhD
    comparative literature • PhD
    dramatic art • MA, PhD
    East Asian languages and cultural studies • MA
    ecology, evolution, and marine biology • MA, PhD
    economics • MA, PhD
    English literature • PhD
    French • MA, PhD
    geography • MA, PhD
    geological sciences • MS, PhD
    geophysics • MS
    Germanic languages and literature • MA, PhD
    Hispanic languages and literature • PhD
    history • MA, PhD
    history of art and architecture • PhD
    humanities and fine arts • MA, MFA, MM, DMA, PhD
    Latin American and Iberian studies • MA
    letters and science • MA, MFA, MM, MS, DMA, PhD
    linguistics • PhD
    marine science • MS, PhD
    mathematics • MA, PhD
    mathematics, life, and physical sciences • MA, MS, PhD
    molecular, cellular, and developmental biology • MA, PhD
    music • MA, MM, DMA, PhD
    performance • MM, DMA
    philosophy • PhD
    physics • PhD
    political science • MA, PhD
    Portuguese • MA
    psychology • MA, PhD
    religious studies • MA, PhD
    social science • MA, PhD
    sociology • MA, PhD
    Spanish • MA
    statistics • MA, PhD

Donald Bren School of Environmental Science and Management
Dr. Dennis J. Aigner, Dean
Program in:
    environmental science and management • MESM, PhD

Graduate School of Education
Jules Zimmer, Dean
Programs in:
    clinical/school/counseling psychology • M Ed, PhD
    education • M Ed, MA, PhD
    school psychology • M Ed

■ UNIVERSITY OF CALIFORNIA, SANTA CRUZ
Santa Cruz, CA 95064
http://www.ucsc.edu/

State-supported, coed, university. CGS member. *Enrollment:* 14,997 graduate, professional, and undergraduate students;

California

1,265 full-time matriculated graduate/professional students (694 women), 103 part-time matriculated graduate/professional students (49 women). *Graduate faculty:* 495 full-time (175 women). *Computer facilities:* 200 computers available on campus for general student use. A campuswide network can be accessed from student residence rooms and from off campus. Internet access is available. *Library facilities:* McHenry Library plus 9 others. *Graduate expenses:* Tuition, nonresident: full-time $12,492. *General application contact:* James M. Moore, Graduate Admissions, Director, 831-459-2301.

Division of Graduate Studies
Robert C. Miller, Vice Chancellor for Research and Dean of Graduate Studies

Division of Arts
Edward Houghton, Dean
Programs in:
  arts • MA, MFA, Certificate
  digital arts/new media • MFA
  music • MA
  theater arts • Certificate

Division of Humanities
Dr. Wlad Godzich, Dean
Programs in:
  history • PhD
  history of consciousness • PhD
  humanities • MA, PhD
  linguistics • MA, PhD
  literature • MA, PhD
  philosophy • PhD

Division of Physical and Biological Sciences
Dr. David Kliger, Dean
Programs in:
  applied mathematics • MA, PhD
  astronomy and astrophysics • PhD
  chemistry • MS, PhD
  earth sciences • MS, PhD
  ecology and evolutionary biology • MA, PhD
  environmental toxicology • MS, PhD
  marine sciences • MS
  mathematics • MA, PhD
  molecular, cellular, and developmental biology • MA, PhD
  ocean sciences • PhD
  physical and biological sciences • MA, MS, PhD, Certificate
  physics • MS, PhD
  science communication • Certificate

Division of Social Sciences
Michael Hutchinson, Dean
Programs in:
  anthropology • MA, PhD
  applied economics • MS
  developmental psychology • PhD
  education • MA, Certificate
  environmental studies • PhD
  experimental psychology • PhD
  international economics • MA, PhD
  politics • PhD
  social psychology • PhD
  social sciences • MA, MS, PhD, Certificate
  sociology • PhD

School of Engineering
Sung Mu Steve Kang, Dean
Programs in:
  bioinformatics • MS, PhD
  computer engineering • MS, PhD
  computer science • MS, PhD
  electrical engineering • MS, PhD
  engineering • MS, PhD

■ UNIVERSITY OF LA VERNE
La Verne, CA 91750-4443
http://www.ulv.edu/

Independent, coed, university. *Enrollment:* 3,604 graduate, professional, and undergraduate students; 1,402 full-time matriculated graduate/professional students (881 women), 1,572 part-time matriculated graduate/professional students (1,051 women). *Graduate faculty:* 71 full-time (35 women), 219 part-time/adjunct (115 women). *Computer facilities:* 150 computers available on campus for general student use. A campuswide network can be accessed from student residence rooms and from off campus. Internet access and online class registration, on-line grade information are available. *Library facilities:* Wilson Library. *Graduate expenses:* Tuition: part-time $425 per hour. Tuition and fees vary according to course level, degree level and program. *General application contact:* Jo Nell Baker, Director, Graduate Admissions and Academic Services, 909-593-3511 Ext. 4244.

College of Arts and Sciences
Dr. Fred Yaffe, Dean
Programs in:
  arts and sciences • MS, Psy D
  clinical-community psychology • Psy D
  counseling • MS
  counseling in higher education • MS
  general counseling • MS
  gerontology • MS
  marriage, family and child counseling • MS
  psychology • Psy D

College of Business and Public Management
Dr. Gordon Badovick, Dean
Programs in:
  accounting • MBA
  business • MBIT
  business administration • MS
  business and public management • MBA, MBA-EP, MBIT, MHA, MPA, MS, DPA
  business organizational management • MS
  counseling • MS
  executive management • MBA-EP
  finance • MBA, MBA-EP
  gerontology administration • MS
  health administration • MHA
  health services management • MBA, MS
  healthcare information management • MHA
  information technology • MBA, MBA-EP
  international business • MBA, MBA-EP
  leadership • MBA-EP
  leadership and management • MS
  managed care • MBA, MHA
  management • MBA, MBA-EP
  marketing • MBA, MBA-EP
  public administration • MS

College of Law
Donald J. Dunn, Dean
Program in:
  law • JD

School of Continuing Education
Dr. James C. Manolis, Dean
Programs in:
  advanced teaching • M Ed
  business • MBA, MBA-EP
  continuing education • M Ed, MBA, MBA-EP, MHA, MS, Credential
  cross cultural language and academic development • Credential
  educational management • M Ed
  health administration • MHA
  leadership and management • MS
  multiple subject • Credential
  reading • M Ed
  school counseling • MS
  single subject • Credential

School of Education and Organizational Leadership
Dr. Leonard Pellicer, Dean
Programs in:
  advanced teaching skills • M Ed
  child development • MS
  child development/child life • MS
  child life • MS
  education • M Ed
  education (special emphasis) • M Ed
  education and organizational leadership • M Ed, MS, Ed D, Credential
  educational management • M Ed, Credential
  multiple subject • Credential
  organizational leadership • Ed D

California

University of La Verne (continued)
  preliminary administrative services • Credential
  professional administrative services • Credential
  pupil personnel services (Credential reading) • M Ed, Credential
  reading and language arts specialist • Credential
  school counseling • MS, Credential
  single subject • Credential
  teacher education • Credential

■ UNIVERSITY OF REDLANDS
Redlands, CA 92373-0999
http://www.redlands.edu/

Independent, coed, comprehensive institution. *Computer facilities:* 563 computers available on campus for general student use. A campuswide network can be accessed from student residence rooms and from off campus. Internet access is available. *Library facilities:* Armacost Library.

Graduate Studies
Program in:
  communicative disorders • MS

School of Music
Program in:
  music • MM

School of Business
Programs in:
  administrative services • MA
  business administration • MBA
  curriculum and instruction • MA
  management and business • MAHRM, MBA
  management and human resources • MAHRM
  pupil personnel services • MA

■ UNIVERSITY OF SAN DIEGO
San Diego, CA 92110-2492
http://www.sandiego.edu/

Independent-religious, coed, university. CGS member. *Enrollment:* 7,262 graduate, professional, and undergraduate students; 1,306 full-time matriculated graduate/professional students (688 women), 999 part-time matriculated graduate/professional students (524 women). *Graduate faculty:* 137 full-time (60 women), 118 part-time/adjunct (43 women). *Computer facilities:* 260 computers available on campus for general student use. A campuswide network can be accessed from student residence rooms and from off campus. Internet access and online class registration are available. *Library facilities:* Helen K. and James S. Copley Library plus 1 other. *Graduate expenses:* Tuition: full-time $14,850; part-time $825 per unit. Required fees: $126. Full-time tuition and fees vary according to class time, course load, degree level and program. *General application contact:* Stephen Pultz, Director of Admissions, 619-260-4524.

Find an in-depth description at www.petersons.com/gradchannel.

College of Arts and Sciences
Dr. Patrick Drinan, Dean
Programs in:
  arts and sciences • MA, MFA, MS, CAS
  dramatic arts • MFA
  history • MA
  international relations • MA
  marine science • MS
  pastoral care and counseling • MA, CAS
  peace and justice studies • MA
  practical theology • MA

Hahn School of Nursing and Health Sciences
Dr. Sally Hardin, Dean
Programs in:
  adult nurse practitioner • MSN, Post Master's Certificate
  case management for vulnerable populations • MSN
  family nurse practitioner • MSN, Post Master's Certificate
  health care systems • MSN
  nursing science • PhD
  pediatric nurse practitioner • MSN, Post Master's Certificate

School of Business Administration
Dr. Curtis Cook, Dean
Programs in:
  accounting and financial management • MS
  business administration • MBA
  executive leadership • MSEL
  global leadership • MSGL
  information technology • MSIT
  international business administration • IMBA
  supply chain management • MS, Certificate

School of Education
Dr. Paula A. Cordeiro, Dean
Programs in:
  counseling • MA
  education • M Ed, MA, MAT, Ed D, Certificate
  educational leadership • M Ed
  leadership studies • MA, Ed D
  learning and teaching • M Ed
  marital and family therapy • MA
  nonprofit leadership and management • Certificate
  teaching • MAT
  teaching and learning • Ed D

School of Law
Daniel B. Rodriguez, Dean
Programs in:
  business and corporate law • LL M
  comparative law • LL M
  general studies • LL M
  international law • LL M
  law • JD
  taxation • LL M, Diploma

■ UNIVERSITY OF SAN FRANCISCO
San Francisco, CA 94117-1080
http://www.usfca.edu/

Independent-religious, coed, university. *Enrollment:* 8,159 graduate, professional, and undergraduate students; 2,763 full-time matriculated graduate/professional students (1,654 women), 662 part-time matriculated graduate/professional students (411 women). *Graduate faculty:* 164 full-time (57 women), 334 part-time/adjunct (123 women). *Computer facilities:* 250 computers available on campus for general student use. A campuswide network can be accessed from student residence rooms and from off campus. Internet access and online class registration are available. *Library facilities:* Gleeson Library plus 2 others. *Graduate expenses:* Tuition: full-time $15,840; part-time $880 per unit. Tuition and fees vary according to degree level, campus/location and program. *General application contact:* 415-422-6563.

Find an in-depth description at www.petersons.com/gradchannel.

College of Arts and Sciences
Dr. Stanley Nel, Dean
Programs in:
  arts and sciences • MA, MFA, MS
  Asia Pacific studies • MA
  biology • MS
  chemistry • MS
  computer science • MS
  economics • MA
  environmental management • MS
  financial economics • MS
  international and development economics • MA
  sport management • MA
  theology • MA
  writing • MA, MFA

College of Professional Studies
Dr. Larry Brewster, Dean
Programs in:
  health services administration • MPA
  human resources and organization development • MHROD
  information systems • MS
  nonprofit administration • MNA
  professional studies • MHROD, MNA, MPA, MS
  public administration • MPA

230 www.petersons.com

California

Masagung Graduate School of Management
Dr. Gary Williams, Dean
Programs in:
 business economics • MBA
 e-business • MBA
 finance and banking • MBA
 international business • MBA
 management • MBA
 marketing • MBA
 professional business administration • MBA
 telecommunications management and policy • MBA

School of Education
Dr. Larry Brewster, Acting Dean
Programs in:
 Catholic school leadership • MA, Ed D
 Catholic school teaching • MA
 counseling • MA
 counseling psychology • Psy D
 education • MA, Ed D, Psy D
 educational technology • MA
 international and multicultural education • MA, Ed D
 learning and instruction • MA, Ed D
 multicultural literature for children and young adults • MA
 organization and leadership • MA, Ed D
 private school administration • Ed D
 teaching English as a second language • MA

School of Law
Jeffrey Brand, Dean
Programs in:
 intellectual property and technology law • LL M
 international transactions and comparative law • LL M
 law • JD, LL M

School of Nursing
Dr. John Lantz, Dean
Programs in:
 advanced practice nursing-nurse practitioner and clinical nurse specialist • MSN
 nursing administration • MSN

■ UNIVERSITY OF SOUTHERN CALIFORNIA
Los Angeles, CA 90089
http://www.usc.edu/

Independent, coed, university. CGS member. *Enrollment:* 31,606 graduate, professional, and undergraduate students; 11,238 full-time matriculated graduate/professional students (5,492 women), 3,453 part-time matriculated graduate/professional students (1,311 women). *Graduate faculty:* 1,450 full-time (439 women), 891 part-time/adjunct (313 women). *Computer facilities:* Computer purchase and lease plans are available. 2,500 computers available on campus for general student use. A campuswide network can be accessed from student residence rooms and from off campus. Internet access and online class registration, online degree progress, grades, financial aid summary are available. *Library facilities:* Doheny Memorial Library plus 20 others. *Graduate expenses:* Tuition: full-time $32,784; part-time $949 per unit. Tuition and fees vary according to course load and program. *General application contact:* J. Michael Thompson, Director of Admissions, 213-740-0070.

Find an in-depth description at www.petersons.com/gradchannel.

Graduate School
Dr. Joseph B. Hellige, Dean and Vice Provost for Academic Programs

Annenberg School for Communication
Dr. Geoffrey Cowan, Dean
Programs in:
 broadcast journalism • MA
 communication • PhD
 • communication management
 global communication • MA
 print journalism • MA
 strategic public relations • MA

College of Letters, Arts and Sciences
Dr. Joseph Aoun, Dean
Programs in:
 american studies and ethnicity • PhD
 anthropology • MA
 applied mathematics • MA, MS, PhD
 art history • MA, PhD, Certificate
 biological anthropology • PhD
 chemical physics • PhD
 chemistry • MA, MS, PhD
 classics • MA, PhD
 clinical psychology • PhD
 comparative literature • MA, PhD
 computational linguistics • MS
 earth sciences • MS, PhD
 East Asian area studies • MA
 East Asian languages and cultures • MA, PhD
 economic development programming • MA
 economics • MA, PhD
 English • MA, PhD
 French • MA, PhD
 geography • MA, MS, PhD
 history • MA, PhD
 international relations • MA, PhD
 letters, arts and sciences • MA, MPW, MS, PhD, Certificate
 linguistics • MA, PhD
 marine environmental biology • PhD
 mathematics • MA, PhD
 molecular and computational biology • PhD
 neuroscience • PhD
 philosophy • MA, PhD
 physics • MA, MS, PhD
 political economy • MA
 political economy and public policy • PhD
 political science • MA, PhD
 professional writing • MPW
 psychology • MA, PhD
 Slavic languages and literatures • MA, PhD
 social anthropology • PhD
 social ethics • MA, PhD
 sociology • MA, PhD
 statistics • MS
 visual anthropology • Certificate

Leonard Davis School of Gerontology
Dr. Edward Schneider, Dean
Program in:
 gerontology • MS, PhD, Certificate

Marshall School of Business
Dr. Yash Gupta, Dean
Programs in:
 accounting • M Acc
 business • M Acc, MBA, MBT, MS, PhD
 business administration • MBA, MS, PhD
 business taxation • MBT
 finance and business economics • MBA
 information and operations management • MS
 international business • MBA

Rossier School of Education
Dr. Karen Symms Gallagher, Dean
Programs in:
 administration and policy • PhD
 college student personnel services • MS
 communication handicapped • MS
 counseling psychology • MS, PhD
 curriculum and instruction • Ed D, PhD
 curriculum and teaching • MS
 education • MS, Ed D, PhD, MFCC
 educational leadership • MS
 educational psychology • PhD
 instructional technology • MS
 international and intercultural education • MS
 language, literacy, and learning • PhD
 learning handicapped • MS
 marriage, family and child counseling • MFCC
 pupil personnel services (K–12) • MS
 teaching English as a second language • MS

School of Architecture
Dr. Robert Timme, Dean
Programs in:
 architecture • M Arch, MBS, ML Arch, AC
 building science • MBS
 historic preservation • AC
 landscape architecture • ML Arch

California

University of Southern California (continued)

School of Cinema-Television
Dr. Elizabeth Daley, Dean
Programs in:
cinema-television • MA, MFA, PhD
critical studies • MA, PhD
film and video production • MFA
film, video, and computer animation • MFA
interactive media • MFA
producing • MFA
screen and television writing • MFA

School of Fine Arts
Ruth Weisberg, Dean
Programs in:
fine arts • MFA, MPAS
public art studies • MPAS

School of Health Affairs
Joseph P. Van Der Meulen, Vice President
Programs in:
biokinesiology • MS, PhD
health affairs • MA, MS, DPT, OTD, PhD
occupational science • PhD
occupational therapy • MA, OTD
physical therapy • MS, DPT

School of Policy, Planning and Development
Dr. Daniel A. Mazmanian, Dean
Programs in:
health administration • MHA
planning • M Pl
planning and development studies • MPDS, DPDS
policy, planning and development • M Pl, MHA, MPA, MPDS, MPP, MRED, DPA, DPDS, PhD, Certificate
public administration • MPA, DPA, PhD, Certificate
public policy • MPP
real estate development • MRED
urban and regional planning • PhD

School of Social Work
Dr. Marilyn L. Flynn, Dean
Program in:
social work • MSW, PhD

School of Theatre
Madeline Puzo, Dean
Programs in:
design • MFA
playwriting • MFA

Thorton School of Music
Robert A. Cutietta, Dean
Programs in:
choral and church music • MM, DMA
composition • MA, MM, DMA, PhD
conducting • MM
early music performance • MA
historical musicology • PhD
jazz studies • MM, DMA
music • MA, MM, MM Ed, DMA, PhD
music education • MM, MM Ed, DMA
music history and literature • MA
performance • MM, DMA

Viterbi School of Engineering
Dr. C.H. Max Nikias, Dean
Programs in:
aerospace engineering • MSAE, PhD, Engr
applied mechanics • MS
astronautics • MSAE
biomedical engineering • MS, PhD
biomedical imaging and telemedicine • MS
chemical engineering • MS, PhD, Engr
civil engineering • MS, PhD, Engr
computer aided engineering • ME, Certificate
computer engineering • MS, PhD
computer networks • MS
computer science • MS, PhD
construction engineering • MS
construction management • MCM
dynamics and control • MSME
earthquake engineering • MS
electrical engineering • MS, PhD, Engr
engineering • MCM, ME, MS, MSAE, MSME, PhD, Certificate, Engr
engineering management • MS
environmental engineering • MS, PhD
industrial and systems engineering • MS, PhD, Engr
manufacturing engineering • MS
materials engineering • MS
materials science • MS, PhD, Engr
mechanical engineering • MSME, PhD, Engr
multimedia and creative technologies • MS
ocean engineering • MS
operations research • MS
petroleum engineering • MS, PhD, Engr
robotics and automation • MS
software engineering • MS
soil mechanics and foundations • MS
structural engineering • MS
structural mechanics • MS
systems architecture and engineering • MS
transportation engineering • MS
VLSI design • MS
water resources • MS

Keck School of Medicine
Dr. Stephen J. Ryan, Dean
Programs in:
medicine • MD, MPAP, MPH, MS, PhD
primary care physician assistant • MPAP

Graduate Programs in Medicine
Dr. Zach W. Hall, Senior Associate Dean for Research
Programs in:
anatomy and cell biology • MS, PhD
applied biostatistics/epidemiology • MS
biochemistry and molecular biology • MS, PhD
biometry/epidemiology • MPH
biostatistics • MS, PhD
cell and neurobiology • MS, PhD
epidemiology • PhD
experimental and molecular pathology • MS
genetic epidemiology and statistical genetics • PhD
health behavior research • MPH, PhD
health communication • MPH
health promotion • MPH
medicine • MPH, MS, PhD
molecular epidemiology • MS, PhD
molecular microbiology and immunology • MS, PhD
pathobiology • PhD
physiology and biophysics • MS, PhD
preventive nutrition • MPH
public health • MPH

Law School
Dr. Matthew L. Spitzer, Dean
Program in:
law • JD, LL M

School of Dentistry
Dr. Harold Slavkin, Dean
Programs in:
craniofacial biology • MS, PhD
dentistry • DDS, MS, PhD, Certificate

School of Pharmacy
Dr. Timothy M. Chan, Dean
Programs in:
molecular pharmacology and toxicology • MS, PhD
pharmaceutical economics and policy • MS, PhD
pharmaceutical sciences • MS, PhD
pharmacy • Pharm D, MS, PhD
regulatory sciences • MS

■ **UNIVERSITY OF THE PACIFIC**
Stockton, CA 95211-0197
http://www.uop.edu/

Independent, coed, university. CGS member. *Enrollment:* 6,121 graduate, professional, and undergraduate students; 2,118 full-time matriculated graduate/professional students (1,106 women), 646 part-time matriculated graduate/professional students (352 women). *Graduate faculty:* 244 full-time (81 women), 205 part-time/adjunct (76 women). *Computer facilities:* Computer purchase and lease plans are available. 274 computers available on campus for general student use. A campuswide network can be accessed from student residence rooms and from off campus. Internet access and online class registration are available. *Library facilities:* Holt Memorial Library plus 1 other. *Graduate expenses:* Tuition: full-time $23,180; part-time $725 per unit. Required fees: $420. *General application contact:* Dr. Robert Brodnick, Director and Assistant Professor, Planning and Research, 209-946-2569.

College of the Pacific
Gary Miller, Dean
Programs in:
 biological sciences • MS
 communication • MA
 psychology • MA
 sport sciences • MA

Conservatory of Music
Dr. Steven Anderson, Dean
Programs in:
 music • MA, MM
 music education • MM
 music therapy • MA

Eberhardt School of Business
Dr. Mark Plovnick, Dean
Program in:
 business • MBA

McGeorge School of Law
Programs in:
 government and public policy • LL M
 international law • LL M
 international waters resources law • LL M
 law • JD
 transnational business practice • LL M

School of Dentistry
Dr. Arthur A. Dugoni, Dean
Programs in:
 advanced education in general dentistry • Certificate
 dentistry • MSD
 international dental studies • DDS
 oral and maxillofacial surgery • Certificate

School of Education
Dr. Jack Nagle, Dean
Programs in:
 curriculum and instruction • M Ed, MA, Ed D
 education • M Ed
 educational administration • MA, Ed D
 educational psychology • MA, Ed D
 school psychology • Ed S
 special education • MA

School of International Studies
Dr. Margee Ensign, Dean
Programs in:
 intercultural relations • MA
 international studies • MA

School of Pharmacy and Health Sciences
Dr. Philip Oppenheimer, Dean
Programs in:
 pharmaceutical sciences • MS, PhD
 pharmacy • Pharm D, MS, DPT, PhD
 physical therapy • MS, DPT
 speech-language pathology • MS

■ **WOODBURY UNIVERSITY**
Burbank, CA 91504-1099
http://www.woodbury.edu/

Independent, coed, comprehensive institution. *Computer facilities:* 116 computers available on campus for general student use. A campuswide network can be accessed from off campus. Internet access is available. *Library facilities:* Los Angeles Times Library. *General application contact:* Graduate Admissions Assistant, 818-767-0888 Ext. 264.

Business Administration Program
Program in:
 business administration • MBA

Colorado

■ **ADAMS STATE COLLEGE**
Alamosa, CO 81102
http://www.adams.edu/

State-supported, coed, comprehensive institution. *Computer facilities:* 261 computers available on campus for general student use. A campuswide network can be accessed from student residence rooms and from off campus. Internet access and online class registration are available. *Library facilities:* Nielsen Library. *General application contact:* Dean of Graduate Studies, 719-587-7936.

Graduate Studies

School of Arts and Letters
Programs in:
 art • MA
 arts and letters • MA

School of Education and Graduate Studies
Programs in:
 counseling • MA
 education and graduate studies • MA
 elementary education • MA
 health, physical education, and recreation • MA
 secondary education • MA
 special education • MA

■ **COLORADO CHRISTIAN UNIVERSITY**
Lakewood, CO 80226
http://www.ccu.edu/

Independent-religious, coed, comprehensive institution. *Enrollment:* 1,583 graduate, professional, and undergraduate students; 95 full-time matriculated graduate/professional students (61 women), 26 part-time matriculated graduate/professional students (17 women). *Graduate faculty:* 32. *Computer facilities:* 141 computers available on campus for general student use. A campuswide network can be accessed from student residence rooms and from off campus. Internet access and online class registration are available. *Library facilities:* Clifton Fowler Library plus 1 other. *Graduate expenses:* Tuition: full-time $6,516; part-time $362 per credit. Required fees: $100. Tuition and fees vary according to program. *General application contact:* Tamara Brod, Executive Director of Graduate Programs, 303-963-3309.

Program in Business Administration
Murray Young, Dean
Program in:
 business administration • MBA

Program in Curriculum and Instruction
Steve Mountjoy, Director
Program in:
 curriculum and instruction • MA

■ **COLORADO STATE UNIVERSITY**
Fort Collins, CO 80523-0015
http://www.colostate.edu/

State-supported, coed, university. CGS member. *Enrollment:* 26,870 graduate, professional, and undergraduate students; 2,605 full-time matriculated graduate/professional students (1,491 women), 3,063 part-time matriculated graduate/professional students (1,435 women). *Graduate faculty:* 901 full-time (245 women), 42 part-time/adjunct (1 woman). *Computer facilities:* 2,530 computers

Colorado

Colorado State University (continued)
available on campus for general student use. A campuswide network can be accessed from student residence rooms and from off campus. Internet access is available. *Library facilities:* William E. Morgan Library plus 3 others. *Graduate expenses:* Tuition, state resident: full-time $4,156. Tuition, nonresident: full-time $14,762. Required fees: $205. Tuition and fees vary according to course load, campus/location, program and reciprocity agreements. *General application contact:* Graduate School, 970-491-6817.

College of Veterinary Medicine and Biomedical Sciences
Dr. Lance Perryman, Dean
Programs in:
  biomedical sciences • MS, PhD
  clinical sciences • MS, PhD
  environmental health • MS, PhD
  immunology • MS, PhD
  microbiology • MS, PhD
  pathology • PhD
  radiological health sciences • MS, PhD
  veterinary medicine • DVM
  veterinary medicine and biomedical sciences • DVM, MS, PhD

Graduate School
Patrick J. Pellicane, Interim Dean
Programs in:
  cell and molecular biology • MS, PhD
  ecology • MS, PhD

College of Agricultural Sciences
Dr. Marc A. Johnson, Dean
Programs in:
  agricultural and resource economics • M Agr, MS, PhD
  agricultural sciences • M Agr, MS, PhD
  animal breeding and genetics • MS, PhD
  animal nutrition • MS, PhD
  animal reproduction • MS, PhD
  animal sciences • M Agr
  crop science • MS, PhD
  entomology • MS, PhD
  floriculture • M Agr, MS, PhD
  horticultural food crops • M Agr, MS, PhD
  integrated resource management • M Agr
  livestock handling • MS, PhD
  meats • MS, PhD
  nursery and landscape management • M Agr, MS, PhD
  plant genetics • MS, PhD
  plant pathology • MS, PhD
  plant pathology and weed science • MS, PhD
  plant physiology • MS, PhD
  production management • MS, PhD
  soil science • MS, PhD
  turf management • M Agr, MS, PhD
  weed science • MS, PhD

College of Applied Human Sciences
Nancy Hartley, Dean
Programs in:
  applied human sciences • M Ed, MS, MSW, PhD
  construction management and information systems • MS
  design and merchandising • MS
  education and human resource studies • M Ed, PhD
  food science • MS, PhD
  health and exercise science • MS
  historic preservation • MS
  human development and family studies • MS
  nutrition • MS, PhD
  occupational therapy • MS
  social work • MSW
  student affairs • MS
  sustainable building • MS

College of Business
Dr. Tom Ingram, Associate Dean
Programs in:
  business • MBA, MS
  business administration • MS

College of Engineering
Dr. Steven Abt, Interim Dean
Programs in:
  atmospheric science • M Eng, MS, PhD
  bioengineering • MS, PhD
  bioresource and agricultural engineering • MS
  bioresource and agriculture engineering • PhD
  chemical engineering • MS, PhD
  electrical and computer engineering • M Eng, MS, PhD
  energy and environmental engineering • MS, PhD
  energy conversion • MS, PhD
  engineering • ME
  engineering management • MS
  environmental engineering • MS, PhD
  heat and mass transfer • MS, PhD
  hydraulics and wind engineering • MS, PhD
  industrial and manufacturing systems engineering • MS, PhD
  mechanical engineering • ME, MS, PhD
  mechanics and materials • MS, PhD
  structural and geotechnical engineering • MS, PhD
  water resources planning and management • MS, PhD
  water resources, hydrologic and environmental sciences • MS, PhD

College of Liberal Arts
Heather Hardy, Dean
Programs in:
  African history • MA
  American history • MA
  anthropology • MA
  applied music • MM
  archival science • MA
  Asian history • MA
  communication development • MA
  conducting • MM
  creative writing • MFA
  drawing • MFA
  economics • MA, PhD
  English • MA
  English as a second language • MA
  English education • MA
  environmental politics and policy • PhD
  European history • MA
  fibers • MFA
  French • MA
  French/TESL • MA
  German • MA
  German/TESL • MA
  graphic design • MFA
  historic preservation • MA
  Latin American history • MA
  liberal arts • MA, MFA, MM, MS, PhD
  literature • MA
  metalsmithing • MFA
  museum studies • MA
  music education • MM
  music therapy • MM
  painting • MFA
  philosophy • MA
  political science • MA, PhD
  printmaking • MFA
  rhetoric and composition • MA
  sculpture • MFA
  sociology • MA, PhD
  Spanish • MA
  Spanish/TESL • MA
  speech communication • MA
  technical communication • MS

College of Natural Resources
Dr. Joyce Berry, Interim Dean
Programs in:
  commercial recreation and tourism • MS
  earth resources • PhD
  fishery and wildlife biology • MS, PhD
  forest sciences • MF, MS, PhD
  geology • MS
  human dimensions in natural resources • PhD
  natural resources • MF, MS, PhD
  rangeland ecosystem science • MS, PhD
  recreation resource management • MS, PhD
  resource interpretation • MS
  watershed science • MS

College of Natural Sciences
Rick Miranda, Dean
Programs in:
  applied social psychology • MS, PhD

Colorado

behavioral neuroscience • PhD
biochemistry and molecular biology • MS, PhD
botany • MS, PhD
chemistry • MS, PhD
cognitive psychology • PhD
computer science • MCS, MS, PhD
counseling psychology • PhD
industrial-organizational psychology • PhD
mathematics • MS, PhD
natural sciences • MCS, MS, PhD
physics • MS, PhD
statistics • MS, PhD
zoology • MS, PhD

■ COLORADO STATE UNIVERSITY-PUEBLO
Pueblo, CO 81001-4901
http://www.colostate-pueblo.edu/

State-supported, coed, comprehensive institution. *Enrollment:* 6,299 graduate, professional, and undergraduate students; 43 full-time matriculated graduate/professional students (18 women), 61 part-time matriculated graduate/professional students (31 women). *Graduate faculty:* 25 full-time (8 women), 3 part-time/adjunct (0 women). *Computer facilities:* 521 computers available on campus for general student use. A campuswide network can be accessed from student residence rooms and from off campus. Internet access is available. *Library facilities:* Colorado State University-Pueblo Library. *Graduate expenses:* Part-time $104 per credit. Tuition, state resident: part-time $156 per credit. Tuition, nonresident: part-time $558 per credit. Tuition and fees vary according to reciprocity agreements. *General application contact:* Jennifer Jensen, Associate Director of Admissions, 719-549-2434.

College of Education, Engineering and Professional Studies
Dr. Hector R. Carrasco, Dean
Programs in:
  education, engineering and professional studies • MS
  industrial and systems engineering • MS

College of Science and Mathematics
Dr. Kristina Proctor, Dean
Program in:
  science and mathematics • MS

Hasan School of Business
Dr. Rex D. Fuller, Dean
Program in:
  business • MBA

■ COLORADO TECHNICAL UNIVERSITY
Colorado Springs, CO 80907-3896
http://www.coloradotech.edu

Proprietary, coed, comprehensive institution. *Computer facilities:* 130 computers available on campus for general student use. A campuswide network can be accessed from off campus. Internet access is available. *Library facilities:* Colorado Technical University Library. *General application contact:* Graduate Admissions, 719-590-6720.

Graduate Studies
Programs in:
  business administration • MBA
  business management • MSM
  business technology • MSM
  communication systems • MSEE
  computer engineering • MSCE
  computer science • DCS
  computer systems security • MSCS
  database management • MSM
  electronic systems • MSEE
  human resources management • MSM
  information technology • MSM
  logistics management • MSM
  management • DM
  organizational leadership • MSM
  project management • MSM
  software engineering • MSCS
  software project management • MSCS

■ REGIS UNIVERSITY
Denver, CO 80221-1099
http://www.regis.edu/

Independent-religious, coed, comprehensive institution. *Graduate faculty:* 575. *Computer facilities:* 300 computers available on campus for general student use. A campuswide network can be accessed from student residence rooms and from off campus. *Library facilities:* Dayton Memorial Library. *Graduate expenses:* Tuition: part-time $460 per credit hour. Part-time tuition and fees vary according to campus/location and program. *General application contact:* 303-458-4300.

Find an in-depth description at www.petersons.com/gradchannel.

Regis College
Dr. Paul Ewald, Dean
Program in:
  education • MA

Rueckert-Hartman School for Health Professions
Dr. Patricia Ladewig, Academic Dean
Programs in:
  clinical leadership for physician assistants • MS
  health services administration • MS
  nursing • MSN
  physical therapy • DPT, TDPT

School for Professional Studies
Dr. Steven Berkshire, Associate Dean
Programs in:
  accounting • MBA
  adult learning, training and development • MLS, Certificate
  business administration • MBA
  computer information technology • MSM
  database technologies • MSCIT, Certificate
  e-commerce engineering • MSCIT, Certificate
  early childhood • M Ed
  educational technology • Certificate
  electronic commerce • MBA
  elementary • M Ed
  ESL • M Ed
  executive international management • Certificate
  executive leadership • Certificate
  finance • MBA
  fine arts • M Ed
  human resource management • MSM
  international business • MBA
  language and communication • MLS
  leadership • Certificate
  licensed professional counselor • MLS
  management of technology • MSCIT
  market strategy • MBA
  networking technologies • MSCIT
  networking technology • Certificate
  nonprofit management • MNM
  object-oriented technologies • MSCIT
  object-oriented technology • Certificate
  operations management • MBA
  organizational leadership • MSM
  program management • Certificate
  project leadership and management • Certificate
  project management • MSM, Certificate
  psychology • MLS
  resource development • Certificate
  secondary • M Ed
  social justice, peace, and reconciliation • Certificate
  social science • MLS
  special education • M Ed
  strategic business • Certificate
  strategic human resource • Certificate
  technical communication • Certificate
  technical management • Certificate

Peterson's Graduate Schools in the U.S. 2006

Colorado

UNIVERSITY OF COLORADO AT BOULDER
Boulder, CO 80309
http://www.colorado.edu/

State-supported, coed, university. CGS member. *Enrollment:* 32,041 graduate, professional, and undergraduate students; 3,664 full-time matriculated graduate/professional students (1,687 women), 947 part-time matriculated graduate/professional students (477 women). *Graduate faculty:* 943 full-time (248 women). *Computer facilities:* 1,525 computers available on campus for general student use. A campuswide network can be accessed from student residence rooms and from off campus. Internet access and online class registration, standard and academic software, student government voting are available. *Library facilities:* Norlin Library plus 5 others. *Graduate expenses:* Tuition, state resident: full-time $2,122. Tuition, nonresident: full-time $9,754. Tuition and fees vary according to course load and program. *General application contact:* Richard Byyny, Chancellor, 303-492-8908.

Graduate School
Carol Lynch, Dean

College of Arts and Sciences
Todd T. Gleeson, Dean
Programs in:
  animal behavior • MA, PhD
  anthropology • MA, PhD
  applied mathematics • MS, PhD
  aquatic biology • MA, PhD
  art history • MA
  arts and sciences • MA, MBS, MFA, MS, PhD
  astrophysical and geophysical fluid dynamics • MS, PhD
  astrophysics • MS, PhD
  atmospheric and oceanic sciences • MS, PhD
  audiology • MA, PhD
  behavioral genetics • MA, PhD
  biochemistry • PhD
  cellular structure and function • MA, PhD
  ceramics • MFA
  chemical physics • PhD
  chemistry • MS, PhD
  Chinese • MA
  classics • MA, PhD
  communication • MA, PhD
  comparative literature • MA, PhD
  dance • MFA
  developmental biology • MA, PhD
  drawing • MFA
  ecology • MA, PhD
  economics • MA, PhD
  English literature • MA, PhD
  environmental studies • MS, PhD
  French • MA, PhD
  geography • MA, PhD
  geology • MS, PhD
  geophysics • PhD
  German • MA
  history • MA, PhD
  international affairs • MA
  Japanese • MA
  kinesiology • PhD
  linguistics • MA, PhD
  liquid crystal science and technology • PhD
  mathematical physics • PhD
  mathematics • MA, MS, PhD
  medical physics • PhD
  microbiology • MA, PhD
  molecular biology • MA, PhD
  museum and field studies • MBS, MS
  neurobiology • MA, PhD
  optical sciences and engineering • PhD
  painting • MFA
  philosophy • MA, PhD
  photography and media arts • MFA
  physical education • MS
  physics • MS, PhD
  plant and animal physiology • MA, PhD
  plant and animal systematics • MA, PhD
  plasma physics • MS, PhD
  political science • MA, PhD
  population biology • MA, PhD
  population genetics • MA, PhD
  printmaking • MFA
  psychology • MA, PhD
  public policy analysis • MA
  religious studies • MA
  sculpture • MFA
  sociology • MA, PhD
  Spanish • MA, PhD
  Spanish literature • MA
  speech-language pathology • MA, PhD
  theatre • MA, PhD

College of Engineering and Applied Science
Robert Davis, Dean
Programs in:
  aerospace engineering sciences • ME, MS, PhD
  building systems • MS, PhD
  chemical engineering • ME, MS, PhD
  computer science • ME, MS, PhD
  construction engineering and management • MS, PhD
  electrical engineering • ME, MS, PhD
  engineering and applied science • ME, MS, PhD
  environmental engineering • MS, PhD
  geoenvironmental engineering • MS, PhD
  geotechnical engineering • MS, PhD
  mechanical engineering • ME, MS, PhD
  operations and logistics • ME
  quality and process • ME
  research and development • ME
  structural engineering • MS, PhD
  telecommunications • ME, MS
  water resource engineering • MS, PhD

College of Music
Daniel P. Sher, Dean
Programs in:
  church music • M Mus
  composition • M Mus, D Mus A
  conducting • M Mus, D Mus A
  music education • M Mus Ed, PhD
  music literature • M Mus
  musicology • PhD
  pedagogy • M Mus, D Mus A
  performance • M Mus, D Mus A

School of Education
Lorrie Shepard, Dean
Programs in:
  education • MA, PhD
  educational and psychological studies • MA, PhD
  instruction and curriculum • MA, PhD
  research and evaluation methodologies • PhD
  social multicultural and bilingual foundations • MA, PhD

School of Journalism and Mass Communication
Paul Voakes, Dean
Programs in:
  communication • PhD
  integrated marketing communications • MA
  mass communication research • MA
  media studies • PhD
  newsgathering • MA

Leeds School of Business
Steven Manaster, Dean
Programs in:
  accounting • MBA, MS
  business administration • MBA, MS, PhD
  business self designed • MBA
  entrepreneurship • MBA
  finance • MBA, PhD
  marketing • MBA, PhD
  operations management • MBA
  organization management • MBA, PhD
  real estate • MBA
  taxation • MS
  technology and innovation management • MBA

School of Law
Harold H. Bruff, Dean
Program in:
  law • JD

UNIVERSITY OF COLORADO AT COLORADO SPRINGS
Colorado Springs, CO 80918
http://www.uccs.edu/

State-supported, coed, comprehensive institution. *Enrollment:* 7,620 graduate, professional, and undergraduate students; 1,440 matriculated graduate/professional students. *Graduate faculty:* 130 full-time (45 women), 59 part-time/adjunct (32 women). *Computer facilities:* 250 computers available on campus for general student use. A campuswide network can be accessed from student residence rooms and from off campus. *Library facilities:* University of Colorado at Colorado Springs Kraemer Family Library. *Graduate expenses:* Tuition, state resident: full-time $3,745; part-time $226 per semester hour. Tuition, nonresident: full-time $13,602; part-time $804 per semester hour. Required fees: $19 per semester hour. $135 per semester. One-time fee: $40 full-time. Tuition and fees vary according to course load and program. *General application contact:* Information Contact, 719-262-3417.

Beth-El College of Nursing
Kathy LaSala, Chair
Programs in:
  adult health nurse practitioner and clinical specialist • MSN
  family practitioner • MSN
  gerontology • MSN
  neonatal nurse practitioner and clinical specialist • MSN
  nursing administration • MSN
  women nurse practitioner • MSN

Graduate School
Dr. David Schmidt, Dean

College of Education
Dr. David E. Nelson, Dean
Programs in:
  counseling and human services • MA
  curriculum and instruction • MA
  educational administration • MA
  educational leadership • MA
  special education • MA

College of Engineering and Applied Science
Dr. Jeremy Haefner, Dean
Programs in:
  applied mathematics • MS
  computer science • MS, PhD
  electrical engineering • MS, PhD
  engineering and applied science • ME, MS, PhD
  engineering management • ME
  information operations • ME
  manufacturing • ME
  mechanical engineering • MS
  software engineering • ME
  space operations • ME
  space systems • MS

College of Letters, Arts and Sciences
Dr. Linda Nolan, Dean
Programs in:
  basic science • MBS
  communications • MA
  geography and environmental studies • MA
  geropsychology • PhD
  history • MA
  letters, arts and sciences • MA, MBS, PhD
  psychology • MA
  sociology • MA

Graduate School of Business Administration
Dr. Gary Klein, Dean
Programs in:
  accounting • MBA
  finance • MBA
  general health care administration • MBA
  information systems • MBA
  international business management • MBA
  marketing • MBA
  service management/technology management • MBA

Graduate School of Public Affairs
Dr. Kathleen Beatty, Dean
Programs in:
  criminal justice • MCJ
  public administration • MPA

UNIVERSITY OF COLORADO AT DENVER
Denver, CO 80217-3364
http://www.cudenver.edu/

State-supported, coed, university. CGS member. *Enrollment:* 15,596 graduate, professional, and undergraduate students; 1,655 full-time matriculated graduate/professional students (925 women), 2,799 part-time matriculated graduate/professional students (1,589 women). *Graduate faculty:* 338 full-time (134 women). *Computer facilities:* 750 computers available on campus for general student use. A campuswide network can be accessed from student residence rooms and from off campus. Internet access and online class registration are available. *Library facilities:* Auraria Library. *Graduate expenses:* Tuition, state resident: part-time $255 per credit hour. Tuition, nonresident: part-time $1,025 per credit hour. *General application contact:* 303-556-2704.

Business School
Ken Bettenhausen, Associate Dean
Programs in:
  accounting • MS
  business • Exec MBA, MBA, MS, MSIB, PhD
  business administration • Exec MBA, MBA
  computer science information systems • PhD
  finance • MS
  health administration • Exec MBA, MS
  information systems management • MS
  international business • MSIB
  management • MS
  marketing • MS

College of Architecture and Planning
Mark Gelernter, Dean
Programs in:
  architecture • M Arch
  architecture and planning • M Arch, MLA, MUD, MURP, PhD
  design and planning • PhD
  landscape architecture • MLA
  urban and regional planning • MURP
  urban design • MUD

Graduate School
Mark Gelernter, Interim Vice Chancellor for Academic and Student Affairs
Programs in:
  arts and media • MS
  recording arts • MS

College of Engineering and Applied Science
Paul Rakowski, Assistant Dean of Student Services
Programs in:
  civil engineering • MS, PhD
  computational biology • PhD
  computer science and engineering • MS
  computer science and information systems • PhD
  electrical engineering • MS
  engineering • M Eng
  engineering and applied science • M Eng, MS, PhD
  mechanical engineering • MS

College of Liberal Arts and Sciences
Prof. Jim Smith, Dean
Programs in:
  anthropology • MA
  applied mathematics • MS, PhD
  applied science • MIS
  biology • MA
  chemistry • MS
  communication • MA
  computer science • MIS
  economics • MA

Colorado

University of Colorado at Denver (continued)
- environmental science • MS
- health and behavioral science • PhD
- history • MA
- humanities • MH
- liberal arts and sciences • MA, MH, MIS, MS, MSS, PhD
- literature • MA
- mathematics • MIS
- political science • MA
- psychology • MA
- social sciences • MSS
- sociology • MA
- teaching English as a second language • MA
- teaching of writing • MA
- technical communication • MS

School of Education
Lynn Rhodes, Dean
Programs in:
- administration, supervision, and curriculum development • MA
- counseling psychology and counselor education • MA
- curriculum and instruction • MA
- early childhood education • MA
- education • MA, PhD, Ed S
- educational administration, curriculum and supervision • Ed S
- educational leadership and innovation • PhD
- educational psychology • MA
- initial professional teacher education • MA
- professional learning and advancement • MA

Graduate School of Public Affairs
Kathleen Beatty, Dean
Programs in:
- agricultural and resource economics • MS, PhD
- criminal justice • MCJ
- public administration • Exec MPA, MPA, PhD
- public affairs • Exec MPA, MCJ, MPA, MS, PhD

■ **UNIVERSITY OF DENVER**
Denver, CO 80208
http://www.du.edu/

Independent, coed, university. CGS member. *Enrollment:* 9,521 graduate, professional, and undergraduate students; 4,903 matriculated graduate/professional students. *Graduate faculty:* 978. *Computer facilities:* 130 computers available on campus for general student use. A campuswide network can be accessed from student residence rooms and from off campus. Internet access and online class registration, online grade reports are available. *Library facilities:* Penrose Library. *Graduate expenses:* Tuition: full-time $24,264. General application contact: 360-871-2706.

Find an in-depth description at www.petersons.com/gradchannel.

College of Education
Dr. Virginia Maloney, Dean
Programs in:
- counseling psychology • MA, PhD
- curriculum and instruction • MA, PhD
- educational psychology • MA, PhD, Ed S
- higher education and adult studies • MA, PhD
- library and information science • MLIS
- school administration • PhD

College of Law
Mary E. Ricketson, Dean
Programs in:
- American and corporative law • LL M
- law • JD, LL M, MRLS, MSLA
- legal administration • MSLA
- natural resources law • LL M, MRLS
- taxation • LL M

Daniels College of Business
James R. Griesemer, Dean
Programs in:
- business • IMBA, M Acc, MBA, MIM, MS
- business administration • MBA
- finance • IMBA, MBA, MS
- general business administration • IMBA, MBA, MS
- hotel, restaurant, and tourism management • IMBA, MBA
- information technology and electronic commerce • IMBA, MBA, MS
- international business/management • IMBA, MBA, MIM
- marketing • IMBA, MBA, MS

School of Accountancy
Dr. Ronald Kucic, Director
Programs in:
- accountancy • M Acc
- accounting • MBA

School of Real Estate and Construction Management
Dr. Mark Levine, Director
Programs in:
- construction management • IMBA, MS
- real estate • IMBA, MBA, MS

Graduate School of International Studies
Dr. Tom Farer, Dean
Programs in:
- global studies • MGS
- international studies • MA, PhD

Graduate School of Professional Psychology
Dr. Peter Buirski, Dean
Programs in:
- clinical psychology • Psy D
- psychology • MA

Graduate School of Social Work
Dr. Christian Molidor, Dean
Program in:
- social work • MSW, PhD

Graduate Studies
Dr. James Moran, Vice Provost
Program in:
- international and intercultural communication • MA

Faculty of Arts and Humanities/Social Sciences
Dr. Gregg Kvistad, Dean
Programs in:
- anthropology • MA
- art history • MA
- art history/museum studies • MA
- arts and humanities/social sciences • MA, MFA, MM, MPP, PhD
- composition • MA
- conducting • MA
- economics • MA
- English • MA, PhD
- French • MA
- German • MA
- history • MA
- Judaic studies • MA
- music • MM
- music education • MA
- music history and literature • MA
- Orff-Schulwerk • MA
- performance • MA
- philosophy • MA
- piano pedagogy • MA
- psychology • PhD
- public policy • MPP
- religious studies • MA
- sociology and criminology • MA
- Spanish • MA
- studio art • MFA
- Suzuki pedagogy • MA
- theory • MA

Faculty of Natural Sciences and Mathematics
Dr. James Fogleman, Interim Dean
Programs in:
- applied mathematics • MA, MS
- biological sciences • MS, PhD
- chemistry • MA, MS, PhD
- computer science • MS
- geography • MA, MS, PhD
- natural sciences and mathematics • MA, MS, PhD
- physics and astronomy • MS, PhD

School of Communication
Dr. Margaret Thompson, Chairperson
Programs in:
- advertising management • MS

communication • MA, MS, PhD
digital media studies • MA
human communication studies • MA, PhD
mass communications • MA
public relations • MS
video production • MA

University College
Dr. James Davis, Dean
Programs in:
alternative dispute resolution • MPS
applied communication • MAC
civic leadership and development • MPS
computer information systems • MCIS, MPS
e-commerce • MPS
environmental policy and management • MEPM
environmental policy and mangement • MPS
geographic information systems • MPS
leadership • MPS
liberal studies • MLS
organizational security • MPS
project management • MPS
technology management • MPS, MoTM
telecommunications • MPS, MTEL
training • MPS

■ UNIVERSITY OF NORTHERN COLORADO
Greeley, CO 80639
http://www.unco.edu/

State-supported, coed, university. CGS member. *Enrollment:* 13,204 graduate, professional, and undergraduate students; 1,122 full-time matriculated graduate/professional students (792 women), 425 part-time matriculated graduate/professional students (303 women). *Graduate faculty:* 195 full-time (79 women). *Computer facilities:* Computer purchase and lease plans are available. 1,100 computers available on campus for general student use. A campuswide network can be accessed from student residence rooms and from off campus. Internet access and online class registration are available. *Library facilities:* James A. Michener Library plus 2 others. *Graduate expenses:* Tuition, state resident: full-time $2,980; part-time $166 per semester. Tuition, nonresident: full-time $12,396; part-time $689 per semester. Required fees: $627; $35 per semester. *General application contact:* Linda Sisson, Graduate Student Admission Coordinator, 970-351-1807.

Find an in-depth description at www.petersons.com/gradchannel.

Graduate School
Dr. Allen Huang, Associate Vice President for Research and Dean of the Graduate School
Programs in:
interdisciplinary education • MA
interdisciplinary studies • MA, MS, DA, Ed D, Ed S

College of Arts and Sciences
Dr. Sandra Flake, Dean
Programs in:
arts and sciences • MA, PhD
biological education • PhD
biological sciences • MA
chemical education • MA, PhD
chemical research • MA
communication • MA
earth sciences • MA
educational mathematics • MA, PhD
English • MA
history • MA
mathematics • MA, PhD
psychology • MA
sociology • MA
Spanish • MA

College of Education
Dr. Eugene Sheehan, Dean
Programs in:
agency counseling • MA
applied statistics and research methods • MS, PhD
counseling psychology • Psy D
counselor education • Ed D
counselor education and counseling psychology • MA, Ed D, Psy D
early childhood education • MA
education • MA, MS, Ed D, PhD, Psy D, Ed S
education of gifted • MA
educational leadership • MA, Ed D, Ed S
educational media • MA
educational psychology • MA, PhD
educational technology • MA, PhD
elementary education • MA, Ed D
elementary school counseling • MA
higher education and student affairs leadership • PhD
reading education • MA, PhD
school psychology • PhD, Ed S
secondary and postsecondary school counseling • MA
special education • MA, Ed D

College of Health and Human Sciences
Dr. Vincent Scalia, Dean
Programs in:
communication disorders • MA
community health • MPH
family nurse practitioner • MS
gerontology • MA
health and human sciences • MA, MPH, MS, Ed D, PhD
nursing education • MS
rehabilitation counseling • MA, PhD
sport and exercise science • MA, Ed D

College of Performing and Visual Arts
Dr. Tim Fleming, Interim Dean
Programs in:
music • MM, MME, DA
performing and visual arts • MA, MM, MME, DA
visual arts • MA

Connecticut

■ CENTRAL CONNECTICUT STATE UNIVERSITY
New Britain, CT 06050-4010
http://www.ccsu.edu/

State-supported, coed, comprehensive institution. CGS member. *Enrollment:* 12,131 graduate, professional, and undergraduate students; 504 full-time matriculated graduate/professional students (322 women), 1,768 part-time matriculated graduate/professional students (1,223 women). *Graduate faculty:* 303 full-time (119 women), 276 part-time/adjunct (119 women). *Computer facilities:* 230 computers available on campus for general student use. A campuswide network can be accessed from student residence rooms and from off campus. Internet access is available. *Library facilities:* Burritt Library plus 1 other. *Graduate expenses:* Tuition, state resident: full-time $3,298. Tuition, nonresident: full-time $9,190. *General application contact:* Kevin Oliva, Graduate Admissions, 860-832-2350.

School of Graduate Studies
Kevin Oliva, Graduate Admissions

School of Arts and Sciences
Dr. Susan Pease, Dean
Programs in:
anesthesia • MS
art education • MS
arts and sciences • MA, MS, Certificate
biological sciences • MA, MS
cell and molecular biology • Certificate
community psychology • MA
computer information technology • MS
criminal justice • MS
data mining • MS
earth science • MS
English • MA
French • MA
general health • MS
general psychology • MA
geography • MS

Connecticut

Central Connecticut State University (continued)
- graphic information design • MA
- health psychology • MA
- history • MA
- international studies • MS
- mathematics • MA, MS
- modern language • MA
- music education • MS
- natural science chemistry • MS
- organizational communication • MS
- physics • MS
- pre health • Certificate
- public history • MS
- Spanish • MA, MS
- Spanish language and Hispanic culture • MA
- teaching English to speakers of other languages • MS

School of Business
Dean
Programs in:
- business • MBA, MS
- business education • MS
- international business administration • MBA

School of Education and Professional Studies
Dr. Ellen Whitford, Dean
Programs in:
- early childhood education • MS
- education and professional studies • MS, Ed D, Sixth Year Certificate
- educational foundations policy/secondary education • MS
- educational leadership • MS, Ed D, Sixth Year Certificate
- educational technology and media • MS
- elementary education • MS
- marriage and family therapy • MS
- physical education • MS
- professional counseling • MS
- reading • MS, Sixth Year Certificate
- school counseling • MS
- special education for special educators • MS
- special education for teachers certified in areas other than education • MS
- student development in higher education • MS

School of Technology
Dr. Zdzislaw Kremens, Dean
Programs in:
- civil construction engineering • MS
- mechanical manufacturing engineering • MS
- technology • MS
- technology education • MS
- technology management • MS

■ **EASTERN CONNECTICUT STATE UNIVERSITY**
Willimantic, CT 06226-2295
http://www.easternct.edu

State-supported, coed, comprehensive institution. *Enrollment:* 5,095 graduate, professional, and undergraduate students; 72 full-time matriculated graduate/professional students (55 women), 307 part-time matriculated graduate/professional students (236 women). *Graduate faculty:* 19 full-time (13 women), 14 part-time/adjunct (8 women). *Computer facilities:* 518 computers available on campus for general student use. A campuswide network can be accessed from student residence rooms and from off campus. Internet access is available. *Library facilities:* J. Eugene Smith Library. *Graduate expenses:* Tuition, state resident: full-time $3,298. Tuition, nonresident: full-time $9,190; part-time $265 per credit. Required fees: $2,397; $35 per term. *General application contact:* Hazel M. Gage, Secretary, 860-465-5292.

School of Education/Professional Studies and Graduate Division
Dr. Patricia A. Kleine, Dean
Programs in:
- accounting • MS
- early childhood education • MS
- education/professional studies • MS
- educational technology • MS
- elementary education • MS
- organizational management • MS
- reading and language arts • MS
- science education • MS
- secondary education • MS

■ **FAIRFIELD UNIVERSITY**
Fairfield, CT 06824-5195
http://www.fairfield.edu/

Independent-religious, coed, comprehensive institution. *Enrollment:* 5,053 graduate, professional, and undergraduate students; 229 full-time matriculated graduate/professional students (141 women), 807 part-time matriculated graduate/professional students (501 women). *Graduate faculty:* 118 full-time (53 women), 51 part-time/adjunct (20 women). *Computer facilities:* Computer purchase and lease plans are available. 150 computers available on campus for general student use. A campuswide network can be accessed from student residence rooms and from off campus. Internet access and online class registration are available. *Library facilities:* Dimenna-Nyselius Library. *Graduate expenses:* Tuition: full-time $10,125; part-time $540 per credit hour. Tuition and fees vary according to program. *General application contact:* Marianne Gumpper, Director of Graduate Admissions, 203-254-4184.

Charles F. Dolan School of Business
Dr. Norman A. Solomon, Dean
Programs in:
- accounting • MBA, CAS
- finance • MBA, CAS
- financial management • MSFM
- general management • MBA
- human resource management • MBA, CAS
- human resource managment • CAS
- information systems and operation management • MBA
- information systems and operations management • CAS
- international business • MBA, CAS
- marketing • MBA, CAS
- taxation • MBA, CAS

College of Arts and Sciences
Dr. Timothy L. Snyder, Dean
Programs in:
- American studies • MA
- arts and sciences • MA, MS
- mathematics and quantitative methods • MS

Graduate School of Education and Allied Professions
Dr. Margaret C. Deignan, Dean
Programs in:
- applied psychology • MA
- community counseling • MA
- computers in education • MA, CAS
- counselor education • CAS
- education and allied professions • MA, CAS
- educational media • MA, CAS
- elementary education • MA
- marriage and family therapy • MA
- school counseling • MA
- school media specialist • CAS
- school psychology • MA, CAS
- special education • MA, CAS
- teaching and foundation • MA, CAS
- TESOL, foreign language and bilingual/multicultural education • MA, CAS

School of Engineering
Dr. Evangelos Hadjimichael, Dean
Programs in:
- electrical and computer engineering • MS
- management of technology • MS
- software engineering • MS

School of Nursing
Dr. Jeanne M. Novotny, Dean
Programs in:
- adult nurse practitioner • MSN, PMC

Connecticut

family nurse practitioner • MSN, PMC
psychiatric nurse practitioner • MSN, PMC

■ **QUINNIPIAC UNIVERSITY**
Hamden, CT 06518-1940
http://www.quinnipiac.edu/

Independent, coed, comprehensive institution. *Enrollment:* 7,121 graduate, professional, and undergraduate students; 1,652 matriculated graduate/professional students. *Graduate faculty:* 71 full-time (32 women), 74 part-time/adjunct (27 women). *Computer facilities:* Computer purchase and lease plans are available. 300 computers available on campus for general student use. A campuswide network can be accessed from student residence rooms and from off campus. Internet access and online class registration are available. *Library facilities:* Arnold Bernhard Library plus 1 other. *Graduate expenses:* Tuition: part-time $500 per credit. Required fees: $25 per credit. *General application contact:* 800-462-1944.

Find an in-depth description at www.petersons.com/gradchannel.

College of Liberal Arts
Dr. Johannes Bergmann, Dean
Programs in:
 biology • MAT
 chemistry • MAT
 elementary school teaching • MAT
 English • MAT
 French • MAT
 history/social studies • MAT
 liberal arts • MAT
 mathematics • MAT
 physics • MAT
 Spanish • MAT

School of Business
Dr. Mark Thompson, Dean
Programs in:
 accounting • MBA
 business • MBA, MHA, MS
 computer information systems • MBA
 economics • MBA
 finance • MBA
 health administration • MHA
 health management • MBA
 information systems • MS
 international business • MBA
 long-term care administration • MHA
 management • MBA
 marketing • MBA

School of Communications
Dr. David Donnelly, Dean
Programs in:
 communications • MS
 e-media • MS
 journalism • MS

School of Health Sciences
Dr. Joseph Woods, Dean
Programs in:
 adult nurse practitioner • MSN
 advanced clinical practice • MSPT
 biomedical sciences • MHS
 family nurse practitioner • MSN
 forensic nursing • MSN
 health sciences • MHS, MOT, MPT, MS, MSN, MSPT
 laboratory management • MHS
 microbiology • MHS
 molecular and cell biology • MS
 occupational therapy • MOT
 orthopedic physical therapy • MSPT
 pathologists' assistant • MHS
 physical therapy • MPT
 physician assistant • MHS

School of Law
Brad Saxton, Dean
Program in:
 law • JD

■ **SACRED HEART UNIVERSITY**
Fairfield, CT 06825-1000
http://www.sacredheart.edu/

Independent-religious, coed, comprehensive institution. *Enrollment:* 5,781 graduate, professional, and undergraduate students; 525 full-time matriculated graduate/professional students (370 women), 1,156 part-time matriculated graduate/professional students (772 women). *Graduate faculty:* 62 full-time (35 women), 81 part-time/adjunct (40 women). *Computer facilities:* Computer purchase and lease plans are available. 330 computers available on campus for general student use. A campuswide network can be accessed from student residence rooms and from off campus. Internet access, Intranet are available. *Library facilities:* Ryan-Matura Library. *Graduate expenses:* Tuition: part-time $405 per credit. Required fees: $311 per term. *General application contact:* Alexis Haakonsen, Dean of Graduate Admissions, 203-365-7619.

Find an in-depth description at www.petersons.com/gradchannel.

Graduate Studies

College of Arts and Sciences
Dr. Claire Paolini, Dean
Programs in:
 arts and sciences • MA, MS, CPS
 chemistry • MS
 computer science • MS, CPS
 e-commerce • CPS
 information technology • MS, CPS
 information technology and network security • CPS
 multimedia • CPS
 religious studies • MA
 web development • CPS

College of Business
Dr. Stephen Brown, Dean
Program in:
 business • MBA

College of Education and Health Professions
Dr. Patricia Walker, Dean
Programs in:
 administration • CAS
 education and health professions • MAT, MS, MSN, MSOT, MSPT, DPT, CAS
 elementary education • MAT
 family nurse practitioner • MSN
 geriatric rehabilitation and wellness • MS
 occupational therapy • MSOT
 patient care services • MSN
 physical therapy • MSPT, DPT
 secondary education • MAT
 teaching • CAS

■ **SAINT JOSEPH COLLEGE**
West Hartford, CT 06117-2700
http://www.sjc.edu/

Independent-religious, women only, comprehensive institution. *Enrollment:* 1,836 graduate, professional, and undergraduate students; 118 full-time matriculated graduate/professional students (103 women), 549 part-time matriculated graduate/professional students (470 women). *Graduate faculty:* 30 full-time (22 women), 45 part-time/adjunct (31 women). *Computer facilities:* 150 computers available on campus for general student use. A campuswide network can be accessed from student residence rooms and from off campus. Internet access is available. *Library facilities:* Pope Pius XII Library plus 1 other. *Graduate expenses:* Tuition: part-time $540 per credit. Required fees: $50 per course. *General application contact:* Emily Morse, Graduate Recruiter, 860-231-5381.

Graduate Division
Dr. Clark Hendley, Vice President of Academic Affairs
Programs in:
 biology • MS
 biology/chemistry • MS
 chemistry • MS
 community counseling • MA
 early childhood education • MA
 education • MA
 family health nurse practitioner • MS
 family health nursing • MS

Connecticut

Saint Joseph College (continued)
  human development/gerontology • Certificate
  marriage and family therapy • MA, Certificate
  nursing • Post Master's Certificate
  psychiatric/mental health nursing • MS
  special education • MA
  spirituality • Certificate

■ SOUTHERN CONNECTICUT STATE UNIVERSITY
New Haven, CT 06515-1355
http://www.southernct.edu/

State-supported, coed, comprehensive institution. CGS member. *Enrollment:* 12,143 graduate, professional, and undergraduate students; 3,053 matriculated graduate/professional students. *Graduate faculty:* 402 full-time (175 women), 337 part-time/adjunct. *Computer facilities:* Computer purchase and lease plans are available. 300 computers available on campus for general student use. A campuswide network can be accessed from student residence rooms and from off campus. Internet access and online class registration are available. *Library facilities:* Hilton C. Buley Library. *Graduate expenses:* Tuition, state resident: full-time $3,298. Tuition, nonresident: full-time $9,190. Full-time tuition and fees vary according to program. *General application contact:* Lisa Galvin, Assistant to the Dean, 203-392-5240.

Find an in-depth description at www.petersons.com/gradchannel.

School of Graduate Studies
Dr. Sandra Holley, Dean

School of Arts and Sciences
Dr. Donna Jean Fredeen, Dean
Programs in:
  art education • MS
  arts and sciences • MA, MS, Diploma
  biology • MS
  biology for nurse anesthetists • MS
  chemistry • MS
  English • MA, MS
  environmental education • MS
  French • MA
  history • MA, MS
  mathematics • MS
  multicultural-bilingual education/teaching English to speakers of other languages • MS
  political science • MS
  psychology • MA
  romance languages • MA
  science education • MS, Diploma
  sociology • MS
  Spanish • MA
  urban studies • MS
  women's studies • MA

School of Business
Dr. Kenneth L. Kraft, Dean
Programs in:
  business • MBA
  business administration • MBA

School of Communication, Information and Library Science
Dr. Edward Harris, Dean
Programs in:
  communication, information and library science • MLS, MS, Diploma
  computer science • MS
  instructional technology • MS
  library science • MLS
  library/information studies • Diploma

School of Education
Dr. James Granfield, Interim Dean
Programs in:
  classroom teacher specialist • Diploma
  community counseling • MS
  counseling • Diploma
  education • MS, MS Ed, Ed D, Diploma
  educational leadership • Ed D, Diploma
  elementary education • MS
  foundational studies • Diploma
  human performance • MS
  physical education • MS
  reading • MS, Diploma
  research, measurement and quantitative analysis • MS
  school counseling • MS
  school health education • MS
  school psychology • MS, Diploma
  special education • MS Ed, Diploma
  sport psychology • MS

School of Health and Human Services
Dr. George Appleby, Interim Dean
Programs in:
  audiology • MS
  health and human services • MFT, MPH, MS, MSN, MSW
  marriage and family therapy • MFT
  nursing administration • MSN
  nursing education • MSN
  public health • MPH
  recreation and leisure studies • MS
  social work • MSW
  speech pathology • MS

■ UNIVERSITY OF BRIDGEPORT
Bridgeport, CT 06601
http://www.bridgeport.edu/

Independent, coed, comprehensive institution. CGS member. *Enrollment:* 3,165 graduate, professional, and undergraduate students; 1,058 full-time matriculated graduate/professional students (529 women), 954 part-time matriculated graduate/professional students (565 women). *Graduate faculty:* 86 full-time (16 women), 220 part-time/adjunct (83 women). *Computer facilities:* 500 computers available on campus for general student use. A campuswide network can be accessed from student residence rooms and from off campus. Internet access is available. *Library facilities:* Wahlstrom Library. *Graduate expenses:* Tuition: full-time $16,012; part-time $445 per credit. Required fees: $55 per term. Tuition and fees vary according to degree level and program. *General application contact:* Barbara L. Maryak, Dean of Admissions, 203-576-4552.

College of Chiropractic
Dr. Francis A. Zolli, Dean
Program in:
  chiropractic • DC

College of Naturopathic Medicine
Dr. Jennifer Brett, Interim Dean
Programs in:
  acupuncture • MS
  naturopathic medicine • ND

Division of Allied Health Technology
Dr. Oscar Rasmussen, Director
Program in:
  allied health technology • MS

Human Nutrition Institute
Dr. Oscar Rasmussen, Director, Division of Allied Health Technology
Program in:
  human nutrition • MS

School of Business
Dr. Y. Paul Huo, Dean
Programs in:
  business • MBA, MS
  business administration • MBA

School of Education and Human Resources
Dr. James J. Ritchie, Dean
Program in:
  education and human resources • MS, Ed D, Diploma

Division of Counseling and Human Resources
Dr. Joseph E. Nechasek, Director
Programs in:
  community agency counseling • MS
  human resource development and counseling • MS

Division of Education
Dr. Allen P. Cook, Associate Dean
Programs in:

computer specialist • MS, Diploma
early childhood education • MS, Diploma
education • MS
educational management • Ed D, Diploma
elementary education • MS, Diploma
international education • MS, Diploma
reading specialist • MS, Diploma
secondary education • MS, Diploma

School of Engineering
Dr. Tarek M. Sobh, Dean
Programs in:
computer engineering • MS
computer science • MS
electrical engineering • MS
engineering and design • MS
mechanical engineering • MS
technology management • MS

■ UNIVERSITY OF CONNECTICUT
Storrs, CT 06269
http://www.uconn.edu/

State-supported, coed, university. CGS member. *Enrollment:* 22,053 graduate, professional, and undergraduate students; 3,298 full-time matriculated graduate/professional students (1,785 women), 2,046 part-time matriculated graduate/professional students (997 women). *Graduate faculty:* 1,105 full-time (324 women). *Computer facilities:* Computer purchase and lease plans are available. 1,318 computers available on campus for general student use. A campuswide network can be accessed from student residence rooms and from off campus. Internet access and online class registration, e-mail are available. *Library facilities:* Homer Babbidge Library plus 3 others. *Graduate expenses:* Tuition, state resident: part-time $3,860 per semester. Tuition, nonresident: part-time $9,036 per semester. *General application contact:* Anne K. Lanzit, Associate Director of Graduate Admissions, 860-486-3617.

Find an in-depth description at www.petersons.com/gradchannel.

Graduate School
Janet L. Greger, Dean and Vice Provost, Research and Graduate Education
Programs in:
biomedical science • PhD
dental science • M Dent Sc
health • M Dent Sc, MPH, MS, PhD
human resource management • MPS
humanitarian services administration • MPS
public health • MPH

College of Agriculture and Natural Resources
Kirklyn M. Kerr, Dean
Programs in:
agricultural and resource economics • MS, PhD
agriculture and natural resources • MS, PhD
animal science • MS, PhD
natural resources • MS, PhD
natural resources management and engineering • MS, PhD
nutritional sciences • MS, PhD
pathobiology • MS, PhD
pathobiology and veterinary science • MS, PhD
plant and soil sciences • MS, PhD
plant science • MS, PhD

College of Liberal Arts and Sciences
Ross D. MacKinnon, Dean
Programs in:
actuarial science • MS, PhD
African studies • MA
anthropology • MA, PhD
applied financial mathematics • MS
applied genomics • MS
applied mathematics • MS
behavioral neuroscience • MA, PhD
biochemistry • MS, PhD
biophysics • MS, PhD
biotechnology • MS, PhD
botany • MS, PhD
cell biology • MS, PhD
chemistry • MS, PhD
clinical • MA, PhD
cognition/instruction • MA, PhD
communication • MA
communication processes and marketing communication • PhD
communication sciences • MA, PhD
comparative literature and cultural studies • MA, PhD
development • MA, PhD
ecological psychology • MA, PhD
ecology • MS, PhD
economics • MA, PhD
English • MA, PhD
entomology • MS, PhD
European studies • MA
experimental • MA, PhD
financial mathematics • MS
French • MA, PhD
general • MA, PhD
genetics • MS, PhD
geography • MS, PhD
geological sciences • MS, PhD
German • MA, PhD
history • MA, PhD
industrial/organizational • MA, PhD
Italian • MA, PhD
language • MA, PhD
Latin American studies • MA
liberal arts and sciences • MA, MPA, MS, PhD
linguistics • MA, PhD
mathematics • MS, PhD
mathematics and computer science • MS
medieval studies • MA, PhD
microbiology • MS, PhD
neurobiology • MS, PhD
neurosciences • MA, PhD
oceanography • MS, PhD
philosophy • MA, PhD
physics • MS, PhD
physiology • MS, PhD
physiology and neurobiology • MS, PhD
political science • MA, PhD
psychology • MA, PhD
public administration • MPA
social • MA, PhD
sociology • MA, PhD
Spanish • MA, PhD
speech, language, and hearing • MA, PhD
statistics • MS, PhD
survey research • MA
zoology • MS, PhD

School of Allied Health and Health Professions
Joseph W. Smey, Dean
Programs in:
allied health • MS
allied health and health professions • MS
physical therapy • MS

School of Business
William Curt Hunter, Dean
Programs in:
accounting • MS, PhD
business administration • Exec MBA, MBA, PhD
finance • PhD
health care management • MBA
human resources management • MBA
management • MBA, PhD
marketing • MBA, PhD

School of Education
Richard L. Schwab, Dean
Programs in:
adult learning • MA, PhD
bilingual and bicultural education • MA, PhD
cognition and instruction • PhD
counseling psychology • MA, PhD
curriculum and instruction • MA, PhD
education • MA, Ed D, PhD
educational administration • MA, Ed D, PhD
educational psychology • MA, PhD
educational studies • MA, PhD
educational technology • MA, PhD
elementary education • MA, PhD
English education • MA, PhD
evaluation and measurement • MA, PhD
exercise science • MA, PhD
foreign languages education • MA, PhD

Connecticut

University of Connecticut (continued)
  gifted and talented education • MA, PhD
  history and social science education • MA, PhD
  kinesiology • MA, PhD
  mathematics education • MA, PhD
  professional higher education administration • MA, PhD
  reading education • MA, PhD
  school psychology • MA, PhD
  science education • MA, PhD
  secondary education • MA, PhD
  social science of sport and leisure • MA, PhD
  special education • MA, PhD

School of Engineering
Amir Faghri, Dean
Programs in:
  aerospace engineering • MS, PhD
  artifical intelligence • MS, PhD
  biomedical engineering • MS, PhD
  chemical engineering • MS, PhD
  chemistry • MS, PhD
  civil engineering • MS, PhD
  computer architecture • MS, PhD
  computer science • MS, PhD
  electrical engineering • MS, PhD
  engineering • M Eng, MS, PhD
  environmental engineering • MS, PhD
  materials science • MS, PhD
  mechanical engineering • MS, PhD
  metallurgy and materials engineering • MS, PhD
  operating systems • MS, PhD
  polymer science • MS, PhD
  robotics • MS, PhD
  software engineering • MS, PhD

School of Fine Arts
David G. Woods, Dean
Programs in:
  art • MFA
  art history • MA
  composition • M Mus
  conducting • M Mus, DMA
  dramatic arts • MA, MFA
  fine arts • M Mus, MA, MFA, DMA, PhD
  historical musicology • MA
  music • M Mus, MA, DMA, PhD
  music education • M Mus, PhD
  music theory and history • PhD
  performance • M Mus, DMA
  theory • MA

School of Human Development and Family Studies
Charles M. Super, Dean
Program in:
  human development and family studies • MA, PhD

School of Nursing
Laura Dzurec, Dean
Program in:
  nursing • MS, PhD

School of Pharmacy
Robert L. McCarthy, Dean
Programs in:
  medicinal and natural products chemistry • MS, PhD
  medicinal chemistry • MS, PhD
  parmaceutical sciences • MS
  pharmaceutical sciences • PhD
  pharmaceutics • MS, PhD
  pharmacology and toxicology • MS, PhD
  pharmacy • MS, PhD

School of Social Work
Kay Davidson, Dean
Program in:
  social work • MSW, PhD

School of Law
Ellen Keane Rutt, Associate Dean of Admissions, Career Services, and Student Finance
Program in:
  law • JD

■ UNIVERSITY OF HARTFORD
West Hartford, CT 06117-1599
http://www.hartford.edu/

Independent, coed, comprehensive institution. CGS member. *Enrollment:* 7,245 graduate, professional, and undergraduate students; 573 full-time matriculated graduate/professional students (331 women), 1,060 part-time matriculated graduate/professional students (637 women). *Graduate faculty:* 134 full-time (48 women), 77 part-time/adjunct (31 women). *Computer facilities:* Computer purchase and lease plans are available. 380 computers available on campus for general student use. A campuswide network can be accessed from student residence rooms and from off campus. Internet access and online class registration, student web pages are available. *Library facilities:* Mortenson Library. *Graduate expenses:* Tuition: full-time $8,370; part-time $465 per credit. Required fees: $220; $190 per credit. *General application contact:* Reneé Murphy, Assistant Director of Graduate Admissions, 860-768-4373.

Barney School of Business
Corine T. Norgaard, Dean
Programs in:
  business • EMBA, MBA, MSAT, Certificate
  business administration • EMBA, MBA
  professional accounting • Certificate
  taxation • MSAT

College of Arts and Sciences
Dr. Joseph C. Voelker, Dean
Programs in:
  arts and sciences • MA, MS, Psy D
  biology • MS
  clinical practices • MA, Psy D
  communication • MA
  general experimental psychology • MA
  neuroscience • MS
  organizational behavior • MS
  psychology • MA
  school psychology • MS

Graduate Institute of Professional Psychology
Dr. John Mehm, Director
Program in:
  clinical psychology • Psy D

College of Education, Nursing, and Health Professions
Dr. Dorothy A. Zeiser, Dean
Programs in:
  community public health nursing • MSN
  counseling • M Ed, MS, Sixth Year Certificate
  early childhood education • M Ed
  education, nursing, and health professions • M Ed, MS, MSN, MSN-OB, MSPT, Ed D, CAGS, Sixth Year Certificate
  educational computing and technology • M Ed
  educational leadership • M Ed, Ed D, CAGS, Sixth Year Certificate
  elementary education • M Ed
  nursing education • MSN
  nursing management • MSN
  nursing/organizational behavior • MSN-OB
  physical therapy • MSPT

College of Engineering, Technology and Architecture
Alan Hadad, Dean
Programs in:
  architecture • M Arch
  engineering • M Eng
  engineering, technology and architecture • M Arch, M Eng

Hartford Art School
Tom Bradley, Associate Dean
Program in:
  art • MFA

Hartt School of Music
Dr. Malcolm Morrison, Dean
Programs in:
  choral conducting • MM Ed
  composition • MM, DMA, Artist Diploma, Diploma
  conducting • MM, DMA, Artist Diploma, Diploma
  early childhood education • MM Ed

Connecticut

instrumental conducting • MM Ed
Kodály • MM Ed
music • CAGS
music education • DMA, PhD
music history • MM
music theory • MM
pedagogy • MM Ed
performance • MM, MM Ed, DMA, Artist Diploma, Diploma
research • MM Ed
technology • MM Ed

■ UNIVERSITY OF NEW HAVEN
West Haven, CT 06516-1916
http://www.newhaven.edu/

Independent, coed, comprehensive institution. CGS member. *Enrollment:* 4,386 graduate, professional, and undergraduate students; 845 full-time matriculated graduate/professional students (495 women), 914 part-time matriculated graduate/professional students (429 women). *Graduate faculty:* 152 full-time, 107 part-time/adjunct. *Computer facilities:* 800 computers available on campus for general student use. A campuswide network can be accessed from student residence rooms and from off campus. Internet access, e-mail are available. *Library facilities:* Marvin K. Peterson Library. *Graduate expenses:* Tuition: part-time $520 per credit. Required fees: $35. Tuition and fees vary according to course load and program. *General application contact:* Pam Sommers, Director of Graduate Admissions, 203-932-7448.

Find an in-depth description at www.petersons.com/gradchannel.

Graduate School
Dr. Ira Kleinfeld, Associate Provost and Dean of Graduate Studies

College of Arts and Sciences
Dr. Dan Nelson, Dean
Programs in:
 arts and sciences • MA, MS, Certificate
 cellular and molecular biology • MS
 community psychology • MA, Certificate
 education • MS
 environmental sciences • MS
 executive tourism and hospitality • MS
 hotel, restaurant, tourism and dietetics administration • MS
 human nutrition • MS
 industrial and organizational psychology • MA, Certificate
 tourism and hospitality management • MS

School of Business
Dr. Zeljan Suster, Dean
Programs in:
 accounting • MBA
 business • EMBA, MBA, MPA, MS
 business administration • EMBA, MBA
 business policy and strategy • MBA
 corporate taxation • MS
 finance • MBA
 finance and financial services • MS
 financial accounting • MS
 health care administration • MS
 health care management • MBA, MPA
 human resources management • MBA
 industrial relations • MS
 international business • MBA
 managerial accounting • MS
 marketing • MBA
 personnel and labor relations • MPA
 public relations • MBA
 public taxation • MS
 sports management • MBA
 taxation • MS
 technology management • MBA

School of Engineering and Applied Science
Dr. Zulma Turo-Ramos, Dean
Programs in:
 applications software • MS
 civil engineering design • Certificate
 electrical engineering • MSEE
 engineering and applied science • EMS, MS, MSEE, MSIE, MSME, Certificate
 engineering management • EMS
 environmental engineering • MS
 industrial engineering • MSIE
 logistics • Certificate
 management information systems • MS
 mechanical engineering • MSME
 operations research • MS
 systems software • MS

School of Public Safety and Professional Studies
Dr. Thomas Johnson, Dean
Programs in:
 advanced investigation • MS
 aviation science • MS
 correctional counseling • MS
 criminal justice management • MS
 criminalistics • MS
 fire science • MS
 forensic science • MS
 industrial hygiene • MS
 occupational safety and health management • MS
 public safety and professional studies • MS
 security management • MS

■ WESTERN CONNECTICUT STATE UNIVERSITY
Danbury, CT 06810-6885
http://www.wcsu.edu/

State-supported, coed, comprehensive institution. *Enrollment:* 6,079 graduate, professional, and undergraduate students; 47 full-time matriculated graduate/professional students (29 women), 749 part-time matriculated graduate/professional students (503 women). *Graduate faculty:* 64 full-time (25 women), 9 part-time/adjunct (3 women). *Computer facilities:* 400 computers available on campus for general student use. A campuswide network can be accessed from student residence rooms and from off campus. Internet access and online class registration are available. *Library facilities:* Ruth Haas Library plus 1 other. *Graduate expenses:* Tuition, state resident: full-time $3,263. Tuition, nonresident: full-time $6,742. *General application contact:* Chris Shankle, Associate Director of Graduate Admissions, 203-837-8244.

Division of Graduate Studies
William Hawkins, Enrollment Management Officer

Ancell School of Business and Public Administration
Dr. Allen Morton, Dean
Programs in:
 accounting • MBA
 business administration • MBA
 business and public administration • MBA, MHA, MS
 health administration • MHA
 justice administration • MS

School of Arts and Sciences
Dr. Linda Vaden-Goad, Dean
Programs in:
 arts and sciences • MA, MFA
 biological and environmental sciences • MA
 earth and planetary sciences • MA
 English • MA
 history • MA
 illustration • MFA
 mathematics and computer science • MA
 painting • MFA
 theoretical mathematics • MA

School of Professional Studies
Dr. Lynne Clark, Dean
Programs in:
 adult nurse practitioner • MSN
 clinical nurse specialist • MSN
 community counseling • MS
 curriculum • MS
 English education • MS
 instructional leadership • Ed D

Connecticut

Western Connecticut State University (continued)
- instructional technology • MS
- mathematics education • MS
- music education • MS
- professional studies • MS, MSN, Ed D
- reading • MS
- school counseling • MS
- special education • MS

■ YALE UNIVERSITY
New Haven, CT 06520
http://www.yale.edu/

Independent, coed, university. CGS member. *Enrollment:* 11,471 graduate, professional, and undergraduate students; 5,420 full-time matriculated graduate/professional students, 184 part-time matriculated graduate/professional students. *Graduate faculty:* 3,330. *Computer facilities:* 350 computers available on campus for general student use. A campuswide network can be accessed from student residence rooms and from off campus. *Library facilities:* Sterling Memorial Library plus 20 others. *Graduate expenses:* Tuition: full-time $25,600; part-time $6,400 per term. *General application contact:* Admissions Information, 203-432-2772.

Divinity School
Dr. Harold W. Attridge, Dean
Program in:
- divinity • M Div, MAR, STM

Graduate School of Arts and Sciences
Programs in:
- African studies • MA
- African-American studies • MA, PhD
- American studies • MA, PhD
- anthropology • MA, PhD
- applied mathematics • M Phil, MS, PhD
- applied mechanics and mechanical engineering • M Phil, MS, PhD
- applied physics • MS, PhD
- archaeological studies • MA
- arts and sciences • M Phil, MA, MS, PhD
- astronomy • MS, PhD
- biophysical chemistry • PhD
- cell biology • PhD
- cellular and molecular physiology • PhD
- chemical engineering • MS, PhD
- classics • PhD
- comparative literature • PhD
- computer science • PhD
- developmental biology • PhD
- East Asian languages and literatures • PhD
- East Asian studies • MA
- ecology and evolutionary biology • PhD
- economics • PhD
- electrical engineering • MS, PhD
- English language and literature • MA, PhD
- environmental sciences • PhD
- experimental pathology • PhD
- forestry • PhD
- French • MA, PhD
- genetics • PhD
- geochemistry • PhD
- geophysics • PhD
- Germanic language and literature • MA, PhD
- history • MA, PhD
- history of art • PhD
- history of medicine and the life sciences • MS, PhD
- immunobiology • PhD
- inorganic chemistry • PhD
- international and development economics • MA
- international relations • MA
- Italian language and literature • PhD
- linguistics • PhD
- mathematics • MS, PhD
- mechanical engineering • M Phil, MS, PhD
- medieval studies • MA, PhD
- meteorology • PhD
- mineralogy and crystallography • PhD
- molecular biology • PhD
- molecular biophysics and biochemistry • MS, PhD
- music • MA, PhD
- Near Eastern languages and civilizations • MA, PhD
- neurobiology • PhD
- neuroscience • PhD
- oceanography • PhD
- organic chemistry • PhD
- paleoecology • PhD
- paleontology and stratigraphy • PhD
- petrology • PhD
- pharmacology • PhD
- philosophy • PhD
- physical chemistry • PhD
- physics • PhD
- plant sciences • PhD
- political science • PhD
- psychology • PhD
- religious studies • PhD
- Renaissance studies • PhD
- Russian and East European studies • MA
- Slavic languages and literatures • PhD
- sociology • PhD
- Spanish and Portuguese • MA, PhD
- statistics • MS, PhD
- structural geology • PhD

School of Architecture
Robert A. M. Stern, Dean
Program in:
- architecture • M Arch, M Env Des

School of Art
Richard Benson, Dean
Programs in:
- graphic design • MFA
- painting/printmaking • MFA
- photography • MFA
- sculpture • MFA

School of Drama
James Bundy, Dean/Artistic Director
Program in:
- drama • MFA, DFA, Certificate

School of Forestry and Environmental Studies
Program in:
- forestry and environmental studies • MES, MF, MFS, DFES, PhD

School of Medicine
Programs in:
- bioinformatics and computational biology • PhD
- biological and biomedical sciences • PhD
- cell biology and molecular physiology • PhD
- immunology • PhD
- medicine • MD, MM Sc, MPH, MS, PhD
- microbiology • PhD
- molecular biophysics and biochemistry • PhD
- molecular cell biology, genetics, and development • PhD
- neuroscience • PhD
- pharmacological sciences and molecular medicine • PhD
- physician associate • MM Sc
- physiology and integrative medical biology • PhD

School of Public Health
Dr. Michael H. Merson, Dean and Chairman
Programs in:
- biostatistics • MPH, MS, PhD
- chronic disease epidemiology • MPH, PhD
- environmental health • MPH, PhD
- epidemiology of microbial diseases • MPH, PhD
- global health • MPH
- health management • MPH
- health policy and administration • MPH, PhD
- parasitology • PhD
- social and behavioral sciences • MPH

School of Music
Robert Blocker, Dean
Program in:
- music • MM, MMA, DMA, AD, Certificate

School of Nursing
Program in:
- nursing • MSN, DN Sc, Post Master's Certificate

Yale Law School
Anthony T. Kronman, Dean
Program in:
 law • JD, LL M, MSL, JSD

Yale School of Management
Jeffrey E. Garten, Dean
Programs in:
 accounting • PhD
 business administration • MBA, PhD
 financial economics • PhD
 management • MBA, PhD
 marketing • PhD

Delaware

■ **DELAWARE STATE UNIVERSITY**
Dover, DE 19901-2277
http://www.dsc.edu/

State-supported, coed, comprehensive institution. *Computer facilities:* 641 computers available on campus for general student use. A campuswide network can be accessed from student residence rooms and from off campus. Internet access and online class registration, online grade access, e-mail are available. *Library facilities:* William C. Jason Library. *General application contact:* Dean of Graduate Studies and Research, 302-857-6800.

Graduate Programs
Programs in:
 applied chemistry • MS
 biology • MS
 biology education • MS
 business administration • MBA
 chemistry • MS
 curriculum and instruction • MA
 education • MA
 mathematics • MS
 physics • MS
 physics teaching • MS
 science education • MA
 social work • MSW
 special education • MA

■ **UNIVERSITY OF DELAWARE**
Newark, DE 19716
http://www.udel.edu/

State-related, coed, university. CGS member. *Enrollment:* 20,501 graduate, professional, and undergraduate students; 2,450 full-time matriculated graduate/professional students (1,197 women), 816 part-time matriculated graduate/professional students (440 women). *Graduate faculty:* 1,068 full-time (384 women), 25 part-time/adjunct (17 women). *Computer facilities:* 900 computers available on campus for general student use. A campuswide network can be accessed from student residence rooms and from off campus. Internet access and online class registration are available. *Library facilities:* Hugh Morris Library plus 4 others. *Graduate expenses:* Tuition, state resident: full-time $5,890; part-time $327 per credit. Tuition, nonresident: full-time $15,420; part-time $857 per credit. Required fees: $968. *General application contact:* Mary Martin, Assistant Provost for Graduate Studies, 302-831-8916.

Alfred Lerner College of Business and Economics
Michael J. Ginzberg, Dean
Programs in:
 accounting • MS
 business administration • MBA
 business and economics • MA, MBA, MS, PhD
 economics • MA, MS, PhD
 economics for entrepreneurship and educators • MA
 information systems and technology management • MS

College of Agriculture and Natural Resources
Dr. Robin Morgan, Dean
Programs in:
 agricultural economics • MS
 agriculture and natural resources • MS, PhD
 animal sciences • MS, PhD
 entomology and applied ecology • MS, PhD
 food sciences • MS
 operations research • MS, PhD
 plant and soil sciences • MS, PhD
 public horticulture • MS
 statistics • MS

College of Arts and Sciences
Dr. Mark W. Huddleston, Dean
Programs in:
 acting • MFA
 applied mathematics • MS, PhD
 art • MA, MFA
 art history • MA, PhD
 arts and sciences • MA, MALS, MFA, MM, MPT, MS, DPT, PhD, Certificate
 behavioral neuroscience • PhD
 biochemistry • MA, MS, PhD
 biotechnology • MS, PhD
 cell and extracellular matrix biology • MS, PhD
 cell and systems physiology • MS, PhD
 chemistry • MA, MS, PhD
 climatology • PhD
 clinical psychology • PhD
 cognitive psychology • PhD
 communication • MA
 computer and information sciences • MS, PhD
 criminology • MA, PhD
 early American culture • MA
 ecology and evolution • MS, PhD
 English and American literature • MA, PhD
 foreign languages and literatures • MA
 foreign languages pedagogy • MA
 geography • MA, MS, PhD
 geology • MS, PhD
 history • MA, PhD
 liberal studies • MALS
 linguistics • MA, PhD
 mathematics • MS, PhD
 microbiology • MS, PhD
 molecular biology and genetics • MS, PhD
 museum studies • Certificate
 music education • MM
 performance • MM
 physical therapy • MPT, DPT
 physics • MA, MS, PhD
 plant biology • MS, PhD
 political science and international relations • MA, PhD
 practicing art conservation • MS
 social psychology • PhD
 sociology • MA, PhD
 stage management • MFA
 technical production • MFA

College of Engineering
Dr. Eric W. Kaler, Dean
Programs in:
 biomechanics and movement science • MS, PhD
 chemical engineering • M Ch E, PhD
 electrical and computer engineering • MS, PhD
 engineering • M Ch E, MAS, MCE, MEM, MMSE, MS, MSME, PhD
 environmental engineering • MAS, MCE, PhD
 geotechnical engineering • MAS, MCE, PhD
 materials science and engineering • MMSE, PhD
 mechanical engineering • MEM, MSME, PhD
 ocean engineering • MAS, MCE, PhD
 railroad engineering • MAS, MCE, PhD
 structural engineering • MAS, MCE, PhD
 transportation engineering • MAS, MCE, PhD
 water resource engineering • MAS, MCE, PhD

Delaware

University of Delaware (continued)

College of Health and Nursing Sciences
Dr. Betty J. Paulanka, Dean
Programs in:
  adult nurse practitioner • MSN, PMC
  cardiopulmonary clinical nurse specialist • MSN, PMC
  cardiopulmonary clinical nurse specialist/adult nurse practitioner • MSN, PMC
  exercise science • MS
  family nurse practitioner • MSN, PMC
  gerontology clinical nurse specialist • MSN, PMC
  gerontology clinical nurse specialist/ geriatric nurse practitioner • PMC
  gerontology clinical nurse specialist/ geriatric nurse practitioner • MSN
  health and nursing sciences • MS, MSN, PMC
  health promotion • MS
  health services administration • MSN, PMC
  human nutrition • MS
  nursing of children clinical nurse specialist • MSN, PMC
  nursing of children clinical nurse specialist/pediatric nurse practitioner • MSN, PMC
  oncology/immune deficiency clinical nurse specialist • MSN, PMC
  oncology/immune deficiency clinical nurse specialist/adult nurse practitioner • MSN, PMC
  perinatal/women's health clinical nurse specialist • MSN, PMC
  perinatal/women's health clinical nurse specialist/women's health nurse practitioner • MSN, PMC
  psychiatric nursing clinical nurse specialist • MSN, PMC

College of Human Services, Education and Public Policy
Dr. Timothy Barnekov, Dean
Programs in:
  college counseling • M Ed
  hospitality information management • MS
  human development and family studies • MS, PhD
  human services, education and public policy • M Ed, MA, MEEP, MI, MPA, MS, Ed D, PhD
  student affairs practice in higher education • M Ed

Center for Energy and Environmental Policy
Dr. John Byrne, Director
Programs in:
  environmental and energy policy • MEEP, PhD
  urban affairs and public policy • MA, PhD

School of Education
Dr. Christopher M. Clark, Director
Programs in:
  curriculum and instruction • M Ed
  education • PhD
  educational leadership • M Ed, Ed D
  exceptional children and youth • M Ed
  instruction • MI
  school counseling • M Ed
  school psychology • MA
  teaching English as a second language (TESL) • MA

School of Urban Affairs and Public Policy
Dr. Jeffrey A. Raffel, Director
Programs in:
  community development and nonprofit leadership • MA
  energy and environmental policy • MA
  governance, planning and management • PhD
  historic preservation • MA
  public administration • MPA
  social and urban policy • PhD
  technology, environment and society • PhD
  urban affairs and public policy • MA, MPA, PhD

College of Marine Studies
Dr. Carolyn A. Thoroughgood, Dean
Programs in:
  marine policy • MS
  marine studies • MMP, MS, PhD
  oceanography • MS, PhD

Delaware Biotechnology Institute
Dr. David S. Weir, Director
Program in:
  biotechnology • PhD

■ WILMINGTON COLLEGE
New Castle, DE 19720-6491
http://www.wilmcoll.edu/

Independent, coed, comprehensive institution. *Enrollment:* 6,954 graduate, professional, and undergraduate students; 684 full-time matriculated graduate/professional students (465 women), 2,191 part-time matriculated graduate/professional students (1,517 women). *Computer facilities:* 500 computers available on campus for general student use. Internet access is available. *Library facilities:* Robert C. and Dorothy M. Peoples Library plus 1 other. *Graduate expenses:* Tuition: full-time $5,187. Tuition and fees vary according to course load and degree level. *General application contact:* Chris Ferguson, Director of Admissions and Financial Aid, 302-328-9407 Ext. 256.

Division of Behavioral Science
James Wilson, Chair
Programs in:
  community counseling • MS
  criminal justice studies • MS
  student affairs and college counseling • MS

Division of Business
Dr. Raj Parikh, Chair
Programs in:
  business administration • MBA
  health care administration • MBA, MS
  human resource management • MS
  management • MS
  public administration • MS
  transport and logistics • MS

Division of Education
Dr. Barbara Raetsch, Chair
Programs in:
  applied education technology • M Ed
  elementary and secondary school counseling • M Ed
  elementary special education • M Ed
  elementary studies • M Ed
  reading • M Ed
  school leadership • M Ed

Division of Information Technology and Advanced Communications
Dr. Jack Nold, Head
Program in:
  information systems technologies • MS

Division of Nursing
Mary Letitia Gallagher, Chair
Programs in:
  adult nurse practitioner • MSN
  family nurse practitioner • MSN
  gerontology • MSN
  leadership • MSN
  nursing • MSN

Program in Innovation and Leadership
Joe Deardorff, Head
Program in:
  innovation and leadership • Ed D

District of Columbia

■ AMERICAN UNIVERSITY
Washington, DC 20016-8001
http://www.american.edu/

Independent-religious, coed, university. CGS member. *Enrollment:* 10,977 graduate, professional, and undergraduate students; 2,788 full-time matriculated

District of Columbia

graduate/professional students (1,749 women), 2,250 part-time matriculated graduate/professional students (1,345 women). *Graduate faculty:* 492 full-time (212 women), 473 part-time/adjunct (206 women). *Computer facilities:* Computer purchase and lease plans are available. 600 computers available on campus for general student use. A campuswide network can be accessed from student residence rooms and from off campus. Internet access and online class registration, online course support, wireless campus are available. *Library facilities:* American University Library plus 1 other. *Graduate expenses:* Tuition: full-time $15,786; part-time $877 per credit hour. Required fees: $300. Tuition and fees vary according to course load and program.

College of Arts and Sciences
Dr. Kay Mussell, Dean
Programs in:
 anthropology • PhD
 applied economics • Certificate
 applied statistics • Certificate
 art history • MA
 arts and sciences • MA, MAT, MFA, MS, PhD, Certificate
 arts management • MA, Certificate
 behavioral neuroscience • PhD
 biology • MA, MS
 chemistry • MS
 clinical psychology • PhD
 computer science • MS
 creative writing • MFA
 dance • MA, Certificate
 dance and health fitness management • Certificate
 development banking • MA
 economics • MA, PhD, Certificate
 environmental science • MS
 ethics and peace • MA
 experimental/biological psychology • MA
 financial economics for public policy • MA
 French studies • MA, Certificate
 general psychology • MA
 health fitness management • MS
 history • MA, PhD
 interdisciplinary studies • MA
 international economic relations • Certificate
 international training and education • MA
 literature • MA
 mathematics • MA
 painting, sculpture and printmaking • MFA
 personality/social psychology • MA
 philosophy • MA
 philosophy and social policy • MA
 physics • Certificate
 professional development • Certificate
 psychology • MA
 public anthropology • MA, Certificate
 Russian studies • MA, Certificate
 social research • Certificate
 sociology • MA, Certificate
 Spanish: Latin American studies • MA, Certificate
 statistics • MS, Certificate
 statistics for policy analysis • MS
 teaching English to speakers of other languages • MA, Certificate
 toxicology • MS, Certificate
 translation • Certificate

School of Education
Dr. Lynn Fox, Dean
Programs in:
 education • MA, MAT, PhD, Certificate
 education administration • PhD
 educational leadership • MA
 educational technology • MA
 elementary education • MAT
 English for speakers of other languages • MAT
 international education • MA
 learning disabilities • MA
 secondary teaching • MAT, Certificate

Kogod School of Business
Dr. Myron Roomkin, Dean
Programs in:
 accounting • MBA
 business • MBA, MS, Certificate
 business administration • MBA
 entrepreneurship and management • MBA
 finance • MBA
 human resource management • MBA
 information resource management • Certificate
 information systems • MS, Certificate
 interdisciplinary • MBA
 international finance • MBA
 international management • MBA
 international marketing • MBA
 management of global information technology • MBA
 marketing • MBA
 marketing information and technology • MBA
 marketing management • MBA
 real estate • MBA
 software process management • Certificate
 system and project management • Certificate
 taxation • MS

School of Communication
Prof. Larry Kirkman, Dean
Programs in:
 broadcast journalism • MA
 communication • MA, MFA
 film and video production • MA, MFA
 interactive journalism • MA
 multimedia development • MA, MFA
 news media studies • MA
 print journalism • MA
 producing for film and video • MA
 public communication • MA
 screenwriting • MFA

School of International Service
Dr. Louis W. Goodman, Dean
Programs in:
 comparative and regional studies • MA
 cross-cultural communication • Certificate
 development management • MS
 environmental policy • MA
 ethics and peace • MA
 global environmental policy • MA
 international communication • MA
 international development • MA
 international development management • Certificate
 international economic policy • MA
 international economic relations • Certificate
 international peace and conflict resolution • MA
 international politics • MA
 international relations • PhD
 international service • MIS
 the Americas • Certificate
 U.S. foreign policy • MA

School of Public Affairs
Dr. William Leo Grande, Dean
Programs in:
 justice, law and society • MS, PhD
 organization development • MSOD
 organizational change • Certificate
 personnel and human resource management • MS
 political science • MA, PhD
 public administration • MPA, PhD
 public affairs • MA, MPA, MPP, MS, MSOD, PhD, Certificate
 public financial management • Certificate
 public management • Certificate
 public policy • MPP

Washington College of Law
Claudio Grossman, Dean
Programs in:
 human rights and the law • Certificate
 international legal studies • LL M
 judicial sciences • SJD
 law • JD
 law and government • LL M

■ THE CATHOLIC UNIVERSITY OF AMERICA
Washington, DC 20064
http://www.cua.edu/

Independent-religious, coed, university. CGS member. *Enrollment:* 5,740 graduate, professional, and undergraduate students; 1,429 full-time matriculated graduate/professional students (740 women), 1,424 part-time matriculated graduate/

District of Columbia

The Catholic University of America (continued)

professional students (734 women). *Graduate faculty:* 336 full-time (115 women), 340 part-time/adjunct (130 women). *Computer facilities:* Computer purchase and lease plans are available. 450 computers available on campus for general student use. A campuswide network can be accessed from student residence rooms and from off campus. Internet access and online class registration are available. *Library facilities:* Mullen Library plus 7 others. *Graduate expenses:* Tuition: full-time $23,600; part-time $895 per credit hour. Required fees: $1,040; $270 per term. One-time fee: $175 part-time. Part-time tuition and fees vary according to campus/location and program. *General application contact:* Diana McCown, Assistant Director of Graduate Admissions, 202-319-5305.

Find an in-depth description at www.petersons.com/gradchannel.

The Benjamin T. Rome School of Music
Murry Sidlin, Dean
Programs in:
 accompanying and chamber music • MM
 chamber music • DMA
 composition • MM, DMA
 instrumental conducting • MM, DMA
 liturgical music • M Lit M, DMA
 music • M Lit M, MA, MM, DMA, PhD
 music education • MM, DMA
 musicology • MA, PhD
 orchestral instruments • MM, DMA
 organ • MM, DMA
 performance • MM, DMA
 piano pedagogy • MM, DMA
 vocal accompanying • DMA
 vocal pedagogy • MM
 vocal performance • MM
 voice pedagogy and performance • DMA

Columbus School of Law
William F. Fox, Dean
Program in:
 law • JD

National Catholic School of Social Service
Dr. James R. Zabora, Dean
Program in:
 social service • MSW, PhD

School of Architecture and Planning
Randall Ott, Dean
Program in:
 architecture and planning • M Arch, M Arch Studies

School of Arts and Sciences
Dr. Lawrence R. Poos, Dean
Programs in:
 accounting • MA
 acting, directing, and playwriting • MFA
 administration, curriculum, and policy studies • MA
 American government • MA, PhD
 anthropology • MA, PhD
 applied experimental psychology • MA, PhD
 arts and sciences • MA, MFA, MS, MTS, PhD, Certificate
 Byzantine studies • MA, Certificate
 Catholic school leadership • MA
 cell and microbial biology • MS, PhD
 cell biology • MS, PhD
 chemistry • MS
 classics • MA
 clinical laboratory science • MS, PhD
 clinical psychology • PhD
 comparative literature • MA, PhD
 congressional studies • MA
 counselor education • MA
 early Christian studies • MA, PhD, Certificate
 economics • MA
 educational administration • PhD
 educational psychology • PhD
 English as a second language • MA
 English language and literature • MA, PhD
 financial management • MA
 French • MA, PhD
 general psychology • MA, PhD
 Greek and Latin • PhD
 history • MA, PhD
 human development • PhD
 human factors • MA
 human resource management • MA
 international affairs • MA
 international political economics • MA
 Irish studies • MA
 Italian • MA
 Latin • MA
 learning and instruction • MA
 medieval studies • MA, PhD, Certificate
 microbiology • MS, PhD
 physics • MS, PhD
 policy studies • PhD
 political theory • MA, PhD
 rhetoric • MA, PhD
 Romance languages and literatures • MA, PhD
 Semitic and Egyptian languages and literature • MA, PhD
 sociology • MA, PhD
 Spanish • MA, PhD
 teacher education • MA
 theatre history and criticism • MA
 world politics • MA, PhD

School of Canon Law
Rev. Msgr. Brian Ferme, Dean
Program in:
 canon law • JCD, JCL

School of Engineering
Dr. Charles C. Nguyen, Dean
Programs in:
 biomedical engineering • MBE, MS Engr, D Engr, PhD
 civil engineering • MCE, D Engr
 construction management • MCE, MS Engr, PhD
 design • D Engr, PhD
 design and robotics • MME, D Engr, PhD
 electrical engineering and computer science • MEE, MS Engr, MSCS, D Engr, PhD
 engineering • MBE, MCE, MEE, MME, MS Engr, MSCS, D Engr, PhD
 engineering management • MS Engr
 environmental engineering • MCE, MS Engr, PhD
 fluid mechanics and thermal science • MME, D Engr, PhD
 geotechnical engineering • MCE
 mechanical design • MME
 ocean and structural acoustics • MME, MS Engr, PhD
 structures and structural mechanics • MCE

School of Library and Information Science
Dr. Martha L. Hale, Dean
Program in:
 library and information science • MSLS

School of Nursing
Dr. Ann Marie T. Brooks, Dean
Programs in:
 advanced practice nursing • MSN
 clinical nursing • DN Sc

School of Philosophy
Rev. Kurt Pritzl, OP, Dean
Program in:
 philosophy • MA, PhD, Ph L

School of Theology and Religious Studies
Rev. Francis Moloney, Dean
Programs in:
 biblical studies • MA, PhD
 church history • MA, PhD
 liturgical studies • MA, PhD
 religion • MA, PhD
 religious education • MA, MRE, PhD
 religious studies • M Div, STB, MA, MRE, D Min, PhD, STD, STL
 theology • M Div, STB, MA, D Min, PhD, STD, STL

■ GALLAUDET UNIVERSITY
Washington, DC 20002-3625
http://www.gallaudet.edu/

Independent, coed, university. CGS member. *Computer facilities:* 240 computers available on campus for general student use. A campuswide network can

District of Columbia

be accessed from student residence rooms and from off campus. Online class registration is available. *Library facilities:* Merrill Learning Center. *General application contact:* Coordinator of Prospective Graduate Student Services, 202-651-5647.

The Graduate School
College of Arts and Sciences
Programs in:
  arts and sciences • MA, MSW, PhD, Psy S
  clinical psychology • PhD
  developmental psychology • MA
  school psychology • MA, Psy S
  social work • MSW

School of Communication
Programs in:
  audiology • Au D
  communication • MA, MS, Au D
  interpretation • MA
  linguistics • MA
  speech and language pathology • MS

School of Education and Human Services
Programs in:
  administration • MS
  administration and supervision • PhD, Ed S
  community counseling • MA
  early childhood education • MA, Ed S
  education and human services • MA, MS, PhD, Certificate, Ed S
  education of deaf and hard of hearing students and multihandicapped deaf and hard of hearing students • MA, Ed S
  elementary education • MA, Ed S
  individualized program of study • PhD
  instructional supervision • Ed S
  integrating technology in the classroom • Certificate
  leadership training • MS
  leisure services administration • MS
  mental health counseling • MA
  parent/infant specialty • MA, Ed S
  school counseling • MA
  secondary education • MA, Ed S
  special education administration • PhD

■ GEORGETOWN UNIVERSITY
Washington, DC 20057
http://www.georgetown.edu/

Independent-religious, coed, university. CGS member. *Computer facilities:* 360 computers available on campus for general student use. A campuswide network can be accessed from student residence rooms and from off campus. Internet access and online class registration, online grade reports are available.

Library facilities: Lauinger Library plus 6 others. *General application contact:* Dean of the Graduate School, 202-687-5974.

Graduate School of Arts and Sciences
Programs in:
  American government • MA, PhD
  analytical chemistry • MS, PhD
  Arab studies • MA, Certificate
  Arabic language, literature, and linguistics • MS, PhD
  arts and sciences • MA, MALS, MAT, MBA, MPP, MS, PhD, Certificate
  bilingual education • Certificate
  biochemistry • MS, PhD
  biology • MS, PhD
  British and American literature • MA
  chemical physics • MS, PhD
  communication, culture, and technology • MA
  comparative government • PhD
  demography • MA
  economics • PhD
  German • MS, PhD
  history • MA, PhD
  inorganic chemistry • MS, PhD
  international relations • PhD
  linguistics • MS, PhD
  national security studies • MA
  organic chemistry • MS, PhD
  philosophy • MA, PhD
  physical chemistry • MS, PhD
  political theory • PhD
  psychology • PhD
  Russian and East European studies • MA
  Spanish • MS, PhD
  teaching English as a second language • MAT, Certificate
  teaching English as a second language and bilingual education • MAT
  theoretical chemistry • MS, PhD

BMW Center for German and European Studies
Dr. Jeffrey J. Anderson, Director
Program in:
  German and European studies • MA

Center for Latin American Studies
Program in:
  Latin American studies • MA

Edmund A. Walsh School of Foreign Service
Program in:
  foreign service • MS

The Georgetown Public Policy Institute
Program in:
  public policy • MPP

McDonough School of Business
Program in:
  business administration • MBA

Programs in Biomedical Sciences
Programs in:
  biochemistry and molecular biology • PhD
  biohazardous threat agents and emerging infectious diseases • MS
  biomedical sciences • MS, PhD
  biostatistics and epidemiology • MS
  cell biology • PhD
  health physics • MS
  microbiology and immunology research • PhD
  neuroscience • PhD
  pathology • MS, PhD
  pharmacology • PhD
  physiology and biophysics • MS, PhD
  radiobiology • MS
  science policy and advocacy for the healthcare arena in a global setting • MS
  teaching microbiology and immunology • MS

School for Summer and Continuing Education
Program in:
  summer and continuing education • MALS

School of Nursing and Health Studies
Program in:
  nursing • MS

Law Center
Programs in:
  advocacy • LL M
  common law studies • LL M
  general • LL M
  international and comparative law • LL M
  labor and employment law • LL M
  law • JD, SJD
  securities regulation • LL M
  taxation • LL M

School of Medicine
Program in:
  medicine • MD

■ THE GEORGE WASHINGTON UNIVERSITY
Washington, DC 20052
http://www.gwu.edu/

Independent, coed, university. CGS member. *Enrollment:* 23,417 graduate, professional, and undergraduate students; 5,686 full-time matriculated graduate/professional students (3,172 women), 6,440 part-time matriculated graduate/professional students (3,335 women). *Graduate faculty:* 1,569 full-time (572 women), 2,932 part-time/adjunct (1,014 women). *Computer facilities:* 550 computers available on campus for general student use. A campuswide network can be accessed from student residence rooms and from off campus. *Library facilities:* Gelman Library plus 2 others. *Graduate expenses:* Tuition: part-time $876 per credit. Required fees: $1 per

District of Columbia

The George Washington University (continued)

credit. Tuition and fees vary according to campus/location. *General application contact:* Kristin Williams, Director, Graduate Enrollment Support Services, 202-994-3900.

Columbian College of Arts and Sciences
William Frawley, Interim Dean
Programs in:
  American studies • MA, PhD
  analytical chemistry • MS, PhD
  anthropology • MA
  applied mathematics • MA, MS
  applied social psychology • PhD
  art history • MA, PhD
  art therapy • MA, Certificate
  arts and sciences • MA, MFA, MFS, MPA, MPP, MS, MSFS, PhD, Psy D, Certificate
  biochemistry • PhD
  biological sciences • MS, PhD
  biostatistics • MS, PhD
  ceramics • MFA
  classical acting • MFA
  clinical psychology • PhD
  cognitive neuropsychology • PhD
  computer fraud investigation and security management • MA, Certificate
  criminal justice • MA
  design • MFA
  economics • MA, PhD
  English • MA, PhD
  epidemiology • MS, PhD
  folklife • MA
  forensic molecular biology • MFS
  forensic sciences • MFS, MSFS
  genomics, proteomics, and bioinformatics • MS
  geography and regional science • MA
  geology • MS, PhD
  geosciences • MS, PhD
  Hinduism and Islam • MA
  historic preservation • MA
  history • MA, PhD
  hominid paleobiology • MS, PhD
  human resource management • MA
  human sciences • PhD
  industrial and engineering statistics • MS
  industrial-organizational psychology • PhD
  inorganic chemistry • MS, PhD
  interior design • MFA
  leadership and coaching • Certificate
  legislative affairs • MA
  material culture • MA
  materials science • MS, PhD
  museum studies • MA, Certificate
  museum training • MA
  organic chemistry • MS, PhD
  organizational management • MA
  painting • MFA
  photography • MFA
  physical chemistry • MS, PhD
  physics • MA, PhD
  political science • MA, PhD
  printmaking • MFA
  professional psychology • Psy D
  pure mathematics • MA, PhD
  sculpture • MFA
  sociology • MA
  speech pathology • MA
  statistics • MS, PhD
  telecommunications • MA
  telecommunications and national security • Certificate
  theatre/design • MFA
  women's studies • MA, Certificate

Graduate School of Political Management
Dr. Christopher Arterton, Dean
Programs in:
  PAC and political management • Certificate
  political management • MA

Institute for Biomedical Sciences
Dr. Stephan Ladisch, Head
Programs in:
  biochemistry and molecular biology • PhD
  genetics • MS, PhD
  immunology • PhD
  molecular and cellular oncology • PhD
  neuroscience • PhD
  pharmacology • PhD

School of Media and Public Affairs
Dr. Jean Folkerts, Director
Program in:
  media and public affairs • MA

School of Public Policy and Public Administration
Programs in:
  budget and public finance • MPA
  environmental and resource policy • MA
  federal policy, politics, and management • MPA
  international development management • MPA
  managing public organizations • MPA
  managing state and local governments and urban policy • MPA
  nonprofit management • MPA
  philosophy and social policy • MA
  policy analysis and evaluation • MPA
  public administration • MPA
  public policy • MA, MPP
  public policy and administration • PhD
  public policy and public administration • MPA
  women's studies • MA

Elliott School of International Affairs
Dr. Harry Harding, Dean
Programs in:
  Asian studies • MA
  European and Eurasian studies • MA
  international affairs • MA, MIPP, MIS
  international development studies • MA
  international policy and practice • MIPP, MIS
  international trade and investment policy • MA
  Latin American studies • MA
  science, technology, and public policy • MA
  security policy studies • MA

Graduate School of Education and Human Development
Dr. Mary Hatwood Futrell, Dean
Programs in:
  counseling • PhD, Ed S
  counseling: school, community and rehabilitation • MA Ed
  curriculum and instruction • MA Ed, Ed D, Ed S
  early childhood special education • MA Ed
  education administration and policy studies • Ed D
  education and human development • M Ed, MA Ed, MAT, Ed D, PhD, Certificate, Ed S
  education policy studies • MA Ed
  educational human development • MA Ed
  educational leadership and administration • MA Ed, Ed S
  educational technology leadership • MA Ed
  elementary education • M Ed
  higher education administration • MA Ed, Ed D, Ed S
  human resource development • MA Ed, Ed D, Ed S
  infant special education • MA Ed
  international education • MA Ed
  museum education • MAT
  secondary education • M Ed
  special education • Ed D, Ed S
  special education of seriously emotionally disturbed students • MA Ed
  transitional special education • MA Ed, Certificate

Law School
Michael K. Young, Dean
Program in:
  law • JD, LL M, SJD

School of Business
Dr. Susan Philips, Dean
Programs in:
  accountancy • M Accy, PhD
  accounting • MBA
  business and public management • M Accy, MBA, MS, MSF, MSIST, MTA, PhD

District of Columbia

business economics and public policy • MBA
destination management • MTA
event management • MTA
finance • MSF, PhD
finance and investments • MBA
human resources management • MBA
information systems management • MBA
international business • MBA, PhD
logistics, operations, and materials management • MBA
management and organization • PhD
management decision making • MBA, PhD
management information systems • MSIST
management of science, technology, and innovation • MBA
marketing • MBA, PhD
organizational behavior and development • MBA
project management • MS
real estate development • MBA
sport management • MTA
strategic management and public policy • PhD
tourism administration • MTA
tourism and hospitality management • MBA
travel marketing • MTA

School of Engineering and Applied Science
Dr. Timothy Tong, Dean
Programs in:
civil and environmental engineering • MS, D Sc, App Sc, Engr
computer science • MS, D Sc, App Sc, Engr
electrical and computer engineering • MS, D Sc, App Sc, Engr
engineering and applied science • MEM, MS, D Sc, App Sc, Engr
engineering management and systems engineering • MEM, MS, D Sc, App Sc, Engr
mechanical and aerospace engineering • MS, D Sc, App Sc, Engr

School of Medicine and Health Sciences
Dr. John F. Williams, Vice President for Academic Affairs
Programs in:
adult nurse practitioner • Post Master's Certificate
advanced family nurse practitioner • Post Master's Certificate
medicine • MD
medicine and health sciences • MD, MSHS, Post Master's Certificate
oral biology • MSHS
physical therapy • MSHS
physician assistant • MSHS

School of Public Health and Health Services
Ruth Katz, Dean
Programs in:
biostatistics • MPH
community-oriented primary care • MPH
environmental and occupational health • Dr PH
epidemiology • MPH
exercise science • MS
health behavior • Dr PH
health information systems • MPH
health management and leadership • MHSA
health policy • MHSA, Dr PH
health promotion • MPH
health services administration • Specialist
international health • Dr PH
international health policy and programs • MPH
international health promotion • MPH
maternal and child health • MPH
microbiology and emerging infectious diseases • MSPH
public health and emergency management • Certificate
public health and health services • MHSA, MPH, MS, MSPH, Dr PH, Certificate, Specialist
public health management • MPH

■ HOWARD UNIVERSITY
Washington, DC 20059-0002
http://www.howard.edu/

Independent, coed, university. CGS member. *Computer facilities:* Computer purchase and lease plans are available. 5,673 computers available on campus for general student use. A campuswide network can be accessed from student residence rooms and from off campus. Internet access and online class registration are available. *Library facilities:* Founders Library plus 8 others. *General application contact:* Associate Dean for Student Relations, 202-806-4676.

College of Dentistry
Dr. Leo E. Rouse, Interim Dean
Programs in:
advanced education program general dentistry • Certificate
dentistry • DDS
general dentistry • Certificate
oral and maxillo surgery • Certificate
orthodontics • Certificate
pediatric dentistry • Certificate

College of Engineering, Architecture, and Computer Sciences
Dr. James H. Johnson, Dean
Program in:
engineering, architecture, and computer sciences • M Eng, MCS, MS, PhD

School of Engineering and Computer Science
Programs in:
chemical engineering • MS
civil engineering • M Eng
electrical engineering • M Eng, PhD
engineering and computer science • M Eng, MCS, MS, PhD
mechanical engineering • M Eng, PhD
systems and computer science • MCS

College of Medicine
Programs in:
biochemistry and molecular biology • PhD
biotechnology • MS
medicine • MD, MS, PhD

College of Pharmacy, Nursing and Allied Health Sciences
Program in:
pharmacy, nursing and allied health sciences • Pharm D, MSN, Certificate

Division of Nursing
Programs in:
nurse practitioner • Certificate
primary family health nursing • MSN

Division of Pharmacy
Program in:
pharmacy • Pharm D

Graduate School of Arts and Sciences
Programs in:
African studies • MA, PhD
analytical chemistry • MS, PhD
anatomy • MS, PhD
applied mathematics • MS, PhD
arts and sciences • M Eng, MA, MAPA, MCS, MFA, MM, MM Ed, MS, PhD
atmospheric • MS, PhD
atmospheric sciences • MS, PhD
biochemistry • MS, PhD
biology • MS, PhD
biophysics • PhD
clinical psychology • PhD
developmental psychology • PhD
economics • MA, PhD
English • MA, PhD
environmental • MS, PhD
exercise physiology • MS
experimental psychology • PhD
French • MA
genetics and human genetics • MS, PhD

Peterson's Graduate Schools in the U.S. 2006

District of Columbia

Howard University (continued)
 history • MA, PhD
 inorganic chemistry • MS, PhD
 mathematics • MS, PhD
 microbiology • PhD
 neuropsychology • PhD
 nutrition • MS, PhD
 organic chemistry • MS, PhD
 personality psychology • PhD
 pharmacology • MS, PhD
 philosophy • MA
 physical chemistry • MS, PhD
 physics • MS, PhD
 physiology • PhD
 political science • MA, PhD
 polymer chemistry • MS, PhD
 psychology • MS
 public administration • MAPA
 public affairs • MA
 recreation and leisure studies • MS
 school and community health education • MS
 social psychology • PhD
 sociology • MA, PhD
 Spanish • MA

Division of Fine Arts
Dr. Tritobia H. Benjamin, Associate Dean
Programs in:
 art history • MA
 ceramics • MFA
 design • MFA
 experimental studio • MFA
 fine arts • MFA
 jazz studies • MM
 music education • MM Ed
 painting • MFA
 performance • MM
 photography • MFA
 printmaking • MFA
 sculpture • MFA

School of Business
Programs in:
 accounting • MBA
 business • MBA
 entrepreneurship • MBA
 finance • MBA
 information systems • MBA
 international business • MBA
 marketing • MBA
 supply chain management • MBA

School of Communications
Dr. Jannette L. Dates, Dean
Programs in:
 communication sciences • PhD
 communications • MA, MFA, MS, PhD
 film • MFA
 intercultural communication • MA, PhD
 mass communication • MA, PhD
 organizational communication • MA, PhD
 speech pathology • MS

School of Divinity
Dr. Bertram Melbourne, Interim Dean
Program in:
 theology • M Div, MARS, D Min

School of Education
Dr. Vinetta C. Jones, Dean
Programs in:
 counseling and guidance • M Ed, MA, CAGS
 counseling psychology • M Ed, MA, PhD, CAGS
 early childhood education • M Ed, MA, MAT, CAGS
 education • M Ed, MA, MAT, MS, Ed D, PhD, CAGS
 educational administration • M Ed, MA, Ed D, CAGS
 educational administration and policy • Ed D
 educational psychology • M Ed, MA, Ed D, PhD, CAGS
 educational supervision • M Ed, MA, CAGS
 elementary education • M Ed
 human development • MS
 reading • M Ed, MA, MAT, CAGS
 school psychology • M Ed, MA, Ed D, PhD, CAGS
 secondary curriculum and instruction • M Ed, MA, MAT, CAGS
 special education • M Ed, MA, CAGS

School of Law
Program in:
 law • JD, LL M

School of Social Work
Program in:
 social work • MSW, PhD

■ SOUTHEASTERN UNIVERSITY
Washington, DC 20024-2788
http://www.seu.edu/

Independent, coed, comprehensive institution. *Computer facilities:* 137 computers available on campus for general student use. A campuswide network can be accessed from off campus. *Library facilities:* The Learning Resources Center plus 1 other. *General application contact:* Director of Admissions, 202-265-5343.

College of Graduate Studies
Programs in:
 accounting • MBA
 business • MBA, MPA, MS, MSMOT
 computer science • MBA, MS
 financial management • MBA
 government program management • MPA, MSMOT
 health services administration • MPA
 international management • MBA
 management • MBA
 management information systems • MBA
 marketing • MBA
 public administration • MPA
 taxation • MS

■ STRAYER UNIVERSITY
Washington, DC 20005-2603
http://www.strayer.edu/

Proprietary, coed, comprehensive institution. *Computer facilities:* 1,500 computers available on campus for general student use. A campuswide network can be accessed. Internet access and online class registration are available. *Library facilities:* Wilkes Library plus 20 others. *General application contact:* Campus Manager, 202-408-2400.

Graduate Studies
Programs in:
 accounting • MS
 business administration • MBA
 communications technology • MS
 information systems • MS
 management information systems • MS

■ TRINITY COLLEGE
Washington, DC 20017-1094
http://www.trinitydc.edu/

Independent-religious, women only, comprehensive institution. *Enrollment:* 1,637 graduate, professional, and undergraduate students; 188 full-time matriculated graduate/professional students (157 women), 438 part-time matriculated graduate/professional students (376 women). *Graduate faculty:* 16 full-time (10 women), 42 part-time/adjunct (25 women). *Computer facilities:* 80 computers available on campus for general student use. A campuswide network can be accessed from student residence rooms and from off campus. Internet access and online class registration are available. *Library facilities:* Sister Helen Sheehan Library plus 1 other. *Graduate expenses:* Tuition: part-time $550 per credit. Tuition and fees vary according to program. *General application contact:* Linda Ashcraft, Assistant Vice President for Graduate Admissions, 202-884-9400.

Find an in-depth description at www.petersons.com/gradchannel.

School of Education
Dr. Suellen Meara, Dean
Programs in:
 counseling • MA

democracy, diversity, and social justice • M Ed
early childhood • MAT
educational administration • MSA
elementary education • MAT
English as a second language • M Ed, MAT
reading instruction • M Ed
secondary education • MAT
special education • MAT

School of Professional Studies
Dr. Bill Steel, Dean for School of Professional Studies
Programs in:
business administration • MBA
communication • MA
Information assurance • MS
organizational management • MSA

■ UNIVERSITY OF THE DISTRICT OF COLUMBIA
Washington, DC 20008-1175
http://www.udc.edu/

District-supported, coed, comprehensive institution. CGS member. *Enrollment:* 5,241 graduate, professional, and undergraduate students; 61 full-time matriculated graduate/professional students (29 women), 111 part-time matriculated graduate/professional students (70 women). *Graduate faculty:* 30. *Computer facilities:* 1,500 computers available on campus for general student use. A campuswide network can be accessed. *Library facilities:* Learning Resources Division Library plus 1 other. *Graduate expenses:* Tuition, district resident: part-time $198 per credit hour. Tuition, nonresident: part-time $329 per credit hour. *General application contact:* LaVerne Hill Flannigan, Processor, Graduate Applications, 202-274-5008.

College of Arts and Sciences
Dr. Rachel Petty, Dean
Programs in:
arts and sciences • MA, MS, MST
early childhood education • MA
English composition and rhetoric • MA
special education • MA
speech and language pathology • MS

Division of Science and Mathematics
Dr. Freddie Dixon, Head
Programs in:
mathematics • MST
science and mathematics • MA, MST

Division of Urban Affairs, Social, and Behavioral Sciences
Dr. Sheila Harmon-Martin, Head
Programs in:
clinical psychology • MS

counseling • MS
urban affairs, social, and behavioral sciences • MS

David A. Clarke School of Law
Katherine S. Broderick, Dean
Program in:
law • JD

School of Business and Public Administration
Dr. Herbert Quigley, Dean
Programs in:
business administration • MBA
business and public administration • MBA, MPA
public administration • MPA

Florida

■ ARGOSY UNIVERSITY/ SARASOTA
Sarasota, FL 34235-8246
http://www.sarasota.edu/

Proprietary, coed, upper-level institution. CGS member. *Graduate faculty:* 35 full-time (15 women), 56 part-time/adjunct (19 women). *Graduate expenses:* Tuition: part-time $450 per credit. *General application contact:* Elmina Taylor, Admissions Representative, 800-331-5995 Ext. 214.

School of Business
Dr. Kathleen Cornett, Dean
Programs in:
accounting • MBA, DBA
finance • MBA
healthcare administration • MBA
human resources • MBA
information systems • DBA
information technology • MBA
international business • MBA, DBA
leadership • MBA
management • DBA
marketing • MBA, DBA

School of Education
Dr. Stanley Imhulse, Dean
Programs in:
curriculum and instruction • MA Ed, Ed D, Ed S
educational leadership • MA Ed, Ed D, Ed S

School of Psychology and Behavioral Sciences
Dr. Douglas Riedmiller, Dean
Programs in:
clinical psychology • Psy D
counseling psychology • Ed D
guidance counseling • MA

mental health counseling • MA
organizational leadership • Ed D
pastoral community counseling • Ed D
school counseling • Ed S

■ BARRY UNIVERSITY
Miami Shores, FL 33161-6695
http://www.barry.edu/

Independent-religious, coed, university. *Computer facilities:* Computer purchase and lease plans are available. 368 computers available on campus for general student use. A campuswide network can be accessed from student residence rooms and from off campus. Internet access is available. *Library facilities:* Monsignor William Barry Memorial Library plus 1 other. *General application contact:* Dean, Enrollment Services, 305-899-3112.

Find an in-depth description at www.petersons.com/gradchannel.

Andreas School of Business
Programs in:
business • MBA
e-commerce • MS
management information systems • Certificate

School of Adult and Continuing Education
Programs in:
adult and continuing education • MS
information technology • MS

School of Arts and Sciences
Programs in:
arts and sciences • EMS, MA, MFA, MS, D Min, Certificate, SSP
broadcasting • Certificate
clinical psychology • MS
communication • EMS, MA
organizational communication • MS
pastoral ministry for Hispanics • MA
pastoral theology • MA
photography • MA, MFA
school psychology • MS, SSP
theology • MA, D Min

School of Education
Programs in:
counseling • MS, PhD, Ed S
education • MAT, MS, PhD, Ed S, PMC
educational computing and technology • MS, PhD, Ed S
educational leadership • MS, Ed S
elementary education • MS, PMC
exceptional student education • MS, PhD, Ed S
guidance and counseling • MS, Ed S
higher education administration • MS, PhD

Florida

Barry University (continued)
  human resource development • MS, PhD
  leadership • PhD
  marriage and family counseling • MS, Ed S
  mental health counseling • MS, Ed S
  Montessori education • MS, Ed S
  pre-kindergarten and primary education • MS
  reading • MS, Ed S
  rehabilitation counseling • MS, Ed S
  teaching • MAT

School of Graduate Medical Sciences
Programs in:
  medical sciences • DPM, MCMS
  physician assistant • MCMS
  podiatric medicine • DPM

School of Human Performance and Leisure Sciences
Programs in:
  athletic training • MS
  biomechanics • MS
  exercise science • MS
  human performance and leisure sciences • MS
  sport management • MS

School of Law
Program in:
  law • JD

School of Natural and Health Sciences
Programs in:
  anesthesiology • MS
  biology • MS
  biomedical sciences • MS
  health services administration • MS
  natural and health sciences • MS
  occupational therapy • MS

School of Nursing
Programs in:
  advanced nursing completion • MSN
  nurse practitioner • MSN
  nursing • MSN, PhD
  nursing administration • MSN, PhD
  nursing education • MSN

School of Social Work
Program in:
  social work • MSW, PhD

■ EMBRY-RIDDLE AERONAUTICAL UNIVERSITY
Daytona Beach, FL 32114-3900
http://www.embryriddle.edu/

Independent, coed, primarily men, comprehensive institution. *Enrollment:* 4,926 graduate, professional, and undergraduate students; 123 full-time matriculated graduate/professional students (34 women), 284 part-time matriculated graduate/professional students (71 women). *Graduate faculty:* 48 full-time (5 women), 3 part-time/adjunct (1 woman). *Computer facilities:* 817 computers available on campus for general student use. A campuswide network can be accessed from student residence rooms and from off campus. Internet access and online class registration are available. *Library facilities:* Jack R. Hunt Memorial Library. *Graduate expenses:* Tuition: full-time $16,740; part-time $930 per credit. Required fees: $660. *General application contact:* Christine Castetter, Graduate Admissions, 800-388-3728.

Daytona Beach Campus Graduate Program
Dr. John Watret, Associate Chancellor for Academic Affairs
Programs in:
  aeronautics • MAS, MBAA, MS Sp C, MSAE, MSE, MSHFS
  aerospace engineering • MSAE
  applied aviation sciences • MAS
  business administration in aviation • MBAA
  human factors engineering • MSHFS
  software engineering • MSE
  space science • MS Sp C
  systems engineering • MSHFS

■ EMBRY-RIDDLE AERONAUTICAL UNIVERSITY, EXTENDED CAMPUS
Daytona Beach, FL 32114-3900
http://www.embryriddle.edu/

Independent, coed, primarily men, comprehensive institution. *Enrollment:* 10,416 graduate, professional, and undergraduate students; 78 full-time matriculated graduate/professional students (20 women), 2,483 part-time matriculated graduate/professional students (391 women). *Graduate faculty:* 58 full-time (7 women), 222 part-time/adjunct (24 women). *Library facilities:* Jack R. Hunt Memorial Library. *Graduate expenses:* Tuition: full-time $6,864; part-time $443 per credit. *General application contact:* Pam Thomas, Director of Admissions and Records, 386-226-6910.

Graduate Resident Centers
Dr. Paul Bankit, Interim Dean
Programs in:
  aeronautical science • MAS
  aviation administration and management • MBAA, MSM
  technical management • MSTM

■ FLORIDA AGRICULTURAL AND MECHANICAL UNIVERSITY
Tallahassee, FL 32307-3200
http://www.famu.edu/

State-supported, coed, university. CGS member. *Enrollment:* 13,013 graduate, professional, and undergraduate students; 1,992 full-time matriculated graduate/professional students (1,365 women), 399 part-time matriculated graduate/professional students (263 women). *Graduate faculty:* 492 full-time (186 women). *Computer facilities:* A campuswide network can be accessed from student residence rooms and from off campus. Internet access is available. *Library facilities:* Coleman Memorial Library plus 5 others. *Graduate expenses:* Tuition, state resident: part-time $192 per credit. Tuition, nonresident: part-time $727 per credit. Tuition and fees vary according to course load. *General application contact:* Dr. Chanta M. Haywood, Dean of Graduate Studies, Research, and Continuing Education, 850-599-3315.

College of Law
Percy R. Luney, Dean
Program in:
  law • JD

Division of Graduate Studies, Research, and Continuing Education
Dr. Chanta M. Haywood, Dean of Graduate Studies, Research, and Continuing Education
Program in:
  nursing • MS

College of Arts and Sciences
Dr. Larry E. Rivers, Dean
Programs in:
  African American history • MASS
  arts and sciences • MASS, MS, MSW, PhD
  biology • MS
  chemistry • MS
  community psychology • MS
  criminal justice • MASS
  economics • MASS
  history • MASS
  history and political sciences • MASS, MSW
  physics • MS, PhD
  political science • MASS
  public administration • MASS
  public management • MASS
  school psychology • MS
  social work • MASS
  sociology • MASS
  software engineering • MS

Florida

College of Education
Dr. Robert Lemons, Dean
Programs in:
  administration and supervision • M Ed, MS Ed, PhD
  adult education • M Ed, MS Ed
  biology • M Ed
  business education • MBE
  chemistry • MS Ed
  early childhood and elementary education • M Ed, MS Ed
  education • M Ed, MBE, MS Ed, PhD
  educational leadership • PhD
  English • MS Ed
  guidance and counseling • M Ed, MS Ed
  health, physical education, and recreation • M Ed, MS Ed
  history • MS Ed
  industrial education • M Ed, MS Ed
  math • MS Ed
  physics • MS Ed

College of Engineering Science, Technology, and Agriculture
Dr. Charles Magee, Dean
Programs in:
  agribusiness • MS
  animal science • MS
  engineering science, technology, and agriculture • MS
  engineering technology • MS
  entomology • MS
  food science • MS
  international programs • MS
  plant science • MS

College of Pharmacy and Pharmaceutical Sciences
Dr. Henry Lewis, Dean
Programs in:
  environmental toxicology • PhD
  medicinal chemistry • MS, PhD
  pharmaceutics • MS, PhD
  pharmacology/toxicology • MS, PhD
  pharmacy administration • MS
  pharmacy and pharmaceutical sciences • Pharm D, MPH, MS, Ex Doc, PhD
  public health • MPH

Environmental Sciences Institute
Dr. Richard Gragg, Interim Director
Program in:
  environmental sciences • MS, PhD

FAMU-FSU College of Engineering
Dr. C. J. Chen, Dean
Programs in:
  biomedical engineering • MS, PhD
  chemical engineering • MS, PhD
  civil engineering • MS, PhD
  electrical engineering • MS, PhD
  engineering • MS, PhD
  environmental engineering • MS, PhD
  industrial engineering • MS, PhD
  mechanical engineering • MS, PhD

School of Allied Health Sciences
Dr. Cynthia Hughes-Harris, Dean
Programs in:
  health administration • MS
  physical therapy • MPT

School of Architecture
Rodner Wright, Dean
Programs in:
  architectural studies • MS Arch
  architecture (professional) • M Arch
  landscape architecture • MLA

School of Business and Industry
Dr. Amos Bradford, Interim Dean
Programs in:
  accounting • MBA
  finance • MBA
  management information systems • MBA
  marketing • MBA

School of Journalism Media and Graphic Arts
Dr. James E. Hawkins, Interim Dean
Program in:
  journalism • MS

■ FLORIDA ATLANTIC UNIVERSITY
Boca Raton, FL 33431-0991
http://www.fau.edu/

State-supported, coed, university. CGS member. *Enrollment:* 25,018 graduate, professional, and undergraduate students; 1,406 full-time matriculated graduate/professional students (769 women), 1,913 part-time matriculated graduate/professional students (1,210 women). *Graduate faculty:* 949 full-time (406 women), 17 part-time/adjunct (9 women). *Computer facilities:* 822 computers available on campus for general student use. A campuswide network can be accessed from student residence rooms and from off campus. Internet access and online class registration are available. *Library facilities:* S. E. Wimberly Library. *Graduate expenses:* Tuition, state resident: full-time $3,777. Tuition, nonresident: full-time $13,953. *General application contact:* Steve Todish, Graduate Studies—Admissions, 561-297-3624.

Charles E. Schmidt College of Science
Dr. Nat Dean, Interim Dean
Programs in:
  applied mathematics and statistics • MS
  biological sciences • MBS, MS, MST
  chemistry and biochemistry • MS, MST, PhD
  environmental sciences • MS
  geography • MA, MAT
  geology • MS
  mathematics • MS, MST, PhD
  physics • MS, MST, PhD
  psychology • MA, PhD
  science • MA, MAT, MBS, MS, MST, PhD

Center for Complex Systems and Brain Sciences
Dr. J. A. Scott Kelso, Director
Program in:
  complex systems and brain sciences • PhD

College of Architecture, Urban and Public Affairs
Dr. Rosalyn Carter, Dean
Programs in:
  architecture, urban and public affairs • MJPM, MNM, MPA, MSW, MURP, PhD
  criminology and criminal justice • MJPM
  urban and regional planning • MURP

School of Public Administration
Dr. Hugh T. Miller, Director
Programs in:
  nonprofit management • MNM
  public administration • MNM, MPA, PhD

School of Social Work
Dr. Michele Hawkins, Director
Program in:
  social work • MSW

College of Business
Dr. Bruce Mallen, Dean
Programs in:
  accounting • MBA
  business • Exec MBA, M Ac, M Tax, MBA, MS, MSIB, MST, PhD
  business administration • Exec MBA
  economics • MS, MST
  electronic commerce • MBA
  finance • MBA
  financial planning • MBA
  global entrepreneurship • MBA
  health administration • MBA
  international business • MBA
  marketing • MBA
  operations management • MBA
  real estate • MBA
  sport management • MBA

School of Accounting
Dr. Carl Borgia, Director
Programs in:
  accounting • M Ac, M Tax
  forensic nursing • M Ac
  taxation • M Tax

College of Education
Dr. Gregory Aloia, Dean
Programs in:
  adult/community education • M Ed, Ed D, Ed S
  art teacher education • M Ed

Peterson's Graduate Schools in the U.S. 2006

Florida

Florida Atlantic University (continued)
  counselor education • M Ed
  curriculum and instruction • M Ed, Ed D, Ed S
  education • M Ed, MA, MAT, MS, MSF, Ed D, Ed S
  educational leadership • M Ed, Ed D, Ed S
  educational psychology • MSF
  educational research • MSF
  educational technology • MSF
  elementary education • M Ed
  emotional handicaps • M Ed
  exceptional student education • M Ed, Ed D
  exercise science and health promotion • M Ed, MS
  family counseling • Ed S
  foundations of education • M Ed
  foundations-educational research • M Ed
  foundations-educational technology • M Ed
  higher education management • M Ed, Ed D
  learning disabilities • M Ed
  mental health counseling • M Ed, Ed S
  mental retardation • M Ed
  multicultural education • MSF
  reading teacher education • M Ed
  rehabilitation counseling • M Ed
  school counseling • Ed S
  science teacher education • M Ed
  special education • Ed D
  speech-language pathology • MS
  varying exceptionalities • M Ed

College of Engineering
Dr. Karl Stevens, Dean
Programs in:
  civil engineering • MS
  computer engineering • MS, PhD
  computer science • MS, PhD
  electrical engineering • MS, PhD
  engineering • MS, PhD
  mechanical engineering • MS, PhD
  ocean engineering • MS, PhD

College of Nursing
Dr. Anne Boykin, Dean
Program in:
  nursing • MS, DNS, Post Master's Certificate

Dorothy F. Schmidt College of Arts and Letters
Dr. William Covino, Interim Dean
Programs in:
  American literature • MA
  anthropology • MA, MAT
  art education • MAT
  arts and letters • MA, MAT, MFA, MLBLST, PhD, Certificate
  ceramics • MFA
  communication • MA
  comparative literature • MA
  comparative studies • PhD
  computer art • MFA
  English literature • MA
  fantasy and science fiction • MA
  French • MA
  German • MA
  graphic design • MFA
  history • MA
  liberal studies • MLBLST
  multicultural literature • MA
  music • MA
  painting • MFA
  political science • MA, MAT
  sociology • MA, MAT
  Spanish • MA
  teaching French • MAT
  teaching German • MAT
  teaching Spanish • MAT
  theatre • MFA

Women's Studies Center
Dr. Mary M. Cameron, Chair and Associate Professor
Program in:
  women's studies • MA, Certificate

■ FLORIDA GULF COAST UNIVERSITY
Fort Myers, FL 33965-6565
http://www.fgcu.edu/

State-supported, coed, comprehensive institution. *Enrollment:* 5,972 graduate, professional, and undergraduate students; 229 full-time matriculated graduate/professional students (148 women), 907 part-time matriculated graduate/professional students (581 women). *Graduate faculty:* 192 full-time (96 women), 195 part-time/adjunct (89 women). *Computer facilities:* 323 computers available on campus for general student use. A campuswide network can be accessed from student residence rooms and from off campus. Internet access and online class registration, online admissions and advising are available. *Library facilities:* Library Services. *Graduate expenses:* Tuition, state resident: part-time $199 per credit hour. Tuition, nonresident: part-time $733 per credit hour. *General application contact:* Larry Stiles, Coordinator, High School, Community College Relations Director, Admissions/Records, 239-590-7891.

College of Arts and Sciences
Dr. José Barreto, Interim Dean
Programs in:
  arts and sciences • MS
  environmental science • MS

College of Business
Dr. Richard Pegnetter, Dean
Programs in:
  accounting and taxation • MS
  business • MBA, MS
  business administration • MBA
  computer and information systems • MS

College of Education
Dr. Lawrence Byrnes, Dean
Programs in:
  behavior disorders • MA
  biology • MAT
  counselor education • M Ed, MA
  education • M Ed, MA, MAT
  educational leadership • M Ed
  educational technology • M Ed, MA
  elementary education • M Ed, MA
  English • MAT
  mathematics • MAT
  mental retardation • MA
  reading education • M Ed
  social sciences • MAT
  specific learning disabilities • MA
  varying exceptionalities • MA

College of Health Professions
Dr. Denise Heinemann, Dean
Programs in:
  health professions • MS, MSN
  health sciences • MS
  physical therapy • MS

School of Nursing
Dr. Karen Miles, Director
Program in:
  nursing • MSN

College of Public and Social Services
Dr. John McGaha, Dean
Programs in:
  criminal justice • MPA
  environmental policy • MPA
  general public administration • MPA
  management • MPA
  public and social services • MPA, MSW
  social work • MSW

■ FLORIDA INSTITUTE OF TECHNOLOGY
Melbourne, FL 32901-6975
http://www.fit.edu/

Independent, coed, university. *Enrollment:* 4,689 graduate, professional, and undergraduate students; 590 full-time matriculated graduate/professional students (252 women), 1,668 part-time matriculated graduate/professional students (619 women). *Graduate faculty:* 198 full-time (28 women), 169 part-time/adjunct (19 women). *Computer facilities:* 400 computers available on campus for general student use. A campuswide network can be accessed from student residence rooms and from off campus. Internet access and online class registration are available. *Library facilities:* Evans

Library. *Graduate expenses:* Tuition: part-time $745 per credit. *General application contact:* Carolyn P. Farrior, Director of Graduate Admissions, 321-674-7118.

Find an in-depth description at www.petersons.com/gradchannel.

Graduate Programs
Antionet Mortara, Director Graduate Programs

College of Engineering
Dr. J. Ronald Bailey, Dean
Programs in:
  aerospace engineering • MS, PhD
  biological oceanography • MS, PhD
  chemical engineering • MS, PhD
  chemical oceanography • MS, PhD
  civil engineering • MS, PhD
  coastal zone management • MS
  computer engineering • MS, PhD
  computer information systems • MS
  computer science • MS, PhD
  electrical engineering • MS, PhD
  engineering • MS, PhD
  engineering management • MS
  environmental resource management • MS
  environmental science • MS, PhD
  geological oceanography • MS, PhD
  mechanical engineering • MS, PhD
  meteorology • MS
  ocean engineering • MS, PhD
  oceanography • MS, PhD
  physical oceanography • MS, PhD
  software engineering • MS
  systems engineering • MS

College of Science and Liberal Arts
Dr. Gordon L. Nelson, Dean
Programs in:
  applied mathematics • MS, PhD
  biological sciences • PhD
  biotechnology • MS
  cell and molecular biology • PhD
  chemistry • MS, PhD
  communication • MS
  computer science education • MS
  ecology • MS
  environmental education • MS
  marine biology • MS
  mathematics education • MS, Ed D, PhD, Ed S
  operations research • MS, PhD
  physics • MS, PhD
  science and liberal arts • MAT, MS, Ed D, PhD, Ed S
  science and mathematics education • MAT
  science education • MS, Ed D, PhD, Ed S
  space science • MS, PhD

School of Aeronautics
Dr. Nathaniel Villaire, Chairman of Graduate Studies
Programs in:
  airport development and management • MSA
  applied aviation safety • MSA
  aviation human factors • MS

School of Extended Graduate Studies
Dr. Ronald L. Marshall, Dean, School of Extended Graduate Studies
Programs in:
  acquisition and contract management • MS, PMBA
  aerospace engineering • MS
  business administration • PMBA
  computer information systems • MS
  computer science • MS
  e-business • PMBA
  electrical engineering • MS
  engineering management • MS
  human resource management • PMBA
  human resources management • MS
  information systems • PMBA
  logistics management • MS
  management • MS
  material acquisition management • MS
  mechanical engineering • MS
  operations research • MS
  project management • MS
  public administration • MPA
  software engineering • MS
  space systems • MS
  space systems management • MS
  systems management • MS

School of Management
Dr. A. Thomas Hollingsworth, Dean
Program in:
  management • MBA

School of Psychology
Dr. Mary Beth Kenkel, Dean
Programs in:
  applied behavior analysis • MS
  clinical psychology • Psy D
  industrial/organizational psychology • MS, PhD

■ FLORIDA INTERNATIONAL UNIVERSITY
Miami, FL 33199
http://www.fiu.edu/~wellness

State-supported, coed, university. CGS member. *Enrollment:* 33,228 graduate, professional, and undergraduate students; 2,467 full-time matriculated graduate/professional students (1,376 women), 2,458 part-time matriculated graduate/professional students (1,480 women). *Graduate faculty:* 977 full-time (353 women), 11 part-time/adjunct (4 women). *Computer facilities:* 600 computers available on campus for general student use. A campuswide network can be accessed from student residence rooms and from off campus. Internet access and online class registration are available. *Library facilities:* University Park Library plus 2 others. *Graduate expenses:* Tuition, state resident: part-time $202 per credit. Tuition, nonresident: part-time $771 per credit. Required fees: $112 per semester. *General application contact:* Carmen Brown, Director of Admissions, 305-348-2363.

Find an in-depth description at www.petersons.com/gradchannel.

College of Arts and Sciences
Dr. R. Bruce Dunlap, Dean
Programs in:
  African-new world studies • MA
  arts and sciences • MA, MFA, MM, MS, PhD
  biological management • MS
  biology • MS, PhD
  chemistry • MS, PhD
  comparative sociology • MA
  creative writing • MFA
  developmental psychology • PhD
  earth sciences • MS, PhD
  economics • MA, PhD
  energy • MS
  English • MA
  forensic science • MS
  general psychology • MS
  history • MA, PhD
  international relations • PhD
  international studies • MA
  Latin American and Caribbean studies • MA
  linguistics • MA
  mathematical sciences • MS
  physics • MS, PhD
  political science • MS, PhD
  pollution • MS
  psychology • MS
  religious studies • MA
  sociology • PhD
  Spanish • MA, PhD
  statistics • MS
  visual arts • MFA

School of Computer Science
Dr. Yi Deng, Director
Program in:
  computer science • MS, PhD

School of Music
Fredrick Kaufman, Director
Programs in:
  music • MM
  music education • MS

College of Business Administration
Dr. Joyce J. Elam, Executive Dean
Programs in:
  business administration • M Acc, MBA, MIB, MS, MSF, MST, PhD
  decision sciences and information systems • PhD
  finance • MSF
  international business • MIB

Florida

Florida International University (continued)

School of Accounting
Dr. Dana Forgione, Director
Programs in:
  accounting • M Acc
  taxation • MST

College of Education
Dr. Linda P. Blanton, Dean
Programs in:
  administration and supervision of vocational education • MS
  adult education • MS, Ed D
  art education • MS, Ed D
  counselor education • MS
  early childhood education • MS
  education • MA, MS, Ed D, Ed S
  educational administration and supervision • Ed D
  educational leadership • MS, Ed S
  elementary education • MS
  emotional disturbances • MS
  English education • MS, Ed D
  English for non-English speakers • MS
  exceptional student education • Ed D
  health education • MS
  higher education administration • Ed D
  home economics education • MS
  human resource development • MS
  international development education • MS, Ed D, Ed S
  mathematics education • MS
  modern language education • MS, Ed D
  non-school based home economics education • MS
  parks and recreation administration • MS
  parks/recreation/sports management • MS
  physical education • MS
  reading education • MS
  school psychology • Ed S
  science education • MS, Ed D
  social studies education • MS
  specific learning disabilities • MS
  urban education • MS
  vocational home economics education • MS
  vocational industrial education • MS

College of Engineering
Dr. Vish Prasad, Acting Dean
Programs in:
  biomedical engineering • MS
  civil engineering • MS, PhD
  computer engineering • MS
  construction management • MS
  electrical engineering • MS, PhD
  engineering • MS, PhD
  environmental and urban systems • MS
  environmental engineering • MS
  industrial engineering • MS
  mechanical engineering • MS, PhD
  telecommunications and networking • MS

College of Health and Urban Affairs
Dr. Ronald M. Berkman, Executive Dean
Programs in:
  dietetics and nutrition • MS, PhD
  health and urban affairs • MHSA, MPA, MPH, MS, MSN, MSW, PhD
  health services administration • MHSA
  public health • MHSA, MPH, MS, PhD

School of Health
Dr. Noma B. Anderson, Director
Programs in:
  communication sciences and disorders • MS
  health • MS
  occupational therapy • MS
  physical therapy • MS

School of Nursing
Dr. Divina Grossman, Director
Program in:
  nursing • MSN, PhD

School of Policy and Management
Dr. Ray Thomlison, Director
Programs in:
  criminal justice • MS
  policy and management • MPA, MS, PhD
  public administration • MPA, PhD

School of Social Work
Dr. Ray Thomlison, Director
Program in:
  social work • MSW, PhD

College of Law
Dr. Leonard Strickman, Dean
Program in:
  law • JD

School of Architecture
Juan A. Bueno, Dean
Programs in:
  architecture • MS
  landscape architecture • MS

School of Hospitality Management
Dr. Joseph West, Dean
Program in:
  hotel and food service management • MS

School of Journalism and Mass Communication
Dr. Lillian Kopenhaver, Interim Dean
Program in:
  mass communication • MS

■ **FLORIDA METROPOLITAN UNIVERSITY–BRANDON CAMPUS**
Tampa, FL 33619
http://www.fmu.edu/

Proprietary, coed, comprehensive institution. *Enrollment:* 1,384 graduate, professional, and undergraduate students; 10 full-time matriculated graduate/professional students (6 women), 81 part-time matriculated graduate/professional students (45 women). *Graduate faculty:* 2 full-time (1 woman), 4 part-time/adjunct (1 woman). *Computer facilities:* 81 computers available on campus for general student use. A campuswide network can be accessed. Internet access is available. *Library facilities:* Tampa College Library. *Graduate expenses:* Tuition: full-time $12,480; part-time $390 per credit hour. One-time fee: $200 full-time. *General application contact:* Dee McKee, Director of Admissions, 813-621-0041 Ext. 106.

Program in Business Administration
Susan Sayles, Chair
Program in:
  business administration • MBA

Program in Criminal Justice
Susan Sayles, Chair
Program in:
  criminal justice • MS

■ **FLORIDA METROPOLITAN UNIVERSITY–NORTH ORLANDO CAMPUS**
Orlando, FL 32810-5674

Proprietary, coed, comprehensive institution. *Computer facilities:* 25 computers available on campus for general student use. A campuswide network can be accessed. Internet access is available. *Library facilities:* Orlando College Library. *General application contact:* Director of Admissions, 407-628-5870 Ext. 108.

Division of Business Administration
Program in:
  business administration • MBA

FLORIDA METROPOLITAN UNIVERSITY–PINELLAS CAMPUS
Clearwater, FL 33759
http://www.fmu.edu/

Proprietary, coed, comprehensive institution. *Computer facilities:* 42 computers available on campus for general student use. A campuswide network can be accessed. Internet access is available. *Library facilities:* Laurel Raffel Memorial Library. *General application contact:* 727-725-2688.

Graduate School of Business
Program in:
business administration • MBA

Program in Criminal Justice
Program in:
criminal justice • MSCJ

FLORIDA METROPOLITAN UNIVERSITY–SOUTH ORLANDO CAMPUS
Orlando, FL 32819
http://www.fmu.edu/

Proprietary, coed, comprehensive institution. *General application contact:* Admissions Director, 407-851-2525 Ext. 111.

Program in Business Administration
Programs in:
accounting • MBA
general management • MBA
human resources • MBA
international management • MBA

FLORIDA METROPOLITAN UNIVERSITY–TAMPA CAMPUS
Tampa, FL 33614-5899
http://www.cci.edu/

Proprietary, coed, comprehensive institution. *Computer facilities:* 113 computers available on campus for general student use. Internet access is available. *Library facilities:* Tampa College Library. *General application contact:* Director of Admission, 813-879-6000 Ext. 129.

Department of Business Administration
Programs in:
accounting • MBA
human resources • MBA
international business • MBA

FLORIDA STATE UNIVERSITY
Tallahassee, FL 32306
http://www.fsu.edu/

State-supported, coed, university. CGS member. *Enrollment:* 36,884 graduate, professional, and undergraduate students; 4,718 full-time matriculated graduate/professional students (2,450 women), 2,133 part-time matriculated graduate/professional students (1,335 women). *Graduate faculty:* 1,003 full-time (320 women), 69 part-time/adjunct (21 women). *Computer facilities:* Computer purchase and lease plans are available. 2,707 computers available on campus for general student use. A campuswide network can be accessed from student residence rooms and from off campus. Internet access and online class registration, course home pages, course search, online fee payment are available. *Library facilities:* Robert Manning Strozier Library plus 6 others. *Graduate expenses:* Tuition, state resident: part-time $196 per credit hour. Tuition, nonresident: part-time $731 per credit hour. Part-time tuition and fees vary according to campus/location. *General application contact:* Melanie Booker, Associate Director for Graduate Admissions, 850-644-3420.

Find an in-depth description at www.petersons.com/gradchannel.

College of Law
Donald J. Weidner, Dean
Program in:
law • JD

Graduate Studies
Dr. Dianne F. Harrison, Associate Vice President for Academic Affairs and Dean of Graduate Studies

College of Arts and Sciences
Dr. Donald J. Foss, Dean
Programs in:
American and Florida studies • MA, Certificate
analytical chemistry • MS, PhD
anthropology • MA, MS, PhD
applied behavioral analysis • MS
applied mathematics • MA, MS, PhD
applied statistics • MS
arts and sciences • MA, MS, PhD, Certificate
biochemistry • MS, PhD
biochemistry, molecular and cell biology • PhD
cell biology • MS, PhD
chemical physics • MS, PhD
classical archaeology • MA
classical civilization • MA, PhD
classics • MA
clinical psychology • PhD
cognitive psychology • PhD
computer and network system administration • MA, MS
computer science • MA, MS, PhD
developmental biology • MS, PhD
ecology • MS, PhD
English • MA, PhD
evolutionary biology • MS, PhD
financial mathematics • PhD
French • MA, PhD
genetics • MS, PhD
geological sciences • MS, PhD
geophysical fluid dynamics • PhD
German • MA
Greek • MA
Greek and Latin • MA
historical administration • MA
history • MA, PhD
history and philosophy of science • MA
humanities • MA, PhD
immunology • MS, PhD
information security • MS
inorganic chemistry • MS, PhD
Italian • MA
Italian studies • MA
Latin • MA
literature • MA, PhD
marine biology • MS, PhD
mathematical sciences • MA, MS
mathematical statistics • MS, PhD
meteorology • MS, PhD
microbiology • MS, PhD
molecular biology • MS, PhD
molecular biophysics • PhD
neuroscience • PhD
oceanography • MS, PhD
organic chemistry • MS, PhD
philosophy • MA, PhD
physical chemistry • MS, PhD
physics • MS, PhD
plant sciences • MS, PhD
pure mathematics • MA, MS, PhD
religion • MA, PhD
Slavic languages and literatures • MA
Slavic languages/Russian • MA
social psychology • PhD
software engineering • MA, MS
Spanish • MA, PhD
writing • MA, PhD

College of Business
Dr. Patrick F. Maroney, Associate Dean for Graduate Programs
Programs in:
accounting • M Acc
business administration • MBA, PhD
insurance • MSM
management information systems • MS

College of Communication
Dr. John K. Mayo, Dean
Programs in:
communication • Adv M, MA, MS, PhD

Florida

Florida State University (continued)
  communication sciences and disorders • Adv M, MS, PhD
  integrated marketing and management communication • MA, MS
  interactive and new communication technology • MA, MS
  mass communication • MA, MS, PhD
  policy and political communications • MA, MS
  rhetorical and communication theory • MA, MS
  speech communication • PhD

College of Education
Dr. Richard Kunkel, Dean
Programs in:
  adapted physical education • MS
  adult education • MS, Ed D, PhD, Ed S
  comprehensive vocational education • PhD, Ed S
  counseling and human systems • MS, Ed S
  counseling psychology • PhD
  early childhood education • MS, Ed D, PhD, Ed S
  education • MS, Ed D, PhD, Ed S
  educational administration/leadership • MS, Ed D, PhD, Ed S
  educational psychology • MS, PhD
  elementary education • MS, Ed D, PhD, Ed S
  emotional disturbance/learning disabilities • MS
  English education • MS, PhD, Ed S
  foundations of education • MS, PhD, Ed S
  health education • MS
  higher education • MS, Ed D, PhD, Ed S
  history and philosophy of education • MS, PhD, Ed S
  institutional research • MS, Ed D, PhD, Ed S
  instructional systems • MS, PhD, Ed S
  international and intercultural education • MS, PhD, Ed S
  learning and cognition • MS, PhD
  mathematics education • MS, PhD, Ed S
  measurement and statistics • MS, PhD
  mental retardation • MS
  multilingual-multicultural education • MS, PhD, Ed S
  open and distance learning • MS
  policy planning and analysis • MS, Ed D, PhD, Ed S
  program evaluation • MS, PhD
  reading education/language arts • MS, Ed D, PhD, Ed S
  recreation administration • MS
  rehabilitation counseling • MS, PhD, Ed S
  school psychology • MS, Ed S

  science education • MS, PhD, Ed S
  social science education • MS, Ed D, PhD, Ed S
  special education • PhD, Ed S
  sports administration • MS, Ed D, PhD, Ed S
  sports psychology • MS, PhD
  teacher education • MS, Ed D, PhD, Ed S
  visual disabilities • MS

College of Human Sciences
Dr. Penny A. Ralston, Dean
Programs in:
  child development • MS, PhD
  exercise science • PhD
  family and consumer sciences education • MS, PhD
  family relations • MS, PhD
  human sciences • MS, PhD
  marriage and family therapy • PhD
  movement science • MS
  nutrition and food science • PhD
  nutrition and food sciences • MS
  textiles and consumer sciences • MS, PhD

College of Social Sciences
Dr. David W. Rasmussen, Dean
Programs in:
  aging studies • MS
  Asian studies • MA
  demography and public health • MS, Certificate
  economics • MS, PhD
  geography • MA, MS, PhD
  health policy research • MPH, MS
  international affairs • MA, MS
  political science • MA, MS, PhD
  public administration and policy • MPA, PhD, Certificate
  Russian and East European studies • MA
  social science • MA, MS
  social sciences • MA, MPA, MPH, MS, MSP, PhD, Certificate
  sociology • MA, MS, PhD
  urban and regional planning • MSP, PhD

FAMU/FSU College of Engineering
Programs in:
  chemical engineering • MS, PhD
  civil engineering • MS, PhD
  electrical engineering • MS, PhD
  engineering • MS, PhD
  environmental engineering • MS, PhD
  industrial engineering • MS, PhD
  mechanical engineering • MS, PhD

School of Criminology and Criminal Justice
Dr. Thomas Blomberg, Acting Dean
Program in:
  criminology and criminal justice • MA, MSC, PhD

School of Information Studies
Dr. Jane B. Robbins, Dean
Program in:
  library and information studies • MS, PhD, Specialist

School of Motion Picture, Television, and Recording Arts
Frank Patterson, Dean
Programs in:
  production • MFA
  professional writing • MFA

School of Music
Jon R. Piersol, Dean
Programs in:
  accompanying • MM
  arts administration • MA
  choral conducting • MM
  composition • MM, DM
  ethnomusicology • MM
  instrumental accompanying • MM
  instrumental conducting • MM
  jazz studies • MM
  music education • MM Ed, Ed D, PhD
  music theory • MM, PhD
  music therapy • MM
  musicology • MM, PhD
  opera • MM
  performance • MM, DM
  piano pedagogy • MM
  vocal accompanying • MM

School of Nursing
Dr. Katherine P. Mason, Dean
Programs in:
  adult nurse practitioner • MN, MSN, Certificate
  case manager • MN, MSN, Certificate
  family nurse practitioner • MN, MSN, Certificate
  nurse educator • MN, MSN, Certificate

School of Social Work
Dr. Bruce A. Thyer, Dean
Programs in:
  clinical social work • MSW
  social policy and administration • MSW
  social work • PhD

School of Theatre
Steven Wallace, Dean
Programs in:
  acting • MFA
  directing • MFA
  lighting, costume, and scenic design • MFA
  technical production • MFA
  theater management • MFA
  theatre • MA, MS, PhD

School of Visual Arts and Dance
Dr. Sally E. McRorie, Dean
Programs in:

art education • MA, MS, Ed D, PhD, Ed S
art history • MA, PhD
dance • MA, MFA
interior design • MA, MFA, MS
museum studies • Certificate
studio art • MFA
visual arts and dance • MA, MFA, MS, Ed D, PhD, Certificate, Ed S

■ JACKSONVILLE UNIVERSITY
Jacksonville, FL 32211-3394
http://www.ju.edu/

Independent, coed, comprehensive institution. *Enrollment:* 2,632 graduate, professional, and undergraduate students; 84 full-time matriculated graduate/professional students (33 women), 334 part-time matriculated graduate/professional students (197 women). *Graduate faculty:* 125 full-time, 139 part-time/adjunct. *Computer facilities:* 450 computers available on campus for general student use. A campuswide network can be accessed from student residence rooms and from off campus. Internet access and online class registration are available. *Library facilities:* Carl S. Swisher Library. *Graduate expenses:* Tuition: full-time $7,110; part-time $395 per credit. Tuition and fees vary according to program. *General application contact:* John P. Grundig, Executive Director of Admissions and Student Development, 904-256-7000.

College of Arts and Sciences
Dr. A. Quinton White, Dean
Programs in:
 arts and sciences • MAT, MSN, Certificate
 orthodontics • Certificate

School of Education
Dr. Harry M. Teitelbaum, Dean
Programs in:
 art education • MAT
 computer sciences • MAT
 early childhood education • Certificate
 elementary education • MAT
 English education • MAT
 exceptional child education • Certificate
 gifted education • Certificate
 integrated learning with educational technology • MAT
 mathematics education • MAT
 music education • MAT
 reading education • MAT
 second career as a teacher • Certificate
 second careers as a teacher • Certificate

School of Nursing
Dr. Linda Miller, Director
Program in:
 nursing • MSN

Davis College of Business
Dr. William L. Rhey, Dean
Programs in:
 business • Exec MBA, MBA
 business administration • Exec MBA, MBA

■ LYNN UNIVERSITY
Boca Raton, FL 33431-5598
http://www.lynn.edu/

Independent, coed, comprehensive institution. *Enrollment:* 1,891 graduate, professional, and undergraduate students; 37 full-time matriculated graduate/professional students (18 women), 311 part-time matriculated graduate/professional students (156 women). *Graduate faculty:* 27 full-time (13 women), 27 part-time/adjunct (9 women). *Computer facilities:* 150 computers available on campus for general student use. A campuswide network can be accessed from student residence rooms and from off campus. Internet access and online class registration are available. *Library facilities:* Eugene M. and Christine E. Lynn Library. *Graduate expenses:* Tuition: full-time $11,040; part-time $660 per credit. *General application contact:* Melissa P. Morri, Graduate Admissions Counselor, 561-237-7900 Ext. 7845.

College of Business and Management
Dr. Ralph Norcio, Dean
Programs in:
 aviation management • MBA
 global leadership • PhD
 health care management • MBA
 hospitality administration • MBA
 international business • MBA
 managerial electronic business • MBA
 marketing • MBA
 mass communication and media management • MBA
 sports and athletics administration • MBA

The Conservatory of Music
Claudio Jaffe, Dean
Program in:
 music performance • Diploma

Ross College of Education and Human Services
Dr. Richard Cohen, Dean
Programs in:
 educational leadership • M Ed
 exceptional student education • M Ed
 global leadership • PhD
 varying exceptionalities • M Ed

■ NOVA SOUTHEASTERN UNIVERSITY
Fort Lauderdale, FL 33314-7796
http://www.nova.edu/

Independent, coed, university. CGS member. *Enrollment:* 23,522 graduate, professional, and undergraduate students; 6,960 full-time matriculated graduate/professional students (4,468 women), 11,339 part-time matriculated graduate/professional students (7,949 women). *Graduate faculty:* 535 full-time, 970 part-time/adjunct. *Computer facilities:* 2,000 computers available on campus for general student use. A campuswide network can be accessed from student residence rooms and from off campus. Internet access and online class registration are available. *Library facilities:* Library, Research, and Information Technology Center plus 4 others. *Graduate expenses:* Tuition: full-time $8,715; part-time $484 per credit. Required fees: $75. Full-time tuition and fees vary according to degree level and program. *General application contact:* Information Contact, 800-541-6682.

Center for Psychological Studies
Dr. Ronald F. Levant, Dean
Programs in:
 clinical psychology • PhD, Psy D, SPS
 mental health counseling • MS
 psychological studies • MS, PhD, Psy D, Psy S, SPS
 psychopharmacology • MS
 school guidance and counseling • MS
 specialist in school psychology • Psy S

Fischler Graduate School of Education and Human Services
Dr. H. Wells Singleton, Provost/Dean
Programs in:
 adult education • Ed D
 child and youth care administration • MS
 child and youth studies • Ed D
 computer science education • MS, Ed S
 computing and information technology • Ed D
 early childhood education administration • MS
 education and human services • MA, MS, Ed D, SLPD, Ed S
 education technology • MS, Ed S
 educational leaders • Ed D
 educational leadership • administration K–12 • MS, Ed S
 educational media • MS, Ed S
 educational technology • MS
 elementary education • MS, Ed S

Florida

Nova Southeastern University (continued)
English • MS, Ed S
family support studies • MS
gifted education • MS
health care education • Ed D
higher education • Ed D
instructional technology and distance education • MS, Ed D
mathematics • MS, Ed S
organizational leadership • Ed D
pre-kindergarten/primary • MS, Ed S
reading • MS, Ed S
science • MS, Ed S
social studies • MS, Ed S
Spanish language • MS
speech-language pathology • MS, SLPD
substance abuse counseling and education • MS
teaching and learning • MA
teaching English to speakers of other languages • MS, Ed S
varying exceptionalities • MS, Ed S
vocational, occupational and technical education • Ed D

Graduate School of Computer and Information Sciences
Dr. Edward Lieblein, Dean
Programs in:
computer information systems • MS, PhD
computer science • MS, PhD
computing technology in education • MS, Ed D, PhD
information science • PhD
information systems • PhD
management information systems • MS

Graduate School of Humanities and Social Sciences
Dr. Honggang Yang, Dean
Programs in:
college student personnel administration • Certificate
conflict analysis and resolution • MS, PhD
criminal justice • MS
cross-disciplinary studies • MA
family systems healthcare • Certificate
family therapy • MS, PhD, Certificate
health care conflict resolution • Certificate
humanities and social sciences • MA, MS, DMFT, PhD, Certificate
marriage and family therapy • DMFT
peace studies • Certificate

Health Professions Division
Dr. Morton Terry, Chancellor
Program in:
health professions • DMD, DO, OD, Pharm D, MBS, MH Sc, MMS, MOT, MPH, MS, Au D, DHSc, DPT, OTD, PhD, TDPT

College of Allied Health and Nursing
Dr. Richard Davis, Dean
Programs in:
allied health and nursing • MH Sc, MMS, MOT, Au D, DHSc, DPT, OTD, PhD, TDPT
audiology • Au D
health science • MH Sc, DHSc
medical science • MMS
occupational therapy • MOT, OTD, PhD
physical therapy • DPT, PhD, TDPT

College of Dental Medicine
Dr. Robert A. Ochin, Dean
Programs in:
craniofacial research • MS
dental medicine • DMD

College of Medical Sciences
Dr. Harold E. Laubach, Dean
Program in:
biomedical sciences • MBS

College of Optometry
Dr. David S. Loshin, Dean
Programs in:
clinical vision research • MS
optometry • OD

College of Osteopathic Medicine
Dr. Anthony J. Silavgni, Dean
Programs in:
osteopathic medicine • DO
public health • MPH

College of Pharmacy
Dr. William Hardigan, Dean
Program in:
pharmacy • Pharm D

H. Wayne Huizenga School of Business and Entrepreneurship
Dr. Randolph A. Pohlman, Dean
Programs in:
accounting • M Acc
business administration • MBA, DBA
health services administration • MBA, MS
human resources management • MSHRM
international business administration • MIBA, DIBA
leadership • MS
public administration • MPA, DPA
taxation • MT

Oceanographic Center
Dr. Richard Dodge, Dean
Programs in:
coastal-zone management • MS
marine biology • MS, PhD
marine biology and oceanography • PhD
marine environmental science • MS
oceanography • PhD

Shepard Broad Law Center
Joseph D. Harbaugh, Dean
Programs in:
law • JD, MHL
mental health law • MHL

■ PALM BEACH ATLANTIC UNIVERSITY
West Palm Beach, FL 33416-4708
http://www.pbac.edu/

Independent-religious, coed, comprehensive institution. *Enrollment:* 2,996 graduate, professional, and undergraduate students; 570 matriculated graduate/professional students. *Graduate faculty:* 44 full-time (15 women), 18 part-time/adjunct (11 women). *Computer facilities:* A campuswide network can be accessed from student residence rooms and from off campus. Internet access and online class registration are available. *Library facilities:* E. C. Blomeyer Library. *Graduate expenses:* Tuition: full-time $5,800; part-time $320 per credit hour. Required fees: $200; $160 per year. Full-time tuition and fees vary according to degree level. Part-time tuition and fees vary according to course load. *General application contact:* Laura A. Leinweber, Director of Graduate and Evening Admissions, 800-281-3466.

MacArthur School of Continuing Education
Dr. Darrell Gwaltney, Dean
Program in:
organizational leadership • MS

Rinker School of Business
Dr. Bob Myers, Dean
Program in:
business • MBA

School of Education and Behavioral Studies
Dr. Dona Thornton, Dean
Programs in:
counseling psychology • MSCP
elementary education • M Ed

School of Ministry
Dr. Kenneth L. Mahanes, Vice President of Religious Life and Dean
Program in:
ministry • MA

School of Pharmacy
Dr. Scott Swigart, Dean
Program in:
pharmacy • Pharm D

Florida

ROLLINS COLLEGE
Winter Park, FL 32789-4499
http://www.rollins.edu/

Independent, coed, comprehensive institution. *Enrollment:* 2,565 graduate, professional, and undergraduate students; 264 full-time matriculated graduate/professional students (129 women), 568 part-time matriculated graduate/professional students (345 women). *Graduate faculty:* 23. *Computer facilities:* 200 computers available on campus for general student use. A campuswide network can be accessed from student residence rooms and from off campus. Internet access is available. *Library facilities:* Olin Library. *Graduate expenses:* Tuition: full-time $19,275. *General application contact:* Information Contact, 407-646-2000.

Crummer Graduate School of Business
Dr. Craig M. McAllaster, Dean
Program in:
 business • MBA

Hamilton Holt School
Dr. Robert Smither, Acting Dean
Programs in:
 corporate communications and technology • MA
 elementary education • M Ed, MAT
 human resources • MA
 liberal studies • MLS
 mental health counseling • MA
 school counseling • MA
 secondary education • MAT

SAINT LEO UNIVERSITY
Saint Leo, FL 33574-6665
http://www.saintleo.edu/

Independent-religious, coed, comprehensive institution. *Enrollment:* 1,518 graduate, professional, and undergraduate students; 262 full-time matriculated graduate/professional students (160 women), 161 part-time matriculated graduate/professional students (91 women). *Graduate faculty:* 15 full-time (4 women), 20 part-time/adjunct (5 women). *Computer facilities:* 750 computers available on campus for general student use. A campuswide network can be accessed from student residence rooms and from off campus. Internet access and online class registration are available. *Library facilities:* Cannon Memorial Library. *Graduate expenses:* Tuition: full-time $5,400; part-time $300 per semester hour. *General application contact:* Martin Smith, Director of Weekend/Graduate Admission, 800-707-8846.

Graduate Business Studies
Dr. T. Lynn Wilson, Director of Weekend/Graduate Admission
Program in:
 business • MBA

Graduate Studies in Education
Dr. John Smith, Director
Program in:
 education • M Ed

ST. THOMAS UNIVERSITY
Miami Gardens, FL 33054-6459
http://www.stu.edu/

Independent-religious, coed, comprehensive institution. *Enrollment:* 2,520 graduate, professional, and undergraduate students; 853 full-time matriculated graduate/professional students (446 women), 496 part-time matriculated graduate/professional students (321 women). *Graduate faculty:* 106. *Computer facilities:* 60 computers available on campus for general student use. A campuswide network can be accessed. *Library facilities:* St. Thomas University Library plus 1 other. *Graduate expenses:* Tuition: part-time $540 per credit. *General application contact:* Cristen L. Scolastico, Graduate Admissions Officer, 305-628-6546.

Find an in-depth description at www.petersons.com/gradchannel.

School of Graduate Studies
Dr. Joseph Iannone, Dean
Programs in:
 accounting • MBA
 business administration • M Acc, MBA, Certificate
 communication arts • MA, Certificate
 educational administration • MS, Certificate
 general management • MSM, Certificate
 guidance and counseling • MS, Certificate
 health management • MBA, MSM, Certificate
 Hispanic media • MA, Certificate
 human resource management • MBA, MSM, Certificate
 international business • MBA, MIB, MSM, Certificate
 justice administration • MSM, Certificate
 management • MBA, MSM
 management accounting • MSM, Certificate
 marriage and family therapy • MS, Certificate
 mental health counseling • MS
 public management • MSM, Certificate
 special education • MS
 sports administration • MBA, Certificate
 sports management • MS

Institute of Pastoral Ministries
Dr. Mercedes Iannone, Director
Program in:
 pastoral ministries • MA, Certificate

School of Law
Robert Butterworth, Dean
Programs in:
 international human rights • LL M
 international taxation • LL M
 law • JD

STETSON UNIVERSITY
DeLand, FL 32723
http://www.stetson.edu/

Independent, coed, comprehensive institution. *Enrollment:* 3,439 graduate, professional, and undergraduate students; 829 full-time matriculated graduate/professional students (464 women), 418 part-time matriculated graduate/professional students (233 women). *Graduate faculty:* 75 full-time (30 women), 56 part-time/adjunct (19 women). *Computer facilities:* 320 computers available on campus for general student use. A campuswide network can be accessed from student residence rooms and from off campus. Internet access is available. *Library facilities:* DuPont-Ball Library plus 2 others. *Graduate expenses:* Tuition: part-time $450 per credit hour. *General application contact:* Pat LeClaire, Office of Graduate Studies, 386-822-7075.

College of Arts and Sciences
Dr. Grady Ballenger, Dean
Programs in:
 arts and sciences • M Ed, MA, MS, Ed S
 career teaching • Ed S
 education • MA
 educational leadership • M Ed, Ed S
 elementary education • M Ed
 exceptional student education • M Ed
 exceptional student education and varying exceptionalities • M Ed
 marriage and family therapy • MS
 mental health counseling • MS
 reading education • M Ed
 school guidance and family consultation • MS

Division of Humanities
Programs in:
 English • MA
 humanities • MA

College of Law
Dr. Darby Dickerson, Dean
Program in:
 law • JD, LL M

Florida

Stetson University (continued)
School of Business Administration
Dr. Paul Dasher, Dean
Programs in:
  accounting • M Acc
  business administration • M Acc, MBA

■ UNIVERSITY OF CENTRAL FLORIDA
Orlando, FL 32816
http://www.ucf.edu/

State-supported, coed, university. CGS member. *Enrollment:* 41,102 graduate, professional, and undergraduate students; 2,734 full-time matriculated graduate/professional students (1,512 women), 3,477 part-time matriculated graduate/professional students (2,020 women). *Graduate faculty:* 964 full-time (373 women), 401 part-time/adjunct (218 women). *Computer facilities:* Computer purchase and lease plans are available. 2,420 computers available on campus for general student use. A campuswide network can be accessed from student residence rooms and from off campus. Internet access and online class registration are available. *Library facilities:* University Library. *Graduate expenses:* Tuition, state resident: full-time $4,968; part-time $171 per credit hour. Tuition, nonresident: full-time $18,630; part-time $713 per credit hour. *General application contact:* Dr. Patricia Bishop, Vice Provost and Dean of Graduate Studies, 407-823-2766.

Find an in-depth description at www.petersons.com/gradchannel.

College of Arts and Sciences
K. L. Seidel, Dean
Programs in:
  actuarial studies • MS
  applied experimental and human factors psychology • PhD
  applied sociology • MA
  arts and sciences • MA, MALS, MFA, MS, PhD, Certificate
  biology • MS
  clinical psychology • MA, MS, PhD
  conservation biology • Certificate
  creative writing • MA
  data mining • MS
  domestic violence • Certificate
  gender studies • Certificate
  history • MA
  industrial chemistry • MS
  industrial/organizational psychology • MS, PhD
  liberal studies • MALS
  literature • MA
  mathematical science • MS
  mathematics • PhD
  Mayan studies • Certificate
  modeling and simulation • MS, PhD
  physics • MS, PhD
  political science • MA
  professional writing • Certificate
  Spanish • MA
  statistical computing • MS
  teaching English as a second language • MA, Certificate
  technical writing • MA
  texts and technology • PhD
  theater • MFA

School of Communication
Dr. M. D. Meeske, Chair
Program in:
  communication • MA

College of Business Administration
Dr. Thomas Keon, Dean
Programs in:
  business administration • MBA
  economics • MAAE
  finance • PhD
  management • MSM
  management information systems • MS
  marketing • PhD
  sport business management • MSBM
  taxation • MST

School of Accounting
Dr. Andrew J. Judd, Director
Program in:
  accounting • MSA

College of Education
Dr. Sandra Robinson, Dean
Programs in:
  art education • M Ed, MA
  counselor education • M Ed, MA, PhD
  curriculum and instruction • Ed D, PhD
  early childhood education • M Ed, MA
  education • PhD
  educational leadership • M Ed, MA, Ed D, Ed S
  educational media • M Ed
  educational research, technology and leadership • PhD
  educational studies • M Ed, MA, Ed S
  educational technology • MA
  elementary education • M Ed, MA, PhD
  English language arts education • M Ed, MA
  exceptional education • M Ed, MA, PhD
  exercise physiology • PhD
  instructional systems • MA
  instructional technology • PhD
  K-8 mathematics and science education • M Ed, MA
  mathematics education • M Ed, MA, PhD
  music education • M Ed, MA
  physical education-exercise physiology • M Ed, MA
  pre-kindergarten handicapped endorsement • Certificate
  reading education • M Ed, MA
  school psychology • Ed S
  science education • M Ed, MA
  social science education • M Ed, MA
  vocational education • M Ed, MA
  world studies education • Certificate
  writing education • Certificate

College of Engineering and Computer Science
Dr. Neal Gallagher, Dean
Programs in:
  aerospace engineering • MSAE
  air pollution control • Certificate
  antennas and propagation • Certificate
  applied operations research • Certificate
  CAD/CAM technology • Certificate
  civil engineering • MS, MSCE, PhD, Certificate
  communications systems • Certificate
  computational methods in mechanics • Certificate
  computer engineering • MS Cp E, PhD, Certificate
  computer science • MS, PhD
  computer-integrated manufacturing • MS
  design for usability • Certificate
  digital signal processing • Certificate
  drinking water treatment • Certificate
  electrical engineering • MSEE, PhD, Certificate
  electronic circuits • Certificate
  engineering • MS, MS Cp E, MS Env E, MSAE, MSCE, MSEE, MSIE, MSME, MSMSE, PhD, Certificate
  engineering management • MS
  environmental engineering • MS, MS Env E, PhD, Certificate
  geotechnical engineering • Certificate
  hazardous waste management • Certificate
  HVAC engineering • Certificate
  industrial engineering • MSIE
  industrial engineering and management systems • PhD
  industrial ergonomics and safety • Certificate
  launch/spacecraft vehicle processing • Certificate
  materials characterization • Certificate
  materials failure analysis • Certificate
  materials science and engineering • MSMSE, PhD
  mechanical engineering • MSME, PhD, Certificate
  operations research • MS

product assurance engineering • MS
project engineering • Certificate
quality assurance • Certificate
simulation systems • MS
structural engineering • Certificate
surface water modeling • Certificate
systems simulations for engineers • Certificate
thermofluids • MSME, PhD
training simulation • Certificate
transportation engineering • Certificate
wastewater treatment • Certificate

College of Health and Public Affairs
Dr. Belinda R. McCarthy, Dean
Programs in:
biomolecular sciences • PhD
communicative disorders • MA
crime analysis • Certificate
criminal justice • MS
health and public affairs • MA, MPA, MS, MSN, MSW, PhD, Certificate, Post-Master's Certificate
health care information systems • Certificate
health services administration • MS
managed care • Certificate
medical group management • Certificate
microbiology • MS
molecular biology • MS
non-profit management • Certificate
physical therapy • MS
public administration • MPA, Certificate
public affairs • PhD
risk quality management • Certificate

School of Nursing
Dr. Jean D'Meza Leuner, Director
Programs in:
adult practitioner • Post-Master's Certificate
family practitioner • Post-Master's Certificate
nursing • MSN
nursing and health profession education • Post-Master's Certificate

School of Social Work
Dr. R. Paul Maiden, Director
Programs in:
aging studies • Certificate
non-profit management • Certificate
social work • MSW

Rosen School of Hospitality Management
Dr. Abraham C. Pizam, Dean
Program in:
hospitality and tourism management • MS

School of Optics
Dr. Eric W. Van Stryland, Director
Programs in:
applied optics • Certificate
lasers • Certificate
optical communication • Certificate
optics • MS, PhD

■ UNIVERSITY OF FLORIDA
Gainesville, FL 32611
http://www.ufl.edu/

State-supported, coed, university. CGS member. *Enrollment:* 47,858 graduate, professional, and undergraduate students; 7,651 full-time matriculated graduate/professional students (3,576 women), 2,277 part-time matriculated graduate/professional students (1,191 women). *Graduate faculty:* 2,873. *Computer facilities:* Computer purchase and lease plans are available. 472 computers available on campus for general student use. A campuswide network can be accessed from student residence rooms and from off campus. Internet access and online class registration are available. *Library facilities:* George A. Smathers Library plus 8 others. *Graduate expenses:* Tuition, state resident: part-time $205 per credit hour. Tuition, nonresident: part-time $775 per credit hour. *General application contact:* Graduate Admissions, 352-392-3261.

Find an in-depth description at www.petersons.com/gradchannel.

College of Dentistry
Dr. Teresa A. Dolan, Dean
Programs in:
dentistry • DMD
endodontics • MS, Certificate
foreign trained dentistry • Certificate
orthodontics • MS, Certificate
periodontics • MS, Certificate
prosthodontics • MS, Certificate

College of Medicine
Dr. C. Craig Tisher, Dean
Programs in:
medicine • MD, MPAS, MPH, MS, PhD
physician assistant studies • MPAS

Interdisciplinary Program in Biomedical Sciences
Dr. Wayne McCormack, Associate Dean of Graduate Education
Programs in:
anatomy and cell biology • PhD
biochemistry and molecular biology • MS, PhD
biomedical sciences • MS, PhD
clinical chemistry • MS
clinical investigation • MS
genetics • PhD
immunology and microbiology • PhD
immunology and molecular pathology • PhD
molecular cell biology • PhD
molecular genetics and microbiology • MS, PhD
neuroscience • MS, PhD
oral biology • PhD
pharmacology and therapeutics • PhD
physiology and functional genomics • PhD
physiology and pharmacology • PhD

College of Pharmacy
Dr. William H. Riffee, Dean
Programs in:
medicinal chemistry • MSP, PhD
pharmaceutics • MSP, PhD
pharmacodynamics • MSP, PhD
pharmacology • PhD
pharmacy • MSP, PhD
pharmacy health care administration • MS, MSP, PhD

College of Veterinary Medicine
Programs in:
forensic toxicology • Certificate
veterinary medical science • MS, PhD
veterinary medicine • DVM, MS, PhD, Certificate

Fredric G. Levin College of Law
Prof. Robert Jerry, Dean
Programs in:
comparative law • LL M!CL
law • JD, LL M, LL M!CL, LL M!T, SJD
taxation • LL M!T

Graduate School
Dr. Kenneth J. Gerhardt, Interim Dean

College of Agricultural and Life Sciences
Dr. Jimmy G. Cheek, Dean
Programs in:
agribusiness • MAB
agricultural education and communication • M Ag, MS, PhD
agriculture and life sciences • M Ag, MAB, MFAS, MFRC, MS, DPM, PhD
agronomy • MS, PhD
animal sciences • M Ag, MS, PhD
cell biology • MS, PhD
entomology and nematology • MS, PhD
environmental horticulture • MS, PhD
fisheries and aquatic science • MFAS, MS, PhD
food and resource economics • M Ag, MS, PhD
food science and human nutrition • MS, PhD

Peterson's Graduate Schools in the U.S. 2006

Florida

University of Florida (continued)
  forest resources and conservation • MFRC, MS, PhD
  fruit crops • MS, PhD
  microbiology • MS, PhD
  microbiology and cell science • M Ag
  plant medicine • DPM
  plant molecular and cellular biology • MS, PhD
  plant pathology • MS, PhD
  soil and water science • M Ag, MS, PhD
  vegetable crops and crop science • MS, PhD
  wildlife ecology and conservation • MS, PhD

College of Design, Construction and Planning
Dr. Jay M. Stein, Interim Dean
Programs in:
  building construction • MBC, MICM, MSBC
  design, construction and planning • M Arch, MAURP, MBC, MICM, MID, MLA, MS, MSAS, MSBC, PhD
  interior design • MID
  landscape architecture • MLA, MS
  urban and regional planning • MAURP

College of Education
Dr. Catherine Emihovich, Dean
Programs in:
  curriculum and instruction • M Ed, MAE, Ed D, PhD, Ed S
  early childhood education • M Ed, MAE, Ed D, PhD, Ed S
  education • M Ed, MAE, Ed D, PhD, Ed S
  educational leadership • M Ed, Ed D, PhD, Ed S
  educational psychology • M Ed, MAE, Ed D, PhD, Ed S
  educational technology • M Ed, MAE, Ed D, PhD, Ed S
  elementary education • M Ed, MAE, Ed D, PhD, Ed S
  English education • M Ed, MAE, Ed D, PhD, Ed S
  foreign language education • M Ed, MAE, Ed D, PhD, Ed S
  higher education administration • Ed D, PhD, Ed S
  marriage and family counseling • M Ed, Ed D, PhD, Ed S
  mathematics education • M Ed, MAE, Ed D, PhD, Ed S
  mental health counseling • M Ed, Ed D, PhD, Ed S
  reading education • M Ed, MAE, Ed D, PhD, Ed S
  research evaluation and methodology • M Ed, MAE, Ed D, PhD
  school counseling and guidance • M Ed, Ed D, Ed S
  school psychology • MAE, Ed D, PhD, Ed S
  science education • M Ed, MAE, Ed D, PhD, Ed S
  social foundations • M Ed, Ed D, PhD
  social studies education • M Ed, MAE, Ed D, PhD, Ed S
  special education • M Ed, MAE, Ed D, PhD, Ed S
  student counseling and guidance • PhD
  student personnel in higher education • M Ed

College of Engineering
Dr. Pramod P. Khargonekar, Dean
Programs in:
  aerospace engineering • ME, MS, PhD, Certificate, Engr
  agricultural and biological engineering • ME, MS, PhD, Engr
  agricultural operations management • MS, PhD
  biomedical engineering • ME, MS, PhD, Certificate, Engr
  chemical engineering • ME, MS, PhD, Engr
  civil engineering • MCE, ME, MS, PhD, Engr
  coastal and oceanographic engineering • ME, MS, PhD, Engr
  computer and information science and engineering • ME, MS, PhD
  electrical and computer engineering • ME, MS, PhD, Engr
  engineering • MCE, ME, MS, PhD, Certificate, Engr
  engineering science and engineering mechanics • ME, MS, PhD, Engr
  environmental engineering sciences • ME, MS, PhD, Engr
  industrial and systems engineering • ME, MS, PhD, Engr
  materials science and engineering • ME, MS, PhD, Engr
  nuclear engineering sciences • ME, PhD, Engr
  nuclear sciences engineering • MS

College of Fine Arts
Dr. Donald McGlothlin, Dean
Programs in:
  art • MFA
  art education • MA
  art history • MA
  fine arts • MA, MFA, MM, PhD
  museology • MA
  music • MA, MM, PhD
  music education • MM, PhD
  theatre and dance • MFA

College of Health and Human Performance
Dr. Jill W. Varnes, Interim Dean
Programs in:
  adapted physical activity • MS
  athletics training/sport medicine • PhD
  biomechanics • PhD
  community health education • MS
  exercise and sport science • MS
  exercise physiology • PhD
  health and human performance • MS, MSRS, PhD
  health behavior • PhD
  health communication • MS
  health program planning and evaluation • MS
  motor learning control • PhD
  natural resource recreation • PhD
  pedagogy of physical activity • MS
  recreation • MSRS
  recreation, parks and tourism • PhD
  school health education • MS
  sport and exercise psychology • PhD
  therapeutic recreation • PhD
  tourism • PhD
  worksite health promotion • MS

College of Journalism and Communications
Dr. Terry Hynes, Dean
Programs in:
  advertising • M Adv
  journalism • MAMC, PhD
  mass communication • MAMC, PhD
  public relations • MAMC, PhD
  telecommunication • MAMC, PhD

College of Liberal Arts and Sciences
Dr. Neil S. Sullivan, Dean
Programs in:
  African studies • Certificate
  anthropology • MA, MAT, PhD
  applied mathematics • MS, PhD
  astronomy • MS, PhD
  botany • M Ag, MS, PhD
  botany education • MST
  chemistry • MS, MST, PhD
  classical studies • MA, PhD
  communication sciences and disorders • MA, PhD
  creative writing • MFA
  English • MA, PhD
  French • MA, MAT, PhD
  geography • MA, MAT, MS, MST, PhD
  geology • MS, PhD
  geology education • MST
  German • MA, PhD
  history • MA, PhD
  international development policy • MA
  international relations • MA, MAT, PhD
  Latin American studies • MA, MAT, Certificate
  liberal arts and sciences • M Ag, M Stat, MA, MAT, MFA, MS, MS Stat, MST, Au D, PhD, Certificate
  linguistics • MA, MAT, PhD
  mathematics • MA, MS, PhD
  mathematics teaching • MAT, MST

Florida

philosophy • MA, MAT, PhD
physics • MS, PhD
physics education • MST
political campaigning • MA, Certificate
political science • MA, MAT, PhD
psychology • MA, MAT, MS, MST, PhD
public affairs • MA, Certificate
religion • MA, PhD
sociology • MA, PhD
Spanish • MA, PhD
statistics • M Stat, MS Stat, PhD
teaching English as a second language • Certificate
zoology • MS, MST, PhD

College of Nursing
Dr. Kathleen A. Long, Dean
Program in:
 nursing • MS Nsg, PhD

College of Public Health and Health Professions
Dr. Robert Frank, Dean
Programs in:
 audiology • Au D
 clinical and health psychology • PhD
 health administration • EMHA, MHA
 health services research • PhD
 occupational therapy • MHS, MOT
 physical therapy • MHS, MPT
 public health • MPH
 public health and health professions • EMHA, MHA, MHS, MOT, MPH, MPT, Au D, PhD
 rehabilitation counseling • MHS
 rehabilitation science • PhD

School of Natural Resources and Environment
Dr. Stephen R. Humphrey, Director
Programs in:
 interdisciplinary ecology • MS, PhD
 natural resources and environment • MS, PhD

Warrington College of Business Administration
Dr. John Kraft, Dean
Programs in:
 accounting • M Acc, PhD
 business administration • M Acc, MA, MAIB, MBA, MS, PhD
 decision and information sciences • MA, MS, PhD
 economics • MA, MS, PhD
 finance • PhD
 finance, real estate and urban analysis • MA
 international business • MAIB
 management • MA, MS
 marketing • MA, MS, PhD

■ **UNIVERSITY OF MIAMI**
Coral Gables, FL 33124
http://www.miami.edu/

Independent, coed, university. CGS member. *Enrollment:* 15,235 graduate, professional, and undergraduate students; 4,340 full-time matriculated graduate/professional students (2,038 women), 905 part-time matriculated graduate/professional students (611 women). *Graduate faculty:* 1,184 full-time (294 women), 5 part-time/adjunct (2 women). *Computer facilities:* Computer purchase and lease plans are available. 1,800 computers available on campus for general student use. A campuswide network can be accessed from student residence rooms and from off campus. Internet access and online class registration, online student account and grade information are available. *Library facilities:* Otto G. Richter Library plus 7 others. *Graduate expenses:* Tuition: full-time $19,526. *General application contact:* 305-284-4154.

Find an in-depth description at www.petersons.com/gradchannel.

Graduate School
Dr. Steven G. Ullmann, Dean
Program in:
 international studies • MA, PhD

College of Arts and Sciences
Dr. James H. Wyche, Vice Provost and Dean
Programs in:
 adult clinical • PhD
 applied developmental psychology • PhD
 art history • MA
 arts and sciences • MA, MALS, MFA, MS, DA, PhD
 behavioral neuroscience • PhD
 biology • MS, PhD
 ceramics/glass • MFA
 chemistry • MS
 child clinical • PhD
 computer science • MS
 English • MA, MFA, PhD
 French • PhD
 genetics and evolution • MS, PhD
 graphic design/multimedia • MFA
 health clinical • PhD
 history • MA, PhD
 inorganic chemistry • PhD
 liberal studies • MALS
 mathematics • MA, MS, DA, PhD
 organic chemistry • PhD
 painting • MFA
 philosophy • MA, PhD
 photography/digital imaging • MFA
 physical chemistry • PhD
 physics • MS, DA, PhD
 printmaking • MFA
 psychology • MS
 sculpture • MFA
 sociology • MA, PhD
 Spanish • PhD
 tropical biology, ecology, and behavior • MS, PhD

College of Engineering
Dr. M. Lewis Temares, Dean
Programs in:
 architectural engineering • MSAE
 biomedical engineering • MSBE, PhD
 civil engineering • MSCE, DA, PhD
 electrical and computer engineering • MSECE, PhD
 engineering • MS, MSAE, MSBE, MSCE, MSECE, MSEVH, MSIE, MSME, MSOES, DA, PhD
 environmental health and safety • MS, MSEVH, MSOES
 ergonomics • PhD
 industrial engineering • MSIE, PhD
 management of technology • MS
 mechanical engineering • MS, MSME, DA, PhD
 occupational ergonomics and safety • MSOES

Rosenstiel School of Marine and Atmospheric Science
Dr. Otis Brown, Dean
Programs in:
 applied marine physics • MS, PhD
 atmospheric science • MS, PhD
 marine affairs • MA, MS
 marine and atmospheric chemistry • MS, PhD
 marine and atmospheric science • MA, MS, PhD
 marine biology and fisheries • MS, PhD
 marine geology and geophysics • MS, PhD
 ocean engineering • MS
 physical oceanography • MS, PhD

School of Architecture
Programs in:
 architecture • M Arch
 computing in design • M Arch
 suburb and town design • M Arch

School of Business Administration
Dr. Harold W. Berkman, Vice Dean
Programs in:
 accounting • MBA
 business administration • MA, MBA, MP Acc, MPA, MS, MS Tax, MSPM, PhD
 computer information systems • MBA, MS
 economic development • MA, PhD
 environmental economics • PhD
 executive and professional • MBA
 finance • MBA
 human resource economics • MA, PhD
 international business • MBA
 international economics • MA, PhD
 macroeconomics • PhD
 management science • MBA, MS, PhD
 marketing • MBA
 political science • MPA

Florida

University of Miami (continued)
  professional accounting • MP Acc
  professional management • MSPM
  taxation • MS Tax

School of Communication
Edward J. Pfister, Dean
Programs in:
  communication • PhD
  communication studies • MA
  film studies • MA
  motion pictures • MFA
  print journalism • MA
  public relations • MA
  Spanish language journalism • MA
  television broadcast journalism • MA

School of Education
Dr. Samuel Yarger, Dean
Programs in:
  advanced professional studies • MS Ed, Ed S
  bilingual and bicultural counseling • Certificate
  counseling • MS Ed, Certificate
  counseling psychology • PhD
  education • MS Ed, PhD, Certificate, Ed S
  educational research and evaluation • MS Ed
  educational research/exercise physiology • PhD
  elementary education • MS Ed, Ed S
  exceptional student education, pre–K disabilities and ESOL • Ed S
  exceptional student education, pre–K disabilities and ESOL • MS Ed
  exceptional student education, reading and ESOL • MS Ed, Ed S
  exercise physiology • MS Ed
  higher education/enrollment management • MS Ed
  marriage and family therapy • MS Ed
  mathematics resource teaching • MS Ed
  mathematics/research teaching • Ed S
  mental health counseling • MS Ed
  pre-K through primary education • MS Ed, Ed S
  reading • MS Ed, PhD, Ed S
  research and evaluation • MS Ed
  special education • PhD
  sport administration • MS Ed
  sports medicine • MS Ed
  teaching and learning • PhD
  teaching English to speakers of other languages • MS Ed, PhD, Ed S

School of Music
Dr. James William Hipp, Dean
Programs in:
  accompanying and chamber music • MM, DMA
  choral conducting • MM, DMA
  composition • MM, DMA
  electronic music • MM
  instrumental conducting • MM, DMA
  instrumental performance • MM, DMA
  jazz composition • DMA
  jazz pedagogy • MM
  jazz performance • MM, DMA
  keyboard performance and pedagogy • MM, DMA
  media writing and production • MM
  multiple woodwinds • MM, DMA
  music • MM, MS, DMA, PhD, Spec M
  music business and entertainment industries • MM
  music education • MM, PhD, Spec M
  music engineering • MS
  music therapy • MM
  musicology • MM
  piano performance • MM, DMA
  studio jazz writing • MM
  vocal performance • MM, DMA

School of Nursing
Dr. Nilda Peragallo, Dean
Programs in:
  community health nursing • MSN
  nursing • PhD
  primary health care • MSN

School of Law
Michael Goodnight, Assistant Dean of Admissions
Programs in:
  comparative law • LL M
  estate planning • LL M
  inter-American law • LL M
  international law • LL M
  law • JD
  ocean and coastal law • LL M
  real property development • LL M
  taxation • LL M

School of Medicine
Dr. John Clarkson, Vice President for Medical Affairs and Dean
Program in:
  medicine • MD, MPH, MSPH, DPT, PhD

Graduate Programs in Medicine
Dr. Richard J. Bookman, Associate Dean for Graduate Studies
Programs in:
  biochemistry and molecular biology • PhD
  biomedical studies • PhD
  epidemiology • PhD
  medicine • MPH, MSPH, DPT, PhD
  microbiology and immunology • PhD
  molecular and cellular pharmacology • PhD
  molecular cell and developmental biology • PhD
  neuroscience • PhD
  physical therapy • DPT, PhD
  physiology and biophysics • PhD
  public health • MPH, MSPH

■ UNIVERSITY OF NORTH FLORIDA
Jacksonville, FL 32224-2645
http://www.unf.edu/

State-supported, coed, comprehensive institution. *Enrollment:* 13,966 graduate, professional, and undergraduate students; 592 full-time matriculated graduate/professional students (397 women), 1,091 part-time matriculated graduate/professional students (721 women). *Graduate faculty:* 295 full-time (116 women). *Computer facilities:* 750 computers available on campus for general student use. A campuswide network can be accessed from student residence rooms and from off campus. Internet access and online class registration, applications software are available. *Library facilities:* Thomas G. Carpenter Library. *Graduate expenses:* Tuition, state resident: full-time $3,050; part-time $169 per semester hour. Tuition, nonresident: full-time $12,672; part-time $704 per semester hour. Required fees: $702; $39 per semester hour. *General application contact:* Jim Owen, Assistant Director of Graduate Studies, 904-620-1360.

Coggin College of Business
Dr. Gary R. Fane, Chair
Programs in:
  accounting • M Acct
  business • M Acct, MBA, MHRM
  business administration • MBA
  human resource management • MHRM

College of Arts and Sciences
Dr. Mark E. Workman, Dean
Programs in:
  applied sociology • MS
  arts and sciences • MA, MAC, MPA, MS, MSCJ
  biology • MA, MS
  counseling psychology • MAC
  creative writing • MA
  criminal justice • MSCJ
  English • MA
  European history • MA
  general psychology • MA
  mathematical sciences • MS
  pratical philosophy and applied ethics • MA
  public administration • MPA
  statistics • MS
  US history • MA

College of Computer Sciences and Engineering
Dr. Neal Coulter, Dean
Program in:
  computer and information sciences • MS

Florida

College of Education and Human Services
Dr. Katherine Kasten, Dean
Programs in:
- administration • M Ed
- counselor education • M Ed
- education and human services • M Ed, Ed D
- educational leadership • M Ed, Ed D
- special education • M Ed

Division of Curriculum and Instruction
Dr. Sandra Gupton, Chair
Programs in:
- elementary education • M Ed
- mathematics education • M Ed
- music education • M Ed
- science education • M Ed
- secondary education • M Ed

College of Health
Dr. Pamela Chally, Dean
Programs in:
- addictions counseling • MSH
- advanced practice nursing • MSN
- aging studies • Certificate
- community health • MPH
- employee health services • MSH
- family nurse practitioner • Certificate
- health • MHA, MPH, MPT, MS, MSH, MSN, Certificate
- health administration • MHA
- health care administration • MSH
- human ecology and nutrition • MSH
- human performance • MSH
- physical therapy • MPT
- rehabilitation counseling • MS

■ UNIVERSITY OF SOUTH FLORIDA
Tampa, FL 33620-9951
http://usfweb.usf.edu/

State-supported, coed, university. CGS member. *Enrollment:* 40,945 graduate, professional, and undergraduate students; 3,588 full-time matriculated graduate/professional students (2,070 women), 3,990 part-time matriculated graduate/professional students (2,521 women). *Graduate faculty:* 1,611 full-time (625 women), 226 part-time/adjunct (87 women). *Computer facilities:* 593 computers available on campus for general student use. A campuswide network can be accessed from student residence rooms and from off campus. Internet access and online class registration are available. *Library facilities:* Tampa Campus Library plus 2 others. *General application contact:* Dr. Kelli MacCormack-Brown, Dean, Graduate School, 813-974-2846.

Find an in-depth description at www.petersons.com/gradchannel.

College of Graduate Studies
Dr. Kelli MacCormack-Brown, Dean, Graduate School
Programs in:
- applied behavior analysis • MA
- cancer biology • PhD

College of Arts and Sciences
Dr. Kathleen Heide, Interim Dean
Programs in:
- Africana studies • MLA
- aging studies • PhD
- American studies • MA
- analytical chemistry • MS, PhD
- applied anthropology • MA, PhD
- applied linguistics • MA
- applied mathematics • PhD
- arts and sciences • MA, MLA, MPA, MS, MSW, Au D, PhD
- aural rehabilitation • MS
- biochemistry • MS, PhD
- biology • PhD
- botany • MS
- clinical psychology • PhD
- communication • MA, PhD
- communication sciences and disorders • PhD
- criminology • MA, PhD
- ecology • PhD
- English • MA, PhD
- environmental science and policy • MS, PhD
- experimental psychology • PhD
- French • MA
- geography • MA
- geology • MA, PhD
- gerontology • MA
- government and international affairs • MA
- hearing science audiology • Au D
- history • MA
- hydrogeology • MA
- industrial/organizational psychology • PhD
- inorganic chemistry • MS, PhD
- liberal arts • MLA
- library and information sciences • MA
- linguistics • MA
- mass communications • MA
- mathematics • MA, PhD
- microbiology • MS
- organic chemistry • MS, PhD
- pathology and deaf education • MS
- philosophy • MA, PhD
- physical chemistry • MS, PhD
- physics • MA, PhD
- physiology • PhD
- polymer chemistry • PhD
- psychology • MA
- public administration • MPA
- rehabilitation and mental health counseling • MA
- religious studies • MA
- social work • MSW
- sociology • MA
- Spanish • MA
- speech language pathology • MS
- women's studies • MA
- zoology • MS

College of Business Administration
Steve Baumgarten, Director, MBA Programs
Programs in:
- accounting • M Acc
- business administration • Exec MBA, M Acc, MA, MBA, MS, PhD
- economics • MA, PhD
- finance • PhD
- information systems • PhD
- management • MS
- management information systems • MS
- marketing • MBA, PhD

College of Education
Colleen S. Kennedy, Dean
Programs in:
- adult education • MA, Ed D, PhD, Ed S
- career and technical education • MA
- college student affairs • M Ed
- counselor education • MA
- early childhood education • M Ed, MAT, PhD
- education • M Ed, MA, MAT, Ed D, PhD, Ed S
- education of the emotionally disturbed • MA
- education of the mentally handicapped • MA
- educational leadership • M Ed, Ed D, Ed S
- educational measurement and research • M Ed, PhD, Ed S
- elementary education • MA, Ed D, PhD, Ed S
- English education • M Ed, MA, PhD
- foreign language education • M Ed, MA
- gifted education (online) • MA
- higher education/community college teaching • MA, PhD, Ed S
- industrial-technical education • MA
- instructional technology • M Ed
- interdisciplinary education • PhD, Ed S
- learning disabilities • MA
- mathematics education • M Ed, MA, PhD, Ed S
- middle school education • M Ed
- physical education • MA
- reading education • M Ed, MA, PhD, Ed S
- school psychology • PhD, Ed S
- science education • M Ed, MA, PhD, Ed S
- second language acquisition/instructional technology • PhD
- secondary education • PhD
- social science education • M Ed, MA
- special education • Ed D, PhD, Ed S
- varying exceptionalities • MA, MAT
- vocational education • Ed D, PhD, Ed S

Peterson's Graduate Schools in the U.S. 2006

Florida

University of South Florida (continued)

College of Engineering
Louis A. Martin-Vega, Dean
Programs in:
 biomedical engineering • MSBE
 chemical engineering • M Ch E, ME, MS Ch E, PhD
 civil and environmental engineering • MEVE, MSEV
 civil engineering • MCE, MSCE, PhD
 computer engineering • M Cp E, MS Cp E
 computer science • MCS, MSCS
 computer science and engineering • PhD
 electrical engineering • ME, MSEE, PhD
 engineering • ME
 engineering management • ME, MIE, MSIE
 engineering science • PhD
 industrial engineering • ME, MIE, MSIE, PhD
 mechanical engineering • ME, MME, MSME, PhD

College of Marine Science
Dr. Peter R. Betzer, Dean
Program in:
 marine science • MS, PhD

College of Nursing
Patricia A. Burns, Dean
Program in:
 nursing • MS, PhD

College of Public Health
Dr. Stanley Graven, Interim Dean
Programs in:
 community and family health • MPH, MSPH, PhD
 environmental and occupational health • MPH, MSPH, PhD
 epidemiology and biostatistics • MPH, MSPH, PhD
 global health
 health policy and management • MHA, MPH, MSPH, PhD
 public health • MHA, MPH, MSPH, PhD
 public health practice • MPH

College of Visual and Performing Arts
Ron Jones, Dean
Programs in:
 art history • MA
 choral conducting • MM
 composition • MM
 instrumental conducting (wind instruments) • MM
 jazz studies • MM
 music education • MA, PhD
 performance • MM
 theory • MM
 visual and performing arts • MA, MM, PhD

School of Architecture and Community Design
Stephen Schreiber, Director
Program in:
 architecture and community design • M Arch

College of Medicine
Dr. Robert S. Belsole, Interim Dean
Program in:
 medicine • MD, MS, PhD

Graduate Programs in Medical Sciences
Dr. Joseph J. Krzanowski, Associate Dean for Research and Graduate Affairs
Programs in:
 anatomy • PhD
 biochemistry and molecular biology • MS, PhD
 medical microbiology and immunology • PhD
 pathology • PhD
 pharmacology and therapeutics • PhD
 physiology and biophysics • PhD

School of Physical Therapy
Martha A. Clendenin, Director
Program in:
 physical therapy • MS

■ THE UNIVERSITY OF TAMPA
Tampa, FL 33606-1490
http://www.utampa.edu/

Independent, coed, comprehensive institution. *Enrollment:* 4,661 graduate, professional, and undergraduate students; 185 full-time matriculated graduate/professional students (89 women), 351 part-time matriculated graduate/professional students (195 women). *Graduate faculty:* 57 full-time (23 women), 22 part-time/adjunct (11 women). *Computer facilities:* Computer purchase and lease plans are available. 454 computers available on campus for general student use. A campuswide network can be accessed from student residence rooms and from off campus. Internet access and online class registration are available. *Library facilities:* Macdonald Library. *Graduate expenses:* Tuition: full-time $6,660. *General application contact:* Barbara P. Strickler, Vice President for Enrollment, 888-646-2738.

John H. Sykes College of Business
Dr. Joseph E. McCann, Dean and Co-Chief Academic Officer
Programs in:
 accounting • MBA
 entrepreneurship • MBA
 information systems management • MBA
 international business • MBA
 management of technology • MSTIM
 marketing • MBA

Nursing Program
Dr. Nancy Ross, Director
Programs in:
 adult nurse practitioner • MSN
 family nurse practitioner • MSN
 nursing administration • MSN
 nursing education • MSN

■ UNIVERSITY OF WEST FLORIDA
Pensacola, FL 32514-5750
http://uwf.edu/

State-supported, coed, comprehensive institution. CGS member. *Enrollment:* 9,452 graduate, professional, and undergraduate students; 345 full-time matriculated graduate/professional students (223 women), 888 part-time matriculated graduate/professional students (591 women). *Graduate faculty:* 180 full-time (74 women), 50 part-time/adjunct (25 women). *Computer facilities:* 900 computers available on campus for general student use. A campuswide network can be accessed from student residence rooms and from off campus. Internet access and online class registration are available. *Library facilities:* Pace Library. *Graduate expenses:* Tuition, state resident: full-time $4,986; part-time $208 per credit hour. Tuition, nonresident: full-time $18,649; part-time $777 per credit hour. Tuition and fees vary according to course load, campus/location and reciprocity agreements. *General application contact:* Matt Hulett, Director of Admissions, 850-474-2230.

College of Arts and Sciences: Arts
Dr. Jane Halonen, Dean
Programs in:
 anthropology • MA
 applied politics • MA
 arts and sciences: arts • MA
 communication arts • MA
 English • MA
 history • MA
 interdisciplinary humanities • MA
 political science • MA
 psychology • MA

College of Arts and Sciences: Sciences
Dr. Jane Halonen, Dean
Programs in:

arts and sciences: sciences • MA, MAT, MS, MST
biology • MS
biology education • MST
coastal zone studies • MS
computer science • MS
general biology • MS, MST
mathematics • MA
mathematics education • MAT
statistics • MA
systems and control engineering • MS

College of Business
Dr. F. Edward Ranelli, Dean
Programs in:
  accounting • MA
  business • MA, MBA
  business administration • MBA

College of Professional Studies
Dr. Janet Pilcher, Dean
Programs in:
  alternative education • M Ed
  career and technical studies • M Ed
  clinical teaching • MA
  curriculum and instruction • M Ed
  elementary education • M Ed
  guidance and counseling • M Ed
  habilitative science • MA
  middle and secondary level education • M Ed
  primary education • M Ed
  professional studies • M Ed, MA, MPA, MS, Ed D, Ed S
  reading • M Ed
  teacher education • M Ed, MA

Division of Administrative Studies
Dr. William Tankersley, Chairperson
Program in:
  public administration • MPA

Division of Graduate Education
Dr. Rex E. Schmid, Chairperson
Programs in:
  curriculum and instruction • Ed D, Ed S
  educational leadership • M Ed, Ed S
  instructional technology • M Ed

Division of Health, Leisure, and Exercise Science
Dr. Stuart W. Ryan, Chairperson
Programs in:
  health and community education • MS
  health, leisure, and sports • MS
  physical education • MS

Georgia

■ ALBANY STATE UNIVERSITY
Albany, GA 31705-2717
http://www.alsnet.peachnet.edu/

State-supported, coed, comprehensive institution. CGS member. *Computer facilities:* 1,000 computers available on campus for general student use. A campuswide network can be accessed from student residence rooms and from off campus. Internet access, email are available. *Library facilities:* James Pendergrast Memorial Library. *General application contact:* Graduate Admissions Counselor, 229-430-5118.

College of Arts and Sciences
Programs in:
  arts and sciences • MPA, MS
  community and economic development • MPA
  criminal justice • MPA, MS
  fiscal management • MPA
  general management • MPA
  health administration and policy • MPA
  human resources management • MPA
  public policy • MPA
  water resource management and policy • MPA

College of Education
Programs in:
  biology • M Ed
  business education • M Ed
  chemistry • M Ed
  early childhood education • M Ed
  education • M Ed, Certificate, Ed S
  educational administration and supervision • M Ed, Certificate, Ed S
  English education • M Ed
  health and physical education • M Ed
  mathematics education • M Ed
  middle grades education • M Ed
  music education • M Ed
  reading education • M Ed
  school counseling • M Ed
  social science education • M Ed
  special education • M Ed

College of Health Professions
Program in:
  nursing • MS

School of Business
Program in:
  water policy • MBA

■ ARMSTRONG ATLANTIC STATE UNIVERSITY
Savannah, GA 31419-1997
http://www.armstrong.edu/

State-supported, coed, comprehensive institution. CGS member. *Enrollment:* 6,653 graduate, professional, and undergraduate students; 250 full-time matriculated graduate/professional students (197 women), 660 part-time matriculated graduate/professional students (510 women). *Graduate faculty:* 120 full-time (63 women), 21 part-time/adjunct (14 women). *Computer facilities:* 160 computers available on campus for general student use. A campuswide network can be accessed from student residence rooms and from off campus. Internet access and online class registration are available. *Library facilities:* Lane Library. *Graduate expenses:* Tuition, state resident: part-time $111 per semester hour. Tuition, nonresident: part-time $443 per semester hour. Required fees: $195 per semester hour. *General application contact:* Nikki Palamiotis, Director of Graduate Enrollment Services, 912-927-5377.

Find an in-depth description at www.petersons.com/gradchannel.

School of Graduate Studies
Dr. Michael Price, Graduate Studies, Executive Director
Programs in:
  adult education • M Ed
  computer science • MS
  criminal justice • MS
  early childhood education • M Ed
  education • M Ed
  elementary education • M Ed
  health services administration • MHSA
  history • MA
  middle grades education • M Ed
  nursing • MSN
  physical therapy • MSPT
  public health • MPH
  secondary education • M Ed
  special education • M Ed
  sports health sciences • MS

■ AUGUSTA STATE UNIVERSITY
Augusta, GA 30904-2200
http://www.aug.edu/

State-supported, coed, comprehensive institution. *Enrollment:* 6,116 graduate, professional, and undergraduate students; 140 full-time matriculated graduate/professional students (92 women), 214 part-time matriculated graduate/professional students (151 women). *Graduate faculty:* 35 full-time (18

Georgia

Augusta State University (continued)
women), 5 part-time/adjunct (3 women). *Computer facilities:* 325 computers available on campus for general student use. A campuswide network can be accessed from off campus. Internet access and online class registration are available. *Library facilities:* Reese Library plus 1 other. *Graduate expenses:* Tuition, state resident: full-time $2,654; part-time $111 per credit hour. Tuition, nonresident: full-time $10,616; part-time $443 per credit hour. Required fees: $190 per semester. *General application contact:* Katherine Sweeney, Director of Admissions and Registrar, 706-737-1405.

Graduate Studies
Dr. Samuel Sullivan, Vice President for Academic Affairs

College of Arts and Sciences
Dr. M. Edward Pettit, Associate Dean
Programs in:
  arts and sciences • MPA, MS
  political science • MPA
  psychology • MS

College of Business Administration
Jackson K. Widener, Dean
Program in:
  business administration • MBA

College of Education
Dr. Richard Harrison, Acting Dean
Programs in:
  counseling/guidance • M Ed, Ed S
  early childhood education • M Ed, Ed S
  education • M Ed, Ed S
  educational leadership • M Ed, Ed S
  middle grades education • M Ed, Ed S
  secondary education • M Ed, Ed S
  special education • M Ed, Ed S

■ **BRENAU UNIVERSITY**
Gainesville, GA 30501-3697
http://www.brenau.edu/

Independent, women only, comprehensive institution. *Enrollment:* 607 graduate, professional, and undergraduate students; 170 full-time matriculated graduate/professional students (151 women), 336 part-time matriculated graduate/professional students (250 women). *Graduate faculty:* 46 full-time (31 women), 56 part-time/adjunct (24 women). *Computer facilities:* 198 computers available on campus for general student use. A campuswide network can be accessed from student residence rooms and from off campus. Internet access and online class registration are available. *Library facilities:* Trustee Library. *Graduate expenses:* Tuition: full-time $5,584; part-time $310 per semester hour. Tuition and fees vary according to course load, campus/location and program. *General application contact:* Michelle Leavell, Graduate Admissions Coordinator, 770-534-6162.

Graduate Programs
Dr. Helen Ray, Dean

School of Business and Mass Communication
Dr. Bill Haney, Dean
Programs in:
  accounting • MBA
  healthcare management • MBA
  leadership development • MBA
  management • MBA
  organizational development • MS

School of Education and Human Development
Dr. William B. Ware, Dean
Programs in:
  early childhood education • M Ed, Ed S
  learning disabilities • M Ed
  middle grades education • M Ed, Ed S
  teaching of selected secondary majors • MAT

School of Fine Arts and Humanities
Dr. Andrea Birch, Dean
Program in:
  conflict resolution • Certificate

School of Health and Science
Dr. Gale Starich, Dean
Programs in:
  family nurse practitioner • MS
  occupational therapy • MS
  psychology • MS

■ **CLARK ATLANTA UNIVERSITY**
Atlanta, GA 30314
http://www.cau.edu/

Independent-religious, coed, university. CGS member. *Computer facilities:* 300 computers available on campus for general student use. A campuswide network can be accessed from off campus. Internet access and online class registration are available. *Library facilities:* Robert W. Woodruff Library. *General application contact:* Graduate Program Assistant, 404-880-8709.

School of Arts and Sciences
Programs in:
  African-American studies • MA
  Africana women's studies • MA, DA
  applied mathematics • MS
  arts and sciences • MA, MPA, MS, DA, PhD
  biology • MS, PhD
  computer and information science • MS
  computer science • MS
  criminal justice • MA
  economics • MA
  English • MA
  history • MA
  humanities • DA
  inorganic chemistry • MS, PhD
  organic chemistry • MS, PhD
  physical chemistry • MS, PhD
  physics • MS
  political science • MA, PhD
  public administration • MPA
  Romance languages • MA
  science education • DA
  sociology • MA

School of Business Administration
Programs in:
  business administration • MBA
  decision science • MBA
  finance • MBA
  marketing • MBA

School of Education
Programs in:
  counseling • MA, PhD
  curriculum • MA, Ed S
  education • MA, Ed D, PhD, Ed S
  education psychology • MA
  educational leadership • MA, Ed D, Ed S
  exceptional student education • MA, Ed S

School of International Affairs and Development
Programs in:
  international affairs and development • PhD
  international business and development • MA
  international development administration • MA
  international development education and planning • MA
  international relations • MA
  regional studies • MA

School of Library and Information Studies
Program in:
  library and information studies • MSLS, SLS

School of Social Work
Program in:
  social work • MSW, PhD

■ **COLUMBUS STATE UNIVERSITY**
Columbus, GA 31907-5645
http://www.colstate.edu/

State-supported, coed, comprehensive institution. *Enrollment:* 6,937 graduate, professional, and undergraduate students;

Georgia

261 full-time matriculated graduate/professional students (152 women), 672 part-time matriculated graduate/professional students (354 women). *Graduate faculty:* 84 full-time (30 women), 35 part-time/adjunct (20 women). *Computer facilities:* 300 computers available on campus for general student use. A campuswide network can be accessed from student residence rooms and from off campus. Internet access and online class registration are available. *Library facilities:* Simon Schwob Memorial Library. *Graduate expenses:* Tuition, state resident: part-time $110 per semester hour. Tuition, nonresident: part-time $443 per semester hour. Required fees: $168 per semester hour. *General application contact:* Katie Thornton, Graduate Admissions Specialist, 706-568-2035.

Graduate Studies
Dr. Martha D. Saunders, Vice President for Academic Affairs

College of Arts and Letters
Dr. William L. Chappell, Dean
Programs in:
 art education • M Ed
 arts and letters • M Ed, MM, MPA
 music education • MM
 public administration • MPA

College of Education
Dr. Thomas E. Harrison, Dean
Programs in:
 community counseling • MS
 early childhood education • M Ed, Ed S
 education • M Ed, MS, Ed S
 educational leadership • M Ed, Ed S
 instructional technology • MS
 middle grades education • M Ed, Ed S
 physical education • M Ed
 school counseling • M Ed, Ed S
 secondary education • M Ed, Ed S
 special education • Ed S

College of Science
Dr. George E. Stanton, Acting Dean
Programs in:
 applied computer science • MS
 environmental science • MS
 science • MS

D. Abbott Turner College of Business
Dr. Linda U. Hadley, Dean
Program in:
 business administration • MBA

■ EMORY UNIVERSITY
Atlanta, GA 30322-1100
http://www.emory.edu/

Independent-religious, coed, university. CGS member. *Enrollment:* 11,362 graduate, professional, and undergraduate students; 4,581 full-time matriculated graduate/professional students (2,551 women), 734 part-time matriculated graduate/professional students (439 women). *Graduate faculty:* 2,332 full-time, 311 part-time/adjunct. *Computer facilities:* 600 computers available on campus for general student use. A campuswide network can be accessed from student residence rooms and from off campus. Internet access and online class registration are available. *Library facilities:* Robert W. Woodruff Library plus 7 others. *Graduate expenses:* Tuition: part-time $1,115 per hour. Required fees: $5 per hour. $125 per term. *General application contact:* Kharen Fulton, Director of Admissions, 404-727-0184.

Find an in-depth description at www.petersons.com/gradchannel.

Candler School of Theology
Matthew L. King, Registrar
Program in:
 theology • M Div, MTS, Th M, Th D

Graduate School of Arts and Sciences
Dr. Bryan Noe, Interim Dean
Programs in:
 anthropology • PhD
 art history • PhD
 arts and sciences • M Ed, MA, MAT, MM, MPH, MS, MSM, MSPH, PhD, Certificate, DAST
 biostatistics • MPH, MSPH, PhD
 chemistry • PhD
 clinical psychology • PhD
 cognition and development • PhD
 comparative literature • Certificate
 economics • PhD
 English • PhD
 film studies • Certificate
 French • PhD
 French and educational studies • PhD
 history • PhD
 Jewish studies • MA
 mathematics • PhD
 mathematics/computer science • MS
 music • MM, MSM
 nursing • PhD
 philosophy • PhD
 physics • PhD
 political science • PhD
 psychobiology • PhD
 public health informatics • MSPH
 sociology • MA, PhD
 Spanish • PhD
 women's studies • Certificate

Division of Biological and Biomedical Sciences
Dr. Keith Wilkinson, Acting Director
Programs in:
 biochemistry, cell and developmental biology • PhD
 biological and biomedical sciences • PhD
 genetics and molecular biology • PhD
 immunology and molecular pathogenesis • PhD
 microbiology and molecular genetics • PhD
 molecular and systems pharmacology • PhD
 neuroscience • PhD
 nutrition and health sciences • PhD
 population biology, ecology and evolution • PhD

Division of Educational Studies
Dr. Eleanor C. Main, Director
Programs in:
 educational studies • MA, PhD, DAST
 middle grades teaching • M Ed, MAT
 secondary teaching • M Ed, MAT

Division of Religion
Dr. Gary Laderman, Director
Program in:
 religion • PhD

Graduate Institute of Liberal Arts
Program in:
 liberal arts • PhD

Nell Hodgson Woodruff School of Nursing
Dr. Marla E. Salmon, Dean
Programs in:
 adult and elder health advanced practice nursing • MSN
 emergency nurse practitioner • MSN
 family nurse practitioner • MSN
 family nurse-midwife • MSN
 leadership in healthcare • MSN
 nurse midwifery • MSN
 nursing administration • MSN
 pediatric advanced nursing practice • MSN
 public health nursing • MSN
 women's health nurse practitioner • MSN

Roberto C. Goizueta Business School
Thomas S. Robertson, Dean
Programs in:
 accounting • PhD
 business • EMBA, MBA, WEMBA, PhD
 finance • PhD
 information systems • PhD
 marketing • PhD
 organization and management • PhD

The Rollins School of Public Health
Dr. Jo Nell A. Usher, Assistant Dean, Student Affairs
Programs in:

Peterson's Graduate Schools in the U.S. 2006

Georgia

Emory University (continued)
  behavioral sciences and health education • MPH
  biostatistics • MPH, MSPH, PhD
  environmental/occupational health • MPH, MSPH
  epidemiology • MPH, MS, MSPH, PhD
  health care outcomes management • MPH
  health policy and management • MPH
  international health • MPH
  maternal and child health epidemiology • MPH
  prevention science • MPH
  public health • MPH, MS, MSPH, PhD
  public health informatics • MSPH
  public nutrition • MSPH

School of Law
Thomas C. Arthur, Dean
Program in:
  law • JD, LL M, Certificate

School of Medicine
Dr. Jonas A. Shulman, Executive Associate Dean, Medical Education and Student Affairs
Programs in:
  anesthesiology/patient monitoring systems • MM Sc
  clinical research • MS
  critical care medicine • MM Sc
  medicine • MD, MM Sc, MS, DPT
  ophthalmic technology • MM Sc
  physical therapy • DPT
  physician assistant • MM Sc
  radiation oncology physics • MM Sc

■ **FORT VALLEY STATE UNIVERSITY**
Fort Valley, GA 31030-4313
http://www.fvsu.edu/

State-supported, coed, comprehensive institution. *Enrollment:* 2,537 graduate, professional, and undergraduate students; 68 full-time matriculated graduate/professional students (46 women), 178 part-time matriculated graduate/professional students (141 women). *Graduate faculty:* 7 full-time (0 women), 11 part-time/adjunct (4 women). *Computer facilities:* 633 computers available on campus for general student use. A campuswide network can be accessed from off campus. On-line grade reports available. *Library facilities:* Henry A. Hunt Memorial Library plus 2 others. *Graduate expenses:* Tuition, state resident: part-time $111 per credit hour. Tuition, nonresident: part-time $402 per credit hour. Required fees: $32 per credit hour. *General application contact:* Wallace Keese, Dean of Admissions and Enrollment Management, 478-825-6307.

College of Graduate Studies and Extended Education
Dr. Seyoum Gelaye, Acting Dean
Programs in:
  animal science • MS
  early childhood education • MS
  environmental health • MPH
  guidance and counseling • MS, Ed S
  mental health counseling • MS
  middle grades education • MS
  vocational rehabilitation counseling • MS

■ **GEORGIA COLLEGE & STATE UNIVERSITY**
Milledgeville, GA 31061
http://www.gcsu.edu/

State-supported, coed, comprehensive institution. *Enrollment:* 5,695 graduate, professional, and undergraduate students; 309 full-time matriculated graduate/professional students (183 women), 627 part-time matriculated graduate/professional students (423 women). *Graduate faculty:* 282. *Computer facilities:* 425 computers available on campus for general student use. A campuswide network can be accessed from student residence rooms and from off campus. Internet access and online class registration are available. *Library facilities:* Ina Dillard Russell Library. *Graduate expenses:* Tuition, state resident: part-time $1,801 per semester. Tuition, nonresident: part-time $7,204 per semester. *General application contact:* Graduate Admissions Specialist, 478-445-6289.

Graduate School
Dr. Mark Pelton, Dean of the Extended University, Research and Graduate Services

The J. Whitney Bunting School of Business
Dr. Faye Gilbert, Dean
Programs in:
  accountancy • MACCT
  business • MBA
  information systems • MIS

School of Education
Dr. Linda Irwin-Devitis, Dean
Programs in:
  administration and supervision • M Ed, Ed S
  behavior disorders • M Ed
  early childhood education • M Ed, Ed S
  education • M Ed, MAT, Ed S
  English education • M Ed
  instructional technology • M Ed
  interrelated teaching • M Ed
  learning disabilities • M Ed
  mathematics education • M Ed
  mental retardation • M Ed
  middle grades education • M Ed, Ed S
  natural science education • M Ed, Ed S
  secondary education • MAT
  social science education • M Ed, Ed S
  special education • M Ed

School of Health Sciences
Dr. Jimmy H. Ishee, Dean
Programs in:
  health and physical education • M Ed, Ed S
  kinesiology • M Ed, Ed S
  music therapy • MMT
  nursing • MSN

School of Liberal Arts and Sciences
Dr. Beth Rushing, Dean
Programs in:
  arts and sciences • MA, MFA, MPA, MS, MSA, MSLS
  biology • MS
  creative writing • MFA
  criminal justice • MS
  English • MA
  history • MA
  logistics • MSA, MSLS
  logistics management • MSA
  logistics systems • MSLS
  public administration • MPA
  public administration and public affairs • MPA, MS
  public affairs • MS

■ **GEORGIA INSTITUTE OF TECHNOLOGY**
Atlanta, GA 30332-0001
http://www.gatech.edu/

State-supported, coed, university. CGS member. *Enrollment:* 16,643 graduate, professional, and undergraduate students; 4,451 full-time matriculated graduate/professional students, 935 part-time matriculated graduate/professional students. *Graduate faculty:* 672 full-time (95 women), 6 part-time/adjunct (1 woman). *Computer facilities:* 180 computers available on campus for general student use. A campuswide network can be accessed from student residence rooms and from off campus. Internet access and online class registration are available. *Library facilities:* Library and Information Center. *Graduate expenses:* Tuition, state resident: part-time $1,925 per semester. Tuition, nonresident: part-time $7,700 per semester. Required fees: $434 per semester. Full-time tuition and fees vary according to program. *General application contact:* Gail Potts, Manager, Graduate Academic and Enrollment Services, 404-894-4612.

Graduate Studies and Research
Programs in:
 algorithms, combinatorics, and optimization • PhD
 statistics • MS Stat

College of Architecture
Thomas D. Galloway, Dean
Programs in:
 architecture • PhD
 economic development • MCRP
 environmental planning and management • MCRP
 geographic information systems • MCRP
 integrated facility management • MS
 integrated project delivery systems • MS
 land development • MCRP
 land use planning • MCRP
 transportation • MCRP
 urban design • MCRP

College of Computing
Programs in:
 algorithms, combinatorics, and optimization • PhD
 computer science • MS, MSCS, PhD
 human computer interaction • MSHCI

College of Engineering
Dr. Jean-Lou Chameau, Dean
Programs in:
 aerospace engineering • MS, MSAE, PhD
 algorithms, combinatorics, and optimization • PhD
 bioengineering • MS Bio E, PhD
 biomedical engineering • MS Bio E
 chemical engineering • MS Ch E, PhD
 civil engineering • MS, MS Bio E, MSCE, PhD
 construction management • MS, MSCE, PhD
 electrical and computer engineering • MS, MSEE, PhD
 engineering • MS, MS Bio E, MS Ch E, MS Env E, MS Poly, MS Stat, MSAE, MSCE, MSEE, MSESM, MSHS, MSIE, MSME, MSNE, MSOR, PhD, Certificate
 engineering science and mechanics • MS, MSESM, PhD
 environmental engineering • MS, MS Env E, PhD
 health systems • MSHS
 industrial and systems engineering • MS, MS Stat, MSIE, PhD
 industrial engineering • MS, MSIE
 materials science and engineering • MS, PhD
 mechanical engineering • MS, MS Bio E, MSME, PhD
 medical physics • MS
 nuclear and radiological engineering • MSNE, PhD
 nuclear and radiological engineering and medical physics • MS, MSNE, PhD
 operations research • MSOR
 paper science and engineering • MS, PhD
 polymer, textile and fiber engineering • MS, PhD
 polymers • MS Poly
 statistics • MS Stat

College of Management
Terry Blum, Dean
Programs in:
 accounting • MBA, PhD
 e-commerce • Certificate
 engineering entrepreneurship • MBA
 entrepreneurship • Certificate
 finance • MBA, PhD
 information technology management • MBA, PhD
 international business • MBA, Certificate
 management • MBA, MS, MSMOT, PhD, Certificate
 management of technology • Certificate
 marketing • MBA, PhD
 operations management • MBA, PhD
 organizational behavior • MBA, PhD
 quantitative and computational finance • MS
 strategic management • MBA, PhD

College of Sciences
Dr. Gary B. Schuster, Dean
Programs in:
 algorithms, combinatorics, and optimization • PhD
 applied biology • MS, PhD
 applied mathematics • MS
 atmospheric chemistry and air pollution • MS, PhD
 atmospheric dynamics and climate • MS, PhD
 bioinformatics • MS, PhD
 biology • MS
 chemistry and biochemistry • MS, MS Chem, PhD
 geochemistry • MS, PhD
 human computer interaction • MSHCI
 hydrologic cycle • MS, PhD
 mathematics • PhD
 ocean sciences • MS, PhD
 orthotics and prosthetics • MS
 physics • MS, PhD
 psychology • MS, MS Psy, PhD
 quantitative and computational finance • MS
 sciences • MS, MS Chem, MS Phys, MS Psy, MS Stat, MSA Phy, MSHCI, PhD
 solid-earth and environmental geophysics • PhD
 solid-earth and evironmental geophysics • MS
 statistics • MS Stat

Ivan Allen College of Policy and International Affairs
Programs in:
 economics • MS
 history of technology • MSHT, PhD
 human computer interaction • MSHCI
 information design and technology • MSIDT
 international affairs • MS Int A
 policy and international affairs • MS, MS Int A, MS Pub P, MSHCI, MSHT, MSIDT, PhD
 public policy • MS Pub P, PhD

■ GEORGIA SOUTHERN UNIVERSITY
Statesboro, GA 30460
http://www.gasou.edu/

State-supported, coed, comprehensive institution. CGS member. *Enrollment:* 15,704 graduate, professional, and undergraduate students; 559 full-time matriculated graduate/professional students (388 women), 1,045 part-time matriculated graduate/professional students (764 women). *Graduate faculty:* 375 full-time (137 women), 26 part-time/adjunct (8 women). *Computer facilities:* 1,425 computers available on campus for general student use. A campuswide network can be accessed from student residence rooms and from off campus. Internet access and online class registration are available. *Library facilities:* Henderson Library. *Graduate expenses:* Tuition, state resident: full-time $1,998; part-time $111 per credit hour. Tuition, nonresident: full-time $7,974; part-time $443 per credit hour. Required fees: $700. Full-time tuition and fees vary according to course load and campus/location. *General application contact:* Office of Graduate Admissions, 912-681-5384.

Jack N. Averitt College of Graduate Studies
Dr. Charles J. Hardy, Dean of Graduate Studies and Research

Allen E. Paulson College of Science and Technology
Dr. Anny Morrobel-Sosa, Dean
Programs in:
 biology • MS
 mathematics • MS
 science and technology • M Tech, MS
 technology • M Tech

College of Business Administration
Dr. Ron Shiffler, Dean
Programs in:
 accounting • M Acc
 business administration • M Acc, MBA, WMBA

Georgia

Georgia Southern University (continued)
College of Education
Dr. Lucindia Chance, Dean
Programs in:
 art education • M Ed
 business education • M Ed
 counselor education • M Ed, Ed S
 curriculum studies • Ed D
 early childhood education • M Ed
 education • M Ed, Ed D, Ed S
 educational administration • Ed D
 educational leadership • M Ed, Ed S
 English education • M Ed
 French education • M Ed
 health and physical education • M Ed
 higher education • M Ed
 instructional technology • M Ed
 mathematics • M Ed
 middle grades education • M Ed
 music education • M Ed
 reading education • M Ed
 school psychology • M Ed, Ed S
 science education • M Ed
 social science education • M Ed
 Spanish education • M Ed
 special education • M Ed
 teaching and learning • Ed S
 technology education • M Ed

College of Health and Human Sciences
Dr. Frederick Whitt, Dean
Programs in:
 health and human sciences • MHSA, MPH, MS, MSN, Certificate
 health services administration • MHSA
 kinesiology • MS
 public health • MPH
 recreation administration • MS
 rural community health nurse specialist • MSN, Certificate
 rural family nurse practitioner • MSN, Certificate
 sport management • MS
 women's health nurse practitioner • Certificate

College of Liberal Arts and Social Sciences
Dr. Katherine Conway-Turner, Dean
Programs in:
 English • MA
 fine arts • MFA
 history • MA
 liberal arts and social sciences • MA, MFA, MM, MPA, MS
 music • MM
 political science • MA
 psychology • MS
 public administration • MPA
 sociology • MA

■ **GEORGIA SOUTHWESTERN STATE UNIVERSITY**
Americus, GA 31709-4693
http://www.gsw.edu/

State-supported, coed, comprehensive institution. *Enrollment:* 2,410 graduate, professional, and undergraduate students; 84 full-time matriculated graduate/professional students (65 women), 230 part-time matriculated graduate/professional students (184 women). *Graduate faculty:* 45 full-time (20 women). *Computer facilities:* 336 computers available on campus for general student use. A campuswide network can be accessed from off campus. Internet access and online class registration are available. *Library facilities:* James Earl Carter Library. *Graduate expenses:* Tuition, state resident: full-time $2,654; part-time $111 per semester hour. Tuition, nonresident: full-time $10,616; part-time $443 per semester hour. Required fees: $554; $38 per semester. Part-time tuition and fees vary according to course load. *General application contact:* Lois R. Oliver, Assistant Registrar and Graduate Admissions Specialist, 229-931-2002.

Graduate Studies
Dr. Anglia Moore, Director of Graduate Studies

School of Business
Dr. John G. Kooti, Dean
Programs in:
 business administration • MBA
 computer information systems • MBA
 social administration • MBA

School of Computer and Information Science
Dr. Boris V. Peltsverger, Interim Dean
Programs in:
 computer information systems • MS
 computer science • MS

School of Education
Dr. Mary Gendernalik Cooper, Dean
Programs in:
 business education • M Ed
 early childhood education • M Ed, Ed S
 health and physical education • M Ed
 middle grades education • M Ed, Ed S
 reading • M Ed
 secondary education • M Ed

■ **GEORGIA STATE UNIVERSITY**
Atlanta, GA 30303-3083
http://www.gsu.edu/

State-supported, coed, university. CGS member. *Computer facilities:* 500 computers available on campus for general student use. A campuswide network can be accessed from student residence rooms and from off campus. *Library facilities:* Pullen Library plus 1 other. *General application contact:* Interim Director of Admissions, 404-651-2469.

Find an in-depth description at www.petersons.com/gradchannel.

Andrew Young School of Policy Studies
Dr. Roy Bahl, Dean
Programs in:
 economics • MA, PhD
 policy studies • MA, MPA, MS, PhD
 public administration • MPA
 public policy • PhD
 urban policy studies • MS

College of Arts and Sciences
Dr. Lauren B. Adamson, Dean
Programs in:
 anthropology • MA
 applied and environmental microbiology • MS, PhD
 applied linguistics • MA
 arts and sciences • M Mu, MA, MA Ed, MAT, MFA, MHP, MS, PhD, Certificate, Ed S
 astronomy • PhD
 cell biology and physiology • MS, PhD
 chemistry • MS, PhD
 communication • MA, PhD
 composition • MA, PhD
 computer science • MS, PhD
 creative writing • MA, MFA, PhD
 English • MA, PhD
 fiction • MFA
 French • MA, Certificate
 geography • MA
 geology • MS
 German • MA, Certificate
 heritage preservation • MHP
 history • MA, PhD
 literature • MA, PhD
 mathematics • MA, MAT, MS
 molecular genetics and biochemistry • MS, PhD
 neurobiology • MS, PhD
 philosophy • MA
 physics • MS, PhD
 poetry • MFA
 political science • MA, PhD
 psychology • PhD
 rhetoric • MA, PhD
 sociology • MA, PhD
 Spanish • MA, Certificate

Georgia

technical and professional writing • MA, PhD
translation and interpretation • Certificate

School of Music
Dr. John Haberlen, Director
Program in:
music • M Mu, PhD, Ed S

Women's Studies Institute
Dr. Linda A. Bell, Director
Program in:
women's studies • MA

College of Education
Programs in:
art education • Ed S
communication disorders • M Ed
counseling • PhD
counseling psychology • PhD
early childhood education • M Ed, PhD, Ed S
education • M Ed, MLM, MS, PhD, Ed S
education of behavior/learning disabled • M Ed
education of the hearing impaired • M Ed
educational leadership • M Ed, PhD, Ed S
educational psychology • MS, PhD
educational research • MS, PhD
English education • M Ed, Ed S
exceptionalities • PhD
exercise science • MS
foreign language education • Ed S
health and physical education • M Ed
higher education • PhD
instructional technology • MS, PhD, Ed S
language and literacy education • M Ed, PhD
library media technology • MLM, PhD, Ed S
library science/media • MLM, MS, PhD, Ed S
mathematics education • M Ed, PhD, Ed S
middle childhood education • M Ed, PhD, Ed S
multiple/severe disabilities • M Ed
music education • Ed S
professional counseling • MS, PhD, Ed S
reading instruction • M Ed, Ed S
rehabilitation counseling • MS, Ed S
research, measurements and statistics • PhD
school counseling • M Ed, Ed S
school psychology • M Ed, PhD, Ed S
science education • M Ed, PhD, Ed S
secondary education • M Ed, PhD, Ed S
social foundations of education • MS, PhD
social science education • Ed S

social studies education • M Ed, PhD
special education • Ed S
sport science • PhD
sports administration • MS
sports medicine • MS
teaching English as a second language • M Ed
urban teacher leadership • MS
vocational education • M Ed

College of Health and Human Sciences
Dr. Susan Kelley, Dean
Programs in:
criminal justice • MS
nursing • MS, PhD
nutrition • MS
physical therapy • MPT
public health • MPH
social work • MSW

School of Nursing
Dr. Patsy L. Ruchala, Associate Director of Graduate Programs
Programs in:
adult health • MS
child health • MS
family nurse practitioner • MS
health promotion, protection and restoration • PhD
perinatal/women's health • MS
psychiatric/mental health • MS

School of Social Work
Dr. James Wolk, Chair
Program in:
community partnerships • MSW

College of Law
Dr. Janice C. Griffith, Dean
Program in:
law • JD

Ernest G. Welch School of Art and Design
Prof. Ralph Gilbert, Director
Programs in:
art education • MA Ed
art history • MA
studio art • MFA

J. Mack Robinson College of Business
Dr. Sidney E. Harris, Dean
Programs in:
actuarial science • MAS, MBA
business • MAS, MBA, MHA, MIB, MPA, MS, MSHA, MSRE, MTX, PhD
business analysis • MBA
computer information systems • MBA, MS, PhD
decision sciences • MS
entrepreneurship • MBA
finance • MBA, MS, PhD
general business administration • MBA
management • MBA, MS, PhD

marketing • MBA, MS, PhD
operations management • PhD
personal financial planning • MBA, MS
real estate • MBA, MSRE, PhD
risk management and insurance • MBA, MS, PhD

Institute of Health Administration
Dr. Andrew T. Sumner, Director
Program in:
health administration • MBA, MHA, MSHA

Institute of International Business
Dr. Karen D. Loch, Director
Program in:
international business • MBA, MIB

School of Accountancy
Dr. Jane Mutchler, Director
Programs in:
accountancy • MBA, MPA, MTX, PhD
taxation • MTX

W. T. Beebe Institute of Personnel and Employee Relations
Dr. Irene M. Duhaime, Director
Program in:
personnel and employee relations • MBA, MS, PhD

■ **KENNESAW STATE UNIVERSITY**
Kennesaw, GA 30144-5591
http://www.kennesaw.edu/

State-supported, coed, comprehensive institution. CGS member. *Enrollment:* 17,477 graduate, professional, and undergraduate students; 511 full-time matriculated graduate/professional students (271 women), 1,239 part-time matriculated graduate/professional students (762 women). *Graduate faculty:* 165 full-time, 48 part-time/adjunct. *Computer facilities:* 542 computers available on campus for general student use. A campuswide network can be accessed from off campus. Internet access and online class registration are available. *Library facilities:* Horace W. Sturgis Library. *Graduate expenses:* Tuition, state resident: part-time $394 per credit hour. Tuition, nonresident: part-time $726 per credit hour. *General application contact:* Selma Aydin, Coordinator of Graduate Admissions, 770-420-4377.

College of Health and Human Services
Dr. Richard Sowell, Dean
Programs in:
health and social service • MSN
primary care nurse practitioner • MSN

Peterson's Graduate Schools in the U.S. 2006

Georgia

Kennesaw State University (continued)
College of Humanities and Social Sciences
Dr. Linda M. Noble, Dean
Programs in:
  conflict management • MSCM
  humanities and social sciences • MAPW, MPA, MSCM
  professional writing • MAPW
  public administration • MPA

College of Science and Mathematics
Dr. Laurence I. Peterson, Dean
Programs in:
  applied computer science • MSaCS
  information systems • MSIS
  science and mathematics • MSIS, MSaCS

Leland and Clarice C. Bagwell College of Education
Dr. Yiping Wan, Dean
Programs in:
  early childhood • M Ed
  education • M Ed
  middle grades • M Ed
  special education • M Ed

Michael J. Coles College of Business
Dr. Timothy Mescon, Dean
Programs in:
  accounting • M Acc, MBA
  business • M Acc, MBA, MBA-EP, MBA-PE
  business administration • MBA, MBA-EP, MBA-PE
  business information systems management • MBA
  entrepreneurship • MBA
  finance • MBA
  human resources management and development • MBA
  marketing • MBA

■ **MERCER UNIVERSITY**
Macon, GA 31207-0003
http://www.mercer.edu/

Independent-religious, coed, comprehensive institution. *Enrollment:* 7,200 graduate, professional, and undergraduate students; 1,668 full-time matriculated graduate/professional students (976 women), 570 part-time matriculated graduate/professional students (342 women). *Graduate faculty:* 113 full-time (50 women), 23 part-time/adjunct (6 women). *Computer facilities:* 140 computers available on campus for general student use. A campuswide network can be accessed from student residence rooms and from off campus.

Internet access is available. *Library facilities:* Jack Tarver Library plus 3 others. *Graduate expenses:* Tuition: full-time $20,529. *General application contact:* 478-301-2700.

Graduate Studies, Cecil B. Day Campus
Georgia Baptist College of Nursing at Mercer
Dr. Susan S. Gunby, Dean
Program in:
  nursing • MSN

James and Carolyn McAfee School of Theology
Dr. R. Alan Culpepper, Dean
Program in:
  theology • M Div, D Min

Southern School of Pharmacy
Dr. Hewitt W. Matthews, Dean
Program in:
  pharmacy • Pharm D, PhD

Stetson School of Business and Economics
Karen S. Goss, Assistant Vice President of Admissions
Program in:
  business administration • MBA, XMBA

Tift College of Education
Dr. Carl R. Martray, Dean
Programs in:
  early childhood education • M Ed, Ed S
  middle grades education • M Ed, Ed S
  reading education • M Ed
  secondary education • M Ed

Graduate Studies, Macon Campus
School of Education
Dr. Carl R. Martray, Dean
Programs in:
  holistic education • M Ed
  secondary education • M Ed

School of Engineering
Dr. M. Dayne Aldridge, Dean
Programs in:
  biomedical engineering • MSE
  computer engineering • MSE
  electrical engineering • MSE
  engineering management • MSE
  mechanical engineering • MSE
  software engineering • MSE
  software systems • MS
  technical communications management • MS
  technical management • MS

Stetson School of Business and Economics
Dr. W. Carl Joiner, Dean
Program in:
  business and economics • MBA

School of Medicine
Dr. Ann C. Jobe, Dean
Program in:
  medicine • MD, MFS, MPH

Walter F. George School of Law
Michael D. Sabbath, Dean
Program in:
  law • JD

■ **NORTH GEORGIA COLLEGE & STATE UNIVERSITY**
Dahlonega, GA 30597-1001
http://www.ngcsu.edu/

State-supported, coed, comprehensive institution. *Enrollment:* 4,517 graduate, professional, and undergraduate students; 130 full-time matriculated graduate/professional students (99 women), 441 part-time matriculated graduate/professional students (337 women). *Graduate faculty:* 99 full-time (46 women), 13 part-time/adjunct (8 women). *Computer facilities:* 125 computers available on campus for general student use. A campuswide network can be accessed from student residence rooms and from off campus. Internet access and online class registration are available. *Library facilities:* Stewart Library. *Graduate expenses:* Tuition, state resident: full-time $2,654. Tuition, nonresident: full-time $8,848. *General application contact:* Dr. Donna Gessell, Director of Graduate Studies, 706-864-1543.

Graduate School
Dr. Donna Gessell, Director of Graduate Studies
Programs in:
  community counseling • MS
  early childhood education • M Ed
  educational administration • Ed S
  family practitioner • MSN
  middle grades education • M Ed
  physical therapy • MS
  public administration • MPA
  secondary education • M Ed
  special education • M Ed

■ **PIEDMONT COLLEGE**
Demorest, GA 30535-0010
http://www.piedmont.edu/

Independent-religious, coed, comprehensive institution. *Enrollment:* 2,159 graduate, professional, and undergraduate students; 395 full-time matriculated graduate/professional students (290 women), 754 part-time matriculated graduate/professional students (647 women). *Graduate faculty:* 16 full-time (7 women), 37 part-time/adjunct (17 women). *Computer facilities:*

Georgia

100 computers available on campus for general student use. A campuswide network can be accessed from student residence rooms and from off campus. Internet access, e-mail are available. *Library facilities:* Arrendale Library. *Graduate expenses:* Tuition: full-time $4,860; part-time $270 per credit hour. *General application contact:* Carol E. Kokesh, Director of Graduate Studies, 706-778-8500 Ext. 1181.

School of Business
Dr. William Piper, Dean
Program in:
 business • MBA

School of Education
Dr. Jane McFerrin, Dean
Programs in:
 early childhood education • MA, MAT
 instruction • Ed S
 secondary education • MA, MAT

■ SAVANNAH STATE UNIVERSITY
Savannah, GA 31404
http://www.savstate.edu/

State-supported, coed, comprehensive institution. *Computer facilities:* 440 computers available on campus for general student use. A campuswide network can be accessed. Internet access is available. *Library facilities:* Asa H. Gordon Library. *General application contact:* Associate Director of Admissions, 912-356-2345.

Program in Marine Science
Program in:
 marine science • MS

Program in Public Administration
Program in:
 public administration • MPA

Program in Social Work
Program in:
 social work • MSW

Program in Urban Studies
Program in:
 urban studies • MS

■ STATE UNIVERSITY OF WEST GEORGIA
Carrollton, GA 30118
http://www.westga.edu/

State-supported, coed, comprehensive institution. CGS member. *Enrollment:* 10,255 graduate, professional, and undergraduate students; 419 full-time matriculated graduate/professional students (299 women), 1,792 part-time matriculated graduate/professional students (1,396 women). *Graduate faculty:* 178 full-time (65 women). *Computer facilities:* 745 computers available on campus for general student use. A campuswide network can be accessed from student residence rooms and from off campus. Internet access and online class registration are available. *Library facilities:* Irvine Sullivan Ingram Library. *Graduate expenses:* Tuition, state resident: full-time $1,998; part-time $111 per semester hour. Tuition, nonresident: full-time $7,974; part-time $443 per semester hour. Required fees: $562; $15 per semester hour. $101 per semester. *General application contact:* Dr. Jack O. Jenkins, Dean, Graduate School, 770-836-6419.

Graduate School
Dr. Jack O. Jenkins, Dean

College of Arts and Sciences
Dr. Richard G. Miller, Dean
Programs in:
 applied computer science • MS
 arts and sciences • M Mus, MA, MPA, MS, MSN
 biology • MS
 English language and literature • MA
 gerontology • MA
 history • MA
 music education • M Mus
 music performance • M Mus
 nursing • MSN
 psychology • MA
 public administration • MPA
 rural and small town planning • MS
 sociology • MA

College of Education
Dr. Kent Layton, Dean
Programs in:
 administration and supervision • M Ed, Ed S
 art education • M Ed
 business education • M Ed, Ed S
 counseling and guidance • M Ed, Ed S
 early childhood education • M Ed, Ed S
 education • M Ed, Ed D, Ed S
 French • M Ed
 learning disabled • Ed S
 media • M Ed, Ed S
 middle grades education • M Ed, Ed S
 physical education • M Ed, Ed S
 reading education • M Ed
 school improvement • Ed D
 secondary education—English • M Ed, Ed S
 secondary education—foreign language • M Ed
 secondary education—mathematics • M Ed, Ed S
 secondary education—science • M Ed, Ed S
 secondary education—social studies • M Ed, Ed S
 Spanish • M Ed
 special education-curriculum specialist and leadership • Ed S
 special education-emotionally handicapped • M Ed, Ed S
 special education-interrelated • M Ed
 speech-language pathology • M Ed

Richards College of Business
Dr. Ara G. Volkan, Interim Chair
Programs in:
 accounting and finance • MP Acc
 business • MBA, MP Acc
 business administration • MBA

■ UNIVERSITY OF GEORGIA
Athens, GA 30602
http://www.uga.edu/

State-supported, coed, university. CGS member. *Enrollment:* 33,878 graduate, professional, and undergraduate students; 4,386 full-time matriculated graduate/professional students (2,404 women), 2,410 part-time matriculated graduate/professional students (1,621 women). *Graduate faculty:* 1,522 full-time (424 women). *Computer facilities:* 2,500 computers available on campus for general student use. A campuswide network can be accessed from student residence rooms and from off campus. Internet access and online class registration, e-mail, web pages are available. *Library facilities:* Ilah Dunlap Little Memorial Library plus 2 others. *Graduate expenses:* Tuition, state resident: part-time $161 per hour. Tuition, nonresident: part-time $690 per hour. One-time fee: $435 part-time. *General application contact:* Dr. Jan Sandor, Director of Graduate Admissions, 706-542-1787.

Find an in-depth description at www.petersons.com/gradchannel.

College of Pharmacy
Dr. Svein Oie, Dean
Programs in:
 experimental therapeutics • MS, PhD
 medicinal chemistry • MS, PhD
 pharmaceutics • MS, PhD
 pharmacology • MS, PhD
 pharmacy • Pharm D, MS, PhD
 pharmacy care administration • MS, PhD
 toxicology • MS, PhD

Georgia

University of Georgia (continued)

College of Veterinary Medicine
Dr. Keith W. Prasse, Dean
Programs in:
  avian medicine • MAM
  medical microbiology • MS, PhD
  medical microbiology and parasitology • MS, PhD
  parasitology • MS, PhD
  pathology • MS, PhD
  pharmacology • MS, PhD
  physiology • MS, PhD
  physiology and pharmacology • MS, PhD
  toxicology • MS, PhD
  veterinary anatomy • MS
  veterinary anatomy and radiology • MS
  veterinary medicine • DVM, MAM, MS, PhD

Graduate School
Dr. Maureen Grasso, Dean

College of Agricultural and Environmental Sciences
Dr. Gale A. Buchanan, Dean
Programs in:
  agricultural and environmental sciences • MA Ext, MADS, MAE, MAL, MCCS, MFT, MPPPM, MS, PhD
  agricultural economics • MAE, MS, PhD
  agricultural engineering • MS
  agricultural leadership • MAL
  agronomy • MS, PhD
  animal and dairy science • PhD
  animal and dairy sciences • MADS
  animal nutrition • PhD
  animal science • MS
  biological and agricultural engineering • PhD
  biological engineering • MS
  crop and soil sciences • MCCS
  dairy science • MS
  entomology • MS, PhD
  environmental economics • MS
  environmental health • MS
  food science • MS, PhD
  food technology • MFT
  horticulture • MS, PhD
  plant pathology • MS, PhD
  plant protection and pest management • MPPPM
  poultry science • MS, PhD
  toxicology • MS, PhD

College of Arts and Sciences
Dr. Wyatt W. Anderson, Dean
Programs in:
  analytical chemistry • MS, PhD
  anthropology • MA, PhD
  applied mathematical science • MAMS
  art • MFA, PhD
  art history • MA
  artificial intelligence • MS
  arts and sciences • MA, MAMS, MAT, MFA, MM, MS, DMA, PhD
  biochemistry and molecular biology • MS, PhD
  cellular biology • MS, PhD
  classical languages • MA
  comparative literature • MA, PhD
  computer science • MS, PhD
  drama • MFA, PhD
  English • MA, MAT, PhD
  French • MA, MAT
  genetics • MS, PhD
  geography • MA, MS, PhD
  geology • MS, PhD
  German • MA
  Greek • MA
  history • MA, PhD
  inorganic chemistry • MS, PhD
  Latin • MA
  linguistics • MA, PhD
  marine sciences • MS, PhD
  mathematics • MA, PhD
  microbiology • MS, PhD
  music • MA, MM, DMA, PhD
  organic chemistry • MS, PhD
  philosophy • MA, PhD
  physical chemistry • MS, PhD
  physics • MS, PhD
  plant biology • MS, PhD
  psychology • MS, PhD
  religion • MA
  Romance languages • MA, MAT, PhD
  sociology • MA, PhD
  Spanish • MA, MAT
  speech communication • MA, PhD
  statistics • MS, PhD

College of Education
Dr. Louis A. Castenell, Dean
Programs in:
  adult education • M Ed, MA, Ed D, PhD, Ed S
  art education • MA Ed, Ed D, Ed S
  college student affairs administration • M Ed
  communication sciences and disorders • M Ed, MA, PhD, Ed S
  counseling and student personnel services • PhD
  counseling psychology • PhD
  early childhood education • M Ed, PhD, Ed S
  education • MA
  education of the gifted • Ed D
  educational administration and policy • M Ed, Ed S
  educational psychology • M Ed, MA, PhD
  elementary and middle school education • M Ed, PhD, Ed S
  elementary education • PhD
  English education • M Ed, Ed S
  exercise science • M Ed, MS, Ed D, PhD
  guidance and counseling • M Ed
  health promotion and behavior • MPH, PhD
  health promotion and behavior and safety education • M Ed
  higher education • Ed D, PhD
  human resource and organization development • M Ed
  human resources and organization development • M Ed
  instructional technology • M Ed, PhD, Ed S
  language education • PhD
  mathematics education • M Ed, Ed D, PhD, Ed S
  middle school education • M Ed, PhD, Ed S
  music education • MM Ed, Ed D, Ed S
  occupational studies • M Ed, MAT, Ed D, PhD, Ed S
  physical education and sport studies • M Ed, MA, Ed D, PhD, Ed S
  reading education • M Ed, MA, Ed D, PhD, Ed S
  recreation and leisure studies • M Ed, MA, Ed D
  safety education • Ed S
  school psychology and school psychometry • Ed S
  science education • M Ed, Ed D, PhD, Ed S
  social foundations of education • PhD
  social science education • M Ed, Ed D, PhD
  special education • M Ed, MA, Ed D, PhD, Ed S
  teaching additional languages • M Ed, Ed S

College of Environment and Design
Dr. John F. Crowley, Dean
Programs in:
  conservation ecology and sustainable development • MS
  ecology • MS, PhD
  environment and design • MHP, MLA, MS, PhD
  historic preservation • MHP
  landscape architecture • MLA

College of Family and Consumer Sciences
Dr. Sharon Y. Nickols, Dean
Programs in:
  child and family development • MFCS, MS, PhD
  family and consumer sciences • MFCS, MS, PhD
  foods and nutrition • MFCS, MS, PhD
  housing and consumer economics • MS, PhD
  textiles, merchandising, and interiors • MS, PhD

Grady School of Journalism and Mass Communication
John Soloski, Dean
Programs in:
  journalism and mass communication • MA
  mass communication • PhD

School of Forest Resources
Dr. James M. Sweeney, Interim Dean
Program in:
  forest resources • MFR, MS, PhD

School of Social Work
Dr. Larry G. Nackerud, Acting Dean
Program in:
  social work • MSW, PhD

Terry College of Business
Dr. P. George Benson, Dean
Programs in:
  accounting • M Acc
  business • M Acc, MA, MBA, MMR, PhD
  business administration • MA, MBA, PhD
  economics • MA, PhD
  marketing research • MMR

School of Law
Rebecca H. White, Acting Dean
Program in:
  law • JD, LL M

School of Public and International Affairs
Dr. Thomas P. Lauth, Dean
Programs in:
  non profit organization • MA
  political science • MA, PhD
  public administration • MPA, DPA
  public and international affairs • MA, MPA, DPA, PhD

■ VALDOSTA STATE UNIVERSITY
Valdosta, GA 31698
http://www.valdosta.edu/

State-supported, coed, university. CGS member. *Enrollment:* 10,547 graduate, professional, and undergraduate students; 406 full-time matriculated graduate/professional students (332 women), 1,048 part-time matriculated graduate/professional students (852 women). *Graduate faculty:* 181 full-time (76 women). *Computer facilities:* 2,400 computers available on campus for general student use. A campuswide network can be accessed from student residence rooms and from off campus. Internet access and online class registration are available. *Library facilities:* Odom Library plus 2 others. *Graduate expenses:* Tuition, state resident: full-time $1,998; part-time $111 per hour. Tuition, nonresident: full-time $7,974; part-time $443 per hour. Required fees: $648. Full-time tuition and fees vary according to campus/location and program. *General application contact:* Dr. Ernestine H. Clark, Dean, 229-333-5694.

Graduate School
Dr. Ernestine H. Clark, Dean
Program in:
  library and information science • MLIS

College of Arts and Sciences
Dr. Linda Calendrillo, Dean
Programs in:
  arts and sciences • MA, MPA, MS
  city management • MPA
  criminal justice • MS
  English • MA
  history • MA
  marriage and family therapy • MS
  public human resources • MPA
  public sector • MPA
  sociology • MS

College of Business Administration
Dr. Kenneth L. Stanley, Dean
Program in:
  business administration • MBA

College of Education
Dr. Phillip Gunter, Dean
Programs in:
  adult and vocational education • Ed D
  business education • M Ed, Ed S
  clinical/counseling psychology • MS
  communication disorders • M Ed
  early childhood education • M Ed, Ed S
  education • M Ed, MME, MS, Ed D, Ed S
  educational leadership • M Ed, Ed D, Ed S
  industrial/organizational psychology • MS
  kinesiology and physical education • M Ed
  middle grades education • M Ed, Ed S
  reading • M Ed, Ed S
  school counseling • M Ed, Ed S
  school psychology • M Ed, Ed S
  secondary education • M Ed, Ed S
  special education • M Ed, Ed S
  vocational education • M Ed

College of Fine Arts
Dr. John Gaston, Dean
Programs in:
  fine arts • MME
  music education • MME

College of Nursing
Dr. Anita Huff, Dean
Programs in:
  administration • MSN
  community health nursing • MSN

Division of Social Work
Dr. Martha Giddings, Director
Program in:
  social work • MSW

Guam

■ UNIVERSITY OF GUAM
Mangilao, GU 96923
http://www.uog.edu/

Territory-supported, coed, comprehensive institution. *Computer facilities:* 150 computers available on campus for general student use. *General application contact:* Dean, Graduate School and Research, 671-735-2173.

Graduate School and Research
College of Arts and Sciences
Programs in:
  arts and sciences • MA, MS
  ceramics • MA
  environmental science • MS
  graphics • MA
  Micronesian studies • MA
  painting • MA
  tropical marine biology • MS

College of Business and Public Administration
Programs in:
  business administration • MBA
  business and public administration • MBA, MPA
  public administration • MPA

College of Education
Programs in:
  administration and supervision • M Ed
  counseling • MA
  education • M Ed, MA
  instructional leadership • MA
  language and literacy • M Ed
  secondary education • M Ed
  special education • M Ed
  teaching English to speakers of other languages • M Ed

Hawaii

■ CHAMINADE UNIVERSITY OF HONOLULU
Honolulu, HI 96816-1578
http://www.chaminade.edu/

Independent-religious, coed, comprehensive institution. *Enrollment:* 1,742 graduate, professional, and undergraduate students; 367 full-time matriculated graduate/professional students (243 women), 257 part-time matriculated graduate/professional students (158 women). *Graduate faculty:* 30. *Computer facilities:* 90 computers available on campus for general student use. A campuswide network can be

Hawaii

Chaminade University of Honolulu (continued)
accessed from student residence rooms and from off campus. Internet access is available. *Library facilities:* Sullivan Library. *Graduate expenses:* Tuition: full-time $9,720; part-time $405 per credit hour. *General application contact:* Dr. Michael Fassiotto, Assistant to the Provost, 808-739-4674.

Graduate Programs
Dr. Michael Fassiotto, Assistant to the Provost
Programs in:
  business administration • MBA
  counseling psychology • MSCP
  criminal justice administration • MSCJA
  pastoral leadership • MPL
  pastoral theology • MPT
  social science via peace education • M Ed

■ HAWAI'I PACIFIC UNIVERSITY
Honolulu, HI 96813-2785
http://www.hpu.edu/

Independent, coed, comprehensive institution. *Computer facilities:* Computer purchase and lease plans are available. 500 computers available on campus for general student use. A campuswide network can be accessed from student residence rooms and from off campus. Internet access and online class registration are available. *Library facilities:* Meader Library plus 2 others. *General application contact:* Admissions Coordinator, 808-544-1135.

Find an in-depth description at www.petersons.com/gradchannel.

College of Business Administration
Programs in:
  accounting • MBA
  e-business • MBA
  economics • MBA
  finance • MBA
  human resource management • MBA
  information systems • MBA
  international business • MBA
  management • MBA
  marketing • MBA
  travel industry management • MBA

College of Communication
Program in:
  communication • MA

College of International Studies
Program in:
  teaching English as a second language • MA

College of Liberal Arts
Program in:
  diplomacy and military studies • MA

College of Professional Studies
Programs in:
  human resource management • MA
  information systems management • MSIS
  information systems technology • MSIS
  management • MA
  organizational change • MA

School of Nursing
Programs in:
  community clinical nurse specialist • MSN
  family nurse practitioner • MSN

■ UNIVERSITY OF HAWAII AT MANOA
Honolulu, HI 96822
http://www.uhm.hawaii.edu/

State-supported, coed, university. CGS member. *Enrollment:* 19,863 graduate, professional, and undergraduate students; 4,855 matriculated graduate/professional students. *Graduate faculty:* 2,360 full-time (675 women), 278 part-time/adjunct (73 women). *Computer facilities:* 1,000 computers available on campus for general student use. A campuswide network can be accessed from student residence rooms and from off campus. Internet access, telephone registration are available. *Library facilities:* Hamilton Library plus 6 others. *Graduate expenses:* Tuition, state resident: full-time $4,464; part-time $186 per credit hour. Tuition, nonresident: full-time $10,608; part-time $442 per credit hour. Tuition and fees vary according to program. *General application contact:* Kenneth Tokuno, Assistant Dean, 808-956-8950.

Graduate Division
Dr. Rolf-Peter Kudritzki, Interim Vice Chancellor for Research and Graduate Education
Programs in:
  cell, molecular, and neurosciences • MS, PhD
  ecology, evolution and conservation biology • MS, PhD
  marine biology • MS, PhD

College of Business Administration
James Wills, Interim Dean
Programs in:
  accountancy • M Acc
  accounting • M Acc
  accounting law • M Acc
  Asian business studies • MBA
  Asian finance • PhD
  business administration • MBA
  China focused business administration • EMBA
  Chinese business studies • MBA
  decision sciences • MBA
  entrepreneurship • MBA
  executive education • EMBA, MHRM
  finance • MBA
  finance and banking • MBA
  global information technology management • PhD
  human resources management • MBA, MHRM
  information management • MBA
  information systems • M Acc
  information technology • MBA
  international accounting • PhD
  international business • MBA
  international management • PhD
  international marketing • PhD
  international organization and strategy • PhD
  Japan focused business administration • EMBA
  Japanese business studies • MBA
  marketing • MBA
  organizational behavior • MBA
  organizational management • MBA
  real estate • MBA
  student-designed track • MBA
  taxation • M Acc
  Vietnam focused business administration • EMBA

College of Education
Dr. Randy A. Hitz, Dean
Programs in:
  counselor education • M Ed
  curriculum and instruction • PhD
  education • M Ed, M Ed T, MS, PhD
  education in teaching • M Ed T
  educational administration • PhD
  educational foundations • PhD
  educational policy studies • PhD
  educational psychology • M Ed, PhD
  educational technology • M Ed
  elementary education • M Ed
  exceptionalities • PhD
  kinesiology and leisure science • MS
  secondary education • M Ed
  special education • M Ed

College of Engineering
Dr. Wai-Fah Chen, Dean
Programs in:
  civil and environmental engineering • MS, PhD
  electrical engineering • MS, PhD
  engineering • MS, PhD
  mechanical engineering • MS, PhD

College of Health Sciences and Social Welfare
Programs in:
  clinical nurse specialist • MS
  health sciences and social welfare • MS, MSW, PhD, Certificate

nurse practitioner • MS
nursing • PhD, Certificate
nursing administration • MS
social welfare • PhD
social work • MSW

College of Tropical Agriculture and Human Resources
Dr. Andrew Hashimoto, Dean
Programs in:
animal sciences • MS
bioengineering • MS
biosystems engineering • MS
botanical sciences • MS, PhD
entomology • MS, PhD
food science • MS
human nutrition, food and animal sciences • MS
molecular biosystems and bioengineering • MS, PhD
natural resources and environmental management • MS, PhD
nutritional science • MS
plant pathology • MS, PhD
tropical agriculture and human resources • MS, PhD
tropical plant and soil sciences • MS, PhD
tropical plant pathology • MS, PhD

Colleges of Arts and Sciences
Programs in:
advanced library and information science • Certificate
American studies • MA, PhD
anthropology • MA, PhD
art • MA
art history • MA
arts and humanities • M Mus, MA, MFA, PhD
arts and sciences • M Mus, MA, MFA, MLI Sc, MLIS, MPA, MS, MURP, PhD, Certificate
Asian and Asian-Western theatre • PhD
botany • MS, PhD
chemistry • MS, PhD
classics • MA
clinical psychology • PhD
communication • MA
communication and information science • PhD
community and culture • MA, PhD
community planning and social policy • MURP
computer science • PhD
dance • MA, MFA
dance and theatre • PhD
East Asian languages and literature • MA, PhD
economics • MA, PhD
English • MA, PhD
English as a second language • MA
environmental planning and management • MURP
French • MA
geography • MA, PhD
German • MA
history • MA, PhD
information and computer sciences • MS
land use and infrastructure planning • MURP
language, linguistics and literature • MA, PhD
library and information science • MLI Sc, MLIS, PhD, Certificate
linguistics • MA, PhD
mathematics • MA, PhD
microbiology • MS, PhD
music • M Mus, MA, PhD
natural sciences • MA, MLI Sc, MLIS, MS, PhD, Certificate
philosophy • MA, PhD
physics and astronomy • MS, PhD
political science • MA, PhD
psychology • MA, PhD
public administration • MPA, Certificate
religion • MA
second language acquisition • PhD
social sciences • MA, MPA, MURP, PhD, Certificate
sociology • MA, PhD
Spanish • MA
speech • MA
theatre • MA, MFA
urban and regional planning in Asia and Pacific • MURP
visual arts • MFA
zoology • MS, PhD

School of Architecture
W. H. Raymond Yeh, Dean
Program in:
architecture • D Arch

School of Hawaiian, Asian and Pacific Studies
Edgar Porter, Interim Dean
Programs in:
Asian studies • MA
Pacific Island studies • MA

School of Ocean and Earth Science and Technology
Klaus Keil, Interim Dean
Programs in:
high-pressure geophysics and geochemistry • MS, PhD
hydrogeology and engineering geology • MS, PhD
marine geology and geophysics • MS, PhD
meteorology • MS, PhD
ocean and earth science and technology • MS, PhD
ocean and resources engineering • MS, PhD
oceanography • MS, PhD
planetary geosciences and remote sensing • MS, PhD
seismology and solid-earth geophysics • MS, PhD
volcanology, petrology, and geochemistry • MS, PhD

School of Travel Industry Management
Dr. Walter Jamieson, Dean
Program in:
travel industry management • MS, Certificate

John A. Burns School of Medicine
Dr. Edwin C. Cadman, Dean
Programs in:
medicine • MD, MPH, MS, PhD
public health sciences and epidemiology • MPH, MS, PhD

Graduate Programs in Biomedical Sciences
Programs in:
anatomy and reproductive biology • MS
biochemistry • MS, PhD
biomedical sciences • MS, PhD
biophysics • MS, PhD
cell and molecular biology • MS, PhD
pharmacology • MS, PhD
physiology • MS, PhD
reproductive biology • PhD
speech pathology and audiology • MS
tropical medicine • MS, PhD

William S. Richardson School of Law
Lawrence C. Foster, Dean
Program in:
law • JD

Idaho

■ BOISE STATE UNIVERSITY
Boise, ID 83725-0399
http://www.boisestate.edu/

State-supported, coed, comprehensive institution. CGS member. *Enrollment:* 18,332 graduate, professional, and undergraduate students; 437 full-time matriculated graduate/professional students (228 women), 1,215 part-time matriculated graduate/professional students (704 women). *Graduate faculty:* 415 full-time (132 women), 242 part-time/adjunct (94 women). *Computer facilities:* 900 computers available on campus for general student use. A campuswide network can be accessed from student residence rooms and from off campus. Internet access and online class registration are available. *Library facilities:* Albertsons Library. *Graduate expenses:* Tuition, state resident: full-time $4,668.

Idaho

Boise State University (continued)
Tuition, nonresident: full-time $11,388.
General application contact: Dr. John R. Pelton, Dean, Graduate College, 208-426-3647.

Graduate College
Dr. John R. Pelton, Dean, Graduate College

College of Arts and Sciences
Dr. Phillip Eastman, Dean
Programs in:
  art • MA
  arts and sciences • MA, MFA, MM, MS, PhD
  biology • MA, MS
  computer science • MS
  creative writing • MFA
  earth science • MS
  English • MA
  fine arts, creative writing • MFA
  fine arts, visual arts • MFA
  geology • MS
  geophysics • MS, PhD
  interdisciplinary studies • MA, MS
  music • MM
  music education • MM
  pedagogy • MM
  performance • MM
  raptor biology • MS
  technical communication • MA
  visual arts • MFA

College of Business and Economics
Dr. Bill Lathen, Dean
Programs in:
  accountancy • MS
  business administration • MBA
  business and economics • MBA, MS
  management information systems • MS

College of Education
Dr. Joyce Lynn Garrett, Dean
Programs in:
  athletic administration • MPE
  curriculum and instruction • MA, Ed D
  early childhood education • MA
  education • MA, MPE, MS, Ed D
  educational technology • MS
  exercise and sport studies • MS
  mathematics education • MS
  physical education • MPE
  reading • MA
  school counseling • MA
  special education • MA

College of Engineering
Dr. Cheryl Schrader, Dean
Programs in:
  civil engineering • MS
  computer engineering • MS
  electrical engineering • MS
  engineering • MS
  instructional and performance technology • MS
  materials science and engineering • MS
  mechanical engineering • MS

College of Health Science
Dr. James Girvan, Associate Dean and Graduate Director
Programs in:
  health science • MHS
  health studies • MHS

College of Social Science and Public Affairs
Dr. Michael B. Blankenship, Dean
Programs in:
  communication • MA
  criminal justice administration • MA
  environmental and natural resources policy and administration • MPA
  general public administration • MPA
  history • MA
  social science and public affairs • MA, MPA, MSW
  social work • MSW
  state and local government policy and administration • MPA

■ IDAHO STATE UNIVERSITY
Pocatello, ID 83209

State-supported, coed, university. CGS member. *Enrollment:* 13,621 graduate, professional, and undergraduate students; 997 full-time matriculated graduate/professional students (529 women), 1,173 part-time matriculated graduate/professional students (730 women). *Graduate faculty:* 261 full-time (75 women), 9 part-time/adjunct (3 women). *Computer facilities:* 562 computers available on campus for general student use. A campuswide network can be accessed from student residence rooms and from off campus. Internet access and online class registration are available. *Library facilities:* Eli M. Oboler Library. *Graduate expenses:* Tuition, state resident: part-time $205 per credit. Tuition, nonresident: full-time $6,600; part-time $300 per credit. Required fees: $4,108. One-time fee: $35 full-time. *General application contact:* Dr. Paul Tate, Dean, 208-282-2150.

Office of Graduate Studies
Dr. Paul Tate, Dean
Programs in:
  biology • MNS
  chemistry • MNS
  general interdisciplinary • M Ed, MA
  geology • MNS
  mathematics • MNS
  physics • MNS
  waste management and environmental science • MS

College of Arts and Sciences
Dr. James Pratt, Dean
Programs in:
  anthropology • MA, MS
  art • MFA
  arts and sciences • MA, MFA, MNS, MPA, MS, DA, PhD, Postbaccalaureate Certificate
  biology • MS, DA, PhD
  chemistry • MNS, MS
  clinical laboratory science • MS
  clinical psychology • PhD
  English • MA, DA
  geology • MS
  geophysics/hydrology • MS
  geotechnology • Postbaccalaureate Certificate
  mathematics • MS, DA
  microbiology • MS
  natural science • MNS
  physics • MS
  political science • MA, DA
  psychology • MS
  public administration • MPA
  sociology • MA
  speech communication • MA
  theatre • MA

College of Business
Dr. William Stratton, Dean
Programs in:
  business administration • MBA, Postbaccalaureate Certificate
  computer information systems • MS

College of Education
Dr. Larry Harris, Dean
Programs in:
  child and family studies • M Ed
  curriculum and instruction • M Ed
  education • M Ed, 5th Year Certificate
  educational administration • M Ed, 6th Year Certificate, Ed S
  educational leadership • Ed D
  human exceptionality • M Ed
  instructional technology • M Ed
  literacy • M Ed
  physical education • MPE
  school psychology • Ed S
  special education • Ed S

College of Engineering
Dr. Jay Kunze, Dean
Programs in:
  engineering and applied science • PhD
  engineering structures and mechanics • MS
  environmental engineering • MS
  measurement and control engineering • MS
  nuclear science and engineering • MS, PhD, Postbaccalaureate Certificate

Idaho

College of Pharmacy
Dr. Joseph Steiner, Dean
Programs in:
  biopharmaceutical analysis • PhD
  biopharmaceutics • PhD
  pharmaceutical chemistry • MS
  pharmaceutical science • PhD
  pharmaceutics • MS
  pharmacognosy • MS
  pharmacokinetics • PhD
  pharmacology • MS, PhD
  pharmacy • Pharm D
  pharmacy administration • MS, PhD

College of Technology
Dr. Ranaye J. Marsh, Dean
Programs in:
  technology • MTD
  training and development • MTD

Kasiska College of Health Professions
Dr. Linda Hatzenbuehler, Dean
Programs in:
  advanced general dentistry • Post-Doctoral Certificate
  audiology • MS, Au D
  counseling • M Coun, Ed S, Postbaccalaureate Certificate
  counselor education and counseling • PhD
  deaf education • MS
  dietetics • Certificate
  family medicine • Post-Master's Certificate
  family-centered practice • Postbaccalaureate Certificate
  health education • MHE
  health professions • M Coun, MHE, MOT, MPAS, MPH, MS, Au D, DPT, PhD, Certificate, Ed S, Post-Doctoral Certificate, Post-Master's Certificate, Postbaccalaureate Certificate
  marriage and family counseling • M Coun
  mental health counseling • M Coun
  nursing • MS, Post-Master's Certificate
  occupational therapy • MOT
  physical therapy • DPT
  physician assistant studies • MPAS
  public health • MPH
  school counseling • M Coun
  speech language pathology • MS
  student affairs and college counseling • M Coun

■ **NORTHWEST NAZARENE UNIVERSITY**
Nampa, ID 83686-5897
http://www.nnu.edu/

Independent-religious, coed, comprehensive institution. *Enrollment:* 1,565 graduate, professional, and undergraduate students; 265 full-time matriculated graduate/professional students (169 women), 144 part-time matriculated graduate/professional students (77 women). *Graduate faculty:* 43 full-time (14 women), 37 part-time/adjunct (16 women). *Computer facilities:* 400 computers available on campus for general student use. A campuswide network can be accessed from student residence rooms and from off campus. Internet access, various software packages are available. *Library facilities:* John E. Riley Library. *Graduate expenses:* Tuition: full-time $3,780; part-time $315 per credit. One-time fee: $25. *General application contact:* Dr. Dennis D. Cartwright, Director, Graduate Studies, 208-467-8366.

Graduate Studies
Dr. Dennis D. Cartwright, Director, Graduate Studies
Programs in:
  business administration • MBA
  christian education • MA
  counseling • MS
  curriculum and instruction • M Ed
  educational leadership • M Ed
  exceptional child • M Ed
  reading education • M Ed
  religion • MA
  school counseling • M Ed
  social work • MSW
  spiritual formation • MA
  teacher education • M Ed

■ **UNIVERSITY OF IDAHO**
Moscow, ID 83844-2282
http://www.uidaho.edu/

State-supported, coed, university. CGS member. *Enrollment:* 12,894 graduate, professional, and undergraduate students; 1,498 full-time matriculated graduate/professional students (608 women), 1,328 part-time matriculated graduate/professional students (598 women). *Graduate faculty:* 435 full-time (104 women), 12 part-time/adjunct (5 women). *Computer facilities:* Computer purchase and lease plans are available. 670 computers available on campus for general student use. A campuswide network can be accessed from student residence rooms and from off campus. Internet access and online class registration, student evaluations of teaching are available. *Library facilities:* University of Idaho Library plus 1 other. *Graduate expenses:* Tuition, state resident: full-time $3,348. Tuition, nonresident: full-time $10,740. Required fees: $540. *General application contact:* Dr. Margrit von Braun, Associate Dean of the College of Graduate Studies, 208-885-6243.

Find an in-depth description at www.petersons.com/gradchannel.

College of Graduate Studies
Dr. Charles R. Hatch, Dean
Programs in:
  environmental science • MS
  interdisciplinary studies • MA, MS
  waste management • MS

College of Agriculture and Life Sciences
Dr. Michael J. Weiss, Dean
Programs in:
  agricultural and extension education • MS
  agricultural economics and rural sociology • MS
  agriculture and life sciences • M Engr, MAT, MS, PhD
  animal physiology • PhD
  biochemistry • MS, PhD
  biological and agricultural engineering • M Engr, MS, PhD
  entomology • MS, PhD
  food science • MS
  food science and toxicology • MAT
  home economics • MS
  microbiology • MS, PhD
  microbiology, molecular biology and biochemistry • MS, PhD
  plant protection • MS, PhD
  plant science • MS, PhD
  soil science • MS, PhD
  veterinary science • MS

College of Business and Economics
Dr. Byron Dangerfield, Dean
Programs in:
  accounting • M Acct, MS
  business and economics • M Acct, MS
  economics • MS

College of Education
Dr. Jeanne S. Christiansen, Dean
Programs in:
  adult education • M Ed, MS, Ed D, PhD, V Ed S
  business education • M Ed, Ed D, PhD
  counseling and human services • M Ed, MS, Ed D, PhD, CHSS
  education • MAT, Ed D, PhD, Ed S
  education administration • M Ed, MS, Ed D, PhD
  educational administration • M Ed
  elementary education • M Ed
  industrial technology education • M Ed, MS, Ed D, PhD
  physical education • M Ed, MS, MSPE, PhD
  professional-technical education • M Ed, MS, Ed D, PhD, Ed Sp PTE
  recreation • MS
  school psychology • Ed D, PhD, SPS
  secondary education • M Ed, MS
  special education • M Ed, MS
  teacher education • Ed S
  teaching, learning and leadership • M Ed, MAT, MS, Ed D, PhD, Ed S
  vocational education • MS

Peterson's Graduate Schools in the U.S. 2006   *www.petersons.com*   **287**

Idaho

University of Idaho (continued)
College of Engineering
Dr. David E. Thompson, Dean
Programs in:
  chemical engineering • M Engr, MAT, MS, PhD
  civil engineering • M Engr, MS, PhD
  computer engineering • M Engr, MS
  computer science • MS, PhD
  electrical engineering • M Engr, MS, PhD
  engineering • M Engr, MAT, MS, PhD
  environmental engineering • M Engr, MS, PhD
  geological engineering • MS
  mechanical engineering • M Engr, MS, PhD
  metallurgical engineering • MS, PhD
  metallurgy • MS
  mining engineering • MS, PhD
  mining engineering metallurgy • MS
  mining engineering: metallurgy • PhD
  nuclear engineering • M Engr, MS, PhD
  systems engineering • M Engr

College of Letters, Arts and Social Sciences
Dr. Joseph R. Zeller, Dean
Programs in:
  anthropology • MA
  architecture • M Arch, MA, MFA
  art • MFA
  art education • MAT
  creative writing • MFA
  English • MA, MAT
  English education • MAT
  French • MAT
  history • MA, PhD
  history education • MAT
  landscape architecture • MS
  letters, arts and social sciences • M Arch, M Mus, MA, MAT, MFA, MPA, MS, PhD
  music • M Mus, MA
  political science • MA, PhD
  psychology • MS
  public administration • MPA
  Spanish • MAT
  teaching English as a second language • MA
  theatre arts • MFA

College of Natural Resources
Steven B. Daley-Laursen, Dean
Programs in:
  fish and wildlife resources • MS, PhD
  fishery resources • MS, PhD
  forest products • MS
  forest resources • MS, PhD
  forestry, wildlife, and range sciences • PhD
  natural resources management and administration • MNR
  range science • MS, PhD
  rangeland ecology and management • MS, PhD
  recreation and park management • MS, PhD
  resource recreation and tourism • MS, PhD
  wildlife resources • MS, PhD

College of Science
Earl H. Bennett, Head
Programs in:
  bioinformatics and computational biology • MS, PhD
  biological sciences • M Nat Sci
  chemistry • MS, PhD
  chemistry education • MAT
  earth science • MAT
  geography • MS, PhD
  geography education • MAT
  geology • MS, PhD
  geophysics • MS
  hydrology • MS
  mathematics • MAT, MS, PhD
  mathematics education • MAT
  physics • MS, PhD
  physics education • MAT
  science • M Nat Sci, MAT, MS, PhD
  statistics • MS

College of Law
Donald L. Burnett, Dean
Program in:
  law • JD

Illinois

■ **ARGOSY UNIVERSITY/ SCHAUMBURG**
Schaumburg, IL 60173
http://www.argosyu.edu/

Proprietary, coed, upper-level institution. CGS member. *Graduate faculty:* 32. *Graduate expenses:* Tuition: part-time $450 per credit hour. Required fees: $40 per term. *General application contact:* Jamal Scott, Director of Admissions, 866-290-2777.

Illinois School of Professional Psychology
Dr. Jim Wasner, Head
Programs in:
  clinical psychology • MA, Psy D
  professional counseling • MA

School of Business
Dr. Rochelle Santopoalo, Head
Programs in:
  accounting • DBA
  finance • MBA
  healthcare administration • MBA
  human resources • MBA
  information systems • DBA
  international business • DBA
  international trade • MBA
  management • DBA
  marketing • MBA, DBA

School of Education
Dr. Kathy McCarville, Head
Programs in:
  curriculum and instruction • MA Ed, Ed D
  curriculum and instruction (K–12 education) • Ed S
  educational leadership • MA Ed, Ed D, Ed S

■ **AURORA UNIVERSITY**
Aurora, IL 60506-4892
http://www.aurora.edu/

Independent, coed, comprehensive institution. *Enrollment:* 3,450 graduate, professional, and undergraduate students; 637 full-time matriculated graduate/professional students (450 women), 1,167 part-time matriculated graduate/professional students (838 women). *Graduate faculty:* 37 full-time (19 women), 41 part-time/adjunct (21 women). *Computer facilities:* 90 computers available on campus for general student use. A campuswide network can be accessed from student residence rooms and from off campus. Internet access is available. *Library facilities:* Charles B. Phillips Library plus 1 other. *Graduate expenses:* Tuition: full-time $8,820; part-time $490 per credit. *General application contact:* Jane Zimmerman, Director of Graduate Recruitment, 800-742-5281.

College of Education
Dr. Mary Daly Lewis, Dean
Programs in:
  curriculum and instruction • Ed D
  education • MAT
  education and administration • Ed D
  educational leadership • MEL

Dunham School of Business
Dr. Lora deLacey, Dean
Program in:
  business • MBA

George Williams College
Dr. Kenneth Millar, Dean

School of Human Services
Programs in:
  administration of leisure services • MS
  outdoor pursuits recreation administration • MS
  outdoor therapeutic recreation administration • MS
  therapeutic recreation administration • MS

Illinois

School of Social Work
Dr. William Buffum, Director
Program in:
 social work • MSW

■ **BENEDICTINE UNIVERSITY**
Lisle, IL 60532-0900
http://www.ben.edu/

Independent-religious, coed, comprehensive institution. *Enrollment:* 2,968 graduate, professional, and undergraduate students; 173 full-time matriculated graduate/professional students (122 women), 677 part-time matriculated graduate/professional students (473 women). *Graduate faculty:* 20 full-time (6 women), 84 part-time/adjunct (40 women). *Computer facilities:* 102 computers available on campus for general student use. A campuswide network can be accessed from student residence rooms and from off campus. *Library facilities:* Benedictine Library. *Graduate expenses:* Tuition: part-time $390 per quarter hour. Full-time tuition and fees vary according to degree level and program. *General application contact:* Kari Gibbons, Director, Admissions, 630-829-6200.

Find an in-depth description at www.petersons.com/gradchannel.

Graduate Programs
Dr. Daniel Julius, Provost and Vice President for Academic Affairs
Programs in:
 business administration • MBA
 clinical exercise physiology • MS
 counseling psychology • MS
 curriculum and instruction and collaborative teaching • M Ed
 elementary education • MA Ed
 leadership and administration • M Ed
 management and organizational behavior • MS
 management information systems • MS
 organizational development • PhD
 public health • MPH
 reading and literacy • M Ed
 secondary education • MA Ed
 special education • MA Ed

■ **BRADLEY UNIVERSITY**
Peoria, IL 61625-0002
http://www.bradley.edu/

Independent, coed, comprehensive institution. CGS member. *Enrollment:* 6,137 graduate, professional, and undergraduate students; 224 full-time matriculated graduate/professional students (113 women), 608 part-time matriculated graduate/professional students (263 women). *Graduate faculty:* 252. *Computer facilities:* 2,000 computers available on campus for general student use. A campuswide network can be accessed from student residence rooms and from off campus. Internet access and online class registration are available. *Library facilities:* Cullom-Davis Library. *Graduate expenses:* Tuition: part-time $460 per semester hour. Tuition and fees vary according to course load. *General application contact:* Sarah E. Gillette, Director, Graduate Admissions, 309-677-2375.

Find an in-depth description at www.petersons.com/gradchannel.

Graduate School
Dean of the Graduate School

College of Communications and Fine Arts
Dr. Jeffrey Huberman, Dean
Programs in:
 ceramics • MA, MFA
 communications and fine arts • MA, MFA
 drawing/illustration • MA, MFA
 interdisciplinary art • MA, MFA
 painting • MA, MFA
 photography • MA, MFA
 printmaking • MA, MFA
 sculpture • MA, MFA
 visual communication and design • MA, MFA

College of Education and Health Sciences
Dr. Joan Sattler, Dean
Programs in:
 curriculum and instruction • MA
 education and health sciences • MA, MPT, MSN
 human development counseling • MA
 leadership in educational administration • MA
 leadership in human services administration • MA
 nursing • MSN
 physical therapy • MPT

College of Engineering and Technology
Dr. Richard Johnson, Dean
Programs in:
 civil engineering and construction • MSCE
 electrical engineering • MSEE
 engineering and technology • MSCE, MSEE, MSIE, MSME, MSMFE
 industrial and manufacturing engineering and technology • MSIE, MSMFE
 mechanical engineering • MSME

College of Liberal Arts and Sciences
Dr. Claire Etaugh, Dean
Programs in:
 biology • MS
 chemistry • MS
 computer information systems • MS
 computer science • MS
 English • MA
 liberal arts and sciences • MA, MLS, MS
 liberal studies • MLS

Foster College of Business Administration
Dr. Rob Baer, Dean
Programs in:
 accounting • MSA
 business administration • MBA, MSA
 executive leadership in business administration • MBA

■ **CHICAGO STATE UNIVERSITY**
Chicago, IL 60628
http://www.csu.edu/

State-supported, coed, comprehensive institution. *Enrollment:* 7,040 graduate, professional, and undergraduate students; 388 full-time matriculated graduate/professional students (257 women), 1,726 part-time matriculated graduate/professional students (1,194 women). *Graduate faculty:* 133 full-time (67 women), 87 part-time/adjunct (49 women). *Computer facilities:* 40 computers available on campus for general student use. *Library facilities:* Paul and Emily Douglas Library. *General application contact:* Daphne G. Townsend, Admissions and Records Officer II, 773-995-2404.

School of Graduate and Professional Studies
Dr. Ellen F. Rosen, Dean of Graduate Studies

College of Arts and Sciences
Dr. Rachel Lindsey, Dean
Programs in:
 arts and sciences • MA, MS, MSW
 biological sciences • MS
 counseling • MA
 criminal justice • MS
 English • MA
 geography • MA
 history, philosophy, and political science • MA
 mathematics and computer science • MS
 social work and sociology • MSW

College of Education
Dr. Sandra Westbrooks, Acting Dean
Programs in:
 bilingual/bicultural education • MS Ed
 early childhood education • MAT, MS Ed

Peterson's Graduate Schools in the U.S. 2006

Illinois

Chicago State University (continued)
    education • MA, MAT, MS, MS Ed
    educational leadership • MA
    elementary education • MAT, MS Ed
    general administration • MA
    higher education administration • MA
    library science and communications media • MS
    physical education • MS Ed
    reading • MS Ed
    secondary education • MAT, MS Ed
    special education • MS Ed
    teaching in non-school settings • MS Ed
    teaching of reading • MS Ed
    technology and education • MS Ed

■ COLUMBIA COLLEGE CHICAGO
Chicago, IL 60605-1996
http://www.colum.edu/

Independent, coed, comprehensive institution. *Enrollment:* 9,915 graduate, professional, and undergraduate students; 343 full-time matriculated graduate/professional students (248 women), 307 part-time matriculated graduate/professional students (231 women). *Graduate faculty:* 9 full-time, 28 part-time/adjunct. *Computer facilities:* 730 computers available on campus for general student use. A campuswide network can be accessed. Internet access is available. *Library facilities:* Columbia College Library. *Graduate expenses:* Tuition: full-time $12,990; part-time $525 per credit hour. Required fees: $390; $85 per term. Tuition and fees vary according to course load and program. *General application contact:* Keith Cleveland, Acting Dean of the Graduate School, 312-344-7261.

Find an in-depth description at www.petersons.com/gradchannel.

Graduate School
Keith Cleveland, Acting Dean of the Graduate School
Programs in:
    architectural studies • MFA
    arts, entertainment, and media management • MA
    creative writing • MFA
    dance/movement therapy • MA, Certificate
    elementary • MAT
    English • MAT
    film and video • MFA
    interdisciplinary arts • MA, MAT
    interdisciplinary book and paper arts • MFA
    interior design • MFA
    multicultural education • MA
    photography • MA, MFA
    poetry • MFA
    public affairs journalism • MA
    teaching of writing • MA
    urban teaching • MA

■ CONCORDIA UNIVERSITY
River Forest, IL 60305-1499
http://www.curf.edu/

Independent-religious, coed, comprehensive institution. CGS member. *Computer facilities:* 70 computers available on campus for general student use. A campuswide network can be accessed from student residence rooms and from off campus. Internet access is available. *Library facilities:* Klinck Memorial Library plus 10 others. *General application contact:* Director of Graduate Admissions, 708-209-3454.

College of Arts and Sciences
Programs in:
    church music • MCM
    community counseling • MA
    gerontology • MA
    human services • MA
    liberal studies • MA
    music • MA
    psychology • MA
    religion • MA

College of Education
Programs in:
    Christian education • MA
    curriculum and instruction • MA
    early childhood education • MA, Ed D
    educational leadership • Ed D
    reading education • MA
    school administration • MA, CAS
    school counseling • MA, CAS
    teaching • MAT
    urban teaching • MA

■ DEPAUL UNIVERSITY
Chicago, IL 60604-2287
http://www.depaul.edu/

Independent-religious, coed, university. *Enrollment:* 23,610 graduate, professional, and undergraduate students; 5,022 full-time matriculated graduate/professional students (2,615 women), 4,003 part-time matriculated graduate/professional students (1,999 women). *Graduate faculty:* 735 full-time (300 women), 1,470 part-time/adjunct (664 women). *Computer facilities:* 850 computers available on campus for general student use. A campuswide network can be accessed from student residence rooms and from off campus. Internet access and online class registration are available. *Library facilities:* John T. Richardson Library plus 2 others. *Graduate expenses:* Tuition: part-time $395 per hour. *General application contact:* 312-362-6709.

Find an in-depth description at www.petersons.com/gradchannel.

Charles H. Kellstadt Graduate School of Business
Robert T. Ryan, Assistant Dean and Director
Programs in:
    business • M Acc, MA, MBA, MS, MSA, MSF, MSHR, MSMA, MSMIS, MST
    business economics • MBA
    economics • MA
    entrepreneurship • MBA
    finance • MBA, MSF
    financial analysis • MBA
    healthcare management • MBA
    human resource management • MBA, MSHR
    international business • MBA
    international marketing and finance • MBA
    leadership/change management • MBA
    management planning and strategy • MBA
    managerial finance • MBA
    marketing • MBA
    marketing analysis • MS
    operations management • MBA
    real estate finance and investment • MBA

School of Accountancy and Management Information Systems
Dr. Ray Whittington, Director
Programs in:
    accountancy • M Acc, MSA
    accountancy and management information systems • M Acc, MBA, MS, MSA, MSMIS, MST
    e-business • MBA, MS
    financial management and control • MBA
    management accounting • MBA
    management information systems • MBA, MSMIS
    taxation • MST

College of Law
Glen Weissenberger, Dean
Program in:
    law • JD, LL M

College of Liberal Arts and Sciences
Michael Mezey, Dean
Programs in:
    advanced practice nursing • MS
    applied physics • MS
    applied statistics • MS
    association management • MS
    biochemistry • MS
    biological sciences • MA, MS

Illinois

chemistry • MS
child clinical psychology • MA, PhD
clinical psychology • MA, PhD
community clinical psychology • MA, PhD
community psychology • PhD
corporate communication • MA
English • MA
experimental psychology • MA, PhD
financial administration management • Certificate
fundraising and philanthropy • MS
general psychology • MS
health administration • Certificate
health law administration • MS
healthcare administration • MS
higher education administration • MS
history • MA
industrial/organizational psychology • MA, PhD
interdisciplinary studies • MA, MS
international studies • MA
liberal arts and sciences • MA, MS, PhD, Certificate
liberal studies • MA
mathematics education • MA
metropolitan planning • MS, Certificate
multicultural communication • MA
new media studies • MA
non-profit administration • MS
nonprofit organization management • MS
nurse anesthesia • MS
philosophy • MA, PhD
polymer chemistry and coatings technology • MS
public administration • MS
public policy • MS
public service management • MS
public services • Certificate
sociology • MA
women's studies • Certificate
writing • MA

School for New Learning
Dr. Russ Rogers, Program Director
Programs in:
applied technology • MA
integrated professional studies • MA

School of Computer Science, Telecommunications, and Information Systems
Dr. Helmut Epp, Dean
Programs in:
computer graphics and animation • MS
computer science • MS, PhD
computer science, telecommunications, and information systems • MA, MBA, MS, MSMIS, PhD
distributed systems • MS
e-commerce technology • MS
human-computer interaction • MS
information systems • MS

management information systems • MS
software engineering • MS
telecommunications systems • MS

School of Education
Dr. Sandra Jackson, Dean
Programs in:
administration and supervision • M Ed, MA
agencies, family concerns, and higher education • M Ed, MA
Catholic school leadership • M Ed, MA
curriculum studies/development • M Ed, MA, Ed D
education • M Ed, MA, Ed D
educational leadership • Ed D
elementary education • M Ed, MA
elementary schools • M Ed, MA
human development and learning • MA
human services management • M Ed, MA
physical education • M Ed, MA
reading and learning disabilities • M Ed, MA
secondary education • M Ed, MA
secondary schools • M Ed, MA

School of Music
Dr. Donald E. Casey, Dean
Programs in:
applied music (performance) • MM, Certificate
composition • MM
music • MM, Certificate
music composition • MM
music education • MM
performance • MM

The Theatre School
John Culbert, Chair
Programs in:
acting • MFA, Certificate
directing • MFA
theatre • MFA, Certificate

■ DOMINICAN UNIVERSITY
River Forest, IL 60305-1099
http://www.dom.edu/

Independent-religious, coed, comprehensive institution. *Enrollment:* 2,900 graduate, professional, and undergraduate students; 355 full-time matriculated graduate/professional students (223 women), 1,334 part-time matriculated graduate/professional students (1,035 women). *Graduate faculty:* 27 full-time (14 women), 44 part-time/adjunct (23 women). *Computer facilities:* 212 computers available on campus for general student use. A campuswide network can be accessed from student residence rooms and from off campus. Internet access and online class registration, email are available. *Library facilities:*

Rebecca Crown Library. *Graduate expenses:* Tuition: part-time $575 per hour. Tuition and fees vary according to program. *General application contact:* Roberta McMahon, Assistant Dean for Graduate Business Programs, 708-524-6507.

Graduate School of Business
Dr. Molly Burke, Dean
Programs in:
accounting • MSA
business administration • MBA
computer information systems • MSCIS
management information systems • MSMIS
organization management • MSOM

Graduate School of Education
Sr. Colleen McNicholas, Dean
Programs in:
curriculum and instruction • MA Ed
early childhood education • MS
education • MAT
educational administration • MA
special education • MS

Graduate School of Library and Information Science
Prudence Dalrymple, Dean
Programs in:
library and information science • MLIS, MSMIS, CSS
management information systems • MSMIS

Graduate School of Social Work
Vimala Pillari, Dean
Program in:
social work • MSW

Institute for Adult Learning
Bryan J. Watkins, Executive Director
Program in:
adult learning • MSOL

■ EASTERN ILLINOIS UNIVERSITY
Charleston, IL 61920-3099
http://www.eiu.edu/

State-supported, coed, comprehensive institution. CGS member. *Enrollment:* 11,522 graduate, professional, and undergraduate students; 652 full-time matriculated graduate/professional students, 1,025 part-time matriculated graduate/professional students. *Graduate faculty:* 448. *Computer facilities:* Computer purchase and lease plans are available. 1,336 computers available on campus for general student use. A campuswide network can be accessed from student residence rooms and from off campus. Internet access and online class registration are available. *Library facilities:* Booth Library. *Graduate*

Illinois

Eastern Illinois University (continued) expenses: Tuition, state resident: part-time $125 per semester hour. Tuition, nonresident: part-time $375 per semester hour. Required fees: $53 per semester hour. $698 per semester. *General application contact:* Ann Shafer, Admissions Counselor, 217-581-7489.

Find an in-depth description at www.petersons.com/gradchannel.

Graduate School
Dr. Robert M. Augustine, Dean

College of Arts and Humanities
James Johnson, Dean
Programs in:
art • MA
arts and humanities • MA
English • MA
historical administration • MA
history • MA
music • MA
speech-communication • MA

College of Education and Professional Studies
Dr. Charles Rohn, Dean
Programs in:
college student affairs • MS
community counseling • MS
education and professional studies • MS, MS Ed, Ed S
educational administration • MS Ed, Ed S
elementary education • MS Ed
physical education • MS
school counseling • MS
special education • MS Ed

College of Sciences
Dr. Mary Ann Hanner, Dean
Programs in:
biological sciences • MS
chemistry • MS
clinical psychology • MA
communication disorders and sciences • MS
economics • MA
mathematics • MA
mathematics and computer science • MA
mathematics education • MA
natural sciences • MS
political science • MA
psychology • MA, SSP
school psychology • SSP

Lumpkin College of Business and Applied Sciences
Dr. Diane Hoadley, Dean
Programs in:
business administration • MBA, Certificate
business and applied sciences • MA, MBA, MS, Certificate
computer technology • Certificate
dietetics • MS
family and consumer sciences • MS
gerontology • MA
quality systems • Certificate
technology • MS
work performance improvement • Certificate

■ **GOVERNORS STATE UNIVERSITY**
University Park, IL 60466-0975
http://www.govst.edu/

State-supported, coed, upper-level institution. *Enrollment:* 5,317 graduate, professional, and undergraduate students; 163 full-time matriculated graduate/professional students (124 women), 2,699 part-time matriculated graduate/professional students (1,911 women). *Graduate faculty:* 147 full-time (55 women), 122 part-time/adjunct (54 women). *Computer facilities:* 165 computers available on campus for general student use. A campuswide network can be accessed from off campus. *Library facilities:* University Library. *Graduate expenses:* Tuition, state resident: part-time $130 per semester hour. Tuition, nonresident: part-time $390 per semester hour. Required fees: $15 per semester hour. *General application contact:* William T. Craig, Associate Director of Admission, 708-534-4492.

College of Arts and Sciences
Dr. Roger Oden, Dean
Programs in:
analytical chemistry • MS
art • MA
arts and sciences • MA, MS
communication studies • MA
computer science • MS
English • MA
environmental biology • MS
instructional and training technology • MA
media communication • MA
political and justice studies • MA

College of Business and Public Administration
Dr. William Nowlin, Dean
Programs in:
accounting • MS
business administration • MBA
business and public administration • MBA, MPA, MS
management information systems • MS
public administration • MPA

College of Education
Dr. Roger V. Bennett, Acting Dean
Programs in:
counseling • MA
early childhood education • MA
education • MA
educational administration and supervision • MA
multi-categorical special education • MA
psychology • MA
reading • MA

College of Health Professions
Dr. Linda Samson, Dean
Programs in:
addictions studies • MHS
communication disorders • MHS
health administration • MHA
health professions • MHA, MHS, MOT, MPT, MSN, MSW
nursing • MSN
occupational therapy • MOT
physical therapy • MPT
social work • MSW

■ **ILLINOIS INSTITUTE OF TECHNOLOGY**
Chicago, IL 60616-3793
http://www.iit.edu/

Independent, coed, university. CGS member. *Enrollment:* 6,167 graduate, professional, and undergraduate students; 2,477 full-time matriculated graduate/professional students (886 women), 1,487 part-time matriculated graduate/professional students (467 women). *Graduate faculty:* 294 full-time (53 women), 283 part-time/adjunct (52 women). *Computer facilities:* Computer purchase and lease plans are available. 650 computers available on campus for general student use. A campuswide network can be accessed from student residence rooms and from off campus. Internet access and online class registration are available. *Library facilities:* Paul V. Galvin Library plus 5 others. *Graduate expenses:* Tuition: part-time $628 per credit. Tuition and fees vary according to course load and program. *General application contact:* Kelly A. Cherwin, Director of Graduate Outreach, 312-567-7974.

Chicago-Kent College of Law
Harold J. Krent, Dean
Programs in:
financial services • LL M
international intellectual property • LL M
international law • LL M
law • JD
taxation • LL M

Graduate College
Kelly A. Cherwin, Dean of Graduate College

Programs in:
  analytical chemistry • M Ch, MS, PhD
  applied mathematics • MS, PhD
  biochemistry • MS
  biology • MBS, MS, PhD
  biotechnology • MS
  cell biology • MS
  chemistry • M Ch, M Chem, MS, PhD
  computer science • MCS, MS, PhD
  financial mathematics • MS
  food safety and technology • MS
  health physics • MHP
  industrial technology and operations • MITO
  information architecture • PhD
  information architecture • MS
  information technology and management • MITM
  inorganic chemistry • MS, PhD
  manufacturing/industrial • MITO
  materials and chemical synthesis • M Ch
  mathematics education • MME, MS, PhD
  microbiology • MS
  molecular biochemistry and biophysics • MS, PhD
  organic chemistry • MS, PhD
  physical chemistry • MS, PhD
  physics • MHP, MS, PhD
  polymer chemistry • MS, PhD
  public administration • MPA
  public works • MPW
  science and letters • M Ch, M Chem, MBS, MCS, MHP, MME, MPA, MPW, MS, MSE, MST, MTSE, PhD
  science education • MS, MSE, PhD
  teaching • MST
  technical communication • MS, PhD
  technical communication and information design • MS
  telecommunications and software engineering • MTSE

Armour College of Engineering
Dr. Hamid Arastoopour, Dean
Programs in:
  architectural engineering • M Arch E
  biomedical engineering • PhD
  biomedical science and engineering • PhD
  chemical engineering • M Ch E, MS, PhD
  civil engineering • MS, PhD
  computer engineering • MS, PhD
  computer/electrical engineering • MS
  construction engineering and management • MCEM
  electrical and computer engineering • MECE
  electrical engineering • MS, PhD
  electricity markets • MEM
  engineering and sciences • M Arch E, M Ch E, M Env E, M Geoenv E, M Trans E, MCEM, MECE, MEM, MFPE, MGE, MGE, MMAE, MME, MMME, MNE, MPW, MS, MSE, MTSE, PhD
  environmental engineering • M Env E, MS, PhD
  environmental management • MS
  food process engineering • MFPE
  food processing engineering • MS
  gas engineering • MGE
  geoenvironmental engineering • M Geoenv E
  geotechnical engineering • MGE
  manufacturing engineering • MME, MS
  materials science and engineering • MMME, MS, PhD
  mechanical and aerospace engineering • MMAE, MS, PhD
  network engineering • MNE
  public works • MPW
  structural engineering • MSE
  telecommunications and software engineering • MTSE
  transportation engineering • M Trans E

College of Architecture
Donna Robertson, Dean
Program in:
  architecture • M Ar, PhD

Institute of Design
Patrick Whitney, Director
Programs in:
  communication design • M Des, PhD
  design methods • MSDM
  design planning • M Des
  design research • PhD
  product design • M Des, PhD
  research • M Des

Institute of Psychology
Dr. M. Ellen Mitchell, Director
Programs in:
  clinical psychology • PhD
  industrial/organizational psychology • PhD
  personnel/human resource development • MS
  psychology • MS
  rehabilitation counseling • MS
  rehabilitation psychology • PhD

Stuart Graduate School of Business
Dr. M. Zia Hassan, Interim Dean
Programs in:
  business • MBA, MS, PhD
  e-business • MBA
  entrepreneurship • MBA
  environmental management • MS
  finance • MBA
  information management • MBA
  international business • MBA
  management science • MBA
  marketing • MBA
  marketing communication • MS
  operations management • MBA
  organization and management • MBA
  quality management • MBA
  strategic management • MBA
  sustainable enterprise • MBA

Center for Financial Markets
Henry H. Perritt, Dean
Program in:
  financial markets • MS

■ ILLINOIS STATE UNIVERSITY
Normal, IL 61790-2200
http://www.ilstu.edu/

State-supported, coed, university. CGS member. *Enrollment:* 20,860 graduate, professional, and undergraduate students; 1,105 full-time matriculated graduate/professional students (695 women), 1,245 part-time matriculated graduate/professional students (812 women). *Graduate faculty:* 609 full-time (231 women), 22 part-time/adjunct (5 women). *Computer facilities:* 2,100 computers available on campus for general student use. A campuswide network can be accessed from student residence rooms and from off campus. Internet access is available. *Library facilities:* Milner Library. *Graduate expenses:* Tuition, state resident: full-time $3,322; part-time $138 per hour. Tuition, nonresident: full-time $6,922; part-time $288 per hour. Required fees: $974; $41 per hour. *General application contact:* Dr. Gary McGinnis, Associate Vice President of Research, Graduate Studies and International Education, 309-438-2583.

Find an in-depth description at www.petersons.com/gradchannel.

Graduate School
Dr. Gary McGinnis, Associate Vice President of Research, Graduate Studies and International Education

College of Applied Science and Technology
Dr. J. Robert Rossman, Dean
Programs in:
  agribusiness • MS
  applied science and technology • MA, MS
  criminal justice sciences • MA, MS
  environmental health and safety • MS
  family and consumer sciences • MA, MS
  health education • MS
  information technology • MS
  physical education • MS
  technology • MS

College of Arts and Sciences
Dr. Roberta Trites, Interim Dean
Programs in:
  arts and sciences • MA, MS, MSW, PhD, SSP
  biological sciences • MS
  biology • PhD

Illinois

Illinois State University (continued)
  biotechnology • MS
  botany • PhD
  chemistry • MS
  communication • MA, MS
  ecology • PhD
  economics • MA, MS
  English • MA, MS, PhD
  English studies • PhD
  French • MA
  French and German • MA
  French and Spanish • MA
  genetics • PhD
  geohydrology • MS
  German • MA
  German and Spanish • MA
  historical archaeology • MA, MS
  history • MA, MS
  mathematics • MA, MS
  mathematics education • PhD
  microbiology • PhD
  physiology • PhD
  politics and government • MA, MS
  psychology • MA, MS
  school psychology • PhD, SSP
  social work • MSW
  sociology • MA, MS
  Spanish • MA
  speech pathology and audiology • MA, MS
  writing • MA, MS
  zoology • PhD

College of Business
Dr. Dixie Mills, Dean
Programs in:
  accounting • MPA, MS
  business • MBA, MPA, MS
  business administration • MBA

College of Education
Dr. Dianne Ashby, Dean
Programs in:
  curriculum and instruction • MS, MS Ed, Ed D
  education • MS, MS Ed, Ed D, PhD
  educational administration and foundations • MS, MS Ed, Ed D, PhD
  educational policies • Ed D
  guidance and counseling • MS, MS Ed
  postsecondary education • Ed D
  reading • MS Ed
  special education • MS, MS Ed, Ed D
  supervision • Ed D

College of Fine Arts
Dr. John Walker, Dean
Programs in:
  art history • MA, MS
  arts technology • MS
  ceramics • MFA, MS
  drawing • MFA, MS
  fibers • MFA, MS
  fine arts • MA, MFA, MM, MM Ed, MS
  glass • MFA, MS
  graphic design • MFA, MS
  metals • MFA, MS
  music • MM, MM Ed
  painting • MFA, MS
  photography • MFA, MS
  printmaking • MFA, MS
  sculpture • MFA, MS
  theatre • MA, MFA, MS

Mennonite College of Nursing
Nancy Ridenour, Dean
Programs in:
  family nurse practitioner • PMC
  nursing • MSN

■ **LEWIS UNIVERSITY**
Romeoville, IL 60446
http://www.lewisu.edu/

Independent-religious, coed, comprehensive institution. *Computer facilities:* 310 computers available on campus for general student use. A campuswide network can be accessed from student residence rooms and from off campus. Internet access and online class registration, e-mail are available. *Library facilities:* Lewis University Library. *General application contact:* Coordinator, 800-897-9000.

College of Arts and Sciences
Programs in:
  administration/education • MA
  arts and sciences • M Ed, MA, MA Ed, MAE, MPSA, MS, CAS
  child and adolescent counseling • MA
  community service • MA
  criminal/social justice • MS
  curriculum and instruction • MA Ed
  education • M Ed, MAE
  educational leadership • MA Ed
  general administrative program • CAS
  higher education/student services • MA
  instructional leadership • MA Ed
  mental health counseling • MA
  organizational management • MA
  pastoral ministry • MA
  public policy • MA
  school counseling and guidance • MA
  special education • MA
  superintendent endorsement program • CAS
  training and development • MA

College of Business
Program in:
  business • MBA

Graduate School of Management
Programs in:
  accounting • MBA
  e-business • MBA
  finance • MBA
  healthcare management • MBA
  human resources management • MBA
  international business • MBA
  management information systems • MBA
  marketing • MBA
  technology and operations management • MBA

College of Nursing and Health Professions
Programs in:
  case management • MSN
  nursing administration • MSN
  nursing and health professions • MSN
  nursing education • MSN

■ **LOYOLA UNIVERSITY CHICAGO**
Chicago, IL 60611-2196
http://www.luc.edu/

Independent-religious, coed, university. CGS member. *Enrollment:* 13,362 graduate, professional, and undergraduate students; 3,671 full-time matriculated graduate/professional students (2,119 women), 1,775 part-time matriculated graduate/professional students (1,284 women). *Graduate faculty:* 1,108 full-time (424 women), 478 part-time/adjunct (257 women). *Computer facilities:* 318 computers available on campus for general student use. A campuswide network can be accessed from student residence rooms and from off campus. Internet access is available. *Library facilities:* Cudahy Library plus 4 others. *Graduate expenses:* Tuition: part-time $578 per credit hour. Tuition and fees vary according to course level and program. *General application contact:* Marianne Gramza, Associate Dean, Graduate School, 312-915-8950.

Find an in-depth description at www.petersons.com/gradchannel.

Graduate School
Dr. William Yost, Dean
Programs in:
  American politics and policy • MA, PhD
  applied social psychology • MA, PhD
  applied sociology • MA
  biochemistry • MS, PhD
  biology • MS
  cell and molecular physiology • MS, PhD
  cell biology, neurobiology and anatomy • MS, PhD
  chemistry • MS, PhD
  clinical psychology • MA, PhD
  computer science • MS
  criminal justice • MA
  developmental psychology • PhD
  English • MA, PhD

Illinois

history • MA, PhD
immunology • MS, PhD
international studies • MA, PhD
mathematics • MS
microbiology • MS, PhD
molecular biology • PhD
neurochemistry • PhD
neuroscience • MS, PhD
organizational development • MSOD
perception • PhD
pharmacology and experimental therapeutics • MS, PhD
philosophy • MA, PhD
political theory and philosophy • MA, PhD
sociology • MA, PhD
Spanish • MA
theology • MA, PhD
virology • MS, PhD

Institute of Human Resources and Industrial Relations
Dr. Homer H. Johnson, Director
Program in:
human resources and industrial relations • MSHR, MSIR

Institute of Pastoral Studies
Dr. Mary Elsbernd, Director
Programs in:
divinity • M Div
pastoral counseling • MA
pastoral studies • MA

Marcella Niehoff School of Nursing
Programs in:
acute care clinical nurse specialist • MSN
acute care nurse practitioner • MSN
adult nurse practitioner • MSN
cardiovascular health and disease clinical nurse specialist • MSN
emergency nurse practitioner • MSN
family nurse practitioner • MSN
health systems management • MSN
nurse midwifery • MSN
nursing • PhD
oncology clinical nurse specialist • MSN
pediatric clinical nurse specialist • MSN
pediatric nurse practitioner • MSN
women's health • MSN
women's health nurse practitioner • MSN

Graduate School of Business
Dr. Sandra LaBlance, Assistant Dean
Programs in:
accountancy • MS
business administration • MBA
human resources and industrial relations • MS
information systems and operations management • MS
information systems management • MS
integrated marketing communications • MS
marketing • MS

School of Education
Dr. Margaret L. Fong, Dean
Programs in:
administration/supervision • M Ed, MA, Ed D, PhD
community counseling • M Ed, MA
comparative-international education • M Ed, MA, Ed D, PhD
counseling psychology • PhD
cultural and educational policy studies • M Ed, MA, Ed D, PhD
curriculum and instruction • M Ed, MA, Ed D
education • M Ed, MA, Ed D, PhD, Ed S
educational psychology • M Ed, MA, PhD
higher education • M Ed, Ed D, PhD
history of education • M Ed, MA, Ed D, PhD
instructional leadership • M Ed
philosophy of education • M Ed, MA, Ed D, PhD
research methods • M Ed, MA, PhD
school counseling • M Ed
school psychology • PhD, Ed S
sociology of education • M Ed, MA, Ed D, PhD
special education • M Ed

School of Law
Nina S. Appel, Dean
Programs in:
business law • LL M, MJ
child and family law • LL M, MJ
health law • LL M, MJ, D Law, SJD
law • JD

School of Social Work
Dr. Joseph A. Walsh, Dean
Program in:
social work • MSW, PhD

Stritch School of Medicine
Dr. Stephen Slogoff, Dean
Program in:
medicine • MD

■ NATIONAL-LOUIS UNIVERSITY
Chicago, IL 60603
http://www.nl.edu/

Independent, coed, university. *Enrollment:* 7,665 graduate, professional, and undergraduate students; 1,480 full-time matriculated graduate/professional students (1,105 women), 3,651 part-time matriculated graduate/professional students (2,939 women). *Graduate faculty:* 284 full-time (190 women), 762 part-time/adjunct (479 women). *Computer facilities:* A campuswide network can be accessed from off campus. Internet access is available. *Library facilities:* NLU Library plus 5 others. *Graduate expenses:* Tuition: part-time $513 per semester hour. Required fees: $40 per term. *General application contact:* Kelly Thompson, Vice President for Enrollment Management, 312-261-3550.

College of Arts and Sciences
Program in:
arts and sciences • M Ad Ed, MA, MS, Ed D, Certificate

Division of Health and Human Services
Programs in:
addictions counseling • MS, Certificate
addictions treatment • Certificate
career counseling and development studies • Certificate
community wellness and prevention • MS, Certificate
counseling • MS, Certificate
eating disorders counseling • Certificate
employee assistance programs • MS, Certificate
gerontology administration • Certificate
gerontology counseling • MS, Certificate
human services administration • MS, Certificate
long-term care administration • Certificate

Division of Language and Academic Development
Programs in:
adult education • M Ad Ed, Ed D, Certificate
adult education and developmental studies • M Ad Ed, Certificate
developmental studies • M Ad Ed

Division of Liberal Arts and Sciences
Programs in:
cultural psychology • MA
health psychology • MA
human development • MA
liberal arts and sciences • MA, MS, Certificate
organizational psychology • MA
psychology • Certificate
written communication • MS

College of Management and Business
Programs in:
business administration • MBA
human resource management and development • MS
management and business • MBA, MS
managerial leadership • MS

National College of Education, McGaw Graduate School
Programs in:
administration and supervision • M Ed, CAS, Ed S

Illinois

National-Louis University (continued)
  curriculum and instruction • M Ed, MS Ed, CAS, Ed S
  curriculum and social inquiry • Ed D
  early childhood administration • M Ed, CAS
  early childhood curriculum and instruction specialist • M Ed, MS Ed, CAS
  early childhood education • M Ed, MAT, CAS
  early childhood leadership and advocacy • M Ed
  education • M Ed, MAT, MS Ed, Ed D, CAS, Ed S
  educational leadership • Ed D
  educational leadership/superintendent endorsement • Ed D
  educational psychology • CAS
  educational psychology/human learning and development • M Ed, MS Ed
  educational psychology/school psychology • M Ed, Ed D, Ed S
  elementary education • MAT
  general special education • M Ed, MS Ed, CAS
  human learning and development • Ed D
  language and literacy • M Ed, MS Ed, CAS
  learning disabilities • M Ed, MS Ed, CAS
  learning disabilities/behavior disorders • M Ed, MAT, MS Ed, CAS
  mathematics education • M Ed, MS Ed, CAS
  reading and language • Ed D
  reading recovery • CAS
  reading specialist • M Ed, MS Ed, CAS
  science education • M Ed, MS Ed, CAS
  secondary education • MAT
  technology in education • M Ed, MS Ed, CAS

■ NORTH CENTRAL COLLEGE
Naperville, IL 60566-7063
http://www.noctrl.edu/

Independent-religious, coed, comprehensive institution. *Enrollment:* 2,458 graduate, professional, and undergraduate students; 63 full-time matriculated graduate/professional students (29 women), 309 part-time matriculated graduate/professional students (161 women). *Graduate faculty:* 18 full-time (10 women), 11 part-time/adjunct (2 women). *Computer facilities:* Computer purchase and lease plans are available. 200 computers available on campus for general student use. A campuswide network can be accessed from student residence rooms and from off campus. Internet access and online class registration, software packages are available. *Library facilities:* Oesterle Library. *Graduate expenses:* Tuition: part-time $408 per credit hour. Tuition and fees vary according to program. *General application contact:* Martha Stolze, Director and Graduate and Continuing Education Admissions, 630-637-5840.

Graduate Programs
Barbara E. Illg, Dean of Graduate and Continuing Education
Programs in:
  business administration • MBA
  computer science • MS
  education • MA Ed
  leadership studies • MLD
  liberal studies • MALS
  management information systems • MS

■ NORTHEASTERN ILLINOIS UNIVERSITY
Chicago, IL 60625-4699
http://www.neiu.edu/

State-supported, coed, comprehensive institution. CGS member. *Computer facilities:* 360 computers available on campus for general student use. A campuswide network can be accessed from off campus. Internet access and online class registration, productivity software are available. *Library facilities:* Ronald Williams Library. *General application contact:* Dean of the Graduate College, 773-442-6010.

Graduate College

College of Arts and Sciences
Programs in:
  arts and sciences • MA, MS
  biology • MS
  chemistry • MS
  composition/writing • MA
  computer science • MS
  earth science • MS
  English • MA
  geography and environmental studies • MA
  gerontology • MA
  history • MA
  linguistics • MA
  literature • MA
  mathematics • MA, MS
  mathematics for elementary school teachers • MA
  music • MA
  political science • MA
  speech • MA

College of Business and Management
Programs in:
  accounting • MBA, MSA
  accounting, business law, and finance • MSA
  finance • MBA
  management • MBA
  marketing • MBA

College of Education
Programs in:
  bilingual/bicultural education • MAT, MSI
  early childhood special education • MA
  educating children with behavior disorders • MA
  educating individuals with mental retardation • MA
  education • M Ed, MA, MAT, MSI
  educational administration and supervision • MA
  educational leadership • MA
  gifted education • MA
  guidance and counseling • MA
  human resource development • MA
  inner city studies • MA
  instruction • MSI
  language arts • MAT, MSI
  reading • MA
  special education • MA
  teaching • MAT
  teaching children with learning disabilities • MA

■ NORTHERN ILLINOIS UNIVERSITY
De Kalb, IL 60115-2854
http://www.niu.edu/

State-supported, coed, university. CGS member. *Enrollment:* 25,260 graduate, professional, and undergraduate students; 5,780 matriculated graduate/professional students. *Graduate faculty:* 672 full-time (248 women), 66 part-time/adjunct (17 women). *Computer facilities:* 1,200 computers available on campus for general student use. A campuswide network can be accessed from student residence rooms and from off campus. *Library facilities:* Founders Memorial Library plus 8 others. *Graduate expenses:* Tuition, state resident: full-time $3,968; part-time $165 per credit hour. Tuition, nonresident: full-time $7,936; part-time $330 per credit hour. Required fees: $1,255; $52 per credit hour. *General application contact:* Graduate School Office, 815-753-0395.

Find an in-depth description at www.petersons.com/gradchannel.

College of Law
LeRoy Pernell, Dean
Program in:
  law • JD

Graduate School
Dr. Rathindra N. Bose, Dean

Illinois

College of Business
Dr. David K. Graf, Dean
Programs in:
  accountancy • MAS, MST
  business • MAS, MBA, MS, MST
  business administration • MBA
  management information systems • MS

College of Education
Dr. Christine Sorensen, Dean
Programs in:
  adult and higher education • MS Ed, Ed D
  counseling • MS Ed, Ed D
  curriculum and instruction • MS Ed, Ed D
  early childhood education • MS Ed
  education • MS, MS Ed, Ed D, Ed S
  educational administration • MS Ed, Ed D, Ed S
  educational psychology • MS Ed, Ed D
  educational research and evaluation • MS
  elementary education • MS Ed
  foundations of education • MS Ed
  instructional technology • MS Ed, Ed D
  literacy education • MS Ed
  physical education • MS Ed
  school business management • MS Ed
  special education • MS Ed
  sport management • MS

College of Engineering and Engineering Technology
Dr. Promod Vohra, Acting Dean
Programs in:
  electrical engineering • MS
  engineering and engineering technology • MS
  industrial engineering • MS
  industrial management • MS
  mechanical engineering • MS

College of Health and Human Sciences
Dr. Shirley Richmond, Dean
Programs in:
  applied family and child studies • MS
  communicative disorders • MA, Au D
  health and human sciences • MA, MPH, MPT, MS, Au D
  nursing • MS
  nutrition and dietetics • MS
  physical therapy • MPT
  public health • MPH

College of Liberal Arts and Sciences
Dr. Frederick Kitterle, Dean
Programs in:
  anthropology • MA
  biological sciences • MS, PhD
  chemistry • MS, PhD
  communication studies • MA
  computer science • MS
  economics • MA, PhD
  English • MA, PhD
  French • MA
  geography • MS
  geology • MS, PhD
  history • MA, PhD
  liberal arts and sciences • MA, MPA, MS, PhD
  mathematical sciences • PhD
  mathematics • MS
  philosophy • MA
  physics • MS, PhD
  political science • MA, PhD
  psychology • MA, PhD
  public administration • MPA
  sociology • MA
  Spanish • MA
  statistics • MS

College of Visual and Performing Arts
Dr. Harold Kafer, Dean
Programs in:
  art • MA, MFA, MS
  music • MM, Performer's Certificate
  theatre and dance • MFA
  visual and performing arts • MA, MFA, MM, MS, Performer's Certificate

■ **NORTH PARK THEOLOGICAL SEMINARY**
Chicago, IL 60625-4895
http://www.northpark.edu/sem/

Independent-religious, coed, graduate-only institution. *Computer facilities:* A campuswide network can be accessed from off campus. Internet access is available. *Library facilities:* North Park Consolidated Library. *General application contact:* Associate Director, 800-964-0101.

Graduate and Professional Programs
Programs in:
  Christian studies • Certificate
  preaching • D Min
  religious education • MACE
  theological studies • MATS
  theology • M Div

■ **NORTH PARK UNIVERSITY**
Chicago, IL 60625-4895
http://www.northpark.edu/

Independent-religious, coed, comprehensive institution. *Computer facilities:* 105 computers available on campus for general student use. A campuswide network can be accessed from student residence rooms and from off campus. *Library facilities:* Consolidated Library plus 4 others. *General application contact:* Vice President for Admissions and Financial Aid, 773-244-5500.

Center for Management Education
Program in:
  management education • MBA, MM

School of Community Development
Program in:
  community development • MA

School of Education
Program in:
  education • MA

School of Nursing
Program in:
  nursing • MS

■ **NORTHWESTERN UNIVERSITY**
Evanston, IL 60208
http://www.northwestern.edu/

Independent, coed, university. CGS member. *Computer facilities:* Computer purchase and lease plans are available. 608 computers available on campus for general student use. A campuswide network can be accessed from student residence rooms and from off campus. Internet access and online class registration are available. *Library facilities:* University Library plus 6 others. *General application contact:* Coordinator of Graduate Admissions, 847-491-8532.

The Graduate School
Programs in:
  biochemistry • PhD
  biochemistry, molecular biology, and cell biology • PhD
  biotechnology • PhD
  cell and molecular biology • PhD
  clinical investigation • MSCI, Certificate
  clinical psychology • PhD
  counseling psychology • MA
  developmental biology and genetics • PhD
  genetic counseling • MS
  hormone action and signal transduction • PhD
  law and social science • Certificate
  liberal studies • MA
  literature • MA
  management and organizations and sociology • PhD
  marital and family therapy • MS
  mathematical methods in social science • MS
  molecular biophysics • PhD
  neuroscience • PhD
  public health • MPH
  structural biology • PhD
  structural biology, biochemistry, and biophysics • PhD

Illinois

Northwestern University (continued)
Center for International and Comparative Studies
Program in:
  international and comparative studies • Certificate

Institute for Neuroscience
Enrico Mugnaini, Director
Program in:
  neuroscience • PhD

Judd A. and Marjorie Weinberg College of Arts and Sciences
Programs in:
  anthropology • PhD
  art history • PhD
  arts and sciences • MA, MFA, MS, PhD, Certificate
  astrophysics • PhD
  brain, behavior and cognition • PhD
  chemistry • PhD
  clinical psychology • PhD
  cognitive psychology • PhD
  comparative literary studies • PhD
  economics • MA, PhD
  eighteenth-century studies • Certificate
  English • MA, PhD
  French • PhD
  French and comparative literature • PhD
  geological sciences • MS, PhD
  German literature and critical thought • PhD
  history • PhD
  Italian studies • Certificate
  linguistics • MA, PhD
  mathematics • PhD
  neurobiology and physiology • MS
  personality • PhD
  philosophy • PhD
  physics • MS, PhD
  political science • MA, PhD
  Slavic languages and literature • PhD
  social psychology • PhD
  sociology • PhD
  statistics • MS, PhD
  visual arts • MFA

Kellogg School of Management
Programs in:
  accounting • PhD
  business administration • MBA
  finance • PhD
  management • MBA, MMM, PhD
  management and organizations • PhD
  managerial economics and strategy • PhD
  manufacturing management • MMM
  marketing • PhD

Program of African Studies
Program in:
  African studies • Certificate

School of Communication
Programs in:
  audiology and hearing sciences • MA, PhD
  clinical audiology • Au D
  communication • MA, MFA, MSC, Au D, PhD
  communication studies • MA, PhD
  communication systems strategy and management • MSC
  directing • MFA
  learning disabilities • MA, PhD
  managerial communication • MSC
  performance studies • MA, PhD
  radio/television/film • MA, MFA, PhD
  speech and language pathology • MA, PhD
  speech and language pathology and learning disabilities • MA
  stage design • MFA
  theatre • MA
  theatre and drama • PhD

School of Education and Social Policy
Mark P. Hoffman, Assistant Dean
Programs in:
  advanced teaching • MS
  education • MS
  education and social policy-learning sciences • MA, PhD
  elementary education and policy • MS
  higher education administration • MS
  human development and social policy • PhD
  learning and organizational change • MS
  secondary teaching • MS

Law School
David Van Zanter, Chair
Programs in:
  executive law • LL M
  international law • JD
  law • JD, LL M

McCormick School of Engineering and Applied Science
Programs in:
  applied mathematics • MS, PhD
  biomedical engineering • MS, PhD
  chemical engineering • MS, PhD
  computer science • MS, PhD
  electrical and computer engineering • MS, PhD
  electronic materials • MS, PhD, Certificate
  engineering and applied science • MEM, MIT, MME, MMM, MPD, MPM, MS, PhD, Certificate
  engineering management • MEM
  environmental engineering and science • MS, PhD
  fluid mechanics • MS, PhD
  geotechnical engineering • MS, PhD
  industrial engineering and management science • MS, PhD
  information technology • MIT
  manufacturing engineering • MME
  materials science and engineering • MS, PhD
  mechanical engineering • MS, PhD
  mechanics of materials and solids • MS, PhD
  operations research • MS, PhD
  project management • MPM
  solid mechanics • MS, PhD
  structural engineering and materials • MS, PhD
  theoretical and applied mechanics • MS, PhD
  transportation systems analysis and planning • MS, PhD

Medill School of Journalism
Programs in:
  advertising/sales promotion • MSMC
  broadcast journalism • MSJ
  direct database and e-commerce marketing • MSMC
  general studies • MSMC
  integrated marketing communications • MSMC
  magazine publishing • MSJ
  new media • MSJ
  public relations • MSMC
  reporting and writing • MSJ

Northwestern Medical School
Programs in:
  cancer biology • PhD
  cell biology • PhD
  clinical investigation • MSCI
  developmental biology • PhD
  evolutionary biology • PhD
  immunology and microbial pathogenesis • PhD
  medicine • MD, MS, MSCI, DPT, PhD
  molecular biology and genetics • PhD
  neurobiology • PhD
  pharmacology and toxicology • PhD
  physical therapy and human movement sciences • DPT
  structural biology and biochemistry • PhD

School of Music
Programs in:
  collaborative arts • DM
  conducting • MM, DM
  jazz pedagogy • MM
  keyboard • MM, DM, CP
  music • MM, DM, PhD, CP
  music cognition • PhD
  music composition • MM, DM
  music education • MM, PhD
  music technology • MM, PhD
  music theory • MM, PhD
  musicology • MM, PhD
  opera production • MM
  performance • MM
  piano performance and pedagogy • MM
  string performance and pedagogy • MM
  strings • MM, DM

strings, winds and percussion • CP
voice • MM, DM, CP
winds and percussion • MM, DM

■ OLIVET NAZARENE UNIVERSITY
Bourbonnais, IL 60914-2271
http://www.olivet.edu/

Independent-religious, coed, comprehensive institution. *Computer facilities:* Computer purchase and lease plans are available. 339 computers available on campus for general student use. A campuswide network can be accessed from student residence rooms and from off campus. Internet access and online class registration are available. *Library facilities:* Benner Library. *General application contact:* Dean of the Graduate School, 815-939-5291.

Graduate School
Programs in:
business administration • MBA
practical ministries • MPM

Division of Education
Programs in:
curriculum and instruction • MAE
elementary education • MAT
secondary education • MAT

Division of Religion and Philosophy
Programs in:
biblical literature • MA
religion • MA
theology • MA

Institute for Church Management
Programs in:
church management • MCM
pastoral counseling • MPC

■ QUINCY UNIVERSITY
Quincy, IL 62301-2699
http://www.quincy.edu/

Independent-religious, coed, comprehensive institution. *Enrollment:* 1,269 graduate, professional, and undergraduate students; 29 full-time matriculated graduate/professional students (17 women), 110 part-time matriculated graduate/professional students (84 women). *Graduate faculty:* 9 full-time (4 women), 5 part-time/adjunct (2 women). *Computer facilities:* 200 computers available on campus for general student use. A campuswide network can be accessed from student residence rooms and from off campus. Internet access and online class registration are available. *Library facilities:* Brenner Library. *Graduate expenses:* Tuition: part-time $325 per semester hour. *General application contact:* Kevin Brown, Director of Admissions, 217-228-5210.

Division of Business
Dr. Richard Magliari, Director, MBA Program
Program in:
business • MBA

Division of Education
Dr. Alice Mills, Chair
Program in:
education • MS Ed

■ ROCKFORD COLLEGE
Rockford, IL 61108-2393
http://www.rockford.edu/

Independent, coed, comprehensive institution. *Enrollment:* 187 full-time matriculated graduate/professional students (100 women), 1,381 part-time matriculated graduate/professional students (801 women). *Graduate faculty:* 33 full-time (11 women), 18 part-time/adjunct (13 women). *Computer facilities:* 65 computers available on campus for general student use. A campuswide network can be accessed from student residence rooms. Internet access is available. *Library facilities:* Howard Colman Library. *Graduate expenses:* Tuition: part-time $530 per credit hour. Required fees: $30 per term. *General application contact:* Glenda Riggins, Administrative Assistant, 815-226-4041.

Graduate Studies
Dr. Debra Dew, Director of MAT Program
Programs in:
art education • MAT
business administration • MBA
elementary education • MAT
English • MAT
history • MAT
learning disabilities • MAT
political science • MAT
reading • MAT
secondary education • MAT
social sciences • MAT

■ ROOSEVELT UNIVERSITY
Chicago, IL 60605-1394
http://www.roosevelt.edu/

Independent, coed, comprehensive institution. *Enrollment:* 7,524 graduate, professional, and undergraduate students; 809 full-time matriculated graduate/professional students (499 women), 2,380 part-time matriculated graduate/professional students (1,670 women). *Graduate faculty:* 211 full-time (83 women), 429 part-time/adjunct. *Computer facilities:* Computer purchase and lease plans are available. 646 computers available on campus for general student use. A campuswide network can be accessed from off campus. Internet access and online class registration are available. *Library facilities:* Murray-Green Library plus 4 others. *Graduate expenses:* Tuition: part-time $624 per semester hour. Required fees: $150 per semester. *General application contact:* Joanne Canyon-Heller, Coordinator of Graduate Admission, 312-281-3250.

Find an in-depth description at www.petersons.com/gradchannel.

Graduate Division
Dean of Graduate Studies

Chicago College of Performing Arts
James Gandre, Dean
Programs in:
directing and dramaturgy • MFA
music • MM
music education • MM Ed
musical theatre • MFA
performing arts • MA, MFA, MM, MM Ed, Diploma
piano pedagogy • Diploma
theatre • MA, MFA
theatre-directing • MA
theatre-performance • MFA

College of Arts and Sciences
Lynn Weiner, Dean
Programs in:
applied economics • MA
arts and sciences • MA, MFA, MPA, MS, MSC, MSIMC, MSJ, MST, Psy D
biotechnology and chemical science • MS
clinical professional psychology • MA, Psy D
communication • MSIMC, MSJ
computer science • MSC
computer science and telecommunications • MSC, MST
creative writing • MFA
economics • MA
English • MA
gerontology • MA
history • MA
industrial/organizational psychology • MA
integrated marketing communications • MSIMC
journalism • MSJ
liberal studies • MA, MFA
mathematical sciences • MS
policy studies • MA, MPA
political science • MA
psychology • MA, Psy D
public administration • MPA
science and mathematics • MS
sociology • MA
Spanish • MA
telecommunications • MST
women's and gender studies • MA

Illinois

Roosevelt University (continued)
College of Education
Dr. George Lowery, Dean
Programs in:
  counseling and human services • MA
  early childhood education/early childhood professions • MA
  education • MA, Ed D
  educational leadership and organizational change • MA, Ed D
  elementary education • MA
  secondary education • MA
  special education • MA
  teacher leadership • MA

Evelyn T. Stone University College
Laura Evans, Dean
Programs in:
  general studies • MGS
  hospitality management • MS
  interdisciplinary studies • MIS
  training and development • MA

Walter E. Heller College of Business Administration
Gordan Patzer, Dean
Programs in:
  accounting • MSA
  business administration • MA, MBA, MSA, MSIB, MSIS
  human resource management • MA
  information systems • MSIS
  international business • MSIB

■ SAINT XAVIER UNIVERSITY
Chicago, IL 60655-3105
http://www.sxu.edu/

Independent-religious, coed, comprehensive institution. *Enrollment:* 5,566 graduate, professional, and undergraduate students; 265 full-time matriculated graduate/professional students (180 women), 2,239 part-time matriculated graduate/professional students (1,814 women). *Graduate faculty:* 152. *Computer facilities:* 306 computers available on campus for general student use. A campuswide network can be accessed from student residence rooms and from off campus. Internet access is available. *Library facilities:* Byrne Memorial Library. *Graduate expenses:* Tuition: part-time $525 per semester hour. *General application contact:* Beth Gierach, Vice President of Enrollment Services, 773-298-3050.

Graduate Studies
Vice President of Academic Affairs

Graham School of Management
Dr. John Eber, Dean
Programs in:
  employee health benefits • Certificate
  finance • MBA, MS
  financial planning • MBA, Certificate
  financial trading and practice • MBA, Certificate
  generalist/administration • MBA
  health administration • MBA, MS
  managed care • Certificate
  management • MBA, MS
  marketing • MBA
  public health • MPH
  taxation • MBA

School of Arts and Sciences
Dr. Lawrence Frank, Dean
Programs in:
  adult counseling • Certificate
  applied computer science in Internet information systems • MS
  arts and sciences • MA, MS, CAS, Certificate
  child/adolescent counseling • Certificate
  core counseling • Certificate
  counseling psychology • MA
  English • CAS
  literary studies • MA
  mathematics and computer science • MA
  speech-language pathology • MS
  teaching of writing • MA
  writing pedagogy • CAS

School of Education
Dr. Beverly Gulley, Dean
Programs in:
  counseling • MA
  counselor education • MA
  curriculum and instruction • MA
  early childhood education • MA
  education • CAS
  educational administration • MA
  elementary education • MA
  field-based education • MA
  general educational studies • MA
  individualized program • MA
  learning disabilities • MA
  reading • MA
  secondary education • MA

School of Nursing
Beth Gierach, Managing Director of Admission
Programs in:
  adult health clinical nurse specialist • MS
  family nurse practitioner • MS, PMC
  leadership in community health nursing • MS
  psychiatric-mental health clinical nurse specialist • MS
  psychiatric-mental health clinical specialist • PMC

■ SOUTHERN ILLINOIS UNIVERSITY CARBONDALE
Carbondale, IL 62901-4701
http://www.siu.edu/siuc/

State-supported, coed, university. CGS member. *Enrollment:* 21,387 graduate, professional, and undergraduate students; 1,648 full-time matriculated graduate/professional students (851 women), 2,632 part-time matriculated graduate/professional students (1,387 women). *Graduate faculty:* 1,074 full-time (262 women), 112 part-time/adjunct. *Computer facilities:* Computer purchase and lease plans are available. 1,681 computers available on campus for general student use. A campuswide network can be accessed from student residence rooms and from off campus. Internet access is available. *Library facilities:* Morris Library plus 1 other. *Graduate expenses:* Tuition, state resident: part-time $478 per hour. Tuition, nonresident: part-time $657 per hour. *General application contact:* Associate Dean of the Graduate School, 618-536-7791.

Graduate School
Dr. John Koropchak, Acting Dean

College of Agriculture
David Shoup, Dean
Programs in:
  agribusiness economics • MS
  agriculture • MS
  animal science • MS
  food and nutrition • MS
  forestry • MS
  horticultural science • MS
  plant and soil science • MS

College of Business and Administration
Dan Worrell, Dean
Programs in:
  accountancy • M Acc, PhD
  business administration • MBA, PhD

College of Education
Keith Hillkirk, Dean
Programs in:
  behavioral analysis and therapy • MS
  communication disorders and sciences • MS
  counselor education • MS Ed, PhD
  curriculum and instruction • MS Ed, PhD
  education • MS, MS Ed, MSW, PhD, Rh D
  educational administration • MS Ed, PhD
  educational psychology • MS Ed, PhD
  health education • MS Ed, PhD
  higher education • MS Ed
  human learning and development • MS Ed
  measurement and statistics • PhD
  physical education • MS Ed
  recreation • MS Ed
  rehabilitation • Rh D
  rehabilitation administration and services • MS

Illinois

rehabilitation counseling • MS
social work • MSW
special education • MS Ed
workforce education and development • MS Ed, PhD

College of Engineering
Dr. George Swisher, Dean
Programs in:
civil engineering and mechanics • MS
electrical engineering • MS
electrical systems • PhD
engineering • MS, PhD
fossil energy • PhD
manufacturing systems • MS
mechanical engineering and energy processes • MS
mechanics • PhD
mining engineering • MS

College of Liberal Arts
Dr. Shirley Clay Scott, Dean
Programs in:
administration of justice • MA
anthropology • MA, PhD
applied linguistics • MA
ceramics • MFA
clinical psychology • MA, MS, PhD
composition • MA, PhD
composition and theory • MM
counseling psychology • MA, MS, PhD
creative writing • MFA
drawing • MFA
economics • MA, MS, PhD
experimental psychology • MA, MS, PhD
fiber/weaving • MFA
foreign languages and literatures • MA
geography • MS, PhD
glass • MFA
history • MA, PhD
history and literature • MM
jewelry • MFA
liberal arts • MA, MFA, MM, MPA, MS, PhD
literature • MA, PhD
metals/blacksmithing • MFA
music education • MM
opera/music theater • MM
painting • MFA
performance • MM
philosophy • MA, PhD
piano pedagogy • MM
political science • MA, PhD
printmaking • MFA
public administration • MPA
rhetoric • MA, PhD
sculpture • MFA
sociology • MA, PhD
speech communication • MA, MS, PhD
speech/theater • PhD
teaching English as a second language • MA
theater • MFA

College of Mass Communication and Media Arts
Dr. Thomas Johnson, Director of Graduate Studies
Program in:
mass communication and media arts • MA, MFA, PhD

College of Science
Jack Parker, Dean
Programs in:
biological sciences • MS
chemistry and biochemistry • MS, PhD
computer science • MS
environmental resources and policy • PhD
geology • MS, PhD
mathematics • MA, MS, PhD
molecular biology, microbiology, and biochemistry • MS, PhD
physics • MS
plant biology • MS, PhD
science • MA, MS, PhD
statistics • MS
zoology • MS, PhD

School of Law
Peter C. Alexander, Dean
Program in:
law • JD

School of Medicine
Dr. Carl J. Getto, Dean and Provost
Programs in:
medicine • MD, MS, PhD
pharmacology • MS, PhD
physiology • MS, PhD

■ **SOUTHERN ILLINOIS UNIVERSITY EDWARDSVILLE**
Edwardsville, IL 62026-0001
http://www.siue.edu/

State-supported, coed, comprehensive institution. CGS member. *Computer facilities:* Computer purchase and lease plans are available. 600 computers available on campus for general student use. A campuswide network can be accessed from student residence rooms and from off campus. Internet access is available. *Library facilities:* Lovejoy Library. *General application contact:* Dean of Graduate School, 618-650-3010.

Find an in-depth description at www.petersons.com/gradchannel.

Graduate Studies and Research
College of Arts and Sciences
Programs in:
American and English literature • MA
art therapy counseling • MA
arts and sciences • MA, MFA, MM, MPA, MS, MSW
biological sciences • MA, MS
ceramics • MFA
chemistry • MS
drawing • MFA
environmental sciences • MS
fiber/fabrics • MFA
geography • MA, MS
history • MA
mass communication • MS
mathematics and statistics • MS
music education • MM
music performance • MM
painting • MFA
physics • MS
printmaking • MFA
public administration • MPA
sculpture • MFA
social work • MSW
sociology • MA
speech communication • MA
teaching English as a second language • MA
teaching of writing • MA

School of Business
Programs in:
accountancy • MSA
business • MA, MBA, MMR, MS, MSA
business administration • MBA
e-business • MBA
economics and finance • MA, MS
management information systems • MBA
marketing research • MBA, MMR

School of Education
Programs in:
clinical adult • MS
community school • MS
education • MA, MS, MS Ed, Certificate, Ed S
educational administration and supervision • MS Ed, Ed S
elementary education • MS Ed
exercise physiology • Certificate
general academic • MA
industrial organizational • MS
instructional technology • MS Ed
kinesiology and health education • MS Ed
pedigogy/administration • Certificate
school psychology • Ed S
secondary education • MS Ed
special education and communication disorders • MS Ed
speech pathology • MS
sports and exercise behavior • Certificate

School of Engineering
Programs in:
civil engineering • MS
computer information systems • MS
electrical engineering • MS
engineering • MS
mechanical engineering • MS

Peterson's Graduate Schools in the U.S. 2006

www.petersons.com 301

Illinois

Southern Illinois University Edwardsville (continued)

School of Nursing
Programs in:
- community health nursing • MS
- medical-surgical nursing • MS
- nurse anesthesia • MS
- nurse practitioner nursing • MS
- psychiatric nursing • MS

School of Dental Medicine
Program in:
- dental medicine • DMD

■ UNIVERSITY OF CHICAGO
Chicago, IL 60637-1513
http://www.uchicago.edu/

Independent, coed, university. CGS member. *Enrollment:* 13,887 graduate, professional, and undergraduate students; 6,632 full-time matriculated graduate/professional students (3,097 women), 1,979 part-time matriculated graduate/professional students (586 women). *Graduate faculty:* 2,179 full-time (632 women), 775 part-time/adjunct (245 women). *Computer facilities:* 1,000 computers available on campus for general student use. A campuswide network can be accessed from student residence rooms and from off campus. *Library facilities:* Joseph Regenstein Library plus 8 others. *General application contact:* Martha Jackson, Manager, Office of Graduate Affairs, 773-702-7813.

Divinity School
Dr. Richard A. Rosengarten, Dean
Program in:
- divinity • M Div, AM, AMRS, PhD

Division of Social Sciences
Prof. John Mark Hansen, Dean
Programs in:
- anthropology • PhD
- economics • PhD
- history • PhD
- human development • PhD
- international relations • AM
- Latin American and Caribbean studies • AM
- Middle Eastern studies • AM
- political science • PhD
- psychology • PhD
- social sciences • AM, MA, PhD
- social thought • PhD
- sociology • PhD

Division of the Biological Sciences
Dr. James Madara, Dean
Programs in:
- biochemistry and molecular biology • PhD
- biological sciences • MS, PhD
- cancer biology • PhD
- cell physiology • PhD
- cellular and molecular physiology • PhD
- cellular differentiation • PhD
- computational neurobiology • PhD
- developmental biology • PhD
- developmental endocrinology • PhD
- developmental genetics • PhD
- developmental neurobiology • PhD
- ecology and evolution • PhD
- evolutionary biology • PhD
- functional and evolutionary biology • PhD
- gene expression • PhD
- genetics • PhD
- health studies • MS
- human genetics • PhD
- immunology • PhD
- medical physics • PhD
- microbiology • PhD
- molecular genetics and cell biology • PhD
- molecular metabolism and nutrition • PhD
- neurobiology • PhD
- neurobiology, pharmacology and physiology • PhD
- ophthalmology and visual science • PhD
- organismal biology and anatomy • PhD
- pathology • PhD
- pharmacological and physiological sciences • PhD

Division of the Humanities
Thomas B. Thuerer, Dean of Students
Programs in:
- ancient Mediterranean world • AM, PhD
- ancient philosophy • AM, PhD
- anthropology and linguistics • PhD
- art history • AM, PhD
- cinema and media studies • AM, PhD
- classical archaeology • AM, PhD
- classical languages and literatures • AM, PhD
- comparative literature • AM, PhD
- conceptual and historical studies of science • AM, PhD
- East Asian languages and civilizations • AM, PhD
- English language and literature • AM, PhD
- French • AM, PhD
- Germanic languages and literatures • AM, PhD
- history of culture • AM, PhD
- humanities • AM, MA, MFA, PhD
- Italian • AM, PhD
- Jewish history and culture • AM, PhD
- Jewish studies • AM
- linguistics • AM, PhD
- music • AM, PhD
- Near Eastern languages and civilizations • AM, PhD
- New Testament and early Christian culture • AM, PhD
- philosophy • AM, PhD
- Slavic languages and literatures • AM, PhD
- South Asian languages and civilizations • AM, PhD
- Spanish • AM, PhD
- visual arts • MFA

Division of the Physical Sciences
Robert Fefferman, Dean
Programs in:
- applied mathematics • SM, PhD
- astronomy and astrophysics • SM, PhD
- atmospheric sciences • SM, PhD
- chemistry • PhD
- computer science • SM, PhD
- earth sciences • SM, PhD
- financial mathematics • MS
- mathematics • SM, PhD
- paleobiology • PhD
- physical sciences • MS, SM, PhD
- physics • PhD
- planetary and space sciences • SM, PhD
- statistics • SM, PhD

Graduate School of Business
Edward A. Snyder, Dean
Programs in:
- business • IMBA, MBA, PhD
- business administration • MBA
- executive business administration • MBA
- international business administration • IMBA

The Irving B. Harris Graduate School of Public Policy Studies
Dr. Susan E. Mayer, Dean
Programs in:
- environmental science and policy • MS
- public policy studies • AM, MPP, PhD

The Law School
Saul Levmore, Dean
Program in:
- law • JD, LL M, MCL, DCL, JSD

Pritzker School of Medicine
Dr. James Madara, Dean
Program in:
- medicine • MD

School of Social Service Administration
Dr. Jeanne Marsh, Acting Dean
Programs in:
- social service administration • PhD
- social work • AM

Illinois

UNIVERSITY OF ILLINOIS AT CHICAGO
Chicago, IL 60607-7128
http://www.uic.edu/grad

State-supported, coed, university. CGS member. *Enrollment:* 25,763 graduate, professional, and undergraduate students; 5,810 full-time matriculated graduate/professional students (3,161 women), 3,337 part-time matriculated graduate/professional students (1,351 women). *Graduate faculty:* 1,319 full-time (326 women), 94 part-time/adjunct (15 women). *Computer facilities:* 1,100 computers available on campus for general student use. A campuswide network can be accessed from student residence rooms and from off campus. *Library facilities:* Richard J. Daley Library plus 7 others. *Graduate expenses:* Tuition, state resident: part-time $941 per semester. Tuition, nonresident: part-time $2,338 per semester. *General application contact:* Jackie Perry, Graduate College Receptionist, 312-413-2550.

College of Dentistry
Bruce E. Graham, Dean
Programs in:
  dentistry • DDS, MS
  oral sciences • MS

College of Medicine
Gerald S. Moss, Dean
Programs in:
  anatomy and cell biology • MS, PhD
  biochemistry and molecular biology • MS, PhD
  genetics • PhD
  health professions education • MHPE
  medicine • MD, MHPE, MS, PhD
  microbiology and immunology • PhD
  molecular genetics • PhD
  pharmacology • PhD
  physiology and biophysics • MS, PhD
  surgery • MS

College of Pharmacy
Rosalie Sagraves, Dean
Programs in:
  forensic science • MS
  medicinal chemistry • MS, PhD
  pharmaceutics • MS, PhD
  pharmacodynamics • MS, PhD
  pharmacognosy • MS, PhD
  pharmacy • Pharm D, MS, PhD
  pharmacy administration • MS, PhD

Center for Pharmaceutical Biotechnology
Program in:
  pharmaceutical biotechnology • MS, PhD

Graduate College
Dr. Clark Hulse, Dean
Program in:
  neuroscience • PhD

College of Applied Health Sciences
Charlotte Tate, Dean
Programs in:
  associated health professions • MAMS, MS, PhD
  biomedical visualization • MAMS
  disability and human development • MS
  disability studies • PhD
  human nutrition and dietetics • MS, PhD
  kinesiology • MS
  occupational therapy • MS
  physical therapy • MS

College of Architecture and Art
Dr. Judith Kirshner, Dean
Programs in:
  architecture • M Arch
  architecture and art • M Arch, MA, MFA, PhD
  art history • MA, PhD
  electronic visualization • MFA
  film animation • MFA
  graphic design • MFA
  industrial design • MFA
  photography • MFA
  studio arts • MFA

College of Business Administration
Wim Wiewel, Dean
Programs in:
  accounting • MS
  business administration • MA, MBA, MS, PhD
  economics • MA, PhD
  management information systems • MS, PhD
  public policy analysis • PhD

College of Education
Victoria Chou, Dean
Programs in:
  curriculum and instruction • PhD
  education • M Ed, PhD
  educational psychology • PhD
  instructional leadership • M Ed
  leadership and administration • M Ed
  policy and administration • PhD
  policy studies in urban education • PhD
  special education • M Ed, PhD

College of Engineering
Lawrence A. Kennedy, Dean
Programs in:
  bioengineering • MS, PhD
  chemical engineering • MS, PhD
  civil and materials engineering • MS, PhD
  computer science • MS, PhD
  electrical and computer engineering • MS, PhD
  engineering • MS, PhD
  industrial engineering • MS
  industrial engineering and operations research • PhD
  mechanical engineering • MS, PhD

College of Liberal Arts and Sciences
Stanley Fish, Dean
Programs in:
  anthropology • MA, PhD
  applied linguistics (teaching English as a second language) • MA
  applied mathematics • MS, DA, PhD
  cell and developmental biology • PhD
  chemistry • MS, PhD
  communication • MA
  computer science • MS, DA, PhD
  criminal justice • MA
  crystallography • MS, PhD
  ecology and evolution • MS, DA, PhD
  English • MA, PhD
  environmental and urban geography • MA
  environmental geology • MS, PhD
  environmental studies • MA
  French • MA
  genetics and development • PhD
  geochemistry • MS, PhD
  geology • MS, PhD
  geomorphology • MS, PhD
  geophysics • MS, PhD
  geotechnical engineering and geosciences • PhD
  Germanic studies • MA, PhD
  Hispanic studies • MA, PhD
  history • MA, MAT, PhD
  hydrogeology • MS, PhD
  language, literacy, and rhetoric • PhD
  liberal arts and sciences • MA, MAT, MS, MST, DA, PhD
  linguistics • MA
  low-temperature and organic geochemistry • MS, PhD
  mass communication • MA
  math and information science for the industry • MS
  mineralogy • MS, PhD
  molecular biology • MS, PhD
  neurobiology • MS, PhD
  paleoclimatology • MS, PhD
  paleontology • MS, PhD
  petrology • MS, PhD
  philosophy • MA, PhD
  physics • MS, PhD
  plant biology • MS, DA, PhD
  political science • MA, PhD
  probability and statistics • MS, DA, PhD
  psychology • PhD
  pure mathematics • MS, DA, PhD
  quaternary geology • MS, PhD
  sedimentology • MS, PhD
  Slavic languages and literatures • PhD
  Slavic studies • MA
  sociology • MA, PhD
  teaching of mathematics • MST
  urban geography • MA
  water resources • MS, PhD

Peterson's Graduate Schools in the U.S. 2006

Illinois

University of Illinois at Chicago (continued)

College of Nursing
Dr. Joan Shaver, Chair/Head
Programs in:
 maternity nursing/nurse midwifery • MS
 nursing • MS, PhD
 nursing research • PhD
 nursing science • PhD
 nursing sciences (medical surgical) • MS
 nursing sciences (nursing administration) • MS
 nursing sciences (psychiatric) • MS
 nursing sciences (public health nursing) • MS
 pediatric nursing • MS
 perinatal nursing • MS

College of Urban Planning and Public Affairs
Robin Hambleton, Dean
Programs in:
 public administration • MPA, PhD
 public policy analysis • PhD
 urban planning and policy • MUPP
 urban planning and public affairs • MPA, MUPP, PhD

Jane Addams College of Social Work
C. F. Hairston, Dean
Program in:
 social work • MSW, PhD

School of Public Health
Dr. Susan Scrimshaw, Dean
Programs in:
 biostatistics • MS, PhD
 community health sciences • MPH, MS, Dr PH, PhD
 environmental and occupational health sciences • MPH, MS, Dr PH, PhD
 epidemiology • MPH, MS, Dr PH, PhD
 health policy administration • MPH, MS, Dr PH, PhD

■ UNIVERSITY OF ILLINOIS AT SPRINGFIELD
Springfield, IL 62703-5407
http://www.uis.edu/

State-supported, coed, upper-level institution. CGS member. *Enrollment:* 4,569 graduate, professional, and undergraduate students; 442 full-time matriculated graduate/professional students (259 women), 1,563 part-time matriculated graduate/professional students (929 women). *Graduate faculty:* 167 full-time (69 women), 132 part-time/adjunct (62 women). *Computer facilities:* 160 computers available on campus for general student use. A campuswide network can be accessed from student residence rooms and from off campus. Internet access is available. *Library facilities:* Brookens Library. *Graduate expenses:* Tuition, state resident: full-time $3,108; part-time $130 per credit. Tuition, nonresident: full-time $9,324; part-time $389 per credit. Required fees: $860. Full-time tuition and fees vary according to student level. *General application contact:* Jeannie M. Jones, Institutional Studies, 217-206-6044.

Graduate Programs
Dr. Michael Chaney, Provost/Vice Chancellor for Academic Affairs

College of Business and Management
Dr. Ronald McNeil, Dean
Programs in:
 accountancy • MA
 business administration • MBA
 business and management • MA, MBA
 management information systems • MA

College of Education and Human Services
Dr. Larry Stonecipher, Dean
Programs in:
 alcoholism and substance abuse • MA
 child and family studies • MA
 education and human services • MA
 educational leadership • MA
 gerontology • MA
 human development counseling • MA
 social services administration • MA

College of Liberal Arts and Sciences
William Bloemer, Dean
Programs in:
 arts and sciences • MA
 biology • MA
 communication • MA
 computer science • MA
 English • MA
 individual option • MA
 public history • MA

College of Public Affairs and Administration
Glen Cope, Dean
Programs in:
 environmental studies • MA
 legal studies • MA
 political studies • MA
 public administration • MPA, DPA
 public affairs and administration • MA, MPA, MPH, DPA
 public affairs reporting • MA
 public health • MPH

■ UNIVERSITY OF ILLINOIS AT URBANA–CHAMPAIGN
Champaign, IL 61820
http://www.uiuc.edu/

State-supported, coed, university. CGS member. *Enrollment:* 40,458 graduate, professional, and undergraduate students; 9,420 full-time matriculated graduate/professional students (4,139 women). *Graduate faculty:* 1,745 full-time (445 women), 117 part-time/adjunct (41 women). *Computer facilities:* Computer purchase and lease plans are available. 3,500 computers available on campus for general student use. A campuswide network can be accessed from student residence rooms and from off campus. Internet access and online class registration are available. *Library facilities:* University Library plus 42 others. *Graduate expenses:* Tuition, state resident: full-time $6,692. Tuition, nonresident: full-time $18,692. *General application contact:* Richard P. Wheeler, Dean, 217-333-6715.

College of Law
Heidi M. Hurd, Dean
Program in:
 law • JD, LL M, MCL, JSD

College of Veterinary Medicine
Herbert Whiteley, Dean
Programs in:
 veterinary biosciences • MS, PhD
 veterinary clinical medicine • MS, PhD
 veterinary medicine • DVM, MS, PhD
 veterinary pathobiology • MS, PhD

Graduate College
Richard P. Wheeler, Dean
Program in:
 • medical scholars

College of Agricultural, Consumer and Environmental Sciences
Robert A. Easter, Dean
Programs in:
 agricultural and consumer economics • MS, PhD
 agricultural engineering • MS, PhD
 agricultural, consumer and environmental sciences • AM, MS, PhD
 animal sciences • MS, PhD
 crop sciences • MS, PhD
 extension education • MS
 food science and human nutrition • MS, PhD
 human and community development • AM, MS, PhD
 natural resources and environmental science • MS, PhD
 nutritional sciences • MS, PhD

College of Applied Life Studies
Tanya Gallagher, Dean
Programs in:
 applied life studies • AM, MS, MSPH, MST, PhD
 community health • MSPH, PhD
 kinesiology • MS, MST, PhD
 leisure studies • MS, PhD
 rehabilitation • MS

Illinois

rehabilitation education services • MS
speech and hearing science • AM, MS, PhD

College of Commerce and Business Administration
Avijit Ghosh, Dean
Programs in:
accountancy • MAS, MS, MSA, PhD
business administration • MBA, MSBA, MSTM, PhD
commerce and business administration • MAS, MBA, MS, MSA, MSBA, MSTM, PhD
economics • MS, PhD
finance • MS, PhD
technology management • MSTM

College of Communications
Ronald E. Yates, Interim Head
Programs in:
advertising • MS
communications • PhD
journalism • MS

College of Education
Susan A. Fowler, Dean
Programs in:
curriculum and instruction • AM, Ed M, MS, Ed D, PhD, AC
education • AM, Ed M, MS, Ed D, PhD, AC
education, organization and leadership • AM, Ed M, MS, Ed D, PhD, AC
educational policy studies • AM, Ed M, MS, Ed D, PhD, AC
educational psychology • AM, Ed M, MS, Ed D, PhD, AC
human resource education • AM, Ed M, MS, Ed D, PhD, AC
special education • AM, Ed M, MS, Ed D, PhD, AC

College of Engineering
Dr. David E. Daniel, Dean
Programs in:
aeronautical and astronautical engineering • MS, PhD
civil engineering • MS, PhD
computer engineering • MS, PhD
computer science • MCS, MS, MST, PhD
electrical engineering • MS, PhD
engineering • MCS, MS, MST, PhD
environmental engineering • MS, PhD
environmental engineering and environmental science • MS, PhD
environmental science • MS, PhD
health physics • MS, PhD
industrial engineering • MS, PhD
materials science and engineering • MS, PhD
mechanical engineering • MS, PhD
nuclear engineering • MS, PhD
physics • MS, PhD
systems engineering and engineering design • MS
theoretical and applied mechanics • MS, PhD

College of Fine and Applied Arts
Kathleen F. Conlin, Dean
Programs in:
architecture • M Arch
art and design • AM, MFA, Ed D, PhD
art education • AM, Ed D
art history • AM, PhD
dance • AM
fine and applied arts • AM, M Arch, M Mus, MFA, MLA, MS, MUP, DMA, Ed D, PhD
industrial design • MFA
landscape architecture • MLA
music • M Mus, MS, DMA, Ed D, PhD
regional planning • PhD
studio arts • MFA
theatre • AM, MFA, PhD
urban and regional planning • MUP

College of Liberal Arts and Sciences
Jesse Delia, Dean
Programs in:
African studies • AM
animal biology • PhD
anthropology • AM, PhD
applied mathematics • MS
applied measurement • MS
astronomy • MS, PhD
atmospheric science • MS, PhD
biochemistry • MS, PhD
bioengineering • PhD
biological psychology • AM, PhD
biophysics and computational biology • PhD
brain and cognition • AM, PhD
cell and structural biology • PhD
chemical and biomolecular engineering • MS, PhD
chemistry • MS, PhD
classics • AM, PhD
clinical psychology • AM, PhD
cognitive psychology • AM, PhD
comparative literature • AM, MAT, PhD
demography • AM, PhD
developmental psychology • AM, PhD
earth sciences • MS, PhD
East Asian languages and cultures • AM, PhD
ecology and evolutionary biology • PhD
English • AM, PhD
English as an international language • AM
entomology • PhD
French • AM, MAT, PhD
geochemistry • MS, PhD
geography • AM, MS, PhD
geology • MS, PhD
geophysics • MS, PhD
Germanic languages and literatures • AM, MAT, PhD
history • AM, PhD
insect pest management • MS

integrative biology • MS, PhD
Italian • AM, PhD
Latin American and Caribbean studies • AM
liberal arts and sciences • AM, MAT, MS, PhD
linguistics • AM, PhD
mathematics • MS, PhD
microbiology • MS, PhD
molecular and cellular biology • MS, PhD
molecular and integrative physiology • MS, PhD
neuroscience • PhD
personnel psychology • MS
philosophy • AM, PhD
physiology and molecular plant biology • PhD
plant biology • MS, PhD
political science • AM, PhD
quantitative psychology • AM, PhD
Russian • AM, MAT, PhD
Russian and East European studies • AM
Slavic languages and literatures • AM, MAT, PhD
social-personality-organizational • AM, PhD
sociology • AM, PhD
Spanish • MAT
speech communication • AM, MAT, PhD
statistics • MS, PhD
teaching of mathematics • MS
visual cognition and human performance • AM, PhD

Graduate School of Library and Information Science
John Unsworth, Dean
Program in:
library and information science • MS, PhD, CAS

Institute of Labor and Industrial Relations
Dr. Peter Feuille, Director
Programs in:
human resources • MHRIR, PhD
labor and industrial relations • MHRIR, PhD

School of Social Work
Wynne S. Korr, Dean
Program in:
social work • MSW, PhD

■ UNIVERSITY OF ST. FRANCIS
Joliet, IL 60435-6169
http://www.stfrancis.edu/

Independent-religious, coed, comprehensive institution. *Enrollment:* 1,988 graduate, professional, and undergraduate students; 299 full-time matriculated graduate/professional students (222 women), 1,436 part-time matriculated graduate/professional

Illinois

University of St. Francis (continued)
students (1,184 women). *Graduate faculty:* 20 full-time (14 women), 112 part-time/adjunct (56 women). *Computer facilities:* 147 computers available on campus for general student use. A campuswide network can be accessed from student residence rooms. Internet access and online class registration are available. *Library facilities:* University of St. Francis Library. *Graduate expenses:* Tuition: part-time $375 per credit hour. Part-time tuition and fees vary according to campus/location and program. *General application contact:* Ron Clement, Director of Admissions, 800-735-7500.

College of Education
Dr. John Gambro, Dean
Programs in:
 educational Leadership • MS
 elementary education certification • M Ed
 secondary education certification • M Ed
 teaching and learning • MS

College of Health Arts, Graduate and Professional Studies
Dr. Lyle Hicks, Dean
Programs in:
 business • MBA
 health services administration • MS
 management • MS
 training and development • MS

Saint Joseph College of Nursing and Allied Health
Dr. Maria Connolly, Dean
Programs in:
 nursing • MSN
 physician assistant studies • MS

■ WESTERN ILLINOIS UNIVERSITY
Macomb, IL 61455-1390
http://www.wiu.edu/

State-supported, coed, comprehensive institution. CGS member. *Enrollment:* 13,469 graduate, professional, and undergraduate students; 771 full-time matriculated graduate/professional students (404 women), 1,048 part-time matriculated graduate/professional students (707 women). *Graduate faculty:* 392 full-time (118 women), 16 part-time/adjunct (3 women). *Computer facilities:* 1,000 computers available on campus for general student use. A campuswide network can be accessed from student residence rooms and from off campus. Internet access and online class registration, course registration are available. *Library facilities:* Leslie Malpass Library plus 4 others. *Graduate expenses:* Part-time $144 per credit hour. Tuition, nonresident: part-time $288 per credit hour. *General application contact:* Dr. Barbara Baily, Director of Graduate Studies/Associate Provost, 309-298-1806.

School of Graduate Studies
Dr. Barbara Baily, Director of Graduate Studies/Associate Provost

College of Arts and Sciences
Dr. Thomas Helm, Acting Dean
Programs in:
 arts and sciences • MA, MS, Certificate, SSP
 biological sciences • MS
 chemistry • MS
 clinical/community mental health • MS
 community development • Certificate
 general psychology • MS
 geography • MA
 history • MA
 literature and language • MA
 mathematics • MS
 physics • MS
 political science • MA
 psychology • MS, SSP
 school psychology • SSP
 sociology • MA
 writing • MA
 zoo and aquarium studies • Certificate

College of Business and Technology
Dr. David Beveridge, Dean
Programs in:
 accountancy • M Acct
 business administration • MBA
 business and technology • M Acct, MA, MBA, MS
 computer science • MS
 economics • MA
 engineering technology • MS

College of Education and Human Services
Dr. Bonnie Smith, Dean
Programs in:
 college student personnel • MS
 counseling • MS Ed
 distance learning • Certificate
 early childhood education • Certificate
 education administration and supervision • MS Ed, Ed S
 education and human services • MA, MAT, MS, MS Ed, Certificate, Ed S
 educational and interdisciplinary studies • MS Ed
 elementary education • MS Ed, Certificate
 graphics application • Certificate
 health education • MS
 health services administration • Certificate
 instructional technology and telecommunications • MS
 language literacy • Certificate
 law enforcement and justice administration • MA
 marriage and family counseling • Certificate
 mathematics • Certificate
 multimedia • Certificate
 physical education • MS
 police executive administration • Certificate
 reading • MS Ed, Certificate
 recreation, park, and tourism administration • MS
 science • Certificate
 secondary education • MAT
 social studies • Certificate
 special education • MS Ed
 sport management • MS
 technology integration in education • Certificate
 training development • Certificate

College of Fine Arts and Communication
Gene J. Kozlowski, Chairperson
Programs in:
 communication • MA
 communication sciences and disorders • MS
 fine arts and communication • MA, MFA, MS
 music • MA
 theatre • MFA

Indiana

■ ANDERSON UNIVERSITY
Anderson, IN 46012-3495
http://www.anderson.edu/

Independent-religious, coed, comprehensive institution. *Computer facilities:* 200 computers available on campus for general student use. A campuswide network can be accessed from student residence rooms and from off campus. Microcomputer software available. *Library facilities:* Robert A. Nicholson Library. *General application contact:* Director of Seminary Advancement, 765-641-4526.

Falls School of Business
Programs in:
 accountancy • MA
 business administration • MBA, DBA

School of Education

School of Theology
Programs in:
 missions • MA
 theology • M Div, MTS, D Min

Indiana

■ BALL STATE UNIVERSITY
Muncie, IN 47306-1099
http://www.bsu.edu/

State-supported, coed, university. CGS member. *Enrollment:* 20,533 graduate, professional, and undergraduate students; 946 full-time matriculated graduate/professional students (537 women), 1,335 part-time matriculated graduate/professional students (793 women). *Graduate faculty:* 750. *Computer facilities:* 1,500 computers available on campus for general student use. A campuswide network can be accessed from student residence rooms and from off campus. *Library facilities:* Bracken Library plus 3 others. *Graduate expenses:* Tuition, state resident: full-time $5,748. Tuition, nonresident: full-time $14,166. *General application contact:* Dr. Deborah W. Balogh, Associate Provost and Dean, 765-285-3716.

Graduate School
Dr. Deborah W. Balogh, Associate Provost and Dean

College of Applied Science and Technology
Dr. Nancy Kingsbury, Dean
Programs in:
 applied gerontology • MA
 applied science and technology • MA, MAE, MS, PhD
 family and consumer sciences • MA, MAE, MS
 human bioenergetics • PhD
 industry and technology • MA, MAE
 nursing • MS
 physical education • MA, MAE, PhD
 wellness management • MA, MS

College of Architecture and Planning
Dr. Joseph Bilello, Dean
Programs in:
 architecture • M Arch
 architecture and planning • M Arch, MLA, MS, MURP
 historic preservation • M Arch, MS
 landscape architecture • MLA
 urban planning • MURP

College of Communication, Information, and Media
Dr. Michael Holmes, Interim Dean
Programs in:
 communication, information, and media • MA, MS
 digital storytelling • MA
 information and communication sciences • MS
 journalism • MA
 public relations • MA
 speech, public address, forensics, and rhetoric • MA

College of Fine Arts
Dr. Robert Kvam, Interim Dean
Programs in:
 art • MA
 art education • MA, MAE
 fine arts • MA, MAE, MM, DA
 music education • MA, MM, DA

College of Sciences and Humanities
Dr. Michael Maggioto, Dean
Programs in:
 actuarial science • MA
 anthropology • MA
 applied linguistics • PhD
 biology • MA, MAE, MS
 biology education • Ed D
 chemistry • MA, MS
 clinical psychology • MA
 cognitive and social processes • MA
 computer science • MA, MS
 earth sciences • MA
 English • MA, PhD
 geology • MA, MS
 health education • MA, MAE
 history • MA
 linguistics • MA, PhD
 linguistics and teaching English to speakers of other languages • MA
 mathematical statistics • MA
 mathematics • MA, MAE, MS
 mathematics education • MAE
 natural resources • MA, MS
 physics • MA, MS
 physiology • MA, MS
 political science • MA
 public administration • MPA
 sciences and humanities • MA, MAE, MPA, MS, Au D, Ed D, PhD
 social sciences • MA
 sociology • MA
 speech pathology and audiology • MA, Au D
 teaching English to speakers of other languages • MA

Miller College of Business
Dr. Lynne D. Richardson, Dean
Programs in:
 accounting • MS
 business • MAE, MBA, MS
 business administration • MBA
 information systems and operations management • MAE

Teachers College
Dr. Roy Weaver, Dean
Programs in:
 adult and community education • MA
 adult education • MA, Ed D
 adult, community, and higher education • Ed D
 counseling psychology • MA, PhD
 curriculum • MAE, Ed S
 curriculum and instruction • MAE, Ed S
 education • MA, MAE, Ed D, PhD, Ed S
 educational administration • MAE, Ed D
 educational psychology • MA, PhD, Ed S
 educational studies • MAE
 elementary education • MAE, Ed D, PhD
 executive development • MA
 junior high/middle school education • MAE
 school psychology • MA, PhD, Ed S
 school superintendency • Ed S
 secondary education • MA
 social psychology • MA
 special education • MA, MAE, Ed D, Ed S
 student affairs administration in higher education • MA
 teaching in elementary education • MAE

■ BUTLER UNIVERSITY
Indianapolis, IN 46208-3485
http://www.butler.edu/

Independent, coed, comprehensive institution. *Enrollment:* 4,424 graduate, professional, and undergraduate students; 229 full-time matriculated graduate/professional students (152 women), 468 part-time matriculated graduate/professional students (223 women). *Graduate faculty:* 83 full-time (26 women), 31 part-time/adjunct (15 women). *Computer facilities:* 250 computers available on campus for general student use. A campuswide network can be accessed from student residence rooms and from off campus. Internet access, e-mail are available. *Library facilities:* Irwin Library System plus 1 other. *Graduate expenses:* Tuition: full-time $5,040; part-time $280 per credit. Full-time tuition and fees vary according to degree level and program. *General application contact:* Kathy Harter, Assistant Director Student Services, 317-940-8100.

College of Business Administration
Dr. Richard Fetter, Dean
Program in:
 business administration • MBA

College of Education
Dr. Robert Rider, Dean
Programs in:
 administration • MS
 elementary education • MS
 reading • MS
 school counseling • MS
 secondary education • MS
 special education • MS

Indiana

Butler University (continued)
College of Liberal Arts and Sciences
Dr. Paul Hanson, Dean
Programs in:
English • MA
history • MA
liberal arts and sciences • MA

College of Pharmacy
Dr. Patricia Chase, Dean
Program in:
pharmaceutical science • Pharm D, MS

Jordan College of Fine Arts
Dr. Peter Alexander, Dean
Programs in:
composition • MM
conducting • MM
fine arts • MM
music • MM
music education • MM
music history • MM
organ • MM
performance • MM

■ INDIANA STATE UNIVERSITY
Terre Haute, IN 47809-1401
http://web.indstate.edu/

State-supported, coed, university. CGS member. *Enrollment:* 11,360 graduate, professional, and undergraduate students; 644 full-time matriculated graduate/professional students (374 women), 1,101 part-time matriculated graduate/professional students (635 women). *Graduate faculty:* 368 full-time (113 women), 91 part-time/adjunct (46 women). *Computer facilities:* 500 computers available on campus for general student use. A campuswide network can be accessed from student residence rooms and from off campus. Internet access is available. *Library facilities:* Cunningham Memorial Library plus 2 others. *Graduate expenses:* Tuition, state resident: full-time $4,356; part-time $242 per credit. Tuition, nonresident: full-time $8,658; part-time $481 per credit. Required fees: $50 per term. *General application contact:* Dr. Kweku Bentil, Dean, School of Graduate Studies, 800-444-GRAD.

Find an in-depth description at www.petersons.com/gradchannel.

School of Graduate Studies
Dr. Kweku Bentil, Dean
Program in:
technology management • PhD

College of Arts and Sciences
Dr. Diane Michelfelder, Dean
Programs in:
arts and sciences • MA, MFA, MM, MME, MPA, MS, PhD, Psy D, CAS
ceramics • MA, MFA
child development and family life • MS
clinical psychology • Psy D
clothing and textiles • MS
communication studies • MA, MS
criminology • MA, MS
dietetics • MS
drawing • MA, MFA
earth sciences • MA, MS
ecology • PhD
economic geography • PhD
English • MA, MS, CAS
European history • MA, MS
family and consumer sciences education • MS
French • MA, MS
general psychology • MA, MS
geography • MA
geology • MS
graphic design • MA, MFA
history of labor and reform movements in the U.S. • MA
life sciences • MS
linguistics/teaching English as a second language • MA, MS
mathematics and computer science • MA, MS
metalry • MA, MFA
microbiology • PhD
music education • MME
music performance • MM
non-west history • MA, MS
nutrition and foods • MS
painting • MA, MFA
photography • MA, MFA
physical geography • PhD
physiology • PhD
political science • MA, MS
printmaking • MA, MFA
public administration • MPA
radio, television and film • MA, MS
science education • MS
sculpture • MA, MFA
Spanish • MA, MS
sports medicine • PhD
TESL/TEFL • CAS
theatre • MA, MS
U.S. history • MA, MS

College of Business
Dr. Ronald Green, Dean
Program in:
business • MBA

College of Education
Dr. Robert Williams, Acting Dean
Programs in:
counseling psychology • MS, PhD
counselor education • PhD
curriculum and instruction • M Ed, PhD
early childhood education • M Ed
education • M Ed, MA, MS, PhD, Ed S
educational administration • PhD, Ed S
educational technology • MS
elementary education • M Ed
literacy • M Ed
marriage and family counseling • MS
school administration and supervision • M Ed
school counseling • M Ed
school psychology • M Ed, PhD, Ed S
special education • MA, MS
speech pathology and audiology • MA, MS
student affairs administration • MS, PhD

School of Health and Human Performance
Dr. Barbara Passmore, Dean
Programs in:
adult fitness • MA, MS
athletic training • MS
coaching • MA, MS
community health promotion • MA, MS
exercise science • MA, MS
health and human performance • MA, MS
master teacher • MA, MS
occupational safety management • MA, MS
recreation and sport management • MA, MS
school health and safety • MA, MS

School of Nursing
Dr. Bonnie Saucier, Dean
Program in:
nursing • MS

School of Technology
Dr. W. Tad Foster, Dean
Programs in:
career and technical education • MS
electronics and computer technology • MS
human resource development • MS
industrial technology • MS
technology • MS, PhD
technology education • MS

■ INDIANA UNIVERSITY BLOOMINGTON
Bloomington, IN 47405-7000
http://www.iub.edu/

State-supported, coed, university. CGS member. *Enrollment:* 38,589 graduate, professional, and undergraduate students; 5,190 full-time matriculated graduate/professional students (2,535 women), 2,619 part-time matriculated graduate/professional students (1,374 women). *Graduate faculty:* 1,156 full-time (315 women), 3 part-time/adjunct (0 women). *Computer facilities:* 1,500 computers

Indiana

available on campus for general student use. A campuswide network can be accessed from student residence rooms and from off campus. Internet access, various software packages are available. *Library facilities:* Indiana University Library plus 32 others. *Graduate expenses:* Tuition, state resident: full-time $4,908; part-time $205 per credit. Tuition, nonresident: full-time $14,298; part-time $596 per credit. Required fees: $661. Tuition and fees vary according to campus/location and program. *General application contact:* 812-855-2666.

Graduate School
George E. Walker, Vice President for Research and Dean

College of Arts and Sciences
Dean
Programs in:
- acting • MFA
- Afro-American studies • MA
- analytical chemistry • PhD
- anthropology • MA, PhD
- apparel studies • MS
- applied linguistics (teaching English as a second language) • MA, Certificate
- applied mathematics–numerical analysis • MA, PhD
- art education • MAT
- arts administration • MA
- arts and sciences • MA, MAT, MFA, MS, PhD, Certificate
- astronomy • MA, PhD
- astrophysics • PhD
- biochemistry and molecular biology • MS, PhD
- biogeochemistry • MS, PhD
- biological chemistry • PhD
- biology and behavior • PhD
- biology teaching • MAT
- Central Eurasian studies • MA, PhD
- ceramics • MFA
- chemistry • MAT, MS
- Chinese language and literature • MA, PhD
- classical studies • MA, MAT, PhD
- clinical science • PhD
- cognitive psychology • PhD
- communication and culture • MA, MAT, PhD
- comparative literature • MA, MAT, PhD
- computer science • MS, PhD
- computer science/cognitive science • PhD
- computer science/logic • PhD
- costume design • MFA
- creative writing • MFA
- cross-cultural studies of crime and justice • MA, PhD
- developmental psychology • PhD
- directing • MFA
- East Asian studies • MA
- East European studies • Certificate
- ecology • MA, PhD
- economics • MA, MAT, PhD
- English • MA, PhD
- English education • MAT
- environmental geosciences • MS, PhD
- evolution, ecology, and behavior • MA, PhD
- evolutionary biology • MA, PhD
- fine arts • MA, MAT, MFA, PhD
- folklore • MA, PhD
- French • MA, MAT, PhD
- French linguistics • MA, PhD
- French literature • MA, PhD
- genetics • PhD
- geobiology, stratigraphy, and sedimentology • MS, PhD
- geochemistry • MS, PhD
- geochemistry, mineralogy, and petrology • MS, PhD
- geography • MA, MAT, PhD
- geophysics • MS, PhD
- geophysics, tectonics, and structural geology • MS, PhD
- German literature and studies • PhD
- German studies • MA, PhD
- graphic design • MFA
- Hispanic linguistics • MA, PhD
- Hispanic literature • MA, PhD
- history • MA, MAT, PhD
- history and philosophy of science • MA, PhD
- history of art • MA, PhD
- inorganic chemistry • PhD
- interior design • MS
- Italian • MA, PhD
- Japanese language and literature • MA, PhD
- jewelry/metalsmithing • MFA
- justice systems and processes • MA, PhD
- Latin American and Caribbean studies • MA
- law and society • MA, PhD
- lighting design • MFA
- linguistics • MA, PhD
- literature • MA, PhD
- Luso-Brazilian literature • MA, PhD
- mass communication • PhD
- mathematics education • MAT
- medieval German studies • PhD
- microbiology • MA, PhD
- molecular, cellular, and developmental biology • PhD
- nature of crime • MA, PhD
- Near Eastern languages and cultures • MA, PhD
- neural sciences • PhD
- painting • MFA
- philosophy • MA, PhD
- photography • MFA
- physical chemistry • PhD
- physics • MAT, MS, PhD
- plant sciences, molecular and organismal biology • MA, PhD
- playwriting • MFA
- political science • MA, PhD
- printmaking • MFA
- probability-statistics • MA, PhD
- religious studies • MA, PhD
- Russian and East European studies • MA
- Russian area studies • Certificate
- scenic design • MFA
- sculpture • MFA
- Slavic languages and literatures • MA, MAT, PhD
- social psychology • PhD
- sociology • MA, PhD
- speech and hearing sciences • MA, MAT, PhD
- teaching French • MAT
- teaching German • MAT
- teaching Spanish • MAT
- technology • MFA
- telecommunications • MA, MS
- textiles • MFA
- theatre and drama • MAT
- theatre history • MA, PhD
- theory • MA, PhD
- West European studies • MA, PhD, Certificate
- zoology • MA, PhD

School of Journalism
Trevor Brown, Dean
Programs in:
- journalism • MA
- mass communication • PhD

Kelley School of Business
Dr. Dan R. Dalton, Dean
Programs in:
- accounting • DBA, PhD
- business • EMBA, MBA, MPA, MS, MSIS, DBA, PhD
- business economics and public policy • DBA, PhD
- decision systems • DBA, PhD
- entrepreneurship • MBA
- finance • MBA, DBA, PhD
- human resources management • MBA
- international business • MBA
- management • MBA, DBA, PhD
- management information systems • MBA, DBA, PhD
- marketing • MBA, DBA, PhD
- operations management • MBA, DBA, PhD
- organizational behavior • DBA, PhD
- production/operations leaders program • MBA
- professional accountancy • MPA
- systems and accounting • MS, MSIS

Medical Sciences Program
Assistant Dean
Programs in:
- anatomy and cell biology • MA, PhD
- pharmacology • MS, PhD
- physiology • MA, PhD

Indiana

Indiana University Bloomington (continued)

School of Education
Gerardo Gonzalez, Dean
Programs in:
  art education • MS Ed
  counseling/counselor education • MS Ed, Ed D, PhD
  curriculum and instruction • Ed D, PhD
  education • MM Ed, MS, MS Ed, D Mus Ed, Ed D, PhD, Ed S
  educational leadership and policy • PhD
  educational psychology • MS Ed, Ed D, PhD
  elementary education • MS Ed, Ed S
  higher education • Ed D, PhD
  higher education and student affairs administration • MS Ed
  history and philosophy of education • MS Ed
  history, philosophy, and policy studies in education • PhD
  instructional systems technology • MS Ed, PhD, Ed S
  international and comparative education • MS Ed
  language education • MS Ed, Ed D, PhD, Ed S
  music education • MM Ed, D Mus Ed
  school administration • MS Ed, Ed D, Ed S
  school psychology • Ed S
  science and environmental education • Ed D
  secondary education • MS Ed, Ed S
  social studies education • MS Ed
  special education • MS Ed, Ed D, PhD, Ed S
  teacher education • MS

School of Health, Physical Education and Recreation
Tony Mobley, Dean
Programs in:
  adapted physical education • MS
  administration • MS
  applied health science • MS
  applied sport science • MS
  athletic administration/sport management • MS
  athletic training • MS
  biomechanics • MS
  clinical exercise physiology • MS
  exercise physiology • MS
  health and safety • HSD, HS Dir
  health behavior • PhD
  health, physical education and recreation • MPH, MS, HSD, PED, PhD, Re D, HS Dir, PE Dir, Re Dir
  human performance • PhD
  leisure behavior • PhD
  motor control • MS
  motor development • MS
  motor learning • MS
  outdoor recreation and resource management • MS
  park and recreation management • MS
  physical education • PED, PE Dir
  public health • MPH
  recreation • Re D, Re Dir
  social science of sport • MS
  sport management • MS
  sports management • MS
  therapeutic recreation • MS

School of Informatics
J. Michael Dunn, Dean
Programs in:
  bioinformatics • MS
  chemical informatics • MS
  human computer interaction • MS
  media arts and sciences • MS

School of Law
Alfred Aman, Dean
Programs in:
  comparative law • MCL
  judicial science • JD
  juridical science • SJD
  law • LL M
  law and social science • PhD

School of Library and Information Science
Dr. Blaise Cronin, Dean
Program in:
  library and information science • MIS, MLS, PhD, Spec

School of Music
Dean
Program in:
  music • MA, MAT, MM, MS, DM, PhD

School of Optometry
Gerald E. Lowther, Dean
Programs in:
  optometry • OD, MS, PhD
  visual sciences and physiological optics • MS, PhD

School of Public and Environmental Affairs
A. James Barnes, Dean
Programs in:
  environmental science • MSES, PhD
  public affairs • EMPA, MPA, PhD
  public and environmental affairs • EMPA, MPA, MSES, PhD
  public policy • PhD

■ INDIANA UNIVERSITY NORTHWEST
Gary, IN 46408-1197

State-supported, coed, comprehensive institution. *Enrollment:* 5,097 graduate, professional, and undergraduate students; 49 full-time matriculated graduate/professional students (31 women), 329 part-time matriculated graduate/professional students (239 women). *Graduate faculty:* 78 full-time (29 women). *Computer facilities:* 250 computers available on campus for general student use. A campuswide network can be accessed from off campus. Internet access and online class registration are available. *Library facilities:* IUN Library. *Graduate expenses:* Tuition, state resident: full-time $3,714; part-time $155 per credit hour. Tuition, nonresident: full-time $8,643; part-time $360 per credit hour. Required fees: $419. Tuition and fees vary according to campus/location and program. *General application contact:* Marilyn Vasquez, Interim Executive Vice Chancellor for Academic Affairs, 219-980-6967.

Program in Social Work
Dr. Grafton Hull, Director
Program in:
  social work • MSW

School of Business and Economics
Dr. Donald A. Coffin, Dean
Programs in:
  accountancy • M Acc
  accounting • Certificate
  business administration • MBA

School of Education
Dr. Stanley E. Wigle, Dean
Programs in:
  elementary education • MS Ed
  secondary education • MS Ed

School of Public and Environmental Affairs
Joseph M. Pellicciotti, Director
Programs in:
  criminal justice • MPA
  health services administration • MPA
  human services administration • MPA
  management of public affairs • MPA
  non-profit management • NPMC
  public management • PMC

■ INDIANA UNIVERSITY–PURDUE UNIVERSITY FORT WAYNE
Fort Wayne, IN 46805-1499
http://www.ipfw.edu/

State-supported, coed, comprehensive institution. CGS member. *Enrollment:* 11,806 graduate, professional, and undergraduate students; 103 full-time matriculated graduate/professional students (60 women), 520 part-time matriculated graduate/professional students (313 women). *Graduate faculty:* 112 full-time (41 women), 26 part-time/adjunct (10 women). *Computer facilities:* 285 computers available on campus for general student use. A campuswide

Indiana

network can be accessed from off campus. Internet access and online class registration, students academic records are available. *Library facilities:* Helmke Library. *Graduate expenses:* Tuition, state resident: full-time $3,443; part-time $191 per credit hour. Tuition, nonresident: full-time $7,760; part-time $431 per credit hour. Required fees: $344; $19 per credit hour. *General application contact:* Sandy Franke, Secretary for Graduate Studies, 260-481-6144.

Division of Public and Environmental Affairs
Dr. Barry Hancock, Assistant Dean and Director
Programs in:
 public affairs • MPA
 public management • Certificate

School of Arts and Sciences
Dr. Marc Lipman, Dean
Programs in:
 applied mathematics • MS
 arts and sciences • MA, MAT, MLS, MS
 biology • MS
 English • MA, MAT
 liberal studies • MLS
 mathematics • MS
 operations research • MS
 professional communication • MA, MS
 sociological practice • MA

School of Business and Management Sciences
Dr. John L. Wellington, Dean
Program in:
 business administration • MBA

School of Education
Dr. Barry Kanpol, Dean
Programs in:
 counselor education • MS Ed
 education • MS Ed
 educational administration • MS Ed
 elementary education • MS Ed
 secondary education • MS Ed

School of Engineering, Technology, and Computer Science
Dr. Gerard Voland, Dean, Interim
Programs in:
 applied computer science • MS
 engineering, technology, and computer science • MS

School of Health Sciences
Dr. James E. Jones, Dean
Programs in:
 health sciences • MS
 nursing administration • MS

■ INDIANA UNIVERSITY–PURDUE UNIVERSITY INDIANAPOLIS
Indianapolis, IN 46202-2896
http://www.indiana.edu/

State-supported, coed, university. *Enrollment:* 29,860 graduate, professional, and undergraduate students; 3,221 full-time matriculated graduate/professional students (1,687 women), 3,327 part-time matriculated graduate/professional students (1,836 women). *Graduate faculty:* 607 full-time (180 women), 3 part-time/adjunct (1 woman). *Computer facilities:* 500 computers available on campus for general student use. A campuswide network can be accessed from off campus. Internet access is available. *Library facilities:* University Library plus 5 others. *Graduate expenses:* Tuition, state resident: full-time $4,658; part-time $194 per credit. Tuition, nonresident: full-time $13,444; part-time $560 per credit. Required fees: $571. Tuition and fees vary according to campus/location and program. *General application contact:* Dr. Sheila Cooper, Director, Graduate Studies and Associate Dean, 317-274-4023.

Center on Philanthropy
Dr. Eugene Tempel, Executive Director
Programs in:
 nonprofit management • MPA
 philanthropic studies • MA

Herron School of Art
Valerie Eickmeier, Dean
Program in:
 art education • MAE

Indiana University School of Medicine
Dr. Robert W. Holden, Dean
Programs in:
 anatomy and cell biology • MS, PhD
 biochemistry and molecular biology • MS, PhD
 cellular and integrative physiology • MS, PhD
 medical and molecular genetics • MS, PhD
 medical biophysics • MS, PhD
 medical neurobiology • MS, PhD
 medicine • MD, MS, PhD
 microbiology and immunology • MS, PhD
 pathology and laboratory medicine • MS, PhD
 pharmacology • MS, PhD
 toxicology • MS, PhD

School of Health and Rehabilitation Sciences
Dr. Mark S. Sothmann, Dean of the School of Allied Health Sciences

Programs in:
 health sciences education • MS
 nutrition and dietetics • MS
 physical therapy • MS
 therapeutic outcomes research • MS

Kelley School of Business
Roger W. Schmenner, Associate Dean, Indianapolis Programs
Program in:
 business • MBA, MPA

School of Dentistry
Lawrence I. Goldblatt, Dean
Programs in:
 dental materials • MS, MSD
 dental sciences • PhD
 dentistry • DDS, MS, MSD, PhD
 diagnostic sciences • MS, MSD
 endodontics • MSD
 operative dentistry • MSD
 oral and maxillofacial surgery • MSD
 oral biology • PhD
 orthodontics • MS, MSD
 pediatric dentistry • MSD
 periodontics • MSD
 preventive dentistry • MS, MSD
 prosthodontics • MSD

School of Education
Dr. Barbara Wilcox, Executive Associate Dean
Programs in:
 counseling and counselor education • MS
 education • MS
 educational leadership and school administration • MS
 elementary education • MS
 higher education and student affairs • MS
 instructional systems technology • MS
 language education • MS
 secondary education • MS
 special education • MS

School of Engineering and Technology
Dr. H. Oner Yurtseven, Dean
Programs in:
 biomedical engineering • MS, MS Bm E, PhD
 electrical and computer engineering • MS, MSECE, PhD
 engineering • MS, MSE
 engineering (interdisciplinary) • MSE
 engineering and technology • MS, MS Bm E, MSE, MSECE, MSME, PhD
 mechanical engineering • MSME

School of Informatics
Dr. Darrell L. Bailey, Associate Dean
Program in:
 media arts and science • MS

Indiana

Indiana University–Purdue University Indianapolis (continued)

School of Liberal Arts
Dr. Herman J. Saatkamp, Dean
Programs in:
 economics • MA
 English • MA
 history • MA
 liberal arts • MA
 public history • MA
 teaching English • MA

School of Library and Information Science
Dr. Blaise Cronin, Dean
Program in:
 library and information science • MIS, MLS

School of Music
Dr. Darrell L. Bailey, Associate Dean
Program in:
 music technology • MS

School of Nursing
Dr. Linda Finke, Associate Dean for Graduate Programs
Programs in:
 acute care nurse practitioner • MSN
 adult clinical nurse specialist • MSN
 adult nurse practitioner • MSN
 clinical nurisng science • PhD
 family nurse practitioner • MSN
 health systems • PhD
 nursing • MSN, PhD
 pediatric • MSN
 pediatric nursing practitioner • MSN
 women's health nurse practitioner • MSN

School of Public and Environmental Affairs
Dr. Mark Rosentraub, Associate Dean
Programs in:
 environmental planning • M Pl
 health administration • MHA
 health planning • M Pl
 planning and public policy • M Pl
 public administration • MPA, Certificate
 public and environmental affairs • M Pl, MHA, MPA, Certificate
 urban development planning • M Pl

School of Science
David L. Stocum, Dean
Programs in:
 applied mathematics • MS, PhD
 applied statistics • MS
 biology • MS, PhD
 chemistry • MS, PhD
 clinical rehabilitation psychology • MS, PhD
 computer science • MS
 geology • MS
 industrial/organizational psychology • MS
 mathematics • MS, PhD
 physics • MS, PhD
 psychobiology of addictions • PhD
 science • MS, PhD

School of Social Work
Michael Patchner, Dean
Program in:
 social work • MSW, PhD

■ INDIANA UNIVERSITY SOUTH BEND
South Bend, IN 46634-7111
http://www.indiana.edu/

State-supported, coed, comprehensive institution. *Enrollment:* 7,280 graduate, professional, and undergraduate students; 177 full-time matriculated graduate/professional students (105 women), 744 part-time matriculated graduate/professional students (485 women). *Graduate faculty:* 128 full-time (58 women), 1 part-time/adjunct (0 women). *Computer facilities:* 200 computers available on campus for general student use. Internet access is available. *Library facilities:* Franklin D. Schurz Library plus 1 other. *Graduate expenses:* Tuition, state resident: part-time $159 per credit hour. Tuition, nonresident: full-time $3,811; part-time $387 per credit hour. International tuition: $9,287 full-time. Tuition and fees vary according to campus/location and program. *General application contact:* Dr. Linda M. Fritshner, Acting Associate Vice Chancellor for Academic Affairs, 574-237-4338.

College of Liberal Arts and Sciences
Dr. Miriam Shillingsburg, Dean
Programs in:
 applied mathematics and computer science • MS
 applied psychology • MA
 liberal arts and sciences • MA, MLS, MS
 liberal studies • MLS

Program in Social Work
Dr. Paul R. Newcomb, Director
Program in:
 social work • MSW

School of Business and Economics
Dr. Bill N. Schwartz, Dean
Programs in:
 accounting • MSA
 business administration • MBA
 business and economics • MBA, MIT, MSA
 management information technologies • MIT

School of Education
Dr. Gwynn Mettetal, Interim Dean
Programs in:
 counseling and human services • MS Ed
 education • MS Ed
 elementary education • MS Ed
 secondary education • MS Ed
 special education • MS Ed

School of Public and Environmental Affairs
Dr. Leda M. Hall, Assistant Dean
Programs in:
 health systems • MPA
 health systems management • Certificate
 nonprofit management • Certificate
 public and community services • MPA
 public management • Certificate
 urban affairs • Certificate

School of the Arts
Dr. Thomas Miller, Dean
Program in:
 music • MM

■ INDIANA UNIVERSITY SOUTHEAST
New Albany, IN 47150-6405
http://www.iu.edu/

State-supported, coed, comprehensive institution. *Enrollment:* 6,408 graduate, professional, and undergraduate students; 26 full-time matriculated graduate/professional students (14 women), 663 part-time matriculated graduate/professional students (426 women). *Graduate faculty:* 101 full-time (45 women). *Computer facilities:* 200 computers available on campus for general student use. A campuswide network can be accessed from off campus. Internet access is available. *Library facilities:* Main library plus 1 other. *Graduate expenses:* Tuition, state resident: full-time $3,779; part-time $157 per credit hour. Tuition, nonresident: full-time $8,644; part-time $360 per credit hour. Required fees: $386. Tuition and fees vary according to campus/location and program. *General application contact:* Dr. Carolyn A. Babione, Graduate Coordinator, 812-941-2594.

School of Business
Dr. Uric Dufrene, Dean
Programs in:
 accounting • Certificate
 business administration • MBA
 economics • Certificate
 finance • Certificate
 general business • Certificate

information and operations
  management • Certificate
management and marketing •
  Certificate
strategic finance • MS

School of Education
Dr. Gloria Murray, Dean
Programs in:
  counselor education • MS Ed
  elementary education • MS Ed
  secondary education • MS Ed

School of Liberal Studies
Dr. Joanna Goldstein, Dean, School of Arts and Letters
Program in:
  liberal studies • MLS

■ INDIANA WESLEYAN UNIVERSITY
Marion, IN 46953-4974
http://www.indwes.edu/

Independent-religious, coed, comprehensive institution. *Enrollment:* 5,133 full-time matriculated graduate/professional students. *Graduate faculty:* 48 full-time, 1,029 part-time/adjunct. *Computer facilities:* 163 computers available on campus for general student use. A campuswide network can be accessed from student residence rooms. Internet access is available. *Library facilities:* Goodman Library. *Graduate expenses:* Tuition: part-time $320 per credit hour. *General application contact:* David McMillan, Assistant Director of Enrollment Management, 765-677-2688.

College of Adult and Professional Studies
Dr. Mark Smith, Vice President
Programs in:
  business administration • MBA
  counseling • MA
  curriculum and instruction • M Ed
  management • MS
  teacher education • M Ed

College of Graduate Studies
Dr. Jim Fuller, Dean
Programs in:
  business administration • MBA
  community counseling • MS
  counseling • MS
  curriculum and instruction • M Ed
  management • MS
  marriage and family counseling • MS
  ministry • MA
  nursing • MS, Post Master's Certificate
  organizational leadership • Ed D

Division of Nursing
Barb Schulz, Interim Director
Programs in:
  community health nursing • MS
  nursing • Post Master's Certificate
  primary care nursing • MS

■ OAKLAND CITY UNIVERSITY
Oakland City, IN 47660-1099
http://www.oak.edu/

Independent-religious, coed, comprehensive institution. *Enrollment:* 1,753 graduate, professional, and undergraduate students; 75 full-time matriculated graduate/professional students (39 women), 190 part-time matriculated graduate/professional students (106 women). *Graduate faculty:* 6 full-time (1 woman), 43 part-time/adjunct (8 women). *Computer facilities:* 92 computers available on campus for general student use. Internet access is available. *Library facilities:* Founders Memorial Library. *Graduate expenses:* Tuition: full-time $2,700; part-time $150 per hour. Required fees: $320. *General application contact:* Counselor for Graduate Admissions, 812-749-1241.

Chapman School of Religious Studies
Dr. Ray Barber, Dean
Program in:
  religious studies • M Div, D Min

School of Adult Degrees
Dr. Ora Johnson, Executive Vice President
Program in:
  management • MS Mgt

School of Education and Technology
Dr. Patricia A. Swails, Dean
Programs in:
  educational leadership • Ed D
  teaching • MA

■ PURDUE UNIVERSITY
West Lafayette, IN 47907
http://www.purdue.edu/

State-supported, coed, university. CGS member. *Computer facilities:* 2,100 computers available on campus for general student use. A campuswide network can be accessed from student residence rooms and from off campus. Internet access is available. *Library facilities:* Hicks Undergraduate Library plus 14 others. *General application contact:* Graduate School Admissions, 765-494-2600.

Graduate School
Programs in:
  biochemistry and molecular biology • PhD
  genetics • MS, PhD
  neuroscience • PhD
  plant biology • PhD

College of Agriculture
Dr. Victor L. Lechtenberg, Dean
Programs in:
  agricultural economics • MS, PhD
  agriculture • EMBA, M Agr, MS, MSF, PhD
  agronomy • MS, PhD
  animal sciences • MS, PhD
  aquaculture, fisheries, aquatic science • MSF
  aquaculture, fisheries, aquatic sciences • MS, PhD
  biochemistry • MS, PhD
  botany and plant pathology • MS, PhD
  entomology • MS, PhD
  food and agricultural business • EMBA
  food science • MS, PhD
  forest biology • MS, MSF, PhD
  horticulture • M Agr, MS, PhD
  natural resources and environmental policy • MS, MSF
  natural resources environmental policy • PhD
  quantitative resource analysis • MS, MSF, PhD
  wildlife science • MS, MSF, PhD
  wood science and technology • MS, MSF, PhD

Krannert Graduate School of Management
Programs in:
  accounting • MS, PhD
  applied optimization • PhD
  applied statistics • PhD
  economics • MS, PhD
  finance • MSM, PhD
  general management • MSM
  human resource management • MS
  industrial administration • MSIA
  management • EMS
  management information systems • MSM, PhD
  management science • MSM
  marketing • MSM, PhD
  operations management • MSM, PhD
  organizational behavior and human resource management • PhD
  quantitative methods • MSM, PhD
  strategic management • MSM, PhD

School of Consumer and Family Sciences
Programs in:
  consumer and family sciences • MS, PhD
  consumer behavior • MS, PhD
  developmental studies • MS, PhD

Indiana

Purdue University (continued)
  family and consumer economics • MS, PhD
  family studies • MS, PhD
  food sciences • MS, PhD
  hospitality and tourism management • MS, PhD
  marriage and family therapy • MS, PhD
  nutrition • MS, PhD
  retail management • MS, PhD
  textile science • MS, PhD

School of Education
Programs in:
  administration • MS Ed, PhD, Ed S
  agricultural and extension education • PhD, Ed S
  agriculture and extension education • MS, MS Ed
  art education • PhD
  consumer and family sciences and extension education • MS Ed, PhD, Ed S
  counseling and development • MS Ed, PhD
  curriculum studies • MS Ed, PhD, Ed S
  education • MS, MS Ed, PhD, Ed S
  education of the gifted • MS Ed
  educational psychology • MS Ed, PhD
  educational technology • MS Ed, PhD, Ed S
  elementary education • MS Ed
  foreign language education • MS Ed, PhD, Ed S
  foundations of education • MS Ed, PhD
  higher education administration • MS Ed, PhD
  industrial technology • PhD, Ed S
  language arts • MS Ed, PhD, Ed S
  literacy • MS Ed, PhD, Ed S
  mathematics/science education • MS, MS Ed, PhD, Ed S
  social studies • MS Ed, PhD
  social studies education • Ed S
  special education • MS Ed, PhD
  vocational/industrial education • MS Ed, PhD, Ed S
  vocational/technical education • MS Ed, PhD, Ed S

School of Health Sciences
Programs in:
  environmental health • MS, PhD
  health physics • MS, PhD
  health sciences • MS, PhD
  industrial hygiene • MS, PhD
  medical physics • MS, PhD
  toxicology • MS, PhD

School of Liberal Arts
Programs in:
  American studies • MA, PhD
  anthropology • MS, PhD
  art and design • MA
  audiology • MS, Au D, PhD
  communication • MA, MS, PhD
  comparative literature • MA, PhD
  creative writing • MFA
  exercise, human physiology of movement and sport • PhD
  French • MA, MAT, PhD
  French education • MAT
  German • MA, MAT, PhD
  German education • MAT
  health and fitness • MS
  health promotion • MS
  health promotion and disease prevention • PhD
  history • MA, PhD
  liberal arts • MA, MAT, MFA, MS, Au D, PhD
  linguistics • MS, PhD
  literature • MA, PhD
  movement and sport science • MS
  pedagogy and administration • MS
  pedagogy of physical activity and health • PhD
  philosophy • MA, PhD
  political science • MA, PhD
  psychological sciences • PhD
  psychology of sport and exercise, and motor behavior • PhD
  sociology • MS, PhD
  Spanish • MA, MAT, PhD
  Spanish education • MAT
  speech and hearing science • MS, PhD
  speech-language pathology • MS, PhD
  theatre • MA, MFA

School of Science
Programs in:
  analytical chemistry • MS, PhD
  applied statistics • MS
  biochemistry • MS, PhD
  biophysics • PhD
  cell and developmental biology • PhD
  chemical education • MS, PhD
  computer sciences • MS, PhD
  earth and atmospheric sciences • MS, PhD
  ecology • MS, PhD
  ecology, evolutionary and population biology • MS, PhD
  evolutionary biology • MS, PhD
  genetics • MS, PhD
  inorganic chemistry • MS, PhD
  mathematics • MS, PhD
  microbiology • MS, PhD
  molecular biology • PhD
  neurobiology • MS, PhD
  organic chemistry • MS, PhD
  physical chemistry • MS, PhD
  physics • MS, PhD
  plant physiology • PhD
  population biology • MS, PhD
  science • MS, PhD
  statistics • PhD
  statistics and computer science • MS
  statistics/computational finance • MS
  theoretical statistics • MS

School of Technology
Program in:
  technology • MS

Schools of Engineering
Dr. Linda P. Katehi, John A. Edwardson Dean of Engineering
Programs in:
  aeronautics and astronautics • MS, MSAAE, MSE, PhD
  agricultural and biological engineering • MS, MSABE, MSE, PhD
  biomedical engineering • MSBME, PhD
  chemical engineering • MS, PhD
  civil engineering • MS, MSCE, MSE, PhD
  computer engineering • MS, PhD
  continuing engineering education • MS, MSE
  electrical engineering • MS, PhD
  engineering • MS, MSAAE, MSABE, MSBME, MSCE, MSCHE, MSE, MSECE, MSIE, MSME, MSMSE, MSNE, PhD
  human factors in industrial engineering • MS, MSIE, PhD
  manufacturing engineering • MS, MSIE, PhD
  materials engineering • MS, MSE, PhD
  mechanical engineering • MS, MSE, MSME, PhD
  nuclear engineering • MS, MSNE, PhD
  operations research • MS, MSIE, PhD
  systems engineering • MS, MSIE, PhD

School of Pharmacy and Pharmacal Sciences
Programs in:
  analytical medicinal chemistry • PhD
  clinical pharmacy • MS, PhD
  computational and biophysical medicinal chemistry • PhD
  industrial and physical pharmacy • PhD
  medicinal and bioorganic chemistry • PhD
  medicinal biochemistry and molecular biology • PhD
  medicinal chemistry and molecular pharmacology • MS, PhD
  molecular pharmacology and toxicology • PhD
  natural products and pharmacognosy • PhD
  nuclear pharmacy • MS
  pharmacy administration • MS, PhD
  pharmacy and pharmacal sciences • Pharm D, MS, PhD
  pharmacy practice • MS, PhD
  radiopharmaceutical chemistry and nuclear pharmacy • PhD

Indiana

School of Veterinary Medicine
Dr. Alan H. Rebar, Dean
Program in:
  veterinary medicine • DVM, MS, PhD

Graduate Programs in Veterinary Medicine
Programs in:
  anatomy • MS, PhD
  basic medical sciences • MS, PhD
  biochemistry and molecular biology • MS, PhD
  comparative epidemiology • MS, PhD
  epidemiology • MS, PhD
  immunology • MS, PhD
  infectious diseases • MS, PhD
  interdisciplinary genetics • PhD
  microbiology • MS, PhD
  molecular virology • MS, PhD
  parasitology • MS, PhD
  pathobiology • MS, PhD
  pharmacology • MS, PhD
  physiology • MS, PhD
  public health epidemiology • MS, PhD
  toxicology • MS, PhD
  veterinary anatomic pathology • MS, PhD
  veterinary clinical pathology • MS, PhD
  veterinary clinical sciences • MS, PhD
  veterinary pathobiology • MS, PhD
  virology • MS, PhD

■ **PURDUE UNIVERSITY CALUMET**
Hammond, IN 46323-2094
http://www.calumet.purdue.edu/

State-supported, coed, comprehensive institution. *Computer facilities:* 250 computers available on campus for general student use. A campuswide network can be accessed. Internet access is available. *Library facilities:* Purdue Calumet Library. *General application contact:* Secretary, Graduate School, 219-989-2257.

Graduate School

School of Education
Programs in:
  counseling and personnel services • MS Ed
  educational administration • MS Ed
  elementary education • MS Ed
  instructional development • MS Ed
  media sciences • MS Ed
  secondary education • MS Ed

School of Engineering, Mathematics, and Science
Programs in:
  biology • MS
  biology teaching • MS
  engineering • MSE
  engineering, mathematics, and science • MAT, MS, MSE
  mathematics • MAT, MS

School of Liberal Arts and Sciences
Programs in:
  communication • MA
  English and philosophy • MA
  history and political science • MA
  liberal arts and sciences • MA, MS
  marriage and family therapy • MS

School of Management
Programs in:
  accountancy • M Acc
  business administration • MBA

School of Nursing
Program in:
  nursing • MS

■ **UNIVERSITY OF EVANSVILLE**
Evansville, IN 47722-0002
http://www.evansville.edu/

Independent-religious, coed, comprehensive institution. *Enrollment:* 2,650 graduate, professional, and undergraduate students; 154 full-time matriculated graduate/professional students (117 women), 10 part-time matriculated graduate/professional students (9 women). *Graduate faculty:* 42. *Computer facilities:* Computer purchase and lease plans are available. 375 computers available on campus for general student use. A campuswide network can be accessed from student residence rooms and from off campus. Internet access and online class registration are available. *Library facilities:* Bower Suhrhoinrich Library plus 1 other. *Graduate expenses:* Tuition: full-time $5,640; part-time $500 per hour. Part-time tuition and fees vary according to course load and program. *General application contact:* Dr. Lynn Penland, Dean, 812-479-2360.

Graduate Programs
Dr. Lynn Penland, Dean
Program in:
  public service administration • MPSA

College of Education and Health Sciences
Programs in:
  education • MPT, MS
  nursing and health sciences • MS
  physical therapy • MPT

■ **UNIVERSITY OF INDIANAPOLIS**
Indianapolis, IN 46227-3697
http://www.uindy.edu/

Independent-religious, coed, comprehensive institution. *Enrollment:* 3,986 graduate, professional, and undergraduate students; 332 full-time matriculated graduate/professional students (251 women), 631 part-time matriculated graduate/professional students (408 women). *Graduate faculty:* 15 full-time (10 women), 79 part-time/adjunct (29 women). *Computer facilities:* 218 computers available on campus for general student use. A campuswide network can be accessed from student residence rooms and from off campus. Internet access is available. *Library facilities:* Krannert Memorial Library. *Graduate expenses:* Tuition: full-time $22,178. Tuition and fees vary according to course level, degree level and program. *General application contact:* Dr. Mary C. Moore, Vice President for Research, Planning and Strategic Partnerships, 317-788-3212.

Graduate Programs
Dr. Mary C. Moore, Vice President for Research, Planning and Strategic Partnerships
Programs in:
  family practice (post-RN) • MSN
  gerontology • MA
  nursing • MSN

College of Arts and Sciences
Dr. David L. Anderson, Dean
Programs in:
  applied sociology • MA
  art • MA
  arts and sciences • MA, MS
  biology • MS
  English language and literature • MA
  history • MA

Krannert School of Physical Therapy
Dr. Elizabeth Domholdt, Dean
Program in:
  physical therapy • MHS, DHS, DPT, TDPT

School of Business
Dr. James Conrad, Dean
Programs in:
  accounting • M Acc
  business administration • MBA

School of Education
Dr. E. Lynne Weisenbach, Dean
Programs in:
  art education • MAT
  biology • MAT
  chemistry • MAT
  earth sciences • MAT
  education • MA, MAT
  elementary education • MA
  English • MAT
  French • MAT
  math • MAT
  physical education • MAT
  physics • MAT

Peterson's Graduate Schools in the U.S. 2006

Indiana

University of Indianapolis (continued)
  secondary education • MA
  social studies • MAT
  Spanish • MAT

School of Occupational Therapy
Dr. Penelope Moyers, Dean
Program in:
  occupational therapy • MHS, MOT, MS, OTD

School of Psychological Sciences
Dr. John McIlvried, Dean
Program in:
  psychological sciences • MA, Psy D

■ **UNIVERSITY OF NOTRE DAME**
Notre Dame, IN 46556
http://www.nd.edu/

Independent-religious, coed, university. CGS member. *Enrollment:* 11,415 graduate, professional, and undergraduate students; 2,865 matriculated graduate/professional students. *Graduate faculty:* 1,067. *Computer facilities:* Computer purchase and lease plans are available. 880 computers available on campus for general student use. A campuswide network can be accessed from student residence rooms and from off campus. Internet access and online class registration are available. *Library facilities:* University Libraries of Notre Dame plus 9 others. *Graduate expenses:* Tuition: full-time $29,375. *General application contact:* Dr. Terrence J. Akai, Director of Graduate Admissions, 574-631-7706.

Find an in-depth description at www.petersons.com/gradchannel.

Graduate School
Dr. Jeffrey C. Kantor, Vice President for Graduate Studies and Research and Dean of the Graduate School

College of Arts and Letters
Dr. Mark W. Roche, Dean
Programs in:
  art history • MA
  arts and letters • M Div, M Ed, MA, MFA, MM, MMS, MTS, PhD
  cognitive psychology • PhD
  counseling psychology • PhD
  creative writing • MFA
  design • MFA
  developmental psychology • PhD
  early Christian studies • MA
  educational initiatives • M Ed
  English • MA, PhD
  French and Francophone studies • MA
  German • MA
  history • MA, PhD
  history and philosophy of science • MA, PhD
  humanities • M Div, MA, MFA, MM, MMS, MTS, PhD
  Iberian and Latin American studies • MA
  international peace studies • MA
  Italian studies • MA
  literature • MA
  medieval studies • MMS, PhD
  music • MA, MM
  philosophy • PhD
  political science • PhD
  quantitative psychology • PhD
  Romance literatures • MA
  social science • M Ed, MA, PhD
  sociology • PhD
  studio art • MFA
  theology • M Div, MA, MTS, PhD

College of Engineering
Dr. Frank P. Incropera, Dean
Programs in:
  aerospace and mechanical engineering • M Eng, PhD
  aerospace engineering • MS Aero E
  bioengineering • MS Bio E
  chemical engineering • MS Ch E, PhD
  civil engineering • MSCE
  civil engineering and geological sciences • PhD
  computer science and engineering • MSCSE
  electrical engineering • MSEE, PhD
  engineering • M Eng, MEME, MS, MS Aero E, MS Bio E, MS Ch E, MS Env E, MSCE, MSCSE, MSEE, MSME, PhD
  environmental engineering • MS Env E
  geological sciences • MS
  mechanical engineering • MEME, MSME

College of Science
Dr. Joseph P. Marino, Dean
Programs in:
  algebra • PhD
  algebraic geometry • PhD
  applied mathematics • MSAM
  aquatic ecology, evolution and environmental biology • MS, PhD
  biochemistry • MS, PhD
  cellular and molecular biology • MS, PhD
  complex analysis • PhD
  differential geometry • PhD
  genetics • MS, PhD
  inorganic chemistry • MS, PhD
  logic • PhD
  organic chemistry • MS, PhD
  partial differential equations • PhD
  physical chemistry • MS, PhD
  physics • PhD
  physiology • MS, PhD
  science • MS, MSAM, PhD
  topology • PhD
  vector biology and parasitology • MS, PhD

School of Architecture
Prof. Norman Crowe, Director of Graduate Studies
Programs in:
  architectural design and urbanism • M Arch
  architecture • M Arch

Law School
Patricia A. O'Hara, Dean
Programs in:
  human rights • LL M, JSD
  international and comparative law • LL M
  law • JD

Mendoza College of Business
Dr. Carolyn Y. Woo, Dean
Programs in:
  accountancy • MS
  administration • MSA
  business • MBA, MS, MSA
  executive education • MBA

■ **UNIVERSITY OF SAINT FRANCIS**
Fort Wayne, IN 46808-3994
http://www.sf.edu/

Independent-religious, coed, comprehensive institution. *Enrollment:* 1,834 graduate, professional, and undergraduate students; 77 full-time matriculated graduate/professional students (58 women), 134 part-time matriculated graduate/professional students (100 women). *Graduate faculty:* 39 full-time (24 women), 15 part-time/adjunct (7 women). *Computer facilities:* 135 computers available on campus for general student use. A campuswide network can be accessed. Internet access and online class registration are available. *Library facilities:* University Library plus 1 other. *Graduate expenses:* Tuition: full-time $6,000; part-time $500 per credit hour. *General application contact:* Derek Campbell, Admissions Counselor, 260-434-7485.

Graduate School
Dr. Marcia Sauter, Chair
Programs in:
  business administration • MBA, MS
  fine art • MA
  general psychology • MS
  mental health counseling • MS
  nursing • MSN
  physician assistant studies • MS
  school counseling • MS Ed
  special education • MS Ed

■ UNIVERSITY OF SOUTHERN INDIANA
Evansville, IN 47712-3590
http://www.usi.edu/

State-supported, coed, comprehensive institution. CGS member. *Enrollment:* 9,899 graduate, professional, and undergraduate students; 97 full-time matriculated graduate/professional students (72 women), 518 part-time matriculated graduate/professional students (376 women). *Graduate faculty:* 83 full-time (33 women). *Computer facilities:* 778 computers available on campus for general student use. A campuswide network can be accessed from student residence rooms and from off campus. Internet access and online class registration are available. *Library facilities:* David L. Rice Library plus 1 other. *Graduate expenses:* Tuition, state resident: full-time $3,335; part-time $185 per credit hour. Tuition, nonresident: full-time $6,588; part-time $366 per credit hour. Required fees: $60; $23 per semester. Tuition and fees vary according to course load. *General application contact:* Dr. Peggy F. Harrel, Director, Graduate Studies, 812-465-7015.

Graduate Studies
Dr. Peggy F. Harrel, Director

School of Business
Dr. R. Eugene Klippel, Dean
Programs in:
  accountancy • MSA
  business • MBA, MSA
  business administration • MBA

School of Education and Human Services
Dr. Thomas Pickering, Dean
Programs in:
  education and human services • MS, MSW
  elementary education • MS
  secondary education • MS
  social work • MSW

School of Liberal Arts
Dr. David L. Glassman, Dean
Programs in:
  liberal arts • MA, MPA
  liberal studies • MA
  public administration • MPA

School of Nursing and Health Professions
Dr. Nadine Coudret, Dean
Programs in:
  health administration • MHA
  nursing • MSN
  nursing and health professions • MHA, MSN, MSOT
  occupational therapy • MSOT

School of Science and Engineering Technology
Dr. Jerome Cain, Dean
Programs in:
  industrial management • MS
  science and engineering • MS

■ VALPARAISO UNIVERSITY
Valparaiso, IN 46383-6493
http://www.valpo.edu/

Independent-religious, coed, comprehensive institution. *Enrollment:* 3,850 graduate, professional, and undergraduate students; 600 full-time matriculated graduate/professional students (318 women), 224 part-time matriculated graduate/professional students (157 women). *Graduate faculty:* 232 full-time, 112 part-time/adjunct. *Computer facilities:* 585 computers available on campus for general student use. A campuswide network can be accessed from student residence rooms and from off campus. Internet access is available. *Library facilities:* Moellering Library plus 1 other. *Graduate expenses:* Tuition: part-time $335 per credit hour. *General application contact:* Dr. David L. Rowland, Dean, Graduate Studies and Continuing Education, 219-464-5313.

Graduate Division
Dr. David L. Rowland, Dean, Graduate Studies and Continuing Education
Programs in:
  clinical mental health counseling • MA
  counseling • MA
  English • MALS
  ethics and values • MALS
  history • MALS
  human behavior and society • MALS
  initial licensure • M Ed
  international commerce and policy • MS
  special education • M Ed, MS Sp Ed
  sports administration • MS
  teaching and learning • M Ed
  theology • MALS
  theology and ministry • MALS
  U.S. culture • MALS

College of Business Administration
Dr. Dean Schroeder, Director
Program in:
  business administration • MBA

College of Nursing
Dr. Janet Brown, Dean
Program in:
  nursing • MSN, Post-Master's Certificate

School of Law
Jay Conison, Dean
Program in:
  law • JD, LL M

Iowa

■ DRAKE UNIVERSITY
Des Moines, IA 50311-4516
http://www.drake.edu/

Independent, coed, university. *Enrollment:* 5,164 graduate, professional, and undergraduate students; 1,281 full-time matriculated graduate/professional students (793 women), 861 part-time matriculated graduate/professional students (526 women). *Graduate faculty:* 80 full-time (36 women), 47 part-time/adjunct (20 women). *Computer facilities:* 360 computers available on campus for general student use. A campuswide network can be accessed from student residence rooms and from off campus. Internet access is available. *Library facilities:* Cowles Library plus 1 other. *Graduate expenses:* Tuition: full-time $20,700; part-time $387 per credit hour. Required fees: $270; $7 per credit hour. Part-time tuition and fees vary according to class time, course load, degree level, program and student level. *General application contact:* Ann J. Martin, Graduate Coordinator, 515-271-3871.

Find an in-depth description at www.petersons.com/gradchannel.

College of Business and Public Administration
Dr. Charles Edwards, Dean
Program in:
  business and public administration • M Acc, MBA, MPA

College of Pharmacy and Health Sciences
Dr. Raylene Rospond, Dean
Programs in:
  pharmacy • Pharm D
  pharmacy and health sciences • Pharm D

Law School
David Walker, Dean
Program in:
  law • JD

School of Education
Dr. Salina Shrofel, Dean
Programs in:
  adult education • MS

Iowa

Drake University (continued)
  adult learning, performance and development • MS
  art • MAT
  biology • MAT
  business • MAT
  chemistry • MAT
  community agency counseling • MSE
  counseling • MSE
  education • MAT, MS, MSE, MST, Ed D, Ed S
  education leadership • MSE, Ed D, Ed S
  effective teaching, learning and leadership • MSE
  elementary education • MST
  English • MAT
  general science • MAT
  guidance counseling • MSE
  history-American • MAT
  history-world • MAT
  journalism • MAT
  mathematics • MAT
  physical science • MAT
  physics • MAT
  secondary education • MAT
  sociology • MAT
  special education • MSE
  speech • MAT
  speech communication • MAT
  teacher education • MSE
  theatre • MAT
  vocational rehabilitation • MS
  vocational rehabilitation administration • MS
  vocational rehabilitation counseling • MS
  vocational rehabilitation placement • MS

■ IOWA STATE UNIVERSITY OF SCIENCE AND TECHNOLOGY
Ames, IA 50011
http://www.iastate.edu/

State-supported, coed, university. CGS member. *Enrollment:* 27,380 graduate, professional, and undergraduate students; 2,695 full-time matriculated graduate/professional students (1,052 women), 2,046 part-time matriculated graduate/professional students (826 women). *Graduate faculty:* 1,413 full-time, 118 part-time/adjunct. *Computer facilities:* Computer purchase and lease plans are available. 2,700 computers available on campus for general student use. A campuswide network can be accessed from student residence rooms and from off campus. Internet access and online class registration, e-mail, network services are available. *Library facilities:* University Library plus 1 other. *Graduate expenses:* Tuition, nonresident: part-time $560 per credit. Required fees: $38 per unit. *General application contact:* 515-294-5836.

Find an in-depth description at www.petersons.com/gradchannel.

College of Veterinary Medicine
Dr. Norman Cheville, Dean
Programs in:
  biomedical sciences • MS, PhD
  veterinary clinical sciences • MS
  veterinary diagnostic and production animal medicine • MS
  veterinary medicine • DVM, MS, PhD
  veterinary microbiology • MS, PhD
  veterinary microbiology and preventive medicine • MS, PhD
  veterinary pathology • MS, PhD
  veterinary preventative medicine • MS

Graduate College
Dr. James R. Bloedel, Dean of the Graduate College
Programs in:
  bioinformatics and computational biology • MS, PhD
  biorenewable resources and technology • MS, PhD
  ecology and evolutionary biology • MS, PhD
  family and consumer sciences • MFCS
  genetics • MS, PhD
  human-computer interaction • MS, PhD
  immunobiology • MS, PhD
  industrial relations • MS
  information assurance • MS
  interdisciplinary graduate studies • MA, MS
  interdisciplinary studies • M Eng, MA, MFCS, MS, PhD
  microbiology • MS, PhD
  molecular, cellular, and developmental biology • MS, PhD
  neuroscience • MS, PhD
  plant physiology • MS, PhD
  systems engineering • M Eng
  toxicology • MS, PhD
  transportation • MS
  water resources • MS, PhD

College of Agriculture
Dr. Catherine E. Woteki, Dean
Programs in:
  agricultural education and studies • MS, PhD
  agricultural meteorology • MS, PhD
  agriculture • M Ag, MS, PhD
  agronomy • MS
  animal breeding and genetics • MS, PhD
  animal ecology • MS, PhD
  animal nutrition • MS, PhD
  animal physiology • MS
  animal psychology • PhD
  animal science • MS, PhD
  biochemistry • MS, PhD
  biophysics • MS, PhD
  crop production and physiology • MS, PhD
  entomology • MS, PhD
  forestry • MS, PhD
  genetics • MS, PhD
  horticulture • MS, PhD
  meat science • MS, PhD
  molecular, cellular, and developmental biology • MS, PhD
  plant breeding • MS, PhD
  plant pathology • MS, PhD
  soil science • MS, PhD
  toxicology • MS, PhD

College of Business
Dr. Labh S. Hira, Interim Dean
Programs in:
  accounting • M Acc
  business • M Acc, MBA, MS
  business administration • MBA, MS
  information systems • MS

College of Design
Mark Engelbrecht, Dean
Programs in:
  architectural studies • MSAS
  architecture • M Arch
  art and design • MA
  art education • MA
  community and regional planning • MCRP
  design • M Arch, MA, MCRP, MFA, MLA, MS, MSAS
  graphic design • MFA
  integrated visual arts • MFA
  interior design • MFA
  landscape architecture • MLA
  transportation • MS

College of Education
Dr. Walter H. Gmelch, Dean
Programs in:
  counselor education • M Ed, MS
  curriculum and instructional technology • M Ed, MS, PhD
  education • M Ed
  educational administration • M Ed, MS
  educational leadership • PhD
  elementary education • M Ed, MS
  exercise and sport science • MS
  health and human performance • PhD
  higher education • M Ed, MS
  historical, philosophical, and comparative studies in education • M Ed, MS
  industrial education and technology • MS, PhD
  organizational learning and human resource development • M Ed, MS
  research and evaluation • MS
  special education • M Ed, MS

Iowa

College of Engineering
Dr. James L. Melsa, Dean
Programs in:
aerospace engineering • M Eng, MS, PhD
agricultural and biosystems engineering • M Eng, MS, PhD
chemical engineering • M Eng, MS, PhD
civil engineering • MS, PhD
computer engineering • MS, PhD
electrical engineering • MS, PhD
engineering • M Eng, MS, PhD
engineering mechanics • M Eng, MS, PhD
industrial engineering • MS, PhD
materials science and engineering • MS, PhD
mechanical engineering • MS, PhD
operations research • MS

College of Family and Consumer Sciences
Dr. Pamela White, Interim Dean
Programs in:
family and consumer science education and studies • M Ed
family and consumer sciences • M Ed, MFCS, MS, PhD
family and consumer sciences education and studies • MS, PhD
food science and technology • MS, PhD
foodservice and lodging management • MFCS, MS, PhD
human development and family studies • MFCS, MS, PhD
marriage and family therapy • PhD
nutrition • MS, PhD
textiles and clothing • MFCS, MS, PhD

College of Liberal Arts and Sciences
Dr. Michael Whiteford, Dean
Programs in:
agricultural economics • MS, PhD
agricultural history and rural studies • PhD
anthropology • MA
applied mathematics • MS, PhD
applied physics • MS, PhD
astrophysics • MS, PhD
chemistry • MS, PhD
cognitive psychology • PhD
computer science • MS, PhD
condensed matter physics • MS, PhD
counseling psychology • PhD
earth science • MS, PhD
ecology, evolution, and organismal biology • MS, PhD
economics • MS, PhD
English • MA
general psychology • MS
genetics, developmental and cell biology • MS, PhD
geology • MS, PhD
high energy physics • MS, PhD
history • MA
history of technology and science • MA, PhD
journalism and mass communication • MS
liberal arts and sciences • MA, MPA, MS, MSM, PhD
mathematics • MS, PhD
meteorology • MS, PhD
nuclear physics • MS, PhD
physics • MS, PhD
political science • MA
public administration • MPA
rhetoric and professional communication • PhD
rural sociology • MS, PhD
school mathematics • MSM
social psychology • PhD
sociology • MS, PhD
statistics • MS, PhD
water resources • MS, PhD

■ **LORAS COLLEGE**
Dubuque, IA 52004-0178
http://www.loras.edu/

Independent-religious, coed, comprehensive institution. *Enrollment:* 1,764 graduate, professional, and undergraduate students; 11 full-time matriculated graduate/professional students (5 women), 99 part-time matriculated graduate/professional students (65 women). *Graduate faculty:* 18 full-time (7 women), 6 part-time/adjunct (2 women). *Computer facilities:* Computer purchase and lease plans are available. 105 computers available on campus for general student use. A campuswide network can be accessed from student residence rooms and from off campus. Internet access is available. *Library facilities:* Academic Resource Center. *Graduate expenses:* Tuition: part-time $400 per credit. *General application contact:* Barb Harrington, Graduate Admissions Coordinator, 563-588-4915.

Graduate Division
Dr. Mary Weck, Director
Programs in:
administration of athletics • MA
clinical psychology • MA
effective teaching • MA
elementary school administration • MA
general physical education • MA
general psychology • MA
literature • MA
ministry • MA
multicategorical resource (7–12) • MA
multicategorical resource (K–6) • MA
multicategorical special class with integration (7–12) • MA
multicategorical special class with integration (K–6) • MA
multidisciplinary studies • MA
secondary school administration • MA
special education • MA
theology • MA

■ **MAHARISHI UNIVERSITY OF MANAGEMENT**
Fairfield, IA 52557
http://www.mum.edu/

Independent, coed, university. *Enrollment:* 790 graduate, professional, and undergraduate students; 526 full-time matriculated graduate/professional students (150 women), 10 part-time matriculated graduate/professional students (6 women). *Graduate faculty:* 36 full-time (10 women), 12 part-time/adjunct (8 women). *Computer facilities:* 120 computers available on campus for general student use. A campuswide network can be accessed from student residence rooms and from off campus. Internet access is available. *Library facilities:* Maharishi University of Management Library plus 1 other. *Graduate expenses:* Tuition: full-time $23,600; part-time $550 per unit. Required fees: $215 per semester. Part-time tuition and fees vary according to course load. *General application contact:* Richard Neate, Director of Admissions, 641-472-1110.

Graduate Studies
Dr. Frederick Travis, Dean of the Graduate School
Programs in:
business administration • MBA, PhD
computer science • MS
Maharishi Vedic science • MA, PhD
physiology with specialization in Maharishi Vedic medicine • MS, PhD
teaching elementary education • MA
teaching secondary education • MA

■ **ST. AMBROSE UNIVERSITY**
Davenport, IA 52803-2898
http://www.sau.edu/

Independent-religious, coed, comprehensive institution. CGS member. *Enrollment:* 3,447 graduate, professional, and undergraduate students; 336 full-time matriculated graduate/professional students (200 women), 628 part-time matriculated graduate/professional students (324 women). *Graduate faculty:* 70 full-time (24 women), 54 part-time/adjunct (9 women). *Computer facilities:* Computer purchase and lease plans are available. 190 computers available on campus for general student use. A campuswide network can be accessed from student residence rooms and from off campus. Internet access and online

Peterson's Graduate Schools in the U.S. 2006

Iowa

St. Ambrose University (continued)
class registration, on-line course syllabi, class listings, grades are available. *Library facilities:* O'Keefe Library plus 1 other. *Graduate expenses:* Tuition: full-time $9,324; part-time $518 per credit hour. One-time fee: $35 full-time. Part-time tuition and fees vary according to degree level, campus/location, program and reciprocity agreements. *General application contact:* Suzanne Humphrey, Assistant Dean for Graduate Studies, 563-333-6308.

College of Arts and Sciences
Dr. Paul Koch, Dean
Programs in:
  arts and sciences • MCJ, MOL, MPS, MSITM, MSW
  criminal justice • MCJ
  information technology management • MSITM
  juvenile justice education • MCJ
  leadership studies • MOL
  pastoral studies • MPS
  social work • MSW

College of Business
Dr. Richard M. Dienesch, Dean
Programs in:
  accounting • M Ac
  business • M Ac, MBA, DBA
  business administration • DBA
  health care • MBA
  management generalist • MBA
  technical management • MBA

College of Education and Health Sciences
Dr. Robert Ristow, Dean
Programs in:
  education and health sciences • M Ed, MOT, DPT
  occupational therapy • MOT
  physical therapy • DPT
  special education • M Ed

■ UNIVERSITY OF DUBUQUE
Dubuque, IA 52001-5099
http://www.dbq.edu/

Independent-religious, coed, comprehensive institution. *Computer facilities:* 220 computers available on campus for general student use. A campuswide network can be accessed from student residence rooms and from off campus. Internet access, intranet are available. *Library facilities:* Charles C. Myer's Library. *General application contact:* Associate Dean for Academic Affairs, 563-589-3205.

Program in Business Administration
Richard Birkenbeuel, Director of Domestic and International MBA Programs
Program in:
  business administration • MBA

Program in Communication
Program in:
  communication • MA

Theological Seminary
Program in:
  theology • M Div, MAR, D Min

■ THE UNIVERSITY OF IOWA
Iowa City, IA 52242-1316
http://www.uiowa.edu/

State-supported, coed, university. CGS member. *Enrollment:* 29,744 graduate, professional, and undergraduate students; 5,722 full-time matriculated graduate/professional students (2,901 women), 3,056 part-time matriculated graduate/professional students (1,503 women). *Graduate faculty:* 1,623 full-time (451 women), 82 part-time/adjunct (12 women). *Computer facilities:* Computer purchase and lease plans are available. 1,200 computers available on campus for general student use. A campuswide network can be accessed from student residence rooms and from off campus. Internet access and online class registration, online degree process, grades, financial aid summary, bills are available. *Library facilities:* Main Library plus 12 others. *Graduate expenses:* Tuition, state resident: full-time $5,038. Tuition, nonresident: full-time $15,072. Tuition and fees vary according to course load and program. *General application contact:* Betty Wood, Assistant Director of Admissions, 319-335-1525.

College of Dentistry
Dr. David C. Johnsen, Dean
Programs in:
  dental public health • MS
  dentistry • DDS, MS, PhD, Certificate
  endodontics • MS, Certificate
  operative dentistry • MS, Certificate
  oral and maxillofacial pathology • Certificate
  oral and maxillofacial radiology • Certificate
  oral and maxillofacial surgery • MS, Certificate
  oral pathology, radiology and medicine • MS, Certificate
  oral science • MS, PhD
  orthodontics • MS, Certificate
  pediatric dentistry • MS, Certificate
  periodontics • MS, Certificate
  preventive and community dentistry • MS
  prosthodontics • MS, Certificate
  stomatology • MS

College of Law
N. William Hines, Dean
Program in:
  law • JD, LL M

College of Pharmacy
Jordan Cohen, Dean
Program in:
  pharmacy • Pharm D, MS, PhD

Graduate College
Dr. John C. Keller, Dean
Programs in:
  applied mathematical and computational sciences • PhD
  genetics • PhD
  immunology • PhD
  molecular biology • PhD
  neuroscience • PhD
  second language acquisition • PhD
  third world development support • MA
  translational biomedicine • MS, PhD
  urban and regional planning • MA, MS

College of Education
Sondra Bowman Damico, Dean
Programs in:
  administration and research • PhD
  art education • MA, PhD
  counseling psychology • PhD
  counselor education • PhD
  curriculum and supervision • MA, PhD
  curriculum supervision • MA
  developmental reading • MA
  early childhood and elementary education • MA, PhD
  early childhood education • MA
  education • MA, MAT, PhD, Ed S
  educational administration • MA, PhD, Ed S
  educational measurement and statistics • MA, PhD
  educational psychology • MA, PhD
  elementary education • MA, PhD
  English education • MA, MAT, PhD
  foreign language education • MA, MAT
  foreign language/ESL education • PhD
  higher education • MA, PhD, Ed S
  language, literature and culture • PhD
  math education • PhD
  mathematics education • MA
  music education • MA, PhD
  rehabilitation counseling • MA, PhD
  school counseling • MA

school psychology • Ed S, PhD
secondary education • MA, MAT, PhD
social foundations • MA, PhD
social studies • MA, PhD
special education • MA, PhD
student affairs • PhD

College of Engineering
Dr. P. Barry Butler, Dean
Programs in:
biomedical engineering • MS, PhD
chemical and biochemical engineering • MS, PhD
civil and environmental engineering • MS, PhD
electrical and computer engineering • MS, PhD
engineering • MS, PhD
engineering design and manufacturing • MS, PhD
ergonomics • MS, PhD
information and engineering management • MS, PhD
mechanical engineering • MS, PhD
operations research • MS, PhD
quality engineering • MS, PhD

College of Liberal Arts and Sciences
Linda Maxson, Dean
Programs in:
African American world studies • MA
American studies • MA, PhD
anthropology • MA, PhD
art • MA, MFA
art history • MA, PhD
Asian civilizations • MA
astronomy • MS
biological sciences • MS, PhD
chemistry • MS, PhD
classics • MA, PhD
communication and mass communication • MA
communication research • MA, PhD
comparative literature • MA, PhD
comparative literature translation • MFA
computer science • MCS, MS, PhD
dance • MFA
development support communication • MA
English • PhD
exercise science • MS, PhD
film and video production • MA, MFA
film studies • MA, PhD
French • MA, PhD
geography • MA, PhD
geoscience • MS, PhD
German • MA, PhD
history • MA, PhD
leisure and recreational sport management • MA
liberal arts • MA, MCS, MFA, MS, MSW, Au D, DMA, PhD
linguistics • MA, PhD
linguistics with TESL • MA
literary criticism • PhD

literary history • PhD
literary studies • MA
mass communication • PhD
mathematics • MS, PhD
music • MA, MFA, DMA, PhD
neural and behavioral sciences • PhD
nonfiction writing • MFA
philosophy • MA, PhD
physics • MS, PhD
political science • MA, PhD
professional journalism • MA
psychology • MA, PhD
psychology of sport and health behavior • MA
psychology of sport and physical activity • PhD
religious studies • MA, PhD
rhetorical studies • MA, PhD
rhetorical theory and stylistics • PhD
Russian • MA
science education • MS, PhD
social work • MSW, PhD
sociology • MA, PhD
Spanish • MA, PhD
speech and hearing science • PhD
speech pathology and audiology • MA, Au D
sports studies • MA, PhD
statistics and actuarial science • MS, PhD
theatre arts • MFA
therapeutic recreation • MA
women's studies • PhD
writer's workshop • MFA

College of Nursing
Melanie Dreher, Dean
Program in:
nursing • MSN, PhD

College of Public Health
Dr. James A. Merchant, Dean
Programs in:
biostatistics • MS, PhD
community and behavioral health • MS, PhD
epidemiology • MS, PhD
health management and policy • MHA, PhD
occupational and environmental health • MS, PhD
public health • MHA, MPH, MS, PhD, Certificate
statistical genetics • PhD, Certificate

Henry B. Tippie College of Business
Prof. Gary C. Fethke, Dean
Programs in:
accountancy • M Ac
accounting • MBA
business • M Ac, MBA, PhD
business administration • PhD
economics • PhD
entrepreneurship • MBA
finance • MBA
individually designed concentration • MBA

management information systems • MBA
management sciences • PhD
marketing • MBA
operations management • MBA
strategic management and consulting • MBA

School of Library and Information Science
David Eichmann, Director
Program in:
library and information science • MA

Roy J. and Lucille A. Carver College of Medicine
Dr. Jean E. Robillard, Dean
Programs in:
biosciences • PhD
clinical investigation • Certificate
medicine • MD, MA, MHA, MPAS, MPH, MPT, MS, DPT, PhD, Certificate
translational biomedical research • MS, PhD

Graduate Programs in Medicine
Programs in:
anatomy and cell biology • PhD
biochemistry • MS, PhD
free radical and radiation biology • MS, PhD
general microbiology and microbial physiology • MS, PhD
immunology • MS, PhD
medicine • MA, MHA, MPAS, MPH, MPT, MS, DPT, PhD
microbial genetics • MS, PhD
pathogenic bacteriology • MS, PhD
pathology • MS
pharmacology • MS, PhD
physical therapy • MA, MPT, DPT
physician assistant • MPAS
physiology and biophysics • PhD
physiology and biophysiology • MS
rehabilitation science • PhD
virology • MS, PhD

■ **UNIVERSITY OF NORTHERN IOWA**
Cedar Falls, IA 50614
http://www.uni.edu/

State-supported, coed, comprehensive institution. CGS member. *Enrollment:* 13,666 graduate, professional, and undergraduate students; 539 full-time matriculated graduate/professional students (355 women), 670 part-time matriculated graduate/professional students (436 women). *Graduate faculty:* 349 full-time (118 women), 10 part-time/adjunct (2 women). *Computer facilities:* Computer purchase and lease plans are available. 1,284 computers available on campus for general student use. A campuswide network can be accessed from student residence rooms and from off campus. Internet access and online

Iowa

University of Northern Iowa (continued) class registration, course registration, student account and grade information are available. *Library facilities:* Rod Library. *Graduate expenses:* Tuition, state resident: full-time $2,519. Tuition, nonresident: full-time $6,056. *General application contact:* Laurie S. Russell, Record Analyst, 319-273-2623.

Graduate College
Dr. John W. Somervill, Dean
Programs in:
  public policy • MPP
  women's studies • MA

College of Business Administration
Dr. Farzad Moussavi, Interim Dean
Programs in:
  accounting • M Acc
  business administration • M Acc, MBA

College of Education
Dr. Jeffrey Cornett, Dean
Programs in:
  communication and training technology • MA
  counseling • MA, MAE, Ed D
  curriculum and instruction • MAE, Ed D
  early childhood education • MAE
  education • MA, MAE, Ed D, Ed S
  education of the gifted • MAE
  educational administration • Ed D
  educational leadership • MAE, Ed D
  educational media • MA
  educational psychology • MAE
  educational technology • MA
  elementary education • MAE
  elementary principal • MAE
  elementary reading and language arts • MAE
  health education • MA
  leisure services • MA, Ed D
  middle school/junior high education • MAE
  physical education • MA
  postsecondary education • MAE
  program administration • MA
  reading • MAE
  reading education • MAE
  school counseling • MAE
  school library media studies • MA
  school psychology • Ed S
  scientific basis of physical education • MA
  secondary principal • MAE
  secondary reading • MAE
  special education • MAE, Ed D
  student affairs • MAE
  teaching/coaching • MA
  youth/human services administration • MA

College of Humanities and Fine Arts
Dr. James F. Lubker, Dean
Programs in:
  art • MA
  art education • MA
  audiology • MA
  communication studies • MA
  composition • MM
  conducting • MM
  English • MA
  French • MA
  German • MA
  humanities and fine arts • MA, MM
  jazz pedagogy • MM
  music • MA
  music education • MM
  music history • MM
  performance • MM
  piano performance and pedagogy • MM
  Spanish • MA
  speech pathology • MA
  teaching English to speakers of other languages • MA
  teaching English to speakers of other languages/French • MA
  teaching English to speakers of other languages/German • MA
  teaching English to speakers of other languages/Spanish • MA
  theatre • MA
  two languages • MA

College of Natural Sciences
Dr. Kichoon Yang, Dean
Programs in:
  biology • MA, MS
  chemistry • MA, MS
  computer science • MA, MS
  environmental science/technology • MS
  industrial technology • MA, DIT
  mathematics • MA
  mathematics for middle grades • MA
  natural sciences • MA, MS, DIT, SP
  science • MA
  science education • MA, SP

College of Social and Behavioral Sciences
Dr. Julia E. Wallace, Dean
Programs in:
  geography • MA
  history • MA
  political science • MA
  psychology • MA
  social and behavioral sciences • MA, MSW
  social work • MSW
  sociology • MA

Kansas

■ BAKER UNIVERSITY
Baldwin City, KS 66006-0065
http://www.bakeru.edu/

Independent-religious, coed, comprehensive institution. *Enrollment:* 821 full-time matriculated graduate/professional students (418 women), 376 part-time matriculated graduate/professional students (270 women). *Graduate faculty:* 11 full-time (5 women), 343 part-time/adjunct (154 women). *Computer facilities:* 129 computers available on campus for general student use. A campuswide network can be accessed from student residence rooms. Internet access is available. *Library facilities:* Collins Library. *Graduate expenses:* Tuition: full-time $9,500; part-time $380 per credit. Required fees: $1,216; $152 per course. One-time fee: $55. Tuition and fees vary according to campus/location and program. *General application contact:* Dr. Donald B. Clardy, Dean, School of Professional and Graduate Studies, 913-491-4432.

School of Professional and Graduate Studies
Dr. Donald B. Clardy, Executive Vice President and Dean
Programs in:
  business • MBA, MSM
  education • MA Ed, MASL
  liberal arts • MLA

■ BENEDICTINE COLLEGE
Atchison, KS 66002-1499
http://www.benedictine.edu/

Independent-religious, coed, comprehensive institution. *Enrollment:* 1,330 graduate, professional, and undergraduate students; 36 full-time matriculated graduate/professional students (11 women), 34 part-time matriculated graduate/professional students (17 women). *Graduate faculty:* 5 full-time (1 woman), 8 part-time/adjunct (2 women). *Computer facilities:* 80 computers available on campus for general student use. A campuswide network can be accessed from student residence rooms and from off campus. Internet access is available. *Library facilities:* Benedictine College Library. *Graduate expenses:* Tuition: full-time $18,000. Tuition and fees vary according to program. *General application contact:* Donna Bonnel, Administrative Assistant of Graduation Programs, 913-367-5340 Ext. 2524.

Executive Master of Business Administration Program
Linda Henry, Administrative Director
Program in:
  executive business administration • EMBA

Program in Business Administration
Dr. Don Hoy, Director
Program in:
  business administration • MBA

Program in Educational Administration
Dr. Dianna Henderson, Director
Program in:
  educational administration • MA

■ EMPORIA STATE UNIVERSITY
Emporia, KS 66801-5087
http://www.emporia.edu/

State-supported, coed, comprehensive institution. CGS member. *Enrollment:* 6,278 graduate, professional, and undergraduate students; 246 full-time matriculated graduate/professional students (160 women), 1,097 part-time matriculated graduate/professional students (794 women). *Graduate faculty:* 196 full-time (62 women), 20 part-time/adjunct (14 women). *Computer facilities:* 410 computers available on campus for general student use. A campuswide network can be accessed from student residence rooms and from off campus. Internet access and online class registration, various software packages are available. *Library facilities:* William Allen White Library. *Graduate expenses:* Tuition, state resident: full-time $2,640; part-time $110 per credit hour. Tuition, nonresident: full-time $8,454; part-time $352 per credit hour. Required fees: $576; $35 per credit hour. Tuition and fees vary according to campus/location. *General application contact:* Mary McKenna, Admissions Coordinator, 800-950-GRAD.

Find an in-depth description at www.petersons.com/gradchannel.

School of Graduate Studies
Dr. Robert J. Grover, Dean

College of Liberal Arts and Sciences
Dr. Rodney Sobieski, Interim Dean
Programs in:
  American history • MAT
  anthropology • MAT
  botany • MS
  chemistry • MS
  earth science • MS
  economics • MAT
  English • MA
  environmental biology • MS
  general biology • MS
  geography • MAT
  history • MA
  liberal arts and sciences • MA, MAT, MM, MS
  mathematics • MS
  microbial and cellular biology • MS
  music education • MM
  performance • MM
  physical science • MS
  physics • MS
  political science • MAT
  social sciences • MAT
  social studies education • MAT
  sociology • MAT
  world history • MAT
  zoology • MS

School of Business
Dr. Robert Hite, Dean
Programs in:
  business • MBA, MS
  business administration • MBA
  business education • MS

School of Library and Information Management
Dr. Diane Bailiff, Interim Dean
Programs in:
  legal information management • MLM
  library and information management • MLS
  library and information science • PhD

The Teachers College
Dr. Teresa Mehring, Dean
Programs in:
  art therapy • MS
  behavior disorders • MS
  clinical psychology • MS
  counselor education • MS
  curriculum and instruction • MS
  early childhood education • MS
  education • MS, Ed S
  educational administration • MS
  elementary education • MS
  general psychology • MS
  gifted, talented, and creative • MS
  health, physical education and recreation • MS
  industrial/organizational psychology • MS
  instructional design and technology • MS
  interrelated special education • MS
  learning disabilities • MS
  mental health counseling • MS
  mental retardation • MS
  psychology • MS
  rehabilitation counseling • MS
  school counseling • MS
  school psychology • MS, Ed S
  special education • MS
  student personnel • MS

■ FORT HAYS STATE UNIVERSITY
Hays, KS 67601-4099
http://www.fhsu.edu/

State-supported, coed, comprehensive institution. CGS member. *Enrollment:* 7,373 graduate, professional, and undergraduate students; 200 full-time matriculated graduate/professional students (116 women), 698 part-time matriculated graduate/professional students (455 women). *Graduate faculty:* 127 full-time (31 women). *Computer facilities:* Computer purchase and lease plans are available. 813 computers available on campus for general student use. A campuswide network can be accessed from student residence rooms and from off campus. Internet access is available. *Library facilities:* Forsyth Library. *Graduate expenses:* Tuition, state resident: part-time $118 per credit hour. Tuition, nonresident: part-time $317 per credit hour. *General application contact:* Dr. Tom Jackson, Dean, 785-628-4236.

Graduate School
Dr. Tom Jackson, Dean

College of Arts and Sciences
Dr. Paul Faber, Dean
Programs in:
  arts and sciences • MA, MFA, MLS, MS, Ed S
  communication • MS
  English • MA
  geology • MS
  history • MA
  liberal studies • MLS
  psychology • MS
  school psychology • Ed S
  studio art • MFA

College of Business and Leadership
Dr. Lawrence Gould, Acting Dean
Programs in:
  accounting • MBA
  business • MBA
  management • MBA

College of Education
Dr. Ed Hammond, Acting Dean
Programs in:
  counseling • MS
  education • MS, Ed S
  education administration • MS, Ed S
  elementary education • MS
  instructional technology • MS
  secondary education • MS
  special education • MS

College of Health and Life Sciences
Dr. Jeff Briggs, Dean
Programs in:
  biology • MS
  health and human performance • MS
  health and life sciences • MS, MSN
  nursing • MSN
  speech-language pathology • MS

■ FRIENDS UNIVERSITY
Wichita, KS 67213
http://www.friends.edu/

Independent, coed, comprehensive institution. *Enrollment:* 472 full-time matriculated graduate/professional

Kansas

Friends University (continued)
students. *Graduate faculty:* 62. *Computer facilities:* 190 computers available on campus for general student use. A campuswide network can be accessed from student residence rooms and from off campus. *Library facilities:* Edmund Stanley Library plus 3 others. *Graduate expenses:* Tuition: part-time $429 per credit hour. *General application contact:* Craig Davis, Director of Graduate Admissions, 800-794-6945 Ext. 5573.

Graduate School
Dr. Al Saber, Dean

Division of Business, Technology, and Leadership
Programs in:
  business law • MS
  business, technology, and leadership • EMBA, MMIS, MS, MSM, MSOD
  executive business administration • EMBA
  management • MSM
  management information systems • MMIS
  organization development • MSOD

Division of Science, Arts, and Education
Programs in:
  Christian ministries • MACM
  elementary education • MAT
  environmental studies • MSES
  family therapy • MSFT
  school leadership • MSL
  science, arts, and education • MACM, MAT, MSES, MSFT, MSL
  secondary education • MAT

■ **KANSAS STATE UNIVERSITY**
Manhattan, KS 66506
http://www.ksu.edu/

State-supported, coed, university. CGS member. *Enrollment:* 23,050 graduate, professional, and undergraduate students; 2,418 full-time matriculated graduate/professional students (1,184 women), 453 part-time matriculated graduate/professional students (201 women). *Graduate faculty:* 1,049. *Computer facilities:* 556 computers available on campus for general student use. A campuswide network can be accessed from student residence rooms and from off campus. Internet access and online class registration are available. *Library facilities:* Hale Library plus 3 others. *Graduate expenses:* Tuition, state resident: part-time $155 per credit hour. Tuition, nonresident: part-time $428 per credit hour. Required fees: $11 per credit hour. *General application contact:* Dr. James Guikema, Associate Dean, 785-532-7927.
Find an in-depth description at www.petersons.com/gradchannel.

College of Veterinary Medicine
Ralph Richardson, Dean
Programs in:
  anatomy • MS
  anatomy and physiology • MS, PhD
  clinical sciences • MS
  diagnostic medicine/pathobiology • MS, PhD
  physiology • MS, PhD
  veterinary medicine • DVM, MS, PhD
  veterinary medicine and surgery • MS

Graduate School
Ron Trewyn, Dean
Programs in:
  food science • MS, PhD
  genetics • MS, PhD

College of Agriculture
Marc Johnson, Dean
Programs in:
  agricultural economics • MAB, MS, PhD
  agriculture • MAB, MS, PhD
  animal nutrition • MS, PhD
  animal reproduction • MS, PhD
  animal sciences and industry • MS, PhD
  crop science • MS, PhD
  entomology • MS, PhD
  genetics • MS, PhD
  grain science and industry • MS, PhD
  horticulture • MS, PhD
  meat science • MS, PhD
  plant pathology • MS, PhD
  range management • MS, PhD
  soil science • MS, PhD
  weed science • MS, PhD

College of Architecture, Planning and Design
Dennis Law, Dean
Programs in:
  architecture • M Arch
  architecture, planning and design • M Arch, MA, MLA, MRCP
  environmental planning and management • MA
  landscape architecture • MLA
  regional and community planning • MRCP

College of Arts and Sciences
Peter Nicholls, Dean
Programs in:
  analytical chemistry • MS
  art • MFA
  arts and sciences • MA, MFA, MM, MPA, MS, PhD
  biochemistry • MS, PhD
  cell biology • MS, PhD
  chemistry • PhD
  developmental biology and physiology • MS, PhD
  economics • MA, PhD
  English • MA
  French • MA
  geography • MA, PhD
  geology • MS
  German • MA
  history • MA, PhD
  inorganic chemistry • MS
  international relations • MA
  kinesiology • MS
  mass communications • MS
  mathematics • MS, PhD
  microbiology and immunology • MS, PhD
  molecular biology and genetics • MS, PhD
  music education • MM
  music history and literature • MM
  organic chemistry • MS
  performance • MM
  performance with pedagogy emphasis • MM
  physical chemistry • MS
  physics • MS, PhD
  political science • MA
  psychology • MS, PhD
  public administration • MPA
  sociology • MA, PhD
  Spanish • MA
  speech • MA
  statistics • MS, PhD
  systematics and ecology • MS, PhD
  theory and composition • MM
  virology and oncology • MS, PhD

College of Business Administration
Yar M. Ebadi, Interim Dean
Programs in:
  accounting • M Acc
  business administration • M Acc, MBA

College of Education
Michael Holen, Dean
Programs in:
  counselor education • PhD
  curriculum and instruction • MS, Ed D, PhD
  education • MS, Ed D, PhD
  educational administration and leadership • MS, Ed D
  foundations and adult education • MS, Ed D, PhD
  school counseling • MS
  special education • MS
  student affairs in higher education • PhD
  student personnel services • MS

College of Engineering
Terry S. King, Dean
Programs in:
  architectural engineering • MS
  bioengineering • MS, PhD

Kansas

biological and agricultural engineering • MS, PhD
chemical engineering • MS, PhD
civil engineering • MS, PhD
communications • MS, PhD
computer engineering • MS, PhD
computer science • MS, PhD
control systems • MS, PhD
electric energy systems • MS, PhD
engineering • PhD
engineering management • MEM
industrial and manufacturing systems engineering • PhD
industrial engineering • MS
instrumentation • MS, PhD
mechanical engineering • MS
nuclear engineering • MS
operations research • MS
signal processing • MS, PhD
software engineering • MSE

College of Human Ecology
Dr. Carol Kellett, Dean
Programs in:
apparel and textiles • MS
dietetics • MS
family studies and human services • MS
food science • MS, PhD
food service and hospitality management • MS, PhD
human ecology • PhD
nutrition • MS, PhD
public health • MS

■ **MIDAMERICA NAZARENE UNIVERSITY**
Olathe, KS 66062-1899
http://www.mnu.edu/

Independent-religious, coed, comprehensive institution. *Enrollment:* 1,952 graduate, professional, and undergraduate students; 246 full-time matriculated graduate/professional students (155 women), 268 part-time matriculated graduate/professional students (227 women). *Graduate faculty:* 11 full-time (5 women), 33 part-time/adjunct (16 women). *Computer facilities:* 85 computers available on campus for general student use. A campuswide network can be accessed from student residence rooms and from off campus. Internet access is available. *Library facilities:* Mabee Library. *Graduate expenses:* Tuition: full-time $13,500. *General application contact:* Melanie Sutherland, Secretary, Graduate Studies in Management, 913-791-3276.

Graduate Studies in Counseling
Dr. Roy Rotz, Director
Program in:
counseling • MAC

Graduate Studies in Education
Dr. Brad D. King, Acting Chair, Division of Education
Programs in:
curriculum and instruction • M Ed
educational technology • MET
special education • MA

Graduate Studies in Management
Dr. Willadee Wehmeyer, Director
Program in:
management • MBA

■ **NEWMAN UNIVERSITY**
Wichita, KS 67213-2097
http://www.newmanu.edu/

Independent-religious, coed, comprehensive institution. *Enrollment:* 2,063 graduate, professional, and undergraduate students; 112 full-time matriculated graduate/professional students (69 women), 174 part-time matriculated graduate/professional students (117 women). *Graduate faculty:* 20 full-time (6 women), 11 part-time/adjunct (7 women). *Computer facilities:* Computer purchase and lease plans are available. 90 computers available on campus for general student use. A campuswide network can be accessed from student residence rooms and from off campus. Internet access is available. *Library facilities:* Ryan Library. *Graduate expenses:* Tuition: part-time $340 per credit hour. *General application contact:* Linda Kay Sabala, Director of Graduate Admissions, 316-942-4291 Ext. 2230.

Program in Business Administration
Dr. Joe Goetz, Dean
Programs in:
entrepreneurship • MBA
international business • MBA
leadership • MBA
management • MBA
technology • MBA

Program in Education
Dr. Guy Glidden, Director
Programs in:
building leadership • MS Ed
curriculum and instruction • MS Ed
elementary/middle-level education • MS Ed
English as a second language • MS Ed
school accountability • MS Ed

Program in Nurse Anesthesia
Dr. Anthony Chipas, Director
Program in:
nurse anesthesia • MS

School of Social Work
Dr. Michael Smith, Dean
Program in:
social work • MSW

■ **PITTSBURG STATE UNIVERSITY**
Pittsburg, KS 66762
http://www.pittstate.edu/

State-supported, coed, comprehensive institution. CGS member. *Computer facilities:* 213 computers available on campus for general student use. A campuswide network can be accessed from student residence rooms and from off campus. Internet access and online class registration are available. *Library facilities:* Leonard H. Axe Library plus 2 others. *General application contact:* Administrative Officer, 620-235-4220.

Graduate School

College of Arts and Sciences
Programs in:
applied communication • MA
applied physics • MS
art education • MA
arts and sciences • MA, MM, MS, MSN
biology • MS
chemistry • MS
communication education • MA
English • MA
history • MA
instrumental music education • MM
mathematics • MS
music history/music literature • MM
nursing • MSN
performance • MM
physics • MS
professional physics • MS
social science • MS
studio art • MA
theatre • MA
theory and composition • MM
vocal music education • MM

College of Education
Programs in:
behavioral disorders • MS
classroom reading teacher • MS
community college and higher education • Ed S
counseling • MS
counselor education • MS
early childhood education • MS
education • MS, Ed S
educational leadership • MS
educational technology • MS
elementary education • MS
learning disabilities • MS
mentally retarded • MS
physical education • MS
psychology • MS
reading • MS
reading specialist • MS
school psychology • Ed S
secondary education • MS
special education teaching • MS

Peterson's Graduate Schools in the U.S. 2006

Kansas

Pittsburg State University (continued)

College of Technology
Programs in:
  engineering technology • MET
  human resource development and technical teacher education • MS, Ed S
  industrial education • Ed S
  technology • MS
  technology education • MS

Kelce College of Business
Programs in:
  accounting • MBA
  business • MBA
  general administration • MBA

■ UNIVERSITY OF KANSAS
Lawrence, KS 66045
http://www.ku.edu

State-supported, coed, university. CGS member. *Enrollment:* 28,580 graduate, professional, and undergraduate students; 4,502 full-time matriculated graduate/professional students (2,451 women), 2,628 part-time matriculated graduate/professional students (1,463 women). *Graduate faculty:* 1,307. *Computer facilities:* 1,100 computers available on campus for general student use. A campuswide network can be accessed from student residence rooms and from off campus. Internet access and online class registration are available. *Library facilities:* Watson Library plus 11 others. *Graduate expenses:* Tuition, state resident: full-time $3,745. Tuition, nonresident: full-time $10,075. Required fees: $574. General application contact: 785-864-4141.

Graduate School
Diana Carlin, Dean

College of Liberal Arts and Sciences
Kim Wilcox, Dean
Programs in:
  American studies • MA, PhD
  anthropology • MA, PhD
  applied behavioral science • MA
  applied mathematics and statistics • MA, PhD
  audiology • PhD
  behavioral psychology • PhD
  biochemistry and biophysics • MA, PhD
  biological sciences • MA, PhD
  botany • MA, PhD
  Brazilian studies • Certificate
  Central American and Mexican studies • Certificate
  chemistry • MS, PhD
  child language • MA, PhD
  Chinese language and literature • MA
  classical languages • MA
  clinical child psychology • MA, PhD
  communication studies • MA, PhD
  computational physics and astronomy • MS
  East Asian cultures • MA
  ecology and evolutionary biology • MA, PhD
  economics • MA, PhD
  English • MA, PhD
  entomology • MA, PhD
  French • MA, PhD
  geography • MA, PhD
  geology • MS, PhD
  German • MA, PhD
  gerontology • MA, PhD
  history • MA, PhD
  history of art • MA, PhD
  human development • MA
  indigenous nations studies • MA
  international studies • MA
  Japanese language and literature • MA
  Latin American studies • MA
  liberal arts and sciences • MA, MPA, MS, PhD, Certificate
  linguistics • MA, PhD
  mathematics • MA, PhD
  microbiology • MA, PhD
  molecular, cellular, and developmental biology • MA, PhD
  museum studies • MA
  philosophy • MA, PhD
  physics • MS, PhD
  political science • MA, PhD
  psychology • MA, PhD
  public administration • MPA
  religious studies • MA
  Russian and East European studies • MA
  Slavic languages and literatures • MA, PhD
  sociology • MA, PhD
  Spanish • MA, PhD
  speech-language pathology • MA, PhD
  systematics and ecology • MA
  theatre and film • MA, PhD

School of Architecture and Urban Design
John C. Gaunt, Dean
Programs in:
  academic track • M Arch
  architecture and urban design • M Arch, MUP
  management track • M Arch
  professional track • M Arch
  urban planning • MUP

School of Business
William L. Fuerst, Head
Programs in:
  accounting and information systems • MAIS, PhD
  business • MS, PhD
  business administration • MBA

School of Education
Angela Lumpkin, Dean
Programs in:
  counseling psychology • MS, PhD
  curriculum and instruction • MA, MS Ed, Ed D, PhD
  education • MA, MS, MS Ed, MSE, Ed D, PhD, Ed S
  education administration • MS Ed
  educational policy and leadership • Ed D, PhD
  educational psychology and research • MS Ed, PhD
  foundations • MS Ed, Ed D, PhD
  higher education • Ed D, PhD
  higher education administration • MS Ed, Ed D, PhD
  physical education • MSE, PhD
  school administration • Ed D, PhD
  school psychology • PhD, Ed S
  special education • MS Ed, Ed D, PhD

School of Engineering
Stuart R. Bell, Dean
Programs in:
  aerospace engineering • ME, MS, DE, PhD
  architectural engineering • MS
  chemical engineering • MS
  chemical/petroleum engineering • PhD
  civil engineering • MCE, MS, DE, PhD
  computer engineering • MS
  computer science • MS, PhD
  construction management • MCM
  electrical engineering • MS, DE, PhD
  engineering • MCE, MCM, ME, MS, DE, PhD
  engineering management • MS
  environmental engineering • MS, PhD
  environmental science • MS, PhD
  mechanical engineering • MS, DE, PhD
  petroleum engineering • MS
  water resources science • MS

School of Fine Arts
Steven K. Hedden, Dean
Programs in:
  art • MFA
  church music • MM, DMA
  composition • MM, DMA
  conducting • MM, DMA
  design • MFA
  fine arts • MA, MFA, MM, MME, DMA, PhD
  music and dance • MM, MME, DMA, PhD
  music education • MME, PhD
  music theory • MM, PhD
  music therapy • MME
  musicology • MM, PhD
  opera • MM
  performance • MM, DMA
  visual arts education • MA

School of Journalism and Mass Communications
James Gentry, Dean
Program in:
journalism • MS

School of Pharmacy
Kenneth L. Audus, Dean
Programs in:
hospital pharmacy • MS
medicinal chemistry • MS, PhD
neurosciences • MS, PhD
pharmaceutical chemistry • MS, PhD
pharmacology • MS, PhD
pharmacy • MS, PhD
toxicology • MS, PhD

Graduate Studies Medical Center
Dr. Allen Rawitch, Vice Chancellor for Academic Affairs and Dean of Graduate Studies
Programs in:
anatomy and cell biology • MA, PhD
biochemistry and molecular biology • MS, PhD
biomedical sciences • MA, MPH, MS, PhD
health policy and management • MHSA
microbiology, molecular genetics and immunology • PhD
molecular and integrative physiology • MS, PhD
pathology and laboratory medicine • MA, PhD
pharmacology • MS, PhD
preventive medicine • MPH
toxicology • MS, PhD

School of Allied Health
Dr. Karen L. Miller, Dean
Programs in:
allied health • MA, MOT, MS, DPT, PhD, Certificate
audiology • MA, PhD
dietetic internship • Certificate
dietetics and nutrition • MS
nurse anesthesia • MS
occupational therapy • MOT, MS
physical therapy education • MS, DPT, PhD
speech-language pathology • MA, PhD
therapeutic science • PhD

School of Nursing
Dr. Karen L. Miller, Dean
Programs in:
nurse educator • PMC
nurse midwife • PMC
nursing • MS, PhD
psychiatric/mental health nurse practitioner • PMC

School of Law
Stephen R. McAllister, Dean
Program in:
law • JD

School of Medicine
Dr. Barbara Atkinson, Executive Dean
Program in:
medicine • MD

School of Social Welfare
Ann Weick, Dean
Program in:
social welfare • MSW, PhD

■ UNIVERSITY OF SAINT MARY
Leavenworth, KS 66048-5082
http://www.smcks.edu/

Independent-religious, coed, comprehensive institution. *Enrollment:* 881 graduate, professional, and undergraduate students; 21 full-time matriculated graduate/professional students (14 women), 268 part-time matriculated graduate/professional students (214 women). *Graduate faculty:* 9 full-time (6 women), 24 part-time/adjunct (15 women). *Computer facilities:* 95 computers available on campus for general student use. A campuswide network can be accessed from student residence rooms. Internet access and online class registration are available. *Library facilities:* De Paul Library. *Graduate expenses:* Tuition: full-time $5,850; part-time $325 per hour. Full-time tuition and fees vary according to course load and program. *General application contact:* Dr. Ron Logan, Graduate Dean, 913-345-8288.

Graduate Programs
Dr. Ron Logan, Graduate Dean
Programs in:
business administration • MBA
curriculum and instruction • MAT
education • MAT
management • MS
psychology • MA
teaching • MAT

■ WASHBURN UNIVERSITY
Topeka, KS 66621
http://www.washburn.edu/

City-supported, coed, comprehensive institution. *Enrollment:* 7,002 graduate, professional, and undergraduate students; 729 full-time matriculated graduate/professional students (394 women), 525 part-time matriculated graduate/professional students (336 women). *Graduate faculty:* 86 full-time (34 women), 49 part-time/adjunct (15 women). *Computer facilities:* 200 computers available on campus for general student use. A campuswide network can be accessed from off campus. Internet access and online class registration are available. *Library facilities:* Mabee Library plus 2 others. *Graduate expenses:* Tuition, state resident: full-time $3,330; part-time $185 per credit hour. Tuition, nonresident: full-time $6,786; part-time $377 per credit hour. Required fees: $62; $31 per semester. Tuition and fees vary according to program. *General application contact:* Gordon McQuere, Dean, 785-231-1010 Ext. 1561.

College of Arts and Sciences
Gordon McQuere, Dean
Programs in:
arts and sciences • M Ed, MA, MLS
clinical psychology • MA
curriculum and instruction • M Ed
educational administration • M Ed
liberal studies • MLS
reading • M Ed
special education • M Ed

School of Applied Studies
Programs in:
applied studies • MCJ, MSW
clinical social work • MSW
criminal justice • MCJ

School of Business
Dr. David L. Sollars, Dean
Program in:
business • MBA

School of Law
Program in:
law • JD

■ WICHITA STATE UNIVERSITY
Wichita, KS 67260
http://www.wichita.edu/

State-supported, coed, university. CGS member. *Enrollment:* 14,896 graduate, professional, and undergraduate students; 1,027 full-time matriculated graduate/professional students (493 women), 1,730 part-time matriculated graduate/professional students (942 women). *Graduate faculty:* 447 full-time (144 women), 153 part-time/adjunct (87 women). *Computer facilities:* 1,500 computers available on campus for general student use. A campuswide network can be accessed from student residence rooms and from off campus. Internet access and online class registration, online grades, e-mail are available. *Library facilities:* Ablah Library plus 2 others. *Graduate expenses:* Tuition, state resident: full-time $2,457; part-time $137 per credit hour. Tuition, nonresident: full-time $7,371; part-time $410 per credit hour. Required fees: $364; $20 per credit hour. Tuition and fees vary according to

Kansas

Wichita State University (continued)
course load. *General application contact:* Dr. Susan K. Kovar, Dean of the Graduate School, 316-978-3095.

Find an in-depth description at www.petersons.com/gradchannel.

Graduate School
Dr. Susan K. Kovar, Dean of the Graduate School

College of Education
Dr. Jon Engelhardt, Dean
Programs in:
- communications sciences • MA, PhD
- counseling • M Ed
- curriculum and instruction • M Ed
- education • M Ed, MA, Ed D, PhD, Ed S
- education administration • M Ed, Ed D
- educational psychology • M Ed
- physical education • M Ed
- school psychology • Ed S
- special education • M Ed
- sports administration • M Ed

College of Engineering
Dr. Walter Horn, Interim Dean
Programs in:
- aerospace engineering • MS, PhD
- electrical engineering • MS, PhD
- engineering • MEM, MS, PhD
- industrial and manufacturing engineering • MEM, MS, PhD
- mechanical engineering • MS, PhD

College of Fine Arts
Dr. Elaine Bernstorf, Dean
Programs in:
- art education • MA
- fine arts • MA, MFA, MM, MME
- music • MM
- music education • MME
- studio arts • MFA

College of Health Professions
Dr. Peter A. Cohen, Dean
Programs in:
- clinical specialization • MSN
- health professions • MPH, MPT, MSN
- nursing administration • MSN
- physical therapy • MPT
- public health • MPH
- teaching of nursing • MSN

Fairmount College of Liberal Arts and Sciences
Dr. William Bischoff, Dean
Programs in:
- anthropology • MA
- applied mathematics • PhD
- biological sciences • MS
- chemistry • MS, PhD
- communication • MA
- community/clinical psychology • PhD
- computer science • MS
- creative writing • MA, MFA
- criminal justice • MA
- English • MA, MFA
- environmental science • MS
- geology • MS
- gerontology • MA
- history • MA
- human factors • PhD
- liberal arts and sciences • MA, MFA, MPA, MS, MSW, PhD
- mathematics • MS
- physics • MS
- political science • MA
- psychology • MA
- public administration • MPA
- social work • MSW
- sociology • MA
- Spanish • MA
- statistics • MS

W. Frank Barton School of Business
Dr. John Beehler, Dean
Programs in:
- accountancy • MPA
- business • EMBA, MBA, MS
- business economics • MA
- economic analysis • MA
- economics • MA
- professional accountancy • MPA

Kentucky

■ BELLARMINE UNIVERSITY
Louisville, KY 40205-0671
http://www.bellarmine.edu/

Independent-religious, coed, comprehensive institution. *Enrollment:* 3,134 graduate, professional, and undergraduate students; 149 full-time matriculated graduate/professional students (95 women), 268 part-time matriculated graduate/professional students (209 women). *Graduate faculty:* 22 full-time (11 women), 4 part-time/adjunct (3 women). *Computer facilities:* 160 computers available on campus for general student use. A campuswide network can be accessed from student residence rooms. Internet access is available. *Library facilities:* W.L. Lyons Brown Library. *Graduate expenses:* Tuition: full-time $5,100. Full-time tuition and fees vary according to class time and program. *General application contact:* Tim A. Sturgeon, Dean of Admission, 502-452-8131.

Annsley Frazier Thornton School of Education
Dr. Maureen R. Norris, Dean
Programs in:
- early elementary education • MA, MAT
- elementary education • MA
- learning and behavior disorders • MA
- middle school education • MA, MAT
- secondary school education • MAT

Donna and Allan Lansing School of Nursing and Health Sciences
Dr. Susan Davis, Dean
Programs in:
- advanced community health nursing • MSN
- nursing administration • MSN
- nursing and health sciences • MSN
- nursing education • MSN

W. Fielding Rubel School of Business
Daniel L. Bauer, Dean
Program in:
- business • EMBA, MBA

■ CAMPBELLSVILLE UNIVERSITY
Campbellsville, KY 42718-2799
http://www.campbellsville.edu/

Independent-religious, coed, comprehensive institution. *Enrollment:* 2,006 graduate, professional, and undergraduate students; 186 full-time matriculated graduate/professional students (101 women), 49 part-time matriculated graduate/professional students (26 women). *Graduate faculty:* 27 full-time (9 women), 6 part-time/adjunct (1 woman). *Computer facilities:* 125 computers available on campus for general student use. Internet access is available. *Library facilities:* Montgomery Library plus 2 others. *Graduate expenses:* Tuition: full-time $4,050; part-time $225 per credit. Required fees: $200; $100 per year. Full-time tuition and fees vary according to program. *General application contact:* Karla Deaton, Assistant Director of Admissions, 270-789-5078.

College of Arts and Sciences
Dr. Mary Wilgus, Dean
Program in:
- social science • MA

School of Business and Economics
Dr. Patricia H. Cowherd, Dean
Program in:
- business administration • MBA

Kentucky

School of Education
Dr. Brenda A. Priddy, Dean
Programs in:
curriculum and instruction • MAE
special education • MASE

School of Music
Dr. J. Robert Gaddis, Dean
Programs in:
church music • MM
music • MA
music education • MM

School of Theology
Dr. John E. Hurtgen, Interim Dean
Program in:
theology • M Th

■ **CUMBERLAND COLLEGE**
Williamsburg, KY 40769-1372
http://www.cumberlandcollege.edu/

Independent-religious, coed, comprehensive institution. *Computer facilities:* 300 computers available on campus for general student use. A campuswide network can be accessed from student residence rooms and from off campus. Internet access and online class registration are available. *Library facilities:* Norma Perkins Hagan Memorial Library. *General application contact:* Director, Graduate Programs in Education, 606-549-2200 Ext. 4432.

Graduate Programs in Education
Programs in:
early childhood education • MA Ed
early elementary K-4 • MA Ed
elementary education • MA Ed
elementary/secondary principalship • Certificate
elementary/secondary teaching • Certificate
middle school 5-8 • MA Ed
middle school education • MA Ed
reading specialist • MA Ed
secondary general education • MA Ed
special education • MA Ed

■ **EASTERN KENTUCKY UNIVERSITY**
Richmond, KY 40475-3102
http://www.eku.edu/

State-supported, coed, comprehensive institution. CGS member. *Enrollment:* 15,951 graduate, professional, and undergraduate students; 493 full-time matriculated graduate/professional students (323 women), 1,891 part-time matriculated graduate/professional students (1,358 women). *Graduate faculty:* 680 full-time (318 women), 347 part-time/adjunct (189 women). *Computer facilities:* Computer purchase and lease plans are available. 1,200 computers available on campus for general student use. A campuswide network can be accessed from student residence rooms and from off campus. Internet access and online class registration are available. *Library facilities:* John Grant Crabbe Library plus 2 others. *Graduate expenses:* Tuition, state resident: full-time $3,550; part-time $197 per credit. Tuition, nonresident: full-time $9,752; part-time $542 per credit. *General application contact:* Dr. Elizabeth Wachtel, Interim Dean, 859-622-1742.

The Graduate School
Dr. Elizabeth Wachtel, Interim Dean

College of Arts and Sciences
Dr. Gary Kuhnhenn, Acting Dean
Programs in:
arts and sciences • MA, MM, MPA, MS, PhD, Psy S
biological sciences • MS
chemistry • MS
choral conducting • MM
clinical psychology • MS
community development • MPA
community health administration • MPA
ecology • MS
English • MA
general public administration • MPA
geology • MS, PhD
history • MA
industrial/organizational psychology • MS
mathematical sciences • MS
performance • MM
political science • MA
school psychology • Psy S
theory/composition • MM

College of Business and Technology
Dr. Robert Rogow, Dean
Programs in:
business administration • MBA
business and technology • MBA, MS
industrial education • MS
industrial technology • MS
occupational training and development • MS
technical administration • MS
technology education • MS

College of Education
Dr. M. Mark Wasicsko, Dean
Programs in:
agricultural education • MA Ed
allied health sciences education • MA Ed
art education • MA Ed
biological sciences education • MA Ed
business education • MA Ed
chemistry education • MA Ed
communication disorders • MA Ed
earth science education • MA Ed
education • MA, MA Ed
elementary education general • MA Ed
English education • MA Ed
general science education • MA Ed
geography education • MA Ed
history education • MA Ed
home economics education • MA Ed
human services • MA
industrial education • MA Ed
instructional leadership • MA Ed
mathematical sciences education • MA Ed
mental health counseling • MA
music education • MA Ed
physical education • MA Ed
physics education • MA Ed
political science education • MA Ed
psychology education • MA Ed
reading • MA Ed
school counseling • MA Ed
school health education • MA Ed
secondary and higher education • MA Ed
sociology education • MA Ed
special education • MA Ed

College of Health Sciences
Dr. David D. Gale, Dean
Programs in:
chemical abuse and dependency • MPH
community health • MPH
community nutrition • MS
environmental health science • MPH
health sciences • MPH, MS, MSN
occupational therapy • MS
physical education • MS
recreation and park administration • MS
rural community health care • MSN
rural health family nurse practitioner • MSN
sports administration • MS

College of Justice and Safety
Dr. Allen Ault, Dean
Programs in:
correctional and juvenile justice studies • MS
criminal justice • MS
criminal justice education • MS
justice and safety • MS
loss prevention and safety • MS
police studies • MS

■ **KENTUCKY STATE UNIVERSITY**
Frankfort, KY 40601
http://www.kysu.edu/

State-related, coed, comprehensive institution. *Enrollment:* 2,306 graduate, professional, and undergraduate students; 80 full-time matriculated graduate/professional students (39 women), 99 part-time matriculated graduate/professional students (44 women). *Graduate faculty:* 8 full-time (2 women).

Peterson's Graduate Schools in the U.S. 2006

Kentucky

Kentucky State University (continued)
Computer facilities: 230 computers available on campus for general student use. A campuswide network can be accessed from off campus. Internet access, e-mail are available. *Library facilities:* Blazer Library. *Graduate expenses:* Tuition, state resident: full-time $3,096. Tuition, nonresident: full-time $9,332. Tuition and fees vary according to course level, degree level and program. *General application contact:* Cornelia F. Calhoun, Assistant to the Dean, 502-597-6117 Ext. 6105.

College of Arts and Sciences
Dr. Paul Bibbins, Dean
Program in:
  aquaculture • MS

School of Public Administration
Dr. Gashaw Lake, Dean
Program in:
  public administration • MPA

■ MOREHEAD STATE UNIVERSITY
Morehead, KY 40351
http://www.moreheadstate.edu/

State-supported, coed, comprehensive institution. *Enrollment:* 9,509 graduate, professional, and undergraduate students; 220 full-time matriculated graduate/professional students (128 women), 729 part-time matriculated graduate/professional students (467 women). *Graduate faculty:* 142 full-time (48 women). *Computer facilities:* 1,000 computers available on campus for general student use. A campuswide network can be accessed from student residence rooms and from off campus. Internet access and online class registration are available. *Library facilities:* Camden Carroll Library. *Graduate expenses:* Tuition, state resident: part-time $203 per hour. Tuition, nonresident: part-time $544 per hour. *General application contact:* Betty R. Cowsert, Graduate Admissions/Records Manager, 606-783-2039.

Graduate Programs
Dr. Deborah Abell, Associate Vice President for Graduate and Undergraduate Programs

Caudill College of Humanities
Dr. Michael Seelig, Dean
Programs in:
  advertising/publications • MA
  art education • MA
  criminology • MA
  electronic media • MA
  English • MA
  general sociology • MA
  gerontology • MA
  humanities • MA, MM
  journalism • MA
  music education • MM
  music performance • MM
  speech • MA
  studio art • MA
  theatre • MA

College of Business
Dr. Robert L. Albert, Dean
Program in:
  business • MBA

College of Education
Dr. Dan Branham, Dean
Programs in:
  adult and higher education • MA, Ed S
  curriculum and instruction • Ed S
  education • MA, MA Ed, MAT, Ed S
  elementary education • MA Ed
  exercise physiology • MA
  guidance and counseling • MA Ed, Ed S
  health, physical education and recreation • MA
  instructional leadership • Ed S
  international education • MA Ed
  middle school education • MA Ed
  reading • MA Ed
  recreation and sports administration • MA
  school administration • MA, Ed S
  secondary education • MA Ed, MAT
  special education • MA Ed, MAT

College of Science and Technology
Dr. Gerald DeMoss, Dean
Programs in:
  biology • MS
  career and technical education • MS
  clinical psychology • MA
  counseling psychology • MA
  experimental/general psychology • MA
  science and technology • MA, MS

■ MURRAY STATE UNIVERSITY
Murray, KY 42071-0009
http://www.murraystate.edu/

State-supported, coed, comprehensive institution. CGS member. *Computer facilities:* 1,500 computers available on campus for general student use. A campuswide network can be accessed from student residence rooms and from off campus. Internet access is available. *Library facilities:* Harry Lee Waterfield Library plus 1 other. *General application contact:* University Coordinator of Graduate Studies, 270-762-3895.

College of Business and Public Affairs
Programs in:
  business administration • MBA
  business and public affairs • MA, MBA, MPA, MPAC, MS
  economics • MS
  mass communications • MA, MS
  organizational communication • MA, MS
  professional accounting • MPAC
  public affairs • MPA
  telecommunications systems management • MS

College of Education
Programs in:
  community and agency counseling • Ed S
  early childhood education • MS
  education • MA, MA Ed, MS, Ed D, PhD, Ed S
  elementary education • MA Ed, Ed S
  guidance and counseling • MA Ed, Ed S
  health, physical education, and recreation • MA
  human development and leadership • MS
  industrial and technical education • MS
  learning disabilities • MA Ed
  middle school education • MA Ed, Ed S
  physical education • MA
  reading and writing • MA Ed
  school administration • MA Ed, Ed S
  secondary education • MA Ed, Ed S
  special education • MA Ed

College of Health Sciences and Human Services
Programs in:
  health sciences and human services • MA, MS, MSN
  nursing • MSN
  occupational safety and health • MS
  recreation and leisure services • MA
  speech language pathology • MS

College of Humanities and Fine Arts
Programs in:
  clinical psychology • MA, MS
  English • MA
  history • MA
  humanities and fine arts • MA, MME, MS
  music education • MME
  psychology • MA, MS
  teaching English to speakers of other languages • MA

College of Science, Engineering and Technology
Programs in:
  biological sciences • MAT, MS, PhD
  chemistry • MAT, MS

geosciences • MA, MS
management of technology • MS
mathematics • MA, MAT, MS
science, engineering and technology • MA, MAT, MS, PhD
water science • MS

School of Agriculture
Program in:
agriculture • MS

■ NORTHERN KENTUCKY UNIVERSITY
Highland Heights, KY 41099
http://www.nku.edu/

State-supported, coed, comprehensive institution. CGS member. *Enrollment:* 13,910 graduate, professional, and undergraduate students; 469 full-time matriculated graduate/professional students (227 women), 1,253 part-time matriculated graduate/professional students (754 women). *Graduate faculty:* 82 full-time (38 women). *Computer facilities:* 600 computers available on campus for general student use. A campuswide network can be accessed from student residence rooms and from off campus. Internet access and online class registration are available. *Library facilities:* Steely Library plus 2 others. *Graduate expenses:* Tuition, state resident: full-time $3,780; part-time $210 per hour. Tuition, nonresident: full-time $8,694; part-time $483 per hour. *General application contact:* Peg Griffin, Graduate Director, 859-572-6364.

Salmon P. Chase College of Law
Gerald A. St. Amand, Dean
Program in:
law • JD

School of Graduate Programs
Dr. Carole A. Beere, Dean
Programs in:
accountancy • M Acc
arts and sciences • MPA, CNM
business administration • MBA
computer science • MSCS
information systems • MSIS
nursing • MSN, Post-Master's Certificate
public administration • MPA, CNM
technology • MST

College of Education
Dr. Rachelle Bruno, Interim Dean
Programs in:
elementary education • MA Ed
instructional leadership • MA
middle school education • MA Ed, MAT
secondary education • MA Ed, MAT

■ SPALDING UNIVERSITY
Louisville, KY 40203-2188
http://www.spalding.edu/

Independent-religious, coed, comprehensive institution. CGS member. *Enrollment:* 940 matriculated graduate/professional students. *Graduate faculty:* 51 full-time (23 women), 80 part-time/adjunct (50 women). *Computer facilities:* 80 computers available on campus for general student use. A campuswide network can be accessed. Internet access is available. *Library facilities:* Spalding Library. *Graduate expenses:* Tuition: part-time $495 per credit hour. Required fees: $15 per credit hour. Part-time tuition and fees vary according to degree level and program.

Find an in-depth description at www.petersons.com/gradchannel.

Graduate Studies
Dr. Randy Strickland, Senior Vice President for Academic Affairs
Programs in:
adult nurse practitioner • MSN
business communication • MS
clinical psychology • MA, Psy D
family nurse practitioner • MSN
health and natural sciences • MS, MSN
leadership in nursing and healthcare • MSN
occupational therapy (advanced-level) • MS
occupational therapy (entry-level) • MS
pediatric nurse practitioner • MSN
social sciences and humanities • MA, MFA, MSW, Psy D
social work • MSW
writing • MFA

College of Education
Dr. Betty Lindsey, Dean
Programs in:
elementary school education • MAT
generic • MA
high school education • MAT
leadership education • Ed D
library media • MA
middle school education • MAT
school administration • MA
school counselor • MA
special education (learning and behavioral disorders) • MAT

■ UNIVERSITY OF KENTUCKY
Lexington, KY 40506-0032
http://www.uky.edu/

State-supported, coed, university. CGS member. *Enrollment:* 25,397 graduate, professional, and undergraduate students; 6,831 matriculated graduate/professional students. *Graduate faculty:* 2,679. *Computer facilities:* 1,400 computers available on campus for general student use. A campuswide network can be accessed from student residence rooms and from off campus. Internet access and online class registration, various software packages are available. *Library facilities:* William T. Young Library plus 15 others. *Graduate expenses:* Tuition, state resident: full-time $4,975; part-time $261 per credit hour. Tuition, nonresident: full-time $12,315; part-time $668 per credit hour. *General application contact:* Dr. Brian Jackson, Associate Dean, 859-257-4905.

College of Dentistry
Dr. Leon A. Assael, Dean
Program in:
dentistry • DMD, MS

College of Law
Allan W. Vestal, Dean
Program in:
law • JD

College of Medicine
Dr. Carol L. Elam, Assistant Dean for Admissions
Programs in:
medicine • MD, MPH, Dr PH
public health • MPH, Dr PH

College of Pharmacy
Dr. Kenneth B. Roberts, Dean
Programs in:
pharmaceutical sciences • MS, PhD
pharmacy • Pharm D, MS, PhD

Graduate School
Dr. Jeannine Blackwell, Dean
Programs in:
biomedical engineering • MSBE, PhD
dentistry • MS
gerontology • PhD
health administration • MHA
nutritional sciences • PhD
public administration • MPA, PhD
toxicology • MS, PhD

College of Architecture
Dr. David Mohney, Dean
Programs in:
architecture • MHP
historic preservation • MHP

College of Communications and Information Studies
Dr. David Johnson, Dean
Programs in:
communication • MA, PhD
communications and information studies • MA, MSLS, PhD
library science • MA, MSLS

Kentucky

University of Kentucky (continued)

Graduate School Program in the College of Social Work
Dr. Kay Hoffman, Dean
Program in:
  social work • MSW, PhD

Graduate School Programs from the College of Arts and Sciences
Dr. Howard Grotch, Dean
Programs in:
  anthropology • MA, PhD
  arts and sciences • MA, MS, MS Ag, PhD
  biological sciences • MS, PhD
  chemistry • MS, PhD
  classical languages and literatures • MA
  English • MA, PhD
  French • MA
  geography • MA, PhD
  geology • MS, PhD
  German • MA
  history • MA, PhD
  mathematics • MA, MS, PhD
  philosophy • MA, PhD
  physics and astronomy • MS, PhD
  political science • MA, PhD
  psychology • MA, PhD
  sociology • MA, MS Ag, PhD
  Spanish • MA, MS
  statistics • MS, PhD

Graduate School Programs from the College of Business and Economics
Dr. Richard Furst, Dean
Programs in:
  accounting • MSACC
  business administration • MBA, PhD
  business and economics • MBA, MS, MSACC, PhD
  economics • MS, PhD

Graduate School Programs from the College of Education
Dr. James Cibulka, Dean
Programs in:
  administration and supervision • M Ed, Ed D, Ed S
  clinical and college teaching • MS Ed
  curriculum and instruction • MA Ed, Ed D
  education • M Ed, MA Ed, MRC, MS, MS Ed, MSVE, Ed D, PhD, Ed S
  educational and counseling psychology • MA Ed, MS Ed, Ed D, PhD, Ed S
  educational policy studies and evaluation • MS Ed, Ed D, PhD
  exercise science • PhD
  instruction and administration • Ed D
  kinesiology • MS, Ed D
  rehabilitation counseling • MRC
  special education • MA Ed, MS Ed, Ed D, Ed S
  vocational education • MA Ed, MS Ed, MSVE, Ed D, Ed S

Graduate School Programs from the College of Engineering
Dr. Thomas W. Lester, Dean
Programs in:
  chemical engineering • MS Ch E, PhD
  civil engineering • MCE, MSCE, PhD
  computer science • MS, PhD
  electrical engineering • MSEE, PhD
  engineering • M Eng, MCE, MME, MS, MS Ch E, MS Min, MSCE, MSEE, MSEM, MSMAE, MSME, MSMSE, PhD
  manufacturing systems engineering • MSMSE
  materials science • MSMAE, PhD
  mechanical engineering • MSME, PhD
  mining engineering • MME, MS Min, PhD

Graduate School Programs from the College of Fine Arts
Dr. Robert Shay, Dean
Programs in:
  art education • MA
  art history • MA
  art studio • MFA
  fine arts • MA, MFA, MM, DMA, PhD
  music • MA, MM, DMA, PhD
  theatre • MA

Graduate School Programs from the College of Health Sciences
Dr. Thomas Robinson, Dean
Programs in:
  clinical sciences • MS, DS
  communication disorders • MSCD
  health physics • MSHP
  health sciences • MS, MSCD, MSHP, MSPAS, MSPT, MSRMP, DS, PhD
  physical therapy • MSPT
  physician assistant studies • MSPAS
  radiological medical physics • MSRMP
  rehabilitation sciences • PhD

Graduate School Programs from the College of Medicine
Dr. E. Wilson, Dean of College of Medicine
Programs in:
  anatomy and neurobiology • PhD
  medical science • MS
  medicine • MS, PhD
  microbiology and immunology • PhD
  molecular and biomedical pharmacology • PhD
  molecular and cellular biochemistry • PhD
  physiology • PhD

Graduate School Programs in the College of Agriculture
Dr. M. Scott Smith, Dean
Programs in:
  agricultural economics • MS, PhD
  agriculture • MS, MS Ag, MSAE, MSFOR, PhD
  animal sciences • MS, PhD
  biosystems and agricultural engineering • MSAE, PhD
  crop science • MS, MS Ag, PhD
  entomology • MS, PhD
  forestry • MSFOR
  plant and soil science • MS
  plant pathology • MS, PhD
  plant physiology • PhD
  soil science • PhD
  veterinary science • MS, PhD

Graduate School Programs in the College of Human Environmental Sciences
Dr. Retia Scott Walker, Dean
Programs in:
  family studies, human development, and resource management • MSFAM, PhD
  hospitality and dietetic administration • MS
  human environmental sciences • MAIDM, MS, MSFAM, MSIDM, PhD
  interior design, merchandising, and textiles • MAIDM, MSIDM

Graduate School Programs in the College of Nursing
Dr. Carolyn Williams, Dean
Program in:
  nursing • MSN, PhD

Patterson School of Diplomacy and International Commerce
Dr. Michael D. Desch, Director of Graduate Studies
Program in:
  diplomacy and international commerce • MA

■ UNIVERSITY OF LOUISVILLE
Louisville, KY 40292-0001
http://www.louisville.edu/

State-supported, coed, university. CGS member. *Enrollment:* 20,825 graduate, professional, and undergraduate students; 3,211 full-time matriculated graduate/professional students (1,723 women), 2,139 part-time matriculated graduate/professional students (1,196 women). *Graduate faculty:* 1,305 full-time (415 women), 524 part-time/adjunct (237 women). *Computer facilities:* Computer purchase and lease plans are available. 265 computers available on campus for general student use. A campuswide network can be accessed from student residence rooms and from off campus. Internet access and online class registration are available. *Library facilities:* William F. Ekstrom Library plus 5 others.

Kentucky

Graduate expenses: Tuition, state resident: full-time $4,842. Tuition, nonresident: full-time $13,338. *General application contact:* Jenny L. Sawyer, Information Contact, 502-852-3101.

Find an in-depth description at www.petersons.com/gradchannel.

Graduate School
Dr. Ronald M. Atlas, Dean

College of Arts and Sciences
J. Blaine Hudson, Acting Dean
Programs in:
 analytical chemistry • MS, PhD
 applied and industrial mathematics • PhD
 art • MA
 art history • MA, PhD
 arts and sciences • MA, MFA, MS, PhD
 biochemistry • MS, PhD
 biology • MS
 chemical physics • PhD
 clinical psychology • PhD
 communication • MA
 creative art • MA
 English • MA
 English literature • MA
 English rhetoric and composition • PhD
 environmental biology • PhD
 experimental psychology • PhD
 French • MA
 history • MA
 humanities • MA, PhD
 inorganic chemistry • MS, PhD
 justice administration • MS
 mathematics • MA
 organic chemistry • MS, PhD
 Pan-African studies • MA
 performance • MFA
 philosophy • MA
 physical chemistry • MS, PhD
 physics • MS
 political science • MA
 production • MFA
 psychology • MA
 sociology • MA
 Spanish • MA
 theatre arts • MA

College of Business and Public Administration
Dr. Alan N. Attaway, Acting Dean
Programs in:
 accountancy • MAC
 business and public administration • MA, MAC, MBA, MPA, MUP, PhD
 labor and public management • MPA
 public administration • MPA
 public policy and administration • MPA
 systems science • MA
 urban and public affairs • PhD
 urban and regional development • MPA
 urban planning • MUP

College of Education and Human Development
Dr. Robert Felner, Dean
Programs in:
 art education • MAT
 college student personnel services • M Ed
 community counseling • M Ed
 counseling psychology • M Ed, PhD
 curriculum and instruction • Ed D
 early elementary education • M Ed, MAT
 education and human development • M Ed, MA, MAT, MS, Ed D, PhD, Ed S
 educational administration • M Ed, PhD, Ed S
 evaluation • M Ed
 exercise physiology • MS
 expressive therapies • MA
 foreign language education • MAT
 higher education • MA, Ed S
 human resource education • M Ed
 instructional technology • M Ed
 interdisciplinary early childhood education • M Ed
 middle school education • M Ed, MAT
 music education • MAT
 occupational training and development • M Ed
 physical education • M Ed, MAT
 reading education • M Ed
 school counseling • M Ed
 school counseling and guidance • M Ed, PhD
 secondary education • M Ed, MAT
 special education • M Ed, PhD
 sport administration • MS

Interdisciplinary Studies
Program in:
 interdisciplinary studies • MA, MS

Raymond A. Kent School of Social Work
Dr. Terry Singer, Dean
Program in:
 social work • MSSW, PhD

School of Music
Dr. Christopher Doane, Dean
Programs in:
 music education • MAT, MME
 music history • MM, PhD
 music history and literature • MM
 music literature • PhD
 music performance • MM
 music theory and composition • MM
 musicology • PhD

School of Nursing
Dr. Mary H. Mundt, Dean
Program in:
 nursing • MSN

School of Public Health
Dr. Richard D. Clover, Dean
Programs in:
 bioinformatics and biostatistics • MS, PhD
 epidemiology: clinical investigation services • MS, PhD
 public health • MS, PhD, Certificate
 public health: clinical investigation • Certificate

Speed Scientific School
Dr. Mickey R. Wilhelm, Acting Dean
Programs in:
 chemical engineering • M Eng, MS, PhD
 civil and environmental engineering • M Eng, MS, PhD
 computer engineering and computer science • M Eng, MS
 computer science • MS
 computer science and engineering • PhD
 electrical and computer engineering • M Eng, MS
 engineering • M Eng, MS, PhD
 engineering management • M Eng
 industrial engineering • M Eng, MS, PhD
 mechanical engineering • M Eng, MS

Louis D. Brandeis School of Law
Laura Rothstein, Dean
Program in:
 law • JD

School of Dentistry
Dr. John N. Williams, Dean
Programs in:
 dentistry • DMD, MS
 oral biology • MS

School of Medicine
Dr. Laura Schweitzer, Dean
Programs in:
 anatomical sciences and neurobiology • MS, PhD
 audiology • Au D
 biochemistry and molecular biology • MS, PhD
 communicative disorders • MS
 medicine • MD, MS, Au D, PhD, Certificate
 microbiology and immunology • MS, PhD
 ophthalmology and visual sciences • PhD
 pharmacology and toxicology • MS, PhD
 physiology and biophysics • MS, PhD

■ **WESTERN KENTUCKY UNIVERSITY**
Bowling Green, KY 42101-3576
http://www.wku.edu/

State-supported, coed, comprehensive institution. CGS member. *Computer facilities:* 1,200 computers available on campus for general student use. A campuswide network can be accessed from student residence rooms and from

Peterson's Graduate Schools in the U.S. 2006

Kentucky

Western Kentucky University (continued) off campus. Internet access and online class registration, on-line grade reports are available. *Library facilities:* Helm-Cravens Library plus 3 others. *General application contact:* Dean, Graduate Studies, 270-745-2446.

Graduate Studies
Program in:
 administration • MA

College of Education and Behavioral Sciences
Programs in:
 business education • MA Ed
 counseling and student affairs • Ed S
 education • Ed S
 education and behavioral sciences • MA, MA Ed, MS, Ed S
 educational administration • MA Ed, Ed S
 elementary education • MA Ed, Ed S
 exceptional child education • MA Ed
 guidance and counseling • MA Ed
 library media education • MS
 literacy • MA Ed
 middle grades education • MA Ed
 psychology • MA
 school administration • Ed S
 school business administration • MA Ed
 school psychology • Ed S
 secondary education • MA Ed, Ed S

College of Health and Human Services
Programs in:
 communication disorders • MS
 early childhood education • MA Ed
 environmental health • MS
 gerontology • MS
 healthcare administration • MHA
 nursing • MSN
 physical education • MS
 public health • MPH
 public health education • MPH
 recreation • MS

Gordon Ford College of Business
Program in:
 business administration • MBA

Ogden College of Science and Engineering
Programs in:
 agriculture • MA Ed, MS
 biology • MA Ed, MS
 chemistry • MA Ed, MS
 computer science • MS
 geography and geology • MS
 mathematics • MA Ed, MS
 science, technology, and health • MA Ed, MS

Potter College of Arts, Humanities and Social Sciences
Programs in:
 art education • MA Ed
 arts and humanities • MA, MA Ed, MPA
 communication • MA
 education • MA
 English • MA Ed
 folk studies • MA
 government • MPA
 historic preservation • MA
 history • MA, MA Ed
 literature • MA
 music • MA Ed
 sociology • MA
 teaching English as a second language • MA
 writing • MA

Louisiana

■ CENTENARY COLLEGE OF LOUISIANA
Shreveport, LA 71104
http://www.centenary.edu/

Independent-religious, coed, comprehensive institution. *Enrollment:* 997 graduate, professional, and undergraduate students; 18 full-time matriculated graduate/professional students (12 women), 134 part-time matriculated graduate/professional students (106 women). *Graduate faculty:* 6 full-time (5 women), 11 part-time/adjunct (7 women). *Computer facilities:* 250 computers available on campus for general student use. A campuswide network can be accessed from student residence rooms and from off campus. Internet access and online class registration are available. *Library facilities:* Magale Library plus 1 other. *Graduate expenses:* Tuition: full-time $2,400; part-time $400 per course. Tuition and fees vary according to program. *General application contact:* Dr. Darrel D. Colson, Provost and Dean of the College, 318-869-5104.

Graduate Programs
Dr. Darrel D. Colson, Provost and Dean of the College
Programs in:
 administration • M Ed
 elementary education • MAT
 secondary education • MAT
 supervision of instruction • M Ed

Frost School of Business
Dr. Christopher L. Martin, Dean
Program in:
 business • MBA

■ GRAMBLING STATE UNIVERSITY
Grambling, LA 71245
http://www.gram.edu/

State-supported, coed, university. CGS member. *Computer facilities:* Computer purchase and lease plans are available. 250 computers available on campus for general student use. A campuswide network can be accessed from student residence rooms and from off campus. Internet access is available. *Library facilities:* A. C. Lewis Memorial Library. *General application contact:* Administrative Assistant, Division of Graduate Studies, 318-274-2158.

Division of Graduate Studies

College of Education
Programs in:
 curriculum and instruction • Ed D
 developmental education • MS, Ed D
 early childhood education • MS
 educational leadership • Ed D
 elementary education • MS
 sports administration • MS

College of Liberal Arts
Programs in:
 criminal justice • MS
 humanities • MA
 mass communication • MA
 public administration • MPA
 social sciences • MAT

College of Science and Technology
Program in:
 natural sciences • MAT

School of Nursing
Program in:
 family nurse practitioner • MSN

School of Social Work
Program in:
 social work • MSW

■ LOUISIANA STATE UNIVERSITY AND AGRICULTURAL AND MECHANICAL COLLEGE
Baton Rouge, LA 70803
http://www.lsu.edu/

State-supported, coed, university. CGS member. *Enrollment:* 31,934 graduate, professional, and undergraduate students; 3,374 full-time matriculated graduate/professional students (1,712 women), 1,281 part-time matriculated graduate/professional students (716 women). *Graduate faculty:* 1,172 full-time (254 women), 23 part-time/adjunct (3 women). *Computer facilities:* 7,000 computers available on campus for general student use. A campuswide network can be

Louisiana

accessed from student residence rooms and from off campus. Internet access and online class registration, e-mail, wireless, grades, payroll, storage are available. *Library facilities:* Troy H. Middleton Library plus 7 others. *Graduate expenses:* Tuition, state resident: part-time $337 per hour. Tuition, nonresident: part-time $577 per hour. *General application contact:* Reneé Renegar, Office of Graduate Admissions, 225-578-1641.

Graduate School
Dr. Pamela Ann Monroe, Associate Dean

College of Agriculture
Dr. Kenneth Koonce, Dean
Programs in:
  agricultural economics and agribusiness • MS, PhD
  agriculture • M App St, MS, MSBAE, PhD
  agronomy • MS, PhD
  animal sciences • MS, PhD
  applied statistics • M App St
  biological and agricultural engineering • MSBAE
  comprehensive vocational education • MS, PhD
  dairy science • MS, PhD
  engineering science • MS, PhD
  entomology • MS, PhD
  extension and international education • MS, PhD
  fisheries • MS
  food science • MS, PhD
  forestry • MS, PhD
  horticulture • MS, PhD
  human ecology • MS, PhD
  industrial education • MS
  plant health • MS, PhD
  vocational agriculture education • MS, PhD
  vocational business education • MS
  vocational home economics education • MS
  wildlife • MS
  wildlife and fisheries science • PhD

College of Art and Design
Frederick G. Ortner, Dean
Programs in:
  architecture • M Arch
  art and design • M Arch, MA, MFA, MLA
  art history • MA
  ceramics • MFA
  graphic design • MFA
  landscape architecture • MLA
  painting and drawing • MFA
  photography • MFA
  printmaking • MFA
  sculpture • MFA
  studio art • MFA

College of Arts and Sciences
Dr. Guillermo Ferreya, Interim Dean
Programs in:
  anthropology • MA
  arts and sciences • MA, MALA, MFA, MS, PhD
  biological psychology • MA, PhD
  clinical psychology • MA, PhD
  cognitive psychology • MA, PhD
  communication sciences and disorders • MA, PhD
  communication studies • MA, PhD
  comparative literature • MA, PhD
  creative writing • MFA
  developmental psychology • MA, PhD
  English • MA, PhD
  French literature and linguistics • MA, PhD
  geography • MA, MS, PhD
  history • MA, PhD
  industrial/organizational psychology • MA, PhD
  liberal arts • MALA
  linguistics • MA, PhD
  mathematics • MS, PhD
  philosophy • MA
  political science • MA, PhD
  school psychology • MA, PhD
  sociology • MA, PhD
  Spanish • MA

College of Basic Sciences
Dr. Kevin Carman, Interim Dean
Programs in:
  astronomy • PhD
  astrophysics • PhD
  basic sciences • MNS, MS, MSSS, PhD
  biochemistry • MS, PhD
  biological science • MS, PhD
  chemistry • MS, PhD
  computer science • MSSS, PhD
  geology and geophysics • MS, PhD
  natural sciences • MNS
  physics • MS, PhD
  systems science • MSSS

College of Education
Dr. Barbara Fuhrmann, Dean
Programs in:
  counseling • M Ed, MA, Ed S
  curriculum and instruction • MA, PhD, Ed S
  education • M Ed, MA, MS, PhD, Ed S
  educational administration • M Ed, MA, PhD, Ed S
  educational technology • MA
  elementary education • M Ed
  higher education • PhD
  kinesiology • MS, PhD
  research methodology • PhD
  secondary education • M Ed

College of Engineering
Dr. Pius J. Egbelu, Dean
Programs in:
  chemical engineering • MS Ch E, PhD
  electrical and computer engineering • MSEE, PhD
  engineering • MS Ch E, MS Pet E, MSCE, MSEE, MSES, MSIE, MSME, PhD
  engineering science • MSES, PhD
  environmental engineering • MSCE, PhD
  geotechnical engineering • MSCE, PhD
  industrial engineering • MSIE
  mechanical engineering • MSME, PhD
  petroleum engineering • MS Pet E, PhD
  structural engineering and mechanics • MSCE, PhD
  transportation engineering • MSCE, PhD
  water resources • MSCE, PhD

College of Music and Dramatic Arts
Dr. Ronald Ross, Dean
Programs in:
  acting • MFA
  directing • MFA
  music • MM, DMA, PhD
  music and dramatic arts • MFA, MM, DMA, PhD
  music education • PhD
  theatre • PhD
  theatre design/technology • MFA

E.J. Ourso College of Business Administration
Dr. Robert T. Sumichrast, Acting Dean
Programs in:
  accounting • MS, PhD
  business administration • PhD
  economics • MS, PhD
  finance • MS
  information systems and decision sciences • MS
  marketing • MS
  public administration • MPA

Manship School of Mass Communication
Dr. John Maxwell Hamilton, Dean
Program in:
  mass communication • MMC, PhD

School of Library and Information Science
Dr. Beth M. Paskoff, Dean
Program in:
  library and information science • MLIS, CAS

School of Social Work
Dr. Mary Ellen Kondrat, Dean
Program in:
  social work • MSW, PhD

School of the Coast and Environment
Dr. Russell L. Chapman, Dean
Programs in:

Peterson's Graduate Schools in the U.S. 2006

Louisiana

Louisiana State University and Agricultural and Mechanical College (continued)
   environmental planning and management • MS
   environmental toxicology • MS
   oceanography and coastal sciences • MS, PhD
   the coast and environment • MS, PhD

Paul M. Hebert Law Center
John J. Costonis, Chancellor
Program in:
   law • JD, LL M, MCL

School of Veterinary Medicine
Dr. Michael G. Groves, Dean
Programs in:
   comparative biomedical sciences • MS, PhD
   pathobiological sciences • MS, PhD
   veterinary clinical sciences • MS
   veterinary medicine • DVM, MS, PhD

■ **LOUISIANA STATE UNIVERSITY IN SHREVEPORT**
Shreveport, LA 71115-2399
http://www.lsus.edu/

State-supported, coed, comprehensive institution. *Computer facilities:* Computer purchase and lease plans are available. A campuswide network can be accessed from off campus. Internet access is available. *Library facilities:* Noel Memorial Library. *General application contact:* Registrar and Director of Admissions, 318-797-5061.

College of Business Administration
Dr. Charlotte A. Jones, Dean
Program in:
   healthcare • MBA

College of Education and Human Development
Programs in:
   counseling psychology • MS
   education and human development • M Ed, MS, SSP
   school psychology • SSP

College of Liberal Arts
Programs in:
   human services administration • MS
   liberal arts • MA, MS

College of Sciences
Dr. Paul Sisson, Chair, Computer Science Department
Program in:
   systems technology • MST

■ **LOUISIANA TECH UNIVERSITY**
Ruston, LA 71272
http://www.latech.edu/

State-supported, coed, university. *Enrollment:* 11,960 graduate, professional, and undergraduate students; 1,146 full-time matriculated graduate/professional students (555 women), 1,081 part-time matriculated graduate/professional students (853 women). *Graduate faculty:* 259 full-time (68 women), 53 part-time/adjunct (32 women). *Computer facilities:* 1,800 computers available on campus for general student use. A campuswide network can be accessed from student residence rooms and from off campus. *Library facilities:* Prescott Memorial Library. *Graduate expenses:* Tuition, state resident: full-time $3,120. Tuition, nonresident: full-time $9,120. Tuition and fees vary according to course load. *General application contact:* Dr. Terry McCouathy, Dean of the Graduate School, 318-257-2924.

Graduate School

College of Administration and Business
Programs in:
   administration and business • MBA, MPA, DBA
   business administration • MBA, DBA
   business economics • MBA, DBA
   finance • MBA, DBA
   management • MBA, DBA
   marketing • MBA, DBA
   professional accountancy • MBA, MPA, DBA

College of Applied and Natural Sciences
Programs in:
   applied and natural sciences • MS
   biological sciences • MS
   dietetics • MS
   human ecology • MS

College of Education
Programs in:
   counseling • MA
   counseling psychology • PhD
   curriculum and instruction • MS, Ed D
   education • M Ed, MA, MS, Ed D, PhD
   educational leadership • Ed D
   health and exercise science • MS
   industrial/organizational psychology • MA
   secondary education • M Ed
   special education • MA

College of Engineering and Science
Dr. Stan Napper, Dean
Programs in:
   applied computational analysis and modeling • PhD
   biomedical engineering • MS, PhD
   chemical engineering • MS, PhD
   chemistry • MS
   civil engineering • MS, PhD
   computer science • MS
   electrical engineering • MS, PhD
   engineering • PhD
   engineering and science • MS, PhD
   industrial engineering • MS, PhD
   manufacturing systems engineering • MS
   mathematics and statistics • MS
   mechanical engineering • MS, PhD
   operations research • MS
   physics • MS

College of Liberal Arts
Programs in:
   art and graphic design • MFA
   English • MA
   history • MA
   interior design • MFA
   liberal arts • MA, MFA
   photography • MFA
   speech • MA
   speech pathology and audiology • MA
   studio art • MFA

■ **LOYOLA UNIVERSITY NEW ORLEANS**
New Orleans, LA 70118-6195
http://www.loyno.edu/

Independent-religious, coed, comprehensive institution. *Enrollment:* 5,518 graduate, professional, and undergraduate students; 776 full-time matriculated graduate/professional students (445 women), 919 part-time matriculated graduate/professional students (603 women). *Graduate faculty:* 30 full-time (9 women), 24 part-time/adjunct (6 women). *Computer facilities:* Computer purchase and lease plans are available. 458 computers available on campus for general student use. A campuswide network can be accessed from student residence rooms and from off campus. Internet access and online class registration are available. *Library facilities:* University Library plus 1 other. *Graduate expenses:* Tuition: part-time $218 per credit hour. Required fees: $45 per semester. One-time fee: $250 part-time. *General application contact:* Deborah C. Stieffel, Dean of Admissions and Enrollment Management, 504-865-3240.

Louisiana

College of Arts and Sciences
Dr. Frank E. Scully, Dean
Programs in:
 arts and sciences • MA, MS
 counseling • MS
 elementary education • MS
 mass communication • MA
 reading education • MS
 religious studies • MA
 secondary education • MS

College of Music
Dr. Edward J. Kvet, Dean
Program in:
 music • MM, MME, MMT

Joseph A. Butt, S.J., College of Business Administration
Dr. J. Patrick O'Brien, Dean
Program in:
 business administration • MBA

School of Law
Brian Bromberger, Dean
Program in:
 law • JD

■ MCNEESE STATE UNIVERSITY
Lake Charles, LA 70609
http://www.mcneese.edu/

State-supported, coed, comprehensive institution. *Computer facilities:* 700 computers available on campus for general student use. A campuswide network can be accessed from student residence rooms and from off campus. Internet access and online class registration are available. *Library facilities:* Frazer Memorial Library plus 2 others. *General application contact:* Director of Admissions, 337-475-5356.

Graduate School

College of Business
Programs in:
 business • MBA
 business administration • MBA

College of Education
Programs in:
 administration and supervision • M Ed, Ed S
 early childhood education • M Ed
 education • M Ed, MA, Ed S
 educational technology • M Ed
 elementary education • M Ed
 health and human performance • M Ed
 psychology • MA
 school counseling • M Ed
 secondary education • M Ed
 special education • M Ed

College of Engineering and Technology
Programs in:
 chemical engineering • M Eng
 civil engineering • M Eng
 electrical engineering • M Eng
 engineering management • M Eng
 mechanical engineering • M Eng

College of Liberal Arts
Programs in:
 creative writing • MFA
 English • MA
 liberal arts • MA, MFA, MM Ed
 music education • MM Ed

College of Nursing
Program in:
 nursing • MSN

College of Science
Programs in:
 biology • MS
 chemistry • PhD
 computer science • MS
 environmental and chemical sciences • MS, PhD
 environmental sciences • MS
 mathematics • MS
 science • MS, PhD
 statistics • MS

■ NICHOLLS STATE UNIVERSITY
Thibodaux, LA 70310
http://www.nicholls.edu

State-supported, coed, comprehensive institution. *Enrollment:* 7,247 graduate, professional, and undergraduate students; 96 full-time matriculated graduate/professional students (62 women), 325 part-time matriculated graduate/professional students (245 women). *Graduate faculty:* 59 full-time (18 women), 7 part-time/adjunct (4 women). *Computer facilities:* 250 computers available on campus for general student use. A campuswide network can be accessed from student residence rooms and from off campus. Internet access is available. *Library facilities:* Allen J. Ellender Memorial Library. *Graduate expenses:* Part-time $341 per course. Tuition, state resident: full-time $2,681. Tuition, nonresident: full-time $8,129. International tuition: $8,249 full-time. Tuition and fees vary according to course load. *General application contact:* Dr. J. B. Stroud, Director, 985-449-7014.

Graduate Studies
Dr. J. B. Stroud, Director

College of Arts and Sciences
Dr. Badiollah R. Asrabadi, Dean
Programs in:
 applied mathematics • MS
 arts and sciences • MS
 marine and environmental biology • MS

College of Business Administration
Dr. Ridley J. Gros, Dean
Program in:
 business administration • MBA

College of Education
Dr. O. Cleveland Hill, Dean
Programs in:
 administration and supervision • M Ed
 counselor education • M Ed
 curriculum and instruction • M Ed
 education • M Ed, MA, SSP
 psychological counseling • MA
 school psychology • SSP

■ NORTHWESTERN STATE UNIVERSITY OF LOUISIANA
Natchitoches, LA 71497
http://www.nsula.edu/

State-supported, coed, comprehensive institution. CGS member. *Enrollment:* 10,505 graduate, professional, and undergraduate students; 254 full-time matriculated graduate/professional students (171 women), 609 part-time matriculated graduate/professional students (495 women). *Graduate faculty:* 66 full-time (41 women), 13 part-time/adjunct (5 women). *Computer facilities:* 748 computers available on campus for general student use. A campuswide network can be accessed from student residence rooms and from off campus. Internet access and online class registration are available. *Library facilities:* Eugene P. Watson Memorial Library. *Graduate expenses:* Tuition, state resident: part-time $845 per semester. Tuition, nonresident: part-time $2,364 per semester. Tuition and fees vary according to course load. *General application contact:* Dr. Martha V. Henderson, Dean, Graduate Studies, Research, and Information Systems, 318-357-5851.

Graduate Studies and Research
Dr. Martha V. Henderson, Dean, Graduate Studies, Research, and Information Systems
Programs in:
 art • MA
 clinical psychology • MS
 English • MA
 health promotion • M Ed
 music • MM
 sport administration • M Ed

Louisiana

Northwestern State University of Louisiana (continued)

College of Education
Dr. Vickie Gentry, Chair
Programs in:
  adult and continuing education • M Ed
  business and distributive education • M Ed
  counseling and guidance • M Ed, Ed S
  early childhood education • M Ed
  educational administration/supervision • M Ed, Ed S
  educational technology • M Ed, Ed S
  elementary teaching • M Ed, Ed S
  health and physical education • M Ed
  home economics education • M Ed
  human services • M Ed, MA, Ed S
  mathematics education • M Ed
  professional secondary studies: alternate certification 5th-year program • M Ed
  reading • M Ed, Ed S
  responsive educators • Certificate
  science education • M Ed
  secondary teaching • M Ed, Ed S
  social sciences education • M Ed
  special education • M Ed, Ed S
  student personnel services • MA

College of Nursing
Dr. Norann Planchock, Director
Program in:
  nursing • MSN

■ SOUTHEASTERN LOUISIANA UNIVERSITY
Hammond, LA 70402
http://www.selu.edu/

State-supported, coed, comprehensive institution. *Enrollment:* 15,662 graduate, professional, and undergraduate students; 490 full-time matriculated graduate/professional students (354 women), 964 part-time matriculated graduate/professional students (778 women). *Graduate faculty:* 172 full-time (85 women), 32 part-time/adjunct (22 women). *Computer facilities:* 819 computers available on campus for general student use. A campuswide network can be accessed from student residence rooms and from off campus. Internet access and online class registration, campus webmail are available. *Library facilities:* Sims Memorial Library. *Graduate expenses:* Tuition, state resident: full-time $2,754; part-time $153 per credit. Tuition, nonresident: full-time $6,750; part-time $375 per credit. International tuition: $6,870 full-time. *General application contact:* Josie Mercante, Associate Director of Admissions, 985-549-2066.

College of Arts and Sciences
Dr. Tammy Bourg, Dean
Programs in:
  applied sociology • MS
  arts and sciences • M Mus, MA, MS
  biology • MS
  English • MA
  history • MA
  music and dramatic arts • M Mus
  organizational communication • MA
  psychology • MA

College of Business and Technology
Dr. Michael Budden, Dean
Program in:
  business administration • MBA

College of Education and Human Development
Dr. Martha Thornhill, Interim Dean
Programs in:
  administration and supervision • M Ed
  counselor education • M Ed
  curriculum and instruction • M Ed
  education and human development • M Ed, MAT
  elementary and special education • MAT
  secondary education • MAT
  special education • M Ed

College of Nursing and Health Sciences
Dr. Donnie Booth, Dean
Programs in:
  communication sciences and disorders • MS
  kinesiology and health studies • MA
  nursing • MSN
  nursing and health sciences • MA, MS, MSN

Program in Integrated Science and Technology
Dr. Michael Kurtz, Dean
Program in:
  integrated science and technology • MS

■ SOUTHERN UNIVERSITY AND AGRICULTURAL AND MECHANICAL COLLEGE
Baton Rouge, LA 70813
http://www.subr.edu/

State-supported, coed, comprehensive institution. CGS member. *Computer facilities:* 1,300 computers available on campus for general student use. A campuswide network can be accessed from student residence rooms and from off campus. Internet access and online class registration are available. *Library facilities:* John B. Cade Library plus 2 others. *General application contact:* Director of Graduate Admissions and Recruitment, 225-771-5390.

Graduate School
Program in:
  science/mathematics education • PhD

College of Agricultural, Family and Consumer Sciences
Program in:
  urban forestry • MS

College of Arts and Humanities
Programs in:
  arts and humanities • MA
  mass communications • MA
  social sciences • MA

College of Business
Programs in:
  accountancy • MPA
  business • MPA

College of Education
Programs in:
  administration and supervision • M Ed
  counselor education • MA
  education • M Ed, MA, MS
  elementary education • M Ed
  media • M Ed
  mental health counseling • MA
  secondary education • M Ed
  therapeutic recreation • MS

College of Sciences
Programs in:
  analytical chemistry • MS
  biochemistry • MS
  biology • MS
  environmental sciences • MS
  information systems • MS
  inorganic chemistry • MS
  mathematics • MS
  micro/minicomputer architecture • MS
  operating systems • MS
  organic chemistry • MS
  physical chemistry • MS
  physics • MS
  rehabilitation counseling • MS
  sciences • MA, MS

Institute for the Study and Rehabilitation of Exceptional Children and Youth
Program in:
  study and rehabilitation of exceptional children and youth • M Ed, PhD

School of Public Policy and Urban Affairs
Programs in:
  public administration • MPA
  public policy • PhD
  public policy and urban affairs • MA, MPA, PhD
  social sciences • MA

Louisiana

School of Nursing
Programs in:
  educator/administrator • PhD
  family health nursing • MSN
  family nurse practitioner • PhD, Post Master's Certificate

Southern University Law Center
Freddie Pitcher, Chancellor
Program in:
  law • JD

■ **SOUTHERN UNIVERSITY AT NEW ORLEANS**
New Orleans, LA 70126-1009
http://www.suno.edu/

State-supported, coed, comprehensive institution. *Computer facilities:* 100 computers available on campus for general student use. *Library facilities:* Leonard Washington Library. *General application contact:* Director of Student Affairs, 504-286-5376.

School of Social Work
Program in:
  social work • MSW

■ **TULANE UNIVERSITY**
New Orleans, LA 70118-5669
http://www.tulane.edu/

Independent, coed, university. CGS member. *Enrollment:* 12,443 graduate, professional, and undergraduate students; 4,364 full-time matriculated graduate/professional students (2,198 women), 694 part-time matriculated graduate/professional students (324 women). *Graduate faculty:* 1,047 full-time, 547 part-time/adjunct. *Computer facilities:* Computer purchase and lease plans are available. 900 computers available on campus for general student use. A campuswide network can be accessed from student residence rooms and from off campus. Internet access and online class registration, wireless access to the Internet are available. *Library facilities:* Howard Tilton Memorial Library plus 8 others. *General application contact:* Dr. Michael Herman, Dean, 504-865-5100.

Find an in-depth description at www.petersons.com/gradchannel.

A. B. Freeman School of Business
Dr. James W. McFarland, Dean
Program in:
  business • EMBA, M Acct, M Fin, MBA, PhD

Graduate School
Dr. Michael Herman, Dean
Programs in:
  anthropology • MA, MS, PhD
  applied mathematics • MS
  art • MFA
  art history • MA
  biology • MS, PhD
  chemistry • MA, MS, PhD
  civic and cultural management • MA
  classical studies • MA
  economics • MA, PhD
  English • MA, PhD
  French and Italian • MA, PhD
  geology • MS, PhD
  history • MA, PhD
  international development and technology transfer • MS, PhD
  liberal arts • MLA
  mathematics • MS, PhD
  music • MA, MFA
  paleontology • PhD
  philosophy • MA, PhD
  physics • MS, PhD
  political science • MA, PhD
  psychology • MS, PhD
  sociology • MA, PhD
  Spanish and Portuguese • MA, PhD
  statistics • MS
  theatre and dance • MFA

Roger Thayer Stone Center for Latin American Studies
Dr. Thomas Reese, Executive Director
Program in:
  Latin American studies • MA, PhD

School of Architecture
Ronald Filson, Interim Dean
Program in:
  architecture • M Arch, MPS

School of Engineering
Dr. Nicholas J. Altiero, Dean
Programs in:
  biomedical engineering • M Eng, MS, MSE, PhD
  chemical engineering • M Eng, MS, MSE, PhD
  civil engineering • M Eng, MS, MSE, PhD
  computer science • M Eng, MS, MSCS, PhD
  electrical engineering • M Eng, MS, MSE, PhD
  engineering • M Eng, MS, MSCS, MSE, PhD
  environmental engineering • M Eng, MS, MSE, PhD
  mechanical engineering • M Eng, MS, MSE, PhD

School of Law
Lawrence Ponoroff, Dean
Programs in:
  admiralty • LL M
  American business law • LL M
  energy and environment • LL M
  international and comparative law • LL M
  law • JD, LL M, PhD

School of Medicine
Dr. Ian Logan Taylor, Dean
Program in:
  medicine • MD, MS, PhD, Diploma

Graduate Programs in Medicine
Dr. Michael Herman, Dean, Graduate School
Programs in:
  biochemistry • MS, PhD
  human genetics • MS, PhD
  medicine • MS, PhD, Diploma
  microbiology and immunology • MS, PhD
  molecular and cellular biology • PhD
  neuroscience • MS, PhD
  pharmacology • MS, PhD
  physiology • MS, PhD
  structural and cellular biology • MS, PhD

School of Public Health and Tropical Medicine
Dr. Pierre Beukens, Dean
Programs in:
  biostatistics • MS, MSPH, PhD, Sc D
  clinical tropical medicine and travelers health • Diploma
  environmental health sciences • MPH, MSPH, Sc D
  epidemiology • MPH, MS, Dr PH, PhD
  health communication/education • MPH
  health systems management • MHA, MMM, MPH, Dr PH
  international health and development • MADH, MPH, Dr PH
  maternal and child health • MPH, Dr PH
  nutrition • MPH
  parasitology • MS, MSPH, PhD, Sc D
  public health and tropical medicine • MPHTM

School of Social Work
Dr. Ronald Marks, Dean
Program in:
  social work • MSW, PhD

■ **UNIVERSITY OF LOUISIANA AT LAFAYETTE**
Lafayette, LA 70504
http://www.louisiana.edu/

State-supported, coed, university. CGS member. *Enrollment:* 16,208 graduate, professional, and undergraduate students; 809 full-time matriculated graduate/professional students (386 women), 504 part-time matriculated graduate/professional students (317 women). *Graduate faculty:* 328 full-time (101

Louisiana

University of Louisiana at Lafayette (continued)
women). *Computer facilities:* 548 computers available on campus for general student use. A campuswide network can be accessed from off campus. Internet access and online class registration are available. *Library facilities:* Edith Garland Dupre Library. *Graduate expenses:* Tuition, state resident: full-time $2,786; part-time $85 per credit. Tuition, nonresident: full-time $8,966; part-time $343 per credit. International tuition: $9,102 full-time. *General application contact:* Dr. C. E. Palmer, Dean, 337-482-6965.

Graduate School
Dr. C. E. Palmer, Dean
Program in:
 counselor education • MS

College of Applied Life Sciences
Dr. Linda Vincent, Dean
Programs in:
 applied life sciences • MS
 human resources • MS

College of Business Administration
Dr. Lewis Gale, IV, Dean
Programs in:
 business administration • MBA
 health care administration • MBA
 health care certification • MBA

College of Education
Dr. Gerald B. Carlson, Dean
Programs in:
 administration and supervision • M Ed
 curriculum and instruction • M Ed
 education • M Ed
 education of the gifted • M Ed

College of Engineering
Dr. Anthony B. Ponter, Dean
Programs in:
 chemical engineering • MSE
 civil engineering • MSE
 computer engineering • MS, PhD
 computer science • MS, PhD
 engineering • MS, MSE, MSET, MSTC, PhD
 engineering and technology management • MSET
 mechanical engineering • MSE
 petroleum engineering • MSE
 telecommunications • MSTC

College of Liberal Arts
Dr. A. David Barry, Dean
Programs in:
 British and American literature • MA
 communicative disorders • MS, PhD
 creative writing • PhD
 francophone studies • PhD
 French • MA
 history and geography • MA
 liberal arts • MA, MS, PhD
 literature • PhD
 mass communications • MS
 psychology • MS
 rehabilitation counseling • MS
 rhetoric • PhD

College of Nursing
Dr. Gail Poirrier, Dean
Program in:
 nursing • MSN

College of Sciences
Dr. Bradd D. Clark, Dean
Programs in:
 biology • MS
 cognitive science • PhD
 computer science • MS, PhD
 environmental and evolutionary biology • PhD
 geology • MS
 mathematics • MS, PhD
 physics • MS
 sciences • MS, PhD

College of the Arts
H. Gordon Brooks, Dean
Programs in:
 architecture • M Arch
 arts • M Arch, MM
 conducting • MM
 pedagogy • MM
 vocal and instrumental performance • MM

■ **UNIVERSITY OF LOUISIANA AT MONROE**
Monroe, LA 71209-0001
http://www.nlu.edu/

State-supported, coed, university. *Enrollment:* 8,571 graduate, professional, and undergraduate students; 558 full-time matriculated graduate/professional students (340 women), 372 part-time matriculated graduate/professional students (279 women). *Graduate faculty:* 101 full-time (36 women), 8 part-time/adjunct (5 women). *Computer facilities:* 1,400 computers available on campus for general student use. A campuswide network can be accessed from off campus. *Library facilities:* Sandel Library. *Graduate expenses:* Tuition, state resident: full-time $2,052. Tuition, nonresident: full-time $8,010. *General application contact:* Dr. Virginia Eaton, Graduate Studies and Research Director, 318-342-1036.

Graduate Studies and Research
Dr. Virginia Eaton, Graduate Studies and Research Director

College of Arts and Sciences
Dr. Carlos Fandal, Dean
Programs in:
 biology • MS
 chemistry • MS
 communication • MA
 criminal justice • MA
 English • MA
 geosciences • MS
 gerontological studies • CGS
 gerontology • MA
 history • MA
 liberal arts • MA, MM, MS, CGS
 music • MM

College of Business Administration
Dr. Kenneth Clow, Dean
Program in:
 business administration • MBA

College of Education and Human Development
Dr. Luke Thomas, Dean
Programs in:
 administration and supervision • M Ed
 counseling • M Ed
 curriculum and instruction • Ed D
 education • M Ed, MA, MS, Ed D, PhD, SSP
 educational leadership • Ed D
 elementary education • M Ed
 exercise science • MS
 marriage and family therapy • MA, PhD
 psychology • MS
 reading • M Ed
 school psychology • SSP
 secondary education • M Ed
 special education • M Ed
 substance abuse counseling • MA

College of Health Sciences
Dr. William M. Bourn, Dean
Programs in:
 communicative disorders • MA
 health sciences • Pharm D, MA, MS, PhD
 pharmaceutical sciences • MS
 pharmacy • Pharm D, PhD

■ **UNIVERSITY OF NEW ORLEANS**
New Orleans, LA 70148
http://www.uno.edu/

State-supported, coed, university. CGS member. *Enrollment:* 17,360 graduate, professional, and undergraduate students; 1,605 full-time matriculated graduate/professional students (849 women), 2,417 part-time matriculated graduate/professional students (1,537 women). *Graduate faculty:* 414 full-time, 299 part-time/adjunct. *Computer facilities:* 1,084 computers available on campus for general student use. A campuswide network can be accessed from student residence rooms and from off campus. Internet access is available. *Library facilities:* Earl K. Long Library. *Graduate expenses:* Tuition, state resident: part-time $488 per semester hour. Tuition, nonresident: part-time $1,826 per semester hour. *General application contact:* Dr. Robert Cashner, Dean, Graduate School, 504-280-6836.

Graduate School
Dr. Robert Cashner, Dean

College of Business Administration
Dr. Paul Hensel, Interim Dean
Programs in:
 accounting • MS
 business administration • MBA, MS, PhD
 financial economics • PhD
 health care management • MS
 hospitality and tourism management • MS
 taxation • MS

College of Education
Dr. James Meza, Dean
Programs in:
 adapted physical education • MA
 counselor education • M Ed, PhD, GCE
 curriculum and instruction • M Ed, PhD, GCE
 education • M Ed, MA, Ed D, PhD, GCE
 educational leadership and foundations • M Ed, PhD, GCE
 exercise physiology • MA
 gerontology • GCE
 health and physical education • GCE
 physical education • M Ed
 science, pedagogy and coaching sport management • MA
 special education • M Ed, Ed D, PhD, GCE

College of Engineering
Dr. Russell Trahan, Dean
Programs in:
 engineering • MS, PhD, Certificate
 engineering and applied sciences • PhD
 engineering management • MS, Certificate
 mechanical engineering • MS

College of Liberal Arts
Dr. Susan Krantz, Interim Dean
Programs in:
 arts administration • MA
 drama and communication • MA, MFA
 English • MA
 fine arts • MFA
 foreign languages • MA
 geography • MA
 history • MA
 liberal arts • MA, MFA, MM, PhD
 music • MM
 political science • MA, PhD
 sociology • MA

College of Sciences
Dr. Joe King, Dean
Programs in:
 biological sciences • MS, PhD
 chemistry • MS, PhD
 computer science • MS
 geology and geophysics • MS
 mathematics • MS
 physics • MS, PhD
 psychology • MS, PhD
 science teaching • MAST
 sciences • MAST, MS, PhD

College of Urban and Public Affairs
Dr. Alan Artibise, Dean
Programs in:
 public administration and policy • MPA
 urban and public affairs • MPA, MS, MURP, PhD
 urban and regional planning • MURP
 urban studies • MS, PhD

■ **XAVIER UNIVERSITY OF LOUISIANA**
New Orleans, LA 70125-1098
http://www.xula.edu/

Independent-religious, coed, comprehensive institution. CGS member. *Enrollment:* 3,913 graduate, professional, and undergraduate students; 757 matriculated graduate/professional students. *Graduate faculty:* 53. *Computer facilities:* 250 computers available on campus for general student use. A campuswide network can be accessed from student residence rooms and from off campus. *Library facilities:* Xavier Library plus 1 other. *Graduate expenses:* Tuition: part-time $210 per semester hour. Required fees: $100 per semester. *General application contact:* Marlene C. Robinson, Director of Graduate Admissions, 504-520-7487.

College of Pharmacy
Dr. Wayne T. Harris, Dean
Program in:
 pharmacy • Pharm D

Graduate School
Dr. Alvin J. Richard, Dean
Programs in:
 administration and supervision • MA
 curriculum and instruction • MA
 elementary education (1–6) • MAT
 guidance and counseling • MA
 secondary education • MAT
 special education (mild/moderate) • MAT

Institute for Black Catholic Studies
Dr. Jamie T. Phelps, Director
Program in:
 pastoral theology • Th M

Maine

■ **HUSSON COLLEGE**
Bangor, ME 04401-2999
http://www.husson.edu/

Independent, coed, comprehensive institution. *Enrollment:* 2,038 graduate, professional, and undergraduate students; 62 full-time matriculated graduate/professional students (42 women), 209 part-time matriculated graduate/professional students (137 women). *Graduate faculty:* 17 full-time (11 women), 44 part-time/adjunct (29 women). *Computer facilities:* 110 computers available on campus for general student use. A campuswide network can be accessed from student residence rooms. Internet access is available. *Library facilities:* Husson College Library. *Graduate expenses:* Tuition: part-time $220 per credit hour. *General application contact:* Dr. Robert M. Smith, Dean of Graduate Studies, 207-941-7062.

Graduate Studies Division
Programs in:
 business • MSB
 family nurse practitioner • MSN
 nursing • MSN
 physical therapy • MSPT
 psychiatric nursing • MSN

■ **SAINT JOSEPH'S COLLEGE OF MAINE**
Standish, ME 04084-5263
http://www.sjcme.edu/

Independent-religious, coed, comprehensive institution. *Enrollment:* 1,704 part-time matriculated graduate/professional students (1,103 women). *Graduate faculty:* 6 full-time (4 women), 43 part-time/adjunct (25 women). *Computer facilities:* Computer purchase and lease plans are available. 71 computers available on campus for general student use. A campuswide network can be accessed from student residence rooms and from off campus. Internet access is available. *Library facilities:* Wellehan Library. *Graduate expenses:* Tuition: part-time $250 per credit. *General application contact:* 800-752-4723.

Department of Nursing
Dr. Margaret Hourigan, Chair
Programs in:
 nursing • MS
 nursing administration and leadership • Certificate
 nursing and health care education • Certificate
 parish nursing • Certificate

Saint Joseph's College of Maine (continued)

Program in Business Administration
Dr. Gregory Gull, Director
Programs in:
  quality leadership • MBA
  resort management • MBA

Program in Health Services Administration
Dr. Alice Rose, Director
Programs in:
  health services administration • MHSA, Certificate
  international health care • Certificate
  long-term care administration • Certificate
  practice management • Certificate

Program in Pastoral Studies
Dr. Rita LaBruzzo, Director
Programs in:
  pastoral ministry • MA
  pastoral studies • MA, Certificate
  pastoral theology • MA

Program in Teacher Education
Dr. Richard Willis, Director
Program in:
  teacher education • MS

■ UNIVERSITY OF MAINE
Orono, ME 04469
http://www.umaine.edu/

State-supported, coed, university. CGS member. *Enrollment:* 11,222 graduate, professional, and undergraduate students; 1,069 full-time matriculated graduate/professional students (648 women), 674 part-time matriculated graduate/professional students (460 women). *Graduate faculty:* 650. *Computer facilities:* Computer purchase and lease plans are available. 520 computers available on campus for general student use. A campuswide network can be accessed from student residence rooms and from off campus. Internet access and online class registration, on-line grade information, e-mail are available. *Library facilities:* Fogler Library plus 2 others. *Graduate expenses:* Tuition, state resident: part-time $235 per credit. Tuition, nonresident: part-time $670 per credit. Tuition and fees vary according to course load. *General application contact:* Scott G. Delcourt, Associate Dean of the Graduate School, 207-581-3218.

Graduate School
Scott G. Delcourt, Associate Dean of the Graduate School
Programs in:
  information systems • MS
  interdisciplinary studies • PhD
  liberal studies • MA
  teaching • MST

Climate Change Institute
Dr. Paul Mayewski, Director
Program in:
  climate change • MS

College of Business, Public Policy and Health
Dr. Daniel E. Innis, Dean
Programs in:
  accounting • MS
  business administration • MBA
  business, public policy and health • MBA, MPA, MS, MSW, PhD, CAS
  nursing • MS, CAS
  public administration • MPA, PhD
  social work • MSW

College of Education and Human Development
Dr. Robert A. Cobb, Dean
Programs in:
  counselor education • M Ed, MA, MS, Ed D, CAS
  educational leadership • M Ed, Ed D, CAS
  elementary education • M Ed, MAT, MS, CAS
  higher education • M Ed, MA, MS, Ed D, CAS
  human development • MS
  human development and family relations • MS
  instructional technology • M Ed
  kinesiology and physical education • M Ed, MS
  literacy education • M Ed, MA, MS, Ed D
  science education • M Ed, MS, CAS
  secondary education • M Ed, MA, MAT, MS, CAS
  social studies education • M Ed, MA, MS, CAS
  special education • M Ed, CAS

College of Engineering
Dr. Larryl K. Matthews, Dean
Programs in:
  biological engineering • MS
  chemical engineering • MS, PhD
  civil engineering • MS, PhD
  computer engineering • MS
  electrical engineering • MS, PhD
  engineering • MS, PhD
  mechanical engineering • MS, PhD
  spatial information science and engineering • MS, PhD

College of Liberal Arts and Sciences
Dr. Ann Leffler, Dean
Programs in:
  chemistry • MS, PhD
  clinical psychology • PhD
  communication • MA
  communication sciences and disorders • MA
  computer science • MS, PhD
  developmental psychology • MA
  economics • MA
  engineering physics • M Eng
  English • MA
  experimental psychology • MA, PhD
  financial economics • MA
  French • MA, MAT
  history • MA, PhD
  liberal arts and sciences • M Eng, MA, MAT, MM, MS, PhD
  mathematics • MA
  music • MM
  physics • MS, PhD
  social psychology • MA
  theatre • MA

College of Natural Sciences, Forestry, and Agriculture
Dr. G. Bruce Wiersma, Dean
Programs in:
  animal sciences • MPS, MS
  biochemistry • MPS, MS
  biochemistry and molecular biology • PhD
  biological sciences • PhD
  botany and plant pathology • MS
  earth sciences • MS, PhD
  ecology and environmental science • MS, PhD
  ecology and environmental sciences • MS, PhD
  entomology • MS
  food and nutritional sciences • PhD
  food science and human nutrition • MS
  forest resources • PhD
  forestry • MF, MS
  horticulture • MS
  marine biology • MS, PhD
  marine policy • MS
  microbiology • MPS, MS, PhD
  natural sciences, forestry, and agriculture • MF, MPS, MS, MWC, PhD
  oceanography • MS, PhD
  plant science • PhD
  plant, soil, and environmental sciences • MS
  resource economics and policy • MS
  resource utilization • MS
  wildlife conservation • MWC
  wildlife ecology • MS, PhD
  zoology • MS, PhD

■ UNIVERSITY OF NEW ENGLAND
Biddeford, ME 04005-9526
http://www.une.edu/

Independent, coed, comprehensive institution. *Enrollment:* 3,192 graduate, professional, and undergraduate students; 872 full-time matriculated graduate/professional students (541 women), 783 part-time matriculated graduate/professional students (609 women).

Graduate faculty: 55 full-time (26 women), 49 part-time/adjunct (24 women). *Computer facilities:* 125 computers available on campus for general student use. A campuswide network can be accessed from student residence rooms and from off campus. Internet access and online class registration are available. *Library facilities:* Ketchum Library plus 1 other. *Graduate expenses:* Tuition: full-time $18,990; part-time $680 per credit hour. *General application contact:* Robert Pecchia, Associate Dean of Admissions, 207-283-0171 Ext. 2297.

College of Arts and Sciences
Jacque Carter, Dean
Programs in:
 arts and sciences • MS Ed, Advanced Certificate
 education • MS Ed
 educational leadership • Advanced Certificate

College of Health Professions
Dr. Vernon Moore, Dean
Programs in:
 health professions • MPA, MS, MSOT, MSPT, MSW, DPT, Certificate
 nurse anesthesia • MS
 occupational therapy • MSOT
 physical therapy • MSPT, DPT
 physician assistant • MPA

School of Social Work
Head
Programs in:
 addictions counseling • Certificate
 gerontology • Certificate
 social work • MSW

College of Osteopathic Medicine
Dr. Stephen Shannon, Dean
Programs in:
 osteopathic medicine • DO, Certificate
 public health • Certificate

■ **UNIVERSITY OF SOUTHERN MAINE**
Portland, ME 04104-9300
http://www.usm.maine.edu/

State-supported, coed, comprehensive institution. CGS member. *Enrollment:* 11,007 graduate, professional, and undergraduate students; 1,203 full-time matriculated graduate/professional students (777 women), 1,191 part-time matriculated graduate/professional students (849 women). *Graduate faculty:* 166. *Computer facilities:* Computer purchase and lease plans are available. 532 computers available on campus for general student use. A campuswide network can be accessed from student residence rooms and from off campus. Internet access and online class registration are available. *Library facilities:* University of Southern Maine Library plus 4 others. *Graduate expenses:* Part-time $215 per credit. Tuition, state resident. part-time $323 per credit. Tuition, nonresident: part-time $602 per credit. Required fees: $18 per credit hour. Tuition and fees vary according to reciprocity agreements. *General application contact:* Mary Sloan, Director of Graduate Admissions, 207-780-4386.

College of Arts and Science
Dr. Luisa Deprez, Dean
Programs in:
 American and New England studies • MA
 biology • MS
 creative writing • MFA
 social work • MSW
 statistics • MS

College of Education and Human Development
Betty Lou Whitford, Dean
Programs in:
 adult education • MS, CAS
 counselor education • MS, CAS
 education and human development • MS, MS Ed, Psy D, CAS, Certificate
 educational leadership • MS Ed, CAS, Certificate
 English as a second language • MS Ed, CAS
 extended teacher education • MS Ed, Certificate
 industrial/technology education • MS Ed
 literacy education • MS Ed, CAS
 school psychology • MS, Psy D
 special education • MS

College of Nursing and Health Professions
Dr. Jane Marie Kirschling, Dean
Programs in:
 adult health nursing • PMC
 clinical nurse specialist adult health care management • MS
 clinical nurse specialist psychiatric-mental health nursing • MS
 family nursing • PMC
 nurse practitioner adult health nursing • MS
 nurse practitioner family nursing • MS
 nurse practitioner psychiatric/mental health nursing • MS
 psychiatric-mental health nursing • PMC

Edmund S. Muskie School of Public Service
Karl R. Braithwaite, Dean
Programs in:
 child and family policy • Certificate
 community planning and development • MCPD, Certificate
 health policy and management • MS, Certificate
 non-profit management • Certificate
 public policy • PhD
 public policy and management • MPPM
 public service • MCPD, MPPM, MS, PhD, Certificate

Program in Occupational Therapy
Program in:
 occupational therapy • MOT

School of Applied Science, Engineering, and Technology
Dr. John R. Wright, Dean
Programs in:
 applied immunology and molecular biology • MS
 applied science, engineering, and technology • MS
 computer science • MS
 manufacturing systems • MS

School of Business
Dr. Jack W. Trifts, Dean
Programs in:
 accounting • MSA
 business administration • MBA

University of Maine School of Law
Colleen A. Khoury, Dean
Program in:
 law • JD

Maryland

■ **BOWIE STATE UNIVERSITY**
Bowie, MD 20715-9465
http://www.bowiestate.edu/

State-supported, coed, comprehensive institution. CGS member. *Enrollment:* 5,454 graduate, professional, and undergraduate students; 317 full-time matriculated graduate/professional students (228 women), 1,149 part-time matriculated graduate/professional students (861 women). *Graduate faculty:* 54 full-time (24 women), 27 part-time/adjunct (14 women). *Computer facilities:* 3,144 computers available on campus for general student use. A campuswide network can be accessed from student residence rooms and from off campus. Internet access and online class registration are available. *Library facilities:* Thurgood Marshall Library. *Graduate expenses:* Tuition, state resident: part-time

Maryland

Bowie State University (continued)
$244 per credit. Tuition, nonresident: part-time $470 per credit. Required fees: $1,054; $527 per term. *General application contact:* Dr. Ida G. Brandon, Graduate Dean, 301-860-3413.

Graduate Programs
Dr. Ida G. Brandon, Dean
Programs in:
 administration of nursing services • MS
 business administration • M Adm Mgt
 business administration and management • MBA
 computer science • MS
 counseling psychology • MA
 educational leadership • Ed D
 elementary education • M Ed
 family nurse practitioner • MS
 guidance and counseling • M Ed
 human resource development • MA
 information systems analyst • Certificate
 management information systems • MS
 nursing education • MS
 organizational communication • MA, Certificate
 public administration • M Adm Mgt
 reading education • M Ed
 school administration and supervision • M Ed
 secondary education • M Ed
 special education • M Ed
 teaching • MAT

■ **COLLEGE OF NOTRE DAME OF MARYLAND**
Baltimore, MD 21210-2476
http://www.ndm.edu/

Independent-religious, women only, comprehensive institution. *Enrollment:* 3,030 graduate, professional, and undergraduate students; 88 full-time matriculated graduate/professional students (75 women), 1,360 part-time matriculated graduate/professional students (1,108 women). *Graduate faculty:* 40 full-time (25 women), 125 part-time/adjunct (100 women). *Computer facilities:* Computer purchase and lease plans are available. 80 computers available on campus for general student use. A campuswide network can be accessed from student residence rooms and from off campus. Internet access, online classroom assignments and information are available. *Library facilities:* Loyola/Notre Dame Library. *Graduate expenses:* Tuition: part-time $360 per credit. *General application contact:* Kathy Nikolaidis, Graduate Admissions Coordinator, 410-532-5317.

Graduate Studies
Sr. Margaret E. Mahoney, Associate Director of Graduate Studies
Programs in:
 communicating in contemporary culture • MA
 leadership in teaching • MA
 liberal studies • MA
 management • MA
 nonprofit management • MA
 studies in aging • MA
 teaching • MA
 teaching English to speakers of other languages • MA

■ **COPPIN STATE UNIVERSITY**
Baltimore, MD 21216-3698
http://www.coppin.edu/

State-supported, coed, comprehensive institution. CGS member. *Enrollment:* 14 full-time matriculated graduate/professional students (10 women), 304 part-time matriculated graduate/professional students (218 women). *Graduate faculty:* 35 full-time (22 women), 28 part-time/adjunct (15 women). *Computer facilities:* 130 computers available on campus for general student use. A campuswide network can be accessed from off campus. Internet access is available. *Library facilities:* Parlett L. Moore Library. *Graduate expenses:* Tuition, state resident: part-time $175 per credit hour. Tuition, nonresident: part-time $318 per credit hour. *General application contact:* Dr. Mary Owens, Dean, Graduate Studies and Research Evaluation, 410-951-3090.

Division of Graduate Studies
Dr. Mary Owens, Dean, Graduate Studies and Research Evaluation

Division of Arts and Sciences
Dr. Clyde Mathura, Dean
Programs in:
 alcohol and substance abuse counseling • MS
 arts and sciences • M Ed, MS
 criminal justice • MS
 human services administration • MS
 rehabilitation counseling • M Ed

Division of Education
Dr. Julius Chapman, Chair
Programs in:
 adult and general education • MS
 curriculum and instruction • M Ed, MA, MS
 reading education • MS
 special education • M Ed
 teacher education • MA
 teaching • MA

Helene Fuld School of Nursing
Dr. Marcella Copes, Dean
Programs in:
 family nurse practitioner • PMC
 nursing • MSN

■ **FROSTBURG STATE UNIVERSITY**
Frostburg, MD 21532-1099
http://www.frostburg.edu/

State-supported, coed, comprehensive institution. *Enrollment:* 5,469 graduate, professional, and undergraduate students; 246 full-time matriculated graduate/professional students (156 women), 579 part-time matriculated graduate/professional students (358 women). *Graduate faculty:* 83 full-time (32 women), 14 part-time/adjunct (5 women). *Computer facilities:* 577 computers available on campus for general student use. A campuswide network can be accessed from student residence rooms and from off campus. Internet access and online class registration are available. *Library facilities:* Lewis J. Ort Library. *Graduate expenses:* Tuition, state resident: full-time $4,212; part-time $234 per credit hour. Tuition, nonresident: full-time $4,878; part-time $271 per credit hour. *General application contact:* Patricia C. Spiker, Director, Graduate Services, 301-687-7053.

Graduate School
Patricia C. Spiker, Director, Graduate Services

College of Business
Dr. Danny Arnold, Dean
Programs in:
 business • MBA
 business administration • MBA

College of Education
Dr. Susan Arisman, Dean
Programs in:
 curriculum and instruction • M Ed
 education • M Ed, MA, MS
 educational administration and supervision • M Ed
 educational technology • M Ed
 elementary • M Ed
 elementary education • M Ed
 elementary teaching • MA
 human performance • MS
 interdisciplinary education • M Ed
 parks and recreational management • MS
 reading • M Ed
 school counseling • M Ed
 secondary • M Ed
 secondary education • M Ed
 secondary teaching • MA
 special education • M Ed

Maryland

College of Liberal Arts and Sciences
Dr. Joseph Hoffman, Dean
Programs in:
 applied computer science • MS
 applied ecology and conservation biology • MS
 counseling psychology • MS
 fisheries and wildlife management • MS
 liberal arts and sciences • MS

■ HOOD COLLEGE
Frederick, MD 21701-8575
http://www.hood.edu/

Independent, coed, comprehensive institution. CGS member. *Computer facilities:* 277 computers available on campus for general student use. A campuswide network can be accessed from student residence rooms and from off campus. Internet access is available. *Library facilities:* Beneficial-Hodson Library and Information Technology Center. *General application contact:* Dean of the Graduate School, 301-696-3600.

Graduate School
Programs in:
 administration and management • MBA
 biomedical science • MS
 computer science • MS
 curriculum and instruction • MS
 educational leadership • MS
 environmental biology • MS
 information technology • MS
 management information technology • MS
 psychology • MA
 regulatory compliance • Certificate
 thanatology • MA, Certificate

■ THE JOHNS HOPKINS UNIVERSITY
Baltimore, MD 21218-2699
http://www.jhu.edu/

Independent, coed, university. CGS member. *Enrollment:* 5,311 full-time matriculated graduate/professional students (2,765 women), 6,265 part-time matriculated graduate/professional students (3,199 women). *Graduate faculty:* 2,970 full-time (1,085 women), 64 part-time/adjunct (31 women). *Computer facilities:* 460 computers available on campus for general student use. A campuswide network can be accessed from student residence rooms and from off campus. Internet access and online class registration are available. *Library facilities:* Milton S. Eisenhower Library plus 6 others. *Graduate expenses:* Tuition: full-time $28,730; part-time $1,490 per course. Part-time tuition and fees vary according to course load, campus/location and program. *General application contact:* Graduate Admissions Office, 410-516-8174.

Find an in-depth description at www.petersons.com/gradchannel.

Bloomberg School of Public Health
Dr. Alfred Sommer, Dean
Programs in:
 biochemistry and molecular biology • PhD
 bioinformatics • MHS
 biostatistics • MHS, Sc M, PhD
 cancer epidemiology • MHS, Sc M, Dr PH, PhD, Sc D
 clinical epidemiology • MHS, Sc M, Dr PH, PhD, Sc D
 clinical investigation • MHS, Sc M, PhD, Certificate
 clinical trials • MHS, Sc M, Dr PH, PhD, Sc D
 disease prevention and control • MHS, PhD, Sc D
 environmental health engineering • MHS, Sc M, PhD, Sc D
 environmental health sciences • MHS, Dr PH
 epidemiology • MHS, Sc M, Dr PH, PhD, Sc D
 finance and administration • MHS
 genetic counseling • Sc M
 genetics • MHS, Sc M, Dr PH, PhD, Sc D
 health and public policy • MHS, PhD, Sc D
 health economics • PhD, Sc D
 health education • MHS
 health policy • MHS
 health policy/prevention policy • PhD, Sc D
 health services research • MHS, PhD, Sc D
 health systems • MHS, PhD, Sc D
 human nutrition • MHS, PhD, Sc D
 infectious disease epidemiology • MHS, Sc M, Dr PH, PhD, Sc D
 international health • Dr PH
 long-term care • PhD, Sc D
 mental health • MHS, Sc M, Dr PH, PhD, Sc D
 molecular microbiology and immunology • MHS, Sc M, PhD
 occupational and environmental health • PhD
 occupational and environmental hygiene • MHS
 occupational/environmental epidemiology • MHS, Sc M, Dr PH, PhD, Sc D
 physiology • Sc M, PhD
 population and family health sciences • MHS, Dr PH, PhD
 public health • MHS, MPH, Sc M, Dr PH, PhD, Sc D, Certificate
 radiation health sciences • MHS, PhD, Sc D
 reproductive biology • MHS, Sc M
 social and behavioral interventions • MHS, PhD, Sc D
 social and behavioral sciences • MHS, Sc M, PhD, Sc D
 toxicological sciences • PhD

G. W. C. Whiting School of Engineering
Dr. Andrew S. Douglas, Interim Dean
Programs in:
 biomedical engineering • MSE, PhD
 chemical and biomolecular engineering • MSE, PhD
 civil engineering • MCE, MSE, PhD
 computer science • MSE, PhD
 discrete mathematics • MA, MSE, PhD
 electrical and computer engineering • MSE, PhD
 engineering • M Ch E, M Mat SE, MA, MCE, MEE, MME, MS, MSE, PhD
 geography and environmental engineering • MA, MS, MSE, PhD
 materials science and engineering • M Mat SE, MSE, PhD
 mechanical engineering • MSE, PhD
 operations research/optimization/decision science • MA, MSE, PhD
 statistics/probability/stochastic processes • MA, MSE, PhD

Part-Time Programs in Engineering and Applied Science
Programs in:
 applied and computational mathematics • MS
 applied biomedical engineering • MS
 applied physics • MS
 chemical engineering • M Ch E
 civil engineering • MCE
 computer science • MS
 electrical and computer engineering • MS
 engineering and applied science • M Ch E, M Mat SE, MCE, MEE, MME, MS, MSE, PhD
 environmental engineering and science • MEE, MS
 information systems and technology • MS
 materials science and engineering • M Mat SE, MSE, PhD
 mechanical engineering • MME
 systems engineering • MS
 technical management • MS

Paul H. Nitze School of Advanced International Studies
Dr. Jessica Einhorn, Dean
Programs in:
 emerging markets • Certificate
 interdisciplinary studies • MA, PhD
 international public policy • MIPP
 international studies • Certificate

Maryland

The Johns Hopkins University (continued)
Peabody Conservatory of Music
Dr. Robert Sirota, Director
Program in:
 music • MM, DMA, AD, GPD

School of Medicine
Dr. Edward D. Miller, Dean of Medical Faculty and Chief Executive Officer
Programs in:
 art as applied to medicine • MA
 medicine • MD, MA, MS, MSE, PhD

Graduate Programs in Medicine
Dr. Peter Maloney, Associate Dean for Graduate Student Affairs
Programs in:
 biochemistry, cellular and molecular biology • PhD
 biological chemistry • PhD
 biophysics and biophysical chemistry • MS, PhD
 cellular and molecular medicine • PhD
 cellular and molecular physiology • PhD
 functional anatomy and evolution • PhD
 human genetics and molecular biology • PhD
 immunology • PhD
 medicine • MA, MS, PhD
 molecular biology and genetics • PhD
 neuroscience • PhD
 pathobiology • PhD
 pharmacology and molecular sciences • PhD
 physiology • PhD

School of Nursing
Dr. Martha N. Hill, Dean
Programs in:
 advanced practice nursing-nurse practitioner • MSN
 clinical nurse specialist • MSN
 clinical nurse specialist and health systems management • MSN
 community health nursing • MSN
 health systems management • MSN
 nurse practitioner • Certificate
 nursing • MSN, PhD, Certificate

School of Professional Studies in Business and Education
Dr. Ralph Fessler, Dean
Program in:
 continuing studies • MAT, MBA, MS, Ed D, CAGS, Certificate, Post Master's Certificate

Division of Business and Management
Dr. Erik Gordon, Interim Associate Dean
Programs in:
 advanced technology • Post Master's Certificate
 business administration • MBA
 electronic commerce • Post Master's Certificate
 electronics business • Post Master's Certificate
 finance • MS
 information and telecommunication systems • Certificate
 information and telecommunication systems for business • MS
 information systems • Post Master's Certificate
 international business • Post Master's Certificate
 investments • Certificate
 leadership development • Certificate
 marketing • MS
 organization development and strategic human resources • MS
 real estate • MS
 seniors housing and care • Certificate
 skilled facilitator • Certificate
 telecommunication systems • Post Master's Certificate
 the business of medicine • Certificate
 the business of nursing • Certificate

Division of Education
Edward Pajak, Interim Associate Dean
Programs in:
 addictions counseling • Post Master's Certificate
 administration and supervision • MS
 adult learning • Certificate
 adult, family and workplace literacy • Certificate
 applied literacy research • Certificate
 assistive technology for communication and social interaction • Certificate
 autism • Certificate
 clinical community counseling • Post Master's Certificate
 counseling • MS, Ed D, CAGS
 counseling at-risk youth • Post Master's Certificate
 databased decision-making and organizational improvement • Certificate
 early intervention/preschool special education specialist • Certificate
 earth/space science • Certificate
 education • MAT, MS, Ed D, CAGS, Certificate, Post Master's Certificate
 elementary education • MAT
 ESL instruction • Certificate
 general education • MS
 gifted education • Certificate
 inclusion • Certificate
 instructional technology for web-based professional development and training • Certificate
 leadership for school, family and community collaboration • Certificate
 leadership in technology integration • Certificate
 organizational counseling • Post Master's Certificate
 program evaluation • Certificate
 reading • MS, Certificate
 school administration and supervision • Certificate
 secondary education • MAT
 severe disabilities • Certificate
 special education • MS, Ed D, CAGS
 spiritual • Post Master's Certificate
 teacher development and leadership • Ed D
 teacher leadership • MS, Certificate
 technology for educators • MS
 technology for internet-based and multimedia instruction • Certificate
 technology-based curriculum design and development • Certificate
 transition planning • Certificate
 visual impairments • Certificate

Division of Public Safety Leadership
Dr. Sheldon Greenberg, Associate Dean
Program in:
 management • MS

Zanvyl Krieger School of Arts and Sciences
Dr. Daniel Weiss, Dean
Programs in:
 anthropology • PhD
 applied economics • MA
 arts and sciences • MA, MLA, MS, PhD, CAGS
 astronomy • PhD
 biochemistry • PhD
 bioinformatics • MS
 biophysics • PhD
 biotechnology • MS
 cell biology • PhD
 chemistry • MA, PhD
 classics • MA, PhD
 cognitive science • PhD
 communications in contemporary society • MA
 developmental biology • PhD
 economics • PhD
 English and American literature • PhD
 environmental sciences and policy • MS
 experimental psychology • PhD
 fiction writing • MA
 French • PhD
 genetic biology • PhD
 geochemistry • MA, PhD
 geology • MA, PhD
 geophysics • MA, PhD
 German • PhD
 government • MA
 groundwater • MA, PhD
 history • PhD
 history of art • MA, PhD
 history of science • PhD
 Italian • PhD

Maryland

liberal arts • MA
mathematics • PhD
molecular biology • PhD
Near Eastern studies • MA
oceanography • MA, PhD
philosophy • MA, PhD
physics • PhD
planetary atmosphere • MA, PhD
poetry • MA
political science • PhD
psychology • PhD
science writing • MA
sociology • PhD
Spanish • PhD
writing • MA

Humanities Center
Michael Fried, Chair
Program in:
comparative literature and intellectual history • PhD

Institute for Public Policy
Dr. Sandra J. Newman, Director
Program in:
public policy • MA

■ LOYOLA COLLEGE IN MARYLAND
Baltimore, MD 21210-2699
http://www.loyola.edu/

Independent-religious, coed, comprehensive institution. *Enrollment:* 6,033 graduate, professional, and undergraduate students; 607 full-time matriculated graduate/professional students (373 women), 2,013 part-time matriculated graduate/professional students (1,232 women). *Graduate faculty:* 200. *Computer facilities:* 292 computers available on campus for general student use. A campuswide network can be accessed from student residence rooms and from off campus. Internet access is available. *Library facilities:* Loyola/Notre Dame Library. *Graduate expenses:* Tuition: part-time $310 per credit. Tuition and fees vary according to degree level, program and student level. *General application contact:* Scott Greatorex, Director, Graduate Admissions, 410-617-5743.

Graduate Programs
Rev. Harold Ridley, SJ, President

College of Arts and Sciences
Dr. James Buckley, Dean
Programs in:
arts and sciences • M Ed, MA, MES, MMS, MS, PhD, Psy D, CAS
clinical psychology • MA, MS, Psy D, CAS
counseling psychology • MA, MS, CAS
curriculum and instruction • M Ed, MA, CAS
education technology • M Ed
educational management and supervision • M Ed, MA, CAS
employee assistance and substance abuse • CAS
engineering science • MES, MS
foundations of education • M Ed, MA, CAS
general psychology • MA, CAS
guidance and counseling • M Ed, MA, CAS
modern studies • MA, MMS
Montessori education • M Ed, CAS
pastoral counseling • MS, PhD, CAS
reading • M Ed, MA, CAS
special education • M Ed, MA, CAS
speech pathology and audiology • MS, CAS
spiritual and pastoral care • MA

The Joseph A. Sellinger S.J. School of Business and Management
John Moran, Associate Dean
Programs in:
business and management • MBA, MIB, MSF, XMBA
decision sciences • MBA
economics • MBA
executive business administration • MBA, XMBA
finance • MBA, MSF
international business • MIB
marketing/management • MBA

■ MORGAN STATE UNIVERSITY
Baltimore, MD 21251
http://www.morgan.edu/

State-supported, coed, university. CGS member. *Enrollment:* 6,621 graduate, professional, and undergraduate students; 309 full-time matriculated graduate/professional students, 325 part-time matriculated graduate/professional students. *Graduate faculty:* 172 full-time, 10 part-time/adjunct. *Computer facilities:* 65 computers available on campus for general student use. A campuswide network can be accessed from student residence rooms and from off campus. Internet access and online class registration, engineering lab supercomputer are available. *Library facilities:* Morris Soper Library. *Graduate expenses:* Tuition, state resident: part-time $215 per credit hour. Tuition, nonresident: part-time $409 per credit hour. Required fees: $48 per credit hour. *General application contact:* Dr. James E. Waller, Admissions and Programs Officer, 443-885-3185.

School of Graduate Studies
Dr. Maurice C. Taylor, Dean, Graduate Studies
Program in:
public health • MPH, Dr PH

College of Liberal Arts
Dr. Burney J. Hollis, Dean
Programs in:
African-American studies • MA
economics • MA
English • MA, PhD
history • MA, PhD
international studies • MA
liberal arts • MA, MS, PhD
music • MA
sociology • MA, MS
telecommunications management • MS

Earl G. Graves School of Business and Management
Dr. Otis A. Thomas, Dean
Programs in:
business administration • MBA, PhD
business and management • MBA, PhD

Institute of Architecture and Planning
Dr. Richard E. Lloyd, Director
Programs in:
architecture • M Arch
city and regional planning • MCRP
landscape architecture • MLA, MSLA

School of Computer, Mathematical, and Natural Sciences
Dr. T. Joan Robinson, Dean
Programs in:
bio-environmental science • PhD
bioinformatics • MS
biology • MS
computer, mathematical, and natural sciences • MA, MS, PhD
mathematics • MA
science • MS

School of Education and Urban Studies
Dr. Patricia L. Welch, Dean
Programs in:
education and urban studies • MAT, MS, Ed D, PhD
educational administration and supervision • MS
elementary and middle school education • MS
elementary education • MAT, MS
high school education • MAT
higher education administration • PhD
higher education-community college leadership • Ed D
math and science education • MS
mathematics education • MS, Ed D
middle school education • MAT
science education • MS, Ed D
teaching • MAT
urban educational leadership • Ed D

Maryland

Morgan State University (continued)
School of Engineering
Dr. Eugene DeLoatch, Dean
Programs in:
  engineering • M Eng, D Eng
  transportation • MS

■ MOUNT SAINT MARY'S UNIVERSITY
Emmitsburg, MD 21727-7799
http://www.msmary.edu/

Independent-religious, coed, comprehensive institution. *Enrollment:* 2,088 graduate, professional, and undergraduate students; 214 full-time matriculated graduate/professional students (35 women), 281 part-time matriculated graduate/professional students (167 women). *Graduate faculty:* 24 full-time (8 women), 30 part-time/adjunct (11 women). *Computer facilities:* Computer purchase and lease plans are available. 135 computers available on campus for general student use. A campuswide network can be accessed from student residence rooms and from off campus. Internet access and online class registration are available. *Library facilities:* Phillips Library. *Graduate expenses:* Tuition: part-time $345 per credit hour. Required fees: $5 per credit hour. Tuition and fees vary according to program. *General application contact:* Linda Martinak, Dean, Division of Continuing Studies, 301-682-8315.

Graduate Seminary
Rev. Kevin Rhoades, Vice President/Rector
Program in:
  theology • M Div, MA

Program in Business
David M. Karn, Director of Academic Services
Program in:
  business • MBA

Program in Education
Elizabeth Monahan, Director
Program in:
  education • M Ed, MAT

■ SALISBURY UNIVERSITY
Salisbury, MD 21801-6837
http://www.ssu.edu/

State-supported, coed, comprehensive institution. *Enrollment:* 6,816 graduate, professional, and undergraduate students; 145 full-time matriculated graduate/professional students (89 women), 262 part-time matriculated graduate/professional students (195 women). *Graduate faculty:* 63 full-time (27 women), 8 part-time/adjunct (5 women). *Computer facilities:* Computer purchase and lease plans are available. 226 computers available on campus for general student use. A campuswide network can be accessed from student residence rooms and from off campus. Internet access and online class registration are available. *Library facilities:* Blackwell Library plus 1 other. *Graduate expenses:* Tuition, state resident: full-time $5,160; part-time $215 per credit hour. Tuition, nonresident: full-time $10,920; part-time $455 per credit hour. *General application contact:* Jane H. Dané, Dean, Enrollment Management, 410-543-6161.

Graduate Division
Programs in:
  applied health physiology • MS
  art • MAT
  biology • MAT
  business administration • MBA
  business education • MAT
  chemistry • MAT
  composition, language and rhetoric • MA
  early childhood education • M Ed
  educational administration • M Ed
  elementary education • M Ed
  English • M Ed, MAT
  French • MAT
  geography • MAT
  history • MA, MAT
  literature • MA
  mathematics • MAT
  mathematics education • MS
  media and technology • MAT
  music • MAT
  nursing • MS
  psychology • MAT
  public school administration • MS Ed
  reading education • MAT
  reading specialist • M Ed
  science • MAT
  secondary education • MAT
  social studies • MAT
  social work • MSW
  Spanish • MAT
  teaching English to speakers of other languages • MA

■ TOWSON UNIVERSITY
Towson, MD 21252-0001
http://www.towson.edu/

State-supported, coed, university. CGS member. *Enrollment:* 17,188 graduate, professional, and undergraduate students; 804 full-time matriculated graduate/professional students (589 women), 2,403 part-time matriculated graduate/professional students (1,818 women). *Graduate faculty:* 484. *Computer facilities:* 1,015 computers available on campus for general student use. A campuswide network can be accessed from student residence rooms and from off campus. Internet access and online class registration are available. *Library facilities:* Cook Library. *Graduate expenses:* Tuition, state resident: part-time $244 per unit. Tuition, nonresident: part-time $510 per unit. Required fees: $61 per unit. *General application contact:* Fran Musotto, Information Contact, 410-704-2501.

Find an in-depth description at www.petersons.com/gradchannel.

Graduate School
Dr. Jin Gong, Dean
Programs in:
  accounting and business advisory services • MS
  applied and industrial mathematics • MS
  applied gerontology • MS
  applied information technology • MS, D Sc
  art education • M Ed
  audiology • Au D
  biology • MS
  clinical psychology • MA
  clinician-administrator transition • Certificate
  communications management • MS
  computer science • MS
  Dalcroze • Certificate
  early childhood education • M Ed
  educational leadership • Certificate
  educational leadership (administrator I certification) • CAS
  educational technology • MS
  elementary education • M Ed
  environmental science • MS, Certificate
  experimental psychology • MA
  geography and environmental planning • MA
  health science • MS
  human resource development • MS
  humanities • MA
  information security and assurance • Certificate
  information systems management • Certificate
  instructional design and training • MS
  instructional technology • Ed D
  Internet application development • Certificate
  internet application development • Certificate
  Kodály • Certificate
  liberal and professional studies • MA
  mathematics education • MS
  music education • MS
  music performance and composition • MM
  networking technologies • Certificate
  nursing • MS, Certificate
  occupational science • Sc D
  occupational therapy • MS
  Orff • Certificate
  organizational change • CAS

Maryland

physician assistant studies • MS
professional writing • MS
reading education • M Ed, CAS
school library media • MS
school psychology • MA, CAS
science education • MS
secondary education • M Ed
social science • MS
software engineering • Certificate
special education certification • M Ed
special education leadership • M Ed
speech-language pathology • MS
strategic public relations and integrated communications • Certificate
studio arts • MFA
teaching • MAT
theatre • MFA
women's studies • MS

■ UNIVERSITY OF BALTIMORE
Baltimore, MD 21201-5779
http://www.ubalt.edu/

State-supported, coed, upper-level institution. *Enrollment:* 4,937 graduate, professional, and undergraduate students; 1,471 full-time matriculated graduate/professional students (787 women), 1,407 part-time matriculated graduate/professional students (863 women). *Graduate faculty:* 214 full-time (63 women), 161 part-time/adjunct (48 women). *Computer facilities:* 135 computers available on campus for general student use. A campuswide network can be accessed from off campus. Internet access is available. *Library facilities:* Langsdale Library plus 1 other. *Graduate expenses:* Tuition, state resident: full-time $6,732; part-time $374 per credit. Tuition, nonresident: full-time $10,242; part-time $569 per credit. Required fees: $414; $50 per credit. Tuition and fees vary according to campus/location. *General application contact:* Reginald Thomas, Associate Director of Admissions, 410-837-4777.

Graduate School
Provost

School of Business
Dr. Ann McCarthy, Dean
Programs in:
  accounting and business advisory services • MS
  business • MBA, MS
  business administration • MBA
  business/finance • MS
  business/management information systems • MS
  business/marketing and venturing • MS
  taxation • MS

The Yale Gordon College of Liberal Arts
Dean
Programs in:
  applied psychology • MS
  communications design • DCD
  creative writing and publishing arts • MFA
  criminal justice • MS
  health systems management • MS
  human services administration • MS
  human-computer interaction • MS
  integrated design • MFA
  interaction design and information technology • MS
  legal and ethical studies • MA
  liberal arts • MA, MFA, MPA, MS, DCD, DPA
  negotiation and conflict • MS
  public administration • MPA, DPA
  publications design • MA

School of Law
Programs in:
  law • JD
  taxation • LL M

■ UNIVERSITY OF MARYLAND
Baltimore, MD 21201
http://www.umaryland.edu/

State-supported, coed, graduate-only institution. CGS member. *Computer facilities:* 125 computers available on campus for general student use. A campuswide network can be accessed from student residence rooms and from off campus. Internet access is available. *Library facilities:* Health Sciences and Human Services Library plus 2 others. *General application contact:* Director, Graduate Enrollment Affairs, 410-706-7131.

Graduate School
Dr. Malinda B. Orlin, Dean of the Graduate School
Programs in:
  biomedical sciences—dental • MS, PhD
  dental hygiene • MS
  gerontology • PhD
  marine-estuarine-environmental sciences • MS, PhD
  medical and research technology • MS
  oral biology • MS
  oral pathology • MS, PhD
  pharmaceutical health service research • PhD
  pharmaceutical sciences • PhD
  pharmacy administration • PhD
  social work • MSW, PhD

Graduate Programs in Medicine
Dr. Donald E. Wilson, Dean and Vice President for Medical Affairs

Programs in:
  anatomy and neurobiology • MS, PhD
  biochemistry • PhD
  epidemiology and preventive medicine • MS, PhD
  human genetics • MS, PhD
  medical pathology • PhD
  medicine • MS, PhD
  membrane biology • PhD
  microbiology and immunology • MS, PhD
  molecular and cell biology • PhD
  neuroscience • PhD
  neuroscience and cognitive sciences • MS, PhD
  pathology • MS
  pharmacology • PhD
  pharmacology and experimental therapeutics • MS
  physical and rehabilitation science • PhD
  physiology • MS, PhD
  reproductive endocrinology • PhD
  toxicology • PhD

School of Nursing
Dr. Janet Allan, Dean
Programs in:
  community health nursing • MS
  direct nursing • PhD
  gerontological nursing • MS
  indirect nursing • PhD
  maternal-child nursing • MS
  medical-surgical nursing • MS
  nursing • PhD
  nursing administration • MS
  nursing education • MS
  nursing health policy • MS
  primary care nursing • MS
  psychiatric nursing • MS

Professional and Advanced Education Programs in Dentistry
Programs in:
  advanced general dentistry • Certificate
  endodontics • Certificate
  oral and experimental pathology • Certificate
  oral biology • MS
  oral-maxillofacial surgery • Certificate
  orthodontics • Certificate
  pediatric dentistry • Certificate
  periodontics • Certificate
  prosthodontics • Certificate

Professional Program in Medicine
Program in:
  medicine • MD

Professional Program in Pharmacy
Dr. Robert S. Beardsley, Associate Dean for Student Affairs
Program in:
  pharmacy • Pharm D

Maryland

University of Maryland (continued)
School of Law
Karen H. Rothenberg, Dean and Marjorie Cook Professor of Law
Program in:
law • JD

■ UNIVERSITY OF MARYLAND, BALTIMORE COUNTY
Baltimore, MD 21250
http://www.umbc.edu/

State-supported, coed, university. CGS member. *Enrollment:* 11,872 graduate, professional, and undergraduate students; 975 full-time matriculated graduate/professional students (524 women), 1,251 part-time matriculated graduate/professional students (679 women). *Graduate faculty:* 460. *Computer facilities:* Computer purchase and lease plans are available. 673 computers available on campus for general student use. A campuswide network can be accessed from student residence rooms and from off campus. Internet access and online class registration, student account and grade information are available. *Library facilities:* Albin O. Kuhn Library and Gallery plus 1 other. *Graduate expenses:* Tuition, state resident: full-time $7,000. Tuition, nonresident: full-time $11,400. Required fees: $1,440. *General application contact:* Graduate School, 410-455-2537.

Find an in-depth description at www.petersons.com/gradchannel.

Graduate School
Dr. Scott A. Bass, Dean and Vice Provost for Research
Programs in:
 administration, planning, and policy • MS
 aging policy for the elderly • PhD
 applied and professional ethics • MA, Certificate
 applied behavioral analysis • MA
 applied developmental psychology • PhD
 applied mathematics • MS, PhD
 applied molecular biology • MS
 applied physics • MS, PhD
 applied sociology • MA, Certificate
 atmospheric physics • MS, PhD
 biochemistry • PhD
 biological sciences • MS, PhD
 chemistry • MS, PhD
 computer/web-based instruction • Postbaccalaureate Certificate
 distance education • Postbaccalaureate Certificate
 early childhood education • MA
 economic policy analysis • MA
 education • MA, MS
 electronic government • Certificate
 elementary education • MA
 English as a second language/bilingual education • MA
 epidemiology of aging • PhD
 French • MA
 German • MA
 historical studies • MA
 imaging and digital arts • MFA
 information systems • MS, PhD
 instructional systems development • MA, Postbaccalaureate Certificate
 intercultural communication • MA
 language, literacy, and culture • PhD
 literacy, language and culture • PhD
 marine-estuarine-environmental sciences • MS, PhD
 medical sociology • MA
 molecular and cell biology • PhD
 neuroscience • PhD
 neurosciences and cognitive sciences • MS, PhD
 policy sciences • MPP, PhD
 post-baccalaureate teacher education • MA
 preventive medicine and epidemiology • MS
 psychology/human services • MA, PhD
 Russian • MA
 secondary education • MA
 sociocultural/behavioral aspects of aging • PhD
 Spanish • MA
 statistics • MS, PhD
 training systems • MA

College of Engineering
Dr. Shlomo Carmi, Dean
Programs in:
 chemical and biochemical engineering • MS, PhD
 computer engineering • MS, PhD
 computer science • MS, PhD
 electrical engineering • MS, PhD
 engineering • MS, PhD
 engineering management • MS
 mechanical engineering • MS, PhD

■ UNIVERSITY OF MARYLAND, COLLEGE PARK
College Park, MD 20742
http://www.maryland.edu/

State-supported, coed, university. CGS member. *Enrollment:* 35,262 graduate, professional, and undergraduate students; 6,503 full-time matriculated graduate/professional students (3,159 women), 3,380 part-time matriculated graduate/professional students (1,716 women). *Graduate faculty:* 2,901 full-time (1,006 women), 755 part-time/adjunct (339 women). *Computer facilities:* Computer purchase and lease plans are available. 791 computers available on campus for general student use. A campuswide network can be accessed from student residence rooms and from off campus. Internet access and online class registration, student account information, financial aid summary are available. *Library facilities:* McKeldin Library plus 6 others. *Graduate expenses:* Tuition, state resident: part-time $349 per credit hour. Tuition, nonresident: part-time $602 per credit hour. *General application contact:* Trudy Lindsey, Director, Graduate Enrollment Management Services, 301-405-4190.

Graduate Studies and Research
Dr. J. Dennis O'Connor, Vice President for Research and Dean
Program in:
 neurosciences and cognitive sciences • PhD

A. James Clark School of Engineering
Dr. Nariman Farvardin, Dean
Programs in:
 aerospace engineering • M Eng
 bioengineering • MS, PhD
 chemical engineering • M Eng
 civil and environmental engineering • M Eng, MS, PhD
 civil engineering • M Eng
 electrical and computer engineering • M Eng, MS, PhD
 electrical engineering • M Eng, MS, PhD
 electronic packaging and reliability • MS, PhD
 engineering • Certificate
 fire protection engineering • M Eng
 manufacturing and design • MS, PhD
 materials science and engineering • M Eng, MS, PhD
 mechanical engineering • M Eng
 mechanics and materials • MS, PhD
 nuclear engineering • ME, MS, PhD
 reliability engineering • M Eng, MS, PhD
 systems engineering • M Eng
 telecommunications • MS
 thermal and fluid sciences • MS, PhD

College of Agriculture and Natural Resources
Dr. Bruce L. Gardner, Interim Dean
Programs in:
 agriculture and natural resources • DVM, MS, PhD
 agriculture economics • MS, PhD
 agronomy • MS, PhD
 animal sciences • MS, PhD
 biological resources engineering • MS, PhD
 food science • MS, PhD
 horticulture • PhD
 natural resource sciences • MS, PhD
 nutrition • MS, PhD
 poultry science • MS, PhD

Maryland

resource economics • MS, PhD
veterinary medical sciences • MS, PhD
veterinary medicine • DVM, MS, PhD

College of Arts and Humanities
Dr. James Harris, Dean
Programs in:
American studies • MA, PhD
art • MFA
art history • MA, PhD
arts and humanities • M Ed, MA, MFA, MM, DMA, Ed D, PhD
classics • MA
communications • MA, PhD
comparative literature • MA, PhD
creative writing • MA, MFA, PhD
dance • MFA
English language and literature • MA, PhD
ethnomusicology • MA
foreign languages and literatures • MA, PhD
French • MA
French language and literature • MA
German • MA
Germanic language and literature • MA, PhD
history • MA, PhD
linguistics • MA, PhD
modern French studies • PhD
music • M Ed, MA, MM, DMA, Ed D, PhD
philosophy • MA, PhD
Russian • MA
Russian language and linguistics • MA
Spanish • MA, PhD
theatre • MA, MFA, PhD
women's studies • MA, PhD

College of Behavioral and Social Sciences
Dr. Edward Montgomery, Dean
Programs in:
American politics • PhD
applied anthropology • MAA
audiology • MA, PhD
behavioral and social sciences • MA, MAA, MS, Au D, PhD
clinical psychology • PhD
comparative politics • PhD
criminology and criminal justice • MA, PhD
developmental psychology • PhD
economics • MA, PhD
experimental psychology • PhD
geography • MA, PhD
hearing and speech sciences • Au D
industrial psychology • MA, MS, PhD
international relations • PhD
language pathology • MA, PhD
neuroscience • PhD
political economy • PhD
political theory • PhD
social psychology • PhD
sociology • MA, PhD
speech • MA, PhD
survey methodology • MS, PhD

College of Computer, Mathematical and Physical Sciences
Dr. Stephen Halperin, Dean
Programs in:
applied mathematics • MS, PhD
astronomy • MS, PhD
chemical physics • MS, PhD
computer science • MS, PhD
computer, mathematical and physical sciences • MA, MS, PhD
geology • MS, PhD
mathematical statistics • MA, PhD
mathematics • MA, PhD
meteorology • MS, PhD
physics • MS, PhD
software engineering • MS

College of Education
Dr. Edna Szymanski, Dean
Programs in:
college student personnel • M Ed, MA
college student personnel administration • PhD
community counseling • CAGS
community/career counseling • M Ed, MA
counseling and personnel services • M Ed, MA, PhD
counseling psychology • PhD
counselor education • PhD
curriculum and educational communications • M Ed, MA, Ed D, PhD
early childhood/elementary education • M Ed, MA, Ed D, PhD
education • M Ed, MA, Ed D, PhD, CAGS
human development • M Ed, MA, Ed D, PhD
measurement • MA, PhD
program evaluation • MA, PhD
reading • M Ed, MA, PhD, CAGS
rehabilitation counseling • M Ed, MA
school counseling • M Ed, MA
school psychology • M Ed, MA, PhD
secondary education • M Ed, MA, Ed D, PhD, CAGS
social foundations of education • M Ed, MA, Ed D, PhD, CAGS
special education • M Ed, MA, PhD, CAGS
statistics • MA, PhD
teaching English to speakers of other languages • M Ed

College of Health and Human Performance
Dr. Robert Gold, Dean
Programs in:
community health education • MPH
family studies • MS, PhD
health and human performance • MA, MPH, MS, PhD
kinesiology • MA, PhD
marriage and family therapy • MS
public/community health • PhD

College of Information Studies
Dr. Bruce Dearstyne, Acting Dean
Program in:
information studies • MIM, MLS, PhD

College of Life Sciences
Dr. Norma M. Allewell, Dean
Programs in:
analytical chemistry • MS, PhD
behavior, ecology, evolution, and systematics • MS, PhD
biochemistry • MS, PhD
biology • MS, PhD
biophysics • PhD
cell biology and molecular genetics • MS, PhD
chemical physics • PhD
chemistry • MS, PhD
entomology • MS, PhD
inorganic chemistry • MS, PhD
life sciences • MLS, MS, PhD
marine-estuarine-environmental sciences • MS, PhD
microbiology • MS, PhD
molecular and cellular biology • PhD
organic chemistry • MS, PhD
physical chemistry • MS, PhD
plant biology • MS, PhD
sustainable development and conservation biology • MS
toxicology • MS, PhD

Phillip Merrill College of Journalism
Thomas Kunkel, Dean
Programs in:
broadcast journalism • MA
journalism • MA
journalism and media studies • PhD
mass communication • PhD
online news • MA
public affairs reporting • MA

Robert H. Smith School of Business
Dr. Howard Frank, Dean
Programs in:
business • MBA, MS, PhD
business administration • MBA
business and management • MS, PhD

School of Architecture
Steven Hurtt, Dean
Programs in:
architecture • M Arch, MCP, MHP, PhD, Certificate
historic preservation • MHP, Certificate
urban and regional planning/design • PhD
urban studies and planning • MCP

School of Public Affairs
Dr. Jacques Gansler, Acting Dean
Programs in:
policy studies • PhD
public affairs • MPM, MPP, PhD
public management • MPM
public policy • MPP

Maryland

■ UNIVERSITY OF MARYLAND EASTERN SHORE
Princess Anne, MD 21853-1299
http://www.umes.edu/

State-supported, coed, university. CGS member. *Computer facilities:* 120 computers available on campus for general student use. A campuswide network can be accessed. *Library facilities:* Frederick Douglass Library. *General application contact:* Admissions and Advisement Coordinator, 410-651-8626.

Find an in-depth description at www.petersons.com/gradchannel.

Graduate Programs
Programs in:
  agriculture education and extension • MS
  applied computer science • MS
  career and technology education • M Ed
  food and agricultural sciences • MS
  guidance and counseling • M Ed
  marine estuarine • MS, PhD
  marine-estuarine-environmental sciences • MS, PhD
  physical therapy • MPT
  special education • M Ed
  teaching • MAT
  toxicology • MS, PhD

■ UNIVERSITY OF MARYLAND UNIVERSITY COLLEGE
Adelphi, MD 20783
http://www.umuc.edu/

State-supported, coed, comprehensive institution. CGS member. *Enrollment:* 25,857 graduate, professional, and undergraduate students; 221 full-time matriculated graduate/professional students (117 women), 7,445 part-time matriculated graduate/professional students (3,721 women). *Graduate faculty:* 62 full-time (22 women), 235 part-time/adjunct (67 women). *Computer facilities:* 375 computers available on campus for general student use. A campuswide network can be accessed from off campus. *Library facilities:* Information and Library Services plus 1 other. *Graduate expenses:* Tuition, state resident: part-time $339 per semester hour. Tuition, nonresident: part-time $553 per semester hour. Tuition and fees vary according to course level and program. *General application contact:* Coordinator, Graduate Admissions, 301-985-7155.

Graduate School of Management and Technology
Dr. Christina A. Hannah, Acting Associate Vice President and Dean of Graduate Studies
Programs in:
  accounting and financial management • MS, Certificate
  accounting and information technology • MS, Certificate
  biotechnology studies • MS, Certificate
  business administration • Exec MBA, MBA
  computer systems management • Exec MS, MS, Certificate
  distance education • MDE, Certificate
  education • M Ed
  electronic commerce • MS, Certificate
  environmental management • MS, Certificate
  health care administration • MS, Certificate
  information technology • Exec MS, MS, Certificate
  international management • Exec MIM, MIM, Certificate
  management • MS, DM, Certificate
  management and technology • Exec MBA, Exec MIM, Exec MS, M Ed, M Sw E, MA, MBA, MDE, MIM, MS, DM, Certificate
  software engineering • M Sw E, Certificate
  teaching • MA
  technology management • Exec MS, MS, Certificate
  telecommunications management • Exec MS, MS, Certificate

Massachusetts

■ AMERICAN INTERNATIONAL COLLEGE
Springfield, MA 01109-3189
http://www.aic.edu/

Independent, coed, comprehensive institution. *Enrollment:* 1,595 graduate, professional, and undergraduate students; 97 full-time matriculated graduate/professional students (60 women), 341 part-time matriculated graduate/professional students (220 women). *Graduate faculty:* 55 full-time (28 women), 60 part-time/adjunct (27 women). *Computer facilities:* 100 computers available on campus for general student use. A campuswide network can be accessed. Internet access is available. *Library facilities:* James J. Shea Jr. Library. *Graduate expenses:* Tuition: full-time $12,120; part-time $505 per credit. Required fees: $225 per term. Full-time tuition and fees vary according to course load. *General application contact:* Joanna McGill, Associate Director for Graduate Admissions, 413-205-3067.

School of Business Administration
Dr. John Rogers, Dean
Program in:
  business administration • MBA

School of Continuing Education and Graduate Studies
Dr. Roland E. Holstead, Dean
Programs in:
  organization development • MSOD
  public administration • MPA

School of Psychology and Education
Dr. Gregory Schmutte, Dean
Programs in:
  administration • M Ed, CAGS
  child development • MA, Ed D
  clinical psychology • MS
  criminal justice studies • MS
  elementary education • M Ed, CAGS
  forensic psychology • MS
  psychology and education • M Ed, MA, MAT, MS, Ed D, CAGS
  reading • M Ed, CAGS
  secondary education • M Ed, CAGS
  special education • M Ed, CAGS
  teaching • MAT

Center for Human Resource Development
Dr. Debra D. Anderson, Director
Program in:
  human resource development • MA, CAGS

■ ANNA MARIA COLLEGE
Paxton, MA 01612
http://www.annamaria.edu/

Independent-religious, coed, comprehensive institution. *Enrollment:* 1,147 graduate, professional, and undergraduate students; 87 full-time matriculated graduate/professional students (43 women), 261 part-time matriculated graduate/professional students (177 women). *Graduate faculty:* 18 full-time (11 women), 55 part-time/adjunct (19 women). *Computer facilities:* 59 computers available on campus for general student use. A campuswide network can be accessed from student residence rooms and from off campus. Internet access, on-line class schedules, student account information are available. *Library facilities:* Mondor-Eagen Library. *Graduate expenses:* Tuition: part-time

Massachusetts

$1,050 per course. *General application contact:* Jennifer Bachour, Continuing Education Coordinator, 508-849-3346.

Graduate Division
Richard Maguire, Dean of Continuing Education
Programs in:
  business administration • MBA, AC
  counseling psychology • MA, CAGS
  criminal justice • MS
  early childhood development • M Ed
  elementary education • M Ed
  emergency response planning • MS
  fire science • MA
  justice administration • MS
  occupational and environmental health and safety • MS
  pastoral ministry • MA
  psychology • MA, CAGS
  reading • M Ed

■ ASSUMPTION COLLEGE
Worcester, MA 01609-1296
http://www.assumption.edu/

Independent-religious, coed, comprehensive institution. *Enrollment:* 2,412 graduate, professional, and undergraduate students; 116 full-time matriculated graduate/professional students (92 women), 184 part-time matriculated graduate/professional students (123 women). *Graduate faculty:* 10 full-time (4 women), 22 part-time/adjunct (8 women). *Computer facilities:* Computer purchase and lease plans are available. 190 computers available on campus for general student use. A campuswide network can be accessed from student residence rooms and from off campus. Internet access is available. *Library facilities:* Emmanuel d'Alzon Library. *Graduate expenses:* Tuition: full-time $9,990; part-time $1,110 per course. Required fees: $60; $20 per semester. Full-time tuition and fees vary according to course load. *General application contact:* Adrian O. Dumas, Director of Graduate Enrollment Management and Services, 508-767-7365.

Find an in-depth description at www.petersons.com/gradchannel.

Graduate School
Dr. MaryLou Anderson, Dean
Programs in:
  business administration • MBA, CPS
  counseling psychology • MA, CAGS
  rehabilitation counseling • MA, CAGS
  special education • MA

■ BENTLEY COLLEGE
Waltham, MA 02452-4705
http://www.bentley.edu/

Independent, coed, comprehensive institution. *Enrollment:* 5,673 graduate, professional, and undergraduate students; 384 full-time matriculated graduate/professional students (156 women), 945 part-time matriculated graduate/professional students (418 women). *Graduate faculty:* 456. *Computer facilities:* A campuswide network can be accessed from student residence rooms and from off campus. Internet access and online class registration are available. *Library facilities:* Soloman R. Baker Library. *Graduate expenses:* Tuition: full-time $25,230. *General application contact:* Paul Vaccaro, Director of Graduate Admissions, 781-891-2108.

The Elkin B. McCallum Graduate School of Business
Dr. Margrethe H. Olson, Dean
Programs in:
  accountancy • FIAMBA
  accounting • MSA, Certificate
  accounting information systems • MSAIS, Certificate
  advanced accountancy • FIAMBA
  business • CIAMBA, FIAMBA, MSA, MSAIS, MSCF, MSF, MSFP, MSGFA, MSHFID, MSIAM, MSIT, MST, Advanced Certificate, Certificate, GBC, GBE, GSS
  business administration • Advanced Certificate
  business communication • FIAMBA
  business data analysis • FIAMBA, Certificate
  business economics • FIAMBA
  business ethics • FIAMBA, Certificate
  corporate finance • MSCF
  e-business • FIAMBA, Certificate
  entrepreneurial studies • FIAMBA
  finance • FIAMBA
  financial planning • MSFP, Advanced Certificate, Certificate
  global financial analysis • MSGFA
  human factors in information design • MSHFID
  information age marketing • MSIAM, Certificate
  information technology • MSIT
  international business • FIAMBA
  management • FIAMBA
  management information systems • FIAMBA
  management of technology • FIAMBA
  marketing • FIAMBA
  operations management • FIAMBA
  taxation • FIAMBA

■ BOSTON COLLEGE
Chestnut Hill, MA 02467-3800
http://www.bc.edu/

Independent-religious, coed, university. CGS member. *Enrollment:* 13,611 graduate, professional, and undergraduate students; 1,623 full-time matriculated graduate/professional students (1,061 women), 1,965 part-time matriculated graduate/professional students (1,060 women). *Graduate faculty:* 647. *Computer facilities:* 200 computers available on campus for general student use. A campuswide network can be accessed from student residence rooms and from off campus. *Library facilities:* Thomas P. O'Neill Library plus 6 others. *Graduate expenses:* Tuition: part-time $810 per credit. *General application contact:* Robert V. Howe, Assistant Dean, 617-552-3265.

Find an in-depth description at www.petersons.com/gradchannel.

The Carroll School of Management
Programs in:
  accounting • MSA
  business administration • MBA
  finance • MSF, PhD
  management • MBA, MSA, MSF, PhD
  organization studies • PhD

Graduate School of Arts and Sciences
Dr. Michael A. Smyer, Dean
Programs in:
  arts and sciences • MA, MS, MST, PhD, CAGS
  biochemistry • MS, PhD
  biology • MS, PhD
  classics • MA
  economics • PhD
  English • MA, PhD, CAGS
  European national studies • MA
  French • MA, PhD
  geology and geophysics • MS
  Greek • MA
  history • MA, PhD
  inorganic chemistry • PhD
  Italian • MA
  Latin • MA
  linguistics • MA
  mathematics • MA
  medieval language • PhD
  medieval studies • MA
  organic chemistry • PhD
  philosophy • MA, PhD
  physical chemistry • PhD
  physics • MS, PhD
  political science • MA, PhD
  psychology • PhD
  Russian and Slavic languages and literature • MA
  science education • MST

Peterson's Graduate Schools in the U.S. 2006

Massachusetts

Boston College (continued)
  Slavic studies • MA
  sociology • MA, PhD
  Spanish • MA, PhD
  theology • MA, PhD

Institute of Religious Education and Pastoral Ministry
Dr. Thomas Groome, Chairperson
Programs in:
  church leadership • MA
  pastoral ministry • MA
  religious education • MA, PhD
  social justice/social ministry • MA
  youth ministry • MA

Graduate School of Social Work
Dr. Alberto Godenzi, Dean
Program in:
  social work • MSW, PhD

Law School
John Garvey, Dean
Program in:
  law • JD

Lynch Graduate School of Education
Rev. Joseph O'Keefe, SJ, Dean
Programs in:
  biology • MST
  Catholic school leadership • M Ed, CAES
  chemistry • MST
  counseling psychology • MA, PhD
  curriculum and instruction • M Ed, PhD, CAES
  developmental and educational psychology • MA, PhD
  early childhood education/teacher option • M Ed
  early childhood/specialist option • MA
  education • M Ed, MA, MAT, MST, Ed D, PhD, CAES
  educational administration • M Ed, Ed D, PhD, CAES
  educational research, measurement, and evaluation • M Ed, PhD, CAES
  elementary teaching • M Ed
  English • MAT
  geology • MST
  higher education administration • MA, PhD
  history • MAT
  Latin and classics • MAT
  mathematics • MST
  moderate special needs • M Ed, CAES
  multiple disabilities and deaf/blindness • M Ed, CAES
  physics • MST
  reading specialist • M Ed, CAES
  religious education • M Ed, CAES
  Romance languages • MAT
  secondary education • M Ed, MAT, MST
  secondary teaching • M Ed
  severe special needs • M Ed
  visual impairment studies • M Ed, CAES

William F. Connell School of Nursing
Dr. Barbara Munro, Dean
Programs in:
  adult health nursing • MS
  community health nursing • MS
  family health • MS
  gerontology • MS
  maternal/child health nursing • MS
  nurse anesthesia • MS
  nursing • PhD
  psychiatric-mental health nursing • MS

■ BOSTON UNIVERSITY
Boston, MA 02215
http://www.bu.edu/

Independent, coed, university. CGS member. *Enrollment:* 29,048 graduate, professional, and undergraduate students; 7,796 full-time matriculated graduate/professional students (4,050 women), 2,965 part-time matriculated graduate/professional students (1,532 women). *Graduate faculty:* 3,400. *Computer facilities:* Computer purchase and lease plans are available. 750 computers available on campus for general student use. A campuswide network can be accessed from student residence rooms and from off campus. Internet access, research and educational networks are available. *Library facilities:* Mugar Memorial Library plus 18 others. *Graduate expenses:* Tuition: full-time $28,512; part-time $891 per credit hour.
Find an in-depth description at www.petersons.com/gradchannel.

College of Communication
John J. Schulz, Dean
Programs in:
  advertising • MS
  broadcast journalism • MS
  business and economics journalism • MS
  communication • MFA, MS
  film production • MFA
  film studies • MFA
  health communication • MS
  mass communication • MS
  photo journalism • MS
  print journalism • MS
  public relations • MS
  science journalism • MS
  screenwriting • MFA
  television • MS
  television management • MS

College of Engineering
Dr. David Campbell, Dean
Programs in:
  aerospace engineering • MS, PhD
  biomedical engineering • MS, PhD
  computer engineering • PhD
  computer systems engineering • MS
  electrical engineering • MS, PhD
  engineering • MS, PhD
  general engineering • MS
  global manufacturing • MS
  manufacturing engineering • PhD
  mechanical engineering • MS, PhD
  photonics • MS
  systems engineering • PhD

College of Fine Arts
Walt Meissner, Acting Dean
Programs in:
  art education • MFA
  arts • MFA, MM, DMA, Artist Diploma, Certificate, Performance Diploma
  collaborative piano • MM, DMA
  composition • MM, DMA
  conducting • MM, Artist Diploma, Performance Diploma
  costume design • MFA
  costume production • MFA
  directing • MFA
  graphic design • MFA
  historical performance • MM, DMA, Artist Diploma, Performance Diploma
  lighting design • MFA
  music education • MM, DMA
  music history and literature • MM
  music theory • MM
  opera performance • Certificate
  painting • MFA
  performance • MM, DMA, Artist Diploma, Performance Diploma
  scene design • MFA
  sculpture • MFA
  studio teaching • MFA
  technical production • MFA, Certificate
  theatre crafts • Certificate
  theatre education • MFA

Graduate School of Arts and Sciences
J. Scott Whittaker, Associate Dean
Programs in:
  African American studies • MA
  African studies • Certificate
  American and New England studies • PhD
  anthropology • PhD
  applied anthropology • MA
  applied linguistics • MA, PhD
  archaeological heritage management • MA
  archaeology • MA, PhD
  art history • MA, PhD
  arts and sciences • MA, MAEP, MAPE, MS, PhD, Certificate

Massachusetts

astronomy • MA, PhD
bioinformatics • MS, PhD
biology • MA, PhD
biostatistics • MA, PhD
cellular biophysics • PhD
chemistry • MA, PhD
classical studies • MA, PhD
cognitive and neural systems • MA, PhD
composition • MA
computer science • MA, PhD
creative writing • MA
earth sciences • MA, PhD
economic policy • MAEP
economics • MA, PhD
energy and environmental analysis • MA
English • MA, PhD
environmental remote sensing and geographic information systems • MA
French language and literature • MA, PhD
geoarchaeology • MA
geography • MA, PhD
Hispanic language and literatures • MA, PhD
history • MA, PhD
international relations • MA
international relations and environmental policy • MA
international relations and environmental policy management • MA
international relations and international communication • MA
mathematical finance • MA
mathematics • MA, PhD
molecular biology, cell biology, and biochemistry • MA, PhD
museum studies • Certificate
music education • MA
music history/theory • PhD
musicology • MA, PhD
neuroscience • MA, PhD
philosophy • MA, PhD
physics • MA, PhD
political economy • MAPE
political science • MA, PhD
preservation studies • MA
psychology • MA, PhD
religious and theological studies • MA, PhD
sociology • MA, PhD
sociology and social work • PhD

Editorial Institute
Archie Burnett, Co-Director
Program in:
  editorial studies • MA, PhD

Henry M. Goldman School of Dental Medicine
Dr. Spencer Frankl, Dean
Programs in:
  advanced general dentistry • CAGS
  dental medicine • DMD, MS, MSD, D Sc, D Sc D, PhD, CAGS
  dental public health • MS, MSD, D Sc D, CAGS
  dentistry • DMD
  endodontics • MSD, D Sc D, CAGS
  implantology • CAGS
  operative dentistry • MSD, D Sc D, CAGS
  oral and maxillofacial surgery • MSD, D Sc D, CAGS
  oral biology • MSD, D Sc, D Sc D, PhD
  orthodontics • MSD, D Sc D, CAGS
  pediatric dentistry • MSD, D Sc D, CAGS
  periodontology • MSD, D Sc D, CAGS
  prosthodontics • MSD, D Sc D, CAGS

Metropolitan College
Dr. Jay Halfond, Dean
Programs in:
  actuarial science • MS
  arts administration • MS
  city planning • MCP
  computer information systems • MS
  computer science • MS
  criminal justice • MCJ
  economics development and tourism management • MSAS
  electronic commerce • MSAS
  financial economics • MSAS
  innovation and technology • MSAS
  liberal arts • MLA
  multinational commerce • MSAS
  telecommunications • MS
  urban affairs • MUA

Sargent College of Health and Rehabilitation Sciences
Dr. Alan M. Jette, Dean
Programs in:
  applied anatomy and physiology • MS, PhD
  audiology • D Sc
  health and rehabilitation sciences • MS, MSOT, MSPT, D Sc, DPT, PhD, CAGS
  movement and rehabilitation sciences • MS
  nutrition • MS
  occupational therapy • MS, MSOT
  physical therapy • MSPT, DPT
  rehabilitation counseling • MS, D Sc, CAGS
  rehabilitation sciences • D Sc
  speech-language pathology • MS, D Sc, CAGS
  therapeutic studies • D Sc

School of Education
Dr. Douglas Sears, Dean
Programs in:
  administration, training, and policy studies • Ed D
  bilingual education • Ed M, CAGS
  counseling • Ed M, CAGS
  counseling psychology • Ed D
  curriculum and teaching • Ed M, MAT, Ed D, CAGS
  developmental studies • Ed M, Ed D, CAGS
  early childhood education • Ed M, Ed D, CAGS
  education • Ed M, MAT, Ed D, CAGS
  education of the deaf • Ed M, CAGS
  educational administration • Ed M
  educational media and technology • Ed M, Ed D, CAGS
  elementary education • Ed M
  English and language arts education • Ed M, Ed D, CAGS
  health education • Ed M, CAGS
  human movement • Ed M, Ed D, CAGS
  human resource education • Ed M, CAGS
  international educational development • Ed M
  Latin and classical studies • MAT
  leisure education • Ed M
  mathematics education • Ed M, MAT, Ed D, CAGS
  modern foreign language education • Ed M, MAT
  policy, planning, and administration • Ed M, CAGS
  reading education • Ed M, Ed D, CAGS
  science education • Ed M, MAT, Ed D, CAGS
  social studies education • Ed M, MAT, Ed D, CAGS
  special education • Ed M, Ed D, CAGS
  teaching of English to speakers of other languages • Ed M, CAGS

School of Law
Ronald A. Cass, Dean
Programs in:
  American law • LL M
  banking law • LL M
  intellectual property law • LL M
  law • JD
  taxation • LL M

School of Management
Louis Lataif, Dean
Programs in:
  accounting • DBA
  advanced accounting • Certificate
  business administration • Exec MBA, MBA, DBA, Certificate
  general management • MBA
  healthcare management • MBA
  information systems • DBA
  international business • Exec MBA
  investment management • MSIM
  management policy • DBA
  marketing • DBA
  operations management • DBA
  organizational behavior • DBA
  public and nonprofit management • MBA

Massachusetts

Boston University (continued)

School of Medicine
Dr. Aram V. Chobanian, Dean
Program in:
medicine • MD, MA, PhD

Division of Graduate Medical Sciences
Dr. Carl Franzblau, Associate Dean
Programs in:
anatomy and neurobiology • MA, PhD
behavioral neurosciences • PhD
biochemistry • MA, PhD
cell and molecular biology • PhD
clinical investigation • MA
experimental pathology • PhD
immunology • PhD
medical nutrition sciences • MA, PhD
medical sciences • MA, PhD
mental health and behavioral medicine • MA
microbiology • MA, PhD
molecular medicine • PhD
pharmacology and experimental therapeutics • MA, PhD
physiology • MA, PhD
physiology and biophysics • MA, PhD

School of Public Health
Dr. Robert F. Meenan, Dean
Programs in:
biostatistics • MA, MPH, PhD
environmental health • MPH, D Sc
epidemiology • M Sc, MPH, D Sc
health behavior, health promotion, and disease prevention • MPH
health law • MPH
health services • M Sc, MPH, D Sc
international health • MPH, Dr PH, Certificate
maternal and child health • MPH
nurse midwifery education • Certificate
public health • M Sc, MA, MPH, D Sc, Dr PH, PhD, Certificate
social behavioral sciences • Dr PH

School of Social Work
Wilma Peebles-Wilkins, Dean
Programs in:
clinical practice with groups • MSW
clinical practice with individuals and families • MSW
macro social work practice • MSW
social work and sociology • PhD

School of Theology
Dr. Robert Neville, Dean
Program in:
theology • M Div, MSM, MTS, STM, D Min, Th D

University Professors Program
Claudio Véliz, Director
Program in:
interdisciplinary studies • MA, PhD

■ BRANDEIS UNIVERSITY
Waltham, MA 02454-9110
http://www.brandeis.edu/

Independent, coed, university. CGS member. *Enrollment:* 4,985 graduate, professional, and undergraduate students; 1,246 full-time matriculated graduate/professional students (670 women), 104 part-time matriculated graduate/professional students (49 women). *Graduate faculty:* 360 full-time (117 women), 181 part-time/adjunct (91 women). *Computer facilities:* Computer purchase and lease plans are available. 104 computers available on campus for general student use. A campuswide network can be accessed from student residence rooms and from off campus. Internet access and online class registration, educational software are available. *Library facilities:* Goldfarb Library plus 2 others. *Graduate expenses:* Tuition: full-time $28,999; part-time $4,867 per course. Required fees: $175. *General application contact:* Margaret Haley, Assistant Dean, Graduate Admissions, 781-736-3406.

Find an in-depth description at www.petersons.com/gradchannel.

Graduate School of Arts and Sciences
Dr. Milton Kornfeld, Associate Dean of Arts and Sciences for Graduate Education
Programs in:
American history • MA, PhD
anthropology • MA, PhD
anthropology and women's studies • MA
arts and sciences • MA, MFA, MS, PhD, Certificate
biochemistry • MS, PhD
biophysics and structural biology • PhD
coexistence and conflict • MA
cognitive neuroscience • PhD
comparative history • MA, PhD
composition and theory • MA, MFA, PhD
English and American literature • PhD
English and women's studies • MA
general psychology • MA
genetic counseling • MS
genetics • PhD
inorganic chemistry • MS, PhD
Jewish communal service • MA
mathematics • MA, PhD
microbiology • PhD
molecular and cell biology • MS, PhD
molecular biology • PhD
music and women's studies • MA, MFA
musicology • MA, MFA, PhD
Near Eastern and Judaic studies • MA, PhD
Near Eastern and Judaic studies and sociology • MA, PhD
Near Eastern and Judaic studies and women's studies • MA
neurobiology • PhD
neuroscience • MS, PhD
organic chemistry • MS, PhD
physical chemistry • MS, PhD
physics • MS, PhD
politics • MA, PhD
postbaccalaureate premedical • Certificate
social policy and sociology • PhD
social/developmental psychology • PhD
sociology • MA, PhD
sociology and women's studies • MA
studio art • Certificate
teaching of Hebrew • MA
theater arts • MFA

Michtom School of Computer Science
Dr. James Pustejovsky, Director of Graduate Studies
Program in:
computer science • MA, PhD, Certificate

The Heller School for Social Policy and Management
Dr. Jack P. Shonkoff, Dean
Programs in:
child, youth, and family services • MBA
health care administration • MBA
human services • MBA
international development • MA
international health policy and management • MA, MS
mission-driven management • MBA
social policy • PhD
sustainable development • MA
sustainable international development • MA, MS

International Business School
Programs in:
finance • MSF
international business • MBAi
international economics and finance • MA, PhD
international finance • MBAi

■ BRIDGEWATER STATE COLLEGE
Bridgewater, MA 02325-0001
http://www.bridgew.edu/

State-supported, coed, comprehensive institution. *Enrollment:* 9,626 graduate, professional, and undergraduate students; 1,900 matriculated graduate/professional students. *Graduate faculty:* 140 full-time.

Massachusetts

Computer facilities: 750 computers available on campus for general student use. A campuswide network can be accessed from student residence rooms and from off campus. Internet access and online class registration, student account information, application software are available. *Library facilities:* Clement Maxwell Library. *Graduate expenses:* Tuition, state resident: part-time $227 per credit. Tuition, nonresident: part-time $451 per credit. *General application contact:* Ray Guillette, Assistant Dean, Graduate and Continuing Education, 508-531-1300.

School of Graduate and Continuing Education
Dr. Edward Minnock, Dean

School of Arts and Sciences
Dr. Howard London, Dean
Programs in:
art • MAT
arts and sciences • MA, MAT, MPA, MS, MSW
biological sciences • MAT
computer science • MS
criminal justice • MS
English • MA, MAT
history • MAT
mathematics • MAT
physical sciences • MAT
physics • MAT
psychology • MA
public administration • MPA
social work • MSW

School of Education and Allied Science
Dr. Anna Bradfield, Dean
Programs in:
counseling • M Ed, CAGS
early childhood education • M Ed
education • M Ed, MAT, MS, CAGS
educational leadership • M Ed, CAGS
elementary education • M Ed
health promotion • M Ed
instructional technology • MS
physical education • MS
reading • M Ed, CAGS
secondary education • MAT
special education • M Ed

School of Management
Programs in:
accounting and finance • MSM
management • MSM

■ CLARK UNIVERSITY
Worcester, MA 01610-1477
http://www.clarku.edu/

Independent, coed, university. CGS member. *Enrollment:* 3,084 graduate, professional, and undergraduate students; 558 full-time matriculated graduate/professional students (327 women), 259 part-time matriculated graduate/professional students (112 women). *Graduate faculty:* 164 full-time (57 women), 115 part-time/adjunct (50 women). *Computer facilities:* 200 computers available on campus for general student use. A campuswide network can be accessed from student residence rooms and from off campus. Internet access, on-line course support are available. *Library facilities:* Robert Hutchings Goddard Library plus 4 others. *Graduate expenses:* Tuition: full-time $26,700. *General application contact:* Denise Robertson, Graduate School Coordinator, 508-793-7676.

Find an in-depth description at www.petersons.com/gradchannel.

Graduate School
Dr. Nancy Budwig, Director
Programs in:
biology • MA, PhD
chemistry • MA, PhD
clinical psychology • PhD
community development and planning • MA
developmental psychology • PhD
economics • PhD
education • MA Ed
English • MA
environmental science and policy • MA
geographic information science for development and environment • MA
geography • PhD
history • MA, CAGS
holocaust history • PhD
international development and social change • MA
physics • MA, PhD
social-personality psychology • PhD
women's studies • PhD

College of Professional and Continuing Education
Dr. Thomas Massey, Director
Programs in:
information technology • MIT
liberal studies • MALA
professional and continuing education • MALA, MIT, MPA, MSPC, CAGS, Certificate
professional communications • MSPC
public administration • MPA, Certificate

Graduate School of Management
Dr. Edward Ottensmeyer, Dean
Programs in:
accounting • MBA
finance • MBA, MSF
global business • MBA
health care management • MBA
management • MBA
management of information technology • MBA
marketing • MBA

■ EASTERN NAZARENE COLLEGE
Quincy, MA 02170-2999
http://www.enc.edu/

Independent-religious, coed, comprehensive institution. *Computer facilities:* 98 computers available on campus for general student use. A campuswide network can be accessed from student residence rooms and from off campus. Internet access is available. *Library facilities:* Nease Library. *General application contact:* Coordinator of Graduate Studies, 617-774-6826.

Graduate Studies
Program in:
marriage and family therapy • MS

Division of Education
Programs in:
early childhood education • M Ed, Certificate
elementary education • M Ed, Certificate
English as a second language • M Ed, Certificate
instructional enrichment and development • M Ed, Certificate
middle school education • M Ed, Certificate
moderate special needs education • M Ed, Certificate
principal • Certificate
program development and supervision • M Ed, Certificate
secondary education • M Ed, Certificate
special education administrator • Certificate
supervisor • Certificate
teacher of reading • M Ed, Certificate

■ ELMS COLLEGE
Chicopee, MA 01013-2839
http://www.elms.edu/

Independent-religious, coed, primarily women, comprehensive institution. *Enrollment:* 971 graduate, professional, and undergraduate students; 9 full-time matriculated graduate/professional students (all women), 96 part-time matriculated graduate/professional students (86 women). *Graduate faculty:* 17 full-time (13 women), 11 part-time/adjunct (7 women). *Computer facilities:* 70 computers available on campus for general student use. A campuswide network can be accessed from student residence rooms and from off campus. Internet access is available. *Library facilities:* Alumnae Library. *Graduate expenses:* Tuition: full-time $8,100; part-time $450 per credit. Required fees: $40; $20 per

Peterson's Graduate Schools in the U.S. 2006

Massachusetts

Elms College (continued)
term. *General application contact:* Joseph P. Wagner, Director of Admission Office, 413-594-2761 Ext. 238.

Division of Education
Dr. Elizabeth Hukowicz, Director
Programs in:
 early childhood education • MAT
 education • M Ed, CAGS
 elementary education • MAT
 English as a second language • MAT
 reading • MAT
 secondary education • MAT
 special education • MAT

Program in Liberal Arts
Dr. Martin Pion, Director of MALA/MAAT Programs
Program in:
 liberal arts • MALA

Religious Studies Department
Dr. Martin Pion, Director of MALA/MAAT Programs
Program in:
 religious studies • MAAT

■ EMERSON COLLEGE
Boston, MA 02116-4624
http://www.emerson.edu/

Independent, coed, comprehensive institution. CGS member. *Enrollment:* 4,385 graduate, professional, and undergraduate students; 781 full-time matriculated graduate/professional students (593 women), 203 part-time matriculated graduate/professional students (141 women). *Graduate faculty:* 140 full-time, 250 part-time/adjunct. *Computer facilities:* 296 computers available on campus for general student use. A campuswide network can be accessed from student residence rooms and from off campus. Internet access and online class registration are available. *Library facilities:* Emerson Library plus 1 other. *Graduate expenses:* Tuition: full-time $16,608; part-time $692 per credit. *General application contact:* 617-824-8610.

Graduate Studies
Dr. Donna Schroth, Director

School of Communication
Dr. Stuart J. Sigman, Dean
Programs in:
 broadcast journalism • MA
 communication • MA, MS
 communication sciences and disorders • MS
 global marketing communication and advertising • MA
 health communication • MA
 integrated journalism • MA
 integrated marketing communication • MA
 organizational and corporate communication • MA
 print/multimedia journalism • MA
 print/multimedia journalism, broadcast journalism, integrated journalism • MA
 speech-language pathology • MS

School of the Arts
Grafton J. Nunes, Dean
Programs in:
 arts • MA, MFA
 audio production • MA
 audio, television/video, and new media production • MA
 creative writing • MFA
 new media production • MA
 publishing and writing • MA
 television/video production • MA
 theatre education • MA

■ EMMANUEL COLLEGE
Boston, MA 02115
http://www.emmanuel.edu/

Independent-religious, coed, comprehensive institution. *Enrollment:* 1,871 graduate, professional, and undergraduate students; 1,095 matriculated graduate/professional students. *Graduate faculty:* 4 full-time, 150 part-time/adjunct. *Computer facilities:* 115 computers available on campus for general student use. A campuswide network can be accessed from student residence rooms. Internet access, software applications are available. *Library facilities:* Cardinal Cushing Library. *Graduate expenses:* Tuition: full-time $8,790; part-time $1,465 per course. *General application contact:* Kate O'Dea, Graduate and Professional Programs, 617-735-9700.

Graduate Programs
Programs in:
 educational leadership • CAGS
 elementary education • MAT
 human resource management • MS, Certificate
 management • MSM
 multi-cultural education • MAT
 school administration • M Ed
 secondary education • MAT

■ FITCHBURG STATE COLLEGE
Fitchburg, MA 01420-2697
http://www.fsc.edu/

State-supported, coed, comprehensive institution. CGS member. *Enrollment:* 4,948 graduate, professional, and undergraduate students; 228 full-time matriculated graduate/professional students (164 women), 602 part-time matriculated graduate/professional students (425 women). *Graduate faculty:* 186. *Computer facilities:* 135 computers available on campus for general student use. A campuswide network can be accessed from student residence rooms and from off campus. Internet access and online class registration are available. *Library facilities:* Hammond Library. *Graduate expenses:* Tuition, nonresident: full-time $3,600; part-time $150 per credit. Required fees: $1,728; $72 per credit. Tuition and fees vary according to course load. *General application contact:* Lynn A. Petrillo, Director of Admissions, 978-665-3144.

Find an in-depth description at www.petersons.com/gradchannel.

Division of Graduate and Continuing Education
Head
Programs in:
 accounting • MBA
 adolescent and family therapy • Certificate
 applied communications • MS, Certificate
 arts in education • M Ed
 child protective services • Certificate
 computer science • MS
 criminal justice • MS
 early childhood education • M Ed
 educational technology • Certificate
 elementary education • M Ed
 elementary school guidance counseling • MS
 fine arts director • Certificate
 forensic nursing • MS, Certificate
 general studies education • M Ed
 guided studies • M Ed
 human resource management • MBA
 interdisciplinary studies • CAGS
 management • MBA
 marriage and family therapy • MS
 mental health counseling • MS
 middle school education • M Ed
 non-licensure • M Ed, CAGS
 occupational education • M Ed
 professional mentoring for teachers • Certificate
 reading specialist • M Ed
 school principal • M Ed, CAGS
 science education • M Ed
 secondary education • M Ed
 secondary school guidance counseling • MS
 substance abuse services • Certificate
 supervisor director • M Ed, CAGS
 teaching biology • MA, MAT
 teaching earth science • MAT
 teaching English • MA, MAT
 teaching history • MA, MAT
 teaching mathematics • MAT

teaching students with moderate disabilities • M Ed
teaching students with severe disabilities • M Ed
technical and professional writing • MS
technology education • M Ed
technology leader • M Ed, CAGS

■ FRAMINGHAM STATE COLLEGE
Framingham, MA 01701-9101
http://www.framingham.edu/

State-supported, coed, comprehensive institution. *Computer facilities:* Computer purchase and lease plans are available. 575 computers available on campus for general student use. A campuswide network can be accessed from student residence rooms and from off campus. Internet access and online class registration, TELNET are available. *Library facilities:* Whittemore Library. *General application contact:* Associate Dean, 508-626-4562.

Graduate Programs
Programs in:
art • M Ed
business administration • MA
counseling • MA
curriculum and instructional technology • M Ed
educational leadership • MA
English • M Ed
food science and nutrition science • MS
health care administration • MA
history • M Ed
human nutrition • MS
human resources administration • MA
literacy and language • M Ed
mathematics • M Ed
public administration • MA
Spanish • M Ed
special education • M Ed
teaching English as a second language • M Ed

■ HARVARD UNIVERSITY
Cambridge, MA 02138
http://www.harvard.edu/

Independent, coed, university. CGS member. *Enrollment:* 20,130 graduate, professional, and undergraduate students; 11,662 full-time matriculated graduate/professional students (5,483 women), 1,028 part-time matriculated graduate/professional students (545 women). *Graduate faculty:* 2,425. *Computer facilities:* A campuswide network can be accessed from student residence rooms and from off campus. Internet access is available. *Library facilities:* Widener Library plus 90 others. *Graduate expenses:* Tuition: full-time $26,066. Full-time tuition and fees vary according to program and student level. *General application contact:* Information Contact, 617-495-1814.

Find an in-depth description at www.petersons.com/gradchannel.

Business School
Programs in:
business • MBA, DBA, PhD
business administration • DBA
business economics • PhD
health policy management • PhD
information and technology management • PhD
organizational behavior • PhD

Divinity School
William A. Graham, Dean
Program in:
divinity • M Div, MTS, Th M, PhD, Th D

Extension School
Michael Shinagel, Dean
Programs in:
applied sciences • CAS
English for graduate and professional studies • DGP
environmental management • CEM
information technology • ALM
liberal arts • ALM
museum studies • CMS
premedical studies • Diploma
public health • CPH
publication and communication • CPC
special studies in administration and management • CSS
technologies of education • CTE

Graduate School of Arts and Sciences
Programs in:
African history • PhD
Akkadian and Sumerian • AM, PhD
American history • PhD
ancient art • PhD
ancient Near Eastern art • PhD
ancient, medieval, early modern, and modern Europe • PhD
anthropology and Middle Eastern studies • PhD
Arabic • AM, PhD
archaeology • PhD
architecture • PhD
Armenian • AM, PhD
arts and sciences • MD, AM, ME, MFS, SM, PhD, Sc D
astronomy • AM, PhD
astrophysics • AM, PhD
baroque art • PhD
biblical history • AM, PhD
biochemical chemistry • AM, PhD
biological anthropology • PhD
biological chemistry and molecular pharmacology • PhD
biological sciences in public health • PhD
biology • PhD
biophysics • PhD
business economics • AM, PhD
Byzantine art • PhD
Byzantine Greek • PhD
cell biology • PhD
chemical physics • PhD
chemistry • AM
Chinese • AM, PhD
Chinese studies • AM
classical archaeology • AM, PhD
classical art • PhD
classical philology • AM, PhD
classical philosophy • PhD
comparative literature • PhD
composition • AM, PhD
critical theory • AM, PhD
descriptive linguistics • AM, PhD
diplomatic history • PhD
earth and planetary sciences • AM, PhD
East Asian history • PhD
economic and social history • PhD
economics • AM, PhD
economics and Middle Eastern studies • PhD
eighteenth-century literature • AM, PhD
experimental pathology • PhD
experimental physics • AM, PhD
fine arts and Middle Eastern studies • PhD
forest science • MFS
French • AM, PhD
genetics • PhD
German • AM, PhD
health policy • PhD
Hebrew • AM, PhD
historical linguistics • AM, PhD
history and East Asian languages • PhD
history and Middle Eastern studies • PhD
history of American civilization • PhD
history of science • AM, PhD
immunology • PhD
Indian art • PhD
Indian philosophy • AM, PhD
Indo-Muslim culture • AM, PhD
Inner Asian and Altaic studies • PhD
inorganic chemistry • AM, PhD
intellectual history • PhD
Iranian • AM, PhD
Irish • AM, PhD
Islamic art • PhD
Italian • AM, PhD
Japanese • AM, PhD
Japanese and Chinese art • PhD
Japanese studies • AM
Jewish history and literature • AM, PhD
Korean • AM, PhD

Massachusetts

Harvard University (continued)
  Korean studies • AM
  landscape architecture • PhD
  Latin American history • PhD
  legal anthropology • AM
  literature: nineteenth-century to the present • AM, PhD
  mathematics • AM, PhD
  medical anthropology • AM
  medical engineering/medical physics • PhD, Sc D
  medieval art • PhD
  medieval Latin • PhD
  medieval literature and language • AM, PhD
  microbiology and molecular genetics • PhD
  modern art • PhD
  modern British and American literature • AM, PhD
  molecular and cellular biology • PhD
  Mongolian • AM, PhD
  Mongolian studies • AM
  musicology • AM
  musicology and ethnomusicology • PhD
  Near Eastern history • PhD
  neurobiology • PhD
  oceanic history • PhD
  oral literature • PhD
  organic chemistry • AM, PhD
  organizational behavior • PhD
  Pali • AM, PhD
  pathology • PhD
  Persian • AM, PhD
  philosophy • PhD
  physical chemistry • AM, PhD
  physics • AM
  Polish • AM, PhD
  political economy and government • PhD
  political science • AM, PhD
  Portuguese • AM, PhD
  psychology • AM, PhD
  public policy • PhD
  regional studies–Middle East • AM
  regional studies-Russia, Eastern Europe, and Central Asia • AM
  Renaissance and modern architecture • PhD
  Renaissance art • PhD
  Renaissance literature • AM, PhD
  Russian • AM, PhD
  Sanskrit • AM, PhD
  Scandinavian • AM, PhD
  Semitic philology • AM, PhD
  Serbo-Croatian • AM, PhD
  Slavic philology • AM, PhD
  social anthropology • AM, PhD
  social change and development • AM
  social psychology • AM, PhD
  sociology • AM, PhD
  Spanish • AM, PhD
  statistics • AM, PhD
  study of religion • AM, PhD
  Syro-Palestinian archaeology • AM, PhD
  theoretical linguistics • AM, PhD
  theoretical physics • AM, PhD
  theory • AM, PhD
  Tibetan • AM, PhD
  Turkish • AM, PhD
  Ukrainian • AM, PhD
  urban planning • PhD
  Urdu • AM, PhD
  Vietnamese • AM, PhD
  Vietnamese studies • AM
  virology • PhD
  Welsh • AM, PhD

Division of Engineering and Applied Sciences
Ventatesh Narayanamurti, Dean
Programs in:
  applied mathematics • ME, SM, PhD
  applied physics • ME, SM, PhD
  computer science • ME, SM, PhD
  computing technology • PhD
  engineering science • ME
  engineering sciences • SM, PhD

Graduate School of Design
Alan Altschuler, Acting Dean
Programs in:
  architecture • M Arch
  design • M Arch, M Des S, MAUD, MLA, MLAUD, MUP, Dr DES
  design studies • M Des S
  landscape architecture • MLA
  urban planning • MUP
  urban planning and design • MAUD, MLAUD

Graduate School of Education
Ellen C. Lagemann, Dean
Programs in:
  administration, planning and social policy • Ed M
  arts in education • Ed M
  community and schools • Ed D
  education • Ed M, Ed D
  education in the community • Ed D
  elementary and secondary education • Ed D
  gender studies • Ed M
  higher education • Ed M, Ed D
  human development and psychology • Ed M, Ed D
  international education • Ed D
  international education policy • Ed M
  language and literacy • Ed M, Ed D
  learning and teaching • Ed M, Ed D
  mid-career mathematics and science (teaching certification) • Ed M
  mind brain and education • Ed M
  philosophy of education and curriculum theory • Ed D
  research • Ed D
  risk and prevention • Ed M
  school leadership • Ed M
  schools and schooling • Ed D
  teaching and curriculum (teaching certification) • Ed M
  technology in education • Ed M
  urban superintendency • Ed D

John F. Kennedy School of Government
Dr. Joseph Nye, Dean
Programs in:
  government • MPA, MPAID, MPP, MPPUP, PhD
  political economy and government • PhD
  public administration • MPA
  public administration and international development • MPAID
  public policy • MPP, PhD
  public policy and urban planning • MPPUP

Law School
Program in:
  law • JD, LL M, SJD

Medical School
Dr. Joseph B. Martin, Dean of the Faculty of Medicine
Program in:
  medicine • MD, M Eng, SM, PhD, Sc D

Division of Health Sciences and Technology
Dr. Joseph Bonventre, Director
Programs in:
  biomedical engineering • M Eng
  biomedical enterprise • SM
  biomedical informatics • SM
  health sciences and technology • MD, M Eng, SM, PhD, Sc D
  medical engineering • PhD
  medical engineering/medical physics • Sc D
  medical physics • PhD
  medical sciences • MD
  speech and hearing bioscience and technology • PhD, Sc D

Division of Medical Sciences
Program in:
  medical sciences • PhD

School of Dental Medicine
Programs in:
  advanced general dentistry • Certificate
  dental medicine • DMD, M Med Sc, D Med Sc, Certificate
  dental public health • Certificate
  endodontics • Certificate
  general practice residency • Certificate
  oral biology • M Med Sc, D Med Sc
  oral pathology • Certificate
  oral surgery • Certificate
  orthodontics • Certificate
  pediatric dentistry • Certificate
  periodontics • Certificate
  prosthodontics • Certificate

School of Public Health
Programs in:
  biostatistics • SM, SD

cancer cell biology • PhD, SD
clinical effectiveness • MPH
environmental epidemiology • SM, DPH, SD
environmental health • SM
environmental science and engineering • SM, SD
epidemiology • SM, DPH, SD
epidemiology/international nutrition • DPH, SD
family and community health • MPH
health and social behavior • SM, DPH, SD
health care management • MPH
health policy and management • SM, DPH, SD
immunology and infectious diseases • DPH, SD
international health • MPH
law and public health • MPH
maternal and child health • SM, DPH, SD
occupational and environmental health • MPH
occupational health • MOH, SM, DPH, SD
physiology • SD
population and international health • SM, DPH, SD
public health • MOH, MPH, SM, DPH, PhD, SD
quantitative methods • MPH

Division of Biological Sciences
Program in:
biological sciences • PhD

■ LESLEY UNIVERSITY
Cambridge, MA 02138-2790
http://www.lesley.edu/

Independent, coed, comprehensive institution. CGS member. *Enrollment:* 6,333 graduate, professional, and undergraduate students; 440 full-time matriculated graduate/professional students (382 women), 4,951 part-time matriculated graduate/professional students (4,262 women). *Graduate faculty:* 88 full-time (65 women), 456 part-time/adjunct (311 women). *Computer facilities:* 170 computers available on campus for general student use. A campuswide network can be accessed from student residence rooms and from off campus. Internet access is available. *Library facilities:* Eleanor DeWolfe Ludcke Library plus 2 others. *Graduate expenses:* Tuition: part-time $595 per credit. *General application contact:* Lois Parker Carmona, Assistant Vice President of Enrollment Management, 617-349-8300.

Find an in-depth description at www.petersons.com/gradchannel.

Graduate School of Arts and Social Sciences
Dr. Julia Halevy, Dean
Programs in:
clinical mental health counseling • MA
counseling psychology • MA, CAGS
creative arts in learning • M Ed, CAGS
creative writing • MFA
critical media studies and culture • MA
development project administration • MA
ecological teaching and learning • MS
environmental education • MS
expressive therapies • MA, PhD, CAGS
fiction • MFA
independent studies • M Ed
independent study • MA
individually designed • MA
intercultural conflict management • MA
intercultural health and human services • MA
intercultural relations • MA, CAGS
intercultural training and consulting • MA
interdisciplinary studies • MA
international education exchange/international student advising • MA
managing culturally diverse human resources • MA
multicultural education • MA
non-fiction • MFA
poetry • MFA
writing for young people • MFA

School of Education
Dr. Mario Borunda, Dean
Programs in:
curriculum and instruction • M Ed, CAGS
early childhood education • M Ed
educational administration • M Ed, CAGS
educational studies • PhD
elementary education • M Ed
individually designed • M Ed
intensive special needs • M Ed
middle school education • M Ed
reading • M Ed, CAGS
science in education • M Ed
special needs • M Ed, CAGS
technology in education • M Ed, CAGS

■ MASSACHUSETTS INSTITUTE OF TECHNOLOGY
Cambridge, MA 02139-4307
http://web.mit.edu/

Independent, coed, university. CGS member. *Enrollment:* 10,340 graduate, professional, and undergraduate students; 5,912 full-time matriculated graduate/professional students (1,721 women), 161 part-time matriculated graduate/professional students (49 women). *Graduate faculty:* 960 full-time (167 women), 14 part-time/adjunct (3 women). *Computer facilities:* Computer purchase and lease plans are available. 950 computers available on campus for general student use. A campuswide network can be accessed from student residence rooms and from off campus. *Library facilities:* MIT Libraries plus 10 others. *Graduate expenses:* Tuition: full-time $29,400. Required fees: $200. *General application contact:* Marilee Jones, Dean of Admissions, 617-253-2917.

Operations Research Center
Dr. James B. Orlin, Co-Director
Program in:
operations research • SM, PhD

School of Architecture and Planning
Programs in:
architecture • M Arch, SM Arch S, SM Vis S, SMBT, PhD
architecture and planning • M Arch, MCP, MS, MSRED, SM Arch S, SM Vis S, SMBT, PhD
city planning • MCP
media arts and sciences • MS, PhD
urban and regional planning • PhD
urban and regional studies • PhD
urban studies and planning • MS

Center for Real Estate
David Geltner, Director
Program in:
real estate • MSRED

School of Engineering
Prof. Thomas L. Magnanti, Dean
Programs in:
aeroacoustics • PhD, Sc D
aerodynamics • PhD, Sc D
aeroelasticity • PhD, Sc D
aeronautics and astronautics • M Eng, SM, EAA
aerospace systems • PhD, Sc D
air craft propulsion • PhD, Sc D
astrodynamics • PhD, Sc D
bioengineering • SM, PhD, Sc D
biological oceanography • PhD, Sc D
biomaterials • PhD, Sc D
biomedical engineering • M Eng, PhD, Sc D
ceramics • PhD, Sc D
chemical engineering • SM, PhD, Sc D
chemical engineering practice • SM, PhD
chemical oceanography • PhD, Sc D
civil and environmental engineering • M Eng, SM, PhD, Sc D, CE, Env E
civil engineering • PhD, Sc D

Massachusetts

Massachusetts Institute of Technology (continued)
  coastal engineering • PhD, Sc D
  computational fluid dynamics • PhD, Sc D
  computer systems • PhD, Sc D
  construction engineering and management • PhD, Sc D
  dynamics energy conversion • PhD, Sc D
  electrical engineering and computer science • M Eng, SM, PhD, Sc D, ECS, EE
  electronic materials • PhD, Sc D
  engineering • M Eng, MST, SM, PhD, Sc D, CE, EAA, ECS, EE, Env E, Mat E, Mech E, Met E, NE, Naval E, Ocean E
  environmental biology • PhD, Sc D
  environmental chemistry • PhD, Sc D
  environmental engineering • PhD, Sc D
  environmental fluid mechanics • PhD, Sc D
  estimation and control • PhD, Sc D
  flight transportation • PhD, Sc D
  fluid mechanics • PhD, Sc D
  gas turbine structures • PhD, Sc D
  gas turbines • PhD, Sc D
  geotechnical and geoenvironmental engineering • PhD, Sc D
  humans and automation • PhD, Sc D
  hydrology • PhD, Sc D
  information technology • PhD, Sc D
  instrumentation • PhD, Sc D
  materials engineering • PhD, Sc D, Mat E
  materials science • PhD, Sc D
  materials science and engineering • M Eng, SM
  mechanical engineering • SM, PhD, Sc D, Mech E
  metallurgical engineering • Met E
  metallurgy • PhD, Sc D
  naval architecture and marine engineering • SM
  naval engineering • Naval E
  navigation and control systems • PhD, Sc D
  nuclear engineering • M Eng, SM, PhD, Sc D, NE
  ocean engineering • M Eng, SM, PhD, Sc D, Ocean E
  ocean systems management • SM
  oceanographic engineering • PhD, Sc D
  physics of fluids • PhD, Sc D
  plasma physics • PhD, Sc D
  polymers • PhD, Sc D
  space propulsion • PhD, Sc D
  structural dynamics • PhD, Sc D
  structures and materials • PhD, Sc D
  structures technology • PhD, Sc D
  toxicology • SM, PhD, Sc D
  transportation • PhD, Sc D
  vehicle design • PhD, Sc D

Engineering Systems Division
Prof. Daniel Roos, Co-Director
Programs in:
  engineering and management • SM
  engineering systems • M Eng, MST, SM, PhD
  logistics • M Eng
  technology and policy • SM, PhD
  transportation • MST

School of Humanities, Arts and Social Sciences
Philip S. Khoury, Dean
Programs in:
  comparative media studies • SM
  economics • MA, PhD
  history and social study of science and technology • PhD
  humanities, arts and social science • MA, SM, PhD
  linguistics • PhD
  philosophy • PhD
  political science • SM, PhD
  science writing • SM
  writing and humanistic studies • SM

School of Science
Prof. Robert J. Silbey, Dean
Programs in:
  atmospheric chemistry • PhD, Sc D
  atmospheric science • SM, PhD, Sc D
  biochemistry • PhD
  biological chemistry • PhD, Sc D
  biological oceanography • PhD
  biophysical chemistry and molecular structure • PhD
  cell biology • PhD
  cellular/molecular neuroscience • PhD
  climate physics and chemistry • PhD, Sc D
  cognitive neuroscience • PhD
  cognitive science • PhD
  computational cognitive science • PhD
  computational neuroscience • PhD
  developmental biology • PhD
  earth and planetary sciences • SM
  genetics/microbiology • PhD
  geochemistry • PhD, Sc D
  geology • PhD, Sc D
  geophysics • PhD, Sc D
  geosystems • SM
  immunology • PhD
  inorganic chemistry • PhD, Sc D
  mathematics • PhD
  neurobiology • PhD
  oceanography • SM, PhD, Sc D
  organic chemistry • PhD, Sc D
  physical chemistry • PhD, Sc D
  physics • SM, PhD, Sc D
  planetary sciences • PhD, Sc D
  science • SM, PhD, Sc D
  systems neuroscience • PhD

Sloan School of Management
Richard L. Schmalensee, Dean
Program in:
  management • MBA, MS, SM, PhD

Whitaker College of Health Sciences and Technology
Programs in:
  biomedical engineering • M Eng
  biomedical enterprise • SM
  biomedical informatics • SM
  health sciences and technology • MD, M Eng, SM, PhD, Sc D
  medical engineering • PhD
  medical engineering and medical physics • Sc D
  medical physics • PhD
  medical sciences • MD
  speech and hearing bioscience and technology • PhD, Sc D

■ NORTHEASTERN UNIVERSITY
Boston, MA 02115-5096
http://www.neu.edu/

Independent, coed, university. CGS member. *Enrollment:* 18,760 graduate, professional, and undergraduate students; 2,825 full-time matriculated graduate/professional students (1,518 women), 1,443 part-time matriculated graduate/professional students (656 women). *Graduate faculty:* 830 full-time (297 women), 316 part-time/adjunct (172 women). *Computer facilities:* A campuswide network can be accessed from student residence rooms and from off campus. Internet access and online class registration are available. *Library facilities:* Snell Library plus 4 others. *Graduate expenses:* Tuition: part-time $790 per credit hour. Tuition and fees vary according to course load and program.

Find an in-depth description at www.petersons.com/gradchannel.

Bouvé College of Health Sciences Graduate School
Dr. Ena Vazquez-Nuttall, Director
Programs in:
  applied behavior analysis • MS
  applied educational psychology • MS
  audiology • MS
  biomedical sciences • MS
  biotechnology • PSM
  cardiopulmonary science (perfusion technology) • MS
  clinical exercise physiology • MS
  college student development and counseling • MS
  counseling psychology • MS, PhD, CAGS
  medical laboratory science • MS, PhD
  medicinal chemistry • MS, PhD
  pharmaceutics • PhD
  pharmacology • MS, PhD
  pharmacy • Pharm D

Massachusetts

pharmacy and health sciences • Pharm D, MS, MS Ed, PSM, PhD, CAGS, CAS
physician assistant • MS
rehabilitation counseling • MS
school counseling • MS
school psychology • MS, PhD, CAGS
special needs and intensive special needs • MS Ed
speech-language pathology • MS
toxicology • MS, PhD

School of Nursing
Dr. Nancy Hoffart, Dean
Programs in:
community health nursing • MS, CAS
critical care-acute care nurse practitioner • MS, CAS
critical care-neonatal nurse practitioner • MS, CAS
nurse anesthesia • MS
nursing • MS, CAS
nursing administration • MS
primary care nursing • MS, CAS
psychiatric-mental health nursing • MS, CAS

College of Arts and Sciences
Dr. Luis M. Falcón, Interim Associate Dean and Director of the Graduate School
Programs in:
American government and politics • MA
analytical chemistry • PhD
architecture • MA
arts and sciences • MA, MAT, MAW, MPA, MS, MSOR, MTPW, PSM, PhD, Certificate
bioinformatics • MS
biology • MS, PhD
biotechnology • MS
chemistry • MS, PhD
cinema studies • Certificate
comparative and international policy and politics • PhD
comparative government and politics • MA
development administration • MPA
economics • MA, PhD
English • MA, PhD
experimental psychology • MA, PhD
health administration and policy • MPA
history • MA, PhD
inorganic chemistry • PhD
international relations • MA
law, policy, and society • MS, PhD
management information systems • MPA
mathematics • MS, PhD
operations research • MSOR
organic chemistry • PhD
physical chemistry • PhD
physics • MS, PhD
political theory • MA
public administration • MA, MPA
public history • MA
public policy • PhD
sociology • MA, PhD
state and local government • MPA
technical and professional writing • MTPW
women's studies • Certificate
writing • MA, MAW

School of Education
Dr. James W. Fraser, Dean/Director
Programs in:
elementary certification • MAT
secondary certification • MAT

School of Journalism
Prof. James Ross, Graduate Coordinator
Program in:
journalism • MA

College of Computer and Information Science
Dr. Larry A. Finkelstein, Dean
Program in:
computer and information science • MS, PhD

College of Criminal Justice
Jack McDevitt, Director
Program in:
criminal justice • MS

College of Engineering
Dr. Yaman Yener, Associate Dean of Engineering for Research and Graduate Studies
Programs in:
chemical engineering • MS, PhD
civil and environmental engineering • MS, PhD
computer engineering • PhD
computer systems engineering • MS
electrical engineering • MS, PhD
engineering • MS, PSM, PhD
engineering management • MS
industrial engineering • MS, PhD
information systems • MS
mechanical engineering • MS, PhD
operations research • MS
telecommunication systems management • MS

Graduate School of Business Administration
Therese M. Hofmann, Associate Dean and Director
Programs in:
business administration • EMBA, MBA, MSF, MST, CAGS
finance • MSF

Graduate School of Professional Accounting
Cynthia Spies, Director
Programs in:
professional accounting • MST, CAGS
taxation • MST, CAGS

School of Law
Emily A. Spieler, Dean
Program in:
law • JD

■ REGIS COLLEGE
Weston, MA 02493
http://www.regiscollege.edu/

Independent-religious, women only, comprehensive institution. *Enrollment:* 1,083 graduate, professional, and undergraduate students; 95 full-time matriculated graduate/professional students (86 women), 188 part-time matriculated graduate/professional students (175 women). *Graduate faculty:* 12 full-time (11 women), 28 part-time/adjunct (20 women). *Computer facilities:* 134 computers available on campus for general student use. A campuswide network can be accessed from student residence rooms. Internet access is available. *Library facilities:* Regis College Library. *Graduate expenses:* Tuition: full-time $19,910; part-time $500 per credit. *General application contact:* Lisa S. Krug, Assistant Director of Admissions, 781-768-7188.

Department of Education
Dr. Leona McCaughey-Oreszak, Program Director
Program in:
education • MAT

Department of Health Product Regulation and Health Policy
Dr. Jane Roman, Director
Program in:
health product regulation and health policy • MS

Department of Management and Leadership
Dr. Phillip Jutras, Director
Program in:
leadership and organizational change • MS

Department of Nursing
Dr. Antoinette Hays, Chair
Program in:
nursing • MS, Certificate

Department of Organizational and Professional Communication
Dr. Joan Murray, Director
Program in:
organizational and professional communication • MS

Massachusetts

■ SALEM STATE COLLEGE
Salem, MA 01970-5353
http://www.salemstate.edu/

State-supported, coed, comprehensive institution. CGS member. *Enrollment:* 9,120 graduate, professional, and undergraduate students; 261 full-time matriculated graduate/professional students (207 women), 823 part-time matriculated graduate/professional students (607 women). *Graduate faculty:* 277 full-time (138 women), 285 part-time/adjunct (151 women). *Computer facilities:* Computer purchase and lease plans are available. 426 computers available on campus for general student use. A campuswide network can be accessed from student residence rooms and from off campus. Internet access is available. *Library facilities:* Salem State College Library. *Graduate expenses:* Tuition, state resident: full-time $2,520; part-time $225 per credit. Tuition, nonresident: full-time $4,140; part-time $315 per credit. Required fees: $1,530. *General application contact:* Dr. Marc Glasser, Dean of the Graduate School, 978-542-6323.

Graduate School
Dr. Marc Glasser, Dean of the Graduate School
Programs in:
bilingual education • M Ed
business administration • MBA
chemistry • MAT
counseling and psychological services • MS
early childhood education • M Ed
education • CAGS
elementary education • M Ed
English • MA, MAT
English as a second language • MAT
geo-information science • MS
geography • MA, MAT
guidance and counseling • M Ed
history • MAT
library media studies • M Ed
mathematics • MAT, MS
middle school education • M Ed
nursing • MSN
reading • M Ed
school administration • M Ed
secondary education • M Ed
social work • MSW
special education • M Ed
teaching English as a second language K-9 • M Ed
technology in education • M Ed

■ SIMMONS COLLEGE
Boston, MA 02115
http://www.simmons.edu/

Independent, women only, university. *Enrollment:* 4,121 graduate, professional, and undergraduate students; 652 full-time matriculated graduate/professional students (584 women), 1,464 part-time matriculated graduate/professional students (1,273 women). *Graduate faculty:* 192. *Computer facilities:* 420 computers available on campus for general student use. A campuswide network can be accessed from student residence rooms and from off campus. Internet access and online class registration are available. *Library facilities:* Beatley Library plus 4 others. *Graduate expenses:* Tuition: full-time $8,640; part-time $720 per credit. Required fees: $20 per semester. Tuition and fees vary according to course load.

Graduate School
Dr. Diane Raymond, Dean

College of Arts and Sciences and Professional Studies
Programs in:
administrator special education • MS Ed, Ed S
arts and sciences and professional studies • MA, MAT, MFA, MS, MS Ed, CAGS, Ed S
assistive technology • MS Ed, Ed S
behavioral education • MS Ed, Ed S
children's literature • MA
communications management • MS
educational leadership • MS Ed, CAGS
elementary school education • MAT
English • MA
gender/cultural studies • MA
general purposes • CAGS
inclusion specialist • MS Ed
language-based learning disabilities • MS Ed, Ed S
moderate disabilities • Ed S
moderate special needs • MS Ed
secondary education • MAT
severe disabilities • Ed S
severe special needs • MS Ed
Spanish • MA
special education • MS Ed, Ed S
supervisor/director special education • MS Ed, Ed S
teacher preparation • MAT, MS Ed, CAGS
teaching English as a second language • MAT
urban education • MS Ed, CAGS
writing for children • MFA

Graduate School of Library and Information Science
Dr. Michele V. Cloonan, Dean
Programs in:
archives/history • MS
library and information science • DA
school library teacher • MS, Certificate

School for Health Studies
Dr. Gerald P. Koocher, Dean
Programs in:
health care administration • MHA, CAGS
health studies • MHA, MS, DPT, CAGS, Certificate
nutrition and health promotion • MS
physical therapy • DPT
primary health care nursing • MS, CAGS
sports nutrition • Certificate

School of Social Work
Dr. Joseph M. Regan, Dean
Program in:
clinical social work • MSW, PhD

Simmons School of Management
Dr. Patricia O'Brien, Dean
Program in:
management • MBA

■ SPRINGFIELD COLLEGE
Springfield, MA 01109-3797
http://www.spfldcol.edu/

Independent, coed, comprehensive institution. *Enrollment:* 3,119 graduate, professional, and undergraduate students; 1,082 full-time matriculated graduate/professional students (766 women), 384 part-time matriculated graduate/professional students (290 women). *Graduate faculty:* 156 full-time (78 women), 98 part-time/adjunct (46 women). *Computer facilities:* Computer purchase and lease plans are available. 95 computers available on campus for general student use. A campuswide network can be accessed from student residence rooms and from off campus. Internet access is available. *Library facilities:* Babson Library. *Graduate expenses:* Tuition: full-time $13,968; part-time $582 per semester hour. Required fees: $25. Tuition and fees vary according to course load. *General application contact:* Donald James Shaw, Director of Graduate Admissions, 413-748-3060.

Find an in-depth description at www.petersons.com/gradchannel.

School of Graduate Studies
Dr. Betty L. Mann, Dean
Programs in:
adapted physical education • M Ed, MPE, MS
advanced level coaching • M Ed, MPE, MS
alcohol rehabilitation/substance abuse counseling • M Ed, MS, CAS
art therapy • M Ed, MS, CAS
athletic administration • M Ed, MPE, MS

Massachusetts

athletic counseling • M Ed, MS, CAS
biomechanics • MS
counseling and secondary education • M Ed, MS
deaf counseling • M Ed, MS, CAS
developmental disabilities • M Ed, MS, CAS
education • M Ed, MS
exercise physiology • MS, DPE
general counseling • M Ed
general counseling and casework • M Ed, MS, CAS
general physical education • DPE, CAS
health care management • MS
health education licensure • MPE, MS
health education licensure program • M Ed
human services • MS
industrial/organizational psychology • MS, CAS
interdisciplinary movement sciences • MS
marriage and family therapy • M Ed, MS, CAS
mental health counseling • M Ed, MS, CAS
occupational therapy • M Ed, MS, CAS
outdoor recreational management • M Ed, MS
physical education licensure • MPE, MS
physical education licensure program • M Ed
physical therapy • MS
physician assistant studies • MS
psychiatric rehabilitation/mental health counseling • M Ed, MS, CAS
recreational management • M Ed, MS
school guidance and counseling • M Ed, MS, CAS
special services • M Ed, MS, CAS
sport management • M Ed, MS
sport performance • M Ed, MPE, MS
sport psychology • MS, DPE
student personnel in higher education • M Ed, MS, CAS
teaching and administration • MS
therapeutic recreational management • M Ed, MS
vocational evaluation and work adjustment • M Ed, MS, CAS

School of Social Work
Dr. Francine Vecchiolla, Dean
Programs in:
advanced generalist • MSW
advanced standing • MSW
practice with children and adolescents • PMC

■ SUFFOLK UNIVERSITY
Boston, MA 02108-2770
http://www.suffolk.edu/

Independent, coed, comprehensive institution. *Enrollment:* 7,804 graduate, professional, and undergraduate students; 1,475 full-time matriculated graduate/professional students (843 women), 2,141 part-time matriculated graduate/professional students (1,094 women). *Graduate faculty:* 187 full-time (69 women), 244 part-time/adjunct (95 women). *Computer facilities:* 400 computers available on campus for general student use. A campuswide network can be accessed from student residence rooms and from off campus. Internet access and online class registration are available. *Library facilities:* Mildred Sawyer Library plus 3 others. *Graduate expenses:* Tuition: part-time $942 per credit. Required fees: $10 per semester. *General application contact:* Judith Reynolds, Director of Graduate Admissions, 617-573-8302.

College of Arts and Sciences
Kenneth S. Greenberg, Dean
Programs in:
administration of higher education • M Ed
adult and organizational learning • MS, CAGS
arts and sciences • M Ed, MA, MS, MSEP, MSIE, PhD, CAGS
clinical-developmental psychology • PhD
communication • MA
computer science • MS
counseling and human relations • M Ed, MS, CAGS
economic policy • MSEP
economics • PhD
educational administration • M Ed
foundations of education • M Ed, CAGS
higher education administration • M Ed, CAGS
human resources • MS, CAGS
instructional design • CAGS
international economics • MSIE
leadership • CAGS
mental health counseling • MS
organizational development • CAGS
organizational learning • CAGS
political science • MS
professional development in teaching programs • CAGS
school counseling • M Ed
secondary school teaching • MS

New England School of Art and Design
Karen Clarke, Program Director
Program in:
interior design • MA

Law School
Gail N. Ellis, Dean of Admissions
Programs in:
civil litigation • JD
financial services • JD
health care/biotechnology law • JD
intellectual property law • JD
international law • JD

Sawyer School of Management
Dr. C. Richard Torrisi, Associate Dean
Programs in:
accounting • MSA, GDPA
banking and financial services • MS
business administration • MBA, APC
disability studies • MPA
executive business administration • EMBA
finance • MSF, CPASF
global business administration • MBA
health administration • MHA, MPA
management • EMBA, MBA, MBAH, MHA, MPA, MS, MSA, MSF, MST, APC, CASPA, CPASF, GDPA
nonprofit management • MPA
public administration • CASPA
public finance and human resources • MPA
state and local government • MPA
taxation • MST

■ TUFTS UNIVERSITY
Medford, MA 02155
http://www.tufts.edu/

Independent, coed, university. CGS member. *Enrollment:* 9,509 graduate, professional, and undergraduate students; 3,717 full-time matriculated graduate/professional students (2,139 women), 900 part-time matriculated graduate/professional students (503 women). *Graduate faculty:* 716 full-time (271 women), 438 part-time/adjunct (194 women). *Computer facilities:* 254 computers available on campus for general student use. A campuswide network can be accessed from student residence rooms and from off campus. Internet access and online class registration are available. *Library facilities:* Tisch Library plus 1 other. *Graduate expenses:* Tuition: full-time $29,949.

Find an in-depth description at www.petersons.com/gradchannel.

Fletcher School of Law and Diplomacy
Stephen W. Bosworth, Dean
Program in:
law and diplomacy • MA, MAHA, MALD, PhD

The Gerald J. and Dorothy R. Friedman School of Nutrition Science and Policy
Lynne Ausman, Student Services
Programs in:
humanitarian assistance • MAHA
nutrition • MS, PhD

Massachusetts

Tufts University (continued)
Graduate School of Arts and Sciences
Robin Kanarek, Dean
Programs in:
 analytical chemistry • MS, PhD
 applied developmental psychology • PhD
 art history • MA
 arts and sciences • MA, MAT, MFA, MPP, MS, PhD, CAGS, Certificate
 bioengineering • Certificate
 biology • MS, PhD
 bioorganic chemistry • MS, PhD
 biotechnology • Certificate
 biotechnology engineering • Certificate
 child development • MA, CAGS
 classical archaeology • MA
 classics • MA
 community development • MA
 community environmental studies • Certificate
 computer science • Certificate
 computer science minor • Certificate
 dance • MA, PhD
 drama • MA
 dramatic literature and criticism • PhD
 early childhood education • MAT
 economics • MA
 education • MA, MAT, CAGS
 elementary education • MAT
 English • MA, PhD
 environmental chemistry • MS, PhD
 environmental management • Certificate
 environmental policy • MA
 epidemiology • Certificate
 ethnomusicology • MA
 French • MA
 German • MA
 health and human welfare • MA
 history • MA, PhD
 housing policy • MA
 human-computer interaction • Certificate
 inorganic chemistry • MS, PhD
 international environment/development policy • MA
 management of community organizations • Certificate
 manufacturing engineering • Certificate
 mathematics • MA, MS, PhD
 microwave and wireless engineering • Certificate
 middle and secondary education • MA, MAT
 museum studies • Certificate
 music history and literature • MA
 music theory and composition • MA
 occupational therapy • Certificate
 organic chemistry • MS, PhD
 philosophy • MA
 physical chemistry • MS, PhD
 physics • MS, PhD
 program evaluation • Certificate
 psychology • MS, PhD
 public policy • MPP
 public policy and citizen participation • MA
 school psychology • MA, CAGS
 secondary education • MA
 studio art • MFA
 theater history • PhD

Sackler School of Graduate Biomedical Sciences
Naomi Rosenberg, Dean
Programs in:
 biochemistry • PhD
 biomedical sciences • MS, PhD
 cell, molecular and developmental biology • PhD
 cellular and molecular physiology • PhD
 genetics • PhD
 immunology • PhD
 molecular microbiology • PhD
 neuroscience • PhD
 pharmacology and experimental therapeutics • PhD

Division of Clinical Care Research
Dr. Harry P. Selker, Program Director
Program in:
 clinical care research • MS, PhD

School of Dental Medicine
Programs in:
 dental medicine • DMD, MS, Certificate
 dentistry • Certificate

School of Engineering
Vincent Manno, Associate Dean for Graduate Studies
Programs in:
 biomedical engineering • MS, PhD
 chemical and biochemical engineering • ME, MS, PhD
 civil engineering • ME, MS, PhD
 computer science • MS, PhD
 electrical engineering • MS, PhD
 engineering • ME, MS, MSEM, PhD
 environmental engineering • ME, MS, PhD
 human factors • MS
 mechanical engineering • ME, MS, PhD

The Gordon Institute
Arthur Winston, Director
Program in:
 engineering management • MSEM

School of Medicine
Dr. Michael Rosenblatt, Dean
Programs in:
 education and policy • MS
 health communication • MS
 medicine • MD, MPH, MS
 pain research • MS
 public health • MPH

School of Veterinary Medicine
Dr. Philip Kosch, Dean
Programs in:
 animals and public policy • MS
 comparative biomedical sciences • PhD
 veterinary medicine • DVM, MS, PhD

■ **UNIVERSITY OF MASSACHUSETTS AMHERST**
Amherst, MA 01003
http://www.umass.edu/

State-supported, coed, university. CGS member. *Enrollment:* 24,310 graduate, professional, and undergraduate students; 2,886 full-time matriculated graduate/professional students (1,433 women), 1,919 part-time matriculated graduate/professional students (1,029 women). *Graduate faculty:* 1,117 full-time (322 women). *Computer facilities:* 450 computers available on campus for general student use. A campuswide network can be accessed from student residence rooms and from off campus. Internet access and online class registration, on-line course and grade information are available. *Library facilities:* W. E. B. Du Bois Library plus 3 others. *Graduate expenses:* Tuition, state resident: full-time $1,320; part-time $110 per credit. Tuition, nonresident: full-time $4,969; part-time $414 per credit. Required fees: $2,626 per term. Tuition and fees vary according to course load. *General application contact:* Jean Ames, Supervisor of Admissions, 413-545-0721.

Find an in-depth description at www.petersons.com/gradchannel.

Graduate School
Dr. John Mullin, Dean
Programs in:
 interdisciplinary studies • MS, PhD
 neuroscience and behavior • MS, PhD
 organismic and evolutionary biology • MS, PhD
 plant biology • MS, PhD

College of Engineering
Dr. Joseph I. Goldstein, Dean
Programs in:
 chemical engineering • MS, PhD
 civil engineering • MS, PhD
 electrical and computer engineering • MS, PhD
 engineering • MS, PhD
 engineering management • MS
 environmental engineering • MS
 industrial engineering and operations research • MS, PhD
 manufacturing engineering • MS
 mechanical engineering • MS, PhD

Massachusetts

College of Humanities and Fine Arts
Dr. Lee Edwards, Dean
Programs in:
  Afro-American studies • MA, PhD
  ancient history • MA
  art • MA, MFA, MS
  art education • MA
  art history • MA
  British Empire history • MA
  Chinese • MA
  comparative literature • MA, PhD
  creative writing • MFA
  English and American literature • MA, PhD
  European (medieval and modern) history • MA, PhD
  French and Francophone studies • MA, MAT
  Germanic languages and literatures • MA, PhD
  Hispanic literatures and linguistics • MA, MAT, PhD
  humanities and fine arts • MA, MAT, MFA, MM, MS, PhD
  interior design • MS
  Islamic history • MA
  Italian studies • MAT
  Japanese • MA
  Latin American history • MA, PhD
  Latin and classical humanities • MAT
  linguistics • MA, PhD
  modern global history • MA
  music • MM, PhD
  philosophy • MA, PhD
  public history • MA
  science and technology history • MA
  studio art • MFA
  theater • MFA
  U.S. history • MA, PhD

College of Natural Resources and the Environment
Dr. Cleve Willis, Director
Programs in:
  entomology • MS, PhD
  food science • MS, PhD
  forestry and wood technology • MS, PhD
  landscape architecture • MLA
  mammalian and avian biology • MS, PhD
  microbiology • MS, PhD
  natural resources and the environment • MLA, MRP, MS, PhD
  plant science • PhD
  regional planning • MRP, PhD
  resource economics • MS, PhD
  soil science • MS, PhD
  wildlife and fisheries conservation • MS, PhD

College of Natural Sciences and Mathematics
Dr. Leon Osterweil, Dean
Programs in:
  applied mathematics • MS
  astronomy • MS, PhD
  biochemistry • MS, PhD
  biological chemistry • PhD
  biology • MA, MS, PhD
  cell and developmental biology • PhD
  chemistry • MS, PhD
  computer science • MS, PhD
  education for engineering and applied science • MS
  geography • MS
  geosciences • MS, PhD
  mathematics and statistics • MS, PhD
  natural sciences and mathematics • MA, MS, PhD
  physics • MS, PhD
  polymer science and engineering • MS, PhD

College of Social and Behavioral Sciences
Dr. Janet Rifkin, Dean
Programs in:
  anthropology • MA, PhD
  clinical psychology • MS, PhD
  communication • MA, PhD
  economics • MA, PhD
  labor studies • MS
  political science • MA, PhD
  public policy and administration • MPA
  social and behavioral sciences • MA, MPA, MS, PhD
  sociology • MA, PhD

Isenberg School of Management
Programs in:
  accounting • MS, PhD
  business administration • PMBA
  hotel, restaurant, and travel administration • MS
  management • MBA, MS, PMBA, PhD
  sport management • MS, PhD

School of Education
Dr. Andrew Effrat, Dean
Programs in:
  cultural diversity and curriculum reform • M Ed, Ed D, CAGS
  early childhood education and development • M Ed, Ed D, CAGS
  education • M Ed, Ed D, PhD, CAGS
  educational administration • M Ed, Ed D, CAGS
  elementary teacher education • M Ed, Ed D, CAGS
  higher education • M Ed, Ed D, CAGS
  international education • M Ed, Ed D, CAGS
  mathematics, science, and instructional technology • M Ed, Ed D, CAGS
  physical education teacher education • M Ed, Ed D, CAGS
  reading and writing • M Ed, Ed D, CAGS
  research and evaluation methods • M Ed, Ed D, CAGS
  school psychology • PhD
  school psychology and school counseling • M Ed, Ed D, CAGS
  science education • Ed D
  secondary teacher education • M Ed, Ed D, CAGS
  social justice education • M Ed, Ed D, CAGS
  special education • M Ed, Ed D, CAGS

School of Nursing
Dr. Eileen T. Breslin, Dean
Program in:
  nursing • MS, PhD

School of Public Health and Health Sciences
Dr. Eileen T. Breslin, Dean
Programs in:
  communication disorders • MA, PhD
  exercise science • MS, PhD
  nutrition • MS
  public health • MPH, MS, PhD
  public health and health sciences • MA, MPH, MS, PhD

■ UNIVERSITY OF MASSACHUSETTS BOSTON
Boston, MA 02125-3393
http://www.umb.edu/

State-supported, coed, university. CGS member. *Enrollment:* 12,394 graduate, professional, and undergraduate students; 690 full-time matriculated graduate/professional students (474 women), 1,416 part-time matriculated graduate/professional students (943 women). *Graduate faculty:* 448 full-time (172 women). *Computer facilities:* Computer purchase and lease plans are available. 260 computers available on campus for general student use. A campuswide network can be accessed from off campus. Internet access and online class registration are available. *Library facilities:* Joseph P. Healey Library. *Graduate expenses:* Tuition, state resident: full-time $4,461. Tuition, nonresident: full-time $9,390. *General application contact:* Peggy Roldan, Graduate Admissions Coordinator, 617-287-6400.

Find an in-depth description at www.petersons.com/gradchannel.

Office of Graduate Studies and Research
Dr. Emily McDermott, Dean of Graduate Studies
Programs in:
  gerontology • MA, MS, PhD, Certificate

Peterson's Graduate Schools in the U.S. 2006

Massachusetts

University of Massachusetts Boston (continued)
- gerontology research • MA
- management in aging services • MA
- public affairs • MS
- public policy • PhD
- women in politics and government • Certificate

College of Liberal Arts
Programs in:
- American studies • MA
- applied sociology • MA
- archival methods • MA
- bilingual education • MA
- clinical psychology • PhD
- English • MA
- English as a second language • MA
- foreign language pedagogy • MA
- historical archaeology • MA
- history • MA
- liberal arts • MA, PhD

College of Management
Dr. Philip Quaglieri, Dean
Programs in:
- business administration • MBA
- management • MBA

College of Nursing and Health Sciences
Dr. Kristine Alster, Acting Dean
Program in:
- nursing • MS, PhD

College of Public and Community Service
Connie Chan, Dean of Graduate Studies
Programs in:
- dispute resolution • MA, Certificate
- human services • MS
- public and community service • MA, MS, Certificate

College of Science and Mathematics
Dr. Christine Armett-Kibel, Dean
Programs in:
- applied physics • MS
- biology • MS
- biotechnology and biomedical science • MS
- chemistry • MS
- computer science • MS, PhD
- environmental biology • PhD
- environmental sciences • MS
- environmental, coastal and ocean sciences • PhD
- molecular, cellular, and organismal biology • PhD
- science and mathematics • MS, PhD

Division of Continuing Education
Dr. Dirk Messelaar, Head
Programs in:
- continuing education • Certificate
- women in politics and government • Certificate

Graduate College of Education
Lester Goodchild, Head
Programs in:
- counseling • M Ed, CAGS
- critical and creative thinking • MA, Certificate
- education • M Ed, Ed D
- educational administration • M Ed, CAGS
- elementary and secondary education/certification • M Ed
- family therapy • M Ed, CAGS
- forensic counseling • M Ed, CAGS
- higher education administration • Ed D
- instructional design • M Ed
- mental health counseling • M Ed, CAGS
- rehabilitation counseling • M Ed, CAGS
- school guidance counseling • M Ed, CAGS
- school psychology • M Ed, CAGS
- special education • M Ed
- teacher certification • M Ed
- urban school leadership • Ed D

■ UNIVERSITY OF MASSACHUSETTS DARTMOUTH
North Dartmouth, MA 02747-2300
http://www.umassd.edu/

State-supported, coed, comprehensive institution. *Enrollment:* 8,284 graduate, professional, and undergraduate students; 290 full-time matriculated graduate/professional students (127 women), 406 part-time matriculated graduate/professional students (227 women). *Graduate faculty:* 229 full-time (78 women), 69 part-time/adjunct (34 women). *Computer facilities:* Computer purchase and lease plans are available. 368 computers available on campus for general student use. A campuswide network can be accessed from student residence rooms and from off campus. Internet access and online class registration are available. *Library facilities:* University of Massachusetts Dartmouth Library. *Graduate expenses:* Tuition, state resident: full-time $2,071; part-time $86 per credit. Tuition, nonresident: full-time $8,099; part-time $337 per credit. Required fees: $248 per credit. One-time fee: $50 full-time. Part-time tuition and fees vary according to course load and program. *General application contact:* Carol Novo, Graduate Admissions Officer, 508-999-8604.

Find an in-depth description at www.petersons.com/gradchannel.

Graduate School
Dr. Richard J. Panofsky, Associate Vice Chancellor for Academic Affairs/Graduate Studies
Program in:
- biomedical engineering/biotechnology • PhD

Charlton College of Business
Dr. Raymond Jackson, Interim Dean
Programs in:
- accounting • Certificate
- business • MBA, Certificate
- business administration • MBA
- management • Certificate

College of Arts and Sciences
Dr. Michael Steinman, Dean
Programs in:
- arts and sciences • MA, MAT, MS, Certificate
- biology • MS
- chemistry • MS
- clinical psychology • MA
- general psychology • MA
- marine biology • MS
- professional writing • MA
- teaching • MAT, Certificate

College of Engineering
Dr. Farhad Azadivar, Dean
Programs in:
- computer engineering • MS, Certificate
- computer science • MS, Certificate
- electrical engineering • MS, PhD, Certificate
- engineering • MS, PhD, Certificate
- mechanical engineering • MS
- physics • MS
- textile chemistry • MS
- textile technology • MS

College of Nursing
Dr. Nancy Dluhy, Interim Dean
Program in:
- nursing • MS, Certificate, PMC

College of Visual and Performing Arts
Dr. John C. Laughton, Dean
Programs in:
- art education • MAE
- artisanry • MFA, Certificate
- fine arts • MFA
- visual and performing arts • MAE, MFA, Certificate
- visual design • MFA

School of Marine Science and Technology
Dr. Brian Rothschild, Director
Program in:
- marine science and technology • MS, PhD

Massachusetts

■ UNIVERSITY OF MASSACHUSETTS LOWELL
Lowell, MA 01854-2881
http://www.uml.edu/

State-supported, coed, university. CGS member. *Computer facilities:* 4,000 computers available on campus for general student use. A campuswide network can be accessed from student residence rooms and from off campus. *Library facilities:* O'Leary Library plus 2 others. *General application contact:* 978-934-2380.

Find an in-depth description at www.petersons.com/gradchannel.

Graduate School

College of Arts and Sciences
Programs in:
 applied mathematics • MS
 applied mechanics • PhD
 applied physics • MS, PhD
 arts and sciences • MA, MM, MMS, MS, MS Eng, PhD, Sc D
 biochemistry • PhD
 biological sciences • MS
 biotechnology • MS
 chemistry • MS, PhD
 community and social psychology • MA
 computational mathematics • PhD
 computer science • MS, PhD, Sc D
 criminal justice • MA
 energy engineering • PhD
 environmental studies • PhD
 mathematics • MS
 music education • MM
 music theory • MM
 performance • MM
 physics • MS, PhD
 polymer sciences • MS, PhD
 radiological sciences and protection • MS, PhD
 regional economic and social development • MS
 sound recording technology • MMS

College of Health Professions
Programs in:
 administration of nursing services • PhD
 adult psychiatric nursing • MS
 advanced practice • MS
 clinical laboratory studies • MS
 family and community health nursing • MS
 gerontological nursing • MS
 health professions • MS, PhD
 health promotion • PhD
 health services administration • MS
 occupational health nursing • MS
 physical therapy • MS

College of Management
Programs in:
 business administration • MBA
 management • MBA, MMS
 manufacturing management • MMS

Graduate School of Education
Dr. Donald E. Pierson, Dean
Programs in:
 administration, planning, and policy • CAGS
 curriculum and instruction • M Ed, CAGS
 educational administration • M Ed
 language arts and literacy • Ed D
 leadership in schooling • Ed D
 math and science education • Ed D
 reading and language • M Ed, CAGS

James B. Francis College of Engineering
Programs in:
 chemical engineering • MS Eng
 chemistry • PhD
 civil engineering • MS Eng
 cleaner production and pollution prevention • MS, Sc D
 computer engineering • MS Eng
 electrical engineering • MS Eng, D Eng
 energy engineering • MS Eng
 engineering • MS, MS Eng, D Eng, PhD, Sc D, Certificate
 environmental risk assessment • Certificate
 environmental studies • MS Eng
 identification and control of ergonomic hazards • Certificate
 industrial hygiene • MS, Sc D
 job stress and healthy job redesign • Certificate
 manufacturing • Certificate
 mechanical engineering • MS Eng, D Eng
 occupational epidemiology • MS, Sc D
 occupational ergonomics • MS, Sc D
 plastics engineering • MS Eng, D Eng
 radiological health physics and general work environment protection • Certificate
 work environmental policy • MS, Sc D

■ WESTERN NEW ENGLAND COLLEGE
Springfield, MA 01119-2654
http://www.wnec.edu/

Independent, coed, comprehensive institution. *Enrollment:* 4,448 graduate, professional, and undergraduate students; 364 full-time matriculated graduate/professional students (167 women), 916 part-time matriculated graduate/professional students (322 women). *Graduate faculty:* 61 full-time (16 women), 80 part-time/adjunct (23 women). *Computer facilities:* 489 computers available on campus for general student use. A campuswide network can be accessed from student residence rooms and from off campus. Internet access is available. *Library facilities:* D'Amour Library plus 1 other. *Graduate expenses:* Tuition: part-time $400 per credit. Part-time tuition and fees vary according to program. *General application contact:* Douglas Kenyon, Director of Continuing Education, 413-782-1249.

School of Arts and Sciences
Dr. Saeed Ghahramani, Dean
Programs in:
 arts and sciences • M Ed, MAET, MAMT, MSCJA
 criminal justice administration • MSCJA
 elementary education • M Ed
 English for teachers • MAET
 mathematics for teachers • MAMT

School of Business
Dr. Stanley Kowalski, Dean
Programs in:
 accounting • MBA, MSA
 business • MBA, MSA
 business administration (general) • MBA
 finance • MBA
 human resources • MBA
 management information systems • MBA
 marketing • MBA

School of Engineering
Dr. Carl E. Rathmann, Dean
Programs in:
 computer and engineering information systems • MSEE
 computer engineering • MSEE
 engineering • MSEE, MSEM, MSME
 mechanical engineering • MSME
 production management • MSEM

School of Law
Dr. Arthur R. Gaudio, Dean
Program in:
 law • JD

■ WESTFIELD STATE COLLEGE
Westfield, MA 01086
http://www.wsc.ma.edu/

State-supported, coed, comprehensive institution. *Enrollment:* 4,938 graduate, professional, and undergraduate students; 310 matriculated graduate/professional students. *Graduate faculty:* 21 full-time (9 women), 29 part-time/adjunct (10 women). *Computer facilities:* 238 computers available on campus for general student use. A campuswide network can be accessed from student residence

Peterson's Graduate Schools in the U.S. 2006

Massachusetts

Westfield State College (continued)
rooms and from off campus. Internet access and online class registration, on-line transcripts, grade reports, billing information are available. *Library facilities:* Ely Library. *Graduate expenses:* Tuition, state resident: part-time $155 per credit. Tuition, nonresident: part-time $165 per credit. *General application contact:* Russ Leary, Admissions Clerk, 413-572-8022.

Division of Graduate Studies and Continuing Education
Dr. Catherine Lilly, Dean
Programs in:
 counseling/clinical psychology • MA
 criminal justice • MS
 early childhood education • M Ed
 elementary education • M Ed
 English • MA
 history • M Ed
 intensive special needs education • M Ed
 mental health counseling/psychology • MA
 middle school education • M Ed
 occupational education • M Ed
 physical education • M Ed
 reading • M Ed
 school administration • M Ed, CAGS
 secondary education • M Ed
 special education • M Ed
 special needs education • CME
 technology for educators • M Ed

■ WHEELOCK COLLEGE
Boston, MA 02215
http://www.wheelock.edu/

Independent, coed, primarily women, comprehensive institution. *Computer facilities:* 120 computers available on campus for general student use. A campuswide network can be accessed from student residence rooms and from off campus. Internet access is available. *Library facilities:* Wheelock College Library. *General application contact:* Director of Graduate Admissions, 617-879-2178.

Graduate School
Program in:
 education • MS, MSW

Division of Arts and Sciences
Program in:
 human development • MS

Division of Child and Family Studies
Programs in:
 family studies • MS
 family support and parent education • MS
 family, culture, and society • MS

Division of Education
Programs in:
 early childhood education • MS
 education leadership • MS
 elementary education • MS
 language, literacy, and reading • MS
 teaching students with moderate disabilities • MS

Division of Social Work
Program in:
 social work • MSW

■ WORCESTER POLYTECHNIC INSTITUTE
Worcester, MA 01609-2280
http://www.wpi.edu/

Independent, coed, university. CGS member. *Enrollment:* 3,789 graduate, professional, and undergraduate students; 423 full-time matriculated graduate/professional students (124 women), 390 part-time matriculated graduate/professional students (90 women). *Graduate faculty:* 201 full-time (31 women), 44 part-time/adjunct (6 women). *Computer facilities:* 1,000 computers available on campus for general student use. A campuswide network can be accessed from student residence rooms and from off campus. Internet access and online class registration are available. *Library facilities:* Gordon Library. *Graduate expenses:* Tuition: part-time $897 per credit. *General application contact:* Michelle Briddon, Administrative Assistant, 508-831-5301.

Find an in-depth description at www.petersons.com/gradchannel.

Graduate Studies and Enrollment
Jeanne M. Gosselin, Director
Programs in:
 applied mathematics • MS
 applied statistics • MS
 biochemistry • MS, PhD
 biology and biotechnology • MS, PhD
 biomedical engineering • M Eng, MS, PhD, Certificate
 chemical engineering • MS, PhD
 chemistry • MS, PhD
 civil and environmental engineering • M Eng, MS, PhD, Advanced Certificate, Certificate
 clinical engineering • M Eng
 computer science • MS, PhD, Advanced Certificate, Certificate
 electrical and computer engineering • MS, PhD, Advanced Certificate, Certificate
 engineering • M Eng, MBA, MME, MS, PhD, Advanced Certificate, Certificate
 financial mathematics • MS
 fire protection engineering • MS, PhD, Advanced Certificate, Certificate
 industrial mathematics • MS
 interdisciplinary studies • MS, PhD
 management • MBA, Certificate
 manufacturing engineering • MS, PhD, Certificate
 marketing and technological innovation • MS
 materials science and engineering • MS, PhD, Certificate
 mathematical science • PhD, Certificate
 mathematics • MME
 mechanical engineering • M Eng, MS, PhD, Advanced Certificate
 operations and information technology • MS
 physics • MS, PhD
 power systems engineering • MS, PhD

■ WORCESTER STATE COLLEGE
Worcester, MA 01602-2597
http://www.worcester.edu/

State-supported, coed, comprehensive institution. *Enrollment:* 5,470 graduate, professional, and undergraduate students; 72 full-time matriculated graduate/professional students (63 women), 733 part-time matriculated graduate/professional students (548 women). *Computer facilities:* 250 computers available on campus for general student use. A campuswide network can be accessed from student residence rooms. Internet access is available. *Library facilities:* Learning Resources Center. *Graduate expenses:* Tuition, nonresident: part-time $150 per credit. Required fees: $1,170; $65 per credit. *General application contact:* Nicole Brown, Assistant Dean of Graduate and Continuing Education, 508-929-8787.

Graduate Studies
Dr. William H. White, Dean of Graduate Studies and Continuing Education
Programs in:
 biotechnology • MS
 community health nursing • MS
 early childhood education • M Ed
 elementary education • M Ed
 English • M Ed
 health care administration • MS
 health education • M Ed
 history • M Ed

Michigan

leadership and administration • M Ed
middle school education • M Ed
non-profit management • MS
occupational therapy • MOT
reading • M Ed
secondary education • M Ed
speech-language pathology • MS
teacher education • M Ed
teacher education in history • M Ed

Michigan

■ ANDREWS UNIVERSITY
Berrien Springs, MI 49104
http://www.andrews.edu/

Independent-religious, coed, university. CGS member. *Enrollment:* 2,995 graduate, professional, and undergraduate students; 549 full-time matriculated graduate/professional students (186 women), 596 part-time matriculated graduate/professional students (200 women). *Graduate faculty:* 162 full-time (49 women), 20 part-time/adjunct (13 women). *Computer facilities:* Computer purchase and lease plans are available. 130 computers available on campus for general student use. A campuswide network can be accessed from student residence rooms and from off campus. Internet access is available. *Library facilities:* James White Library plus 2 others. *Graduate expenses:* Tuition: full-time $15,230; part-time $620 per credit. Required fees: $350. *General application contact:* Carolyn Hurst, Supervisor of Graduate Admission, 800-253-2874.

School of Graduate Studies
Dr. Lyndon G. Furst, Dean
Program in:
 architecture • M Arch

College of Arts and Sciences
Dr. William Richardson, Dean
Programs in:
 allied health • MSMT
 arts and sciences • M Mus, MA, MAT, MS, MSA, MSMT, MSW, DPT, Dr Sc PT
 biology • MAT, MS
 communication • MA
 community services management • MSA
 English • MA, MAT
 history • MA, MAT
 international development • MSA
 mathematics and physical science • MS
 modern languages • MAT
 music • M Mus, MA
 nursing • MS
 nutrition • MS
 physical therapy • DPT, Dr Sc PT
 social work • MSW

College of Technology
Dr. Verlya Benson, Head
Programs in:
 software engineering • MS
 technology • MS

School of Business
Dr. Ann Gibson, Dean
Programs in:
 business • MBA, MSA
 management and marketing • MBA, MSA

School of Education
Dr. James R. Jeffery, Dean
Programs in:
 community counseling • MA
 counseling psychology • PhD
 curriculum and instruction • MA, Ed D, PhD, Ed S
 education • MA, MAT, MS, Ed D, PhD, Ed S
 educational administration and leadership • MA, Ed D, PhD, Ed S
 educational and developmental psychology • MA, Ed D, PhD
 educational psychology • Ed D, PhD
 elementary education • MAT
 leadership • Ed D, PhD
 reading • MA
 school counseling • MA
 school psychology • Ed S
 secondary education • MAT
 special education • MS
 special education/learning disabilities • MS
 teacher education • MAT

Seventh-day Adventist Theological Seminary
Dr. John K. McVay, Dean
Programs in:
 ministry • M Div, D Min
 pastoral ministry • MA
 religious education • MA, Ed D, PhD, Ed S
 theology • M Th, Th D

■ AQUINAS COLLEGE
Grand Rapids, MI 49506-1799
http://www.aquinas.edu/

Independent-religious, coed, comprehensive institution. *Enrollment:* 2,338 graduate, professional, and undergraduate students; 175 full-time matriculated graduate/professional students (120 women), 335 part-time matriculated graduate/professional students (235 women). *Graduate faculty:* 35 full-time (21 women), 41 part-time/adjunct (25 women). *Computer facilities:* 176 computers available on campus for general student use. A campuswide network can be accessed from student residence rooms and from off campus. Internet access is available. *Library facilities:* Woodhouse Library. *Graduate expenses:* Tuition: part-time $386 per credit. *General application contact:* Lynn Atkins-Rykert, Executive Assistant, School of Management, 616-632-2924 Ext. 8000.

Graduate School of Management
Cynthia VanGelderen, Dean
Program in:
 management • M Mgt

School of Education
Dr. V. James Garofalo, Dean
Program in:
 education • MAT, ME, MS

■ CENTRAL MICHIGAN UNIVERSITY
Mount Pleasant, MI 48859
http://www.cmich.edu/

State-supported, coed, university. CGS member. *Enrollment:* 27,758 graduate, professional, and undergraduate students; 974 full-time matriculated graduate/professional students (602 women), 6,994 part-time matriculated graduate/professional students (4,290 women). *Graduate faculty:* 705 full-time (247 women). *Computer facilities:* Computer purchase and lease plans are available. 1,585 computers available on campus for general student use. A campuswide network can be accessed from student residence rooms and from off campus. Internet access and online class registration are available. *Library facilities:* Park Library plus 1 other. *Graduate expenses:* Tuition, state resident: part-time $200 per credit hour. Tuition, nonresident: part-time $397 per credit hour. *General application contact:* Judith Prince, Director of Graduate Admissions, 989-774-1059.

Find an in-depth description at www.petersons.com/gradchannel.

College of Extended Learning
Dr. D. Terry Rawls, Interim Dean
Programs in:
 audiology • Au D
 educational administration • MA
 educational technology • MA
 extended learning • MA, MSA, Au D, DHA, Certificate
 general administration • MSA
 health administration • DHA
 health services administration • MSA, Certificate
 hospitality and tourism • MSA, Certificate
 human resources administration • MSA, Certificate
 humanities • MA

Michigan

Central Michigan University (continued)
  information resource management • MSA, Certificate
  international administration • MSA, Certificate
  leadership • MSA, Certificate
  public administration • MSA, Certificate
  school principalship • MA
  software engineering administration • MSA, Certificate
  vehicle design and manufacturing administration • MSA, Certificate

College of Graduate Studies
Dr. James Hageman, Dean

College of Business Administration
Dr. John Schleede, Dean
Programs in:
  accounting • MBA
  business administration • MA, MBA, MBE, MS
  business education • MBE
  economics • MA
  finance and law • MBA
  information systems • MS
  management • MBA
  marketing and hospitality services administration • MBA

College of Communication and Fine Arts
Dr. Sue Ann Martin, Dean
Programs in:
  art • MA, MFA
  broadcast and cinematic arts • MA
  communication and fine arts • MA, MFA, MM
  interpersonal and public communication • MA
  music education and supervision • MM
  music performance • MM
  oral interpretation • MA
  theatre • MA

College of Education and Human Services
Dr. Karen Adams, Dean
Programs in:
  community leadership • MA
  counseling • MA
  education and human services • MA, MS, Ed D, Ed S
  educational administration • MA, Ed S
  educational leadership • Ed D
  educational technology • MA
  elementary education • MA
  human development and family studies • MA
  library, media, and technology • MA
  middle level education • MA
  nutrition and dietetics • MS
  professional counseling • MA
  reading improvement • MA
  recreation and park administration • MA
  school guidance personnel • MA
  school principalship • MA
  secondary education • MA
  special education • MA
  teaching senior high • MA
  therapeutic recreation • MA

College of Health Professions
Dr. Marvis Lary, Dean
Programs in:
  athletic administration • MA
  audiology • Au D
  coaching • MA
  exercise science • MA
  health professions • MA, MS, Au D, DPT
  health promotion and program management • MA
  physical therapy • DPT
  physician assistant • MS
  speech and language pathology • MA
  sport administration • MA
  teaching • MA

College of Humanities and Social and Behavioral Sciences
Dr. Gary Shapiro, Dean
Programs in:
  applied experimental psychology • PhD
  clinical psychology • PhD
  composition and communication • MA
  creative writing • MA
  English language and literature • MA
  general, applied, and experimental psychology • MS, PhD
  general/experimental psychology • MS
  history • MA, PhD
  humanities and social and behavioral sciences • MA, MPA, MS, PhD, S Psy S
  industrial/organizational psychology • MA, PhD
  political science • MA
  public administration • MPA
  public management • MPA
  school psychology • PhD, S Psy S
  social and criminal justice • MA
  sociology • MA
  Spanish • MA
  state and local government • MPA
  teaching English to speakers of other languages • MA

College of Science and Technology
Dr. Robert E. Kohrman, Dean
Programs in:
  biology • MS
  chemistry • MS
  computer science • MS
  conservation biology • MS
  industrial education • MA
  industrial management and technology • MA
  mathematics • MA, MAT, PhD
  physics • MS
  science and technology • MA, MAT, MS, PhD
  teaching chemistry • MA

Interdisciplinary Programs
Programs in:
  general administration • MSA
  health service administration • MSA
  hospitality and tourism administration • MSA
  human resource administration • MSA
  humanities • MA
  information resource administration • MSA
  interdisciplinary studies • MA, MSA
  international administration • MSA
  leadership • MSA
  organizational communications • MSA
  public administration • MSA
  recreation and park administration • MSA
  software engineering • MSA
  sports administration • MSA

■ CORNERSTONE UNIVERSITY
Grand Rapids, MI 49525-5897
http://www.cornerstone.edu/

Independent-religious, coed, comprehensive institution. *Computer facilities:* 531 computers available on campus for general student use. A campuswide network can be accessed from student residence rooms and from off campus. Internet access is available. *Library facilities:* Miller Library. *General application contact:* Graduate Admissions Representative, 616-222-1442.

Grand Rapids Theological Seminary
Programs in:
  chaplaincy ministries • M Div
  counseling ministries • M Div, MA
  educational ministries • M Div, MA
  historical theology • MA, Th M
  intercultural ministries • MA
  intercultural studies • M Div
  interdisciplinary studies • MA
  New Testament • MA, Th M
  Old Testament • MA, Th M
  pastoral ministries • M Div
  systematic theology • MA, Th M

■ EASTERN MICHIGAN UNIVERSITY
Ypsilanti, MI 48197
http://www.emich.edu/

State-supported, coed, comprehensive institution. CGS member. *Enrollment:* 24,129 graduate, professional, and undergraduate students; 5,750

Michigan

matriculated graduate/professional students (3,899 women). *Graduate faculty:* 678 full-time. *Computer facilities:* Computer purchase and lease plans are available. 1,500 computers available on campus for general student use. A campuswide network can be accessed from student residence rooms and from off campus. Internet access is available. *Library facilities:* Bruce T. Halle Library. *Graduate expenses:* Tuition, state resident: full-time $4,324. Tuition, nonresident: full-time $8,769. Required fees: $496. Tuition and fees vary according to course level. *General application contact:* Mary Ann Shichtman, Associate Director of Admissions, 734-487-3400.

Find an in-depth description at www.petersons.com/gradchannel.

Graduate School
Dr. Robert Holkeboer, Associate Vice President for Research and Graduate Studies

College of Arts and Sciences
Dr. Linda Pritchard, Dean
Programs in:
applied economics • MA
art • MA
art education • MA
arts administration • MA
arts and sciences • M Math, MA, MFA, MLS, MPA, MS, PhD
biology • MS
chemistry • MS
children's literature • MA
clinical psychology • PhD
clinical/behavioral services • MS, PhD
communication • MA
computer science • M Math
criminology and criminal justice • MA
development, trade and planning • MA
drama/theatre for the young • MA, MFA
economics • MA
English • MA
English linguistics • MA
fine arts • MFA
foreign languages • MA
French • MA
general psychology • MS
general science • MS
geography • MA, MS
German • MA
historic preservation • MS
history • MA
interpretation/performance studies • MA
language and international trade • MA
literature • MA
mathematics education • M Math
music • MA
physics • MS
physics education • MS
psychology • MS
public administration • MPA
social science • MA, MLS
social science and American culture • MLS
sociology • MA
Spanish • MA
Spanish (bilingual-bicultural education) • MA
statistics • M Math
studio art • MA
teaching English to speakers of other languages • MA
theatre arts • MA
women's studies • MLS
written communication • MA

College of Business
Dr. P. Nick Blanchard, Interim Dean
Programs in:
accounting • MSA
accounting and taxation • MBA
accounting, financial, and operational control • MBA
business • MBA, MSA, MSHROD, MSIS
business administration • MBA
computer information systems • MBA
computer-based information systems • MSIS
finance • MBA
human resources management and organizational development • MSHROD
international business • MBA
management of human resources • MBA
management organizational development • MBA
marketing • MBA
production and operations management • MBA
strategic quality management • MBA

College of Education
Dr. Jerry Robbins, Dean
Programs in:
advanced counseling • MA
community counseling • MA
curriculum and instruction • MA
early childhood education • MA
education • MA, MS, Ed D, Sp Ed
educational leadership • MA, Ed D, Sp Ed
educational psychology • MA
elementary education • MA
guidance and counseling • MA, Sp Ed
K–12 curriculum • MA
middle school education • MA
physical education • MS
reading • MA
school counseling • MA, Sp Ed
secondary curriculum • MA
secondary school teaching • MA
social foundations of education • MA
special education • MA, Sp Ed
speech and language pathology • MA

College of Health and Human Services
Dr. Polly Buchanan, Interim Dean
Programs in:
health and human services • MOT, MS, MSN, MSW
human, environmental, and consumer resources • MS
nursing education • MSN
occupational therapy • MOT, MS
social work • MSW

College of Technology
Dr. John Dugger, Dean
Programs in:
business education • MBE
industrial technology • MS
liberal studies in technology • MLS
polymer technology • MS
technology • MA, MBE, MLS, MS
technology education • MA

■ FERRIS STATE UNIVERSITY
Big Rapids, MI 49307
http://www.ferris.edu/

State-supported, coed, comprehensive institution. *Enrollment:* 11,821 graduate, professional, and undergraduate students; 661 full-time matriculated graduate/professional students (393 women), 332 part-time matriculated graduate/professional students (183 women). *Graduate faculty:* 77 full-time (33 women), 110 part-time/adjunct (47 women). *Computer facilities:* 1,610 computers available on campus for general student use. A campuswide network can be accessed from student residence rooms and from off campus. Internet access and online class registration are available. *Library facilities:* Ferris Library for Information, Technology and Education. *Graduate expenses:* Tuition, state resident: full-time $11,400; part-time $5,700 per semester. Tuition, nonresident: full-time $22,800; part-time $11,400 per semester. *General application contact:* Craig Westman, Associate Dean Enrollment Services/Director Admissions and Records, 231-591-2100.

College of Business
Dr. Bill Boras, Department Chair
Programs in:
application development • MSISM
database administration • MSISM
e-business • MSISM
information systems • MBA
networking • MSISM
quality management • MBA
security • MSISM

Michigan

Ferris State University (continued)

College of Education and Human Services
Michelle Johnston, Dean
Program in:
  education and human services • M Ed, MS, MSCTE

School of Criminal Justice
Dr. Frank Crowe, Director
Program in:
  criminal justice administration • MS

School of Education
Dr. Susanne Chandler, Director
Programs in:
  administration • MSCTE
  curriculum and instruction • M Ed
  education technology • MSCTE
  instructor • MSCTE
  post-secondary administration • MSCTE
  training and development • MSCTE

College of Pharmacy
Dr. Ian Mathison, Dean
Program in:
  pharmacy • Pharm D

Michigan College of Optometry
Dr. Kevin L. Alexander, Dean
Program in:
  optometry • OD

■ GRAND RAPIDS THEOLOGICAL SEMINARY OF CORNERSTONE UNIVERSITY
Grand Rapids, MI 49525-5897
http://grts.cornerstone.edu/

Independent-religious, coed, graduate-only institution. *Graduate faculty:* 11 full-time (1 woman), 4 part-time/adjunct (0 women). *Computer facilities:* A campuswide network can be accessed from student residence rooms and from off campus. Internet access and online class registration are available. *Library facilities:* Miller Library. *Graduate expenses:* Tuition: part-time $326 per credit hour. *General application contact:* Dallas Lenear, Director of Admissions, 616-222-1422 Ext. 1559.

Graduate Programs
Dr. Robert W. Nienhuis, Executive Vice President
Programs in:
  biblical counseling • MA
  chaplaincy • M Div
  Christian education • M Div, MA
  intercultural studies • MA
  missions • M Div
  New Testament • MA, Th M
  Old Testament • MA, Th M
  pastoral studies • M Div
  systematic theology • MA
  theology • Th M

■ GRAND VALLEY STATE UNIVERSITY
Allendale, MI 49401-9403
http://www.gvsu.edu/

State-supported, coed, comprehensive institution. CGS member. *Enrollment:* 21,429 graduate, professional, and undergraduate students; 587 full-time matriculated graduate/professional students, 1,963 part-time matriculated graduate/professional students. *Graduate faculty:* 178 full-time, 82 part-time/adjunct. *Computer facilities:* 2,600 computers available on campus for general student use. A campuswide network can be accessed from student residence rooms and from off campus. Internet access and online class registration, transcript, degree audit, credit card payments, grades are available. *Library facilities:* James H. Zumberge Library plus 2 others. *Graduate expenses:* Tuition, state resident: part-time $272 per credit hour. Tuition, nonresident: part-time $586 per credit hour. *General application contact:* Tracey James-Heer, Associate Director for Graduate Recruitment, 616-331-2025.

Find an in-depth description at www.petersons.com/gradchannel.

College of Community and Public Service
Dr. Erika G. King, Dean
Program in:
  community and public service • MHA, MPA, MS

School of Criminal Justice
Dr. Terry L. Fisk, Director
Program in:
  criminal justice • MS

School of Public and Nonprofit Administration
Dr. Danny L. Balfour, Director
Program in:
  public and nonprofit administration • MHA, MPA

College of Education
Dr. Elaine C. Collins, Interim Dean
Programs in:
  adult and higher education • M Ed
  early childhood developmental delay • M Ed
  early childhood education • M Ed
  education • M Ed
  education of the gifted and talented • M Ed
  educational leadership • M Ed
  educational technology • M Ed
  elementary education • M Ed
  emotional impairment • M Ed
  learning disabilities • M Ed
  middle and high school education • M Ed
  reading/language arts • M Ed
  school counseling • M Ed
  special education administration • M Ed
  teaching English to speakers of other languages • M Ed

Division of Arts and Humanities
Jon Jellema, Dean
Program in:
  arts and humanities • MS

School of Communications
Dr. Alex Nesterenko, Director
Program in:
  communications • MS

Russell B. Kirkhof School of Nursing
Dr. Phyllis Gendler, Dean
Programs in:
  advanced practice • MSN
  case management • MSN
  nursing administration • MSN
  nursing education • MSN

School of Social Work
Dr. Rodney Mulder, Dean
Program in:
  social work • MSW

Science and Mathematics Division
Dr. P. Douglas Kindschi, Dean
Programs in:
  health science • MS
  information systems • MS
  science and mathematics • MPAS, MS, MSE, MSOT, DPT
  software engineering • MS

College of Health Professions
Dr. Jane Toot, Dean
Programs in:
  health professions • MPAS, MS, MSOT, DPT
  occupational therapy • MSOT
  physical therapy • MS, DPT
  physician assistant studies • MPAS

Seymour and Esther Padnos School of Engineering
Dr. Hugh Jack, Director
Programs in:
  electrical and computer engineering • MSE
  manufacturing engineering • MSE
  manufacturing operations • MSE
  mechanical engineering • MSE

Michigan

Seidman College of Business
Dr. John Reifel, Dean
Programs in:
 accounting • MS Acct
 business • MBA, MS Acct, MST
 business administration • MBA
 taxation • MST

■ **LAWRENCE TECHNOLOGICAL UNIVERSITY**
Southfield, MI 48075-1058
http://www.ltu.edu/

Independent, coed, university. *Enrollment:* 4,241 graduate, professional, and undergraduate students; 19 full-time matriculated graduate/professional students (8 women), 1,264 part-time matriculated graduate/professional students (422 women). *Graduate faculty:* 43 full-time (13 women), 97 part-time/adjunct (15 women). *Computer facilities:* 60 computers available on campus for general student use. A campuswide network can be accessed from student residence rooms. Internet access and online class registration, degree audit, black board, SCT Banner (student information) are available. *Library facilities:* Lawrence Technological University Library plus 1 other. *Graduate expenses:* Tuition: part-time $526 per credit hour. *General application contact:* Jane Rohrback, Director of Admissions, 248-204-3160.

College of Architecture and Design
David Chasco, Interim Dean
Program in:
 architecture and design • M Arch

College of Arts and Sciences
Dr. James Rodgers, Dean
Programs in:
 computer science • MS
 science education • MSE
 technical communication • MS

College of Engineering
Dr. Laird Johnston, Dean
Programs in:
 automotive engineering • MAE
 civil engineering • MCE
 construction engineering management • MS
 electrical and computer engineering • MS
 manufacturing systems • MEMS, DE
 mechanical engineering • MS

College of Management
Dr. Lou DeGennaro, Dean
Programs in:

 business administration • MBA
 industrial operations • MS
 information systems • MS
 information technology • DM

■ **MADONNA UNIVERSITY**
Livonia, MI 48150-1173
http://www.munet.edu/

Independent-religious, coed, comprehensive institution. *Enrollment:* 4,276 graduate, professional, and undergraduate students; 682 matriculated graduate/professional students. *Graduate faculty:* 56 full-time, 27 part-time/adjunct. *Computer facilities:* 175 computers available on campus for general student use. A campuswide network can be accessed from student residence rooms and from off campus. Internet access is available. *Library facilities:* Madonna University Library. *Graduate expenses:* Tuition: part-time $350 per semester hour. *General application contact:* Sandra Kellums, Coordinator of Graduate Admissions, 734-432-5667.

Department of English
Dr. Andrew Domzalski, Director
Program in:
 teaching English to speakers of other languages • MATESOL

Department of Psychology
Dr. Robert Cohen, Chairperson
Program in:
 clinical psychology • MSCP

Program in Health Services
Dr. Ted Biermann, Dean
Program in:
 health services • MSHS

Program in Hospice
Dr. Kelly Rhoades, Director
Program in:
 hospice • MSH

Program in Nursing
Dr. Nancy O'Connor, Chairperson
Programs in:
 adult health: chronic health conditions • MSN
 adult nurse practitioner • MSN
 nursing administration • MSN

Programs in Education
Dr. Robert Kimball, Dean
Programs in:
 Catholic school leadership • MSA
 educational leadership • MSA
 learning disabilities • MAT
 literacy education • MAT
 teaching and learning • MAT

School of Business
Dr. Stuart Arends, Dean of Business School

Programs in:
 business administration • MBA
 international business • MSBA
 leadership studies • MSBA
 leadership studies in criminal justice • MSBA
 quality and operations management • MSBA

■ **MARYGROVE COLLEGE**
Detroit, MI 48221-2599
http://www.marygrove.edu/

Independent-religious, coed, primarily women, comprehensive institution. *Computer facilities:* Computer purchase and lease plans are available. 115 computers available on campus for general student use. A campuswide network can be accessed from student residence rooms. Internet access is available. *General application contact:* Director of Graduate Studies, 313-864-8000 Ext. 445.

Graduate Division
Programs in:
 educational leadership • MA
 pastoral ministry • MA

Education Unit
Programs in:
 adult learning • MA
 art of teaching • MAT
 griot • M Ed
 reading education • M Ed
 sage • M Ed

Human Resource Management Unit
Program in:
 human resource management • MA

■ **MICHIGAN STATE UNIVERSITY**
East Lansing, MI 48824
http://www.msu.edu/

State-supported, coed, university. CGS member. *Enrollment:* 44,542 graduate, professional, and undergraduate students; 6,846 full-time matriculated graduate/professional students (3,679 women), 2,843 part-time matriculated graduate/professional students (1,806 women). *Graduate faculty:* 1,925 full-time (564 women), 19 part-time/adjunct (4 women). *Computer facilities:* Computer purchase and lease plans are available. 2,000 computers available on campus for general student use. A campuswide network can be accessed from student residence rooms and from off campus. Internet access and online class registration are available. *Library facilities:* Main Library plus 14 others. *Graduate expenses:* Tuition, state resident: part-time

Peterson's Graduate Schools in the U.S. 2006

Michigan

Michigan State University (continued)
$291 per hour. Tuition, nonresident: part-time $589 per hour. *General application contact:* Dr. Karen Klomparens, Dean of the Graduate School, 517-355-0301.

Find an in-depth description at www.petersons.com/gradchannel.

College of Human Medicine
Dr. Glenn Craig Davis, Dean
Programs in:
  anatomy • MS
  biochemistry • MS, PhD
  bioethics, humanities, and society • MA
  epidemiology • MS, PhD
  human medicine • MD, MA, MS, PhD
  microbiology • MS, PhD
  pharmacology/toxicology • MS, PhD
  pharmacology/toxicology-environmental toxicology • PhD
  physiology • MS, PhD
  zoology • MS

College of Osteopathic Medicine
Dr. William D. Strampel, Dean
Program in:
  osteopathic medicine • DO, MS, PhD

Graduate Studies in Osteopathic Medicine
Dr. Veronica M. Maher, Associate Dean, Graduate Studies
Programs in:
  anatomy • MS, PhD
  biochemistry • MS, PhD
  microbiology • PhD
  pathology • MS, PhD
  pharmacology/toxicology • MS, PhD
  physiology • MS, PhD

College of Veterinary Medicine
Dr. Lonnie J. King, Dean
Programs in:
  comparative medicine and integrative biology • MS, PhD
  food safety • MS
  food safety and toxicology • MS
  industrial microbiology • PhD
  large animal clinical sciences • MS, PhD
  microbiology • MS, PhD
  microbiology and molecular genetics • MS, PhD
  pathobiology and diagnostic investigation • MS, PhD
  pathology • MS, PhD
  pharmacology/ toxicology • MS, PhD
  small animal clinical sciences • MS
  veterinary medicine • DVM, MS, PhD

Center for Integrative Toxicology
Dr. Lawrence J. Fischer, Director
Programs in:
  animal science • PhD
  biochemistry and molecular biology • PhD
  chemical engineering • PhD
  chemistry • PhD
  crop and soil sciences • PhD
  entomology • PhD
  environmental engineering • PhD
  environmental geosciences • PhD
  fisheries and wildlife • PhD
  food science • PhD
  forestry • PhD
  human nutrition • PhD
  microbiology • PhD
  pathology • PhD
  pharmacology and toxicology • PhD
  resource development • PhD
  zoology • PhD

Graduate School
Dr. Karen Klomparens, Dean of the Graduate School

College of Agriculture and Natural Resources
Dr. Jeffrey D. Armstrong, Dean
Programs in:
  agricultural economics • MS, PhD
  agricultural technology and systems management • MS, PhD
  agriculture and natural resources • MS, PhD
  animal science • MS, PhD
  animal science-environmental toxicology • PhD
  biosystems engineering • MS, PhD
  community, agriculture, recreation, and resource studies • MS, PhD
  construction management • MS
  crop and soil sciences • MS, PhD
  crop and soil sciences-environmental toxicology • PhD
  entomology • MS, PhD
  entomology-environmental toxicology • PhD
  fisheries and wildlife • MS, PhD
  forestry • MS, PhD
  forestry-environmental toxicology • PhD
  horticulture • MS, PhD
  integrated pest management • MS
  packaging • MS, PhD
  plant breeding and genetics • MS, PhD
  plant breeding and genetics-crop and soil sciences • MS, PhD
  plant breeding and genetics-forestry • MS, PhD
  plant breeding and genetics-horticulture • MS, PhD
  plant pathology • MS, PhD

College of Arts and Letters
Dr. Wendy K. Wilkins, Dean
Programs in:
  African-American and African studies • MA, PhD
  American studies • MA, PhD
  applied Spanish linguistics • MA
  arts and letters • M Mus, MA, MFA, DMA, PhD
  critical studies in the teaching of English • MA
  digital rhetoric and professional writing • MA
  English • PhD
  French • MA
  French language and literature • PhD
  German studies • MA
  Hispanic cultural studies • PhD
  Hispanic literatures • MA
  history • MA, PhD
  history-secondary school teaching • MA
  linguistics • MA, PhD
  literature in English • MA
  music • PhD
  music composition • M Mus, DMA
  music conducting • M Mus, DMA
  music education • M Mus
  music performance • M Mus, DMA
  music theory • M Mus
  music therapy • M Mus
  musicology • MA
  philosophy • MA, PhD
  piano pedagogy • M Mus
  rhetoric and writing • PhD
  studio art • MFA
  teaching English to speakers of other languages • MA
  theatre • MA, MFA

College of Communication Arts and Sciences
Dr. Charles Salmon, Acting Dean
Programs in:
  advertising • MA
  audiology and speech sciences • MA, PhD
  communication • MA, PhD
  communication arts and sciences • PhD
  health communication • MA
  journalism • MA
  public relations • MA
  telecommunication • MA
  telecommunication, information studies, and media • MA

College of Education
Dr. Carole Ames, Dean
Programs in:
  counseling • MA
  curriculum and teaching • MA
  curriculum, teaching and education policy • PhD, Ed S
  education • MA, MS, PhD, Ed S
  educational policy • PhD
  educational technology • MA
  higher, adult and lifelong education • MA, PhD
  K-12 educational administration • MA, PhD, Ed S
  K-12 school and postsecondary leadership • MA
  kinesiology • MS, PhD

Michigan

learning, technology and culture • PhD
literacy education • MA
literacy instruction • MA
measurement and quantitative methods • MA, PhD
rehabilitation counseling • MA
rehabilitation counselor education • PhD
school psychology • PhD, Ed S
science and mathematics education • MA
special education • MA, PhD
student affairs administration • MA
teaching and learning with technology • MA
technology and learning • MA

College of Engineering
Dr. Janie Fouke, Dean
Programs in:
chemical engineering • MS, PhD
civil engineering • MS, PhD
computer science • MS, PhD
electrical engineering • MS, PhD
engineering • MS, PhD
engineering mechanics • MS, PhD
environmental engineering • MS, PhD
environmental engineering–environmental toxicology • PhD
materials science and engineering • MS, PhD
mechanical engineering • MS, PhD

College of Human Ecology
Dr. William Abbett, Acting Dean
Programs in:
child development • MA
community services • MS
family and child ecology • PhD
family studies • MA
food science • MS, PhD
food science—environmental toxicology • PhD
human ecology • MA, MS, PhD
human environment: design and management • PhD
human nutrition • MS, PhD
human nutrition–environmental toxicology • PhD
interior design and facilities management • MA
marriage and family therapy • MA
merchandising management • MS
youth development • MA

College of Natural Science
Dr. George E. Leroi, Dean
Programs in:
applied mathematics • MS, PhD
applied statistics • MS
astrophysics and astronomy • MS, PhD
biochemistry and molecular biology • MS, PhD
biochemistry and molecular biology–environmental toxicology • PhD
biological science • MS
biomedical laboratory operations • MS
cell and molecular biology • MS, PhD
cellular and molecular biology • PhD
chemical physics • PhD
chemistry • MS, PhD
chemistry–environmental toxicology • PhD
clinical laboratory sciences • MS
computational chemistry • MS
crop and soil sciences • PhD
environmental geosciences • MS, PhD
environmental geosciences–environmental toxicology • PhD
general science • MAT
genetics • PhD
geological sciences • MS, PhD
industrial mathematics • MS
mathematics • MAT, MS, PhD
mathematics education • PhD
microbiology and molecular genetics • PhD
natural science • MA, MAT, MS, PhD
neuroscience • MS, PhD
physical science • MS
physics • MS, PhD
plant biology • MS, PhD
plant breeding and genetics—botany and plant pathology • MS, PhD
plant physiology • PhD
statistics • MA, MS, PhD
zoo and aquarium management • MS
zoology • MS, PhD
zoology–environmental toxicology • PhD

College of Nursing
Dr. Marilyn Rothert, Dean
Program in:
nursing • MSN, PhD

College of Social Science
Dr. Marietta Baba, Dean
Programs in:
anthropology • MA, PhD
clinical social work • MSW
criminal justice • MS, PhD
economics • MA, PhD
environmental design • MA
forensic science • MS
geographic information science • MS
geography • MA, PhD
labor relations and human resources • MLHR
organizational and community practice • MSW
political science • MA, PhD
professional applications in anthropology • MA
psychology • MA, PhD
public administration • MPA
social science • PhD
social science-global applications • MA
social work • PhD
sociology • MA, PhD
urban and regional planning—urban studies • MURP

Eli Broad Graduate School of Management
Dr. Robert B. Duncan, Dean
Programs in:
accounting • MS
business administration • MBA, PhD
finance • MS
food service management • MS
hospitality business • MS
integrative management • MBA
logistics • MS
management • MBA, MS, PhD
manufacturing and engineering management • MS
manufacturing and innovation • MS

■ MICHIGAN TECHNOLOGICAL UNIVERSITY
Houghton, MI 49931-1295
http://www.mtu.edu/

State-supported, coed, university. CGS member. *Enrollment:* 6,565 graduate, professional, and undergraduate students; 631 full-time matriculated graduate/professional students (214 women), 169 part-time matriculated graduate/professional students (52 women). *Graduate faculty:* 303 full-time (60 women), 16 part-time/adjunct (5 women). *Computer facilities:* 1,555 computers available on campus for general student use. A campuswide network can be accessed from student residence rooms and from off campus. Internet access and online class registration are available. *Library facilities:* J. R. Van Pelt Library. *Graduate expenses:* Tuition, nonresident: full-time $9,552; part-time $398 per credit. Required fees: $768. *General application contact:* Jill E. Pietila, Coordinator, Graduate Admissions, 906-487-2327.

Find an in-depth description at www.petersons.com/gradchannel.

Graduate School
Dr. J. Bruce Rafert, Dean of the Graduate School

College of Engineering
Dr. Robert O. Warrington, Dean
Programs in:
chemical engineering • MS, PhD
civil engineering • ME, MS, PhD
computational science and engineering • PhD
electrical engineering • ME, MS, PhD
engineering • ME, MS, PhD

Peterson's Graduate Schools in the U.S. 2006

Michigan

Michigan Technological University (continued)
- engineering mechanics • MS
- environmental engineering • ME, MS, PhD
- environmental engineering science • MS
- geological engineering • MS, PhD
- geology • MS, PhD
- geophysics • MS
- materials science and engineering • MS, PhD
- mechanical engineering • MS, PhD
- mechanical engineering-engineering mechanics • PhD
- mining engineering • MS, PhD
- sensing and signal processing • PhD
- structural engineering • PhD

College of Sciences and Arts
Dr. Maximilian J. Seel, Dean
Programs in:
- applied science education • MS-ASE
- biological sciences • MS, PhD
- chemistry • MS, PhD
- computer science • MS, PhD
- engineering physics • PhD
- environmental policy • MS
- industrial archaeology • MS, PhD
- mathematical sciences • PhD
- mathematics • MS
- physics • MS, PhD
- rhetoric and technical writing • MS, PhD
- sciences and arts • MS, MS-ASE, PhD

School of Business and Economics
Dr. Keith W. Lantz, Dean
Programs in:
- business administration • MS
- business and economics • MS, MSBA
- mineral economics • MS

School of Forest Resources and Environmental Science
Dr. Glenn D. Mroz, Interim Dean
Programs in:
- applied ecology • MS
- forest ecology and management • MS
- forest molecular genetics and biotechnology • PhD
- forest science • PhD
- forestry • MS

■ NORTHERN MICHIGAN UNIVERSITY
Marquette, MI 49855-5301
http://www.nmu.edu/

State-supported, coed, comprehensive institution. CGS member. *Computer facilities:* Computer purchase and lease plans are available. 9,000 computers available on campus for general student use. A campuswide network can be accessed from student residence rooms and from off campus. Internet access and online class registration are available. *Library facilities:* Lydia Olson Library plus 1 other. *General application contact:* Dean of Graduate Studies, 906-227-2300.

College of Graduate Studies

College of Arts and Sciences
Programs in:
- administrative services • MA
- arts and sciences • MA, MFA, MPA, MS
- biochemistry • MS
- biology • MS
- chemistry • MS
- creative writing • MFA
- literature • MA
- mathematics education • MS
- pedagogy • MA
- public administration • MPA
- science education • MS
- writing • MA

College of Professional Studies
Programs in:
- administration and supervision • MA Ed, Ed S
- behavioral sciences and human services • MA, MA Ed, MS, MSN, Ed S
- communication disorders • MA
- criminal justice • MS
- elementary education • MA Ed
- exercise science • MS
- nursing • MSN
- psychology • MS
- secondary education • MA Ed
- special education • MA Ed

■ OAKLAND UNIVERSITY
Rochester, MI 48309-4401
http://www.oakland.edu/

State-supported, coed, university. CGS member. *Enrollment:* 16,575 graduate, professional, and undergraduate students; 1,062 full-time matriculated graduate/professional students (649 women), 2,325 part-time matriculated graduate/professional students (1,395 women). *Graduate faculty:* 448 full-time (177 women), 90 part-time/adjunct (45 women). *Computer facilities:* 640 computers available on campus for general student use. A campuswide network can be accessed from student residence rooms and from off campus. Internet access and online class registration are available. *Library facilities:* Kresge Library plus 1 other. *Graduate expenses:* Tuition, state resident: full-time $7,032; part-time $293 per credit. Tuition, nonresident: full-time $12,804; part-time $534 per credit. *General application contact:* Christina J. Grabowski, Associate Director of Graduate Study and Lifelong Learning, 248-370-3167.

Find an in-depth description at www.petersons.com/gradchannel.

Graduate Study and Lifelong Learning
Christina J. Grabowski, Associate Director of Graduate Study and Lifelong Learning

College of Arts and Sciences
Dr. David Downing, Dean
Programs in:
- applied mathematical science • PhD
- applied statistics • MS, PhD
- arts and sciences • MA, MM, MPA, MS, PhD, Certificate
- biological sciences • MA, MS
- cellular biology of aging • MS
- chemistry • MS, PhD
- English • MA
- health and environmental chemistry • PhD
- history • MA
- industrial applied mathematics • MS
- liberal studies • MA
- linguistics • MA
- mathematics • MA
- medical physics • PhD
- music • MM
- physics • MS
- public administration • MPA
- statistical methods • Certificate

School of Business Administration
Dr. John C. Gardner, Dean
Programs in:
- accounting • M Acc
- business administration • MBA, Certificate
- information technology management • MS

School of Education and Human Services
Dr. Mary L. Otto, Dean
Programs in:
- counseling • MA, PhD
- curriculum, instruction and leadership • M Ed, PhD, Certificate
- early childhood education • M Ed, PhD, Certificate
- education and human services • M Ed, MA, MAT, MTD, PhD, Certificate, Ed S
- educational specialist • Ed S
- microcomputer applications in education • Certificate
- reading • MAT, PhD, Certificate
- special education • M Ed
- training and development • MTD

School of Engineering and Computer Science
Dr. Pieter A. Frick, Dean
Programs in:
- computer science • MS
- electrical and computer engineering • MS
- embedded systems • MS
- engineering and computer science • MS, PhD

Michigan

engineering management • MS
information systems engineering • MS
mechanical engineering • MS, PhD
software engineering • MS
systems engineering • MS, PhD

School of Health Sciences
Dr. Kenneth R. Hightower, Interim Dean
Programs in:
complementary wellness • Certificate
exercise science • MS
health sciences • MS, DPT, Dr Sc PT, Certificate
orthopedic manual physical therapy • Certificate
pediatric rehabilitation • Certificate
physical therapy • MS, DPT, Dr Sc PT

School of Nursing
Dr. Linda Thompson, Dean
Programs in:
adult health • MSN
family nurse practitioner • MSN, Certificate
nurse anesthetist • MSN, Certificate
nursing • MSN, Certificate

■ SAGINAW VALLEY STATE UNIVERSITY
University Center, MI 48710
http://www.svsu.edu/

State-supported, coed, comprehensive institution. *Enrollment:* 9,168 graduate, professional, and undergraduate students; 109 full-time matriculated graduate/professional students (74 women), 1,479 part-time matriculated graduate/professional students (1,078 women). *Graduate faculty:* 108 full-time (48 women), 14 part-time/adjunct (8 women). *Computer facilities:* Computer purchase and lease plans are available. 851 computers available on campus for general student use. A campuswide network can be accessed from student residence rooms and from off campus. Internet access is available. *Library facilities:* Zahnow Library. *Graduate expenses:* Tuition, state resident: part-time $239 per credit hour. Tuition, nonresident: part-time $473 per credit hour. Required fees: $20 per credit hour. *General application contact:* Barb Sageman, Director, Graduate Admissions, 989-249-1696.

College of Arts and Behavioral Sciences
Dr. Donald Bachand, Dean
Programs in:
arts and behavioral sciences • MA
communication and multimedia • MA
leadership in public administration • MA

College of Business and Management
Dr. Paul J. Uselding, Dean
Program in:
business and management • MBA

College of Education
Dr. Steve P. Barbus, Dean
Programs in:
chief business officers • M Ed
early childhood education • MAT
education • M Ed, MAT, Ed S
education leadership • Ed S
educational administration and supervision • M Ed
elementary classroom teaching • MAT
learning and behavioral disorders • MAT
middle school • MAT
middle school classroom teaching • MAT
principalship • M Ed
reading • MAT
secondary classroom teaching • MAT
secondary school • MAT
superintendency • M Ed

College of Science, Engineering, and Technology
Dr. Ron Williams, Dean
Programs in:
science, engineering, and technology • MS
technological processes • MS

Crystal M. Lange College of Nursing and Health Sciences
Dr. Janet Blecke, Dean
Programs in:
client care management • MSN
clinical nurse specialist • MSN
nurse practitioner • MSN
nursing • MSN
nursing education • MSN

■ SIENA HEIGHTS UNIVERSITY
Adrian, MI 49221-1796
http://www.sienahts.edu

Independent-religious, coed, comprehensive institution. *Computer facilities:* 75 computers available on campus for general student use. A campuswide network can be accessed from student residence rooms and from off campus. Internet access is available. *General application contact:* Dean, Graduate College, 517-264-7663.

Graduate College
Programs in:
agency counseling • MA
community counseling • Spt
curriculum and instruction • MA
early childhood education • MA
elementary education • MA
elementary education/reading • MA
human resource development • MA
middle school education • MA
Montessori education • MA
school counseling • MA
secondary education • MA
secondary education/reading • MA

■ SPRING ARBOR UNIVERSITY
Spring Arbor, MI 49283-9799
http://www.arbor.edu/

Independent-religious, coed, comprehensive institution. *Enrollment:* 3,531 graduate, professional, and undergraduate students; 628 full-time matriculated graduate/professional students (462 women), 280 part-time matriculated graduate/professional students (202 women). *Graduate faculty:* 8 full-time (2 women), 88 part-time/adjunct (29 women). *Computer facilities:* 147 computers available on campus for general student use. A campuswide network can be accessed from student residence rooms and from off campus. Internet access is available. *Library facilities:* Hugh A. White Library plus 1 other. *Graduate expenses:* Tuition: part-time $320 per credit hour. Tuition and fees vary according to program. *General application contact:* Dale N. Glinz, Graduate Recruiter, Admissions Office.

School of Adult Studies
Programs in:
counseling • MAC
family studies • MAFS
organizational management • MAOM
religion • M Div

School of Business and Management
Program in:
business and management • MBA

School of Education
Program in:
education • MAE

■ UNIVERSITY OF DETROIT MERCY
Detroit, MI 48219-0900
http://www.udmercy.edu/

Independent-religious, coed, university. *Computer facilities:* 250 computers available on campus for general student use. A campuswide network can be accessed from student residence rooms and from off campus. Internet access is available. *Library facilities:* McNichols Campus

Michigan

University of Detroit Mercy (continued)
Library plus 3 others. *General application contact:* Vice President, Enrollment Management, 313-993-1245.

College of Business Administration
Programs in:
  business administration • MBA, MSCIS
  computer information systems • MSCIS

College of Engineering and Science
Programs in:
  automotive engineering • DE
  chemical engineering • ME, DE
  civil and environmental engineering • ME
  computer science • MSCS
  electrical engineering • ME, DE
  elementary mathematics education • MATM
  engineering and science • M Eng Mgt, MATM, ME, MS, MSCS, DE
  engineering management • M Eng Mgt
  junior high mathematics education • MATM
  macromolecular chemistry • MS
  manufacturing engineering • DE
  mechanical engineering • ME, DE
  polymer engineering • ME
  secondary mathematics education • MATM
  teaching of mathematics • MATM

College of Health Professions
Programs in:
  family nurse practitioner • MSN, Certificate
  health professions • MS, MSN, Certificate
  health services administration • MS
  health systems management • MSN
  nurse anesthesiology • MS
  physician assistant • MS

College of Liberal Arts and Education
Programs in:
  addiction counseling • MA
  addiction studies • Certificate
  clinical psychology • MA, PhD
  community counseling • MA
  counseling • MA
  criminal justice • MA
  curriculum and instruction • MA
  early childhood education • MA
  educational administration • MA
  emotionally impaired • MA
  industrial/organizational psychology • MA
  learning disabilities • MA
  liberal arts and education • MA, MALS, MS, PhD, Certificate, Spec
  liberal studies • MALS
  religious studies • MA
  school counseling • MA
  school psychology • Spec
  security administration • MS
  special education • MA
  teaching and learning • MA

School of Architecture
Program in:
  architecture • M Arch

School of Dentistry
Programs in:
  dentistry • DDS, MS, Certificate
  endodontics • MS, Certificate
  orthodontics • MS, Certificate

School of Law
Program in:
  law • JD

■ UNIVERSITY OF MICHIGAN
Ann Arbor, MI 48109
http://www.umich.edu/

State-supported, coed, university. CGS member. *Enrollment:* 39,031 graduate, professional, and undergraduate students; 12,576 full-time matriculated graduate/professional students (5,592 women), 1,938 part-time matriculated graduate/professional students (751 women). *Graduate faculty:* 3,468 full-time (1,096 women), 979 part-time/adjunct (481 women). *Computer facilities:* Computer purchase and lease plans are available. 2,600 computers available on campus for general student use. A campuswide network can be accessed from student residence rooms and from off campus. Internet access and online class registration are available. *Library facilities:* University Library plus 20 others. *Graduate expenses:* Tuition, state resident: full-time $7,463. Tuition, nonresident: full-time $13,913. Full-time tuition and fees vary according to course load, degree level and program. *General application contact:* Admissions Office, 734-764-8129.

A. Alfred Taubman College of Architecture and Urban Planning
Douglas S. Kelbaugh, Dean
Programs in:
  architecture • M Arch, M Sc, PhD
  architecture and urban planning • M Arch, M Sc, MUD, MUP, PhD, Certificate
  real estate development • Certificate
  urban and regional planning • MUP, PhD, Certificate
  urban design • MUD
  urban planning • MUP
  urban, technological, and environmental planning • PhD

College of Pharmacy
James W. Richards, Dean
Programs in:
  medicinal chemistry • PhD
  pharmaceutical sciences • PhD
  pharmacy • Pharm D, PhD
  social and administrative sciences • PhD

Horace H. Rackham School of Graduate Studies
Steven L. Kunkel, Interim Dean of the Graduate School
Programs in:
  biophysics • PhD
  education and psychology • PhD
  English and education • PhD
  medical and biological illustration • MFA
  modern Middle Eastern and North African studies • AM
  neuroscience • PhD
  survey methodology • MS, PhD, Certificate

College of Engineering
Stephen W. Director, Dean
Programs in:
  aerospace engineering • M Eng, MS, MSE, PhD
  applied physics • PhD
  atmospheric and space sciences • PhD
  automotive engineering • M Eng
  biomedical engineering • MS, MSE, PhD
  chemical engineering • MSE, PhD, Ch E
  civil engineering • MSE, PhD, CE
  computer science and engineering • MS, MSE, PhD
  concurrent marine design • M Eng
  construction engineering and management • M Eng, MSE
  electrical engineering • MS, MSE, PhD
  electrical engineering systems • MS, MSE, PhD
  engineering • M Eng, MS, MSE, D Eng, PhD, CE, Certificate, Ch E, Mar Eng, Nav Arch, Nuc E
  environmental engineering • MSE, PhD
  financial engineering • MS
  geoscience and remote sensing • PhD
  industrial and operations engineering • MS, MSE, PhD
  integrated microsystems • M Eng
  macromolecular science and engineering • MS, MSE, PhD
  manufacturing • M Eng, D Eng
  materials science and engineering • MS, PhD
  mechanical engineering • MSE, PhD

Michigan

naval architecture and marine engineering • MS, MSE, PhD, Mar Eng, Nav Arch
nuclear engineering • Nuc E
nuclear engineering and radiological sciences • MSE, PhD
nuclear science • MS, PhD
pharmaceutical engineering • M Eng
plastics engineering • M Eng
space and planetary physics • PhD
space engineering • M Eng

College of Literature, Science, and the Arts
Terrence McDonald
Programs in:
American culture • AM, PhD
analytical chemistry • PhD
ancient Israel/Hebrew Bible • AM, PhD
anthropology • PhD
anthropology and history • PhD
applied economics • AM
applied statistics • AM
Arabic • AM, PhD
Armenian • AM, PhD
Asian languages and cultures • MA, PhD
astronomy • MS, PhD
biopsychology • PhD
chemical biology • PhD
Chinese studies • AM
classical art and archaeology • PhD
classical studies • PhD
clinical psychology • PhD
cognition and perception • PhD
communication studies • PhD
comparative literature • PhD
creative writing • MFA
Czech • AM, PhD
developmental psychology • PhD
early Christian studies • AM, PhD
ecology and evolutionary biology • MS, PhD
economics • AM, PhD
Egyptology • AM, PhD
English and education • PhD
English and women's studies • PhD
English language and literature • PhD
film and video studies • Certificate
French • PhD
general linguistics • PhD
geology • MS, PhD
German • AM, PhD
Greek • AM
Greek and Roman history • PhD, Certificate
Hebrew • AM, PhD
history • PhD
history and women's studies • PhD
history of art • PhD
inorganic chemistry • PhD
Islamic studies • AM, PhD
Japanese studies • AM
Latin • AM
linguistics and Germanic languages and literatures • PhD
linguistics and Romance languages and literatures • PhD
literature, science, and the arts • AM, MA, MAT, MFA, MS, PhD, Certificate
mass communication • PhD
material chemistry • PhD
mathematics • AM, MS, PhD
Mesopotamian and ancient Near Eastern studies • AM, PhD
mineralogy • MS, PhD
molecular, cellular, and developmental biology • MS, PhD
oceanography: marine geology and geochemistry • MS, PhD
organic chemistry • PhD
organizational psychology • PhD
Persian • AM, PhD
personality psychology • PhD
philosophy • AM, PhD
physical chemistry • PhD
physics • MS, PhD
Polish • AM, PhD
political science • AM, PhD
psychology and women's studies • PhD
public policy and sociology • PhD
Romance linguistics • PhD
Russian • AM, PhD
Russian and East European studies • AM, Certificate
Serbo-Croatian • AM, PhD
Slavic linguistics • AM, PhD
social psychology • PhD
social work and economics • PhD
social work and political science • PhD
social work and sociology • PhD
sociology • PhD
South Asian studies • AM
Southeast Asian studies • AM
Spanish • PhD
statistics • AM, PhD
teaching Latin • MAT
teaching of Arabic as a foreign Language • AM
Turkish • AM, PhD
Ukrainian • AM, PhD
women's studies • Certificate
women's studies and sociology • PhD

Division of Kinesiology
Dr. Beverly D. Ulrich, Dean
Programs in:
kinesiology • MS, PhD
sport management • AM

Gerald R. Ford School of Public Policy
Program in:
public policy • MPA, MPP, PhD

School of Art and Design
Programs in:
art and design • AM, MFA
biomedical visualization • MFA

School of Education
Karen Wixson, Dean
Programs in:
academic affairs and student development • PhD
curriculum development • MA
early childhood education • MA, PhD
education • AM, MA, MS, PhD
educational administration and policy • PhD
educational foundation, administration, policy, and research methods • MA
educational foundations and policy • PhD
elementary education • MA, MS, PhD
English education • MA
higher education • AM
individually designed concentration • PhD
learning technologies • MA, MS, PhD
literacy, language, and culture • MA, PhD
mathematics education • MA, MS, PhD
organizational behavior and management • PhD
public policy • PhD
public policy in postsecondary education • AM
research, evaluation, and assessment • PhD
science education • MA, MS, PhD
secondary education • MA, MS, PhD
social studies education • MA
special education • PhD
student development, support, and academic affairs • AM
teaching and teacher education • PhD

School of Information
Programs in:
archives and records management • MS
human-computer interaction • MS
information • PhD
information economics, management and policy • MS
library and information services • MS

School of Music
Karen L. Wolff, Dean
Programs in:
composition • MA, MM, A Mus D
composition and theory • PhD
conducting • MM, A Mus D
design • MFA
media arts • MA
modern dance performance and choreography • MFA
music • MA, MFA, MM, A Mus D, PhD, Spec M
music education • MM, PhD, Spec M
musicology • MA, PhD
performance • MM, A Mus D, Spec M
theatre • PhD
theory • MA, PhD

Peterson's Graduate Schools in the U.S. 2006

Michigan

University of Michigan (continued)

School of Nursing
Dr. Ada Sue Hinshaw, Dean
Programs in:
  adult acute care nurse practitioner • MS
  adult primary care/adult nurse practitioner • MS
  community care/home care • MS
  community health nursing • MS
  family nurse practitioner • MS
  gerontology nurse practitioner • MS
  gerontology nursing • MS
  infant, child, adolescent health nurse practitioner • MS
  medical-surgical nursing • MS
  nurse midwifery • MS
  nurse practitioner • MS
  nursing • MS, PhD
  nursing business and health systems • MS
  occupational health nursing • MS
  parent-child nursing • MS
  psychiatric mental health nurse practitioner • MS
  psychiatric mental health nursing • MS

Law School
Evan H. Caminker, Dean
Programs in:
  comparative law • MCL
  law • JD, LL M, SJD

Medical School
Dr. Allen S. Lichter, Dean
Programs in:
  bioinformatics • MS, PhD
  biological chemistry • PhD
  biomedical sciences • MS, PhD
  cell and developmental biology • MS, PhD
  cellular and molecular biology • PhD
  human genetics • MS, PhD
  immunology • PhD
  medicine • MD, MS, PhD
  microbiology and immunology • PhD
  pathology • PhD
  pharmacology • PhD
  physiology • PhD

School of Dentistry
Program in:
  dentistry • DDS, MS, PhD, Certificate

School of Natural Resources and Environment
Programs in:
  industrial ecology • Certificate
  landscape architecture • MLA, PhD
  natural resources and environment • PhD
  resource ecology and management • MS, PhD
  resource policy and behavior • MS, PhD
  spatial analysis • Certificate

School of Public Health
Noreen M. Clark, Dean
Programs in:
  biostatistics • MPH, MS, PhD
  clinical research design and statistical analysis • MS
  dental public health • MPH
  environmental health • MPH, MS, Dr PH, PhD
  epidemiologic science • PhD
  epidemiology • MPH, Dr PH
  health behavior and health education • MPH, PhD
  health management and policy • MHSA, MPH
  health services organization and policy • PhD
  hospital and molecular epidemiology • MPH
  human nutrition • MPH, MS
  industrial hygiene • MS, PhD
  international health • MPH
  occupational health • MPH, MS, PhD
  occupational medicine • MPH
  public health • MHSA, MPH, MS, Dr PH, PhD
  toxicology • MPH, MS, PhD

School of Social Work
Programs in:
  social work • MSW, PhD
  social work and social science • PhD

University of Michigan Business School
Dr. Robert J. Dolan, Dean
Programs in:
  business • M Acc, MBA
  business administration • PhD

■ **UNIVERSITY OF MICHIGAN–DEARBORN**
Dearborn, MI 48128-1491
http://www.umd.umich.edu/

State-supported, coed, comprehensive institution. *Enrollment:* 9,021 graduate, professional, and undergraduate students; 252 full-time matriculated graduate/professional students (120 women), 2,164 part-time matriculated graduate/professional students (936 women). *Graduate faculty:* 299 full-time (101 women), 259 part-time/adjunct (139 women). *Computer facilities:* 350 computers available on campus for general student use. A campuswide network can be accessed from off campus. Internet access is available. *Library facilities:* Mardigian Library. *Graduate expenses:* Tuition, state resident: part-time $357 per credit hour. Tuition, nonresident: part-time $820 per credit hour. Required fees: $107. *General application contact:* Julie Tigani, Graduate Coordinator, 313-593-1494.

Find an in-depth description at www.petersons.com/gradchannel.

College of Arts, Sciences, and Letters
Dr. Kathryn Anderson-Levitt, Dean
Programs in:
  applied and computational mathematics • MS
  arts, sciences, and letters • MA, MS
  environmental science • MS
  health psychology • MS
  liberal studies • MA

College of Engineering and Computer Science
Dr. Subrata Sengupta, Dean
Programs in:
  automotive systems engineering • MSE
  computer and information science • MS
  computer engineering • MSE
  electrical engineering • MSE
  engineering • MS, MSE, D Eng
  engineering management • MS
  industrial and systems engineering • MSE
  information systems and technology • MS
  manufacturing systems engineering • MSE, D Eng
  mechanical engineering • MSE
  software engineering • MS

School of Education
Dr. John Poster, Dean
Programs in:
  education • M Ed, MA, MPA, Certificate
  educational administration • Certificate
  emotional impairments endorsement • M Ed
  inclusion specialist • M Ed
  learning disabilities endorsement • M Ed
  nonprofit leadership • Certificate
  performance improvement and instructional design • MA, Certificate
  public administration • MPA
  teaching • MA

School of Management
Dr. Gary Waissi, Dean
Programs in:
  accounting • MS
  finance • MS
  management • MBA

Michigan

■ UNIVERSITY OF MICHIGAN–FLINT
Flint, MI 48502-1950
http://www.flint.umich.edu/

State-supported, coed, comprehensive institution. *Enrollment:* 6,152 graduate, professional, and undergraduate students; 101 full-time matriculated graduate/professional students (76 women), 473 part-time matriculated graduate/professional students (264 women). *Graduate faculty:* 55 full-time (26 women), 17 part-time/adjunct (7 women). *Computer facilities:* 213 computers available on campus for general student use. A campuswide network can be accessed from off campus. Internet access and online class registration are available. *Library facilities:* Frances Willson Thompson Library. *Graduate expenses:* Tuition, nonresident: full-time $8,472; part-time $471 per credit. Required fees: $274; $137 per term. Full-time tuition and fees vary according to program. Part-time tuition and fees vary according to course load. *General application contact:* Ann Briggs, Administrative Associate, 810-762-3171.

Graduate Programs
Dr. Vahid Lotfi, Associate Provost and Dean of Graduate Programs
Programs in:
 American culture • MLS
 public administration • MPA

School of Education and Human Services
Dr. Robert Hahn, Interim Dean
Programs in:
 early childhood education specialization • MA
 education • MA Ed
 elementary with teacher certification • MA
 literacy (K–12 specialization) • MA
 urban and multicultural specialization • MA

School of Health Professions and Studies
Dr. Augustine D. Agho, Dean
Programs in:
 anesthesia • MSA
 health education • MS
 health professions and studies • MS, MSA, MSN, DPT
 nursing • MSN
 physical therapy • DPT

School of Management
Dr. Douglas Moon, Interim Dean
Program in:
 management • MBA

■ WAYNE STATE UNIVERSITY
Detroit, MI 48202
http://www.wayne.edu/

State-supported, coed, university. CGS member. *Enrollment:* 33,091 graduate, professional, and undergraduate students; 7,284 full-time matriculated graduate/professional students (3,806 women), 5,657 part-time matriculated graduate/professional students (3,394 women). *Graduate faculty:* 990. *Computer facilities:* 1,800 computers available on campus for general student use. A campuswide network can be accessed from student residence rooms and from off campus. Internet access and online class registration are available. *Library facilities:* David Adamany Undergraduate Library plus 6 others. *Graduate expenses:* Tuition, state resident: part-time $263 per credit hour. Tuition, nonresident: part-time $580 per credit hour. Required fees: $21 per credit hour. *General application contact:* Susan Zwieg, Director, 313-577-3596.

Graduate School
Dr. Hilary Ratner, Dean
Programs in:
 alcohol and drug abuse studies • Certificate
 archives administration • Certificate
 developmental disabilities • Certificate
 gerontology • Certificate
 infant mental health • Certificate
 interdisciplinary studies • PhD
 library and information science • MLIS, Spec
 molecular and cellular toxicology • MS, PhD
 molecular biology and genetics • MS, PhD

College of Education
Dr. Paula Wood, Dean
Programs in:
 art education • M Ed
 bilingual/bicultural education • M Ed
 career and technical education • M Ed
 counseling • M Ed, MA, Ed D, PhD, Ed S
 curriculum and instruction • Ed D, PhD, Ed S
 early childhood education • M Ed
 education • M Ed, MA, MAT, Ed D, PhD, Ed S
 educational evaluation and research • M Ed, Ed D, PhD
 educational leadership • M Ed
 educational leadership and policy studies • Ed D, PhD
 educational psychology • M Ed, Ed D
 elementary education • M Ed, MAT
 English education-secondary • M Ed
 general administration and supervision • Ed D, PhD, Ed S
 health education • M Ed
 higher education • Ed D, PhD
 instructional technology • M Ed, Ed D, PhD, Ed S
 mathematics education • M Ed
 physical education • M Ed
 PK–12 education • MAT
 reading • M Ed, Ed S
 reading education • Ed D
 recreation and park services • MA
 rehabilitation counseling and community inclusion • MA
 school and community psychology • MA, Ed S
 science education • M Ed
 secondary education • MAT
 social studies • M Ed
 special education • M Ed, Ed D, PhD, Ed S
 sports administration • MA

College of Engineering
Dr. Ralph Kummler, Dean
Programs in:
 biomedical engineering • MS, PhD
 chemical engineering • MS, PhD
 civil and environmental engineering • MS, PhD
 computer engineering • MS, PhD
 electrical engineering • MS, PhD
 engineering • MS, PhD, Certificate
 engineering management • MS
 engineering technology • MS
 environmental auditing • Certificate
 hazardous materials management on public lands • Certificate
 hazardous waste • MS, Certificate
 hazardous waste control • Certificate
 hazardous waste management • MS
 industrial engineering • MS, PhD
 manufacturing engineering • MS
 materials science and engineering • MS, PhD, Certificate
 mechanical engineering • MS, PhD
 operations research • MS
 polymer engineering • Certificate

College of Fine, Performing and Communication Arts
Jack Kay, Interim Dean
Programs in:
 art • MA, MFA
 art history • MA
 choral conducting • MM
 communication studies • MA, PhD
 composition • MM
 design and merchandising • MA
 fine, performing and communication arts • MA, MFA, MM, PhD, Certificate
 music • MA
 music education • MM
 orchestral studies • Certificate
 performance • MM
 public relations and organizational communication • MA

Peterson's Graduate Schools in the U.S. 2006

Michigan

Wayne State University *(continued)*
  radio-TV-film • MA, PhD
  speech communication • MA, PhD
  theatre • MA, MFA, PhD
  theory • MM

College of Liberal Arts
Robert Thomas, Dean
Programs in:
  anthropology • MA, PhD
  archival administration • Certificate
  classics • MA
  comparative literature • MA
  criminal justice • MPA
  economics • MA, PhD
  English • MA, PhD
  French • MA
  German • MA
  history • MA, PhD
  Italian • MA
  language learning • MA
  liberal arts • MA, MPA, MS, PhD, Certificate
  linguistics • MA
  modern languages • PhD
  Near Eastern studies • MA
  philosophy • MA, PhD
  political science • MA, PhD
  public administration • MPA
  sociology • MA, PhD
  Spanish • MA

College of Nursing
Dr. Barbara Redman, Dean
Programs in:
  adult acute care nursing • MSN
  adult primary care nursing • MSN
  advanced practice nursing with women, neonates and children • MSN
  community health nursing • MSN
  nursing • MSN, PhD, Certificate
  nursing education • Certificate
  psychiatric mental health nurse practitioner • MSN

College of Science
Robert Thomas, Dean
Programs in:
  applied mathematics • MA, PhD
  audiology • MS
  biological sciences • MA, MS, PhD
  chemistry • MA, MS, PhD
  clinical psychology • PhD
  cognitive psychology • PhD
  computer science • MA, MS, PhD
  developmental psychology • PhD
  electronics and computer control systems • MS
  geology • MS
  human development • MA
  industrial/organizational psychology • PhD
  mathematics • MA, PhD
  molecular biotechnology • MS
  nutrition and food science • MA, MS, PhD, Certificate
  physics • MA, MS, PhD
  psychology • MA, PhD
  science • MA, MS, PhD, Certificate
  scientific computing • Certificate
  social psychology • PhD
  speech-language pathology • MA, PhD
  statistics • MA, PhD

College of Urban, Labor and Metropolitan Affairs
Robin Boyle, Interim Dean
Programs in:
  dispute resolution • MADR, Certificate
  economic development • Certificate
  geography • MA
  industrial relations • MAIR
  interdisciplinary studies • MIS
  urban planning • MUP
  urban, labor and metropolitan affairs • MA, MADR, MAIR, MIS, MUP, Certificate

Eugene Applebaum College of Pharmacy and Health Sciences
Beverly J. Schmoll, Dean
Programs in:
  clinical laboratory sciences • MS, Certificate
  health systems pharmacy management • MS
  industrial toxicology • Certificate
  nurse anesthesia • MS
  occupational health sciences • MS
  occupational safety • Certificate
  occupational therapy • MS
  pharmaceutical sciences • MS, PhD
  pharmacy • Pharm D
  pharmacy and health sciences • Pharm D, MS, MSPT, PhD, Certificate
  physical therapy • MSPT
  physician assistant studies • MS

Law School
Frederica Lombard, Interim Dean
Program in:
  law • JD, LL M

School of Business Administration
Dr. Harvey Kahalas, Dean
Programs in:
  business administration • MBA
  taxation • MS

School of Social Work
Phyllis Vroom, Dean
Programs in:
  social work • MSW
  social work practice with families and couples • Certificate

School of Medicine
Dr. John D. Crissman, Dean
Program in:
  medicine • MD, MS, PhD, Certificate

Graduate Programs in Medicine
Dr. Kenneth C. Palmer, Assistant Dean
Programs in:
  anatomy and cell biology • MS, PhD
  basic medical science • MS
  biochemistry • MS, PhD
  cancer biology • MS, PhD
  cellular and clinical neurobiology • PhD
  community health • MS
  community health services • Certificate
  immunology and microbiology • MS, PhD
  medical physics • PhD
  medical research • MS
  medicine • MS, PhD, Certificate
  pathology • PhD
  pharmacology • MS, PhD
  physical medicine and rehabilitation sciences • MS
  physiology • MS, PhD
  radiological physics • MS

■ WESTERN MICHIGAN UNIVERSITY
Kalamazoo, MI 49008-5202
http://www.wmich.edu/

State-supported, coed, university. CGS member. *Computer facilities:* 2,000 computers available on campus for general student use. A campuswide network can be accessed from student residence rooms and from off campus. *Library facilities:* Waldo Library plus 4 others. *General application contact:* Admissions and Orientation, 616-387-2000.

Find an in-depth description at www.petersons.com/gradchannel.

Graduate College

College of Arts and Sciences
Programs in:
  anthropology • MA
  applied behavior analysis • MA, PhD
  applied economics • PhD
  applied mathematics • MS
  arts and sciences • MA, MDA, MFA, MPA, MS, DPA, PhD, Ed S
  biological sciences • MS, PhD
  biostatistics • MS
  chemistry • MA, PhD
  clinical psychology • MA, PhD
  comparative religion • MA, PhD
  computational mathematics • MS
  creative writing • MFA
  development administration • MDA
  earth science • MS
  economics • MA
  English • MA, PhD
  experimental analysis of behavior • PhD
  experimental psychology • MA

geography • MA
geology • MS, PhD
graph theory and computer science • PhD
history • MA, PhD
industrial/organizational psychology • MA
mathematics • MA, PhD
mathematics education • MA, PhD
medieval studies • MA
molecular biotechnology • MS
organizational communication • MA
philosophy • MA
physics • MA, PhD
political science • MA, PhD
professional writing • MA
public affairs and administration • MPA, DPA
school psychology • PhD, Ed S
science studies • MA, PhD
sociology • MA, PhD
Spanish • MA
statistics • MS, PhD

College of Education
Programs in:
administration • MA
athletic training • MA
career and technical education • MA
coaching and sports studies • MA
counseling psychology • PhD
counselor education • MA, Ed D, PhD
counselor education and counseling psychology • MA, PhD
counselor psychology • MA
early childhood education • MA
education • MA, Ed D, PhD, Ed S
education and professional development • MA
educational leadership • MA, Ed D, PhD, Ed S
educational studies • MA, Ed D
educational technology • MA
elementary education • MA
evaluation, measurement, and research • MA, PhD
exercise science • MA
family and consumer sciences • MA
human resources development • MA
marriage and family therapy • MA
middle school education • MA
motor development • MA
physical education • MA
reading • MA
socio-cultural foundations and educational thought • MA
special education for handicapped children • MA

College of Engineering and Applied Sciences
Programs in:
computer engineering • MSE, PhD
computer science • MS, PhD
construction management • MS
electrical engineering • MSE, PhD
engineering and applied sciences • MS, MSE, PhD
engineering management • MS
industrial engineering • MSE
manufacturing engineering • MS
materials science and engineering • MS
mechanical engineering • MSE, PhD
operations research • MS
paper and printing science and engineering • MS, PhD

College of Fine Arts
Programs in:
fine arts • MA, MFA, MM
graphic design • MFA
music • MA, MM
performing arts administration • MFA
textile design • MA, MFA

College of Health and Human Services
Programs in:
audiology • MA
blind rehabilitation • MA
health and human services • MA, MS, MSW
occupational therapy • MS
physician assistant • MS
social work • MSW
speech pathology • MA

Haworth College of Business
Programs in:
accountancy • MSA
business • MBA, MSA
business administration • MBA

Minnesota

■ AUGSBURG COLLEGE
Minneapolis, MN 55454-1351
http://www.augsburg.edu/

Independent-religious, coed, comprehensive institution. *Enrollment:* 3,172 graduate, professional, and undergraduate students; 213 full-time matriculated graduate/professional students (160 women), 98 part-time matriculated graduate/professional students (77 women). *Graduate faculty:* 31 full-time (24 women), 13 part-time/adjunct (6 women). *Computer facilities:* 260 computers available on campus for general student use. A campuswide network can be accessed from student residence rooms and from off campus. Internet access and online class registration are available. *Library facilities:* James G. Lindell Library. *Graduate expenses:* Tuition: part-time $1,500 per course. *General application contact:* Carrie Carroll, Director, Weekend College and Graduate Admissions, 612-330-1101 Ext. 1792.

Program in Education
Vicki Olson, Professor
Program in:
education • MAE

Program in Leadership
Dr. Norma Noonan, Director
Program in:
leadership • MA

Program in Physicians Assistant Studies
Dawn B. Ludwig, Director
Program in:
physicians assistant studies • MS

Program in Social Work
Dr. Tony Bibus, Director
Program in:
social work • MSW

Program in Transcultural Community Health Nursing
Dr. Ruth C. Enestvedt, Director
Program in:
transcultural community health nursing • MA

■ BEMIDJI STATE UNIVERSITY
Bemidji, MN 56601-2699
http://www.bemidjistate.edu/

State-supported, coed, comprehensive institution. *Enrollment:* 5,024 graduate, professional, and undergraduate students; 14 full-time matriculated graduate/professional students (8 women), 115 part-time matriculated graduate/professional students (70 women). *Graduate faculty:* 84 part-time/adjunct (34 women). *Computer facilities:* 600 computers available on campus for general student use. A campuswide network can be accessed from student residence rooms and from off campus. Internet access and online class registration are available. *Library facilities:* A. C. Clark Library. *Graduate expenses:* Tuition, state resident: part-time $217 per credit. Tuition, nonresident: part-time $344 per credit. Required fees: $7 per credit. $245 per semester. *General application contact:* Dr. Martin K. Tadlock, Dean, 218-755-3732.

Graduate Studies
Dr. Martin K. Tadlock, Dean

College of Professional Studies
Programs in:
education • MS
industrial education • MS
physical education • MS
professional studies • MS
special education • MS

Minnesota

Bemidji State University (continued)
College of Social and Natural Sciences
Dr. Ranae Womack, Dean
Programs in:
   biology • MS
   environmental studies • MS
   mathematics • MS
   science • MS

Division of Arts and Letters
Dr. Nancy Erickson, Dean
Programs in:
   arts and letters • MA, MS
   English • MA, MS

■ BETHEL UNIVERSITY
St. Paul, MN 55112-6999
http://www.bethel.edu/

Independent-religious, coed, comprehensive institution. *Enrollment:* 3,303 graduate, professional, and undergraduate students; 133 full-time matriculated graduate/professional students (95 women), 239 part-time matriculated graduate/professional students (171 women). *Graduate faculty:* 62 full-time (34 women), 37 part-time/adjunct (17 women). *Computer facilities:* Computer purchase and lease plans are available. 110 computers available on campus for general student use. A campuswide network can be accessed from student residence rooms and from off campus. Online class registration is available. *Library facilities:* Bethel College Library plus 1 other. *Graduate expenses:* Tuition: part-time $340 per credit. One-time fee: $25 part-time. *General application contact:* Rachelle Holm, Director of Admissions, 651-635-8000.

Center for Graduate and Continuing Studies
Dr. Carl Polding, Dean
Programs in:
   applied ethnomusicology • Certificate
   child and adolescent mental health • Certificate
   Christian health ministry • MA
   communication • MA
   counseling psychology • MA
   ethnomusicology • MA
   gerontology • MA
   health systems • MA
   instructional leadership (K–12) • M Ed
   nursing education • MA, Certificate
   organizational leadership • MA
   post-secondary teaching • Certificate
   secondary education • MA
   special education • M Ed
   teaching k-12 reading • Certificate

■ COLLEGE OF ST. CATHERINE
St. Paul, MN 55105-1789
http://www.stkate.edu/

Independent-religious, women only, comprehensive institution. *Enrollment:* 4,807 graduate, professional, and undergraduate students; 664 full-time matriculated graduate/professional students (558 women), 462 part-time matriculated graduate/professional students (425 women). *Graduate faculty:* 93 full-time (74 women). *Computer facilities:* Computer purchase and lease plans are available. 350 computers available on campus for general student use. A campuswide network can be accessed from student residence rooms and from off campus. Internet access, transcript are available. *Library facilities:* St. Catherine Library plus 2 others. *Graduate expenses:* Tuition: part-time $530 per credit. Tuition and fees vary according to program. *General application contact:* 651-690-6933.

Graduate Program
Susan Cochrane, Dean of Professional Studies
Programs in:
   education • MA
   holistic health studies • MA
   library and information science • MA
   nursing • MA
   occupational therapy • MA
   organizational leadership • MA
   physical therapy • MPT, DPT
   social work • MSW
   theology • MA

■ THE COLLEGE OF ST. SCHOLASTICA
Duluth, MN 55811-4199
http://www.css.edu/

Independent-religious, coed, comprehensive institution. *Computer facilities:* 145 computers available on campus for general student use. A campuswide network can be accessed from student residence rooms and from off campus. Internet access is available. *Library facilities:* College of St. Scholastica Library plus 1 other. *General application contact:* Graduate Administrative Assistant, 218-723-6285.

Graduate Studies
Programs in:
   education • M Ed
   educational media and technology • M Ed
   exercise physiology • MA
   health information management • MA
   management • MA
   nursing • MA
   occupational therapy • MA
   physical therapy • MA

■ HAMLINE UNIVERSITY
St. Paul, MN 55104-1284
http://www.hamline.edu/

Independent-religious, coed, comprehensive institution. *Computer facilities:* A campuswide network can be accessed from student residence rooms and from off campus. Internet access and online class registration are available. *Library facilities:* Bush Library plus 1 other. *General application contact:* Assistant Director, Graduate Admission, 651-523-2900.

Graduate Liberal Studies Program
Program in:
   liberal studies • MALS, MFA, CALS

Graduate School of Education
Program in:
   education • MA Ed, MAESL, MAT, Ed D

Graduate School of Public Administration and Management
Programs in:
   management • MAM
   nonprofit management • MANM
   public administration • MAPA

School of Law
Jon M. Garon, Dean
Program in:
   law • JD, LL M

■ MAYO GRADUATE SCHOOL
Rochester, MN 55905
http://www.mayo.edu/mgs/gs.html

Independent, coed, graduate-only institution. *Graduate faculty:* 227 full-time (25 women). *Computer facilities:* A campuswide network can be accessed from off campus. Internet access is available. *Library facilities:* Plummer Library plus 7 others. *General application contact:* Melissa L. Thomforde, Admissions Coordinator, 507-538-1160.

Graduate Programs in Biomedical Sciences
Dr. Diane F. Jelinek, Dean
Programs in:
   biochemistry • PhD
   biomedical engineering • PhD

biomedical sciences • MD, PhD
immunology • PhD
molecular biology • PhD
molecular neuroscience • PhD
pharmacology • PhD
tumor biology • MD, PhD
virology and gene therapy • PhD

■ METROPOLITAN STATE UNIVERSITY
St. Paul, MN 55106-5000
http://www.metrostate.edu

State-supported, coed, comprehensive institution. *Computer facilities:* 420 computers available on campus for general student use. A campuswide network can be accessed from off campus. Internet access and online class registration are available. *Library facilities:* Library and Information Services. *General application contact:* Recruiter/Admissions Adviser, 612-659-7258.

College of Arts and Sciences
Program in:
technical communication • MS

College of Management
Programs in:
finance • MBA
human resource management • MBA
information management • MMIS
international business • MBA
law enforcement • MPNA
management information systems • MBA
marketing • MBA
nonprofit management • MPNA
organizational studies • MBA
public administration • MPNA
purchasing management • MBA
systems management • MMIS

School of Nursing
Program in:
nursing • MSN

■ MINNESOTA STATE UNIVERSITY MANKATO
Mankato, MN 56001
http://www.mnsu.edu/

State-supported, coed, comprehensive institution. CGS member. *Enrollment:* 14,065 graduate, professional, and undergraduate students; 594 full-time matriculated graduate/professional students (371 women), 1,080 part-time matriculated graduate/professional students (686 women). *Graduate faculty:* 405 full-time (150 women), 120 part-time/adjunct (58 women). *Computer facilities:* 900 computers available on campus for general student use. A campuswide network can be accessed from student residence rooms and from off campus.

Internet access and online class registration are available. *Library facilities:* Memorial Library. *Graduate expenses:* Tuition, state resident: part-time $226 per credit hour. Tuition, nonresident: part-time $339 per credit hour. Tuition and fees vary according to reciprocity agreements. *General application contact:* Joni Roberts, Admissions Coordinator, 507-389-5244.

College of Graduate Studies
Dr. Terrance Flaherty, Chairperson
Program in:
multidisciplinary studies • MS

College of Allied Health and Nursing
Dr. Sharon Aodalen, Interim Dean
Programs in:
allied health and nursing • MA, MS, MSN, MT, SP
communication disorders • MS
community health • MS
family consumer science • MS, MT
family nursing • MSN
health science • MS, MT
human performance • MA, MS, MT, SP
managed care • MSN
rehabilitation counseling • MS

College of Arts and Humanities
Dr. Jane F. Earley, Dean
Programs in:
art education • MS
arts and humanities • MA, MAT, MFA, MM, MS, MT
creative writing • MFA
English • MA, MS
French • MAT, MS
German • MAT
music • MM, MT
Spanish • MAT, MS
speech communication • MA, MS, MT
studio art • MA
teaching art • MAT, MT
teaching English • MS, MT
theatre arts • MA, MFA

College of Education
Dr. Joanne Brandt, Interim Dean
Programs in:
computer services administration • MS
counseling and student personnel • MS
curriculum and instruction • MAT, MT
early childhood education • MS
early education for exceptional children • MS
education • MA, MAT, MS, MT, Certificate, SP
education of the gifted and talented • MS
education technology • MS
educational administration • Certificate

educational leadership • MS, Certificate, SP
elementary education • MS, SP
elementary school administration • MS, SP
emotional disturbance • MS
experiential education • MS
general educational administration • MS
higher education administration • MS
learning disabilities • MS
library media education • MS, SP
mental retardation • MS
reading consultant • MS
secondary administration • MS, SP
secondary teaching • MA, MS, SP
severely handicapped • MS
vocational-technical administration • MS

College of Science, Engineering and Technology
Dr. John Frey, Dean
Programs in:
biology • MS
chemistry • MA, MS
computer science • MS
computers • MS
ecology • MS
economic and political systems • MS
electrical engineering and electronic engineering technology • MSE
environmental science • MS
human ecosystems • MS
manufacturing • MS
mathematics • MA, MS
mathematics: computer science • MS
mechanical engineering • MS
physical science • MS
physics and astronomy • MS, MT
science, engineering and technology • MA, MS, MSE, MT
statistics • MS
teaching mathematics • MT
technology • MS

College of Social and Behavioral Sciences
Dr. Susan Coultrap-McQuin, Acting Dean
Programs in:
anthropology • MS
clinical psychology • MA
geography • MA, MS, MT
gerontology • MS
history • MA, MS
industrial psychology • MA
political science • MA, MS, MT
psychology • MT
public administration • MAPA
social and behavioral sciences • MA, MAPA, MS, MT
social studies • MS
sociology • MA, MT
sociology: corrections • MS
teaching history • MS, MT
urban and regional studies • MA
women's studies • MS

Minnesota

■ MINNESOTA STATE UNIVERSITY MOORHEAD
Moorhead, MN 56563-0002
http://www.mnstate.edu/

State-supported, coed, comprehensive institution. *Enrollment:* 7,695 graduate, professional, and undergraduate students; 104 full-time matriculated graduate/professional students (86 women), 167 part-time matriculated graduate/professional students (127 women). *Graduate faculty:* 141. *Computer facilities:* 450 computers available on campus for general student use. A campuswide network can be accessed from student residence rooms and from off campus. Internet access and online class registration are available. *Library facilities:* Livingston Lord Library. *Graduate expenses:* Tuition, state resident: full-time $3,727. Tuition, nonresident: full-time $7,452. Required fees: $516. Full-time tuition and fees vary according to program. *General application contact:* Karla Wenger, Graduate Studies Office, 218-477-2344.

Graduate Studies
Dr. Dorothy Suomala, Director of Graduate Studies
Programs in:
 arts and humanities • MA, MFA, MLA, MS
 creative writing • MFA
 liberal studies • MLA
 music • MA
 music education • MS
 public, human services, and health administration • MS
 school psychology • MS, Psy S
 social and natural sciences • MS, Psy S
 speech-language pathology • MS

College of Education and Human Services
Dr. Dorothy Suomala, Interim Dean of Education and Human Services
Programs in:
 counseling and student affairs • MS
 curriculum and instruction • MS
 educational administration • MS, Ed S
 nursing • MS
 reading • MS
 special education • MS

■ ST. CLOUD STATE UNIVERSITY
St. Cloud, MN 56301-4498
http://www.stcloudstate.edu/

State-supported, coed, comprehensive institution. CGS member. *Enrollment:* 15,925 graduate, professional, and undergraduate students; 957 matriculated graduate/professional students (545 women). *Graduate faculty:* 452 full-time (142 women), 71 part-time/adjunct (31 women). *Computer facilities:* Computer purchase and lease plans are available. 1,244 computers available on campus for general student use. A campuswide network can be accessed from student residence rooms and from off campus. Internet access and online class registration are available. *Library facilities:* James W. Miller Learning Resources Center. *Graduate expenses:* Tuition, state resident: part-time $203 per credit. Tuition, nonresident: part-time $317 per credit. Required fees: $24 per credit. Tuition and fees vary according to campus/location and reciprocity agreements. *General application contact:* Dr. Dennis Nunes, Dean of Graduate Studies, 320-255-2113.

School of Graduate Studies
Dr. Dennis Nunes, Dean

College of Education
Dr. Joane McKay, Dean
Programs in:
 behavior analysis • MS
 child and family studies • MS
 college student development • MS
 community counseling • MS
 curriculum and instruction • MS
 educable mentally handicapped • MS
 education • MS, Spt
 educational administration • MS
 educational leadership and community psychology • Spt
 emotionally disturbed • MS
 exercise science • MS
 gifted and talented • MS
 information media • MS
 learning disabled • MS
 physical education • MS
 rehabilitation counseling • MS
 school counseling • MS
 social responsibility • MS
 special education • MS
 sports management • MS
 trainable mentally retarded • MS

College of Fine Arts and Humanities
Dr. Roland Specht-Jarvis, Dean
Programs in:
 art • MA
 communication disorders • MS
 conducting and literature • MM
 English • MA, MS
 fine arts and humanities • MA, MM, MS
 mass communication • MS
 music education • MM
 piano pedagogy • MM
 teaching English as a second language • MA

College of Science and Engineering
Dr. A. I. Musah, Dean
Programs in:
 biological sciences • MA, MS
 computer science • MS
 electrical engineering • MS
 engineering management • MEM
 environmental and technological studies • MS
 mathematics • MS
 mechanical engineering • MS
 science and engineering • MA, MEM, MS

College of Social Sciences
Dr. Richard Lewis, Dean
Programs in:
 applied economics • MS
 criminal justice administration • MS
 criminal justice counseling • MS
 geography • MS
 gerontology • MS
 history • MA, MS
 industrial-organizational psychology • MS
 public and nonprofit institutions • MS
 public safety executive leadership • MS
 social sciences • MA, MS

G.R. Herberger College of Business
Dr. Michael Pesch, Graduate Director
Programs in:
 management and finance • MBA
 marketing and general business • MBA

■ SAINT MARY'S UNIVERSITY OF MINNESOTA
Winona, MN 55987-1399
http://www.smumn.edu/

Independent-religious, coed, comprehensive institution. *Enrollment:* 4,996 graduate, professional, and undergraduate students; 503 full-time matriculated graduate/professional students (304 women), 2,789 part-time matriculated graduate/professional students (1,913 women). *Graduate faculty:* 32 full-time (9 women), 416 part-time/adjunct (200 women). *Computer facilities:* 356 computers available on campus for general student use. A campuswide network can be accessed from student residence rooms and from off campus. Internet access and online class registration are available. *Library facilities:* Fitzgerald Library. *Graduate expenses:* Tuition: part-time $255 per credit. *General application contact:* Jim Stevens, Director of Admissions, 612-728-5207.

Minnesota

Graduate School
James M. Bedtke, Vice President, Graduate and Special Programs
Programs in:
- arts administration • MA
- business • MS
- counseling and psychological services • MA
- criminal justice • MS
- developmental disabilities • MA
- education • MA
- education in teaching and learning • M Ed
- educational administration • MA, Certificate, Ed S
- educational leadership • Ed D
- geographic information systems • Certificate
- human and health services administration • MA
- human development • MA
- human resources • MA
- instruction • MA, Certificate
- international business • MA
- management • MA
- marriage and family therapy • Certificate
- natural resources • MS
- nurse anesthesia • MS
- philanthropy and development • MA
- project management • MS
- public administration • MS
- telecommunications • MS

Institute of Pastoral Ministries
Dr. Gregory Sobolewski, Director
Program in:
- pastoral ministries • MA, Certificate

■ UNIVERSITY OF MINNESOTA, DULUTH
Duluth, MN 55812-2496
http://www.d.umn.edu/

State-supported, coed, comprehensive institution. *Enrollment:* 10,114 graduate, professional, and undergraduate students; 616 full-time matriculated graduate/professional students (373 women), 135 part-time matriculated graduate/professional students (48 women). *Graduate faculty:* 247 full-time (61 women), 64 part-time/adjunct (20 women). *Computer facilities:* 680 computers available on campus for general student use. A campuswide network can be accessed from student residence rooms and from off campus. Internet access and online class registration are available. *Library facilities:* University of Minnesota Duluth Library. *Graduate expenses:* Tuition, state resident: part-time $614 per credit. Tuition, nonresident: part-time $1,205 per credit. *General application contact:* Dr. Steven C. Hedman, Associate Dean for Research, 218-726-6839.

Graduate School
Dr. Steven C. Hedman, Associate Dean for Research
Program in:
- toxicology • MS, PhD

College of Education and Human Service Professions
Dr. Paul Deputy, Dean
Programs in:
- communication sciences and disorders • MA
- education and human service professions • MA, MSW
- social work • MSW

College of Liberal Arts
Dr. Linda Krug, Dean
Programs in:
- English • MA
- liberal arts • MA, MLS
- sociology/anthropology • MLS

College of Science and Engineering
Dr. James Riehl, Dean
Programs in:
- applied and computational mathematics • MS
- biology • MS
- chemistry • MS
- computer science • MS
- electrical and computer engineering • MSECE
- engineering management • MSEM
- environmental health and safety • MEHS
- geological sciences • MS
- physics • MS
- science and engineering • MEHS, MS, MSECE, MSEM

School of Business and Economics
Kjell Knudsen, Dean
Programs in:
- business administration • MBA
- business and economics • MBA

School of Fine Arts
Dr. Jack Bowman, Dean
Programs in:
- fine arts • MFA, MM
- graphic design • MFA
- music education • MM
- performance • MM

School of Medicine
Dr. Richard J. Ziegler, Dean
Programs in:
- anatomy and cell biology • MS, PhD
- biochemistry and molecular biology • MS, PhD
- medical microbiology and immunology • MS, PhD
- medicine • MD, MS, PhD
- pharmacology • MS, PhD
- physiology • MS, PhD

■ UNIVERSITY OF MINNESOTA, TWIN CITIES CAMPUS
Minneapolis, MN 55455-0213
http://www.umn.edu/tc/

State-supported, coed, university. CGS member. *Enrollment:* 49,474 graduate, professional, and undergraduate students; 9,763 matriculated graduate/professional students (5,131 women). *Graduate faculty:* 2,288. *Computer facilities:* A campuswide network can be accessed from student residence rooms and from off campus. E-mail available. *Library facilities:* Wilson Library plus 17 others. *Graduate expenses:* Tuition, state resident: full-time $3,681; part-time $614 per credit. Tuition, nonresident: full-time $7,231; part-time $1,205 per credit. *General application contact:* 612-625-3014.

Carlson School of Management
Dr. Lawrence Benveniste, Dean
Programs in:
- accounting • MBA, PhD
- business administration • MBA, PhD
- business taxation • MBT
- entrepreneurship • MBA
- finance • MBA, PhD
- healthcare management • MBA
- human resources and industrial relations • MA, PhD
- information and decision sciences • MBA, PhD
- international business • MBA
- management • EMBA, MA, MBA, MBT, MHA, MS, MSMOT, PhD
- marketing and logistics management • MBA, PhD
- operations and management science • MBA, PhD
- strategic management and organization • MBA, PhD
- supply chain management • MBA

College of Pharmacy
Programs in:
- medicinal chemistry • MS, PhD
- pharmaceutics • MS, PhD
- pharmacy • Pharm D, MS, PhD
- social and administrative pharmacy • MS, PhD

College of Veterinary Medicine
Dr. Jeffrey Klausner, Dean
Programs in:
- molecular veterinary biosciences • MS, PhD
- veterinary medicine • MS, PhD

Graduate School
Dr. Victor Bloomfield, Interim Dean
Programs in:

Minnesota

University of Minnesota, Twin Cities Campus (continued)
  biophysical sciences and medical physics • MS, PhD
  genetic counseling • MS
  health informatics • MHI, MS, PhD
  molecular, cellular, developmental biology and genetics • PhD
  neuroscience • MS, PhD
  pharmacology • MS, PhD
  scientific computation • MS, PhD

College of Agricultural, Food, and Environmental Sciences
Dr. Charles C. Muscoplat, Dean
Programs in:
  agricultural and applied economics • MS, PhD
  agricultural, food, and environmental sciences • MA, MBAE, MS, MSBAE, PhD
  animal science • MS, PhD
  applied plant sciences • MS, PhD
  biosystems and agricultural engineering • MBAE, MSBAE, PhD
  entomology • MS, PhD
  food science • MS, PhD
  microbial ecology • MS, PhD
  nutrition • MS, PhD
  plant pathology • MS, PhD
  rhetoric and scientific and technical communication • MA, PhD
  scientific and technical communication • MS
  soil, water, and climate • MS, PhD

College of Architecture and Landscape Architecture
Programs in:
  architecture • M Arch
  architecture and landscape architecture • M Arch, MLA, MS
  landscape architecture • MLA, MS

College of Biological Sciences
Programs in:
  biological sciences • MBS, MS, PhD
  ecology, evolution, and behavior • MS, PhD
  plant biological sciences • MS, PhD

College of Education and Human Development
Dr. Steven Yussen, Dean
Programs in:
  adapted physical education • MA, PhD
  adult education • M Ed, MA, Ed D, PhD, Certificate
  agricultural, food and environmental education • M Ed, MA, Ed D, PhD
  art education • M Ed, MA, PhD
  biomechanics • MA
  biomechanics and neural control • PhD
  business and industry education • M Ed, MA, Ed D, PhD
  business education • M Ed
  child psychology • MA, PhD
  children's literature • M Ed, MA, PhD
  Chinese • M Ed
  coaching • Certificate
  comparative and international development education • MA, PhD
  counseling and student personnel psychology • MA, PhD, Ed S
  curriculum and instruction • MA, PhD
  developmental adapted physical education • M Ed
  disability policy and services • Certificate
  early childhood education • M Ed, MA, PhD
  earth science • M Ed
  education and human development • M Ed, MA, Ed D, PhD, Certificate, Ed S
  educational administration • MA, Ed D, PhD
  educational psychology • PhD
  elementary education • M Ed, MA, PhD
  elementary special education • M Ed
  English • M Ed
  English as a second language • M Ed
  English education • MA, PhD
  environmental education • M Ed
  evaluation studies • MA, PhD
  exercise physiology • MA, PhD
  family education • M Ed, MA, Ed D, PhD
  French • M Ed
  German • M Ed
  Hebrew • M Ed
  higher education • MA, PhD
  human factors/ergonomics • MA, PhD
  human resource development • M Ed, MA, Ed D, PhD, Certificate
  instructional systems and technology • M Ed, MA, PhD
  international/comparative sport • MA, PhD
  Japanese • M Ed
  kinesiology • M Ed, MA, PhD
  language arts • MA, PhD
  language immersion education • Certificate
  leisure services/management • MA, PhD
  life sciences • M Ed
  literacy education • MA
  marketing education • M Ed
  mathematics • M Ed
  mathematics education • MA, PhD
  middle school science • M Ed
  motor development • MA, PhD
  motor learning/control • MA, PhD
  outdoor education/recreation • MA, PhD
  physical education • M Ed
  postsecondary administration • Ed D
  program evaluation • Certificate
  psychological foundations of education • MA, PhD, Ed S
  reading education • MA, PhD
  recreation, park, and leisure studies • M Ed, MA, PhD
  school psychology • MA, PhD, Ed S
  school-to-work • Certificate
  science • M Ed
  science education • MA, PhD
  second languages and cultures • M Ed
  second languages and cultures education • MA, PhD
  social studies • M Ed
  social studies education • MA, PhD
  Spanish • M Ed
  special education • M Ed, MA, PhD, Ed S
  sport and exercise science • M Ed
  sport management • M Ed, MA, PhD
  sport psychology • MA, PhD
  sport sociology • MA, PhD
  staff development • Certificate
  talent development and gifted education • Certificate
  teacher leadership • M Ed
  teaching • M Ed
  technical education • Certificate
  technology education • M Ed, MA
  technology enhanced learning • Certificate
  therapeutic recreation • MA, PhD
  work, community, and family education • M Ed, MA, Ed D, PhD
  writing education • M Ed, MA, PhD
  youth development leadership • M Ed

College of Human Ecology
Programs in:
  design, housing, and apparel • MA, MFA, MS, PhD
  family social science • MA, PhD
  human ecology • MA, MFA, MS, MSW, PhD
  social work • MSW, PhD

College of Liberal Arts
Steven J. Rosenstone, Dean
Programs in:
  American studies • PhD
  ancient and medieval art and archaeology • MA, PhD
  anthropology • MA, PhD
  art • MFA
  art history • MA, PhD
  audiology • Au D, PhD
  biological psychopathology • PhD
  classics • MA, PhD
  clinical psychology • PhD
  cognitive and biological psychology • PhD
  communication studies • MA, PhD
  comparative literature • PhD
  comparative studies in discourse and society • PhD
  counseling psychology • PhD
  design technology • MFA
  differential psychology/behavior genetics • PhD

Minnesota

directing • MFA
East Asian studies • MA
economics • PhD
English • MA, MFA, PhD
French • MA, PhD
geographic information science • MGIS
geography • MA, PhD
Germanic studies: German and Scandinavian • PhD
Germanic studies: German track • MA, PhD
Germanic studies: medieval • MA, PhD
Germanic studies: Scandinavian track • MA
Germanic studies: teaching German • MA
Greek • MA, PhD
health journalism • MA
hearing science • PhD
Hispanic and Luso-Brazilian literatures and linguistics • PhD
Hispanic linguistics • MA
history • MA, PhD
industrial/organizational psychology • PhD
Italian • MA
Latin • MA, PhD
liberal arts • MA, MFA, MGIS, MM, MS, Au D, DMA, PhD
linguistics • MA, PhD
mass communication • MA, PhD
music • MA, MM, DMA, PhD
personality research • PhD
philosophy • MA, PhD
political science • MA, PhD
Portuguese • MA
psychometric methods • MA, PhD
Russian area studies • MA
school psychology • PhD
social psychology • PhD
sociology • MA, PhD
Spanish • MA
speech science • PhD
speech-language pathology • MA, PhD
statistics • MS, PhD
theater arts and dance • PhD

College of Natural Resources
Dr. Susan Stafford, Dean
Programs in:
conservation biology • MS, PhD
natural resources • MS, PhD
natural resources science and management • MS, PhD
wildlife conservation • MS, PhD

Hubert H. Humphrey Institute of Public Affairs
J. Brian Atwood, Dean
Programs in:
advanced policy analysis methods • MPP
economic and community development • MPP
environmental and ecological planning • MURP
foreign policy • MPP
housing and community development • MURP
land use and urban design • MURP
public affairs • MPA, MPP, MS, MURP
public and nonprofit leadership and management • MPP
regional, economic and workforce development • MURP
science technology and environmental policy • MPP
science, technology, and environmental policy • MS
social policy • MPP
transportation planning • MURP
women and public policy • MPP

Institute of Technology
Programs in:
aerospace engineering • M Aero E, MS, PhD
astronomy • MS, PhD
astrophysics • MS, PhD
biomedical engineering • MS, PhD
chemical engineering • M Ch E, MS Ch E, PhD
chemistry • MS, PhD
civil engineering • MCE, MS, PhD
computer and information sciences • MCIS, MS, PhD
computer engineering • M Comp E, MS
electrical and computer engineering • MEE, MSEE, PhD
geological engineering • M Geo E, MS, PhD
geology • MS, PhD
geophysics • MS, PhD
history of science and technology • MA, PhD
industrial engineering • MSIE, PhD
infrastructure systems engineering • MS
management of technology • MSMOT
materials science and engineering • M Mat SE, MS Mat SE, PhD
mathematics • MS, PhD
mechanical engineering • MSME, PhD
mechanics • MS, PhD
physics • MS, PhD
software engineering • MS
technology • M Aero E, M Ch E, M Comp E, M Geo E, M Mat SE, MA, MCE, MCIS, MEE, MS, MS Ch E, MS Mat SE, MSEE, MSIE, MSME, MSMOT, PhD

School of Nursing
Sandra Edwardson, Dean
Programs in:
adolescent nursing • MS
adult health clinical nurse specialist • MS
advanced clinical specialist in gerontology • MS
children with special health care needs • MS
family nurse practitioner • MS
gerontological nurse practitioner • MS
midwifery • MS
nurse anesthetist • MS
nursing • MS, PhD
nursing education • MS
nursing management • MS
pediatric clinical nurse specialist • MS
pediatric nurse practitioner • MS
psychiatric mental health clinical nurse specialist • MS
public health nursing • MS
women's health nurse practitioner • MS

Law School
Alex M. Johnson, Dean
Program in:
law • JD, LL M

Medical School
Program in:
medicine • MD, MA, MS, PhD

Graduate Programs in Medicine
Programs in:
biochemistry, molecular biology and biophysics • PhD
cellular and integrative physiology • MS, PhD
clinical laboratory sciences • MS
experimental surgery • MS
history of medicine • MA, PhD
medicine • MA, MS, PhD
microbial engineering • MS
microbiology, immunology and cancer biology • PhD
otolaryngology • MS, PhD
physical therapy • MS
rehabilitation science • PhD
surgery • MS, PhD

School of Dentistry
Programs in:
dentistry • DDS, MS, PhD
endodontics • MS
oral biology • MS, PhD
oral health services for older adults • MS
orthodontics • MS
pediatric dentistry • MS
periodontology • MS
prosthodontics • MS
temporal mandibular joint • MS

School of Public Health
Dr. Mark P. Becker, Dean
Programs in:
biostatistics • MPH, MS, PhD
clinical research • MS
community health education • MPH
core concepts • Certificate

Minnesota

University of Minnesota, Twin Cities Campus (continued)
  environmental and occupational epidemiology • MPH, MS, PhD
  environmental chemistry • MS, PhD
  environmental health policy • MPH, MS, PhD
  environmental infectious diseases • MPH, MS, PhD
  environmental toxicology • MPH, MS, PhD
  epidemiology • MPH, PhD
  food safety and biosecurity • Certificate
  general environmental health • MPH, MS
  health services research, policy, and administration • MS, PhD
  industrial hygiene • MPH, MS, PhD
  maternal and child health • MPH
  occupational health and safety • Certificate
  occupational health nursing • MPH, MS, PhD
  occupational medicine • MPH
  preparedness, response and recovery • Certificate
  public health • MA, MPH, MS, PhD, Certificate
  public health administration • MPH
  public health nutrition • MPH
  public health practice • MPH

■ UNIVERSITY OF ST. THOMAS
St. Paul, MN 55105-1096
http://www.stthomas.edu/

Independent-religious, coed, university. *Enrollment:* 11,037 graduate, professional, and undergraduate students; 985 full-time matriculated graduate/professional students (544 women), 4,108 part-time matriculated graduate/professional students (2,056 women). *Graduate faculty:* 160 full-time (58 women), 267 part-time/adjunct (87 women). *Computer facilities:* 1,249 computers available on campus for general student use. A campuswide network can be accessed from student residence rooms and from off campus. Internet access and online class registration are available. *Library facilities:* O'Shaughnessy-Frey Library plus 2 others. *Graduate expenses:* Tuition: part-time $533 per credit hour. Tuition and fees vary according to degree level and program. *General application contact:* Dr. Angeline Barretta-Herman, Associate Vice President for Academic Affairs, 651-962-6033.

Find an in-depth description at www.petersons.com/gradchannel.

Graduate Studies
Dr. Thomas R. Rochon, Executive Vice President for Academic Affairs
Programs in:
  law • JD
  social work • MSW

College of Arts and Sciences
Dr. Thomas B. Connery, Dean of the College of Arts and Sciences
Programs in:
  art history • MA
  arts and sciences • MA
  Catholic studies • MA
  English • MA
  music education • MA

College of Business
Dr. Chistopher P. Puto, Dean
Programs in:
  accounting • MBA
  business • MBA, MBC, MS
  business administration • MBA
  business communication • MBC
  electronic commerce • MBA
  environmental management • MBA
  finance • MBA
  financial services management • MBA
  franchise management • MBA
  government contracts • MBA
  health care management • MBA
  human resource management • MBA
  information management • MBA
  insurance and risk management • MBA
  management • MBA
  manufacturing systems • MBA
  marketing • MBA
  medical group management • MBA
  nonprofit management • MBA
  real estate • MBA
  real estate appraisal • MS
  sports and entertainment management • MBA
  venture management • MBA

Graduate School of Applied Science and Engineering
Programs in:
  applied science and engineering • MMSE, MS, MSDD, MSS, Certificate
  engineering and technology management • Certificate
  manufacturing systems • MS
  manufacturing systems engineering • MMSE
  software engineering • MS, MSDD, MSS, Certificate
  technology management • MS

Graduate School of Professional Psychology
Dr. Jean M. Birbilis, Interim Dean
Programs in:
  counseling psychology • MA, Psy D
  family psychology • Certificate

Saint Paul Seminary School of Divinity
Bp. Frederick Campbell, Rector
Programs in:
  divinity • M Div, MA, D Min
  ministry • D Min
  pastoral studies • MA
  religious education • MA
  theology • MA

School of Education
Dr. Miriam Q. Williams, Dean
Programs in:
  advanced curriculum design • Certificate
  autism spectrum disorders • Certificate
  critical pedagogy • Ed D
  curriculum and instruction • MA, Ed S
  education • MA, MAT, Ed D, Certificate, Ed S
  educational leadership and administration • MA, Ed D, Certificate, Ed S
  gifted, creative, talented • Certificate
  learning technology • MA, Certificate
  organization learning and development • MA, Ed D, Certificate
  Orton Gillingham reading • Certificate
  reading • MA
  reading and language technology • Certificate
  special education • MA
  teacher education • MAT

■ WALDEN UNIVERSITY
Minneapolis, MN 55401
http://www.waldenu.edu/

Proprietary, coed, upper-level institution. CGS member. *Graduate faculty:* 10 full-time (5 women), 400 part-time/adjunct (207 women). *Graduate expenses:* Tuition: part-time $254 per quarter hour. Tuition and fees vary according to degree level and program. *General application contact:* Seth Saunders, Director of Student Enrollment, 866-4-WALDEN.

Find an in-depth description at www.petersons.com/gradchannel.

Graduate Programs
Dr. Paula Peinovich, President
Programs in:
  education • MS, PhD
  health services • PhD
  human services • PhD
  management • MBA, PhD
  professional psychology • MS, PhD
  public administration • MPA, PhD
  public health • MPH, MS, PhD

■ WINONA STATE UNIVERSITY
Winona, MN 55987-5838
http://www.winona.msus.edu/

State-supported, coed, comprehensive institution. *Enrollment:* 8,236 graduate, professional, and undergraduate students; 109 full-time matriculated graduate/professional students (90 women), 318 part-time matriculated graduate/professional students (205 women). *Graduate faculty:* 66 full-time (43 women). *Computer facilities:* Computer purchase and lease plans are available. 1,400 computers available on campus for general student use. A campuswide network can be accessed from student residence rooms and from off campus. Internet access and online class registration are available. *Library facilities:* The Library. *Graduate expenses:* Tuition, state resident: full-time $3,261; part-time $204 per credit. Tuition, nonresident: full-time $4,912; part-time $307 per credit. Required fees: $405; $25 per credit. *General application contact:* Dr. Ron Elcombe, Director of Graduate Studies, 507-457-5088.

Graduate Studies
Dr. Ron Elcombe, Director of Graduate Studies

College of Education
Dr. Carol Anderson, Dean
Programs in:
  counselor education • MS
  education • MS
  educational leadership • Ed S
  elementary school administration • MS
  general school administration • MS
  learning disabilities • MS
  mild to moderate mentally handicapped • MS
  secondary school administration • MS
  special education • MS

College of Liberal Arts
Dr. Joe Gow, Dean
Programs in:
  English • MA, MS
  liberal arts • MA, MS

College of Nursing
Dr. Timothy Gaspar, Graduate Director
Program in:
  nursing • MS

Mississippi

■ ALCORN STATE UNIVERSITY
Alcorn State, MS 39096-7500
http://www.alcorn.edu/

State-supported, coed, comprehensive institution. CGS member. *Enrollment:* 3,309 graduate, professional, and undergraduate students; 146 full-time matriculated graduate/professional students (99 women), 364 part-time matriculated graduate/professional students (270 women). *Graduate faculty:* 64 full-time (21 women), 12 part-time/adjunct (4 women). *Computer facilities:* 500 computers available on campus for general student use. A campuswide network can be accessed from student residence rooms and from off campus. Online class registration is available. *Library facilities:* John Dewey Boyd Library. *Graduate expenses:* Tuition, state resident: full-time $3,192. Tuition, nonresident: full-time $7,698. *General application contact:* Lula Russell, Administrative Assistant to the Dean, School of Graduate Studies, 601-877-6122.

School of Graduate Studies
Dr. Irene Harris Johnson, Dean

School of Agriculture and Applied Science
Napoleon Moses, Dean
Programs in:
  agricultural economics • MS Ag
  agronomy • MS Ag
  animal science • MS Ag

School of Arts and Sciences
Programs in:
  arts and sciences • MS
  biology • MS
  computer and information sciences • MS

School of Business
Dr. John Gill, Dean
Program in:
  business • MBA

School of Nursing
Dr. Frances C. Henderson, Dean
Program in:
  rural nursing • MSN

School of Psychology and Education
Dr. Josephine M. Posey, Dean
Programs in:
  agricultural education • MS Ed
  elementary education • MS Ed, Ed S
  guidance and counseling • MS Ed
  industrial education • MS Ed
  secondary education • MS Ed
  special education • MS Ed

■ DELTA STATE UNIVERSITY
Cleveland, MS 38733-0001
http://www.deltast.edu/

State-supported, coed, comprehensive institution. *Enrollment:* 3,785 graduate, professional, and undergraduate students; 204 full-time matriculated graduate/professional students (118 women), 425 part-time matriculated graduate/professional students (320 women). *Graduate faculty:* 120 full-time (42 women), 26 part-time/adjunct (9 women). *Computer facilities:* 300 computers available on campus for general student use. A campuswide network can be accessed from student residence rooms and from off campus. Internet access and online class registration, e-mail are available. *Library facilities:* W. B. Roberts Library plus 1 other. *Graduate expenses:* Part-time $156 per hour. Tuition, state resident: full-time $3,348; part-time $256 per hour. Tuition, nonresident: full-time $7,965; part-time $412 per hour. *General application contact:* Tyrone Jackson, Director of Graduate Studies, 662-846-4875.

Graduate Programs
Dr. John Thornell, Provost and Vice President for Academic Affairs

College of Arts and Sciences
Collier Parker, Dean
Programs in:
  arts and sciences • M Ed, MM Ed, MSCD, MSCJ, MSNS, MSW
  biological sciences • MSNS
  community development • MSCD
  criminal justice • MSCJ
  English education • M Ed
  history education • M Ed
  mathematics education • M Ed
  music education • MM Ed
  social science education • M Ed
  social work • MSW

College of Business
Dr. Billy Moore, Dean
Programs in:
  business • MBA, MCA
  commercial aviation • MCA
  management • MBA
  marketing • MBA

College of Education
Dr. Lynn House, Dean
Programs in:
  administration • M Ed
  administration and supervision • M Ed, Ed S
  education • M Ed, Ed D, Ed S
  elementary education • M Ed, Ed S
  elementary principalship • M Ed
  elementary supervision • M Ed
  guidance and counseling • M Ed
  physical education and recreation • M Ed
  professional studies • Ed D
  secondary principalship • M Ed
  secondary supervision • M Ed
  special education • M Ed

School of Nursing
Dr. Maureen Gruich, Dean
Program in:
  nursing • MSN

Mississippi

■ JACKSON STATE UNIVERSITY
Jackson, MS 39217
http://www.jsums.edu/

State-supported, coed, university. CGS member. *Computer facilities:* A campuswide network can be accessed from off campus. Internet access is available. *Library facilities:* H. T. Sampson Library plus 1 other. *General application contact:* Dean of the Graduate School, 601-968-2455.

Graduate School

School of Allied Health
Program in:
 allied health • MS

School of Business
Programs in:
 accounting • MPA
 business • M Bus Ed, MBA, MPA, MSSM, PhD
 business administration • MBA
 business education • M Bus Ed
 systems management • MSSM

School of Education
Programs in:
 community and agency counseling • MS
 early childhood education • MS Ed, Ed D
 education • MS, MS Ed, Ed D, PhD, Ed S
 education administration • Ed S
 educational administration • MS Ed, PhD
 elementary education • MS Ed, Ed S
 guidance and counseling • MS, MS Ed, Ed S
 health, physical education and recreation • MS Ed
 rehabilitative counseling service • MS Ed
 secondary education • MS Ed, Ed S
 special education • MS Ed, Ed S

School of Liberal Arts
Programs in:
 clinical psychology • PhD
 criminology and justice service • MA
 English • MA
 history • MA
 liberal arts • MA, MAT, MM Ed, MPPA, MS, PhD
 mass communications • MS
 music education • MM Ed
 political science • MA
 public policy and administration • MPPA, PhD
 sociology • MA
 teaching English • MAT
 urban and regional planning • MS

School of Science and Technology
Programs in:
 biology education • MST
 chemistry • MS, PhD
 computer science • MS
 environmental science • MS, PhD
 hazardous materials management • MS
 industrial arts education • MS Ed
 mathematics • MS
 mathematics education • MST
 science and technology • MS, MS Ed, MST, PhD
 science education • MST

School of Social Work
Program in:
 social work • MSW, PhD

■ MISSISSIPPI COLLEGE
Clinton, MS 39058

Independent-religious, coed, comprehensive institution. *Computer facilities:* 207 computers available on campus for general student use. A campuswide network can be accessed from student residence rooms and from off campus. Internet access is available. *Library facilities:* Leland Speed Library plus 1 other. *General application contact:* Graduate Dean, 601-925-3260.

Graduate School

College of Arts and Sciences
Programs in:
 administration of justice • MSS
 applied music performance • MM
 art • MA, MFA
 arts and sciences • M Ed, MA, MCS, MFA, MLS, MM, MS, MSC, MSS, MSS
 biology • MCS
 chemistry • MCS
 communication • MSC
 computer science • MS
 conducting • MM
 counseling psychology • MS
 English • M Ed, MA
 history • M Ed, MA, MSS
 liberal studies • MLS
 mathematics • MCS, MS
 music education • MM
 political science • MSS
 psychology • MS
 psychometry • M Ed
 social sciences • M Ed, MSS
 sociology • MSS
 theory and composition • MM
 vocal pedagogy • MM

School of Business Administration
Programs in:
 accounting • MBA
 business administration • MBA
 health services administration • MHSA

School of Education
Programs in:
 art education • M Ed
 biology education • M Ed
 business education • M Ed
 computer science education • M Ed
 counseling psychology • MCP
 education • M Ed, MCP, Ed S
 educational leadership • M Ed
 elementary education • M Ed
 guidance and counseling • M Ed, Ed S
 mathematics education • M Ed
 sciences education • M Ed
 secondary education • M Ed

School of Law
James H. Rosenblatt, Dean
Program in:
 law • JD

■ MISSISSIPPI STATE UNIVERSITY
Mississippi State, MS 39762
http://www.msstate.edu/

State-supported, coed, university. CGS member. *Enrollment:* 16,173 graduate, professional, and undergraduate students; 1,697 full-time matriculated graduate/professional students (783 women), 1,637 part-time matriculated graduate/professional students (902 women). *Graduate faculty:* 1,043 full-time (300 women), 140 part-time/adjunct (75 women). *Computer facilities:* 2,000 computers available on campus for general student use. A campuswide network can be accessed from student residence rooms and from off campus. Internet access and online class registration, wireless network with partial campus coverage are available. *Library facilities:* Mitchell Memorial Library plus 2 others. *Graduate expenses:* Tuition, state resident: full-time $3,874; part-time $215 per hour. Tuition, nonresident: full-time $8,780; part-time $488 per hour. International tuition: $9,105 full-time. Tuition and fees vary according to course load. *General application contact:* Diane D. Wolfe, Director of Admissions, 662-325-2224.

Bagley College of Engineering
Dr. A. Wayne Bennett, Dean
Programs in:
 aerospace engineering • MS
 biological engineering • MS
 biomedical engineering • MS, PhD
 civil engineering • MS
 computer engineering • MS, PhD
 computer science • MS, PhD
 electrical engineering • MS, PhD
 engineering • PhD
 engineering mechanics • MS
 industrial engineering • MS, PhD
 mechanical engineering • MS, PhD

David C. Swalm School of Chemical Engineering
Dr. Kirk H. Schulz, Director
Programs in:
chemical engineering • MS
engineering • PhD

College of Agriculture and Life Sciences
Dr. Vance Watson, Dean and Vice President
Programs in:
agribusiness management • MABM
agricultural economics • PhD
agricultural pest management • MS
agriculture and extension education • MS
agriculture and life sciences • MABM, MLA, MS, PhD
agronomy • MS, PhD
biochemistry • MS
entomology • MS, PhD
food science and technology • MS, PhD
horticulture • MS, PhD
landscape architecture • MLA
molecular biology • PhD
plant pathology • MS, PhD
poultry science • MS
weed science • MS, PhD

College of Arts and Sciences
Dr. Philip B. Oldham, Dean
Programs in:
applied anthropology • MA
arts and sciences • MA, MFA, MPPA, MS, PhD
biological sciences • MS, PhD
chemistry • MS, PhD
clinical psychology • MS
cognitive science • PhD
electronic visualization • MFA
engineering physics • PhD
English • MA
experimental psychology • MS
French • MA
French/German • MA
geosciences • MS
German • MA
history • MA, PhD
mathematical sciences • PhD
mathematics • MS
physics • MS
political science • MA
public policy and administration • MPPA, PhD
sociology • MS, PhD
Spanish • MA
Spanish/French • MA
Spanish/German • MA
statistics • MS

College of Business and Industry
Dr. Sara M. Freedman, Dean
Programs in:
applied economics • PhD
business administration • MBA, PhD
business and industry • MA, MBA, MPA, MSBA, MSIS, MTX, PhD
economics • MA
finance • MSBA
information systems • MSIS
project management • MBA

School of Accountancy
Dr. Dan P. Hollingsworth, Director
Program in:
accountancy • MPA, MTX

College of Education
Dr. Roy Ruby, Dean
Programs in:
counselor education • MS, PhD, Ed S
curriculum and instruction • PhD
education • MS, MSIT, Ed D, PhD, Ed S
educational psychology • MS, PhD, Ed S
elementary education • MS, Ed D, PhD, Ed S
exercise science • MS
health education/health promotion • MS
instructional technology • MSIT
secondary education • MS, Ed D, PhD, Ed S
special education • MS, Ed S
sports administration • MS
teaching/coaching • MS
technology • MS, Ed D, PhD, Ed S
workforce education leadership • MS

College of Forest Resources
Dr. Bob L. Karr, Dean
Programs in:
forest products • MS
forest resources • MS, PhD
forestry • MS
wildlife and fisheries science • MS

College of Veterinary Medicine
Dr. John U. Thomson, Dean
Programs in:
environmental toxicology • PhD
veterinary medical science • MS, PhD
veterinary medicine • DVM, MS, PhD

School of Architecture
Prof. James L. West, Dean
Program in:
architecture • MS

■ MISSISSIPPI UNIVERSITY FOR WOMEN
Columbus, MS 39701-9998
http://www.muw.edu/

State-supported, coed, primarily women, comprehensive institution. *Computer facilities:* 250 computers available on campus for general student use. A campuswide network can be accessed from student residence rooms and from off campus. Internet access, various software packages are available. *Library facilities:* John Clayton Fant Memorial Library. *General application contact:* Director, Graduate School, 601-329-7150.

Graduate School

Division of Education and Human Sciences
Programs in:
gifted studies • M Ed
instructional management • M Ed
speech/language pathology • MS

Division of Health and Kinesiology
Program in:
health education • MS

Division of Nursing
Program in:
nursing • MSN, Certificate

■ UNIVERSITY OF MISSISSIPPI
Oxford, University, MS 38677
http://www.olemiss.edu/

State-supported, coed, university. CGS member. *Enrollment:* 13,804 graduate, professional, and undergraduate students; 1,785 full-time matriculated graduate/professional students (866 women), 372 part-time matriculated graduate/professional students (244 women). *Graduate faculty:* 514. *Computer facilities:* 3,500 computers available on campus for general student use. A campuswide network can be accessed from student residence rooms and from off campus. *Library facilities:* J. D. Williams Library plus 3 others. *Graduate expenses:* Tuition, state resident: part-time $218 per hour. Tuition, nonresident: part-time $273 per hour. *General application contact:* Dr. Donald R. Cole, Associate Dean of Graduate School, 662-915-7474.

Graduate School
Dr. Maurice Eftink, Acting Dean

College of Liberal Arts
Dr. Glenn Hopkins, Dean
Programs in:
anthropology • MA
art education • MA
art history • MA
biology • MS, PhD
chemistry • MS, DA, PhD
classics • MA
clinical psychology • PhD
creative writing • MFA
economics • MA, PhD
English • MA, PhD
experimental psychology • PhD
fine arts • MFA
French • MA
German • MA
history • MA, PhD

Mississippi

University of Mississippi (continued)
- journalism • MA
- liberal arts • MA, MFA, MM, MS, MSS, DA, PhD
- mathematics • MA, MS, PhD
- music • MM, DA
- philosophy • MA
- physics • MA, MS, PhD
- political science • MA, PhD
- psychology • MA
- sociology • MA, MSS
- Southern studies • MA
- Spanish • MA
- theatre arts • MFA

School of Accountancy
Dr. Morris Stocks, Dean
Programs in:
- accountancy • M Acc, PhD
- taxation accounting • M Tax

School of Applied Sciences
Dr. Linda Chitwood, Dean
Programs in:
- applied sciences • MA, MS, PhD
- communicative disorders • MS
- exercise science • MA, MS
- exercise science and leisure management • PhD
- leisure management • MA
- park and recreation management • MA
- wellness • MS

School of Business Administration
Dr. Michael Harvey, Dean
Programs in:
- business administration • MBA, PhD
- systems management • MS

School of Education
Dr. James Chambless, Dean
Programs in:
- counselor education • M Ed, PhD, Specialist
- curriculum and instruction • M Ed, Ed D, Ed S
- education • PhD
- educational leadership • PhD
- educational leadership and counselor education • M Ed, MA, Ed D, Ed S
- higher education/student personnel • MA
- secondary education • MA

School of Engineering
Dr. Kai-Fong Lee, Dean
Programs in:
- computational engineering science • MS, PhD
- engineering science • MS, PhD

School of Pharmacy
Dr. Barbara G. Wells, Dean
Programs in:
- medicinal chemistry • MS, PhD
- pharmaceutics • MS, PhD
- pharmacognosy • MS, PhD
- pharmacology • MS, PhD
- pharmacy • Pharm D, MS, PhD
- pharmacy administration • MS, PhD
- toxicology • PhD

School of Law
Dr. Samuel Davis, Dean
Program in:
- law • JD

■ UNIVERSITY OF SOUTHERN MISSISSIPPI
Hattiesburg, MS 39406-0001
http://www.usm.edu/

State-supported, coed, university. CGS member. *Enrollment:* 14,894 graduate, professional, and undergraduate students; 1,286 full-time matriculated graduate/professional students (739 women), 1,393 part-time matriculated graduate/professional students (909 women). *Graduate faculty:* 396 full-time (142 women), 32 part-time/adjunct (18 women). *Computer facilities:* 600 computers available on campus for general student use. Internet access is available. *Library facilities:* Cook Memorial Library plus 4 others. *Graduate expenses:* Tuition, state resident: part-time $1,967 per semester. Tuition, nonresident: part-time $4,376 per semester. *General application contact:* Dr. Bradley Bond, Assistant Provost, 601-266-4369.

Graduate School
Dr. Bradley Bond, Assistant Provost

College of Arts and Letters
Dr. Elliott A. Pood, Dean
Programs in:
- anthropology • MA
- art • MFA
- art education • MAE
- arts and letters • MA, MAE, MATL, MFA, MM, MME, MS, DMA, DME, PhD
- church music • MM
- conducting • MM
- English • MA, PhD
- foreign languages and literatures • MATL
- history • MA, MS, PhD
- history and literature • MM
- mass communication • MA, MS, PhD
- music education • MME, DME, PhD
- performance • MM
- performance and pedagogy • DMA
- philosophy • MA
- political science • MA, MS
- public relations • MS
- speech communication • MA, MS, PhD
- theatre and dance • MFA
- theory and composition • MM
- woodwind performance • MM

College of Business and Economic Development
Dr. Harold Doty, Dean
Programs in:
- business administration • MBA
- business and economic development • MBA, MPA, MS, PhD
- economic development • MS
- economics, finance, and international business • MS, PhD
- international development • PhD
- professional accountancy • MPA
- workforce training and development • MS

College of Education and Psychology
Dr. W. Lee Pierce, Interim Dean
Programs in:
- adult education • M Ed, Ed D, PhD, Ed S
- alternative secondary teacher education • MAT
- business technology education • MS
- early childhood education • M Ed, Ed S
- early intervention • MS
- education and psychology • M Ed, MA, MAT, MLIS, MS, Ed D, PhD, Ed S, SLS
- education of the gifted • M Ed, Ed D, PhD, Ed S
- educational administration • M Ed, Ed D, PhD, Ed S
- elementary education • M Ed, Ed D, PhD, Ed S
- family and consumer studies • MS
- instructional technology • MS
- library and information science • MLIS, SLS
- marriage and family therapy • MS
- psychology • M Ed, MA, MS, PhD, Ed S
- reading • M Ed, MS, Ed S
- secondary education • M Ed, MS, Ed D, PhD, Ed S
- special education • M Ed, Ed D, PhD, Ed S
- technical occupational education • MS

College of Health
Dr. Joan Exline, Interim Dean
Programs in:
- adult health nursing • MSN
- community health nursing • MSN
- ethics • PhD
- family nurse practitioner • MSN
- health • MA, MPH, MS, MSN, MSW, Ed D, PhD
- health education • MPH
- health policy/administration • MPH
- human performance • MS, Ed D, PhD
- leadership • PhD
- medical technology • MS
- nursing service administration • MSN
- nutrition and food systems • MS, PhD

occupational/environmental health • MPH
policy analysis • PhD
psychiatric nursing • MSN
public health nutrition • MPH
recreation • MS
social work • MSW
speech and hearing sciences • MA, MS, PhD
sport administration • MS

College of Science and Technology
Dr. Rex Gandy, Dean
Programs in:
administration of justice • PhD
analytical chemistry • MS, PhD
biochemistry • MS, PhD
coastal sciences • MS, PhD
computer science • MS
corrections • MA, MS
engineering technology • MS
environmental biology • MS, PhD
geography • MS
geology • MS
hydrographic science • MS
inorganic chemistry • MS, PhD
juvenile justice • MA, MS
law enforcement • MA, MS
marine biology • MS, PhD
marine science • MS, PhD
mathematics • MS
microbiology • MS, PhD
molecular biology • MS, PhD
organic chemistry • MS, PhD
physical chemistry • MS, PhD
physics and astronomy • MS
polymers and materials engineering • MS, PhD
science and mathematics education • M Ed, MS, Ed D, PhD
science and technology • M Ed, MA, MS, Ed D, PhD
scientific computing • PhD

■ **WILLIAM CAREY COLLEGE**
Hattiesburg, MS 39401-5499
http://www.wmcarey.edu/

Independent-religious, coed, comprehensive institution. *Enrollment:* 2,586 graduate, professional, and undergraduate students; 368 full-time matriculated graduate/professional students (271 women), 547 part-time matriculated graduate/professional students (460 women). *Graduate faculty:* 41 full-time (22 women), 25 part-time/adjunct (19 women). *Computer facilities:* 30 computers available on campus for general student use. A campuswide network can be accessed from student residence rooms and from off campus. Internet access is available. *Library facilities:* I. E. Rouse Library. *Graduate expenses:* Tuition: full-time $3,780; part-time $210 per credit hour. Tuition and fees vary according to program. *General application contact:* Dr. Tommy King, Dean of Graduate Admissions, 601-318-6774.

Graduate School
Dr. Cloyd L. Ezell, Vice President of Academic Affairs
Programs in:
counseling psychology • MS
industrial and organizational psychology • MS

School of Business
Dr. Hubert L. Keasler, Dean
Program in:
business • MBA

School of Education
Dr. Bonnie Holder, Dean
Programs in:
art education • M Ed
art of teaching • M Ed
elementary education • Ed S
English education • M Ed
mild/moderate disabilities • M Ed

School of Nursing
Dr. Mary Stewart, Interim Dean
Program in:
nursing • MSN

Missouri

■ **AVILA UNIVERSITY**
Kansas City, MO 64145-1698
http://www.avila.edu/

Independent-religious, coed, comprehensive institution. *Enrollment:* 1,683 graduate, professional, and undergraduate students; 126 full-time matriculated graduate/professional students (104 women), 202 part-time matriculated graduate/professional students (127 women). *Graduate faculty:* 20 full-time (13 women), 27 part-time/adjunct (15 women). *Computer facilities:* 68 computers available on campus for general student use. A campuswide network can be accessed from student residence rooms. Internet access is available. *Library facilities:* Hooley Bundshu Library. *Graduate expenses:* Tuition: full-time $5,625; part-time $375 per credit hour. Required fees: $12 per credit hour. *General application contact:* Don Miller, Coordinator, MBA Admissions, 816-501-3601.

Graduate Programs
Sr. Marie Joan Harris, Provost and Vice President for Academic Affairs

Division of Business and Economics
Wendy L. Acker, MBA Director
Program in:
business and economics • MBA

Division of Education and Psychology
Chairperson
Programs in:
counseling psychology • MS
education • MA

■ **CENTRAL MISSOURI STATE UNIVERSITY**
Warrensburg, MO 64093
http://www.cmsu.edu/

State-supported, coed, comprehensive institution. CGS member. *Enrollment:* 10,351 graduate, professional, and undergraduate students; 255 full-time matriculated graduate/professional students (142 women), 1,188 part-time matriculated graduate/professional students (717 women). *Graduate faculty:* 312 full-time (109 women), 10 part-time/adjunct (3 women). *Computer facilities:* 1,230 computers available on campus for general student use. A campuswide network can be accessed from student residence rooms and from off campus. Internet access and online class registration are available. *Library facilities:* James C. Kirkpatrick Library. *Graduate expenses:* Tuition, state resident: part-time $198 per credit hour. Tuition, nonresident: part-time $396 per credit hour. Required fees: $12 per credit hour. *General application contact:* Dr. Novella Perrin, Dean of Graduate Studies/Assistant Vice-President for Academic Affairs, 660-543-4092.

Find an in-depth description at www.petersons.com/gradchannel.

School of Graduate Studies
Dr. Novella Perrin, Dean of Graduate Studies/Assistant Vice President for Academic Affairs

College of Applied Sciences and Technology
Dr. Alice Greife, Dean
Programs in:
agriculture technology • MS
applied sciences and technology • MS, MSE, Ed S
aviation safety • MS
fire science • MS
human services/ technology and occupation education • Ed S
human services/industrial arts and technology • Ed S
human services/public services • Ed S
industrial hygiene • MS
industrial management • MS
industrial safety management • MS

Missouri

Central Missouri State University (continued)
industrial, vocational, and technical education • MS
loss control • MS
occupational safety management • MS
public safety • MS
rural and family nursing • MS
safety management • MS
secondary education/business and office education • MSE
security • MS
technology and occupation/technology education • MS
transportation safety • MS

College of Arts and Sciences
Dr. Charles McAdams, Chair
Programs in:
applied mathematics • MS
arts and sciences • MA, MS, MSE
biology • MS
communication/mass communication • MA
English • MA
English education • MSE
history • MA
mathematics • MS
mathematics education • MSE
music • MA
speech communication • MA
teaching English as a second language • MA
theatre • MA

College of Education and Human Services
Dr. Rick Sluder, Interim Dean
Programs in:
administration • Ed S
adult education • MSE
criminal justice • MS
curriculum and instruction • Ed S
education and human services • MA, MS, MSE, Ed S
education technology • MSE
education, administration and higher education • MS, MSE, Ed S
elementary education • MSE
human services • Ed S
human services-public services • Ed S
human services/learning resources • Ed S
K–12 education • MSE
library information technology • MS
library science and information services • MS
physical education/exercise and sports science • MS
psychology • MS
reading • MSE
school administration • MSE
secondary education • MSE
social gerontology • MS
sociology • MA
special education • MSE, Ed S
special education/human services • Ed S

speech pathology and audiology • MS
student personnel administration • MS

Harmon College of Business Administration
Dr. George Wilson, Dean
Programs in:
accounting • MA
business administration • MBA
economics • MA
information technology • MS

■ DRURY UNIVERSITY
Springfield, MO 65802-3791
http://www.drury.edu/

Independent, coed, comprehensive institution. *Computer facilities:* 323 computers available on campus for general student use. A campuswide network can be accessed from student residence rooms and from off campus. Internet access and online class registration, digital imaging lab are available. *Library facilities:* F. W. Olin Library plus 1 other. *General application contact:* Director of Teacher Education, 417-873-7271.

Breech School of Business Administration
Programs in:
business administration • MBA
business and international management • MBA

Graduate Programs in Education
Programs in:
elementary education • M Ed
gifted education • M Ed
human services • M Ed
middle school teaching • M Ed
physical education • M Ed
secondary education • M Ed

Program in Communication
Program in:
communication • MA

Program in Criminology/Criminal Justice
Programs in:
criminal justice • MS
criminology • MA

■ FONTBONNE UNIVERSITY
St. Louis, MO 63105-3098
http://www.fontbonne.edu/

Independent-religious, coed, comprehensive institution. *Enrollment:* 2,538 graduate, professional, and undergraduate students; 357 full-time matriculated graduate/professional students (251 women), 418 part-time matriculated graduate/professional students (333 women). *Graduate faculty:* 64 full-time (39 women), 230 part-time/adjunct (141 women). *Computer facilities:* 120 computers available on campus for general student use. A campuswide network can be accessed from student residence rooms and from off campus. Internet access and online class registration are available. *Library facilities:* Fontbonne Library. *Graduate expenses:* Tuition: part-time $435 per credit. Required fees: $16 per credit. *General application contact:* Peggy Musen, Associate Dean of Enrollment Management and Director of Admissions, 314-889-1400.

Graduate Programs
Programs in:
art • MA
business administration • MBA
computer education • MS
early intervention in deaf education • MA
education • MA
family and consumer sciences • MA
fine arts • MFA
options in business administration • MBA
options in management • MM
speech language pathology • MS
taxation • MST

■ LINCOLN UNIVERSITY
Jefferson City, MO 65102
http://www.lincolnu.edu/

State-supported, coed, comprehensive institution. *Enrollment:* 3,128 graduate, professional, and undergraduate students; 61 full-time matriculated graduate/professional students (30 women), 117 part-time matriculated graduate/professional students (78 women). *Graduate faculty:* 5 full-time (3 women), 26 part-time/adjunct (6 women). *Computer facilities:* 175 computers available on campus for general student use. A campuswide network can be accessed from off campus. Internet access is available. *Library facilities:* Inman Page Library. *Graduate expenses:* Tuition, state resident: part-time $162 per semester hour. Tuition, nonresident: part-time $312 per semester hour. Required fees: $478; $5 per semester hour. $20 per semester. *General application contact:* Dr. Linda S. Bickel, Dean of the School for Graduate Studies and Continuing Education, 573-681-5247.

School for Graduate Studies and Continuing Education
Dr. Linda S. Bickel, Dean of the School for Graduate Studies and Continuing Education

Missouri

College of Business and Professional Studies
Dr. Kojo Quartey, Dean
Programs in:
  accounting • MBA
  business • MBA
  management • MBA

College of Liberal Arts, Education and Journalism
Dr. Patrick Henry, Dean
Programs in:
  educational leadership • Ed S
  elementary and secondary teaching • M Ed
  guidance and counseling • M Ed
  history • MA
  liberal arts, education and journalism • M Ed, MA, Ed S
  school administration and supervision • M Ed
  social science • MA
  sociology • MA
  sociology/criminal justice • MA
  special education • M Ed

■ **LINDENWOOD UNIVERSITY**
St. Charles, MO 63301-1695
http://www.lindenwood.edu/

Independent-religious, coed, comprehensive institution. *Computer facilities:* Computer purchase and lease plans are available. 160 computers available on campus for general student use. A campuswide network can be accessed from student residence rooms and from off campus. Internet access is available. *Library facilities:* Butler Library. *General application contact:* Dean of Admissions, 636-949-4933.

Graduate Programs
Programs in:
  administration • MSA
  business administration • MBA
  corporate communication • MS
  counseling psychology • MA
  criminal justice and administration • MS
  gerontology • MA
  health management • MS
  human resource management • MS
  human service agency management • MS
  management • MSA
  marketing • MSA
  mass communication • MS
  valuation sciences • MS
  writing • MFA

Division of Arts and Communication Arts
Programs in:
  arts management • MA
  communication arts • MA
  studio art • MFA
  theatre arts • MA, MFA

Division of Business Administration
Programs in:
  accounting • MBA, MS
  business administration • MBA
  finance • MBA, MS
  human resource management • MBA
  human resources • MS
  human services agency management • MA
  international business • MBA, MS
  management • MBA, MS
  management information systems • MBA, MS
  managing business to business • MA
  managing human resources • MA
  managing international business • MA
  managing investment management • MA
  managing leadership • MA
  managing marketing • MA
  managing organizational behavior • MA
  managing sales • MA
  marketing • MBA, MS
  public management • MBA, MS
  sport management • MA

Division of Education
Programs in:
  education • MA, Ed S
  educational administration • MA
  library media • MA

■ **MARYVILLE UNIVERSITY OF SAINT LOUIS**
St. Louis, MO 63141-7299
http://www.maryville.edu/

Independent, coed, comprehensive institution. *Enrollment:* 3,301 graduate, professional, and undergraduate students; 193 full-time matriculated graduate/professional students (164 women), 403 part-time matriculated graduate/professional students (289 women). *Graduate faculty:* 39 full-time (25 women), 47 part-time/adjunct (32 women). *Computer facilities:* 250 computers available on campus for general student use. A campuswide network can be accessed from student residence rooms and from off campus. Internet access, e-mail, specialized software, university catalog, schedules are available. *Library facilities:* Maryville University Library. *Graduate expenses:* Tuition: full-time $15,200; part-time $465 per credit hour. Required fees: $45 per semester. *General application contact:* MaryAnn Chastain, Director of Adult Student Recruitment, 314-529-9334.

The John E. Simon School of Business
Dr. Pamela Horwitz, Dean
Programs in:
  accounting • MBA, PGC
  business studies • PGC
  e-business • MBA, PGC
  information systems • MBA, PGC
  international business • MBA, PGC
  management • MBA, PGC
  marketing • MBA, PGC

School of Education
Dr. Kathe Rasch, Dean
Programs in:
  art education • MA Ed
  early childhood education • MA Ed
  elementary education • MA Ed
  elementary education/English • MA Ed
  elementary education/psychology • MA Ed
  environmental education • MA Ed
  gifted education • MA Ed
  middle grades education • MA Ed
  reading specialist • MA Ed
  secondary education • MA Ed

School of Health Professions
Dr. Mary Ellen Finch, Interim Dean
Programs in:
  health administration • MHA
  health professions • MARC, MHA, MMT, MOT, MPT, MSN
  music therapy • MMT
  nursing • MSN
  occupational therapy • MOT
  physical therapy • MPT
  rehabilitation counseling • MARC

■ **NORTHWEST MISSOURI STATE UNIVERSITY**
Maryville, MO 64468-6001
http://www.nwmissouri.edu/

State-supported, coed, comprehensive institution. *Enrollment:* 166 full-time matriculated graduate/professional students (82 women), 317 part-time matriculated graduate/professional students (213 women). *Graduate faculty:* 128 full-time (41 women). *Computer facilities:* 2,450 computers available on campus for general student use. A campuswide network can be accessed from student residence rooms and from off campus. Internet access is available. *Library facilities:* B. D. Owens Library plus 1 other. *Graduate expenses:* Tuition, state resident: full-time $1,815; part-time $202 per credit. Tuition, nonresident: full-time $3,177; part-time $354 per credit. Tuition and fees vary according to course level and course load. *General application contact:* Dr. Frances Shipley, Dean of Graduate School, 660-562-1145.

Graduate School
Dr. Frances Shipley, Dean of Graduate School

Missouri

Northwest Missouri State University (continued)

College of Arts and Sciences
Dr. Frank C. Veeman, Interim Dean
Programs in:
 agriculture • MS
 arts and sciences • MA, MS, MS Ed
 biology • MS
 English • MA
 English with speech emphasis • MA
 geographic information sciences • MS
 history • MA
 teaching agriculture • MS Ed
 teaching English with speech emphasis • MS Ed
 teaching history • MS Ed
 teaching mathematics • MS Ed
 teaching music • MS Ed

College of Education and Human Services
Dr. Max Ruhl, Dean
Programs in:
 counseling psychology • MS
 early childhood education • MS Ed
 education and human services • MS, MS Ed, Ed S
 educational leadership • MS Ed, Ed S
 educational leadership: elementary • MS Ed
 educational leadership: secondary • MS Ed
 elementary education • MS Ed
 elementary principalship • Ed S
 guidance and counseling • MS Ed
 health and physical education • MS Ed
 learning disabilities: elementary • MS Ed
 learning disabilities: elementary/secondary • MS Ed
 learning disabilities: secondary • MS Ed
 learning disabled and mentally handicapped • MS Ed
 mentally handicapped: elementary • MS Ed
 mentally handicapped: elementary/secondary • MS Ed
 mentally handicapped: secondary • MS Ed
 middle school education • MS Ed
 reading education • MS Ed
 science education teaching • MS Ed
 secondary education • MS Ed
 secondary individualized prescribed programs • MS Ed
 secondary principalship • Ed S
 special education • MS Ed
 superintendency • Ed S
 teaching secondary • MS Ed

Melvin and Valorie Booth College of Business and Professional Studies
Dr. Ron DeYoung, Dean
Programs in:
 accounting • MBA
 agricultural economics • MBA
 business administration • MBA
 business and professional studies • MBA, MS, MS Ed
 health management • MBA
 management information systems • MBA
 school computer studies • MS
 teaching instructional technology • MS Ed

■ PARK UNIVERSITY
Parkville, MO 64152-3795
http://www.park.edu/

Independent, coed, comprehensive institution. *Enrollment:* 11,868 graduate, professional, and undergraduate students; 54 full-time matriculated graduate/professional students, 361 part-time matriculated graduate/professional students. *Graduate faculty:* 17 full-time (6 women), 25 part-time/adjunct (10 women). *Computer facilities:* 143 computers available on campus for general student use. A campuswide network can be accessed from student residence rooms. Internet access and online class registration are available. *Library facilities:* McAfee Memorial Library. *Graduate expenses:* Tuition: full-time $3,240; part-time $270 per hour. *General application contact:* Thomas E. Gee, Director of Graduate Admissions, 816-421-1125 Ext. 236.

■ ROCKHURST UNIVERSITY
Kansas City, MO 64110-2561
http://www.rockhurst.edu/

Independent-religious, coed, comprehensive institution. CGS member. *Enrollment:* 2,764 graduate, professional, and undergraduate students; 279 full-time matriculated graduate/professional students (173 women), 499 part-time matriculated graduate/professional students (239 women). *Graduate faculty:* 48 full-time (24 women), 24 part-time/adjunct (12 women). *Computer facilities:* 500 computers available on campus for general student use. A campuswide network can be accessed from student residence rooms and from off campus. Internet access is available. *Library facilities:* Greenlease Library. *Graduate expenses:* Tuition: part-time $465 per credit hour. Required fees: $25 per term. Part-time tuition and fees vary according to program. *General application contact:* Director of Graduate Recruitment, 816-501-4100.

Helzberg School of Management
Dr. James Daley, Dean
Program in:
 management • MBA

School of Graduate and Professional Studies
Dr. Robin Bowen, Interim Dean
Programs in:
 arts and sciences • M Ed, MOT, MPT, MS, DPT
 communication sciences and disorders • MS
 education • M Ed
 occupational therapy education • MOT
 physical therapy • MPT, DPT

■ SAINT LOUIS UNIVERSITY
St. Louis, MO 63103-2097
http://imagine.slu.edu/

Independent-religious, coed, university. CGS member. *Enrollment:* 11,217 graduate, professional, and undergraduate students; 2,530 full-time matriculated graduate/professional students (1,415 women), 1,596 part-time matriculated graduate/professional students (967 women). *Graduate faculty:* 1,294 full-time (471 women), 420 part-time/adjunct (192 women). *Computer facilities:* Computer purchase and lease plans are available. 6,500 computers available on campus for general student use. A campuswide network can be accessed from student residence rooms and from off campus. Internet access and online class registration are available. *Library facilities:* Pius XII Memorial Library plus 2 others. *Graduate expenses:* Tuition: part-time $690 per credit hour. Required fees: $59 per semester. Tuition and fees vary according to program. *General application contact:* Gary Behrman, Associate Dean of the Graduate School, 314-977-3827.

Find an in-depth description at www.petersons.com/gradchannel.

Graduate School
Donald G. Brennan, PhD, Dean
Programs in:
 anatomy and neurobiology • MS-R, PhD
 biochemistry and molecular biology • PhD
 economics • MA
 international business and marketing • PhD
 medicine • MS-R, PhD
 molecular microbiology and immunology • PhD
 pathology • PhD
 pharmacological and physiological science • PhD

Center for Advanced Dental Education
Dr. Rolf Behrents, Executive Director
Program in:
  advanced dental education • MS, MS-R

Center for Health Care Ethics
Rev. Gerard Magill, PhD, Executive Director
Program in:
  health care ethics • PhD

College of Arts and Sciences
Rev. Michael K. May, SJ, Interim Dean
Programs in:
  American studies • MA, MA-R, MS, MS-R, PhD
  applied experimental psychology • MS-R, PhD
  arts and sciences • M Pr Met, MA, MA-R, MS, MS-R, PhD
  biology • MS, MS-R, PhD
  chemistry • MS, MS-R

College of Public Service
Dr. James F. Gilsinian, Dean
Program in:
  communication sciences and disorders • MA, MA-R

Parks College of Engineering and Aviation
Dr. Bjong Wolf Yeigh, Dean
Program in:
  aerospace engineering • MS, MS-R

School of Nursing
Dr. Joan Hrubetz, Dean
Programs in:
  nursing • MSN, MSN-R, PhD, Certificate

School of Public Health
Dr. Andrew Balas, Dean
Programs in:
  behavioral science in health education • MPH
  biostatistics • MPH
  biostatistics and epidemiology • MPH
  community health • MPH
  environmental and occupational health • MPH
  environmental health and epidemiology • MPH
  epidemiology • MPH
  health management and policy • MHA
  public health studies • PhD

John Cook School of Business
Dr. Ellen Harshman, Dean
Programs in:
  accounting • M Acct
  business • EMIB, M Acct, M Fin, MBA, PhD
  finance • M Fin

Boeing Institute of International Business
Dr. Seung H. Kim, Director
Program in:
  executive international business • EMIB

School of Allied Health Professions
Dr. Charlotte Royeen, Dean
Programs in:
  allied health professions • MMS, MOT, MS, MSPT, DPT
  nutrition and dietetics • MS
  occupational science and occupational therapy • MOT
  physical therapy • MSPT, DPT
  physician assistant • MMS

School of Law
Dr. Jeffrey E. Lewis, Dean
Program in:
  law • JD, LL M

School of Medicine
Dr. Patricia L. Monteleone, Dean
Program in:
  medicine • MD

School of Social Service
Susan C. Tebb, PhD, Dean
Program in:
  social service • MSW

■ SOUTHEAST MISSOURI STATE UNIVERSITY
Cape Girardeau, MO 63701-4799
http://www.semo.edu/

State-supported, coed, comprehensive institution. CGS member. *Enrollment:* 9,570 graduate, professional, and undergraduate students; 186 full-time matriculated graduate/professional students (124 women), 901 part-time matriculated graduate/professional students (698 women). *Graduate faculty:* 226 full-time (88 women). *Computer facilities:* Computer purchase and lease plans are available. 650 computers available on campus for general student use. A campuswide network can be accessed from student residence rooms and from off campus. Internet access and online class registration are available. *Library facilities:* Kent Library. *Graduate expenses:* Tuition, state resident: full-time $4,061; part-time $180 per credit hour. Tuition, nonresident: full-time $7,514; part-time $324 per credit hour. One-time fee: $257. *General application contact:* Dr. Fred Janzow, Dean of the School of Graduate and University Studies, 573-651-2192.

School of Graduate and University Studies
Dr. Fred Janzow, Dean
Programs in:
  art education • MA
  biology • MNS
  business education • MA
  chemistry • MNS
  communication disorders • MA
  community counseling • MA
  community wellness and leisure services • MS
  counseling education • Ed S
  criminal justice • MS
  educational administration • MA, Ed D, Ed S
  educational studies • MA
  elementary education • MA
  English • MA
  exceptional child education • MA
  geosciences • MNS
  guidance and counseling • MA
  history • MA
  home economics • MA
  human environmental studies • MA
  mathematics • MNS
  middle level education • MA
  music education • MME
  nursing • MSN
  nutrition and exercise science • MS
  political science, philosophy and religion • MPA
  school counseling • MA
  science education • MNS
  social studies • MA
  teaching English to speakers of other languages • MA

Harrison College of Business
Kenneth Heischmidt, Director
Programs in:
  accounting • MBA
  environmental management • MBA
  finance • MBA
  general management • MBA
  industrial management • MBA
  international business • MBA

School of Polytechnic Studies
Dr. Randall Shaw, Dean
Program in:
  industrial management • MS

■ SOUTHWEST BAPTIST UNIVERSITY
Bolivar, MO 65613-2597
http://www.sbuniv.edu/

Independent-religious, coed, comprehensive institution. *Enrollment:* 3,563 graduate, professional, and undergraduate students; 288 full-time matriculated graduate/professional students (218 women), 522 part-time matriculated graduate/professional students (417 women). *Graduate faculty:* 16 full-time (7 women), 71 part-time/adjunct (35 women). *Computer facilities:* 130 computers available on campus for

Missouri

Southwest Baptist University (continued)
general student use. A campuswide network can be accessed from off campus. Internet access is available. *Library facilities:* Harriett K. Hutchens Library. *Graduate expenses:* Tuition: part-time $135 per credit hour. *General application contact:* Dr. Gordon Dutile, Provost, 417-328-1601.

Graduate Studies
Dr. Gordon Dutile, Provost
Programs in:
 education • MS
 educational administration • MS, Ed S
 health administration • MBA
 physical therapy • MSPT

■ SOUTHWEST MISSOURI STATE UNIVERSITY
Springfield, MO 65804-0094
http://www.smsu.edu/

State-supported, coed, comprehensive institution. CGS member. *Enrollment:* 18,930 graduate, professional, and undergraduate students; 968 full-time matriculated graduate/professional students (554 women), 1,340 part-time matriculated graduate/professional students (908 women). *Graduate faculty:* 400 full-time (123 women), 87 part-time/adjunct (20 women). *Computer facilities:* Computer purchase and lease plans are available. 1,800 computers available on campus for general student use. A campuswide network can be accessed from student residence rooms and from off campus. Internet access is available. *Library facilities:* Meyer Library plus 3 others. *Graduate expenses:* Tuition, state resident: full-time $2,862. Tuition, nonresident: full-time $5,724. *General application contact:* Tobin Bushman, Coordinator of Admissions and Recruitment, 417-836-5335.

Find an in-depth description at www.petersons.com/gradchannel.

Graduate College
Frank A. Einhellig, Associate Vice President for Academic Affairs and Dean
Programs in:
 community analysis • MSAS
 environmental management • MSAS

College of Arts and Letters
Dr. Curtis P. Lawrence, Dean
Programs in:
 arts and letters • MA, MM, MS Ed
 communication and mass media • MA, MS Ed
 English • MS Ed
 English and writing • MA
 music • MM, MS Ed
 theatre • MA
 theatre and dance • MS Ed

College of Business Administration
Dr. Ronald Bottin, Dean
Programs in:
 accountancy • M Acc
 business administration • M Acc, MBA, MHA, MS
 computer information systems • MS
 health administration • MHA

College of Education
Dr. David L. Hough, Dean
Programs in:
 counseling • MS
 director of special education • Ed S
 director of vocational education • Ed S
 early childhood education • MS Ed
 education • MAT, MS, MS Ed, Ed S
 educational administration • MS Ed, Ed S
 elementary education • MS Ed
 elementary principal • Ed S
 instructional media technology • MS Ed
 middle school education • MS Ed
 reading education • MS Ed
 secondary education • MS Ed
 secondary principal • Ed S
 special education • MS Ed
 superintendent • Ed S
 teaching • MAT
 vocational education • MS Ed

College of Health and Human Services
Dr. Cynthia Pemberton, Dean
Programs in:
 audiology • Au D
 cell and molecular biology • MS
 communication sciences and disorders • MS
 health and human services • MPH, MPT, MS, MS Ed, MSN, MSW, Au D
 health promotion and wellness management • MS
 health, physical education, and recreation • MS Ed
 nurse anesthesia • MS
 nursing • MSN
 physical therapy • MPT
 physician assistant studies • MS
 psychology • MS, MS Ed
 public health • MPH
 social work • MSW

College of Humanities and Public Affairs
Dr. Lorene H. Stone, Dean
Programs in:
 defense and strategic studies • MS
 history • MA, MS Ed
 humanities and public affairs • MA, MIAA, MPA, MS, MS Ed
 international affairs and administration • MIAA
 public administration • MPA
 religious studies • MA

College of Natural and Applied Sciences
Dr. Lawrence E. Banks, Dean
Programs in:
 agriculture • MS Ed
 biology • MS
 biology education • MS Ed
 chemistry • MS
 earth science • MS Ed
 fruit science • MS
 geography • MS Ed
 geography, geology and planning • MNAS
 materials science • MS
 mathematics • MS
 natural and applied sciences • MNAS, MS, MS Ed
 natural science • MS Ed
 plant science • MS
 resource planning • MS
 secondary education • MS Ed

■ TRUMAN STATE UNIVERSITY
Kirksville, MO 63501-4221
http://www.truman.edu/

State-supported, coed, comprehensive institution. CGS member. *Enrollment:* 5,833 graduate, professional, and undergraduate students; 173 full-time matriculated graduate/professional students (128 women), 36 part-time matriculated graduate/professional students (24 women). *Graduate faculty:* 151. *Computer facilities:* Computer purchase and lease plans are available. 840 computers available on campus for general student use. A campuswide network can be accessed from student residence rooms and from off campus. Internet access is available. *Library facilities:* Pickler Memorial Library. *Graduate expenses:* Tuition, state resident: full-time $3,726; part-time $207 per credit. Tuition, nonresident: full-time $6,660; part-time $370 per credit. *General application contact:* Crista Chappell, Graduate Office Secretary, 660-785-4109.

Find an in-depth description at www.petersons.com/gradchannel.

Graduate School
Dr. Maria Di Stefano, Dean of Graduate Studies

Division of Business and Accountancy
Dr. James Bailey, Head
Program in:
 accounting • M Ac

Division of Education
Dr. Sam Minner, Head
Programs in:
  counseling • MA
  education • MA, MAE

Division of Fine Arts
Robert Jones, Head
Program in:
  music • MA

Division of Human Potential and Performance
Dr. Fontaine Piper, Head
Program in:
  communication disorders • MA

Division of Language and Literature
Dr. Heinz Woehlk, Head
Program in:
  English • MA

Division of Science
Dr. Scott Ellis, Head
Program in:
  biology • MS

Division of Social Science
Dr. Seymour Patterson, Head
Program in:
  history • MA

■ UNIVERSITY OF MISSOURI–COLUMBIA
Columbia, MO 65211
http://www.missouri.edu/

State-supported, coed, university. CGS member. *Enrollment:* 26,805 graduate, professional, and undergraduate students; 3,622 full-time matriculated graduate/professional students (1,861 women), 2,742 part-time matriculated graduate/professional students (1,635 women). *Graduate faculty:* 1,477 full-time (439 women), 50 part-time/adjunct (27 women). *Computer facilities:* 1,176 computers available on campus for general student use. A campuswide network can be accessed from student residence rooms and from off campus. Internet access and online class registration, telephone registration are available. *Library facilities:* Ellis Library plus 11 others. *Graduate expenses:* Tuition, state resident: full-time $5,205. Tuition, nonresident: full-time $14,058. *General application contact:* Stephanie White-Thorn, Coordinator of Graduate Student Affairs, 573-882-3292.

College of Veterinary Medicine
Dr. Joe Kornegay, Dean
Programs in:
  laboratory animal medicine • MS
  pathobiology • MS, PhD
  veterinary biomedical sciences • MS
  veterinary clinical sciences • MS
  veterinary medicine • DVM
  veterinary medicine and surgery • MS
  veterinary pathobiology • MS, PhD

Graduate School
Dr. Suzanne Ortega, Dean
Programs in:
  dispute resolution • LL M
  genetics • PhD
  health administration • MHA
  health informatics • MHA
  health services management • MHA

College of Agriculture, Food and Natural Resources
Dr. Thomas T. Payne, Dean
Programs in:
  agricultural economics • MS, PhD
  agricultural education • MS, PhD
  agriculture, food and natural resources • MS, PhD
  agronomy • MS, PhD
  animal sciences • MS, PhD
  entomology • MS, PhD
  food science • MS, PhD
  foods and food systems management • MS
  horticulture • MS, PhD
  human nutrition • MS
  nutrition • MS, PhD
  plant pathology and microbiology • MS, PhD
  rural sociology • MS, PhD

College of Arts and Sciences
Dr. Richard Schwartz, Dean
Programs in:
  analytical chemistry • MS, PhD
  anthropology • MA, PhD
  applied mathematics • MS
  art • MFA
  art history and archaeology • MA, PhD
  arts and sciences • MA, MFA, MM, MS, MST, PhD
  cellular, molecular and developmental biology • MA, PhD
  classical studies • MA, PhD
  communication • MA, PhD
  economics • MA, PhD
  English • MA, PhD
  evolutionary biology and ecology • MA, PhD
  French • MA, PhD
  geography • MA
  geological sciences • MS, PhD
  German • MA
  history • MA, PhD
  inorganic chemistry • MS, PhD
  literature • MA
  mathematics • MA, MST, PhD
  music • MA, MM
  neurobiology and behavior • MA, PhD
  organic chemistry • MS, PhD
  philosophy • MA, PhD
  physical chemistry • MS, PhD
  physics and astronomy • MS, PhD
  political science • MA, PhD
  psychological sciences • MA, MS, PhD
  religious studies • MA
  sociology • MA, PhD
  Spanish • MA, PhD
  statistics • MA, PhD
  teaching • MA
  theatre • MA, PhD

College of Business
Dr. Bruce Walker, Dean
Programs in:
  accountancy • M Acc, PhD
  business • M Acc, MBA, PhD

College of Education
Dr. Richard Andrews, Dean
Programs in:
  administration and supervision of special education • PhD
  agricultural education • M Ed, PhD, Ed S
  art education • M Ed, PhD, Ed S
  behavior disorders • M Ed, PhD
  business and office education • M Ed, PhD, Ed S
  counseling psychology • M Ed, MA, PhD, Ed S
  curriculum development of exceptional students • M Ed, PhD
  early childhood education • M Ed, PhD, Ed S
  early childhood special education • M Ed, PhD
  education • M Ed, MA, Ed D, PhD, Ed S
  education administration • M Ed, MA, Ed D, PhD, Ed S
  educational psychology • M Ed, MA, PhD, Ed S
  educational technology • M Ed, Ed S
  elementary education • M Ed, PhD, Ed S
  English education • M Ed, PhD, Ed S
  foreign language education • M Ed, PhD, Ed S
  general special education • M Ed, MA, PhD
  health education and promotion • M Ed, PhD
  higher and adult education • M Ed, MA, Ed D, PhD, Ed S
  information science and learning technology • PhD
  learning and instruction • M Ed
  learning disabilities • M Ed, PhD
  library science • MA
  marketing education • M Ed, PhD, Ed S
  mathematics education • M Ed, PhD, Ed S
  mental retardation • M Ed, PhD
  music education • M Ed, PhD, Ed S
  reading education • M Ed, PhD, Ed S

Missouri

University of Missouri–Columbia (continued)
  school psychology • M Ed, MA, PhD, Ed S
  science education • M Ed, PhD, Ed S
  social studies education • M Ed, PhD, Ed S
  vocational education • M Ed, PhD, Ed S

College of Engineering
Dr. James Thompson, Dean
Programs in:
  agricultural engineering • MS
  biological engineering • MS, PhD
  chemical engineering • MS, PhD
  civil engineering • MS, PhD
  computer science • MS, PhD
  electrical and computer engineering • MS, PhD
  engineering • MS, PhD
  environmental engineering • MS, PhD
  geotechnical engineering • MS, PhD
  industrial and manufacturing systems engineering • MS, PhD
  mechanical and aerospace engineering • MS, PhD
  nuclear engineering • MS, PhD
  structural engineering • MS, PhD
  transportation and highway engineering • MS
  water resources • MS, PhD

College of Human Environmental Science
Dr. Stephen R. Jorgensen, Dean
Programs in:
  consumer and family economics • MS
  design with digital media • MA, MS
  environmental design • MS
  exercise physiology • MA, PhD
  human development and family studies • MA, MS, PhD
  human environmental science • MA, MS, PhD
  nutritional sciences • MS, PhD
  textiles and apparel management • MA, MS

Harry S. Truman School of Public Affairs
Guy B. Adams, Director of Graduate Studies
Program in:
  public affairs • MPA

School of Journalism
Dr. Esther Thorson, Associate Dean
Program in:
  journalism • MA, PhD

School of Natural Resources
Dr. Harold Gene Garrett, Director
Programs in:
  atmospheric science • MS
  fisheries and wildlife • MS, PhD
  forestry • MS, PhD
  natural resources • MS, PhD
  parks, recreation and tourism • MS
  soil science • PhD
  spo scoemce • MS
  stmospheric science • PhD

School of Social Work
Dr. Judith Davenport, Director of Graduate Studies
Program in:
  social work • MSW

Sinclair School of Nursing
Dr. Roxanne W. McDaniel, Director of Graduate Studies
Program in:
  nursing • MS, PhD

School of Health Professions
Dr. Richard E. Oliver, Dean
Programs in:
  communication science and disorders • MHS
  diagnostic medical ultrasound • MHS
  health professions • MHS, MPT
  physical therapy • MPT

School of Law
Dr. R. Lawrence Dessem, Dean
Program in:
  law • JD, LL M

School of Medicine
Dr. William M. Crist, Dean
Program in:
  medicine • MD, MS, MSPH, PhD

Graduate Programs in Medicine
Programs in:
  biochemistry • MS, PhD
  family and community medicine • MSPH
  medicine • MS, MSPH, PhD
  molecular microbiology and immunology • MS, PhD
  pharmacology • MS, PhD
  physiology • MS, PhD

■ **UNIVERSITY OF MISSOURI–KANSAS CITY**
Kansas City, MO 64110-2499
http://www.umkc.edu/

State-supported, coed, university. CGS member. *Enrollment:* 14,226 graduate, professional, and undergraduate students; 2,533 full-time matriculated graduate/professional students (1,417 women), 2,526 part-time matriculated graduate/professional students (1,557 women). *Graduate faculty:* 508. *Computer facilities:* 400 computers available on campus for general student use. A campuswide network can be accessed from student residence rooms and from off campus. Internet access and online class registration are available. *Library facilities:* Miller-Nichols Library plus 3 others. *General application contact:* Jennifer Deltaemers, Director of Admissions, 816-235-1111.

Bloch School of Business and Public Administration
Dr. O. Homer Erekson, Dean
Programs in:
  accountancy accounting • MS
  business administration • MBA
  public affairs • MPA, PhD

College of Arts and Sciences
Dr. Bryan LeBeau, Dean
Programs in:
  acting • MFA
  analytical chemistry • MS, PhD
  art history • MA, PhD
  arts and sciences • MA, MFA, MS, MSW, PhD
  criminal justice and criminology • MS
  design technology • MFA
  economics • MA, PhD
  English • MA, PhD
  geosciences • PhD
  history • MA, PhD
  inorganic chemistry • MS, PhD
  mathematics and statistics • MA, MS, PhD
  organic chemistry • MS, PhD
  physical chemistry • MS, PhD
  physics • MS, PhD
  political science • MA, PhD
  polymer chemistry • MS, PhD
  psychology • MA, PhD
  Romance languages and literatures • MA
  sociology • MA, PhD
  studio art • MA
  theatre • MA
  urban environmental geology • MS

School of Social Work
Dr. Kathylene F. Siska, Director
Program in:
  social work • MSW

Conservatory of Music
Dr. Randall G. Pembrook, Dean
Programs in:
  composition • MM, DMA
  conducting • MM, DMA
  music • MA
  music education • MME, PhD
  music history and literature • MM
  music theory • MM
  performance • MM, DMA

School of Biological Sciences
Dr. Lawrence A. Dreyfus, Dean
Programs in:
  biology • MA
  cell biology and biophysics • PhD
  cellular and molecular biology • MS
  molecular biology and biochemistry • PhD

School of Computing and Engineering
Dr. William Osborne, PE, PhD, Dean
Programs in:
  civil engineering • MS

Missouri

computer science • MS, PhD
electrical engineering • ME, MS
engineering • PhD
mechanical engineering • MS

School of Dentistry
Dr. Michael Reed, Dean
Programs in:
advanced education in dentistry • Graduate Dental Certificate
dental hygiene education • MS
dental specialties • Graduate Dental Certificate
dentistry • DDS
diagnostic sciences • Graduate Dental Certificate
oral and maxillofacial surgery • Graduate Dental Certificate
oral biology • MS, PhD
orthodontics and dentofacial orthopedics • Graduate Dental Certificate
pediatric dentistry • Graduate Dental Certificate
periodontics • Graduate Dental Certificate
prosthodontics • Graduate Dental Certificate

School of Education
Dr. Linda Edwards, Interim Dean
Programs in:
counseling and guidance • MA, Ed S
counseling psychology • PhD
curriculum and instruction • MA, Ed S
education • PhD
educational research and psychology • MA
reading education • MA, Ed S
special education • MA

School of Graduate Studies
Dr. Ronald MacQuarrie, Vice Provost/Dean
Program in:
interdisciplinary studies • PhD

School of Law
Dr. Jeffrey Berman, Interim Dean
Program in:
law • JD, LL M

School of Medicine
Dr. Betty Drees, Dean
Program in:
medicine • MD

School of Nursing
Dr. Lora Lacey-Haun, Dean
Programs in:
adult clinical nurse specialist • MSN
family nurse practitioner • MSN
neonatal nurse practitioner • MSN
nurse administrator • MSN
nurse educator • MSN
nursing • PhD
pediatric nurse practitioner • MSN

School of Pharmacy
Dr. Robert W. Piepho, Dean
Programs in:
pharmaceutical sciences • MS, PhD
pharmacy • Pharm D

■ UNIVERSITY OF MISSOURI–ROLLA
Rolla, MO 65409-0910
http://www.umr.edu/

State-supported, coed, university. *Enrollment:* 5,459 graduate, professional, and undergraduate students; 970 full-time matriculated graduate/professional students (210 women), 322 part-time matriculated graduate/professional students (61 women). *Graduate faculty:* 238 full-time (13 women), 4 part-time/adjunct (0 women). *Computer facilities:* 800 computers available on campus for general student use. A campuswide network can be accessed from student residence rooms and from off campus. Internet access and online class registration are available. *Library facilities:* Curtis Laws Wilson Library. *Graduate expenses:* Tuition, state resident: full-time $5,871. Tuition, nonresident: full-time $13,114. Required fees: $820. Tuition and fees vary according to course load. *General application contact:* Julie Sibley, Admissions Coordinator, 573-341-4315.

Graduate School
Dr. Y. T. Shah, Provost

College of Arts and Sciences
Dr. Paula Lutz, Dean
Programs in:
applied and environmental biology • MS
applied mathematics • MS
arts and sciences • MS, MST, PhD
biological sciences • MS
chemistry • MS, PhD
chemistry education • MST
computer science • MS, PhD
mathematics • MST, PhD
mathematics education • MST
physics • MS, PhD

School of Engineering
Dr. O. Robert Mitchell, Dean
Programs in:
aerospace engineering • MS, PhD
chemical and biological engineering • MS, PhD
civil engineering • MS, PhD
computer engineering • MS, DE, PhD
construction engineering • MS, DE, PhD
electrical engineering • MS, DE, PhD
engineering • M Eng, MS, DE, PhD
engineering management • MS, PhD
environmental engineering • MS
fluid mechanics • MS, DE, PhD
geotechnical engineering • MS, DE, PhD
hydrology and hydraulic engineering • MS, DE, PhD
manufacturing engineering • M Eng, MS
mechanical engineering • MS, DE, PhD
sanitary engineering and environmental health • MS, DE, PhD
structural analysis and design • MS, DE, PhD
structural engineering • MS
structural methods • DE, PhD
systems engineering • MS

School of Management and Information Systems
Dr. Arlan Dekock, Dean
Program in:
information science and technology • MS

School of Materials, Energy, and Earth Resources
Dr. Mariesa Crow, Transitional Dean
Programs in:
ceramic engineering • MS, PhD
geochemistry • MS, PhD
geological engineering • MS, DE, PhD
geology • MS, PhD
geology and geophysics • MS, PhD
geophysics • MS, PhD
groundwater and environmental geology • MS, PhD
materials, energy, and earth resources • MS, DE, PhD
metallurgical engineering • MS, PhD
mining engineering • MS, DE, PhD
nuclear engineering • MS, DE, PhD
petroleum engineering • MS, DE, PhD

■ UNIVERSITY OF MISSOURI–ST. LOUIS
St. Louis, MO 63121
http://www.umsl.edu/

State-supported, coed, university. CGS member. *Enrollment:* 15,605 graduate, professional, and undergraduate students; 590 full-time matriculated graduate/professional students (376 women), 2,049 part-time matriculated graduate/professional students (1,390 women). *Graduate faculty:* 388. *Computer facilities:* Computer purchase and lease plans are available. 750 computers available on campus for general student use. A campuswide network can be accessed from student residence rooms and from off campus. Internet access and online class registration are available. *Library facilities:* Thomas Jefferson Library plus 2

Missouri

University of Missouri–St. Louis (continued)
others. *Graduate expenses:* Tuition, state resident: part-time $237 per credit hour. Tuition, nonresident: part-time $639 per credit hour. Required fees: $10 per credit hour. *General application contact:* Graduate Admissions, 314-516-5458.

Find an in-depth description at www.petersons.com/gradchannel.

College of Optometry
Dr. Larry J. Davis, Dean
Programs in:
optometry • OD, MS, PhD
vision science • MS, PhD

Graduate School
Dr. Judith Walker de Félix, Associate Vice Chancellor for Academic Affairs
Programs in:
communication • MA
fine arts and communication • MA, MME
gerontological social work • Certificate
gerontology • MS, Certificate
health policy • MPPA
music education • MME
nonprofit organization management • MPPA
nonprofit organization management and leadership • Certificate
public policy analysis • MPPA
public policy processes • MPPA
public sector human resources management • MPPA

College of Arts and Sciences
Dr. Mark Burkholder, Dean
Programs in:
advanced social perspective • MA
American literature • MA
American politics • MA
applied mathematics • MA, PhD
applied physics • MS
arts and sciences • MA, MFA, MS, MSW, PhD, Certificate
astrophysics • MS
biology • MS, PhD
biotechnology • Certificate
chemistry • MS, PhD
clinical psychology • PhD
clinical psychology respecialization • Certificate
community conflict intervention • MA
comparative politics • MA
computer science • MS
creative writing • MFA
criminology and criminal justice • MA, PhD
English • MA
English literature • MA
experimental psychology • PhD
general economics • MA
general psychology • MA
historical agencies • MA
industrial/organizational psychology • PhD
international politics • MA
linguistics • MA
managerial economics • Certificate
museum studies • MA, Certificate
philosophy • MA
physics • PhD
political process and behavior • MA
political science • PhD
program design and evaluation research • MA
public administration and public policy • MA
social policy planning and administration • MA
social work • MSW
telecommunications science • Certificate
tropical biology and conservation • Certificate
urban and regional politics • MA
women's and gender studies • Certificate

College of Business Administration
Karl Kottemann, Assistant Director
Programs in:
accounting • MBA
auditing/systems • M Acc
business administration • Certificate
electronic commerce • Certificate
finance • MBA
human resource management • Certificate
information resources management • Certificate
management • MBA
management information systems • MSMIS, PhD, Certificate
marketing • MBA
marketing management • Certificate
quantitative management science • MBA
taxation • M Acc, Certificate
telecommunications management • Certificate

College of Nursing
Dr. Connie Koch, Interim Dean
Program in:
nursing • MSN, PhD

School of Education
Dr. Kathleen Haywood, Director of Graduate Studies
Programs in:
adult education • M Ed, Ed D, PhD
community education • M Ed
counseling • M Ed, Ed D, PhD
curriculum and instruction • M Ed, Ed D, PhD
early childhood special education • M Ed
education leadership and policy studies • M Ed
educational leadership and policy studies • Ed D, PhD
educational psychology, research, and evaluation • M Ed, Ed D, PhD
elementary administration • M Ed
elementary education • M Ed, Ed D, PhD
elementary reading • M Ed, Ed D, PhD
elementary school counseling • M Ed
emotionally disturbed education • M Ed
general counseling • M Ed
higher education administration • Ed D, PhD
institutional research • Certificate
learning disabilities • M Ed
mentally retarded education • M Ed
reading • M Ed, Ed D, PhD
school psychology • Certificate
secondary administration • M Ed
secondary education • M Ed, Ed D, PhD
secondary school counseling • M Ed
special education • M Ed

■ WASHINGTON UNIVERSITY IN ST. LOUIS
St. Louis, MO 63130-4899
http://www.admissions.wustl.edu/

Independent, coed, university. CGS member. *Enrollment:* 13,020 graduate, professional, and undergraduate students; 4,104 full-time matriculated graduate/professional students (1,936 women), 1,279 part-time matriculated graduate/professional students (524 women). *Graduate faculty:* 1,733 full-time (464 women), 739 part-time/adjunct (214 women). *Computer facilities:* Computer purchase and lease plans are available. 2,500 computers available on campus for general student use. A campuswide network can be accessed from student residence rooms and from off campus. Internet access and online class registration, e-mail are available. *Library facilities:* John M. Olin Library plus 13 others. *Graduate expenses:* Tuition: full-time $28,300; part-time $1,180 per credit. *General application contact:* 314-935-6880.

Find an in-depth description at www.petersons.com/gradchannel.

George Warren Brown School of Social Work
Program in:
social work • MSW, PhD

Graduate School of Arts and Sciences
Dr. Robert E. Thach, Dean
Programs in:

Missouri

American history • MA, PhD
anthropology • MA, PhD
art history • MA, PhD
arts and sciences • MA, MA Ed, MAT, MFAW, MM, PhD
Asian history • MA, PhD
Asian language • MA
Asian studies • MA
British history • MA, PhD
chemistry • MA, PhD
Chinese • MA, PhD
Chinese and comparative literature • PhD
classical archaeology • MA, PhD
classics • MA, MAT
clinical psychology • PhD
comparative literature • MA, PhD
earth and planetary sciences • MA
East Asian studies • MA
economics • MA, PhD
educational research • PhD
elementary education • MA Ed
English and American literature • MA, PhD
European history • MA, PhD
French • MA, PhD
general experimental psychology • MA, PhD
geochemistry • PhD
geology • MA, PhD
geophysics • PhD
Germanic languages and literature • MA, PhD
history • PhD
Islamic and Near Eastern studies • MA
Japanese • MA, PhD
Japanese and comparative literature • PhD
Jewish studies • MA
Jewish, Islamic, and Near Eastern studies • MA
Latin American history • MA, PhD
mathematics • MA, PhD
mathematics education • MAT
Middle Eastern history • MA, PhD
movement science • PhD
music • MA, MM, PhD
performing arts • MA
philosophy • MA, PhD
philosophy/neuroscience/psychology • PhD
physics • MA, PhD
planetary sciences • PhD
political economy and public policy • MA
political science • MA, PhD
Romance languages • MA, PhD
secondary education • MA Ed, MAT
social psychology • MA, PhD
social work • PhD
Spanish • MA, PhD
statistics • MA, PhD
writing • MFAW

Division of Biology and Biomedical Sciences
Programs in:
 biochemistry • PhD
 chemical biology • PhD
 computational biology • PhD
 developmental biology • PhD
 ecology • PhD
 environmental biology • PhD
 evolution, ecology and population biology • PhD
 evolutionary biology • PhD
 genetics • PhD
 immunology • PhD
 molecular biophysics • PhD
 molecular cell biology • PhD
 molecular genetics • PhD
 molecular microbiology and microbial pathogenesis • PhD
 neurosciences • PhD
 plant biology • PhD

Henry Edwin Sever Graduate School of Engineering and Applied Science
Christopher I. Byrnes, Dean
Programs in:
 biomedical engineering • MS, D Sc
 chemical engineering • MS, D Sc
 civil engineering • MSCE
 computer engineering • MS, D Sc
 computer science • MS, D Sc
 construction engineering • MCE
 construction management • MCM
 electrical engineering • MS, D Sc
 engineering and applied science • MCE, MCE, MCM, MEM, MIM, MS, MSCE, MSE, MSEE, MSEE, MTM, D Sc
 environmental engineering • MS, D Sc
 mechanical and aerospace engineering • MS, D Sc
 structural engineering • MSE, D Sc
 systems science and mathematics • MS, D Sc
 transportation and urban systems engineering • D Sc

John M. Olin School of Business
Stuart I. Greenbaum, Dean
Programs in:
 business • EMBA, PhD
 business administration • MBA

School of Architecture
Cynthia Weese, Dean
Programs in:
 architecture • M Arch, MUD
 urban design • MUD

School of Art
Jeff Pike, Dean
Programs in:
 ceramics • MFA
 painting • MFA
 photography • MFA
 printmaking/drawing • MFA
 sculpture • MFA

School of Law
Joel L. Seligman, Dean
Program in:
 law • JD, LL M, MJS, JSD

School of Medicine
Dr. William A. Peck, Dean
Programs in:
 audiology • Au D
 deaf education • MS
 genetic epidemiology • MS, Certificate
 health administration • MHA
 medicine • MD, MA, MHA, MHS, MS, MSOT, Au D, DPT, OTD, PhD, Certificate, PPDPT
 movement science • PhD
 occupational therapy • MSOT, OTD
 physical therapy • MHS, DPT, PhD, PPDPT
 speech and hearing sciences • MA, PhD

■ **WEBSTER UNIVERSITY**
St. Louis, MO 63119-3194
http://www.webster.edu/

Independent, coed, comprehensive institution. *Enrollment:* 4,560 full-time matriculated graduate/professional students, 11,121 part-time matriculated graduate/professional students. *Graduate faculty:* 88 full-time (34 women), 1,638 part-time/adjunct (410 women). *Computer facilities:* 330 computers available on campus for general student use. A campuswide network can be accessed. Internet access and online class registration are available. *Library facilities:* Eden-Webster Library. *Graduate expenses:* Tuition: full-time $7,740; part-time $430 per credit. Tuition and fees vary according to degree level, campus/location and program. *General application contact:* Matt Nolan, Director of Graduate and Evening Student Admissions, 314-968-7089.

College of Arts and Sciences
Dr. David Carl Wilson, Dean
Programs in:
 arts and sciences • MA, MS, MSN, Certificate
 counseling • MA
 family systems nursing • MSN
 gerontology • MA
 international relations • MA
 legal studies • MA
 nurse anesthesia • MS
 paralegal studies • Certificate

Leigh Gerdine College of Fine Arts
Peter Sargent, Dean
Programs in:
 art • MA

Missouri

Webster University (continued)
  arts management and leadership • MFA
  church music • MM
  composition • MM
  conducting • MM
  fine arts • MA, MFA, MM
  jazz studies • MM
  music education • MM
  performance • MM
  piano • MM

School of Business and Technology
Dr. Benjamin Ola Akande, Dean
Programs in:
  business • MA, MBA
  business and organizational security management • MA
  business and technology • MA, MBA, MS, DM, Certificate
  computer distributed systems • Certificate
  computer resources and information management • MA, MBA
  computer science • MS
  computer science/distributed systems • MS
  environmental management • MS
  finance • MA, MBA
  health care management • MA
  health services management • MA, MBA
  human resources development • MA, MBA
  human resources management • MA
  international business • MA, MBA
  management • MA, MBA, DM
  marketing • MA, MBA
  procurement and acquisitions management • MA, MBA
  public administration • MA
  real estate management • MBA
  security management • MA, MBA
  space systems management • MA, MBA, MS
  telecommunications management • MA, MBA

School of Communications
Debra Carpenter, Dean
Program in:
  media communication • MA

School of Education
Dr. Brenda Fyfe, Dean
Programs in:
  communications • MAT
  early childhood education • MAT
  education • MAT, Ed S
  Education Leadership • Ed S
  education technology • MAT
  mathematics education • MAT
  multidisciplinary studies • MAT
  science education • MAT
  social science education • MAT
  special education • MAT

■ WILLIAM WOODS UNIVERSITY
Fulton, MO 65251-1098
http://www.williamwoods.edu/

Independent-religious, coed, comprehensive institution. *Enrollment:* 2,670 graduate, professional, and undergraduate students; 1,304 full-time matriculated graduate/professional students (845 women). *Graduate faculty:* 18 full-time (5 women), 347 part-time/adjunct (140 women). *Computer facilities:* Computer purchase and lease plans are available. 105 computers available on campus for general student use. A campuswide network can be accessed from student residence rooms. Internet access is available. *Library facilities:* Dulany Library. *Graduate expenses:* Tuition: full-time $8,820; part-time $245 per credit. One-time fee: $100 part-time. *General application contact:* Linda Rembish, Administrative Assistant, 800-995-3199.

Graduate and Adult Studies
Dr. Betty R. Tutt, Academic Dean
Programs in:
  accounting • MBA
  administration • M Ed
  curriculum and instruction • M Ed
  education • M Ed, Ed S
  health management • MBA
  human resources • MBA
  initial certification • M Ed

Montana

■ MONTANA STATE UNIVERSITY–BILLINGS
Billings, MT 59101-0298
http://www.msubillings.edu/

State-supported, coed, comprehensive institution. *Enrollment:* 4,670 graduate, professional, and undergraduate students; 194 full-time matriculated graduate/professional students (139 women), 335 part-time matriculated graduate/professional students (243 women). *Graduate faculty:* 62 full-time (23 women). *Computer facilities:* 500 computers available on campus for general student use. A campuswide network can be accessed from student residence rooms and from off campus. Internet access and online class registration, on-line degree programs are available. *Library facilities:* Montana State University-Billings Library. *Graduate expenses:* Tuition, state resident: full-time $3,770; part-time $206 per credit. Tuition, nonresident: full-time $9,290; part-time $513 per credit. Required fees: $3,733; $204 per credit. $1,223 per semester. Tuition and fees vary according to course level, course load, degree level and reciprocity agreements. *General application contact:* Dr. George White, Director of Graduate Studies and Research, 406-657-2238.

College of Allied Health Professions
Dr. Carl Hanson, Dean
Programs in:
  allied health professions • MHA, MS, MSRC
  athletic training • MS
  health administration • MHA
  rehabilitation counseling • MSRC
  sport management • MS

College of Arts and Sciences
Dr. Tasneem Khaleel, Chair
Programs in:
  arts and sciences • MS
  psychology • MS
  public relations • MS

College of Education and Human Services
Director of Graduate Studies and Research
Programs in:
  advanced studies • MS Sp Ed
  early childhood education • M Ed
  education and human services • M Ed, MS Sp Ed, Certificate
  educational technology • M Ed
  general curriculum • M Ed
  interdisciplinary studies • M Ed
  reading • M Ed
  school counseling • M Ed
  secondary education • M Ed
  special education • MS Sp Ed
  special education generalist • MS Sp Ed
  teaching • Certificate

■ MONTANA STATE UNIVERSITY–BOZEMAN
Bozeman, MT 59717
http://www.montana.edu/

State-supported, coed, university. CGS member. *Enrollment:* 12,135 graduate, professional, and undergraduate students; 447 full-time matriculated graduate/professional students (195 women), 691 part-time matriculated graduate/professional students (312 women). *Graduate faculty:* 548 full-time (174 women), 253 part-time/adjunct (150 women). *Computer facilities:* 850 computers available on campus for general student use. A campuswide network can be accessed from student residence

Montana

rooms and from off campus. Internet access and online class registration, e-mail are available. *Library facilities:* Renne Library plus 1 other. *Graduate expenses:* Tuition, state resident: full-time $3,907; part-time $163 per credit. Tuition, nonresident: full-time $12,383; part-time $516 per credit. Required fees: $890; $445 per term. Tuition and fees vary according to course load and program. *General application contact:* Dr. Bruce McLeod, Dean, Graduate Studies, 406-994-4145.

College of Graduate Studies
Dr. Bruce McLeod, Dean, Graduate Studies

College of Agriculture
Dr. Jeffrey S. Jacobsen, Interim Dean
Programs in:
 agricultural education • MS
 agriculture • MS, PhD
 animal and range sciences • MS, PhD
 applied economics • MS
 entomology • MS
 land rehabilitation (interdisciplinary) • MS
 land resources and environmental sciences • MS, PhD
 plant pathology • MS
 plant science • MS, PhD
 veterinary molecular biology • MS, PhD

College of Arts and Architecture
Jerry Bancroft, Dean
Programs in:
 architecture • M Arch
 art • MFA
 arts and architecture • M Arch, MFA
 science and natural history filmmaking • MFA

College of Business
Dr. Richard J. Semenik, Dean
Program in:
 professional accountancy • MP Ac

College of Education, Health, and Human Development
Dr. Greg Weisenstein, Dean
Programs in:
 education • M Ed, Ed D, Ed S
 education, health, and human development • M Ed, MS, Ed D, PhD, Ed S
 health and human development • MS

College of Engineering
Dr. Robert Marley, Dean
Programs in:
 chemical engineering • MS
 civil engineering • MS
 computer sciences • MS, PhD
 construction engineering management • MCEM
 electrical engineering • MS
 engineering • PhD
 environmental engineering • MS
 industrial and management engineering • MS
 land rehabilitation (interdisciplinary) • MS
 mechanical engineering • MS
 project engineering and management • MPEM

College of Letters and Science
Dr. Sara Jayne Steen, Dean
Programs in:
 biochemistry • MS, PhD
 biological sciences • MS, PhD
 chemistry • MS, PhD
 earth sciences • MS, PhD
 English • MA
 fish and wildlife biology • PhD
 fish and wildlife management • MS
 history • MA
 land rehabilitation (interdisciplinary) • MS
 letters and science • MA, MPA, MS, PhD
 mathematics • MS, PhD
 microbiology • MS, PhD
 Native American studies • MA
 physics • MS, PhD
 psychology • MS
 public administration • MPA
 statistics • MS, PhD

College of Nursing
Dr. Jean Ballantyne, Interim Dean
Program in:
 nursing • MN

■ **MONTANA STATE UNIVERSITY–NORTHERN**
Havre, MT 59501-7751
http://www.msun.edu/

State-supported, coed, comprehensive institution. *Enrollment:* 7 full-time matriculated graduate/professional students (6 women), 81 part-time matriculated graduate/professional students (56 women). *Graduate faculty:* 5 full-time (2 women), 1 part-time/adjunct (0 women). *Computer facilities:* 140 computers available on campus for general student use. A campuswide network can be accessed from student residence rooms and from off campus. Internet access and online class registration are available. *Library facilities:* Vande Bogart Libraries. *Graduate expenses:* Tuition, state resident: part-time $228 per credit. *General application contact:* Dr. Will Rawn, Interim Dean, College of Arts and Science, Education, and Nursing, 406-265-4169.

College of Education and Graduate Programs
Dr. Will Rawn, Interim Dean, College of Arts and Science, Education, and Nursing

Programs in:
 counselor education • M Ed
 elementary education • M Ed
 general science • M Ed
 learning development • M Ed

■ **UNIVERSITY OF GREAT FALLS**
Great Falls, MT 59405
http://www.ugf.edu/

Independent-religious, coed, comprehensive institution. *Enrollment:* 801 graduate, professional, and undergraduate students; 62 full-time matriculated graduate/professional students (45 women), 57 part-time matriculated graduate/professional students (49 women). *Graduate faculty:* 14 full-time (6 women), 10 part-time/adjunct (4 women). *Computer facilities:* 110 computers available on campus for general student use. A campuswide network can be accessed from student residence rooms. Internet access and online class registration are available. *Library facilities:* University of Great Falls Library. *Graduate expenses:* Tuition: full-time $7,600; part-time $475 per credit. Required fees: $440; $90 per term. Tuition and fees vary according to course load. *General application contact:* Dr. Deborah J. Kottel, Dean of Graduate Studies Division, 406-791-5339.

Graduate Studies Division
Dr. Deborah J. Kottel, Dean
Programs in:
 addictions counseling • MAC
 chemical dependent services • MHSA
 counseling psychology • MSC
 criminal justice administration • MCJ
 curriculum and instruction • MAT
 elementary education • M Ed, MAT
 family services • MHSA
 guidance and counseling • M Ed
 information systems • MIS
 marriage and family counseling • MSC
 school psychology • MSP
 secondary education • MAT

■ **THE UNIVERSITY OF MONTANA–MISSOULA**
Missoula, MT 59812-0002
http://www.umt.edu/

State-supported, coed, university. CGS member. *Enrollment:* 13,352 graduate, professional, and undergraduate students; 1,007 full-time matriculated graduate/professional students (505 women), 500 part-time matriculated graduate/professional students (300 women). *Graduate faculty:* 539 full-time (180 women), 109 part-time/adjunct (51

Montana

The University of Montana–Missoula (continued)

women). *Computer facilities:* 545 computers available on campus for general student use. A campuswide network can be accessed from student residence rooms and from off campus. Internet access and online class registration are available. *Library facilities:* Maureen and Mike Mansfield Library plus 2 others. *Graduate expenses:* Tuition, state resident: full-time $1,848; part-time $221 per credit. Tuition, nonresident: full-time $4,880; part-time $333 per credit. Required fees: $2,200. *General application contact:* Dr. David A. Strobel, Dean of the Graduate School, 406-243-2572.

Find an in-depth description at www.petersons.com/gradchannel.

Graduate School
Dr. David A. Strobel, Dean of the Graduate School
Programs in:
  individual interdisciplinary programs (IIP) • PhD
  interdisciplinary studies • MIS

College of Arts and Sciences
Dr. Jerry Fetz, Dean
Programs in:
  anthropology • PhD
  arts and sciences • MA, MFA, MPA, MS, MST, PhD, Ed S
  chemistry • MS, PhD
  chemistry teaching • MST
  clinical psychology • PhD
  communication studies • MA
  computer science • MS
  creative writing • MFA
  criminology • MA
  cultural heritage • MA
  economics • MA
  English literature • MA
  English teaching • MA
  environmental studies • MS
  experimental psychology • PhD
  fiction • MFA
  French • MA
  geography • MA
  geology • MS, PhD
  German • MA
  history • MA, PhD
  linguistics • MA
  mathematics • MA, PhD
  non-fiction • MFA
  poetry • MFA
  political science • MA
  public administration • MPA
  rural and environmental change • MA
  school psychology • MA, Ed S
  Spanish • MA
  teaching ethics • MA

College of Forestry and Conservation
Dr. Perry Brown, Dean
Programs in:
  ecosystem management • MEM, MS
  fish and wildlife biology • PhD
  forestry • MS, PhD
  recreation management • MS
  resource conservation • MS
  wildlife biology • MS

Division of Biological Sciences
Dr. Don Christian, Associate Dean
Programs in:
  biochemistry and microbiology • MS, PhD
  biological sciences • MS, PhD
  organismal biology and ecology • MS, PhD

School of Education
Programs in:
  counselor education • M Ed, MA, Ed D, Ed S
  curriculum and instruction • M Ed, MA, Ed D
  education • M Ed, MA, MS, Ed D, Ed S
  exercise and performance psychology • MS
  exercise science • MS
  health promotion • MS
  school administration and supervision • M Ed, Ed D, Ed S

School of Fine Arts
Dr. Shirley Howell, Dean
Programs in:
  fine arts • MA, MFA
  music • MM

School of Journalism
Dr. Jerry Brown, Dean
Program in:
  journalism • MA

School of Pharmacy and Allied Health Sciences
Dr. David Forbes, Dean
Programs in:
  pharmaceutical sciences • MS
  pharmacology • PhD
  pharmacy and allied health sciences • MS, DPT, PhD
  physical therapy • DPT
  toxicology • MS, PhD

School of Business Administration
Dr. Larry Gianchetta, Dean
Programs in:
  accounting • M Acct
  business • MBA
  business administration • M Acct, MBA

School of Law
E. Edwin Eck, Dean
Program in:
  law • JD

Nebraska

■ BELLEVUE UNIVERSITY
Bellevue, NE 68005-3098
http://www.bellevue.edu/

Independent, coed, comprehensive institution. *Enrollment:* 5,110 graduate, professional, and undergraduate students; 856 full-time matriculated graduate/professional students (515 women), 321 part-time matriculated graduate/professional students (128 women). *Graduate faculty:* 62 full-time (24 women), 36 part-time/adjunct (10 women). *Computer facilities:* 450 computers available on campus for general student use. A campuswide network can be accessed from off campus. Internet access and online class registration are available. *Library facilities:* Freeman/Lozier Library plus 1 other. *Graduate expenses:* Tuition: full-time $7,080; part-time $295 per credit hour. Required fees: $180. *General application contact:* Ed Rauchut, Executive Assistant to the President, 402-293-3701.

Find an in-depth description at www.petersons.com/gradchannel.

Graduate School
Dr. Mary Hawkins, Provost
Programs in:
  business • MBA
  computer information systems • MS
  health care administration • MS
  human services • MS
  leadership • MA
  management • MA

■ CHADRON STATE COLLEGE
Chadron, NE 69337
http://www.csc.edu/

State-supported, coed, comprehensive institution. *Enrollment:* 2,711 graduate, professional, and undergraduate students; 45 full-time matriculated graduate/professional students (25 women), 105 part-time matriculated graduate/professional students (71 women). *Graduate faculty:* 72 full-time (17 women). *Computer facilities:* 200 computers available on campus for general student use. A campuswide network can be accessed from student residence rooms and from off campus. Internet access and online class registration are available. *Library facilities:* Reta King Library. *Graduate expenses:* Tuition, state resident: full-time $1,980; part-time $110 per credit hour. Tuition, nonresident: full-time $3,960; part-time $220 per credit hour. Required

Nebraska

fees: $213; $34 per credit hour. Tuition and fees vary according to campus/location. *General application contact:* Dr. David Welch, Dean, Professional and Graduate Studies, 308-432-6330.

School of Education and Graduate Studies
Dr. David Welch, Dean, Professional and Graduate Studies
Programs in:
 business • MA Ed
 business and economics • MBA
 counseling • MA Ed
 educational administration • MS Ed, Sp Ed
 elementary education • MS Ed
 history • MA Ed
 language and literature • MA Ed
 secondary administration • MS Ed
 secondary education • MS Ed

■ CONCORDIA UNIVERSITY
Seward, NE 68434-1599
http://www.cune.edu/

Independent-religious, coed, comprehensive institution. *Computer facilities:* 75 computers available on campus for general student use. A campuswide network can be accessed from student residence rooms and from off campus. Internet access and online class registration, academic plans, human resource data are available. *Library facilities:* Link Library. *General application contact:* Dean of Graduate Studies, 402-643-7464.

Graduate Programs in Education
Programs in:
 curriculum and instruction • M Ed
 early childhood education • M Ed
 education • M Ed, MPE, MS
 educational administration • M Ed
 family life ministry • MS
 literacy education • M Ed
 parish education • MPE

■ CREIGHTON UNIVERSITY
Omaha, NE 68178-0001
http://www.creighton.edu/

Independent-religious, coed, university. CGS member. *Computer facilities:* Computer purchase and lease plans are available. 520 computers available on campus for general student use. A campuswide network can be accessed from student residence rooms and from off campus. Internet access and online class registration, online grade information are available. *Library facilities:* Reinert Alumni Memorial Library plus 2 others. *General application contact:* Dean, Graduate School, 402-280-2870.

Graduate School
College of Arts and Sciences
Programs in:
 arts and sciences • MA, MCS, MLS, MS
 atmospheric sciences • MS
 Christian spirituality • MA
 computer sciences • MCS
 educational administration • MS
 guidance and counseling • MS
 international relations • MA
 liberal studies • MLS
 ministry • MA
 physics • MS
 theology • MA

Eugene C. Eppley College of Business Administration
Programs in:
 business administration • MBA
 electronic commerce • MS
 information technology • MS

School of Dentistry
Program in:
 dentistry • DDS

School of Law
Patrick J. Borchers, Dean
Program in:
 law • JD

School of Medicine
Dr. Cam E. Enarson, Dean
Programs in:
 biomedical sciences • MS, PhD
 medical microbiology and immunology • MS, PhD
 medicine • MD, MS, PhD
 pharmaceutical sciences • MS
 pharmacology • MS, PhD

School of Nursing
Program in:
 nursing • MS

School of Pharmacy and Health Professions
Programs in:
 occupational therapy • OTD
 pharmaceutical sciences • MS
 pharmacy • Pharm D
 pharmacy and health professions • Pharm D, MS, DPT, OTD
 physical therapy • DPT

■ DOANE COLLEGE
Crete, NE 68333-2430
http://www.doane.edu/

Independent-religious, coed, comprehensive institution. *Computer facilities:* 200 computers available on campus for general student use. A campuswide network can be accessed from student residence rooms and from off campus. Internet access and online class registration are available. *Library facilities:* Perkins Library. *General application contact:* Dean of Graduate Studies in Education, 402-464-1223.

Program in Counseling
Program in:
 counseling • MAC

Program in Education
Programs in:
 curriculum and instruction • M Ed
 educational leadership • M Ed

Program in Management
Program in:
 management • MAM

■ PERU STATE COLLEGE
Peru, NE 68421
http://www.peru.edu/

State-supported, coed, comprehensive institution. *Enrollment:* 1,671 graduate, professional, and undergraduate students; 5 full-time matriculated graduate/professional students (3 women), 155 part-time matriculated graduate/professional students (111 women). *Graduate faculty:* 5 full-time (2 women), 5 part-time/adjunct (4 women). *Computer facilities:* 120 computers available on campus for general student use. A campuswide network can be accessed from student residence rooms. Internet access is available. *Library facilities:* Peru State College Library. *Graduate expenses:* Tuition, state resident: part-time $110 per credit hour. Tuition, nonresident: part-time $220 per credit hour. Required fees: $20 per credit hour. $20 per semester. *General application contact:* Todd Drew, Dean, Graduate School, 402-872-2258.

Graduate Studies
Todd Drew, Dean, Graduate School
Program in:
 education • MS Ed

■ UNIVERSITY OF NEBRASKA AT KEARNEY
Kearney, NE 68849-0001
http://www.unk.edu/

State-supported, coed, comprehensive institution. CGS member. *Enrollment:* 129 full-time matriculated graduate/professional students (95 women), 567 part-time matriculated graduate/professional students (377 women). *Graduate faculty:* 95 full-time (38 women). *Computer facilities:* 277 computers available on campus for general student use. A campuswide network can be accessed from student residence rooms and from off campus. Internet access and online class registration, online grade reports are available. *Library*

Peterson's Graduate Schools in the U.S. 2006 — www.petersons.com — 411

Nebraska

University of Nebraska at Kearney (continued)
facilities: Calvin T. Ryan Library. *Graduate expenses:* Tuition, state resident: full-time $2,318; part-time $129 per credit. Tuition, nonresident: full-time $4,793; part-time $266 per credit. Required fees: $572; $44 per credit. One-time fee: $16 full-time. Tuition and fees vary according to course load and campus/location. *General application contact:* Dr. Kenneth Nikels, Graduate Dean, 308-865-8500.

College of Graduate Study
Dr. Kenneth Nikels, Dean

College of Business and Technology
Dr. Galen Hadley, Interim Dean
Programs in:
business administration • MBA
business and technology • MBA

College of Education
Dr. Marilyn Hadley, Dean
Programs in:
adapted physical education • MA Ed
counseling • MS Ed, Ed S
curriculum and instruction • MS Ed
education • MA Ed, MS Ed, Ed S
educational administration • MA Ed, Ed S
exercise science • MA Ed
instructional technology • MS Ed
master teacher • MA Ed
reading education • MA Ed
school psychology • Ed S
special education • MA Ed
speech pathology • MS Ed
supervisor of educational media • MA Ed

College of Fine Arts and Humanities
Dr. William Jurma, Dean
Programs in:
art education • MA Ed
creative writing • MA
fine arts and humanities • MA, MA Ed
French • MA Ed
German • MA Ed
literature • MA
music education • MA Ed
Spanish • MA Ed

College of Natural and Social Sciences
Dr. Francis Harrold, Dean
Programs in:
biology • MS
history • MA
natural and social sciences • MA, MS, MS Ed
science education • MS Ed

■ **UNIVERSITY OF NEBRASKA AT OMAHA**
Omaha, NE 68182
http://www.unomaha.edu/

State-supported, coed, university. CGS member. *Enrollment:* 13,997 graduate, professional, and undergraduate students; 610 full-time matriculated graduate/professional students (366 women), 1,821 part-time matriculated graduate/professional students (1,143 women). *Graduate faculty:* 298 full-time (97 women). *Computer facilities:* 64 computers available on campus for general student use. A campuswide network can be accessed from student residence rooms and from off campus. Internet access and online class registration are available. *Library facilities:* University Library. *Graduate expenses:* Tuition, state resident: full-time $3,504. Tuition, nonresident: full-time $9,216. Required fees: $516. *General application contact:* Penny Harmoney, Director, Graduate Studies, 402-554-2341.

Graduate Studies and Research
Dr. Thomas Bragg, Dean for Graduate Studies
Program in:
public health • MPH

College of Arts and Sciences
Dr. Shelton Hendricks, Dean
Programs in:
advanced writing • Certificate
arts and sciences • MA, MAT, MS, PhD, Certificate, Ed S
biology • MA, MS
communication • MA
developmental psychobiology • PhD
English • MA
experimental child psychology • PhD
geographic information science • Certificate
geography • MA
history • MA
industrial/organizational psychology • MS, PhD
mathematics • MA, MAT, MS
political science • MS
psychology • MA
school psychology • MS, Ed S
sociology • MA
teaching English to speakers of other languages • Certificate

College of Business Administration
Dr. Louis Pol, Associate
Programs in:
accounting • M Acc
business administration • EMBA, M Acc, MA, MBA, MS
economics • MA, MS

College of Education
Dr. John Langan, Chairperson
Programs in:
community counseling • MA, MS
counseling gerontology • MA, MS
education • MA, MS, Ed D, Certificate, Ed S
educational administration and supervision • MS, Ed D, Ed S
elementary education • MA, MS
health, physical education, and recreation • MA, MS
instruction in urban schools • Certificate
instructional technology • Certificate
reading education • MS
rehabilitation counseling • MA, MS
school counseling-elementary • MA, MS
school counseling-secondary • MA, MS
secondary education • MA, MS
special education • MS
speech-language pathology • MA, MS
student affairs practice in higher education • MA, MS

College of Fine Arts
Dr. Robert Welk, Interim Dean
Programs in:
fine arts • MA, MM
music • MM
theatre • MA

College of Information Science and Technology
Dr. David Hinton, Dean
Programs in:
computer science • MA, MS
information science and technology • MA, MS, PhD
information technology • PhD
management information systems • MS

College of Public Affairs and Community Service
Dr. Burton J. Reed, Chairperson
Programs in:
criminal justice • MA, MS, PhD
gerontology • MA, Certificate
public administration • MPA, PhD
public affairs and community service • MA, MPA, MS, MSW, PhD, Certificate
social work • MSW
urban studies • MS

■ **UNIVERSITY OF NEBRASKA–LINCOLN**
Lincoln, NE 68588
http://www.unl.edu/

State-supported, coed, university. CGS member. *Computer facilities:* Computer purchase and lease plans are available. 600 computers available on campus for general student use. A campuswide network can be accessed from student residence rooms and from off campus. Internet access and online class registration are available. *Library facilities:* Love Memorial Library plus 10 others. *General application contact:* Executive Associate Dean of Graduate Studies, 402-472-2875.

College of Law
Programs in:
law • JD, MLS
legal studies • MLS

Graduate College
Programs in:
museum studies • MA, MS
survey research and methodology • MS
toxicology • MS, PhD

College of Agricultural Sciences and Natural Resources
Programs in:
agricultural economics • MS, PhD
agricultural leadership, education and communication • MS
agricultural sciences and natural resources • M Ag, MA, MS, PhD
agriculture • M Ag
agronomy • MS, PhD
animal science • MS, PhD
biochemistry • MS, PhD
biometry • MS
entomology • MS, PhD
food science and technology • MS, PhD
horticulture • MS, PhD
mechanized systems management • MS
natural resources • MS
nutrition • MS, PhD
veterinary and biomedical sciences • MS, PhD

College of Architecture
Programs in:
architecture • M Arch, MS
community and regional planning • MCRP

College of Arts and Sciences
Programs in:
analytical chemistry • PhD
anthropology • MA
arts and sciences • M Sc T, MA, MAT, MS, PhD
astronomy • MS, PhD
biological sciences • MA, MS, PhD
chemistry • MS
classics and religious studies • MA
communication studies and theatre arts • PhD
communications studies • MA
computer engineering • PhD
computer science • MS, PhD
English • MA, PhD
French • MA, PhD
geography • MA, PhD
geosciences • MS, PhD
German • MA, PhD
history • MA, PhD
inorganic chemistry • PhD
mathematics and statistics • M Sc T, MA, MAT, MS, PhD
organic chemistry • PhD
philosophy • MA, PhD
physical chemistry • PhD
physics • MS, PhD
political science • MA, PhD
psychology • MA, PhD
sociology • MA, PhD
Spanish • MA, PhD

College of Business Administration
Programs in:
accountancy • PhD
actuarial science • MS
business • MA, MBA, PhD
business administration • MA, MBA, MPA, MS, PhD
economics • MA, PhD
finance • MA, PhD
management • MA, PhD
marketing • MA, PhD

College of Education and Human Sciences
Programs in:
family and consumer sciences • MS
human resources and family sciences • PhD
nutritional science and dietetics • MS
textiles, clothing and design • MA, MS

College of Education and Human Services
Programs in:
administration, curriculum and instruction • Ed D, PhD
community and human resources • Ed D, PhD
curriculum and instruction • M Ed, MA, MST, Ed S
education • M Ed, MA, MPE, MS, MST, Ed D, PhD, Certificate, Ed S
educational administration • M Ed, MA, Ed D, Certificate
educational psychology • MA, Ed S
health, physical education, and recreation • M Ed, MPE
psychological and cultural studies • Ed D, PhD
special education • M Ed, MA
special education and communication disorders • Ed S
speech-language pathology and audiology • MS

College of Engineering and Technology
Programs in:
agricultural and biological systems engineering • MS
agricultural science • MEE, MS
architectural engineering • MAE
chemical engineering • MS
civil engineering • MS
electrical engineering • MS
engineering • M Eng, PhD
engineering and technology • M Eng, MAE, MEE, MS, PhD
engineering mechanics • MS
environmental engineering • MS
industrial and management systems engineering • MS
manufacturing systems engineering • MS
mechanical engineering • MS

College of Fine and Performing Arts
Programs in:
art and art history • MFA
fine and performing arts • MFA, MM, DMA
music • MM, DMA
theatre arts • MFA

College of Journalism and Mass Communications
Program in:
journalism and mass communications • MA

■ WAYNE STATE COLLEGE
Wayne, NE 68787
http://www.wsc.edu/

State-supported, coed, comprehensive institution. CGS member. *Enrollment:* 3,317 graduate, professional, and undergraduate students; 36 full-time matriculated graduate/professional students (19 women), 395 part-time matriculated graduate/professional students (268 women). *Graduate faculty:* 82 part-time/adjunct (47 women). *Computer facilities:* 200 computers available on campus for general student use. A campuswide network can be accessed from student residence rooms and from off campus. Internet access and online class registration are available. *Library facilities:* U. S. Conn Library plus 1 other. *Graduate expenses:* Part-time $110 per credit hour. Tuition, nonresident: part-time $220 per credit hour. Required fees: $33 per credit hour. Tuition and fees vary according to course load. *General application contact:* Dr. Paul Theobald, Dean, 402-375-7389.

Departments of Communication Arts and Language and Literature
Dr. James O'Donnell, Dean
Programs in:
communication arts • MSE
English as a second language • MSE
English education • MSE

School of Business and Technology
Dr. Vaughn Benson, Dean
Program in:
business and technology • MBA

Nebraska

Wayne State College (continued)
School of Education and Counseling
Dr. Paul Theobald, Dean
Programs in:
  consumer science education • MSE
  counseling • MSE
  counselor education • MSE
  curriculum and instruction • MSE
  education and counseling • MSE, Ed S
  education technology • MSE
  educational administration • MSE, Ed S
  elementary administration • MSE
  elementary and secondary administration • MSE
  elementary education • MSE
  guidance and counseling • MSE
  health and physical education/health • MSE
  industrial technology education • MSE
  mathematics education • MSE
  music education • MSE
  school counseling • MSE
  science education • MSE
  secondary administration • MSE
  social science education • MSE
  special education • MSE

Nevada

■ UNIVERSITY OF NEVADA, LAS VEGAS
Las Vegas, NV 89154-9900
http://www.unlv.edu/

State-supported, coed, university. CGS member. *Enrollment:* 25,749 graduate, professional, and undergraduate students; 1,428 full-time matriculated graduate/professional students (772 women), 1,716 part-time matriculated graduate/professional students (1,042 women). *Graduate faculty:* 698 full-time (205 women), 169 part-time/adjunct (48 women). *Computer facilities:* 1,600 computers available on campus for general student use. A campuswide network can be accessed from student residence rooms and from off campus. Internet access and online class registration are available. *Library facilities:* Lied Library. *Graduate expenses:* Tuition, state resident: part-time $115 per credit. Tuition, nonresident: part-time $242 per credit. Required fees: $8 per semester. Tuition and fees vary according to course load. *General application contact:* Karen Maldonado, Administrative Assistant I, 702-895-3320.
Find an in-depth description at www.petersons.com/gradchannel.

Graduate College
Dr. Gale Sinatra, Interim Dean, Graduate College

College of Business
Dr. Richard Flaherty, Dean
Programs in:
  accounting • MS
  business • MA, MBA, MS
  business administration • MBA
  economics • MA
  management information systems • MS

College of Education
Dr. Gene Hall, Dean
Programs in:
  assessment and evaluation techniques for the exceptional • Ed D
  education • M Ed, MS, Ed D, PhD, Ed S
  educational administration • M Ed, Ed D, PhD, Ed S
  educational computing and technology • M Ed, MS
  educational leadership • MS
  educational psychology • M Ed, MS, PhD
  emotional disturbance • Ed D
  English/language arts • M Ed, MS
  general elementary curriculum • M Ed, MS
  general secondary education • M Ed, MS
  general special education • Ed D
  health promotion • M Ed
  instructional and curricular studies • Ed D, PhD, Ed S
  language and literacy education • M Ed, MS
  learning disabilities • Ed D
  library science and audiovisual education • M Ed, MS
  mathematics education • M Ed, MS
  mental retardation • Ed D
  middle school education • M Ed, MS
  postsecondary education • M Ed, MS
  school psychology • Ed S
  special education • M Ed, MS, PhD, Ed S
  teaching English as a second language • M Ed, MS
  vocational education • M Ed, MS

College of Fine Arts
Dr. Jeffrey Koep, Dean
Programs in:
  acting • MA
  applied music (performance) • MM
  architecture • M Arch
  art • MFA
  composition/theory • MM
  dance • MM
  design and technical • MA
  directing • MA
  fine arts • M Arch, MA, MFA, MM, DMA
  music education • MM
  performance studies • DMA
  playwriting • MA
  screenwriting • MFA
  theatre arts • MFA

College of Health Sciences
Dr. Carolyn Sabo, Dean
Programs in:
  exercise physiology • MS
  family nurse practitioner • MS
  geriatric nurse practitioner • MS
  health physics • MS
  health sciences • MS
  kinesiology • MS
  pediatric nurse practitioner • MS
  physical therapy • MS

College of Liberal Arts
Dr. James Frey, Dean
Programs in:
  anthropology • MA, PhD
  clinical psychology • PhD
  creative writing • MFA
  English • PhD
  English and American literature • MA
  ethics and policy studies • MA
  experimental psychology • PhD
  French • MA
  general psychology • MA
  history • MA, PhD
  language studies • MA
  liberal arts • MA, MFA, PhD
  political science • MA
  sociology • MA, PhD
  Spanish • MA
  writing • MA

College of Science
Dr. Ronald Yasbin, Dean
Programs in:
  applied mathematics • MS
  applied statistics • MS
  biochemistry • MS
  biological sciences • MS, PhD
  chemistry • MS
  geoscience • MS, PhD
  physics • MS, PhD
  pure mathematics • MS
  science • MAS, MS, PhD
  water resources management • MS

Greenspun College of Urban Affairs
Dr. Martha Watson, Dean
Programs in:
  community agency counseling • MS
  criminal justice • MA
  environmental science • MS, PhD
  marriage and family counseling • MS
  mass communications • MA
  public administration • MPA
  rehabilitation counseling • MS
  social work • MSW
  urban affairs • MA, MPA, MS, MSW, PhD

Howard R. Hughes College of Engineering
Dr. Eric Sandgren, Dean
Programs in:

Nevada

civil and environmental engineering • MSE, PhD
computer science • MS, PhD
electrical and computer engineering • MSE, PhD
engineering • MS, MSE, PhD
mechanical engineering • MSE, PhD

William F. Harrah College of Hotel Administration
Dr. Stuart Mann, Dean
Programs in:
hospitality administration • MHA, PhD
hotel administration • MS
leisure studies • MS

William S. Boyd School of Law
Richard J. Morgan, Dean
Program in:
law • JD

■ UNIVERSITY OF NEVADA, RENO
Reno, NV 89557
http://www.unr.edu/

State-supported, coed, university. CGS member. *Enrollment:* 15,534 graduate, professional, and undergraduate students; 1,838 full-time matriculated graduate/professional students (1,085 women), 506 part-time matriculated graduate/professional students (295 women). *Graduate faculty:* 574 full-time (177 women), 76 part-time/adjunct (25 women). *Computer facilities:* Computer purchase and lease plans are available. 200 computers available on campus for general student use. A campuswide network can be accessed from student residence rooms and from off campus. Internet access and online class registration are available. *Library facilities:* Getchell Library plus 5 others. *Graduate expenses:* Tuition, state resident: part-time $119 per credit. Tuition, nonresident: part-time $127 per credit. Required fees: $20 per term. Tuition and fees vary according to course load. *General application contact:* John C. Green, Admissions and Registrar Specialist, 775-784-6869 Ext. 3075.

Graduate School
Dr. Marsha Read, Associate Dean of the Graduate School
Programs in:
atmospheric sciences • MS, PhD
biology • MS
chemical physics • PhD
chemistry • MS, PhD
earth sciences and engineering • MS, PhD, EM, Geol E
ecology, evolution, and conservation biology • PhD
environmental sciences and health • MS, PhD
geochemistry • MS, PhD
geography • MS
geological engineering • MS, Geol E
geology • MS, PhD
geophysics • MS, PhD
hydrogeology • MS, PhD
hydrology • MS, PhD
judicial studies • MJS
land use planning • MS
mathematics • MS
mining engineering • MS, EM
molecular biosciences and biotechnology • MS, PhD
physics • MS, PhD
science • MATM, MS, PhD, EM, Geol E
teaching mathematics • MATM

College of Agriculture and Natural Resources
Dr. David Trawley, Dean
Programs in:
agriculture and natural resources • MS, PhD
animal science • MS
biochemistry • MS, PhD
environmental and natural resource science • MS
resource and applied economics • MS

College of Business Administration
Dr. H. Michael Reed, Dean
Programs in:
accounting • M Acc
business administration • M Acc, MA, MBA, MS
economics • MA, MS

College of Education
Dr. William E. Sparkman, Dean
Programs in:
counseling and educational psychology • M Ed, MA, MS, Ed D, PhD, Ed S
curriculum and instruction • Ed D, PhD
education • M Ed, MA, MS, Ed D, PhD, Ed S
educational leadership • M Ed, MA, MS, Ed D, PhD, Ed S
educational specialties • MA, MS, Ed S
elementary education • M Ed, MA, MS, Ed S
secondary education • M Ed, MS, Ed S
special education • M Ed
ssecondary education • MA
teaching English as a second language • MA

College of Engineering
Dr. Theodore Batchman, Dean
Programs in:
chemical engineering • MS, PhD
civil engineering • MS, PhD
computer engineering • MS
computer science • MS
computer science and engineering • PhD
electrical engineering • MS, PhD
engineering • MS, PhD, Met E
mechanical engineering • MS, PhD
metallurgical engineering • MS, PhD, Met E

College of Human and Community Sciences
Dr. Jean L. Perry, Dean
Programs in:
human and community sciences • MPH, MS, MSW
human development and family studies • MS
nursing • MS
nutrition • MS
public health • MPH
social work • MSW

College of Liberal Arts
Dr. Eric Herzik, Dean
Programs in:
anthropology • MA, PhD
Basque studies • PhD
English • MA, MATE, PhD
French • MA
German • MA
history • MA, PhD
liberal arts • MA, MATE, MM, MPA, MS, PhD
music • MA, MM
philosophy • MA
political science • MA, PhD
psychology • MA, PhD
public administration • MPA
public administration and policy • MPA
social psychology • PhD
sociology • MA
Spanish • MA
speech communications • MA

Donald W. Reynolds School of Journalism
Dr. Jennifer Greer, Dean
Program in:
journalism • MA

School of Medicine
Dr. Stephen McFarlane, Dean
Program in:
medicine • MD, MS, PhD

Graduate Programs in Medicine
Dr. Linda Brinkley, Dean of the Graduate School
Programs in:
biomedical engineering • MS, PhD
cellular and molecular pharmacology and physiology • MS, PhD
medicine • MS, PhD
speech pathology • PhD
speech pathology and audiology • MS

New Hampshire

■ ANTIOCH NEW ENGLAND GRADUATE SCHOOL
Keene, NH 03431-3552
http://www.antiochne.edu/

Independent, coed, graduate-only institution. *Graduate faculty:* 57 full-time (36 women), 68 part-time/adjunct (36 women). *Computer facilities:* 12 computers available on campus for general student use. A campuswide network can be accessed from off campus. Internet access, e-mail, intranet services are available. *Library facilities:* Antioch New England Graduate School Library. *Graduate expenses:* Tuition: part-time $5,650 per semester. *General application contact:* Leatrice A. Johnson, Director of Admissions, 603-357-6265 Ext. 287.

Find an in-depth description at www.petersons.com/gradchannel.

Graduate School
Peter S. Temes, President
Programs in:
  clinical psychology • Psy D
  community health care management • Certificate
  conservation biology • MS
  counseling psychology • MA
  dance/movement therapy • M Ed, MA
  educational administration and supervision • M Ed
  environmental advocacy • MS
  environmental education • MS
  environmental studies • MS, PhD
  experienced educators • M Ed
  human services administration • MHSA
  integrated learning • M Ed
  management • MS
  marriage and family therapy • MA
  resource management and administration • MS
  substance abuse counseling • M Ed
  substance abuse/addictions counseling • M Ed, MA
  teacher certification in biology (7th–12th grade) • MS
  teacher certification in general science (5th–9th grade) • MS
  Waldorf teacher training • M Ed

Interdisciplinary Studies
Program in:
  interdisciplinary studies • MA

■ DARTMOUTH COLLEGE
Hanover, NH 03755
http://www.dartmouth.edu/

Independent, coed, university. CGS member. *Enrollment:* 5,683 graduate, professional, and undergraduate students; 1,501 full-time matriculated graduate/professional students (584 women), 84 part-time matriculated graduate/professional students (46 women). *Graduate faculty:* 265 full-time (53 women). *Computer facilities:* 200 computers available on campus for general student use. A campuswide network can be accessed from student residence rooms and from off campus. Internet access and online class registration are available. *Library facilities:* Baker-Berry Library plus 10 others. *Graduate expenses:* Tuition: full-time $28,965. *General application contact:* Gary Hutchins, Assistant Dean/School of Arts and Sciences, 603-646-2107.

Find an in-depth description at www.petersons.com/gradchannel.

Dartmouth Medical School
Program in:
  medicine • MD

School of Arts and Sciences
Dr. Carol Folt, Dean of Graduate Studies
Programs in:
  arts and sciences • AM, MALS, MPH, MS, PhD
  biochemistry • PhD
  biology • PhD
  chemistry • PhD
  cognitive neuroscience • PhD
  comparative literature • AM
  computer science • MS, PhD
  earth sciences • MS, PhD
  electro-acoustic music • AM
  evaluative clinical sciences • MS, PhD
  genetics • PhD
  liberal studies • MALS
  mathematics • PhD
  pharmacology and toxicology • PhD
  physics and astronomy • MS, PhD
  physiology • PhD
  psychology • PhD
  public health • MPH

The Neuroscience Center
Program in:
  neuroscience • PhD

Thayer School of Engineering
Dr. Lewis M. Duncan, Dean
Programs in:
  biomedical engineering • MS, PhD
  biotechnology and biochemical engineering • MS, PhD
  computer engineering • MS, PhD
  electrical engineering • MS, PhD
  engineering • MEM, MS, PhD
  engineering management • MEM
  engineering physics • MS, PhD
  manufacturing systems • MS, PhD
  materials sciences and engineering • MS, PhD
  mechanical engineering • MS, PhD

Tuck School of Business at Dartmouth
Paul Danos, Dean
Program in:
  business • MBA

■ KEENE STATE COLLEGE
Keene, NH 03435
http://www.keene.edu/

State-supported, coed, comprehensive institution. *Enrollment:* 4,920 graduate, professional, and undergraduate students; 44 full-time matriculated graduate/professional students (27 women), 80 part-time matriculated graduate/professional students (58 women). *Graduate faculty:* 13 full-time (6 women), 6 part-time/adjunct (5 women). *Computer facilities:* Computer purchase and lease plans are available. 386 computers available on campus for general student use. A campuswide network can be accessed from student residence rooms and from off campus. Internet access, e-mail, personal web pages are available. *Library facilities:* Mason Library. *Graduate expenses:* Tuition, state resident: full-time $4,750; part-time $220 per credit. Tuition, nonresident: full-time $10,808; part-time $240 per credit. Required fees: $1,760; $71 per credit. *General application contact:* Peggy Richmond, Director of Admissions, 603-358-2276.

Division of Graduate and Professional Studies
Dr. David Hill, Acting Dean
Programs in:
  curriculum and instruction • M Ed
  educational administration • M Ed
  educational leadership • PMC
  school counselor • M Ed, PMC
  special education • M Ed, PMC

■ PLYMOUTH STATE UNIVERSITY
Plymouth, NH 03264-1595
http://www.plymouth.edu/

State-supported, coed, comprehensive institution. *Enrollment:* 4,910 graduate, professional, and undergraduate students; 20 full-time matriculated graduate/professional students (16 women), 1,031 part-time matriculated graduate/professional students (737 women). *Graduate faculty:* 73 full-time (33 women), 95 part-time/adjunct (54 women). *Computer facilities:* Computer purchase and lease plans are available. 500 computers available on campus for general student use. A campuswide network can be accessed from student residence rooms and from off campus.

New Hampshire

Internet access and online class registration are available. *Library facilities:* Lamson Library *Graduate expenses:* Tuition, state resident: part-time $340 per credit. Tuition, nonresident: part-time $374 per credit. *General application contact:* Cheryl B. Baker, Education Coordinator, 603-535-2737.

Division of Graduate Studies and Community Outreach
Dr. Dennise M. Maslakowski, Associate Vice President
Programs in:
  advanced graduate studies • CAGS
  athletic training • M Ed
  business • MBA
  counselor education • M Ed
  education • CAGS
  educational leadership • M Ed
  elementary education • M Ed
  English education • M Ed
  health education • M Ed
  k-12 education • M Ed
  mathematics education • M Ed
  reading and writing specialist • M Ed
  secondary education • M Ed
  special education administration • M Ed
  special education k-12 • M Ed

■ **RIVIER COLLEGE**
Nashua, NH 03060-5086
http://www.rivier.edu/

Independent-religious, coed, comprehensive institution. *Enrollment:* 2,317 graduate, professional, and undergraduate students; 119 full-time matriculated graduate/professional students (85 women), 444 part-time matriculated graduate/professional students (341 women). *Graduate faculty:* 26 full-time (12 women), 20 part-time/adjunct (2 women). *Computer facilities:* 93 computers available on campus for general student use. A campuswide network can be accessed from student residence rooms and from off campus. *Library facilities:* Regina Library plus 1 other. *Graduate expenses:* Tuition: part-time $393 per credit. *General application contact:* Diane Monahan, Director of Graduate Admissions, 603-897-8129.

Find an in-depth description at www.petersons.com/gradchannel.

School of Graduate Studies
Dr. Albert DeCiccio, Dean
Programs in:
  arts and sciences • M Ed, MA, MAT, MBA, MS, CAGS
  business administration • MBA
  computer information systems • MS
  computer science • MS

  counseling and psychotherapy • MA
  counselor education • M Ed
  curriculum and instruction • M Ed
  early childhood education • M Ed
  educational administration • M Ed
  elementary education • M Ed
  emotional and behavioral disorders • M Ed
  English • MA, MAT
  general education • M Ed
  health care administration • MBA
  human resources management • MS
  leadership and learning • CAGS
  learning disabilities • M Ed
  mathematics • MAT
  modern languages • MAT
  nursing • MS
  nursing education • MS
  reading • M Ed
  secondary education • M Ed
  social studies education • MAT
  Spanish • MAT
  writing and literature • MA

■ **UNIVERSITY OF NEW HAMPSHIRE**
Durham, NH 03824
http://www.unh.edu/

State-supported, coed, university. CGS member. *Enrollment:* 14,431 graduate, professional, and undergraduate students; 1,120 full-time matriculated graduate/professional students (644 women), 1,204 part-time matriculated graduate/professional students (701 women). *Graduate faculty:* 605 full-time. *Computer facilities:* A campuswide network can be accessed from student residence rooms and from off campus. Internet access and online class registration are available. *Library facilities:* Dimond Library plus 4 others. *Graduate expenses:* Full-time $7,070. Tuition, state resident: full-time $10,605. Tuition, nonresident: full-time $17,430. Required fees: $15. *General application contact:* Graduate Admissions Office, 603-862-3000.

Find an in-depth description at www.petersons.com/gradchannel.

Graduate School
Dr. Harry J. Richards, Associate Dean
Programs in:
  college teaching • MST
  earth and environmental science • PhD
  environmental education • MS
  natural resources and environmental studies • PhD

College of Engineering and Physical Sciences
Dr. Arthur Greenberg, Dean
Programs in:
  applied mathematics • MS
  chemical engineering • MS, PhD
  chemistry • MS, MST, PhD
  civil engineering • MS, PhD
  computer science • MS, PhD
  earth sciences • MS
  electrical engineering • MS, PhD
  engineering and physical sciences • MS, MST, PhD
  hydrology • MS
  materials science • MS, PhD
  mathematics • MS, MST, PhD
  mathematics education • PhD
  mechanical engineering • MS, PhD
  ocean engineering • MS, PhD
  ocean mapping • MS
  physics • MS, PhD
  statistics • MS
  systems design • PhD

College of Liberal Arts
Dr. Marilyn Hoskin, Dean
Programs in:
  adult and occupational education • MAOE
  counseling • M Ed, MA
  early childhood education • M Ed
  education • PhD
  educational administration • M Ed, CAGS
  elementary education • M Ed, MAT
  English • PhD
  English education • MST
  history • MA, PhD
  language and linguistics • MA
  liberal arts • M Ed, MA, MALS, MAOE, MAT, MFA, MPA, MST, PhD, CAGS
  liberal studies • MALS
  literacy and schooling • PhD
  literature • MA
  museum studies • MA
  music education • MA
  music history • MA
  painting • MFA
  political science • MA
  psychology • PhD
  public administration • MPA
  reading • M Ed
  secondary education • M Ed, MAT
  sociology • MA, PhD
  Spanish • MA
  special education • M Ed
  special needs • M Ed
  teacher leadership • M Ed
  writing • MA

College of Life Sciences and Agriculture
Dr. Andrew Rosenberg, Dean
Programs in:
  animal and nutritional sciences • PhD
  animal science • MS
  biochemistry and molecular biology • MS, PhD
  environmental conservation • MS
  forestry • MS
  genetics • MS, PhD

New Hampshire

University of New Hampshire (continued)
  life sciences and agriculture • MS, PhD
  microbiology • MS, PhD
  nutritional sciences • MS
  plant biology • MS, PhD
  resource administration • MS
  resource economics • MS
  soil science • MS
  water resources management • MS
  wildlife • MS
  zoology • MS, PhD

School of Health and Human Services
Dr. James McCarthy, Dean
Programs in:
  early childhood intervention • MS
  family studies • MS
  health and human services • MPH, MS, MSW
  kinesiology • MS
  language and literature disabilities • MS
  marriage and family therapy • MS
  nursing • MS
  occupational therapy • MS
  public health: ecology • MPH
  public health: nursing • MPH
  public health: policy and management • MPH
  recreation administration • MS
  social work • MSW
  therapeutic recreation • MS

Whittemore School of Business and Economics
Dr. Steve Bolander, Dean
Programs in:
  accounting • MS
  business administration • MBA
  business and economics • MA, MBA, MS, MSMOT, PhD
  economics • MA, PhD
  executive business administration • MBA
  health management • MBA
  management of technology • MBA

New Jersey

■ THE COLLEGE OF NEW JERSEY
Ewing, NJ 08628
http://www.tcnj.edu/

State-supported, coed, comprehensive institution. CGS member. *Enrollment:* 6,912 graduate, professional, and undergraduate students; 151 full-time matriculated graduate/professional students (116 women), 822 part-time matriculated graduate/professional students (656 women). *Computer facilities:* 800 computers available on campus for general student use. A campuswide network can be accessed from student residence rooms and from off campus. Internet access and online class registration are available. *Library facilities:* Roscoe L. West Library. *Graduate expenses:* Part-time $422 per credit. Tuition, state resident: full-time $7,610. Tuition, nonresident: full-time $10,652. Required fees: $1,244; $66 per credit. *General application contact:* Dr. J. Paul Stephens, Director, Office of Graduate Studies, 609-771-2300.

Find an in-depth description at www.petersons.com/gradchannel.

Graduate Division
Dr. Suzanne Pasch, Dean of Graduate Studies

School of Culture and Society
Dr. Susan Albertine, Dean
Programs in:
  applied spanish studies • MA
  culture and society • MA
  English • MA

School of Education
Dr. Terence O'Connor, Dean
Programs in:
  community counseling: human services • MA
  community counseling: substance abuse and addiction • MA, Certificate
  developmental reading • M Ed
  education • M Ed, MA, MAT, MS, Certificate, Ed S
  education administration • MAT
  educational leadership • M Ed
  educational technology • MS
  elementary education • M Ed, MAT
  elementary teaching • MAT
  English as a second language • M Ed
  health • MAT
  health education • M Ed, MAT
  instructional computing coordinator • Certificate
  marriage and family therapy • Ed S
  overseas education • MAT
  physical education • M Ed, MAT
  reading certification • Certificate
  school counseling • MA
  school personnel licensure: preschool–grade 3 • M Ed
  secondary education • M Ed, MAT
  special education • M Ed, MAT
  special education with learning disabilities • M Ed
  speech pathology • MA
  teaching English as a second language • M Ed, Certificate

School of Nursing
Dr. Susan Bakewell-Sachs, Dean
Programs in:
  nursing • MSN, Certificate
  school nurse certification • Certificate

■ FAIRLEIGH DICKINSON UNIVERSITY, COLLEGE AT FLORHAM
Madison, NJ 07940-1099
http://www.fdu.edu/

Independent, coed, comprehensive institution. *Enrollment:* 3,743 graduate, professional, and undergraduate students; 393 full-time matriculated graduate/professional students (254 women), 704 part-time matriculated graduate/professional students (437 women). *Graduate faculty:* 300 full-time, 400 part-time/adjunct. *Computer facilities:* 300 computers available on campus for general student use. A campuswide network can be accessed from student residence rooms and from off campus. *Library facilities:* Friendship Library plus 1 other. *Graduate expenses:* Tuition: part-time $700 per credit. *General application contact:* Thomas M. Shea, University Director of International and Graduate Admissions, 973-443-8905.

Find an in-depth description at www.petersons.com/gradchannel.

Maxwell Becton College of Arts and Sciences
Dr. Barbara Salmore, Dean
Programs in:
  arts and sciences • MA, MFA, MS, Certificate
  biology • MS
  chemistry • MS
  clinical/counseling psychology • MA
  corporate and organizational communication • MA
  creative writing • MFA
  industrial/organizational psychology • MA
  organizational behavior • MA
  organizational leadership • Certificate

New College of General and Continuing Studies
Kenneth T. Vehrkens, Dean
Program in:
  public administration • MPA

School of Hotel, Restaurant and Tourism Management
Dr. Richard Wisch, Director
Program in:
  hospitality management studies • MS

Samuel J. Silberman College of Business
Dr. David Steele, Dean
Programs in:
  accounting • MS
  business • MBA, MS, Certificate
  business administration • MBA

New Jersey

entrepreneurial studies • MBA, Certificate
evolving technology • Certificate
finance • MBA, Certificate
healthcare management studies • MBA, Certificate
human resource management • MBA
human resource management studies • MBA
international business • MBA, Certificate
management • MBA, Certificate
marketing • MBA
pharmaceutical-chemical studies • MBA, Certificate
taxation • MS, Certificate

■ FAIRLEIGH DICKINSON UNIVERSITY, METROPOLITAN CAMPUS
Teaneck, NJ 07666-1914
http://www.fdu.edu/

Independent, coed, comprehensive institution. *Enrollment:* 7,118 graduate, professional, and undergraduate students; 736 full-time matriculated graduate/professional students (364 women), 1,316 part-time matriculated graduate/professional students (764 women). *Graduate faculty:* 300 full-time, 400 part-time/adjunct. *Computer facilities:* 210 computers available on campus for general student use. A campuswide network can be accessed from student residence rooms and from off campus. *Library facilities:* Weiner Library plus 2 others. *Graduate expenses:* Tuition: part-time $700 per credit. Required fees: $872; $390 per year. *General application contact:* Thomas Shea, University Director of International and Graduate Admissions, 201-692-2554.

Find an in-depth description at www.petersons.com/gradchannel.

New College of General and Continuing Studies
Kenneth T. Vehrkens, Dean

Public Administration Institute
Dr. William Roberts, Director
Programs in:
  administrative science • MAS, Certificate
  public administration • MPA, Certificate
  public non-profit management • Certificate

School of Hotel, Restaurant and Tourism Management
Dr. Richard Wisch, Director
Program in:
  hospitality management studies • MS

Samuel J. Silberman College of Business
Dr. David Steele, Dean
Programs in:
  accounting • MS, Certificate
  business • MBA, MS, Certificate
  business administration • MBA
  entrepreneurial studies • MBA, Certificate
  finance • MBA, Certificate
  human resource management • MBA, Certificate
  international business • MBA
  management • MBA, Certificate
  management information systems • Certificate
  marketing • MBA, Certificate

Center for Healthcare Management Studies
Dr. Donald Zimmerman, Director
Programs in:
  chemical studies • Certificate
  pharmaceutical-chemical studies • MBA, Certificate

Institute for Global Business Education
Dr. Ron Heim, Director
Program in:
  global management • MBA

University College: Arts, Sciences, and Professional Studies
Dr. John Snyder, Dean
Programs in:
  arts, sciences, and professional studies • MA, MAT, MS, MSEE, MSN, PhD, Psy D, Certificate
  computer science • MS
  e-commerce • MS
  English and comparative literature • MA
  management information systems • MS
  systems science • MS

Henry P. Becton School of Nursing and Allied Health
Dr. Minerva Guttman, Director
Programs in:
  medical technology • MS
  nursing • MSN, Certificate

Peter Sammartino School of Education
Dr. Mary Farrell, Interim Director
Programs in:
  dyslexia specialist • Certificate
  education for certified teachers • MA
  educational leadership • MA
  instructional technology • Certificate
  learning disabilities • MA
  literacy/reading • Certificate
  multilingual education • MA
  teacher of the handicapped • Certificate
  teaching • MAT

School of Computer Sciences and Engineering
Dr. Alfredo Tan, Director
Programs in:
  computer engineering • MS
  computer science • MS
  database administration • Certificate
  e-commerce • MS
  electrical engineering • MSEE
  information systems • Certificate
  management information systems • MS

School of History, Political, and International Studies
Dr. Faramarz S. Fatemi, Director
Programs in:
  history • MA
  international studies • MA
  political science • MA

School of Natural Sciences
Dr. David Flory, Director
Programs in:
  biology • MS
  science • MA

School of Psychology
Dr. Christopher Capuano, Director
Programs in:
  clinical psychology • PhD
  clinical psychopharmacology • MA
  general-theoretical psychology • MA, Certificate
  school psychology • MA, Psy D

■ GEORGIAN COURT UNIVERSITY
Lakewood, NJ 08701-2697
http://www.georgian.edu/

Independent-religious, women only, comprehensive institution. *Enrollment:* 2,976 graduate, professional, and undergraduate students; 94 full-time matriculated graduate/professional students (77 women), 690 part-time matriculated graduate/professional students (582 women). *Graduate faculty:* 45 full-time (25 women), 61 part-time/adjunct (24 women). *Computer facilities:* 172 computers available on campus for general student use. A campuswide network can be accessed from student residence rooms. Internet access, intranet are available. *Library facilities:* The Sister Mary Joseph Cunningham Library. *Graduate expenses:* Tuition: full-time $8,496; part-time $472 per credit. Required fees: $200 per semester. Tuition and fees vary according to course load. *General application contact:* Kathie DeBona, Director of Admissions, 732-364-2200 Ext. 2760.

School of Arts and Humanities
Dr. Connie Chismar, Dean
Program in:
  theology • MA, Certificate

Peterson's Graduate Schools in the U.S. 2006

New Jersey

Georgian Court University (continued)
School of Business
Dr. Siamack Shojai, Dean
Program in:
business • MBA

School of Education
Dr. John Groves, Dean
Programs in:
administration, supervision, and curriculum planning • MA
early intervention studies • Certificate
education • MA
instructional technology • MA, Certificate
special education • MA
substance awareness coordinator • Certificate

School of Sciences and Mathematics
Dr. Linda James, Dean
Programs in:
biology • MS
counseling psychology • MA
holistic health • Certificate
holistic health studies • MA
mathematics • MA
professional counselor • Certificate
school psychology • Certificate

■ KEAN UNIVERSITY
Union, NJ 07083
http://www.kean.edu/

State-supported, coed, comprehensive institution. CGS member. *Enrollment:* 12,978 graduate, professional, and undergraduate students; 542 full-time matriculated graduate/professional students (413 women), 1,552 part-time matriculated graduate/professional students (1,226 women). *Graduate faculty:* 367 full-time (169 women). *Computer facilities:* 2,000 computers available on campus for general student use. A campuswide network can be accessed from student residence rooms and from off campus. Internet access and online class registration are available. *Library facilities:* Nancy Thompson Library plus 1 other. *Graduate expenses:* Tuition, state resident: full-time $7,488; part-time $312 per credit. Tuition, nonresident: full-time $9,528; part-time $397 per credit. Required fees: $1,814; $76 per credit. *General application contact:* Joanne Morris, Director of Graduate Admissions, 908-737-3355.

Find an in-depth description at www.petersons.com/gradchannel.

College of Arts, Humanities and Social Sciences
Dr. Cathleen Londino, Acting Dean
Programs in:
arts, humanities and social sciences • MA, MSW, Diploma, PMC
behavioral sciences • MA, PMC
business and industry counseling • MA, PMC
communication studies • MA
educational psychology • MA
graphic communication technology management • MA
human behavior and organizational psychology • MA
liberal studies • MA
marriage and family therapy • MA, Diploma
psychological services • MA
school psychology • MA, Diploma
social work • MSW

School of Visual and Performing Arts
Richard Buncamper, Graduate Coordinator
Program in:
fine arts education • MA

College of Business and Public Administration
Dr. David Yamoah, Dean
Programs in:
accounting • MS
business and public administration • MPA, MS, MSMIS
environmental management • MPA
health services administration • MPA
management information systems • MSMIS
public administration • MPA

College of Education
Dr. Ana Maria Schuhmann, Dean
Programs in:
administration in early childhood and family studies • MA
adult literacy • MA
advanced curriculum and teaching • MA
alcohol and drug abuse counseling • MA
basic skills • MA
bilingual education • Certificate
bilingual/bicultural education • MA
business and industry counseling • MA, PMC
classroom instruction • MA
community/agency counseling • MA
counselor education • MA, PMC
developmental disabilities • MA
earth science • MA
education • MA, Certificate, PMC
education for family living • MA
educational administration • MA, Certificate
educational media specialist • MA
educational technology • MA
elementary education • MA
emotionally disturbed and socially maladjusted • MA
English as a second language • Certificate
exercise science • MA
instruction and curriculum • MA, Certificate
learning disabilities • MA
mathematics/science/computer education • MA
pre-school handicapped • MA
preschool-third grade • Certificate
principals and supervisors • MA
reading specialist • Certificate
reading specialization • MA, Certificate
school business administration • MA, Certificate
school counseling • MA
special education • MA
speech language pathology • MA
speech pathology • MA
supervisor • Certificate
supervisors • MA
teaching • MA
teaching English as a second language • MA
teaching of reading • Certificate

School of Natural, Applied and Health Sciences
Dr. Roxie James, Dean
Programs in:
biotechnology • MS
clinical management • MSN
community health • MSN
computing, statistics and mathematics • MS
mathematics education • MA
natural, applied and health sciences • MA, MS, MSN
nursing • MSN
occupational therapy • MS

■ MONMOUTH UNIVERSITY
West Long Branch, NJ 07764-1898
http://www.monmouth.edu/

Independent, coed, comprehensive institution. *Enrollment:* 6,212 graduate, professional, and undergraduate students; 503 full-time matriculated graduate/professional students (367 women), 1,158 part-time matriculated graduate/professional students (739 women). *Graduate faculty:* 102 full-time (44 women), 27 part-time/adjunct (11 women). *Computer facilities:* 520 computers available on campus for general student use. A campuswide network can be accessed from student residence rooms and from off campus. Internet access is available. *Library facilities:* Murry and Leonie Guggenheim Memorial Library. *Graduate expenses:* Tuition: full-time $10,386; part-time $577 per credit.

Required fees: $142 per term. *General application contact:* Kevin Roane, Director, Office of Graduate Admission, 732-571-3452.

Find an in-depth description at www.petersons.com/gradchannel.

Graduate School
Dr. Datta V. Naik, Dean
Programs in:
 community and international development • MSW
 computer science • MS
 corporate and public communication • MA
 criminal justice administration • MA, Certificate
 history • MA
 human resources communication • Certificate
 liberal arts • MA
 media studies • Certificate
 practice with families and children • MSW
 professional counseling • PMC
 psychological counseling • MA
 public relations • Certificate
 software development • Certificate
 software engineering • MS, Certificate

The Marjorie K. Unterberg School of Nursing and Health Studies
Dr. Janet Mahoney, Director
Programs in:
 advanced practice nursing • Post-Master's Certificate
 nursing • MSN
 school nursing • Certificate
 substance awareness coordinator • Certificate

School of Business Administration
Edward Christensen, Associate Dean
Programs in:
 accounting • MBA
 business administration • MBA
 health care management • MBA, Certificate

School of Education
Dr. William Stanley, Dean
Programs in:
 educational counseling • MS Ed
 elementary education • MAT
 learning disabilities-teacher consultant • Certificate
 principal studies • MS Ed
 reading specialist • MS Ed, Certificate
 special education • MS Ed
 supervisor • Certificate
 teacher of the handicapped • Certificate

■ MONTCLAIR STATE UNIVERSITY
Upper Montclair, NJ 07043-1624
http://www.montclair.edu/

State-supported, coed, comprehensive institution. CGS member. *Enrollment:* 15,204 graduate, professional, and undergraduate students; 711 full-time matriculated graduate/professional students (491 women), 3,118 part-time matriculated graduate/professional students (2,218 women). *Graduate faculty:* 458 full-time, 538 part-time/adjunct. *Computer facilities:* 650 computers available on campus for general student use. A campuswide network can be accessed from student residence rooms and from off campus. Internet access is available. *Library facilities:* Sprague Library. *Graduate expenses:* Tuition, state resident: full-time $8,771; part-time $323 per credit. Tuition, nonresident: full-time $10,365; part-time $470 per credit. Required fees: $42 per credit. Tuition and fees vary according to degree level and program. *General application contact:* Dr. Carla M. Narrett, Dean of the Graduate School, 973-655-5147.

Find an in-depth description at www.petersons.com/gradchannel.

The Graduate School
Dr. Carla M. Narrett, Dean of the Graduate School

College of Education and Human Services
Dr. Ada Beth Cutler, Dean
Programs in:
 administration and supervision • MA
 art • MAT
 biological science • MAT
 coaching and sports administration • MA
 counseling and guidance • MA
 critical thinking • M Ed
 early childhood education (P–3) • MAT
 early childhood special education • M Ed
 earth science • MAT
 education • M Ed, Ed D
 education and human services • M Ed, MA, MAT, Ed D, Certificate
 educator/trainer • MA
 elementary education (K–8) • MAT
 English • MAT
 exercise science • MA
 family life education • MA
 family relations/child development • MA
 French • MAT
 health and physical education • MAT
 health education • MA, MAT, Certificate
 home economics • MAT
 home economics education • MA
 home management/consumer economics • MA
 human services • MA
 learning disabilities • M Ed
 mathematics • MAT
 mathematics education • Ed D
 music • MAT
 nutrition and exercise science • Certificate
 nutrition education • MA
 philosophy for children • M Ed, Ed D
 physical education • MA, MAT
 physical science • MAT
 reading • MA
 social studies • MAT
 Spanish • MAT
 teacher of ESL • MAT
 teacher of students with disabilities • MAT
 teaching • MAT
 teaching and supervision of physical education • MA

College of Humanities and Social Sciences
Dr. Richard Gigliotti, Dean
Programs in:
 applied linguistics • MA
 applied sociology • MA
 child advocacy • Certificate
 child/adolescent clinical psychology • MA
 clinical psychology for Spanish/English bilinguals • MA
 dispute resolution • MA
 early childhood special education • MA
 economics • MA
 educational psychology • MA
 English • MA
 French • MA
 history • MA
 humanities and social sciences • MA, Certificate
 industrial and organizational psychology • MA
 law office management and technology • MA
 learning disabilities • MA
 legal studies • MA
 paralegal • Certificate
 psychology • MA
 Spanish • MA
 speech/language pathology • MA
 teaching English to speakers of other languages • MA

College of Science and Mathematics
Dr. Robert Prezant, Dean
Programs in:
 applied mathematics • MS
 applied statistics • MS
 biology • MS

New Jersey

Montclair State University (continued)
  chemistry • MS
  computer science • MS
  environmental management • MA, D Env M
  environmental studies • MS
  geoscience • MS, Certificate
  informatics • MS
  mathematics • MS
  mathematics education • MS
  molecular biology • Certificate
  object oriented computing • Certificate
  pure and applied mathematics • MS
  science and mathematics • MA, MS, D Env M, Certificate
  statistics • MS
  water resource management • Certificate

School of Business
Dr. Alan Oppenheim, Dean
Programs in:
  accounting • MBA
  business • MA, MBA
  business economics • MBA
  finance • MBA
  international business • MBA
  management • MBA
  management information systems • MBA
  marketing • MBA
  social science • MA

School of the Arts
Dr. Geoffrey Newman, Dean
Programs in:
  art education • MA
  art history • MA
  arts • MA, MFA
  music education • MA
  music therapy • MA
  organizational communication • MA
  performance • MA
  public relations • MA
  speech communication • MA
  studio arts • MA, MFA
  theatre • MA
  theory/composition • MA

■ **NEW JERSEY CITY UNIVERSITY**
Jersey City, NJ 07305-1597
http://www.njcu.edu/

State-supported, coed, comprehensive institution. *Enrollment:* 9,361 graduate, professional, and undergraduate students; 93 full-time matriculated graduate/professional students (56 women), 1,410 part-time matriculated graduate/professional students (1,020 women). *Graduate faculty:* 136. *Computer facilities:* 1,400 computers available on campus for general student use. *Library facilities:* Congressman Frank J. Guarini Library. *Graduate expenses:* Tuition, state resident: full-time $7,036; part-time $293 per credit. Tuition, nonresident: full-time $12,312; part-time $513 per credit. Required fees: $1,154; $48 per credit. *General application contact:* Dr. Catherine Shevey, Director of Graduate Studies, 201-200-3409.

Graduate and Continuing Education
Dr. Catherine Shevey, Director of Graduate Studies

College of Arts and Sciences
Dr. Lisa Fiol-Mata, Dean
Programs in:
  art • MA, MFA
  art education • MA
  arts and sciences • MA, MFA, MM, PD
  counseling • MA
  educational psychology • MA, PD
  mathematics education • MA
  music education • MA
  performance in music • MM
  school psychology • PD

College of Education
Dr. Muriel Rand, Dean
Programs in:
  basics and urban studies • MA
  bilingual/bicultural education and English as a second language • MA
  early childhood education • MA
  education • MA
  educational technology • MA
  elementary and secondary education • MA
  elementary school reading • MA
  reading specialist • MA
  secondary school reading • MA
  special education • MA
  urban education • MA

College of Professional Studies
Dr. Sandra Bloomberg, Dean
Programs in:
  accounting • MS
  community health education • MS
  criminal justice • MS
  health administration • MS
  holistic medicine • MS
  professional studies • MA, MS
  urban medicine • MS

■ **NEW JERSEY INSTITUTE OF TECHNOLOGY**
Newark, NJ 07102
http://www.njit.edu/

State-supported, coed, university. CGS member. *Enrollment:* 8,770 graduate, professional, and undergraduate students; 1,261 full-time matriculated graduate/professional students (416 women), 1,797 part-time matriculated graduate/professional students (544 women). *Graduate faculty:* 404 full-time (61 women), 230 part-time/adjunct (41 women). *Computer facilities:* 4,500 computers available on campus for general student use. A campuswide network can be accessed from student residence rooms and from off campus. *Library facilities:* Van Houten Library plus 1 other. *Graduate expenses:* Tuition, state resident: full-time $9,620; part-time $520 per credit. Tuition, nonresident: full-time $13,542; part-time $715 per credit. Tuition and fees vary according to course load. *General application contact:* Kathryn Kelly, Director of Admissions, 973-596-3300.

Office of Graduate Studies
Dr. Ron Kane, Dean of Graduate Studies
Programs in:
  applied mathematics • MS
  applied physics • MS, PhD
  applied statistics • MS
  biology • MS, PhD
  biomedical engineering • MS, PhD
  chemical engineering • MS, PhD
  chemistry • MS, PhD
  civil engineering • MS, PhD
  computer engineering • MS, PhD
  electrical engineering • MS, PhD
  engineering • MS, PhD, Engineer
  engineering management • MS
  engineering science • MS
  environmental engineering • MS, PhD
  environmental policy studies • MS, PhD
  environmental science • MS, PhD
  history • MA, MAT
  history of technology, environment and medicine • MA
  industrial engineering • MS, PhD
  Internet engineering • MS
  manufacturing engineering • MS
  materials science and engineering • MS, PhD
  mathematics science • PhD
  mechanical engineering • MS, PhD, Engineer
  occupational safety and health engineering • MS
  occupational safety and industrial hygiene • MS
  pharmaceutical engineering • MS
  professional and technical communication • MS
  public health • MS
  science and liberal arts • MA, MAT, MS, PhD
  transportation • MS, PhD

College of Computing Science
Dr. Stephen B. Seidman, Dean
Programs in:
  computational biology • MS
  computer science • MS, PhD
  information systems • MS, PhD
  telecommunication • MS

New Jersey

School of Architecture
Urs P. Gauchat, Dean
Programs in:
architecture • M Arch, MS
infrastructure planning • MIP
urban systems • PhD

School of Management
Dr. Mark Somers, Dean
Programs in:
management of business administration • MBA
management of technology • MS, PhD

■ PRINCETON UNIVERSITY
Princeton, NJ 08544-1019
http://www.princeton.edu/

Independent, coed, university. CGS member. *Enrollment:* 6,849 graduate, professional, and undergraduate students; 1,991 full-time matriculated graduate/professional students (755 women). *Graduate faculty:* 846 full-time (208 women), 227 part-time/adjunct (47 women). *Computer facilities:* Computer purchase and lease plans are available. 500 computers available on campus for general student use. A campuswide network can be accessed from student residence rooms and from off campus. Internet access and online class registration, academic applications and courseware are available. *Library facilities:* Harvey S. Firestone Memorial Library plus 14 others. *Graduate expenses:* Tuition: full-time $29,910. Required fees: $810. *General application contact:* Janice Yip, Director of Graduate Admission, 609-258-3034.

Graduate School
William B. Russel, Dean
Programs in:
ancient history • PhD
ancient Near Eastern studies • PhD
anthropology • PhD
applied and computational mathematics • PhD
applied physics • M Eng, MSE, PhD
astrophysical sciences • PhD
atmospheric and oceanic sciences • PhD
biology • PhD
chemical engineering • M Eng, MSE, PhD
chemistry • PhD
Chinese and Japanese art and archaeology • PhD
classical archaeology • PhD
classical art and archaeology • PhD
classical philosophy • PhD
community college history teaching • PhD
comparative literature • PhD
composition • PhD
computational methods • M Eng, MSE
computer science • M Eng, MSE, PhD
demography • PhD, Certificate
demography and public affairs • PhD
dynamics and control systems • M Eng, MSE, PhD
East Asian civilizations • PhD
East Asian studies • PhD
economics • PhD
economics and demography • PhD
electrical engineering • M Eng, MSE, PhD
energy and environmental policy • M Eng, MSE, PhD
energy conversion, propulsion, and combustion • M Eng, MSE, PhD
English • PhD
environmental engineering and water resources • PhD
financial engineering • M Eng
flight science and technology • M Eng, MSE, PhD
fluid mechanics • M Eng, MSE, PhD
French and Italian • PhD
geological and geophysical sciences • PhD
Germanic languages and literatures • PhD
history • PhD
history of science • PhD
history, archaeology and religions of the ancient world • PhD
industrial chemistry • MS
Islamic studies • PhD
mathematical physics • PhD
mathematics • PhD
mechanics, materials, and structures • M Eng, MSE, PhD
molecular biology • PhD
molecular biophysics • PhD
musicology • PhD
Near Eastern studies • MA
neuroscience • PhD
operations research and financial engineering • MSE, PhD
philosophy • PhD
physics • PhD
physics and chemical physics • PhD
plasma physics • PhD
plasma science and technology • MSE, PhD
political philosophy • PhD
politics • PhD
polymer sciences and materials • MSE, PhD
psychology • PhD
religion • PhD
Slavic languages and literatures • PhD
sociology • PhD
sociology and demography • PhD
Spanish and Portuguese languages and cultures • PhD
statistics and operations research • MSE, PhD
transportation systems • MSE, PhD

Bendheim Center for Finance
Rene Carmona, Director of Graduate Studies
Program in:
finance • M Fin

School of Architecture
Prof. Stan Allen, Dean
Program in:
architecture • M Arch, PhD

Woodrow Wilson School of Public and International Affairs
John Templeton, Director of Graduate Admissions
Program in:
public and international affairs • MPA, MPA-URP, MPP, PhD

■ RIDER UNIVERSITY
Lawrenceville, NJ 08648-3001
http://www.rider.edu/

Independent, coed, comprehensive institution. *Enrollment:* 5,509 graduate, professional, and undergraduate students; 205 full-time matriculated graduate/professional students (147 women), 677 part-time matriculated graduate/professional students (450 women). *Graduate faculty:* 75 full-time, 63 part-time/adjunct. *Computer facilities:* Computer purchase and lease plans are available. 403 computers available on campus for general student use. A campuswide network can be accessed from student residence rooms and from off campus. Internet access is available. *Library facilities:* Franklin F. Moore Library plus 1 other. *Graduate expenses:* Tuition: full-time $20,590; part-time $415 per credit hour. Required fees: $200; $35 per course. Tuition and fees vary according to course load and program. *General application contact:* Christine Zelenak, Director of Graduate Admissions, 609-896-5036.

College of Business Administration
Thomas Charles Kelly, Associate Dean
Programs in:
accountancy • M Acc
business administration • M Acc, MBA

Department of Graduate Education and Human Services
Dr. Sandra Stein, Chair
Programs in:
business education • Certificate
counseling services • MA, Ed S
curriculum, instruction and supervision • MA
educational administration • MA
elementary education • Certificate

New Jersey

Rider University (continued)
  English education • Certificate
  foreign language education • Certificate
  human services administration • MA
  mathematics education • Certificate
  reading specialist • MA
  reading/language arts • MA
  school psychology • Ed S
  science education • Certificate
  social studies education • Certificate
  special education • MA
  teacher certification • Certificate

Westminster Choir College of Rider University
Dr. James Goldsworthy, Associate Dean
Programs in:
  choral conducting • MM
  composition • MM
  music education • MM, MME
  organ performance • MM
  piano accompanying and coaching • MM
  piano pedagogy and performance • MM
  sacred music • MM
  vocal pedagogy and performance • MM

■ **ROWAN UNIVERSITY**
Glassboro, NJ 08028-1701
http://www.rowan.edu/

State-supported, coed, comprehensive institution. CGS member. *Enrollment:* 9,667 graduate, professional, and undergraduate students; 178 full-time matriculated graduate/professional students (97 women), 694 part-time matriculated graduate/professional students (505 women). *Graduate faculty:* 47 full-time (22 women), 29 part-time/adjunct (14 women). *Computer facilities:* 350 computers available on campus for general student use. A campuswide network can be accessed from student residence rooms and from off campus. Internet access is available. *Library facilities:* Keith and Shirley Campbell Library plus 2 others. *Graduate expenses:* Tuition, state resident: full-time $8,476; part-time $385 per credit hour. Tuition, nonresident: full-time $13,576; part-time $617 per credit hour. Required fees: $1,438; $65 per credit hour. Tuition and fees vary according to degree level. *General application contact:* Dr. Jay Kuder, Dean, Graduate Studies, 856-256-4050.
Find an in-depth description at www.petersons.com/gradchannel.

Graduate School
Dr. Jay Kuder, Dean

College of Business
Dr. Edward Schoen, Dean
Programs in:
  business • MBA
  business administration • MBA

College of Communication
Dr. Craig Monroe, Dean
Programs in:
  public relations • MA
  writing • MA

College of Education
Dr. Carol Sharp, Dean
Programs in:
  art education • MA
  biological science education • MA
  education • MA, MST, Ed D, Ed S
  educational leadership • Ed D
  educational technology • MA
  elementary education • MA, MST
  environmental education • MA
  environmental education and conservation • MA
  higher education administration • MA
  learning disabilities • MA
  mathematics education • MA
  music education • MA
  physical science education • MA
  reading education • MA
  school administration • MA
  school administration-business administration • MA
  school and public librarianship • MA
  school psychology • MA, Ed S
  science education • MA
  special education • MA, MST
  student personnel services • MA
  subject matter teaching • MA
  supervision and curriculum development • MA
  teaching-secondary • MST

College of Engineering
Dr. Dianne Dorland, Dean
Program in:
  engineering • MS

College of Fine and Performing Arts
Dr. Donald Gephardt, Dean
Programs in:
  fine and performing arts • MA, MM
  music • MM
  theatre • MA

College of Liberal Arts and Sciences
Dr. Jay Harper, Dean
Programs in:
  liberal arts and sciences • MA
  mathematics • MA
  mental health counseling and applied psychology • MA

■ **RUTGERS, THE STATE UNIVERSITY OF NEW JERSEY, CAMDEN**
Camden, NJ 08102-1401
http://camden-www.rutgers.edu/

State-supported, coed, university. *Enrollment:* 5,485 graduate, professional, and undergraduate students; 684 full-time matriculated graduate/professional students (311 women), 764 part-time matriculated graduate/professional students (366 women). *Graduate faculty:* 225 full-time (81 women), 157 part-time/adjunct (65 women). *Computer facilities:* 184 computers available on campus for general student use. A campuswide network can be accessed from student residence rooms and from off campus. Internet access, online grade reports are available. *Library facilities:* Paul Robeson Library plus 2 others. *Graduate expenses:* Tuition, state resident: full-time $10,030. Tuition, nonresident: full-time $14,202. *General application contact:* Kathryn B. Gallagher, Admissions Counselor, 856-225-6105.

Graduate School
Dr. Margaret Marsh, Dean
Programs in:
  American and public history • MA
  biology • MS
  chemistry • MS
  criminal justice • MA
  English • MA
  health care management and policy • MPA
  international public service and development • MPA
  liberal studies • MA
  mathematics • MS
  physical therapy • MPT
  public management • MPA

School of Business
Milton Leontiades, Dean
Program in:
  business • M Ac, MBA

School of Law
Rayman L. Solomon, Dean
Program in:
  law • JD

■ **RUTGERS, THE STATE UNIVERSITY OF NEW JERSEY, NEWARK**
Newark, NJ 07102
http://www.newark.rutgers.edu/

State-supported, coed, university. CGS member. *Enrollment:* 10,465 graduate, professional, and undergraduate students; 1,392 full-time matriculated graduate/professional students (657 women),

New Jersey

2,289 part-time matriculated graduate/professional students (1,036 women). *Graduate faculty:* 424 full-time (167 women), 210 part-time/adjunct (92 women). *Computer facilities:* 708 computers available on campus for general student use. A campuswide network can be accessed from student residence rooms and from off campus. Internet access, online grade reports are available. *Library facilities:* John Cotton Dana Library plus 4 others. *Graduate expenses:* Tuition, state resident: full-time $10,030. Tuition, nonresident: full-time $14,202. *General application contact:* Bruce C. Neimeyer, Director of Admissions, 973-353-5205.

Find an in-depth description at www.petersons.com/gradchannel.

Graduate School
Dr. Sterling L. Bland, Associate Dean
Programs in:
 accounting • PhD
 accounting information systems • PhD
 American political system • MA
 analytical chemistry • MS, PhD
 applied physics • MS, PhD
 biochemistry • MS, PhD
 biology • MS, PhD
 cognitive neuroscience • PhD
 cognitive science • PhD
 computational biology • MS
 computer information systems • PhD
 criminal justice • PhD
 English • MA
 environmental geology • MS
 environmental science • MS, PhD
 finance • PhD
 global affairs • MS, PhD
 health care administration • MPA
 history • MA, MAT
 human resources administration • MPA
 information technology • PhD
 inorganic chemistry • MS, PhD
 integrative neuroscience • PhD
 international business • PhD
 international relations • MA
 jazz history and research • MA
 liberal studies • MALS
 management science • PhD
 marketing • PhD
 mathematical sciences • PhD
 nursing • MS
 organic chemistry • MS, PhD
 organization management • PhD
 perception • PhD
 physical chemistry • MS, PhD
 psychobiology • PhD
 public administration • PhD
 public management • MPA
 public policy analysis • MPA
 social cognition • PhD
 urban systems • PhD
 urban systems and issues • MPA

Center for Global Change and Governance
Program in:
 global affairs • MS, PhD

School of Criminal Justice
Program in:
 criminal justice • MA, PhD

Rutgers Business School: Graduate Programs-Newark/New Brunswick
Dr. Howard Tuckman, Dean
Programs in:
 accounting • PhD
 accounting information systems • PhD
 business • M Accy, MBA, MQF, PhD, Certificate
 business environment • MBA
 customized concentration • MBA
 finance • PhD
 finance and economics • MBA, MQF
 global business • MBA
 government financial management • Certificate
 governmental accounting • M Accy
 individualized study • PhD
 information technology • PhD
 international business • PhD
 management and business strategy • MBA
 management science • PhD
 management science and information systems • MBA
 marketing • MBA
 organizational management • PhD
 professional accounting • MBA
 supply chain manaegment • PhD
 taxation • M Accy

School of Law
Program in:
 law • JD

■ **RUTGERS, THE STATE UNIVERSITY OF NEW JERSEY, NEW BRUNSWICK/PISCATAWAY**
New Brunswick, NJ 08901-1281
http://www.rutgers.edu/

State-supported, coed, university. CGS member. *Enrollment:* 35,318 graduate, professional, and undergraduate students; 3,946 full-time matriculated graduate/professional students (2,291 women), 4,007 part-time matriculated graduate/professional students (2,707 women). *Graduate faculty:* 1,920 full-time (640 women), 658 part-time/adjunct (307 women). *Computer facilities:* 1,450 computers available on campus for general student use. A campuswide network can be accessed from student residence rooms and from off campus. Internet access, online grade reports are available. *Library facilities:* Archibald S. Alexander Library plus 14 others. *Graduate expenses:* Tuition, state resident: full-time $10,030. Tuition, nonresident: full-time $14,202. *General application contact:* Dr. Donald J. Taylor, Director of Graduate Admissions, 732-932-7711.

Edward J. Bloustein School of Planning and Public Policy
James W. Hughes, Dean
Programs in:
 planning and public policy • MCRP, MCRS, MPAP, MPH, MPP, Dr PH, PhD
 public health • MPH, Dr PH, PhD
 public policy • MPAP, MPP
 urban planning and policy development • MCRP, MCRS, PhD

Ernest Mario School of Pharmacy
John L. Colaizzi, Dean
Program in:
 pharmacy • Pharm D

Graduate School
Programs in:
 African diaspora • PhD
 agricultural economics • MS
 air resources • MS, PhD
 American political institutions • PhD
 analytical chemistry • MS, PhD
 anthropology • MA, PhD
 applied mathematics • MS, PhD
 applied microbiology • MS, PhD
 aquatic biology • MS, PhD
 aquatic chemistry • MS, PhD
 art history • MA, PhD
 astronomy • MS, PhD
 atmospheric science • MS, PhD
 bilingualism and second language acquisition • MA, PhD
 biochemistry • MS, PhD
 biological chemistry • PhD
 biomedical engineering • MS, PhD
 biophysics • PhD
 biopsychology and behavioral neuroscience • PhD
 bioresource engineering • MS
 cell biology • MS, PhD
 cellular and molecular pharmacology • PhD
 ceramic and materials science and engineering • MS, PhD
 chemical and biochemical engineering • MS, PhD
 chemistry and physics of aerosol and hydrosol systems • MS, PhD
 chemistry education • MST
 civil and environmental engineering • MS, PhD
 classics • MA, MAT, PhD
 clinical microbiology • MS, PhD
 clinical psychology • PhD
 cognitive psychology • PhD
 communication, information, and library studies • PhD

Peterson's Graduate Schools in the U.S. 2006

New Jersey

Rutgers, The State University of New Jersey, New Brunswick/Piscataway (continued)

  communications and solid-state electronics • MS, PhD
  comparative literature • MA, PhD
  comparative politics • PhD
  composition • MA, PhD
  computational fluid dynamics • MS, PhD
  computational molecular biology • PhD
  computer engineering • MS, PhD
  computer science • MS, PhD
  condensed matter physics • MS, PhD
  control systems • MS, PhD
  design and dynamics • MS, PhD
  developmental biology • MS, PhD
  digital signal processing • MS, PhD
  diplomatic history • PhD
  direct intervention in interpersonal situations • PhD
  early American history • PhD
  early modern European history • PhD
  ecology and evolution • MS, PhD
  economics • MA, PhD
  elementary particle physics • MS, PhD
  endocrine control of growth and metabolism • MS, PhD
  entomology • MS, PhD
  environmental chemistry • MS, PhD
  environmental microbiology • MS, PhD
  environmental toxicology • MS, PhD
  exposure assessment • PhD
  fate and effects of pollutants • MS, PhD
  fluid mechanics • MS, PhD
  food science • M Phil, MS, PhD
  French • MA, PhD
  French studies • MAT
  geography • MA, MS, PhD
  geological sciences • MS, PhD
  German • PhD
  global/comparative history • PhD
  heat transfer • MS, PhD
  historic preservation • PhD
  history • PhD
  history of technology, environment and health • PhD
  horticulture • MS, PhD
  immunology • MS, PhD
  industrial and systems engineering • MS, PhD
  industrial pharmacy • MS, PhD
  industrial relations and human resources • PhD
  industrial-occupational toxicology • MS, PhD
  information technology • MS
  inorganic chemistry • MS, PhD
  interdisciplinary developmental psychology • PhD
  interdisciplinary health psychology • PhD
  intermediate energy nuclear physics • MS
  international relations • PhD
  Italian • MA
  Italian history • PhD
  Italian literature and literary criticism • MA, PhD
  language, literature and civilization • MAT
  Latin American history • PhD
  linguistics • PhD
  literature • MA, PhD
  literatures in English • PhD
  manufacturing systems • MS
  mathematics • MS, PhD
  mechanics • MS, PhD
  medicinal chemistry • MS, PhD
  medieval history • PhD
  microbial biochemistry • MS, PhD
  modern American history • PhD
  modern British history • PhD
  modern European history • PhD
  molecular and cell biology • PhD
  molecular biology • MS, PhD
  molecular biology and biochemistry • MS, PhD
  molecular genetics • MS, PhD
  museum studies • MA
  music history • MA, PhD
  neuroscience • PhD
  nuclear physics • MS, PhD
  nutrition of ruminant and nonruminant animals • MS, PhD
  nutritional sciences • MS, PhD
  nutritional toxicology • MS, PhD
  oceanography • MS, PhD
  operations research • PhD
  organic chemistry • MS, PhD
  pathology • MS, PhD
  pharmaceutical chemistry • MS, PhD
  pharmaceutical toxicology • MS, PhD
  pharmaceutics • MS, PhD
  philosophy • PhD
  physical chemistry • MS, PhD
  physical metallurgy • MS, PhD
  physics • MST
  physiology and neurobiology • PhD
  plant ecology • MS, PhD
  plant genetics • PhD
  plant physiology • MS, PhD
  political and cultural history • PhD
  political economy • PhD
  political theory • PhD
  pollution prevention and control • MS, PhD
  polymer science • MS, PhD
  production and management • MS
  public law • PhD
  quality and productivity management • MS
  quality and reliability engineering • MS
  reproductive endocrinology and neuroendocrinology • MS, PhD
  social policy analysis and administration • PhD
  social psychology • PhD
  social work • PhD
  sociology • MA, PhD
  solid mechanics • MS, PhD
  Spanish • MA, MAT, PhD
  Spanish-American literature • MA, PhD
  statistics • MS, PhD
  structure and plant groups • MS, PhD
  surface science • PhD
  theoretical physics • MS, PhD
  translation • MA
  virology • MS, PhD
  water and wastewater treatment • MS, PhD
  water resources • MS, PhD
  women and politics • PhD
  women's and gender studies • MA, PhD
  women's history • PhD

BioMaps Institute (Biology at the Inter-face of the Mathematical and Physcial Sciences)
Program in:
  biology • PhD

Eagleton Institute of Politics
Program in:
  politics • MS

Graduate School of Applied and Professional Psychology
Dr. Stanley B. Messer, Dean
Programs in:
  applied and professional psychology • Psy M, Psy D
  clinical psychology • Psy M, Psy D
  organizational psychology • Psy M, Psy D
  school psychology • Psy M, Psy D

Graduate School of Education
Dr. Richard DeLisi, Acting Dean
Programs in:
  adult and continuing education • Ed M, Ed D
  counseling psychology • Ed M
  early childhood/elementary education • Ed M, Ed D
  education • Ed M, Ed D, PhD
  education administration • Ed M
  educational administration and supervision • Ed M, Ed D
  educational policy • PhD
  educational psychology • PhD
  educational statistics, measurement and evaluation • Ed M
  English as a second language education • Ed M, Ed D
  English education • Ed M
  language education • Ed M, Ed D
  learning cognition and development • Ed M
  literacy education • Ed M, Ed D, PhD
  mathematics education • Ed M, Ed D, PhD

New Jersey

reading education • Ed M
school business administration • Ed M
science education • Ed M, Ed D
social and philosophical foundations of education • Ed M, Ed D
social studies education • Ed M, Ed D
special education • Ed M, Ed D

Mason Gross School of the Arts
George B. Stauffer, Dean
Programs in:
acting • MFA
arts • MFA, MM, DMA, AD
collaborative piano • MM, DMA
design • MFA
directing • MFA
drawing • MFA
jazz studies • MM
music • MM, DMA, AD
music education • MM
painting • MFA
playwriting • MFA
sculpture • MFA
stage management • MFA

Programs in Engineering
Program in:
engineering • MS, PhD

School of Communication, Information and Library Studies
Programs in:
communication and information studies • MCIS
library and information science • MLS

School of Management and Labor Relations
Dr. Barbara A. Lee, Dean
Programs in:
human resource management • MHRM
labor and employment relations • MLER
management and labor relations • MHRM, MLER

School of Social Work
Program in:
social work • MSW, PhD

■ SAINT PETER'S COLLEGE
Jersey City, NJ 07306-5997
http://www.spc.edu/

Independent-religious, coed, comprehensive institution. *Computer facilities:* 150 computers available on campus for general student use. A campuswide network can be accessed from student residence rooms and from off campus. Internet access is available. *Library facilities:* Theresa and Edward O'Toole Library plus 1 other. *General application contact:* Graduate Admissions Coordinator, 201-915-9220.

Find an in-depth description at www.petersons.com/gradchannel.

Graduate Programs in Education
Programs in:
administration and supervision • MA
elementary teacher • Certificate
reading specialist • MA
supervisor of instruction • Certificate
teaching • MA, Certificate
urban education • MA

MBA Programs
Programs in:
finance • MBA
international business • MBA
management • MBA
management information systems • MBA
marketing • MBA

Nursing Program
Program in:
nursing • MSN

Program in Accountancy
Program in:
accountancy • MS, Certificate

■ SETON HALL UNIVERSITY
South Orange, NJ 07079-2697
http://www.shu.edu/

Independent-religious, coed, university. CGS member. *Computer facilities:* Computer purchase and lease plans are available. 300 computers available on campus for general student use. A campuswide network can be accessed from student residence rooms and from off campus. Internet access and online class registration are available. *Library facilities:* Walsh Library plus 1 other.

Find an in-depth description at www.petersons.com/gradchannel.

College of Arts and Sciences
Programs in:
analytical chemistry • MS, PhD
arts and sciences • MA, MHA, MPA, MS, PhD
Asian studies • MA
behavioral neuroscience • MS
biochemistry • MS, PhD
biology • MS
chemistry • MS
corporate and public communication • MA
English • MA
experimental psychology • MS
inorganic chemistry • MS, PhD
Jewish-Christian studies • MA
microbiology • MS
molecular biosciences • PhD
museum professions • MA
organic chemistry • MS, PhD
physical chemistry • MS, PhD

Center for Public Service
Programs in:
arts administration • MPA
health policy and management • MPA
healthcare administration • MHA
nonprofit organization management • MPA
public service: leadership, governance, and policy • MPA

College of Education and Human Services
Programs in:
bilingual education • MA, Ed S
Catholic school leadership • MA
Catholic school teaching EPICS • MA
counseling psychology • PhD
counselor preparation • MA
education and human services • MA, MS, Ed D, Exec Ed D, PhD, Ed S
education media specialist • MA
elementary education • MA
English as a second language • MA, Ed S
higher education administration • PhD
human resource training and development • MA
instructional design • MA, Ed S
K–12 administration and supervision • Ed D, Exec Ed D, Ed S
marriage and family counseling • MS, PhD, Ed S
professional development • MA, Ed S
psychological studies • MA
school psychology • Ed S
secondary education • MA

College of Nursing
Dr. Phyllis Hansell, Dean
Programs in:
acute care nurse practitioner • MSN
adult nurse practitioner • MSN
advanced practice in acute care nursing • MSN
advanced practice in primary health care • MSN
gerontological nurse practitioner • MSN
nursing • MA, MSN
nursing administration • MSN
nursing case management • MSN
nursing education • MA
pediatric nurse practitioner • MSN
school nurse practitioner • MSN
women's health nurse practitioner • MSN

Immaculate Conception Seminary School of Theology
Programs in:
pastoral ministry • M Div, MA
theology • MA, Certificate

Peterson's Graduate Schools in the U.S. 2006

www.petersons.com **427**

New Jersey

Seton Hall University (continued)
John C. Whithead School of Diplomacy and International Relations
Ursula Sanjamino, Assistant Dean of Graduate Studies
Program in:
 diplomacy and international relations • MA

School of Graduate Medical Education
Dr. David L. Felten, Dean
Programs in:
 athletic training • MS
 audiology • Sc D
 health sciences • MS, PhD
 medical education • MS, DPT, PhD, Sc D
 occupational therapy • MS
 physician assistant • MS
 post-professional physical therapy • DPT
 professional physical therapy • DPT
 speech-language pathology • MS

School of Law
Patrick E. Hobbs, Dean
Program in:
 law • JD, LL M, MSJ

Stillman School of Business
Dr. Karen E. Boroff, Dean
Programs in:
 accounting • MBA, MS, Post-Graduate Certificate
 business • MBA, MS, Certificate, Post-Graduate Certificate
 finance • MBA, Post-Graduate Certificate
 financial markets, institutions and instruments • MBA
 healthcare management • MBA
 information systems • MBA, Post-Graduate Certificate
 international business • MBA, Post-Graduate Certificate
 management • MBA, Post-Graduate Certificate
 marketing • MBA, Post-Graduate Certificate
 pharmaceutical management • MBA
 professional accounting • MS
 sport management • MBA, Post-Graduate Certificate
 taxation • Post-Graduate Certificate

■ STEVENS INSTITUTE OF TECHNOLOGY
Hoboken, NJ 07030
http://www.stevens-tech.edu/

Independent, coed, university. *Computer facilities:* Computer purchase and lease plans are available. 1,700 computers available on campus for general student use. A campuswide network can be accessed from student residence rooms and from off campus. Internet access and online class registration, online grade and account information are available. *Library facilities:* S. C. Williams Library. *General application contact:* Dean of the Graduate School, 201-216-5234.

Find an in-depth description at www.petersons.com/gradchannel.

Graduate School
Program in:
 interdisciplinary sciences and engineering • M Eng, MS, PhD

Charles V. Schaefer Jr. School of Engineering
Programs in:
 advanced manufacturing • Certificate
 air pollution technology • Certificate
 analysis of polymer processing methods • Certificate
 biochemical engineering • M Eng, PhD, Engr
 building energy systems • Certificate
 civil engineering • M Eng, PhD, Certificate, Engr
 coastal and ocean engineering • M Eng, PhD, Engr
 computational methods in fluid mechanics and heat transfer • Certificate
 computer and communications security • Certificate
 computer and information engineering • M Eng, PhD, Engr
 computer architecture and digital system design • M Eng, PhD, Engr
 computer engineering • M Eng, PhD, Certificate, Engr
 concurrent design management • M Eng
 concurrent engineering • PhD, Certificate
 construction accounting/estimating • Certificate
 construction engineering • M Eng, PhD, Certificate, Engr
 construction law/disputes • Certificate
 construction management • MS
 construction/quality management • Certificate
 controls in aerospace and robotics • Certificate
 design and production management • MS, Certificate
 digital systems and VLSI design • Certificate
 electrical engineering • M Eng, MS, PhD, Certificate, Engr
 engineering • M Eng, MS, PhD, Certificate, Engr
 environmental compatibility in engineering • Certificate
 environmental engineering • M Eng, PhD, Certificate
 environmental process • M Eng, PhD, Certificate
 finite-element analysis • Certificate
 fundamentals of modern chemical engineering • Certificate
 geotechnical engineering • Certificate
 geotechnical/geoenvironmental engineering • M Eng, PhD, Engr
 groundwater and soil pollution control • M Eng, PhD, Certificate
 image and signal processing • M Eng, PhD, Engr
 information networks • Certificate
 inland and coastal environmental hydrodynamics • M Eng, PhD, Certificate
 integrated production design • Certificate
 maritime systems • M Eng
 materials engineering • M Eng, PhD
 materials science • MS, PhD
 mechanical engineering • M Eng, PhD, Engr
 mechanism design • Certificate
 ocean engineering • M Eng, PhD
 polymer engineering • M Eng, PhD, Engr
 polymer processing • Certificate
 power generation • Certificate
 process control • M Eng, PhD, Engr
 process engineering • M Eng, PhD, Certificate, Engr
 robotics and automation • M Eng, PhD, Engr
 robotics and control • Certificate
 robotics/control/instrumentation • M Eng, PhD, Engr
 satellite communications engineering • Certificate
 signal and image processing • M Eng, PhD, Engr
 software engineering • M Eng, PhD, Engr
 stress analysis and design • Certificate
 structural analysis of materials • Certificate
 structures • M Eng, PhD, Engr
 surface modification of materials • Certificate
 telecommunications engineering • M Eng, PhD, Engr
 telecommunications management • MS, PhD, Certificate
 vibration and noise control • Certificate
 water quality • Certificate

School of Applied Sciences and Liberal Arts
Programs in:
 advanced programming: theory, design and verification • Certificate
 algebra • PhD
 analysis • PhD
 applied mathematics • MS, PhD
 applied optics • Certificate
 applied sciences and liberal arts • M Eng, MS, PhD, Certificate
 applied statistics • MS, Certificate

artificial intelligence and robotics • MS, PhD
chemistry • MS, PhD, Certificate
computer and information systems • MS, PhD
computer architecture and digital system design • MS, PhD
database systems • Certificate
elements of computer science • Certificate
engineering physics • M Eng
information systems • MS, Certificate
mathematics • MS, PhD
network and graph theory • Certificate
physics • MS, PhD
software design • MS, PhD
software engineering • Certificate
surface physics • Certificate
theoretical computer science • MS, PhD, Certificate
wireless communications • Certificate

Wesley J. Howe School of Technology Management
Programs in:
computer science • MS
construction management • MS
design and production management • MS, Certificate
e-commerce • MS, Certificate
general management • MS
information management • MIM, MS, PhD, Certificate
management planning • MS
network planning and evaluation • MS, PhD
project management • MS, PhD, Certificate
technology applications in science education • Certificate
technology management • EMTM, MIM, MS, MTM, PhD, Certificate
technology management marketing • MS, PhD
telecommunications management • MS, Certificate

■ **THOMAS EDISON STATE COLLEGE**
Trenton, NJ 08608-1176
http://www.tesc.edu/

State-supported, coed, comprehensive institution. CGS member. *Enrollment:* 10,233 graduate, professional, and undergraduate students; 222 part-time matriculated graduate/professional students (108 women). *Computer facilities:* A campuswide network can be accessed from off campus. Internet access and online class registration are available. *Graduate expenses:* Tuition, nonresident: part-time $342 per credit. *General application contact:* Gregg Dye, Coordinator of Graduate Advisement, 888-442-8372.

Find an in-depth description at www.petersons.com/gradchannel.

The Graduate School
Dr. Sonja Eveslage, Dean of the Graduate School/Associate Vice President of New Program Development
Programs in:
human resources management • MSHRM
insurance • MSM
liberal studies • MAPS
management • MSM
project management • MSM
public sector auditing • MSM
substance abuse • MSM

■ **WILLIAM PATERSON UNIVERSITY OF NEW JERSEY**
Wayne, NJ 07470-8420
http://www.wpunj.edu/

State-supported, coed, comprehensive institution. CGS member. *Computer facilities:* 700 computers available on campus for general student use. A campuswide network can be accessed from student residence rooms and from off campus. Internet access and online class registration are available. *Library facilities:* David and Lorraine Cheng Library. *General application contact:* Graduate Admissions Counselor, 973-720-3579.

Find an in-depth description at www.petersons.com/gradchannel.

College of Business
Program in:
business • MBA

College of Education
Programs in:
counseling • M Ed
counseling services • M Ed
education • M Ed, MAT
educational leadership • M Ed
elementary education • M Ed, MAT
reading • M Ed
special education • M Ed

College of Science and Health
Programs in:
biotechnology • MS
general biology • MA
limnology and terrestrial ecology • MA
molecular biology • MA
nursing • MSN
physiology • MA
science and health • MA, MS, MSN
speech pathology • MS

College of the Arts and Communication
Programs in:
art • MFA
arts and communication • MA, MFA, MM
media studies • MA
music • MM
visual arts • MA

College of the Humanities and Social Sciences
Programs in:
applied clinical psychology • MA
English • MA
history • MA
humanities and social sciences • MA
sociology • MA

New Mexico

■ **COLLEGE OF SANTA FE**
Santa Fe, NM 87505-7634
http://www.csf.edu

Independent, coed, comprehensive institution. *Enrollment:* 1,761 graduate, professional, and undergraduate students; 139 full-time matriculated graduate/professional students (101 women), 233 part-time matriculated graduate/professional students (167 women). *Computer facilities:* 180 computers available on campus for general student use. A campuswide network can be accessed from student residence rooms and from off campus. Internet access is available. *Library facilities:* Fogelson Library Center plus 2 others. *Graduate expenses:* Tuition: full-time $5,796; part-time $322 per credit. Required fees: $195; $8 per credit. $70 per semester. *General application contact:* Judy Kares, Director, Evening and Weekend Degree Program, 505-473-6177.

Department of Business Administration
Dr. Ali Arshad, Chair
Program in:
business administration • MBA

Department of Education
Dr. Kate Friesner, Chair
Programs in:
at-risk youth • MA
curriculum and instruction • MA
multicultural special education • MA

New Mexico

COLLEGE OF THE SOUTHWEST
Hobbs, NM 88240-9129
http://www.csw.edu/

Independent, coed, comprehensive institution. *Enrollment:* 894 graduate, professional, and undergraduate students; 46 full-time matriculated graduate/professional students (40 women), 115 part-time matriculated graduate/professional students (93 women). *Graduate faculty:* 9 full-time (8 women), 3 part-time/adjunct (2 women). *Computer facilities:* 35 computers available on campus for general student use. A campuswide network can be accessed. Internet access is available. *Library facilities:* Scarborough Memorial Library plus 1 other. *Graduate expenses:* Tuition: part-time $220 per semester hour. *General application contact:* Linda Chapman, Special Events Coordinator, 505-392-6561 Ext. 1069.

School of Education and Professional Studies
Dr. Elizabeth Posey, Dean
Programs in:
curriculum and instruction • MS
educational administration • MS
educational counseling • MS
educational diagnostician • MS

EASTERN NEW MEXICO UNIVERSITY
Portales, NM 88130
http://www.enmu.edu/

State-supported, coed, comprehensive institution. CGS member. *Enrollment:* 3,706 graduate, professional, and undergraduate students; 29 full-time matriculated graduate/professional students (17 women), 397 part-time matriculated graduate/professional students (280 women). *Graduate faculty:* 72 full-time (30 women), 6 part-time/adjunct (1 woman). *Computer facilities:* 437 computers available on campus for general student use. A campuswide network can be accessed from student residence rooms and from off campus. Internet access and online class registration are available. *Library facilities:* Golden Library. *Graduate expenses:* Tuition, state resident: full-time $2,064; part-time $86 per credit hour. Tuition, nonresident: full-time $7,620; part-time $318 per credit hour. Required fees: $29 per credit hour. *General application contact:* Dr. Phillip Shelley, Dean, Graduate School, 505-562-2147.

Graduate School
Dr. Phillip Shelley, Dean

College of Business
Dr. Gerry Huybregts, Dean
Program in:
business • MBA

College of Education and Technology
Dr. Steven Russell, Dean
Programs in:
counseling • MA
education • M Ed
education and technology • M Ed, M Sp Ed, MA, MS
physical education • MS
school guidance • M Ed
special education • M Sp Ed

College of Liberal Arts and Sciences
Dr. Thurman Elder, Dean
Programs in:
anthropology • MA
biology • MS
chemistry • MS
communication • MA
English • MA
liberal arts and sciences • MA, MS
mathematical sciences • MA
psychology • MA
speech pathology and audiology • MS

NEW MEXICO HIGHLANDS UNIVERSITY
Las Vegas, NM 87701
http://www.nmhu.edu/

State-supported, coed, comprehensive institution. CGS member. *Enrollment:* 3,960 graduate, professional, and undergraduate students; 401 full-time matriculated graduate/professional students (295 women), 561 part-time matriculated graduate/professional students (387 women). *Graduate faculty:* 113 full-time (48 women), 3 part-time/adjunct (1 woman). *Computer facilities:* 500 computers available on campus for general student use. A campuswide network can be accessed from student residence rooms and from off campus. Internet access and online class registration are available. *Library facilities:* Donnelly Library. *Graduate expenses:* Tuition, state resident: full-time $2,328; part-time $97 per hour. Tuition, nonresident: full-time $9,672. One-time fee: $50 full-time; $20 part-time. *General application contact:* Dr. Linda S. LaGrange, Dean of Graduate Studies, 505-454-3194.

Graduate Studies
Dr. Linda S. LaGrange, Dean of Graduate Studies

College of Arts and Sciences
Dr. Roy Lujan, Dean
Programs in:
administration • MA
anthropology • MA
applied chemistry • MS
applied sociology • MA
arts and sciences • MA, MS
biology • MS
cognitive science • MA, MS
computer graphics • MA, MS
design studies • MA
digital audio and video production • MA
English • MA
environmental science and management • MS
Hispanic language and literature • MA
historical and cross-cultural perspective • MA
history and political science • MA
multimedia systems • MS
networking technology • MA, MS
political and governmental processes • MA
psychology • MS

School of Business
Dr. Margaret Young, Director
Program in:
business • MBA

School of Education
Dr. Nick Sanchez, Director
Programs in:
curriculum and instruction • MA
education administration • MA
guidance and counseling • MA
human performance, leisure and sport • MA
special education • MA

School of Social Work
Dr. Roberto Villa, Dean
Program in:
social work • MSW

NEW MEXICO INSTITUTE OF MINING AND TECHNOLOGY
Socorro, NM 87801
http://www.nmt.edu/

State-supported, coed, university. *Enrollment:* 1,798 graduate, professional, and undergraduate students; 254 full-time matriculated graduate/professional students (88 women), 74 part-time matriculated graduate/professional students (26 women). *Graduate faculty:* 96 full-time (14 women), 36 part-time/adjunct (7 women). *Computer facilities:* 225 computers available on campus for general student use. A campuswide network can be accessed from student residence rooms and from off campus. Internet access and online class registration are available. *Library facilities:* New Mexico Tech Library plus 1 other. *Graduate expenses:* Tuition, state resident: full-time $2,276; part-time $126 per credit.

New Mexico

Tuition, nonresident: full-time $9,170; part-time $509 per credit. Required fees: $924; $27 per credit. $214 per term. Part-time tuition and fees vary according to course load. *General application contact:* Dr. David B. Johnson, Dean of Graduate Studies, 505-835-5513.

Find an in-depth description at www.petersons.com/gradchannel.

Graduate Studies
Dr. David B. Johnson, Dean
Programs in:
  advanced mechanics • MS
  applied math • PhD
  astrophysics • MS, PhD
  atmospheric physics • MS, PhD
  biochemistry • MS
  biology • MS
  chemistry • MS
  computer science • MS, PhD
  electrical engineering • MS
  engineering management • MEM
  environmental chemistry • PhD
  environmental engineering • MS
  explosives engineering • MS
  explosives technology and atmospheric chemistry • PhD
  geochemistry • MS, PhD
  geology • MS, PhD
  geology and geochemistry • MS, PhD
  geophysics • MS, PhD
  hydrology • MS, PhD
  instrumentation • MS
  material engineering • MS, PhD
  mathematical physics • PhD
  mathematics • MS
  mining and mineral engineering • MS
  operations research • MS
  petroleum engineering • MS, PhD
  science teaching • MST

■ NEW MEXICO STATE UNIVERSITY
Las Cruces, NM 88003-8001
http://www.nmsu.edu/

State-supported, coed, university. CGS member. *Enrollment:* 16,174 graduate, professional, and undergraduate students; 1,606 full-time matriculated graduate/professional students (785 women), 1,415 part-time matriculated graduate/professional students (905 women). *Graduate faculty:* 500 full-time (147 women), 109 part-time/adjunct (26 women). *Computer facilities:* 500 computers available on campus for general student use. A campuswide network can be accessed from student residence rooms and from off campus. Internet access and online class registration are available. *Library facilities:* New Mexico State University Library plus 1 other. *Graduate expenses:* Tuition, state resident: full-time $2,670; part-time $151 per credit. Tuition, nonresident: full-time $10,596; part-time $481 per credit. Required fees: $954. *General application contact:* Jennifer Nanez, Recruitment Officer, 505-646-3498.

Find an in-depth description at www.petersons.com/gradchannel.

Graduate School
Dr. Linda Lacey, Dean
Programs in:
  interdisciplinary studies • MA, MS, PhD
  molecular biology • MS, PhD

College of Agriculture and Home Economics
Dr. Jerry Schickedanz, Dean
Programs in:
  agricultural economics • MS
  agriculture and extension education • MA
  agriculture and home economics • M Ag, MA, MS, PhD
  animal science • M Ag, MS, PhD
  economics • MA
  entomology, plant pathology and weed science • MS
  family and consumer sciences • MS
  general agronomy • MS, PhD
  horticulture • MS
  range science • M Ag, MS, PhD
  wildlife science • MS

College of Arts and Sciences
Dr. Waded Cruzado-Salas, Dean
Programs in:
  anthropology • MA
  art • MA, MFA
  arts and sciences • MA, MAG, MCJ, MFA, MM, MPA, MS, PhD
  astronomy • MS, PhD
  biology • MS, PhD
  chemistry and biochemistry • MS, PhD
  communication studies • MA
  computer science • MS, PhD
  creative writing • MFA
  criminal justice • MCJ
  English • MA, PhD
  geography • MAG
  geological sciences • MS
  government • MA, MPA
  history • MA
  mathematical sciences • MS, PhD
  music • MM
  physics • MS, PhD
  psychology • MA, PhD
  sociology • MA
  Spanish • MA

College of Business Administration and Economics
Dr. Garrey Carruthers, Dean
Programs in:
  accounting and business computer systems • M Acct
  business administration • MBA, PhD
  business administration and economics • M Acct, MA, MBA, MS, PhD
  economics • MA
  experimental statistics • MS

College of Education
Dr. Robert Moulton, Dean
Programs in:
  counseling and guidance • MA, Ed S
  counseling psychology • PhD
  curriculum and instruction • MAT, Ed D, PhD, Ed S
  education • MA, MAT, Ed D, PhD, Ed S
  educational administration • MA, PhD
  educational management and development • Ed D
  general education • MA
  reading • Ed S
  special education/communication disorders • MA

College of Engineering
Dr. William McCarthy, Interim Dean
Programs in:
  chemical engineering • MS Ch E, PhD
  civil engineering • MSCE, PhD
  electrical and computer engineering • MSEE
  engineering • MS Ch E, MS Env E, MSCE, MSEE, MSIE, MSME, PhD
  environmental engineering • MS Env E
  industrial engineering • MSIE, PhD
  mechanical engineering • MSME, PhD

College of Health and Social Services
Dr. Jeffrey Brandon, Dean
Programs in:
  health and social services • MPH, MSN, MSW
  health science • MPH
  nursing • MSN
  social work • MSW

■ UNIVERSITY OF NEW MEXICO
Albuquerque, NM 87131-2039
http://www.unm.edu/

State-supported, coed, university. CGS member. *Enrollment:* 25,686 graduate, professional, and undergraduate students; 3,752 full-time matriculated graduate/professional students (2,075 women), 2,176 part-time matriculated graduate/professional students (1,279 women). *Graduate faculty:* 1,444 full-time (557 women), 588 part-time/adjunct (287 women). *Computer facilities:* 382 computers available on campus for general student use. A campuswide network can be accessed from student residence rooms and from off campus. Internet

New Mexico

University of New Mexico (continued)
access and online class registration are available. *Library facilities:* The University of New Mexico General Library plus 7 others. *Graduate expenses:* Tuition, state resident: full-time $1,802; part-time $152 per credit hour. Tuition, nonresident: full-time $6,135; part-time $513 per credit hour. Tuition and fees vary according to program. *General application contact:* Edwina Chavez-Salazar, Enrollment Management Specialist, 505-277-2711.

Find an in-depth description at www.petersons.com/gradchannel.

Graduate School
Dr. Teresita E. Aguilar, Dean
Program in:
  water resources • MWR

College of Arts and Sciences
Dr. Reed Way Dasenbrock, Dean
Programs in:
  American studies • MA, PhD
  anthropology • MA, MS, PhD
  arts and sciences • MA, MS, PhD
  biology • MS, PhD
  chemistry • MS, PhD
  clinical psychology • MS, PhD
  communication • MA, PhD
  comparative literature and cultural studies • MA
  earth and planetary sciences • MS, PhD
  economics • MA, PhD
  English • MA, PhD
  French • MA
  French studies • PhD
  geography • MS
  German studies • MA
  history • MA, PhD
  Latin American studies • MA, PhD
  linguistics • MA, PhD
  mathematics • MS, PhD
  optical sciences • PhD
  philosophy • MA, PhD
  physics • MS, PhD
  political science • MA, PhD
  Portuguese • MA
  psychology • MS, PhD
  sociology • MA, PhD
  Spanish • MA
  Spanish and Portuguese • PhD
  speech and hearing sciences • MS
  statistics • MS, PhD

College of Education
Dr. Viola E. Florez, Dean
Programs in:
  art education • MA
  counselor education • MA, PhD
  education • MA, MS, Ed D, PhD, EDSPC
  educational leadership • MA, Ed D, EDSPC
  educational linguistics • Ed D, PhD
  educational psychology • MA, PhD
  elementary education • MA
  family studies • MA, PhD
  health education • MS
  language, literacy and sociocultural studies • MA, Ed D, PhD
  multicultural teacher and childhood education • Ed D, PhD, EDSPC
  nutrition • MS
  organizational learning and instructional technologies • MA, PhD, EDSPC
  physical education • MS, Ed D, PhD
  recreation • MA, EDSPC
  special education • MA, Ed D, PhD, EDSPC

College of Fine Arts
Dr. James S. Moy, Dean
Programs in:
  art history • MA, PhD
  dramatic writing • MFA
  fine arts • M Mu, MA, MFA, PhD
  music • M Mu
  studio arts • MFA
  theater and dance • MA

College of Nursing
Dr. Karen Carlson, Dean
Program in:
  nursing • MSN, EDSPC

College of Pharmacy
Dr. John Pieper, Dean
Programs in:
  pharmaceutical sciences • MS, PhD
  pharmacy • Pharm D, MS, PhD

School of Architecture and Planning
Dr. Roger L. Schluntz, Dean
Programs in:
  architecture • M Arch
  architecture and planning • M Arch, MCRP, MLA
  community and regional planning • MCRP
  landscape architecture • MLA

School of Engineering
Dr. Joseph L. Cecchi, Dean
Programs in:
  chemical engineering • MS, PhD
  civil engineering • MS
  computer science • MS, PhD
  electrical engineering • MS
  engineering • PhD
  hazardous waste engineering • MEHWE
  manufacturing engineering • MEME
  mechanical engineering • MS
  nuclear engineering • MS, PhD
  optical sciences • PhD

School of Public Administration
Dr. Kenneth Baker, Interim Director
Program in:
  public administration • MPA

Robert O. Anderson Graduate School of Management
Dr. Charles Crespy, Dean
Programs in:
  accounting • M Acc, MBA
  financial management • MBA
  financial, international and technology management • MBA
  human resources management • MBA
  international management • MBA
  international management in Latin America • MBA
  management information systems • MBA
  management of technology • MBA
  marketing management • MBA
  marketing, information and decision sciences • MBA
  operations management • MBA
  organizational studies • MBA
  policy and planning • MBA
  tax accounting • MBA

School of Law
Suellyn Scarnecchia, Dean
Program in:
  law • JD

School of Medicine
Programs in:
  biochemistry and molecular biology • MS, PhD
  cell biology and physiology • MS, PhD
  medicine • MD, Pharm D, MOT, MPH, MPT, MS, PhD
  molecular genetics and microbiology • MS, PhD
  neuroscience • MS, PhD
  occupational therapy • MOT
  pathology • MS, PhD
  physical therapy • MPT
  public health • MPH
  toxicology • MS, PhD

■ WESTERN NEW MEXICO UNIVERSITY
Silver City, NM 88062-0680
http://www.wnmu.edu/

State-supported, coed, comprehensive institution. *Enrollment:* 93 full-time matriculated graduate/professional students (56 women), 486 part-time matriculated graduate/professional students (346 women). *Graduate faculty:* 35 full-time (18 women), 32 part-time/adjunct (19 women). *Computer facilities:* 85 computers available on campus for general student use. Internet access and online class registration, online classes in Spanish are available. *Library facilities:* Miller Library plus 2 others. *Graduate expenses:* Tuition, state resident: full-time $2,007. Tuition, nonresident: full-time $6,939. Required fees: $100; $70 per term. Tuition and fees vary according to campus/location. *General application contact:* Michael Alecksen, Director of Admissions, 505-538-6106.

Graduate Division
Dr. Faye N. Vowell, Dean
Programs in:
 business • MBA
 interdisciplinary programs • MA

School of Education
Dr. Jerry Harmon, Dean
Programs in:
 counselor education • MA
 elementary education • MAT
 reading • MAT
 school administration • MA
 secondary education • MAT
 special education • MAT

New York

■ ADELPHI UNIVERSITY
Garden City, NY 11530
http://www.adelphi.edu/

Independent, coed, university. *Enrollment:* 7,355 graduate, professional, and undergraduate students; 882 full-time matriculated graduate/professional students (702 women), 2,328 part-time matriculated graduate/professional students (1,848 women). *Graduate faculty:* 228. *Computer facilities:* Computer purchase and lease plans are available. 525 computers available on campus for general student use. A campuswide network can be accessed from student residence rooms and from off campus. Internet access and online class registration, payment, grades, drop/add classes, check application status are available. *Library facilities:* Swirbul Library plus 1 other. *Graduate expenses:* Tuition: full-time $19,550; part-time $590 per credit hour. Required fees: $700; $200 per semester. *General application contact:* Christine Murphy, Director of Admissions, 516-877-3050.

Derner Institute of Advanced Psychological Studies
Dr. Louis Primavera, Dean
Programs in:
 clinical psychology • PhD, Post-Doctoral Certificate
 general psychology • MA

Graduate School of Arts and Sciences
Gayle Insler, Dean
Programs in:
 art and art history • MA
 arts and sciences • MA, MS
 biology • MS
 English • MA
 environmental studies • MS

School of Business
Dr. Anthony F. Libertella, Dean
Programs in:
 accounting • MBA
 business • MBA, MS, Certificate
 corporate finance • MBA
 finance • MS
 human resource management • Certificate
 management for non-business majors • Certificate
 management for women • Certificate
 management information systems • MBA
 management/human resource management • MBA
 marketing/e-commerce • MBA

School of Education
Dr. Elaine Sands, Dean
Programs in:
 bilingual education • MA, MS
 communication sciences and disorders • MS, DA
 education • MA, MS, DA, Certificate
 educational leadership and technology • MA, Certificate
 elementary education • MA, Certificate
 health studies • MA, Certificate
 physical education and human performance science • MA, Certificate
 reading • MS, Certificate
 secondary education • MA
 special education • MS, Certificate
 teaching English to speakers of other languages • MA, Certificate

School of Nursing
Dr. Marilyn Klainberg, Interim Dean
Program in:
 nursing • MS, Certificate

School of Social Work
Dr. Brooke Spiro, Dean
Programs in:
 social welfare • DSW
 social work • MSW

■ ALFRED UNIVERSITY
Alfred, NY 14802-1205
http://www.alfred.edu/

Independent, coed, university. CGS member. *Enrollment:* 2,367 graduate, professional, and undergraduate students; 197 full-time matriculated graduate/professional students (98 women), 115 part-time matriculated graduate/professional students (71 women). *Graduate faculty:* 89 full-time (26 women), 6 part-time/adjunct (2 women). *Computer facilities:* Computer purchase and lease plans are available. A campuswide network can be accessed from student residence rooms and from off campus. Internet access is available. *Library facilities:* Herrick Memorial Library plus 1 other. *Graduate expenses:* Tuition: full-time $25,944; part-time $600 per credit hour. Required fees: $780. One-time fee: $132 part-time. Full-time tuition and fees vary according to program. *General application contact:* Cathleen R. Johnson, Coordinator of Graduate Admissions, 607-871-2141.

Find an in-depth description at www.petersons.com/gradchannel.

Graduate School
Dr. Alastair Cormack, Director of Graduate School
Programs in:
 community services administration • MPS
 electrical engineering • MS
 mechanical engineering • MS
 school psychology • MA, Psy D, CAS

College of Business
Lori Hollenbeck, Director of MBA Program
Program in:
 business • MBA

Division of Education
Dr. James Curl, Chair
Programs in:
 counseling • MS Ed
 literacy teacher • MS Ed

New York State College of Ceramics
Programs in:
 biomedical materials engineering science • MS
 ceramic engineering • MS
 ceramics • MFA, PhD
 electronic integrated arts • MFA
 glass art • MFA
 glass science • MS, PhD
 materials science • MS
 sculpture • MFA

■ BERNARD M. BARUCH COLLEGE OF THE CITY UNIVERSITY OF NEW YORK
New York, NY 10010-5585
http://www.baruch.cuny.edu/

State and locally supported, coed, comprehensive institution. *Enrollment:* 15,126 graduate, professional, and undergraduate students; 778 full-time matriculated graduate/professional students, 1,886 part-time matriculated graduate/professional students. *Graduate faculty:* 269 full-time (67 women), 55 part-time/adjunct (14 women). *Computer facilities:* 1,294 computers available on campus for general student use. A

New York

Bernard M. Baruch College of the City University of New York (continued)
campuswide network can be accessed. Internet access and online class registration are available. *Library facilities:* The William and Anita Newman Library plus 1 other. *Graduate expenses:* Tuition, state resident: full-time $7,500; part-time $330 per credit. Tuition, nonresident: full-time $15,540; part-time $555 per credit. Required fees: $218; $72 per semester. Tuition and fees vary according to course load and program. *General application contact:* Frances Murphy, Office of Graduate Admissions, 646-312-1300.

Find an in-depth description at www.petersons.com/gradchannel.

School of Public Affairs
Stan Altman, Dean
Programs in:
  educational administration and supervision • MS Ed, SAS
  higher education administration • MS Ed
  public administration • MPA
  public affairs • MPA, MS Ed, SAS

Weissman School of Arts and Sciences
Programs in:
  applied mathematics for finance • MS
  arts and sciences • MA, MS
  business journalism • MA
  corporate communication • MA

Zicklin School of Business
John Elliot, Vice President and Dean
Programs in:
  accounting • MBA, MS, PhD
  business • EMBA, MBA, MS, PhD, Certificate
  business administration • EMBA
  computer information systems • MBA, MS, PhD
  economics • MBA
  entrepeneurship • MBA
  finance • MBA, MS, PhD
  general business • MBA
  general management and policy • MBA
  health care administration • MBA
  human resources management • MBA
  industrial and labor relations • MS
  industrial and organizational psychology • MBA, MS, PhD, Certificate
  international business • MBA
  management planning systems • PhD
  management science • MBA
  marketing • MBA, MS, PhD
  operations research • MBA, MS
  organization and policy studies • PhD
  organizational behavior • MBA
  statistics • MBA, MS
  taxation • MBA, MS

■ BROOKLYN COLLEGE OF THE CITY UNIVERSITY OF NEW YORK
Brooklyn, NY 11210-2889
http://www.brooklyn.cuny.edu/

State and locally supported, coed, comprehensive institution. CGS member. *Enrollment:* 15,513 graduate, professional, and undergraduate students; 413 full-time matriculated graduate/professional students (284 women), 3,227 part-time matriculated graduate/professional students (2,174 women). *Graduate faculty:* 214 full-time (83 women), 188 part-time/adjunct (92 women). *Computer facilities:* 800 computers available on campus for general student use. A campuswide network can be accessed from off campus. Internet access and online class registration are available. *Library facilities:* Brooklyn College Library plus 1 other. *Graduate expenses:* Tuition, state resident: full-time $5,440; part-time $230 per credit. Tuition, nonresident: full-time $10,200; part-time $425 per credit. Required fees: $280; $103 per term. *General application contact:* Michael Lovaglio, Assistant Director of Graduate Admissions, 718-951-5001.

Find an in-depth description at www.petersons.com/gradchannel.

Division of Graduate Studies
Dr. Louise Hainline, Acting Dean
Programs in:
  accounting • MA
  acting • MFA
  applied biology • MA
  applied chemistry • MA
  applied geology • MA
  applied physics • MA
  art history • MA, PhD
  audiology • MS
  biology • MA, PhD
  chemistry • MA, PhD
  community health • MA, MPH, MS
  community health education • MA
  computer and information science • MA, PhD
  computer science and health science • MS
  creative writing • MFA
  criticism • MA
  criticism and history • MA
  design and technical production • MFA
  digital art • MFA
  directing • MFA
  dramaturgy • MFA
  drawing and painting • MFA
  economics • MA
  economics and computer and information science • MPS
  economics/accounting • MA
  English • MA, PhD
  exercise science and rehabilitation • MS
  experimental psychology • MA
  fiction • MFA
  French • MA
  geology • MA, PhD
  health care management • MA, MPH
  health care policy and administration • MA, MPH
  history • MA, PhD
  industrial and organizational psychology • MA
  information systems • MS
  Judaic studies • MA
  liberal studies • MA
  management and programming • MFA
  mathematics • MA, PhD
  modern languages and literature • PhD
  nutrition • MS
  nutrition sciences • MS
  performance and interactive media • CAS
  performing arts management • MFA
  photography • MFA
  physical education • MS, MS Ed
  physics • MA, PhD
  playwriting • MFA
  poetry • MFA
  political science • MA, PhD
  political science, urban policy and administration • MA
  printmaking • MFA
  psychology • PhD
  public health • MPH
  sculpture • MFA
  secondary mathematics education • MA
  sociology • MA, PhD
  Spanish • MA
  speech • MA, MS Ed, PhD
  speech pathology • MS
  television and radio • MFA
  television production • MFA
  thanatology • MA
  theater • PhD
  theater history • MA
  tv/radio management • MS

Conservatory of Music
Dr. Nancy Hager, Chairperson
Programs in:
  composition • MM
  music • DMA, PhD
  music education • MA
  musicology • MA
  performance practice • MM

School of Education
Dr. Deborah Shanley, Dean
Programs in:
  art teacher • MA
  bilingual education • MS Ed
  bilingual special education • MS Ed
  biology teacher • MA

biology, chemistry, physics, earth science • MS Ed
birth-grade 2 • MS Ed
birth-grade 6 • MS Ed
chemistry teacher • MA
children with emotional handicaps • MS Ed
children with neuropsychological learning disabilities • MS Ed
children with retarded mental development • MS Ed
education • MA, MS Ed, CAS
education leaderships • CAS
English teacher • MA
French teacher • MA
general science • MS Ed
grades 5-12 • MS Ed
guidance and counseling • MS Ed, CAS
guidance and counseling-bilingual • MS Ed
health and nutrition science/health teacher • MS Ed
health and nutrition sciences: health teacher • MS Ed
home economics education • MS Ed
liberal arts • MS Ed
math specialist • MS Ed
mathematics • MS Ed
mathematics teacher • MA
music education • CAS
music teacher • MA, MS Ed
physical education teacher • MS Ed
physics teacher • MA
school psychologist • MS Ed, CAS
school psychologist-bilingual • CAS
science/environmental education • MS Ed
social studies teacher • MA
Spanish teacher • MA
speech teacher • MA
teacher of students with disabilities • MS Ed

■ BUFFALO STATE COLLEGE, STATE UNIVERSITY OF NEW YORK
Buffalo, NY 14222-1095
http://www.buffalostate.edu/

State-supported, coed, comprehensive institution. CGS member. *Enrollment:* 11,157 graduate, professional, and undergraduate students; 369 full-time matriculated graduate/professional students (287 women), 1,420 part-time matriculated graduate/professional students (1,000 women). *Graduate faculty:* 274 full-time (92 women), 57 part-time/adjunct (20 women). *Computer facilities:* 900 computers available on campus for general student use. A campuswide network can be accessed from student residence rooms and from off campus. Internet access is available. *Library facilities:* E. H. Butler Library. *Graduate expenses:* Tuition, state resident: full-time $2,550; part-time $213 per credit hour. Tuition, nonresident: full-time $4,208; part-time $351 per credit hour. Required fees: $17 per credit hour. *General application contact:* Graduate Studies and Research, 716-878-5601.

Graduate Studies and Research
Dr. Richard S. Podemski, Dean
Program in:
  multidisciplinary studies • MA, MS

Faculty of Applied Science and Education
Dr. Richard Lee, Interim Dean
Programs in:
  adult education • MS, Certificate
  applied science and education • MPS, MS, MS Ed, CAS, Certificate
  business and marketing education • MS Ed
  career and technical education • MS Ed
  childhood education (grades 1–6) • MS Ed
  creative studies • MS
  criminal justice • MS
  early childhood and childhood curriculum and instruction • MS Ed
  early childhood education (birth–grade 2) • MS Ed
  educational computing • MS Ed
  educational leadership and facilitation • CAS
  elementary education • MS Ed
  human resources development • Certificate
  industrial technology • MS
  literacy specialist • MPS, MS Ed
  literacy specialist (birth–grade 6) • MS Ed
  literacy specialist • (grades 5–12) • MPS
  special education • MS Ed
  special education: adolescents • MS Ed
  special education: childhood • MS Ed
  special education: early childhood • MS Ed
  speech language pathology • MS Ed
  student personnel administration • MS
  teaching bilingual exceptional individuals • MS Ed
  technology education • MS Ed

Faculty of Arts and Humanities
Dr. Emile C. Netzhammer, Dean
Programs in:
  art conservation • CAS
  art education • MS Ed
  arts and humanities • MA, MS Ed, CAS
  conservation of historic works and art works • MA
  English • MA
  secondary education • MS Ed

Faculty of Natural and Social Sciences
Dr. Lawrence G. Flood, Dean
Programs in:
  applied economics • MA
  biology • MA
  chemistry • MA
  history • MA
  mathematics education • MS Ed
  natural and social sciences • MA, MS Ed
  secondary education • MS Ed
  secondary education physics • MS Ed

■ CANISIUS COLLEGE
Buffalo, NY 14208-1098
http://www.canisius.edu/

Independent-religious, coed, comprehensive institution. *Enrollment:* 5,095 graduate, professional, and undergraduate students; 757 full-time matriculated graduate/professional students (334 women), 803 part-time matriculated graduate/professional students (380 women). *Graduate faculty:* 70 full-time (18 women), 101 part-time/adjunct (38 women). *Computer facilities:* Computer purchase and lease plans are available. 325 computers available on campus for general student use. A campuswide network can be accessed from student residence rooms and from off campus. Internet access and online class registration, online accounts are available. *Library facilities:* Andrew L. Bouwhuis Library plus 1 other. *Graduate expenses:* Tuition: part-time $558 per credit hour. Required fees: $132; $11 per credit hour. One-time fee: $90 full-time. *General application contact:* Dr. Herbert J. Nelson, Vice President for Academic Affairs, 716-888-2120 Ext. 109.

Graduate Division
Dr. Herbert J. Nelson, Vice President for Academic Affairs

College of Arts and Sciences
Dr. Paula McNutt, Dean
Programs in:
  arts and sciences • MS
  organizational communication and development • MS

Richard J. Wehle School of Business
Laura McEwen, Director, Graduate Business Programs
Programs in:
  business • MBA, MBAPA, MS
  business administration • MBA, MBAPA
  professional accounting • MBAPA
  telecommunications management • MS

New York

Canisius College (continued)
School of Education and Human Services
Dr. Margaret C. McCarthy, Dean
Programs in:
 college student personnel administration • MS
 counseling and human services • MS, CAS
 education and human services • MS, MS Ed, CAS, SAS
 educational administration • MS, SAS
 health and human performance • MS
 physical education • MS
 reading • MS Ed
 secondary education • MS
 special education—preparation of teachers of the deaf • MS
 sport administration • MS
 teacher education • MS Ed

■ CITY COLLEGE OF THE CITY UNIVERSITY OF NEW YORK
New York, NY 10031-9198
http://www.ccny.cuny.edu/

State and locally supported, coed, university. *Enrollment:* 12,400 graduate, professional, and undergraduate students; 229 full-time matriculated graduate/professional students (110 women), 3,333 part-time matriculated graduate/professional students (1,956 women). *Graduate faculty:* 491 full-time (145 women), 475 part-time/adjunct (240 women). *Computer facilities:* 3,000 computers available on campus for general student use. A campuswide network can be accessed from off campus. Internet access is available. *Library facilities:* Morris Raphael Cohen Library plus 3 others. *Graduate expenses:* Tuition, state resident: full-time $5,440; part-time $230 per credit. Tuition, nonresident: part-time $425 per credit. Required fees: $63 per semester. *General application contact:* 212-650-6977.

Find an in-depth description at www.petersons.com/gradchannel.

Graduate School
Joseph Barba, Assistant Provost for Graduate Studies and Research

College of Liberal Arts and Science
Programs in:
 advertising design • MFA
 applied urban anthropology • MA
 art history • MA
 art history and museum studies • MA
 biochemistry • MA, PhD
 biology • MA, PhD
 ceramic design • MFA
 chemistry • MA, PhD
 clinical psychology • PhD
 creative writing • MA
 earth and environmental science • PhD
 earth systems science • MA
 economics • MA
 English and American literature • MA
 experimental cognition • PhD
 fine arts • MFA
 general psychology • MA
 history • MA
 humanities and arts • MA, MFA
 international relations • MA
 language and literacy • MA
 liberal arts and science • MA, MFA, PhD
 mathematics • MA
 media arts production • MFA
 museum studies • MA
 music • MA
 painting • MFA
 physics • MA, PhD
 printmaking • MFA
 science • MA, PhD
 sculpture • MFA
 social science • MA, PhD
 sociology • MA
 Spanish • MA
 wood and metal design • MFA

School of Architecture and Environmental Studies
George Ranalli, Dean
Programs in:
 architecture • M Arch, PD
 urban design • MUP

School of Education
Dr. Alfred Posamentier, Dean
Programs in:
 administration and supervision • MS, AC
 adolescent mathematics education • MA, AC
 bilingual education • MS
 childhood education • MS
 education • MA, MS, AC
 elementary education • MS
 English education • MA
 middle school mathematics education • MS
 science education • MA
 social studies education • AC
 teaching students with disabilities • MA

School of Engineering
Dr. Muntaz G. Kassir, Associate Dean for Graduate Studies
Programs in:
 biomedical engineering • ME, PhD
 chemical engineering • ME, MS, PhD
 civil engineering • ME, MS, PhD
 computer sciences • MS, PhD
 electrical engineering • ME, MS, PhD
 engineering • ME, MS, PhD
 mechanical engineering • ME, MS, PhD

■ CITY UNIVERSITY OF NEW YORK SCHOOL OF LAW AT QUEENS COLLEGE
Flushing, NY 11367-1358
http://www.law.cuny.edu/

State and locally supported, coed, graduate-only institution. *Graduate faculty:* 31 full-time (17 women), 10 part-time/adjunct (4 women). *Computer facilities:* 85 computers available on campus for general student use. A campuswide network can be accessed from off campus. Internet access is available. *Library facilities:* City University of New York School of Law Library. *Graduate expenses:* Tuition, state resident: full-time $20,487. Tuition, nonresident: full-time $25,940. *General application contact:* Yvonne Cherena-Pacheco, Assistant Dean for Enrollment Management and Director of Admissions, 718-340-4210.

Professional Program
Kristin Booth Glen, Dean
Program in:
 law • JD

■ CLARKSON UNIVERSITY
Potsdam, NY 13699
http://www.clarkson.edu/

Independent, coed, university. *Enrollment:* 3,105 graduate, professional, and undergraduate students; 349 full-time matriculated graduate/professional students (109 women), 33 part-time matriculated graduate/professional students (14 women). *Graduate faculty:* 175 full-time (34 women), 20 part-time/adjunct (7 women). *Computer facilities:* Computer purchase and lease plans are available. 400 computers available on campus for general student use. A campuswide network can be accessed from student residence rooms and from off campus. Internet access is available. *Library facilities:* Andrew S. Schuler Educational Resources Center plus 1 other. *Graduate expenses:* Tuition: full-time $19,272; part-time $803 per credit. Tuition and fees vary according to course load. *General application contact:* Donna Brockway, Assistant to Dean/Foreign Student Advisor, 315-268-6447.

Graduate School
Center for Health Science
Dr. Samuel B. Feitelberg, Associate Dean of Health Sciences
Programs in:
 basic science • MS
 health science • MPT, MS
 physical therapy • MPT

New York

Interdisciplinary Studies
Programs in:
  computer science • MS
  engineering and global operations management • MS
  environmental science and engineering • MS, PhD
  information technology • MS

School of Arts and Sciences
Dr. David L. Powers, Dean
Programs in:
  analytical chemistry • MS, PhD
  arts and sciences • MS, PhD
  inorganic chemistry • MS, PhD
  mathematics • MS, PhD
  organic chemistry • MS, PhD
  physical chemistry • MS, PhD
  physics • MS, PhD

School of Business
Dr. Timothy F. Sugrue, Dean
Programs in:
  business • MBA, MS
  business administration • MBA
  human resource management • MS
  management information systems • MS
  manufacturing management • MS

School of Engineering
Dr. Subrahmanyam S. Venkata, Dean
Programs in:
  chemical engineering • ME, MS, PhD
  civil and environmental engineering • PhD
  civil engineering • ME, MS
  computer engineering • ME, MS
  electrical and computer engineering • PhD
  electrical engineering • ME, MS
  engineering • ME, MS, PhD
  engineering science • MS, PhD
  mechanical engineering • ME, MS, PhD

■ **COLLEGE OF MOUNT SAINT VINCENT**
Riverdale, NY 10471-1093
http://www.mountsaintvincent.edu/

Independent, coed, comprehensive institution. *Enrollment:* 1,626 graduate, professional, and undergraduate students; 24 full-time matriculated graduate/professional students (17 women), 321 part-time matriculated graduate/professional students (245 women). *Graduate faculty:* 4 full-time (2 women), 26 part-time/adjunct (20 women). *Computer facilities:* A campuswide network can be accessed from student residence rooms and from off campus. E-mail available. *Library facilities:* Elizabeth Seton Library. *Graduate expenses:* Tuition: full-time $13,920; part-time $580 per credit. *General application*

contact: Dr. Norman Puffett, Associate Dean, Graduate Studies and Continuing Education, 718-405-3320.

Division of Nursing
Dr. Susan Apold, Chairperson
Programs in:
  adult nurse practitioner • MSN, PMC
  family nurse practitioner • MSN, PMC
  nursing administration • MSN
  nursing for the adult and aged • MSN

Program in Allied Health Studies
Dr. Rita Scher Dytell, Director
Programs in:
  allied health studies • MS
  counseling • Certificate
  health care management • Certificate
  health care systems • Certificate

Program in Education
Dr. Ron Scapp, Director
Programs in:
  instructional technology and global perspectives • Certificate
  middle level education • Certificate
  multicultural studies • Certificate
  urban and multicultural education • MS Ed

■ **THE COLLEGE OF NEW ROCHELLE**
New Rochelle, NY 10805-2308
http://cnr.edu/

Independent, coed, primarily women, comprehensive institution. CGS member. *Enrollment:* 2,450 graduate, professional, and undergraduate students; 205 full-time matriculated graduate/professional students (174 women), 1,268 part-time matriculated graduate/professional students (1,068 women). *Graduate faculty:* 28 full-time (18 women), 74 part-time/adjunct (51 women). *Computer facilities:* Computer purchase and lease plans are available. 120 computers available on campus for general student use. A campuswide network can be accessed from off campus. Internet access and online class registration are available. *Library facilities:* Gill Library. *Graduate expenses:* Tuition: part-time $440 per credit. Required fees: $30 per term. *General application contact:* Dr. Nancy Brown, Dean of the Graduate School, 914-654-5320.

Find an in-depth description at www.petersons.com/gradchannel.

Graduate School
Dr. Nancy Brown, Dean of the Graduate School

Programs in:
  acute care nurse practitioner • MS, Certificate
  clinical specialist in holistic nursing • MS, Certificate
  family nurse practitioner • MS, Certificate
  nursing and health care management • MS
  nursing education • Certificate

Division of Art and Communication Studies
Head
Programs in:
  art education • MA
  art museum education • Certificate
  art therapy • MS
  communication studies • MS, Certificate
  fine art • MS
  graphic art • MS
  studio art • MS

Division of Education
Dr. John J. Koster, Division Head
Programs in:
  bilingual education • Certificate
  creative teaching and learning • MS Ed, Certificate
  elementary education/early childhood education • MS Ed
  literacy education • MS Ed
  reading/special education • MS Ed
  school administration and supervision • MS Ed, Certificate, PD
  special education • MS Ed
  speech-language pathology • MS
  teaching English as a second language • MS Ed
  teaching English as a second language and multilingual/multicultural education • MS Ed, Certificate

Division of Human Services
Dr. Marie Ribarich, Head
Programs in:
  career development • MS, Certificate
  community-school psychology • MS
  gerontology • MS, Certificate
  guidance and counseling • MS
  thanatology • Certificate

■ **THE COLLEGE OF SAINT ROSE**
Albany, NY 12203-1419
http://www.strose.edu/

Independent, coed, comprehensive institution. CGS member. *Computer facilities:* 322 computers available on campus for general student use. A campuswide network can be accessed from student residence rooms and from off campus. Internet access and online class registration are available. *Library facilities:* Neil Hellman Library plus 1 other. *General*

Peterson's Graduate Schools in the U.S. 2006

www.petersons.com 437

New York

The College of Saint Rose (continued)
application contact: Dean of Graduate and Adult and Continuing Education Admissions, 518-454-5136.

Find an in-depth description at www.petersons.com/gradchannel.

Graduate Studies

School of Arts and Humanities
Programs in:
 art education • MS Ed, Certificate
 arts and humanities • MA, MS Ed, Certificate
 English • MA
 history/political science • MA
 music • MA
 music education • MS Ed, Certificate
 public communications • MA

School of Business
Programs in:
 accounting • MS
 business • MBA, MS, Certificate
 business administration • MBA
 not-for-profit management • Certificate

School of Education
Programs in:
 adolescent education • MS Ed, Certificate
 applied technology education • MS Ed, Certificate
 bilingual pupil personnel services • Certificate
 biology • MS Ed
 business and marketing education • MS Ed, Certificate
 chemistry • MS Ed
 childhood education • MS Ed
 college student personnel • MS Ed
 college student services administration • MS Ed
 communication disorders • MS Ed
 community counseling • MS Ed
 counseling • MS Ed
 early childhood education • MS Ed
 education • MS, MS Ed, Certificate
 educational administration and supervision • MS Ed, Certificate
 educational computing • Certificate
 educational psychology • MS Ed
 elementary education • MS Ed
 elementary education (K–6) • MS Ed
 English • MS Ed
 literacy: birth—grade 6 • MS Ed, Certificate
 literacy: grades 5-12 • MS Ed, Certificate
 mathematics • MS Ed
 reading • MS Ed, Certificate
 school administrator and supervisor • Certificate
 school counseling • MS Ed
 school psychology • MS, Certificate
 secondary education • MS Ed, Certificate
 social studies • MS Ed
 Spanish • MS Ed
 special education • MS Ed
 teacher education • MS Ed, Certificate

School of Mathematics and Sciences
Programs in:
 computer information systems • MS
 mathematics and sciences • MS

■ COLLEGE OF STATEN ISLAND OF THE CITY UNIVERSITY OF NEW YORK
Staten Island, NY 10314-6600
http://www.csi.cuny.edu/

State and locally supported, coed, comprehensive institution. *Enrollment:* 12,422 graduate, professional, and undergraduate students; 87 full-time matriculated graduate/professional students (55 women), 946 part-time matriculated graduate/professional students (742 women). *Graduate faculty:* 67 full-time (29 women), 19 part-time/adjunct (10 women). *Computer facilities:* 140 computers available on campus for general student use. A campuswide network can be accessed from off campus. Internet access and online class registration are available. *Library facilities:* College of Staten Island Library. *Graduate expenses:* Tuition, state resident: full-time $5,440; part-time $230 per credit. Tuition, nonresident: full-time $10,200; part-time $425 per credit. Required fees: $154 per semester. Tuition and fees vary according to course load. *General application contact:* Mary Beth Reilly, Director of Admissions, 718-982-2010.

Find an in-depth description at www.petersons.com/gradchannel.

Graduate Programs
Dr. David Podell, Vice President for Academic Affairs and Provost
Programs in:
 adult health nursing • MS
 biology • MS
 cinema and media studies • MA
 computer science • MS, PhD
 educational supervision and administration • 6th Year Certificate
 elementary education • MS Ed
 English • MA
 environmental science • MS
 gerontological nursing • MS
 history • MA
 liberal studies • MA
 physical therapy • MS
 polymer chemistry • PhD
 secondary education • MS Ed
 special education • MS Ed

Center for Developmental Neuroscience and Developmental Disabilities
Dr. Ekkehart Trenkner, Deputy Director
Programs in:
 biology • PhD
 learning processes • PhD
 neuroscience • MS, PhD
 neuroscience, mental retardation, and developmental disabilities • MS
 psychology • PhD

■ COLUMBIA UNIVERSITY
New York, NY 10027
http://www.columbia.edu/

Independent, coed, university. CGS member. *Graduate faculty:* 3,221 full-time (1,142 women), 949 part-time/adjunct (366 women). *Graduate expenses:* Tuition: full-time $14,820. *General application contact:* Information Contact, 212-854-1754.

Find an in-depth description at www.petersons.com/gradchannel.

College of Physicians and Surgeons
Dr. Herbert Pardes, Dean, Faculty of Medicine
Programs in:
 medicine • MD, M Phil, MA, MS, DN Sc, DPT, PhD, Adv C
 occupational therapy (professional) • MS
 occupational therapy administration or education (post-professional) • MS
 physical therapy • DPT

Graduate School of Arts and Sciences at the College of Physicians and Surgeons
Programs in:
 anatomy • M Phil, MA, PhD
 anatomy and cell biology • PhD
 biochemistry and molecular biophysics • M Phil, PhD
 biomedical sciences • M Phil, MA, PhD
 biophysics • PhD
 cellular, molecular and biophysical studies • M Phil, MA, PhD
 genetics • M Phil, MA, PhD
 medical informatics • M Phil, MA, PhD
 medicine • M Phil, MA, PhD
 neurobiology and behavior • M Phil, PhD
 pathobiology • M Phil, MA, PhD
 pharmacology • M Phil, MA, PhD
 pharmacology-toxicology • M Phil, MA, PhD
 physiology and cellular biophysics • M Phil, MA, PhD

New York

Institute of Human Nutrition
Dr. Richard J. Deckelbaum, Director
Program in:
  nutrition • M Phil, MA, MS, PhD

Fu Foundation School of Engineering and Applied Science
Zvi Galil, Dean
Programs in:
  applied physics • MS, PhD
  applied physics and applied mathematics • Eng Sc D
  biomedical engineering • MS, Eng Sc D
  chemical engineering • MS, Eng Sc D, PhD, Engr
  civil engineering • MS, Eng Sc D, PhD, Engr
  computer science • MS, PhD, CSE
  earth resources engineering • MS, PhD
  electrical engineering • MS, Eng Sc D, PhD, EE
  engineering and applied science • ME, MS, Eng Sc D, PhD, CSE, EE, Engr
  financial engineering • MS
  industrial engineering • MS, Eng Sc D, PhD, Engr
  materials science and engineering • MS, Eng Sc D, PhD
  mechanical engineering • ME, MS, Eng Sc D, PhD
  mechanics • MS, Eng Sc D, PhD, Engr
  medical physics • MS
  minerals engineering and materials science • Eng Sc D, PhD, Engr
  operations research • MS, Eng Sc D, PhD
  solid state science and engineering • MS, Eng Sc D, PhD
  telecommunications • MS

Graduate School of Architecture, Planning, and Preservation
Programs in:
  advanced architectural design • MS
  architecture • M Arch, PhD
  architecture and urban design • MS
  architecture, planning, and preservation • M Arch, MS, PhD
  historic preservation • MS
  real estate development • MS
  urban planning • MS, PhD

Graduate School of Arts and Sciences
Dr. Henry C. Pinkham, Dean
Programs in:
  African-American studies • MA
  American studies • MA
  arts and sciences • M Phil, MA, MS, DMA, PhD, Certificate
  climate and society • MA
  conservation biology • MA
  East Asian regional studies • MA
  East Asian studies • MA
  French cultural studies • MA
  human rights studies • MA
  Islamic culture studies • MA
  Jewish studies • MA
  medieval studies • MA
  modern European studies • MA
  quantitative methods in the social sciences • MA
  Russian, Eurasian and East European regional studies • MA
  South Asian studies • MA
  sustainable development • PhD
  theatre • M Phil, MA, PhD
  Yiddish studies • MA

Division of Humanities
Programs in:
  archaeology • M Phil, MA, PhD
  art history and archaeology • M Phil, MA, PhD
  classics • M Phil, MA, PhD
  comparative literature • M Phil, MA, PhD
  East Asian languages and cultures • M Phil, MA, PhD
  English literature • M Phil, MA, PhD
  French and Romance philology • M Phil, PhD
  Germanic languages • M Phil, MA, PhD
  Hebrew language and literature • M Phil, MA, PhD
  humanities • M Phil, MA, DMA, PhD
  Italian • M Phil, MA, PhD
  Jewish studies • M Phil, MA, PhD
  literature-writing • M Phil, MA, PhD
  Middle Eastern languages and cultures • M Phil, MA, PhD
  modern art • MA
  music • M Phil, MA, DMA, PhD
  Oriental studies • M Phil, MA, PhD
  philosophy • M Phil, MA, PhD
  religion • M Phil, MA, PhD
  Romance languages • MA
  Russian literature • M Phil, MA, PhD
  Slavic languages • M Phil, MA, PhD
  Spanish and Portuguese • M Phil, MA, PhD

Division of Natural Sciences
Programs in:
  astronomy • M Phil, MA, PhD
  atmospheric and planetary science • M Phil, PhD
  biological sciences • M Phil, MA, PhD
  chemical physics • M Phil, PhD
  conservation biology • Certificate
  ecology and evolutionary biology • PhD
  environmental policy • Certificate
  experimental psychology • M Phil, MA, PhD
  geochemistry • M Phil, MA, PhD
  geodetic sciences • M Phil, MA, PhD
  geophysics • M Phil, MA, PhD
  inorganic chemistry • M Phil, MS, PhD
  mathematics • M Phil, MA, PhD
  natural sciences • M Phil, MA, MS, PhD, Certificate
  oceanography • M Phil, MA, PhD
  organic chemistry • M Phil, MS, PhD
  philosophical foundations of physics • MA
  physics • M Phil, PhD
  psychobiology • M Phil, MA, PhD
  social psychology • M Phil, MA, PhD
  statistics • M Phil, MA, PhD

Division of Social Sciences
Programs in:
  American history • M Phil, MA, PhD
  anthropology • M Phil, MA, PhD
  economics • M Phil, MA, PhD
  history • M Phil, MA, PhD
  political science • M Phil, MA, PhD
  social sciences • M Phil, MA, PhD
  sociology • M Phil, MA, PhD

Graduate School of Business
Prof. Meyer Feldberg, Dean
Programs in:
  accounting • MBA
  business • PhD
  business administration • EMBA, MBA
  decision, risk, and operations • MBA
  entrepreneurship • MBA
  finance and economics • MBA
  global business administration • EMBA
  human resource management • MBA
  international business • MBA
  management • MBA
  marketing • MBA
  media, entertainment and communications • MBA
  real estate • MBA
  social enterprise • MBA

Graduate School of Journalism
Program in:
  journalism • MS, PhD

Joseph L. Mailman School of Public Health
Programs in:
  biostatistics • MPH, MS, Dr PH, PhD
  environmental health sciences • MPH, Dr PH, PhD
  epidemiology • MPH, MS, Dr PH, PhD
  health policy and management • Exec MPH, MPH
  population and family health • MPH
  public health • MPH, Dr PH
  sociomedical sciences • MPH, Dr PH, PhD

New York

Columbia University (continued)
School of Dental and Oral Surgery
Programs in:
 clinical specialty • MA
 dental and oral surgery • DDS, MA, MS

School of International and Public Affairs
Dr. Lisa Anderson, Dean
Programs in:
 environmental science and policy • MPA
 international affairs • MIA
 international and public affairs • MIA, MPA, Certificate
 public policy and administration • MPA

East Asian Institute
Dr. Charles K. Armstrong, Director
Program in:
 Asian studies • Certificate

Harriman Institute
Dr. Catherine T. Nepomnyaschchy, Director

Institute for the Study of Europe
Dr. John Micgiel, Director
Program in:
 Europe • Certificate

Institute of African Studies
Prof. Mahmood Mamdani, Director
Program in:
 African studies • Certificate

Institute of Latin American and Iberian Studies
Dr. Albert Fishlow, Director
Program in:
 Latin American and Iberian studies • Certificate

Institute on East Central Europe
Dr. John Micgiel, Director
Program in:
 East Central Europe • Certificate

Middle East Institute
Dr. Rashidi Khalidi, Director
Program in:
 Middle East studies • Certificate

Southern Asian Institute
Dr. Vidya Dehejia, Director
Program in:
 Southern Asian studies • Certificate

School of Law
David W. Leebron, Dean of Faculty of Law
Program in:
 law • JD, LL M, JSD

School of Nursing
Dr. Mary O'Neil Mundinger, Dean
Programs in:
 acute care nurse practitioner • MS, Adv C
 adult nurse practitioner • MS, Adv C
 family nurse practitioner • MS, Adv C
 geriatric nurse practitioner • MS, Adv C
 HIV nursing • MS, Adv C
 informatics • MS
 neonatal nurse practitioner • MS, Adv C
 nurse anesthesia • MS, Adv C
 nurse midwifery • MS
 nursing • MS, DN Sc, Adv C
 nursing science • DN Sc
 oncology nursing • MS, Adv C
 pediatric nurse practitioner • MS, Adv C
 psychiatric-community mental health nursing • MS, Adv C
 women's health nurse practitioner • MS, Adv C

School of Social Work
Dr. Jeanette Takamura, Dean
Program in:
 social work • MSSW, PhD

School of the Arts
Bruce Ferguson, Dean
Programs in:
 arts • MFA
 digital media • MFA
 directing • MFA
 fiction • MFA
 nonfiction • MFA
 painting • MFA
 photography • MFA
 poetry • MFA
 printmaking • MFA
 producing • MFA
 screen writing • MFA
 sculpture/new genres • MFA

Theater Arts Division
Steven Chaikelson, Chair
Programs in:
 acting • MFA
 directing • MFA
 dramaturgy • MFA
 playwriting • MFA
 stage management • MFA
 theater management • MFA

■ CORNELL UNIVERSITY
Ithaca, NY 14853-0001
http://www.cornell.edu/

Independent, coed, university. CGS member. *Enrollment:* 19,620 graduate, professional, and undergraduate students; 5,965 full-time matriculated graduate/professional students (2,498 women). *Graduate faculty:* 1,484 full-time (360 women), 80 part-time/adjunct (15 women). *Computer facilities:* Computer purchase and lease plans are available. 2,500 computers available on campus for general student use. A campuswide network can be accessed from student residence rooms and from off campus. Internet access and online class registration are available. *Library facilities:* Olin Library plus 17 others. *Graduate expenses:* Tuition: full-time $28,630. One-time fee: $50 full-time. *General application contact:* Graduate School Application Requests, Caldwell Hall, 607-255-4884.

College of Veterinary Medicine
Dr. Donald F. Smith, Dean
Program in:
 veterinary medicine • DVM

Cornell Law School
Stewart J. Schawb, Dean
Program in:
 law • JD, LL M

Graduate School
Dr. Alison G. Power, Dean
Programs in:
 acarology • MS, PhD
 advanced composites and structures • M Eng
 advanced materials processing • M Eng, MS, PhD
 aerospace engineering • M Eng, MS, PhD
 African history • MA, PhD
 African studies • MPS
 African-American literature • PhD
 African-American studies • MPS
 agricultural economics • MPS, MS, PhD
 agricultural education • MAT
 agriculture and life sciences • M Eng, MAT, MFS, MLA, MPS, MS, PhD
 agronomy • MPS, MS, PhD
 algorithms • M Eng, PhD
 American art • PhD
 American history • MA, PhD
 American literature after 1865 • PhD
 American literature to 1865 • PhD
 American politics • PhD
 American studies • PhD
 analytical chemistry • PhD
 ancient art and archaeology • PhD
 ancient history • MA, PhD
 ancient Near Eastern studies • MA, PhD
 ancient philosophy • PhD
 animal breeding • MS, PhD
 animal cytology • MS, PhD
 animal genetics • MS, PhD
 animal nutrition • MPS, MS, PhD
 animal science • MPS, MS, PhD
 apiculture • MS, PhD
 apparel design • MA, MPS
 applied economics • PhD
 applied entomology • MS, PhD
 applied linguistics • MA, PhD
 applied logic and automated reasoning • M Eng, PhD
 applied mathematics • PhD

New York

applied mathematics and computational methods • M Eng, MS, PhD
applied physics • PhD
applied probability and statistics • PhD
applied research in human-environment relations • MS
applied statistics • MPS
aquatic entomology • MS, PhD
aquatic science • MPS, MS, PhD
Arabic and Islamic studies • MA, PhD
archaeological anthropology • PhD
artificial intelligence • M Eng, PhD
arts and sciences • MA, MFA, MPA, MPS, MS, DMA, PhD
Asian art • PhD
Asian religions • MA, PhD
astronomy • PhD
astrophysics • PhD
atmospheric science • MS, PhD
atmospheric sciences • MPS, MS, PhD
baroque art • PhD
basic analytical economics • PhD
behavioral biology • MS, PhD
behavioral physiology • MS, PhD
biblical studies • MA, PhD
bio-organic chemistry • PhD
biochemical engineering • M Eng, MS, PhD
biochemistry • PhD
biological anthropology • PhD
biological control • MS, PhD
biological engineering • M Eng, MPS, MS, PhD
biology (7–12) • MAT
biomechanical engineering • M Eng, MS, PhD
biomedical engineering • MS, PhD
biometry • MS, PhD
biophysical chemistry • PhD
biophysics • PhD
biopsychology • PhD
cardiovascular and respiratory physiology • MS, PhD
cell biology • PhD
cellular and molecular medicine • MS, PhD
cellular and molecular toxicology • MS, PhD
cellular immunology • MS, PhD
chemical biology • PhD
chemical physics • PhD
chemical reaction engineering • M Eng, MS, PhD
chemistry (7–12) • MAT
Chinese linguistics • MA, PhD
Chinese philology • MA, PhD
classical and statistical thermodynamics • M Eng, MS, PhD
classical archaeology • PhD
classical Chinese literature • MA, PhD

classical Japanese literature • MA, PhD
classical myth • PhD
classical rhetoric • PhD
collective bargaining, labor law and labor history • MILR, MPS, MS, PhD
colonial and postcolonial literature • PhD
combustion • M Eng, MS, PhD
communication • MPS, MS, PhD
communication research methods • MS, PhD
community and regional society • MS
community and regional sociology • MPS, PhD
community development process • MPS
community nutrition • MPS, MS, PhD
comparative and functional anatomy • MS, PhD
comparative biomedical sciences • MS, PhD
comparative literature • PhD
comparative politics • PhD
composition • DMA
computer engineering • M Eng, PhD
computer graphics • M Eng, PhD
computer science • M Eng, PhD
computer vision • M Eng, PhD
concurrency and distributed computing • M Eng, PhD
consumer policy • PhD
controlled environment agriculture • MPS, PhD
controlled environment horticulture • MS
creative writing • MFA
cultural studies • PhD
curriculum and instruction • MPS, MS, PhD
cytology • MS, PhD
dairy science • MPS, MS, PhD
decision theory • MS, PhD
development policy • MPS
developmental and reproductive biology • MS, PhD
developmental biology • MS, PhD
developmental psychology • PhD
drama and the theatre • PhD
dramatic literature • PhD
dynamics and space mechanics • MS, PhD
early modern European history • MA, PhD
earth science (7–12) • MAT
East Asian linguistics • MA, PhD
East Asian studies • MA
ecological and environmental plant pathology • MPS, MS, PhD
ecology • MS, PhD
econometrics and economic statistics • PhD
economic and social statistics • MILR, MS, PhD
economic development • MPS

economic development and planning • PhD
economic geology • M Eng, MS, PhD
economic theory • PhD
economy and society • MA, PhD
ecotoxicology and environmental chemistry • MS, PhD
electrical engineering • M Eng, PhD
electrical systems • M Eng, PhD
electrophysics • M Eng, PhD
endocrinology • MS, PhD
energy • M Eng, MPS, MS, PhD
energy and power systems • M Eng, MS, PhD
engineering • M Eng, MPS, MS, PhD
engineering geology • M Eng, MS, PhD
engineering management • M Eng, MS, PhD
engineering physics • M Eng
engineering statistics • MS, PhD
English history • MA, PhD
English linguistics • MA, PhD
English poetry • PhD
English Renaissance to 1660 • PhD
environmental and comparative physiology • MS, PhD
environmental archaeology • MA
environmental engineering • M Eng, MPS, MS, PhD
environmental fluid mechanics and hydrology • M Eng, MS, PhD
environmental geophysics • M Eng, MS, PhD
environmental information science • MPS, MS, PhD
environmental management • MPS
environmental systems engineering • M Eng, MS, PhD
epidemiological plant pathology • MPS, MS, PhD
evaluation • PhD
evolutionary biology • PhD
experimental design • MS, PhD
experimental physics • MS, PhD
extension, and adult education • MPS, MS, PhD
facilities planning and management • MS
family and social welfare policy • PhD
fiber science • MS, PhD
field crop science • MPS, MS, PhD
fishery science • MPS, MS, PhD
fluid dynamics, rheology and biorheology • M Eng, MS, PhD
fluid mechanics • M Eng, MS, PhD
food chemistry • MPS, MS, PhD
food engineering • MPS, MS, PhD
food microbiology • MPS, MS, PhD
food processing engineering • M Eng, MPS, MS, PhD
food processing waste technology • MPS, MS, PhD
food science • MFS, MPS, MS, PhD

New York

Cornell University (continued)
forest science • MPS, MS, PhD
French history • MA, PhD
French linguistics • PhD
French literature • PhD
gastrointestinal and metabolic physiology • MS, PhD
gender and life course • MA, PhD
general geology • M Eng, MS, PhD
general linguistics • MA, PhD
general space sciences • PhD
genetics • PhD
geobiology • M Eng, MS, PhD
geochemistry and isotope geology • M Eng, MS, PhD
geohydrology • M Eng, MS, PhD
geomorphology • M Eng, MS, PhD
geophysics • M Eng, MS, PhD
geotechnical engineering • M Eng, MS, PhD
geotectonics • M Eng, MS, PhD
German area studies • MA, PhD
German history • MA, PhD
German intellectual history • MA, PhD
Germanic linguistics • MA, PhD
Germanic literature • MA, PhD
Greek and Latin language and linguistics • PhD
Greek language and literature • PhD
greenhouse crops • MPS, MS, PhD
health administration • MHA
health management and policy • PhD
heat and mass transfer • M Eng, MS, PhD
heat transfer • M Eng, MS, PhD
Hebrew and Judaic studies • MA, PhD
Hispanic literature • PhD
histology • MS, PhD
historical archaeology • MA
history and philosophy of science and technology • MA, PhD
history of science • MA, PhD
horticultural business management • MPS, MS, PhD
horticultural physiology • MPS, MS, PhD
hospitality management • MMH
hotel administration • MS, PhD
housing and design • MS
human development and family studies • PhD
human ecology • MA, MHA, MPS, MS, PhD
human experimental psychology • PhD
human factors and ergonomics • MS
human nutrition • MPS, MS, PhD
human resource studies • MILR, MPS, MS, PhD
human-environment relations • MS
immunochemistry • MS, PhD
immunogenetics • MS, PhD
immunopathology • MS, PhD
Indo-European linguistics • MA, PhD
industrial and labor relations problems • MILR, MPS, MS, PhD
industrial organization and control • PhD
infection and immunity • MS, PhD
infectious diseases • MS, PhD
information organization and retrieval • M Eng, PhD
infrared astronomy • PhD
inorganic chemistry • PhD
insect behavior • MS, PhD
insect biochemistry • MS, PhD
insect ecology • MS, PhD
insect genetics • MS, PhD
insect morphology • MS, PhD
insect pathology • MS, PhD
insect physiology • MS, PhD
insect systematics • MS, PhD
insect toxicology and insecticide chemistry • MS, PhD
integrated pest management • MS, PhD
interior design • MA, MPS
international agriculture • M Eng, MPS, MS, PhD
international agriculture and development • MPS
international and comparative labor • MILR, MPS, MS, PhD
international communication • MS, PhD
international economics • PhD
international food science • MPS, MS, PhD
international nutrition • MPS, MS, PhD
international planning • MPS
international population • MPS
international relations • PhD
Italian linguistics • PhD
Italian literature • PhD
Japanese linguistics • MA, PhD
kinetics and catalysis • M Eng, MS, PhD
Korean literature • MA, PhD
labor economics • MILR, MPS, MS, PhD
landscape architecture • MLA
landscape horticulture • MPS, MS, PhD
Latin American archaeology • MA
Latin American history • MA, PhD
Latin language and literature • PhD
lesbian, bisexual, and gay literature studies • PhD
literary criticism and theory • PhD
local government organizations and operations • MPS
local roads • M Eng, MPS, MS, PhD
machine systems • M Eng, MPS, MS, PhD
manufacturing systems engineering • PhD
marine geology • MS, PhD
materials and manufacturing engineering • M Eng, MS, PhD
materials chemistry • PhD
materials engineering • M Eng, PhD
materials science • M Eng, PhD
mathematical programming • PhD
mathematical statistics • MS, PhD
mathematics (7–12) • MAT
mechanical systems and design • M Eng, MS, PhD
mechanics of materials • MS, PhD
medical and veterinary entomology • MS, PhD
medieval and Renaissance Latin literature • PhD
medieval archaeology • MA, PhD
medieval art • PhD
medieval Chinese history • MA, PhD
medieval history • MA, PhD
medieval literature • PhD
medieval music • PhD
medieval philology and linguistics • PhD
medieval philosophy • PhD
Mediterranean and Near Eastern archaeology • MA
membrane and epithelial physiology • MS, PhD
methodology • MA, PhD
methods of social research • MPS, MS, PhD
microbiology • PhD
mineralogy • M Eng, MS, PhD
modern art • PhD
modern Chinese history • MA, PhD
modern Chinese literature • MA, PhD
modern European history • MA, PhD
modern Japanese history • MA, PhD
modern Japanese literature • MA, PhD
molecular and cell biology • PhD
molecular and cellular physiology • MS, PhD
molecular biology • PhD
molecular plant pathology • MPS, MS, PhD
monetary and macroeconomics • PhD
multiphase flows • M Eng, MS, PhD
musicology • PhD
mycology • MPS, MS, PhD
neural and sensory physiology • MS, PhD
neurobiology • MS, PhD
nineteenth century • PhD
nuclear engineering • M Eng, MS, PhD
nuclear science • MS, PhD
nursery crops • MPS, MS, PhD
nutrition of horticultural crops • MPS, MS, PhD
nutritional and food toxicology • MS, PhD
nutritional biochemistry • MPS, MS, PhD
Old and Middle English • PhD
old Norse • MA, PhD
operating systems • M Eng, PhD

operations research and industrial engineering • M Eng
organic chemistry • PhD
organizational behavior • MILR, MPS, MS, PhD
organizations • MA, PhD
organometallic chemistry • PhD
paleobotany • MS, PhD
paleontology • M Eng, MS, PhD
parallel computing • M Eng, PhD
performance practice • DMA
personality and social psychology • PhD
petroleum geology • M Eng, MS, PhD
petrology • M Eng, MS, PhD
pharmacology • MS, PhD
philosophy • PhD
phonetics • MA, PhD
phonological theory • MA, PhD
physical chemistry • PhD
physics • MS, PhD
physics (7–12) • MAT
physiological genomics • MS, PhD
physiology of reproduction • MPS, MS, PhD
planetary geology • M Eng, MS, PhD
planetary studies • PhD
plant breeding • MPS, MS, PhD
plant cell biology • MS, PhD
plant disease epidemiology • MPS, MS, PhD
plant ecology • MS, PhD
plant genetics • MPS, MS, PhD
plant molecular biology • MS, PhD
plant morphology, anatomy and biomechanics • MS, PhD
plant pathology • MPS, MS, PhD
plant physiology • MS, PhD
plant propagation • MPS, MS, PhD
plant protection • MPS
policy analysis • MA, PhD
political methodology • PhD
political sociology/social movements • MA, PhD
political thought • PhD
polymer chemistry • PhD
polymer science • MS, PhD
polymers • M Eng, MS, PhD
pomology • MPS, MS, PhD
population and development • MPS, MS, PhD
population medicine and epidemiology sciences • PhD
population medicine and epidemiology • MS
Precambrian geology • M Eng, MS, PhD
premodern Islamic history • MA, PhD
premodern Japanese history • MA, PhD
probability • MS, PhD
program development and planning • MPS
programming environments • M Eng, PhD

programming languages and methodology • M Eng, PhD
prose fiction • PhD
public affairs • MPA
public finance • PhD
public garden management • MPS, MS, PhD
public policy • MPA, PhD
Quaternary geology • M Eng, MS, PhD
racial and ethnic relations • MA, PhD
radio astronomy • PhD
radiophysics • PhD
remote sensing • M Eng, MS, PhD
Renaissance art • PhD
Renaissance history • MA, PhD
reproductive physiology • MS, PhD
resource economics • MPS, MS, PhD
resource policy and management • MPS, MS, PhD
Restoration and eighteenth century • PhD
restoration ecology • MPS, MS, PhD
risk assessment, management and public policy • MS, PhD
robotics • M Eng, PhD
rock mechanics • M Eng, MS, PhD
Romance linguistics • MA, PhD
rural and environmental sociology • MPS, MS, PhD
Russian history • MA, PhD
sampling • MS, PhD
science and environmental communication • MS, PhD
science and technology policy • MPS
scientific computing • M Eng, PhD
second language acquisition • MA, PhD
sedimentology • M Eng, MS, PhD
seismology • M Eng, MS, PhD
semantics • MA, PhD
sensory evaluation • MPS, MS, PhD
Slavic linguistics • MA, PhD
social networks • MA, PhD
social psychology • MA, PhD
social psychology of communication • MS, PhD
social stratification • MA, PhD
social studies of science and technology • MA, PhD
sociocultural anthropology • PhD
sociolinguistics • MA, PhD
soil and water engineering • M Eng, MPS, MS, PhD
soil science • MPS, MS, PhD
solid mechanics • MS, PhD
South Asian linguistics • MA, PhD
South Asian studies • MA
Southeast Asian art • PhD
Southeast Asian history • MA, PhD
Southeast Asian linguistics • MA, PhD
Southeast Asian studies • MA
Spanish linguistics • PhD
state, economy and society • MS
state, economy, and society • MPS, PhD

statistical computing • MS, PhD
statistics • MPS, MS, PhD
stochastic processes • MS, PhD
Stone Age archaeology • MA
stratigraphy • M Eng, MS, PhD
structural and functional biology • MS, PhD
structural engineering • M Eng, MS, PhD
structural geology • M Eng, MS, PhD
structural mechanics • M Eng, MS
structures and environment • M Eng, MPS, MS, PhD
surface science • M Eng, MS, PhD
syntactic theory • MA, PhD
systematic botany • MS, PhD
systems engineering • M Eng
taxonomy of ornamental plants • MPS, MS, PhD
textile science • MS, PhD
theatre history • PhD
theatre theory and aesthetics • PhD
theoretical astrophysics • PhD
theoretical chemistry • PhD
theoretical physics • MS, PhD
theory and criticism • PhD
theory of computation • M Eng, PhD
theory of music • MA
transportation engineering • MS, PhD
transportation systems engineering • M Eng
turfgrass science • MPS, MS, PhD
twentieth century • PhD
urban horticulture • MPS, MS, PhD
uses and effects of communication • MS, PhD
vegetable crops • MPS, MS, PhD
water resource systems • M Eng, MS, PhD
weed science • MPS, MS, PhD
wildlife science • MPS, MS, PhD
women's literature • PhD

Field of Environmental Management
Program in:
  environmental management • MPS

Graduate Field in the Law School
Director of Graduate Studies
Program in:
  law • LL M, JSD

Graduate Field of Management
Director of Graduate Studies
Programs in:
  accounting • PhD
  behavioral decision theory • PhD
  finance • PhD
  management information systems • PhD
  marketing • PhD
  organizational behavior • PhD
  production and operations management • PhD

New York

Cornell University (continued)
Graduate Fields of Architecture, Art and Planning
Programs in:
   architectural design • M Arch
   architectural science • MS
   architecture, art and planning • M Arch, MA, MFA, MLA, MPSRE, MRP, MS, PhD
   building technology and environmental science • MS
   city and regional planning • MRP, PhD
   computer graphics • MS
   creative visual arts • MFA
   environmental planning and design • MRP, PhD
   environmental studies • MA, MS, PhD
   historic preservation planning • MA
   history of architecture • MA, PhD
   history of urban development • MA, PhD
   international development planning • MRP, PhD
   international spatial problems • MA, MS, PhD
   location theory • MA, MS, PhD
   multiregional economic analysis • MA, MS, PhD
   peace science • MA, MS, PhD
   planning methods • MA, MS, PhD
   planning theory and systems analysis • MRP, PhD
   real estate • MPSRE
   regional economics and development planning • MRP, PhD
   regional science • MRP, PhD
   social and health systems planning • MRP, PhD
   theory and criticism of architecture • M Arch
   urban and regional economics • MA, MS, PhD
   urban and regional theory • MRP, PhD
   urban design • M Arch
   urban planning history • MRP, PhD

Professional Field of the Johnson Graduate School of Management
Robert J. Swieringa, Dean
Program in:
   management • MBA

■ **DOWLING COLLEGE**
Oakdale, NY 11769-1999
http://www.dowling.edu/

Independent, coed, comprehensive institution. *Enrollment:* 6,247 graduate, professional, and undergraduate students; 1,044 full-time matriculated graduate/professional students (581 women), 2,113 part-time matriculated graduate/professional students (1,447 women). *Computer facilities:* 118 computers available on campus for general student use. A campuswide network can be accessed. Internet access and online class registration are available. *Library facilities:* Dowling College Library. *Graduate expenses:* Tuition: part-time $565 per credit. Required fees: $770; $258 per term. *General application contact:* Amy Stier, Director of Enrollment Services for Admissions, 631-244-5010.

Graduate Programs in Education
Dr. Clyde Payne, Associate Provost
Programs in:
   computers in education • PD
   educational administration • Ed D, PD
   human development and learning • MS Ed
   literacy • MS Ed
   literacy/special education • MS Ed
   school administration and supervision • PD
   school district administration • PD
   secondary education • MS Ed
   special education • MS Ed

Programs in Arts and Sciences
Dr. Richard Resch, Provost
Programs in:
   integrated math and science • MS
   liberal studies • MA

School of Business
Ward Deutschman, Associate Provost
Programs in:
   aviation management • MBA, Certificate
   banking and finance • MBA, Certificate
   general management • MBA
   public management • MBA, Certificate
   total quality management • MBA, Certificate

■ **FORDHAM UNIVERSITY**
New York, NY 10458
http://www.fordham.edu/

Independent-religious, coed, university. CGS member. *Enrollment:* 14,731 graduate, professional, and undergraduate students; 3,355 full-time matriculated graduate/professional students (2,088 women), 3,284 part-time matriculated graduate/professional students (1,985 women). *Graduate faculty:* 502 full-time, 416 part-time/adjunct. *Computer facilities:* 617 computers available on campus for general student use. A campuswide network can be accessed from student residence rooms and from off campus. Internet access and online class registration are available. *Library facilities:* Walsh Library plus 3 others. *Graduate expenses:* Tuition: part-time $690 per credit. *General application contact:* Anthony J. DeCarlo, Director of Graduate Admissions, 718-817-4418.

Find an in-depth description at www.petersons.com/gradchannel.

Graduate School of Arts and Sciences
Dr. Nancy A. Busch, Dean
Programs in:
   arts and sciences • MA, MS, PhD, CIF
   biblical studies • MA, PhD
   biological sciences • MS, PhD
   classical Greek and Latin literature • MA
   classical Greek literature • MA
   classical Latin literature • MA
   classical philology • PhD
   clinical psychology • PhD
   computer science • MS
   criminology • MA
   developmental psychology • PhD
   economics • MA, PhD
   English language and literature • MA, PhD
   historical theology • MA, PhD
   history • MA, PhD
   humanities and sciences • MA
   international political economy and development • MA, CIF
   medieval Latin • PhD
   medieval studies • MA
   philosophical resources • MA
   philosophy • MA, PhD
   political science • MA
   psychometrics • PhD
   public communications • MA
   sociology • MA, PhD
   systematics • MA, PhD

Graduate School of Education
Dr. Regis Bernhardt, Dean
Program in:
   education • MAT, MS, MSE, MST, Ed D, PhD, Adv C

Division of Curriculum and Teaching
Dr. Joanna Ultry, Chairperson
Programs in:
   adult education • MS, MSE
   bilingual teacher education • MSE
   curriculum and teaching • MSE
   early childhood education • MSE
   elementary education • MST
   language, literacy, and learning • PhD
   reading education • MSE, Adv C
   secondary education • MAT, MSE
   special education • MSE, Adv C
   teaching English as a second language • MSE

Division of Educational Leadership, Administration and Policy
Dr. Bruce Cooper, Chairperson
Programs in:

New York

administration and supervision • MSE, Adv C
administration and supervision for church leaders • PhD
educational administration and supervision • Ed D, PhD
human resource program administration • MS

Division of Psychological and Educational Services
Dr. Eric Chen, Chairman
Programs in:
counseling and personnel services • MSE, Adv C
counseling psychology • PhD
educational psychology • MSE, PhD
school psychology • PhD
urban and urban bilingual school psychology • Adv C

Graduate School of Religion and Religious Education
Rev. Vincent M. Novak, SJ, Dean
Programs in:
pastoral counseling and spiritual care • MA
religion and religious education • MA, PD
religious education • MS, PhD, PD
spiritual direction • Certificate

Graduate School of Social Service
Dr. Peter B. Vaughan, Dean
Program in:
social work • MSW, PhD

Graduate Schools of Business
Dr. Sharon P. Smith, Dean
Programs in:
accounting • MBA
communications and media management • MBA
finance • MBA
information and communication systems • MBA
information systems • MS
management systems • MBA
marketing • MBA
media management • MS
taxation • MS

School of Law
Michael R. Lanzarone, Associate Dean
Programs in:
banking, corporate and finance law • LL M
international business and trade law • LL M
law • JD

■ **HOFSTRA UNIVERSITY**
Hempstead, NY 11549
http://www.hofstra.edu/

Independent, coed, university. CGS member. *Enrollment:* 13,221 graduate, professional, and undergraduate students; 2,163 full-time matriculated graduate/professional students (1,323 women), 1,449 part-time matriculated graduate/professional students (1,008 women). *Graduate faculty:* 196 full-time (84 women), 148 part-time/adjunct (65 women). *Computer facilities:* Computer purchase and lease plans are available. 1,130 computers available on campus for general student use. A campuswide network can be accessed from student residence rooms. Internet access and online class registration are available. *Library facilities:* Axinn Library plus 1 other. *Graduate expenses:* Tuition: full-time $10,800; part-time $600 per credit. Required fees: $910; $155 per semester. Tuition and fees vary according to course load and program. *General application contact:* Dr. Tina Montgomery-Sneed, Dean of Graduate Admissions, 516-463-4876.

Find an in-depth description at www.petersons.com/gradchannel.

College of Liberal Arts and Sciences
Dr. Bernard J. Firestone, Dean
Program in:
liberal arts and sciences • MA, MS, PhD, Psy D, Post-Doctoral Certificate, Post-Master's Certificate

Division of Humanities
Programs in:
applied linguistics • MA
audiology • MA
bilingualism • MA
English and creative writing • MA
English literature • MA
humanities • MA
Spanish • MA
speech-language pathology • MA
teacher of students with speech and language disabilities • Post-Master's Certificate

Division of Natural Sciences, Mathematics, Engineering, and Computer Science
Programs in:
applied mathematics • MS
biology • MA, MS
computer science • MA, MS
engineering management • MS
human cytogenetics • MS
mathematics • MA
natural sciences, mathematics, engineering, and computer science • MA, MS

Division of Social Sciences
Programs in:
applied organizational psychology • PhD
clinical and school psychology • PhD, Post-Doctoral Certificate
industrial/organizational psychology • MA
school-community psychology • Psy D
social sciences • MA, PhD, Psy D, Post-Doctoral Certificate

Frank G. Zarb School of Business
Dr. Ralph Polimeni, Dean
Programs in:
accounting • MBA, MS
accounting information systems • MS
business • EMBA, MBA, MS, Advanced Certificate
business administration • EMBA
business computer information systems • MBA
computer information systems • MS, Advanced Certificate
corporate accounting • Advanced Certificate
finance • MBA, MS, Advanced Certificate
human resource management • MS, Advanced Certificate
international business • MBA, Advanced Certificate
management • EMBA, MBA
marketing • MBA, MS, Advanced Certificate
marketing research • MS
taxation • MBA, MS, Advanced Certificate

New College
Heidi Contreras, Senior Assistant Dean
Program in:
interdisciplinary studies • MA

School of Communication
Dr. Sybil A. DelGaudio, Dean
Programs in:
communication • MA
speech communication and rhetorical studies • MA

School of Education and Allied Human Services
Dr. James R. Johnson, Dean
Programs in:
addiction studies • CAS
advanced literacy studies • PD
advanced literacy studies (grades 5–12) • PD
adventure education • CAS
art education • MA, MS Ed
bilingual education • MA
bilingual extension • CAS
business education • MS Ed
counseling • MS Ed, Advanced Certificate, CAS, PD
creative arts therapy • MA, MS Ed
creative arts therapy and special education (birth–grade 2) • MS Ed
creative arts therapy and special education (grades 1–12) • MS Ed

New York

Hofstra University (continued)
- divorce mediation • CAS
- early childhood education • MA, MS Ed
- early childhood special education • MS Ed, Advanced Certificate
- education and allied human services • MA, MHA, MS, MS Ed, Ed D, PhD, Advanced Certificate, CAS, PD
- educational administration • MS Ed, Ed D, CAS
- educational administration and policy studies • MS Ed
- educational and policy leadership • Ed D
- elementary education • MA, MS Ed
- elementary education-math/science/technology • MA
- elementary special education • MS Ed
- English education • MA, MS Ed
- family therapy • CAS
- fine arts education • MA, MS Ed
- foreign language education • MA, MS Ed
- foundations of education • MA, CAS
- French • MA, MS Ed
- German • MA, MS Ed
- gerontology • MS, Advanced Certificate
- gifted education • Advanced Certificate
- health administration • MA, MHA
- health education • MS
- inclusive early childhood special education • MS Ed
- inclusive elementary special education • MS Ed
- literacy studies • MA, MS Ed, CAS, PD
- literacy studies (birth–grade 6) • MS Ed, CAS
- literacy studies (grades 5–12) • MS Ed, CAS
- literacy studies and special education • MS Ed
- literacy studies/early childhood special education • MS Ed
- managed care • PD
- marriage and family therapy • MA, CAS, PD
- math education • MA, MS Ed
- middle level education • MA, CAS
- middle school extension (grades 5–6) • CAS
- middle school extension (grades 7–9) • CAS
- music education • MA, MS Ed
- physical education • MS
- reading, language, and cognition • Ed D, PhD
- rehabilitation administration • PD
- rehabilitation counseling • MS Ed, PD
- Russian • MA, MS Ed
- school counselor • MS Ed
- school counselor-bilingual extension • Advanced Certificate
- science education • MA, MS Ed
- science education (biology, chemistry, physics, earth science) • MS Ed
- science education (biology, chemistry, physics, geology) • MA
- secondary education • MA
- sex counseling • CAS
- social studies education • MA, MS Ed
- Spanish • MA, MS Ed
- special education • MA, MS Ed, Advanced Certificate
- special education assessment and diagnosis • Advanced Certificate
- teaching of writing (birth–grade 6) • MA
- teaching of writing (grades 5–12) • MA
- TESL • MS Ed, CAS
- TESL/bilingual education • MA, MS Ed, CAS
- wind conducting • MA

School of Law
Dr. Marshall E. Tracht, Vice Dean
Programs in:
- American legal studies • LL M
- international law • LL M
- law • JD

■ HUNTER COLLEGE OF THE CITY UNIVERSITY OF NEW YORK
New York, NY 10021-5085
http://www.hunter.cuny.edu/

State and locally supported, coed, comprehensive institution. *Enrollment:* 20,797 graduate, professional, and undergraduate students; 872 full-time matriculated graduate/professional students (698 women), 2,967 part-time matriculated graduate/professional students (2,319 women). *Graduate faculty:* 299 full-time (161 women), 172 part-time/adjunct (122 women). *Computer facilities:* 600 computers available on campus for general student use. A campuswide network can be accessed. Internet access is available. *Library facilities:* Hunter College Library. *Graduate expenses:* Tuition, state resident: part-time $230 per credit. Tuition, nonresident: part-time $425 per credit. *General application contact:* William Zlata, Director for Graduate Admissions, 212-772-4482.

Graduate School
William Zlata, Director of Admissions

School of Arts and Sciences
Dr. Judith Friedlander, Acting Dean
Programs in:
- analytical geography • MA
- anthropology • MA
- applied and evaluative psychology • MA
- applied mathematics • MA
- applied social research • MS
- art history • MA
- arts and sciences • MA, MFA, MS, MSSR, MSW, MUP, DSW, PhD, Certificate
- biochemistry • MA
- biological sciences • MA, PhD
- biopsychology and comparative psychology • MA
- British and American literature • MA
- communications • MA
- creative writing • MFA
- earth system science • MA
- economics • MA
- English education • MA
- environmental and social issues • MA
- fine arts • MFA
- French • MA
- French education • MA
- geographic information science • Certificate
- geographic information systems • MA
- history • MA
- integrated media arts • MFA
- Italian • MA
- Italian education • MA
- mathematics for secondary education • MA
- music • MA
- music education • MA
- physics • MA, PhD
- pure mathematics • MA
- social work • MSW, DSW
- social, cognitive, and developmental psychology • MA
- sociology • MSSR
- Spanish • MA
- Spanish education • MA
- studio art • MFA
- teaching earth science • MA
- teaching Latin • MA
- theater • MA
- urban affairs • MS
- urban planning • MUP

School of Education
Dr. Shirley Cohen, Acting Dean
Programs in:
- bilingual education • MS
- biology education • MA
- blind or visually impaired • MS Ed
- chemistry education • MA
- corrective reading (K–12) • MS Ed
- deaf or hard of hearing • MS Ed
- early childhood education • MS
- earth science • MA
- education • MA, MS, MS Ed, AC
- educational supervision and administration • AC
- elementary education • MS
- English education • MA
- French education • MA
- Italian education • MA
- literacy • MS

New York

mathematics education • MA
music education • MA
physics education • MA
rehabilitation counseling • MS Ed
school counselor • MS Ed
severe/multiple disabilities • MS Ed
social studies education • MA
Spanish education • MA
special education • MS Ed
teaching English as a second language • MA

Schools of the Health Professions
Lauren N. Sherwen, Dean
Programs in:
audiology • MS
environmental and occupational health • MS
environmental and occupational health sciences • MS
health professions • MPH, MPT, MS, AC
physical therapy • MPT
public health • MPH
speech language pathology • MS
teacher of speech and hearing handicapped • MS

Hunter-Bellevue School of Nursing
Dr. Diane Rendon, Director
Programs in:
adult nurse practitioner • MS
community health nursing • MS
gerontological nurse practitioner • MS
maternal child-health nursing • MS
medical/surgical nursing • MS
nursing • MS, AC
pediatric nurse practitioner • MS, AC
psychiatric nursing • MS

■ IONA COLLEGE
New Rochelle, NY 10801-1890
http://www.iona.edu/

Independent-religious, coed, comprehensive institution. *Enrollment:* 4,388 graduate, professional, and undergraduate students; 95 full-time matriculated graduate/professional students (49 women), 887 part-time matriculated graduate/professional students (536 women). *Graduate faculty:* 68 full-time (18 women), 59 part-time/adjunct (17 women). *Computer facilities:* Computer purchase and lease plans are available. 500 computers available on campus for general student use. A campuswide network can be accessed from student residence rooms and from off campus. Internet access and online class registration are available. *Library facilities:* Ryan Library plus 2 others. *Graduate expenses:* Tuition: part-time $540 per credit. Required fees: $65 per term. *General application contact:* Thomas Delahunt, Vice Provost for Enrollment Management, 914-633-2603.

Find an in-depth description at www.petersons.com/gradchannel.

Hagan School of Business
Dr. Nicholas J. Beutell, Dean
Programs in:
business • MBA, PMC
financial management • MBA, PMC
human resource management • MBA, PMC
information and decision technology management • MBA, PMC
international business • PMC
management • MBA, PMC
marketing • MBA, PMC

School of Arts and Science
Dr. Alexander R. Eodice, Dean
Programs in:
arts and science • MA, MS, MS Ed, MST, Certificate, PMC
biology education • MS Ed, MST
business education • MST
communication • PMC
computer science • MS
criminal justice • MS
educational administration • MS Ed
educational technology • MS, Certificate
English • MA
English education • MS Ed, MST
family counseling • MS, Certificate
health service administration • MS, Certificate
history • MA
journalism • MS
mathematics education • MS Ed, MST
multicultural education • MS Ed
pastoral counseling • MS
psychology • MA
school counseling • MA
school psychologist • MA
science • MS Ed
social studies education • MS Ed, MST
Spanish • MA
Spanish education • MS Ed, MST
teaching elementary education • MST
telecommunications • MS, Certificate

■ ITHACA COLLEGE
Ithaca, NY 14850-7020
http://www.ithaca.edu/

Independent, coed, comprehensive institution. CGS member. *Enrollment:* 6,496 graduate, professional, and undergraduate students; 218 full-time matriculated graduate/professional students (155 women), 13 part-time matriculated graduate/professional students (2 women). *Graduate faculty:* 119 full-time (50 women), 10 part-time/adjunct (7 women). *Computer facilities:* Computer purchase and lease plans are available. 624 computers available on campus for general student use. A campuswide network can be accessed from student residence rooms and from off campus. Internet access and online class registration are available. *Library facilities:* Ithaca College Library. *Graduate expenses:* Tuition: full-time $16,704; part-time $696 per credit hour. *General application contact:* Dr. Garry Brodhead, Associate Provost and Dean of Graduate Studies, 607-274-3527.

Find an in-depth description at www.petersons.com/gradchannel.

Graduate Studies
Dr. Garry Brodhead, Associate Provost and Dean

Roy H. Park School of Communications
Program in:
communications • MS

School of Business
Dr. Robert A. Ullrich, Dean
Programs in:
business • MBA
management • MBA

School of Health Sciences and Human Performance
Dr. Steven Siconolfi, Dean
Programs in:
exercise and sport sciences • MS
health sciences and human performance • MS
occupational therapy • MS
physical therapy • MS
speech pathology • MS
teacher of the speech and hearing handicapped • MS

School of Music
Dr. Arthur Ostrander, Dean
Programs in:
composition • MM
conducting • MM
music • MM, MS
music education • MM, MS
music theory • MM
performance • MM
strings, woodwinds, or brasses • MM
Suzuki pedagogy • MM

■ LEHMAN COLLEGE OF THE CITY UNIVERSITY OF NEW YORK
Bronx, NY 10468-1589
http://www.lehman.cuny.edu/

State and locally supported, coed, comprehensive institution. *Computer facilities:* 600 computers available on campus for general student use. Internet access is available. *Library facilities:*

New York

Lehman College of the City University of New York (continued)
Lehman College Library plus 1 other. *General application contact:* Deputy Director of Admissions and Recruitment, 718-960-8856.

Division of Arts and Humanities
Programs in:
  art • MA, MFA
  arts and humanities • MA, MAT, MFA
  English • MA
  history • MA
  music • MAT
  Spanish • MA
  speech-language pathology and audiology • MA

Division of Education
Programs in:
  bilingual special education • MS Ed
  business education • MS Ed
  early childhood education • MS Ed
  early special education • MS Ed
  education • MA, MS Ed
  elementary education • MS Ed
  emotional handicaps • MS Ed
  English education • MS Ed
  guidance and counseling • MS Ed
  learning disabilities • MS Ed
  mathematics 7–12 • MS Ed
  mental retardation • MS Ed
  reading teacher • MS Ed
  science education • MS Ed
  social studies 7–12 • MA
  special education • MS Ed
  teaching English to speakers of other languages • MS Ed

Division of Natural and Social Sciences
Programs in:
  accounting • MS
  adult health nursing • MS
  approved preprofessional practice • MS
  biology • MA
  clinical nutrition • MS
  community nutrition • MS
  computer science • MS
  health education and promotion • MA
  health N–12 teacher • MS Ed
  mathematics • MA
  natural and social sciences • MA, MS, MS Ed, PhD
  nursing of older adults • MS
  nutrition • MS
  parent-child nursing • MS
  pediatric nurse practitioner • MS
  plant sciences • PhD
  recreation • MA, MS Ed
  recreation education • MA, MS Ed

■ LE MOYNE COLLEGE
Syracuse, NY 13214-1399
http://www.lemoyne.edu/

Independent-religious, coed, comprehensive institution. *Enrollment:* 3,403 graduate, professional, and undergraduate students; 83 full-time matriculated graduate/professional students (62 women), 417 part-time matriculated graduate/professional students (245 women). *Graduate faculty:* 25 full-time (11 women), 17 part-time/adjunct (7 women). *Computer facilities:* 325 computers available on campus for general student use. A campuswide network can be accessed from student residence rooms and from off campus. Internet access and online class registration, ECHO (campus-wide portal) are available. *Library facilities:* Noreen Reale Falcone Library. *Graduate expenses:* Tuition: full-time $8,316; part-time $462 per credit hour. Tuition and fees vary according to program.

Department of Business
Dr. Joan K. Myers, Interim Director
Program in:
  business • MBA

Department of Education
Dr. Robert P. Anderson, Interim Chair, Education Department and Director of Graduate Education
Program in:
  education • MS Ed, MST

■ LONG ISLAND UNIVERSITY, BROOKLYN CAMPUS
Brooklyn, NY 11201-8423
http://www.liu.edu/

Independent, coed, university. *Enrollment:* 8,008 graduate, professional, and undergraduate students; 1,160 full-time matriculated graduate/professional students (774 women), 1,468 part-time matriculated graduate/professional students (1,054 women). *Graduate faculty:* 322. *Computer facilities:* 345 computers available on campus for general student use. A campuswide network can be accessed from student residence rooms and from off campus. *Library facilities:* Salena Library. *Graduate expenses:* Tuition: part-time $658 per credit. *General application contact:* Edward Dettling, Director of Graduate Admissions, 718-488-1011.

Arnold and Marie Schwartz College of Pharmacy and Health Sciences
Dr. Stephen M. Gross, Dean
Programs in:
  cosmetic science • MS
  drug regulatory affairs • MS
  industrial pharmacy • MS
  pharmaceutics • PhD
  pharmaceutics and industrial pharmacy • MS, PhD
  pharmacology/toxicology • MS
  pharmacology/toxicology/medicinal chemistry • MS
  pharmacy administration • MS
  pharmacy and health sciences • MS, PhD
  pharmacy practice • MS
  social and administrative sciences • MS

Richard L. Conolly College of Liberal Arts and Sciences
Dr. David Cohen, Dean
Programs in:
  biology • MS
  chemistry • MS
  clinical psychology • PhD
  economics • MA
  English literature • MA
  history • MS
  liberal arts and sciences • MA, MS, PhD, Certificate
  media arts • MA
  political science • MA
  professional and creative writing • MA
  psychology • MA
  speech-language pathology • MS
  teaching of writing • MA
  United Nations studies • Certificate
  urban studies • MA

School of Business, Public Administration and Information Sciences
Dr. Kathleen Waldron, Dean
Programs in:
  accounting • MS
  business administration • MBA
  business, public administration and information sciences • MBA, MPA, MS
  computer science • MS
  human resources management • MS
  public administration • MPA
  taxation • MS

School of Education
Dr. David Ramirez, Dean
Programs in:
  bilingual education • MS Ed
  computers in education • MS
  counseling and development • MS, MS Ed, Certificate
  education • MS, MS Ed, Certificate
  elementary education • MS Ed

New York

leadership and policy • MS
mathematics education • MS Ed
reading • MS Ed
school psychology • MS Ed
secondary education • MS Ed
special education • MS Ed
teaching English to speakers of other languages • MS Ed

School of Health Professions
Dr. Stephen M. Gross, Dean
Programs in:
adapted physical education • MS
athletic training and sports sciences • MS
community mental health • MS
exercise physiology • MS
family health • MS
health management • MS
health professions • MS, DPT, TDPT
health sciences • MS
physical therapy • DPT, TDPT

School of Nursing
Dr. Dawn Kilts, Dean
Programs in:
adult nurse practitioner • MS, Certificate
nurse executive • MS
nursing • MS, Certificate

■ LONG ISLAND UNIVERSITY, C.W. POST CAMPUS
Brookville, NY 11548-1300
http://www.cwpost.liunet.edu/cwis/cwp/post.html

Independent, coed, comprehensive institution. *Enrollment:* 8,425 graduate, professional, and undergraduate students; 1,105 full-time matriculated graduate/professional students (796 women), 2,604 part-time matriculated graduate/professional students (1,851 women). *Graduate faculty:* 322 full-time (140 women), 740 part-time/adjunct (353 women). *Computer facilities:* 357 computers available on campus for general student use. A campuswide network can be accessed from student residence rooms and from off campus. Internet access is available. *Library facilities:* B. Davis Schwartz Memorial Library. *Graduate expenses:* Tuition: part-time $658 per credit. Tuition and fees vary according to course load, degree level and program. *General application contact:* Beth Carson, Director of Graduate Admissions, 516-299-2900.

Find an in-depth description at www.petersons.com/gradchannel.

College of Information and Computer Science
Dr. Michael E. D. Koenig, Dean
Programs in:
computer science education • MS
information and computer science • MS, PhD, Certificate
information systems • MS
management engineering • MS

Palmer School of Library and Information Science
Programs in:
archives • Certificate
information studies • PhD
library and information science • MS
records management • Certificate
school library media specialist • MS

College of Liberal Arts and Sciences
Dr. Katherine Hill-Miller, Dean
Programs in:
adolescent education/childhood education: English • MS
adolescent education: English/literacy • MS
applied behavior analysis • Advanced Certificate
applied mathematics • MS
biology • MS
biology secondary education • MS
clinical psychology • Psy D
English • MA
English secondary education • MS
environmental studies • MS
experimental psychology • MA, Advanced Certificate
history • MA
interdisciplinary studies • MA, MS
liberal arts and sciences • MA, MS, Psy D, Advanced Certificate
mathematics education • MS
mathematics for secondary school teachers • MS
political science/international studies • MA
Spanish • MA
Spanish education • MS

College of Management
Dr. Robert J. Sanator, Dean
Program in:
management • MBA, MPA, MS, Certificate

School of Business (MBA Programs)
Salvatore F. Cordo, MBA Director
Programs in:
business administration • Certificate
finance • MBA, Certificate
general business administration • MBA
international business • MBA, Certificate
logistical supply chain • Certificate
management • MBA, Certificate
management information systems • MBA
marketing • MBA

School of Professional Accountancy
Dr. Lawrence P. Kalbers, Director
Programs in:
accounting • MS
taxation • MS

School of Public Service
Programs in:
criminal justice • MS
fraud examination • MS
gerontology • Certificate
health care administration • MPA
health care administration/gerontology • MPA
nonprofit management • MPA, Certificate
public administration • MPA
public service • MPA, MS, Certificate
security administration • MS

School of Education
Dr. Robert Manheimer, Dean
Programs in:
adolescent education • MS
adolescent education: biology • MS
adolescent education: earth science • MS
adolescent education: English • MS
adolescent education: mathematics • MS
adolescent education: social studies • MS
adolescent education: Spanish • MS
art education • MS
bilingual education • MS
childhood • MS
childhood education/literacy • MS
childhood education/special education • MS
computers in education • MS
early childhood • MS
early childhood/literacy • MS
early childhood/special education • MS
education • MA, MS, MS Ed, PD
literacy • MS, MS Ed
mental health counseling • MS
music education • MS
school administration and supervision • MS Ed
school business administration • PD
school counseling • MS
school district administration • PD
special education • MS Ed
speech-language pathology • MA

School of Health Professions and Nursing
Dr. Theodora T. Grauer, Dean
Programs in:
advanced practice nursing • MS
cardiovascular perfusion • MS, Certificate
clinical laboratory management • MS
dietetic internship • Certificate
family nurse practitioner • MS, Certificate

Peterson's Graduate Schools in the U.S. 2006

New York

Long Island University, C.W. Post Campus (continued)
  health professions and nursing • MS, Certificate
  hematology • MS
  immunology • MS
  medical biology • MS
  medical chemistry • MS
  microbiology • MS
  nutrition • MS

School of Visual and Performing Arts
Lynn Croton, Dean
Programs in:
  art • MA
  art education • MS
  clinical art therapy • MA
  fine art and design • MFA
  interactive multimedia arts • MA
  music • MA
  music education • MS
  theatre • MA
  visual and performing arts • MA, MFA, MS

■ MANHATTAN COLLEGE
Riverdale, NY 10471
http://www.manhattan.edu/

Independent-religious, coed, comprehensive institution. *Enrollment:* 3,233 graduate, professional, and undergraduate students; 73 full-time matriculated graduate/professional students (33 women), 314 part-time matriculated graduate/professional students (161 women). *Graduate faculty:* 61. *Computer facilities:* 375 computers available on campus for general student use. A campuswide network can be accessed from student residence rooms and from off campus. Internet access and online class registration are available. *Library facilities:* O'Malley Library plus 1 other. *Graduate expenses:* Tuition: part-time $575 per credit. Tuition and fees vary according to program. *General application contact:* Dr. Weldon Jackson, Provost, 718-862-7303.

Find an in-depth description at www.petersons.com/gradchannel.

Graduate Division
Dr. Weldon Jackson, Provost

School of Education
Dr. Elizabeth Kosky, Director, Graduate Education Programs
Programs in:
  5 year dual childhood/special education • Diploma
  administration and supervision • MS Ed, Diploma
  counseling • MA, Diploma
  dual childhood/special education • Diploma
  special education • MS Ed, Diploma

School of Engineering
Dr. Richard H. Heist, Dean
Programs in:
  chemical engineering • MS
  civil engineering • MS
  computer engineering • MS
  electrical engineering • MS
  environmental engineering • ME, MS
  mechanical engineering • MS

■ MANHATTANVILLE COLLEGE
Purchase, NY 10577-2132
http://www.manhattanville.edu/

Independent, coed, comprehensive institution. *Computer facilities:* Computer purchase and lease plans are available. 155 computers available on campus for general student use. A campuswide network can be accessed from student residence rooms and from off campus. Internet access and online class registration are available. *Library facilities:* Manhattanville College Library. *General application contact:* Graduate Admissions, 914-694-3425.

Find an in-depth description at www.petersons.com/gradchannel.

Graduate Programs
Programs in:
  leadership and strategic management • MS
  liberal studies • MA
  management communications • MS
  organization development and human resources management • MS
  writing • MA

School of Education
Dr. Shelly Wepner, Dean of Faculty, School of Education
Programs in:
  art education • MAT
  biology • MAT
  biology and special education • MPS
  chemistry • MAT
  chemistry and special education • MPS
  childhood and early childhood education • MAT
  childhood education • MAT
  childhood education and special education • MPS
  early childhood education (birth–grade 2) • MAT
  education • MAT, MPS
  educational leadership • MPS
  English • MAT
  English and special education • MPS
  literacy • MPS
  literacy (birth–grade 6) • MPS
  literacy (birth–grade 6) and special education (grades 1–6) • MPS
  literacy and special education • MPS
  math • MAT
  math and special education • MPS
  math, science and technology • MAT
  music education • MAT
  second language • MAT
  social studies • MAT
  social studies and special education • MPS
  special education • MPS
  special education (birth–grade 2) • MPS
  special education (birth–grade 6) • MPS
  teaching English as a second language • MPS

■ MARIST COLLEGE
Poughkeepsie, NY 12601-1387
http://www.marist.edu/

Independent, coed, comprehensive institution. *Enrollment:* 5,616 graduate, professional, and undergraduate students; 127 full-time matriculated graduate/professional students (78 women), 736 part-time matriculated graduate/professional students (370 women). *Graduate faculty:* 43 full-time (16 women), 34 part-time/adjunct (12 women). *Computer facilities:* Computer purchase and lease plans are available. 501 computers available on campus for general student use. A campuswide network can be accessed from student residence rooms and from off campus. Internet access is available. *Library facilities:* Marist College Library. *Graduate expenses:* Tuition: full-time $9,540; part-time $530 per credit. Required fees: $30 per semester. *General application contact:* Dr. Dennis DeLong, Assistant Associate Vice President/Dean, Graduate and Continuing Education, 845-575-3000 Ext. 2892.

Graduate Programs
Dr. Artin Arslanian, Academic Vice President

School of Computer Science and Mathematics
Dr. Roger Norton, Dean
Program in:
  computer science • MS

School of Management
Dr. Andres Fortino, Dean
Programs in:
  business administration • MBA, PGC
  management • MBA, MPA, Certificate, PGC
  public administration • MPA, Certificate

New York

School of Social and Behavioral Sciences
Margaret Calista, Dean
Programs in:
 counseling psychology • MA
 education psychology • MA
 learning and technology • Adv C
 school psychology • MA, Adv C

Program in Organizational Communication and Leadership
Dr. Mary S. Alexander, Director
Program in:
 organizational communication and leadership • MA

■ MERCY COLLEGE
Dobbs Ferry, NY 10522-1189
http://www.mercynet.edu/

Independent, coed, comprehensive institution. CGS member. *Computer facilities:* 138 computers available on campus for general student use. A campuswide network can be accessed from off campus. Internet access is available. *Library facilities:* Mercy College Library. *General application contact:* Director of Admissions, 914-674-7600.

Find an in-depth description at www.petersons.com/gradchannel.

Division of Business and Accounting
Dr. Tom Milton, Chairperson
Programs in:
 banking • MS
 business administration • MBA
 direct marketing • MS
 finance • MBA
 human resource management • MS
 international business • MBA
 internet business systems • MS
 management • MBA
 marketing • MBA
 organizational leadership • MS
 securities • MS

Division of Education
Dr. William Prattella, Chairperson
Programs in:
 administration and supervision • PD
 education • MS
 learning technology • MS
 reading education • MS
 school administration and supervision • MS
 teaching English to speakers of other languages • MS
 urban education • MS

Division of Health Professions
Dr. Richard MacIntyre, Head
Programs in:
 acupuncture and Oriental medicine • MPS
 adult nurse practitioner • MS
 communication disorders • MS
 family clinical nurse specialist • MS
 nursing • MS
 occupational therapy • MS
 physical therapy • MS
 physician assistant • MPS

Division of Literature, Language, and Communication
Dr. Joel Feimer, Program Director
Program in:
 English literature • MA

Division of Social and Behavioral Sciences
Diana Juettner, Chair
Programs in:
 alcohol and substance abuse counseling • AC
 family counseling • AC
 health services management • MPA, MS
 psychology • MS
 retirement counseling • AC
 school counseling • MS
 school psychology • MS

■ MOLLOY COLLEGE
Rockville Centre, NY 11571-5002
http://www.molloy.edu/

Independent, coed, comprehensive institution. *Enrollment:* 3,007 graduate, professional, and undergraduate students; 295 part-time matriculated graduate/professional students (282 women). *Graduate faculty:* 16 full-time (all women), 2 part-time/adjunct (both women). *Computer facilities:* 246 computers available on campus for general student use. A campuswide network can be accessed. Internet access is available. *Library facilities:* James Edward Tobin Library. *Graduate expenses:* Tuition: part-time $555 per credit. Required fees: $200 per semester. One-time fee: $55 part-time. *General application contact:* Dr. Freida Pemberton, Director, Graduate Program, 516-678-5000 Ext. 6820.

Department of Nursing
Dr. Freida Pemberton, Director, Graduate Nursing Program
Programs in:
 adult nurse practitioner • Advanced Certificate
 clinical nurse specialist: adult health • Advanced Certificate
 family nurse practitioner • Advanced Certificate
 nurse practitioner psychiatry • Advanced Certificate
 nursing • MS
 nursing administration • Advanced Certificate
 nursing administration and infomatics • Advanced Certificate
 nursing education • Advanced Certificate
 nursing informatics • Advanced Certificate
 pediatric nurse practitioner • Advanced Certificate

■ MOUNT SAINT MARY COLLEGE
Newburgh, NY 12550-3494
http://www.msmc.edu/

Independent, coed, comprehensive institution. *Enrollment:* 2,606 graduate, professional, and undergraduate students; 108 full-time matriculated graduate/professional students (81 women), 351 part-time matriculated graduate/professional students (288 women). *Graduate faculty:* 18 full-time (12 women), 26 part-time/adjunct (21 women). *Computer facilities:* 286 computers available on campus for general student use. A campuswide network can be accessed from student residence rooms and from off campus. Internet access and online class registration, intranet are available. *Library facilities:* Curtin Memorial Library plus 1 other. *Graduate expenses:* Tuition: full-time $8,910; part-time $495 per credit. *General application contact:* Graduate Coordinator, 845-561-0800.

Division of Business
David R. Rant, Coordinator
Programs in:
 business • MBA
 financial planning • MBA

Division of Education
Dr. Lucy DiPaola, Chairperson
Programs in:
 adolescence and special education • MS Ed
 adolescence education • MS Ed
 childhood and special education • MS Ed
 childhood education • MS Ed
 literacy and special education • MS Ed
 literacy/childhood • MS Ed
 middle school (5–6) • MS Ed
 middle school (7–9) • MS Ed
 special education (1–6) • MS Ed
 special education (7–12) • MS Ed

Division of Nursing
Sr. Leona DeBoer, Coordinator
Programs in:
 adult nurse practitioner • MS
 clinical nurse specialist-adult health • MS

New York

■ NAZARETH COLLEGE OF ROCHESTER
Rochester, NY 14618-3790
http://www.naz.edu/

Independent, coed, comprehensive institution. *Enrollment:* 3,062 graduate, professional, and undergraduate students; 336 full-time matriculated graduate/professional students (287 women), 729 part-time matriculated graduate/professional students (574 women). *Graduate faculty:* 93. *Computer facilities:* 150 computers available on campus for general student use. A campuswide network can be accessed from student residence rooms and from off campus. Internet access is available. *Library facilities:* Lorette Wilmot Library. *Graduate expenses:* Tuition: part-time $498 per credit hour. *General application contact:* Dr. Kay F. Marshman, Associate Vice President for Graduate Studies, 585-389-2815.

Graduate Studies
Dr. Kay F. Marshman, Associate Vice President for Graduate Studies
Programs in:
  art education • MS Ed
  art therapy • MS
  business education • MS Ed
  communication sciences and disorders • MS
  computer education • MS Ed
  early childhood education • MS Ed
  educational technology • MS Ed
  elementary education • MS Ed
  general secondary education • MS Ed
  gerontological nurse practitioner • MS
  inclusive education-adolescence level • MS Ed
  inclusive education-childhood level • MS Ed
  inclusive education-early childhood level • MS Ed
  liberal studies • MA
  literacy education • MS Ed
  management • MS
  music education • MS Ed
  social work • MSW
  special education • MS Ed
  teaching English to speakers of other languages • MS Ed

■ NEW SCHOOL UNIVERSITY
New York, NY 10011-8603
http://www.newschool.edu/

Independent, coed, university. *Graduate faculty:* 87 full-time (31 women), 410 part-time/adjunct (154 women). *Graduate expenses:* Tuition: part-time $1,140 per credit. Required fees: $115 per term. *General application contact:* Christy Kalan, Director of Enrollment Management, 212-229-5154.

Find an in-depth description at www.petersons.com/gradchannel.

Actors Studio Drama School
Sam Schacht, Dean
Programs in:
  acting • MFA
  directing • MFA
  playwriting • MFA

Graduate Faculty of Political and Social Science
Dr. Benjamin Lee, Dean
Programs in:
  anthropology • MA, DS Sc, PhD
  clinical psychology • PhD
  economics • MA, DS Sc, PhD
  general psychology • MA, PhD
  historical studies • MA, PhD
  liberal studies • MA
  philosophy • MA, DS Sc, PhD
  political and social science • MA, DS Sc, PhD
  political science • MA, DS Sc, PhD
  sociology • MA, DS Sc, PhD

Mannes College of Music
Joel Lester, Dean
Program in:
  music performance • MM, PD

New School
Dr. Ann Louise Shapiro, Dean
Programs in:
  communication theory • MA
  creative writing • MFA
  global management, trade, and finance • MA, MS
  international development • MA, MS
  international media and communication • MA, MS
  international politics and diplomacy • MA, MS
  media studies • MA
  service, civic, and non-profit management • MA, MS

Parsons School of Design
H. Randolph Swearer, Dean
Programs in:
  architecture • M Arch
  design • M Arch, MA, MFA, MS Ed
  design and technology • MFA
  history of decorative arts • MA
  lighting design • MFA
  painting • MFA
  photography and related technologies • MFA
  sculpture • MFA

Robert J. Milano Graduate School of Management and Urban Policy
Dr. Edward J. Blakely, Dean
Programs in:
  health services management and policy • MS
  human resources management • MS, Adv C
  management and urban policy • MS, PhD, Adv C
  medical group practice management • Adv C
  nonprofit management • MS
  organizational change management • MS
  public and urban policy • PhD
  urban policy analysis and management • MS

■ NEW YORK INSTITUTE OF TECHNOLOGY
Old Westbury, NY 11568-8000
http://www.nyit.edu/

Independent, coed, university. CGS member. *Enrollment:* 9,387 graduate, professional, and undergraduate students; 2,128 full-time matriculated graduate/professional students (1,061 women), 1,354 part-time matriculated graduate/professional students (654 women). *Graduate faculty:* 255 full-time (75 women), 684 part-time/adjunct (247 women). *Computer facilities:* 815 computers available on campus for general student use. A campuswide network can be accessed from student residence rooms and from off campus. Internet access, e-mail are available. *Library facilities:* George and Gertrude Wisser Memorial Library plus 4 others. *Graduate expenses:* Tuition: part-time $598 per credit. One-time fee: $50 part-time. *General application contact:* Jacquelyn Nealon, Dean of Admissions and Financial Aid, 516-686-7925.

Ellis College
Dr. Geoffrey M. Cox, Vice President of Academic Affairs
Programs in:
  accounting and information systems • MBA
  e-commerce • MBA
  finance • MBA
  global management • MBA
  healthcare administration • MBA
  human resources management • MBA
  leadership • MBA
  management of information systems • MBA
  management of technology • MBA
  marketing • MBA
  professional accounting • MBA

project management • MBA
risk management • MBA
strategy and economics • MBA

Graduate Division
Dr. Alexandra W. Logue, Vice President for Academic Affairs

School of Allied Health and Life Sciences
Dr. Barbara Ross-Lee, Dean
Programs in:
 allied health and life sciences • MPS, MS, DPT
 clinical nutrition • MS
 human relations • MPS
 occupational therapy • MS
 physical therapy • MS, DPT

School of Architecture
Judith DiMaio, Dean
Program in:
 urban and regional design • M Arch

School of Arts, Sciences, and Communication
Dr. Roger Yu, Dean
Programs in:
 arts, sciences, and communication • MA
 communication arts • MA

School of Education and Professional Services
Dr. Jacqueline Kress, Dean
Programs in:
 distance learning • Advanced Certificate
 district leadership and technology • Professional Diploma
 education and professional services • MS, Advanced Certificate, Professional Diploma
 elementary education • MS
 instructional technology • MS
 mental health counseling and school counseling • MS
 multimedia • Advanced Certificate
 school counseling • MS
 school leadership and technology • Professional Diploma

School of Engineering and Technology
Dr. Heskia Heskiaoff, Dean
Programs in:
 computer science • MS
 electrical engineering and computer engineering • MS
 energy management • MS
 energy technology • Advanced Certificate
 engineering and technology • MS, Advanced Certificate
 environmental management • Advanced Certificate
 environmental technology • MS
 facilities management • Advanced Certificate

School of Management
Dr. David R. Decker, Dean
Programs in:
 accounting • Advanced Certificate
 business administration • MBA
 finance • Advanced Certificate
 human resources administration • Advanced Certificate
 human resources management and labor relations • MS
 international business • Advanced Certificate
 labor relations • Advanced Certificate
 management • MBA, MS, Advanced Certificate
 management of information systems • Advanced Certificate
 marketing • Advanced Certificate

New York College of Osteopathic Medicine
Dr. Barbara Ross-Lee, Dean
Program in:
 osteopathic medicine • DO

■ NEW YORK UNIVERSITY
New York, NY 10012-1019
http://www.nyu.edu/

Independent, coed, university. CGS member. *Enrollment:* 38,188 graduate, professional, and undergraduate students; 10,761 full-time matriculated graduate/professional students (6,139 women), 7,275 part-time matriculated graduate/professional students (4,227 women). *Graduate faculty:* 3,083 full-time (1,137 women), 2,519 part-time/adjunct. *Computer facilities:* Computer purchase and lease plans are available. 1,400 computers available on campus for general student use. A campuswide network can be accessed from student residence rooms and from off campus. Internet access and online class registration are available. *Library facilities:* Elmer H. Bobst Library plus 11 others. *Graduate expenses:* Tuition: full-time $22,056; part-time $919 per credit. Required fees: $1,664; $49 per credit. Tuition and fees vary according to course load and program. *General application contact:* New York University Information, 212-998-1212.

Find an in-depth description at www.petersons.com/gradchannel.

College of Dentistry
Dr. Michael C. Alfano, Dean
Programs in:
 clinical research • MS
 dentistry • DDS, MS, Advanced Certificate
 endodontics • Advanced Certificate
 general dentistry • Advanced Certificate
 oral and maxillofacial surgery • Advanced Certificate
 orthodontics • Advanced Certificate
 pediatric dentistry • Advanced Certificate
 periodontics • Advanced Certificate
 prosthodontics • Advanced Certificate
 prosthodontics (implantology) • Advanced Certificate

Gallatin School of Individualized Study
Dr. E. Frances White, Dean
Program in:
 individualized study • MA

Graduate School of Arts and Science
Catharine R. Stimpson, Dean
Programs in:
 Africana studies • MA
 American studies • MA, PhD
 anthropology • MA, PhD
 anthropology and French studies • PhD
 applied economic analysis • Advanced Certificate
 archival management and historical editing • Advanced Certificate
 arts and science • MA, MFA, MS, PhD, Advanced Certificate
 biochemistry • MS, PhD
 biology • PhD
 biomaterials • MS
 biomedical journalism • MS
 cell biology • MS, PhD
 chemistry • MS, PhD
 classics • MA, PhD
 clinical psychology • PhD
 cognition and perception • PhD
 community psychology • PhD
 comparative literature • MA, PhD
 creative writing • MFA
 early music performance • Advanced Certificate
 economics • MA, PhD
 English and American literature • MA, PhD
 French studies and politics • PhD
 French studies and sociology • PhD
 French studies/history • PhD
 French studies/journalism • MA
 general biology • MS
 general psychology • MA
 Germanic languages and literatures • MA, PhD
 Hebrew and Judaic studies • MA, PhD
 Hebrew and Judaic studies/history • PhD
 Hebrew and Judaic studies/museum studies • MA
 history • MA, PhD
 humanities and social thought • MA

New York

New York University (continued)
- industrial/organizational psychology • MA, PhD
- international politics and international business • MA
- Italian • MA, PhD
- Italian studies • MA
- journalism • MA
- journalism (cultural reporting and criticism) • MA
- Latin American and Caribbean studies • MA
- Latin American and Caribbean studies/journalism • MA
- linguistics • MA, PhD
- microbiology • MS, PhD
- Middle Eastern studies/history • PhD
- museum studies • Advanced Certificate
- music (ethnomusicology) • MA, PhD
- music (theory, composition and musicology) • MA, PhD
- Near Eastern studies • MA
- Near Eastern Studies/history • MA
- Near Eastern studies/journalism • MA
- parasitology • MS, PhD
- pathology • MS, PhD
- pharmacology • MS, PhD
- philosophy • MA, PhD
- physics • MS, PhD
- physiology and neuroscience • MS, PhD
- poetics and theory • Advanced Certificate
- politics • MA, PhD
- politics (Near Eastern studies) • PhD
- Portuguese • MA, PhD
- psychotherapy and psychoanalysis • Advanced Certificate
- public history • MA, Advanced Certificate
- religion • Advanced Certificate
- religious studies • MA
- Romance languages and literatures • MA
- Russian literature • MA
- science and environmental reporting • Advanced Certificate
- Slavic literature • MA
- social theory • Advanced Certificate
- social/personality psychology • PhD
- sociology • MA, PhD
- Spanish • MA, PhD
- world history • MA

Center for European Studies
Martin Schain, Director
Program in:
- European studies • MA

Center for French Civilization and Culture
Judith Miller, Chair
Programs in:
- French • PhD
- French civilization and culture • MA, PhD, Advanced Certificate
- French language and civilization • MA
- French literature • MA
- French studies • MA, PhD, Advanced Certificate
- French studies and anthropology • PhD
- French studies and history • PhD
- French studies and journalism • MA
- French studies and politics • PhD
- French studies and sociology • PhD
- Romance languages and literatures • MA

Center for Latin American and Caribbean Studies
George Yudice, Director
Programs in:
- Latin American and Caribbean studies • MA
- Latin American and Caribbean studies (museum studies) • MA
- Latin American and Caribbean studies/journalism • MA

Center for Neural Science
Daniel Sanes, Chairman
Program in:
- neural science • PhD

Courant Institute of Mathematical Sciences
Charles Newman, Associate Director
Programs in:
- atmosphere-ocean science and mathematics • PhD
- computer science • MS, PhD
- information systems • MS
- mathematics • MS, PhD
- mathematics and statistics/operations research • MS
- mathematics in finance • MS
- scientific computing • MS

Hagop Kevorkian Center for Near Eastern Studies
Timothy Mitchell, Chair
Programs in:
- Middle Eastern studies • MA, PhD
- Middle Eastern studies/history • PhD
- Near Eastern studies • MA
- Near Eastern studies (museum studies) • MA
- Near Eastern studies/journalism • MA

Institute for Law and Society
Lewis Kornhauser, Director
Program in:
- law and society • MA, PhD

Institute of Fine Arts
Mariet Westermann, Chair
Programs in:
- classical art and archaeology • PhD
- history of art and archaeology • MA, PhD
- Near Eastern art and archaeology • PhD

Nelson Institute of Environmental Medicine
Dr. Max Costa, Director
Program in:
- environmental health sciences • MS, PhD

Leonard N. Stern School of Business
Thomas F. Cooley, Dean
Programs in:
- accounting • MBA, PhD
- business • MBA, PhD, APC
- economics • MBA, PhD
- finance • MBA, PhD
- information systems • MBA, PhD
- management • PhD
- management and organizations • MBA, APC
- marketing • MBA, PhD
- operations management • MBA, PhD
- statistics • MBA, PhD

Robert F. Wagner Graduate School of Public Service
Prof. Ellen Schall, Dean
Programs in:
- advanced management program for clinicians • MS
- financial management • MPA
- health policy analysis • MPA
- health services management • MPA
- housing • Advanced Certificate
- infrastructure management • MS
- international public service management • MS
- public administration • PhD
- public and nonprofit management and policy • MPA, Advanced Certificate
- public economics • Advanced Certificate
- public service • MPA, MS, MUP, PhD, Advanced Certificate
- quantitative analysis and computer applications for policy and planning • Advanced Certificate
- urban planning • MUP

School of Continuing and Professional Studies
Dr. David F. Finney, Dean
Programs in:
- continuing and professional studies • MS, Advanced Certificate
- energy policy/environment/oil • MS
- global studies • MS
- human rights and humanitarian assistance • MS
- international affairs • MS
- international law, dispute settlement, and institutions • MS
- private sector: international business, economics, and development • MS

New York

Center for Hospitality, Tourism and Travel Administration
Dr. Lalia Rach, Associate Dean
Programs in:
  customer relationship management • Advanced Certificate
  hospitality industry studies • MS, Advanced Certificate
  sports business • MS, Advanced Certificate
  tourism and travel management • MS, Advanced Certificate

Center for Instructional Design and Online Learning
Robert Manney, Director
Program in:
  instructional design • MS

Real Estate Institute
D. Kenneth Patton, Associate Dean
Programs in:
  construction management • MS, Advanced Certificate
  real estate • Advanced Certificate

School of Law
Richard L. Revesz, Dean
Programs in:
  law • JD, LL M, JSD
  law and business • Advanced Certificate
  tax • Advanced Certificate

School of Medicine
Dr. Robert M. Glickman, Dean
Program in:
  medicine • MD, PhD

Sackler Institute of Graduate Biomedical Sciences
Dr. Joel D. Oppenheim, Senior Associate Dean for Graduate Studies
Programs in:
  biochemistry • PhD
  biomedical sciences • PhD
  cell biology • PhD
  immunology • PhD
  medical and molecular parasitology • PhD
  microbiology • PhD
  molecular oncology • PhD
  neuroscience • PhD
  pathology • PhD
  pharmacology • PhD
  physiology • PhD
  structural biology • PhD

School of Social Work
Suzanne England, Dean
Program in:
  social work • MSW, PhD

The Steinhardt School of Education
Dr. Mary Brabeck, Dean
Programs in:
  administration and management of technology and industry oriented programs • Ed D, PhD, Advanced Certificate
  adolescence special education • MA
  advanced occupational therapy • MA
  applied psychology • MA, PhD, Psy D, Advanced Certificate
  art education • MA, Ed D, PhD
  art therapy • MA
  arts and humanities education • MA, PhD
  bilingual education • MA, PhD, Advanced Certificate
  biology and general science: intermediate • MA
  biology and general science: secondary • MA
  biology grades 7-12 • MA
  business education • MA, Ed D, PhD, Advanced Certificate
  chemistry and general science: intermediate • MA
  chemistry and general science: secondary • MA
  chemistry grades 7-12 • MA
  childhood and bilingual special education • MA
  childhood education • MA, PhD, Advanced Certificate
  childhood special education • MA
  community health education • Ed D, PhD
  community public health • MPH, Ed D, PhD
  costume studies • MA
  counseling and guidance • MA, PhD, Advanced Certificate
  counseling psychology • PhD
  counselor education • MA, PhD, Advanced Certificate
  dance education • MA, Ed D, PhD
  drama therapy • MA
  early childhood and elementary education • MA, PhD, Advanced Certificate
  early childhood education • MA, PhD, Advanced Certificate
  early childhood special education • MA
  education • MA, MFA, MM, MPH, MS, DA, DPT, Ed D, PhD, Psy D, Advanced Certificate
  education and Jewish studies • PhD
  educational administration • MA, Ed D, PhD, Advanced Certificate
  educational communication and technology • MA, Ed D, PhD, Advanced Certificate
  educational psychology • MA
  educational theatre • MA, Ed D, PhD, Advanced Certificate
  educational theatre in colleges and communities • MA
  educational theatre with English 7-12 • MA
  English education • MA, PhD, Advanced Certificate
  environmental conservation education • MA
  food management • MA
  food studies • MA
  food studies and food management • MA, PhD
  for-profit sector • MA
  foreign language education • MA, Advanced Certificate
  foreign language education/TESOL • MA
  graphic communications management and technology • MA, Ed D, PhD, Advanced Certificate
  higher education • MA, Ed D, PhD
  history of education • MA, PhD
  international community health education • Ed D, PhD
  international education • MA, PhD, Advanced Certificate
  international public health • MPH
  literacy • MA
  literacy 5-12 • MA
  literacy 8-6 • MA
  mathematics education • MA, PhD
  media ecology • MA, PhD
  middle childhood special education • MA
  multilingual/multicultural studies • MA, PhD, Advanced Certificate
  music business • MA
  music education • MA, Ed D, PhD, Advanced Certificate
  music performance and composition • MA, PhD
  music technology • MM
  music therapy • MA, DA
  nutrition and dietetics • MS, PhD
  occupational therapy • MA
  performing arts administration • MA
  philosophy of education • MA, PhD
  physical therapists pathokinesiology • MA
  physical therapy • DPT
  physics and general science: intermediate • MA
  physics and general science: secondary • MA
  physics grades 7-12 • MA
  practicing physical therapist • DPT
  professional child/school psychology • Psy D
  psychological development • PhD
  public health nutrition • MPH
  research in occupational therapy • PhD
  research in physical therapy • PhD
  school psychologist • Advanced Certificate
  school psychology • PhD
  science education • MA
  severe disabilities • Advanced Certificate
  social studies • MA
  social studies education • MA
  sociology of education • MA, PhD

Peterson's Graduate Schools in the U.S. 2006

New York

New York University (continued)
  special education • MA, Advanced Certificate
  special education learning consultant • Advanced Certificate
  speech and interpersonal communication • MA, Advanced Certificate
  speech-language pathology and audiology • MA, PhD
  student personnel administration in higher education • MA
  studio art • MA, MFA
  teachers of business subjects in higher education • MA, Ed D, PhD, Advanced Certificate
  teaching and learning • Ed D, PhD
  teaching educational theatre, all grades • MA
  teaching English to speakers of other languages • MA, PhD, Advanced Certificate
  visual arts administration • MA
  visual culture • MA
  workplace learning • Advanced Certificate

Division of Nursing
Dr. Terry Fulmer, Chairperson
Programs in:
  advance practice nursing: adult primary care nurse practitioner • MA
  advanced practice nursing: adult acute care nurse practitioner • MA, Advanced Certificate
  advanced practice nursing: adult acute care/home health nursing • Advanced Certificate
  advanced practice nursing: adult care/home health nursing • Advanced Certificate
  advanced practice nursing: adult primary care nurse practitioner • Advanced Certificate
  advanced practice nursing: adult primary care/geriatrics • MA, Advanced Certificate
  advanced practice nursing: children with special needs • Advanced Certificate
  advanced practice nursing: geriatrics • MA, Advanced Certificate
  advanced practice nursing: holistic nursing • MA, Advanced Certificate
  advanced practice nursing: home health nursing • Advanced Certificate
  advanced practice nursing: mental health • MA, Advanced Certificate
  advanced practice nursing: pediatrics • MA, Advanced Certificate
  advanced practice nursing: pediatrics/children with special needs • MA
  midwifery • MA, Advanced Certificate
  nursing • MA, PhD, Advanced Certificate
  nursing administration • MA, Advanced Certificate
  nursing informatics • MA, Advanced Certificate
  palliative care • MA, Advanced Certificate
  research and theory development in nursing science • PhD
  teaching of nursing • MA

Tisch School of the Arts
Mary Schmidt Campbell, Dean
Programs in:
  acting • MFA
  arts • MA, MFA, MPS, PhD
  cinema studies • MA, PhD
  dance • MFA
  design • MFA
  dramatic writing • MFA
  film and television • MFA
  interactive telecommunications • MPS
  moving image archiving and preservation • MA
  musical theatre writing • MFA
  performance studies • MA, PhD

■ **NIAGARA UNIVERSITY**
Niagara Falls, Niagara University, NY 14109
http://www.niagara.edu/

Independent-religious, coed, comprehensive institution. *Enrollment:* 3,548 graduate, professional, and undergraduate students; 506 full-time matriculated graduate/professional students (329 women), 308 part-time matriculated graduate/professional students (212 women). *Graduate faculty:* 27 full-time (10 women), 24 part-time/adjunct (11 women). *Computer facilities:* 150 computers available on campus for general student use. A campuswide network can be accessed from student residence rooms. Internet access is available. *Library facilities:* Our Lady of Angels Library. *Graduate expenses:* Tuition: full-time $3,780; part-time $420 per credit hour. Required fees: $50; $25 per semester. Tuition and fees vary according to program. *General application contact:* John Hammill, Director of Graduate Admissions, 716-286-8769.

Graduate Division of Arts and Sciences
Dr. Nancy McGlen, Dean
Programs in:
  arts and sciences • MS
  criminal justice administration • MS

Graduate Division of Business Administration
Dr. Philip Scherer, Director
Programs in:
  business • MBA
  commerce • MBA

Graduate Division of Education
Dr. Debra A. Colley, Dean
Programs in:
  administration and supervision • MS Ed, Certificate
  biology • MAT
  elementary education • MS Ed
  foundations and teaching • MA, MS Ed
  inclusive education • MS Ed
  literacy instruction • MS Ed
  mental health counseling • MS Ed, Certificate
  school business administration • MS Ed, Certificate
  school counseling • MS Ed, Certificate
  school psychology • MS
  secondary education • MS Ed
  teacher education • MS Ed

■ **NYACK COLLEGE**
Nyack, NY 10960-3698
http://www.nyackcollege.edu/

Independent-religious, coed, comprehensive institution. *Enrollment:* 2,814 graduate, professional, and undergraduate students; 33 full-time matriculated graduate/professional students (18 women), 4 part-time matriculated graduate/professional students (3 women). *Graduate faculty:* 83 full-time, 101 part-time/adjunct. *Computer facilities:* 180 computers available on campus for general student use. A campuswide network can be accessed. Internet access is available. *Library facilities:* The Bailey Library plus 2 others. *Graduate expenses:* Tuition: part-time $625 per credit. *General application contact:* Bethany Ilsley, Director of Admissions, 800-33-NYACK.

Graduate and Professional Programs

School of Business
George Stratis, Dean of the School of Business
Programs in:
  accounting • MBA
  business administration • MBA

School of Education
Bennett Schepens, Dean of the School of Education
Program in:
  inclusive education • MSE

■ **PACE UNIVERSITY**
New York, NY 10038
http://www.pace.edu/

Independent, coed, university. CGS member. *Enrollment:* 13,962 graduate, professional, and undergraduate students; 594 full-time matriculated graduate/

New York

professional students (345 women), 2,304 part-time matriculated graduate/professional students (1,254 women). *Graduate faculty:* 189 full-time, 139 part-time/adjunct. *Computer facilities:* 234 computers available on campus for general student use. A campuswide network can be accessed from student residence rooms and from off campus. *Library facilities:* Henry Birnbaum Library plus 3 others. *Graduate expenses:* Tuition: part-time $710 per credit. Tuition and fees vary according to course load and program. *General application contact:* Alan Young, Director of Admissions, 212-346-1652.

Find an in-depth description at www.petersons.com/gradchannel.

Dyson College of Arts and Sciences
Dr. Michael Roberts, Acting Dean
Programs in:
 arts and sciences • MA, MS, MS Ed, Psy D
 forensic science • MS
 psychology • MA
 publishing • MS
 school psychology • MS Ed
 school-clinical child psychology • Psy D
 school-community psychology • MA, Psy D

Lienhard School of Nursing
Dr. Harriet Feldman, Dean
Program in:
 nursing • MS, Advanced Certificate

Lubin School of Business
Dr. Arthur Centonze, Dean
Programs in:
 banking and finance • MBA
 business • MBA, MS, DPS, APC
 corporate economic planning • MBA
 corporate financial management • MBA
 economics • MS
 financial economics • MBA
 financial management • MBA
 health systems management • MBA
 information systems • MBA
 international business • MBA
 international economics • MBA
 investment management • MBA, MS
 management • MBA
 management science • MBA
 managerial accounting • MBA
 marketing management • MBA
 marketing research • MBA
 operations management • MBA
 professional studies • DPS
 public accounting • MBA, MS
 taxation • MBA, MS

School of Computer Science and Information Systems
Dr. Susan Merritt, Dean
Programs in:
 computer communications and networks • Certificate
 computer science • MS
 computing studies • DPS
 information systems • MS
 object-oriented programming • Certificate
 telecommunications • MS, Certificate

School of Education
Dr. Janet McDonald, Dean
Programs in:
 administration and supervision • MS Ed
 curriculum and instruction • MS
 education • MST
 school business management • Certificate

■ PACE UNIVERSITY, PLEASANTVILLE/BRIARCLIFF CAMPUS
Pleasantville, NY 10570
http://www.pace.edu/

Independent, coed, comprehensive institution. *Enrollment:* 14 full-time matriculated graduate/professional students (12 women), 87 part-time matriculated graduate/professional students (81 women). *Graduate faculty:* 9 full-time (all women), 21 part-time/adjunct (14 women). *Computer facilities:* 128 computers available on campus for general student use. A campuswide network can be accessed from student residence rooms and from off campus. *Library facilities:* Mortola Library plus 3 others. *Graduate expenses:* Tuition: part-time $710 per credit. Tuition and fees vary according to course load and program. *General application contact:* Joanna Broda, Director of Admissions, 914-422-4283.

Lienhard School of Nursing
Dr. Harriet Feldman, Dean
Program in:
 nursing • MS, Advanced Certificate

■ PACE UNIVERSITY, WHITE PLAINS CAMPUS
White Plains, NY 10606
http://www.pace.edu/

Independent, coed, graduate-only institution. *Graduate faculty:* 77 full-time, 83 part-time/adjunct. *Computer facilities:* 68 computers available on campus for general student use. A campuswide network can be accessed from student residence rooms and from off campus. Internet access is available. *Graduate expenses:* Tuition: part-time $710 per credit. Tuition and fees vary according to course load and program. *General application contact:* Joanna Broda, Director of Admissions, 914-422-4283.

Dyson College of Arts and Sciences
Dr. Michael Roberts, Acting Dean
Programs in:
 arts and sciences • MPA, MS
 counseling-substance abuse • MS
 environmental science • MS
 government management • MPA
 health care administration • MPA
 nonprofit management • MPA

Lubin School of Business
Dr. Arthur Centonze, Dean
Programs in:
 banking and finance • MBA
 business • MBA, MS, APC
 corporate economic planning • MBA
 corporate financial management • MBA
 economics • MS
 financial economics • MBA
 financial management • MBA
 health systems management • MBA
 information systems • MBA
 international business • MBA
 international economics • MBA
 investment management • MBA, MS
 management • MBA
 management science • MBA, MS
 managerial accounting • MBA
 marketing management • MBA
 marketing research • MBA
 operations management • MBA
 personal financial planning • MS
 public accounting • MBA, MS
 taxation • MBA, MS

School of Computer Science and Information Systems
Dr. Susan Merritt, Dean
Programs in:
 computer communications and networks • Certificate
 computer science • MS
 computing studies • DPS
 information systems • MS
 object-oriented programming • Certificate
 telecommunications • MS, Certificate

School of Education
Dr. Janet McDonald, Dean
Programs in:
 administration and supervision • MS Ed
 curriculum and instruction • MS
 education • MST
 school business management • Certificate

New York

Pace University, White Plains Campus (continued)
School of Law
David S. Cohen, Dean
Programs in:
  comparative legal studies • LL M
  environmental law • LL M, SJD
  law • JD

■ POLYTECHNIC UNIVERSITY, BROOKLYN CAMPUS
Brooklyn, NY 11201-2990
http://www.poly.edu/

Independent, coed, university. CGS member. *Enrollment:* 2,846 graduate, professional, and undergraduate students; 493 full-time matriculated graduate/professional students (117 women), 484 part-time matriculated graduate/professional students (108 women). *Graduate faculty:* 71 full-time (11 women), 71 part-time/adjunct (8 women). *Computer facilities:* Computer purchase and lease plans are available. 1,330 computers available on campus for general student use. A campuswide network can be accessed from student residence rooms and from off campus. Internet access is available. *Library facilities:* Bern Dibner Library plus 1 other. *Graduate expenses:* Tuition: full-time $16,416; part-time $855 per credit. Required fees: $320 per term. *General application contact:* Anthea Jeffrey, Graduate Admissions, 718-260-3200.

Find an in-depth description at www.petersons.com/gradchannel.

Department of Applied Mathematics
Dr. Erwin Lutwak, Head
Program in:
  mathematics • MS, PhD

Department of Chemical Engineering, Chemistry and Materials Science
Dr. Jovan Mijovic, Head
Programs in:
  biomedical engineering • MS
  chemical engineering • MS, PhD
  chemistry • MS
  informatics in chemistry and biology • MS
  materials chemistry • PhD
  polymer science and engineering • MS

Department of Civil and Environmental Engineering
Dr. Roger Roess, Head
Programs in:
  civil engineering • MS, PhD
  environmental engineering • MS
  environmental health science • MS
  transportation management • MS
  transportation planning and engineering • MS

Department of Computer and Information Science
Dr. Stuart Steele, Head
Program in:
  computer science • MS, PhD

Department of Electrical Engineering
Dr. Henry Bertoni, Head
Programs in:
  computer engineering • MS
  electrical engineering • MS, PhD
  electrophysics • MS
  systems engineering • MS
  telecommunication networks • MS
  wireless communications • MS

Department of Humanities and Social Sciences
Dr. Harold Sjursen, Head
Programs in:
  environment behavior studies • MS
  history of science • MS
  humanities • MS
  social sciences • MS
  specialized journalism • MS
  technical and professional communication • MS

Department of Management
Dr. Barry Blecherman, Associate Dean
Programs in:
  financial engineering • MS
  management • MS
  management of technology • MS
  operations management • MS
  organizational behavior • MS
  telecommunications and information management • MS

Department of Mechanical, Aerospace and Manufacturing Engineering
Dr. Said Nourbaksh, Head
Programs in:
  industrial engineering • MS
  manufacturing engineering • MS
  materials science • MS
  mechanical engineering • MS, PhD

Program in Physics
Dr. Edward Wolf, Head
Program in:
  physics • MS, PhD

■ POLYTECHNIC UNIVERSITY, WESTCHESTER GRADUATE CENTER
Hawthorne, NY 10532-1507
http://west.poly.edu/~www/

Independent, coed, graduate-only institution. *Graduate faculty:* 71 full-time (11 women), 71 part-time/adjunct (8 women). *Computer facilities:* 30 computers available on campus for general student use. A campuswide network can be accessed from off campus. Internet access is available. *Library facilities:* Dibner Library. *Graduate expenses:* Tuition: part-time $855 per credit. Required fees: $320 per term. *General application contact:* Anthea Jeffrey, Graduate Admissions, 718-260-3200.

Graduate Programs
LaVerne Clark, Director of Campus Operations
Programs in:
  chemical engineering • MS
  chemistry • MS
  computer engineering • MS
  computer science • MS, PhD
  electrical engineering • MS, PhD
  information systems engineering • MS
  telecommunication networks • MS

Department of Management
Dr. Barry Blecherman, Associate Dean
Programs in:
  capital markets • MS
  computational finance • MS
  financial engineering • MS, AC
  financial technology • MS
  financial technology management • AC
  information management • AC
  management • MS

■ PRATT INSTITUTE
Brooklyn, NY 11205-3899
http://www.pratt.edu/

Independent, coed, comprehensive institution. *Computer facilities:* 250 computers available on campus for general student use. A campuswide network can be accessed from student residence rooms and from off campus. Internet access and online class registration are available. *Library facilities:* Pratt Institute Library. *General application contact:* Director of Graduate Admissions, 718-636-3669.

School of Architecture
Programs in:

architecture • M Arch, MS, MSCRP, MSUD, MSUESM
city and regional planning • MSCRP
facilities management • MS
urban design • MSUD
urban environmental systems management • MSUESM

School of Art and Design
Programs in:
art and design • MFA, MID, MPS, MS
art and design education • MS
art history • MS
art therapy and creativity development • MPS
art therapy-special education • MPS
arts and cultural management • MPS
ceramics • MFA
communications design • MS
computer graphics design and interactive media • MFA
dance therapy • MPS
design management • MPS
industrial design • MID
interior design • MS
metals • MFA
new forms • MFA
package design • MS
painting • MFA
photography • MFA
printmaking • MFA
sculpture • MFA
theory and criticism • MS

School of Information and Library Science
Program in:
information and library science • MS, Adv C

■ PURCHASE COLLEGE, STATE UNIVERSITY OF NEW YORK
Purchase, NY 10577-1400
http://www.purchase.edu/

State-supported, coed, comprehensive institution. *Computer facilities:* 350 computers available on campus for general student use. A campuswide network can be accessed from student residence rooms and from off campus. Internet access, e-mail are available. *Library facilities:* Purchase College Library. *General application contact:* Counselor, 914-251-6310.

Conservatory of Dance
Programs in:
choreography • MFA
performance and pedagogy • MFA

Conservatory of Music
Programs in:
composition • MFA
instrumental • MFA
voice • MFA

Conservatory of Theatre Arts and Film
Programs in:
theatre design • MFA
theatre technology • MFA

Division of Humanities
Program in:
art history • MA

School of Art and Design
Program in:
art and design • MFA

■ QUEENS COLLEGE OF THE CITY UNIVERSITY OF NEW YORK
Flushing, NY 11367-1597
http://www.qc.edu/

State and locally supported, coed, comprehensive institution. CGS member. *Enrollment:* 16,993 graduate, professional, and undergraduate students; 491 full-time matriculated graduate/professional students (344 women), 4,818 part-time matriculated graduate/professional students (3,443 women). *Graduate faculty:* 495 full-time (172 women), 555 part-time/adjunct (269 women). *Computer facilities:* 1,000 computers available on campus for general student use. A campuswide network can be accessed from off campus. Internet access is available. *Library facilities:* Benjamin S. Rosenthal Library plus 1 other. *Graduate expenses:* Tuition, state resident: full-time $7,130; part-time $230 per credit. Tuition, nonresident: full-time $11,880; part-time $425 per credit. Required fees: $66; $38 per semester. *General application contact:* Mario Caruso, Director of Graduate Admissions, 718-997-5200.

Find an in-depth description at www.petersons.com/gradchannel.

Division of Graduate Studies
Dr. Joanne Miller, Dean of Research and Graduate Services

Arts Division
Dr. Tamara Evans, Dean
Programs in:
applied linguistics • MA
art history • MA
arts • MA, MFA, MS Ed
creative writing • MA
English language and literature • MA
fine arts • MFA
French • MA
Italian • MA
media studies • MA
music • MA
Spanish • MA
speech pathology • MA
teaching English to speakers of other languages • MS Ed

Division of Education
Dr. Penny Hammrich, Acting Dean
Programs in:
administration and supervision • AC
art • MS Ed
bilingual education • MS Ed
biology • MS Ed, AC
chemistry • MS Ed, AC
childhood education • MA
counselor education • MS Ed
early childhood education • MA
earth sciences • MS Ed, AC
education • MA, MS Ed, AC
elementary education • MS Ed, AC
English • MS Ed, AC
French • MS Ed, AC
Italian • MS Ed, AC
literacy • MS Ed
mathematics • MS Ed, AC
music • MS Ed, AC
physics • MS Ed, AC
school psychology • MS Ed, AC
social studies • MS Ed, AC
Spanish • MS Ed, AC
special education • MS Ed

Mathematics and Natural Sciences Division
Dr. Thomas Strekas, Dean
Programs in:
biochemistry • MA
biology • MA
chemistry • MA
clinical behavioral applications in mental health settings • MA
computer science • MA
earth and environmental science • MA
home economics • MS Ed
mathematics • MA
mathematics and natural sciences • MA, MS Ed
physical education and exercise sciences • MS Ed
physics • MA
psychology • MA

Social Science Division
Dr. Donald Scott, Dean
Programs in:
accounting • MS
history • MA
liberal studies • MALS
library and information studies • MLS, AC
social science • MA, MALS, MASS, MLS, MS, AC
social sciences • MASS
sociology • MA
urban studies • MA

■ RENSSELAER POLYTECHNIC INSTITUTE
Troy, NY 12180-3590
http://www.rpi.edu/

Independent, coed, university. CGS member. *Enrollment:* 8,265 graduate, professional, and undergraduate students;

New York

Rensselaer Polytechnic Institute (continued)

1,212 full-time matriculated graduate/professional students (356 women), 676 part-time matriculated graduate/professional students (191 women). *Graduate faculty:* 383 full-time (62 women), 96 part-time/adjunct (21 women). *Computer facilities:* Computer purchase and lease plans are available. 500 computers available on campus for general student use. A campuswide network can be accessed from student residence rooms and from off campus. Internet access and online class registration are available. *Library facilities:* Folsom Library plus 1 other. *Graduate expenses:* Tuition: full-time $27,700; part-time $1,320 per credit. Required fees: $1,470. *General application contact:* Teresa C. Duffy, Dean of Enrollment Management, 518-276-6216.

Find an in-depth description at www.petersons.com/gradchannel.

Graduate School
Dr. Thomas Apple, Dean of Graduate Education

Lally School of Management and Technology
Dr. Denis Fred Simon, Dean
Programs in:
- finance • MBA, MS
- management • PhD
- management and technology • MBA, MS, PhD
- management information systems • MBA, MS
- new product development and marketing • MBA
- new production and operations management • MS
- product development and marketing • MS
- production and operations management • MBA
- technological entrepreneurship • MBA, MS

School of Architecture
Prof. Peter Parsons, Director, Graduate Programs in Architecture
Programs in:
- architecture • M Arch
- building conservation • MS
- building science • MS
- building sciences • MS
- informatics and architecture • MS
- lighting • MS

School of Engineering
Dr. William A. Baeslack, Dean
Programs in:
- aerospace engineering • M Eng, MS, D Eng, PhD
- biomedical engineering • MS, PhD
- ceramics and glass science • M Eng, MS, PhD
- chemical and biological engineering • M Eng, MS, D Eng, PhD
- civil engineering • M Eng, MS, D Eng, PhD
- composites • M Eng, MS, PhD
- computer and systems engineering • M Eng, MS, D Eng, PhD
- decision sciences and engineering systems • PhD
- electric power engineering • M Eng, MS, D Eng, PhD
- electrical engineering • M Eng, MS, D Eng, PhD
- electronic materials • M Eng, MS, PhD
- engineering • M Eng, MS, D Eng, PhD
- engineering physics • MS, PhD
- engineering science • MS, PhD
- environmental engineering • M Eng, MS, D Eng, PhD
- geotechnical engineering • M Eng, MS, D Eng, PhD
- industrial and management engineering • M Eng, MS, PhD
- manufacturing systems engineering • M Eng, MS, PhD
- mechanical engineering • M Eng, MS, D Eng, PhD
- mechanics • M Eng, MS, PhD
- mechanics of composite materials and structures • M Eng, MS, D Eng, PhD
- metallurgy • M Eng, MS, PhD
- nuclear engineering • M Eng, MS, D Eng, PhD
- nuclear engineering and science • PhD
- operations research and statistics • M Eng, MS, PhD
- polymers • M Eng, MS, PhD
- structural engineering • M Eng, MS, D Eng, PhD
- transportation engineering • M Eng, MS, D Eng, PhD

School of Humanities and Social Sciences
Dr. John P. Harrington, Dean
Programs in:
- cognitive science • PhD
- communication and rhetoric • MS, PhD
- ecological economics • PhD
- ecological economics, values, and policy • MS
- economics • MS
- electronic arts • MFA
- humanities and social sciences • MFA, MS, PhD
- science and technology studies • MS, PhD
- technical communication • MS

School of Science
Dr. Joseph E. Flaherty, Dean
Programs in:
- analytical chemistry • MS, PhD
- applied mathematics • MS
- applied science • MS
- biochemistry • MS, PhD
- biophysics • MS, PhD
- cell biology • MS, PhD
- computer science • MS, PhD
- developmental biology • MS, PhD
- environmental chemistry • MS, PhD
- geochemistry • MS, PhD
- geology • MS, PhD
- geophysics • MS, PhD
- information technology • MS
- inorganic chemistry • MS, PhD
- mathematics • MS, PhD
- microbiology • MS, PhD
- molecular biology • MS, PhD
- multidisciplinary science • MS, PhD
- natural sciences • MS
- organic chemistry • MS, PhD
- petrology • MS, PhD
- physical chemistry • MS, PhD
- physics • MS, PhD
- polymer chemistry • MS, PhD
- science • MS, PhD

■ ROBERTS WESLEYAN COLLEGE
Rochester, NY 14624-1997
http://www.roberts.edu/

Independent-religious, coed, comprehensive institution. *Computer facilities:* 160 computers available on campus for general student use. A campuswide network can be accessed from student residence rooms and from off campus. Internet access and online class registration, campus Intranet are available. *Library facilities:* Ora A. Sprague Library. *General application contact:* Admissions Secretary, Office Manager for Adult and Graduate Education, 716-594-6600.

Division of Business and Management
Programs in:
- business and management • MS
- organizational management • MS

Division of Social Work and Social Sciences
Programs in:
- child and family services • MSW
- physical and mental health services • MSW

Division of Teacher Education
Program in:
- teacher education • M Ed, Advanced Certificate

New York

ROCHESTER INSTITUTE OF TECHNOLOGY
Rochester, NY 14623-5603
http://www.rit.edu/

Independent, coed, comprehensive institution. CGS member. *Enrollment:* 14,685 graduate, professional, and undergraduate students; 1,058 full-time matriculated graduate/professional students (415 women), 1,122 part-time matriculated graduate/professional students (420 women). *Computer facilities:* 2,500 computers available on campus for general student use. A campuswide network can be accessed from student residence rooms and from off campus. Internet access and online class registration, student account information are available. *Library facilities:* Wallace Memorial Library. *Graduate expenses:* Tuition: full-time $22,965; part-time $644 per hour. Required fees: $174; $29 per quarter. *General application contact:* Diane Ellison, Director, Graduate Enrollment Services, 585-475-7284.

Find an in-depth description at www.petersons.com/gradchannel.

Graduate Enrollment Services
Diane Ellison, Director, Graduate Enrollment Services

College of Applied Science and Technology
Dr. Wiley McKinzie, Dean
Programs in:
  applied science and technology • MS, AC
  computer integrated manufacturing • MS
  cross-disciplinary professional studies • MS
  environmental management • MS
  health systems administration • MS, AC
  health systems-finance • AC
  hospitality-tourism management • MS
  human resources development • MS
  integrated health systems • AC
  multidisciplinary studies • MS, AC
  packaging science • MS
  senior living management • AC
  service management • MS
  technical information design • AC
  telecom engineering technology • MS
  training and instructional design • MS

College of Business
Dr. Thomas D. Hopkins, Dean
Programs in:
  accounting • MBA, MS
  business • Exec MBA, MBA, MS
  business administration • MBA
  executive business administration • Exec MBA
  finance • MS
  international business • MS

College of Engineering
Dr. Harvey Palmer, Dean
Programs in:
  applied statistics • MS
  computer engineering • MS
  electrical engineering • MSEE
  engineering • ME, MS, MSEE, MSME, PhD, AC
  engineering management • ME
  industrial engineering • ME
  manufacturing engineering • ME
  manufacturing leadership • MS
  mechanical engineering • MSME
  microelectronic manufacturing engineering • ME, MS
  microsystems engineering • PhD
  product development • MS
  statistical quality • AC
  systems engineering • ME

College of Imaging Arts and Sciences
Dr. Joan Stone, Dean
Programs in:
  art education • MST
  ceramics • MFA, MST
  computer graphics design • MFA
  fine arts • MFA, MST
  fine arts studio • MST
  glass • MFA, MST
  graphic arts publishing • MS
  graphic arts systems • MS
  graphic design • MFA, MST
  imaging arts • MFA
  imaging arts and sciences • MFA, MS, MST
  industrial design • MFA, MST
  medical illustration • MFA
  metal crafts and jewelry • MFA, MST
  painting • MFA
  printing technology • MS
  woodworking and furniture design • MFA, MST

College of Liberal Arts
Dr. Andrew Moore, Dean
Programs in:
  communication and media technologies • MS
  liberal arts • MS, AC
  public policy • MS
  school psychology • MS, AC
  school psychology and deafness • AC

College of Science
Dr. Ian Gatley, Dean
Programs in:
  bioinformatics • MS
  chemistry • MS
  clinical chemistry • MS
  color science • MS
  imaging science • MS, PhD
  industrial and applied mathematics • MS
  materials science and engineering • MS
  science • MS, PhD

Golisano College of Computing and Information Sciences
Jorge Diaz-Herrara, Dean
Programs in:
  computer science • MS
  computing and information sciences • MS, AC
  information technology • MS
  interactive multimedia development • AC
  software development and management • MS

National Technical Institute for the Deaf
Dr. Alan Hurwitz, Dean
Program in:
  secondary education • MS

THE ROCKEFELLER UNIVERSITY
New York, NY 10021-6399
http://www.rockefeller.edu/

Independent, coed, graduate-only institution. CGS member. *Graduate faculty:* 252 full-time (90 women), 203 part-time/adjunct (51 women). *Computer facilities:* 26 computers available on campus for general student use. A campuswide network can be accessed from student residence rooms and from off campus. Internet access is available. *Library facilities:* Rockefeller University Library. *General application contact:* Dr. Sidney Strickland, Dean of Graduate Studies, 212-327-8086.

Program in Biomedical Sciences
Dr. Sidney Strickland, Dean of Graduate Studies
Program in:
  biomedical sciences • PhD

SAGE GRADUATE SCHOOL
Troy, NY 12180-4115
http://www.sage.edu/

Independent, coed, graduate-only institution. *Graduate faculty:* 36 full-time (28 women), 38 part-time/adjunct (20 women). *Computer facilities:* 355 computers available on campus for general student use. A campuswide network can be accessed from student residence rooms and from off campus. Internet access is available. *Library facilities:* James Wheelock Clark Library plus 1 other. *Graduate expenses:* Tuition: full-time $7,920; part-time $440 per credit hour. *General application contact:* Melissa M. Coon, Director of Admissions, 518-244-6878.

Find an in-depth description at www.petersons.com/gradchannel.

New York

Sage Graduate School (continued)
Graduate School
Dr. John A. Tribble, Dean

Division of Education
Dr. Connell G. Frazer, Dean
Programs in:
 biology • MAT
 childhood education • MS Ed
 childhood special education • MS Ed
 English • MAT
 guidance and counseling • MS, PMC
 health education • MS
 literacy • MS Ed
 literacy/childhood special education • MS Ed
 mathematics • MAT
 school health education • MS
 secondary education • MS Ed
 social studies • MAT
 teaching • MAT

Division of Health and Rehabilitation Sciences
Program in:
 physical therapy • PhD

Division of Management, Communications and Legal Studies
Dr. Michael Hall, Director
Programs in:
 communications • MBA, MS
 finance • MBA
 gerontology • MS
 health education • MS
 human resources management • MBA
 human services administration • MS
 management • MS
 management, communications and legal studies • MBA, MS
 marketing • MBA
 nutrition and dietetics • MS
 organizational management • MS
 public management • MS

Division of Nursing
Dr. Glenda Kelman, Chair
Programs in:
 adult health • MS
 adult nurse practitioner • MS
 community health nursing • MS
 family nurse practitioner • MS
 nursing • PMC
 nursing-medical surgical • MS
 psychiatric–mental health nurse practitioner • MS
 psychology mental health • MS

Division of Psychology
Dr. Sam Hill, Chair
Programs in:
 chemical dependence • MA
 child care and children's services • MA
 community counseling • MA
 community health • MA
 community psychology • MA
 forensic psychology • MA
 general psychology • MA
 visual art therapy • MA

■ **ST. BONAVENTURE UNIVERSITY**
St. Bonaventure, NY 14778-2284
http://www.sbu.edu/

Independent-religious, coed, comprehensive institution. CGS member. *Enrollment:* 2,806 graduate, professional, and undergraduate students; 265 full-time matriculated graduate/professional students (181 women), 250 part-time matriculated graduate/professional students (154 women). *Graduate faculty:* 65 full-time (17 women), 28 part-time/adjunct (9 women). *Computer facilities:* 200 computers available on campus for general student use. A campuswide network can be accessed from student residence rooms and from off campus. Internet access and online class registration are available. *Library facilities:* Friedsam Library. *Graduate expenses:* Tuition: part-time $590 per credit. Tuition and fees vary according to course load. *General application contact:* Connie Cayse Horan, Information Contact, 716-375-2021.

School of Graduate Studies
School of Arts and Sciences
Programs in:
 arts and sciences • MA
 English • MA
School of Business
Programs in:
 accounting • Adv C
 accounting and finance • MBA
 finance • Adv C
 management • Adv C
 management and marketing • MBA
 marketing • Adv C
 professional leadership • Adv C
School of Education
Programs in:
 counseling education • Adv C
 counseling education-agency • MS, MS Ed
 counseling education-school • MS, MS Ed
 education • MS, MS Ed, Adv C
 educational leadership • MS Ed, Adv C
 literacy • MS Ed
School of Franciscan Studies
Program in:
 Franciscan studies • MA, Adv C

■ **ST. JOHN FISHER COLLEGE**
Rochester, NY 14618-3597
http://www.sjfc.edu/

Independent-religious, coed, comprehensive institution. *Enrollment:* 3,152 graduate, professional, and undergraduate students; 147 full-time matriculated graduate/professional students (102 women), 509 part-time matriculated graduate/professional students (355 women). *Graduate faculty:* 52 full-time (22 women), 19 part-time/adjunct (10 women). *Computer facilities:* 260 computers available on campus for general student use. A campuswide network can be accessed from student residence rooms and from off campus. Internet access and online class registration are available. *Library facilities:* Charles V. Lavery Library plus 1 other. *Graduate expenses:* Tuition: full-time $18,720; part-time $520 per credit. Required fees: $25 per term. *General application contact:* Shannon Cleverley, Director, Graduate Admissions, 585-385-8161.

Office of Academic Affairs
Dr. Ronald J. Ambrosetti, Vice President for Academic Affairs and Provost
Programs in:
 childhood and adolescence • MS Ed
 educational administration • MS Ed
 human resources development • MS
 human service administration • MS
 international studies • MS
 literacy • MS
 management • MBA
 mathematics/science/technology education • MS
 nursing • MS, Certificate
 special education • MS
 taxation • MS

■ **ST. JOHN'S UNIVERSITY**
Jamaica, NY 11439
http://www.stjohns.edu/

Independent-religious, coed, university. CGS member. *Enrollment:* 19,777 graduate, professional, and undergraduate students; 1,849 full-time matriculated graduate/professional students (1,068 women), 2,742 part-time matriculated graduate/professional students (1,763 women). *Graduate faculty:* 587 full-time (203 women), 743 part-time/adjunct (306 women). *Computer facilities:* 950 computers available on campus for general student use. A campuswide network can be accessed from student residence rooms and from off campus. Internet access and online class registration, various software packages are available. *Library facilities:* St. John's University Library plus 2 others. *Graduate expenses:* Tuition: full-time $15,840; part-time $8,320 per year. Tuition and fees vary according to course load, degree level,

New York

program and student level. *General application contact:* Matthew Whelan, Director, Office of Admission, 718-990-2000.

Find an in-depth description at www.petersons.com/gradchannel.

College of Pharmacy and Allied Health Professions
Dr. Robert Mangione, Dean
Programs in:
 clinical pharmacy • MS
 cosmetic sciences • MS
 industrial pharmacy • MS, PhD
 medical technology • MS
 medicinal chemistry • MS, PhD
 pharmaceutical marketing • MS
 pharmaceutical sciences • MS, PhD
 pharmacology • MS, PhD
 pharmacotherapeutics • MS
 pharmacy • Pharm D, MS, PhD
 pharmacy administration • MS
 pharmacy and administrative sciences • MS
 pharmacy and allied health professions • Pharm D, MS, PhD
 toxicology • MS, PhD

College of Professional Studies
Dr. Kathleen MacDonald, Dean
Programs in:
 criminal justice and legal studies • MPS
 professional studies • MPS

The Peter J. Tobin College of Business
Richard Highfield, Dean
Programs in:
 accounting • MBA, MS, Adv C
 business • MBA, MS, Adv C
 computer information systems and decision sciences • MBA, Adv C
 economics • MBA, Adv C
 finance • MBA, Adv C
 international business • MBA
 management • MBA, Adv C
 marketing • MBA, Adv C
 taxation • MBA, Adv C

School of Risk Management and Actuarial Science
Dr. James Barrese, Chair
Program in:
 risk management and actuarial science • MBA, MS

St. John's College of Liberal Arts and Sciences
Dr. Jeffrey Fagen, Dean
Programs in:
 algebra • MA
 analysis • MA
 applied mathematics • MA
 biological sciences • MS, PhD
 chemistry • MS
 clinical psychology • MA, PhD
 clinical psychology-child • MA, PhD
 clinical psychology-general • MA, PhD
 computer science • MA
 criminology and justice • MA
 English • MA, DA
 general experimental psychology • MA
 geometry-topology • MA
 government and politics • MA
 history • MA
 international law and diplomacy • Adv C
 liberal arts and sciences • M Div, MA, MLS, MS, DA, PhD, Psy D, Adv C
 library and information science • MLS, Adv C
 logic and foundations • MA
 modern world history • DA
 priestly studies • M Div
 probability and statistics • MA
 school psychology • MS, Psy D
 sociology • MA
 Spanish • MA
 speech pathology and audiology • MA
 theology • MA

Institute of Asian Studies
Dr. Abraham Ho, Director
Programs in:
 Asian and African cultural studies • Adv C
 Asian studies • Adv C
 Chinese studies • MA, Adv C
 East Asian culture studies • Adv C
 East Asian studies • MA

The School of Education
Dr. Jerrold Ross, Dean
Programs in:
 administration and supervision • MS Ed, Ed D, PD
 bilingual school counseling • MS Ed
 bilingual special education • MS Ed, PD
 bilingual/multicultural education/teaching English to speakers of other languages • MS Ed
 education • MS Ed, Ed D, PD
 instructional leadership • Ed D, PD
 reading special education • MS Ed
 reading specialist • MS Ed, PD
 rehabilitation counseling • MS Ed, PD
 school counseling • MS Ed, PD
 special education • MS Ed, PD
 special education/bilingual special education/reading special education • MS Ed, PD
 student development practice in higher education • MS Ed, PD
 teaching children with disabilities • MS Ed, PD

Division of Early Childhood, Childhood and Adolescent Education
Dr. William Sanders, Chair
Programs in:
 adolescent education • MS Ed, PD
 childhood education • MS Ed
 early childhood education • MS Ed

School of Law
Joseph W. Bellacosa, Dean
Programs in:
 bankruptcy • LL M
 law • JD

■ ST. THOMAS AQUINAS COLLEGE
Sparkill, NY 10976
http://www.stac.edu/

Independent, coed, comprehensive institution. *Enrollment:* 2,394 graduate, professional, and undergraduate students; 91 full-time matriculated graduate/professional students (64 women), 155 part-time matriculated graduate/professional students (104 women). *Graduate faculty:* 18 full-time (10 women), 18 part-time/adjunct (7 women). *Computer facilities:* 200 computers available on campus for general student use. A campuswide network can be accessed from student residence rooms and from off campus. Internet access is available. *Library facilities:* Lougheed Library plus 1 other. *Graduate expenses:* Tuition: full-time $8,910. Required fees: $320. *General application contact:* Tracey Howard-Ubelhoer, Director of Admissions, 845-398-4102.

Division of Business Administration
Michael Murphy, Chairperson
Programs in:
 business administration • MBA
 finance • MBA
 management • MBA
 marketing • MBA

Division of Teacher Education
Dr. Meenakshi Gajria, Chairperson
Programs in:
 adolescence education • MST
 childhood and special education • MST
 childhood education • MST
 reading • MS Ed, PMC
 special education • MS Ed, PMC
 teacher education • MS Ed, MST, PMC
 teaching • MS Ed

■ STATE UNIVERSITY OF NEW YORK AT BINGHAMTON
Binghamton, NY 13902-6000
http://www.binghamton.edu/

State-supported, coed, university. CGS member. *Computer facilities:* Computer

Peterson's Graduate Schools in the U.S. 2006

New York

State University of New York at Binghamton (continued)
purchase and lease plans are available. 6,228 computers available on campus for general student use. A campuswide network can be accessed from student residence rooms and from off campus. Internet access and online class registration are available. *Library facilities:* Glenn G. Bartle Library plus 1 other. *General application contact:* Vice Provost and Dean of the Graduate School, 607-777-2070.

Graduate School
Program in:
  public administration • MPA

Decker School of Nursing
Program in:
  nursing • MS, PhD, Certificate

School of Arts and Sciences
Programs in:
  analytical chemistry • PhD
  anthropology • MA, PhD
  applied physics • MS
  art • MA, MFA
  art history • MA, PhD
  arts and sciences • MA, MM, MS, PhD, Certificate
  behavioral neuroscience • MA, PhD
  biological sciences • MA, PhD
  chemistry • MA, MS
  clinical psychology • MA, PhD
  cognitive and behavioral science • MA, PhD
  comparative literature • MA, PhD
  computer science • MA, PhD
  economics • MA, PhD
  economics and finance • MA, PhD
  English • MA, PhD
  French • MA
  geography • MA
  geological sciences • MA, PhD
  history • MA, PhD
  inorganic chemistry • PhD
  Italian • MA
  music • MA, MM
  organic chemistry • PhD
  philosophy • MA, PhD
  physical chemistry • PhD
  physics • MA, MS
  political science • MA, PhD
  probability and statistics • MA, PhD
  public policy • MA, PhD
  sociology • MA, PhD
  Spanish • MA, Certificate
  theater • MA
  translation • Certificate
  translation research and instruction • Certificate

School of Education and Human Development
Programs in:
  biology education • MAT, MS Ed, MST
  early childhood and elementary education • MS Ed
  earth science education • MAT, MS Ed, MST
  education and human development • MASS, MAT, MS Ed, MST, Ed D
  educational theory and practice • Ed D
  English education • MAT, MS Ed, MST
  French education • MAT, MST
  mathematical sciences education • MAT, MS Ed, MST
  physics • MAT, MS Ed, MST
  reading education • MS Ed
  social science • MASS
  social studies • MAT, MS Ed, MST
  Spanish education • MAT, MST
  special education • MS Ed

School of Management
Programs in:
  accounting • MS, PhD
  business administration • MBA, PhD
  health care professional executive • MBA
  management • MBA, MS, PhD

Thomas J. Watson School of Engineering and Applied Science
Programs in:
  computer science • M Eng, MS, PhD
  electrical engineering • M Eng, MS, PhD
  engineering and applied science • M Eng, MS, MSAT, PhD
  mechanical engineering • M Eng, MS, PhD
  systems science and industrial engineering • M Eng, MS, MSAT, PhD

■ **STATE UNIVERSITY OF NEW YORK AT NEW PALTZ**
New Paltz, NY 12561
http://www.newpaltz.edu/

State-supported, coed, comprehensive institution. *Enrollment:* 7,908 graduate, professional, and undergraduate students; 525 full-time matriculated graduate/professional students (358 women), 1,307 part-time matriculated graduate/professional students (892 women). *Graduate faculty:* 116 full-time, 90 part-time/adjunct. *Computer facilities:* 600 computers available on campus for general student use. A campuswide network can be accessed from student residence rooms and from off campus. Internet access and online class registration, e-mail are available. *Library facilities:* Sojourner Truth Library. *Graduate expenses:* Tuition, state resident: full-time $6,900; part-time $288 per credit hour. Tuition, nonresident: full-time $10,500; part-time $438 per credit hour. Tuition and fees vary according to program. *General application contact:* Dr. Phyllis R. Freeman, Dean, 845-257-3285.

Graduate School
Dr. Phyllis R. Freeman, Dean

Faculty of Education
Dr. Robert Michael, Dean
Programs in:
  childhood education (1–6) • MST
  early childhood (B–2) • MS Ed
  education • MAT, MPS, MS Ed, MST, CAS
  educational administration • MS Ed, CAS
  English as a second language • MS Ed
  environmental (1–6) • MS Ed
  humanistic (1–6) • MS Ed
  humanistic/multicultural education • MPS
  math, science, and technology (1–6) • MS Ed
  reading/literacy • MS Ed
  secondary education • MAT, MS Ed
  special education • MS Ed
  special education (1–6) • MS Ed

Faculty of Fine and Performing Arts
Dr. Kurt Daw, Dean
Programs in:
  ceramics • MA, MFA
  fine and performing arts • MA, MFA, MS Ed
  intermedia design • MFA
  metal • MA, MFA
  painting • MA
  painting/drawing • MFA
  printmaking • MA, MFA
  sculpture • MA, MFA
  visual arts education • MS Ed

Faculty of Liberal Arts and Sciences
Dr. Gerald Benjamin, Dean
Programs in:
  biology • MA, MAT, MS Ed
  communication disorders • MS
  English • MA, MAT, MS Ed
  gerontological nursing • MS
  liberal arts and sciences • MA, MAT, MS, MS Ed
  psychology • MA
  sociology • MA

School of Business
Dr. Hadi Salavitabar, Dean
Programs in:
  accounting • MBA
  finance • MBA
  international business • MBA
  marketing • MBA

School of Science and Engineering
Dr. John Harrington, Dean
Programs in:
  chemistry • MA, MAT, MS Ed
  computer science • MS

electrical and computer engineering • MS
geological sciences • MA, MAT, MS Ed
mathematics • MA, MAT, MS Ed
science and engineering • MA, MAT, MS, MS Ed

■ STATE UNIVERSITY OF NEW YORK AT OSWEGO
Oswego, NY 13126
http://www.oswego.edu/

State-supported, coed, comprehensive institution. *Enrollment:* 8,465 graduate, professional, and undergraduate students; 363 full-time matriculated graduate/professional students (237 women), 587 part-time matriculated graduate/professional students (401 women). *Graduate faculty:* 81 full-time, 30 part-time/adjunct. *Computer facilities:* Computer purchase and lease plans are available. 600 computers available on campus for general student use. A campuswide network can be accessed from student residence rooms and from off campus. Internet access and online class registration are available. *Library facilities:* Penfield Library plus 1 other. *Graduate expenses:* Tuition, state resident: full-time $7,100; part-time $296 per credit. Tuition, nonresident: full-time $10,800; part-time $450 per credit. Required fees: $540. *General application contact:* Dr. Jack Y. Narayan, Dean of Graduate Studies, 315-312-3152.

Graduate Studies
Dr. Jack Y. Narayan, Dean

Division of Arts and Sciences
Dr. Sara Varhus, Dean
Programs in:
  art • MA
  arts and sciences • MA, MS
  chemistry • MS
  English • MA
  history • MA

School of Business
Dr. Lanny A. Karns, Dean
Programs in:
  business • MBA
  business administration • MBA

School of Education
Dr. Linda Markert, Dean
Programs in:
  art education • MAT
  counseling services • MS, CAS
  education • MAT, MS, MS Ed, CAS
  elementary education • MS Ed
  human services/counseling • MS
  instructional administration • MS Ed, CAS
  reading education • MS Ed
  school psychology • MS, CAS
  secondary education • MS Ed
  special education • MS Ed
  technology • MS Ed
  vocational teacher preparation • MS Ed

■ STATE UNIVERSITY OF NEW YORK AT PLATTSBURGH
Plattsburgh, NY 12901-2681
http://www.plattsburgh.edu/

State-supported, coed, comprehensive institution. *Enrollment:* 6,047 graduate, professional, and undergraduate students; 240 full-time matriculated graduate/professional students (176 women), 262 part-time matriculated graduate/professional students (183 women). *Graduate faculty:* 54 full-time (22 women), 1 part-time/adjunct (0 women). *Computer facilities:* Computer purchase and lease plans are available. 450 computers available on campus for general student use. A campuswide network can be accessed from student residence rooms and from off campus. Internet access and online class registration are available. *Library facilities:* Feinberg Library. *Graduate expenses:* Tuition, state resident: full-time $6,900; part-time $288 per credit. Tuition, nonresident: full-time $10,500; part-time $438 per credit. Required fees: $513; $40 per credit. One-time fee: $16 full-time. *General application contact:* Richard Higgins, Director of Graduate Admissions, 518-564-2040.

Center for Lifelong Learning
Dr. Ray Guydosh, Interim Dean
Program in:
  liberal studies • MA

Faculty of Arts and Science
Dr. Kathleen Lavoie, Dean
Programs in:
  arts and science • MA, CAS
  school psychology • MA, CAS

Faculty of Professional Studies
Dr. Gretchen Beebe, Interim Dean
Programs in:
  college/agency counseling • MS
  curriculum and instruction • MS Ed
  elementary education • MST
  elementary education Pre K-6 • MS Ed
  English 7-9 • MS Ed, MST
  English Pre K-6 • MS Ed, MST
  general science 7-9 • MS Ed, MST
  general science Pre K-6 • MS Ed
  general science Pre-K • MST
  mathematics 7-9 • MS Ed, MST
  mathematics Pre K-6 • MS Ed, MST
  professional studies • MA, MS, MS Ed, MST, CAS
  reading teacher • MS Ed
  school administrator and supervisor • CAS
  school counseling • MS Ed
  school counselor • CAS
  social studies 7-9 • MS Ed, MST
  social studies Pre K-6 • MS Ed, MST
  special education • MS Ed
  speech-language pathology • MA

■ STATE UNIVERSITY OF NEW YORK COLLEGE AT BROCKPORT
Brockport, NY 14420-2997
http://www.brockport.edu/

State-supported, coed, comprehensive institution. CGS member. *Enrollment:* 8,742 graduate, professional, and undergraduate students; 392 full-time matriculated graduate/professional students (279 women), 1,055 part-time matriculated graduate/professional students (652 women). *Graduate faculty:* 152 full-time (67 women), 76 part-time/adjunct (35 women). *Computer facilities:* 750 computers available on campus for general student use. A campuswide network can be accessed from student residence rooms and from off campus. Internet access and online class registration are available. *Library facilities:* Drake Memorial Library. *Graduate expenses:* Tuition, state resident: full-time $6,910; part-time $288 per credit hour. Tuition, nonresident: full-time $10,500; part-time $438 per credit hour. Required fees: $26 per credit. *General application contact:* Sue A. Smithson, Graduate Admissions Secretary, 585-395-5465.

Find an in-depth description at www.petersons.com/gradchannel.

School of Arts and Performance
Dr. Francis X. Short, Interim Dean
Programs in:
  arts and performance • MA, MFA, MS Ed
  communication • MA
  dance • MA, MFA
  physical education • MS Ed
  visual studies • MFA

School of Letters and Sciences
Dr. Stuart Appelle, Dean
Programs in:
  biological sciences • MS
  computational science • MS
  English • MA
  history • MA

New York

State University of New York College at Brockport (continued)
  letters and sciences • MA, MS
  liberal studies • MA
  mathematics • MA
  psychology • MA

School of Professions
Dr. Chirstine Murray, Dean
Programs in:
  bilingual education • MS Ed
  biology education • MS Ed
  chemistry education • MS Ed
  childhood literacy • MS Ed
  counselor education • MS Ed, CAS
  earth science education • MS Ed
  elementary education • MS Ed
  English education • MS Ed
  health science • MS Ed
  mathematics education • MS Ed
  physics education • MS Ed
  public administration • MPA
  recreation and leisure studies • MS
  school administration and supervision • MS Ed, CAS
  school business administration • CAS
  school district administration • CAS
  secondary education • MS Ed
  social studies education • MS Ed
  social work • MSW
  special education: childhood • MS Ed

■ **STATE UNIVERSITY OF NEW YORK COLLEGE AT CORTLAND**
Cortland, NY 13045
http://www.cortland.edu/

State-supported, coed, comprehensive institution. *Enrollment:* 7,337 graduate, professional, and undergraduate students; 291 full-time matriculated graduate/professional students, 1,250 part-time matriculated graduate/professional students. *Graduate faculty:* 58 full-time. *Computer facilities:* 832 computers available on campus for general student use. A campuswide network can be accessed from student residence rooms and from off campus. *Library facilities:* Memorial Library. *Graduate expenses:* Tuition, state resident: full-time $2,592; part-time $288 per credit. Tuition, nonresident: full-time $3,942; part-time $438 per credit. Required fees: $36 per credit. Part-time tuition and fees vary according to course load and campus/location. *General application contact:* Assistant Director of Graduate Studies, 607-753-4800.

Graduate Studies
Dr. Yvonne M. Murnane, Director of Graduate Studies

School of Arts and Sciences
Dr. Mark Prus, Dean
Programs in:
  American civilization and culture • CAS
  arts and sciences • MA, MAT, MS Ed, CAS
  biology • MAT, MS Ed
  chemistry • MAT, MS Ed
  earth science • MAT, MS Ed
  English • MS Ed
  French • MS Ed
  history • MA, MS Ed
  mathematics • MAT, MS Ed
  physics • MAT, MS Ed
  second language education • MS Ed
  social studies • MS Ed
  Spanish • MS Ed

School of Education
Dr. Edward Caffarella, Dean
Programs in:
  childhood/early child education • MS Ed, MST
  educational leadership • CAS
  literacy • MS Ed
  teaching students with disabilities • MS Ed

School of Professional Studies
Dr. Christopher Malone, Head
Programs in:
  exercise science and sport studies • MS
  health education • MS Ed, MST
  physical education • MS Ed
  professional studies • MS, MS Ed, MST
  recreation and leisure studies • MS, MS Ed

■ **STATE UNIVERSITY OF NEW YORK COLLEGE AT FREDONIA**
Fredonia, NY 14063-1136
http://www.fredonia.edu/

State-supported, coed, comprehensive institution. *Computer facilities:* 500 computers available on campus for general student use. A campuswide network can be accessed from student residence rooms and from off campus. *Library facilities:* Reed Library. *General application contact:* Dean of Graduate Studies, 716-673-3808.

Graduate Studies
Programs in:
  biology • MS, MS Ed
  chemistry • MS, MS Ed
  English • MA, MS Ed
  mathematics • MS Ed
  social sciences • MA, MS
  speech pathology and audiology • MS, MS Ed

School of Education
Programs in:
  educational administration • CAS
  elementary education • MS Ed
  reading • MS Ed
  secondary education • MS Ed

School of Music
Programs in:
  music • MM
  music education • MM

■ **STATE UNIVERSITY OF NEW YORK COLLEGE AT GENESEO**
Geneseo, NY 14454-1401
http://www.geneseo.edu/

State-supported, coed, comprehensive institution. *Enrollment:* 5,550 graduate, professional, and undergraduate students; 52 full-time matriculated graduate/professional students (46 women), 126 part-time matriculated graduate/professional students (105 women). *Graduate faculty:* 38 full-time (23 women), 10 part-time/adjunct (7 women). *Computer facilities:* Computer purchase and lease plans are available. 900 computers available on campus for general student use. A campuswide network can be accessed from student residence rooms and from off campus. Internet access and online class registration are available. *Library facilities:* Milne Library plus 1 other. *Graduate expenses:* Tuition, state resident: full-time $6,900; part-time $288 per credit hour. Tuition, nonresident: full-time $10,500; part-time $351 per credit hour. Required fees: $22 per credit hour. Part-time tuition and fees vary according to course load. *General application contact:* Dr. Susan Bailey, Dean of the College, 585-245-5546.

Graduate Studies
Dr. Susan Bailey, Dean of the College
Program in:
  communicative disorders and sciences • MA

School of Education
Dr. Mary Ellen Schmidt, Chairperson
Programs in:
  elementary education • MS Ed
  reading • MPS, MS Ed
  secondary education • MS Ed
  special education • MS Ed

■ **STATE UNIVERSITY OF NEW YORK COLLEGE AT ONEONTA**
Oneonta, NY 13820-4015
http://www.oneonta.edu/

State-supported, coed, comprehensive institution. *Enrollment:* 5,724 graduate, professional, and undergraduate students; 61 full-time matriculated graduate/professional students (47 women), 107 part-time matriculated graduate/professional students (86 women). *Graduate faculty:* 144 part-time/adjunct. *Computer facilities:* Computer purchase and lease plans are available. 600 computers available on campus for general student use. A campuswide network can be accessed from student residence rooms and from off campus. Internet access and online class registration are available. *Library facilities:* Milne Library. *Graduate expenses:* Tuition, state resident: full-time $5,100; part-time $213 per semester hour. Tuition, nonresident: full-time $8,416; part-time $351 per semester hour. Required fees: $666. *General application contact:* Dr. Carolyn Haessig, Director, 607-436-2523.

Graduate Studies
Dr. Carolyn Haessig, Director
Programs in:
   biology • MA
   earth science • MA
   history museum studies • MA

Division of Education
Dr. Joanne Curran, Associate Dean
Programs in:
   adolescence education • MS Ed
   childhood education • MS Ed
   educational psychology and counseling • MS Ed, CAS
   elementary and reading education • MS Ed
   family and consumer science education • MS Ed
   literacy education • MS Ed
   school counselor K-12 • MS Ed, CAS

■ STATE UNIVERSITY OF NEW YORK COLLEGE AT POTSDAM
Potsdam, NY 13676
http://www.potsdam.edu/

State-supported, coed, comprehensive institution. *Enrollment:* 4,307 graduate, professional, and undergraduate students; 550 full-time matriculated graduate/professional students (398 women), 275 part-time matriculated graduate/professional students (204 women). *Graduate faculty:* 48 full-time (11 women), 19 part-time/adjunct (7 women). *Computer facilities:* Computer purchase and lease plans are available. 400 computers available on campus for general student use. A campuswide network can be accessed from student residence rooms and from off campus. Internet access and online class registration, online access to grades and financial aid status are available. *Library facilities:* F. W. Crumb Memorial Library plus 1 other. *Graduate expenses:* Tuition, state resident: full-time $6,900; part-time $288 per credit hour. Tuition, nonresident: full-time $10,500; part-time $438 per credit hour. Required fees: $710; $29 per credit hour. One-time fee: $5 part-time. *General application contact:* Dr. William Amoriell, Dean of Education and Graduate Studies, 315-267-2515.

Crane School of Music
Dr. Alan Solomon, Dean
Programs in:
   composition • MM
   history and literature • MM
   music education • MM
   music theory • MM
   performance • MM

School of Arts and Sciences
Dr. Galen K. Pletcher, Dean
Programs in:
   arts and sciences • MA
   English • MA
   mathematics • MA

School of Education
Dr. William Amoriell, Dean of Education and Graduate Studies
Programs in:
   education • MS Ed, MST
   educational technology • MS Ed
   elementary education • MS Ed, MST
   professional education • MS Ed
   reading education • MS Ed
   secondary education • MS Ed, MST
   special education • MS Ed

■ STATE UNIVERSITY OF NEW YORK COLLEGE OF ENVIRONMENTAL SCIENCE AND FORESTRY
Syracuse, NY 13210-2779
http://www.esf.edu/

State-supported, coed, university. *Enrollment:* 2,016 graduate, professional, and undergraduate students; 287 full-time matriculated graduate/professional students (137 women), 167 part-time matriculated graduate/professional students (59 women). *Graduate faculty:* 115 full-time (20 women), 32 part-time/adjunct (15 women). *Computer facilities:* 150 computers available on campus for general student use. A campuswide network can be accessed from student residence rooms and from off campus. Internet access and online class registration are available. *Library facilities:* F. Franklin Moon Library plus 1 other. *Graduate expenses:* Part-time $288 per credit hour. Tuition, nonresident: part-time $438 per credit hour. Required fees: $300; $5 per credit hour. $18 per semester. One-time fee: $25 full-time. *General application contact:* Dr. Dudley J. Raynal, Dean, Instruction and Graduate Studies, 315-470-6599.

Find an in-depth description at www.petersons.com/gradchannel.

Faculty of Chemistry
Dr. John P. Hassett, Chair
Programs in:
   biochemistry • MS, PhD
   environmental and forest chemistry • MS, PhD
   organic chemistry of natural products • MS, PhD
   polymer chemistry • MS, PhD

Faculty of Construction Management and Wood Products Engineering
Dr. Robert W. Meyer, Chair
Program in:
   environmental and resources engineering • MPS, MS, PhD

Faculty of Environmental and Forest Biology
Dr. Neil H. Ringler, Chair
Programs in:
   chemical ecology • MPS, MS, PhD
   conservation biology • MPS, MS, PhD
   ecology • MPS, MS, PhD
   entomology • MPS, MS, PhD
   environmental interpretation • MPS, MS, PhD
   environmental physiology • MPS, MS, PhD
   fish and wildlife biology • MPS, MS, PhD
   forest pathology and mycology • MPS, MS, PhD
   plant science and biotechnology • MPS, MS, PhD

Faculty of Environmental Resources and Forest Engineering
Dr. James M. Hassett, Chair
Program in:
   environmental and resources engineering • MPS, MS, PhD

Faculty of Environmental Studies
Dr. Richard Smardon, Chair
Programs in:
   environmental and community land planning • MPS, MS, PhD
   environmental and natural resources policy • PhD
   environmental communication and participatory processes • MPS, MS, PhD
   environmental policy and democratic processes • MPS, MS, PhD
   environmental systems and risk management • MPS, MS, PhD
   water and wetland resource studies • MPS, MS, PhD

New York

State University of New York College of Environmental Science and Forestry (continued)

Faculty of Forest and Natural Resources Management
Dr. Chad P. Dawson, Chair
Programs in:
  environmental and natural resource policy • MS, PhD
  environmental and natural resources policy • MPS
  forest management and operations • MF
  forestry ecosystems science and applications • MPS, MS, PhD
  natural resources management • MPS, MS, PhD
  quantitative methods and management in forest science • MPS, MS, PhD
  recreation and resource management • MPS, MS, PhD
  watershed management and forest hydrology • MPS, MS, PhD

Faculty of Landscape Architecture
Richard S. Hawks, Chair
Programs in:
  community design and planning • MLA, MS
  cultural landscape studies and conservation • MLA, MS
  landscape and urban ecology • MLA, MS

Faculty of Paper Science and Engineering
Dr. Thomas E. Amidon, Chair
Program in:
  environmental and resources engineering • MPS, MS, PhD

■ STATE UNIVERSITY OF NEW YORK EMPIRE STATE COLLEGE
Saratoga Springs, NY 12866-4391
http://www.esc.edu/

State-supported, coed, comprehensive institution. *Enrollment:* 10,252 graduate, professional, and undergraduate students; 34 full-time matriculated graduate/professional students (20 women), 336 part-time matriculated graduate/professional students (214 women). *Graduate faculty:* 6 full-time (2 women), 109 part-time/adjunct (45 women). *Computer facilities:* 100 computers available on campus for general student use. A campuswide network can be accessed from off campus. Internet access and online class registration are available. *Graduate expenses:* Tuition, state resident: part-time $288 per credit. Tuition, nonresident: part-time $438 per credit.

Required fees: $85 per credit. $50 per term. Part-time tuition and fees vary according to course load, degree level and program. *General application contact:* Cammie Baker-Clancy, Assistant Director, 518-587-2100 Ext. 393.

Graduate Studies
Dr. Robert Carey, Dean
Programs in:
  business administration • MBA
  business and policy studies • MA
  labor and policy studies • MA
  liberal studies • MA
  social policy • MA
  teaching • MA

■ STATE UNIVERSITY OF NEW YORK INSTITUTE OF TECHNOLOGY
Utica, NY 13504-3050
http://www.sunyit.edu/

State-supported, coed, comprehensive institution. *Enrollment:* 2,682 graduate, professional, and undergraduate students; 165 full-time matriculated graduate/professional students (63 women), 354 part-time matriculated graduate/professional students (164 women). *Graduate faculty:* 65. *Computer facilities:* 250 computers available on campus for general student use. A campuswide network can be accessed from student residence rooms and from off campus. Internet access and online class registration, various other software applications are available. *Library facilities:* SUNY Institute of Technology at Utica/Rome Library. *Graduate expenses:* Tuition, state resident: full-time $6,900; part-time $288 per credit hour. Tuition, nonresident: full-time $10,500; part-time $438 per credit hour. Required fees: $764; $31 per credit hour. Tuition and fees vary according to program. *General application contact:* Marybeth Lyons, Director of Admissions, 315-792-7500.

Find an in-depth description at www.petersons.com/gradchannel.

School of Arts and Sciences
Dr. Linda Weber, Interim Dean
Programs in:
  applied sociology • MS
  information design and technology • MS

School of Information Systems and Engineering Technology
Dean
Programs in:
  advanced technology • MS
  computer and information science • MS
  telecommunications • MS

School of Management
Dr. Stephen Havlovic, Interim Dean
Programs in:
  accountancy • MS
  business administration in technology management • MBA
  health services administration • MS
  technology management • MBA

School of Nursing and Health Systems
Dr. Esther Bankert, Interim Dean
Programs in:
  adult nurse practitioner • MS, CAS
  family nurse practitioner • MS, CAS
  nursing administration • MS, CAS

■ STONY BROOK UNIVERSITY, STATE UNIVERSITY OF NEW YORK
Stony Brook, NY 11794
http://www.sunysb.edu/

State-supported, coed, university. CGS member. *Enrollment:* 22,344 graduate, professional, and undergraduate students; 4,247 full-time matriculated graduate/professional students (2,175 women), 2,845 part-time matriculated graduate/professional students (1,897 women). *Graduate faculty:* 1,191 full-time (346 women), 404 part-time/adjunct (162 women). *Computer facilities:* 2,587 computers available on campus for general student use. A campuswide network can be accessed from student residence rooms and from off campus. Internet access and online class registration are available. *Library facilities:* Frank Melville, Jr. Building Library plus 6 others. *Graduate expenses:* Tuition, state resident: full-time $6,900; part-time $288 per credit hour. Tuition, nonresident: full-time $10,500; part-time $438 per credit hour. Required fees: $22. *General application contact:* Dr. Kent Marks, Director, Admissions and Records, 631-632-4723.

Find an in-depth description at www.petersons.com/gradchannel.

Graduate School
Dr. Lawrence B. Martin, Dean

College of Arts and Sciences
Dr. James Staros, Dean
Programs in:
  anthropology • MA, PhD
  art history and criticism • MA, PhD
  arts and sciences • MA, MAPP, MAT, MFA, MM, MS, DA, DMA, PhD
  astronomy • MS, PhD
  biochemistry and molecular biology • PhD
  biochemistry and structural biology • PhD

New York

biological and biomedical sciences • PhD
biological sciences • MA
biopsychology • PhD
cellular and developmental biology • PhD
chemistry • MAT, MS, PhD
clinical psychology • PhD
dramaturgy • MFA
earth and space science • MS, PhD
earth and space sciences • MS, PhD
earth science • MAT
ecology and evolution • PhD
economics • MA, PhD
English • MA, PhD
experimental psychology • DA
foreign languages • DA
French • MA, MAT, DA
genetics • PhD
German • MA, MAT, DA
Germanic languages and literatures • MA
Hispanic languages and literature • MA, DA, PhD
history • MA, MAT, PhD
immunology and pathology • PhD
Italian • MA, MAT, DA
linguistics • MA, PhD
mathematics • MA, PhD
molecular and cellular biology • MA, PhD
music • MA, PhD
music history, theory and composition • MA, PhD
music performance • MM, DMA
neuroscience • PhD
philosophy • MA, PhD
physics • MA, MAT, MS, PhD
political science • MA, PhD
psychology • MA
public policy • MAPP
Romance languages and literatures • MA
Russian • MAT, DA
Slavic languages and literatures • MA
social/health psychology • PhD
sociology • MA, PhD
studio art • MFA
teaching English to speakers of other languages • MA, DA
theatre • MA

College of Engineering and Applied Sciences
Dr. Yacov Shamash, Dean
Programs in:
applied mathematics and statistics • MS, PhD
biomedical engineering • MS, PhD, Certificate
computer science • MS, PhD
educational computing • MS, Advanced Certificate
electrical and computer engineering • MS, PhD
engineering and applied sciences • MBA, MS, PhD, Advanced Certificate, Certificate
environmental and waste management • MS, Advanced Certificate
global industrial management • MS
industrial management • Advanced Certificate, Certificate
management and policy • MS
materials science and engineering • MS, PhD
mechanical engineering • MS, PhD
medical physics • PhD
optoelectromechanical systems engineering • MS
software engineering • Certificate
technological systems management • MS
technology management • MBA, MS

Institute for Terrestrial and Planetary Atmospheres
Minghua Zhang, Director
Program in:
terrestrial and planetary atmospheres • PhD

Marine Sciences Research Center
Dr. David O. Conover, Dean and Director
Program in:
marine and atmospheric sciences • MS, PhD

Health Sciences Center
Dr. Norman H. Edelman, Vice President
Programs in:
community health • MPH
evaluation sciences • MPH
family violence • MPH
health economics • MPH
health sciences • DDS, MD, MPH, MS, MSW, DPT, PhD, Advanced Certificate, Certificate
population health • MPH
substance abuse • MPH

School of Dental Medicine
Dr. Barry R. Rifkin, Dean
Programs in:
dental medicine • DDS
endodontics • Certificate
oral biology and pathology • PhD
orthodontics • Certificate
periodontics • Certificate

School of Health Technology and Management
Dr. Craig A. Lehmann, Dean
Programs in:
community health • Advanced Certificate
health care management • Advanced Certificate
health care policy and management • MS
occupational therapy • MS
physical therapy • MS, DPT

School of Medicine
Programs in:
anatomical sciences • PhD
medicine • MD, PhD
molecular and cellular pharmacology • PhD
molecular microbiology • PhD
physiology and biophysics • PhD

School of Nursing
Dr. Lenora J. McClean, Dean
Programs in:
adult health nurse practitioner • Certificate
adult health/primary care nursing • MS
child health nurse practitioner • Certificate
child health nursing • MS
family nurse practitioner • MS, Certificate
gerontological nursing • MS
mental health nurse practitioner • Certificate
mental health/psychiatric nursing • MS
neonatal nurse practitioner • Certificate
neonatal nursing • MS
nurse-midwifery • MS, Certificate
nursing • MS, Certificate
perinatal/women's health nurse practitioner • Certificate
perinatal/women's health nursing • MS

School of Social Welfare
Dr. Frances L. Brisbane, Dean
Programs in:
social welfare • PhD
social work • MSW

School of Professional Development and Continuing Studies
Dr. Paul J. Edelson, Dean
Programs in:
biology 7-12 • MAT
chemistry-grade 7-12 • MAT
coaching • Certificate
computer integrated engineering • Certificate
cultural studies • Certificate
earth science-grade 7-12 • MAT
educational computing • Certificate
English-grade 7-12 • MAT
environmental systems management • Certificate
environmental/occupational health and safety • Certificate
French-grade 7-12 • MAT
German-grade 7-12 • MAT
human resource management • Certificate
industrial management • Certificate
information systems management • Certificate
Italian-grade 7-12 • MAT

New York

Stony Brook University, State University of New York (continued)
  liberal studies • MA
  liberal studies online • MA
  Long Island regional studies • Certificate
  operation research • Certificate
  physics-grade 7-12 • MAT
  Russian-grade 7-12 • MAT
  school administration and supervision • Certificate
  school district administration • Certificate
  social science and the professions • MPS
  social studies 7-12 • MAT
  waste management • Certificate
  women's studies • Certificate

■ SYRACUSE UNIVERSITY
Syracuse, NY 13244-0003
http://www.syracuse.edu/

Independent, coed, university. CGS member. *Enrollment:* 15,598 graduate, professional, and undergraduate students; 2,817 full-time matriculated graduate/professional students (1,405 women), 1,612 part-time matriculated graduate/professional students (848 women). *Graduate faculty:* 864 full-time (290 women), 498 part-time/adjunct. *Computer facilities:* 1,200 computers available on campus for general student use. A campuswide network can be accessed from student residence rooms and from off campus. Internet access and online class registration, online services, networked client and server computing are available. *Library facilities:* E. S. Bird Library plus 6 others. *Graduate expenses:* Tuition: full-time $13,356; part-time $742 per credit. Required fees: $482. *General application contact:* The Graduate Enrollment Management Center, 315-443-4492.

College of Law
Program in:
  law • JD

Graduate School
Dr. John Mercer, Dean

College of Arts and Sciences
Dr. Cathryn Newton, Dean
Programs in:
  applied statistics • MS
  art history • MA
  arts and sciences • MA, MFA, MS, PhD, CAS
  audiology • MS, PhD
  biology • MS, PhD
  chemistry • MS, PhD
  clinical psychology • PhD
  college science teaching • PhD
  composition and cultural rhetoric • PhD
  creative writing • MFA
  English • MA, PhD
  experimental psychology • PhD
  French language, literature and culture • MA
  geology • MA, MS, PhD
  linguistic studies • MA
  mathematics • MS, PhD
  philosophy • MA, PhD
  physics • MS, PhD
  religion • MA, PhD
  school psychology • PhD
  social psychology • PhD
  Spanish language, literature and culture • MA
  speech pathology • MS, PhD
  structural biology, biochemistry and biophysics • PhD
  women's studies • CAS

College of Human Services and Health Professions
Dr. Bruce Lagay, Dean
Programs in:
  child and family studies • MA, MS, PhD
  human services and health professions • MA, MS, MSW, PhD
  marriage and family therapy • MA, PhD
  nutrition science and food management • MA, MS
  social work • MSW

College of Visual and Performing Arts
Carole Brzozowski, Dean
Programs in:
  advertising design • MA
  art media studies • MFA
  art photography process • MFA
  art video • MFA
  arts education • MS
  ceramics • MFA
  computer arts • MFA
  conducting • M Mus
  fashion and design technologies • MA, MS
  fashion design • MFA
  fiber structure interlocking • MFA
  film • MFA
  history of arts • MFA
  illustration • MA
  metalsmithing • MFA
  museum studies • MA, MFA
  music composition • M Mus
  music theory • M Mus
  organ • M Mus
  painting • MFA
  percussion • M Mus
  piano • M Mus
  printmaking • MFA
  sculpture • MFA
  speech communication • MA, MS
  strings • M Mus
  studio arts • MFA
  surface pattern design • MFA
  textile design • MFA
  theory • M Mus
  visual and performing arts • M Mus, MA, MFA, MS
  visual communications • MA
  voice • M Mus
  wind instruments • M Mus

L. C. Smith College of Engineering and Computer Science
Dr. Eric F. Spina, Dean
Programs in:
  aerospace engineering • MS, PhD
  bioengineering • ME, MS, PhD
  chemical engineering • MS, PhD
  civil engineering • MS, PhD
  computer and information science • PhD
  computer engineering • MS, PhD, CE
  computer science • MS
  electrical engineering • MS, PhD, EE
  engineering and computer science • ME, MS, PhD, CE, EE
  engineering management • MS
  environmental engineering • MS
  environmental engineering science • MS
  manufacturing engineering • MS
  mechanical and aerospace engineering • PhD
  mechanical engineering • MS
  neuroscience • MS
  systems and information science • MS

Maxwell School of Citizenship and Public Affairs
Mitchel Wallerstein, Dean
Programs in:
  anthropology • MA, PhD
  citizenship and public affairs • MA, MPA, MS Sc, PhD, CAS
  economics • MA, PhD
  geography • MA, PhD
  health services management and policy • CAS
  history • MA, PhD
  international relations • MA
  political science • MA, PhD
  public administration • MA, MPA, PhD, CAS
  social sciences • MS Sc, PhD
  sociology • MA, PhD

School of Architecture
Mark Robbins, Dean
Program in:
  architecture • M Arch

School of Education
Dr. Louise Wilkinson, Dean
Programs in:
  art education • MS, CAS
  childhood education • MS
  counselor education • MS, PhD, CAS
  cultural foundations of education • MS, PhD, CAS
  disability studies • CAS

early childhood special education • MS
education • M Mu, MS, Ed D, PhD, CAS
educational leadership • MS, Ed D, PhD, CAS
elementary education • MS, CAS
English education • PhD, CAS
exercise science • MS, PhD
higher education • PhD
inclusive special education (grades 1–6) • MS
inclusive special education (grades 7–12) • MS
instructional design, development, and evaluation • PhD, CAS
learning disabilities • MS
literacy education • MS
mathematics education • MS, PhD
music education • M Mu, MS
reading education • PhD, CAS
rehabilitation counseling • MS
science education • MS, PhD, CAS
social studies education • MS, CAS
special education • PhD
teaching and curriculum • MS, PhD, CAS

School of Information Studies
Dr. Raymond F. von Dran, Dean
Programs in:
digital libraries • CAS
information and library science • MS
information management • MS, CAS
information security management • CAS
information systems and telecommunications management • CAS
information transfer • PhD
library and information science • MS, CAS
school media • MS, CAS
telecommunications and network management • MS

S. I. Newhouse School of Public Communications
David M. Rubin, Dean
Programs in:
advertising • MA
broadcast journalism • MS
communications management • MS
magazine, newspaper and online journalism • MA
mass communications • PhD
media management • MS
media studies • MA
new media • MS
photography • MS
public communications • MA, MS, PhD
public relations • MS
television-radio-film • MA

Martin J. Whitman School of Management
Sandra N. Hurd, Interim Dean
Programs in:
accounting • PhD
business administration • MBA, PhD
finance • PhD
management • MBA, MS Acct, MSF, PhD
management information systems • PhD
managerial statistics • PhD
marketing • PhD
operations management • PhD
organizational behavior • PhD
strategy and human resources • PhD
supply chain management • PhD

■ **TEACHERS COLLEGE COLUMBIA UNIVERSITY**
New York, NY 10027-6696
http://www.tc.columbia.edu/

Independent, coed, graduate-only institution. *Graduate faculty:* 153 full-time (88 women), 227 part-time/adjunct. *Computer facilities:* 165 computers available on campus for general student use. A campuswide network can be accessed from student residence rooms and from off campus. Internet access and online class registration are available. *Library facilities:* Milbank Memorial Library. *Graduate expenses:* Tuition: full-time $20,180. *General application contact:* Thomas Rock, Director of Admissions, 212-678-3083.

Find an in-depth description at www.petersons.com/gradchannel.

Graduate Faculty of Education
Arthur Levine, President
Programs in:
administration and supervision in special education • Ed M, MA, Ed D, PhD
adult education • MA, Ed D
anthropology • Ed M, MA, Ed D, PhD
applied educational psychology—school psychology • Ed M, MA, Ed D, PhD
applied linguistics • Ed M, MA, Ed D
applied physiology • Ed M, MA, MS, Ed D
art and art education • Ed M, MA, Ed D, Ed DCT
arts administration • MA
audiology • Ed M, MS, Ed D, PhD
behavioral disorders • MA, Ed D, PhD
bilingual and bicultural education • MA
blind and visual impairment • MA, Ed D
clinical psychology • MA, PhD
college teaching and academic leadership • Ed D
communications • Ed M, MA, Ed D
comparative and international education • Ed M, MA, Ed D, PhD
computing in education • MA
counseling psychology • Ed M, Ed D, PhD
curriculum and teaching • Ed M, MA, Ed D
curriculum and teaching in physical education • Ed M, MA, Ed D
dance and dance education • MA
developmental psychology • MA, Ed D, PhD
early childhood education • Ed M, MA, Ed D
early childhood special education • Ed M, MA
economics and education • Ed M, MA, Ed D, PhD
education • Ed M, MA, MS, Ed D, Ed DCT, PhD
educational administration • Ed M, MA, Ed D, PhD
educational media/instructional technology • Ed M, MA, Ed D
educational psychology-human cognition and learning • Ed M, MA, Ed D, PhD
elementary/childhood education, preservice • MA
giftedness • MA, Ed D
health education • MA, MS, Ed D
hearing impairment • MA, Ed D
higher education • Ed M, MA, Ed D, PhD
history and education • Ed M, MA, Ed D, PhD
inquiry in educational administration • Ed D
interdisciplinary studies • Ed M, MA, Ed D
international educational development • Ed M, MA, Ed D, PhD
learning disabilities • Ed M, MA, Ed D
mathematics education • Ed M, MA, MS, Ed D, Ed DCT, PhD
measurement, evaluation, and statistics • MA, MS, Ed D, PhD
mental retardation • MA, Ed D, PhD
motor learning/movement science • Ed M, MA, Ed D
music and music education • Ed M, MA, Ed D, Ed DCT
neuroscience and education • Ed M, Ed D
nurse executive • Ed M, MA, Ed D
nursing, professional role • Ed M, MA, Ed D
nutrition and education • Ed M, MS, Ed D
nutrition education • Ed M, MS, Ed D

New York

Teachers College Columbia University (continued)
- nutrition education and public health nutrition • Ed M, MS, Ed D
- organizational psychology • MA, Ed D, PhD
- philosophy and education • Ed M, MA, Ed D, PhD
- physical disabilities • MA, Ed D, PhD
- politics and education • Ed M, MA, Ed D, PhD
- reading specialist • MA
- reading/learning disability • Ed M
- religion and education • Ed M, MA, Ed D
- research in special education • Ed D
- science education • Ed M, MA, MS, Ed D, Ed DCT, PhD
- social and organizational psychology • MA, Ed D, PhD
- social psychology • Ed D, PhD
- social studies education • Ed M, MA, Ed D, PhD
- sociology and education • Ed M, MA, Ed D, PhD
- special education • Ed M, MA, Ed D
- speech-language pathology • Ed M, MS, Ed D, PhD
- student personnel administration • Ed M, MA, Ed D
- teaching English to speakers of other languages • Ed M, MA, Ed D
- teaching of English and English education • Ed M, MA, Ed D, PhD
- teaching of sign language • MA
- teaching of Spanish • Ed M, MA, Ed D, Ed DCT, PhD

■ TOURO COLLEGE
New York, NY 10010
http://www.touro.edu/

Independent, coed, comprehensive institution. *Computer facilities:* 350 computers available on campus for general student use. A campuswide network can be accessed from off campus. Internet access and online class registration are available. *Library facilities:* Touro College Library plus 14 others.

Barry Z. Levine School of Health Sciences
Programs in:
- biomedical sciences • MS
- health information management • Certificate
- occupational therapy • MS
- physical therapy • MS

Jacob D. Fuchsberg Law Center
Programs in:
- law • JD
- U.S. law for foreign lawyers • LL M

School of Jewish Studies
Program in:
- Jewish studies • MA

■ UNIVERSITY AT ALBANY, STATE UNIVERSITY OF NEW YORK
Albany, NY 12222-0001
http://www.albany.edu/

State-supported, coed, university. CGS member. *Enrollment:* 16,998 graduate, professional, and undergraduate students; 2,513 full-time matriculated graduate/professional students (1,519 women), 2,080 part-time matriculated graduate/professional students (1,311 women). *Graduate faculty:* 558 full-time, 328 part-time/adjunct. *Computer facilities:* 500 computers available on campus for general student use. A campuswide network can be accessed from student residence rooms and from off campus. Internet access is available. *Library facilities:* University Library plus 2 others. *Graduate expenses:* Tuition, state resident: part-time $288 per credit. Tuition, nonresident: part-time $438 per credit. Required fees: $495 per semester. *General application contact:* Jeffrey Collins, Director, Graduate Admissions, 518-442-3980.

College of Arts and Sciences
Joan Wick-Pelletier, Dean
Programs in:
- African studies • MA
- Afro-American studies • MA
- anthropology • MA, PhD
- art • MA, MFA
- arts and sciences • MA, MFA, MRP, MS, PhD, Certificate
- atmospheric science • MS, PhD
- biodiversity, conservation, and policy • MS
- biopsychology • PhD
- chemistry • MS, PhD
- clinical psychology • PhD
- communication • MA
- computer science • MS, PhD
- demography • Certificate
- ecology, evolution, and behavior • MS, PhD
- economics • MA, PhD, Certificate
- English • MA, PhD
- forensic molecular biology • MS
- French • MA, PhD
- general/experimental psychology • PhD
- geographic information systems and spatial analysis • Certificate
- geography • MA, Certificate
- geology • MS, PhD
- history • MA, PhD
- industrial/organizational psychology • PhD
- Italian • MA
- Latin American and Caribbean studies • MA, Certificate
- liberal studies • MA
- mathematics • PhD
- molecular, cellular, developmental, and neural biology • MS, PhD
- philosophy • MA, PhD
- physics • MS, PhD
- psychology • MA
- public history • Certificate
- regional planning • MRP
- Russian • MA, Certificate
- Russian translation • Certificate
- secondary teaching • MA
- social/personality psychology • PhD
- sociology • MA, PhD
- sociology and communication • PhD
- Spanish • MA, PhD
- statistics • MA
- theatre • MA
- urban policy • Certificate
- women's studies • MA

Nelson A. Rockefeller College of Public Affairs and Policy
Dr. Frank J. Thompson, Dean
Programs in:
- administrative behavior • PhD
- comparative and development administration • MPA, PhD
- human resources • MPA
- legislative administration • MPA
- planning and policy analysis • CAS
- policy analysis • MPA
- political science • MA, PhD
- program analysis and evaluation • PhD
- public affairs and policy • MA
- public finance • MPA, PhD
- public management • MPA, PhD

School of Business
Paul Leonard, Interim Dean
Programs in:
- accounting • MS
- business • MBA, MS, PhD
- finance • MBA
- human resource systems • MBA
- management science and information systems • MBA
- marketing • MBA
- organizational studies • PhD
- taxation • MS

School of Criminal Justice
Julie Horney, Dean
Program in:
- criminal justice • MA, PhD

School of Education
Susanne K. Phillips, Dean
Programs in:
- counseling psychology • MS, PhD, CAS
- curriculum and instruction • MS, Ed D, CAS
- curriculum planning and development • MA

New York

education • MA, MS, Ed D, PhD, Psy D, CAS
educational administration • MS, PhD, CAS
educational communications • MS, CAS
educational psychology • Ed D
educational psychology and statistics • MS
measurements and evaluation • Ed D
reading • MS, Ed D, CAS
rehabilitation counseling • MS
school counselor • CAS
school psychology • Psy D, CAS
special education • MS
statistics and research design • Ed D

School of Information Science and Policy
Peter Bloniarz, Dean
Programs in:
information science • MS, PhD
information science and policy • CAS
library science • MLS

School of Public Health
Dr. Peter Levin, Dean
Programs in:
biochemistry, molecular biology, and genetics • MS, PhD
biometry and statistics • MS, PhD
cell and molecular structure • MS, PhD
environmental and occupational health • MS, PhD
environmental chemistry • MS, PhD
epidemiology • MS, PhD
health policy, management, and behavior • MS
immunobiology and immunochemistry • MS, PhD
molecular pathogenesis • MS, PhD
neuroscience • MS, PhD
public health • MPH, MS, Dr PH, PhD
toxicology • MS, PhD

School of Social Welfare
Katharine Briar-Lawson, Dean
Program in:
social welfare • MSW, PhD

■ **UNIVERSITY AT BUFFALO, THE STATE UNIVERSITY OF NEW YORK**
Buffalo, NY 14260
http://www.buffalo.edu/

State-supported, coed, university. CGS member. *Enrollment:* 27,255 graduate, professional, and undergraduate students; 6,958 full-time matriculated graduate/professional students (3,436 women), 2,136 part-time matriculated graduate/professional students (1,214 women). *Graduate faculty:* 1,214 full-time (356 women), 958 part-time/adjunct (340 women). *Computer facilities:* 2,391 computers available on campus for general student use. A campuswide network can be accessed from student residence rooms and from off campus. Internet access and online class registration are available. *Library facilities:* Lockwood Library plus 7 others. *Graduate expenses:* Tuition, state resident: full-time $7,110. Tuition, nonresident: full-time $10,920. Tuition and fees vary according to program. *General application contact:* Katherine Gerstle Ferguson, Associate Vice Provost, 716-645-5908.

Find an in-depth description at www.petersons.com/gradchannel.

Graduate School
Dr. Myron A. Thompson, Associate Provost and Executive Director of the Graduate School
Programs in:
cancer pathology and prevention • PhD
cancer research and biomedical sciences • MS, PhD
cellular and molecular biology • PhD
immunology • PhD
molecular and cellular biophysics and biochemistry • PhD
molecular pharmacology and cancer therapeutics • PhD
natural and biomedical sciences • MS

College of Arts and Sciences
Dr. Uday P. Sukhatme, Dean
Programs in:
American studies • MA, PhD
anthropology • MA, PhD
art history • MA
arts and sciences • MA, MFA, MM, MS, Au D, PhD, Certificate
audiology • Au D
behavioral neuroscience • PhD
biological sciences • MA, MS, PhD
chemistry • MA, PhD
classics • MA, PhD
clinical psychology • PhD
cognitive psychology • PhD
communicative disorders and sciences • MA, PhD
comparative literature • MA, PhD
economics • MA, PhD
English • MA, PhD
financial economics • Certificate
fine arts • MFA
French • MA, PhD
general psychology • MA
geographic information science • Certificate
geography • MA, PhD
geology • MA, MS, PhD
health services • Certificate
historical musicology and music theory • PhD
history • MA, PhD
humanities • MA
information and Internet economics • Certificate
international economics • Certificate
law and regulation • Certificate
linguistics • MA, PhD
mathematics • MA, PhD
media study • MFA
medicinal chemistry • MS, PhD
music composition • MA, PhD
music education • MM
music history • MA, PhD
music performance • MM
music theory • MA, PhD
natural science • MS
new media design • Certificate
philosophy • MA, PhD
physics • MS, PhD
political science • MA, PhD
social sciences • MS
social-personality • PhD
sociology • MA, PhD
Spanish • MA, PhD
transportation and business geographics • Certificate
urban and regional economics • Certificate

Graduate School of Education
Mary H. Gresham, Dean
Programs in:
adolescence education • Certificate
biology • Ed M
chemistry • Ed M
childhood education • Ed M
counseling/school psychology • PhD
counselor education • PhD
early childhood and childhood education with bilingual extension • Ed M
early childhood education • Ed M
Earth science • Ed M
education • Ed M, MA, MS, Ed D, PhD, Certificate
education technology specialist • Ed M
educational administration • Ed M, Ed D, PhD
educational psychology • MA, PhD
educational technology • Certificate
elementary education • Ed D, PhD
English • Ed M
English education • PhD
English for speakers of other languages • Ed M
foreign and second language education • PhD
French • Ed M
general education • Ed M
German • Ed M
higher education • PhD
higher education administration • Ed M
Italian • Ed M
Japanese • Ed M
Latin • Ed M
literary specialist • Ed M
mathematics • Ed M
mathematics education • PhD

Peterson's Graduate Schools in the U.S. 2006

www.petersons.com **473**

New York

University at Buffalo, The State University of New York (continued)
  mentoring teachers • Certificate
  music education • Ed M, Certificate
  physics • Ed M
  reading education • PhD
  rehabilitation counseling • MS
  Russian • Ed M
  school administrator and supervisor • Certificate
  school business and human resource administration • Certificate
  school counseling • Ed M, Certificate
  school psychology • MA
  science education • PhD
  social foundations • PhD
  social studies • Ed M
  Spanish • Ed M
  special education • PhD
  specialist in education administration • Certificate
  teaching and leading for diversity • Certificate
  teaching English to speakers of other languages • Ed M

Law School
R. Nils Olsen, Dean
Programs in:
  criminal law • LL M
  international law • LL M
  law • JD

School of Architecture and Planning
Brian Carter, Dean
Programs in:
  architecture • M Arch
  architecture and planning • M Arch, MUP
  planning • MUP

School of Dental Medicine
Dr. Richard N. Buchanan, Dean
Programs in:
  biomaterials • MS
  combined prosthodontics • Certificate
  dental medicine • DDS, MS, PhD, Certificate
  endodontics • Certificate
  fixed prosthodontics • Certificate
  oral and maxillofacial pathology • Certificate
  oral and maxillofacial surgery • Certificate
  oral biology • PhD
  oral sciences • MS
  orthodontics • MS, Certificate
  pediatric dentistry • Certificate
  periodontics • Certificate
  removable prosthodontics • Certificate
  restorative dentistry • MS, Certificate
  temporomandibular disorders and oralfacial pain • Certificate

School of Engineering and Applied Sciences
Dr. Mark H. Karwan, Dean
Programs in:
  aerospace engineering • M Eng, MS, PhD
  chemical and biological engineering • M Eng, MS, PhD
  civil engineering • M Eng, MS, PhD
  computer science and engineering • MS, PhD
  electrical engineering • M Eng, MS, PhD
  engineering and applied sciences • M Eng, MS, PhD
  engineering science • MS
  industrial engineering • M Eng, MS, PhD
  mechanical engineering • M Eng, MS, PhD

School of Informatics
Dr. W. David Penniman, Dean
Programs in:
  communication • MA, PhD
  informatics • MA, MLS, PhD, Certificate
  library and information studies • MLS, PhD, Certificate

School of Management
John M. Thomas, Dean
Programs in:
  accounting • MS
  business administration • MBA
  management • PhD
  management information systems • MS
  organizational leadership, change, and development • MS
  supply chains and operations management • MS

School of Medicine and Biomedical Sciences
Dr. Margaret Paroski, Dean and Vice President for Health Affairs
Programs in:
  anatomical sciences • MA, PhD
  biochemical pharmacology • MS, PhD
  biochemistry • MA, PhD
  biomedical sciences • PhD
  biophysics • MS, PhD
  biotechology • MS
  medicine • MD
  medicine and biomedical sciences • MD, MA, MS, PhD
  microbiology and immunology • MA, PhD
  neuroscience • MS, PhD
  pathology • MA, PhD
  pharmacology • MA, PhD
  physiology • MA, PhD

School of Nursing
Dr. Mecca S. Cranley, Dean
Programs in:
  acute care nurse practitioner • MS, Certificate
  adult health nursing • MS, Certificate
  child health nursing • MS
  family nursing • MS
  geriatric nurse practitioner • MS, Certificate
  maternal and women's health nurse practitioner • Certificate
  maternal and women's health nursing • MS
  nurse anesthetist • MS
  nursing • DNS
  nursing education • Certificate
  pediatric nurse practitioner • Certificate
  psychiatric/mental health nurse practitioner • Certificate
  psychiatric/mental health nursing • MS

School of Pharmacy and Pharmaceutical Sciences
Dr. Wayne K. Anderson, Dean
Programs in:
  pharmaceutical sciences • MS, PhD
  pharmacy • Pharm D
  pharmacy and pharmaceutical sciences • Pharm D, MS, PhD

School of Public Health and Health Professions
Dr. Maurizio Trevisan, Dean
Programs in:
  biostatistics • MA, PhD
  epidemiology • MS
  epidemiology and community health • PhD
  exercise science • MS, PhD
  nutrition • MS
  occupational therapy • MS
  physical therapy • DPT
  public health • MPH
  public health and health professions • MA, MPH, MS, DPT, PhD, Certificate
  rehabilitation science • PhD

School of Social Work
Dr. Andrew Safyer, Interim Dean
Program in:
  social work • MSW, PhD

■ **UNIVERSITY OF ROCHESTER**
Rochester, NY 14627-0250
http://www.rochester.edu/

Independent, coed, university. CGS member. *Enrollment:* 8,543 graduate, professional, and undergraduate students; 2,883 full-time matriculated graduate/professional students (1,231 women), 1,078 part-time matriculated graduate/professional students (618 women). *Graduate faculty:* 2,009. *Computer facilities:* 260 computers available on campus for general student use. A campuswide network can be accessed from student residence rooms and from off campus. *Library facilities:* Rush Rhees Library plus 5 others. *Graduate expenses:* Tuition: part-time $880 per credit hour. Required fees: $522. *General application contact:* Bruce Jacobs, Dean of Graduate Studies, 585-275-3540.

The College, Arts and Sciences
Thomas LeBlanc, Vice Provost and Dean of the Faculty
Programs in:
  arts and sciences • MA, MS, PhD
  biology • MS, PhD
  brain and cognitive sciences • MS, PhD
  chemistry • MS, PhD
  clinical psychology • PhD
  computer science • MS, PhD
  developmental psychology • PhD
  economics • MA, PhD
  English • MA, PhD
  geological sciences • MS, PhD
  history • MA, PhD
  mathematics • MA, MS, PhD
  philosophy • MA, PhD
  physics • MA, MS, PhD
  physics and astronomy • PhD
  political science • MA, PhD
  psychology • MA
  social-personality psychology • PhD
  visual and cultural studies • MA, PhD

The College, School of Engineering and Applied Sciences
Kevin Parker, Dean
Programs in:
  biomedical engineering • MS, PhD
  chemical engineering • MS, PhD
  electrical and computer engineering • MS, PhD
  engineering and applied sciences • MS, PhD
  materials science • MS, PhD
  mechanical engineering • MS, PhD

Institute of Optics
Wayne Knox, Director
Program in:
  optics • MS, PhD

Eastman School of Music
James Undercofler, Director
Programs in:
  composition • MA, MM, DMA, PhD
  conducting • MM, DMA
  education • MA, PhD
  jazz studies/contemporary media • MM
  music education • MM, DMA
  musicology • MA, PhD
  pedagogy of music theory • MA
  performance and literature • MM, DMA
  piano accompanying and chamber music • MM, DMA
  theory • MA, PhD

Margaret Warner Graduate School of Education and Human Development
Raffaella Borasi, Dean
Program in:
  education and human development • MAT, MS, Ed D, PhD

School of Medicine and Dentistry
Dr. David Guzick, Dean
Programs in:
  medicine • MD
  medicine and dentistry • MD, MA, MPH, MS, PhD, Certificate

Graduate Programs in Medicine and Dentistry
Paul La Celle, Senior Associate Dean
Programs in:
  biochemistry • MS, PhD
  biophysics • MS, PhD
  epidemiology • MS, PhD
  genetics, genomics and development • MS, PhD
  health services research and policy • PhD
  marriage and family therapy • MS
  medical statistics • MS
  medicine and dentistry • MA, MPH, MS, PhD
  microbiology • MS, PhD
  neurobiology and anatomy • MS, PhD
  neuroscience • MS, PhD
  oral biology • MS
  pathology • MS, PhD
  pharmacology • MS, PhD
  physiology • MS, PhD
  public health • MPH
  statistics • MA, PhD
  toxicology • MS, PhD

School of Nursing
Dr. Patricia Chiverton, Dean
Program in:
  nursing • MS, PhD, Certificate

William E. Simon Graduate School of Business Administration
Mark Zupan, Dean
Program in:
  business administration • MBA, MS, PhD

■ WAGNER COLLEGE
Staten Island, NY 10301-4495
http://www.wagner.edu/

Independent, coed, comprehensive institution. *Enrollment:* 2,218 graduate, professional, and undergraduate students; 183 full-time matriculated graduate/professional students (105 women), 209 part-time matriculated graduate/professional students (144 women). *Graduate faculty:* 27 full-time (16 women), 27 part-time/adjunct (14 women). *Computer facilities:* 150 computers available on campus for general student use. A campuswide network can be accessed from student residence rooms and from off campus. Internet access is available. *Library facilities:* August Horrmann Library. *Graduate expenses:* Tuition: part-time $780 per credit. *General application contact:* 718-390-3411.

Division of Graduate Studies
Dr. Jeffrey Glanz, Dean of Graduate Studies
Programs in:
  accounting • MS
  adolescent education • MS Ed
  advanced physician assistant studies • MS
  childhood education • MS Ed
  early childhood education (birth–grade 2) • MS Ed
  family nurse practitioner • Certificate
  finance • MBA
  health care administration • MBA
  international business • MBA
  literacy (B–6) • MS Ed
  management • Exec MBA, MBA
  marketing • MBA
  microbiology • MS
  middle level education (5–9) • MS Ed
  nursing • MS

■ YESHIVA UNIVERSITY
New York, NY 10033-3201
http://www.yu.edu/

Independent, coed, university. CGS member. *Computer facilities:* 142 computers available on campus for general student use. Internet access is available. *Library facilities:* Mendel Gottesman Library plus 6 others. *General application contact:* Associate Director of Admissions, 212-960-5277.

Albert Einstein College of Medicine
Program in:
  medicine • MD, PhD

Sue Golding Graduate Division of Medical Sciences
Programs in:
  anatomy • PhD
  biochemistry • PhD
  cell and developmental biology • PhD
  cell biology • PhD
  developmental and molecular biology • PhD
  medical sciences • PhD
  microbiology and immunology • PhD
  molecular genetics • PhD
  molecular pharmacology • PhD
  neuroscience • PhD
  pathology • PhD
  physiology and biophysics • PhD

New York

Yeshiva University (continued)
Azrieli Graduate School of Jewish Education and Administration
Program in:
 Jewish education and administration • MS, Ed D, Specialist

Benjamin N. Cardozo School of Law
David Rudenstine, Dean
Programs in:
 general law • LL M
 intellectual property law • LL M
 law • JD

Bernard Revel Graduate School of Jewish Studies
Program in:
 Jewish studies • MA, PhD

Ferkauf Graduate School of Psychology
Dr. Lawrence J. Siegel, Dean
Programs in:
 clinical psychology • Psy D
 developmental psychology • PhD
 general psychology • MA
 health psychology • PhD
 psychology • MA, PhD, Psy D
 school/clinical-child psychology • Psy D

Wurzweiler School of Social Work
Dr. Sheldon R. Gelman, Dean
Program in:
 social work • MSW, PhD

North Carolina

■ APPALACHIAN STATE UNIVERSITY
Boone, NC 28608
http://www.appstate.edu/

State-supported, coed, comprehensive institution. CGS member. *Enrollment:* 14,343 graduate, professional, and undergraduate students; 836 full-time matriculated graduate/professional students (551 women), 673 part-time matriculated graduate/professional students (482 women). *Graduate faculty:* 413 full-time (150 women), 31 part-time/adjunct (17 women). *Computer facilities:* 500 computers available on campus for general student use. A campuswide network can be accessed from student residence rooms. Internet access is available. *Library facilities:* Carol Grotnes Belk Library plus 1 other. *Graduate expenses:* Tuition, state resident: full-time $1,668; part-time $208 per credit. Tuition, nonresident: full-time $11,176; part-time $1,397 per credit. Required fees: $1,361; $196 per term. *General application contact:* Dr. E. D. Huntley, Senior Associate Dean for Graduate Studies, 828-262-2130.

Cratis D. Williams Graduate School
Dean of Graduate Studies and Research
Program in:
 information systems • Certificate

College of Arts and Sciences
Dean
Programs in:
 Appalachian studies • MA
 applied physics • MS
 arts and sciences • MA, MPA, MS, CAS
 biology • MA, MS
 clinical psychology • MA
 computer science • MS
 English • MA
 English education • MA
 general experimental psychology • MA
 geography • MA
 gerontology • MA
 health psychology • MA
 history • MA
 industrial and organizational psychology • MA
 mathematics • MA
 mathematics education • MA
 political science • MA
 public administration • MPA
 public history • MA
 romance languages • MA
 school psychology • MA, CAS
 social sciences • MA

College of Education
Dr. Charles Duke, Dean
Programs in:
 communication disorders • MA
 community counseling • MA
 curriculum specialist • MA
 early childhood education • MA
 education • MA, MLS, MSA, Ed D, Ed S
 educational leadership • Ed D
 educational media • MA, Ed S
 elementary education • MA
 higher education • MA, Ed S
 instructional technology • MA, Ed S
 library science • MA, MLS, Ed S
 marriage and family therapy • MA
 reading education • MA
 school administration • MSA
 school counseling • MA, Ed S
 secondary education • MA
 special education • MA
 speech pathology • MA
 student development • MA, Ed S

College of Fine and Applied Arts
Dr. Mark Estepp, Dean
Programs in:
 child development • MA
 exercise science • MS
 family and consumer science • MA
 fine and applied arts • MA, MS
 industrial education • MA
 industrial technology • MA
 master teacher • MA
 physical education • MA
 sport management • MA
 sports management • MA

John A. Walker College of Business
Dr. Lyle Schoenfeldt, Dean
Programs in:
 accounting • MS
 business • MBA, MS
 business administration • MBA

School of Music
Dr. William Harbinson, Dean
Programs in:
 music education • MM
 music performance • MM

■ CAMPBELL UNIVERSITY
Buies Creek, NC 27506
http://www.campbell.edu/

Independent-religious, coed, university. *Enrollment:* 3,975 graduate, professional, and undergraduate students; 955 full-time matriculated graduate/professional students (527 women), 680 part-time matriculated graduate/professional students (417 women). *Graduate faculty:* 103 full-time (36 women), 37 part-time/adjunct (7 women). *Computer facilities:* 256 computers available on campus for general student use. A campuswide network can be accessed from student residence rooms and from off campus. Internet access is available. *Library facilities:* Carrie Rich Memorial Library plus 3 others. *Graduate expenses:* Tuition: part-time $305 per semester hour. *General application contact:* James S. Farthing, Director of Graduate Admissions for Business and Education, 910-893-1200 Ext. 1318.

Graduate and Professional Programs
Dr. M. Dwaine Greene, Vice President for Academic Affairs and Provost

Divinity School
Dr. Michael Glenn Cogdill, Dean
Programs in:
 Christian education • MA
 divinity • M Div
 ministry • D Min

Lundy-Fetterman School of Business
Dr. Ben Hawkins, Dean
Program in:
 business • MBA, MTIM

North Carolina

Norman Adrian Wiggins School of Law
Willis Whichard, Dean
Program in:
  law • JD

School of Education
Dr. Karen P. Nery, Dean
Programs in:
  administration • MSA
  community counseling • MA
  elementary education • M Ed
  English education • M Ed
  interdisciplinary studies • M Ed
  mathematics education • M Ed
  middle grades education • M Ed
  physical education • M Ed
  school counseling • M Ed
  secondary education • M Ed
  social science education • M Ed

School of Pharmacy
Dr. Ronald W. Maddox, Dean
Programs in:
  clinical research • MS
  pharmaceutical science • MS
  pharmacy • Pharm D

■ DUKE UNIVERSITY
Durham, NC 27708-0586
http://www.duke.edu/

Independent-religious, coed, university. CGS member. *Enrollment:* 12,398 graduate, professional, and undergraduate students; 6,209 full-time matriculated graduate/professional students (2,879 women), 227 part-time matriculated graduate/professional students (163 women). *Graduate faculty:* 2,185. *Computer facilities:* Computer purchase and lease plans are available. 600 computers available on campus for general student use. A campuswide network can be accessed from student residence rooms and from off campus. Internet access and online class registration are available. *Library facilities:* Perkins Library plus 11 others. *Graduate expenses:* Tuition: full-time $23,280; part-time $835 per unit. *General application contact:* Bertie S. Belvin, Associate Dean for Academic Services, 919-684-3913.

Find an in-depth description at www.petersons.com/gradchannel.

Divinity School
Dr. L. Gregory Jones, Dean
Program in:
  theology • M Div, MCM, MTS, Th M

Fuqua School of Business
Douglas T. Breeden, Dean
Programs in:
  business • CCMBA, GEMBA, MBA, WEMBA, PhD
  health sector management • MBA

Graduate School
Lewis M. Siegel, Dean
Programs in:
  art and art history • PhD
  bioinformatics and genome technology • PhD
  biological chemistry • PhD, Certificate
  biological psychology • PhD
  biology • PhD
  business administration • PhD
  cell biology • PhD
  cellular and molecular biology • PhD
  chemistry • PhD
  classical studies • PhD
  clinical psychology • PhD
  cognitive psychology • PhD
  computer science • MS, PhD
  crystallography of macromolecules • PhD
  developmental biology • PhD, Certificate
  developmental psychology • PhD
  East Asian studies • AM, Certificate
  ecology • PhD, Certificate
  economics • AM, PhD
  English • PhD
  enzyme mechanisms • PhD
  experimental psychology • PhD
  French • PhD
  genetics • PhD
  geology • MS, PhD
  German studies • PhD
  gross anatomy and physical anthropology • PhD
  health psychology • PhD
  history • AM, PhD
  human social development • PhD
  humanities • AM
  immunology • PhD
  Latin American studies • PhD
  liberal studies • AM
  lipid biochemistry • PhD
  literature • PhD
  mathematics • PhD
  medieval and Renaissance studies • Certificate
  membrane structure and function • PhD
  molecular biophysics • Certificate
  molecular cancer biology • PhD
  molecular genetics • PhD
  molecular genetics and microbiology • PhD
  music composition • AM, PhD
  musicology • AM, PhD
  natural resource economics/policy • AM, PhD
  natural resource science/ecology • AM, PhD
  natural resource systems science • AM, PhD
  neuroanatomy • PhD
  neurobiology • PhD
  neurochemistry • PhD
  nucleic acid structure and function • PhD
  pathology • PhD
  performance practice • AM, PhD
  pharmacology • PhD
  philosophy • AM, PhD
  physical anthropology • PhD
  physics • PhD
  political science • AM, PhD
  protein structure and function • PhD
  religion • MA, PhD
  Slavic languages and literatures • AM
  social/cultural anthropology • PhD
  sociology • AM, PhD
  Spanish • PhD
  teaching • MAT
  toxicology • PhD, Certificate
  women's studies • Certificate

Center for Demographic Studies
Dr. Ken Manton, Director
Program in:
  demographic studies • PhD

Center for International Development
Dr. Francis Lethem, Director of Graduate Studies
Program in:
  international development • MA, Certificate

Institute of Statistics and Decision Sciences
Alan Gelfand, Director of Graduate Studies
Program in:
  statistics and decision sciences • PhD

School of Engineering
Dr. Kristina M. Johnson, Dean
Programs in:
  biomedical engineering • MS, PhD
  civil and environmental engineering • MS, PhD
  electrical and computer engineering • MS, PhD
  engineering • MEM, MS, PhD
  engineering management • MEM
  environmental engineering • MS, PhD
  materials science • MS, PhD
  mechanical engineering • MS, PhD

Terry Sanford Institute of Public Policy
Fritz Mayer, Director
Program in:
  public policy • MPP

Nicholas School of the Environment and Earth Sciences
Programs in:
  coastal environmental management • MEM
  environmental health and security • MEM
  environmental science and policy • PhD
  environmental toxicology, chemistry, and risk assessment • MEM
  forest resource management • MF

North Carolina

Duke University (continued)
  global environmental change • MEM
  resource ecology • MEM
  resource economics and policy • MEM
  water and air resources • MEM

School of Law
Dennis Shields, Associate Dean, Admissions and Financial Aid
Program in:
  law • JD, LL M, MLS, SJD

School of Medicine
Dr. Edward C. Halperin, Vice Dean of Medical Education
Programs in:
  clinical leadership program • MHS
  clinical research • MHS
  medicine • MD, MHS, DPT
  pathologists' assistant • MHS
  physician assistant • MHS

Physical Therapy Division
Dr. Jan K. Richardson, Director of Graduate Studies
Program in:
  physical therapy • DPT

School of Nursing
Dr. Mary T. Champagne, Dean
Programs in:
  adult acute care • Certificate
  adult cardiovascular • Certificate
  adult oncology/HIV • Certificate
  adult primary care • Certificate
  clinical nurse specialist • MSN
  clinical research management • MSN, Certificate
  family • Certificate
  gerontology • Certificate
  health and nursing ministries • MSN, Certificate
  health systems leadership and outcomes • Certificate
  leadership in community based long term care • MSN, Certificate
  neonatal • Certificate
  neonatal/pediatric in rural health • MSN, Certificate
  nurse anesthetist • MSN, Certificate
  nurse practitioner • MSN
  nursing and healthcare leadersip • MSN
  nursing education • MSN
  nursing informatics • MSN, Certificate
  pediatric • Certificate
  pediatric acute care • Certificate

■ EAST CAROLINA UNIVERSITY
Greenville, NC 27858-4353
http://www.ecu.edu/

State-supported, coed, university. CGS member. *Enrollment:* 21,756 graduate, professional, and undergraduate students; 1,874 full-time matriculated graduate/professional students (1,156 women), 1,781 part-time matriculated graduate/professional students (1,120 women). *Graduate faculty:* 526 full-time (131 women), 4 part-time/adjunct (0 women). *Computer facilities:* Computer purchase and lease plans are available. 1,425 computers available on campus for general student use. A campuswide network can be accessed from student residence rooms and from off campus. Internet access and online class registration are available. *Library facilities:* J. Y. Joyner Library plus 1 other. *Graduate expenses:* Tuition, state resident: full-time $1,991; part-time $249 per hour. Tuition, nonresident: full-time $12,232; part-time $1,529 per hour. Required fees: $1,221; $153 per hour. *General application contact:* Dr. Paul D. Tschetter, Interim Dean of Graduate School, 252-328-6012.

Find an in-depth description at www.petersons.com/gradchannel.

Brody School of Medicine
Dr. Cynda Johnson, Dean
Programs in:
  anatomy and cell biology • PhD
  biochemistry • PhD
  interdisciplinary biological sciences • PhD
  medicine • MD, MPH, PhD
  microbiology and immunology • PhD
  pharmacology • PhD
  physiology • PhD
  public health • MPH

Graduate Medical Education
Program in:
  medicine • MD

Graduate School
Dr. Paul D. Tschetter, Interim Dean of Graduate School
Programs in:
  art • MA, MA Ed, MFA
  coastal resources management • PhD
  fine arts and communication • MA, MA Ed, MFA, MM
  music education • MM
  music therapy • MM
  performance • MM
  theory and composition • MM

College of Business
Dr. Rick Niswander, Director of Graduate Studies
Program in:
  business • MBA, MSA

College of Education
Dr. Marilyn Sheerer, Dean
Programs in:
  adult education • MA Ed
  behavior/emotional disabilities • MA Ed
  counselor education • MS, Ed S
  education • MA, MA Ed, MLS, MS, MSA, Ed D, CAS, Ed S
  educational administration and supervision • Ed S
  educational leadership • Ed D
  elementary education • MA Ed
  English education • MA Ed
  higher education administration • Ed D
  information technologies • MS
  instruction technology specialist • MA Ed
  learning disabilities • MA Ed
  library science • MLS, CAS
  low incidence disabilities • MA Ed
  mathematics • MA Ed
  mental retardation • MA Ed
  middle grade education • MA Ed
  reading education • MA Ed
  school administration • MSA
  science education • MA, MA Ed
  social studies education • MA Ed
  supervision • MA Ed
  vocation education • MA Ed

College of Health and Human Performance
Dr. Glen Gilbert, Dean
Programs in:
  bioenergetics • PhD
  environmental health • MS
  exercise and sport science • MA, MA Ed
  health and human performance • MA, MA Ed, MS, PhD
  health education • MA, MA Ed
  recreation and leisure services administration • MS
  therapeutic recreation administration • MS

College of Human Ecology
Dr. Karla Hughes, Dean
Programs in:
  child development and family relations • MS
  criminal justice • MS
  human ecology • MS, MSW
  marriage and family therapy • MS
  nutrition • MS
  social work • MSW

College of Technology and Computer Science
Dr. Ralph Rogers, Dean
Programs in:
  computer network professional • Certificate
  computer science • MS
  industrial technology • MS
  information assurance • Certificate
  occupational safety • MS
  technology and computer science • MS, PhD, Certificate
  technology management • PhD
  website developer • Certificate

North Carolina

School of Allied Health Sciences
Dr. Stephen Thomas, Interim Dean
Programs in:
  allied health sciences • MPT, MS, MSOT, PhD
  communication sciences and disorders • PhD
  occupational therapy • MSOT
  physical therapy • MPT
  physician assistant studies • MS
  rehabilitation counseling • MS
  speech, language and auditory pathology • MS
  substance abuse and clinical counseling • MS
  vocational evaluation • MS

School of Nursing
Dr. Sylvia Brown, Director of Graduate Studies
Program in:
  nursing • MSN, PhD

Thomas Harriot College of Arts and Sciences
Dr. Keats Sparrow, Dean
Programs in:
  American history • MA
  anthropology • MA
  applied and biomedical physics • MS
  applied mathematics • MA
  applied resource economics • MS
  arts and sciences • MA, MA Ed, MPA, MS, PhD
  biology • MS
  chemistry • MS
  clinical psychology • MA
  English • MA
  European history • MA
  general psychology • MA
  geography • MA
  geology • MS
  international studies • MA
  maritime history • MA
  mathematics • MA
  medical physics • MS
  molecular biology/biotechnology • MS
  physics • PhD
  public administration • MPA
  sociology • MA

■ ELON UNIVERSITY
Elon, NC 27244-2010
http://www.elon.edu/

Independent-religious, coed, comprehensive institution. CGS member. *Enrollment:* 4,584 graduate, professional, and undergraduate students; 65 full-time matriculated graduate/professional students (42 women), 88 part-time matriculated graduate/professional students (37 women). *Graduate faculty:* 53 full-time (25 women), 8 part-time/adjunct (7 women). *Computer facilities:* Computer purchase and lease plans are available. 500 computers available on campus for general student use. A campuswide network can be accessed from student residence rooms and from off campus. Internet access and online class registration, e-mail are available. *Library facilities:* Carol Grotnes Belk. *Graduate expenses:* Tuition: part-time $1,050 per course. *General application contact:* Art Fadde, Director of Graduate Admissions, 800-334-8448 Ext. 3.

Program in Business Administration
Dr. Kevin J. O'Mara, Director
Program in:
  business administration • MBA

Program in Education
Dr. Judith B. Howard, Director
Programs in:
  elementary education • M Ed
  special education • M Ed

Program in Physical Therapy
Dr. Elizabeth A. Rogers, Chair
Program in:
  physical therapy • DPT

■ FAYETTEVILLE STATE UNIVERSITY
Fayetteville, NC 28301-4298

State-supported, coed, comprehensive institution. CGS member. *Computer facilities:* 325 computers available on campus for general student use. A campuswide network can be accessed from student residence rooms and from off campus. Internet access and online class registration, access to student information are available. *Library facilities:* Charles W. Chestnut Library. *General application contact:* Director of the Graduate Center, 910-672-1498.

Graduate School
Programs in:
  biology • MA Ed, MS
  business administration • MBA
  educational leadership • Ed D
  elementary education • MA Ed
  English • MA
  history • MA, MA Ed
  mathematics • MA Ed, MS
  middle grades • MA Ed
  political science • MA, MA Ed
  psychology • MA
  school administration • MSA
  sociology • MA Ed
  special education • MA Ed

■ GARDNER-WEBB UNIVERSITY
Boiling Springs, NC 28017
http://www.gardner-webb.edu/

Independent-religious, coed, comprehensive institution. *Enrollment:* 3,964 graduate, professional, and undergraduate students; 184 full-time matriculated graduate/professional students (80 women), 975 part-time matriculated graduate/professional students (601 women). *Graduate faculty:* 46 full-time (20 women), 13 part-time/adjunct (5 women). *Computer facilities:* 150 computers available on campus for general student use. A campuswide network can be accessed from student residence rooms and from off campus. Internet access and online class registration are available. *Library facilities:* Dover Memorial Library. *Graduate expenses:* Tuition: part-time $230 per hour. *General application contact:* Dr. Darlene J. Gravett, Dean, Graduate School, 704-406-4723.

Graduate School
Dr. Darlene J. Gravett, Dean
Programs in:
  elementary education • MA
  English • MA
  English education • MA
  mental health counseling • MA
  middle grades education • MA
  school administration • MA
  school counseling • MA
  sport science and pedagogy • MA

Graduate School of Business
Dr. Anthony Negbenebor, Director
Program in:
  business • M Acc, MBA

M. Christopher White School of Divinity
Dr. Robert W. Canoy, Acting Dean
Programs in:
  Christian education • M Div
  church music • M Div
  ministry • D Min
  missiology • M Div
  pastoral care and counseling • M Div
  pastoral ministry • M Div

■ MEREDITH COLLEGE
Raleigh, NC 27607-5298
http://www.meredith.edu/

Independent, women only, comprehensive institution. CGS member. *Enrollment:* 2,152 graduate, professional, and undergraduate students; 7 full-time matriculated graduate/professional students (all women), 104 part-time matriculated graduate/professional students (88 women). *Graduate faculty:* 19 full-time (13 women), 12 part-time/adjunct (10 women). *Computer facilities:* Computer purchase and lease plans are available. 140 computers available on campus for general student use. A campuswide network can be accessed from student residence rooms. Internet access, wireless connectivity in most

North Carolina

Meredith College (continued)
buildings are available. *Library facilities:* Carlyle Campbell Library plus 1 other. *Graduate expenses:* Tuition: part-time $410 per credit hour. *General application contact:* Deborah Horvitz, Director, John E. Weems Graduate School, 919-760-8423.

John E. Weems Graduate School
Deborah Horvitz, Director
Programs in:
 education • M Ed
 music • MM
 nutrition • MS

School of Business
Dr. Sidney Adkins, Dean
Program in:
 business administration • MBA

■ **NORTH CAROLINA AGRICULTURAL AND TECHNICAL STATE UNIVERSITY**
Greensboro, NC 27411
http://www.ncat.edu/

State-supported, coed, university. CGS member. *Computer facilities:* 250 computers available on campus for general student use. A campuswide network can be accessed from off campus. Internet access and online class registration are available. *Library facilities:* F. D. Bluford Library plus 1 other. *General application contact:* Interim Dean of the Graduate School, 336-334-7920.

Find an in-depth description at www.petersons.com/gradchannel.

Graduate School

College of Arts and Sciences
Programs in:
 art education • MS
 arts and sciences • MA, MS, MSW
 biology • MS
 chemistry • MS
 English • MA
 English and Afro-American literature • MA
 history education • MS
 mathematics education • MS
 social science education • MS
 sociology and social work • MSW

College of Engineering
Programs in:
 architectural, agricultural, civil and environmental engineering • MSAE, MSCE, MSE
 chemical engineering • MSE
 computer science • MSCS
 electrical engineering • MSEE, PhD
 engineering • MSAE, MSCE, MSCS, MSE, MSEE, MSISE, MSME, PhD
 industrial and systems engineering • MSISE, PhD
 mechanical engineering • MSME, PhD

School of Agriculture and Environmental and Allied Sciences
Programs in:
 agricultural economics • MS
 agricultural education • MS
 agriculture and environmental and allied sciences • MS
 food and nutrition • MS
 plant science • MS

School of Education
Programs in:
 adult education • MS
 biology education • MS
 chemistry education • MS
 early childhood education • MS
 education • MS
 educational administration • MS
 educational media • MS
 elementary education • MS
 English education • MS
 guidance and counseling • MS
 health and physical education • MS
 history education • MS
 human resources • MS
 intermediate education • MS
 reading • MS
 social science education • MS

School of Technology
Programs in:
 industrial arts education • MS
 industrial technology • MS, MSIT
 safety and driver education • MS
 technology • MS, MSIT
 technology education • MS
 vocational-industrial education • MS

■ **NORTH CAROLINA CENTRAL UNIVERSITY**
Durham, NC 27707-3129
http://www.nccu.edu/

State-supported, coed, comprehensive institution. CGS member. *Enrollment:* 7,191 graduate, professional, and undergraduate students; 779 full-time matriculated graduate/professional students (510 women), 803 part-time matriculated graduate/professional students (627 women). *Graduate faculty:* 207 full-time (105 women), 131 part-time/adjunct (67 women). *Computer facilities:* Computer purchase and lease plans are available. 450 computers available on campus for general student use. A campuswide network can be accessed from student residence rooms and from off campus. Internet access and online class registration are available. *Library facilities:* Shepherd Library plus 1 other. *Graduate expenses:* Tuition, state resident: full-time $3,366. Tuition, nonresident: full-time $12,872. *General application contact:* Dr. Lucy Reuben, Vice Chancellor for Academic Affairs and Provost, 919-560-6230.

Division of Academic Affairs
Dr. Lucy Reuben, Vice Chancellor For Academic Affairs

College of Arts and Sciences
Dr. Mattie Moss, Dean
Programs in:
 arts and sciences • MA, MPA, MS
 biology • MS
 chemistry • MS
 criminal justice • MS
 earth sciences • MS
 English • MA
 general physical education • MS
 history • MA
 human sciences • MS
 mathematics • MS
 psychology • MA
 public administration • MPA
 recreation administration • MS
 sociology • MA
 special physical education • MS
 therapeutic recreation • MS

School of Business
Dr. H. James Williams, Head
Program in:
 business • MBA

School of Education
Dr. Cecelia Steppe-Jones, Interim Dean
Programs in:
 agency counseling • MA
 career counseling • MA
 development leadership and professional studies • MA
 education • M Ed, MA
 education of the emotionally handicapped • M Ed
 education of the mentally handicapped • M Ed
 elementary education • M Ed, MA
 instructional media • MA
 school counseling • MA
 speech pathology and audiology • M Ed

School of Law
Janice Mills, Dean
Program in:
 law • JD, LL B

School of Library and Information Sciences
Dr. Robert Ballard, Dean
Program in:
 library and information sciences • MIS, MLS

NORTH CAROLINA STATE UNIVERSITY
Raleigh, NC 27695
http://www.ncsu.edu/

State-supported, coed, university. CGS member. *Enrollment:* 29,854 graduate, professional, and undergraduate students; 3,995 full-time matriculated graduate/professional students (1,701 women), 1,661 part-time matriculated graduate/professional students (804 women). *Graduate faculty:* 1,686 full-time (356 women), 1,027 part-time/adjunct (142 women). *Computer facilities:* Computer purchase and lease plans are available. 4,600 computers available on campus for general student use. A campuswide network can be accessed from student residence rooms and from off campus. Internet access is available. *Library facilities:* D. H. Hill Library plus 4 others. *Graduate expenses:* Tuition, state resident: part-time $396 per hour. Tuition, nonresident: part-time $1,895 per hour. *General application contact:* Office of Graduate Admissions, 919-515-2871.

College of Veterinary Medicine
Dr. Oscar J. Fletcher, Dean
Programs in:
- cell biology and morphology • MS, PhD
- epidemiology and population medicine • MS, PhD
- immunology • MS, PhD
- microbiology and immunology • MS, PhD
- pathology • MS, PhD
- pharmacology • MS, PhD
- specialized veterinary medicine • MS
- veterinary medicine • DVM, MLS, MS, MVPH, PhD
- veterinary public health • MVPH

Department of Biomedical Engineering
Dr. H. Troy Nagle, Founding Chair and Professor
Program in:
- biomedical engineering • MS, PhD

Graduate School
Dr. Robert S. Sowell, Dean

College of Agriculture and Life Sciences
Dr. Johnny C. Wynne, Interim Dean
Programs in:
- agricultural and resource economics • M Econ, MS, PhD
- agricultural education • MAEE, MS
- agriculture and life sciences • M Econ, M Tox, MAEE, MB, MBAE, MFG, MFM, MFS, MG, MMB, MN, MP, MS, PhD
- animal science • MS, PhD
- biochemistry • MS, PhD
- bioinformatics • MB, PhD
- biological and agricultural engineering • MBAE, MS, PhD
- botany • MS, PhD
- crop science • MS, PhD
- entomology • MS, PhD
- extension education • MAEE, MS
- financial mathematics • MFM
- food science • MFS, MS, PhD
- functional genomics • MFG, MS, PhD
- genetics • MG, MS, PhD
- horticultural science • MS, PhD
- immunology • MS, PhD
- microbial biotechnology • MMB
- microbiology • MS, PhD
- nutrition • MN, MS, PhD
- physiology • MP, MS, PhD
- plant pathology • MS, PhD
- poultry science • MS
- soil science • MS, PhD
- toxicology • M Tox, MS, PhD
- zoology • MS, PhD

College of Design
Prof. Marvin Malecha, Dean
Programs in:
- architecture • M Arch
- art and design • MAD
- design • M Arch, MAD, MGD, MID, MLA, PhD
- graphic design • MGD
- industrial design • MID
- landscape architecture • MLA

College of Education
Kathryn M. Moore, Dean
Programs in:
- adult and community college education • M Ed, MS
- adult and community colleges education • Ed D
- agency counseling • M Ed, MS
- agricultural education • M Ed, MS
- counselor education • M Ed, MS, PhD
- curriculum and instruction • M Ed, MS, PhD
- education • M Ed, MS, MSA, Ed D, PhD, Certificate
- educational administration and supervision • Ed D
- educational research and policy analysis • PhD
- health occupations education • M Ed, MS
- higher education administration • M Ed, MS, Ed D
- mathematics education • M Ed, MS, PhD
- middle grades education • M Ed, MS
- occupational education • M Ed, MS, Ed D
- school administration • MSA
- science education • M Ed, MS, PhD
- special education • M Ed, MS
- technology education • M Ed, MS, Ed D
- training and development • M Ed, MS

College of Engineering
Dr. Nino A. Masnari, Dean
Programs in:
- aerospace engineering • MS, PhD
- chemical engineering • M Ch E, MS, PhD
- civil engineering • MCE, MS, PhD
- computer engineering • MS, PhD
- computer networking • MS
- computer science • MC Sc, MS, PhD
- electrical engineering • MS, PhD
- engineering • M Ch E, M Eng, MBAE, MC Sc, MCE, MIE, MIMS, MME, MMSE, MNE, MOR, MS, MSIE, PhD, PD
- industrial engineering • MIE, MSIE, PhD
- integrated manufacturing systems engineering • MIMS
- materials science and engineering • MMSE, MS, PhD
- mechanical engineering • MME, MS, PhD
- nuclear engineering • MNE, MS, PhD
- operations research • MOR, MS, PhD

College of Humanities and Social Sciences
Linda P. Brady, Dean
Programs in:
- creative writing • MFA
- English • MA
- French language and literature • MA
- history • MA
- humanities and social sciences • M Soc, MA, MAIS, MFA, MPA, MS, PhD
- international studies • MAIS
- liberal studies • MA
- organizational communication • MS
- psychology • MS, PhD
- public administration • MPA, PhD
- public history • MA
- rural sociology • MS
- sociology • M Soc, PhD
- Spanish language and literature • MA
- technical communication • MS

College of Management
Dr. Jon W. Bartley, Interim Dean
Programs in:
- accounting • MAC
- business administration • MBA
- economics • M Econ, MA, PhD
- financial management • MBA
- information technology management • MBA
- marketing management • MBA
- product innovation management • MBA
- supply chain management • MBA
- technology commercialization • MBA

North Carolina

North Carolina State University (continued)

College of Natural Resources
Larry A. Nielsen, Dean
Programs in:
 fisheries and wildlife sciences • MFWS, MS
 forestry • MF, MS, PhD
 geographic information systems • MS
 maintenance management • MRRA, MS
 natural resources • MF, MFWS, MNR, MRRA, MS, MWPS, PhD
 parks, recreation and tourism management • PhD
 recreation planning • MRRA, MS
 recreation resources administration/public administration • MRRA
 recreation/park management • MRRA, MS
 sports management • MRRA, MS
 travel and tourism management • MS
 wood and paper science • MS, MWPS, PhD

College of Physical and Mathematical Sciences
Dr. Daniel L. Solomon, Dean
Programs in:
 applied mathematics • MS, PhD
 biomathematics • M Biomath, MS, PhD
 chemistry • MCH, MS, PhD
 ecology • PhD
 marine, earth, and atmospheric sciences • MS, PhD
 mathematics • MS, PhD
 meteorology • MS, PhD
 oceanography • MS, PhD
 physical and mathematical sciences • M Biomath, M Stat, MCH, MS, PhD
 physics • MS, PhD
 statistics • M Stat, MS, PhD

College of Textiles
A. Blanton Godfrey, Dean
Programs in:
 fiber and polymer sciences • PhD
 textile and apparel technology and management • MS, MT
 textile chemistry • MS
 textile engineering • MS
 textile technology management • PhD
 textiles • MS, MT, PhD

■ PFEIFFER UNIVERSITY
Misenheimer, NC 28109-0960
http://www.pfeiffer.edu/

Independent-religious, coed, comprehensive institution. *Enrollment:* 2,027 graduate, professional, and undergraduate students; 845 full-time matriculated graduate/professional students (495 women). *Graduate faculty:* 20 full-time (6 women), 20 part-time/adjunct (6 women). *Computer facilities:* 90 computers available on campus for general student use. A campuswide network can be accessed from student residence rooms and from off campus. Internet access, e-mail are available. *Library facilities:* Gustavus A. Pfeiffer Library. *Graduate expenses:* Tuition: full-time $5,500. *General application contact:* Michael Utsman, Assistant Dean, 704-521-9116 Ext. 253.

Program in Business Administration
Dr. Robert K. Spear, Director of the MBA Program
Programs in:
 business administration • MBA
 organizational management • MS

School of Religion and Christian Education
Kay Kilbourne, Coordinator
Program in:
 religion and Christian education • MACE

■ QUEENS UNIVERSITY OF CHARLOTTE
Charlotte, NC 28274-0002
http://www.queens.edu/

Independent-religious, coed, comprehensive institution. *Enrollment:* 1,964 graduate, professional, and undergraduate students; 433 matriculated graduate/professional students. *Graduate faculty:* 22 full-time (12 women), 9 part-time/adjunct (4 women). *Computer facilities:* Computer purchase and lease plans are available. 125 computers available on campus for general student use. A campuswide network can be accessed from student residence rooms. Internet access and online class registration are available. *Library facilities:* Everett Library plus 1 other. *Graduate expenses:* Tuition: part-time $235 per credit hour. Tuition and fees vary according to program. *General application contact:* Robert Mobley, Director of PMBA Admissions, 704-337-2224.

College of Arts and Sciences
Dr. Michael Tarabek, Dean
Program in:
 creative writing • MFA

Hayworth College
Dr. Darrel Miller, Dean
Programs in:
 elementary education • MAT
 organizational communications • MA

Division of Nursing
Dr. Joan McGill, Chair
Program in:
 nursing management • MSN

McColl Graduate School of Business
Peter Browning, Dean
Program in:
 business • EMBA, MBA

■ THE UNIVERSITY OF NORTH CAROLINA AT CHAPEL HILL
Chapel Hill, NC 27599
http://www.unc.edu/

State-supported, coed, university. CGS member. *Enrollment:* 26,359 graduate, professional, and undergraduate students; 8,387 full-time matriculated graduate/professional students (4,677 women), 3,004 part-time matriculated graduate/professional students (1,772 women). *Graduate faculty:* 1,810 full-time (470 women), 613 part-time/adjunct (329 women). *Computer facilities:* Computer purchase and lease plans are available. 600 computers available on campus for general student use. A campuswide network can be accessed from student residence rooms and from off campus. Internet access and online class registration, online grade reports are available. *Library facilities:* Davis Library plus 14 others. *Graduate expenses:* Tuition, state resident: full-time $3,163. Tuition, nonresident: full-time $15,161. *General application contact:* Cheryl Thomas, Director of Admissions and Enrollment Services, 919-966-2611.

Find an in-depth description at www.petersons.com/gradchannel.

Graduate School
Dr. Linda Dykstra, Dean
Programs in:
 materials science • MS, PhD
 public policy • PhD
 Russian and east European studies • MA

College of Arts and Sciences
Programs in:
 acting • MFA
 anthropology • MA, PhD
 art history • MA, PhD
 arts and sciences • MA, MFA, MPA, MRP, MS, MSRA, PhD, Certificate
 athletic training • MA
 biological psychology • PhD
 botany • MA, MS, PhD
 cell biology, development, and physiology • MA, MS, PhD
 cell motility and cytoskeleton • PhD
 chemistry • MA, MS, PhD
 city and regional planning • MRP
 classical archaeology • MA, PhD
 classics • MA, PhD
 clinical psychology • PhD

cognitive psychology • PhD
communication studies • MA, PhD
comparative literature • MA, PhD
computer science • MS, PhD
costume production • MFA
developmental psychology • PhD
ecology • MA, MS, PhD
ecology and behavior • MA, MS, PhD
economics • MS, PhD
English • MA, PhD
exercise physiology • MA
folklore • MA
French • MA, PhD
genetics and molecular biology • MA, MS, PhD
geography • MA, PhD
geological sciences • MS, PhD
history • MA, PhD
Italian • MA, PhD
Latin American studies • Certificate
linguistics • MA, PhD
literature and linguistics • MA, PhD
marine sciences • MS, PhD
mathematics • MA, MS, PhD
morphology, systematics, and evolution • MA, MS, PhD
music • MA, PhD
operations research • MS, PhD
philosophy • MA, PhD
physics • MS, PhD
planning • PhD
Polish literature • PhD
political science • MA, PhD
Portuguese • MA, PhD
public administration • MPA
public policy analysis • PhD
quantitative psychology • PhD
recreation and leisure studies • MSRA
religious studies • MA, PhD
Romance languages • MA, PhD
Romance philology • MA, PhD
Russian literature • MA, PhD
Serbo-Croatian literature • PhD
Slavic linguistics • MA, PhD
social psychology • PhD
sociology • MA, PhD
Spanish • MA, PhD
sport administration • MA
statistics • MS, PhD
studio art • MFA
technical production • MFA
trans-Atlantic studies • MA

School of Education
Dr. Thomas James, Dean
Programs in:
culture, curriculum and change • PhD
culture, curriculum, and change • MA
curriculum and instruction • Ed D
early childhood, families, and literacy studies • MA, PhD
education • M Ed, MA, MAT, MSA, Ed D, PhD
education for experienced teachers • M Ed
education for experienced teachers, early childhood intervention and family studies (birth–K) • M Ed
educational leadership • Ed D
educational psychology • M Ed
educational psychology measurements, and evaluation • PhD
educational psychology, measurement, and evaluation • MA
English (Grades 9–12) • MAT
French (Grades K–12) • MAT
German (Grades K–12) • MAT
Japanese (Grades K–12) • MAT
Latin (Grades 9–12) • MAT
mathematics (Grades 9–12) • MAT
music (Grades K–12) • MAT
school administration • MSA
school counseling • M Ed
school psychology • M Ed, MA, PhD
science (Grades 9–12) • MAT
social studies/social science (Grades 9–12) • MAT
Spanish (Grades K–12) • MAT

School of Information and Library Science
Dr. Joanne Gard Marshall, Dean
Program in:
information and library science • MSIS, MSLS, PhD, CAS

School of Journalism and Mass Communication
Dr. Richard R. Cole, Dean
Program in:
mass communication • MA, PhD

School of Public Health
Dr. Margaret B. Dardess, Interim Dean
Programs in:
air, radiation and industrial hygiene • MPH, MS, MSEE, MSPH, PhD
aquatic and atmospheric sciences • MPH, MS, MSPH, PhD
biostatistics • MPH, MS, Dr PH, PhD
environmental engineering • MPH, MS, MSEE, MSPH, PhD
environmental health sciences • MPH, MS, MSPH, PhD
environmental management and policy • MPH, MS, MSPH, PhD
epidemiology • MPH, MSPH, Dr PH, PhD
health behavior and health education • MPH, Dr PH, PhD
health care and prevention • MPH
health policy and administration • MHA, MPH, MSPH, Dr PH, PhD
leadership • MPH
maternal and child health • MPH, MSPH, Dr PH, PhD
nutrition • MPH, Dr PH, PhD
nutritional biochemistry • MS
occupational health nursing • MPH
professional practice program • MPH
public health • MHA, MPH, MS, MSEE, MSPH, Dr PH, PhD
public health nursing • MPH

School of Social Work
Dr. Jack Richman, Interim Dean
Program in:
social work • MSW, PhD

Kenan-Flagler Business School
Steve Jones, Dean
Programs in:
accounting • PhD
business • MAC, MBA, PhD
business administration • MBA, PhD
finance • PhD
marketing • PhD
operations management • PhD
organizational behavior • PhD
strategy • PhD

School of Dentistry
Dr. John Stamm, Dean
Programs in:
dentistry • MS
oral biology • PhD
oral epidemiology • PhD

School of Law
Gene R. Nichol, Dean and Professor
Program in:
law • JD

School of Medicine
Dr. Jeffrey Houpt, Dean
Programs in:
allied health sciences • MPT, MS, Au D, PhD
biochemistry and biophysics • MS, PhD
biomedical engineering • MS, PhD
cell and developmental biology • PhD
cell and molecular physiology • PhD
experimental pathology • PhD
genetics and molecular biology • MS, PhD
human movement science • MS, PhD
immunology • MS, PhD
medicine • MD, MPT, MS, Au D, PhD
microbiology • MS, PhD
microbiology and immunology • MS, PhD
neurobiology • PhD
occupational science • MS
pathology and laboratory medicine • PhD
pharmacology • PhD
physical therapy • MPT, MS
rehabilitation psychology and counseling • MS, PhD
speech and hearing sciences • MS, Au D, PhD
toxicology • MS, PhD

School of Nursing
Program in:
nursing • MSN, PhD

The University of North Carolina at Chapel Hill (continued)
School of Pharmacy
Dr. Robert A. Blouin, Dean
Program in:
  pharmacy • MS, PhD

■ THE UNIVERSITY OF NORTH CAROLINA AT CHARLOTTE
Charlotte, NC 28223-0001
http://www.uncc.edu/

State-supported, coed, university. CGS member. *Enrollment:* 19,605 graduate, professional, and undergraduate students; 970 full-time matriculated graduate/professional students (528 women), 2,004 part-time matriculated graduate/professional students (1,189 women). *Graduate faculty:* 484 full-time (152 women), 148 part-time/adjunct (48 women). *Computer facilities:* Computer purchase and lease plans are available. 1,100 computers available on campus for general student use. A campuswide network can be accessed from student residence rooms and from off campus. Internet access and online class registration are available. *Library facilities:* J. Murrey Atkins Library. *Graduate expenses:* Tuition, state resident: full-time $1,979. Tuition, nonresident: full-time $12,111. Required fees: $1,201. Tuition and fees vary according to course load. *General application contact:* Dr. Thomas L. Reynolds, Dean and Associate Provost, 704-687-3372.

Graduate School
Dr. Thomas L. Reynolds, Dean and Associate Provost

Belk College of Business Administration
Dr. Claude C. Lilly, Dean
Programs in:
  accounting • M Acc
  business administration • M Acc, MBA, MS
  economics • MS
  mathematical finance • MS

College of Architecture
Kenneth A. Lambla, Dean
Program in:
  architecture • M Arch

College of Arts and Sciences
Dr. Schley R. Lyons, Dean
Programs in:
  applied math • PhD
  applied mathematics • MS
  applied physics • MS
  art administration • MA
  arts and sciences • MA, MPA, MS, PhD
  biology • MA, MS, PhD
  chemistry • MS
  communication studies • MA
  community/clinical psychology • MA
  criminal justice • MS
  earth sciences • MS
  English • MA
  English education • MA
  geography • MA
  geography/community planning • MA
  gerontology • MA
  history • MA
  industrial/organizational psychology • MA
  liberal studies • MA
  mathematics • MA, MS
  mathematics education • MA
  optical science and engineering • MS, PhD
  psychology • MA
  public administration • MPA
  public policy • PhD
  religious studies • MA
  sociology • MA
  Spanish • MA

College of Education
Dr. Mary Lynne Calhoun, Dean
Programs in:
  child and family studies • M Ed
  community and school counseling • MA
  counseling • PhD
  curriculum and instruction • PhD
  curriculum and supervision • M Ed
  education • M Ed, MA, MAT, MSA, Ed D, PhD, CAS
  educational administration • CAS
  educational leadership • Ed D
  elementary education • M Ed
  general teacher education • MAT
  instructional systems technology • M Ed
  middle school and secondary education • M Ed
  reading, language and literacy • M Ed
  school administration • MSA
  special education • M Ed, PhD
  teaching English as a second language • M Ed

College of Health and Human Services
Dr. Karen Schmaling, Dean
Programs in:
  family nurse practitioner • MSN
  health and human services • MHA, MS, MSN, MSW
  health behavior and administration • MHA
  health promotion • MS
  nursing • MSN
  nursing adult health • MSN
  nursing and health administration • MSN
  nursing-anesthesia • MSN
  nursing-community health • MSN
  nursing-mental health • MSN
  social work • MSW

College of Information Technology
Dr. Mirsad Hadzikadic, Dean
Programs in:
  computer science • MS
  information technology • MS, PhD

The William States Lee College of Engineering
Dr. Robert E. Johnson, Dean
Programs in:
  civil engineering • MSCE
  electrical and computer engineering • MSEE, PhD
  engineering • ME, MS, MSCE, MSE, MSEE, MSME, PhD
  engineering management • MS
  mechanical engineering and engineering science • MSME, PhD

■ THE UNIVERSITY OF NORTH CAROLINA AT GREENSBORO
Greensboro, NC 27412-5001
http://www.uncg.edu/

State-supported, coed, university. CGS member. *Enrollment:* 14,328 graduate, professional, and undergraduate students; 1,113 full-time matriculated graduate/professional students (727 women), 2,515 part-time matriculated graduate/professional students (1,712 women). *Graduate faculty:* 543 full-time (241 women), 65 part-time/adjunct (23 women). *Computer facilities:* Computer purchase and lease plans are available. 500 computers available on campus for general student use. A campuswide network can be accessed from student residence rooms and from off campus. Internet access and online class registration are available. *Library facilities:* Jackson Library plus 1 other. *Graduate expenses:* Tuition, state resident: part-time $1,887 per unit. Tuition, nonresident: part-time $12,862 per unit. *General application contact:* Michelle Harkleroad, Director of Graduate Admissions, 336-334-4886.

Find an in-depth description at www.petersons.com/gradchannel.

Graduate School
Dr. James Peterson, Dean
Program in:
  liberal studies • MALS

College of Arts and Sciences
Timothy Johnston, Dean
Programs in:
  acting • MFA

art • M Ed
arts and sciences • M Ed, MA, MFA, MPA, MS, PhD, Certificate
biology • M Ed, MS
chemistry • M Ed, MS
clinical psychology • MA, PhD
cognitive psychology • MA, PhD
communication studies • M Ed, MA
computer science • MA
creative writing • MFA
developmental psychology • MA, PhD
directing • MFA
drama • M Ed, MFA
English • M Ed, MA, PhD, Certificate
French • M Ed, MA
geography • MA
historic preservation • Certificate
history • M Ed, MA
Latin • M Ed
mathematical science • M Ed, MA
museum studies • Certificate
nonprofit management • Certificate
political science • MA
public affairs • MPA, Certificate
social psychology • MA, PhD
sociology • MA
Spanish • M Ed, MA
studio arts • MFA
technical writing • Certificate
theater design • MFA
theater education • M Ed
theater for youth • MFA
women's studies • Certificate

Joseph M. Bryan School of Business and Economics
James K. Weeks, Dean
Programs in:
accounting • MS
applied economics • MA
business administration • MBA, Certificate
business and economics • MA, MBA, MS, Certificate
information systems and operations management • MS
international business administration • Certificate

School of Education
Dr. David Armstrong, Dean
Programs in:
counseling and development • MS, Ed D, PhD
cross categorical • M Ed
curriculum and instruction • M Ed
curriculum and teaching • PhD
deaf education • M Ed, MA
education • M Ed, MA, MLIS, MS, MSA, Ed D, PhD, Ed S, PMC
educational leadership • Ed D, PhD, Ed S
educational research, measurement and evaluation • M Ed, PhD
gerontological counseling • PMC
higher education • M Ed, Ed S

interdisciplinary studies in preschool education • M Ed
library and information studies • MLIS
marriage and family counseling • PMC
school administration • MSA
school counseling • PMC
special education • M Ed
supervision • M Ed

School of Health and Human Performance
David Perrin, Dean
Programs in:
dance • MA, MFA
exercise and sports science • M Ed, MS, Ed D, PhD
health and human performance • M Ed, MA, MFA, MPH, MS, Ed D, PhD
parks and recreation management • MS
public health education • MPH
speech pathology and audiology • MA

School of Human Environmental Sciences
Laura S. Sims, Dean
Programs in:
human development and family studies • M Ed, MS, PhD
human environmental sciences • M Ed, MS, MSW, PhD
human nutrition • M Ed, MS, PhD
interior architecture • MS
social work • MSW
textile products design and marketing • M Ed, MS, PhD

School of Music
Dr. John J. Deal, Dean
Programs in:
composition • MM
education • MM
music education • PhD
performance • MM, DMA

School of Nursing
Dr. Lynne Pearcey, Dean
Programs in:
administration of nursing in health agencies • MSN
gerontological nurse practitioner • PMC
nurse anesthesia • MSN, PMC

■ **THE UNIVERSITY OF NORTH CAROLINA AT PEMBROKE**
Pembroke, NC 28372-1510
http://www.uncp.edu/

State-supported, coed, comprehensive institution. CGS member. *Enrollment:* 4,722 graduate, professional, and undergraduate students; 68 full-time matriculated graduate/professional students (34 women), 401 part-time matriculated graduate/professional students (278 women). *Graduate faculty:* 27 full-time (9 women), 2 part-time/adjunct (1 woman). *Computer facilities:* 380 computers available on campus for general student use. A campuswide network can be accessed from student residence rooms and from off campus. Internet access is available. *Library facilities:* Sampson-Livermore Library. *Graduate expenses:* Tuition, state resident: part-time $384 per semester. Tuition, nonresident: part-time $2,767 per semester. Required fees: $138 per semester. Tuition and fees vary according to course load. *General application contact:* Dr. Kathleen C. Hilton, Dean of Graduate Studies, 910-521-6271.

Graduate Studies
Dr. Kathleen C. Hilton, Dean of Graduate Studies
Programs in:
art education • MA
English education • MA
mathematics education • MA
physical education • MA
public administration • MPA
school counseling • MA
science education • MA
service agency counseling • MA
social studies education • MA

School of Business
Dr. Eric Dent, Dean
Program in:
business administration • MBA

School of Education
Dr. Warren Baker, Dean
Programs in:
elementary education • MA Ed
middle grades education • MA Ed
reading education • MA Ed
school administration • MSA

■ **THE UNIVERSITY OF NORTH CAROLINA AT WILMINGTON**
Wilmington, NC 28403-3297
http://www.uncwil.edu/

State-supported, coed, comprehensive institution. CGS member. *Enrollment:* 10,929 graduate, professional, and undergraduate students; 325 full-time matriculated graduate/professional students (195 women), 483 part-time matriculated graduate/professional students (299 women). *Graduate faculty:* 279 full-time (86 women), 5 part-time/adjunct (0 women). *Computer facilities:* Computer purchase and lease plans are available. 778 computers available on campus for general student use. A campuswide network can be accessed from student residence rooms and from

North Carolina

The University of North Carolina at Wilmington (continued)
off campus. Internet access and online class registration are available. *Library facilities:* William M. Randall Library. *Graduate expenses:* Tuition, state resident: full-time $2,282. Tuition, nonresident: full-time $11,980. Required fees: $1,659. Tuition and fees vary according to course load. *General application contact:* Dr. Robert D. Roer, Dean, Graduate School, 910-962-4117.

College of Arts and Sciences
Dr. JoAnn Seiple, Dean
Programs in:
  arts and sciences • MA, MALS, MFA, MPA, MS, PhD
  biology • MS
  chemistry • MS
  creative writing • MFA
  English • MA
  geology • MS
  history • MA
  liberal studies • MALS
  marine biology • MS, PhD
  marine science • MS
  mathematical sciences • MA, MS
  psychology • MA
  public administration • MPA

School of Business
Dr. Lawrence Clark, Dean
Programs in:
  accountancy • MSA
  business • MBA, MSA
  business administration • MBA

School of Education
Dr. Cathy L. Barlow, Dean
Programs in:
  curricular/instruction supervisor • M Ed
  education • M Ed, MAT, MS, MSA
  educational administration and supervision • M Ed
  elementary education • M Ed
  instructional technology • MS
  middle grades education • M Ed
  reading education • M Ed
  school administration • MSA
  secondary education • M Ed
  special education • M Ed
  teaching • MAT

School of Nursing
Dr. Virginia W. Adams, Dean
Program in:
  nursing • MSN

■ WAKE FOREST UNIVERSITY
Winston-Salem, NC 27109
http://www.wfu.edu/

Independent, coed, university. CGS member. *Enrollment:* 6,451 graduate, professional, and undergraduate students; 2,407 matriculated graduate/professional students. *Graduate faculty:* 1,448. *Computer facilities:* Computer purchase and lease plans are available. 150 computers available on campus for general student use. A campuswide network can be accessed from student residence rooms and from off campus. Internet access and online class registration, personal computer are available. *Library facilities:* Z. Smith Reynolds Library plus 3 others. *Graduate expenses:* Tuition: full-time $26,500. *General application contact:* Dr. Gordon A. Melson, Dean of the Graduate School, 336-758-5301.

Find an in-depth description at www.petersons.com/gradchannel.

Babcock Graduate School of Management
Ajay Patel, Interim Dean
Programs in:
  business administration • MBA
  management • MBA

Graduate School
Dr. Gordon A. Melson, Dean
Programs in:
  accountancy • MSA
  analytical chemistry • MS, PhD
  biology • MS, PhD
  computer science • MS
  English • MA
  health and exercise science • MS
  inorganic chemistry • MS, PhD
  liberal studies • MALS
  mathematics • MA
  organic chemistry • MS, PhD
  pastoral counseling • MA
  physical chemistry • MS, PhD
  physics • MS, PhD
  psychology • MA
  religion • MA
  secondary education • MA Ed
  speech communication • MA

School of Law
Robert K. Walsh, Dean
Program in:
  law • JD, LL M

School of Medicine
Dr. William B. Applegate, Dean
Program in:
  medicine • MD, MS, PhD

Graduate Programs in Medicine
Dr. Gordon A. Melson, Dean of the Graduate School
Programs in:
  biochemistry • PhD
  cancer biology • PhD
  clinical epidemiology and health services research • MS
  comparative medicine • MS
  medicine • MS, PhD
  microbiology and immunology • PhD
  molecular and cellular pathobiology • MS, PhD
  molecular genetics • PhD
  molecular medicine • MS, PhD
  neurobiology and anatomy • PhD
  neuroscience • PhD
  pharmacology • PhD
  physiology • PhD

Virginia Tech-Wake Forest University School of Biomedical Engineering and Sciences
Dr. Elaine P. Scott, Interim Director
Program in:
  biomedical engineering and sciences • MS, PhD

■ WARREN WILSON COLLEGE
Swannanoa, Asheville, NC 28815-9000
http://www.warren-wilson.edu/

Independent-religious, coed, comprehensive institution. *Enrollment:* 851 graduate, professional, and undergraduate students; 88 full-time matriculated graduate/professional students (65 women). *Graduate faculty:* 22 full-time (8 women). *Computer facilities:* 68 computers available on campus for general student use. A campuswide network can be accessed from student residence rooms and from off campus. Internet access, word processing, software are available. *Library facilities:* Pew Learning Center and Ellison Library. *Graduate expenses:* Tuition: full-time $10,200. *General application contact:* Peter Turchi, Director, 828-771-3715.

MFA Program for Writers
Peter Turchi, Director
Program in:
  creative writing • MFA

■ WESTERN CAROLINA UNIVERSITY
Cullowhee, NC 28723
http://www.wcu.edu/

State-supported, coed, comprehensive institution. CGS member. *Enrollment:* 7,561 graduate, professional, and undergraduate students; 452 full-time matriculated graduate/professional students (262 women), 1,022 part-time matriculated graduate/professional students (643 women). *Graduate faculty:* 311 full-time (113 women). *Computer facilities:* 575 computers available on campus for general student use. A campuswide network can be accessed from student residence rooms and from off campus. Internet access and online class registration, e-mail are available. *Library facilities:* Hunter Library. *Graduate expenses:* Tuition, state resident: full-time $1,426. Tuition, nonresident: full-time $10,787. Required fees: $1,558. *General application contact:* Josie Bewsey, Assistant to the Dean, 828-227-7398.

Find an in-depth description at www.petersons.com/gradchannel.

Graduate School
Dr. Abdul M. Turay, Dean

College of Applied Science
Dr. Noelle Kehrberg, Dean
Programs in:
 applied science • MHS, MPT, MS, MSN
 engineering technology • MS
 health sciences • MHS
 nursing • MSN
 physical therapy • MPT

College of Arts and Sciences
Dr. Robert Vartabedian, Dean
Programs in:
 American history • MA
 applied mathematics • MS
 art education • MA Ed, MAT
 arts and sciences • MA, MA Ed, MAT, MFA, MPA, MS
 biology • MAT, MS
 chemistry • MAT, MS
 comprehensive education • MA Ed
 comprehensive education—art • MA Ed
 comprehensive education-biology • MA Ed
 comprehensive education-chemistry • MA Ed
 comprehensive education-English • MA Ed
 comprehensive education-mathematics • MA Ed
 English • MA, MAT
 history • MA
 mathematics • MAT
 music • MA
 public affairs • MPA
 social sciences • MAT
 studio art • MFA

College of Business
Dr. Leroy Kauffman, Dean
Programs in:
 accountancy • M Ac
 business administration • MBA
 entrepreneurship • ME
 project management • MPM

College of Education and Allied Professions
Dr. A. Michael Dougherty, Dean
Programs in:
 art education • MAT
 behavioral disorders • MA Ed
 biology • MAT
 chemistry • MAT
 clinical psychology • MA
 communication disorders • MS

 community college education • MA Ed
 community counseling • MS
 comprehensive education • MA Ed
 comprehensive education-elementary education • MA Ed
 comprehensive education-reading • MA Ed
 comprehensive education-special education • MA Ed, MS
 counseling • M Ed, MA Ed, MS
 education and allied professions • M Ed, MA, MA Ed, MAT, MS, MSA, Ed D, Ed S
 educational leadership • Ed D, Ed S
 educational supervision • MA Ed
 elementary education • MA Ed
 English • MAT
 family and consumer sciences • MAT
 general special education • MA Ed, MAT
 human resource development • MS
 learning disabilities • MA Ed
 mathematics • MAT
 mental retardation • MA Ed
 middle grades education • MA Ed, MAT
 physical education • MA Ed, MAT
 reading • MAT
 reading education • M Ed, MA Ed, MAT
 school administration • MSA
 school counseling • M Ed, MA Ed
 school psychology • MA
 secondary education • MA Ed, MAT
 social sciences • MAT
 special education-learning disabilities • MAT

North Dakota

■ MINOT STATE UNIVERSITY
Minot, ND 58707-0002
http://www.minotstateu.edu/

State-supported, coed, comprehensive institution. *Enrollment:* 3,825 graduate, professional, and undergraduate students; 58 full-time matriculated graduate/professional students (52 women), 173 part-time matriculated graduate/professional students (125 women). *Graduate faculty:* 73 full-time (29 women), 52 part-time/adjunct (31 women). *Computer facilities:* 400 computers available on campus for general student use. A campuswide network can be accessed from student residence rooms and from off campus. Internet access and online class registration are available. *Library facilities:* Gordon B. Olson Library. *Graduate expenses:* Part-time $171 per semester hour. Tuition, state resident: part-time $220 per semester hour. Tuition, nonresident: part-time $423 per semester hour. *General application contact:* Renee Olson, Administrative Assistant, 701-858-3250 Ext. 3150.

Graduate School
Rod Hewlett, Dean
Programs in:
 audiology • MS
 criminal justice • MS
 education of the deaf • MS
 elementary education • M Ed
 learning disabilities • MS
 management • MS
 mathematics • MAT
 music education • MME
 school psychology • Ed Sp
 science • MAT
 special education strategist • MS
 speech-language pathology • MS

■ NORTH DAKOTA STATE UNIVERSITY
Fargo, ND 58105
http://www.ndsu.edu/

State-supported, coed, university. CGS member. *Enrollment:* 11,623 graduate, professional, and undergraduate students; 1,466 full-time matriculated graduate/professional students (655 women). *Graduate faculty:* 432 full-time (65 women), 21 part-time/adjunct (6 women). *Computer facilities:* 500 computers available on campus for general student use. A campuswide network can be accessed from student residence rooms and from off campus. Internet access is available. *Library facilities:* North Dakota State University Library plus 3 others. *Graduate expenses:* Tuition, nonresident: full-time $4,071. Required fees: $493. *General application contact:* Dr. David A. Wittrock, Interim Dean, 701-231-7033.

Find an in-depth description at www.petersons.com/gradchannel.

The Graduate School
Dr. David A. Wittrock, Interim Dean
Programs in:
 food safety • MS, PhD
 natural resources management • MS, PhD
 nursing • MS
 transportation and logistics • PhD

College of Agriculture, Food Systems, and Natural Resources
Dr. James R. Venette, Associate Dean for Academic Programs
Programs in:

North Dakota

North Dakota State University (continued)

- agribusiness and applied economics • MS
- agriculture, food systems, and natural resources • MS, PhD
- animal science • MS, PhD
- cellular and molecular biology • PhD
- crop and weed sciences • MS
- entomology • MS, PhD
- environment and conservation science • MS, PhD
- horticulture • MS
- international agribusiness • MS
- microbiology • MS
- natural resources management • MS, PhD
- plant pathology • MS, PhD
- plant sciences • PhD
- range science • MS, PhD
- soil sciences • MS, PhD
- veterinary sciences • MS

College of Arts, Humanities and Social Sciences
Dr. Thomas J. Riley, Dean
Programs in:
- communication • PhD
- criminal justice • PhD
- emergency management • MS, PhD
- English • MA, MS
- history • MA, MS, PhD
- humanities and social sciences • MA, MS, PhD
- mass communication • MA, MS
- social science • MA, MS
- social sciences • MS
- speech communication • MA, MS

College of Business Administration
Dr. Jay Leitch, Dean
Program in:
- business administration • MBA

College of Engineering and Architecture
Dr. Otto J. Helweg, Dean
Programs in:
- agricultural and biosystems engineering • MS, PhD
- civil engineering • MS, PhD
- electrical engineering • MS, PhD
- engineering • PhD
- engineering and architecture • MS, PhD
- environmental engineering • MS, PhD
- industrial and manufacturing engineering • PhD
- industrial engineering and management • MS
- manufacturing engineering • MS
- mechanical engineering • MS, PhD
- natural resource management • MS, PhD
- transportation and logistics • PhD
- transportation logistics (logistics systems) • PhD

College of Human Development and Education
Dr. Virginia L. Clark, Dean
Programs in:
- agricultural education • M Ed, MS
- agricultural extension education • MS
- athletic administration • M Ed
- child development and family science • MS
- counselor education • M Ed, MS
- education • M Ed, MS, PhD, Ed S
- educational administration • M Ed, MS, Ed S
- exercise sciences • MS
- family and consumer sciences education • M Ed, MS
- gerontology • PhD
- human development • PhD
- human development and education • M Ed, MS, PhD, Ed S
- nutrition • MS
- pedagogy • M Ed, MS
- physical education and athletic administration • M Ed, MS
- sport pedagogy • MS
- sports recreation management • MS

College of Pharmacy
Dr. Charles D. Peterson, Dean
Programs in:
- pharmaceutical sciences • MS, PhD
- pharmacy • MS, PhD

College of Science and Mathematics
Dr. Alan R. White, Dean
Programs in:
- applied mathematics • MS, PhD
- applied statistics • MS
- biochemistry • MS, PhD
- botany • MS, PhD
- cellular and molecular biology • PhD
- chemistry • MS, PhD
- clinical psychology • MS, PhD
- computer science • MS, PhD
- computer science and statistics • MS
- environmental and conservation sciences • PhD
- general psychology • MS
- genomics • PhD
- mathematics • MS, PhD
- natural resources management • MS
- operations research • MS
- physics • MS, PhD
- polymers and coatings • MS, PhD
- psychology • MS
- science and mathematics • MS, PhD, Certificate
- software engineering • MS, PhD, Certificate
- statistics • PhD
- zoology • MS, PhD

■ UNIVERSITY OF MARY
Bismarck, ND 58504-9652
http://www.umary.edu/

Independent-religious, coed, comprehensive institution. *Enrollment:* 2,619 graduate, professional, and undergraduate students; 450 full-time matriculated graduate/professional students (277 women), 197 part-time matriculated graduate/professional students (145 women). *Graduate faculty:* 21 full-time (14 women), 144 part-time/adjunct (67 women). *Computer facilities:* 250 computers available on campus for general student use. A campuswide network can be accessed from student residence rooms. Internet access and online class registration are available. *Library facilities:* University of Mary Library. *Graduate expenses:* Tuition: part-time $365 per credit. *General application contact:* Dr. Kathy Perrin, Director of Graduate Studies, 701-355-8119.

Department of Occupational Therapy
Stacie Lynn Iken, Interim Program Director
Program in:
- occupational therapy • MS

Department of Physical Therapy
Joellen Marie Roller, Program Director
Program in:
- physical therapy • MPT

Division of Nursing
Deborah K. Swanson Banik, Director
Programs in:
- family nurse practitioner • MSN
- nurse management • MSN
- nursing educator • MSN

Program in Business Administration
David Heringer, Vice President of Enrollment Services
Program in:
- business administration • MBA

Program in Education
Rebecca Yunker Salveson, Director
Programs in:
- college teaching • MS Ed
- early childhood education • MS Ed
- early childhood special education • MS Ed
- elementary education administration • MS Ed
- elementary teaching • MS Ed
- reading emphasis • MS Ed
- secondary education administration • MS Ed
- secondary teaching • MS Ed
- special education • MS Ed

Program in Management
David Heringer, Vice President of Enrollment Services
Program in:
- management • M Mgmt

■ UNIVERSITY OF NORTH DAKOTA
Grand Forks, ND 58202
http://www.und.nodak.edu/

State-supported, coed, university. CGS member. *Enrollment:* 13,034 graduate, professional, and undergraduate students; 2,437 matriculated graduate/professional students. *Graduate faculty:* 497. *Computer facilities:* Computer purchase and lease plans are available. 1,000 computers available on campus for general student use. A campuswide network can be accessed from student residence rooms and from off campus. Internet access is available. *Library facilities:* Chester Fritz Library plus 2 others. *Graduate expenses:* Tuition, state resident: part-time $235 per credit. Tuition, nonresident: part-time $535 per credit. Tuition and fees vary according to course level, course load, program and reciprocity agreements. *General application contact:* Kristin A. Ellwanger, Admissions Officer, 701-777-2945.

Graduate School
Dr. Joseph N. Benoit, Dean
Program in:
  earth system science and policy • MEM, MS, PhD

College of Arts and Sciences
Dr. Bruce Dearden, Interim Dean
Programs in:
  arts and sciences • M Ed, M Mus, MA, MFA, MS, DA, PhD
  botany • MS, PhD
  chemistry • MS, PhD
  clinical psychology • PhD
  communication • MA, PhD
  communication sciences and disorders • PhD
  criminal justice • PhD
  ecology • MS, PhD
  English • MA, PhD
  entomology • MS, PhD
  environmental biology • MS, PhD
  experimental psychology • PhD
  fisheries/wildlife • MS, PhD
  genetics • MS, PhD
  geography • MA, MS
  history • MA, DA, PhD
  linguistics • MA
  mathematics • M Ed, MS
  music • M Mus
  music education • M Mus
  physics • MS, PhD
  psychology • MA
  sociology • MA
  speech-language pathology • MS
  theatre arts • MA
  visual arts • MFA
  zoology • MS, PhD

College of Business and Public Administration
Dr. Dennis J. Elbert, Dean
Programs in:
  business administration • MBA
  business and public administration • MBA, MPA, MS
  career and technical education • MS
  public administration • MPA
  technology education • MS

College of Education and Human Development
Dr. Dan R. Rice, Dean
Programs in:
  counseling • MA
  counseling psychology • PhD
  early childhood education • MS
  education and human development • M Ed, MA, MS, MSW, Ed D, PhD, Specialist
  education/general studies • MS
  educational leadership • M Ed, MS, Ed D, PhD, Specialist
  elementary education • Ed D, PhD
  instructional design and technology • M Ed, MS
  kinesiology • MS
  measurement and statistics • Ed D, PhD
  reading education • M Ed, MS
  secondary education • Ed D, PhD
  social work • MSW
  special education • Ed D, PhD

College of Nursing
Dr. Ginny W. Guido, Director
Program in:
  nursing • MS, PhD

John D. Odegard School of Aerospace Sciences
Bruce A. Smith, Dean
Programs in:
  aerospace sciences • MS
  atmospheric sciences • MS
  aviation • MS
  computer science • MS
  space studies • MS

School of Engineering and Mines
Dr. John L. Watson, Dean
Programs in:
  chemical engineering • M Engr, MS
  civil engineering • M Engr
  electrical engineering • M Engr, MS
  engineering • PhD
  engineering and mines • M Engr, MA, MS, PhD
  environmental engineering • M Engr, MS
  geological engineering • MS
  geology • MA, MS, PhD
  mechanical engineering • M Engr, MS
  sanitary engineering • M Engr

School of Law
Paul LeBel, Dean
Program in:
  law • JD

School of Medicine
Dr. H. David Wilson, Dean
Programs in:
  anatomy • MS, PhD
  biochemistry • MS, PhD
  clinical laboratory science • MS
  medicine • MD, MOT, MPAS, MPT, MS, DPT, PhD
  microbiology and immunology • MS, PhD
  occupational therapy • MOT
  pharmacology • MS, PhD
  physical therapy • MPT, DPT
  physician assistant • MPAS
  physiology • MS, PhD

Ohio

■ ANTIOCH UNIVERSITY MCGREGOR
Yellow Springs, OH 45387-1609
http://www.mcgregor.edu/

Independent, coed, upper-level institution. *Computer facilities:* 49 computers available on campus for general student use. A campuswide network can be accessed from off campus. Internet access is available. *Library facilities:* Olive Kettering Library. *General application contact:* Enrollment Services Officer, 937-769-1818.

Graduate Programs
Programs in:
  conflict resolution • MA
  liberal and professional studies • MA
  management • MA
  teacher education • M Ed

■ ASHLAND UNIVERSITY
Ashland, OH 44805-3702
http://www.ashland.edu/

Independent-religious, coed, comprehensive institution. CGS member. *Enrollment:* 6,835 graduate, professional, and undergraduate students; 1,136 full-time matriculated graduate/professional students (604 women), 1,637 part-time matriculated graduate/professional students (1,023 women). *Graduate faculty:* 96 full-time (40 women), 208 part-time/adjunct (101 women). *Computer facilities:* 90 computers available on campus for general student use. A campuswide network can be accessed from student residence rooms and from off campus. *Library facilities:* Ashland

Ohio

Ashland University (continued)
Library plus 2 others. *Graduate expenses:* Tuition: part-time $347 per credit hour. Part-time tuition and fees vary according to degree level and program. *General application contact:* Dr. John P. Sikula, Associate Provost, 419-289-5751.

College of Business Administration and Economics
Dr. Paul A. Sears, Dean
Program in:
business administration and economics • MBA

College of Education
Dr. Frank E. Pettigrew, Dean
Program in:
education • M Ed, Ed D

Doctoral Studies in Educational Leadership
Dr. W. Gregory Gerrick, Director
Program in:
educational leadership • Ed D

Graduate Studies in Education
Dr. Ann C. Shelly, Director and Chair
Programs in:
administration • M Ed
classroom instruction • M Ed
curriculum and instruction • M Ed
curriculum specialist • M Ed
early childhood education • M Ed
early childhood intervention specialist • M Ed
economics education • M Ed
education foundations • M Ed
educational administration and leadership • M Ed
intervention specialist-mild/moderate • M Ed
intervention specialist-moderate/intensive • M Ed
literacy • M Ed
middle school education • M Ed
principalship • M Ed
pupil personnel services • M Ed
school business manager • M Ed
school treasurer • M Ed
sport education • M Ed
superintendency • M Ed
talent development education • M Ed
technology education • M Ed

■ BALDWIN-WALLACE COLLEGE
Berea, OH 44017-2088
http://www.bw.edu/

Independent-religious, coed, comprehensive institution. *Enrollment:* 4,692 graduate, professional, and undergraduate students; 399 full-time matriculated graduate/professional students (237 women), 431 part-time matriculated graduate/professional students (324 women). *Graduate faculty:* 30 full-time (12 women), 31 part-time/adjunct (10 women). *Computer facilities:* Computer purchase and lease plans are available. 450 computers available on campus for general student use. A campuswide network can be accessed from student residence rooms. Internet access is available. *Library facilities:* Ritter Library plus 2 others. *Graduate expenses:* Tuition: part-time $470 per credit. *General application contact:* Winifred W. Gerhardt, Director of Admission for the Evening and Weekend College, 440-826-2222.

Graduate Programs
Mary Lou Higgerson, Dean of the College

Division of Business Administration
Dr. Peter Rea, Chairperson, Business Administration
Programs in:
accounting • MBA
business administration-systems management • MBA
entrepreneurship • MBA
executive management • MBA
health care executive management • MBA
human resources • MBA
international management • MBA

Division of Education
Karen Kaye, Chair
Programs in:
educational technology • MA Ed
mild/moderate educational needs • MA Ed
post-administration • MA Ed
pre-administration • MA Ed
reading • MA Ed

■ BOWLING GREEN STATE UNIVERSITY
Bowling Green, OH 43403
http://www.bgsu.edu/

State-supported, coed, university. CGS member. *Enrollment:* 18,534 graduate, professional, and undergraduate students; 1,516 full-time matriculated graduate/professional students (882 women), 1,150 part-time matriculated graduate/professional students (750 women). *Graduate faculty:* 608 full-time. *Computer facilities:* 6,240 computers available on campus for general student use. A campuswide network can be accessed from student residence rooms and from off campus. Internet access and online class registration are available. *Library facilities:* Jerome Library plus 7 others. *Graduate expenses:* Tuition, state resident: part-time $436 per hour. Tuition, nonresident: part-time $768 per hour. *General application contact:* Terry L. Lawrence, Assistant Dean for Graduate Admissions and Studies, 419-372-7710.
Find an in-depth description at www.petersons.com/gradchannel.

Graduate College
Dr. Heinz Bulmahn, Vice Provost for Research and Dean

College of Arts and Sciences
Dr. Donald Nieman, Dean
Programs in:
American culture studies • MA, MAT, PhD
applied biology • Specialist
applied philosophy • PhD
applied statistics • MS
art • MA
arts and sciences • MA, MAT, MFA, MPA, MS, PhD, Ed S, Specialist
biological sciences • MAT, MS, PhD
chemistry • MAT, MS
clinical psychology • MA, PhD
communication studies • MA, PhD
computer science • MS
creative writing • MFA
criminology/deviant behavior • MA, PhD
demography and population studies • MA, PhD
developmental psychology • MA, PhD
English • MA, PhD
experimental psychology • MA, PhD
family studies • MA, PhD
French • MA, MAT
French education • MAT
geology • MAT, MS
German • MA, MAT
history • MA, MAT, PhD
industrial/organizational psychology • MA, PhD
mathematics • MA, MAT, PhD
mathematics supervision • Ed S
philosophy • MA
photochemical sciences • PhD
physics • MAT, MS
physics and astronomy • MAT
popular culture • MA
public administration • MPA
quantitative psychology • MA, PhD
social psychology • MA, PhD
Spanish • MA, MAT
Spanish education • MAT
statistics • MA, MAT, PhD
studio art • MFA
teaching English as a second language • MA
theatre • MA, PhD

College of Business Administration
Dr. Robert Edmister, Dean
Programs in:
accountancy • M Acc
applied statistics • MS
business • MBA

business administration • M Acc, MA, MBA, MOD, MS
economics • MA
organization development • MOD

College of Education and Human Development
Dr. Josué Cruz, Dean
Programs in:
administrative supervision • Sp Ed As
business education • M Ed
classroom technology • M Ed
college student personnel • MA
curriculum and teaching • M Ed
developmental kinesiology • M Ed
education and human development • M Ed, MA, MFCS, MRC, Ed D, PhD, Ed S, Sp Ed, Sp Ed As, Sp Sch Psych
education and intervention services • M Ed, MA, MRC, Ed S, Sp Ed, Sp Sch Psych
educational administration and supervision • M Ed, Ed S
food and nutrition • MFCS
guidance and counseling • M Ed, MA
higher education administration • PhD
human development and family studies • MFCS
leadership and policy studies • M Ed, MA, Ed D, PhD, Ed S, Sp Ed As
leadership studies • Ed D
mathematics supervision • Ed S
reading • M Ed, Ed S
recreation and leisure • M Ed
rehabilitation counseling • MRC
school psychology • M Ed, Sp Ed, Sp Sch Psych
special education • M Ed
sport administration • M Ed

College of Health and Human Services
Dr. Linda Petrosino, Dean
Programs in:
communication disorders • MS, PhD
criminal justice • MSCJ
health and human services • MPH, MS, MSCJ, PhD
public health • MPH

College of Musical Arts
Dr. Richard Kennell, Dean
Programs in:
composition • MM
music education • MM
music history • MM
music theory • MM
performance • MM

College of Technology
Dr. Ernie Savage, Dean
Programs in:
manufacturing technology • MIT
technology • M Ed, MIT
visual communication and technology education • M Ed

Interdisciplinary Studies
Program in:
interdisciplinary studies • MA, MS, PhD

■ CAPITAL UNIVERSITY
Columbus, OH 43209-2394
http://www.capital.edu/

Independent-religious, coed, comprehensive institution. *Enrollment:* 3,959 graduate, professional, and undergraduate students; 668 full-time matriculated graduate/professional students (312 women), 461 part-time matriculated graduate/professional students (221 women). *Graduate faculty:* 157. *Computer facilities:* 100 computers available on campus for general student use. A campuswide network can be accessed from student residence rooms and from off campus. Internet access is available. *Library facilities:* Blackmore Library. *Graduate expenses:* Tuition, state resident: part-time $694 per credit hour. Part-time tuition and fees vary according to program.

Law School
Steven C. Bahls, Dean
Programs in:
business • LL M
business and taxation • LL M
law • JD, LL M, MT
taxation • LL M, MT

School of Management
Program in:
management • MBA

School of Nursing
Dr. Elaine F. Haynes, Dean and Professor
Programs in:
administration • MSN
family and community health nursing • MSN
legal studies • MSN
parish nursing • MSN
school health nursing • MSN
theological studies • MSN

■ CASE WESTERN RESERVE UNIVERSITY
Cleveland, OH 44106
http://www.cwru.edu/

Independent, coed, university. CGS member. *Enrollment:* 9,186 graduate, professional, and undergraduate students; 3,606 full-time matriculated graduate/professional students (1,586 women), 1,411 part-time matriculated graduate/professional students (702 women). *Graduate faculty:* 1,949 full-time (550 women). *Computer facilities:* Computer purchase and lease plans are available.

100 computers available on campus for general student use. A campuswide network can be accessed from student residence rooms and from off campus. Internet access and online class registration, software library, CD-ROM databases are available. *Library facilities:* University Library plus 6 others. *Graduate expenses:* Tuition: full-time $26,900. *General application contact:* Susan M. Benedict, Assistant Dean of Graduate Studies, 216-368-4390.

Frances Payne Bolton School of Nursing
Dr. May L. Wykle, Dean
Programs in:
acute care cardiac • MSN
acute care nurse practitioner • MSN
acute care/flight nurse • MSN
adult practitioner • MSN
community health • MSN
community health nursing • MSN
family nurse practitioner • MSN
gerontological nurse practitioner • MSN
graduate entry/pre-licensure option • ND
infection control • MSN
medical-surgical nursing • MSN
neonatal practitioner • MSN
nurse anesthesia • MSN
nurse midwifery • MSN
nurse practitioner • MSN
nursing • MSN, ND, PhD
nursing informatics • MSN
pediatric nurse practitioner • MSN
post-licensure option • ND
psychiatric-mental health nurse practitioner • MSN
women's health nurse practitioner • MSN

Mandel School of Applied Social Sciences
Dr. Grover Cleveland Gilmore, Dean
Programs in:
nonprofit organizations • MNO, CNM
social administration • MSSA
social welfare • PhD

School of Dental Medicine
Dr. Jerold S. Goldberg, Dean
Programs in:
advanced general dentistry • Certificate
dental medicine • DMD, MSD, Certificate
dentistry • DMD, MSD, Certificate
endodontics • MSD, Certificate
oral surgery • Certificate
orthodontics • MSD, Certificate
pedodontics • Certificate
periodontics • MSD, Certificate

Ohio

Case Western Reserve University (continued)

School of Graduate Studies
Dr. Lenore A. Kola, Dean
Programs in:
- acting • MFA
- analytical chemistry • MS, PhD
- anthropology • MA, PhD
- applied mathematics • MS, PhD
- art education • MA
- art history • MA, PhD
- art history and museum studies • MA, PhD
- astronomy • MS, PhD
- bioethics • MA, PhD
- biology • MS, PhD
- clinical psychology • PhD
- comparative literature • MA
- contemporary dance • MFA
- early music • D Mus A
- English and American literature • MA, PhD
- experimental psychology • PhD
- French • MA, PhD
- geological sciences • MS, PhD
- gerontology • Certificate
- history • MA, PhD
- inorganic chemistry • MS, PhD
- mathematics • MS, PhD
- mental retardation • PhD
- museum studies • MA
- music • MA, PhD
- music education • MA, PhD
- organic chemistry • MS, PhD
- physical chemistry • MS, PhD
- physics • MS, PhD
- political science • MA, PhD
- sociology • PhD
- speech-language pathology • MA, PhD
- statistics • MS, PhD
- theater • MFA

The Case School of Engineering
Joseph M. Mansour, Department Chair
Programs in:
- aerospace engineering • MS, PhD
- biomedical engineering • MS, PhD
- ceramics and materials science • MS
- chemical engineering • MS, PhD
- civil engineering • MS, PhD
- computer engineering • MS, PhD
- computing and information science • MS, PhD
- electrical engineering • MS, PhD
- engineering • ME, MEM, MS, PhD
- engineering mechanics • MS
- fluid and thermal engineering sciences • MS, PhD
- integration of management and engineering • MEM
- macromolecular science • MS, PhD
- materials science and engineering • MS, PhD
- mechanical engineering • MS, PhD
- systems and control engineering • MS, PhD

School of Law
Gerald Korngold, Dean
Programs in:
- law • JD
- U.S. legal studies • LL M

School of Medicine
Dr. Ralph I. Horwitz, Dean
Programs in:
- biomedical sciences • PhD
- clinical research • MS
- medicine • MD, MA, MPH, MS, PhD

Graduate Programs in Medicine
Dr. Lenore A. Kola, Dean, Graduate Studies
Programs in:
- anesthesiology • MS
- applied anatomy • MS
- biochemical research • MS
- biochemistry • MS, PhD
- biological anthropology • MS, PhD
- biophysics and bioengineering • PhD
- biostatistics • MS, PhD
- cell biology • MS, PhD
- cell physiology • PhD
- cellular biology • MS, PhD
- developmental biology • PhD
- dietetics • MS
- environmental toxicology • MS, PhD
- epidemiology • MS, PhD
- exercise physiology • MS
- genetic counseling • MS
- human, molecular, and developmental genetics and genomics • PhD
- immunology • MS, PhD
- medicine • MPH, MS, PhD
- microbiology • PhD
- molecular biology • PhD
- molecular toxicology • MS, PhD
- molecular virology • PhD
- neurobiology • PhD
- neuroscience • PhD
- nutrition • MS, PhD
- pathology • MS, PhD
- pharmacology • MS, PhD
- physiology and biophysics • PhD
- physiology and biotechnology • MS
- public health • MPH
- public health nutrition • MS
- systems physiology • PhD

Weatherhead School of Management
Myron L. Room Kin, Dean
Programs in:
- accountancy • M Acc, PhD
- banking and finance • MBA, PhD
- economics • MBA
- information systems • MBA, MSM, PhD
- labor and human resource policy • MBA, PhD
- management • MS, EDM
- management policy • MBA, PhD
- marketing • MBA, PhD
- operations research • PhD
- organizational behavior and analysis • MBA, MS, PhD

Mandel Center for Nonprofit Organizations
Susan Lajoie Eagan, Director
Program in:
- nonprofit organizations • MNO, CNM

■ CLEVELAND STATE UNIVERSITY
Cleveland, OH 44115
http://www.csuohio.edu/

State-supported, coed, university. CGS member. *Enrollment:* 16,014 graduate, professional, and undergraduate students; 2,046 full-time matriculated graduate/professional students (1,062 women), 2,860 part-time matriculated graduate/professional students (1,719 women). *Graduate faculty:* 398 full-time (137 women), 69 part-time/adjunct (20 women). *Computer facilities:* Computer purchase and lease plans are available. 600 computers available on campus for general student use. A campuswide network can be accessed. Internet access and online class registration are available. *Library facilities:* University Library plus 1 other. *Graduate expenses:* Full-time $8,258; part-time $344 per credit hour. Tuition, nonresident: full-time $16,352; part-time $681 per credit hour. *General application contact:* Dr. William C. Bailey, Director of Graduate Admissions and Associate Dean, College of Graduate Studies, 216-687-9370.

Find an in-depth description at www.petersons.com/gradchannel.

Cleveland-Marshall College of Law
Steven H. Steinglass, Dean
Program in:
- law • JD, LL M

College of Graduate Studies
Dr. Mark A. Tumeo, Vice Provost for Research and Dean, College of Graduate Studies

College of Arts and Sciences
Dr. Earl Anderson, Interim Dean
Programs in:
- analytical chemistry • MS, PhD
- applied mathematics • MS
- applied optics • MS
- art history • MA
- arts and sciences • MA, MACTM, MM, MOT, MPT, MS, MSW, PhD, Certificate, Psy S
- bioethics • MA, Certificate
- biological, geological, and environmental sciences • MS, PhD
- clinical and counseling psychology • MA

Ohio

clinical chemistry • MS, PhD
clinical/bioanalytical • PhD
communication • MACTM
composition • MM
condensed matter physics • MS
consumer/industrial research • MA
diversity management • MA
economics • MA
education and performance • MM
English • MA
health sciences • MS
history • MA
inorganic chemistry • MS
mathematics • MA
medical physics • MS
music history • MM
occupational therapy • MOT
organic chemistry • MS
physical chemistry • MS
physical therapy • MPT
research psychology • MA
school psychology • Psy S
social studies • MA
social work • MSW
sociology • MA
Spanish • MA
speech and hearing • MA
structural analysis • MS, PhD

College of Education and Human Services
Dr. James McLoughlin, Dean
Programs in:
administration • PhD
adult learning and development • M Ed, Certificate
community agency counseling • M Ed
community health education • M Ed
counseling • PhD
counselor education • M Ed
curriculum and instruction • M Ed
education and human services • M Ed, MSN, PhD, Certificate, Ed S
educational administration and supervision • M Ed, Ed S
exercise science • M Ed
forensic nursing • MSN
human performance • M Ed
leadership and lifelong learning • PhD
learning and development • PhD
pedagogy • M Ed
policy studies • PhD
population health nursing • MSN
school and professional counseling • M Ed, Ed S
school health education • M Ed
sport and exercise psychology • M Ed
sport management • M Ed
sport management/exercise science • M Ed

Fenn College of Engineering
Dr. John H. Hemann, Interim Dean
Programs in:
applied biomedical engineering • D Eng
chemical engineering • MS, D Eng
civil engineering • MS, D Eng
electrical and computer engineering • MS, D Eng
engineering • D Eng
engineering mechanics • MS
environmental engineering • MS
industrial engineering • MS
mechanical engineering • MS, D Eng

James J. Nance College of Business Administration
Dr. Robert F. Scherer, Dean
Programs in:
business administration • MBA, DBA
data-driven marketing planning • Certificate
e-commerce • MBA
finance • DBA
financial accounting/audit • MAC
health care administration • MBA, MPA
labor relations and human resources • MLRHR
management and labor relations • DBA
management and organization analysis • MCIS
marketing • MBA, DBA
operations management and business statistics • MBA
production/operations management • DBA
public health • MPH
systems programming • MCIS
tax program • MAC

Maxine Goodman Levin College of Urban Affairs
Dr. Mark Rosentraub, Dean
Programs in:
environmental studies • MAES
non-profit management • Certificate
public administration • MPA, PhD
urban affairs • MA, MAES, MPA, MS, MUPDD, PhD, Certificate
urban economic development • Certificate
urban planning, design, and development • MUPDD
urban real estate development and finance • Certificate
urban studies • MA, MS, PhD

■ COLLEGE OF MOUNT ST. JOSEPH
Cincinnati, OH 45233-1670
http://www.msj.edu/

Independent-religious, coed, comprehensive institution. *Enrollment:* 2,110 graduate, professional, and undergraduate students; 21 full-time matriculated graduate/professional students (17 women), 213 part-time matriculated graduate/professional students (172 women). *Graduate faculty:* 20 full-time (13 women). *Computer facilities:* Computer purchase and lease plans are available. 251 computers available on campus for general student use. A campuswide network can be accessed from student residence rooms and from off campus. Internet access and online class registration, computer-aided instruction are available. *Library facilities:* Archbishop Alter Library. *Graduate expenses:* Tuition: full-time $16,000; part-time $400 per credit hour. Required fees: $140; $50 per year. Tuition and fees vary according to program. *General application contact:* Peggy Minnich, Director of Admission, 513-244-4814.

Find an in-depth description at www.petersons.com/gradchannel.

Education Department
Dr. Clarissa Enio Rosas, Chair
Programs in:
art • MA Ed
inclusive childhood education • MA Ed
professional development • MA Ed
professional foundations • MA Ed
reading • MA Ed
special education • MA Ed

Interdisciplinary Program in Organizational Leadership
Dr. John Weiler, Chair
Program in:
organizational leadership • MS

Physical Therapy Department
Dr. Darla Vale, Chair, Health Science
Program in:
physical therapy • MPT

Religious Studies Department
Dr. John Trokan, Chair
Programs in:
religious studies • MA
spiritual and pastoral care • MA

■ FRANCISCAN UNIVERSITY OF STEUBENVILLE
Steubenville, OH 43952-1763
http://www.franuniv.edu/

Independent-religious, coed, comprehensive institution. *Enrollment:* 2,281 graduate, professional, and undergraduate students; 174 full-time matriculated graduate/professional students (91 women), 263 part-time matriculated graduate/professional students (156 women). *Graduate faculty:* 8 full-time (2 women), 33 part-time/adjunct (10 women). *Computer facilities:* 126 computers available on campus for general student use. A campuswide network can be accessed. Internet access is available. *Library facilities:* John Paul II

Ohio

Franciscan University of Steubenville (continued)
Library. *Graduate expenses:* Tuition: full-time $8,820. *General application contact:* Mark McGuire, Director of Graduate Enrollment, 800-783-6220.

Graduate Programs
Dr. Stephen Miletic, Dean of Faculty
Programs in:
    administration • MS Ed
    business • MBA
    counseling • MA
    nursing • MSN
    philosophy • MA
    teaching • MS Ed
    theology and Christian ministry • MA

■ HEIDELBERG COLLEGE
Tiffin, OH 44883-2462
http://www.heidelberg.edu/

Independent-religious, coed, comprehensive institution. *Enrollment:* 1,243 graduate, professional, and undergraduate students; 15 full-time matriculated graduate/professional students (14 women), 175 part-time matriculated graduate/professional students (120 women). *Graduate faculty:* 7 full-time (3 women), 7 part-time/adjunct (4 women). *Computer facilities:* 125 computers available on campus for general student use. A campuswide network can be accessed from student residence rooms and from off campus. Internet access and online class registration are available. *Library facilities:* Beeghly Library plus 1 other. *Graduate expenses:* Tuition: part-time $315 per credit hour. *General application contact:* 419-448-2288.

Program in Business
Dr. Henry G. Rennie, Director of Graduate Studies in Business
Program in:
    business administration • MBA

Program in Counseling
Dr. Jo-Ann Lipford Sanders, Director of Graduate Studies in Counseling
Program in:
    counseling • MA

Program in Education
Dr. Jim Getz, Director of Graduate Studies in Education
Program in:
    education • MA

■ JOHN CARROLL UNIVERSITY
University Heights, OH 44118-4581
http://www.jcu.edu/

Independent-religious, coed, comprehensive institution. CGS member. *Enrollment:* 4,242 graduate, professional, and undergraduate students; 192 full-time matriculated graduate/professional students (130 women), 519 part-time matriculated graduate/professional students (323 women). *Graduate faculty:* 140 full-time (41 women), 42 part-time/adjunct (23 women). *Computer facilities:* 210 computers available on campus for general student use. A campuswide network can be accessed from student residence rooms and from off campus. Internet access and online class registration are available. *Library facilities:* Grasselli Library. *Graduate expenses:* Tuition: part-time $600 per semester hour. Tuition and fees vary according to program. *General application contact:* Revona Spicuzza, Admissions Secretary, 216-397-1925.

Graduate School
Dr. Mary E. Beadle, Dean
Programs in:
    administration • M Ed, MA
    biology • MA, MS
    chemistry • MS
    clinical counseling • Certificate
    communications management • MA
    community counseling • MA
    educational and school psychology • M Ed, MA
    English • MA
    history • MA
    humanities • MA
    mathematics • MA, MS
    physics • MS
    professional teacher education • M Ed, MA
    religious studies • MA
    school based adolescent-young adult education • M Ed
    school based early childhood education • M Ed
    school based middle childhood education • M Ed
    school based multi-age education • M Ed
    school counseling • M Ed, MA

John M. and Mary Jo Boler School of Business
Dr. Darrell Radson, Associate Dean
Programs in:
    accountancy • MS
    business • MBA

■ KENT STATE UNIVERSITY
Kent, OH 44242-0001
http://www.kent.edu/

State-supported, coed, university. CGS member. *Enrollment:* 23,536 graduate, professional, and undergraduate students; 2,247 full-time matriculated graduate/professional students (1,350 women), 2,185 part-time matriculated graduate/professional students (1,515 women). *Graduate faculty:* 807. *Computer facilities:* 1,680 computers available on campus for general student use. A campuswide network can be accessed from student residence rooms and from off campus. Internet access is available. *Library facilities:* Kent Library plus 5 others. *Graduate expenses:* Tuition, state resident: part-time $334 per hour. Tuition, nonresident: part-time $627 per hour. *General application contact:* Division of Research and Graduate Studies, 330-672-2661.

College of Arts and Sciences
Programs in:
    analytical chemistry • MS, PhD
    anthropology • MA
    applied mathematics • MA, MS, PhD
    arts and sciences • MA, MLS, MPA, MS, PhD
    biochemistry • MS, PhD
    botany • MS
    chemical physics • MS, PhD
    chemistry • MA, MS, PhD
    clinical psychology • MA, PhD
    comparative literature • MA
    computer science • MA, MS, PhD
    ecology • MS, PhD
    English for teachers • MA
    experimental psychology • MA, PhD
    French • MA
    geography • MA, PhD
    geology • MS, PhD
    German • MA
    history • MA, PhD
    inorganic chemistry • MS, PhD
    Japanese • MA
    justice studies • MA
    Latin • MA
    liberal studies • MLS
    literature • PhD
    literature and writing • MA
    organic chemistry • MS, PhD
    philosophy • MA
    physical chemistry • MS, PhD
    physics • MA, MS, PhD
    physiology • MS, PhD
    political science • MA
    public administration • MPA
    public policy • PhD
    pure mathematics • MA, MS, PhD
    rhetoric and composition • PhD
    Russian • MA
    sociology • MA, PhD
    Spanish • MA

teaching English as a second language • MA
translation • MA

College of Communication and Information
Program in:
visual communication design • MA, MFA

School of Communication Studies
Program in:
communication studies • MA, PhD

School of Journalism and Mass Communication
Program in:
journalism and mass communication • MA

School of Library and Information Science
Program in:
library and information science • MLS, MS

College of Fine and Professional Arts
Program in:
fine and professional arts • M Arch, MA, MFA, MLS, MM, MPH, MS, Au D, PhD, Certificate

Hugh A. Glauser School of Music
Mary Sue Hyatt, Interim Director
Programs in:
composition • MA
conducting • MM
ethnomusicology • MA
music education • MM, PhD
musicology • MA
musicology-ethnomusicology • PhD
performance • MM
theory • MA
theory and composition • PhD

Northeastern Ohio Universities Public Health Program
Program in:
public health • MPH

School of Architecture and Environmental Design
Program in:
architecture • M Arch

School of Art
Programs in:
art education • MA
art history • MA
crafts • MA, MFA
fine arts • MA, MFA

School of Exercise, Leisure and Sport
Programs in:
exercise physiology • PhD
physical education • MA

School of Family and Consumer Studies
Programs in:
family life professional • MA
gerontology • MA, Certificate
nutrition • MS
nutrition and gerontology • MS

School of Speech Pathology and Audiology
Program in:
speech pathology and audiology • MA, Au D, PhD

School of Theatre and Dance
Programs in:
acting • MFA
design and technology • MFA
theatre • MA, MFA

College of Nursing
Head
Programs in:
clinical nursing • MSN
nursing • PhD
nursing administration • MSN
nursing education • MSN
parent-child nursing • MSN

Graduate School of Education
Dr. David A. England, Dean
Programs in:
community counseling • M Ed, MA
counseling • Ed S
counseling and human development services • PhD
cultural foundations • M Ed, MA, PhD
curriculum and instruction • M Ed, MA, PhD, Ed S
early childhood education • M Ed, MA, MAT
early childhood intervention • M Ed, MA
education • M Ed, MA, MAT, PhD, Ed S
educational administration • M Ed, MA, PhD, Ed S
educational foundations • M Ed, MA, PhD
educational psychology • M Ed, MA, PhD
evaluation and measurement • M Ed, MA, PhD
gifted education • M Ed, MA
health education and promotion • M Ed, MA, PhD
hearing impaired education • M Ed, MA
higher education administration and student personnel • M Ed, MA, PhD, Ed S
instructional technology • M Ed, MA
K–12 leadership • M Ed, MA, PhD, Ed S
learning and development • M Ed, MA
middle childhood education • M Ed, MA
mild/moderate • M Ed, MA
moderate/intensive • M Ed, MA
reading • M Ed, MA
rehabilitation counseling • M Ed, MA, Ed S
school counseling • M Ed, MA
school psychology • M Ed, PhD, Ed S
secondary education • M Ed, MA, MAT
special education • M Ed, MA, PhD, Ed S
vocational and technical education • M Ed, MA, Ed S
vocational education • M Ed, MA, Ed S

Graduate School of Management
Dr. Donald R. Williams, Associate Dean
Programs in:
accounting • MS, PhD
business administration • MBA
economics • MA
finance • PhD
financial engineering • MSFE
management • MA, MBA, MS, MSFE, PhD
management systems • PhD
marketing • PhD

Program in Biological Anthropology
Program in:
biological anthropology • PhD

School of Biomedical Sciences
Programs in:
biomedical sciences • MS, PhD
cellular and molecular biology • MS, PhD
neuroscience • MS, PhD
pharmacology • MS, PhD
physiology • MS, PhD

School of Technology
Program in:
technology • M Tech, MA

■ LAKE ERIE COLLEGE
Painesville, OH 44077-3389
http://www.lec.edu/

Independent, coed, comprehensive institution. *Computer facilities:* 104 computers available on campus for general student use. A campuswide network can be accessed from student residence rooms and from off campus. Internet access and online class registration are available. *Library facilities:* Lincoln Library plus 2 others. *General application contact:* 440-639-7879.

Ohio

Lake Erie College (continued)
Division of Education
Programs in:
 education • MS Ed
 effective teaching • MS Ed
 reading • MS Ed

Division of Management Studies
Programs in:
 general management • MBA
 management healthcare administration • MBA

■ MALONE COLLEGE
Canton, OH 44709-3897
http://www.malone.edu/

Independent-religious, coed, comprehensive institution. *Enrollment:* 2,206 graduate, professional, and undergraduate students; 19 full-time matriculated graduate/professional students (12 women), 240 part-time matriculated graduate/professional students (160 women). *Graduate faculty:* 30 full-time (13 women), 42 part-time/adjunct (22 women). *Computer facilities:* 197 computers available on campus for general student use. A campuswide network can be accessed from student residence rooms and from off campus. Internet access is available. *Library facilities:* Everett L. Cattell Library. *Graduate expenses:* Tuition: part-time $360 per semester hour. One-time fee: $25 part-time. Part-time tuition and fees vary according to program. *General application contact:* Jeffrey A. Bartolet, Recruiter, 330-471-8447.

Program in Counselor Education
Dr. Daniel R. Merz, Director
Programs in:
 community counseling • MA
 school counseling • MA

School of Business
Dr. Thomas A. Kratzer, Dean
Program in:
 business • MBA

School of Education
Dr. Christine A. Krol, Dean
Programs in:
 curriculum and instruction • MA
 curriculum, instruction, and professional development • MA
 instructional technology • MA
 intervention specialist • MA
 reading • MA

School of Nursing
Dr. Loretta M. Reinhart, Dean
Programs in:
 clinical nurse specialist • MSN
 family nurse practitioner • MSN

School of Theology
Dr. Larry D. Reinhart, Dean
Programs in:
 Christian ministries • MA
 leadership in the Christian church • MA

■ MIAMI UNIVERSITY
Oxford, OH 45056
http://www.muohio.edu/

State-related, coed, university. CGS member. *Enrollment:* 16,795 graduate, professional, and undergraduate students; 1,085 full-time matriculated graduate/professional students (614 women), 288 part-time matriculated graduate/professional students (219 women). *Graduate faculty:* 625 full-time (197 women), 41 part-time/adjunct (13 women). *Computer facilities:* 1,000 computers available on campus for general student use. A campuswide network can be accessed from student residence rooms and from off campus. Internet access and online class registration are available. *Library facilities:* King Library plus 3 others. *Graduate expenses:* Full-time $9,346. International tuition: $19,924 full-time. Full-time tuition and fees vary according to course level and campus/location. *General application contact:* Dr. John M. Hughes, Associate Provost for Research and Dean of the Graduate School, 513-529-4125.

Find an in-depth description at www.petersons.com/gradchannel.

Graduate School
Dr. John M. Hughes, Associate Provost for Research and Dean of the Graduate School

College of Arts and Sciences
Dr. John Skillings, Dean
Programs in:
 analytical chemistry • MS, PhD
 arts and sciences • MA, MAT, MGS, MS, MS Stat, MTSC, PhD
 biochemistry • MS, PhD
 biological sciences • MAT
 botany • MA, MS, PhD
 chemical education • MS, PhD
 chemistry • MS, PhD
 clinical psychology • PhD
 comparative religion • MA
 composition and rhetoric • MA, PhD
 creative writing • MA
 criticism • PhD
 English and American literature and language • PhD
 English education • MAT
 experimental psychology • PhD
 French • MA
 geography • MA
 geology • MA, MS, PhD
 gerontology • MGS
 history • MA, PhD
 inorganic chemistry • MS, PhD
 library theory • PhD
 literature • MA, MAT, PhD
 mass communication • MA
 mathematics • MA, MAT, MS
 mathematics/operations research • MS
 microbiology • MS, PhD
 organic chemistry • MS, PhD
 philosophy • MA
 physical chemistry • MS, PhD
 physics • MS
 political science • MA, MAT, PhD
 social psychology • PhD
 Spanish • MA
 speech communication • MA
 speech pathology and audiology • MA, MS
 statistics • MS Stat
 technical and scientific communication • MTSC
 zoology • MA, MS, PhD

Institute of Environmental Sciences
Dr. Gene Willeke, Director
Program in:
 environmental sciences • M En S

Richard T. Farmer School of Business Administration
Dr. Roger Jenkins, Dean
Programs in:
 accountancy • M Acc
 business administration • MBA
 economics • MA
 finance • MBA
 general management • MBA
 management information systems • MBA
 marketing • MBA
 quality and process improvement • MBA

School of Education and Allied Professions
Dr. Barbara Schirmer, Acting Dean
Programs in:
 adolescent education • MAT
 child and family studies • MS
 college student personnel services • MS
 curriculum and teacher leadership • M Ed
 education and allied professions • M Ed, MA, MAT, MS, Ed D, PhD, Ed S
 educational administration • Ed D, PhD
 educational leadership • M Ed, MS
 educational psychology • M Ed
 elementary education • M Ed, MAT
 elementary mathematics education • M Ed
 physical education, health, and sports studies • MS

reading education • M Ed
school psychology • MS, Ed S
secondary education • M Ed, MAT
special education • M Ed, MA

School of Engineering and Applied Science
Dr. Marek Dollár, Dean
Programs in:
computer science • MCS
computer science and systems analysis • MCS
paper science and engineering • MS
software development • Certificate

School of Fine Arts
Dr. Curtis Ellison, Interim Dean
Programs in:
architecture • M Arch
art education • MA
fine arts • M Arch, MA, MFA, MM
music education • MM
music performance • MM
studio art • MFA
theatre • MA

■ THE OHIO STATE UNIVERSITY
Columbus, OH 43210
http://www.osu.edu/

State-supported, coed, university. CGS member. *Enrollment:* 50,731 graduate, professional, and undergraduate students; 9,987 full-time matriculated graduate/professional students (5,065 women), 2,639 part-time matriculated graduate/professional students (1,474 women). *Graduate faculty:* 2,876. *Computer facilities:* 1,000 computers available on campus for general student use. A campuswide network can be accessed from student residence rooms and from off campus. Internet access and online class registration are available. *Library facilities:* Main Library plus 12 others. *Graduate expenses:* Tuition, state resident: full-time $7,233. Tuition, nonresident: full-time $18,489. *General application contact:* Marie Taris, Director, Graduate, International, and Professional Schools Admissions, 614-292-9444.

College of Dentistry
Jan E. Kronmiller, Dean
Programs in:
dentistry • DDS, MS, PhD
oral biology • PhD

College of Medicine and Public Health
Programs in:
medicine • MD
medicine and public health • MD, MHA, MOT, MPH, MPT, MS, PhD

Graduate Programs in the Basic Medical Sciences
Programs in:
allied medicine • MS
anatomy • MS, PhD
basic medical sciences • MHA, MOT, MPH, MPT, MS, PhD
experimental pathobiology • MS
health administration • MHA
integrated biomedical science • PhD
molecular virology, immunology and medical genetics • MS
neuroscience • PhD
occupational therapy • MOT
pathology assistant • MS
pharmacology • MS
physical therapy • MPT
physiology • MS
public health • MPH, MS, PhD

College of Optometry
Programs in:
optometry • OD, MS, PhD
vision science • MS, PhD

College of Pharmacy
Dr. Robert W. Brueggemeier, Chair
Programs in:
health-system pharmacy administration • MS
medicinal chemistry and pharmacognosy • MS, PhD
pharmaceutical administration • MS, PhD
pharmaceutics • MS, PhD
pharmacology • MS, PhD
pharmacy • MS, PhD
pharmacy practice and administration • MS, PhD

College of Veterinary Medicine
Glen F. Hoffsis, Dean
Programs in:
anatomy and cellular biology • MS, PhD
pathobiology • MS, PhD
pharmacology • MS, PhD
toxicology • MS, PhD
veterinary biosciences • MS, PhD
veterinary clinical sciences • MS, PhD
veterinary medicine • DVM, MS, PhD
veterinary physiology • MS, PhD
veterinary preventive medicine • MS, PhD

Graduate School
Dr. Susan L. Huntington, Vice Provost for Graduate Studies and Dean
Program in:
Slavic and East European studies • MA

College of Biological Sciences
Dr. Joan Herbers, Dean
Programs in:
biochemistry • MS, PhD
biological sciences • MS, PhD
biophysics • MS, PhD
cell and developmental biology • MS, PhD
entomology • MS, PhD
environmental science • MS, PhD
evolution, ecology, and organismal biology • MS, PhD
genetics • MS, PhD
microbiology • MS, PhD
molecular biology • MS, PhD
molecular, cellular and developmental biology • MS, PhD
plant biology • MS, PhD

College of Education
Dr. Donna Evans, Dean
Programs in:
education • M Ed, MA, PhD, Certificate
educational administration • Certificate
educational policy and leadership • M Ed, MA, PhD
physical activity and educational services • M Ed, MA, PhD
teaching and learning • M Ed, MA, PhD

College of Engineering
Dr. James C. Williams, Dean
Programs in:
aeronautical and astronautical engineering • MS, PhD
architecture • M Arch, M Land Arch, MCRP, PhD
biomedical engineering • MS, PhD
chemical engineering • MS, PhD
city and regional planning • MCRP, PhD
civil engineering • MS, PhD
computer and information science • MS, PhD
electrical engineering • MS, PhD
engineering • M Arch, M Land Arch, MCRP, MS, PhD
engineering mechanics • MS, PhD
geodetic science and surveying • MS, PhD
industrial and systems engineering • MS, PhD
landscape architecture • M Land Arch
materials science and engineering • MS, PhD
mechanical engineering • MS, PhD
nuclear engineering • MS, PhD
welding engineering • MS, PhD

College of Food, Agricultural, and Environmental Sciences
Dr. Bobby D. Moser, Dean
Programs in:
agricultural economics and rural sociology • MS, PhD
agricultural education • MS, PhD
animal sciences • MS, PhD
food science and nutrition • MS, PhD
food, agricultural, and biological engineering • MS, PhD

Ohio

The Ohio State University (continued)
  food, agricultural, and environmental sciences • MS, PhD
  horticulture and crop science • MS, PhD
  plant pathology • MS, PhD
  soil science • MS, PhD
  vocational education • PhD

College of Human Ecology
David W. Andrews, Dean
Programs in:
  family and consumer sciences education • M Ed, MS, PhD
  family relations and human development • MS, PhD
  family resource management • MS, PhD
  food service management • MS, PhD
  foods • MS, PhD
  human ecology • M Ed, MS, PhD
  nutrition • MS, PhD
  textiles and clothing • MS, PhD

College of Humanities
Dr. Jacqueline Royster, Dean
Programs in:
  African-American and African studies • MA
  comparative studies • MA, PhD
  East Asian languages and literatures • MA, PhD
  English • MA, MFA, PhD
  French and Italian • MA, PhD
  Germanic languages and literatures • MA, PhD
  Greek and Latin • MA, PhD
  history • MA, PhD
  humanities • MA, MFA, PhD, Certificate
  Latin American studies • Certificate
  linguistics • MA, PhD
  Near Eastern languages and cultures • MA
  philosophy • MA, PhD
  Russian area studies • Certificate
  Slavic and East European languages and literatures • MA, PhD
  Spanish and Portuguese • MA, PhD
  women's studies • MA, PhD

College of Mathematical and Physical Sciences
Dr. Richard R. Freeman, Dean
Programs in:
  astronomy • MS, PhD
  biostatistics • PhD
  chemical physics • MS, PhD
  chemistry • MS, PhD
  geological sciences • MS, PhD
  mathematical and physical sciences • M Appl Stat, MA, MS, PhD
  mathematics • MA, MS, PhD
  physics • MS, PhD
  statistics • M Appl Stat, MS, PhD

College of Nursing
Dr. Elizabeth R. Lenz, Dean
Program in:
  nursing • MS, PhD

College of Social and Behavioral Sciences
Dr. Randall Ripley, Dean
Programs in:
  anthropology • MA, PhD
  atmospheric sciences • MS, PhD
  clinical psychology • PhD
  cognitive/experimental psychology • PhD
  communication • PhD
  counseling psychology • PhD
  developmental psychology • PhD
  economics • MA, PhD
  geography • MA, PhD
  journalism and communication • MA
  Latin American studies • Certificate
  mental retardation and developmental disabilities • PhD
  political science • MA, PhD
  psychobiology • PhD
  public policy and management • MA, MPA, PhD
  quantitative psychology • PhD
  Russian area studies • Certificate
  social and behavioral sciences • MA, MPA, MS, PhD, Certificate
  social psychology • PhD
  sociology • MA, PhD
  speech and hearing science • MA, PhD

College of Social Work
Tony Tripodi, Dean
Program in:
  social work • MSW, PhD

College of the Arts
Karen A. Bell, Dean
Programs in:
  art • MA, MFA
  art education • MA, PhD
  arts • M Mus, MA, MFA, DMA, PhD
  arts policy and administration • MA
  dance • MA, MFA
  history of art • MA, PhD
  industrial, interior, and visual communication design • MA, MFA
  music • M Mus, MA, DMA, PhD
  theatre • MA, MFA, PhD

Max M. Fisher College of Business
Joseph A. Alutto, Dean
Programs in:
  accounting and management information systems • M Acc, MA, PhD
  business • M Acc, MA, MBA, MLHR, PhD
  business administration • MA, MBA, PhD
  labor and human resources • MLHR, PhD

Moritz College of Law
Nancy H. Rogers, Dean
Program in:
  law • JD

■ **OHIO UNIVERSITY**
Athens, OH 45701-2979
http://www.ohio.edu/

State-supported, coed, university. CGS member. *Enrollment:* 20,394 graduate, professional, and undergraduate students; 1,780 full-time matriculated graduate/professional students (907 women), 470 part-time matriculated graduate/professional students (254 women). *Graduate faculty:* 836 full-time (259 women), 148 part-time/adjunct (58 women). *Computer facilities:* 1,500 computers available on campus for general student use. A campuswide network can be accessed from student residence rooms and from off campus. *Library facilities:* Alden Library. *Graduate expenses:* Tuition, state resident: full-time $2,651; part-time $328 per credit. Tuition, nonresident: full-time $5,095; part-time $632 per credit. Tuition and fees vary according to program. *General application contact:* 740-593-2800.

College of Osteopathic Medicine
Dr. John A. Brose, Dean
Program in:
  osteopathic medicine • DO

Graduate Studies
Dr. Michael J. Mumper, Associate Provost for Graduate Studies
Program in:
  interdisciplinary studies • PhD

Center for International Studies
Dr. Josep Rota, Director
Programs in:
  African studies • MA
  communications and development studies • MA
  development studies • MA
  international studies • MA
  Latin American studies • MA
  Southeast Asian studies • MA

College of Arts and Sciences
Dr. Leslie Flemming, Dean
Programs in:
  applied economics • MA
  applied linguistics/TESOL • MA
  arts and sciences • MA, MPA, MS, MSS, MSW, PhD
  biological sciences • MS, PhD
  chemistry and biochemistry • MS, PhD
  clinical psychology • PhD
  English language and literature • MA, PhD
  environmental and plant biology • MS, PhD
  environmental geochemistry • MS
  environmental geology • MS
  environmental studies • MS

environmental/hydrology • MS
experimental psychology • PhD
financial economics • MA
French • MA
geography • MA
geology • MS
geology education • MS
geomorphology/surficial processes • MS
geophysics • MS
history • MA, PhD
hydrogeology • MS
mathematics • MS, PhD
microbiology • MS, PhD
molecular and cellular biology • MS, PhD
neuroscience • MS, PhD
organizational psychology • PhD
philosophy • MA
physics • MS, PhD
political science • MA
public administration • MPA
sedimentology • MS
social sciences • MSS
social work • MSW
sociology • MA
Spanish • MA
structure/tectonics • MS
zoology • MS, PhD

College of Business
Dr. Edward B. Yost, Director, Graduate Programs
Programs in:
business • EMBA, MBA
business administration • EMBA, MBA

College of Communication
Dr. Kathy Krendl, Dean
Programs in:
communication • MA, MCTP, MS, PhD
communication studies • MA, PhD
communications systems management • MCTP
journalism • MS, PhD
telecommunications • MA, PhD
visual communication • MA

College of Education
Dr. James L. Heap, Dean
Programs in:
adolescent to young adult education • M Ed
college student personnel • M Ed
community/agency counseling • M Ed
computer education and technology • M Ed
counselor education • PhD
cultural studies • M Ed
curriculum and instruction • M Ed, PhD
education • M Ed, Ed D, PhD
educational administration • M Ed, Ed D

educational research and evaluation • M Ed, PhD
higher education • M Ed, PhD
instructional technology • PhD
mathematics education • PhD
middle child education • M Ed
middle level education • PhD
reading and language arts • PhD
reading education • M Ed
rehabilitation counseling • M Ed
school counseling • M Ed
secondary mathematics education • M Ed
social studies education • PhD
special education • M Ed, PhD

College of Fine Arts
Dr. Raymond Tymas-Jones, Dean
Programs in:
art education • MA
art history • MFA
art history/studio • MFA
ceramics • MFA
conducting • MM
film • MA, MFA
fine arts • MA, MFA, MM, PhD
history • MM
interdisciplinary arts • PhD
literature • MM
music education • MM
painting • MFA
performance • MM
photography • MFA
printmaking • MFA
sculpture • MFA
theater • MA, MFA
theory • MM

College of Health and Human Services
Dr. Gary Neiman, Dean
Programs in:
athletics/training education • MS
audiology • Au D, PhD
child development and family life • MSHCS
coaching education • MS
food and nutrition • MSHCS
health and human services • MA, MBA, MHA, MS, MSA, MSHCS, MSP Ex, Au D, DPT, PhD
health sciences • MHA
hearing, speech and language sciences • PhD
physical education pedagogy • MS
physical therapy • DPT
physiology of exercise • MSP Ex
recreation studies • MS
speech language pathology • MA, PhD
sports administration and facility management • MBA, MSA

Russ College of Engineering and Technology
Dr. Dennis Irwin, Interim Dean
Programs in:
chemical engineering • MS, PhD

computer science • MS
electrical engineering • MS, PhD
engineering and technology • MS, PhD
environmental • MS
geotechnical and environmental engineering • MS, PhD
industrial and manufacturing systems engineering • MS
intelligent systems • PhD
manufacturing engineering • MS
materials processing • PhD
mechanical engineering • MS, PhD
structures • MS
transportation • MS
water resources and structures • MS

■ UNION INSTITUTE & UNIVERSITY
Cincinnati, OH 45206-1925
http://www.tui.edu/

Independent, coed, university. *Enrollment:* 2,910 graduate, professional, and undergraduate students; 1,622 full-time matriculated graduate/professional students (1,092 women). *Graduate faculty:* 151. *Computer facilities:* A campuswide network can be accessed from off campus. Internet access is available. *Library facilities:* Gary Library plus 1 other. *Graduate expenses:* Tuition: full-time $15,750. Required fees: $108. Full-time tuition and fees vary according to course load, degree level, campus/location and program. *General application contact:* Dr. Emily Harbold, Associate Vice President, 800-486-3116.

Program in Education (Vermont Campus)
Dr. Brian Webb, Assistant Vice President, Academic Affairs
Program in:
education • M Ed

Program in Interdisciplinary Studies (Vermont Campus)
Dr. Brian Webb, Assistant Vice President, Academic Affairs
Program in:
interdisciplinary studies • MA

Program in Visual Art (Vermont Campus)
Dr. Brian Webb, Assistant Vice President, Academic Affairs
Program in:
visual art • MFA

Program in Writing (Vermont Campus)
Dr. Brian Webb, Assistant Vice President, Academic Affairs
Program in:
writing • MFA

Ohio

Union Institute & University (continued)

School of Interdisciplinary Arts and Sciences
Dr. Richard Green, Executive Vice President and Dean, Graduate Studies
Program in:
  interdisciplinary studies • PhD

School of Professional Psychology
Dr. Tom Jackson, Assistant Dean
Program in:
  interdisciplinary studies • PhD

■ THE UNIVERSITY OF AKRON
Akron, OH 44325-0001
http://www.uakron.edu/

State-supported, coed, university. CGS member. *Enrollment:* 24,335 graduate, professional, and undergraduate students; 2,253 full-time matriculated graduate/professional students (1,133 women), 1,671 part-time matriculated graduate/professional students (1,057 women). *Graduate faculty:* 508 full-time (171 women), 372 part-time/adjunct (178 women). *Computer facilities:* 2,450 computers available on campus for general student use. A campuswide network can be accessed from student residence rooms and from off campus. Internet access and online class registration, wireless campus, library has laptops for student checkout are available. *Library facilities:* Bierce Library plus 3 others. *Graduate expenses:* Tuition, state resident: part-time $277 per credit hour. Tuition, nonresident: part-time $476 per credit hour. *General application contact:* Dr. Giannina D'Agruma, Interim Director, Graduate Programs, 330-972-6266.

Graduate School
Dr. George R. Newkome, Vice President for Research and Dean of the Graduate School

Buchtel College of Arts and Sciences
Dr. Roger Creel, Dean
Programs in:
  applied cognitive aging • MA, PhD
  applied mathematics • MS
  applied politics • MA
  arts and sciences • MA, MPA, MS, PhD
  biology • MS
  chemistry • MS, PhD
  composition • MA
  computer science • MS
  counseling psychology • MA, PhD
  earth science • MS
  economics • MA
  environmental • MS
  geography • MS
  geology • MS
  geophysics • MS
  history • MA, PhD
  industrial/gerontological • PhD
  industrial/organizational psychology • MA, PhD
  labor and industrial relations • MA
  literature • MA
  mathematics • MS
  physics • MS
  political science • MA
  psychology • MA
  public administration • MPA
  sociology • MA, PhD
  Spanish • MA
  statistics • MS
  urban planning • MA
  urban studies • MA, PhD
  urban studies and public affairs • PhD

College of Business Administration
Jim Barnett, Dean
Programs in:
  accountancy • MS
  accounting • MBA
  accounting-information systems • MS
  business administration • MBA, MS, MT
  electronic business • MBA
  entrepreneurship • MBA
  finance • MBA
  international business • MBA
  international business for international executive • MBA
  management • MBA
  management of technology • MBA
  management-human resources • MS
  management-information systems • MS
  marketing • MBA
  quality management • MBA
  taxation • MT

College of Education
Dr. Elizabeth Stroble, Dean
Programs in:
  administrative specialist • MA, MS
  classroom guidance for teachers • MA, MS
  community counseling • MA, MS
  counseling in secondary schools • MA, MS
  counseling psychology • PhD
  education • MA, MS, Ed D, PhD
  educational administration • MA, MS, Ed D
  educational foundations and leadership • MA, MS, Ed D
  elementary education • MA, MS, PhD
  elementary education—literacy • MA
  elementary education with licensure • MS
  exercise physiology/adult fitness • MA, MS
  guidance and counseling • PhD
  higher education administration • MA, MS
  marriage and family therapy • MA, MS
  outdoor education • MA, MS
  physical education K–12 • MA, MS
  principalship • MA, MS
  school counseling • MA, MS
  school psychology • MS
  secondary education • MA, MS, PhD
  secondary education with licensure • MS
  special education • MA, MS
  sports science/coaching • MA, MS
  superintendent • MA, MS
  technical education • MS
  technical education guidance • MS
  technical education instructional technology • MS
  technical education teaching • MS
  technical education training • MS

College of Engineering
Dr. George Haritos, Dean
Programs in:
  biomedical engineering • MS, PhD
  chemical engineering • MS, PhD
  civil engineering • MS, PhD
  electrical engineering • MS, PhD
  engineering • MS, PhD
  engineering (management specialization) • MS
  engineering (polymer specialization) • MS
  engineering-applied mathematics • PhD
  mechanical engineering • MS, PhD

College of Fine and Applied Arts
Dr. Mark Auburn, Dean
Programs in:
  arts administration • MA
  audiology • Au D
  child and family development • MA
  child development • MA
  child life • MA
  clothing, textiles and interiors • MA
  communication • MA
  composition • MM
  family development • MA
  fine and applied arts • MA, MM, MS, Au D
  food science • MA
  music education • MM
  music history and literature • MM
  music technology • MM
  nutrition and dietetics • MS
  performance • MM
  social work • MS
  speech-language pathology • MA
  theatre arts • MA
  theory • MM

College of Nursing
Dr. Irene Glanville, Coordinator
Programs in:
  nursing • MSN, PhD
  public health • MPH

Ohio

College of Polymer Science and Polymer Engineering
Dr. Frank Kelley, Dean
Programs in:
  polymer engineering • MS, PhD
  polymer science • MS, PhD

School of Law
Richard L. Aynes, Dean
Program in:
  law • JD

■ UNIVERSITY OF CINCINNATI
Cincinnati, OH 45221
http://www.uc.edu/

State-supported, coed, university. CGS member. *Computer facilities:* 325 computers available on campus for general student use. A campuswide network can be accessed from student residence rooms and from off campus. Internet access and online class registration are available. *Library facilities:* Langsam Library plus 7 others. *General application contact:* Vice President and University Dean, 513-556-2872.

College of Law
Program in:
  law • JD

Division of Research and Advanced Studies
Program in:
  neuroscience • PhD

College-Conservatory of Music
Programs in:
  arts administration • MA
  choral conducting • MM, DMA
  composition • MM, DMA
  directing • MFA
  keyboard studies • MM, DMA, AD
  music • MA, MFA, MM, DMA, PhD, AD
  music education • MM
  music history • MM
  music theory • MM, PhD
  musicology • PhD
  orchestral conducting • MM, DMA
  performance • MM, DMA, AD
  theater design and production • MFA
  theater performance • MFA
  wind conducting • MM, DMA

College of Allied Health Sciences
Programs in:
  allied health sciences • MA, MPT, MS, Au D, PhD
  blood transfusion medicine • MS
  cellular therapies • MS
  communication sciences and disorders • MA, Au D, PhD
  medical genetics • MS
  nutritional science • MS
  rehabilitation science • MPT

College of Business
Dr. Frederick A. Russ, Dean and Professor of Marketing
Programs in:
  accounting • MBA
  accounting management/ organizational behavior • PhD
  business • MBA, MS, PhD
  construction management • MBA
  e-business • MBA
  finance • MBA, PhD
  general accounting • MS
  information systems • MBA, MS
  international business • MBA
  management • MBA, PhD
  management of advanced technology and innovation • MBA
  marketing • MBA, PhD
  operations management • MBA, PhD
  quantitative analysis • MBA, MS, PhD
  real estate • MBA
  taxation • MS

College of Design, Architecture, Art, and Planning
Programs in:
  architecture • M Arch, MS Arch
  art education • MA
  art history • MA
  community planning • MCP
  design, architecture, art, and planning • M Arch, M Des, MA, MCP, MFA, MS Arch, PhD
  fashion design • M Des
  fine arts • MFA
  graphic design • M Des
  industrial design • M Des
  interior design • M Des
  planning • MCP

College of Education
Programs in:
  community health • M Ed
  counselor education • Ed D, CAGS
  criminal justice • MS, PhD
  curriculum and instruction • M Ed, Ed D
  early childhood education • M Ed
  education • M Ed, MA, MS, Ed D, PhD, CAGS, Ed S
  educational administration • M Ed, Ed S
  educational foundations • M Ed, Ed D
  educational studies • M Ed, Ed D, Ed S
  elementary education • M Ed
  health promotion and education • M Ed
  human services • M Ed, MA, Ed D, PhD, CAGS
  mental health • MA
  reading/literacy • M Ed, Ed D
  school counseling • M Ed
  school psychology • M Ed, PhD
  secondary education • M Ed
  special education • M Ed, Ed D
  urban educational leadership • Ed D

College of Engineering
Programs in:
  aerospace engineering • MS, PhD
  bioinformatics • MS, PhD
  ceramic science and engineering • MS, PhD
  chemical engineering • MS, PhD
  civil engineering • MS, PhD
  computer engineering • MS
  computer science • MS
  computer science and engineering • PhD
  electrical engineering • MS, PhD
  engineering • MS, PhD
  environmental engineering • MS, PhD
  environmental sciences • MS, PhD
  health physics • MS
  industrial engineering • MS, PhD
  materials science and engineering • MS, PhD
  materials science and metallurgical engineering • MS, PhD
  mechanical engineering • MS, PhD
  medical imaging • MS, PhD
  metallurgical engineering • MS, PhD
  nuclear engineering • MS, PhD
  polymer science and engineering • MS, PhD
  tissue engineering • MS, PhD

College of Medicine
Programs in:
  cell and molecular biology • PhD
  cell biophysics • PhD
  environmental and industrial hygiene • MS, PhD
  environmental and occupational medicine • MS
  epidemiology and biostatistics • MS, PhD
  flex option • PhD
  immunobiology • MS, PhD
  medical physics • MS
  medicine • MD, MS, D Sc, PhD
  molecular and developmental biology • MS, PhD
  molecular genetics, biochemistry and microbiology • MS, PhD
  occupational safety and ergonomics • MS, PhD
  pathology • PhD
  pharmacology • PhD
  physiology • PhD
  teratology • MS, PhD
  toxicology • MS, PhD

College of Nursing
Dr. Andrea Lindell, Dean
Programs in:
  adult health acute nurse practitioner • MSN
  adult health nursing • MSN
  adult health-ambulatory • MSN
  clinical nurse specialist • MSN
  community health nursing • MSN
  family nurse practitioner • MSN

Ohio

University of Cincinnati (continued)
  family nurse practitioner/psychiatric nurse practitioner • MSN
  neonatal nurse practitioner • MSN
  nurse anesthesia • MSN
  nurse midwifery • MSN
  nursing • PhD
  nursing administration • MSN
  occupational health • MSN
  parent/child nursing • MSN
  pediatric nurse practitioner • MSN
  psychiatric nursing • MSN
  woman's health • MSN
  women's health nurse practitioner • MSN

College of Pharmacy
Programs in:
  pharmaceutical sciences • MS, PhD
  pharmacy • Pharm D, MS, PhD
  pharmacy practice • Pharm D

McMicken College of Arts and Sciences
Programs in:
  analytical chemistry • MS, PhD
  anthropology • MA
  applied economics • MA
  applied mathematics • MS, PhD
  arts and sciences • MA, MALER, MAT, MS, PhD, Certificate
  biochemistry • MS, PhD
  biological sciences • MS, PhD
  classics • MA, PhD
  clinical psychology • PhD
  communication • MA
  English • MA, PhD
  experimental psychology • PhD
  French • MA
  geography • MA, PhD
  geology • MS, PhD
  German studies • MA, PhD
  history • MA, PhD
  inorganic chemistry • MS, PhD
  interdisciplinary studies • PhD
  labor and employment relations • MALER
  mathematics education • MAT
  organic chemistry • MS, PhD
  philosophy • MA, PhD
  physical chemistry • MS, PhD
  physics • MS, PhD
  political science • MA, PhD
  polymer chemistry • MS, PhD
  pure mathematics • MS, PhD
  Romance languages and literatures • PhD
  sensors • PhD
  sociology • MA, PhD
  Spanish • MA
  statistics • MS, PhD
  women's studies • MA, Certificate

School of Social Work
Program in:
  social work • MSW

■ **UNIVERSITY OF DAYTON**
Dayton, OH 45469-1300
http://www.udayton.edu/

Independent-religious, coed, university. CGS member. *Enrollment:* 10,284 graduate, professional, and undergraduate students; 1,642 full-time matriculated graduate/professional students (838 women), 1,536 part-time matriculated graduate/professional students (996 women). *Graduate faculty:* 177 full-time (53 women), 121 part-time/adjunct. *Computer facilities:* Computer purchase and lease plans are available. 1,000 computers available on campus for general student use. A campuswide network can be accessed from student residence rooms and from off campus. Internet access and online class registration are available. *Library facilities:* Roesch Library plus 1 other. *Graduate expenses:* Tuition: full-time $6,060; part-time $505 per hour. Required fees: $50; $25 per term. Tuition and fees vary according to degree level, campus/location, program and student's religious affiliation. *General application contact:* Nancy A. Wilson, Assistant to the Vice President for Graduate Studies and Research, 937-229-2390.

Graduate School
Dr. Thomas Skill, Associate Provost and Interim Dean of the Graduate School

College of Arts and Sciences
Dr. Paul J. Morman, Dean
Programs in:
  applied mathematics • MS
  arts and sciences • MA, MCS, MPA, MS, PhD
  biology • MS, PhD
  chemistry • MS
  clinical psychology • MA
  communication • MA
  computer science • MCS
  English • MA
  experimental/human factors • MA
  general psychology • MA
  pastoral ministry • MA
  physics • MS
  public administration • MPA
  theological studies • MA
  theology • PhD

School of Business Administration
Dr. Patricia W. Meyers, Dean
Program in:
  business administration • MBA

School of Education and Allied Professions
Dr. Thomas J. Lasley, Dean
Programs in:
  adolescent/young adult • MS Ed
  art education • MS Ed
  college student personnel • MS Ed
  community counseling • MS Ed
  early childhood education • MS Ed
  education and allied professions • MS Ed, PhD, Ed S
  educational leadership • MS Ed, PhD
  exercise sports science • MS Ed
  higher education administration • MS Ed
  human development services • MS Ed
  inclusive early childhood • MS Ed
  interdisciplinary education • MS Ed
  intervention specialist education, mild/moderate • MS Ed
  literacy • MS Ed
  middle childhood • MS Ed
  physical education • MS Ed
  school counseling • MS Ed
  school psychology • MS Ed
  teacher as child/youth development specialist • MS Ed
  teacher as leader • MS Ed
  technology in education • MS Ed

School of Engineering
Dr. Joseph E. Saliba, Dean
Programs in:
  aerospace engineering • MSAE, DE, PhD
  chemical engineering • MS Ch E
  electrical and computer engineering • MSEE, DE, PhD
  electro-optics • MSEO, PhD
  engineering • MS Ch E, MS Mat E, MSAE, MSCE, MSE, MSEE, MSEM, MSEM, MSEO, MSME, MSMS, DE, PhD
  engineering management • MSEM
  engineering mechanics • MSEM
  environmental engineering • MSCE
  management science • MSMS
  materials engineering • MS Mat E, DE, PhD
  mechanical engineering • MSME, DE, PhD
  soil mechanics • MSCE
  structural engineering • MSCE
  transport engineering • MSCE

School of Law
Lisa A. Kloppenberg, Dean
Program in:
  law • JD

■ **THE UNIVERSITY OF FINDLAY**
Findlay, OH 45840-3653
http://www.findlay.edu/

Independent-religious, coed, comprehensive institution. CGS member. *Enrollment:* 4,712 graduate, professional, and undergraduate students; 502 full-time matriculated graduate/professional students (300 women), 778 part-time matriculated graduate/professional

Ohio

students (480 women). *Computer facilities:* Computer purchase and lease plans are available. 200 computers available on campus for general student use. A campuswide network can be accessed from student residence rooms and from off campus. Internet access and online class registration are available. *Library facilities:* Shafer Library. *Graduate expenses:* Tuition: part-time $349 per semester hour. One-time fee: $30 part-time. *General application contact:* Nancy Leatherman, Administrative Assistant to the VP for Academic Affairs, 419-434-4553.

Graduate College
Dr. Marie Louden-Hanes, Graduate Dean
Programs in:
 administration • MA Ed
 early childhood • MA Ed
 elementary education • MA Ed
 professional studies • MA, MA Ed, MALS, MBA, MOT, MPT, MSEM
 special education • MA Ed
 technology • MA Ed

College of Liberal Arts
Dr. Dale R. Brougher, Dean
Programs in:
 bilingual and multicultural education • MA
 liberal arts • MA, MALS
 liberal studies • MALS
 teaching English to speakers of other languages • MA

College of Science
Dr. Daniel J. May, Graduate Director
Programs in:
 environmental management • MSEM
 occupational therapy • MOT
 physical therapy • MPT
 science • MOT, MPT, MSEM

MBA Program
Dr. Theodore C. Alex, Dean
Programs in:
 financial management • MBA
 human resource management • MBA
 international management • MBA
 management • MBA
 marketing • MBA
 public management • MBA

■ UNIVERSITY OF RIO GRANDE
Rio Grande, OH 45674
http://www.rio.edu/

Independent, coed, comprehensive institution. *Enrollment:* 2,076 graduate, professional, and undergraduate students; 350 matriculated graduate/professional students. *Graduate faculty:* 9 full-time (3 women), 6 part-time/adjunct (2 women). *Computer facilities:* 225 computers available on campus for general student use. A campuswide network can be accessed from student residence rooms and from off campus. Internet access is available. *Library facilities:* Jeanette Albiez Davis Library plus 2 others. *Graduate expenses:* Tuition: full-time $7,678; part-time $349 per hour. *General application contact:* Dreama Hudson, Graduate Secretary, 740-245-7167.

Graduate School
Dr. Greg Miller, Coordinator
Program in:
 classroom teaching • M Ed

■ UNIVERSITY OF TOLEDO
Toledo, OH 43606-3390

State-supported, coed, university. CGS member. *Enrollment:* 20,594 graduate, professional, and undergraduate students; 808 full-time matriculated graduate/professional students (420 women), 1,521 part-time matriculated graduate/professional students (871 women). *Graduate faculty:* 491. *Computer facilities:* 2,800 computers available on campus for general student use. A campuswide network can be accessed from student residence rooms and from off campus. Internet access and online class registration, online transcripts, student account and grade information are available. *Library facilities:* Carlson Library plus 3 others. *Graduate expenses:* Part-time $3,817 per semester. Tuition, state resident: part-time $8,177 per semester. Required fees: $502 per semester. *General application contact:* Information Contact, 419-530-4723.

Find an in-depth description at www.petersons.com/gradchannel.

College of Law
Phillip J. Closius, Dean
Program in:
 law • JD

Graduate School
Dr. Martin A. Abraham, Dean of the Graduate School

College of Arts and Sciences
Dr. David Stern, Dean
Programs in:
 analytical chemistry • MS, PhD
 anthropology • MAE
 applied mathematics • MS
 arts and sciences • EMBA, MA, MAE, MES, MLS, MME, MMP, MPA, MS, PhD
 biological chemistry • MS, PhD
 biology • MS, PhD
 biology (ecology track) • MS, PhD
 clinical psychology • PhD
 economics • MA
 English language and literature • MA
 experimental psychology • MA, PhD
 French • MA
 geography • MA
 geology • MS
 German • MA
 history • MA, PhD
 inorganic chemistry • MS, PhD
 liberal studies • MLS
 mathematics • MA, PhD
 music education • MME
 organic chemistry • MS, PhD
 performance • MMP
 philosophy • MA
 physical chemistry • MS, PhD
 physics • MES, MS, PhD
 planning • MA
 political science • MA
 public administration • MPA
 science education • MES
 sociology • MA, MAE
 Spanish • MA
 statistics • MS

College of Business Administration
Dr. Thomas G. Gutteridge, Dean
Programs in:
 accounting • MBA, MSA
 business administration • EMBA, MBA, MSA, DME
 business administration-general • MBA
 decision sciences • MBA
 finance and business economics • MBA
 information systems • MBA
 management • MBA
 manufacturing management • DME
 marketing • MBA
 operations management • MBA

College of Education
Dr. Thomas J. Switzer, Dean
Programs in:
 business education • ME, DE, PhD, Ed S
 curriculum and instruction • ME, DE, PhD, Ed S
 early childhood education • DE, PhD, Ed S
 early childhood, physical and special education • ME
 education • MAE, ME, MES, MME, DE, PhD, Ed S
 education and economics • MAE
 education and English • MAE
 education and French • MAE
 education and German • MAE
 education and history • MAE
 education and mathematics • MAE
 education and political science • MAE
 education and sociology • MAE
 education and Spanish • MAE
 education theory and social foundations • ME

Peterson's Graduate Schools in the U.S. 2006

Ohio

University of Toledo (continued)
    educational administration and supervision • ME, Ed S
    educational education and supervision • DE
    educational media • DE, PhD, Ed S
    educational psychology • ME, DE, PhD
    educational research and measurement • DE, PhD
    educational sociology • DE, PhD
    elementary education • DE, PhD, Ed S
    English as a second language • MAE
    foundations of education • DE, PhD
    higher education • ME, PhD
    history of education • DE, PhD
    music education • MME
    philosophy of education • DE, PhD
    secondary education • ME, DE, PhD, Ed S
    special education • ME, DE, PhD, Ed S
    vocational education • ME, Ed S

College of Engineering
Dr. Nagi Naganathan, Dean
Programs in:
    bioengineering • MS, PhD
    chemical engineering • MS
    civil engineering • MS
    computer science • MS
    ecology • PhD
    electrical engineering • MS
    engineering • PhD
    engineering sciences • PhD
    general engineering • MS
    industrial engineering • MS
    mechanical engineering • MS

College of Health and Human Services
Dr. Jerome M. Sulivan, Dean
Programs in:
    community counseling • MA
    counselor education and supervision • PhD
    criminal justice • MA
    exercise science • MSX, PhD
    health education • PhD
    physical education • PhD
    public health and rehabilitative services • MPH
    recreation and leisure studies • MA
    school counseling • MA
    school psychology • Ed S
    speech language pathology • MA

College of Pharmacy
Dr. Wayne P. Hoss, Vice Dean Graduate Studies and Research
Programs in:
    administrative pharmacy • MSPS
    industrial pharmacy • MSPS
    medicinal and biological chemistry • MS, PhD
    pharmaceutical science • MSPS
    pharmacology • MSPS
    pharmacy • Pharm D, MS, MSPS, PhD

■ URSULINE COLLEGE
Pepper Pike, OH 44124-4398
http://www.ursuline.edu/

Independent-religious, women only, comprehensive institution. *Enrollment:* 1,409 graduate, professional, and undergraduate students; 89 full-time matriculated graduate/professional students (75 women), 225 part-time matriculated graduate/professional students (201 women). *Graduate faculty:* 14 full-time (12 women), 6 part-time/adjunct (3 women). *Computer facilities:* 107 computers available on campus for general student use. A campuswide network can be accessed from student residence rooms. Internet access is available. *Library facilities:* Ralph M. Besse Library. *Graduate expenses:* Tuition: part-time $620 per credit hour. Required fees: $50 per semester. Full-time tuition and fees vary according to program, reciprocity agreements and student's religious affiliation. *General application contact:* Dr. Catherine Hackney, Dean of Graduate Studies, 440-646-8119.

Graduate Studies
Dr. Catherine Hackney, Dean of Graduate Studies
Programs in:
    art therapy • MA
    education • MA
    liberal studies • MALS
    management • MM
    ministry • MA
    non-public educational administration • MA
    nursing • MSN

■ WALSH UNIVERSITY
North Canton, OH 44720-3396
http://www.walsh.edu/

Independent-religious, coed, comprehensive institution. *Enrollment:* 1,801 graduate, professional, and undergraduate students; 90 full-time matriculated graduate/professional students (67 women), 138 part-time matriculated graduate/professional students (84 women). *Graduate faculty:* 22 full-time (14 women), 15 part-time/adjunct (6 women). *Computer facilities:* 115 computers available on campus for general student use. A campuswide network can be accessed from student residence rooms and from off campus. Internet access is available. *Library facilities:* Walsh University Library. *Graduate expenses:* Tuition: full-time $8,100; part-time $450 per credit. *General application contact:* Brett D. Freshour, Dean of Enrollment Management, 330-490-7286.

Graduate Programs
Dr. Laurence Bove, Academic Dean
Programs in:
    business administration • MBA
    education • MA
    mental health counseling • MA
    physical therapy • M Sc
    school counseling • MA

■ WRIGHT STATE UNIVERSITY
Dayton, OH 45435
http://www.wright.edu/

State-supported, coed, university. CGS member. *Enrollment:* 15,694 graduate, professional, and undergraduate students; 2,169 full-time matriculated graduate/professional students (1,162 women), 1,365 part-time matriculated graduate/professional students (896 women). *Graduate faculty:* 749 full-time (232 women), 354 part-time/adjunct (195 women). *Computer facilities:* 450 computers available on campus for general student use. A campuswide network can be accessed from student residence rooms and from off campus. *Library facilities:* Paul Laurence Dunbar Library plus 2 others. *Graduate expenses:* Tuition, state resident: full-time $8,112; part-time $255 per quarter hour. Tuition, nonresident: full-time $14,127; part-time $442 per quarter hour. International tuition: $14,283 full-time. Tuition and fees vary according to course load, degree level and program. *General application contact:* John Kimble, Associate Director of Graduate Admissions and Records, 937-775-2957.

School of Graduate Studies
Dr. Joseph F. Thomas, Dean and Vice President
Program in:
    interdisciplinary studies • MA, MS

College of Education and Human Services
Dr. Gregory R. Bernhardt, Dean
Programs in:
    adolescent young adult • M Ed, MA
    advanced curriculum and instruction • Ed S
    advanced educational leadership • Ed S
    business, technology, and vocational education • M Ed, MA
    career, technology and vocational education • M Ed, MA
    chemical dependency • MRC
    classroom teacher education • M Ed, MA
    computer/technology education • M Ed, MA

Ohio

counseling • M Ed, MA, MS
curriculum and instruction: teacher leader • MA
early childhood education • M Ed, MA
education and human services • M Ed, MA, MRC, MS, Ed S
educational administrative specialist: teacher leader • M Ed
educational administrative specialist: vocational education administration • M Ed, MA
educational leadership • M Ed, MA
gifted educational needs • M Ed, MA
health, physical education, and recreation • M Ed, MA
higher education-adult education • Ed S
intervention specialist • M Ed, MA
library/media • M Ed, MA
middle childhood • M Ed
middle childhood education • MA
mild to moderate educational needs • M Ed, MA
moderate to intensive educational needs • M Ed, MA
multi-age • M Ed, MA
pupil personnel services • M Ed, MA
rehabilitation counseling • MRC
severe disabilities • MRC
student affairs in higher education-administration • M Ed, MA
superintendent • Ed S
vocational education • M Ed, MA

College of Engineering and Computer Science
Dr. James E. Brandeberry, Dean, Dean and Director, Engineering Ph.D. Program
Programs in:
biomedical and human factors engineering • MSE
biomedical engineering • MSE
computer engineering • MSCE
computer science • MS
computer science and engineering • PhD
electrical engineering • MSE
engineering • PhD
engineering and computer science • MS, MSCE, MSE, PhD
human factors engineering • MSE
materials science and engineering • MSE
mechanical and materials engineering • MSE
mechanical engineering • MSE

College of Liberal Arts
Dr. Mary Ellen Mazey, Dean
Programs in:
composition and rhetoric • MA
criminal justice and social problems • MA
English • MA
history • MA
humanities • M Hum

international and comparative politics • MA
liberal arts • M Hum, M Mus, MA, MPA
literature • MA
music education • M Mus
performance • M Mus
public administration • MPA
teaching English to speakers of other languages • MA

College of Nursing and Health
Dr. Patricia A. Martin, Dean
Programs in:
acute care nurse practitioner • MS
administration of nursing and health care systems • MS
adult health • MS
child and adolescent health • MS
community health • MS
family nurse practitioner • MS
nurse practitioner • MS
nursing and health • MS
school nurse • MS

College of Science and Mathematics
Dr. Michele Wheatly, Dean
Programs in:
anatomy • MS
applied mathematics • MS
applied statistics • MS
biochemistry and molecular biology • MS
biological sciences • MS
biomedical sciences • PhD
chemistry • MS
earth science education • MST
environmental geochemistry • MS
environmental geology • MS
environmental sciences • MS
geological sciences • MS
geophysics • MS
human factors and industrial/organizational psychology • MS, PhD
hydrogeology • MS
mathematics • MS
medical physics • MS
microbiology and immunology • MS
petroleum geology • MS
physics • MS
physics education • MST
physiology and biophysics • MS
science and mathematics • MS, MST, PhD

Raj Soin College of Business
Dr. Berkwood Farmer, Dean
Programs in:
accountancy • M Acc
accounting • MBA
business • M Acc, MBA, MS
business economics • MBA
finance • MBA
flexible business • MBA
health care management • MBA
international business • MBA
logistics management • MS

management information technology • MBA
management, innovation and change • MBA
marketing • MBA
project management • MBA
social and applied economics • MS
supply chain management • MBA

School of Medicine
Dr. Howard Part, Dean
Programs in:
aerospace medicine • MS
health promotion and education • MPH
medicine • MD, MPH, MS, PhD
pharmacology and toxicology • MS
public health management • MPH
public health nursing • MPH

School of Professional Psychology
Dr. John R. Rudisill, Dean
Program in:
clinical psychology • Psy D

■ XAVIER UNIVERSITY
Cincinnati, OH 45207
http://www.xu.edu/

Independent-religious, coed, comprehensive institution. *Enrollment:* 6,626 graduate, professional, and undergraduate students; 657 full-time matriculated graduate/professional students (420 women), 1,512 part-time matriculated graduate/professional students (831 women). *Graduate faculty:* 109 full-time (52 women), 124 part-time/adjunct (61 women). *Computer facilities:* 200 computers available on campus for general student use. A campuswide network can be accessed from student residence rooms and from off campus. Internet access and online class registration are available. *Library facilities:* McDonald Library plus 1 other. *Graduate expenses:* Tuition: part-time $405 per credit hour. One-time fee: $50 part-time. Full-time tuition and fees vary according to degree level, campus/location and program. General application contact: John Cooper, Director of Graduate Services, 513-745-3357.

College of Arts and Sciences
Dr. Janice B. Walker, Dean
Programs in:
arts and sciences • MA
English • MA
humanities • MA
theology • MA

College of Social Sciences
Dr. Neil Heighberger, Dean
Programs in:

Ohio

Xavier University (continued)
  clinical psychology • Psy D
  community counseling • MA
  criminal justice • MS
  educational administration • M Ed
  elementary education • M Ed
  forensic nursing • MSN
  health services administration • MHSA
  healthcare law • MSN
  human resource development • M Ed
  Montessori • M Ed
  multicultural literature for children • M Ed
  nursing administration • MSN
  psychology • MA
  reading specialist • M Ed
  school counseling • MA
  school nursing • MSN
  secondary education • M Ed
  social sciences • M Ed, MA, MHSA, MS, MSN, Psy D
  special education • M Ed
  sport administration • M Ed

Williams College of Business
Dr. Ali Malekzadeh, Dean
Programs in:
  accounting • MBA
  business • Exec MBA, MBA
  business administration • Exec MBA, MBA
  e-commerce • MBA
  entrepreneurship • MBA
  finance • MBA
  human resources • MBA
  international business • MBA
  management information systems • MBA
  marketing • MBA

■ **YOUNGSTOWN STATE UNIVERSITY**
Youngstown, OH 44555-0001
http://www.ysu.edu/

State-supported, coed, comprehensive institution. CGS member. *Enrollment:* 12,850 graduate, professional, and undergraduate students; 351 full-time matriculated graduate/professional students (204 women), 909 part-time matriculated graduate/professional students (605 women). *Graduate faculty:* 245 full-time, 103 part-time/adjunct. *Computer facilities:* 1,619 computers available on campus for general student use. A campuswide network can be accessed from student residence rooms and from off campus. Internet access and online class registration are available. *Library facilities:* Maag Library. *Graduate expenses:* Tuition, state resident: full-time $4,194; part-time $233 per credit. Tuition, nonresident: full-time $8,352; part-time $464 per credit. Required fees: $42 per credit. Tuition and fees vary according to course load and reciprocity agreements.

General application contact: Dr. Peter J. Kasvinsky, Dean of Graduate Studies and Research, 330-941-3091.

Graduate School
College of Arts and Sciences
Programs in:
  arts and sciences • MA, MS, Certificate
  biological sciences • MS
  chemistry • MS
  economics • MA
  English • MA
  environmental studies • MS
  history • MA
  industrial/institutional management • Certificate
  mathematics • MS
  risk management • Certificate

College of Education
Programs in:
  counseling • MS Ed
  early and middle childhood education • MS Ed
  education • MS Ed, Ed D
  educational administration • MS Ed
  educational leadership • Ed D
  gifted and talented education • MS Ed
  secondary education • MS Ed
  special education • MS Ed
  teaching—elementary education • MS Ed
  teaching—secondary reading • MS Ed

College of Fine and Performing Arts
Programs in:
  fine and performing arts • MM
  music education • MM
  music history and literature • MM
  music theory and composition • MM
  performance • MM

College of Health and Human Services
Programs in:
  criminal justice • MS
  health and human services • MHHS
  nursing • MSN
  physical therapy • MPT
  public health • MPH

Warren P. Williamson Jr. College of Business Administration
Programs in:
  accounting • MBA
  business administration • EMBA, MBA
  executive business administration • EMBA
  finance • MBA
  management • MBA
  marketing • MBA

William Rayen College of Engineering
Programs in:
  civil, chemical, and environmental engineering • MSE
  electrical engineering • MSE
  engineering • MSE
  mechanical and industrial engineering • MSE

Oklahoma

■ **CAMERON UNIVERSITY**
Lawton, OK 73505-6377
http://www.cameron.edu/

State-supported, coed, comprehensive institution. CGS member. *Enrollment:* 5,632 graduate, professional, and undergraduate students; 116 full-time matriculated graduate/professional students (80 women), 253 part-time matriculated graduate/professional students (175 women). *Graduate faculty:* 47 full-time (20 women), 14 part-time/adjunct (6 women). *Computer facilities:* 350 computers available on campus for general student use. A campuswide network can be accessed. *Library facilities:* Cameron University Library. *Graduate expenses:* Tuition, state resident: full-time $2,034; part-time $113 per credit hour. Tuition, nonresident: full-time $4,824; part-time $268 per credit hour. International tuition: $4,874 full-time. Required fees: $25; $10 per term. One-time fee: $2 full-time. *General application contact:* Suzanne Cartwright, Graduate Admissions Coordinator, 580-581-2987.

School of Graduate Studies
Dr. Lloyd Dawe, Dean
Programs in:
  behavioral sciences • MS
  business administration • MBA
  education • M Ed
  instructional leadership • MS
  teaching • MAT

■ **EAST CENTRAL UNIVERSITY**
Ada, OK 74820-6899
http://www.ecok.edu/

State-supported, coed, comprehensive institution. CGS member. *Enrollment:* 4,442 graduate, professional, and undergraduate students; 158 full-time matriculated graduate/professional students (109 women), 338 part-time matriculated graduate/professional students (250 women). *Graduate faculty:* 48. *Computer facilities:* 40 computers available on campus for general student use. A campuswide network can be accessed. *Library facilities:* Linscheid Library. *Graduate expenses:* Tuition, state resident: part-time $85 per semester hour.

Tuition, nonresident: part-time $240 per semester hour. *General application contact:* Dr. Alvin O. Turner, Acting Dean, School of Graduate Studies, 580-310-5709 Ext. 709.

School of Graduate Studies
Dr. Alvin O. Turner, Acting Dean
Programs in:
  administration • MSHR
  counseling • MSHR
  criminal justice • MSHR
  education • M Ed
  psychology • MSPS
  rehabilitation counseling • MSHR

■ NORTHEASTERN STATE UNIVERSITY
Tahlequah, OK 74464-2399
http://www.nsuok.edu/

State-supported, coed, comprehensive institution. *Enrollment:* 9,297 graduate, professional, and undergraduate students; 710 matriculated graduate/professional students. *Graduate faculty:* 121 full-time (35 women), 10 part-time/adjunct (5 women). *Computer facilities:* 534 computers available on campus for general student use. A campuswide network can be accessed from student residence rooms and from off campus. Internet access is available. *Library facilities:* John Vaughn Library. *Graduate expenses:* Tuition, state resident: part-time $85 per credit hour. Tuition, nonresident: part-time $240 per credit hour. Required fees: $24 per credit hour. $18 per semester. *General application contact:* Margie Railey, Administrative Assistant, 918-456-5511.

College of Optometry
Dr. George E. Foster, Dean
Program in:
  optometry • OD

Graduate College
Dr. Donna B. Wood, Interim Dean

College of Arts and Letters
Dr. Kathryn Robinson, Dean
Programs in:
  arts and letters • MA
  communication • MA
  English • MA

College of Behavioral and Social Sciences
Dr. Lyle Haskins, Dean
Programs in:
  American studies • MA
  behavioral and social sciences • M Ed, MA, MS
  counseling psychology • MS
  criminal justice • MS
  school counseling • M Ed

College of Business and Industry
Dr. Penny Dotson, Dean
Programs in:
  accounting and financial analysis • MS
  business administration • MBA
  business and industry • MBA, MS
  industrial management • MS

College of Education
Dr. Kay Grant, Head
Programs in:
  college teaching • MS
  early childhood education • M Ed
  education • M Ed, MS
  health and human performance • MS
  reading • M Ed
  school administration • M Ed
  special education • M Ed
  special education/speech language pathology • MS
  teaching • M Ed

■ NORTHWESTERN OKLAHOMA STATE UNIVERSITY
Alva, OK 73717-2799
http://www.nwosu.edu/

State-supported, coed, comprehensive institution. *Enrollment:* 2,126 graduate, professional, and undergraduate students; 37 full-time matriculated graduate/professional students (30 women), 130 part-time matriculated graduate/professional students (99 women). *Graduate faculty:* 25 full-time (13 women), 12 part-time/adjunct (7 women). *Computer facilities:* 131 computers available on campus for general student use. A campuswide network can be accessed from off campus. Internet access and online class registration are available. *Library facilities:* J. W. Martin Library plus 1 other. *Graduate expenses:* Tuition, state resident: full-time $2,640. Tuition, nonresident: full-time $6,360. One-time fee: $15 full-time. *General application contact:* Dr. Rodney C. Murrow, Director of Graduate Studies, 580-327-8589.

School of Education, Psychology, and Health and Physical Education
Dr. James Bowen, Dean
Programs in:
  adult education management and administration • M Ed
  counseling psychology • MCP
  education: non-certificate option • M Ed
  elementary education • M Ed
  guidance and counseling K–12 • M Ed
  reading specialist • M Ed
  secondary education • M Ed

■ OKLAHOMA CITY UNIVERSITY
Oklahoma City, OK 73106-1402
http://www.okcu.edu/

Independent-religious, coed, comprehensive institution. *Enrollment:* 3,668 graduate, professional, and undergraduate students; 1,235 full-time matriculated graduate/professional students (494 women), 640 part-time matriculated graduate/professional students (299 women). *Graduate faculty:* 161 full-time (64 women), 121 part-time/adjunct (53 women). *Computer facilities:* 264 computers available on campus for general student use. A campuswide network can be accessed from student residence rooms and from off campus. Internet access and online class registration are available. *Library facilities:* Dulaney Browne Library plus 1 other. *Graduate expenses:* Tuition: full-time $11,660; part-time $530 per hour. Required fees: $360. Tuition and fees vary according to course level and degree level. *General application contact:* Dr. Dennis Dunham, Dean of Enrollment Management, 800-633-7242.

Meinders School of Business
Dr. Bart Ward, Dean
Programs in:
  accounting • MSA
  arts management • MBA
  finance • MBA
  health administration • MBA
  information systems management • MBA
  integrated marketing communications • MBA
  international business • MBA
  management • MBA
  management and business sciences • MBA, MSA
  marketing • MBA
  public administration • MBA

Petree College of Arts and Sciences
Dr. Roberta Olson, Dean
Programs in:
  art • MLA
  arts and sciences • M Ed, MA, MCJA, MLA, MS
  international studies • MLA
  leadership management • MLA
  literature • MLA
  philosophy • MLA
  writing • MLA

Division of Education
Dr. Donna C. Richardson, Director
Programs in:
  curriculum and instruction • M Ed
  early childhood education • M Ed

Oklahoma

Oklahoma City University (continued)
  education • M Ed, MA
  elementary education • M Ed
  teaching English as a second language • MA

Division of Mathematics and Science
Dr. Molisa Derk, Program Director
Program in:
  computer science • MS

Division of Social Sciences
Dr. Jody Horn, Director
Program in:
  criminal justice administration • MCJA

Division of Theatre
Judith Palladino, Chairperson
Programs in:
  costume design • MA
  technical theatre • MA
  theatre • MA
  theatre for young audiences • MA

School of Law
Dr. Larry Hellman, Dean
Program in:
  law • JD

School of Music
Mark Parker, Dean
Programs in:
  music composition • MM
  musical theatre • MM
  opera performance • MM
  performance • MM

School of Religion and Church Vocations
Dr. Mark Davies, Interim Dean
Programs in:
  church business management • MAR
  religious education • M Rel
  religious studies • MAR

■ **OKLAHOMA STATE UNIVERSITY**
Stillwater, OK 74078
http://www.okstate.edu/

State-supported, coed, university. CGS member. *Enrollment:* 23,577 graduate, professional, and undergraduate students; 1,829 full-time matriculated graduate/professional students (734 women), 2,262 part-time matriculated graduate/professional students (1,016 women). *Graduate faculty:* 1,206 full-time (336 women), 168 part-time/adjunct (82 women). *Computer facilities:* 2,000 computers available on campus for general student use. A campuswide network can be accessed from student residence rooms and from off campus. Internet access and online class registration are available. *Library facilities:* Edmon Low Library plus 4 others. *Graduate expenses:* Tuition, state resident: full-time $3,752; part-time $118 per credit hour. Tuition, nonresident: full-time $10,346; part-time $393 per credit hour. Tuition and fees vary according to course load. *General application contact:* Dr. Al Carlozzi, Interim Dean, 405-744-6368.
Find an in-depth description at www.petersons.com/gradchannel.

College of Veterinary Medicine
Dr. Michael Lorenz, Dean
Programs in:
  veterinary biomedical sciences • MS, PhD
  veterinary medicine • DVM, MS, PhD

Graduate College
Dr. Al Carlozzi, Interim Dean
Programs in:
  biophotonics • MS, PhD
  environmental sciences • MS, PhD
  international studies • MS
  natural and applied science • MS
  plant science • PhD

College of Agricultural Sciences and Natural Resources
Dr. Samuel E. Curl, Dean
Programs in:
  agricultural economics • M Ag, MS, PhD
  agricultural education, communication and 4H • M Ag, MS, Ed D, PhD
  agricultural sciences and natural resources • M Ag, M Bio E, MS, Ed D, PhD
  agronomy • M Ag, MS, PhD
  animal breeding • PhD
  animal nutrition • PhD
  animal sciences • M Ag, MS
  biochemistry and molecular biology • MS, PhD
  biosystems engineering • M Bio E
  crop science • PhD
  entomology • MS, PhD
  environmental and natural resources • MS, PhD
  food and bioprocessing • MS, PhD
  food science • MS, PhD
  forestry • M Ag, MS
  horticulture • M Ag, MS
  plant pathology • MS, PhD
  soil science • PhD

College of Arts and Sciences
Bruce C. Crauder, Interim Dean
Programs in:
  applied history • MA
  applied mathematics • MS
  arts and sciences • MA, MM, MS, Ed D, PhD
  botany • MS, PhD
  chemistry • MS, PhD
  clinical psychology • PhD
  communications sciences and disorders • MS
  computer science • MS, PhD
  corrections • MS
  creative writing • MA, PhD
  experimental psychology • PhD
  fire and emergency management administration • MS
  general psychology • MS
  geography • MS
  geology • MS
  history • MA, PhD
  literature • MA, PhD
  mass communication • MS, Ed D
  mathematics • MS, Ed D, PhD
  microbiology and molecular genetics • MS, PhD
  music pedagogy • MM
  philosophy • MA
  photonics • MS, PhD
  physics • MS, PhD
  political science • MA
  sociology • MS, PhD
  statistics • MS, PhD
  technical writing • MA, PhD
  theatre • MA
  wildlife and fisheries ecology • MS, PhD
  zoology • MS, PhD

College of Business Administration
Dr. James Lumpkin, Dean
Programs in:
  accounting • MS, PhD
  business administration • MBA, MS, PhD
  economics and legal studies in business • MS, PhD
  finance • MBA, PhD
  management • MBA
  management information systems • PhD
  management information systems/accounting information systems • MS
  management science • PhD
  management science and information systems • MBA
  marketing • MBA
  operations management • PhD
  telecommunications management • MS, PhD

College of Education
Dr. Ann C. Lotven, Dean
Programs in:
  applied behavioral studies • MS, Ed D, PhD
  counseling and student personnel • MS, PhD
  curriculum and educational leadership • MS, PhD, Ed S
  education • MS, Ed D, PhD, Ed S
  educational administration • MS, Ed S
  educational psychology • PhD
  health • MS, Ed D
  higher education • MS, Ed D
  leisure sciences • MS, Ed D
  physical education • MS, Ed D

Oklahoma

physical education and leisure sciences • Ed D
technical education • MS, Ed D, Ed S
trade and industrial education • MS, Ed D, Ed S

College of Engineering, Architecture and Technology
Dr. Karl N. Reid, Dean
Programs in:
architectural engineering • M Arch E
architecture • M Arch, M Arch E
chemical engineering • MS, PhD
civil engineering • M En, MS, PhD
control systems engineering • MSCSE
electrical and computer engineering • M En, MS, PhD
engineering and technology • MSETM
engineering, architecture and technology • M Arch, M Arch E, M Bio E, M En, MIE Mgmt, MS, MSCSE, MSETM, MSHCA, PhD
environmental engineering • M En, MS, PhD
health care administration • MSHCA
industrial engineering and management • M En, MIE Mgmt, MS, PhD
manufacturing systems engineering • M En
mechanical engineering • MS, PhD

College of Human Environmental Sciences
Dr. Patricia Knaub, Dean
Programs in:
design, housing and merchandising • MS, PhD
family relations and child development • MS
hotel and restaurant administration • MS
human development and family science • PhD
human environmental sciences • MS, PhD
nutritional sciences • MS, PhD

■ ORAL ROBERTS UNIVERSITY
Tulsa, OK 74171-0001
http://www.oru.edu/

Independent-religious, coed, comprehensive institution. *Enrollment:* 4,117 graduate, professional, and undergraduate students; 372 full-time matriculated graduate/professional students (171 women), 382 part-time matriculated graduate/professional students (211 women). *Graduate faculty:* 33 full-time (5 women), 20 part-time/adjunct (5 women). *Computer facilities:* 253 computers available on campus for general student use. A campuswide network can be accessed from student residence rooms and from off campus.

Internet access is available. *Library facilities:* John D. Messick Resources Center plus 1 other. *Graduate expenses:* Tuition: part-time $295 per credit hour. *General application contact:* Steve Kime, 918-495-6236.

School of Business
Dr. David Dyson, Dean
Programs in:
accounting • MBA
finance • MBA
human resource management • M Man, MBA
marketing • MBA
non-profit management • M Man, MBA

School of Education
Dr. David Hand, Dean
Programs in:
Christian school administration (K–12) • MA Ed, Ed D
Christian school administration (post-secondary) • MA Ed, Ed D
Christian school curriculum development • MA Ed
early childhood education • MA Ed
public school administration (K–12) • MA Ed, Ed D
public school teaching • MA Ed
teaching English as a second language • MA Ed

School of Theology and Missions
Dr. Thomson K. Mathew, Dean
Programs in:
biblical literature • MA
Christian counseling • MA
Christian education • MA
divinity • M Div
missions • MA
practical theology • MA
theological/historical studies • MA
theology • D Min

■ SOUTHEASTERN OKLAHOMA STATE UNIVERSITY
Durant, OK 74701-0609
http://www.sosu.edu/

State-supported, coed, comprehensive institution. *Enrollment:* 4,203 graduate, professional, and undergraduate students; 121 full-time matriculated graduate/professional students (67 women), 228 part-time matriculated graduate/professional students (145 women). *Graduate faculty:* 97 full-time (33 women), 8 part-time/adjunct (3 women). *Computer facilities:* 398 computers available on campus for general student use. A campuswide network can be accessed. Internet access and online class registration are available. *Library facilities:* Henry G. Bennett Memorial Library. *Graduate expenses:* Tuition, state resident: part-time $85 per credit hour. Tuition, nonresident: part-time $240 per credit hour. Required fees: $29 per credit hour. $43 per semester. One-time fee: $20. Tuition and fees vary according to course level and degree level. *General application contact:* Becky Hightower, Graduate Secretary, 580-745-2200.

Graduate School
Dr. Doug McMillan, Interim Dean

School of Arts and Sciences
Dr. Stan Rice, Graduate Coordinator
Program in:
technology • MT

School of Behavioral Sciences
Dr. Charla Hall, Coordinator
Program in:
guidance and counseling • MBS

School of Business
Dr. Buddy Gaster, Interim Dean
Program in:
business • MBA, MS

School of Education
Dr. Muhammad Betz, Chair
Programs in:
educational administration • M Ed
educational instruction and leadership • M Ed
educational technology • M Ed
elementary education • M Ed
school counseling • M Ed
secondary education • M Ed

■ SOUTHERN NAZARENE UNIVERSITY
Bethany, OK 73008
http://www.snu.edu/

Independent-religious, coed, comprehensive institution. *Enrollment:* 2,199 graduate, professional, and undergraduate students; 373 full-time matriculated graduate/professional students (199 women), 26 part-time matriculated graduate/professional students (5 women). *Graduate faculty:* 18 full-time (6 women), 36 part-time/adjunct (16 women). *Computer facilities:* 55 computers available on campus for general student use. A campuswide network can be accessed from student residence rooms and from off campus. Internet access is available. *Library facilities:* R. T. Williams Learning Resources Center. *General application contact:* Dr. W. Davis Berryman, Dean of Graduate College, 405-491-6316.

School of Business
Program in:
business • MBA, MS Mgt

Oklahoma

Southern Nazarene University (continued)

School of Education
Program in:
education • MA

School of Psychology
Programs in:
counseling psychology • MSCP
marriage and family therapy • MA

■ **SOUTHWESTERN OKLAHOMA STATE UNIVERSITY**
Weatherford, OK 73096-3098
http://www.swosu.edu/

State-supported, coed, comprehensive institution. *Computer facilities:* 270 computers available on campus for general student use. A campuswide network can be accessed from student residence rooms and from off campus. Internet access is available. *Library facilities:* Al Harris Library. *General application contact:* Dean, School of Education and Graduate Studies, 580-774-3285.

Graduate School

School of Arts and Sciences
Programs in:
arts and sciences • MM
education • MM
performance • MM

School of Business
Program in:
business • MBA

School of Education
Programs in:
agency counseling • M Ed
art • M Ed
early childhood education • M Ed
education • M Ed
educational administration • M Ed
elementary education • M Ed
English • M Ed
health, physical education and recreation • M Ed
mathematics • M Ed
natural sciences • M Ed
psychometry • M Ed
school counseling • M Ed
social sciences • M Ed
special education • M Ed
technology • M Ed

School of Pharmacy
Program in:
pharmacy • Pharm D

■ **UNIVERSITY OF CENTRAL OKLAHOMA**
Edmond, OK 73034-5209
http://www.cwc.cc.wy.us/

State-supported, coed, comprehensive institution. CGS member. *Computer facilities:* 250 computers available on campus for general student use. A campuswide network can be accessed from student residence rooms and from off campus. Internet access is available. *Library facilities:* Max Chambers Library. *General application contact:* Dean, College of Graduate Studies and Research, 405-974-3341.

College of Graduate Studies and Research

College of Arts, Media, and Design
Programs in:
arts, media, and design • MFA, MM
design and interior design • MFA
music education • MM
performance • MM

College of Business Administration
Program in:
business administration • MBA

College of Education
Programs in:
adult education • M Ed
community services • M Ed
counseling psychology • MS
early childhood education • M Ed
education • M Ed, MA, MS
elementary education • M Ed
family and child studies • MS
family and consumer science education • MS
general education • M Ed
gerontology • M Ed
guidance and counseling • M Ed
instructional media • M Ed
interior design • MS
nutrition-food management • MS
professional health occupations • M Ed
psychology • MA
reading • M Ed
school administration • M Ed
secondary education • M Ed
special education • M Ed
speech-language pathology • M Ed

College of Liberal Arts
Programs in:
composition skills • MA
contemporary literature • MA
creative writing • MA
criminal justice management and administration • MA
history • MA
international affairs • MA
liberal arts • MA
museum studies • MA
political science • MA
social studies teaching • MA
Southwestern studies • MA
teaching English as a second language • MA
traditional studies • MA
urban affairs • MA

College of Mathematics and Science
Programs in:
applied mathematical sciences • MS
biology • MS
chemistry • MS
industrial and applied physics • MS
mathematics and science • MS

■ **UNIVERSITY OF OKLAHOMA**
Norman, OK 73019-0390
http://www.ou.edu/

State-supported, coed, university. CGS member. *Enrollment:* 24,483 graduate, professional, and undergraduate students; 3,307 full-time matriculated graduate/professional students (1,603 women), 2,973 part-time matriculated graduate/professional students (1,572 women). *Graduate faculty:* 973 full-time (276 women), 127 part-time/adjunct (44 women). *Computer facilities:* Computer purchase and lease plans are available. 2,187 computers available on campus for general student use. A campuswide network can be accessed from student residence rooms and from off campus. Internet access and online class registration are available. *Library facilities:* Bizzell Memorial Library plus 8 others. *Graduate expenses:* Tuition, state resident: full-time $2,774; part-time $116 per credit hour. Tuition, nonresident: full-time $9,571; part-time $399 per credit hour. Required fees: $953; $33 per credit hour. Full-time tuition and fees vary according to course level, course load and program. *General application contact:* Patricia Lynch, Director of Admissions, 405-325-2251.

Find an in-depth description at www.petersons.com/gradchannel.

College of Law
Dr. Andrew M. Coats, Dean
Program in:
law • JD

Graduate College
Lee William, Dean
Program in:
interdisciplinary studies • MA, MS, PhD

College of Architecture
Bob G. Fillpot, Dean
Programs in:

Oklahoma

architecture • M Arch, MLA, MRCP, MS
construction science • MS
landscape architecture • MLA
regional and city planning • MRCP

College of Arts and Sciences
Dr. Paul B. Bell, Dean
Programs in:
anthropology • MA, PhD
arts and sciences • M Nat Sci, MA, MHR, MLIS, MPA, MS, MSW, PhD, Certificate
astrophysics • MS, PhD
botany • MS, PhD
chemistry and biochemistry • MS, PhD
communication • MA, PhD
economics • MA, PhD
English • MA, PhD
French • MA, PhD
German • MA
health and exercise science • MS
history • MA, PhD
history of science • MA, PhD
human relations • MHR
international studies • MA
knowledge management • MS
library and information studies • MLIS
mathematics • MA, MS, PhD
microbiology • MS, PhD
philosophy • MA, PhD
physics • MS, PhD
political science • MA, PhD
psychology • MS, PhD
public administration • MPA
school library media specialist • Certificate
social work • MSW
sociology • MA, PhD
Spanish • MA, PhD
sport management • MS
zoology • M Nat Sci, MS, PhD

College of Education
Dr. Joan Karen Smith, Dean
Programs in:
adult and higher education • M Ed, PhD
community counseling • M Ed
counseling psychology • PhD
education • Certificate
educational administration, curriculum and supervision • M Ed, Ed D, PhD
educational leadership and policy studies • M Ed, Ed D, PhD
historical, philosophical, and social foundations of education • M Ed, PhD
instructional leadership and academic curriculum • M Ed, PhD
instructional psychology • M Ed, PhD
school counseling • M Ed
special education • M Ed, PhD

College of Engineering
Dr. Arthur Porter, Dean
Programs in:
aerospace engineering • MS, PhD
air • M Env Sc
bioengineering • MS, PhD
chemical engineering • MS, PhD
civil engineering • MS, PhD
computer science • MS, PhD
electrical and computer engineering • MS, PhD
engineering • M Env Sc, MS, D Engr, PhD
engineering physics • MS, PhD
environmental engineering • MS
environmental science • M Env Sc, PhD
geological engineering • MS
geotechnical engineering • MS
groundwater management • M Env Sc
hazardous solid waste • M Env Sc
industrial engineering • MS, PhD
mechanical engineering • MS, PhD
natural gas engineering • MS
occupational safety and health • M Env Sc
petroleum and geological engineering • PhD
petroleum engineering • MS
process design • M Env Sc
structures • MS
telecommunication systems • MS
transportation • MS
water quality resources • M Env Sc

College of Fine Arts
Marvin Lamb, Dean
Programs in:
acting • MFA
art • MA, MFA
art history • MA
ceramics • MFA
choral conducting • M Mus
conducting • M Mus Ed, DMA
dance • MFA
design • MFA
directing • MFA
drama • MA
film and video • MFA
fine arts • M Mus, M Mus Ed, MA, MFA, DMA, PhD
instrumental • M Mus Ed
instrumental conducting • M Mus
music • M Mus
music composition • M Mus, DMA
music education • M Mus Ed, PhD
music theory • M Mus
organ • M Mus, DMA
painting • MFA
performance and composition • DMA
photography • MFA
piano • M Mus, DMA
printmaking • MFA
vice • M Mus, DMA
visual communications • MFA
vocal–general • M Mus Ed
wind/percussion/string • M Mus, DMA

College of Geosciences
Dr. John T. Snow, Dean
Programs in:
geography • MA, PhD
geology • MS, PhD
geophysics • MS
geosciences • MA, MS, MS Metr, PhD
meteorology • MS Metr, PhD

College of Liberal Studies
Dr. James Pappas, Dean
Program in:
liberal studies • MLS

Gaylord College of Journalism and Mass Communication
Charles Self, Dean
Programs in:
advertising and public relations • MA
information gathering and distribution • MA
journalism and mass communication • MA
mass communication management and policy • MA
professional writing • MA, MPW
telecommunication and new technology • MA

Michael F. Price College of Business
Dr. Dennis Logue, Dean
Programs in:
accounting • M Acc
business administration • MBA, PhD
management • MS
management information systems • MS

■ **UNIVERSITY OF TULSA**
Tulsa, OK 74104-3189
http://www.utulsa.edu/

Independent-religious, coed, university. CGS member. *Enrollment:* 4,072 graduate, professional, and undergraduate students; 1,069 full-time matriculated graduate/professional students (453 women), 308 part-time matriculated graduate/professional students (138 women). *Graduate faculty:* 212 full-time (62 women), 7 part-time/adjunct (4 women). *Computer facilities:* Computer purchase and lease plans are available. 900 computers available on campus for general student use. A campuswide network can be accessed from student residence rooms and from off campus. Internet access is available. *Library facilities:* McFarlin Library plus 1 other. *Graduate expenses:* Tuition: full-time $10,584; part-time $588 per credit hour. Required fees: $60; $3 per credit hour. *General application contact:* Dr. Janet A. Haggerty, Dean of Research and Graduate Studies, 918-631-2336.

Find an in-depth description at www.petersons.com/gradchannel.

Peterson's Graduate Schools in the U.S. 2006

Oklahoma

University of Tulsa (continued)
College of Law
Programs in:
  American Indian and indigenous law • LL M
  comparative and international law • LL M
  law • JD

Graduate School
Dr. Janet A. Haggerty, Dean of Research and Graduate Studies

College of Arts and Sciences
Dr. Dale Thomas Benediktson, Dean
Programs in:
  anthropology • MA
  art • MA, MFA
  arts and sciences • MA, MFA, MS, MSMSE, MTA, PhD
  clinical psychology • MA, PhD
  education • MA
  English language and literature • MA, PhD
  history • MA
  industrial/organizational psychology • MA, PhD
  math/science education • MSMSE
  speech-language pathology • MS
  teaching arts • MTA

College of Business Administration
Dr. W. Gale Sullenburger, Dean
Programs in:
  business administration • M Tax, MBA, METM, MS
  chemical engineering • METM
  computer science • METM
  corporate finance • MS
  electrical engineering • METM
  geological science • METM
  international finance • MS
  investment and portfolio management • MS
  mathematics • METM
  mechanical engineering • METM
  petroleum engineering • METM
  risk management/financial engineering • MS
  taxation • M Tax

College of Engineering and Natural Sciences
Dr. Steve J. Bellovich, Dean
Programs in:
  biological sciences • MS, PhD
  chemical engineering • ME, MSE, PhD
  chemistry • MS
  computer science • MS, PhD
  electrical engineering • ME, MSE
  engineering and natural sciences • ME, METM, MS, MSE, PhD
  geosciences • MS, PhD
  mathematical sciences • MS
  mechanical engineering • ME, MSE, PhD
  petroleum engineering • ME, MSE, PhD

Oregon

■ CONCORDIA UNIVERSITY
Portland, OR 97211-6099
http://www.cu-portland.edu/

Independent-religious, coed, comprehensive institution. *Computer facilities:* 60 computers available on campus for general student use. A campuswide network can be accessed from student residence rooms and from off campus. Internet access is available. *Library facilities:* Concordia Library plus 1 other. *General application contact:* Director of Graduate Admissions, 503-280-8501.

College of Education
Programs in:
  curriculum and instruction (elementary) • M Ed
  educational administration • M Ed
  elementary education • MAT
  secondary education • MAT

■ EASTERN OREGON UNIVERSITY
La Grande, OR 97850-2899
http://www.eou.edu/

State-supported, coed, comprehensive institution. *Enrollment:* 3,287 graduate, professional, and undergraduate students; 66 full-time matriculated graduate/professional students (46 women), 118 part-time matriculated graduate/professional students (73 women). *Graduate faculty:* 12 full-time (6 women), 7 part-time/adjunct (3 women). *Computer facilities:* Computer purchase and lease plans are available. 125 computers available on campus for general student use. A campuswide network can be accessed from student residence rooms and from off campus. Internet access and online class registration are available. *Library facilities:* Pierce Library plus 1 other. *Graduate expenses:* Tuition, nonresident: part-time $200 per credit hour. *General application contact:* Dr. Danny Ray Mielke, Coordinator of Graduate Studies, 541-962-3399.

School of Education and Business
Dr. Michael Jaeger, Dean
Programs in:
  education • MS
  education and business • MS, MTE
  elementary education • MTE
  secondary education • MTE

■ GEORGE FOX UNIVERSITY
Newberg, OR 97132-2697
http://www.georgefox.edu/

Independent-religious, coed, university. *Computer facilities:* 1,300 computers available on campus for general student use. A campuswide network can be accessed from student residence rooms and from off campus. Internet access and online class registration are available. *Library facilities:* Murdock Learning Resource Center plus 1 other. *General application contact:* Director of Admission, 800-765-4369.

Find an in-depth description at www.petersons.com/gradchannel.

Graduate and Professional Studies
Programs in:
  business administration • MBA
  counseling • MA
  marriage and family therapy • MA
  organizational leadership • MAOL
  teacher education • M Ed, MAT, Ed D

George Fox Evangelical Seminary
Programs in:
  Christian education • MA
  divinity • M Div
  ministry • D Min
  theological studies • MA

Graduate School of Clinical Psychology
Programs in:
  clinical psychology • Psy D
  psychology • MA

■ MARYLHURST UNIVERSITY
Marylhurst, OR 97036-0261
http://www.marylhurst.edu/

Independent-religious, coed, comprehensive institution. *Enrollment:* 1,212 graduate, professional, and undergraduate students; 93 full-time matriculated graduate/professional students (65 women), 242 part-time matriculated graduate/professional students (147 women). *Graduate faculty:* 5 full-time (2 women), 76 part-time/adjunct (37 women). *Computer facilities:* 40 computers available on campus for general student use. A campuswide network can be accessed. Internet access and online class registration are available. *Library facilities:* Shoen Library. *Graduate expenses:* Tuition: full-time $8,964; part-time $332 per credit hour. Required fees: $6 per credit hour. Full-time tuition and fees vary according to course load and program. *General application contact:* Marylee King, Dean of Admissions, 800-634-9982 Ext. 4430.

Graduate Program in Applied Theology
Dr. Jerry Roussell, Chair-Religious Studies Department
Program in:
 theology • MAAT

Graduate Program in Art Therapy Counseling
Christine Turner, Chairperson
Programs in:
 art therapy • PGC
 art therapy counseling • MA
 counseling • PGC

Graduate Program in Management
Bert Desmond, Chair
Program in:
 management • MBA

Master of Arts in Interdisciplinary Studies
Dr. Debrah B. Bokowski, Chair
Programs in:
 gerontology • MA
 liberal arts • MA
 organizational communications • MA
 spiritual traditions • MA

■ OREGON STATE UNIVERSITY
Corvallis, OR 97331
http://osu.orst.edu/

State-supported, coed, university. CGS member. *Enrollment:* 18,979 graduate, professional, and undergraduate students; 2,499 full-time matriculated graduate/professional students (1,194 women), 881 part-time matriculated graduate/professional students (476 women). *Graduate faculty:* 1,383 full-time (484 women), 182 part-time/adjunct (85 women). *Computer facilities:* 2,251 computers available on campus for general student use. A campuswide network can be accessed from student residence rooms and from off campus. Internet access and online class registration are available. *Library facilities:* Valley Library. *Graduate expenses:* Tuition, state resident: full-time $8,139; part-time $301 per credit. Tuition, nonresident: full-time $14,376; part-time $532 per credit. Required fees: $1,227. *General application contact:* Dr. Sally K. Francis, Dean of the Graduate School, Interim, 541-737-4881.

College of Pharmacy
Dr. Wayne A. Kradjan, Dean
Program in:
 pharmacy • Pharm D, MAIS, MS, PhD

College of Veterinary Medicine
Dr. Howard Gelberg, Dean
Programs in:
 comparative veterinary medicine • PhD
 microbiology • MS
 pathology • MS
 toxicology • MS
 veterinary medicine • DVM, MS, PhD

Graduate School
Dr. Sally K. Francis, Dean
Programs in:
 college student service administration • Ed M, MS
 interdisciplinary studies • MAIS
 molecular and cellular biology • MS, PhD
 plant physiology • MS, PhD

College of Agricultural Sciences
Dr. Thayne R. Dutson, Dean
Programs in:
 agricultural and resource economics • M Agr, MAIS, MS, PhD
 agricultural education • M Agr, MAIS, MAT, MS
 agricultural sciences • M Ag, M Agr, MA, MAIS, MAT, MS, PhD
 agriculture • M Agr
 animal science • M Agr, MAIS, MS, PhD
 crop science • M Agr, MAIS, MS, PhD
 economics • MS, PhD
 fisheries science • M Agr, MAIS, MS, PhD
 food science and technology • M Agr, MAIS, MS, PhD
 genetics • MA, MAIS, MS, PhD
 horticulture • M Ag, MAIS, MS, PhD
 poultry science • M Agr, MAIS, MS, PhD
 rangeland resources • M Agr, MAIS, MS, PhD
 soil science • M Agr, MAIS, MS, PhD
 toxicology • MS, PhD
 wildlife science • MAIS, MS, PhD

College of Business
Dr. Ilene K. Kleinsorge, Dean
Program in:
 business • MAIS, MBA, Certificate

College of Engineering
Ronald L. Adams, Dean
Programs in:
 bioengineering • MS, PhD
 chemical engineering • MS, PhD
 civil engineering • MS, PhD
 electrical engineering and computer science • MA, MAIS, MS, PhD
 engineering • M Engr, M Oc E, MA, MAIS, MS, PhD
 industrial engineering • MS, PhD
 manufacturing engineering • M Engr
 materials science • MAIS, MS
 mechanical engineering • MS, PhD
 nuclear engineering • MS, PhD
 ocean engineering • M Oc E
 radiation health physics • MS, PhD

College of Forestry
Hal J. Salwasser, Dean
Programs in:
 economics • MS, PhD
 forest engineering • MAIS, MF, MS, PhD
 forest products • MAIS, MF, MS, PhD
 forest resources • MAIS, MF, MS, PhD
 forest science • MAIS, MF, MS, PhD
 forestry • MAIS, MF, MS, PhD
 wood science and technology • MF, MS, PhD

College of Health and Human Sciences
Dr. Tammy Bray, Dean
Programs in:
 apparel, interiors, housing, and merchandising • MA, MAIS, MS, PhD
 environmental health management • MAIS, MS
 exercise and sport science • MS, PhD
 gerontology • MAIS
 health • MS, PhD
 health and human sciences • MA, MAIS, MAT, MPH, MS, PhD
 health education • MAIS, MAT, MS
 healthcare administration • MS
 human development and family studies • MS, PhD
 human performance • MAIS, MS, PhD
 movement studies in disabilities • MAIS, MS
 nutrition and food management • MAIS, MS, PhD
 physical education • MAT
 public health • MPH

College of Liberal Arts
Dr. Kay F. Schaffer, Dean
Programs in:
 anthropology • MAIS
 applied anthropology • MA
 economics • MA, MS, PhD
 English • MA, MAIS, MFA
 history • MA, MS, PhD
 liberal arts • MA, MAIS, MAT, MFA, MS, PhD
 music education • MAT

Oregon

Oregon State University (continued)
College of Oceanic and Atmospheric Sciences
Dr. Mark R. Abbott, Dean
Programs in:
  atmospheric sciences • MA, MS, PhD
  geophysics • MA, MS, PhD
  marine resource management • MA, MS
  oceanography • MA, MS, PhD

College of Science
Dr. Sherman H. Bloomer, Dean
Programs in:
  advanced mathematics education • MAT
  analytical chemistry • MS, PhD
  applied statistics • MA, MS, PhD
  biochemistry and biophysics • MA, MAIS, MS, PhD
  biology education • MAT
  biometry • MA, MS, PhD
  chemistry • MA, MAIS
  chemistry education • MAT
  ecology • MA, MAIS, MS, PhD
  environmental sciences • MA, MS, PhD
  environmental statistics • MA, MS, PhD
  general science • MA, MS, PhD
  genetics • MA, MAIS, MS, PhD
  geography • MA, MAIS, MS, PhD
  geology • MA, MAIS, MS, PhD
  inorganic chemistry • MS, PhD
  integrated science education • MAT
  mathematical statistics • MA, MS, PhD
  mathematics • MA, MAIS, MS, PhD
  mathematics education • MA, MAT, MS, PhD
  microbiology • MA, MAIS, MS, PhD
  molecular and cellular biology • MA, MAIS, MS, PhD
  mycology • MA, MAIS, MS, PhD
  nuclear and radiation chemistry • MS, PhD
  operations research • MA, MAIS, MS
  organic chemistry • MS, PhD
  physical chemistry • MS, PhD
  physics • MA, MS, PhD
  physics education • MAT
  plant pathology • MA, MAIS, MS, PhD
  plant physiology • MA, MAIS, MS, PhD
  science • MA, MAIS, MAT, MS, PhD
  science education • MA, MAT, MS, PhD
  statistics • MA, MS, PhD
  structural botany • MA, MAIS, MS, PhD
  systematics • MA, MAIS, MS, PhD
  zoology • MA, MAIS, MS, PhD

School of Education
Dr. Sam Stern, Dean
Programs in:
  adult education • Ed M, MAIS
  counseling • MS, PhD
  education • Ed M, MAIS, MAT, MS, Ed D, PhD
  elementary education • MAT
  family and consumer sciences • MAT, MS
  general education • Ed M, MAIS, MS, Ed D, PhD
  professional technical education • MAT
  teacher education • MAT

■ PACIFIC UNIVERSITY
Forest Grove, OR 97116-1797
http://www.pacificu.edu/

Independent, coed, comprehensive institution. *Enrollment:* 2,420 graduate, professional, and undergraduate students; 968 full-time matriculated graduate/professional students (619 women), 203 part-time matriculated graduate/professional students (143 women). *Graduate faculty:* 86 full-time (44 women), 47 part-time/adjunct (26 women). *Computer facilities:* Computer purchase and lease plans are available. 150 computers available on campus for general student use. A campuswide network can be accessed from student residence rooms and from off campus. Internet access, email, web space are available. *Library facilities:* Scott Memorial Library. *Graduate expenses:* Tuition: full-time $19,000. Required fees: $500. Tuition and fees vary according to degree level, program and student level. *General application contact:* Jon-Erik Larsen, Director of Graduate and Professional Admissions, 503-352-2218 Ext. 2321.

College of Education
Dr. Guy E. Mills, Dean
Programs in:
  early childhood education • MAT
  education • MAE
  elementary education • MAT
  high school education • MAT
  middle school education • MAT
  school counseling • M Ed
  special education • MAT
  visual function in learning • M Ed

College of Optometry
Dr. Leland W. Carr, Dean
Programs in:
  clinical optometry • MS
  optometry • OD, MS

School of Occupational Therapy
Dr. John A. White, Director
Program in:
  occupational therapy • MOT

School of Physical Therapy
Dr. Daiva A. Banaitis, Director
Programs in:
  entry level • DPT
  post-professional • DPT

School of Physician Assistant Studies
Christine Legler, Director
Program in:
  physician assistant studies • MHS, MS

School of Professional Psychology
Dr. Michel Hersen, Dean
Programs in:
  clinical psychology • Psy D
  counseling psychology • MA

■ PORTLAND STATE UNIVERSITY
Portland, OR 97207-0751
http://www.pdx.edu/

State-supported, coed, university. CGS member. *Enrollment:* 23,117 graduate, professional, and undergraduate students; 2,048 full-time matriculated graduate/professional students (1,267 women), 2,089 part-time matriculated graduate/professional students (1,165 women). *Graduate faculty:* 652 full-time (274 women), 487 part-time/adjunct (235 women). *Computer facilities:* 425 computers available on campus for general student use. A campuswide network can be accessed from student residence rooms and from off campus. Internet access and online class registration are available. *Library facilities:* Branford P. Millar Library. *Graduate expenses:* Tuition, state resident: full-time $6,588. Tuition, nonresident: full-time $12,060; part-time $298 per credit. Required fees: $1,041; $19 per credit. $35 per term. *General application contact:* Sam Collie, Director of Admissions and Records, 503-725-3511.

Graduate Studies
Dr. William H. Feyerherm, Vice Provost for Graduate Studies and Research
Programs in:
  computational intelligence • Certificate
  computer modeling and simulation • Certificate
  systems science • MS
  systems science/anthropology • PhD
  systems science/business administration • PhD
  systems science/civil engineering • PhD

Oregon

systems science/economics • PhD
systems science/engineering management • PhD
systems science/general • PhD
systems science/mathematical sciences • PhD
systems science/mechanical engineering • PhD
systems science/psychology • PhD
systems science/sociology • PhD

College of Engineering and Computer Science
Dr. Robert D. Dryden, Dean
Programs in:
civil and environmental engineering • MS
civil and environmental engineering management • M Eng
civil engineering • M Eng
computer science • MS, PhD
electrical and computer engineering • MS, PhD
engineering and computer science • M Eng, ME, MS, MSE, PhD, Certificate
engineering and technology management • M Eng, MS, PhD
environmental sciences and resources • PhD
manufacturing engineering • ME
mechanical engineering • MS, PhD
systems engineering • M Eng
systems engineering fundamentals • Certificate
systems science/civil engineering • PhD

College of Liberal Arts and Sciences
Dr. Marvin Kaiser, Dean
Programs in:
anthropology • MA, PhD
applied economics • MA, MS
biology • MA, MS, PhD
chemistry • MA, MS, PhD
conflict resolution • MA, MS
economics • PhD
English • MA, MAT
environmental management • MEM
environmental sciences/biology • PhD
environmental sciences/chemistry • PhD
environmental sciences/civil engineering • PhD
environmental sciences/economics • PhD
environmental sciences/geography • PhD
environmental sciences/geology • PhD
environmental sciences/physics • PhD
environmental studies • MS
foreign literature and language • MA
French • MA
general arts and letters education • MAT, MST
general economics • MA, MS

general science education • MAT, MST
general social science education • MAT, MST
general speech communication • MA, MS
geography • MA, MS, PhD
geology • MA, MS, PhD
German • MA
history • MA
liberal arts and sciences • MA, MAT, MEM, MS, MST, PhD
mathematical sciences • MA, MAT, MS, MST, PhD
mathematics education • PhD
physics • MA, MS, PhD
psychology • MA, MS, PhD
science/geology • MAT, MST
sociology • MA, MS, PhD
Spanish • MA
speech and hearing sciences • MA, MS
teaching English to speakers of other languages • MA

College of Urban and Public Affairs
Dr. Lawrence Wallack, Dean
Programs in:
administration of justice • MS, PhD
gerontology • Certificate
government • MA, MAT, MPA, MPH, MS, MST, PhD
health administration • MPA, MPH
health administration and policy • MPH
health education • MA, MS
health education and health promotion • MPH
political science • MA, MAT, MS, MST, PhD
public administration • MPA
public administration and policy • PhD
urban and public affairs • MA, MAT, MPA, MPH, MS, MST, MURP, MUS, PhD, Certificate
urban and regional planning • MURP
urban studies • MUS, PhD
urban studies and planning • MURP, MUS, PhD
urban studies: regional science • PhD

Graduate School of Social Work
Dr. James Ward, Dean
Programs in:
social work • MSW
social work and social research • PhD

School of Business Administration
Dr. Scott Dawson, Dean
Programs in:
business administration • MBA, MIM, MSFA, PhD
financial analysis • MSFA
international management • MIM

School of Education
Dr. Phyllis Edmundson, Dean
Programs in:

counselor education • MA, MS
early childhood education • MA, MS
education • M Ed, MA, MS
educational administration and leadership • MA, MS, Ed D
educational leadership: curriculum and instruction • Ed D
educational media/school librarianship • MA, MS
elementary education • M Ed, MAT, MST
postsecondary education • Ed D
reading • MA, MS
secondary education • M Ed, MAT, MST
special education • MA, MS

School of Fine and Performing Arts
Dr. Robert Sylvester, Dean
Programs in:
ceramics • MFA
conducting • MMC
fine and performing arts • MA, MAT, MFA, MMC, MMP, MST
music education • MAT, MST
painting • MFA
performance • MMP
sculpture • MFA
theater arts • MA

■ **SOUTHERN OREGON UNIVERSITY**
Ashland, OR 97520
http://www.sou.edu/

State-supported, coed, comprehensive institution. *Enrollment:* 5,506 graduate, professional, and undergraduate students; 215 full-time matriculated graduate/professional students (151 women), 327 part-time matriculated graduate/professional students (233 women). *Graduate faculty:* 189 full-time (77 women), 148 part-time/adjunct (72 women). *Computer facilities:* 400 computers available on campus for general student use. A campuswide network can be accessed. *Library facilities:* Southern Oregon University Library. *Graduate expenses:* Tuition, state resident: full-time $7,326. Tuition, nonresident: full-time $12,573. *General application contact:* Mara Affre, Director of Admissions, 541-552-6411.

Graduate Office
Dr. John Laughlin, Dean

School of Arts and Letters
Dr. Edwin Battistella, Dean
Program in:
music • MA, MS

School of Business
Dr. John Laughlin, Dean
Program in:
business • MA Ed, MIM, MS Ed

Oregon

Southern Oregon University (continued)
School of Sciences
Dr. Joseph Graf, Dean
Programs in:
 environmental education • MA, MS
 mathematics/computer science • MA, MS
 science • MA, MS

School of Social Science, Health and Physical Education
Dr. Kenneth Kempner, Dean
Programs in:
 applied psychology • MAP
 elementary education • MA Ed, MS Ed
 human service-organizational training and development • MA, MS
 secondary education • MA Ed, MS Ed
 social science • MA, MS
 social science, health and physical education • MA, MA Ed, MAP, MAT, MS, MS Ed
 teaching • MAT

■ UNIVERSITY OF OREGON
Eugene, OR 97403
http://www.uoregon.edu/

State-supported, coed, university. CGS member. *Enrollment:* 19,992 graduate, professional, and undergraduate students; 2,974 full-time matriculated graduate/professional students (1,546 women), 1,097 part-time matriculated graduate/professional students (617 women). *Graduate faculty:* 715 full-time (273 women), 188 part-time/adjunct (106 women). *Computer facilities:* 1,250 computers available on campus for general student use. A campuswide network can be accessed from student residence rooms and from off campus. Internet access and online class registration are available. *Library facilities:* Knight Library plus 6 others. *Graduate expenses:* Tuition, state resident: part-time $8,910 per term. Tuition, nonresident: part-time $13,689 per term. *General application contact:* 541-346-5129.

Graduate School
Marian Friestad, Associate Dean
Program in:
 applied information management • MS

Charles H. Lundquist College of Business
Philip J. Romero, Dean
Programs in:
 accounting • M Actg, PhD
 business • M Actg, MA, MBA, MS, PhD
 decision sciences • MA, MS
 finance • PhD
 management • PhD
 management: general business • MBA
 marketing • PhD

College of Arts and Sciences
Joe Stone, Dean
Programs in:
 anthropology • MA, MS, PhD
 arts and sciences • MA, MFA, MS, PhD
 Asian studies • MA
 biochemistry • MA, MS, PhD
 chemistry • MA, MS, PhD
 Chinese • MA, PhD
 classical civilization • MA
 classics • MA
 clinical psychology • PhD
 cognitive psychology • MA, MS, PhD
 comparative literature • MA, PhD
 computer and information science • MA, MS, PhD
 creative writing • MFA
 developmental psychology • MA, MS, PhD
 ecology and evolution • MA, MS, PhD
 economics • MA, MS, PhD
 English • MA, PhD
 environmental science, studies, and policy • PhD
 environmental studies • MA, MS
 exercise and movement science • MS, PhD
 French • MA
 geography • MA, MS, PhD
 geological sciences • MA, MS, PhD
 Germanic languages and literatures • MA, PhD
 Greek • MA
 history • MA, PhD
 independent study: folklore • MA, MS
 international studies • MA
 Italian • MA
 Japanese • MA, PhD
 Latin • MA
 linguistics • MA, PhD
 marine biology • MA, MS, PhD
 mathematics • MA, MS, PhD
 molecular, cellular and genetic biology • PhD
 neuroscience and development • PhD
 philosophy • MA, PhD
 physics • MA, MS, PhD
 physiological psychology • MA, MS, PhD
 political science • MA, MS, PhD
 psychology • MA, MS, PhD
 Romance languages • MA, PhD
 Russian and East European Studies • MA
 social/personality psychology • MA, MS, PhD
 sociology • MA, MS, PhD
 Spanish • MA
 theater arts • MA, MFA, MS, PhD

College of Education
Martin J. Kaufman, Dean
Program in:
 education • M Ed, MA, MS, D Ed, PhD

School of Architecture and Allied Arts
Robert Melnick, Dean
Programs in:
 architecture • M Arch
 architecture and allied arts • M Arch, MA, MCRP, MFA, MI Arch, MLA, MPA, MS, PhD
 art history • MA, PhD
 arts management • MA, MS
 community and regional planning • MCRP
 fine and applied arts • MFA
 historic preservation • MS
 interior architecture • MI Arch
 landscape architecture • MLA
 public policy and management • MA, MPA, MS

School of Journalism and Communication
Timothy W. Gleason, Dean
Program in:
 journalism • MA, MS, PhD

School of Music
C. Brad Foley, Dean
Programs in:
 composition • M Mus, DMA, PhD
 conducting • M Mus
 dance • MA, MS
 jazz studies • M Mus
 music • MA
 music education • M Mus, DMA, PhD
 music history • PhD
 music theory • PhD
 performance • M Mus, DMA
 piano pedagogy • M Mus

School of Law
Laird Kirkpatrick, Dean
Program in:
 law • JD

■ UNIVERSITY OF PORTLAND
Portland, OR 97203-5798
http://www.up.edu/

Independent-religious, coed, comprehensive institution. *Enrollment:* 3,263 graduate, professional, and undergraduate students; 143 full-time matriculated graduate/professional students (89 women), 326 part-time matriculated graduate/professional students (195 women). *Graduate faculty:* 84 full-time (26 women), 11 part-time/adjunct (5 women). *Computer facilities:* 200 computers available on campus for general student use. A campuswide network can be accessed from student residence rooms and from off campus.

Internet access and online class registration are available. *Library facilities:* Wilson M. Clark Library plus 1 other. *Graduate expenses:* Tuition: part-time $610 per semester hour. *General application contact:* Dr. Patricia L. Chadwick, Assistant to the Provost and Dean of the Graduate School, 503-943-7107.

Graduate School
Dr. Patricia L. Chadwick, Assistant to the Provost and Dean of the Graduate School

College of Arts and Sciences
Dr. Marlene Moore, Dean
Programs in:
  arts and sciences • MA, MFA, MS
  communication studies • MA
  drama • MFA
  management communication • MS
  music • MA
  pastoral ministry • MA

Dr. Robert B. Pamplin, Jr. School of Business
Dr. Larry Lewis, Dean
Program in:
  business • MBA

School of Education
Dr. Maria Ciriello, OP, Dean
Programs in:
  early childhood education • M Ed, MA, MAT
  education • M Ed, MA, MAT
  religious education • M Ed, MA
  secondary education • M Ed, MA, MAT
  special education • M Ed, MA

School of Engineering
Dr. Zia Yamayee, Dean
Program in:
  engineering • ME

School of Nursing
Dr. Terry Misener, Dean
Programs in:
  family nurse practitioner • Post Master's Certificate
  leadership in health care systems • Post Master's Certificate
  nursing • MS
  nursing education • Post Master's Certificate

■ WESTERN OREGON UNIVERSITY
Monmouth, OR 97361-1394
http://www.wou.edu/

State-supported, coed, comprehensive institution. *Computer facilities:* 277 computers available on campus for general student use. A campuswide network can be accessed from student residence rooms and from off campus.

Internet access is available. *Library facilities:* Wayne and Lynn Hamersly Library. *General application contact:* Director of Admissions, 503-838-8211.

Graduate Programs
College of Education
Programs in:
  bilingual education • MS Ed
  deaf education • MS Ed
  early childhood education • MS Ed
  education • MAT, MS Ed
  health • MS Ed
  humanities • MAT, MS Ed
  information technology • MS Ed
  initial licensure • MAT
  learning disabilities • MS Ed
  mathematics • MAT, MS Ed
  multihandicapped education • MS Ed
  rehabilitation counseling • MS Ed
  science • MAT, MS Ed
  social science • MAT, MS Ed
  teacher education • MAT, MS Ed

College of Liberal Arts and Sciences
Programs in:
  correctional administration • MA, MS
  liberal arts and sciences • MA, MS

Pennsylvania

■ ARCADIA UNIVERSITY
Glenside, PA 19038-3295
http://www.arcadia.edu/

Independent-religious, coed, comprehensive institution. CGS member. *Computer facilities:* Computer purchase and lease plans are available. 110 computers available on campus for general student use. A campuswide network can be accessed from student residence rooms and from off campus. Internet access is available. *Library facilities:* Landman Library. *General application contact:* 215-572-2910.

Find an in-depth description at www.petersons.com/gradchannel.

Graduate Studies
Programs in:
  allied health • MSHE, MSPH
  art education • M Ed, MA Ed
  biology education • MA Ed
  chemistry education • MA Ed
  child development • CAS
  computer education • M Ed, CAS
  computer education 7–12 • MA Ed
  counseling • MAC
  early childhood education • M Ed, CAS
  educational leadership • M Ed, CAS
  educational psychology • CAS
  elementary education • M Ed, CAS
  English • MAE
  English education • MA Ed
  environmental education • MA Ed, CAS
  fine arts, theater, and music • MAH
  genetic counseling • MSGC
  history education • MA Ed
  history, philosophy, and religion • MAH
  international peace and conflict management • MAIPCR
  language arts • M Ed, CAS
  literature and language • MAH
  mathematics education • M Ed, MA Ed, CAS
  medical science and community health • MM Sc, MSHE, MSPH
  music education • MA Ed
  physical therapy • DPT
  psychology • MA Ed
  pupil personnel services • CAS
  reading • M Ed, CAS
  school library science • M Ed
  science education • M Ed, CAS
  secondary education • M Ed, CAS
  special education • M Ed, Ed D, CAS
  theater arts • MA Ed
  written communication • MA Ed

■ BLOOMSBURG UNIVERSITY OF PENNSYLVANIA
Bloomsburg, PA 17815-1301
http://www.bloomu.edu/

State-supported, coed, comprehensive institution. CGS member. *Enrollment:* 8,282 graduate, professional, and undergraduate students; 298 full-time matriculated graduate/professional students (201 women), 353 part-time matriculated graduate/professional students (260 women). *Graduate faculty:* 196 full-time (69 women). *Computer facilities:* 800 computers available on campus for general student use. A campuswide network can be accessed from student residence rooms and from off campus. Internet access and online class registration are available. *Library facilities:* Andruss Library. *Graduate expenses:* Tuition, state resident: full-time $5,518; part-time $307 per credit. Tuition, nonresident: full-time $8,830; part-time $491 per credit. Required fees: $1,200. *General application contact:* Carol Arnold, Administrative Assistant, 570-389-4015.

School of Graduate Studies
Dr. James F. Matta, Dean of Graduate Studies

Pennsylvania

Bloomsburg University of Pennsylvania (continued)

College of Business
Dr. David Long, Dean
Programs in:
business • M Ed, MBA
business administration • MBA
business education • M Ed

College of Liberal Arts
Dr. Hsien-Tung Liu, Dean
Programs in:
art history • MA
exercise science and adult fitness • MS
liberal arts • MA, MS
studio art • MA

College of Professional Studies
Dr. Ann L. Lee, Dean
Programs in:
audiology • Au D
curriculum and instruction • M Ed
early childhood education • MS
education • M Ed, MS
education of deaf/hard of hearing • MS
elementary education • M Ed
health sciences • MS, MSN, Au D
nursing • MSN
professional studies • M Ed, MS, MSN, Au D
reading • M Ed
special education • MS
speech language pathology • MS

College of Science and Technology
Dr. Robert Marande, Dean
Programs in:
biology • MS
biology education • M Ed
instructional technology • MS
science and technology • M Ed, MS

■ CABRINI COLLEGE
Radnor, PA 19087-3698
http://www.cabrini.edu/

Independent-religious, coed, comprehensive institution. *Enrollment:* 2,203 graduate, professional, and undergraduate students; 50 full-time matriculated graduate/professional students (35 women), 438 part-time matriculated graduate/professional students (316 women). *Graduate faculty:* 9 full-time (4 women), 29 part-time/adjunct (15 women). *Computer facilities:* 195 computers available on campus for general student use. A campuswide network can be accessed from student residence rooms. Internet access is available. *Library facilities:* Holy Spirit Library. *Graduate expenses:* Tuition: part-time $447 per credit. Required fees: $45 per term. Tuition and fees vary according to course load. *General application contact:* Dr. Leslie Petty, Assistant Dean for Academic Affairs, 610-902-8592.

Graduate and Professional Studies
Dr. Leslie Petty, Assistant Dean for Academic Affairs
Programs in:
education • M Ed
educational leadership • Certificate
instructional systems technology • MS
organization leadership • MS
Project Management • Certificate

■ CALIFORNIA UNIVERSITY OF PENNSYLVANIA
California, PA 15419-1394
http://www.cup.edu/

State-supported, coed, comprehensive institution. CGS member. *Enrollment:* 6,428 graduate, professional, and undergraduate students; 476 full-time matriculated graduate/professional students (304 women), 570 part-time matriculated graduate/professional students (367 women). *Graduate faculty:* 72 full-time (29 women), 27 part-time/adjunct (14 women). *Computer facilities:* 720 computers available on campus for general student use. A campuswide network can be accessed from student residence rooms and from off campus. Internet access is available. *Library facilities:* Manderino Library. *Graduate expenses:* Tuition, state resident: full-time $5,518; part-time $307 per credit. Tuition, nonresident: full-time $8,830; part-time $491 per credit. Required fees: $1,000. *General application contact:* Dr. Thomas G. Kinsey, Dean of Graduate Studies, 724-938-4187.

School of Graduate Studies
Dr. Thomas G. Kinsey, Dean
Program in:
technology management • MSBA

School of Education
Geraldine Jones, Dean
Programs in:
communication disorders • MS
education • M Ed, MAT, MS, MSW
educational administration • M Ed
educational studies • MAT
elementary education • M Ed
exercise science: injury prevention and health promotion • MS
guidance and counseling • M Ed, MS
mentally and/or physically handicapped education • M Ed
reading specialist • M Ed
reading specialist and reading supervision • M Ed
school psychology • MS
social work • MSW
technology education • M Ed

School of Liberal Arts
Dr. Richard Helldobler, Acting Dean
Programs in:
communication • MA
earth science • MS
geography • M Ed, MA
liberal arts • M Ed, MA, MS
social science • MA

School of Science and Technology
Dr. Leonard Colelli, Dean
Programs in:
biology • M Ed, MS
business administration • MS
computer science • M Ed
mathematics • M Ed
multimedia technology • MS
science and technology • M Ed, MS

■ CARLOW COLLEGE
Pittsburgh, PA 15213-3165
http://www.carlow.edu/

Independent-religious, coed, primarily women, comprehensive institution. *Computer facilities:* 250 computers available on campus for general student use. A campuswide network can be accessed from student residence rooms and from off campus. Internet access and online class registration, applications software, e-mail are available. *Library facilities:* Grace Library. *General application contact:* Secretary, Graduate Studies, 412-578-6092.

Division of Education
Programs in:
art education • M Ed
early childhood education • M Ed
early childhood supervision • M Ed
educational leadership • M Ed

Division of Management
Program in:
management and technology • MS

Division of Nursing
Programs in:
case management/leadership • Certificate
home health advanced practice nursing • MSN, Certificate
nursing case management/leadership • MSN
nursing leadership • MSN

Division of Professional Leadership
Programs in:
health service education • MS
nonprofit management • MS
training and development • MS

Division of Social Services
Program in:
professional counseling • MSPC

Pennsylvania

■ CARNEGIE MELLON UNIVERSITY
Pittsburgh, PA 15213-3891
http://www.cmu.edu/

Independent, coed, university. CGS member. *Enrollment:* 9,756 graduate, professional, and undergraduate students; 3,045 full-time matriculated graduate/professional students (924 women), 1,227 part-time matriculated graduate/professional students (357 women). *Graduate faculty:* 1,550 full-time (328 women), 198 part-time/adjunct (84 women). *Computer facilities:* 450 computers available on campus for general student use. A campuswide network can be accessed from student residence rooms and from off campus. Internet access and online class registration are available. *Library facilities:* Hunt Library plus 2 others. *Graduate expenses:* Tuition: full-time $28,200; part-time $392 per unit. Required fees: $220.

Carnegie Institute of Technology
Programs in:
architecture-engineering construction management • MS
bioengineering • MS, PhD
biomedical engineering • MS, PhD
chemical engineering • M Ch E, MS, PhD
civil and environmental engineering • MS, PhD
civil engineering • MS
civil engineering and management • MS
civil engineering/engineering and public policy • PhD
colloids, polymers and surfaces • MS
electrical and computer engineering • MS, PhD
engineering • MS, PhD
engineering and public policy • PhD
environmental engineering • MS, PhD
environmental management and science • MS, PhD
materials science and engineering • MS, PhD
mechanical engineering • ME, MS, PhD
product development • MPD
technology • M Ch E, ME, MPD, MS, PhD

Information Networking Institute
Programs in:
information networking • MS
information security technology and management • MS

College of Fine Arts
Programs in:
art • MFA
fine arts • M Des, M Sc, MAM, MET, MFA, MM, MPD, MSA, PhD

School of Architecture
Programs in:
architecture • MSA
building performance and diagnostics • M Sc, PhD
computational design • M Sc, PhD

School of Design
Prof. Daniel Boyarski, Head
Programs in:
communication planning and information design • M Des
design • PhD
design theory • PhD
interaction design • M Des
new product development • PhD
product development • MPD
typography and information design • PhD

School of Drama
Programs in:
design • MFA
directing • MFA
dramatic writing • MFA
performance technology and management • MFA

School of Music
Programs in:
composition • MM
conducting • MM
music education • MM
performance • MM

College of Humanities and Social Sciences
Programs in:
behavioral decision theory • PhD
cognitive neuropsychology • PhD
cognitive psychology • PhD
communication planning and design • M Des
computer-assisted language learning • MCALL
design • MAPW
developmental psychology • PhD
English • MA
history • MA, MS
history and policy • MA, PhD
humanities and social sciences • M Des, MA, MAPW, MCALL, MS, PhD
literary and cultural studies • MA, PhD
logic and computation • MS
logic, computation and methodology • PhD
mathematical finance • PhD
organization science • PhD
philosophy • MA, MS
professional writing • MAPW
research • MAPW
rhetoric • MA, PhD
rhetorical theory • MAPW
science writing • MAPW
second language acquisition • PhD
social and cultural history • PhD
social and decision science • PhD
social/personality psychology • PhD
statistics • MS, PhD
technical • MAPW

Center for Innovation in Learning
Program in:
instructional science • PhD

Graduate School of Industrial Administration
Programs in:
accounting • PhD
algorithms, combinatorics, and optimization • MS, PhD
business management and software engineering • MBMSE
civil engineering and industrial management • MS
computational finance • MSCF
economics • MS, PhD
electronic commerce • MS
environmental engineering and management • MEEM
finance • PhD
financial economics • PhD
industrial administration • MBA, PhD
information systems • PhD
management of manufacturing and automation • MOM, PhD
manufacturing • MOM
marketing • PhD
mathematical finance • PhD
operations research • PhD
organizational behavior and theory • PhD
political economy • PhD
production and operations management • PhD
public policy and management • MS, MSED
software engineering and business management • MS

H. John Heinz III School of Public Policy and Management
Programs in:
arts management • MAM
health care policy and management • MSHCPM
information systems management • MISM
medical management • MMM
public management • MPM
public policy analysis • PhD
public policy and management • MAM, MIS, MISM, MMM, MPM, MS, MSED, MSHCPM, PhD
sustainable economic development • MIS

Mellon College of Science
Programs in:
algorithms, combinatorics, and optimization • PhD
biochemistry • PhD
biophysics • PhD
cell biology • PhD
chemical instrumentation • MS

Peterson's Graduate Schools in the U.S. 2006

Pennsylvania

Carnegie Mellon University (continued)
  chemistry • MS, PhD
  colloids, polymers and surfaces • MS
  computational biology • MS, PhD
  developmental biology • PhD
  genetics • PhD
  mathematical finance • PhD
  mathematical sciences • MS, DA, PhD
  molecular biology • PhD
  neurobiology • PhD
  physics • PhD
  polymer science • MS
  pure and applied logic • PhD
  science • MS, DA, PhD

School of Computer Science
Programs in:
  algorithms, combinatorics, and optimization • PhD
  computer science • PhD
  entertainment technology • MET
  human-computer interaction • MHCI, PhD
  knowledge discovery and data mining • MS
  pure and applied logic • PhD
  software engineering • MSE, PhD

Language Technologies Institute
Program in:
  language technologies • MLT, PhD

Robotics Institute
Program in:
  robotics • MS, PhD

■ CHESTNUT HILL COLLEGE
Philadelphia, PA 19118-2693
http://www.chc.edu/

Independent-religious, coed, primarily women, comprehensive institution. *Enrollment:* 1,555 graduate, professional, and undergraduate students; 88 full-time matriculated graduate/professional students (78 women), 525 part-time matriculated graduate/professional students (430 women). *Graduate faculty:* 9 full-time (3 women), 68 part-time/adjunct (46 women). *Computer facilities:* Computer purchase and lease plans are available. 101 computers available on campus for general student use. Internet access, e-mail are available. *Library facilities:* Logue Library. *Graduate expenses:* Tuition: part-time $400 per credit. *General application contact:* Sr. Ann Harkin, SSJ, Secretary, 215-248-7170.

Find an in-depth description at www.petersons.com/gradchannel.

School of Graduate Studies
Sr. Roseann Quinn, SSJ, Dean of the Graduate Division

Programs in:
  administration of human services • MS
  adult and aging services • CAS
  applied spirituality • CAS
  applied technology/instruction design • MS
  applied technology/leadership and technology • MS
  applied technology/technology and education • MS
  clinical pastoral education • CAS
  clinical psychology • Psy D
  counseling psychology and human services • MA, MS, CAS
  e-communication • CAS
  early childhood education • M Ed
  education and technology • CAS
  educational leadership • M Ed
  elementary education • M Ed
  holistic spirituality • MA
  holistic spirituality and healthcare • MA
  holistic spirituality and spiritual direction • MA
  holistic spirituality/health care • CAS
  instructional design • CAS
  instructional technology specialist • CAS
  leadership and technology • CAS
  leadership development • CAS
  multimedia design • CAS
  online learning • CAS
  restructured environments • CAS
  spirituality • CAS
  supervision of spiritual directors • CAS
  video • CAS

■ CHEYNEY UNIVERSITY OF PENNSYLVANIA
Cheyney, PA 19319-0200
http://www.cheyney.edu/

State-supported, coed, comprehensive institution. *Enrollment:* 1,536 graduate, professional, and undergraduate students; 91 full-time matriculated graduate/professional students (64 women), 194 part-time matriculated graduate/professional students (138 women). *Graduate faculty:* 8 full-time (4 women), 8 part-time/adjunct (3 women). *Computer facilities:* 200 computers available on campus for general student use. A campuswide network can be accessed from student residence rooms and from off campus. Internet access and online class registration, various software packages are available. *Library facilities:* Leslie Pickney Hill Library. *Graduate expenses:* Tuition, state resident: full-time $2,759; part-time $307 per credit. Tuition, nonresident: full-time $4,415; part-time $491 per credit. Required fees: $120 per term. *General application contact:* Dr. George Calhoun, Executive Dean of Graduate Studies, 215-560-7034.

School of Education
Dr. Chistine Gilchrist, Dean
Programs in:
  adult and continuing education • MS
  early childhood education • Certificate
  education • M Ed, MAT, MS, Certificate
  educational administration and supervision • M Ed, Certificate
  educational administration of adult and continuing education • M Ed, MS
  elementary and secondary principalship • Certificate
  elementary education • M Ed, MAT
  mathematics education • Certificate
  special education • M Ed, MS

■ CLARION UNIVERSITY OF PENNSYLVANIA
Clarion, PA 16214
http://www.clarion.edu/

State-supported, coed, comprehensive institution. CGS member. *Enrollment:* 6,497 graduate, professional, and undergraduate students; 538 matriculated graduate/professional students. *Graduate faculty:* 71. *Computer facilities:* 400 computers available on campus for general student use. A campuswide network can be accessed from student residence rooms and from off campus. Internet access and online class registration are available. *Library facilities:* Carlson Library. *Graduate expenses:* Tuition, state resident: full-time $5,518; part-time $307 per credit. Tuition, nonresident: full-time $8,830; part-time $491 per credit. Required fees: $63 per term. *General application contact:* Dr. Brenda Dédé, Assistant Vice President for Academic Affairs, 814-393-2337.

Find an in-depth description at www.petersons.com/gradchannel.

College of Graduate Studies
Dr. Brenda Dédé, Assistant Vice President for Academic Affairs

College of Arts and Sciences
Dr. Stephen Johnson, Interim Dean
Programs in:
  arts and sciences • MA, MS
  biology • MS
  communication • MS
  English • MA

College of Business Administration
Dr. Sarah Bower, Dean
Program in:
  business administration • MBA

Pennsylvania

College of Education and Human Services
Dr. Gail Grejda, Graduate Coordinator
Programs in:
communication sciences and disorders • MS
education • M Ed
education and human services • M Ed, MS, MSLS, CAS
library science • MSLS, CAS
reading • M Ed
rehabilitative sciences • MS
science education • M Ed
special education • MS

School of Nursing
Dr. Mary Kavoosi, Director
Program in:
nursing • MSN

■ COLLEGE MISERICORDIA
Dallas, PA 18612-1098
http://www.miseri.edu/

Independent-religious, coed, comprehensive institution. *Computer facilities:* 50 computers available on campus for general student use. A campuswide network can be accessed from student residence rooms and from off campus. Internet access is available. *Library facilities:* Mary Kintz Bevevina Library. *General application contact:* Coordinator of Part-Time Undergraduate and Graduate Programs, 570-674-6451.

Division of Health Sciences
Programs in:
health sciences • MSN, MSOT, MSPT, MSSLP
nursing • MSN
occupational therapy • MSOT
physical therapy • MSPT
speech-language pathology • MSSLP

Division of Professional Studies
Programs in:
education/curriculum • MS
organizational management • MS
professional studies • MS

■ DESALES UNIVERSITY
Center Valley, PA 18034-9568
http://www.desales.edu

Independent-religious, coed, comprehensive institution. *Enrollment:* 2,914 graduate, professional, and undergraduate students; 421 full-time matriculated graduate/professional students, 703 part-time matriculated graduate/professional students. *Graduate faculty:* 138. *Computer facilities:* 200 computers available on campus for general student use. A campuswide network can be accessed from student residence rooms and from off campus.

Internet access is available. *Library facilities:* Trexler Library. *Graduate expenses:* Tuition: part-time $7,350 per semester. *General application contact:* Dr. Robert Blumenstein, Dean of Graduate Education, 610-282-1100 Ext. 1237.

Graduate Division
Dr. Robert Blumenstein, Dean of Graduate Education
Programs in:
bilingual/ESL studies • Certificate
biology • M Ed
business administration • MBA
chemistry • M Ed
computers in education (K-12) • M Ed
computers in education (K-8) • M Ed
English • M Ed
family nurse practitioner • MSN
information systems • MSIS
instructional technology specialist • Certificate
mathematics • M Ed
physician assistant studies • MSPAS
special education • M Ed, Certificate
TESOL • M Ed

■ DREXEL UNIVERSITY
Philadelphia, PA 19104-2875
http://www.drexel.edu/

Independent, coed, university. CGS member. *Computer facilities:* 6,500 computers available on campus for general student use. A campuswide network can be accessed from student residence rooms and from off campus. Internet access and online class registration, campuswide wireless network are available. *Library facilities:* W. W. Hagerty Library. *General application contact:* Director of Graduate Admissions, 215-895-6700.

Find an in-depth description at www.petersons.com/gradchannel.

College of Arts and Sciences
Programs in:
arts and sciences • MA, MS, PhD
biological science • MS, PhD
chemistry • MS, PhD
clinical psychology • MA, MS, PhD
communication • MS
environmental policy • MS
environmental science • MS, PhD
food science • MS
forensic psychology • PhD
health psychology • PhD
law-psychology • PhD
mathematics • MS, PhD
neuropsychology • PhD
nutrition and food sciences • MS, PhD
nutrition science • PhD
physics • MS, PhD
publication management • MS
science, technology and society • MS

College of Business and Administration
Programs in:
accounting • MS
business administration • MBA, PhD, APC
business and administration • MBA, MS, PhD, APC
decision sciences • MS
finance • MS
marketing • MS
taxation • MS

College of Engineering
Programs in:
biochemical engineering • MS
chemical engineering • MS, PhD
civil engineering • MS, PhD
computer engineering • MS
computer science • MS, PhD
electrical and computer engineering • PhD
electrical engineering • MSEE, PhD
engineering • MS, MSEE, MSSE, PhD
engineering geology • MS
engineering management • MS, PhD
environmental engineering • MS, PhD
manufacturing engineering • MS, PhD
materials engineering • MS, PhD
mechanical engineering and mechanics • MS, PhD
software engineering • MSSE
telecommunications engineering • MSEE

College of Information Science and Technology
Programs in:
information science and technology • PhD
information studies • PhD, CAS
information systems • MSIS
library and information science • MS

College of Media Arts and Design
Programs in:
architecture • M Arch
arts administration • MS
design • MS
fashion design • MS
interior design • MS
media arts • MS
performing arts • MS

College of Medicine
Program in:
medicine • MD, MBS, MLAS, MMS, MS, PhD, Certificate

Pennsylvania

Drexel University (continued)
Biomedical Graduate Programs
Programs in:
 biochemistry • MS, PhD
 biomedical sciences • MBS, MLAS, MMS, MS, PhD, Certificate
 laboratory animal science • MLAS
 medical science • MBS, MMS, Certificate
 microbiology and immunology • MS, PhD
 molecular and cell biology • MS, PhD
 molecular and human genetics • MS, PhD
 molecular pathobiology • PhD
 neuroscience • PhD
 pharmacology and physiology • MS, PhD
 radiation • MS
 radiation biology • MS
 radiation physics • PhD
 radiation science • PhD
 radiopharmaceutical science • MS, PhD

College of Nursing and Health Professions
Programs in:
 advanced physician assistant studies • MHS
 art therapy • MA
 couples and family therapy • PhD
 dance/movement therapy • MA
 emergency and public safety service • MS
 family therapy • MFT
 hand/upper quarter rehabilitation • MHS, MS, PhD
 movement science • MHS, MS, PhD
 music therapy • MA
 nurse anesthesia • MSN
 nursing • MSN
 nursing and health professions • MA, MFT, MHS, MS, MSN, DPT, PhD, Certificate
 orthopedics • MHS, MS, PhD
 pediatrics • MHS, MS, PhD
 physical therapy • DPT, Certificate

School of Biomedical Engineering, Science and Health Systems
Programs in:
 biomedical engineering • MS, PhD
 biomedical science • MS, PhD
 biostatistics • MS
 clinical/rehabilitation engineering • MS

School of Education
Programs in:
 educational leadership and learning technology • PhD
 science of instruction • MS

School of Public Health
Program in:
 public health • MPH

■ **DUQUESNE UNIVERSITY**
Pittsburgh, PA 15282-0001
http://www.duq.edu/

Independent-religious, coed, university. CGS member. *Enrollment:* 9,701 graduate, professional, and undergraduate students; 2,518 full-time matriculated graduate/professional students (1,464 women), 1,459 part-time matriculated graduate/professional students (891 women). *Computer facilities:* 650 computers available on campus for general student use. A campuswide network can be accessed from student residence rooms and from off campus. Internet access is available. *Library facilities:* Gumberg Library plus 1 other. *Graduate expenses:* Tuition: part-time $626 per credit. Required fees: $62 per credit. Tuition and fees vary according to degree level and program. *General application contact:* Dr. Ralph L. Pearson, Provost and Academic Vice President, 412-396-6054.

Find an in-depth description at www.petersons.com/gradchannel.

Bayer School of Natural and Environmental Sciences
Dr. David Seybert, Dean
Programs in:
 biochemistry • MS, PhD
 biology • MS, PhD
 chemistry • MS, PhD
 environmental management • Certificate
 environmental science • Certificate
 environmental science and management • MS
 natural and environmental sciences • MS, PhD, Certificate

Graduate School of Liberal Arts
Dr. Constance D. Ramirez, Dean
Programs in:
 archival, museum, and editing studies • MA
 clinical psychology • PhD
 communication • MA
 computational mathematics • MA
 developmental psychology • PhD
 English • MA, PhD
 health care ethics • MA, DHCE, PhD, Certificate
 history • MA
 liberal arts • M Phil, MA, MALS, MS, DHCE, PhD, Certificate
 liberal studies • M Phil, MALS
 multimedia technology • MS, Certificate
 pastoral ministry • MA
 philosophy • MA, PhD
 religious education • MA
 rhetoric • PhD
 systematic theology • PhD
 theology • MA

Graduate Center for Social and Public Policy
Dr. Richard Colignon, Director
Programs in:
 conflict resolution and peace studies • Certificate
 social and public policy • MA, Certificate

John F. Donahue Graduate School of Business
James C. Stalder, Dean
Programs in:
 business administration • MBA
 information systems management • MS
 taxation • MS

John G. Rangos, Sr. School of Health Sciences
Dr. Gregory H. Frazer, Dean
Programs in:
 health management systems • MHMS
 occupational therapy • MOT
 physical therapy • MPT, DPT
 physician assistant • MPA
 rehabilitation science • MS, PhD
 speech–language pathology • MS

Mary Pappert School of Music
Dr. Edward Kocher, Dean
Programs in:
 music education • MM
 music performance • MM, AD
 music technology • AD
 music theory/composition • MM
 sacred music • MM

School of Education
Programs in:
 community counseling • MS Ed
 counselor education • MS Ed, Ed D
 counselor education and supervision • Ed D
 early childhood education • MS Ed
 education • MS Ed, Ed D, PhD, CAGS
 educational leaders • Ed D
 educational studies • MS Ed
 elementary education • MS Ed
 instructional leadership excellence • Ed D
 instructional technology • MS Ed, Ed D
 marriage and family therapy • MS Ed
 reading and language arts • MS Ed
 school administration • MS Ed
 school administration and supervision • MS Ed
 school counseling • MS Ed
 school psychology • MS Ed, PhD, CAGS
 school supervision • MS Ed
 secondary education • MS Ed
 special education • MS Ed

Pennsylvania

School of Law
Nicholas P. Cafardi, Dean
Program in:
 law • JD

School of Nursing
Dr. Eileen Zungolo, Dean and Professor
Programs in:
 family nurse practitioner • MSN
 nursing • MSN, PhD
 nursing administration • MSN
 nursing education • MSN

School of Pharmacy
Dr. R. Pete Vanderveen, Dean
Program in:
 pharmacy • Pharm D, MS, PhD

Graduate School of Pharmaceutical Sciences
Dr. Aleem Gangjee, Director
Programs in:
 medicinal chemistry • MS, PhD
 pharmaceutical administration • MS
 pharmaceutical chemistry • MS, PhD
 pharmaceutics • MS, PhD
 pharmacology/toxicology • MS, PhD

■ EASTERN UNIVERSITY
St. Davids, PA 19087-3696
http://www.eastern.edu/

Independent-religious, coed, comprehensive institution. *Computer facilities:* 60 computers available on campus for general student use. A campuswide network can be accessed from student residence rooms and from off campus. Internet access is available. *Library facilities:* Warner Library plus 1 other. *General application contact:* Director of Graduate Admissions, 610-341-5972.

Graduate Business Programs
Programs in:
 business administration • MBA
 economic development • MBA, MS
 nonprofit management • MBA, MS

Graduate Education Programs
Programs in:
 English as a second or foreign language • Certificate
 multicultural education • M Ed
 school health services • M Ed

Programs in Counseling
Programs in:
 community/clinical counseling • MA
 educational counseling • MA, MS
 marriage and family • MA
 school counseling • MA
 school psychology • MS
 student development • MA

■ EAST STROUDSBURG UNIVERSITY OF PENNSYLVANIA
East Stroudsburg, PA 18301-2999
http://www.esu.edu/

State-supported, coed, comprehensive institution. *Enrollment:* 6,162 graduate, professional, and undergraduate students; 284 full-time matriculated graduate/professional students (185 women), 531 part-time matriculated graduate/professional students (372 women). *Graduate faculty:* 89 full-time (33 women), 21 part-time/adjunct (11 women). *Computer facilities:* 708 computers available on campus for general student use. A campuswide network can be accessed from off campus. Internet access and online class registration are available. *Library facilities:* Kemp Library. *Graduate expenses:* Tuition, state resident: full-time $5,618; part-time $307 per credit. Tuition, nonresident: full-time $8,980; part-time $491 per credit. Required fees: $1,106; $62 per credit. *General application contact:* Dr. James A. Fagin, Dean of Graduate Studies and Faculty Research, 570-423-3536.

Find an in-depth description at www.petersons.com/gradchannel.

Graduate School
Dr. James A. Fagin, Dean

School of Arts and Sciences
Dr. Bonnie Neumann, Dean
Programs in:
 arts and sciences • M Ed, MA, MS
 biology • M Ed, MS
 computer science • MS
 general science • M Ed, MS
 history • M Ed, MA
 political science • M Ed, MA

School of Health Sciences and Human Performance
Dr. Mark Kilker, Dean
Programs in:
 cardiac rehabilitation and exercise science • MS
 community health education • MPH
 health and physical education • M Ed
 health education • MS
 health sciences and human performance • M Ed, MPH, MS
 physical education • MS
 speech pathology and audiology • MS

School of Professional Studies
Dr. Sam Hausfather, Dean
Programs in:
 elementary education • M Ed
 instructional technology • M Ed
 professional and secondary education • M Ed
 professional studies • M Ed
 reading • M Ed
 special education • M Ed

■ EDINBORO UNIVERSITY OF PENNSYLVANIA
Edinboro, PA 16444
http://www.edinboro.edu/

State-supported, coed, comprehensive institution. *Enrollment:* 8,045 graduate, professional, and undergraduate students; 433 full-time matriculated graduate/professional students (299 women), 583 part-time matriculated graduate/professional students (402 women). *Graduate faculty:* 66 full-time (34 women), 3 part-time/adjunct (2 women). *Computer facilities:* Computer purchase and lease plans are available. 700 computers available on campus for general student use. A campuswide network can be accessed from student residence rooms and from off campus. Internet access and online class registration, e-mail are available. *Library facilities:* Baron-Forness Library plus 1 other. *Graduate expenses:* Tuition, state resident: full-time $5,518; part-time $307 per credit. Tuition, nonresident: full-time $8,830; part-time $491 per credit. Required fees: $19 per credit. $39 per term. *General application contact:* Dr. Mary Margaret Bevevino, Dean of Graduate Studies, 814-732-2856.

Graduate Studies
Dr. Mary Margaret Bevevino, Dean of Graduate Studies

School of Education
Dr. R. Scott Baldwin, Dean of Education
Programs in:
 behavior management • Certificate
 character education • Certificate
 counseling • MA, Certificate
 counseling and human development • MA, Certificate
 early childhood • M Ed
 education • M Ed, MA, Certificate
 educational psychology • M Ed
 elementary education • M Ed
 elementary education clinical • M Ed
 elementary school administration • M Ed, Certificate
 language arts • M Ed
 mathematics • M Ed
 reading • M Ed, Certificate
 reading specialist • Certificate
 school administration • M Ed, Certificate
 school psychology • Certificate

Peterson's Graduate Schools in the U.S. 2006 *www.petersons.com* **523**

Pennsylvania

Edinboro University of Pennsylvania (continued)
- science • M Ed
- secondary education • M Ed
- secondary school administration • M Ed, Certificate
- social studies • M Ed
- special education • M Ed

School of Liberal Arts
Dr. Terry L. Smith, Dean of Liberal Arts
Programs in:
- art • MA
- ceramics • MFA
- clinical psychology • MA
- communication studies • MA
- fine arts • MFA
- jewelry • MFA
- liberal arts • MA, MFA, MSW
- painting • MFA
- printmaking • MFA
- sculpture • MFA
- social sciences • MA
- social work • MSW
- speech-language pathology • MA

School of Science, Management and Technology
Dr. Eric Randall, Dean
Programs in:
- biology • MS
- family nurse practitioner • MSN
- information technology • MS, Certificate
- science, management and technology • MS, MSN, Certificate

■ **GANNON UNIVERSITY**
Erie, PA 16541-0001
http://www.gannon.edu/

Independent-religious, coed, comprehensive institution. *Computer facilities:* 229 computers available on campus for general student use. A campuswide network can be accessed from student residence rooms and from off campus. Internet access is available. *Library facilities:* Nash Library plus 1 other. *General application contact:* Director of Admissions, 814-871-7240.

School of Graduate Studies

College of Humanities, Business, and Education
Programs in:
- accounting • Certificate
- business • MBA, Certificate
- business administration • MBA, Certificate
- counseling psychology • MS, PhD
- curriculum and instruction • M Ed
- early intervention • MS, Certificate
- education • M Ed, MS, PhD, Certificate
- educational computing technology • M Ed
- English • M Ed, MA
- finance • Certificate
- gerontology • Certificate
- human resources management • Certificate
- humanities • M Ed, MA, MPA, MS, PhD, Certificate
- humanities, business, and education • M Ed, MA, MBA, MPA, MS, PhD, Certificate
- pastoral studies • MA, Certificate
- public administration • MPA, Certificate
- reading • M Ed, Certificate
- secondary education • M Ed

College of Sciences, Engineering, and Health Sciences
Programs in:
- administration • MSN
- anesthesia • MSN
- electrical engineering • MS
- embedded software engineering • MS
- engineering and computer science • MS
- family nurse practitioner • MSN, Certificate
- gerontology • MSN
- health sciences • MOT, MPT, MS, Certificate
- mechanical engineering • MS
- medical-surgical nursing • MSN
- natural sciences/environmental education • M Ed, Certificate
- occupational therapy • MOT
- physical therapy • MPT
- physician assistant • MS
- sciences • M Ed, Certificate
- sciences, engineering, and health sciences • M Ed, MOT, MPT, MS, MSN, Certificate

■ **GENEVA COLLEGE**
Beaver Falls, PA 15010-3599
http://www.geneva.edu/

Independent-religious, coed, comprehensive institution. *Computer facilities:* 150 computers available on campus for general student use. A campuswide network can be accessed from off campus. *Library facilities:* McCartney Library plus 5 others. *General application contact:* Director of Graduate Student Services, 724-847-6697.

Program in Business Administration
Program in:
- business administration • MBA

Program in Counseling
Programs in:
- marriage and family • MA
- mental health • MA
- school counseling • MA

Program in Higher Education
Dr. David S. Guthrie, Director
Programs in:
- campus ministry • MA
- college teaching • MA
- educational leadership • MA
- student affairs administration • MA

Program in Organizational Leadership
Program in:
- organizational leadership • MS

Program in Special Education
Program in:
- special education • M Ed

■ **GRATZ COLLEGE**
Melrose Park, PA 19027
http://www.gratzcollege.edu/

Independent-religious, coed, comprehensive institution. *Enrollment:* 696 graduate, professional, and undergraduate students; 22 full-time matriculated graduate/professional students (16 women), 658 part-time matriculated graduate/professional students (508 women). *Graduate faculty:* 8 full-time (4 women), 116 part-time/adjunct (93 women). *Computer facilities:* 2 computers available on campus for general student use. A campuswide network can be accessed from off campus. *Library facilities:* Tuttleman Library. *Graduate expenses:* Tuition: full-time $11,000; part-time $499 per credit. Required fees: $700; $50 per year. *General application contact:* Dr. Jill K. Sigman, Director of Admissions, 215-635-7300 Ext. 140.

Find an in-depth description at www.petersons.com/gradchannel.

Graduate Programs
Dr. Jerome Kutnick, Dean for Academic Affairs
Programs in:
- classical studies • MA
- education • MA
- Israel studies • Certificate
- Jewish communal studies • MA, Certificate
- Jewish education • MA, Certificate
- Jewish music • MA, Certificate
- Jewish studies • MA
- Judaica librarianship • Certificate
- modern studies • MA

■ **GWYNEDD-MERCY COLLEGE**
Gwynedd Valley, PA 19437-0901
http://www.gmc.edu/

Independent-religious, coed, comprehensive institution. *Enrollment:* 2,615 graduate, professional, and

Pennsylvania

undergraduate students; 57 full-time matriculated graduate/professional students (41 women), 381 part-time matriculated graduate/professional students (300 women). *Graduate faculty:* 11 full-time (8 women), 25 part-time/adjunct (14 women). *Computer facilities:* 97 computers available on campus for general student use. A campuswide network can be accessed from student residence rooms and from off campus. Internet access is available. *Library facilities:* Lourdes Library plus 1 other. *Graduate expenses:* Tuition: part-time $395 per credit. *General application contact:* 800-342-5462.

School of Education
Dr. Lorraine Cavaliere, Dean
Programs in:
  educational administration • MS
  mental health counseling • MS
  reading • MS
  school counseling • MS
  special education • MS
  teaching, master teacher • MS

School of Nursing
Dr. Andrea Hollingsworth, Dean
Programs in:
  clinical nurse specialist • MSN
  nurse practitioner • MSN

■ HOLY FAMILY UNIVERSITY
Philadelphia, PA 19114-2094
http://www.holyfamily.edu/

Independent-religious, coed, comprehensive institution. *Computer facilities:* 148 computers available on campus for general student use. A campuswide network can be accessed. Internet access is available. *Library facilities:* Holy Family College Library plus 1 other. *General application contact:* Dean, Graduate Studies, 215-637-7700 Ext. 3230.

Graduate School

School of Arts and Sciences
Program in:
  counseling psychology • MS

School of Business
Programs in:
  human resources management • MS
  information systems management • MS

School of Education
Programs in:
  education • M Ed
  elementary education • M Ed
  reading specialist • M Ed
  secondary education • M Ed

School of Nursing
Program in:
  nursing • MSN

■ IMMACULATA UNIVERSITY
Immaculata, PA 19345
http://www.immaculata.edu/

Independent-religious, coed, comprehensive institution. *Enrollment:* 3,381 graduate, professional, and undergraduate students; 73 full-time matriculated graduate/professional students (64 women), 640 part-time matriculated graduate/professional students (504 women). *Graduate faculty:* 44. *Computer facilities:* Computer purchase and lease plans are available. 215 computers available on campus for general student use. A campuswide network can be accessed from student residence rooms and from off campus. Internet access is available. *Library facilities:* Gabriele Library. *Graduate expenses:* Tuition: part-time $440 per credit hour. Tuition and fees vary according to course level. *General application contact:* Sr. Ann M. Heath, Dean, 610-647-4400 Ext. 3211.

Find an in-depth description at www.petersons.com/gradchannel.

College of Graduate Studies
Sr. Ann M. Heath, Dean
Programs in:
  clinical psychology • Psy D
  counseling psychology • MA, Certificate
  cultural and linguistic diversity • MA
  educational leadership and administration • MA, Ed D
  elementary education • Certificate
  intermediate unit director • Certificate
  music therapy • MA
  nursing • MSN
  nutrition education • MA
  nutrition education/approved pre-professional practice program • MA
  organization leadership • MA
  school principal • Certificate
  school psychology • Psy D
  school superintendent • Certificate
  secondary education • Certificate
  special education • Certificate

■ INDIANA UNIVERSITY OF PENNSYLVANIA
Indiana, PA 15705-1087
http://www.iup.edu/

State-supported, coed, university. CGS member. *Enrollment:* 13,868 graduate, professional, and undergraduate students; 800 full-time matriculated graduate/professional students (500 women), 949 part-time matriculated graduate/professional students (610 women). *Graduate faculty:* 346 full-time (136 women). *Computer facilities:* Computer purchase and lease plans are available. 3,500 computers available on campus for general student use. A campuswide network can be accessed from student residence rooms and from off campus. Internet access and online class registration are available. *Library facilities:* Stapleton Library. *Graduate expenses:* Tuition, state resident: full-time $5,518; part-time $307 per credit. Tuition, nonresident: full-time $8,830; part-time $491 per credit. Required fees: $31 per credit. $111 per semester. Tuition and fees vary according to degree level. *General application contact:* Donna Griffith, Assistant Dean, 724-357-2222.

Find an in-depth description at www.petersons.com/gradchannel.

Graduate School and Research
Dr. Alicia Linzey, Dean

College of Education and Educational Technology
Dr. John Butzow, Dean
Programs in:
  administration and leadership studies • D Ed
  adult education and communication technology • MA
  communications technology • MA
  community counseling • MA
  counselor education • M Ed
  curriculum and instruction • M Ed, D Ed
  early childhood education • M Ed
  education • M Ed, Certificate
  education and educational technology • M Ed, MA, MS, D Ed, Certificate
  education of exceptional persons • M Ed
  educational psychology • M Ed, Certificate
  literacy • M Ed
  principal • Certificate
  reading • M Ed
  school psychology • D Ed, Certificate
  speech-language pathology • MS
  student affairs in higher education • MA

College of Fine Arts
Michael Hood, Dean
Programs in:
  art • MA, MFA
  fine arts • MA, MFA
  music • MA
  music education • MA
  music history and literature • MA
  music theory and composition • MA
  performance • MA

Pennsylvania

Indiana University of Pennsylvania (continued)

College of Health and Human Services
Dr. Carleen Zoni, Dean
Programs in:
  aquatics administration and facilities management • MS
  exercise science • MS
  food and nutrition • MS
  health and human services • MA, MS, Certificate
  industrial and labor relations • MA
  nursing • MS
  safety sciences • MS, Certificate
  sport management • MS
  sport science • MS

College of Humanities and Social Sciences
Dr. Brenda Carter, Dean
Programs in:
  administration and leadership studies • PhD
  composition and teaching English to speakers of other languages • MA, MAT, PhD
  criminology • MA, PhD
  generalist • MA
  geography • MA, MS
  history • MA
  humanities and social sciences • MA, MAT, MS, PhD
  literature • MA
  literature and criticism • MA, PhD
  public affairs • MA
  rhetoric and linguistics • PhD
  sociology • MA
  teaching English • MAT
  teaching English to speakers of other languages • MA

College of Natural Sciences and Mathematics
Dr. John S. Eck, Dean
Programs in:
  applied mathematics • MS
  biology • MS
  chemistry • MA, MS
  clinical psychology • Psy D
  elementary and middle school mathematics education • M Ed
  mathematics education • M Ed
  natural sciences and mathematics • M Ed, MA, MS, Psy D
  physics • MA, MS
  psychology • MA

Eberly College of Business and Information Technology
Dr. Robert Camp, Dean
Programs in:
  business • M Ed, MBA
  business administration • MBA
  business/workforce development • M Ed

■ KING'S COLLEGE
Wilkes-Barre, PA 18711-0801
http://www.kings.edu/

Independent-religious, coed, comprehensive institution. *Enrollment:* 2,204 graduate, professional, and undergraduate students; 38 full-time matriculated graduate/professional students (25 women), 102 part-time matriculated graduate/professional students (89 women). *Graduate faculty:* 11 full-time (6 women), 8 part-time/adjunct (5 women). *Computer facilities:* Computer purchase and lease plans are available. 273 computers available on campus for general student use. A campuswide network can be accessed from student residence rooms and from off campus. Internet access is available. *Library facilities:* D. Leonard Corgan Library. *Graduate expenses:* Tuition: full-time $22,760; part-time $560 per credit. Required fees: $800. *General application contact:* Dr. Elizabeth S. Lott, Director of Graduate Programs, 570-208-5991.

Program in Physician Assistant Studies
Dr. Elizabeth S. Lott, Director of Graduate Programs
Program in:
  physician assistant studies • MSPAS

Program in Reading
Dr. Elizabeth S. Lott, Director of Graduate Programs
Program in:
  reading • M Ed

William G. McGowan School of Business
Dr. John J. Ryan, Interim Director
Program in:
  health care administration • MS

■ KUTZTOWN UNIVERSITY OF PENNSYLVANIA
Kutztown, PA 19530-0730
http://www.kutztown.edu/

State-supported, coed, comprehensive institution. CGS member. *Enrollment:* 9,008 graduate, professional, and undergraduate students; 242 full-time matriculated graduate/professional students (154 women), 708 part-time matriculated graduate/professional students (521 women). *Graduate faculty:* 15 full-time (7 women), 71 part-time/adjunct (32 women). *Computer facilities:* 650 computers available on campus for general student use. A campuswide network can be accessed from student residence rooms and from off campus. Internet access and online class registration are available. *Library facilities:* Rohrbach Library. *Graduate expenses:* Tuition, state resident: full-time $5,518; part-time $307 per credit. Tuition, nonresident: full-time $8,830; part-time $491 per credit. Required fees: $1,098. *General application contact:* Dr. Charles Cullum, Dean of Graduate Studies and Extended Learning, 610-683-4201.

Find an in-depth description at www.petersons.com/gradchannel.

College of Graduate Studies and Extended Learning
Dr. Charles Cullum, Dean of Graduate Studies and Extended Learning
Programs in:
  agency counseling • MA
  counselor education • M Ed
  marital and family therapy • MA
  student affairs in higher education • M Ed

College of Business
Dr. Eileen Shultz, Dean
Programs in:
  business • MBA
  business administration • MBA

College of Education
Dr. Regis Bernhardt, Dean
Programs in:
  biology • M Ed
  curriculum and instruction • M Ed
  early childhood education • Certificate
  education • M Ed, MLS, Certificate
  elementary education • M Ed, Certificate
  English • M Ed
  instructional technology • M Ed, Certificate
  library science • MLS, Certificate
  mathematics • M Ed
  reading • M Ed
  secondary education • Certificate
  social studies • M Ed
  special education • Certificate

College of Liberal Arts and Sciences
Dr. Edward Simpson, Dean
Programs in:
  electronic media • MS
  English • MA
  liberal arts and sciences • MA, MPA, MS, MSW, Certificate
  mathematics and computer science • MS
  public administration • MPA
  school nursing • Certificate
  social work • MSW

College of Visual and Performing Arts
Dr. William Mowder, Dean
Programs in:
  art education • M Ed, Certificate
  visual and performing arts • M Ed, Certificate

Pennsylvania

■ LA ROCHE COLLEGE
Pittsburgh, PA 15237-5898
http://www.laroche.edu/

Independent-religious, coed, comprehensive institution. *Enrollment:* 1,771 graduate, professional, and undergraduate students; 101 full-time matriculated graduate/professional students (48 women), 119 part-time matriculated graduate/professional students (82 women). *Graduate faculty:* 7 full-time (5 women), 11 part-time/adjunct (5 women). *Computer facilities:* 200 computers available on campus for general student use. A campuswide network can be accessed from student residence rooms and from off campus. Internet access and online class registration are available. *Library facilities:* John J. Wright Library. *Graduate expenses:* Tuition: full-time $8,730; part-time $485 per credit. *General application contact:* Director of Admissions for Graduate and Continuing Education, 412-536-1265.

Find an in-depth description at www.petersons.com/gradchannel.

Graduate Studies
Dr. Howard Ishiyama, Vice President for Academic Affairs and Graduate Dean
Programs in:
community health nursing • MSN
family nurse practitioner • MSN
human resources management • MS
nurse anesthesia • MS
nursing management • MSN

■ LA SALLE UNIVERSITY
Philadelphia, PA 19141-1199
http://www.lasalle.edu/

Independent-religious, coed, comprehensive institution. *Computer facilities:* 350 computers available on campus for general student use. A campuswide network can be accessed from student residence rooms and from off campus. Internet access and online class registration are available. *Library facilities:* Connelly Library. *General application contact:* Director of Marketing/Graduate Enrollment, 215-951-1946.

School of Arts and Sciences
Programs in:
arts and sciences • MA, MS, Psy D
bilingual/bicultural studies (Spanish) • MA
Central and Eastern European studies • MA
clinical psychology • Psy D
clinical-counseling psychology • MA
computer information science • MS
education • MA
family psychology • Psy D
information technology leadership • MS
pastoral studies • MA
professional communication • MA
rehabilitation psychology • Psy D
religion • MA
theological studies • MA

School of Business Administration
Program in:
business administration • MBA, MS, Certificate

School of Nursing
Programs in:
adult health and illness, clinical nurse specialist • MSN
clinical research • Certificate
nursing administration • MSN
nursing education • Certificate
nursing informatics • Certificate
primary care of adults-nurse practitioner • MSN
public health nursing • MSN
school nurse • Certificate
speech-language-hearing science • MS
wound, ostomy, and continence nursing • MSN, Certificate

■ LEBANON VALLEY COLLEGE
Annville, PA 17003-1400
http://www.lvc.edu/

Independent-religious, coed, comprehensive institution. *Enrollment:* 1,906 graduate, professional, and undergraduate students; 248 part-time matriculated graduate/professional students (144 women). *Graduate faculty:* 3 full-time (1 woman), 27 part-time/adjunct (8 women). *Computer facilities:* 175 computers available on campus for general student use. A campuswide network can be accessed from student residence rooms and from off campus. Internet access and online class registration are available. *Library facilities:* Bishop Library. *Graduate expenses:* Tuition: part-time $345 per credit hour. *General application contact:* Dr. Nancy J. Aumann, Director of Graduate Studies and Continuing Education, 717-867-6213.

Graduate Studies and Continuing Education
Dr. Nancy J. Aumann, Director of Graduate Studies and Continuing Education
Programs in:
business administration • MBA
music education • MME
science education • MSE

■ LEHIGH UNIVERSITY
Bethlehem, PA 18015-3094
http://www.lehigh.edu/

Independent, coed, university. CGS member. *Enrollment:* 6,732 graduate, professional, and undergraduate students; 909 full-time matriculated graduate/professional students (382 women), 1,144 part-time matriculated graduate/professional students (544 women). *Graduate faculty:* 430 full-time (100 women), 117 part-time/adjunct (47 women). *Computer facilities:* 572 computers available on campus for general student use. A campuswide network can be accessed from student residence rooms and from off campus. Internet access and online class registration are available. *Library facilities:* E. W. Fairchild-Martindale Library plus 1 other. *Graduate expenses:* Tuition: full-time $16,920; part-time $940 per credit hour. Required fees: $200. Tuition and fees vary according to degree level and program.

College of Arts and Sciences
Dr. Carl Moses, Interim Dean
Programs in:
American studies • MA
applied mathematics • MS, PhD
arts and sciences • MA, MS, DA, PhD
biochemistry • PhD
chemistry • MS, DA, PhD
earth and environmental sciences • MS, PhD
English • MA, PhD
experimental psychology • MS, PhD
history • MA, PhD
integrative biology • PhD
mathematics • MS, PhD
molecular biology • PhD
photonics • MS
physics • MS, PhD
political science • MA
sociology and anthropology • MA
statistics • MS

College of Business and Economics
Kathleen A. Trexler, Associate Dean and Director
Programs in:
accounting • MS
accounting and information analysis • MS
analytical finance • MS
business • PhD
business administration • MBA
economics • MS, PhD
entreprenuership • Certificate
health and bio-pharmaceutical economics • MS
organizational leadership • Certificate
project management • Certificate
supply chain management • Certificate

Pennsylvania

Lehigh University (continued)
College of Education
Dr. Sally A. White, Dean
Programs in:
  counseling and human services • M Ed
  counseling psychology • M Ed, PhD, Certificate
  education • M Ed, MA, MS, Ed D, PhD, Certificate, Ed S
  educational leadership • M Ed, Ed D, Certificate
  educational technology • MS, Ed D
  elementary education • M Ed, Certificate
  school counseling • M Ed, Certificate
  school psychology • PhD, Certificate, Ed S
  secondary education • M Ed, MA, Certificate
  special education • M Ed, PhD, Certificate
  technology–based teacher education • M Ed, Certificate
  technology-based teacher education • MA

P.C. Rossin College of Engineering and Applied Science
Dr. John P. Coulter, Associate Dean of Graduate Studies and Research
Programs in:
  analytical finance • MS
  applied mathematics • MS, PhD
  chemical engineering • M Eng, MS, PhD
  civil and environmental engineering • M Eng, MS, PhD
  computer engineering • MS, PhD
  computer science • MS, PhD
  electrical engineering • M Eng, MS, PhD
  engineering • MS
  engineering and applied science • M Eng, MS, PhD
  industrial engineering • M Eng, MS, PhD
  information and systems engineering • MS
  management science • MS
  manufacturing systems • MS
  materials science and engineering • M Eng, PhD
  mechanical engineering • M Eng, MS, PhD
  mechanics • M Eng, MS, PhD
  photonics • MS
  quality engineering • MS

Center for Polymer Science and Engineering
Dr. Raymond A. Pearson, Director
Program in:
  polymer science and engineering • MS, PhD

■ **LINCOLN UNIVERSITY**
Lincoln University, PA 19352
http://www.lincoln.edu/

State-related, coed, comprehensive institution. *Computer facilities:* Computer purchase and lease plans are available. 210 computers available on campus for general student use. A campuswide network can be accessed from student residence rooms and from off campus. Internet access is available. *Library facilities:* Langston Hughes Memorial Library. *General application contact:* Acting Director, Graduate Program in Human Services, 610-932-8300 Ext. 3360.

Graduate Program in Human Services
Program in:
  human services • M Hum Svcs

■ **LOCK HAVEN UNIVERSITY OF PENNSYLVANIA**
Lock Haven, PA 17745-2390
http://www.lhup.edu/

State-supported, coed, comprehensive institution. *Enrollment:* 4,908 graduate, professional, and undergraduate students; 114 full-time matriculated graduate/professional students (71 women), 76 part-time matriculated graduate/professional students (59 women). *Graduate faculty:* 5 full-time (2 women), 22 part-time/adjunct (7 women). *Computer facilities:* 270 computers available on campus for general student use. A campuswide network can be accessed from student residence rooms and from off campus. Internet access and online class registration are available. *Library facilities:* Stevenson Library. *Graduate expenses:* Tuition, state resident: full-time $5,518; part-time $307 per credit. Tuition, nonresident: full-time $8,830; part-time $491 per credit. Required fees: $822; $89 per credit. Tuition and fees vary according to course load. *General application contact:* C. Ginger Frankenberger, Secretary, Enrollment Services Office, 570-893-2124.

Office of Graduate Studies
Dr. Sue Malin, Director
Programs in:
  curriculum and instruction • M Ed
  liberal arts • MLA
  physician assistant in rural primary care • MHS

■ **MANSFIELD UNIVERSITY OF PENNSYLVANIA**
Mansfield, PA 16933
http://www.mansfield.edu/

State-supported, coed, comprehensive institution. *Enrollment:* 3,520 graduate, professional, and undergraduate students; 88 full-time matriculated graduate/professional students (59 women), 264 part-time matriculated graduate/professional students (223 women). *Graduate faculty:* 42 full-time (19 women), 13 part-time/adjunct (11 women). *Computer facilities:* Computer purchase and lease plans are available. 550 computers available on campus for general student use. A campuswide network can be accessed from student residence rooms and from off campus. Internet access is available. *Library facilities:* North Hall Library. *Graduate expenses:* Tuition, state resident: full-time $2,759. Tuition, nonresident: full-time $4,415. Tuition and fees vary according to course load. *General application contact:* Dr. Nancy J. Cooledge, Director of Teacher Education, 570-662-4565.

Graduate Studies
Dr. Nancy J. Cooledge, Director of Teacher Education
Programs in:
  art education • M Ed
  band conducting • MA
  choral conducting • MA
  elementary education • M Ed
  performance • MA
  school library and information technologies • MS
  secondary education • MS

■ **MARYWOOD UNIVERSITY**
Scranton, PA 18509-1598
http://www.marywood.edu/

Independent-religious, coed, comprehensive institution. *Enrollment:* 3,136 graduate, professional, and undergraduate students; 398 full-time matriculated graduate/professional students (310 women), 652 part-time matriculated graduate/professional students (495 women). *Graduate faculty:* 39 full-time (25 women). *Computer facilities:* 367 computers available on campus for general student use. A campuswide network can be accessed from student residence rooms and from off campus. Internet access and online class registration are available. *Library facilities:* Learning Resources Center plus 1 other. *Graduate expenses:* Tuition: part-time $584 per credit. *General application contact:* Deborah M. Flynn, Coordinator of Admissions, 570-340-6002.

Pennsylvania

Academic Affairs
Dr. Patricia Ann Matthews, Vice President for Academic Affairs
Programs in:
  addiction • MA
  advertising design • MFA
  art education • MA
  art therapy • MA
  business administration • MS
  child clinical/school psychology • MA
  church music • MA
  clay • MA, MFA
  clinical psychology • Psy D
  clinical services • MA
  communication arts • MA
  counselor education-elementary • MS
  counselor education-secondary • MS
  creative arts and management • MA, MBA, MFA, MS
  criminal justice • MPA, MS
  e-business • MS
  early childhood intervention • MS
  education • M Ed
  education and human development • M Ed, MA, MAT, MS, PhD, Psy D
  elementary education • MAT, MS
  fibers • MFA
  finance and investments • MBA
  foods and nutrition • MS
  general • MA
  general management • MBA
  general theoretical psychology • MA
  graphic design • MFA
  health and human services • MHSA, MPA, MS, MSW, PhD
  health communication • MS
  health services administration • MHSA
  human development • PhD
  human development (health promotion) • PhD
  human development (social work) • PhD
  information sciences • MS
  instructional technology • MS
  interdisciplinary • MA
  liberal arts and sciences • MS
  library science/information science • MS
  long term care • MHSA
  managed care • MHSA
  management information systems • MBA, MS
  media management • MA
  mental health counseling • MA
  metals • MFA
  music education • MA
  musicology • MA
  nursing administration • MS
  painting • MA, MFA
  photography • MFA
  physician assistant studies • MS
  printmaking • MA, MFA
  production • MA
  psychology • MA
  public administration • MPA
  reading education • MS
  school leadership • MS
  social work • MSW
  special education • MS
  special education administration and supervision • MS
  speech language pathology • MS
  studio art • MA
  visual arts • MFA

■ MILLERSVILLE UNIVERSITY OF PENNSYLVANIA
Millersville, PA 17551-0302
http://www.millersville.edu/

State-supported, coed, comprehensive institution. CGS member. *Enrollment:* 7,861 graduate, professional, and undergraduate students; 103 full-time matriculated graduate/professional students (79 women), 418 part-time matriculated graduate/professional students (298 women). *Graduate faculty:* 212 full-time (99 women), 91 part-time/adjunct (50 women). *Computer facilities:* Computer purchase and lease plans are available. 470 computers available on campus for general student use. A campuswide network can be accessed from student residence rooms and from off campus. Internet access and online class registration are available. *Library facilities:* Helen A. Ganser Library. *Graduate expenses:* Tuition, state resident: full-time $5,518; part-time $307 per credit. Tuition, nonresident: full-time $8,830; part-time $491 per credit. Required fees: $81 per credit. Tuition and fees vary according to course load. *General application contact:* Dr. Steven R. Centola, Acting Dean of Graduate Studies, Professional Training and Education, 717-872-3030.

Graduate School
Dr. Steven R. Centola, Acting Dean of Graduate Studies, Professional Training and Education

School of Education
Dr. Jane S. Bray, Dean
Programs in:
  athletic coaching • M Ed
  athletic management • M Ed
  clinical psychology • MS
  counseling and human development • M Ed
  early childhood education • M Ed
  education • M Ed, MS
  elementary education • M Ed
  industrial arts/technology education • M Ed
  leadership for teaching and learning • M Ed
  psychology • MS
  reading education • M Ed
  reading/language arts education • M Ed
  school counseling • M Ed
  school psychology • MS
  special education • M Ed
  sport management • M Ed

School of Humanities and Social Sciences
Dr. John N. Short, Acting Dean
Programs in:
  art education • M Ed
  business administration • MBA
  English • MA
  English education • M Ed
  French • M Ed, MA
  German • M Ed, MA
  history • MA
  humanities and social sciences • M Ed, MA, MBA
  Spanish • M Ed, MA

School of Science and Mathematics
Dr. Robert T. Smith, Acting Dean
Programs in:
  biology • MS
  mathematics • M Ed
  nursing • MSN
  science and mathematics • M Ed, MS, MSN

■ THE PENNSYLVANIA STATE UNIVERSITY AT ERIE, THE BEHREND COLLEGE
Erie, PA 16563-0001
http://www.psu.edu/

State-related, coed, comprehensive institution. *Enrollment:* 3,683 graduate, professional, and undergraduate students; 118 matriculated graduate/professional students. *Graduate faculty:* 50. *Computer facilities:* Computer purchase and lease plans are available. 448 computers available on campus for general student use. A campuswide network can be accessed from student residence rooms and from off campus. Internet access and online class registration are available. *Graduate expenses:* Tuition, state resident: full-time $1,036; part-time $443 per credit. Tuition, nonresident: full-time $17,082; part-time $712 per credit. *General application contact:* Ann M. Burbules, Graduate Admissions Counselor, 814-898-6100.

Graduate School
Dr. John D. Burke, CEO and Dean
Programs in:
  business administration • MBA
  manufacturing systems engineering • M Eng
  project management • MPM

Peterson's Graduate Schools in the U.S. 2006

Pennsylvania

■ THE PENNSYLVANIA STATE UNIVERSITY GREAT VALLEY CAMPUS
Malvern, PA 19355-1488
http://www.gv.psu.edu/

State-related, coed, graduate-only institution. *Graduate faculty:* 42 full-time (15 women), 58 part-time/adjunct (14 women). *Computer facilities:* 343 computers available on campus for general student use. A campuswide network can be accessed. Internet access and online class registration are available. *Library facilities:* Great Valley Library. *Graduate expenses:* Tuition, state resident: part-time $540 per credit. Tuition, nonresident: part-time $925 per credit. *General application contact:* Dr. Kathy Mingioni, Assistant Director of Admissions, 610-648-3315.

Find an in-depth description at www.petersons.com/gradchannel.

Graduate Studies and Continuing Education
Dr. William D. Milheim, Campus Executive Officer and Associate Dean

College of Education
Dr. Arlene Mitchell, Academic Division Head
Programs in:
curriculum and instruction • M Ed
instructional systems • M Ed, MS
special education • M Ed, MS

School of Graduate Professional Studies
Programs in:
biotechnology and health industry management • MBA
business administration • MBA
graduate professional studies • M Eng, MBA, MLD, MS, MSE
information science • MS
leadership development • MLD
software engineering • MSE
systems engineering • M Eng

■ THE PENNSYLVANIA STATE UNIVERSITY HARRISBURG CAMPUS OF THE CAPITAL COLLEGE
Middletown, PA 17057-4898
http://www.psu.edu/

State-related, coed, comprehensive institution. *Enrollment:* 3,441 graduate, professional, and undergraduate students; 1,437 matriculated graduate/professional students. *Graduate faculty:* 228. *Computer facilities:* Computer purchase and lease plans are available. 132 computers available on campus for general student use. A campuswide network can be accessed from student residence rooms and from off campus. Internet access and online class registration are available. *Graduate expenses:* Tuition, state resident: full-time $10,010; part-time $417 per credit. Tuition, nonresident: full-time $16,512; part-time $668 per credit. *General application contact:* Dr. Thomas I. Streveler, Director of Enrollment Services, 717-948-6250.

Find an in-depth description at www.petersons.com/gradchannel.

Graduate School
Dr. Madlyn L. Hanes, Provost and Dean

School of Behavioral Sciences and Education
Dr. Ernest K. Dishner, Professor
Programs in:
adult education • D Ed
applied behavior analysis • MA
applied clinical psychology • MA
applied psychological research • MA
behavioral sciences and education • M Ed, MA, D Ed
community psychology and social change • MA
health education • M Ed
teaching and curriculum • M Ed
training and development • M Ed

School of Business Administration
Dr. Mukund S. Kulkarni, Associate Professor
Programs in:
business administration • MBA, MSIS
information systems • MSIS

School of Humanities
Dr. Kathryn D. Robinson, Professor
Programs in:
American studies • MA
humanities • MA

School of Public Affairs
Dr. Steven A. Peterson, Professor of Politics
Programs in:
criminal justice • MA
health administration • MHA
public administration • MPA, PhD
public affairs • MA, MHA, MPA, PhD

School of Science, Engineering and Technology
Dr. Omid Ansary, Director
Programs in:
computer science • MS
electrical engineering • M Eng
engineering science • M Eng
environmental engineering • M Eng
environmental pollution control • M Eng, MEPC, MS

■ THE PENNSYLVANIA STATE UNIVERSITY UNIVERSITY PARK CAMPUS
State College, University Park, PA 16802-1503
http://www.psu.edu/

State-related, coed, university. CGS member. *Enrollment:* 41,795 graduate, professional, and undergraduate students; 6,203 matriculated graduate/professional students. *Graduate faculty:* 2,872. *Computer facilities:* 3,589 computers available on campus for general student use. A campuswide network can be accessed from student residence rooms and from off campus. Internet access and online class registration are available. *Library facilities:* Pattee Library plus 7 others. *Graduate expenses:* Tuition, state resident: full-time $10,010; part-time $417 per credit. Tuition, nonresident: full-time $19,830; part-time $826 per credit. Full-time tuition and fees vary according to course level, course load, campus/location and program. *General application contact:* Cynthia E. Nicosia, Director of Graduate Enrollment Services, 814-865-1795.

Find an in-depth description at www.petersons.com/gradchannel.

Graduate School
Dr. Eva J. Pell, Vice President, Research and Dean of the Graduate School
Programs in:
acoustics • M Eng, MS, PhD
bioengineering • MS, PhD
biotechnology • MS
ecology • MS, PhD
environmental pollution control • M Eng, MEPC, MS
genetics • MS, PhD
integrative biosciences • MS, PhD
mass communications • PhD
materials • MS, PhD
nutrition • M Ed, MS, PhD
physiology • MS, PhD
plant physiology • MS, PhD
quality and manufacturing management • MMM
science and biotechnology • MS

College of Agricultural Sciences
Dr. Robert D. Steele, Dean
Programs in:
agricultural and biological engineering • MS, PhD
agricultural and extension education • M Ed, MS, D Ed, PhD
agricultural sciences • M Agr, M Ed, MFR, MS, D Ed, PhD

agricultural, environmental and regional economics • M Agr, MS, PhD
agronomy • M Agr, MS, PhD
animal science • M Agr, MS, PhD
community and economic development • MS
entomology • M Agr, MS, PhD
food science • MS, PhD
forest resources • M Agr, MFR, MS, PhD
horticulture • M Agr, MS, PhD
pathobiology • MS, PhD
plant pathology • M Agr, MS, PhD
rural sociology • M Agr, MS, PhD
soil science • M Agr, MS, PhD
wildlife and fisheries sciences • M Agr, MFR, MS, PhD
youth and family education • M Ed

College of Arts and Architecture
Dr. Richard W. Durst, Dean
Programs in:
architecture • M Arch, MS
art • MA, MFA
art education • M Ed, MS, PhD
art history • MA, PhD
arts and architecture • M Arch, M Ed, M Mus, MA, MFA, MLA, MME, MS, PhD
ceramics • MFA
composition/theory • M Mus
conducting • M Mus
drawing/painting • MFA
graphic design • MFA
landscape architecture • MLA
metals • MFA
music and music education • M Mus, MA, MME, PhD
music education • MME, PhD
music theory • MA
music theory and history • MA
musicology • MA
performance • M Mus
photography • MFA
piano pedagogy and performance • M Mus
printmaking • MFA
sculpture • MFA
theatre arts • MFA
voice performance and pedagogy • M Mus

College of Communications
Dr. Douglas A. Anderson, Dean
Programs in:
communications • MA, PhD
mass communications • PhD
media studies • MA
telecommunications studies • MA

College of Earth and Mineral Sciences
Dr. Eric A. Barron, Dean
Programs in:
ceramic science • MS, PhD
earth and mineral sciences • M Eng, MS, PhD
fuel science • MS, PhD
geo-environmental engineering • MS, PhD
geochemistry • MS, PhD
geography • MS, PhD
geology • MS, PhD
geophysics • MS, PhD
industrial health and safety • MS
metals science and engineering • MS, PhD
meteorology • MS, PhD
mineral processing • MS, PhD
mining engineering • M Eng, MS, PhD
oil and gas engineering management • M Eng
petroleum and natural gas engineering • MS, PhD
polymer science • MS, PhD

College of Education
Dr. David H. Monk, Dean
Programs in:
adult education • M Ed, D Ed
bilingual education • M Ed, MS, D Ed, PhD
counseling psychology • PhD
counselor education • M Ed, MS, D Ed, PhD
early childhood education • M Ed, MS, D Ed, PhD
education • M Ed, MA, MS, D Ed, PhD
educational leadership • M Ed, MS, D Ed, PhD
educational psychology • MS, PhD
educational theory and policy • MA, PhD
elementary counseling • M Ed, MS
elementary education • M Ed, MS, D Ed, PhD
higher education • M Ed, D Ed, PhD
instructional systems • M Ed, MS, D Ed, PhD
language arts and reading • M Ed, MS, D Ed, PhD
school psychology • M Ed, MS, PhD
science education • M Ed, MS, D Ed, PhD
social studies education • MS, D Ed, PhD
special education • M Ed, MS, PhD
supervisor and curriculum development • M Ed, MS, D Ed, PhD
workforce education and development • M Ed, MS, D Ed, PhD

College of Engineering
Dr. David N. Wormley, Dean
Programs in:
aerospace engineering • M Eng, MS, PhD
architectural engineering • M Eng, MAE, MS, PhD
chemical engineering • MS, PhD
civil engineering • M Eng, MS, PhD
computer science and engineering • M Eng, MS, PhD
electrical engineering • M Eng, MS, PhD
engineering • M Eng, MAE, MS, PhD
engineering mechanics • M Eng, MS
engineering science • MS
engineering science and mechanics • PhD
environmental engineering • M Eng, MS, PhD
industrial engineering • M Eng, MS, PhD
manufacturing engineering • M Eng
mechanical engineering • M Eng, MS, PhD
nuclear engineering • M Eng, MS, PhD
structural engineering • M Eng, MS, PhD
transportation and highway engineering • M Eng, MS, PhD
water resources engineering • M Eng, MS, PhD

College of Health and Human Development
Dr. Raymond T. Coward, Dean
Programs in:
biobehavioral health • MS, PhD
communication sciences and disorders • M Ed, MS, PhD
health and human development • M Ed, MHA, MHRIM, MS, PhD
health policy and administration • MHA, MS, PhD
hotel, restaurant, and institutional management • MHRIM, MS, PhD
hotel, restaurant, and recreation management • M Ed, MHRIM, MS, PhD
human development and family studies • MS, PhD
human nutrition • M Ed
kinesiology • MS, PhD
leisure studies • M Ed, MS, PhD
nursing • MS, PhD
nutrition • MS, PhD

College of Liberal Arts
Dr. Susan Welch, Dean
Programs in:
anthropology • MA, PhD
applied linguistics • PhD
classical American philosophy • MA, PhD
clinical psychology • MS, PhD
cognitive psychology • MS, PhD
communication arts and sciences • MA, PhD
comparative literature • MA, PhD
contemporary European philosophy • MA, PhD
crime, law, and justice • MA, PhD
developmental psychology • MS, PhD
economics • MA, PhD
English • M Ed, MA, MFA, PhD
French • MA, PhD
German • MA, PhD

Pennsylvania

The Pennsylvania State University University Park Campus (continued)
  history • M Ed, MA, PhD
  history of philosophy • MA, PhD
  industrial relations and human resources • MS
  industrial/organizational psychology • MS, PhD
  liberal arts • M Ed, MA, MFA, MS, PhD
  political science • MA, PhD
  psychobiology • MS, PhD
  Russian and comparative literature • MA
  social psychology • MS, PhD
  sociology • MA, PhD
  Spanish • M Ed, MA, PhD
  teaching English as a second language • MA

Eberly College of Science
Dr. Daniel J. Larson, Dean
Programs in:
  applied statistics • MAS
  astronomy and astrophysics • MS, PhD
  biochemistry, microbiology, and molecular biology • MS, PhD
  biology • MS, PhD
  cell and developmental biology • PhD
  chemistry • MS, PhD
  mathematics • M Ed, MA, D Ed, PhD
  molecular evolutionary biology • MS, PhD
  physics • M Ed, MS, D Ed, PhD
  science • M Ed, MA, MAS, MS, D Ed, PhD
  statistics • MA, MS, PhD

The Mary Jean and Frank P. Smeal College of Business Administration
Dr. Judy D. Olian, Dean
Programs in:
  accounting • MS, PhD
  business administration • MBA, MS, PhD
  business administration, executive • MBA
  business logistics • MS
  finance • PhD
  management and organization • PhD
  management science/operations/logistics • PhD
  marketing • PhD
  real estate • PhD
  supply chain and information systems • MS, PhD

School of Information Sciences and Technology
Dr. James B. Thomas, Dean
Program in:
  information sciences and technology • MS, PhD

■ **PHILADELPHIA UNIVERSITY**
Philadelphia, PA 19144-5497
http://www.philau.edu/

Independent, coed, comprehensive institution. *Enrollment:* 3,093 graduate, professional, and undergraduate students; 112 full-time matriculated graduate/professional students (84 women), 339 part-time matriculated graduate/professional students (192 women). *Graduate faculty:* 37 full-time (8 women), 50 part-time/adjunct (12 women). *Computer facilities:* 400 computers available on campus for general student use. A campuswide network can be accessed from student residence rooms and from off campus. Internet access, on-line registration for advanced workshops and seminars are available. *Library facilities:* Paul J. Gutman Library plus 1 other. *Graduate expenses:* Tuition: part-time $587 per credit. *General application contact:* William H. Firman, Director of Graduate Admissions, 215-951-2943.

School of Business
Dr. Elmore Alexander, Dean
Programs in:
  accounting • MBA
  business • MBA, MS
  business administration • MBA
  finance • MBA
  health care management • MBA
  international business • MBA
  marketing • MBA
  taxation • MS

School of Design and Communication
Programs in:
  design and communication • MS
  digital design • MS
  instructional design and technology • MS

School of Science and Health
Matt Dane Baker, Interim Dean
Programs in:
  midwifery • MS
  occupational therapy • MS
  physician assistant studies • MS
  science and health • MS

School of Textiles and Materials Science
Dr. David Brookstein, Dean of School of Textiles and Materials Technology
Programs in:
  fashion-apparel studies • MS
  textile design • MS
  textile engineering • MS
  textiles and materials science • MS

■ **POINT PARK UNIVERSITY**
Pittsburgh, PA 15222-1984
http://www.ppc.edu/

Independent, coed, comprehensive institution. *Enrollment:* 3,226 graduate, professional, and undergraduate students; 192 full-time matriculated graduate/professional students (108 women), 204 part-time matriculated graduate/professional students (110 women). *Graduate faculty:* 31 full-time, 75 part-time/adjunct. *Computer facilities:* 183 computers available on campus for general student use. A campuswide network can be accessed from student residence rooms and from off campus. Internet access is available. *Library facilities:* The Library Center. *Graduate expenses:* Tuition: full-time $10,054; part-time $457 per credit. Required fees: $15 per credit. *General application contact:* Kathryn B. Ballas, Director, Adult Enrollment, 412-392-3812.

School of Business
Margaret Gilfillan, Associate Professor
Program in:
  business • MBA

■ **ROBERT MORRIS UNIVERSITY**
Moon Township, PA 15108-1189
http://www.robert-morris.edu/

Independent, coed, comprehensive institution. *Enrollment:* 4,816 graduate, professional, and undergraduate students; 1,081 part-time matriculated graduate/professional students (508 women). *Graduate faculty:* 52 full-time (11 women), 31 part-time/adjunct (8 women). *Computer facilities:* 300 computers available on campus for general student use. A campuswide network can be accessed from student residence rooms and from off campus. Internet access and online class registration are available. *Library facilities:* Robert Morris University Library. *Graduate expenses:* Tuition: part-time $486 per credit. Part-time tuition and fees vary according to degree level and program. *General application contact:* Kellie L. Laurenzi, Assistant Dean, Enrollment Services, 412-262-8235.

Find an in-depth description at www.petersons.com/gradchannel.

Graduate Studies
Dr. William J. Katip, Senior Vice President for Academic and Student Affairs

School of Business
Dr. Derya A. Jacobs, Acting Dean
Programs in:
  accounting • MS
  business administration and management • MBA
  finance • MS
  nonprofit management • MS
  sport management • MS
  taxation • MS

School of Communications and Information Systems
Dr. David L. Jamison, Dean
Programs in:
  business education • MS
  communications and information systems • MS
  information systems and communications • D Sc
  information systems management • MS
  instructional leadership • MS
  Internet information systems • MS

School of Engineering, Mathematics, Science, and Nursing
Dr. Yildirim Omurtag, Dean
Programs in:
  engineering management • MS
  engineering, mathematics, science, and nursing • MS
  nursing • MS

■ SAINT FRANCIS UNIVERSITY
Loretto, PA 15940-0600
http://www.sfcpa.edu/

Independent-religious, coed, comprehensive institution. *Computer facilities:* 60 computers available on campus for general student use. A campuswide network can be accessed from student residence rooms. *Library facilities:* Pasquerella Library. *General application contact:* Assistant Vice President for Academic Affairs, 814-472-3085.

Business Administration Program
Program in:
  business administration • MBA

Department of Education and Educational Leadership
Dr. Elizabeth Gensante, Director, Graduate Education
Programs in:
  education • M Ed
  leadership • M Ed

Department of Occupational Therapy
Program in:
  occupational therapy • MOT

Department of Physical Therapy
Program in:
  physical therapy • MPT

Department of Physician Assistant Sciences
Albert Simon, Chair
Program in:
  physician assistant sciences • MPAS

Graduate School of Human Resource Management and Industrial Relations
Dr. Philip Benham, Director
Program in:
  human resource management and industrial relations • MHRM

Medical Science Program
Program in:
  medical science • MMS

Occupational Therapy Program
Program in:
  occupational therapy • MOT

■ SAINT JOSEPH'S UNIVERSITY
Philadelphia, PA 19131-1395
http://www.sju.edu/

Independent-religious, coed, comprehensive institution. *Enrollment:* 7,565 graduate, professional, and undergraduate students; 521 full-time matriculated graduate/professional students (310 women), 1,843 part-time matriculated graduate/professional students (1,048 women). *Graduate faculty:* 110 full-time (43 women), 111 part-time/adjunct (50 women). *Computer facilities:* Computer purchase and lease plans are available. 180 computers available on campus for general student use. A campuswide network can be accessed from student residence rooms and from off campus. Internet access and online class registration are available. *Library facilities:* Francis A. Drexel Library plus 1 other. *Graduate expenses:* Tuition: part-time $645 per credit. Part-time tuition and fees vary according to class time, course load, degree level and program. *General application contact:* Susan P. Kassab, Director of Admissions, 610-660-1306.

College of Arts and Sciences
Dr. Robert H. Palestini, Dean
Programs in:
  arts and sciences • MA, MS, Ed D, Certificate, Post-Master's Certificate
  biology • MA, MS
  computer science • MS
  criminal justice • MS
  education • MS, Certificate
  educational leadership • Ed D
  elementary education • MS
  environmental protection • MS
  gerontological counseling • MS
  health administration • MS
  health education • MS
  human services administration • MS
  instructional technology • MS
  mathematics education • MS
  nurse anesthesia • MS
  professional education • MS
  psychology • MS
  public safety • MS, Post-Master's Certificate
  reading • MS
  secondary education • MS
  special education • MS
  training and organization development • MS
  writing studies • MA

Erivan K. Haub School of Business
Dr. Joseph A. DiAngelo, Dean
Programs in:
  accounting • MBA
  business • EMBA, MBA, MS, Post Master's Certificate
  business administration • EMBA
  executive food marketing • MS
  executive pharmaceutical marketing • MBA, Post Master's Certificate
  finance • MBA
  financial services • MS
  general business • MBA
  health and medical services administration • MBA
  human resource management • MS
  information systems • MBA
  international business • MBA
  international marketing • MBA
  management • MBA
  marketing • MBA

■ SHIPPENSBURG UNIVERSITY OF PENNSYLVANIA
Shippensburg, PA 17257-2299
http://www.ship.edu/

State-supported, coed, comprehensive institution. CGS member. *Enrollment:* 7,607 graduate, professional, and undergraduate students; 230 full-time matriculated graduate/professional students (130 women), 628 part-time matriculated graduate/professional students (409 women). *Graduate faculty:* 141 full-time (51 women), 11 part-time/adjunct (5 women). *Computer facilities:* 527 computers available on campus for general student use. A campuswide network can be accessed from student residence rooms and from off campus. Internet access, personal web pages are available. *Library facilities:* Ezra Lehman Memorial Library plus 1 other. *Graduate expenses:* Tuition, state resident: full-time

Peterson's Graduate Schools in the U.S. 2006   www.petersons.com   **533**

Pennsylvania

Shippensburg University of Pennsylvania (continued)
$5,518; part-time $307 per credit hour. Tuition, nonresident: full-time $8,830; part-time $491 per credit hour. Required fees: $25 per credit hour. $162 per semester. Tuition and fees vary according to course load. *General application contact:* Renee Payne, Associate Dean of Graduate Admissions, 717-477-1213.

Find an in-depth description at www.petersons.com/gradchannel.

School of Graduate Studies
Dr. James G. Coolsen, Dean of Graduate Studies and Associate Provost
Program in:
 business administration • MBA

College of Arts and Sciences
Dr. John Benhart, Interim Dean
Programs in:
 applied history • MA
 arts and sciences • MA, MPA, MS
 biology • MS
 communication studies • MS
 computer science • MS
 geoenvironmental studies • MS
 information systems • MS
 organizational development and leadership • MS
 psychology • MS
 public administration • MPA

College of Education and Human Services
Dr. Robert B. Bartos, Dean
Programs in:
 Adlerian studies • Certificate
 administration of justice • MS
 advanced study in counseling • Certificate
 aging • Certificate
 applied gerontology • MS
 counseling • MS
 curriculum and instruction • M Ed
 education and human services • M Ed, MS, Certificate
 guidance and counseling • M Ed
 reading specialist • M Ed
 school administration • M Ed
 special education • M Ed

■ SLIPPERY ROCK UNIVERSITY OF PENNSYLVANIA
Slippery Rock, PA 16057-1383
http://www.sru.edu/

State-supported, coed, comprehensive institution. *Enrollment:* 7,789 graduate, professional, and undergraduate students; 317 full-time matriculated graduate/professional students (207 women), 355 part-time matriculated graduate/professional students (249 women). *Graduate faculty:* 74 full-time (33 women), 3 part-time/adjunct (1 woman). *Computer facilities:* Computer purchase and lease plans are available. 940 computers available on campus for general student use. A campuswide network can be accessed from student residence rooms and from off campus. Internet access and online class registration are available. *Library facilities:* Bailey Library. *Graduate expenses:* Tuition, state resident: full-time $5,518; part-time $307 per credit hour. Tuition, nonresident: full-time $8,830; part-time $491 per credit hour. Required fees: $1,620; $106 per credit hour. Tuition and fees vary according to course load and program. *General application contact:* Dr. Duncan M. Sargent, Director of Graduate Studies, 724-738-2051 Ext. 2116.

Find an in-depth description at www.petersons.com/gradchannel.

Graduate Studies (Recruitment)
Dr. Duncan M. Sargent, Director of Graduate Studies

College of Business, Information, and Social Sciences
Dr. Bruce Russell, Dean
Program in:
 business, information, and social sciences • MS

College of Education
Dr. C. Jay Hertzog, Dean
Programs in:
 community counseling • MA
 early childhood education • M Ed
 education • M Ed, MA, MS
 elementary guidance and counseling • M Ed
 master teacher • M Ed
 math/science • M Ed
 reading • M Ed
 secondary education in math/science • M Ed
 secondary guidance and counseling • M Ed
 sport management • MS
 student personnel • MA
 supervision • M Ed

College of Health, Environment, and Science
Dr. Jane Fulton, Dean
Programs in:
 environmental education • M Ed
 exercise and rehabilitative sciences • MS
 health, environment, and science • M Ed, MS, MSN, DPT
 nursing • MSN
 physical therapy • DPT
 resource management • MS
 sustainable systems • MS

College of Humanities, Fine and Performing Arts
Dr. William McKinney, Dean
Programs in:
 English • MA
 history • MA
 humanities, fine and performing arts • MA

■ TEMPLE UNIVERSITY
Philadelphia, PA 19122-6096
http://www.temple.edu/

State-related, coed, university. CGS member. *Computer facilities:* 2,000 computers available on campus for general student use. A campuswide network can be accessed from student residence rooms and from off campus. Internet access and online class registration, student account and grade information are available. *Library facilities:* Paley Library plus 11 others. *General application contact:* Coordinator, Graduate Admissions and Recruitment, 215-204-1380.

Find an in-depth description at www.petersons.com/gradchannel.

Graduate School

College of Education
Programs in:
 adult and organizational development • Ed M
 counseling psychology • Ed M, PhD
 early childhood education and elementary education • MS
 education • Ed M, MS, Ed D, PhD
 educational administration • Ed M, Ed D
 educational psychology • Ed M, PhD
 kinesiology • PhD
 math/science education • Ed D
 physical education • Ed M
 reading and language education • MS, Ed D
 school psychology • Ed M, PhD
 secondary education • MS
 special education • MS
 urban education • Ed M, Ed D
 vocational education • MS

College of Liberal Arts
Programs in:
 African-American studies • MA, PhD
 anthropology • MA, PhD
 clinical psychology • PhD
 cognitive psychology • PhD
 creative writing • MA
 criminal justice • MA, PhD
 developmental psychology • PhD
 English • MA, PhD
 experimental psychology • PhD
 geography • MA
 history • MA, PhD
 liberal arts • MA, MLA, PhD

philosophy • MA, PhD
political science • MA, PhD
religion • MA, PhD
social and organizational psychology • PhD
sociology • MA, PhD
Spanish • MA, PhD
urban studies • MA

College of Science and Technology
Programs in:
applied and computational mathematics • MA, PhD
biology • MA, PhD
chemistry • MA, PhD
civil and environmental engineering • MSE
computer and information sciences • MS, PhD
electrical and computer engineering • MSE
engineering • PhD
environmental health sciences • MS
geology • MA
mechanical engineering • MSE
physics • MA, PhD
pure mathematics • MA, PhD
science and technology • MA, MS, MSE, PhD

Esther Boyer College of Music
Programs in:
composition • MM, DMA
dance • M Ed, MFA, PhD
music • M Ed, MFA, MM, MMT, DMA, PhD
music education • MM, PhD
music history • MM
music performance • MM, DMA
music theory • MM
music therapy • MMT, PhD

Fox School of Business and Management
Dr. M. Moshe Porat, Dean
Programs in:
accounting • MBA, PhD
accounting and financial management • MS
actuarial science • MS
business administration • EMBA, IMBA, MBA, MS
business and management • EMBA, IMBA, MA, MBA, MS, PhD
e-business • MBA, MS
economics • MA, MBA, PhD
finance • MBA, MS, PhD
general and strategic management • MBA, PhD
healthcare financial management • MS
healthcare management • MBA, PhD
human resource administration • MBA, MS, PhD
international business • IMBA
international business administration • PhD
management information systems • MBA, MS, PhD
management science/operations management • MBA, MS
management science/operations research • PhD
marketing • MBA, MS, PhD
risk management and insurance • MBA
risk, insurance, and health-care management • PhD
statistics • MBA, MS, PhD
tourism • PhD

School of Communications and Theater
Programs in:
acting • MFA
broadcasting, telecommunications and mass media • MA
communications and theater • MA, MFA, MJ, PhD
design • MFA
directing • MFA
film and media arts • MFA
journalism • MJ
mass media and communication • PhD

School of Social Administration
Programs in:
social administration • MSW
social work • MSW

School of Tourism and Hospitality Management
Programs in:
sport and recreation administration • Ed M
tourism and hospitality management • Ed M, MTHM

Tyler School of Art
Programs in:
art • M Ed, MA, MFA, PhD
art education • M Ed
art history • MA, PhD
ceramics • MFA
fibers • MFA
glass • MFA
metalworking • MFA
painting/drawing • MFA
photography • MFA
printmaking • MFA
sculpture • MFA
visual design • MFA

Health Sciences Center
Program in:
health sciences • DMD, DPM, MD, Pharm D, Ed M, MA, MOT, MPH, MPT, MS, MSN, PhD, Certificate

College of Health Professions
Dr. Donna Weiss, Associate Dean
Programs in:
applied communication • MA
communication sciences • PhD
community health education • MPH
environmental health • MS
health professions • Ed M, MA, MOT, MPH, MPT, MS, MSN, PhD
health studies • Ed M, MPH, PhD
linguistics • MA
nursing • MSN
occupational therapy • MOT, MS
physical therapy • MPT, MS, PhD
school health education • Ed M
speech, language, and hearing • MA
therapeutic recreation • Ed M

School of Dentistry
Thomas E. Rams, Associate Dean for Advanced Education
Programs in:
advanced education in general dentistry • Certificate
dentistry • DMD, MS, Certificate
endodontology • Certificate
oral and maxillofacial surgery • Certificate
oral biology • MS
orthodontics • Certificate
periodontology • Certificate
prosthodontics • Certificate

School of Medicine
Programs in:
anatomy and cell biology • PhD
biochemistry • MS, PhD
medicine • MD, MS, PhD
microbiology and immunology • MS, PhD
molecular biology and genetics • PhD
pathology and laboratory medicine • PhD
pharmacology • MS, PhD
physiology • MS, PhD

School of Pharmacy
Programs in:
medicinal and pharmaceutical chemistry • MS, PhD
pharmaceutics • MS, PhD
pharmacy • Pharm D, MS, PhD
quality assurance/regulatory affairs • MS

School of Podiatric Medicine
Program in:
podiatric medicine • DPM

James E. Beasley School of Law
Programs in:
law • JD
taxation • LL M
transnational law • LL M
trial advocacy • LL M

Program in Community and Regional Planning
Program in:
community and regional planning • MS

Pennsylvania

■ UNIVERSITY OF PENNSYLVANIA
Philadelphia, PA 19104
http://www.upenn.edu/

Independent, coed, university. CGS member. *Enrollment:* 19,428 graduate, professional, and undergraduate students; 9,226 full-time matriculated graduate/professional students (4,482 women), 1,733 part-time matriculated graduate/professional students (976 women). *Graduate faculty:* 2,440 full-time (650 women), 2,963 part-time/adjunct (935 women). *Computer facilities:* 1,575 computers available on campus for general student use. A campuswide network can be accessed from student residence rooms and from off campus. Internet access and online class registration are available. *Library facilities:* Van Pelt-Dietrich Library plus 13 others. *Graduate expenses:* Tuition: full-time $28,040; part-time $3,550 per course. Required fees: $1,750; $214 per course. Tuition and fees vary according to degree level, program and student level. *General application contact:* Karen Lawrence, Assistant Vice Provost for Graduate Education, 215-898-1842.

Find an in-depth description at www.petersons.com/gradchannel.

Annenberg School for Communication
Joseph Turow, Graduate Dean
Program in:
 communication • MAC, PhD

School of Design
David Leatherbarrow, Graduate Dean
Programs in:
 architecture • M Arch
 city and regional planning • MCP, PhD, Certificate
 conservation and heritage management • Certificate
 design • M Arch, MCP, MFA, MLA, MS, PhD, Certificate
 fine arts • MFA
 historic conservation • Certificate
 historic preservation • MS
 landscape architecture and regional planning • MLA
 landscape studies • Certificate
 real estate design and development • Certificate
 urban design • Certificate

Law School
Michael A. Fitts, Dean
Program in:
 law • JD, LL CM, LL M, SJD

School of Arts and Sciences
Dr. Walter Licht, Associate Dean
Programs in:
 American civilization • AM, PhD
 ancient history • AM, PhD
 anthropology • AM, MS, PhD
 art and archaeology of the Mediterranean world • AM, PhD
 arts and sciences • AM, M Bioethics, MA, MBA, MES, MGA, MLA, MS, PhD
 Asian and Middle Eastern studies • AM, PhD
 bioethics • M Bioethics
 biology • PhD
 chemistry • MS, PhD
 classical studies • AM, PhD
 comparative literature • AM, PhD
 criminology • MA, MS, PhD
 demography • AM, PhD
 East Asian languages and civilization • AM, PhD
 ecology, evolution and biodiversity • PhD
 economics • AM, PhD
 English • AM, PhD
 folklore and folklife • AM, PhD
 French • AM, PhD
 geology • MS, PhD
 Germanic languages • AM, PhD
 history • AM, PhD
 history and sociology of science • AM, PhD
 history of art • AM, PhD
 international studies • AM
 Italian • AM, PhD
 linguistics • AM, PhD
 literary theory • AM, PhD
 mathematics • AM, PhD
 medical physics • MS
 music • AM, PhD
 near eastern languages and civilization • AM, PhD
 neurobiology and physiology • PhD
 organizational dynamics • MS
 philosophy • AM, PhD
 physics • PhD
 plant and microbial biology • PhD
 political science • AM, PhD
 psychology • PhD
 religious studies • PhD
 sociology • AM, PhD
 South Asian regional studies • AM, PhD
 Spanish • AM, PhD

College of General Studies
Programs in:
 environmental studies • MES
 individualized study • MLA

Fels Center of Government
Program in:
 government • MGA

Joseph H. Lauder Institute of Management and International Studies
Programs in:
 international studies • MA
 management and international studies • MBA

School of Dental Medicine
Program in:
 dental medicine • DMD

School of Engineering and Applied Science
Norm Badler, Graduate Dean
Programs in:
 applied mechanics • MSE, PhD
 bioengineering • MSE, PhD
 biotechnology • MS
 chemical engineering • MSE, PhD
 computer and information science • MCIT, MSE, PhD
 electrical and systems engineering • MSE, PhD
 engineering and applied science • EMBA, MCIT, MS, MSE, PhD, AC
 management of technology • EMBA
 materials science and engineering • MSE, PhD
 mechanical engineering • MSE, PhD
 telecommunications and networking • MSE

School of Medicine
Dr. Arthur M. Rubenstein, Dean
Program in:
 medicine • MD, MS, MSCE, PhD

Biomedical Graduate Studies
Dr. Susan R. Ross, Director
Programs in:
 biochemistry and molecular biophysics • PhD
 biomedical studies • MS, PhD
 biostatistics • MS, PhD
 cell biology and physiology • PhD
 cell growth and cancer • PhD
 developmental biology • PhD
 gene therapy • PhD
 genetics and gene regulation • PhD
 immunology • PhD
 microbiology • PhD
 microbiology and virology • PhD
 neuroscience • PhD
 parasitology • PhD
 pharmacology • PhD

Center for Clinical Epidemiology and Biostatistics
Dr. Harold I. Feldman, Director
Programs in:
 clinical epidemiology • MSCE
 epidemiology • PhD

School of Nursing
Anne Keane, Graduate Dean
Programs in:
 acute care nurse practitioner • MSN

Pennsylvania

administration/consulting • MSN
adult and special populations • MSN
adult oncology nurse practitioner • MSN
adult/health nurse practitioner • MSN
child and family • MSN
family health nurse practitioner • MSN, Certificate
geropsychiatrics • MSN
health leadership • MSN
neonatal nurse practitioner • MSN
nurse midwifery • MSN
nursing • MSN, PhD, Certificate
nursing and health care administration • MSN, PhD
pediatric acute/chronic care nurse practitioner • MSN
pediatric critical care nurse practitioner • MSN
pediatric nurse practitioner • MSN
pediatric oncology nurse practitioner • MSN
perinatal advanced practice nurse specialist • MSN
primary care • MSN
women's healthcare nurse practitioner • MSN

School of Social Work
Richard Gelles, Dean
Programs in:
  social welfare • PhD
  social work • MSW, PhD

School of Veterinary Medicine
Dr. Alan M. Kelly, Dean
Program in:
  veterinary medicine • VMD

Wharton School
Programs in:
  accounting • AM, MS, PhD
  business • AM, MBA, MS, PhD
  business and public policy • AM, MS, PhD
  finance • AM, MS, PhD
  health care systems • AM, MS, PhD
  insurance and risk management • MS, PhD
  insurance and risk managment • AM
  management • AM, MS, PhD
  marketing • AM, MS, PhD
  operations and information management • MBA, PhD
  operations and information management operations research • AM, MS, PhD
  real estate • AM, MS, PhD
  statistics • AM, MS, PhD

Wharton Executive MBA Division
Program in:
  executive business administration • MBA

Wharton MBA Division
Program in:
  business administration • MBA

■ **UNIVERSITY OF PITTSBURGH**
Pittsburgh, PA 15260
http://www.pitt.edu/

State-related, coed, university. CGS member. *Enrollment:* 26,795 graduate, professional, and undergraduate students; 6,421 full-time matriculated graduate/professional students (3,296 women), 2,961 part-time matriculated graduate/professional students (1,827 women). *Graduate faculty:* 3,377 full-time (1,195 women), 723 part-time/adjunct (373 women). *Computer facilities:* 600 computers available on campus for general student use. A campuswide network can be accessed from student residence rooms and from off campus. Internet access, online class listings are available. *Library facilities:* Hillman Library plus 26 others. *Graduate expenses:* Tuition, state resident: full-time $11,744; part-time $479 per credit. Tuition, nonresident: full-time $22,910; part-time $941 per credit. Required fees: $560. Tuition and fees vary according to degree level and program.

Find an in-depth description at www.petersons.com/gradchannel.

Center for Neuroscience
Dr. Alan Sved, Co-Director, Graduate Program
Programs in:
  neurobiology • PhD
  neuroscience • PhD

Graduate School of Public and International Affairs
Dr. Carolyn Ban, Dean
Programs in:
  criminal justice • MPPM
  development planning • MPPM
  environmental management and policy • MPPM
  international development • MPPM
  international political economy • MPPM
  international security studies • MPPM
  management of non profit organizations • MPPM
  metropolitan management and regional development • MPPM
  personnel and labor relations • MPPM
  policy analysis and evaluation • MPPM
  public and international affairs • MID, MPA, MPIA, MPPM, PhD

Division of International Development
Dr. Paul J. Nelson, Director, International Development Division
Programs in:
  development planning and environmental sustainability • MPIA
  governmental organizations and civil society • MPIA
  international development • MID

Division of Public and Urban Affairs
Dr. Leon Haley, Director, Public and Urban Affairs Division
Programs in:
  policy research and analysis • MPA
  public and urban affairs • MPA
  public management and policy • MPA
  urban and regional affairs • MPA

Doctoral Program in Public and International Affairs
Dr. Phyllis Coontz, Doctoral Program Coordinator
Programs in:
  development policy • PhD
  foreign and security policy • PhD
  international political economy • PhD
  public administration • PhD
  public policy • PhD

International Affairs Division
Dr. Martin Staniland, Director, International Affairs Division
Programs in:
  global political economy • MPIA
  security and intelligence studies • MPIA

Graduate School of Public Health
Dr. Bernard D. Goldstein, Dean
Programs in:
  behavioral and community health sciences • MPH, Certificate
  biostatistics • MPH, MS, Dr PH, PhD
  environmental and occupational health • MPH, MS, PhD
  epidemiology • MPH, MS, Dr PH, PhD
  genetic counseling • MS
  health administration • Dr PH
  health policy and management • MHA
  human genetics • MS, PhD
  infectious diseases and microbiology • MPH, MS, Dr PH, PhD
  occupational and environmental medicine • MPH
  occupational medicine • MPH
  public health • MHA, MPH, MS, Dr PH, PhD, Certificate
  public health/aging • Certificate

Joseph M. Katz Graduate School of Business
Dr. Frederick W. Winter, Dean
Programs in:
  business • EMBA, MBA, MS, PhD
  business administration • EMBA, MBA, PhD
  international business • MBA

Peterson's Graduate Schools in the U.S. 2006

Pennsylvania

University of Pittsburgh (continued)
  international business administration • MBA
  management of information systems • MS

School of Arts and Sciences
Dr. Steven Husted, Associate Dean, Graduate Studies and Research
Programs in:
  anthropology • MA, PhD
  applied mathematics • MA, MS
  applied statistics • MA, MS
  arts and sciences • MA, MFA, MS, PM Sc, PMS, PhD, Certificate
  bioethics • MA
  chemistry • MS, PhD
  classics • MA, PhD
  communication • MA, PhD
  computer science • MS, PhD
  cultural and critical studies • PhD
  East Asian studies • MA
  ecology and evolution • MS, PhD
  English • MA
  financial mathematics • PMS
  French • MA, PhD
  geographical information systems • PM Sc
  geology and planetary science • MS, PhD
  Germanic languages and literatures • MA, PhD
  Hispanic languages and literatures • MA, PhD
  history • MA, PhD
  history and philosophy of science • MA, PhD
  history of art and architecture • MA, PhD
  intelligent systems • MS, PhD
  Italian • MA
  linguistics • MA, PhD
  mathematics • MA, MS, PhD
  molecular biophysics • PhD
  molecular, cellular, and developmental biology • PhD
  music • MA, PhD
  performance pedagogy • MFA
  philosophy • MA, PhD
  physics • MS, PhD
  political science • MA, PhD
  psychology • MS, PhD
  religion • PhD
  religious studies • MA
  Slavic languages and literatures • MA, PhD
  sociology • MA, PhD
  statistics • MA, MS, PhD
  TESOL • Certificate
  theatre and performance studies • MA, PhD
  women's studies • Certificate
  writing • MFA

Center for Latin American Studies
Kathleen M. DeWalt, Director
Program in:
  Latin American studies • Certificate

Department of Economics
Dr. Jean-Françedil;ois Richard, Department Chair
Program in:
  economics • PhD

School of Dental Medicine
Dr. Thomas W. Braun, Dean
Programs in:
  advanced education in general dentistry • Certificate
  anesthesiology • Certificate
  dental medicine • DMD, MD, MDS, Certificate
  endodontics • Certificate
  oral and maxillofacial surgery • MD, Certificate
  orthodontics • Certificate
  orthodontics and dentofacial orthopedics • Certificate
  pediatric dentistry • Certificate
  periodontics • MDS, Certificate
  prosthodontics • Certificate

School of Education
Dr. Alan Lesgold, Dean
Programs in:
  applied developmental psychology • MS, PhD
  cognitive studies • PhD
  deaf and hard of hearing • M Ed
  developmental movement • MS
  early childhood education • M Ed
  early education of disabled students • M Ed
  education • M Ed, MA, MAT, MS, Ed D, PhD
  education of students with mental and physical disabilities • M Ed
  education of the visually impaired • M Ed
  elementary education • M Ed, MAT
  English/communications education • M Ed, MAT, Ed D, PhD
  exercise physiology • MS, PhD
  foreign languages education • M Ed, MAT, Ed D, PhD
  general special education • M Ed
  higher education • M Ed, Ed D
  higher education management • M Ed, Ed D
  international development education • MA, PhD
  international developmental education • M Ed
  mathematics education • M Ed, MAT, Ed D
  movement science • MS, PhD
  reading education • M Ed, Ed D, PhD
  research methodology • M Ed, MA, PhD
  school leadership • M Ed, Ed D
  science education • M Ed, MAT, MS, Ed D
  secondary education • M Ed, MAT, MS, Ed D, PhD
  social and comparative analysis • M Ed, MA, PhD
  social studies education • M Ed, MAT, Ed D, PhD
  social, philosophical, and historical foundations of education • M Ed, MA, PhD
  special education • M Ed, Ed D, PhD

School of Engineering
Dr. Gerald D. Holder, Dean
Programs in:
  bioengineering • MSBENG, PhD
  chemical engineering • MS Ch E, PhD
  civil and environmental engineering • MSCEE, PhD
  electrical engineering • MSEE, PhD
  engineering • MS Ch E, MS Met E, MSBENG, MSCEE, MSEE, MSIE, MSME, MSMSE, MSPE, PhD, Certificate
  industrial engineering • MSIE, PhD
  materials science and engineering • MSMSE, PhD
  mechanical engineering • MSME, PhD
  metallurgical engineering • MS Met E, PhD
  petroleum engineering • MSPE

School of Health and Rehabilitation Sciences
Dr. Clifford E. Brubaker, Dean
Programs in:
  communication science and disorders • MA, MS, Au D, PhD
  health and rehabilitation sciences • MS
  occupational therapy • MOT
  physical therapy • DPT
  rehabilitation engineering • Certificate
  rehabilitation science • PhD
  rehabilitation technology • Certificate

School of Information Sciences
Dr. Ronald L. Larsen, Dean
Programs in:
  information sciences • MLIS, MSIS, MST, PhD, Certificate
  library and information science • MLIS, PhD, Certificate
  telecommunications • MST, PhD, Certificate

School of Law
David J. Herring, Dean
Programs in:
  business law • MSL
  civil litigation • Certificate
  constitutional law • MSL
  criminal justice • MSL
  disabilities law • MSL
  dispute resolution • MSL
  education law • MSL
  elder and estate planning law • MSL

Pennsylvania

employment and labor law • MSL
environment and real estate law • MSL
environmental law • Certificate
family law • MSL
general law and jurisprudence • MSL
health law • MSL
intellectual property and technology • MSL
intellectual property and technology law • Certificate
international and comparative law • LL M, MSL
international law • Certificate
law • JD, LL M, MA, MSL, Certificate
personal injury and civil litigation • MSL
regulatory law • MSL
self-designed • MSL

School of Medicine
Programs in:
biochemistry and molecular genetics • MS, PhD
biomedical informatics • MS, PhD, Certificate
biomedical sciences • PhD
cell biology and molecular physiology • MS, PhD
cellular and molecular pathology • MS, PhD
clinical research • MS, Certificate
immunology • MS, PhD
medical education • MS, Certificate
medical research • Certificate
medicine • MD, MS, PhD, Certificate
molecular pharmacology • PhD
molecular virology and microbiology • MS, PhD
neurobiology • MS, PhD

School of Nursing
Dr. Jacqueline Dunbar-Jacob, Dean
Programs in:
acute care nurse practitioner • MSN
administration • MSN
adult nurse practitioner • MSN
anesthesia nursing • MSN
family nurse practitioner • MSN
informatics • MSN
medical/surgical clinical nurse specialist • MSN
nursing • MSN, PhD
nursing education • MSN
pediatric nurse practitioner • MSN
psychiatric and mental health clinical nurse specialist • MSN
psychiatric primary care nurse practitioner • MSN
research • MSN

School of Pharmacy
Dr. Patricia Dowley Kroboth, Interim Dean
Programs in:
pharmaceutical sciences • MS, PhD
pharmacy • Pharm D

School of Social Work
Dr. Larry E. Davis, Dean
Programs in:
employee assistance • Certificate
family and marital therapy • Certificate
gerontology • Certificate
social work • MSW, PhD, Certificate

■ THE UNIVERSITY OF SCRANTON
Scranton, PA 18510
http://www.scranton.edu/

Independent-religious, coed, comprehensive institution. CGS member. *Enrollment:* 4,679 graduate, professional, and undergraduate students; 253 full-time matriculated graduate/professional students (166 women), 345 part-time matriculated graduate/professional students (212 women). *Graduate faculty:* 147 full-time (55 women), 24 part-time/adjunct (12 women). *Computer facilities:* 837 computers available on campus for general student use. A campuswide network can be accessed from student residence rooms and from off campus. Internet access and online class registration are available. *Library facilities:* Harry and Jeanette Weinberg Memorial Library plus 1 other. *Graduate expenses:* Tuition: part-time $590 per credit. Required fees: $25 per term. *General application contact:* James L. Goonan, Director of Admissions, 570-941-6304.

Graduate School
Dr. Duncan Perry, Dean
Programs in:
accounting • MBA
adult health nursing • MS
biochemistry • MA, MS
chemistry • MA, MS
clinical chemistry • MA, MS
community counseling • MS
curriculum and instruction • MS
early childhood education • MS
educational administration • MS
elementary education • MS
enterprise management technology • MBA
family nurse practitioner • MS, PMC
finance • MBA
general business administration • MBA
health administration • MHA
history • MA
human resources • MS
human resources administration • MS
human resources development • MS
international business • MBA
management information systems • MBA
marketing • MBA

nurse anesthesia • MS, PMC
occupational therapy • MS
operations management • MBA
organizational leadership • MS
physical therapy • MPT
professional counseling • CAGS
reading education • MS
rehabilitation counseling • MS
school counseling • MS
secondary education • MS
software engineering • MS
special education • MS
theology • MA

■ VILLANOVA UNIVERSITY
Villanova, PA 19085-1699
http://www.villanova.edu/

Independent-religious, coed, comprehensive institution. CGS member. *Enrollment:* 10,619 graduate, professional, and undergraduate students; 1,451 full-time matriculated graduate/professional students (683 women), 1,635 part-time matriculated graduate/professional students (726 women). *Graduate faculty:* 1,067. *Computer facilities:* 800 computers available on campus for general student use. A campuswide network can be accessed from student residence rooms and from off campus. Internet access and online class registration are available. *Library facilities:* Falvey Library plus 2 others. *Graduate expenses:* Tuition: part-time $750 per credit. *General application contact:* Dr. Gerald Long, Dean, Graduate School of Liberal Arts and Sciences, 610-519-7090.

Find an in-depth description at www.petersons.com/gradchannel.

College of Commerce and Finance
Dr. Stephen A. Stumpf, Dean
Programs in:
accounting and professional consultancy • M Ac
business administration • MBA
commerce and finance • EMBA, LL M, M Ac, MBA, MT
executive business administration • EMBA

College of Engineering
Dr. Barry C. Johnson, Dean
Programs in:
chemical engineering • M Ch E
civil engineering • MCE
computer engineering • MSCE, Certificate
electrical engineering • MSEE
electro-mechanical systems • Certificate
engineering • Certificate
machinery dynamics • Certificate

Peterson's Graduate Schools in the U.S. 2006

Pennsylvania

Villanova University (continued)
  manufacturing • Certificate
  mechanical engineering • MME
  thermofluid systems • Certificate
  transportation engineering • MSTE
  water resources and environmental engineering • MSWREE

College of Nursing
Dr. Marguerite K. Schlag, Assistant Dean and Director, Graduate Program
Programs in:
  adult nurse practitioner • MSN, Post Master's Certificate
  clinical case management • MSN, Post Master's Certificate
  geriatric nurse practitioner • MSN, Post Master's Certificate
  health care administration • MSN
  nurse anesthetist • MSN, Post Master's Certificate
  nursing • PhD
  nursing education • MSN, Post Master's Certificate
  pediatric nurse practitioner • MSN, Post Master's Certificate

Graduate School of Liberal Arts and Sciences
Dr. Gerald Long, Dean
Programs in:
  applied statistics • MS
  biology • MA, MS
  chemistry • MS
  classics • MA
  community counseling • MS
  computing sciences • MS
  counseling and human relations • MS
  criminal justice administration • MS
  educational leadership • MA
  elementary school counseling • MS
  elementary teacher education • MA
  English • MA
  history • MA
  human resource development • MS
  liberal arts and sciences • MA, MPA, MS, PhD
  liberal studies • MA
  mathematical sciences • MA
  philosophy • MA, PhD
  political science • MA
  psychology • MS
  public administration • MPA
  secondary school counseling • MS
  secondary teacher education • MA
  Spanish • MA
  theatre • MA
  theology • MA

School of Law
Mark A. Sargent, Dean
Programs in:
  law • JD, LL M, MT
  taxation • LL M, MT

■ WAYNESBURG COLLEGE
Waynesburg, PA 15370-1222
http://www.waynesburg.edu/

Independent-religious, coed, comprehensive institution. *Computer facilities:* 150 computers available on campus for general student use. A campuswide network can be accessed from student residence rooms and from off campus. Internet access is available. *Library facilities:* Waynesburg College Library. *General application contact:* Director, 412-854-3600.

Graduate and Professional Studies
Program in:
  business administration • MBA

■ WEST CHESTER UNIVERSITY OF PENNSYLVANIA
West Chester, PA 19383
http://www.wcupa.edu/

State-supported, coed, comprehensive institution. CGS member. *Enrollment:* 12,695 graduate, professional, and undergraduate students; 511 full-time matriculated graduate/professional students (376 women), 1,622 part-time matriculated graduate/professional students (1,140 women). *Graduate faculty:* 226. *Computer facilities:* 700 computers available on campus for general student use. A campuswide network can be accessed from student residence rooms and from off campus. Internet access and online class registration are available. *Library facilities:* Francis Harvey Green Library plus 1 other. *Graduate expenses:* Tuition, state resident: full-time $5,518; part-time $307 per credit. Tuition, nonresident: full-time $8,830; part-time $491 per credit. Required fees: $902; $52 per credit. One-time fee: $35 part-time. *General application contact:* 610-436-2943.

Find an in-depth description at www.petersons.com/gradchannel.

Graduate Studies
Dr. Cheryl Vermey, Dean

College of Arts and Sciences
Dr. Charlie Hurt, Dean
Programs in:
  arts and sciences • M Ed, MA, MS, MSA, Certificate
  biology • MS
  chemistry • M Ed, MS
  clinical chemistry • MS
  clinical psychology • MA
  communication studies • MA
  computer science • MS, Certificate
  English • MA
  French • M Ed, MA
  general psychology • MA
  German • M Ed
  gerontology • Certificate
  history • M Ed, MA
  industrial organizational psychology • MA
  Latin • M Ed
  long term care • MSA
  mathematics • MA
  philosophy • MA
  physical science • MA
  Spanish • M Ed, MA
  teaching English as a second language • MA

School of Business and Public Affairs
Dr. Christopher Fiorentino, Dean
Programs in:
  business and public affairs • MA, MBA, MS, MSA, MSW
  criminal justice • MS
  economics/finance • MBA
  executive business administration • MBA
  general business • MBA
  geography • MA
  health services • MSA
  human research management • MSA
  individualized • MSA
  leadership for women • MSA
  long-term care • MSA
  management • MBA
  public administration • MSA
  regional planning • MSA
  social work • MSW
  sport and athletic administration • MSA
  sport and athletic training • MSA
  technology and electronic commerce • MBA
  training and development • MSA

School of Education
Dr. Tony Johnson, Dean
Programs in:
  counseling and educational psychology • M Ed, MS
  early childhood and special education • M Ed
  educational research • MS
  elementary education • M Ed
  elementary school counseling • M Ed
  higher education counseling • MS
  literacy • M Ed
  professional and secondary education • M Ed, MS
  reading • M Ed
  secondary education • M Ed
  secondary school counseling • M Ed
  special education • M Ed
  teaching and learning with technology • Certificate

Pennsylvania

School of Health Sciences
Dr. Donald E. Barr, Dean
Programs in:
 communicative disorders • MA
 driver education • Certificate
 environmental health • MS
 exercise and sport physiology • MS
 gerontology • MS
 health sciences • M Ed, MA, MS, MSA, MSN, Certificate
 health services • MSA
 nursing • MSN
 nursing education • MSN
 physical education • MS
 public health • MS
 safety • Certificate
 school health • M Ed
 sport and athletic administration • MSA

School of Music
Dr. Timothy Blair, Dean
Programs in:
 accompanying • MM
 composition • MM
 music • MA, MM
 music education • MM
 music history • MA
 music theory • MM
 performance • MM
 piano pedagogy • MM

■ **WIDENER UNIVERSITY**
Chester, PA 19013-5792
http://www.widener.edu/

Independent, coed, comprehensive institution. CGS member. *Computer facilities:* Computer purchase and lease plans are available. 310 computers available on campus for general student use. A campuswide network can be accessed from student residence rooms and from off campus. Internet access is available. *Library facilities:* Wolfgram Memorial Library. *General application contact:* Associate Provost for Graduate Studies, 610-499-4351.

Find an in-depth description at www.petersons.com/gradchannel.

College of Arts and Sciences
Programs in:
 arts and sciences • MA, MPA
 criminal justice • MA
 liberal studies • MA
 public administration • MPA

Graduate Programs in Engineering
John H. Dixon, Director of Graduate and Special Programs
Programs in:
 chemical engineering • M Eng
 civil engineering • M Eng
 computer and software engineering • M Eng
 engineering management • M Eng
 management and technology • MSMT
 mechanical engineering • M Eng
 telecommunications engineering • M Eng

School of Business Administration
Programs in:
 accounting information systems • MS
 business administration • MBA, MHA, MHR, MS
 health and medical services administration • MBA, MHA
 human resource management • MHR, MS
 taxation • MS

School of Human Service Professions
Program in:
 human service professions • M Ed, MS, MSW, DPT, Ed D, Psy D

Center for Education
Programs in:
 adult education • M Ed
 counseling in higher education • M Ed
 counselor education • M Ed
 early childhood education • M Ed
 educational foundations • M Ed
 educational leadership • M Ed
 educational psychology • M Ed
 elementary education • M Ed
 English and language arts • M Ed
 health education • M Ed
 higher education leadership • Ed D
 home and school visitor • M Ed
 human sexuality • M Ed
 mathematics education • M Ed
 middle school education • M Ed
 principalship • M Ed
 reading and language arts • Ed D
 reading education • M Ed
 school administration • Ed D
 science education • M Ed
 social studies education • M Ed
 special education • M Ed
 technology education • M Ed

Center for Social Work Education
Program in:
 social work education • MSW

Institute for Graduate Clinical Psychology
Program in:
 clinical psychology • Psy D

Institute for Physical Therapy Education
Program in:
 physical therapy education • MS, DPT

School of Law
Program in:
 law • JD

School of Law at Wilmington
Programs in:
 corporate law and finance • LL M
 health law • LL M, MJ, D Law
 juridical science • SJD
 law • JD

School of Nursing
Program in:
 nursing • MSN, DN Sc, PMC

■ **WILKES UNIVERSITY**
Wilkes-Barre, PA 18766-0002
http://www.wilkes.edu/

Independent, coed, comprehensive institution. *Enrollment:* 4,390 graduate, professional, and undergraduate students; 372 full-time matriculated graduate/professional students (229 women), 1,963 part-time matriculated graduate/professional students (1,346 women). *Graduate faculty:* 104 full-time, 159 part-time/adjunct. *Computer facilities:* 700 computers available on campus for general student use. A campuswide network can be accessed from student residence rooms and from off campus. Internet access and online class registration are available. *Library facilities:* Eugene S. Farley Library. *Graduate expenses:* Tuition: part-time $650 per credit hour. Required fees: $13 per credit hour. Tuition and fees vary according to program. *General application contact:* Kathleen Diekhaus, Coordinator of Graduate Studies, 570-408-4160.

Graduate Programs
Dr. Maravene Loeschke, Provost
Programs in:
 arts, humanities and social sciences • MS Ed
 classroom technology • MS Ed
 educational computing • MS Ed
 educational development and strategies • MS Ed
 educational leadership • MS Ed
 electrical engineering • MSEE
 elementary education • MS Ed
 instructional technology • MS Ed
 mathematics • MS, MS Ed
 secondary education • MS Ed
 special education • MS Ed

College of Pharmacy and Nursing
Dr. Bernard Graham, Dean
Programs in:
 nursing • MSN
 pharmacy and nursing • Pharm D, MSN

Division of Business Administration and Accounting
Dr. Richard Raspen, Director
Programs in:

Peterson's Graduate Schools in the U.S. 2006

Pennsylvania

Wilkes University (continued)
   accounting • MBA
   finance • MBA
   health care • MBA
   human resource management • MBA
   international business • MBA
   marketing • MBA

■ YORK COLLEGE OF PENNSYLVANIA
York, PA 17405-7199
http://www.ycp.edu/

Independent, coed, comprehensive institution. *Enrollment:* 5,515 graduate, professional, and undergraduate students; 25 full-time matriculated graduate/professional students, 222 part-time matriculated graduate/professional students. *Graduate faculty:* 17 full-time (3 women), 1 part-time/adjunct (0 women). *Computer facilities:* 250 computers available on campus for general student use. A campuswide network can be accessed from student residence rooms and from off campus. Internet access and online class registration are available. *Library facilities:* Schmidt Library plus 1 other. *Graduate expenses:* Tuition: part-time $362 per credit. Required fees: $122 per term. Tuition and fees vary according to course load. *General application contact:* John F. Barbor, MBA Coordinator, 717-815-1491.

Department of Business Administration
John F. Barbor, MBA Coordinator
Program in:
   business administration • MBA

Department of Nursing
Lynn Warner, Coordinator
Program in:
   nursing • MS

Puerto Rico

■ BAYAMÓN CENTRAL UNIVERSITY
Bayamón, PR 00960-1725
http://www.ucb.edu.pr/

Independent-religious, coed, comprehensive institution. *Computer facilities:* 130 computers available on campus for general student use. A campuswide network can be accessed. Internet access is available. *Library facilities:* BCU Library plus 1 other. *General application contact:* Director of Admissions, 787-786-3030 Ext. 2100.

Graduate Programs
Programs in:
   accounting • MBA
   administration and supervision • MA Ed
   biblical studies • MA
   divinity • M Div
   education of the autistic • MA Ed
   elementary education (K–3) • MA Ed
   elementary education (K–6) • MA Ed
   general business • MBA
   guidance and counseling • MA Ed
   management • MBA
   marketing • MBA
   pastoral theology • MA
   pre-elementary teacher • MA Ed
   psychology • MA
   religious studies • MA
   special education • MA Ed
   specific learning disabled • MA Ed
   theological studies • MA
   theology • MA

■ INTER AMERICAN UNIVERSITY OF PUERTO RICO, METROPOLITAN CAMPUS
San Juan, PR 00919-1293
http://metro.inter.edu/

Independent, coed, comprehensive institution. CGS member. *Computer facilities:* 400 computers available on campus for general student use. A campuswide network can be accessed from student residence rooms and from off campus. Internet access and online class registration are available. *Library facilities:* Centro de Acceso a la Informacion plus 1 other. *General application contact:* Graduate Coordinator, 787-250-1912.

Faculty of Education
Programs in:
   administration and supervision • MA
   education • Ed D
   elementary education • MA
   guidance and counseling • MA
   health and physical education • MA
   higher education • MA Ed
   occupational education • MA
   special education • MA Ed
   teaching of science • MA Ed
   vocational evaluation • MA

Faculty of Liberal Arts
Programs in:
   humanistic studies • MA, PhD
   Spanish • MA
   teaching English as a second language • MA
   theological studies • PhD

Faculty of Science and Technology
Programs in:
   educational computing • MA
   medical technology • MS
   open information systems • MS

School of Criminal Justice
Program in:
   criminal justice • MA

School of Law
Program in:
   law • JD

School of Psychology
Program in:
   psychology • MA

School of Social Work
Program in:
   social work • MA

■ INTER AMERICAN UNIVERSITY OF PUERTO RICO, SAN GERMÁN CAMPUS
San Germán, PR 00683-5008
http://www.sg.inter.edu/

Independent, coed, university. *Enrollment:* 6,210 graduate, professional, and undergraduate students; 315 full-time matriculated graduate/professional students, 693 part-time matriculated graduate/professional students. *Graduate faculty:* 36 full-time (19 women), 47 part-time/adjunct (19 women). *Computer facilities:* 1,600 computers available on campus for general student use. A campuswide network can be accessed. Internet access and online class registration are available. *Library facilities:* Juan Cancio Ortiz Library. *Graduate expenses:* Tuition: part-time $170 per credit. *General application contact:* Dr. Carlos E. Irizarry, Director of Graduate Studies Center, 787-264-1912 Ext. 7357.

Graduate Studies Center
Dr. Carlos E. Irizarry, Director of Graduate Studies Center
Programs in:
   accounting • MBA
   administration and supervision • MA
   applied mathematics • MA
   art • MFA
   business education • MA
   ceramics • MFA
   counseling psychology • MA, PhD
   drawing • MFA
   environmental sciences • MS
   finance • MBA
   guidance and counseling • MA
   human resources • MBA, PhD

Puerto Rico

industrial relations • MBA
interregional and international business • PhD
labor relations • PhD
library and information sciences • MLS
management information systems • MBA
marketing • MBA
painting • MFA
photography • MFA
physical education and scientific analysis of human body movement • MA
printmaking • MFA
quality organizational design • MBA
school psychology • MS, PhD
science education • MA
sculpture • MFA
special education • MA
teaching English as a second language • MA

■ PONTIFICAL CATHOLIC UNIVERSITY OF PUERTO RICO
Ponce, PR 00717-0777
http://www.pucpr.edu/

Independent-religious, coed, university. *Enrollment:* 7,468 graduate, professional, and undergraduate students; 732 full-time matriculated graduate/professional students (426 women), 1,161 part-time matriculated graduate/professional students (823 women). *Graduate faculty:* 65 full-time (32 women), 42 part-time/adjunct (15 women). *Computer facilities:* 419 computers available on campus for general student use. A campuswide network can be accessed from off campus. Internet access is available. *Library facilities:* Encarnacion Valdes Library plus 1 other. *General application contact:* Ana O. Bonilla, Director of Admissions, 787-841-2000 Ext. 1000.

College of Arts and Humanities
Prof. Alfonso Santiago, Chairperson
Programs in:
 arts and humanities • MA
 divinity • MA
 Hispanic studies • MA
 history • MA

College of Business Administration
Dr. Kenya Carrasquillo, Chairperson
Programs in:
 accounting • MBA
 business administration • PhD
 finance • MBA
 human resources • MBA
 merchandising • MBA
 office administration • MBA

College of Education
Dr. Myvian Zayas, Chairperson
Programs in:
 commercial education • MRE
 curriculum instruction • M Ed
 education • PhD
 education-general • MRE
 English as a second language • MRE
 religious education • MA Ed
 scholar psychology • MRE

College of Sciences
Carmen Velázquez, Dean
Programs in:
 chemistry • MS
 medical-surgical nursing • MS
 mental health and psychiatric nursing • MS
 obstetric nursing • MS
 sciences • MS

Institute of Graduate Studies in Behavioral Science and Community Affairs
Dr. Nilde Cordoline, Director
Programs in:
 clinical psychology • MS
 clinical social work • MSW
 criminology • MA
 industrial psychology • MS
 psychology • PhD
 public administration • MA

School of Law
Charles Cuprill, Dean
Program in:
 law • JD

■ UNIVERSIDAD DEL TURABO
Turabo, PR 00778-3030

Independent, coed, comprehensive institution. *Computer facilities:* A campuswide network can be accessed from off campus. Internet access is available. *General application contact:* Admissions Officer, 787-746-3009.

Graduate Programs
Programs in:
 accounting • MBA
 bilingual education • MA
 criminal justice studies • MPA
 education administration and supervision • MA
 environmental studies • MES
 human resources • MBA
 human services administration • MPA
 logistics and materials management • MBA
 management • MBA
 marketing • MBA
 school libraries administration • MA
 special education • MA
 teaching English as a second language • MA

■ UNIVERSIDAD METROPOLITANA
Río Piedras, PR 00928-1150
http://www.suagm.edu/umet/

Independent, coed, comprehensive institution. *Computer facilities:* 50 computers available on campus for general student use. Internet access is available. *General application contact:* Director, 787-766-1717 Ext. 6416.

Graduate Programs in Education
Programs in:
 curriculum and teaching • MA
 educational administration and supervision • MA
 fitness management • MA
 managing leisure services • MA
 pre-school centers administration • MA
 pre-school education • MA
 special education • MA
 teaching of physical education • MA

School of Business Administration
Programs in:
 accounting • MBA
 human resources • MA
 management • MBA
 marketing • MBA
 public accounting • Certificate

School of Environmental Affairs
Programs in:
 conservation and management of natural resources • MEM
 environmental education • MA
 environmental planning • MEM
 environmental risk and assessment management • MEM

■ UNIVERSITY OF PUERTO RICO, MAYAGÜEZ CAMPUS
Mayagüez, PR 00681-9000
http://www.uprm.edu

Commonwealth-supported, coed, university. *Computer facilities:* 1,066 computers available on campus for general student use. A campuswide network can be accessed from off campus. Internet access and online class registration are available. *Library facilities:* General Library plus 1 other. *General application contact:* Director of Graduate Studies, 787-265-3809.

Graduate Studies

College of Agricultural Sciences
Programs in:
 agricultural economics • MS
 agricultural education • MS
 agricultural extension • MS

Peterson's Graduate Schools in the U.S. 2006

Puerto Rico

University of Puerto Rico, Mayagüez Campus (continued)
  agricultural sciences • MS
  animal industry • MS
  crop protection • MS
  crops • MS
  food technology • MS
  horticulture • MS
  soils • MS

College of Arts and Sciences
Programs in:
  applied mathematics • MS
  arts and sciences • MA, MMS, MS, PhD
  biological oceanography • MMS, PhD
  biology • MS
  chemical oceanography • MMS, PhD
  chemistry • MS
  computational sciences • MS
  English • MA
  geological oceanography • MMS, PhD
  geology • MS
  Hispanic studies • MA
  physical oceanography • MMS, PhD
  physics • MS
  pure mathematics • MS
  statistics • MS

College of Business Administration
Program in:
  business administration • MBA

College of Engineering
Programs in:
  chemical engineering • M Ch E, MS
  civil engineering • MCE, MS, PhD
  computer engineering • M Co E, MS
  electrical engineering • MEE, MS
  engineering • M Ch E, M Co E, MCE, MEE, MME, MMSE, MS, PhD
  industrial engineering • MMSE
  mechanical engineering • MME, MS

■ **UNIVERSITY OF PUERTO RICO, RÍO PIEDRAS**
San Juan, PR 00931
http://upracd.upr.clu.edu:9090/

Commonwealth-supported, coed, university. CGS member. *Enrollment:* 1,654 full-time matriculated graduate/professional students (1,082 women), 2,405 part-time matriculated graduate/professional students (1,687 women). *Graduate faculty:* 1,172 full-time (586 women), 336 part-time/adjunct (147 women). *Computer facilities:* 170 computers available on campus for general student use. A campuswide network can be accessed from student residence rooms. Internet access is available. *Library facilities:* Jose M. Lazaro Library plus 10 others. *Graduate expenses:* Tuition, commonwealth resident: part-time $75 per credit. Tuition, nonresident: full-time $1,200; part-time $218 per credit. International tuition: $3,500 full-time. Required fees: $70; $35 per term. *General application contact:* Cruz B. Valentin-Arbelo, Admission Office Director, 787-764-0000 Ext. 5653.

College of Education
Dr. Nivia A. Fernández, Dean
Programs in:
  biology education • M Ed
  chemistry education • M Ed
  child education • M Ed
  curriculum and teaching • Ed D
  education • M Ed, Ed D
  educational research and evaluation • M Ed
  English education • M Ed
  family ecology and nutrition • M Ed
  guidance and counseling • M Ed, Ed D
  history education • M Ed
  mathematics education • M Ed
  physics education • M Ed
  school administration and supervision • M Ed, Ed D
  secondary education • M Ed
  Spanish education • M Ed
  special education • M Ed
  teaching English as a second language • M Ed

College of Humanities
Dr. José Rafael Iguina, Acting Dean
Programs in:
  comparative literature • MA
  English • MA, PhD
  Hispanic studies • MA, PhD
  history • MA, PhD
  humanities • MA, PhD, Certificate
  linguistics • MA
  philosophy • MA
  translation • MA, Certificate

College of Social Sciences
Dr. Carlos Severino-Valdés, Acting Dean
Programs in:
  economics • MA
  psychology • MA, PhD
  social sciences • MA, MPA, MRC, MSW, PhD
  sociology • MA

Beatriz Lassalle Graduate School of Social Work
Dr. Norma Rodriguez, Director
Program in:
  social work • MSW, PhD

Graduate School of Rehabilitation Counseling
Director
Program in:
  rehabilitation counseling • MRC

School of Public Administration
Dr. Palmira Rios, Interim Director
Program in:
  public administration • MPA

Faculty of Natural Sciences
Dr. María Socorro Rivera-Baez, Acting Dean
Programs in:
  applied physics • MS
  biology • MS, PhD
  chemistry • MS, PhD
  mathematics • MS, PhD
  natural sciences • MS, PhD
  physics • MS
  physics-chemical • PhD

Graduate School of Business Administration
Dr. Jorge Ayala, Coordinator of Master Programs
Program in:
  business administration • MBA, PhD

Graduate School of Librarianship
Dr. Consuelo Figueras-Alvarez, Director
Programs in:
  librarianship • Post-Graduate Certificate
  librarianship and information services • MLS

Graduate School of Planning
Dr. Elías R. Gutierrez, Director
Program in:
  planning • MP

School of Architecture
Dr. Enrique Vivoni, Coordinator of Master Programs
Program in:
  architecture • M Arch

School of Law
Dr. Efrén Rivera-Ramos, Dean
Program in:
  law • JD, LL M

School of Public Communication
Dr. Eliseo Colón, Director
Program in:
  public communication • MA

■ **UNIVERSITY OF THE SACRED HEART**
San Juan, PR 00914-0383
http://www.sagrado.edu/

Independent-religious, coed, comprehensive institution. *Enrollment:* 5,210 graduate, professional, and undergraduate students; 21 full-time matriculated graduate/professional students (16 women), 629 part-time matriculated graduate/professional students (466 women). *Graduate faculty:*

19 full-time (10 women), 42 part-time/adjunct (29 women). *Computer facilities:* 500 computers available on campus for general student use. A campuswide network can be accessed from off campus. *Library facilities:* Maria Teresa Guevara Library plus 1 other. *Graduate expenses:* Tuition: full-time $4,455; part-time $165 per credit. *General application contact:* Alfredo Carrasquillo, Information Contact, 787-728-1515 Ext. 2314.

Graduate Programs
Dr. Lydia Espinet, Dean, Academic and Student Affairs
Programs in:
advertising • MA
contemporary culture and means • MA
human resource management • MBA
instruction systems and education technology • M Ed
journalism and mass communication • MA
management information systems • MBA
marketing • MBA
medical technology • Certificate
natural science • Certificate
non-profit organization • MS
occupational health • MS
public relations • MA
taxation • MBA

Rhode Island

■ BROWN UNIVERSITY
Providence, RI 02912
http://www.brown.edu/

Independent, coed, university. CGS member. *Computer facilities:* Computer purchase and lease plans are available. 400 computers available on campus for general student use. A campuswide network can be accessed from student residence rooms and from off campus. Internet access and online class registration are available. *Library facilities:* John D. Rockefeller Library plus 5 others. *General application contact:* Admission Office, 401-863-2600.

Graduate School
Programs in:
American civilization • AM, PhD
anthropology • AM, PhD
art history • AM, PhD
biochemistry • PhD
chemistry • Sc M, PhD
classics • AM, PhD
cognitive science • Sc M, PhD
comparative literature • AM, PhD
comparative study of development • AM
computer science • Sc M, PhD
economics • AM, PhD
Egyptology • AM, PhD
elementary education 1-6 • MAT
English literature and language • AM, PhD
French studies • AM, PhD
geological sciences • MA, Sc M, PhD
German • AM, PhD
Hispanic studies • AM, PhD
history • AM, PhD
history of mathematics • AM, PhD
Italian studies • AM, PhD
Judaic studies • AM, PhD
linguistics • AM, PhD
mathematics • M Sc, MA, PhD
music • AM, PhD
old world archaeology and art • AM, PhD
philosophy • AM, PhD
physics • Sc M, PhD
political science • AM, PhD
population studies • PhD
psychology • AM, Sc M, PhD
religious studies • AM, PhD
Russian • AM, PhD
secondary biology • MAT
secondary English • MAT
secondary social studies/history • MAT
Slavic languages • AM, PhD
sociology • AM, PhD
theatre arts • AM
writing • MFA

A. Alfred Taubman Center for Public Policy and American Institutions
Program in:
public policy and American institutions • MPA, MPP

Center for Environmental Studies
Harold Ward, Director
Program in:
environmental studies • AM

Center for Old World Archaeology and Art
Program in:
old world archaeology and art • AM, PhD

Center for Portuguese and Brazilian Studies
Programs in:
Brazilian studies • AM
Luso-Brazilian studies • PhD
Portuguese studies and bilingual education • AM

Division of Applied Mathematics
Program in:
applied mathematics • Sc M, PhD

Division of Biology and Medicine
Dr. Donald Marsh, Dean
Programs in:
artificial organs/biomaterials/cellular technology • MA, Sc M, PhD
biochemistry • M Med Sc, Sc M, PhD
biology • MA, PhD
biology and medicine • M Med Sc, MA, MPH, MS, Sc M, PhD
biomedical engineering • MS, PhD
biostatistics • MS, PhD
cancer biology • PhD
cell biology • M Med Sc, Sc M, PhD
developmental biology • M Med Sc, Sc M, PhD
ecology and evolutionary biology • PhD
epidemiology • MS, PhD
health services research • MS, PhD
immunology • M Med Sc, Sc M, PhD
immunology and infection • PhD
medical science • PhD
molecular microbiology • M Med Sc, Sc M, PhD
molecular pharmacology and physiology • MA, Sc M, PhD
neuroscience • PhD
pathobiology • Sc M
public health • MPH
statistical science • MS, PhD
toxicology and environmental pathology • PhD

Division of Engineering
Programs in:
aerospace engineering • Sc M, PhD
biomedical engineering • Sc M
electrical sciences • Sc M, PhD
fluid mechanics, thermodynamics, and chemical processes • Sc M, PhD
materials science • Sc M, PhD
mechanics of solids and structures • Sc M, PhD

Program in Medicine
Program in:
medicine • MD

■ JOHNSON & WALES UNIVERSITY
Providence, RI 02903-3703
http://www.jwu.edu/

Independent, coed, comprehensive institution. *Enrollment:* 9,868 graduate, professional, and undergraduate students; 459 full-time matriculated graduate/professional students (218 women), 189 part-time matriculated graduate/professional students (99 women). *Graduate faculty:* 15 full-time, 18 part-time/adjunct. *Computer facilities:* 340 computers available on campus for general student use. A campuswide network can be accessed from student residence rooms and from off campus. Internet access is available. *Library facilities:* Johnson & Wales University Library plus 2 others. *Graduate expenses:* Tuition: part-time $234 per credit hour. *General*

Rhode Island

Johnson & Wales University (continued) application contact: Dr. Allan G. Freedman, Director of Graduate Admissions, 401-598-1015.

Find an in-depth description at www.petersons.com/gradchannel.

The Alan Shawn Feinstein Graduate School
Dr. Frank Pontarelli, Dean
Programs in:
  accounting • MBA
  business administration • MAT
  educational leadership • Ed D
  finance • MBA
  food service • MAT
  hospitality administration • MBA
  international trade • MBA
  marketing • MBA
  organizational leadership • MBA

■ PROVIDENCE COLLEGE
Providence, RI 02918
http://www.providence.edu/

Independent-religious, coed, comprehensive institution. *Enrollment:* 5,258 graduate, professional, and undergraduate students; 122 full-time matriculated graduate/professional students (75 women), 453 part-time matriculated graduate/professional students (282 women). *Graduate faculty:* 33 full-time (10 women), 60 part-time/adjunct (25 women). *Computer facilities:* 160 computers available on campus for general student use. A campuswide network can be accessed from student residence rooms and from off campus. Internet access and online class registration are available. *Library facilities:* Phillips Memorial Library. *Graduate expenses:* Tuition: full-time $5,495. *General application contact:* Dr. Thomas F. Flaherty, Dean, 401-865-2247.

Graduate School
Dr. Thomas F. Flaherty, Dean
Programs in:
  administration • M Ed
  biblical studies • MA
  business administration • MBA
  education literacy • M Ed
  elementary administration • M Ed
  guidance and counseling • M Ed
  history • MA
  mathematics • MAT
  pastoral ministry • MA
  religious education • MA
  religious studies • MA
  secondary administration • M Ed
  special education • M Ed

■ RHODE ISLAND COLLEGE
Providence, RI 02908-1991
http://www.ric.edu/

State-supported, coed, comprehensive institution. *Enrollment:* 8,923 graduate, professional, and undergraduate students; 246 full-time matriculated graduate/professional students (211 women), 534 part-time matriculated graduate/professional students (439 women). *Graduate faculty:* 196 full-time (77 women), 39 part-time/adjunct (19 women). *Computer facilities:* 350 computers available on campus for general student use. A campuswide network can be accessed from off campus. *Library facilities:* Adams Library. *Graduate expenses:* Tuition, state resident: part-time $194 per credit hour. Tuition, nonresident: part-time $410 per credit hour. Required fees: $50 per semester. *General application contact:* Dean of Graduate Studies, 401-456-8700.

Find an in-depth description at www.petersons.com/gradchannel.

School of Graduate Studies
Dean

Center for Management and Technology
Dr. James Schweikart, Director
Programs in:
  accounting information systems • MP Ac
  management and technology • MP Ac

Faculty of Arts and Sciences
Dr. Richard R. Weiner, Dean
Programs in:
  art • MA
  art education • MA, MAT
  art education and studio art • MA, MAT
  art media studies • MA
  art studio • MA
  arts and sciences • MA, MAT, MFA, MM, CAGS
  biology • MA, MAT
  English • MA, MAT
  French • MA, MAT
  general science • MAT
  history • MA, MAT
  mathematics • MA, MAT, CAGS
  music • MM
  music education • MAT
  physical science • MAT
  psychology • MA
  Spanish • MAT
  theatre • MFA

Feinstein School of Education and Human Development
Dr. James A. Bucci, Dean
Programs in:
  agency counseling • MA, CAGS
  bilingual/bicultural education • M Ed
  counselor education • M Ed, MA, CAGS
  curriculum • CAGS
  early childhood education • M Ed
  education • PhD
  education and human development • M Ed, MA, MAT, PhD, CAGS
  educational administration • M Ed, CAGS
  educational psychology • MA
  elementary education • M Ed, MAT
  English as a second language • M Ed, MAT
  health education • M Ed
  reading education • M Ed, CAGS
  school psychology • CAGS
  secondary education • M Ed
  special education • M Ed, CAGS
  teaching of the handicapped • M Ed, CAGS
  technology education • M Ed

School of Social Work
Dr. George Metrey, Dean
Program in:
  social work • MSW

■ SALVE REGINA UNIVERSITY
Newport, RI 02840-4192
http://www.salve.edu/

Independent-religious, coed, comprehensive institution. *Enrollment:* 2,357 graduate, professional, and undergraduate students; 45 full-time matriculated graduate/professional students (35 women), 285 part-time matriculated graduate/professional students (162 women). *Graduate faculty:* 12 full-time (3 women), 27 part-time/adjunct (10 women). *Computer facilities:* 163 computers available on campus for general student use. A campuswide network can be accessed from student residence rooms and from off campus. Internet access is available. *Library facilities:* McKillop Library. *Graduate expenses:* Tuition: part-time $330 per credit. *General application contact:* Karen E. Johnson, Graduate Admissions Counselor, 401-341-2153.

Find an in-depth description at www.petersons.com/gradchannel.

Graduate School
Dr. Lance Carluccio, Dean of Graduate Studies
Programs in:

administration of justice • MS, Certificate
business administration • MBA
business studies • Certificate
expressive art therapies • CAGS
expressive arts as a healing modality • Certificate
health services administration • MS, Certificate
holistic counseling • MA
human development • Certificate
human resource management • Certificate
humanities • MA, PhD, CAGS
information systems • Certificate
international relations • MA, Certificate
management • MS, Certificate
mental health • CAGS
organizational development • Certificate

■ UNIVERSITY OF RHODE ISLAND
Kingston, RI 02881
http://www.uri.edu

State-supported, coed, university. CGS member. *Enrollment:* 14,791 graduate, professional, and undergraduate students; 3,493 matriculated graduate/professional students. *Computer facilities:* 552 computers available on campus for general student use. A campuswide network can be accessed from off campus. *Library facilities:* University Library plus 1 other. *Graduate expenses:* Tuition, state resident: full-time $4,338; part-time $281 per credit. Tuition, nonresident: full-time $12,438; part-time $704 per credit. Required fees: $1,840. *General application contact:* Harold D. Bibb, Associate Dean of the Graduate School, 401-874-2262.

Graduate School
Janett Trubatah, Vice Provost for Graduate Studies, Research and Outreach

Alan Shawn Feinstein College of Continuing Education
John McCray, Vice Provost
Programs in:
 clinical laboratory sciences • MS
 continuing education • Exec MBA, MS

College of Arts and Sciences
Winifed Brownell, Dean
Programs in:
 arts and sciences • MA, MM, MPA, MS, PhD, Certificate
 biological sciences • MS, PhD
 chemistry • MS, PhD
 clinical psychology • PhD
 computer science and statistics • MS, PhD
 English • MA, PhD
 experimental psychology • PhD
 French • MA
 history • MA
 international development studies • Certificate
 mathematics • MS, PhD
 music • MM
 philosophy • MA
 physics • MS, PhD
 political science • MA
 public policy and administration • MPA
 school psychology • MS, PhD
 Spanish • MA

College of Business Administration
Dr. Edward Mazze, Dean
Programs in:
 accounting • MS
 applied mathematics • PhD
 finance • MBA
 international business • MBA
 international sports management • MBA
 management • MBA
 management science • MBA
 marketing • MBA

College of Engineering
Bahram Nassersharif, Dean
Programs in:
 chemical engineering • MS, PhD
 design/systems • MS, PhD
 electrical and computer engineering • MS, PhD
 engineering • MS, PhD
 environmental engineering • MS, PhD
 fluid mechanics • MS, PhD
 geotechnical engineering • MS, PhD
 industrial engineering • MS
 manufacturing engineering • MS
 ocean engineering • MS, PhD
 solid mechanics • MS, PhD
 structural engineering • MS, PhD
 thermal sciences • MS, PhD
 transportation engineering • MS, PhD

College of Human Science and Services
W. Lynn McKinney, Dean
Programs in:
 adult education • MA
 communicative disorders • MA, MS
 elementary education • MA
 guidance and counseling • MS
 health • MS
 home economics education • MS
 human science and services • MA, MS
 marriage and family therapy • MS
 physical education • MS
 physical therapy • MS
 reading • MA
 recreation • MS
 secondary education • MA
 textiles, fashion merchandising and design • MS

College of Nursing
Dayle Joseph, Dean
Programs in:
 nursing • PhD
 nursing service administration • MS
 teaching of nursing • MS

College of Pharmacy
Donald Letendre, Dean
Programs in:
 applied pharmaceutical sciences • MS, PhD
 biomedical sciences • MS, PhD
 medicinal chemistry • MS, PhD
 pharmaceutics • MS, PhD
 pharmacognosy • MS, PhD
 pharmacology and toxicology • MS, PhD
 pharmacy • Pharm D, MS, PhD
 pharmacy administration • MS
 pharmacy practice • Pharm D

College of the Environment and Life Sciences
Jeffrey Seemann, Dean
Programs in:
 animal science • MS
 biochemistry • MS, PhD
 community planning and area development • MCP
 entomology • MS, PhD
 environment and life sciences • MA, MCP, MMA, MS, PhD
 food and nutrition science • MS, PhD
 food science and technology, nutrition and dietetics • MS, PhD
 geosciences • MS
 marine affairs • MA, MMA
 microbiology • MS, PhD
 plant pathology • MS, PhD
 plant pathology-entomology • MS, PhD
 plant science • MS, PhD
 resource economics and marine resources • MS, PhD

Graduate Library School
Dr. W. Michael Havener, Director
Program in:
 library science • MLIS

Graduate School of Oceanography
David Farmer, Dean
Program in:
 oceanography • MS, PhD

Labor Research Center
Dr. Richard Scholl, Director
Program in:
 labor and industrial relations • MS

South Carolina

■ CHARLESTON SOUTHERN UNIVERSITY
Charleston, SC 29423-8087
http://www.charlestonsouthern.edu/

Independent-religious, coed, comprehensive institution. *Enrollment:* 2,990 graduate, professional, and undergraduate students; 21 full-time matriculated graduate/professional students (10 women), 277 part-time matriculated graduate/professional students (167 women). *Graduate faculty:* 20 full-time (7 women), 10 part-time/adjunct (6 women). *Computer facilities:* 190 computers available on campus for general student use. A campuswide network can be accessed. Internet access and online class registration, online course work are available. *Library facilities:* L. Mendel Rivers Library. *Graduate expenses:* Tuition: full-time $7,213; part-time $216 per credit hour. One-time fee: $80 part-time. *General application contact:* Debbie Williamson, Vice President for Enrollment Management, 843-863-7050.

Program in Business
Dr. Bill Bowers, Director of the MBA Program
Programs in:
  accounting • MBA
  finance • MBA
  health care administration • MBA
  information systems • MBA
  organizational development • MBA

Program in Criminal Justice
Dr. Beth H. McConnell, Chair, Department of Criminal Justice and Director of Graduate Studies in Criminal Justice
Program in:
  criminal justice • MSCJ

Programs in Education
Dr. Gary O. Leonard, Director of Graduate Studies in Education
Programs in:
  administration and supervision • M Ed
  elementary education • M Ed
  English • MAT
  science • MAT
  secondary education • M Ed
  social studies • MAT

■ THE CITADEL, THE MILITARY COLLEGE OF SOUTH CAROLINA
Charleston, SC 29409
http://www.citadel.edu

State-supported, coed, primarily men, comprehensive institution. *Enrollment:* 3,695 graduate, professional, and undergraduate students; 174 full-time matriculated graduate/professional students (113 women), 641 part-time matriculated graduate/professional students (357 women). *Graduate faculty:* 52 full-time (20 women), 26 part-time/adjunct (7 women). *Computer facilities:* 350 computers available on campus for general student use. A campuswide network can be accessed from student residence rooms and from off campus. Internet access and online class registration are available. *Library facilities:* Daniel Library. *Graduate expenses:* Tuition, state resident: full-time $1,854; part-time $206 per credit hour. Tuition, nonresident: full-time $3,447; part-time $383 per credit hour. Required fees: $15 per term. *General application contact:* Patricia Ezell, Assistant Dean, College of Graduate and Professional Studies, 843-953-5089.

College of Graduate and Professional Studies
Brig. Gen. Harrison Carter, Acting Dean
Programs in:
  biology education • MAE
  business administration • MBA
  computer and information science • MS
  educational administration • M Ed, Ed S
  English • MA
  guidance and counseling • M Ed
  health and physical education • M Ed
  history • MA
  mathematics education • MAE
  psychology • MA
  reading • M Ed
  school psychology • Ed S
  secondary education • MAT
  social studies education • MAE

■ CLEMSON UNIVERSITY
Clemson, SC 29634
http://www.clemson.edu/

State-supported, coed, university. CGS member. *Enrollment:* 17,016 graduate, professional, and undergraduate students; 1,918 full-time matriculated graduate/professional students (683 women), 907 part-time matriculated graduate/professional students (493 women). *Graduate faculty:* 864 full-time (207 women), 133 part-time/adjunct (39 women). *Computer facilities:* 1,000 computers available on campus for general student use. A campuswide network can be accessed from student residence rooms and from off campus. Internet access and online class registration, wireless network are available. *Library facilities:* Robert Muldrow Cooper Library plus 1 other. *Graduate expenses:* Tuition, state resident: full-time $7,432. Tuition, nonresident: full-time $14,732. *General application contact:* Dr. Mark A. McKnew, Associate Dean of the Graduate School, 861-656-3195.

Find an in-depth description at www.petersons.com/gradchannel.

Graduate School
Dr. Bonnie J. Holaday, Dean
Program in:
  policy studies • PhD, Certificate

College of Agriculture, Forestry and Life Sciences
Dr. Calvin Schoulties, Interim Dean
Programs in:
  agricultural and applied economics • MS
  agricultural education • M Ag Ed
  agriculture, forestry and life sciences • M Ag Ed, M Engr, MFR, MS, PhD
  animal physiology • MS, PhD
  applied economics • PhD
  aquaculture, fisheries, and wildlife • MS, PhD
  biochemistry • MS, PhD
  biosystems engineering • M Engr, MS, PhD
  entomology • MS, PhD
  environmental toxicology • MS, PhD
  food technology • PhD
  food, nutrition, and culinary science • MS
  forest resources • MFR, MS, PhD
  genetics • MS, PhD
  microbiology • MS, PhD
  plant and environmental sciences • MS, PhD
  zoology • MS, PhD

College of Architecture, Arts, and Humanities
Dr. Janice Schach, Dean
Programs in:
  architecture • M Arch, MS
  architecture, arts, and humanities • M Arch, MA, MCRP, MCSM, MFA, MFAC, MS
  construction science and management • MCSM
  digital production arts • MFAC
  English • MA
  environmental planning • MCRP
  historic preservation • MS
  history • MA
  land development planning • MCRP
  professional communication • MA
  visual arts • MFA

South Carolina

College of Business and Behavioral Science
Dr. Jerry Trapnell, Dean
Programs in:
  accountancy • MP Acc
  applied economics • PhD
  applied psychology • MS
  applied sociology • MS
  business administration • MBA
  business and behavioral science • M E!Com, MA, MBA, MP Acc, MPA, MS, PhD
  economics • MA
  electronic commerce • M E!Com
  graphic communications • MS
  human factors • MS
  industrial management • MS, PhD
  industrial/organizational psychology • PhD
  management science • PhD
  public administration • MPA

College of Engineering and Science
Dr. Thomas M. Keinath, Dean
Programs in:
  applied and pure mathematics • MS, PhD
  astronomy and astrophysics • MS, PhD
  atmospheric physics • MS, PhD
  bioengineering • MS, PhD
  biophysics • MS, PhD
  ceramic and materials engineering • MS, PhD
  chemical engineering • MS, PhD
  chemistry • MS, PhD
  civil engineering • M Engr, MS, PhD
  computational mathematics • MS, PhD
  computer engineering • MS, PhD
  computer science • MS, PhD
  electrical engineering • M Engr, MS, PhD
  engineering and science • M Engr, MS, PhD
  environmental engineering and science • M Engr, MS, PhD
  hydrogeology • MS
  industrial engineering • MS, PhD
  management science • PhD
  materials science and engineering • MS, PhD
  mechanical engineering • MS, PhD
  operations research • MS, PhD
  physics • MS, PhD
  statistics • MS, PhD
  textiles, fiber and polymer science • MS, PhD

College of Health, Education, and Human Development
Dr. Larry Allen, Interim Dean
Programs in:
  administration and supervision • M Ed, Ed S
  administration and supervision for the two-year college • MCTE
  career and technology education • MCTE, Ed D
  counselor education • M Ed
  curriculum and instruction • PhD
  educational leadership • PhD
  elementary education • M Ed
  English • M Ed
  health, education, and human development • M Ed, MAT, MCTE, MHA, MHRD, MPRTM, MS, Ed D, PhD, Ed S
  history and government • M Ed
  human resource development • MHRD
  industrial technology education • MCTE
  mathematics • M Ed
  middle grades education • MAT
  natural sciences • M Ed
  nursing • MS
  parks, recreation, and tourism management • MPRTM, MS, PhD
  public health • MHA
  reading • M Ed
  secondary education • M Ed
  special education • M Ed
  vocational and technical education • MCTE, Ed D

■ COLLEGE OF CHARLESTON
Charleston, SC 29424-0001
http://www.cofc.edu/

State-supported, coed, comprehensive institution. *Enrollment:* 11,536 graduate, professional, and undergraduate students; 290 full-time matriculated graduate/professional students (219 women), 346 part-time matriculated graduate/professional students (234 women). *Graduate faculty:* 151 full-time (52 women), 40 part-time/adjunct (18 women). *Computer facilities:* Computer purchase and lease plans are available. 300 computers available on campus for general student use. A campuswide network can be accessed from student residence rooms and from off campus. Internet access and online class registration are available. *Library facilities:* Robert Scott Small Library plus 1 other. *Graduate expenses:* Tuition, state resident: full-time $2,175; part-time $238 per credit hour. Tuition, nonresident: full-time $4,902; part-time $541 per credit hour. Required fees: $2 per credit hour. $15 per term. One-time fee: $45 full-time. *General application contact:* Leah Hinds, Assistant Director of Admissions, 843-953-7354.

Find an in-depth description at www.petersons.com/gradchannel.

Graduate School
Dr. Hugh Haynsworth, Dean of Graduate Studies

School of Business and Economics
Dr. Robert Pitts, Dean
Programs in:
  accountancy • MS
  business and economics • MS

School of Education
Dr. Frances Welch, Dean
Programs in:
  early childhood education • M Ed, MAT
  education • M Ed, MAT
  elementary education • M Ed, MAT
  languages • M Ed
  science and mathematics for teachers • M Ed
  special education • M Ed, MAT

School of Humanities and Social Sciences
Dr. Samuel M. Hines, Dean
Programs in:
  bilingual legal interpreting • MA
  English • MA
  history • MA
  humanities and social sciences • MA, MPA
  public administration • MPA

School of Sciences and Mathematics
Dr. Gordon Jones, Dean
Programs in:
  computer and information sciences • MS
  environmental studies • MS
  marine biology • MS
  mathematics • MS
  sciences and mathematics • MS

■ CONVERSE COLLEGE
Spartanburg, SC 29302-0006
http://www.converse.edu/

Independent, women only, comprehensive institution. *Enrollment:* 1,124 graduate, professional, and undergraduate students; 85 full-time matriculated graduate/professional students (59 women), 873 part-time matriculated graduate/professional students (708 women). *Graduate faculty:* 72 full-time (39 women), 15 part-time/adjunct (8 women). *Computer facilities:* 65 computers available on campus for general student use. A campuswide network can be accessed from student residence rooms and from off campus. Internet access is available. *Library facilities:* Mickel Library. *Graduate expenses:* Tuition: part-time $260 per credit hour. *General application contact:* Dr. Thomas R. McDaniel, Acting Dean, 864-596-9082.

South Carolina

Converse College (continued)

Carroll McDaniel Petrie School of Music
Joseph Hopkins, Dean
Programs in:
  instrumental performance • M Mus
  music education • M Mus
  piano pedagogy • M Mus
  vocal performance • M Mus

Department of Education
Dr. Thomas R. McDaniel, Acting Dean
Programs in:
  administration and supervision • Ed S
  biology • MAT
  chemistry • MAT
  curriculum and instruction • Ed S
  early childhood education • MAT
  educable mental disabilities • MAT
  education • MAT, Ed S
  elementary education • M Ed, MAT
  English • M Ed, MAT, MLA
  gifted education • M Ed
  history • MLA
  leadership • M Ed
  learning disabilities • MAT
  liberal arts • MLA
  marriage and family therapy • Ed S
  mathematics • M Ed, MAT
  natural sciences • M Ed
  political science • MLA
  secondary education • M Ed, MAT
  social sciences • M Ed, MAT
  special education • M Ed, MAT

■ FRANCIS MARION UNIVERSITY
Florence, SC 29501-0547
http://www.fmarion.edu/

State-supported, coed, comprehensive institution. *Enrollment:* 3,590 graduate, professional, and undergraduate students; 37 full-time matriculated graduate/professional students (28 women), 175 part-time matriculated graduate/professional students (133 women). *Graduate faculty:* 101 full-time (18 women), 5 part-time/adjunct (3 women). *Computer facilities:* 409 computers available on campus for general student use. A campuswide network can be accessed from student residence rooms and from off campus. Internet access and online class registration, blackboard are available. *Library facilities:* James A. Rogers Library plus 1 other. *Graduate expenses:* Tuition, state resident: full-time $5,147; part-time $515 per credit hour. Tuition, nonresident: full-time $10,294; part-time $1,029 per credit hour. Required fees: $135; $68 per semester. Part-time tuition and fees vary according to course load. *General application contact:* Rannie Gamble, Administrative Manager, 843-661-1286.

Graduate Programs
Provost's Office
Programs in:
  applied clinical psychology • MS
  applied community psychology • MS
  school psychology • MS

School of Business
Dr. M. Barry O'Brien, Dean
Programs in:
  business • MBA
  health management • MBA

School of Education
Dr. James R. Faulkenberry, Dean
Programs in:
  early childhood education • M Ed
  elementary education • M Ed
  learning disabilities • M Ed, MAT
  remediation education • M Ed
  secondary education • M Ed

■ LANDER UNIVERSITY
Greenwood, SC 29649-2099
http://www.lander.edu/

State-supported, coed, comprehensive institution. *Enrollment:* 2,950 graduate, professional, and undergraduate students; 10 full-time matriculated graduate/professional students (9 women), 56 part-time matriculated graduate/professional students (54 women). *Graduate faculty:* 7 full-time (5 women), 5 part-time/adjunct (4 women). *Computer facilities:* 125 computers available on campus for general student use. A campuswide network can be accessed from student residence rooms and from off campus. Internet access and online class registration are available. *Library facilities:* Jackson Library. *Graduate expenses:* Tuition, state resident: full-time $2,955; part-time $247 per semester hour. Tuition, nonresident: full-time $6,125; part-time $510 per semester hour. *General application contact:* Dr. Robert Taylor, Director of Graduate Studies, School of Education, 864-388-8225.

School of Education
Dr. Danny McKenzie, Dean
Programs in:
  elementary education • M Ed
  teaching • MAT

■ SOUTH CAROLINA STATE UNIVERSITY
Orangeburg, SC 29117-0001
http://www.scsu.edu/

State-supported, coed, comprehensive institution. CGS member. *Enrollment:* 4,466 graduate, professional, and undergraduate students; 233 full-time matriculated graduate/professional students (191 women), 265 part-time matriculated graduate/professional students (220 women). *Graduate faculty:* 50 full-time (31 women), 26 part-time/adjunct (14 women). *Computer facilities:* 300 computers available on campus for general student use. A campuswide network can be accessed. Internet access is available. *Library facilities:* Miller F. Whittaker Library plus 1 other. *Graduate expenses:* Tuition, state resident: part-time $2,785 per semester. Tuition, nonresident: part-time $5,425 per semester. *General application contact:* Dr. Gail Joyner-Fleming, Interim Dean of the School of Graduate Studies, 803-533-3769.

School of Graduate Studies
Dr. Gail Joyner-Fleming, Interim Dean
Program in:
  agribusiness • MS

School of Applied Professional Sciences
Dr. Leola Adams, Dean
Programs in:
  applied professional sciences • MA, MS
  individual and family development • MS
  nutritional sciences • MS
  rehabilitation counseling • MA
  speech/language pathology • MA

School of Education
Programs in:
  early childhood and special education • M Ed
  early childhood education • MAT
  education • M Ed, MAT, Ed D, Ed S
  educational leadership • Ed D, Ed S
  elementary counselor education • M Ed
  elementary education • M Ed, MAT
  engineering • MAT
  general science • MAT
  mathematics • MAT
  secondary counselor education • M Ed
  secondary education • M Ed
  special education • M Ed

■ SOUTHERN WESLEYAN UNIVERSITY
Central, SC 29630-1020
http://www.swu.edu/

Independent-religious, coed, comprehensive institution. *Enrollment:* 2,430 graduate, professional, and undergraduate students; 453 full-time matriculated graduate/professional students (306 women). *Graduate faculty:* 23 full-time (4 women), 34 part-time/adjunct (8 women). *Computer facilities:* 78 computers available on campus for general student use. A campuswide network can be accessed from student residence rooms and from off campus.

Internet access is available. *Library facilities:* Rickman Library. *Graduate expenses:* Tuition: full-time $7,080. Required fees: $125. *General application contact:* Jeanne Bolt, Regional Enrollment Manager, 800-264-5327.

Program in Business Administration
Dr. Jim Mahony, Chair
Program in:
 business administration • MBA

Program in Christian Ministries
Dr. Mari Gonlag, Director
Program in:
 Christian ministries • M Min

Program in Education
Dr. Ray Locy, Head
Program in:
 education • M Ed

Program in Management
Dr. Jim Mahony, Chair
Program in:
 management • MSM

■ UNIVERSITY OF SOUTH CAROLINA
Columbia, SC 29208
http://www.sc.edu/

State-supported, coed, university. CGS member. *Enrollment:* 25,288 graduate, professional, and undergraduate students; 3,474 full-time matriculated graduate/professional students (2,012 women), 3,383 part-time matriculated graduate/professional students (2,374 women). *Graduate faculty:* 1,387 full-time (406 women), 324 part-time/adjunct (139 women). *Computer facilities:* 11,000 computers available on campus for general student use. A campuswide network can be accessed from student residence rooms and from off campus. Internet access and online class registration are available. *Library facilities:* Thomas Cooper Library plus 7 others. *Graduate expenses:* Tuition, state resident: part-time $308 per hour. Tuition, nonresident: part-time $655 per hour. *General application contact:* Dale Moore, Director of Graduate Admissions, 803-777-4243.

Find an in-depth description at www.petersons.com/gradchannel.

College of Pharmacy
Programs in:
 pharmaceutical sciences • MS, PhD
 pharmacy • Pharm D, MS, PhD

The Graduate School
Dr. Gordon B. Smith, Dean
Program in:
 gerontology • Certificate

College of Education
Dr. Les Sternberg, Dean
Programs in:
 art education • IMA, MAT
 business education • IMA, MAT
 community and adult education • M Ed
 counseling education • PhD, Ed S
 curriculum and instruction • Ed D
 early childhood education • M Ed, MAT, PhD
 education • IMA, M Ed, MA, MAT, MS, MT, Ed D, PhD, Certificate, Ed S
 educational administration • M Ed, MA, PhD, Ed S
 educational psychology, research • M Ed, PhD
 educational technology • M Ed
 elementary education • M Ed, MAT, PhD
 English • MAT
 foreign language • MAT
 foundations in education • PhD
 health education • MAT
 health education administration • Ed D
 higher education and student affairs • M Ed
 higher education leadership • Certificate
 language and literacy • M Ed, PhD
 mathematics • MAT
 physical education • IMA, MAT, MS, PhD
 science • IMA, MAT
 secondary education • IMA, M Ed, MA, MAT, MT, PhD
 social studies • IMA, MAT
 special education • M Ed, MAT, PhD
 teaching • Ed S
 theatre and speech • IMA, MAT

College of Engineering and Information Technology
Dr. Ralph E. White, Dean
Programs in:
 chemical engineering • ME, MS, PhD
 civil engineering • ME, MS, PhD
 computer science and engineering • ME, MS, PhD
 electrical engineering • ME, MS, PhD
 engineering and information technology • ME, MS, PhD
 mechanical engineering • ME, MS, PhD
 software engineering • MS

College of Hospitality, Retail, and Sport Management
Programs in:
 hospitality • MHRTA
 hospitality, retail, and sport management • MHRTA

College of Liberal Arts
Dr. John V. Skvoretz, Interim Dean
Programs in:
 anthropology • MA
 archives • MA
 art education • IMA, MA, MAT
 art history • MA
 art studio • MA
 clinical/community psychology • PhD
 creative writing • MFA
 criminology and criminal justice • MCJ
 English • MA, PhD
 English education • MAT
 experimental psychology • MA, PhD
 foreign languages • MAT
 geography • MA, MS, PhD
 geography education • IMA
 German • MA
 historic preservation • MA
 history • MA, PhD
 history education • IMA, MAT
 international studies • MA, PhD
 liberal arts • IMA, MA, MAT, MCJ, MFA, MMA, MPA, MS, PhD, Certificate
 linguistics • MA, PhD
 media arts • MMA
 museum • MA
 museum management • Certificate
 philosophy • MA, PhD
 political science • MA, PhD
 public administration • MPA
 public history • MA, Certificate
 religious studies • MA
 school psychology • PhD
 sociology • MA, PhD
 studio art • MFA
 teaching English as a foreign language • Certificate
 theater • IMA, MA, MAT, MFA
 women's studies • Certificate

College of Mass Communications and Information Studies
Programs in:
 library and information science • MLIS, Certificate, Specialist
 mass communication and information studies • MLIS, Certificate, Specialist

College of Nursing
Dr. Mary Ann Parsons, Dean
Programs in:
 acute care nurse practitioner • MSN
 adult nurse practitioner • MSN
 advanced practice nursing in clinical and psychiatric mental health • Certificate

Peterson's Graduate Schools in the U.S. 2006

South Carolina

University of South Carolina (continued)
  advanced practice nursing in primary care and women's health • Certificate
  clinical nursing • MSN
  clinical/acute care nurse practitioner • Certificate
  community mental health and psychiatric health nursing • MSN
  family nurse practitioner • MSN
  health nursing • MSN
  nursing • ND
  nursing administration • MSN
  nursing science • PhD
  pediatric nurse practitioner • MSN
  primary care • Certificate
  psychiatric mental health nurse practitioner • Certificate
  women's health • Certificate
  women's health nurse practitioner • MSN

College of Science and Mathematics
Dr. Gary Crawley, Dean
Programs in:
  applied statistics • CAS
  biology • MS, PhD
  biology education • IMA, MAT
  chemistry and biochemistry • IMA, MAT, MS, PhD
  ecology, evolution and organismal biology • MS, PhD
  environmental geoscience • PMS
  geological sciences • MS, PhD
  marine science • MS, PhD
  mathematics • MA, MS, PhD
  mathematics education • M Math, MAT
  molecular, cellular, and developmental biology • MS, PhD
  physics and astronomy • IMA, MAT, MS, PMS, PhD
  science and mathematics • IMA, M Math, MA, MAT, MIS, MS, PMS, PhD, CAS
  statistics • MIS, MS, PhD

College of Social Work
Program in:
  social work • MSW, PhD

The Darla Moore School of Business
Joel A. Smith, Dean
Programs in:
  accountancy • M Acc
  business administration • PMBA, PhD
  business measurement and assurance • M Acc
  economics • MA, PhD
  human resources • MHR
  international business administration • IMBA

Norman J. Arnold School of Public Health
Dr. Donna L. Richter, Interim Dean
Programs in:
  alcohol and drug studies • Certificate
  biostatistics • MPH, MSPH, Dr PH, PhD
  communication sciences and disorders • MCD, MSP, PhD
  environmental health science • MS
  environmental quality • MPH, MSPH, PhD
  epidemiology • MPH, MSPH, Dr PH, PhD
  exercise science • MS, DPT, PhD
  general public health • MPH
  hazardous materials management • MPH, MSPH, PhD
  health education administration • Ed D
  health promotion and education • MAT, MPH, MS, MSPH, Dr PH, PhD
  health services policy and management • MHA, MPH, Dr PH, PhD
  industrial hygiene • MPH, MSPH, PhD
  public health • MAT, MCD, MHA, MPH, MS, MSP, MSPH, DPT, Dr PH, Ed D, PhD, Certificate
  school health education • Certificate

School of Journalism and Mass Communications
Program in:
  journalism and mass communications • MA, MMC, PhD

School of Music
Dr. Jãmal J. Rossi, Dean
Programs in:
  composition • MM, DMA
  conducting • MM, DMA
  jazz studies • MM
  music education • MM Ed, PhD
  music history • MM
  music performance • Certificate
  music theory • MM
  opera theater • MM
  performance • MM, DMA
  piano pedagogy • MM, DMA

School of the Environment
Dr. Bruce C. Coull, Dean
Programs in:
  earth and environmental resources management • MEERM
  environment • MEERM

School of Law
Burnele V. Powell, Dean
Program in:
  law • JD

School of Medicine
Dr. Larry R. Faulkner, Dean
Programs in:
  biomedical science • MBS, PhD
  genetic counseling • MS
  medicine • MD, MBS, MNA, MRC, MS, PhD, Certificate
  nurse anesthesia • MNA
  psychiatric rehabilitation • Certificate
  rehabilitation counseling • MRC, Certificate

■ WINTHROP UNIVERSITY
Rock Hill, SC 29733
http://www.winthrop.edu/

State-supported, coed, comprehensive institution. *Enrollment:* 6,558 graduate, professional, and undergraduate students; 316 full-time matriculated graduate/professional students (195 women), 405 part-time matriculated graduate/professional students (281 women). *Graduate faculty:* 156 full-time (69 women), 72 part-time/adjunct (46 women). *Computer facilities:* 250 computers available on campus for general student use. A campuswide network can be accessed from student residence rooms and from off campus. Internet access is available. *Library facilities:* Dacus Library. *Graduate expenses:* Tuition, state resident: full-time $3,203; part-time $268 per credit hour. Tuition, nonresident: full-time $5,891; part-time $492 per credit hour. Required fees: $10 per semester. *General application contact:* Sharon B. Johnson, Director of Graduate Studies, 800-411-7041.

College of Arts and Sciences
Dr. Thomas F. Moove, Dean
Programs in:
  arts and sciences • M Math, MA, MLA, MS, SSP
  biology • MS
  English • MA
  history • MA
  human nutrition • MS
  liberal arts • MLA
  mathematics • M Math
  psychology • MS, SSP
  Spanish • MA

College of Business Administration
Dr. Roger Weikle, Dean
Programs in:
  business administration • MBA, MS, Certificate
  software development • MS
  software project management • Certificate

College of Education
Dr. Patricia Graham, Dean
Programs in:
  agency counseling • M Ed
  education • M Ed, MAT, MS
  educational leadership • M Ed
  elementary education • M Ed
  middle level education • M Ed
  physical education • MS
  reading education • M Ed
  school counseling • M Ed
  secondary education • M Ed, MAT
  special education • M Ed

College of Visual and Performing Arts
Dr. Andrew Svedlow, Dean
Programs in:
  art • MFA
  art administration • MA
  art education • MA
  conducting • MM
  music education • MME
  performance • MM
  visual and performing arts • MA, MFA, MM, MME

South Dakota

■ MOUNT MARTY COLLEGE
Yankton, SD 57078-3724
http://www.mtmc.edu/

Independent-religious, coed, comprehensive institution. *Enrollment:* 1,185 graduate, professional, and undergraduate students; 73 full-time matriculated graduate/professional students (36 women). *Graduate faculty:* 2 full-time (1 woman), 1 part-time/adjunct (0 women). *Computer facilities:* Computer purchase and lease plans are available. 21 computers available on campus for general student use. A campuswide network can be accessed from student residence rooms and from off campus. Internet access is available. *Library facilities:* Mount Marty College Library. *Graduate expenses:* Tuition: full-time $15,000. Required fees: $600. *General application contact:* Larry Lee Dahlen, Director of Nurse Anesthesia Program, 605-322-8090.

Graduate Studies Division
Larry Lee Dahlen, Director of Nurse Anesthesia Program
Program in:
  nursing anesthesia • MS

■ NORTHERN STATE UNIVERSITY
Aberdeen, SD 57401-7198
http://www.northern.edu/

State-supported, coed, comprehensive institution. *Enrollment:* 3,083 graduate, professional, and undergraduate students; 127 matriculated graduate/professional students. *Graduate faculty:* 83 full-time (21 women). *Computer facilities:* 900 computers available on campus for general student use. A campuswide network can be accessed from student residence rooms and from off campus.

Internet access and online class registration are available. *Library facilities:* Beulah Williams Library. *Graduate expenses:* Tuition, state resident: full-time $2,616; part-time $109 per credit. Tuition, nonresident: full-time $7,739; part-time $322 per credit. Required fees: $1,636; $68 per credit. One-time fee: $35 part-time. Full-time tuition and fees vary according to course load, degree level and reciprocity agreements. *General application contact:* Tammy K. Griffith, Senior Secretary, 605-626-2558.

Division of Graduate Studies in Education
Dr. Ruth A. Johnson, Head
Programs in:
  e-learning design and instruction • MS Ed
  education • MS, MS Ed
  educational studies • MS Ed
  elementary classroom teaching • MS Ed
  elementary school administration • MS Ed
  guidance and counseling • MS Ed
  health, physical education, and coaching • MS Ed
  language and literacy • MS Ed
  secondary classroom teaching • MS Ed
  secondary school administration • MS Ed
  special education • MS Ed

Center for Statewide E-Learning
Dr. Erika Tallman, Director
Program in:
  e-learning technology and administration • MS

■ SOUTH DAKOTA STATE UNIVERSITY
Brookings, SD 57007
http://www.sdstate.edu/

State-supported, coed, university. CGS member. *Computer facilities:* 278 computers available on campus for general student use. A campuswide network can be accessed from student residence rooms and from off campus. Internet access is available. *Library facilities:* H. M. Briggs Library. *General application contact:* Dean of the Graduate School, 605-688-4181.

Graduate School

College of Agriculture and Biological Sciences
Programs in:
  agriculture and biological sciences • MS, PhD
  agronomy • MS, PhD
  animal science • MS, PhD
  biological sciences • PhD
  biology • MS
  dairy science • MS, PhD
  economics • MS
  entomology • MS
  microbiology • MS
  plant pathology • MS
  rural sociology • MS, PhD
  wildlife and fisheries sciences • MS

College of Arts and Science
Programs in:
  analytical chemistry • MS, PhD
  arts and science • MA, MS, PhD
  biochemistry • MS, PhD
  chemistry • MS, PhD
  communication studies and theatre • MS
  English • MA
  geography • MS
  health, physical education and recreation • MS
  inorganic chemistry • MS, PhD
  journalism • MS
  organic chemistry • MS, PhD
  physical chemistry • MS, PhD

College of Education and Counseling
Programs in:
  counseling and human resource development • MS
  curriculum and instruction • M Ed
  education and counseling • M Ed, MS
  educational administration • M Ed

College of Engineering
Programs in:
  agricultural engineering • MS, PhD
  atmospheric, environmental, and water resources • PhD
  electrical engineering • MS
  engineering • MS
  industrial management • MS
  mathematics • MS
  mechanical engineering • MS
  physics • MS

College of Family and Consumer Sciences
Program in:
  family and consumer sciences • MS

College of Nursing
Program in:
  nursing • MS

College of Pharmacy
Programs in:
  pharmaceutical sciences • MS
  pharmacy • Pharm D, MS

■ UNIVERSITY OF SIOUX FALLS
Sioux Falls, SD 57105-1699
http://www.usiouxfalls.edu/

Independent-religious, coed, comprehensive institution. *Computer facilities:* 142 computers available on

South Dakota

University of Sioux Falls (continued) campus for general student use. A campuswide network can be accessed from student residence rooms and from off campus. Internet access is available. *Library facilities:* Norman B. Mears Library. *General application contact:* Director of Graduate Studies, 605-331-6710.

Program in Business Administration
Program in:
business administration • MBA

Program in Education
Programs in:
leadership • M Ed
reading • M Ed
technology • M Ed

■ THE UNIVERSITY OF SOUTH DAKOTA
Vermillion, SD 57069-2390
http://www.usd.edu/

State-supported, coed, university. *Computer facilities:* 750 computers available on campus for general student use. A campuswide network can be accessed from student residence rooms and from off campus. Internet access is available. *Library facilities:* I. D. Weeks Library plus 2 others. *General application contact:* Administrative Assistant, 605-677-6287.

Find an in-depth description at www.petersons.com/gradchannel.

Graduate School
Programs in:
administrative studies • MS
interdisciplinary studies • MA

College of Arts and Sciences
Programs in:
arts and sciences • MA, MNS, MPA, MS, PhD
audiology • MA
biology • MA, MNS, MS, PhD
chemistry • MA, MNS
clinical psychology • MA, PhD
computer science • MA
English • MA, PhD
history • MA
human factors • MA, PhD
mathematics • MA, MNS
political science • MA
public administration • MPA
sociology • MA
speech communication • MA
speech-language pathology • MA

College of Fine Arts
Programs in:
art • MFA
fine arts • MA, MFA, MM
mass communications • MA
music • MM
theatre • MA, MFA

School of Business
Programs in:
accounting • MP Acc
business • MBA, MP Acc
business administration • MBA

School of Education
Programs in:
counseling and psychology in education • MA, Ed D, PhD, Ed S
curriculum and instruction • Ed D, Ed S
education • MA, MS, Ed D, PhD, Ed S
educational administration • MA, Ed D, Ed S
elementary education • MA
health, physical education and recreation • MA
secondary education • MA
special education • MA
technology for education and training • MS, Ed S

School of Law
Barry R. Vickrey, Dean
Program in:
law • JD

School of Medicine
Dr. Robert Talley, Dean
Programs in:
cardiovascular research • MA, PhD
cellular and molecular biology • MA, PhD
medicine • MD, MA, MS, PhD
molecular microbiology and immunology • MA, PhD
neuroscience • MA, PhD
occupational therapy • MS
physical therapy • MS
physician assistant studies • MS
physiology and pharmacology • MA, PhD

Tennessee

■ AUSTIN PEAY STATE UNIVERSITY
Clarksville, TN 37044-0001
http://www.apsu.edu/

State-supported, coed, comprehensive institution. CGS member. *Enrollment:* 7,623 graduate, professional, and undergraduate students; 188 full-time matriculated graduate/professional students (133 women), 247 part-time matriculated graduate/professional students (190 women). *Graduate faculty:* 84 full-time (42 women), 13 part-time/adjunct (7 women). *Computer facilities:* 600 computers available on campus for general student use. A campuswide network can be accessed from student residence rooms and from off campus. Internet access and online class registration are available. *Library facilities:* Felix G. Woodward Library. *Graduate expenses:* Tuition, state resident: full-time $4,206; part-time $222 per credit hour. Tuition, nonresident: full-time $12,138; part-time $566 per credit hour. Required fees: $872; $41 per credit hour. *General application contact:* Dr. Charles Pinder, Dean, College of Graduate Studies, 931-221-7414.

Graduate School
Dr. Charles Pinder, Dean, College of Graduate Studies

College of Arts and Letters
James Diehr, Dean
Programs in:
arts and letters • M Mu, MA, MA Ed
communication arts • MA
English • MA, MA Ed
music • M Mu
music education • M Mu

College of Professional Programs and Social Sciences
Dr. Thomas Buttery, Dean
Programs in:
administration and supervision • MA Ed, Ed S
clinical psychology • MA
counseling and guidance • Ed S
curriculum and instruction • MA Ed
elementary education • MA Ed, Ed S
guidance and counseling • MS
health and human performance • MA Ed, MS
psychological science • MA
reading • MA Ed
school psychology • MA, Ed S
secondary education • Ed S
social sciences • MA, MA Ed, MS, Ed S
special education • MA

College of Science and Mathematics
Gaines Hunt, Dean
Programs in:
biology • MS
science and mathematics • MS

■ BELMONT UNIVERSITY
Nashville, TN 37212-3757
http://www.belmont.edu/

Independent-religious, coed, comprehensive institution. *Enrollment:* 3,629 graduate, professional, and undergraduate students; 277 full-time matriculated graduate/professional students (205 women), 363 part-time matriculated graduate/professional students (220 women). *Graduate faculty:* 77 full-time (41 women), 47 part-time/adjunct (28 women). *Computer facilities:* 350 computers available on campus for general student use. A campuswide

Tennessee

network can be accessed from student residence rooms and from off campus. Internet access and online class registration, individual student information via BANNER web are available. *Library facilities:* Lila D. Bunch Library. *Graduate expenses:* Tuition: full-time $7,400; part-time $390 per hour. Full-time tuition and fees vary according to degree level, program and student level. *General application contact:* Dr. Kathryn Baugher, Dean of Enrollment Services, 615-460-6785.

College of Arts and Sciences
Dr. Larry M. Hall, Dean
Programs in:
  arts and sciences • M Ed, MA, MAT
  literature • MA
  writing • MA

School of Education
Dr. Trevor F. Hutchins, Associate Dean
Programs in:
  education • MAT
  elementary education • M Ed
  English • M Ed
  history • M Ed
  mathematics • M Ed
  middle grade education • M Ed
  science • M Ed
  secondary education • M Ed
  sports administration • M Ed
  technology • M Ed

College of Health Sciences
Dr. Debra B. Wollaber, Dean
Program in:
  health sciences • MSN, MSOT, DPT, OTD

School of Nursing
Dr. Leslie J. Higgins, Director, Graduate Program
Program in:
  nursing • MSN

School of Occupational Therapy
Dr. Lorry Kleinfeld, Associate Dean
Program in:
  occupational therapy • MSOT, OTD

School of Physical Therapy
Dr. David G. Greathouse, Associate Dean
Program in:
  physical therapy • DPT

College of Visual and Performing Arts
Dr. Cynthia R. Curtis, Dean
Program in:
  visual and performing arts • MM

School of Music
Dr. Robert Gregg, Director
Programs in:
  church music • MM
  composition • MM
  music education • MM
  pedagogy • MM
  performance • MM

Jack C. Massey Graduate School of Business
Dr. Patrick Raines, Dean
Program in:
  business • M Acc, MBA

■ CARSON-NEWMAN COLLEGE
Jefferson City, TN 37760
http://www.cn.edu/

Independent-religious, coed, comprehensive institution. *Enrollment:* 2,115 graduate, professional, and undergraduate students; 89 full-time matriculated graduate/professional students (67 women), 84 part-time matriculated graduate/professional students (62 women). *Graduate faculty:* 7 full-time (4 women), 20 part-time/adjunct (12 women). *Computer facilities:* 200 computers available on campus for general student use. A campuswide network can be accessed from student residence rooms and from off campus. Internet access is available. *Library facilities:* Stephens-Burnett Library plus 1 other. *Graduate expenses:* Tuition: part-time $200 per hour. *General application contact:* Jane W. McGill, Graduate Admissions and Services Adviser, 865-471-3460.

Department of Nursing
Dr. Patricia Kraft, Dean and Chair
Program in:
  family nurse practitioner • MSN

Graduate Program in Education
Dr. Margaret A. Hypes, Chair
Programs in:
  curriculum and instruction • M Ed
  elementary education • MAT
  school counseling • M Ed
  secondary education • MAT
  teaching English as a second language • MATESL

■ CHRISTIAN BROTHERS UNIVERSITY
Memphis, TN 38104-5581
http://www.cbu.edu/

Independent-religious, coed, comprehensive institution. *Enrollment:* 1,929 graduate, professional, and undergraduate students; 63 full-time matriculated graduate/professional students (37 women), 284 part-time matriculated graduate/professional students (178 women). *Graduate faculty:* 17 full-time (6 women), 10 part-time/adjunct (6 women). *Computer facilities:* 300 computers available on campus for general student use. A campuswide network can be accessed from student residence rooms and from off campus. Internet access and online class registration, online class listings, e-mail, course assignments are available. *Library facilities:* Plough Memorial Library and Media Center. *Graduate expenses:* Tuition: part-time $475 per credit. *General application contact:* Information Contact, 901-321-3200.

Graduate Programs
Information Contact

School of Arts
Dr. Kristin Pruitt, Dean
Program in:
  liberal arts • M Ed

School of Business
Dr. Thomas Dukes, Dean
Program in:
  business • MBA

School of Engineering
Dr. Sinipong Malasri, Dean
Program in:
  engineering • MEM

■ CUMBERLAND UNIVERSITY
Lebanon, TN 37087-3408
http://www.cumberland.edu/

Independent, coed, comprehensive institution. *Enrollment:* 1,420 graduate, professional, and undergraduate students; 29 full-time matriculated graduate/professional students (17 women), 470 part-time matriculated graduate/professional students (383 women). *Graduate faculty:* 15 full-time (5 women), 18 part-time/adjunct (12 women). *Computer facilities:* 150 computers available on campus for general student use. A campuswide network can be accessed from student residence rooms and from off campus. Internet access is available. *Library facilities:* Doris and Harry Vise Library. *Graduate expenses:* Tuition: full-time $12,384; part-time $516 per semester hour. Required fees: $25 per semester. Tuition and fees vary according to program. *General application contact:* Melinda Y. Bone, Vice President for Enrollment Management, 615-444-2562 Ext. 1225.

Division of Graduate Studies
Dr. J. M. Galloway, Dean of Graduate Studies

Tennessee

Cumberland University (continued)
Programs in:
  business administration • MBA
  education • MAE
  human relations management • MS
  public service administration • MS

■ EAST TENNESSEE STATE UNIVERSITY
Johnson City, TN 37614
http://www.etsu.edu/

State-supported, coed, university. CGS member. *Enrollment:* 11,624 graduate, professional, and undergraduate students; 1,138 full-time matriculated graduate/professional students (719 women), 861 part-time matriculated graduate/professional students (565 women). *Graduate faculty:* 460 full-time (164 women), 56 part-time/adjunct (13 women). *Computer facilities:* Computer purchase and lease plans are available. 550 computers available on campus for general student use. A campuswide network can be accessed. Internet access and online class registration are available. *Library facilities:* Sherrod Library plus 2 others. *Graduate expenses:* Tuition, state resident: part-time $222 per hour. Tuition, nonresident: part-time $344 per hour. Required fees: $264 per hour. *General application contact:* Jeffrey Powers-Beck, Assistant Dean, 423-439-4221.

Find an in-depth description at www.petersons.com/gradchannel.

James H. Quillen College of Medicine
Dr. Ronald Franks, Vice President for Health Affairs, Dean
Programs in:
  anatomy • MS, PhD
  biochemistry • MS, PhD
  biophysics • MS, PhD
  medicine • MD, MS, PhD
  microbiology • MS, PhD
  pharmacology • MS, PhD
  physiology • MS, PhD

School of Graduate Studies
Dr. Wesley Brown, Dean

College of Arts and Sciences
Dr. Gordon K. Anderson, Dean
Programs in:
  applied sociology • MA
  art education • MA
  art history • MA
  arts and sciences • M Mu Ed, MA, MFA, MS, MSW
  biology • MS
  chemistry • MS
  clinical psychology • MA
  communication • MA
  criminal justice and criminology • MA
  English • MA
  general psychology • MA
  general sociology • MA
  history • MA
  mathematics • MS
  microbiology • MS
  music • M Mu Ed
  social work • MSW
  studio art • MA, MFA

College of Business and Technology
Dr. Linda Garceau, Dean
Programs in:
  accountancy • M Acc
  business administration • MBA, Certificate
  business and technology • M Acc, MBA, MCM, MPM, MS, Certificate
  city management • MCM
  clinical nutrition • MS
  community development • MPM
  computer science • MS
  engineering technology • MS
  general administration • MPM
  health care management • Certificate
  industrial arts/technology education • MS
  information systems science • MS
  municipal service management • MPM
  software engineering • MS
  urban and regional economic development • MPM
  urban and regional planning • MPM

College of Education
Dr. Hal Knight, Dean
Programs in:
  7-12 • MAT
  administrative endorsement • M Ed, Ed D, Ed S
  advanced practitioner • M Ed
  classroom leadership • Ed D
  classroom technology • M Ed
  community agency counseling • M Ed, MA
  comprehensive concentration • M Ed
  counseling • M Ed, MA
  early childhood education • M Ed, MA
  early childhood general • M Ed
  early childhood special education • M Ed
  early childhood teaching • M Ed
  education • M Ed, MA, MAT, Ed D, Ed S
  educational communication • M Ed
  educational leadership • M Ed, Ed D, Ed S
  educational media/educational technology • M Ed
  elementary and secondary (school counseling) • M Ed, MA
  elementary education • M Ed, MAT
  exercise physiology • MA
  fitness leadership • MA
  K-12 • MAT
  marriage and family therapy • M Ed, MA
  modified concentration • M Ed
  physical education • M Ed, MA
  post secondary and private sector leadership • Ed D
  reading and storytelling • M Ed, MA
  reading education • M Ed, MA
  school leadership • Ed D
  school library media • M Ed
  school system leadership • Ed S
  secondary education • M Ed, MAT
  sports management • MA
  sports sciences • MA
  teacher leadership • Ed S

College of Nursing
Dr. Patricia Smith, Dean
Programs in:
  advanced nursing practice • Post Master's Certificate
  health care management • Certificate
  nursing • MSN, DSN

College of Public and Allied Health
Dr. Wilsie Bishop, Dean
Programs in:
  audiology • MS, Au D
  communicative disorders • MS
  community health • MPH
  environmental health • MSEH
  gerontology • Certificate
  health care management • Certificate
  physical therapy • MPT
  public and allied health • MPH, MPT, MS, MSEH, Au D, Certificate
  public health • MPH
  public health administration • MPH
  special education audiology pre-K-12 • MS
  special education speech pathology pre-K-12 • MS
  speech pathology • MS

Division of Cross-Disciplinary Studies
Dr. Rick E. Osborn, Associate Dean
Program in:
  liberal studies • MALS

■ FREED-HARDEMAN UNIVERSITY
Henderson, TN 38340-2399
http://www.fhu.edu/

Independent-religious, coed, comprehensive institution. *Enrollment:* 1,966 graduate, professional, and undergraduate students; 132 full-time matriculated graduate/professional students (87 women), 387 part-time matriculated graduate/professional students (241 women). *Graduate faculty:* 22 full-time (5 women), 10 part-time/adjunct (5 women). *Computer facilities:* Computer purchase and lease plans are available. 250 computers available on campus for general student use. A campuswide network can be accessed from student residence rooms and from off campus. Internet access is available. *Library facilities:* Loden-Daniel Library. *Graduate expenses:* Tuition: part-time $265 per hour. *General application contact:* Dr. Samuel T. Jones, Vice President for Academic Affairs, 731-989-6004.

Program in Counseling
Dr. Mike Cravens, Graduate Director
Program in:
 counseling • MS

Program in Education
Dr. Elizabeth Saunders, Graduate Director
Programs in:
 curriculum and instruction • M Ed
 school counseling • M Ed

School of Biblical Studies
Dr. Earl Edwards, Director of Graduate Studies
Programs in:
 biblical studies • M Min, MA
 ministry • M Min
 New Testament • MA

■ LINCOLN MEMORIAL UNIVERSITY
Harrogate, TN 37752-1901
http://www.lmunet.edu/

Independent, coed, comprehensive institution. *Computer facilities:* 150 computers available on campus for general student use. A campuswide network can be accessed from student residence rooms. Internet access is available. *Library facilities:* Carnegie Library. *General application contact:* Senior Assistant, Graduate Office, 423-869-6374.

Program in Business Administration
Program in:
 business administration • MBA

Program in Education
Programs in:
 administration and supervision • M Ed, Ed S
 counseling and guidance • M Ed
 curriculum and instruction • M Ed, Ed S

■ LIPSCOMB UNIVERSITY
Nashville, TN 37204-3951
http://www.lipscomb.edu/

Independent-religious, coed, comprehensive institution. *Enrollment:* 2,661 graduate, professional, and undergraduate students; 59 full-time matriculated graduate/professional students (29 women), 154 part-time matriculated graduate/professional students (60 women). *Graduate faculty:* 23 full-time (2 women), 12 part-time/adjunct (2 women). *Computer facilities:* 232 computers available on campus for general student use. A campuswide network can be accessed from student residence rooms and from off campus. Internet access and online class registration are available. *Library facilities:* Beaman Library plus 1 other. *Graduate expenses:* Tuition: part-time $453 per semester hour. Required fees: $16 per semester hour. $15 per semester. *General application contact:* Dr. James Thomas, Director of Graduate Bible Studies, 615-269-1000 Ext. 5761.

MBA Program
Dr. Perry G. Moore, Director
Program in:
 business administration • MBA

Program in Bible Studies
Dr. Terry Briley, Director
Programs in:
 biblical studies • MA, MAR
 divinity • M Div

Program in Education
Dr. Carolyn Tucker, Director
Program in:
 education • M Ed

■ MIDDLE TENNESSEE STATE UNIVERSITY
Murfreesboro, TN 37132
http://www.mtsu.edu/

State-supported, coed, university. CGS member. *Enrollment:* 21,744 graduate, professional, and undergraduate students; 1,748 matriculated graduate/professional students. *Graduate faculty:* 470. *Computer facilities:* 2,300 computers available on campus for general student use. A campuswide network can be accessed from student residence rooms and from off campus. Internet access and online class registration are available. *Library facilities:* James E. Walker Library. *Graduate expenses:* Tuition, state resident: full-time $4,206. Tuition, nonresident: full-time $12,138. *General application contact:* Dr. Donald L. Curry, Dean and Vice Provost for Research, 615-898-2840.

College of Graduate Studies
Dr. Donald L. Curry, Vice Provost for Research and Dean

College of Basic and Applied Sciences
Dr. Thomas Cheatham, Dean
Programs in:
 aerospace education • M Ed
 airport/airline management • MS
 asset management • MS
 aviation administration • MS
 basic and applied sciences • M Ed, MS, MST, MVTE, DA
 biology • MS, MST
 chemistry • MS, DA
 computer science • MS
 engineering technology and industrial studies • MS, MVTE
 mathematics • MS
 mathematics education • MST
 natural science • MS

College of Business
Dr. James E. Burton, Dean
Programs in:
 accounting • MS
 business • MA, MBA, MBE, MS, DA
 business education • MBE
 computer information systems • MS
 economics • MA, DA
 industrial relations • MA
 information systems • MS
 management and marketing • MBA

College of Education and Behavioral Science
Dr. Gloria Bonner, Dean
Programs in:
 administration and supervision • M Ed, Ed S
 child development and family studies • MS
 criminal justice administration • MCJ
 curriculum and instruction • M Ed, Ed S
 curriculum specialist • M Ed, Ed S
 early childhood education • M Ed
 education and behavioral science • M Ed, MA, MCJ, MS, DA, Ed S
 elementary education • M Ed, Ed S
 exercise science and health promotion • MS
 health, physical education, recreation and safety • MS
 industrial/organizational psychology • MA
 middle school education • M Ed
 nutrition and food science • MS
 physical education • DA
 psychology • MA
 reading • M Ed
 school counseling • M Ed, Ed S
 school psychology • Ed S
 secondary education • M Ed, Ed S
 special education • M Ed

College of Liberal Arts
Dr. John McDaniel, Dean
Programs in:
 English • MA, DA
 foreign languages and literatures • MAT

Tennessee

Middle Tennessee State University (continued)
- historic preservation • DA
- history • MA, DA
- liberal arts • MA, MAT, DA
- music • MA
- sociology • MA

College of Mass Communications
Dr. Anantha Babbili, Dean
Program in:
- mass communications • MS

■ MILLIGAN COLLEGE
Milligan College, TN 37682
http://www.milligan.edu/

Independent-religious, coed, comprehensive institution. *Enrollment:* 838 graduate, professional, and undergraduate students; 35 full-time matriculated graduate/professional students, 31 part-time matriculated graduate/professional students. *Graduate faculty:* 7 full-time (4 women), 5 part-time/adjunct (2 women). *Computer facilities:* Computer purchase and lease plans are available. 119 computers available on campus for general student use. A campuswide network can be accessed from student residence rooms and from off campus. Internet access is available. *Library facilities:* P. H. Welshimer Memorial Library. *Graduate expenses:* Tuition: part-time $260 per hour. *General application contact:* Carrie Davidson, Director of Graduate Admissions, 423-461-8306.

Area of Teacher Education
Dr. Billye Joyce Fine, Director of Teacher Education
Program in:
- teacher education • M Ed

Program in Occupational Therapy
Dr. Christy Isbell, Program Director and Associate Professor
Program in:
- occupational therapy • MSOT

■ TENNESSEE STATE UNIVERSITY
Nashville, TN 37209-1561
http://www.tnstate.edu/

State-supported, coed, comprehensive institution. CGS member. *Enrollment:* 9,024 graduate, professional, and undergraduate students; 544 full-time matriculated graduate/professional students (356 women), 1,098 part-time matriculated graduate/professional students (772 women). *Graduate faculty:* 208 full-time (62 women), 35 part-time/adjunct (15 women). *Computer facilities:* 320 computers available on campus for general student use. A campuswide network can be accessed from student residence rooms and from off campus. *Library facilities:* Martha M. Brown/Lois H. Daniel Library plus 1 other. *General application contact:* Dr. Helen Barrett, Dean of the Graduate School, 615-963-5901.

Graduate School
Dr. Helen Barrett, Dean

College of Arts and Sciences
Dr. William Lawson, Dean
Programs in:
- arts and sciences • MA, MCJ, MS, PhD
- biological sciences • MS, PhD
- chemistry • MS
- criminal justice • MCJ
- English • MA
- mathematics • MS
- music education • MS

College of Business
Dr. Tilden J. Curry, Dean
Program in:
- business • MBA

College of Education
Dr. Leslie Drummonds, Dean
Programs in:
- counseling and guidance • MS
- counseling psychology • PhD
- curriculum and instruction • Ed D
- curriculum planning • Ed D
- education • M Ed, MA Ed, MS, Ed D, PhD
- educational administration • M Ed, MA Ed, Ed D
- elementary education • M Ed, MA Ed, Ed D
- human performance and sports science • MA Ed
- psychology • MS, PhD
- school psychology • MS, PhD
- special education • M Ed, MA Ed, Ed D

College of Engineering, Technology, and Computer Science
Dr. Decatur B. Rogers, Dean
Program in:
- engineering, technology, and computer science • ME, PhD

Institute of Government
Dr. Ann-Marie Rizzo, Director
Program in:
- public administration • MPA, PhD

School of Agriculture and Family Services
Dr. Troy Wakefield, Dean
Program in:
- agriculture and family services • MS, PhD

School of Allied Health Professions
Dr. Kathleen McEnerney, Dean
Program in:
- allied health professions • M Ed

School of Nursing
Dr. Mary Graham, Dean
Program in:
- nursing • MS, PhD

■ TENNESSEE TECHNOLOGICAL UNIVERSITY
Cookeville, TN 38505
http://www.tntech.edu/

State-supported, coed, university. CGS member. *Enrollment:* 9,107 graduate, professional, and undergraduate students; 526 full-time matriculated graduate/professional students (258 women), 818 part-time matriculated graduate/professional students (551 women). *Graduate faculty:* 341 full-time (62 women). *Computer facilities:* 600 computers available on campus for general student use. A campuswide network can be accessed from student residence rooms and from off campus. Internet access and online class registration are available. *Library facilities:* Angelo and Jennette Volpe Library and Media Center. *Graduate expenses:* Tuition, state resident: full-time $7,410; part-time $263 per semester hour. Tuition, nonresident: full-time $19,134; part-time $607 per semester hour. *General application contact:* Dr. Francis O. Otuonye, Associate Vice President for Research and Graduate Studies, 931-372-3233.

Graduate School
Dr. Francis O. Otuonye, Associate Vice President for Research and Graduate Studies

College of Arts and Sciences
Dr. Jack Armistead, Dean
Programs in:
- arts and sciences • MA, MS, PhD
- chemistry • MS
- computer science • MS
- English • MA
- environmental biology • MS
- environmental sciences • PhD
- fish, game, and wildlife management • MS
- mathematics • MS

College of Business Administration
Dr. Bob G. Wood, Interim Director
Program in:
- business administration • MBA

Tennessee

College of Education
Dr. Darrell Garber, Dean
Programs in:
   curriculum • MA, Ed S
   early childhood education • MA, Ed S
   education • MA, PhD, Ed S
   educational psychology • MA, Ed S
   educational psychology and student personnel • MA, Ed S
   elementary education • MA, Ed S
   exceptional learning • PhD
   health and physical education • MA
   instructional leadership • MA, Ed S
   library science • MA
   reading • MA, Ed S
   secondary education • MA, Ed S
   special education • MA, Ed S

College of Engineering
Dr. Glen Johnson, Dean
Programs in:
   chemical engineering • MS, PhD
   civil engineering • MS, PhD
   electrical engineering • MS, PhD
   engineering • MS, PhD
   industrial engineering • MS, PhD
   mechanical engineering • MS, PhD

■ TREVECCA NAZARENE UNIVERSITY
Nashville, TN 37210-2877
http://www.trevecca.edu/

Independent-religious, coed, comprehensive institution. *Enrollment:* 1,911 graduate, professional, and undergraduate students; 572 full-time matriculated graduate/professional students (377 women), 101 part-time matriculated graduate/professional students (55 women). *Graduate faculty:* 23 full-time (9 women), 39 part-time/adjunct (12 women). *Computer facilities:* 200 computers available on campus for general student use. A campuswide network can be accessed from student residence rooms and from off campus. Internet access is available. *Library facilities:* Mackey Library. *Graduate expenses:* Tuition: full-time $5,364; part-time $298 per credit. Tuition and fees vary according to degree level and program. *General application contact:* Dr. Stephen M. Pusey, Vice President of Academic Affairs, 615-248-1258.

Graduate Division
Dr. Stephen M. Pusey, Vice President of Academic Affairs

Division of Natural and Applied Sciences
Dr. Mike Moredock, Chair
Programs in:
   natural and applied sciences • MS
   physician assistant • MS

Division of Social and Behavioral Sciences
Dr. Peter Wilson, Chair
Programs in:
   counseling • MA
   counseling psychology • MA
   marriage and family therapy • MMFT

School of Business and Management
Dr. Jim Hiatt, Dean
Programs in:
   business administration • MBA
   business and management • MBA, MSM
   management • MSM

School of Education
Dr. Esther Swink, Dean
Programs in:
   educational leadership • M Ed
   instructional effectiveness • M Ed
   library and information science • MLI Sc
   professional practics • D Ed

School of Religion and Philosophy
Dr. Tim Green, Dean
Programs in:
   religion and philosophy • MA
   religious studies • MA

■ TUSCULUM COLLEGE
Greeneville, TN 37743-9997
http://www.tusculum.edu/

Independent-religious, coed, comprehensive institution. *Enrollment:* 2,132 graduate, professional, and undergraduate students; 218 full-time matriculated graduate/professional students (144 women). *Graduate faculty:* 20 full-time (6 women), 15 part-time/adjunct (6 women). *Computer facilities:* 102 computers available on campus for general student use. A campuswide network can be accessed from student residence rooms and from off campus. Internet access is available. *Library facilities:* Albert Columbus Tate Library plus 2 others. *Graduate expenses:* Tuition: full-time $6,360; part-time $265 per semester hour. *General application contact:* Information Contact, 423-693-1177 Ext. 330.

Graduate School
Dr. Denise Wood, Dean
Programs in:
   adult education • MA Ed
   K–12 • MA Ed
   organizational management • MAOM

■ UNION UNIVERSITY
Jackson, TN 38305-3697
http://www.uu.edu/

Independent-religious, coed, comprehensive institution. *Enrollment:* 2,774 graduate, professional, and undergraduate students; 537 full-time matriculated graduate/professional students (364 women), 79 part-time matriculated graduate/professional students (65 women). *Graduate faculty:* 69. *Computer facilities:* 236 computers available on campus for general student use. A campuswide network can be accessed from student residence rooms and from off campus. Internet access is available. *Library facilities:* Emma Waters Summar Library plus 1 other. *Graduate expenses:* Tuition: part-time $240 per semester hour. *General application contact:* Robbie Graves, Director of Enrollment Services, 731-661-5008.

Institute for International and Intercultural Studies
Dr. Cynthia Powell Jayne, Director
Program in:
   international and intercultural studies • MAIS

McAfee School of Business Administration
Program in:
   business administration • MBA

School of Education and Human Studies
Dr. Tom R. Rosebrough, Dean
Programs in:
   education • M Ed, MA Ed
   education administration generalist • Ed S
   educational leadership • Ed D
   educational supervision • Ed S

School of Nursing
Dr. Cathy Parrett, Director
Programs in:
   nursing administration • MSN, PMC
   nursing education • MSN, PMC

■ THE UNIVERSITY OF MEMPHIS
Memphis, TN 38152
http://www.memphis.edu/

State-supported, coed, university. CGS member. *Enrollment:* 19,911 graduate, professional, and undergraduate students; 4,702 matriculated graduate/professional students. *Graduate faculty:* 516 full-time (156 women), 63 part-time/adjunct (28 women). *Computer facilities:* 2,000 computers available on campus for general student use. A campuswide network can be accessed from off campus. Internet access and online class registration are available. *Library facilities:*

Tennessee

The University of Memphis (continued)
McWherter Library plus 6 others. *Graduate expenses:* Tuition, state resident: full-time $5,142. Tuition, nonresident: full-time $13,296. *General application contact:* Dr. Dianne Horgan, Associate Dean of Graduate School, 901-678-2531.

Find an in-depth description at www.petersons.com/gradchannel.

Cecil C. Humphreys School of Law
Rodney K. Smith, Interim Dean
Program in:
- law • JD

Graduate School
Dr. Dianne Horgan, Associate Dean of Graduate School
Programs in:
- clinical nutrition • MS
- consumer science and education • MS

College of Arts and Sciences
Dr. Henry A. Kurtz, Dean
Programs in:
- anthropology • MA
- applied mathematics • MS
- applied statistics • PhD
- arts and sciences • MA, MCRP, MFA, MHA, MPA, MS, PhD
- bioinformatics • MS
- biology • MS, PhD
- chemistry • MS, PhD
- city and regional planning • MCRP
- clinical psychology • PhD
- computer science • PhD
- computer sciences • MS
- creative writing • MFA
- criminology and criminal justice • MA
- earth sciences • PhD
- English • MA
- experimental psychology • PhD
- French • MA
- geography • MA, MS
- geology • MS
- geophysics • MS
- health administration • MHA
- history • MA, PhD
- mathematics • MS, PhD
- nonprofit administration • MPA
- philosophy • MA, PhD
- physics • MS
- political science • MA
- psychology • MS
- public management and policy • MPA
- school psychology • MA, PhD
- sociology • MA
- Spanish • MA
- statistics • MS, PhD
- urban affairs and public policy • MA, MCRP, MHA, MPA
- urban management and planning • MPA
- writing and language studies • PhD

College of Communication and Fine Arts
Dr. Richard R. Ranta, Dean
Programs in:
- applied music • M Mu
- art history • MA
- ceramics • MFA
- communication • MA
- communication and fine arts • M Mu, MA, MFA, DMA, PhD
- communication arts • PhD
- composition • M Mu, DMA
- Egyptian art and archaeology • MA
- film and video production • MA
- general art history • MA
- general journalism • MA
- graphic design • MFA
- interior design • MFA
- journalism administration • MA
- music education • M Mu, DMA
- music history • M Mu
- musicology • PhD
- Orff-Schulwerk • M Mu
- painting • MFA
- performance • DMA
- piano pedagogy • M Mu
- printmaking/photography • MFA
- sacred music • M Mu, DMA
- sculpture • MFA
- Suzuki pedagogy-piano/strings • M Mu
- theatre • MFA

College of Education
Dr. Ric A. Hovda, Dean
Programs in:
- adult education • Ed D
- clinical nutrition • MS
- community education • Ed D
- counseling and personnel services • MS, Ed D
- counseling psychology • PhD
- early childhood education • MAT, MS, Ed D
- education • Ed S
- educational leadership • Ed D
- educational psychology and research • MS, Ed D, PhD
- elementary education • MAT
- exercise and sport science • MS
- health promotion • MS
- higher education • Ed D
- instruction and curriculum • MS, Ed D
- instruction design and technology • MS, Ed D
- leadership • MS
- physical education teacher education • MS
- policy studies • Ed D
- reading • MS, Ed D
- school administration and supervision • MS
- secondary education • MAT
- special education • MAT, MS, Ed D
- sport and leisure commerce • MS

Fogelman College of Business and Economics
Dr. John J. Pepin, Dean
Programs in:
- accounting • MBA, MS, PhD
- accounting systems • MS
- business and economics • MA, MBA, MS, PhD
- economics • MBA, PhD
- executive business administration • MBA
- finance • PhD
- finance, insurance, and real estate • MBA, MS
- international business administration • MBA
- management • MBA, MS, PhD
- management information systems • MBA, MS, PhD
- management science • MBA
- marketing • MBA, MS
- marketing and supply chain management • PhD
- real estate development • MS
- taxation • MS

Herff College of Engineering
Dr. Richard C. Warder, Dean
Programs in:
- automatic control systems • MS
- biomedical engineering • MS, PhD
- biomedical systems • MS
- civil engineering • PhD
- communications and propagation systems • MS
- design and mechanical engineering • MS
- electrical engineering • PhD
- electronics engineering technology • MS
- energy systems • MS
- engineering • MS, PhD
- engineering computer systems • MS
- environmental engineering • MS
- foundation engineering • MS
- industrial engineering • MS
- manufacturing engineering technology • MS
- mechanical engineering • PhD
- mechanical systems • MS
- power systems • MS
- structural engineering • MS
- transportation engineering • MS
- water resources engineering • MS

School of Audiology and Speech-Language Pathology
Dr. Maurice Mendel, Dean
Program in:
- audiology and speech-language pathology • MA, Au D, PhD

■ THE UNIVERSITY OF TENNESSEE
Knoxville, TN 37996
http://www.tennessee.edu/

State-supported, coed, university. CGS member. *Computer facilities:* Computer purchase and lease plans are available. 1,500 computers available on campus for general student use. A campuswide network can be accessed from student residence rooms and from off campus. Internet access and online class registration are available. *Library facilities:* John C. Hodges Library plus 6 others. *General application contact:* Director of Graduate Admissions and Records, 865-974-3251.

College of Law
Dr. Karen R. Britton, Director of Admissions and Career Services
Program in:
  law • JD

Graduate School
Programs in:
  aviation systems • MS
  comparative and experimental medicine • MS, PhD

College of Agricultural Sciences and Natural Resources
Programs in:
  agribusiness • MS
  agricultural economics • MS
  agricultural education • MS
  agricultural extension education • MS
  agricultural sciences and natural resources • MS, PhD
  animal anatomy • PhD
  biosystems engineering • MS, PhD
  biosystems engineering technology • MS
  breeding • MS, PhD
  entomology • MS, PhD
  floriculture • MS
  food science and technology • MS, PhD
  forestry • MS
  intergrated pest management and bioactive natural products • PhD
  landscape design • MS
  management • MS, PhD
  nutrition • MS, PhD
  physiology • MS, PhD
  plant pathology • MS, PhD
  public horticulture • MS
  rural sociology • MS
  turfgrass • MS
  wildlife and fisheries science • MS
  woody ornamentals • MS

College of Architecture and Design
Dr. Jan Simek, Interim Dean
Program in:
  architecture and design • M Arch

College of Arts and Sciences
Programs in:
  accompanying • MM
  American history • PhD
  analytical chemistry • MS, PhD
  applied linguistics • PhD
  applied mathematics • MS
  archaeology • MA, PhD
  arts and sciences • M Math, MA, MFA, MM, MPA, MS, MSP, PhD
  audiology • MA, PhD
  behavior • MS, PhD
  biochemistry and cellular and molecular biology • MS, PhD
  biological anthropology • MA, PhD
  botany • MS, PhD
  ceramics • MFA
  chemical physics • PhD
  choral conducting • MM
  clinical psychology • PhD
  composition • MM
  computer science • MS, PhD
  costume design • MFA
  criminology • MA, PhD
  cultural anthropology • MA, PhD
  drawing • MFA
  ecology • MS, PhD
  energy, environment, and resource policy • MA, PhD
  English • MA, PhD
  environmental chemistry • MS, PhD
  environmental planning • MSP
  European history • PhD
  evolutionary biology • MS, PhD
  experimental psychology • MA, PhD
  French • MA, PhD
  genome science and technology • MS, PhD
  geography • MS, PhD
  geology • MS, PhD
  German • MA, PhD
  graphic design • MFA
  hearing science • PhD
  history • MA
  inorganic chemistry • MS, PhD
  instrumental conducting • MM
  inter-area studies • MFA
  Italian • PhD
  jazz • MM
  land-use planning • MSP
  lighting design • MFA
  mathematical ecology • PhD
  mathematics • M Math, MS, PhD
  media arts • MFA
  medical ethics • MA, PhD
  microbiology • MS, PhD
  modern foreign languages • PhD
  music education • MM
  music theory • MM
  musicology • MM
  organic chemistry • MS, PhD
  painting • MFA
  performance • MFA, MM
  philosophy • MA, PhD
  physical chemistry • MS, PhD
  physics • MS, PhD
  piano pedagogy and literature • MM
  plant physiology and genetics • MS, PhD
  political economy • MA, PhD
  political science • MA, PhD
  polymer chemistry • MS, PhD
  Portuguese • PhD
  printmaking • MFA
  psychology • MA
  public administration • MPA
  real estate development planning • MSP
  religious studies • MA
  Russian • PhD
  scene design • MFA
  sculpture • MFA
  Spanish • MA, PhD
  speech and hearing science • PhD
  speech and language pathology • PhD
  speech and language science • PhD
  speech pathology • MA
  theatre technology • MFA
  theoretical chemistry • PhD
  transportation planning • MSP
  watercolor • MFA
  zooarchaeology • MA, PhD

College of Business Administration
Programs in:
  accounting • M Acc, PhD
  business administration • M Acc, MA, MBA, MS, PhD
  economics • MA, PhD
  finance • MBA, PhD
  industrial statistics • MS
  industrial/organizational psychology • PhD
  logistics and transportation • MBA, PhD
  management • PhD
  management science • MS, PhD
  marketing • MBA, PhD
  operations management • MBA
  professional business administration • MBA
  statistics • MS, PhD
  systems • M Acc
  taxation • M Acc

College of Communications
Programs in:
  advertising • MS, PhD
  broadcasting • MS, PhD
  communications • MS, PhD
  information sciences • PhD
  journalism • MS, PhD
  public relations • MS, PhD
  speech communication • MS, PhD

College of Education
Programs in:
  adult education • MS
  art education • MS
  college student personnel • MS
  counseling education • PhD
  counseling psychology • PhD
  cultural studies in education • PhD
  curriculum • MS, Ed S
  curriculum education research and evaluation • PhD
  curriculum, educational research and evaluation • Ed D
  early childhood education • PhD
  early childhood special education • MS
  education • MS, Ed D, PhD, Ed S
  education of deaf and hard of hearing • MS

Tennessee

The University of Tennessee (continued)
  education psychology • PhD
  educational administration and policy studies • Ed D, PhD
  educational administration and supervision • MS, Ed S
  educational psychology • Ed D
  elementary education • MS, Ed S
  elementary teaching • MS
  English education • MS, Ed S
  exercise science • MS, PhD
  foreign language/ESL education • MS, Ed S
  individual and collaborative learning • MS
  industrial technology • PhD
  instructional technology • MS, Ed D, Ed S
  literacy, language education and ESL education • PhD
  literacy, language education, and ESL education • Ed D
  mathematics education • MS, Ed S
  mental health counseling • MS
  modified and comprehensive special education • MS
  reading education • MS, Ed S
  rehabilitation counseling • MS
  school counseling • MS, Ed S
  school psychology • PhD, Ed S
  science education • MS, Ed S
  secondary teaching • MS
  social foundations • MS
  social science education • MS, Ed S
  socio-cultural foundations of sports and education • PhD
  special education • Ed S
  sport management • MS
  sport studies • MS
  teacher education • Ed D, PhD

College of Engineering
Programs in:
  aerospace engineering • MS, PhD
  applied artificial intelligence • MS
  biomedical engineering • MS, PhD
  chemical engineering • MS, PhD
  civil engineering • MS, PhD
  composite materials • MS, PhD
  computational mechanics • MS, PhD
  electrical engineering • MS, PhD
  engineering • MS, PhD
  engineering management • MS
  engineering science • MS, PhD
  environmental engineering • MS
  fluid mechanics • MS, PhD
  industrial engineering • PhD
  manufacturing systems engineering • MS
  materials science and engineering • MS, PhD
  mechanical engineering • MS, PhD
  nuclear engineering • MS, PhD
  optical engineering • MS, PhD
  polymer engineering • MS, PhD
  product development and manufacturing • MS
  solid mechanics • MS, PhD
  traditional industrial engineering • MS

College of Human Ecology
Programs in:
  child and family studies • MS, PhD
  community health • PhD
  community health education • MPH
  early childhood education • MS
  gerontology • MPH
  health planning/administration • MPH
  health promotion and health education • MS
  hospitality management • MS
  human ecology • MPH, MS, PhD
  human resource development • PhD
  nutrition • MS
  nutrition science • PhD
  public health • MPH
  recreation administration • MS
  recreation, tourism, and hospitality management • MS
  retail and consumer sciences • MS
  retailing and consumer sciences • PhD
  safety • MS
  teacher licensure • MS
  textile science • MS, PhD
  textiles, retailing and consumer sciences • MS
  therapeutic recreation • MS
  tourism • MS
  training and development • MS

College of Nursing
Program in:
  nursing • MSN, PhD

College of Social Work
Programs in:
  clinical social work practice • MSSW
  social welfare management and community practice • MSSW
  social work • PhD

College of Veterinary Medicine
Program in:
  veterinary medicine • DVM

School of Information Sciences
Program in:
  information sciences • MS

■ THE UNIVERSITY OF TENNESSEE AT CHATTANOOGA
Chattanooga, TN 37403-2598
http://www.utc.edu/

State-supported, coed, comprehensive institution. CGS member. *Enrollment:* 8,528 graduate, professional, and undergraduate students; 469 full-time matriculated graduate/professional students (297 women), 862 part-time matriculated graduate/professional students (515 women). *Graduate faculty:* 129 full-time (49 women), 27 part-time/adjunct (15 women). *Computer facilities:* 300 computers available on campus for general student use. A campuswide network can be accessed from student residence rooms and from off campus. Internet access and online class registration are available. *Library facilities:* Lupton Library. *Graduate expenses:* Tuition, state resident: full-time $2,228; part-time $764 per credit. Tuition, nonresident: full-time $6,054; part-time $2,039 per credit. *General application contact:* Dr. Deborah E. Arfken, Dean of Graduate Studies, 423-425-1740.

Graduate Division
Dr. Deborah E. Arfken, Dean of Graduate Studies

College of Arts and Sciences
Dr. Herbert Burhenn, Dean
Programs in:
  arts and sciences • MA, MM, MPA, MS, MSCJ
  criminal justice • MSCJ
  English • MA
  environmental sciences • MS
  industrial/organizational psychology • MS
  music • MM
  public administration • MPA
  research psychology • MS

College of Business Administration
Dr. Richard P. Casavant, Dean
Programs in:
  accountancy • M Acc
  business administration • MBA
  economics • MBA
  finance • MBA
  marketing • MBA
  operations/production • MBA
  organizational management • MBA

College of Education and Applied Professional Studies
Dr. Mary Tanner, Dean
Programs in:
  administration • MSN
  adult health • MSN
  athletic training • MS
  counseling • M Ed
  education • MSN
  education and applied professional studies • M Ed, MS, MSN, MSPT, DPT, Ed S
  educational specialist • Ed S
  educational technology • Ed S
  elementary education • M Ed
  family nurse practitioner • MSN
  health and human performance • MS
  nurse anesthesia • MSN
  physical therapy • MSPT, DPT
  school leadership • M Ed
  school psychology • Ed S
  secondary education • M Ed
  special education • M Ed

Tennessee

College of Engineering and Computer Sciences
Dr. Phil M. Kazemersky, Acting Dean
Programs in:
computer science • MS
engineering • MS
engineering management • MS

THE UNIVERSITY OF TENNESSEE AT MARTIN
Martin, TN 38238-1000
http://www.utm.edu/

State-supported, coed, comprehensive institution. *Enrollment:* 5,810 graduate, professional, and undergraduate students; 366 matriculated graduate/professional students (247 women). *Graduate faculty:* 135. *Computer facilities:* 185 computers available on campus for general student use. A campuswide network can be accessed from student residence rooms and from off campus. *Library facilities:* Paul Meek Library plus 1 other. *Graduate expenses:* Tuition, state resident: part-time $251 per credit hour. Tuition, nonresident: part-time $676 per credit hour. *General application contact:* Linda L. Arant, Administrative Services Assistant, 731-587-7012.

Graduate Studies
Dr. Victoria S. Seng, Assistant Vice Chancellor and Dean of Graduate Studies

College of Agriculture and Applied Sciences
Dr. James Byford, Dean
Programs in:
agricultural operations management • MSAOM
agriculture and applied sciences • MSAOM, MSFCS
child development and family relations • MSFCS
food science and nutrition • MSFCS

College of Business and Public Affairs
Dr. Ernest Moser, Dean
Programs in:
accounting • M Ac
business administration • MBA
business and public affairs • M Ac, MBA

College of Education and Behavioral Sciences
Dr. Mary Lee Hall, Dean
Programs in:
advanced elementary • MS Ed
advanced secondary • MS Ed
community mental health • MS Ed
education • MS Ed
educational administration and supervision • MS Ed
initial licensure elementary • MS Ed
initial licensure K-12 • MS Ed
initial licensure secondary • MS Ed
school counseling • MS Ed

VANDERBILT UNIVERSITY
Nashville, TN 37240-1001
http://www.vanderbilt.edu/

Independent, coed, university. CGS member. *Enrollment:* 11,092 graduate, professional, and undergraduate students; 1,878 full-time matriculated graduate/professional students (881 women), 86 part-time matriculated graduate/professional students (34 women). *Graduate faculty:* 2,346 full-time, 1,655 part-time/adjunct. *Computer facilities:* 400 computers available on campus for general student use. A campuswide network can be accessed from student residence rooms and from off campus. Productivity and educational software available. *Library facilities:* Jean and Alexander Heard Library plus 7 others. *Graduate expenses:* Tuition: part-time $1,155 per semester hour. Required fees: $1,538. *General application contact:* Information Contact, 615-343-2727.

Divinity School
Program in:
divinity • M Div, MTS

Graduate School
Programs in:
analytical chemistry • MAT, MS, PhD
anthropology • MA, PhD
astronomy • MS
biochemistry • MS, PhD
biological sciences • MS, PhD
biomedical informatics • MS, PhD
cancer biology • MS, PhD
cell and developmental biology • MS, PhD
cellular and molecular pathology • PhD
classical studies • MA, MAT, PhD
comparative literature • MA, PhD
economics • MA, MAT, PhD
educational leadership • MS, PhD
English • MA, MAT, PhD
fine arts • MA, MAT
French • MA, MAT, PhD
geology • MS
German • MA, MAT, PhD
history • MA, MAT, PhD
inorganic chemistry • MAT, MS, PhD
Latin American studies • MA
liberal arts and science • MLAS
mathematics • MA, MAT, MS, PhD
microbiology and immunology • MS, PhD
molecular physiology and biophysics • PhD
neuroscience • PhD
nursing science • PhD
organic chemistry • MAT, MS, PhD
pharmacology • PhD
philosophy • MA, PhD
physical chemistry • MAT, MS, PhD
physics • MA, MAT, MS, PhD
policy development and program evaluation • MS, PhD
political science • MA, MAT, PhD
Portuguese • MA
psychology • MA, PhD
religion • MA, PhD
sociology • MA, PhD
Spanish • MA, MAT, PhD
Spanish and Portuguese • PhD
special education • MS, PhD
teaching and learning • MS, PhD
theoretical chemistry • MAT, MS, PhD

Law School
Kent D. Syverud, Dean
Program in:
law • JD, LL M

Owen Graduate School of Management
Dr. William G. Christie, Dean
Programs in:
business administration • MBA
executive business administration • MBA
finance • PhD
management • MBA, PhD
marketing • PhD
operations management • PhD
organization studies • PhD

Peabody College
Dr. Camilla P. Benbow, Dean
Programs in:
child studies • M Ed
curriculum and instructional leadership • M Ed
early childhood education • M Ed
education • M Ed, MPP, Ed D, PhD
education policy • MPP
educational leadership and policy • Ed D
elementary education • M Ed
English education • M Ed
higher education • M Ed
higher education, leadership and policy • Ed D
human development counseling • M Ed
human resource development • M Ed
human, organizational and community development • M Ed
international education policy and management • M Ed
mathematics education • M Ed
organizational leadership • M Ed
psychological sciences • PhD
reading education • M Ed
school administration • M Ed

Tennessee

Vanderbilt University (continued)
science education • M Ed
secondary education • M Ed
special education • M Ed
technology and education • M Ed

School of Engineering
Dr. Kenneth F. Galloway, Dean
Programs in:
biomedical engineering • M Eng, MS, PhD
chemical engineering • M Eng, MS, PhD
civil engineering • M Eng, MS, PhD
computer science • M Eng, MS, PhD
electrical engineering • M Eng, MS, PhD
engineering • M Eng, MS, PhD
environmental engineering • M Eng, MS, PhD
environmental management • MS, PhD
management of technology • M Eng, MS, PhD
materials science • M Eng, MS, PhD
mechanical engineering • M Eng, MS, PhD

School of Medicine
Dr. Steven G. Gabbe, Dean
Programs in:
audiology • PhD
biomedical and biological sciences • PhD
chemical and physical biology • PhD
clinical investigation • MS
hearing and speech sciences • MS
medical physics • MS
medicine • MD, MPH, MS, PhD

School of Nursing
Programs in:
adult acute care nurse practitioner • MSN
adult/correctional health nurse practitioner • MSN
family nurse practitioner • MSN
gerontology nurse practitioner • MSN
health systems management • MSN
neonatal nurse practitioner • MSN
nurse midwifery • MSN
nursing science • PhD
occupational health/adult health nurse practitioner • MSN
pediatric nurse practitioner • MSN
psychiatric-mental health nurse practitioner • MSN
women's health nurse practitioner • MSN

Texas

■ ABILENE CHRISTIAN UNIVERSITY
Abilene, TX 79699-9100
http://www.acu.edu/

Independent-religious, coed, comprehensive institution. CGS member. *Enrollment:* 4,648 graduate, professional, and undergraduate students; 240 full-time matriculated graduate/professional students (110 women), 213 part-time matriculated graduate/professional students (78 women). *Graduate faculty:* 12 full-time (0 women), 85 part-time/adjunct (21 women). *Computer facilities:* 700 computers available on campus for general student use. A campuswide network can be accessed from student residence rooms and from off campus. Internet access and online class registration are available. *Library facilities:* Brown Library. *Graduate expenses:* Tuition: full-time $10,200; part-time $425 per hour. Required fees: $540; $17 per hour. $5 per semester. *General application contact:* Dr. Carol G. Williams, Graduate Dean, 325-674-2223.

Graduate School
Dr. Carol G. Williams, Graduate Dean
Program in:
liberal arts • MLA

Center for Conflict Resolution
Dr. Joe L. Cope, Graduate Adviser
Program in:
conflict resolution • Certificate

College of Arts and Sciences
Dr. Colleen Durrington, Dean
Programs in:
arts and sciences • M Ed, MA, MS, Certificate
clinical psychology • MS
communication sciences and disorders • MS
composition/rhetoric • MA
counseling psychology • MS
educational diagnosis • M Ed
elementary teaching • M Ed
family studies • MS
general psychology • MS
gerontology • MS, Certificate
human communication • MA
literature • MA
organizational and human resource development • MS
reading specialist • M Ed
school counselor • M Ed
school principalship • M Ed
school psychology • MS
secondary teaching • M Ed
writing • MA

College of Biblical Studies
Dr. Jack Reese, Dean
Programs in:
biblical studies • M Div, MA, MACM, MMFT, D Min
Christian ministry • MACM
divinity • M Div
history and theology • MA
marriage and family therapy • MMFT
ministry • D Min
missions • MA
New Testament • MA
Old Testament • MA

College of Business Administration
Bill Fowler, Department Chair
Program in:
business administration • M Acc

School of Nursing
Dr. Jan Noles, Dean
Program in:
nursing • MSN

■ ANGELO STATE UNIVERSITY
San Angelo, TX 76909
http://www.angelo.edu/

State-supported, coed, comprehensive institution. CGS member. *Enrollment:* 6,043 graduate, professional, and undergraduate students; 130 full-time matriculated graduate/professional students (81 women), 268 part-time matriculated graduate/professional students (178 women). *Graduate faculty:* 107 full-time (42 women), 2 part-time/adjunct (0 women). *Computer facilities:* 500 computers available on campus for general student use. A campuswide network can be accessed from student residence rooms and from off campus. Internet access and online class registration are available. *Library facilities:* Porter Henderson Library plus 1 other. *Graduate expenses:* Tuition, state resident: part-time $204 per semester hour. Tuition, nonresident: part-time $440 per semester hour. *General application contact:* Jackie Droll, Coordinator of Graduate Admissions, 325-942-2169.

Find an in-depth description at www.petersons.com/gradchannel.

Graduate School
Dr. Carol B. Diminnie, Dean of Graduate School
Program in:
interdisciplinary studies • MA, MS

Texas

College of Business and Professional Studies
Dr. Michael Butler, Dean
Programs in:
 accounting • MBA
 business and professional studies • MBA, MPAC, MS
 kinesiology • MS
 management • MBA
 professional accountancy • MPAC

College of Liberal and Fine Arts
Dr. Charles A. Endress, Interim Dean
Programs in:
 communications systems management • MA
 English • MA
 history • MA
 liberal and fine arts • MA, MPA, MS
 psychology • MS
 public administration • MPA

College of Sciences
Dr. David H. Loyd, Dean
Programs in:
 animal science • MS
 biology • MS
 medical-surgical nursing • MSN
 physical therapy • MPT
 sciences • MPT, MS, MSN

School of Education
Dr. John J. Miazga, Dean of the School of Education
Programs in:
 education • M Ed, MA
 educational diagnostics • M Ed
 guidance and counseling • M Ed
 instructional technology • MA
 reading specialist • M Ed
 school administration • M Ed

■ **BAYLOR UNIVERSITY**
Waco, TX 76798
http://www.baylor.edu/

Independent-religious, coed, university. CGS member. *Enrollment:* 13,937 graduate, professional, and undergraduate students; 1,792 full-time matriculated graduate/professional students (751 women), 421 part-time matriculated graduate/professional students (232 women). Graduate faculty: 350. *Computer facilities:* Computer purchase and lease plans are available. 1,500 computers available on campus for general student use. A campuswide network can be accessed from student residence rooms and from off campus. Internet access and online class registration are available. *Library facilities:* Moody Memorial Library plus 8 others. *Graduate expenses:* Tuition: part-time $698 per hour. *General application contact:* Suzanne Keener, Administrative Assistant, 254-710-3588.

George W. Truett Seminary
Dr. Paul W. Powell, Dean
Program in:
 theology • M Div, D Min

Graduate School
Dr. Larry Lyon, Dean

Academy of Health Sciences
Col. Darwin L. Fretwell, Dean
Programs in:
 health care administration • MHA
 health sciences • MHA, MPT, DPT, Dr Sc PT
 physical therapy • MPT, DPT, Dr Sc PT

College of Arts and Sciences
Dr. Wallace Daniel, Dean
Programs in:
 American studies • MA
 applied sociology • PhD
 arts and sciences • MA, MES, MFA, MIJ, MPPA, MS, MSCP, MSCSD, MSL, MSW, PhD, Psy D
 biology • MA, MS, PhD
 chemistry • MS, PhD
 church-state studies • MA, PhD
 clinical psychology • MSCP, Psy D
 communication sciences and disorders • MA, MSCSD
 communication studies • MA
 directing • MFA
 earth science • MA
 English • MA, PhD
 environmental biology • MS
 environmental studies • MES, MS
 geology • MS, PhD
 history • MA
 international journalism • MIJ
 international studies • MA
 journalism • MA
 limnology • MSL
 mathematics • MS, PhD
 museum studies • MA
 neuroscience • MA, PhD
 philosophy • MA, PhD
 physics • MA, MS, PhD
 political science • MA
 public policy and administration • MPPA
 religion • MA, PhD
 social work • MSW
 sociology • MA
 Spanish • MA
 theater arts • MA

Hankamer School of Business
Dr. Gary Carini, Director of Graduate Programs
Programs in:
 accounting • M Acc, MT
 business • M Acc, MA, MBA, MBAIM, MIM, MS, MS Eco, MSIS, MT
 business administration • MBA
 economics • MS Eco
 information systems • MSIS
 information systems management • MBA
 international economics • MA, MS
 international management • MBA, MBAIM, MIM

Institute of Biomedical Studies
Dr. Darden Powers, Director
Program in:
 biomedical studies • MS, PhD

Institute of Statistics
Dr. Tom Bratcher, Graduate Program Director
Program in:
 statistics • MA, PhD

Louise Herrington School of Nursing of Baylor University
Dr. Pauline Johnson, Graduate Program Director
Programs in:
 family nurse practitioner • MSN
 neonatal nurse practitioner • MSN
 nursing administration and management • MSN

School of Education
Dr. Robert Yinger, Dean
Programs in:
 curriculum and instruction • MA, MS Ed, Ed D, Ed S
 education • MA, MS Ed, Ed D, PhD, Ed S
 educational administration • MS Ed, Ed D, Ed S
 educational psychology • MA, MS Ed, PhD, Ed S
 health, human performance and recreation • MS Ed

School of Engineering and Computer Science
Dr. Greg Speegle, Graduate Program Director
Program in:
 computer science • MS

School of Music
Dr. Harry Elzinga, Graduate Program Director
Programs in:
 church music • MM
 composition • MM
 conducting • MM
 music education • MM
 music history and literature • MM
 music theory • MM
 performance • MM
 piano accompanying • MM
 piano pedagogy and performance • MM

School of Law
Dr. Bradley J. B. Toben, Dean
Program in:
 law • JD

Texas

■ DALLAS BAPTIST UNIVERSITY
Dallas, TX 75211-9299
http://www.dbu.edu/

Independent-religious, coed, comprehensive institution. *Enrollment:* 4,538 graduate, professional, and undergraduate students; 261 full-time matriculated graduate/professional students (180 women), 833 part-time matriculated graduate/professional students (544 women). *Graduate faculty:* 92 full-time (36 women), 287 part-time/adjunct (131 women). *Computer facilities:* 182 computers available on campus for general student use. A campuswide network can be accessed from student residence rooms and from off campus. Internet access and online class registration are available. *Library facilities:* Vance Memorial Library. *Graduate expenses:* Tuition: full-time $6,786; part-time $377 per credit hour. *General application contact:* Sarah R. Brancaccio, Director of Graduate Programs, 214-333-5242.

College of Adult Education
Jeremy B. Dutschke, Dean
Programs in:
 adult education • MA, MLA
 arts • MLA
 business • MA
 Christian ministry • MLA
 counseling • MA
 criminal justice • MA
 English • MLA
 fine arts • MLA
 higher education • MA
 history • MLA
 leadership • MA
 political science • MLA
 professional development • MA

College of Humanities and Social Sciences
Dr. Michael E. Williams, Dean
Programs in:
 counseling • MA
 humanities and social sciences • MA

Dorothy M. Bush College of Education
Dr. Charles Carona, Dean
Programs in:
 early childhood education • M Ed
 education • M Ed, MAT
 educational organization and administration • M Ed
 elementary reading education • M Ed
 general elementary education • M Ed
 reading specialist • M Ed
 school counseling • M Ed
 teaching • MAT

Graduate School of Business
Dr. Denny Dowd, Acting Dean
Programs in:
 accounting • MBA
 business • MA, MBA
 conflict resolution management • MA, MBA
 E. business • MBA
 finance • MBA
 general management • MA
 health care management • MA, MBA
 human resource management • MA
 international business • MBA
 management • MBA
 management information systems • MBA
 marketing • MBA
 technology and engineering management • MBA

School of Leadership and Christian Education
Dr. Bernie Spooner, Dean
Programs in:
 adult ministry • MA
 Baptist student ministry • MA
 business ministry • MA
 children's ministry • MA
 counseling ministry • MA
 education ministry • MA
 higher education • M Ed
 leadership and Christian education • M Ed, MA
 worship ministry • MA
 youth ministry • MA

■ HARDIN-SIMMONS UNIVERSITY
Abilene, TX 79698-0001
http://www.hsutx.edu/

Independent-religious, coed, comprehensive institution. *Enrollment:* 2,361 graduate, professional, and undergraduate students; 174 full-time matriculated graduate/professional students (94 women), 189 part-time matriculated graduate/professional students (102 women). *Graduate faculty:* 78 full-time (22 women), 23 part-time/adjunct (3 women). *Computer facilities:* 250 computers available on campus for general student use. A campuswide network can be accessed from student residence rooms and from off campus. Internet access is available. *Library facilities:* Richardson Library plus 1 other. *Graduate expenses:* Tuition: full-time $7,020; part-time $390 per hour. Required fees: $650; $110 per year. Tuition and fees vary according to course load, degree level and program. *General application contact:* Dr. Gary Stanlake, Dean of Graduate Studies, 325-670-1298.

Graduate School
Dr. Gary Stanlake, Dean of Graduate Studies
Programs in:
 English • MA
 entry level physical therapy • DPT
 environmental management • MS
 family psychology • MA
 history • MA

Irvin School of Education
Dr. Pam Williford, Dean
Programs in:
 advanced physical education • M Ed
 counseling and human development • M Ed
 education • M Ed
 gifted education • M Ed
 reading specialist • M Ed
 sports and recreation management • M Ed

Logsdon Seminary
Dr. Thomas Brisco, Dean
Programs in:
 family ministry • MA
 religion • MA
 theology • M Div

School of Business
Dr. Charles Walts, Director
Program in:
 business • MBA

School of Music
Dr. Leigh Anne Hunsaker, Director
Programs in:
 church music • MM
 music education • MM
 music performance • MM
 theory-composition • MM

School of Nursing
Dr. Janet Noles, Dean
Programs in:
 advanced healthcare delivery • MSN
 family nurse practitioner • MSN

■ HOUSTON BAPTIST UNIVERSITY
Houston, TX 77074-3298
http://www.hbu.edu/

Independent-religious, coed, comprehensive institution. *Enrollment:* 2,340 graduate, professional, and undergraduate students; 101 full-time matriculated graduate/professional students (70 women), 209 part-time matriculated graduate/professional students (130 women). *Graduate faculty:* 44 full-time (15 women), 26 part-time/adjunct (12 women). *Computer facilities:* 93 computers available on campus for general student use. A campuswide network can be accessed from off campus. Internet access is available. *Library facilities:* Moody Library. *Graduate expenses:* Tuition: part-time $1,140 per semester hour. *General application contact:* David Melton, Associate Vice President, 281-649-3208.

College of Arts and Humanities
Dr. James Taylor, Dean
Programs in:
arts and humanities • MATS, MLA
liberal arts • MLA
theological studies • MATS

College of Business and Economics
Dr. Ray Newman, Dean
Programs in:
business administration • MBA, MSM
business and economics • MBA, MSHRM, MSM, MSMIS
human resources management • MSHRM
management, information systems • MSMIS

College of Education and Behavioral Sciences
Dr. Joseph D. Brown, Dean
Programs in:
bilingual education • M Ed
Christian counseling • MACC
counselor education • M Ed
curriculum and instruction • M Ed
education and behavioral sciences • M Ed, MACC, MAP
educational administration • M Ed
educational diagnostican • M Ed
psychology • MAP
reading education • M Ed

College of Nursing
Programs in:
health administration • MSHA
nursing • MSHA

■ **LAMAR UNIVERSITY**
Beaumont, TX 77710

State-supported, coed, university. CGS member. *Enrollment:* 10,379 graduate, professional, and undergraduate students; 659 full-time matriculated graduate/professional students (192 women), 536 part-time matriculated graduate/professional students (298 women). *Graduate faculty:* 164 full-time (51 women), 20 part-time/adjunct (9 women). *Computer facilities:* 120 computers available on campus for general student use. A campuswide network can be accessed from student residence rooms and from off campus. *Library facilities:* Mary and John Gray Library. *Graduate expenses:* Tuition, state resident: part-time $170 per semester hour. Tuition, nonresident: part-time $351 per semester hour. Required fees: $174 per semester hour. One-time fee: $10 part-time. *General application contact:* Sandy Drane, Coordinator of Graduate Admissions, 409-880-8356.

Find an in-depth description at www.petersons.com/gradchannel.

College of Graduate Studies
Dr. James W. Westgate, Associate Vice President for Research and Dean

College of Arts and Sciences
Dr. Brenda S. Nichols, Dean
Programs in:
applied criminology • MS
arts and sciences • MA, MPA, MS, MSN
biology • MS
chemistry • MS
community/clinical psychology • MS
English • MA
history • MA
industrial/organizational psychology • MS
nursing administration • MSN
public administration • MPA

College of Business
Dr. Enrique R. Venta, Associate Dean
Programs in:
accounting • MBA
information systems • MBA
management • MBA

College of Education and Human Development
Dr. R. Carl Westerfield, Dean
Programs in:
counseling and development • M Ed, Certificate
education administration • M Ed, Certificate
education and human development • M Ed, MS, Certificate
family and consumer science • MS
kinesiology • MS
mid-management administration • Certificate
school superintendent • Certificate
supervision • M Ed
supervisor • Certificate
technology application • Certificate
vocational home economics • Certificate

College of Engineering
Dr. Jack Hopper, Chair
Programs in:
chemical engineering • ME, MES, DE
civil engineering • ME, MES, DE
computer science • MS
electrical engineering • ME, MES, DE
engineering • ME, MEM, MES, MS, DE
engineering management • MEM
environmental engineering • MS
environmental studies • MS
industrial engineering • ME, MES, DE
mathematics • MS
mechanical engineering • ME, MES, DE

College of Fine Arts and Communication
Dr. Russ A. Schultz, Dean
Programs in:
art history • MA
audiology • MS
deaf education • MS, Ed D
fine arts and communication • MA, MM, MM Ed, MS, Ed D
music education • MM Ed
music performance • MM
photography • MA
speech language pathology • MS
studio art • MA
theatre • MS
visual design • MA

■ **LETOURNEAU UNIVERSITY**
Longview, TX 75607-7001
http://www.letu.edu/

Independent-religious, coed, comprehensive institution. *Enrollment:* 3,597 graduate, professional, and undergraduate students; 50 full-time matriculated graduate/professional students (26 women), 372 part-time matriculated graduate/professional students (185 women). *Graduate faculty:* 8 full-time (0 women), 32 part-time/adjunct (3 women). *Library facilities:* Margaret Estes Resource Center. *Graduate expenses:* Tuition: full-time $8,210; part-time $421 per credit hour. *General application contact:* Chris Fontaine, Director of Enrollment Management, 903-233-3250.

Graduate and Professional Studies
Dr. Robert W. Hudson, Vice President for Graduate and Professional Studies
Programs in:
business administration • MBA
health care • MBA

■ **MIDWESTERN STATE UNIVERSITY**
Wichita Falls, TX 76308
http://www.mwsu.edu/

State-supported, coed, comprehensive institution. *Enrollment:* 6,483 graduate, professional, and undergraduate students; 118 full-time matriculated graduate/professional students (71 women), 553 part-time matriculated graduate/professional students (341 women). *Graduate faculty:* 67 full-time (24 women), 8 part-time/adjunct (4 women). *Computer facilities:* 425 computers available on campus for general student use. A campuswide network can be accessed from student residence rooms and from off campus. Internet access and online

Texas

Midwestern State University (continued)
class registration are available. *Library facilities:* Moffett Library. *Graduate expenses:* Tuition, state resident: full-time $2,276; part-time $76 per credit. Tuition, nonresident: full-time $6,524; part-time $312 per credit. Required fees: $1,048; $125 per credit. Tuition and fees vary according to program and reciprocity agreements. *General application contact:* Barbara Ramos Merkle, Director of Admissions, 800-842-1922.

Graduate Studies
Dr. Emerson Capps, Graduate Dean

College of Business Administration
Dr. Martha Harvey, Interim Dean
Programs in:
 business administration • MBA
 health services administration • MBA

College of Education
Dr. Grant Simpson, Dean
Programs in:
 curriculum and instruction • ME
 education • M Ed, MA, ME
 educational leadership • ME
 general counseling • MA
 human resource development • MA
 reading education • M Ed
 school counseling • M Ed
 special education • M Ed
 training and development • MA

College of Health Sciences and Human Services
Dr. Susan Sportsman, Dean
Programs in:
 family nurse practitioner • MSN
 health sciences and human services • MA, MHA, MPA, MSK, MSN, MSR
 health services administration • MHA, MSN
 kinesiology • MSK
 nurse educator • MSN
 public administration • MPA
 public administration (administrative justice) • MPA
 public administration (health services administration with certificate) • MPA
 public administration (health services) • MPA
 radiologic administration • MSR
 radiologic education • MSR
 radiologic services • MSR

College of Liberal Arts
Dr. Michael Collins, Dean
Programs in:
 English • MA
 history • MA
 liberal arts • MA
 political science • MA
 psychology • MA

College of Science and Mathematics
Dr. Norman Horner, Dean
Programs in:
 biology • MS
 computer science • MS

■ OUR LADY OF THE LAKE UNIVERSITY OF SAN ANTONIO
San Antonio, TX 78207-4689
http://www.ollusa.edu/

Independent-religious, coed, comprehensive institution. *Enrollment:* 3,245 graduate, professional, and undergraduate students; 347 full-time matriculated graduate/professional students (274 women), 935 part-time matriculated graduate/professional students (671 women). *Graduate faculty:* 124 full-time (64 women), 157 part-time/adjunct (71 women). *Computer facilities:* 200 computers available on campus for general student use. A campuswide network can be accessed from off campus. *Library facilities:* Saint Florence Library plus 2 others. *Graduate expenses:* Tuition: part-time $514 per credit hour. Required fees: $48 per semester. *General application contact:* 210-434-6711 Ext. 2314.

College of Arts and Sciences
Ric Slocum, Dean
Programs in:
 English • MA
 English communication arts • MA
 language and literature • MA

School of Business
Dr. Lois Graff, Dean
Programs in:
 general • MBA
 health care management • MBA

School of Education and Clinical Studies
Dr. Jacquelyn Alexander, Dean
Programs in:
 communication and learning disorders • MA
 counseling psychology • MS, Psy D
 curriculum and instruction • M Ed
 human sciences • MA
 leadership studies • PhD
 learning resources • M Ed
 marriage and family therapy • MS
 principal • M Ed
 school counseling • M Ed
 school psychology • MS
 sociology • MA
 special education • MA

Worden School of Social Service
Dr. James Allen, Dean
Program in:
 social service • MSW

■ PRAIRIE VIEW A&M UNIVERSITY
Prairie View, TX 77446-0519
http://www.pvamu.edu/

State-supported, coed, comprehensive institution. *Enrollment:* 7,808 graduate, professional, and undergraduate students; 698 full-time matriculated graduate/professional students (482 women), 1,068 part-time matriculated graduate/professional students (765 women). *Graduate faculty:* 151 full-time (40 women), 41 part-time/adjunct (18 women). *Computer facilities:* 504 computers available on campus for general student use. A campuswide network can be accessed from student residence rooms. E-mail available. *Library facilities:* John B. Coleman Library. *Graduate expenses:* Tuition, state resident: part-time $50 per credit hour. Tuition, nonresident: part-time $282 per credit hour. Required fees: $36 per credit hour. $51 per term. *General application contact:* Dr. William H. Parker, Dean of the Graduate School, 936-857-2312.

Graduate School
Dr. William H. Parker, Dean of the Graduate School

College of Agriculture and Human Sciences
Dr. Elizabeth Noel, Dean
Programs in:
 agricultural economics • MS
 animal sciences • MS
 interdisciplinary human sciences • MS
 marriage and family therapy • MS
 soil science • MS

College of Arts and Sciences
Dr. Edward Martin, Dean
Programs in:
 arts and sciences • MA, MS
 biology • MS
 chemistry • MS
 English • MA
 mathematics • MS
 sociology • MA

College of Business
Dr. Munir Quddus, Dean
Programs in:
 accounting • MS
 general business administration • MBA

College of Education
Dr. M. Paul Mehta, Dean
Programs in:
 counseling • MA, MS Ed
 curriculum and instruction • M Ed, MS Ed
 education • M Ed, MA, MA Ed, MS Ed, PhD

educational leadership • PhD
health education • MA Ed, MS Ed
physical education • MA Ed, MS Ed
school administration • M Ed, MS Ed
school supervision • M Ed, MS Ed
special education • M Ed, MS Ed

College of Engineering
Dr. Milton R. Bryant, Dean
Programs in:
 computer information systems • MSCIS
 computer science • MSCS
 electrical engineering • MSEE, PhDEE
 engineering • MS Engr

College of Nursing
Dr. Betty N. Adams, Dean
Program in:
 nursing • MSN

School of Architecture
Dr. Ikhlas Sabouni, Dean
Programs in:
 architecture • M Arch
 community development • MCD

School of Juvenile Justice and Psychology
Dr. Elaine Rodney, Dean
Programs in:
 juvenile forensic psychology • MSJFP
 juvenile justice • MSJJ, PhD

■ **RICE UNIVERSITY**
Houston, TX 77251-1892
http://www.rice.edu/

Independent, coed, university. CGS member. *Enrollment:* 4,959 graduate, professional, and undergraduate students; 1,999 matriculated graduate/professional students. *Graduate faculty:* 434 full-time, 150 part-time/adjunct. *Computer facilities:* 600 computers available on campus for general student use. A campuswide network can be accessed from student residence rooms and from off campus. Internet access is available. *Library facilities:* Fondren Library. *Graduate expenses:* Tuition: full-time $19,700; part-time $1,096 per hour. *General application contact:* Paul Andrew Emig, Executive Assistant, 713-348-4002.

Graduate Programs
Jordan Konisky, Vice Provost for Research and Graduate Studies
Program in:
 education • MAT

George R. Brown School of Engineering
C. Sidney Burrus, Dean of Engineering
Programs in:
 bioengineering • MS, PhD
 biostatistics • PhD
 chemical engineering • M Ch E, MS, PhD
 circuits, controls, and communication systems • MS, PhD
 civil engineering • MCE, MS, PhD
 computational and applied mathematics • MA, MCAM, MCSE, PhD
 computational finance • PhD
 computer science • MCS, MS, PhD
 computer science and engineering • MS, PhD
 computer science in bioinformatics • MCS
 electrical engineering • MEE
 engineering • M Ch E, M Stat, MA, MCAM, MCE, MCS, MCSE, MEE, MEE, MES, MME, MMS, MS, PhD
 environmental engineering • MEE, MES, MS, PhD
 environmental science • MEE, MES, MS, PhD
 lasers, microwaves, and solid-state electronics • MS, PhD
 materials science • MMS, MS, PhD
 mechanical engineering • MME, MS, PhD
 statistics • M Stat, MA, PhD

Jesse H. Jones Graduate School of Management
Dr. Gilbert R. Whitaker, Dean
Program in:
 business administration • EMBA, MBA

School of Architecture
Lars Lerup, Dean
Programs in:
 architecture • M Arch, D Arch
 urban design • M Arch UD

School of Humanities
Gary Wihl, Dean
Programs in:
 English • MA, PhD
 French studies • MA, PhD
 history • MA, PhD
 humanities • MA, PhD
 linguistics • MA, PhD
 philosophy • MA, PhD
 religious studies • PhD
 Spanish • MA

School of Social Sciences
Robert M. Stein, Dean
Programs in:
 anthropology • MA, PhD
 cognitive sciences • MA, PhD
 economics • MA, PhD
 industrial-organizational/social psychology • MA, PhD
 political science • MA, PhD
 psychology • MA, PhD
 social sciences • MA, PhD

Shepherd School of Music
Dr. Robert Yekovich, Dean
Programs in:
 composition • MM, DMA
 conducting • MM
 history • MM
 performance • MM, DMA
 theory • MM

Wiess School of Natural Sciences
Dr. Kathleen S. Matthews, Dean
Programs in:
 biochemistry and cell biology • MA, PhD
 chemistry • MA
 earth science • MA, PhD
 ecology and evolutionary biology • MA, PhD
 environmental analysis and decision-making • MS
 geophysics • MS
 inorganic chemistry • PhD
 mathematics • MA, PhD
 nanoscale physics • MS
 natural sciences • MA, MS, PhD
 organic chemistry • PhD
 physical chemistry • PhD
 physics • MA
 physics and astronomy • MS, PhD

Rice Quantum Institute
Dr. Peter Nordlander, Executive Director
Program in:
 applied physics • MS, PhD

■ **ST. EDWARD'S UNIVERSITY**
Austin, TX 78704
http://www.stedwards.edu/

Independent-religious, coed, comprehensive institution. *Enrollment:* 4,443 graduate, professional, and undergraduate students; 146 full-time matriculated graduate/professional students (83 women), 752 part-time matriculated graduate/professional students (442 women). *Graduate faculty:* 16 full-time (11 women), 65 part-time/adjunct (20 women). *Computer facilities:* 498 computers available on campus for general student use. A campuswide network can be accessed from student residence rooms and from off campus. Internet access and online class registration are available. *Library facilities:* Scarborough-Phillips Library. *Graduate expenses:* Tuition: full-time $9,144; part-time $508 per credit. Full-time tuition and fees vary according to program. *General application contact:* Bridget Sowinski, Graduate Admissions Coordinator, 512-428-1061.

College of Professional and Graduate Studies
Dr. John Houghton, Vice President

Texas

St. Edward's University (continued)
Graduate School of Management
Marsha Kelliher, Dean
Programs in:
  accounting • MBA
  business management • MBA
  computer information science • MS
  conflict resolution • Certificate
  e-commerce • MBA, Certificate
  entrepreneurship • MBA, Certificate
  finance—general • MBA, Certificate
  global business • MBA, Certificate
  healthcare management • MA, MBA
  human resource management • MBA, Certificate
  human services • MA
  management • MA, MBA, MS, Certificate
  management information systems • MBA, Certificate
  marketing • MBA, Certificate
  operations management • MBA, Certificate
  organizational leadership and ethics • MS
  personal financial planner • MBA, Certificate
  sports management • MBA, Certificate

New College
Dr. H. Ramsey Fowler, Dean
Programs in:
  counseling • MA
  liberal arts • MLA, Certificate

ST. MARY'S UNIVERSITY OF SAN ANTONIO
San Antonio, TX 78228-8507
http://www.stmarytx.edu/

Independent-religious, coed, comprehensive institution. *Enrollment:* 4,118 graduate, professional, and undergraduate students; 963 full-time matriculated graduate/professional students (452 women), 573 part-time matriculated graduate/professional students (298 women). *Graduate faculty:* 97 full-time (33 women), 39 part-time/adjunct (9 women). *Computer facilities:* 100 computers available on campus for general student use. A campuswide network can be accessed from student residence rooms and from off campus. *Library facilities:* Academic Library plus 1 other. *Graduate expenses:* Tuition: full-time $9,216; part-time $512 per credit hour. Required fees: $500; $250 per term. Tuition and fees vary according to degree level. *General application contact:* Dr. Ronald D. Merrell, Dean of the Graduate School, 210-436-3101.

Graduate School
Dr. Ronald D. Merrell, Dean
Programs in:
  Catholic principalship • Certificate
  Catholic school administrators • Certificate
  Catholic school leadership • MA, Certificate
  Catholic school teachers • Certificate
  clinical psychology • MA, MS
  communication studies • MA
  community counseling • MA
  computer information systems • MS
  computer science • MS
  counseling • Sp C
  counseling education and supervision • PhD
  educational leadership • MA, Certificate
  electrical engineering • MS
  electrical/computer engineering • MS
  engineering administration • MS
  engineering computer applications • MS
  engineering management • MS
  engineering systems management • MS
  English literature and language • MA
  financial economics • MA
  history • MA
  industrial engineering • MS
  industrial psychology • MA, MS
  inter-American administration • MPA
  international relations • MA
  Latin American and U.S. Latino history • MA
  marriage and family relations • Certificate
  marriage and family therapy • MA, PhD
  mental health • MA
  mental health and substance abuse counseling • Certificate
  operations research • MS
  pastoral ministry • MA
  political communications and applied science • MA
  political economy • MA
  political science • MA
  principalship (mid-management) • Certificate
  public administration • MPA
  public management • MPA
  reading • MA
  school psychology • MA
  software engineering • MS
  substance abuse • MA
  theology • MA

School of Business Administration
Dr. Monica Parzinger, Director
Programs in:
  accounting • M Acc
  finance • MBA
  international business • MBA
  management • MBA
  taxation • M Acc

School of Law
Robert William Piatt, Dean
Program in:
  law • JD

SAM HOUSTON STATE UNIVERSITY
Huntsville, TX 77341
http://www.shsu.edu/

State-supported, coed, university. *Enrollment:* 13,460 graduate, professional, and undergraduate students; 417 full-time matriculated graduate/professional students (253 women), 1,289 part-time matriculated graduate/professional students (919 women). *Computer facilities:* 455 computers available on campus for general student use. A campuswide network can be accessed from student residence rooms and from off campus. Internet access and online class registration are available. *Library facilities:* Newton Gresham Library. *Graduate expenses:* Tuition, state resident: part-time $243 per semester hour. Tuition, nonresident: part-time $479 per semester hour. *General application contact:* Dr. Mitchell Muehsam, Dean of Graduate Studies and Associate Vice President for Academic Affairs, 936-294-1971.

College of Arts and Sciences
Dr. Brian Chapman, Dean
Programs in:
  agricultural business • MS
  agricultural education • M Ed, MA
  agricultural mechanization • MS
  agriculture • MS
  art • MFA
  arts and sciences • M Ed, MA, MFA, MM, MS
  biology • MA, MS
  ceramics • MA, MFA
  chemistry • MS
  computing and information science • MS
  dance • MFA
  drawing • MA, MFA
  English • MA
  history • MA
  industrial education • M Ed, MA
  industrial technology • MA
  jewelry • MA
  mathematics • MA, MS
  painting • MA, MFA
  physics • MS
  political science • MA
  printmaking • MA, MFA
  sculpture • MA, MFA
  social research • MA
  sociology • MA
  statistics • MS
  studio art • MA
  vocational education • M Ed

School of Music
Dr. Rod Cannon, Chair
Programs in:
  conducting • MM
  elementary • M Ed
  instrumental • M Ed
  Kodály pedagogy • M Ed, MM
  music • MM
  music education • M Ed, MM
  musicology • MM
  performance • MM
  theory and composition • MM
  vocal • M Ed

College of Business Administration
Dr. R. Dean Lewis, Dean
Programs in:
  business administration • MBA
  finance • MS
  general business and finance • MS

College of Criminal Justice
Dr. Richard Ward, Dean
Programs in:
  criminal justice • MS, PhD
  criminal justice and criminology • MA
  criminal justice management • MS
  forensic science • MS

College of Education and Applied Science
Dr. Genevieve Brown, Dean
Programs in:
  administration • M Ed, MA
  clinical psychology • MA
  correctional education • M Ed
  counseling • M Ed, MA
  counselor education • MA, PhD
  early childhood education • M Ed
  education and applied science • M Ed, MA, MLS, Ed D, PhD
  educational leadership • Ed D
  elementary education • M Ed, MA
  family and consumer sciences • MA
  forensic psychology • PhD
  health and kinesiology • M Ed, MA
  instructional leadership • M Ed, MA
  library science • MLS
  psychology • MA
  reading • M Ed, MA
  school psychology • MA
  secondary education • M Ed, MA
  special education • M Ed, MA

■ SOUTHERN METHODIST UNIVERSITY
Dallas, TX 75275

Independent-religious, coed, university. CGS member. *Enrollment:* 11,161 graduate, professional, and undergraduate students; 2,032 full-time matriculated graduate/professional students (866 women), 2,830 part-time matriculated graduate/professional students (1,095 women). *Graduate faculty:* 566 full-time (172 women). *Computer facilities:* 409 computers available on campus for general student use. A campuswide network can be accessed from student residence rooms and from off campus. *Library facilities:* Central University Library plus 7 others. *Graduate expenses:* Tuition: full-time $11,362; part-time $874 per credit. Required fees: $112 per credit. Tuition and fees vary according to course load and program. *General application contact:* Dr. U. Narayan Bhat, Dean of Research and Graduate Studies, 214-768-4345.

Find an in-depth description at www.petersons.com/gradchannel.

Cox School of Business
Dr. Albert W. Niemi, Dean
Programs in:
  accounting • MSA
  business • Exec MBA, MBA

Dedman College
Dr. Jasper Neel, Dean
Programs in:
  anthropology • PhD
  applied economics • MA
  applied geophysics • MS
  archaeology • PhD
  biological sciences • MA, MS, PhD
  chemistry • MS
  clinical and counseling psychology • MA
  clinical science • PhD
  computational and applied mathematics • MS, PhD
  economics • MA, PhD
  English • MA
  exploration geophysics • MS
  geology • MS, PhD
  geophysics • MS, PhD
  history • MA, PhD
  liberal arts • MLA
  medical anthropology • MA, PhD
  medieval studies • MA
  physics • MS, PhD
  religious studies • MA, PhD
  statistical science • MS, PhD

Dedman School of Law
John B. Attanasio, Dean
Programs in:
  comparative and international law • LL M
  law • JD, LL M, SJD
  taxation • LL M

Meadows School of the Arts
Carole Brandt, Dean
Programs in:
  acting • MFA
  art history • MA
  arts • MA, MFA, MM, MMT, MSM, Certificate
  choreographic theory and practice • MFA
  conducting • MM
  design • MFA
  directing • MFA
  music composition • MM
  music education • MM
  music history • MM
  music theory • MM
  music therapy • MMT
  performance • MM, Certificate
  piano performance and pedagogy • MM
  sacred music • MSM
  studio art • MFA

Division of Arts Administration
Dr. Gregory Poggi, Chair

Division of Cinema—Television
Rick Worland, Chair
Program in:
  TV—radio • MA

Perkins School of Theology
Dr. William B. Lawrence, Dean
Program in:
  theology • M Div, CMM, MSM, MTS, D Min

School of Engineering
Dr. Geoffrey Orsak, Graduate and Executive Admissions
Programs in:
  applied science • MS, PhD
  civil engineering • MS, PhD
  computer engineering • MS Cp E, PhD
  computer science • MS, PhD
  electrical engineering • MSEE, PhD
  electronic and optical packaging • MS
  engineering • MS, MS Cp E, MSEE, MSEM, MSIEM, MSME, DE, PhD
  engineering management • MSEM, DE
  environmental engineering • MS
  environmental science • MS
  facilities management • MS
  information engineering and management • MSIEM
  manufacturing systems management • MS
  mechanical engineering • MSME, PhD
  operations research • MS, PhD
  software engineering • MS
  systems engineering • MS
  telecommunications • MS

■ STEPHEN F. AUSTIN STATE UNIVERSITY
Nacogdoches, TX 75962
http://www.sfasu.edu/

State-supported, coed, comprehensive institution. *Enrollment:* 11,408 graduate, professional, and undergraduate students; 622 full-time matriculated graduate/professional students (382 women), 997

Texas

Stephen F. Austin State University (continued)
part-time matriculated graduate/professional students (664 women). *Graduate faculty:* 359 full-time (119 women), 74 part-time/adjunct (18 women). *Computer facilities:* Computer purchase and lease plans are available. 1,000 computers available on campus for general student use. A campuswide network can be accessed from student residence rooms and from off campus. Internet access and online class registration are available. *Library facilities:* Ralph W. Steen Library. *Graduate expenses:* Tuition, state resident: part-time $46 per hour. Tuition, nonresident: part-time $282 per hour. Required fees: $71 per hour. Tuition and fees vary according to reciprocity agreements. *General application contact:* Dr. David Jeffrey, Associate Vice President for Graduate Studies and Research, 936-468-2807.

Graduate School
Dr. David Jeffrey, Associate Vice President for Graduate Studies and Research

College of Applied Arts and Science
Dr. James O. Standley, Dean
Programs in:
  applied arts and science • MA, MIS, MSW
  communication • MA
  interdisciplinary studies • MIS
  mass communication • MA
  social work • MSW

College of Business
Dr. Violet Rogers, Interim Dean
Programs in:
  business • MBA
  computer science • MS
  management and marketing • MBA
  professional accountancy • MPAC

College of Education
Dr. John Jacobson, Dean
Programs in:
  agriculture • MS
  athletic training • MS
  counseling • MA
  early childhood education • M Ed
  education • M Ed, MA, MS, Ed D
  educational leadership • Ed D
  elementary education • M Ed
  human sciences • MS
  physical education • M Ed
  school psychology • MA
  secondary education • M Ed
  special education • M Ed
  speech pathology • MS

College of Fine Arts
Dr. Richard Berry, Dean
Programs in:
  art • MA
  design • MFA
  drawing • MFA
  fine arts • MA, MFA, MM
  music • MA, MM
  painting • MFA
  sculpture • MFA

College of Forestry
Dr. Scott Beasley, Dean
Program in:
  forestry • MF, MS, PhD

College of Liberal Arts
Dr. Robert Herbert, Dean
Programs in:
  English • MA
  history • MA
  liberal arts • MA, MPA
  psychology • MA
  public administration • MPA

College of Sciences and Mathematics
Dr. Thomas Atchison, Dean
Programs in:
  biology • MS
  biotechnology • MS
  chemistry • MS
  environmental science • MS
  geology • MS, MSNS
  mathematics • MS
  mathematics education • MS
  physics • MS
  sciences and mathematics • MS, MSNS
  statistics • MS

■ SUL ROSS STATE UNIVERSITY
Alpine, TX 79832
http://www.sulross.edu/

State-supported, coed, comprehensive institution. *Computer facilities:* 200 computers available on campus for general student use. A campuswide network can be accessed from student residence rooms and from off campus. Internet access is available. *Library facilities:* Bryan Wildenthal Memorial Library. *General application contact:* Dean of Admissions and Records, 915-837-8050.

Division of Agricultural and Natural Resource Science
Programs in:
  agricultural and natural resource science • M Ag, MS
  animal science • M Ag, MS
  range and wildlife management • M Ag, MS

Rio Grande College of Sul Ross State University
Programs in:
  business administration • MBA
  teacher education • M Ed

School of Arts and Sciences
Programs in:
  art education • M Ed
  art history • M Ed
  arts and sciences • M Ed, MA, MS
  biology • MS
  English • MA
  geology and chemistry • MS
  history • MA
  political science • MA
  psychology • MA
  public administration • MA
  studio art • M Ed

School of Professional Studies
Programs in:
  bilingual education • M Ed
  counseling • M Ed
  criminal justice • MS
  educational diagnostics • M Ed
  elementary education • M Ed
  industrial arts • M Ed
  international trade • MBA
  management • MBA
  physical education • M Ed
  professional studies • M Ed, MBA, MS
  reading specialist • M Ed
  school administration • M Ed
  secondary education • M Ed
  supervision • M Ed

■ TARLETON STATE UNIVERSITY
Stephenville, TX 76402
http://www.tarleton.edu/

State-supported, coed, comprehensive institution. *Enrollment:* 8,845 graduate, professional, and undergraduate students; 253 full-time matriculated graduate/professional students (144 women), 1,094 part-time matriculated graduate/professional students (703 women). *Graduate faculty:* 104 full-time (20 women). *Computer facilities:* 600 computers available on campus for general student use. A campuswide network can be accessed from student residence rooms and from off campus. Internet access and online class registration are available. *Library facilities:* Dick Smith Library plus 1 other. *Graduate expenses:* Tuition, state resident: part-time $99 per credit hour. Tuition, nonresident: part-time $325 per credit hour. One-time fee: $52 part-time. *General application contact:* Dr. Linda M. Jones, Dean, 254-968-9104.

College of Graduate Studies and Academic Affairs
Dr. Linda M. Jones, Dean

College of Agriculture and Human Sciences
Dr. Don Cawthon, Acting Dean
Programs in:
  agriculture • MS
  animal sciences • MS

College of Business Administration
Dr. Ruby Barker, Dean
Programs in:
  business administration • MBA
  computer and information systems • MS
  human resource management • MS
  management • MS

College of Education
Dr. Jill Burk, Dean
Programs in:
  counseling • M Ed
  counseling and psychology • M Ed
  counseling psychology • M Ed
  curriculum and instruction • M Ed
  education • M Ed, Certificate
  educational administration • M Ed, Certificate
  educational psychology • M Ed
  health and physical education • M Ed, Certificate
  reading • Certificate
  secondary education • M Ed, Certificate
  special education • Certificate

College of Liberal and Fine Arts
Dr. Don Zelman, Dean
Programs in:
  criminal justice • MCJ, MS
  English and languages • MA
  history • MA
  liberal and fine arts • MA, MCJ, MS
  political science • MA

College of Sciences and Technology
Dr. Rueben Walter, Dean
Programs in:
  arts and sciences • MS
  biological sciences • MS
  environmental science • MS
  mathematics • MS

■ TEXAS A&M INTERNATIONAL UNIVERSITY
Laredo, TX 78041-1900
http://www.tamiu.edu/

State-supported, coed, comprehensive institution. *Enrollment:* 4,078 graduate, professional, and undergraduate students; 135 full-time matriculated graduate/professional students (58 women), 836 part-time matriculated graduate/professional students (557 women). *Graduate faculty:* 65 full-time (17 women), 7 part-time/adjunct (1 woman). *Computer facilities:* 200 computers available on campus for general student use. A campuswide network can be accessed from off campus. *Library facilities:* Sue and Radcliff Killam Library. *Graduate expenses:* Tuition, state resident: part-time $158 per hour. Tuition, nonresident: part-time $394 per hour. *General application contact:* Maria R. Rosillo, Director of Admissions, 956-326-2200.

Division of Graduate Studies
Dr. Dan Jones, Dean
Programs in:
  biology • MAIS
  mathematics • MAIS

College of Arts and Sciences
Dr. Nasser Momayezi, Dean
Programs in:
  arts and sciences • MA, MAIS, MPAD, MSCJ
  counseling psychology • MA
  criminal justice • MSCJ
  English • MA
  history • MA
  math and physical science • MAIS
  political science • MA
  public administration • MPAD
  sociology • MA
  Spanish • MA

College of Business Administration
Dr. Michael Patrick, Interim Dean
Programs in:
  business administration • MBA, MPA, MSIS
  information systems • MSIS
  international banking • MBA
  international trade • MBA
  professional accountancy • MPA

College of Education
Dr. Humberto Gonzalez, Dean
Programs in:
  administration • MS Ed
  bilingual education • MS Ed
  counseling education • MS Ed
  curriculum and instruction • MS Ed
  early childhood education • MS Ed
  reading • MS Ed
  special education • MS

■ TEXAS A&M UNIVERSITY
College Station, TX 77843
http://www.tamu.edu/

State-supported, coed, university. CGS member. *Enrollment:* 44,813 graduate, professional, and undergraduate students; 6,678 full-time matriculated graduate/professional students (2,579 women), 2,069 part-time matriculated graduate/professional students (1,039 women). *Graduate faculty:* 1,643 full-time (323 women), 71 part-time/adjunct (17 women). *Computer facilities:* 1,500 computers available on campus for general student use. A campuswide network can be accessed from student residence rooms and from off campus. Internet access and online class registration are available. *Library facilities:* Sterling C. Evans Library plus 4 others. *Graduate expenses:* Tuition, state resident: full-time $3,420. Tuition, nonresident: full-time $9,084. Required fees: $1,861. *General application contact:* Graduate Admissions, 979-845-1044.

College of Agriculture and Life Sciences
Dr. Edward A. Hiler, Dean
Programs in:
  agricultural economics • MAB, MS, PhD
  agricultural education • M Ed, MS, Ed D, PhD
  agriculture • M Agr
  agriculture and life sciences • M Agr, M Ed, M Eng, MAB, MS, DE, Ed D, PhD
  agronomy • M Agr, MS, PhD
  animal breeding • MS, PhD
  animal science • M Agr, MS, PhD
  biochemistry • MS, PhD
  biological and agricultural engineering • M Agr, M Eng, MS, DE, PhD
  biophysics • MS
  dairy science • M Agr, MS
  entomology • M Agr, MS, PhD
  food science and technology • M Agr, MS, PhD
  forestry • MS, PhD
  genetics • MS, PhD
  horticulture • PhD
  horticulture and floriculture • M Agr, MS
  molecular and environmental plant sciences • MS, PhD
  natural resource development • M Agr
  natural resources development • M Agr
  nutrition • MS, PhD
  physiology of reproduction • MS, PhD
  plant breeding • MS, PhD
  plant pathology • MS, PhD
  plant protection • M Agr
  poultry science • M Agr, MS, PhD
  rangeland ecology and management • M Agr, MS, PhD
  recreation and resources development • M Agr
  recreation, park, and tourism sciences • MS, PhD
  soil science • MS, PhD
  wildlife and fisheries sciences • M Agr, MS, PhD

Faculty of Genetics
Dr. Linda Guarino, Chair
Program in:
  genetics • MS, PhD

Texas

Texas A&M University (continued)

College of Architecture
J. Thomas Regan, Dean
Programs in:
- architecture • M Arch, MS, MS Arch, PhD
- construction management • MS
- land development • MSLD
- landscape architecture • MLA
- urban and regional science • PhD
- urban planning • MUP

College of Education
Jane Conoley, Dean
Programs in:
- counseling psychology • PhD
- curriculum instructions and foundations • MS
- curriculum, instructions and foundations • M Ed, Ed D, PhD
- education • M Ed, MS, Ed D, PhD
- educational administration and human resource development • M Ed, MS, Ed D, PhD
- educational technology • M Ed
- gifted and talented education • M Ed, MS
- health education • M Ed, MS, Ed D, PhD
- Hispanic bilingual education • M Ed, PhD
- intelligence, creativity, and giftedness • PhD
- kinesiology • M Ed, MS, Ed D, PhD
- learning, development, and instruction • M Ed, MS, PhD
- licensing specialist in school psychology • MS
- math • M Ed, MS, Ed D, PhD
- multicultural/urban/ESL/international education • M Ed, MS, PhD
- physical education • M Ed, Ed D
- reading/language arts/English • M Ed, MS, Ed D, PhD
- research, measurement and statistics • MS
- research, measurement, and statistics • M Ed, PhD
- school counseling • M Ed
- school psychology • MS, PhD
- science • M Ed, MS, Ed D, PhD
- social studies • M Ed, MS, Ed D, PhD
- special education • M Ed, PhD

College of Engineering
Dr. G. Kemble Bennett, Dean
Programs in:
- aerospace engineering • M Eng, MS, PhD
- biomedical engineering • M Eng, MS, D Eng, PhD
- chemical engineering • M Eng, MS, PhD
- computer engineering • M En, MS, PhD
- computer science • MCS, MS, PhD
- construction engineering and project management • M Eng, MS, D Eng, PhD
- electrical engineering • M Eng, MS, PhD
- engineering • M En, M Eng, MCS, MID, MS, D Eng, DE, PhD
- engineering mechanics • M Eng, MS, PhD
- environmental engineering • M Eng, MS, D Eng, PhD
- geotechnical engineering • M Eng, MS, D Eng, PhD
- health physics • MS
- health physics/radiological health • MS
- hydraulic engineering • M Eng, MS, PhD
- hydrology • M Eng, MS, PhD
- industrial engineering • M Eng, MS, PhD
- materials engineering • M Eng, MS, D Eng, PhD
- mechanical engineering • M Eng, MS, D Eng, PhD
- nuclear engineering • M Eng, MS, PhD
- ocean engineering • M Eng, MS, D Eng, PhD
- petroleum engineering • M Eng, MS, D Eng, PhD
- public works engineering and management • M Eng, MS, PhD
- structural engineering and structural mechanics • M Eng, MS, D Eng, PhD
- transportation engineering • M Eng, MS, D Eng, PhD
- water resources engineering • M Eng, MS, D Eng, PhD

College of Geosciences
Dr. Bjorn Kjerfve, Dean
Programs in:
- atmospheric sciences • MS, PhD
- geography • MS, PhD
- geology and geophysics • MS, PhD
- geosciences • MGS, MS, PhD
- oceanography • MS, PhD

College of Liberal Arts
Dr. Charles A. Johnson, Dean
Programs in:
- anthropology • MA, PhD
- behavioral neuroscience • MS, PhD
- clinical psychology • MS, PhD
- cognitive psychology • MS, PhD
- communication • MA, PhD
- developmental psychology • MS, PhD
- economics • MS, PhD
- English • MA, PhD
- history • MA, PhD
- industrial/organizational psychology • MS, PhD
- liberal arts • MA, MS, PhD
- philosophy • MA, PhD
- political science • MA, PhD
- science and technology journalism • MS
- social psychology • MS, PhD
- sociology • MS, PhD
- Spanish • MA

College of Science
H. Joseph Newton, Dean
Programs in:
- applied physics • PhD
- biology • MS, PhD
- botany • MS, PhD
- chemistry • MS, PhD
- mathematics • MS, PhD
- microbial genetics and genomics • PhD
- microbiology • MS, PhD
- molecular and cell biology • PhD
- neuroscience • MS, PhD
- physics • MS, PhD
- science • MS, PhD
- statistics • MS, PhD
- zoology • MS, PhD

College of Veterinary Medicine
Dr. H. Richard Adams, Dean
Programs in:
- anatomy • MS, PhD
- epidemiology • MS
- genetics • MS, PhD
- physiology • MS, PhD
- reproductive biology • PhD
- toxicology • MS, PhD
- veterinary anatomy and public health • MS, PhD
- veterinary large animal medicine and surgery • MS, PhD
- veterinary medical science • MS
- veterinary medicine • DVM, MS, PhD
- veterinary medicine and surgery • MS
- veterinary microbiology • MS, PhD
- veterinary parasitology • MS
- veterinary pathology • MS, PhD
- veterinary physiology and pharmacology • MS, PhD
- veterinary public health • MS
- veterinary science • MS
- veterinary small animal medicine and surgery • MS

George Bush School of Government and Public Service
Richard A. Chilcoat, Dean
Programs in:
- government and public service • MA, MPSA
- international affairs • MA

Intercollegiate Faculty of Nutrition
Dr. Robert S. Chapkin, Chair
Program in:
- nutrition • MS, PhD

Interdisciplinary Faculty in Toxicology
Dr. Timothy D. Phillips, Chair
Program in:
- toxicology • MS, PhD

Texas

Interdisciplinary Faculty of Biotechnology
Dr. Linda Guarino, Chair
Program in:
  biotechnology • MBIOT

Mays Business School
Dr. Jerry R. Strawser, Dean
Programs in:
  accounting • MS, PhD
  business • EMBA, MBA, MLERE, MS, PhD
  business administration • EMBA, MBA
  finance • MS, PhD
  human resource management • MS
  land economics and real estate • MLERE
  management • PhD
  management information systems • MS, PhD
  management science • PhD
  marketing • MS, PhD
  production and operations management • PhD

■ **TEXAS A&M UNIVERSITY–COMMERCE**
Commerce, TX 75429-3011
http://www.tamu-commerce.edu/

State-supported, coed, university. CGS member. *Computer facilities:* 405 computers available on campus for general student use. A campuswide network can be accessed from student residence rooms and from off campus. Internet access and online class registration are available. *Library facilities:* Gee Library. *General application contact.* Graduate Admissions Adviser, 843-886-5167.

Graduate School

College of Arts and Sciences
Programs in:
  agricultural education • M Ed, MS
  agricultural sciences • M Ed, MS
  art • MA, MS
  art history • MA
  arts and sciences • M Ed, MA, MFA, MM, MS, MSW, Ed D, PhD
  biological and earth sciences • M Ed, MS
  chemistry • M Ed, MS
  college teaching of English • PhD
  computer science • MS
  English • MA, MS
  fine arts • MFA
  history • MA, MS
  mathematics • MA, MS
  music • MA, MS
  music composition • MA, MM
  music education • MA, MM, MS
  music literature • MA
  music performance • MA, MM
  music theory • MA, MM

physics • M Ed, MS
social sciences • M Ed, MS
social work • MSW
sociology • MA, MS
Spanish • MA
studio art • MA
theatre • MA, MS

College of Business and Technology
Programs in:
  business administration • MBA
  business and technology • MA, MBA, MS
  economics • MA, MS
  industry and technology • MS

College of Education and Human Services
Programs in:
  counseling • M Ed, MS, Ed D
  early childhood education • M Ed, MA, MS
  education • M Ed, MA, MS, Ed D, PhD
  educational administration • M Ed, MS, Ed D
  educational psychology • PhD
  elementary education • M Ed, MS
  health, kinesiology and sports studies • M Ed, MS, Ed D
  higher education • MS
  learning technology and information systems • M Ed, MS
  psychology • MA, MS
  reading • M Ed, MA, MS
  secondary education • M Ed, MS
  special education • M Ed, MA, MS
  supervision of curriculum and instruction: elementary education • Ed D
  supervision, curriculum, and instruction • Ed D
  training and development • MS

■ **TEXAS A&M UNIVERSITY–CORPUS CHRISTI**
Corpus Christi, TX 78412-5503
http://www.tamucc.edu/

State-supported, coed, comprehensive institution. CGS member. *Enrollment:* 7,860 graduate, professional, and undergraduate students; 397 full-time matriculated graduate/professional students (244 women), 1,133 part-time matriculated graduate/professional students (751 women). *Graduate faculty:* 215 full-time (78 women), 51 part-time/adjunct (32 women). *Computer facilities:* 500 computers available on campus for general student use. A campuswide network can be accessed from student residence rooms and from off campus. Internet access and online class registration are available. *Library facilities:* Mary and Jeff Bell Library. *Graduate expenses:* Tuition, state resident: part-time $58 per credit hour. Tuition, nonresident: part-time $294 per credit hour. *General application contact:* Maria Martinez, Records Evaluator, 361-825-5740.

Graduate Studies and Research
Dr. Sandra Harper, Provost

College of Arts and Humanities
Dr. Paul Hain, Dean
Programs in:
  arts • MA, MFA
  English • MA
  history • MA
  psychology • MA
  public administration • MPA

College of Business Administration
Dr. Moustafa H. Abdelsamad, Dean
Programs in:
  accounting • M Acc
  management • MBA

College of Education
Dr. Dee Hopkins, Dean
Programs in:
  curriculum and instruction • MS
  early childhood education • MS
  educational administration • MS
  educational administration and supervision • MS
  educational leadership • Ed D
  educational technology • MS
  elementary education • MS
  guidance and counseling • MS
  occupational education • MS
  reading • MS
  school counseling • Ed D
  secondary education • MS
  special education • MS

College of Science and Technology
Dr. Diana Marinez, Dean
Programs in:
  biology • MS
  computer science • MS
  environmental sciences • MS
  mariculture • MS
  nursing administration • MSN
  science and technology • MS, MSN

■ **TEXAS A&M UNIVERSITY–KINGSVILLE**
Kingsville, TX 78363
http://www.tamuk.edu/

State-supported, coed, university. *Computer facilities:* 600 computers available on campus for general student use. A campuswide network can be accessed from student residence rooms and from off campus. *Library facilities:* James C. Jernigan Library. *General application contact:* Dean, College of Graduate Studies, 361-593-2808.

Find an in-depth description at www.petersons.com/gradchannel.

Peterson's Graduate Schools in the U.S. 2006

Texas

Texas A&M University–Kingsville (continued)

College of Graduate Studies

College of Agriculture and Home Economics
Programs in:
 agribusiness • MS
 agricultural education • MS
 agriculture and home economics • MS, PhD
 animal sciences • MS
 human sciences • MS
 plant and soil sciences • MS, PhD
 range and wildlife management • MS
 wildlife science • PhD

College of Arts and Sciences
Programs in:
 applied geology • MS
 art • MA, MS
 arts and sciences • MA, MM, MS
 biology • MS
 chemistry • MS
 communication • MS
 English • MA, MS
 gerontology • MS
 history and political science • MA, MS
 mathematics • MS
 music education • MM
 psychology • MA, MS
 sociology • MA, MS
 Spanish • MA

College of Business Administration
Program in:
 business administration • MBA, MS

College of Education
Programs in:
 adult education • M Ed
 bilingual education • MA, MS, Ed D
 early childhood education • M Ed
 education • M Ed, MA, MS, Ed D, PhD
 elementary education • MA, MS
 English as a second language • M Ed
 guidance and counseling • MA, MS
 health and kinesiology • MA, MS
 higher education administration leadership • PhD
 reading • MS
 school administration • MA, MS, Ed D
 secondary education • MA, MS
 special education • M Ed
 supervision • MA, MS

College of Engineering
Programs in:
 chemical engineering • ME, MS
 civil engineering • ME, MS
 computer science • MS
 electrical engineering • ME, MS
 engineering • ME, MS, PhD
 environmental engineering • ME, MS, PhD
 industrial engineering • ME, MS
 mechanical engineering • ME, MS
 natural gas engineering • ME, MS

■ TEXAS A&M UNIVERSITY–TEXARKANA
Texarkana, TX 75505-5518
http://www.tamut.edu/

State-supported, coed, upper-level institution. *Enrollment:* 1,480 graduate, professional, and undergraduate students; 123 full-time matriculated graduate/professional students (93 women), 274 part-time matriculated graduate/professional students (188 women). *Computer facilities:* 133 computers available on campus for general student use. A campuswide network can be accessed from off campus. Internet access and online class registration are available. *Library facilities:* John F. Moss Library plus 1 other. *Graduate expenses:* Tuition, state resident: part-time $113 per semester hour. Tuition, nonresident: part-time $349 per semester hour. *General application contact:* Patricia E. Black, Director of Admissions and Registrar, 903-223-3068.

Graduate Studies and Research
Dr. David Allard, Dean
Program in:
 counseling psychology • MS

College of Arts and Sciences and Education
Dr. Gene Mueller, Dean
Programs in:
 adult education • MS
 educational administration • M Ed
 elementary education • M Ed, MA, MS
 interdisciplinary studies • MA, MS
 secondary education • M Ed, MA, MS
 special education • M Ed, MA, MS

College of Business
Dr. Alfred Ntoko, Dean
Programs in:
 accounting • MSA
 business administration • MBA, MS

■ TEXAS CHRISTIAN UNIVERSITY
Fort Worth, TX 76129-0002
http://www.tcu.edu/

Independent-religious, coed, university. CGS member. *Enrollment:* 8,275 graduate, professional, and undergraduate students; 585 full-time matriculated graduate/professional students, 757 part-time matriculated graduate/professional students. *Graduate faculty:* 291. *Computer facilities:* Computer purchase and lease plans are available. 4,225 computers available on campus for general student use. A campuswide network can be accessed from student residence rooms and from off campus. Internet access and online class registration are available. *Library facilities:* Mary Couts Burnett Library. *Graduate expenses:* Tuition: part-time $640 per credit hour. Tuition and fees vary according to program. *General application contact:* Admissions, TCU Graduate Studies Office, 817-257-7515.

AddRan College of Humanities and Social Sciences
Dr. Mary Volcansek, Dean
Programs in:
 English • MA, PhD
 history • MA, PhD
 humanities and social sciences • MA, PhD

Brite Divinity School
Dr. D. Newell Williams, President
Programs in:
 Biblical interpretation • PhD
 Christian service • MACS
 divinity • M Div, D Min
 pastoral theology and pastoral counseling • PhD
 theological studies • MTS, CTS
 theology • Th M

College of Communication
Dr. William T. Slater, Dean
Programs in:
 advertising/public relations • MS
 communication • MS
 communication in human relations • MS
 news-editorial • MS

College of Fine Arts
Dr. Scott Sullivan, Dean
Programs in:
 art history • MA
 fine arts • M Mus, MA, MFA, MM Ed, Artist Diploma
 studio art • MFA

School of Music
Dr. Richard Gipson, Director
Programs in:
 conducting • M Mus
 music education • MM Ed
 musicology • M Mus
 organ performance • M Mus
 piano • Artist Diploma
 piano pedagogy • M Mus
 piano performance • M Mus
 string performance • M Mus
 theory/composition • M Mus
 vocal performance • M Mus
 voice pedagogy • M Mus
 wind and percussion performance • M Mus

College of Health and Human Sciences
Dr. Rhonda Keen-Payne, Dean
Programs in:

health and human sciences • MS, MSN, MSNA
kinesiology • MS
nurse anesthesia • MSNA
speech-language pathology • MS

Harris School of Nursing
Dr. Paulette Burns, Director
Program in:
adult nursing • MSN

College of Science and Engineering
Dr. Michael McCracken, Dean
Programs in:
biology • MA, MS
chemistry • MA, MS, PhD
earth sciences • MS
ecology • MS
environmental sciences • MS
geology • MS
mathematics • MAT
physics • PhD
psychology • MS, PhD
science and engineering • MA, MAT, MS, PhD

Graduate Studies and Research
Dr. Don Coerver, Director
Program in:
liberal arts • MLA

M. J. Neeley School of Business
Dr. Bob Lusch, Dean
Programs in:
accounting • M Ac
business administration • MBA
international management • MIM

School of Education
Dr. Sam Deitz, Dean
Programs in:
counseling • M Ed
education • M Ed, Certificate
educational administration • M Ed
educational foundations • M Ed
elementary education • M Ed, Certificate
school counseling • Certificate
secondary education • M Ed, Certificate
special education • M Ed

■ TEXAS SOUTHERN UNIVERSITY
Houston, TX 77004-4584
http://www.tsu.edu/

State-supported, coed, university. CGS member. *Enrollment:* 10,891 graduate, professional, and undergraduate students; 1,329 full-time matriculated graduate/professional students (799 women), 634 part-time matriculated graduate/professional students (434 women). *Graduate faculty:* 142 full-time (56 women), 65 part-time/adjunct (24 women). *Computer facilities:* 410 computers available on campus for general student use. A campuswide network can be accessed. Internet access and online class registration are available. *Library facilities:* Robert J. Terry Library plus 2 others. *Graduate expenses:* Tuition, state resident: full-time $1,656. Tuition, nonresident: full-time $5,940. Required fees: $1,314; $689 per semester. Tuition and fees vary according to course load and degree level. *General application contact:* Dr. Richard Pitre, Dean of the Graduate School, Acting, 713-313-7232.

College of Pharmacy and Health Sciences
Dr. Barbara Hayes, Dean
Program in:
pharmacy and health sciences • Pharm D, MHCA

Graduate School
Dr. Richard Pitre, Dean of the Graduate School, Acting

College of Education
Dr. Jay Cummings, Dean
Programs in:
bilingual education • M Ed
business education • M Ed
counseling • M Ed, Ed D
counseling education • Ed D
curriculum, instruction, and urban education • Ed D
early childhood education • M Ed
education • M Ed, MS, Ed D
educational administration • M Ed, Ed D
elementary education • M Ed
health education • MS
higher education administration • Ed D
mid-management superintending • Ed D
physical education • MS
reading education • M Ed
research education and certification • Ed D
research education and education • Ed D
secondary education • M Ed
special education • M Ed

College of Liberal Arts and Behavioral Sciences
Dr. Merline Pitre, Dean
Programs in:
city planning • MCP
English • MA, MS
history • MA
human services and consumer sciences • MS
humanities, fine arts and social sciences • MA, MCP, MPA, MS
journalism • MA
music • MA
psychology • MA
public administration • MPA
sociology • MA
speech communications • MA
telecommunications • MA

Jesse H. Jones School of Business
Dr. Joseph Boyd, Dean
Programs in:
business • MBA
business administration • MBA

School of Science and Technology
Dr. Mitchell Allen, Interim Dean
Programs in:
biology • MS
chemistry • MS
constructional technology • M Ed
educational technology • M Ed
environmental toxicology • MS, PhD
mathematics • MA, MS
science and technology • M Ed, MA, MS, PhD
transportation • MS

Thurgood Marshall School of Law
McKen V. Carrington, Acting Dean
Program in:
law • JD

■ TEXAS STATE UNIVERSITY-SAN MARCOS
San Marcos, TX 78666
http://www.swt.edu/

State-supported, coed, university. CGS member. *Enrollment:* 26,306 graduate, professional, and undergraduate students; 1,371 full-time matriculated graduate/professional students (874 women), 1,911 part-time matriculated graduate/professional students (1,235 women). *Graduate faculty:* 325 full-time (132 women), 78 part-time/adjunct (43 women). *Computer facilities:* Computer purchase and lease plans are available. 750 computers available on campus for general student use. A campuswide network can be accessed from student residence rooms and from off campus. Internet access is available. *Library facilities:* Alkek Library. *Graduate expenses:* Tuition, state resident: full-time $2,484; part-time $138 per semester hour. Tuition, nonresident: full-time $6,732; part-time $374 per semester hour. Required fees: $948; $31 per semester hour. $195 per term. Tuition and fees vary according to course load. *General application contact:* Dr. J. Michael Willoughby, Dean of Graduate School, 512-245-2581.

Graduate School
Dr. J. Michael Willoughby, Dean
Programs in:
interdisciplinary studies in applied sociology • MAIS

Texas

Texas State University-San Marcos (continued)
- interdisciplinary studies in biology • MSIS
- interdisciplinary studies in criminal justice • MSIS
- interdisciplinary studies in education administration and psychological services • MAIS
- interdisciplinary studies in elementary mathematics, science, and technology • MSIS
- interdisciplinary studies in health, physical education, and recreation • MAIS
- interdisciplinary studies in modern languages • MAIS
- interdisciplinary studies in occupational education • MAIS, MSIS
- interdisciplinary studies in political science • MAIS
- interdisciplinary studies in psychology • MAIS
- international studies • MA

College of Applied Arts
Dr. Jaime Chahin, Dean
Programs in:
- agriculture education • M Ed
- applied arts • M Ed, MS, MSCJ
- criminal justice • MSCJ
- family and child studies • MS
- management of vocational/technical education • M Ed

College of Business Administration
Dr. Denise Smart, Dean
Programs in:
- accounting • M Acy
- business administration • M Acy, MBA

College of Education
Dr. John Beck, Dean
Programs in:
- counseling and guidance • M Ed
- developmental education • MA
- early childhood education • M Ed, MA
- education • M Ed, MA, MSRLS
- educational administration • M Ed, MA
- elementary education • M Ed, MA
- elementary education-bilingual/bicultural • M Ed, MA
- health and physical education • MA
- health education • M Ed
- physical education • M Ed
- professional counseling • MA
- reading education • M Ed
- recreation and leisure services • MSRLS
- school psychology • MA
- secondary education • M Ed, MA
- special education • M Ed

College of Fine Arts and Communication
Dr. T. Richard Cheatham, Dean
Programs in:
- communication studies • MA
- fine arts and communication • MA, MM
- mass communication • MA
- music education • MM
- music performance • MM
- theatre arts • MA

College of Health Professions
Dr. Ruth Welborn, Dean
Programs in:
- communication disorders • MA, MSCD
- health professions • MA, MHA, MSCD, MSHP, MSPT, MSW
- health services research • MSHP
- healthcare administration • MHA
- healthcare human resources • MSHP
- physical therapy • MSPT
- social work • MSW

College of Liberal Arts
Dr. Ann Marrie Ellis, Dean
Programs in:
- applied geography • MAG
- creative writing • MFA
- environmental geography • PhD
- environmental geography, geography education, and geography information science • PhD
- geographic information science • MAG
- geography • MAG, MS
- geography education • PhD
- health psychology • MA
- history • M Ed, MA
- information science • PhD
- land/area studies • MAG
- legal studies-alternative dispute resolution • MA
- legal studies-environmental law • MA
- legal studies-legal administration • MA
- liberal arts • M Ed, MA, MAG, MFA, MPA, MS, PhD
- literature • MA
- political science • MA
- public administration • MPA
- resource and environmental studies • MAG
- sociology • MA, MS
- Spanish • MA
- technical communication • MA

College of Science
Dr. Gregory B. Passty, Acting Dean
Programs in:
- aquatic biology • MS
- biochemistry • MS
- biology • M Ed, MA, MS
- chemistry • MA, MS
- computer science • MA, MS
- industrial mathematics • MS
- industrial technology • MST
- mathematics • MA
- middle school mathematics teaching • M Ed
- physics • MS
- science • M Ed, MA, MS, MST
- software engineering • MS
- wildlife ecology • MS

■ TEXAS TECH UNIVERSITY
Lubbock, TX 79409
http://www.texastech.edu/

State-supported, coed, university. CGS member. *Enrollment:* 28,549 graduate, professional, and undergraduate students; 2,706 full-time matriculated graduate/professional students (1,163 women), 1,526 part-time matriculated graduate/professional students (819 women). *Graduate faculty:* 828 full-time (222 women), 55 part-time/adjunct (11 women). *Computer facilities:* Computer purchase and lease plans are available. 3,000 computers available on campus for general student use. A campuswide network can be accessed from student residence rooms and from off campus. Internet access and online class registration, online degree plans, accounts, transcripts, schedules are available. *Library facilities:* Texas Tech Library plus 3 others. *Graduate expenses:* Tuition, state resident: full-time $3,312. Tuition, nonresident: full-time $8,976. Required fees: $1,745. Tuition and fees vary according to program. *General application contact:* Dr. Ann P. McGlynn, Assistant Dean of Graduate Admissions and Recruitment, 806-742-2787.

Find an in-depth description at www.petersons.com/gradchannel.

Graduate School
Dr. John Borrelli, Dean
Programs in:
- accounting • PhD
- accounting information systems • MS Acct
- accounting information systems assurance • MS Acct
- accounting information systems design control • MS Acct
- agricultural business • MBA
- audit/financial reporting • MS Acct
- business administration • MBA, MS, MS Acct, MSA, MSBA, PhD, Certificate
- business statistics • MSBA, PhD
- controllership • MS Acct
- e-business • MBA
- entrepreneurial family studies • MBA
- entrepreneurial skills • MBA
- finance • MBA
- general business • MBA

Texas

global entrepreneurship • MBA
health operations management controllership • MSA
health organization management • MBA, Certificate
health organization management/controllership • MSA
heritage management • MS
high performance management • MBA
home health organization management • MS
interdisciplinary studies • MA, MPA, MS, PhD
international business • MBA
management • PhD
management information systems • MBA, MS, MSBA, PhD
marketing • MBA, MSBA, PhD
museum science • MA
production and operations management • MSBA, PhD
taxation • MS Acct
telecommunications • MSBA

College of Agricultural Sciences and Natural Resources
Dr. Marvin R. Cepica, Interim Dean
Programs in:
agricultural and applied economics • MS, PhD
agricultural business management • M Agr
agricultural education • MS, Ed D
agricultural sciences and natural resources • M Agr, MLA, MS, Ed D, PhD
agriculture • M Agr
agronomy • PhD
animal science • MS, PhD
crop science • MS
entomology • MS
fisheries science • MS, PhD
food technology • MS
horticulture • MS
landscape architecture • MLA
range science • MS, PhD
soil science • MS
wildlife science • MS, PhD

College of Architecture
David Andrew Vernooy, Dean
Programs in:
architecture • M Arch, MS, PhD
land-use planning, management, and design • PhD

College of Arts and Sciences
Dr. Jane L. Winer, Dean
Programs in:
anthropology • MA
applied linguistics • MA
applied physics • MS, PhD
arts and sciences • MA, MPA, MS, PhD
atmospheric sciences • MS
biological informatics • MS
biology • MS, PhD
biotechnology • MS
chemistry • MS, PhD
classics • MA
clinical psychology • PhD
communication studies • MA
counseling psychology • MA, PhD
economics • MA, PhD
English • MA, PhD
environmental toxicology • MS, PhD
exercise and sport sciences • MS
general experimental • MA, PhD
geoscience • MS, PhD
German • MA
history • MA, PhD
mass communications • MA
mathematics • MA, MS, PhD
microbiology • MS
philosophy • MA
physics • MS, PhD
political science • MA, PhD
psychology • MA, PhD
public administration • MPA
Romance languages-French • MA
Romance languages-Spanish • MA
romance languages-Spanish • PhD
sociology • MA
sports health • MS
statistics • MS
technical communication • MA
technical communication and rhetoric • PhD
zoology • MS, PhD

College of Education
Dr. Sheryl Santos, Dean
Programs in:
bilingual education • M Ed
counselor • Certificate
counselor education • M Ed, Ed D
curriculum and instruction • M Ed, Ed D, Certificate
education • M Ed, Ed D, PhD, Certificate
education diagnostician • Certificate
educational leadership • M Ed, Ed D
educational psychology • M Ed, Ed D
elementary education • M Ed
gifted and talented • Certificate
higher education • M Ed, Ed D, PhD
information processing technologist • Certificate
instructional technology • M Ed, Ed D
language and literacy education • M Ed
principal • Certificate
secondary education • M Ed
special education • M Ed, Ed D
special education counselor • Certificate
superintendent • Certificate
visually handicapped • Certificate

College of Engineering
Dr. James L. Smith, Interim Dean
Programs in:
chemical engineering • MS Ch E, PhD
civil engineering • MSCE, PhD
computer science • MS, PhD
electrical and computer engineering • MSEE, PhD
engineering • M Engr, MENVEGR, MS, MS Ch E, MS Pet E, MSCE, MSEE, MSETM, MSIE, MSME, MSMSE, MSSEM, PhD
environmental engineering • MENVEGR
environmental technology and management • MSETM
industrial engineering • MSIE, PhD
manufacturing systems and engineering • MSMSE
mechanical engineering • MSME, PhD
petroleum engineering • MS Pet E, PhD
software engineering • MS
systems and engineering management • MSSEM

College of Human Sciences
Linda C. Hoover, Dean
Programs in:
environmental design • MS
environmental design and consumer economics • PhD
family and consumer sciences education • MS, PhD
family financial planning • MS
food and nutrition • MS, PhD
hospitality administration • PhD
hotel, restaurant and institutional management • MS
human development and family studies • MS, PhD
human sciences • MS, PhD
marriage and family therapy • MS, PhD
restaurant, hotel, and institutional management • MS, PhD

College of Visual and Performing Arts
Dr. Garry W. Owens, Dean
Programs in:
art • MFA
art education • MAE
composition • DMA
conducting • DMA
fine arts • MFA, PhD
music education • MM Ed
music history and literature • MM
music performance • MM
music theory • MM
performance • DMA
piano pedagogy • DMA
theatre arts • MA, MFA
visual and performing arts • MA, MAE, MFA, MM, MM Ed, DMA, PhD

School of Law
Walter Burl Huffman, Dean
Program in:
law • JD

Texas

■ TEXAS WESLEYAN UNIVERSITY
Fort Worth, TX 76105-1536
http://www.txwesleyan.edu/

Independent-religious, coed, comprehensive institution. *Enrollment:* 2,734 graduate, professional, and undergraduate students; 781 full-time matriculated graduate/professional students (417 women), 447 part-time matriculated graduate/professional students (233 women). *Graduate faculty:* 37 full-time (11 women), 40 part-time/adjunct (13 women). *Computer facilities:* 65 computers available on campus for general student use. A campuswide network can be accessed. Internet access is available. *Library facilities:* Eunice and James L. West Library plus 1 other. *Graduate expenses:* Tuition: part-time $405 per credit hour. Tuition and fees vary according to program. *General application contact:* Carolyn Hall, Director of Transfer/Graduate Admission, 817-531-4458.

Graduate Programs
Dr. Allen Henderson, Interim Provost
Programs in:
  business administration • MBA, MSHA
  education • M Ed, MAT, MS Ed
  geriatrics • MSHA
  health administration • MSHA
  nurse anesthesia • MHS, MSNA
  public health • MSHA

School of Law
Fred Slabach, Dean
Program in:
  law • JD

■ TEXAS WOMAN'S UNIVERSITY
Denton, TX 76201
http://www.twu.edu/

State-supported, coed, primarily women, university. CGS member. *Enrollment:* 9,709 graduate, professional, and undergraduate students; 1,463 full-time matriculated graduate/professional students (1,297 women), 2,078 part-time matriculated graduate/professional students (1,846 women). *Graduate faculty:* 389 full-time, 411 part-time/adjunct. *Computer facilities:* 400 computers available on campus for general student use. A campuswide network can be accessed from student residence rooms and from off campus. Internet access is available. *Library facilities:* Blagg-Huey Library. *Graduate expenses:* Tuition, state resident: part-time $66 per credit. Tuition, nonresident: part-time $302 per credit. Full-time tuition and fees vary according to reciprocity agreements. *General application contact:* Holly Kiser, Coordinator of Graduate Admissions, 940-898-3188.

Find an in-depth description at www.petersons.com/gradchannel.

Graduate School
Dr. Jennifer L. Martin, Dean of the Graduate School

College of Arts and Sciences
Dr. Richard Rodean, Interim Dean
Programs in:
  art • MA, MFA
  arts and sciences • MA, MBA, MFA, MS, PhD
  biology • MS
  biology teaching • MS
  business administration • MBA
  chemistry • MS
  chemistry teaching • MS
  counseling psychology • MA, PhD
  dance • MA, MFA, PhD
  drama • MA
  English • MA
  government • MA
  history • MA
  mathematics • MA, MS
  mathematics teaching • MS
  molecular biology • PhD
  music • MA
  music and drama • MA
  rhetoric • PhD
  school psychology • MA, PhD
  science teaching • MS
  sociology • MA, PhD
  visual arts • MA, MFA
  women's studies • MA

College of Health Sciences
Dr. Jean Pyfer, Dean
Programs in:
  education of the deaf • MS
  exercise and sports nutrition • MS
  food science • MS
  health care administration • MHA
  health sciences • MA, MHA, MOT, MS, Ed D, PhD
  health studies • MS, Ed D, PhD
  institutional administration • MS
  kinesiology • MS, PhD
  nutrition • MS, PhD
  occupational therapy • MA, MOT, PhD
  physical therapy • MS, PhD
  speech-language pathology • MS

College of Nursing
Dr. Lucille Travis, Interim Dean
Programs in:
  administration • MS
  clinical specialist • MS
  nurse practitioner • MS
  nursing education • MS
  nursing science • PhD

College of Professional Education
Dr. April Miller, Dean
Programs in:
  child development • MS, PhD
  counseling and development • MS
  early childhood education • M Ed, MA, MS, Ed D
  education administration • M Ed, MA
  elementary education • M Ed, MA
  family studies • MS, PhD
  family therapy • MS, PhD
  library science • MA, MLS, PhD
  professional education • M Ed, MA, MAT, MLS, MS, Ed D, PhD
  reading education • M Ed, MA, MS, Ed D, PhD
  special education • M Ed, MA, PhD
  teaching • MAT

■ TRINITY UNIVERSITY
San Antonio, TX 78212-7200
http://www.trinity.edu/

Independent-religious, coed, comprehensive institution. CGS member. *Enrollment:* 2,633 graduate, professional, and undergraduate students; 134 full-time matriculated graduate/professional students (89 women), 92 part-time matriculated graduate/professional students (56 women). *Graduate faculty:* 32 full-time (11 women), 7 part-time/adjunct (3 women). *Computer facilities:* 100 computers available on campus for general student use. A campuswide network can be accessed from student residence rooms and from off campus. Internet access is available. *Library facilities:* Elizabeth Huth Coates Library. *Graduate expenses:* Tuition: full-time $18,420; part-time $767 per semester hour. *General application contact:* Dr. Mary E. Stefl, Chair, 210-999-8424.

Department of Business Administration
Dr. Petrea K. Sandlin, Director of the Accounting Program
Program in:
  accounting • MS

Department of Education
Dr. Paul Kelleher, Chair
Programs in:
  school administration • M Ed
  school psychology • MA
  teacher education • MAT

Department of Health Care Administration
Dr. Mary E. Stefl, Chair
Program in:
  health care • MS

UNIVERSITY OF HOUSTON
Houston, TX 77204
http://www.uh.edu/

State-supported, coed, university. CGS member. *Enrollment:* 35,066 graduate, professional, and undergraduate students; 4,618 full-time matriculated graduate/professional students (2,433 women), 2,781 part-time matriculated graduate/professional students (1,490 women). *Graduate faculty:* 631 full-time (155 women), 349 part-time/adjunct (130 women). *Computer facilities:* 825 computers available on campus for general student use. A campuswide network can be accessed from student residence rooms and from off campus. Internet access and online class registration are available. *Library facilities:* M.D. Anderson Library plus 5 others. *Graduate expenses:* Tuition, state resident: full-time $1,656; part-time $92 per credit hour. Tuition, nonresident: full-time $5,904; part-time $328 per credit hour. Required fees: $1,704. *General application contact:* Susanna Finnell, Director of Admissions, 713-743-1010.

Bauer College of Business
Dr. Arthur Warga, Dean
Programs in:
 accountancy • MS Accy
 accounting • PhD
 business • MBA, MS, MS Accy, MS Admin, PhD
 decision and information sciences • MBA, PhD
 finance • MS, PhD
 management • PhD
 marketing and entrepreneurship • PhD

College of Architecture
Joseph Mashburn, Dean
Program in:
 architecture • M Arch

College of Education
Robert K. Wimpelberg, Dean
Programs in:
 allied health • M Ed, Ed D
 art education • M Ed
 bilingual education • M Ed
 counseling psychology • M Ed, PhD
 curriculum and instruction • Ed D
 early childhood education • M Ed
 education • M Ed, MS, Ed D, PhD
 education of the gifted • M Ed
 educational administration • M Ed, Ed D
 educational psychology • M Ed
 educational psychology and individual differences • PhD
 elementary education • M Ed
 exercise science • MS
 health education • M Ed
 higher education • M Ed
 historical, social, and cultural foundations of education • M Ed, Ed D
 mathematics education • M Ed
 physical education • M Ed, Ed D
 reading and language arts education • M Ed
 science education • M Ed
 second language education • M Ed
 secondary education • M Ed
 social studies education • M Ed
 special education • M Ed, Ed D
 teaching • M Ed

College of Liberal Arts and Social Sciences
Dr. John Antel, Interim Dean
Programs in:
 anthropology • MA
 applied English linguistics • MA
 clinical psychology • PhD
 economics • MA, PhD
 English and American literature • MA, PhD
 French • MA
 graphic communications • MFA
 history • MA, PhD
 industrial/organizational psychology • PhD
 interior design • MFA
 liberal arts and social sciences • MA, MFA, MM, DMA, PhD
 literature and creative writing • MA, MFA, PhD
 painting • MFA
 philosophy • MA
 photography • MFA
 political science • MA, PhD
 public history • MA
 sculpture • MFA
 social psychology • PhD
 sociology • MA
 Spanish • MA, PhD
 speech language pathology • MA

Moores School of Music
David Ashley White, Director
Programs in:
 accompanying • MM
 applied music • MM
 composition • MM, DMA
 conducting • DMA
 music education • MM, DMA
 music literature • MM
 music performance and pedagogy • MM
 music theory • MM
 performance • DMA

School of Communication
Garth Jowett, Chairperson
Programs in:
 mass communication studies • MA
 public relations studies • MA
 speech communication • MA

School of Theatre
Sidney Berger, Director
Program in:
 theatre • MA, MFA

College of Natural Sciences and Mathematics
Dr. John L. Bear, Dean
Programs in:
 applied mathematics • MSAM
 biochemistry • MS, PhD
 biology • MS, PhD
 chemistry • MS, PhD
 computer science • MS, PhD
 geology • MS, PhD
 geophysics • MS, PhD
 mathematics • MSM, PhD
 natural sciences and mathematics • MS, MSAM, MSM, PhD
 physics • MS, PhD

College of Optometry
Jerald Strickland, Dean
Programs in:
 optometry • OD
 physiological optics/vision science • MS Phys Op, PhD

College of Pharmacy
Dr. M. F. Lokhandwala, Dean
Programs in:
 hospital pharmacy • MSPHR
 medical chemistry and pharmacology • MS
 pharmaceutics • MS, PhD
 pharmacology • MS, PhD
 pharmacy • Pharm D
 pharmacy administration • MSPHR

College of Technology
Uma G. Gupta, Dean
Programs in:
 construction management • MT
 manufacturing systems • MT
 microcomputer systems • MT
 occupational technology • MSOT

Conrad N. Hilton College of Hotel and Restaurant Management
Dr. Agnes DeFranco, Interim Dean
Program in:
 hotel and restaurant management • MHM

Cullen College of Engineering
Dr. Raymond W. Flumerfelt, Dean
Programs in:
 aerospace engineering • MS, PhD
 biomedical engineering • MS
 chemical engineering • M Ch E, MS Ch E, PhD
 civil and environmental engineering • MCE, MS Env E, MSCE, PhD
 computer and systems engineering • MS, PhD

Texas

University of Houston (continued)
  electrical and computer engineering • MEE, MSEE, PhD
  engineering • M Ch E, MCE, MEE, MIE, MME, MS, MS Ch E, MS Env E, MSCE, MSEE, MSIE, MSME, PhD
  environmental engineering • MS, PhD
  industrial engineering • MIE, MSIE, PhD
  materials engineering • MS, PhD
  mechanical engineering • MME, MSME
  petroleum engineering • MS

Graduate School of Social Work
Dr. Ira C. Colby, Dean
Program in:
  social work • MSW, PhD

Law Center
Nancy B. Rapoport, Dean
Program in:
  law • JD, LL M

■ UNIVERSITY OF HOUSTON–CLEAR LAKE
Houston, TX 77058-1098
http://www.cl.uh.edu/

State-supported, coed, upper-level institution. CGS member. *Enrollment:* 7,776 graduate, professional, and undergraduate students; 1,257 full-time matriculated graduate/professional students (690 women), 2,593 part-time matriculated graduate/professional students (1,602 women). *Graduate faculty:* 179 full-time (76 women), 70 part-time/adjunct (37 women). *Computer facilities:* 383 computers available on campus for general student use. A campuswide network can be accessed from off campus. Internet access and online class registration are available. *Library facilities:* Neumann Library. *Graduate expenses:* Tuition, state resident: full-time $2,484; part-time $414 per course. Tuition, nonresident: full-time $6,318; part-time $1,053 per course. Required fees: $12 per course. $199 per semester. *General application contact:* Rose Sklar, Director of Enrollment Services, 281-283-2540.

Find an in-depth description at www.petersons.com/gradchannel.

School of Business and Public Administration
Dr. William Theodore Cummings, Dean
Programs in:
  accounting • MS
  business administration • MBA
  business and public administration • MA, MBA, MHA, MS
  environmental management • MS
  finance • MS
  healthcare administration • MHA
  human resource management • MA
  management information systems • MS
  professional accounting • MS
  public management • MA

School of Education
Dr. Dennis Spuck, Dean
Programs in:
  counseling • MS
  curriculum and instruction • MS
  early childhood education • MS
  education • MS
  educational management • MS
  instructional technology • MS
  multicultural studies • MS
  reading • MS
  school library and information science • MS

School of Human Sciences and Humanities
Dr. Bruce Palmer, Dean
Programs in:
  behavioral sciences • MA
  clinical psychology • MA
  criminology • MA
  cross-cultural studies • MA
  family therapy • MA
  fitness and human performance • MA
  history • MA
  human sciences and humanities • MA, MS
  humanities • MA
  literature • MA
  school psychology • MA
  studies of the future • MS

School of Science and Computer Engineering
Dr. Charles McKay, Dean
Programs in:
  biological sciences • MS
  chemistry • MS
  computer engineering • MS
  computer information systems • MS
  computer science • MS
  environmental science • MS
  mathematical sciences • MS
  physical science • MS
  science and computer engineering • MS
  software engineering • MS
  statistics • MS
  system engineering • MS

■ UNIVERSITY OF HOUSTON–VICTORIA
Victoria, TX 77901-4450
http://www.vic.uh.edu/

State-supported, coed, upper-level institution. *Enrollment:* 2,411 graduate, professional, and undergraduate students; 314 full-time matriculated graduate/professional students (194 women), 958 part-time matriculated graduate/professional students (628 women). *Graduate faculty:* 69 full-time (24 women). *Computer facilities:* 150 computers available on campus for general student use. A campuswide network can be accessed from off campus. Internet access and online class registration are available. *Library facilities:* VC/UHV Library plus 1 other. *Graduate expenses:* Tuition, state resident: full-time $3,552; part-time $148 per semester hour. Tuition, nonresident: full-time $8,112; part-time $338 per semester hour. Required fees: $35 per semester hour. Tuition and fees vary according to course load. *General application contact:* Minnie Urbano, Enrollment Management and Recruitment Coordinator, 361-570-4135.

School of Arts and Sciences
Dr. Dan Jaeckle, Dean
Programs in:
  arts and sciences • MA, MAIS
  interdisciplinary studies • MAIS
  psychology • MA

School of Business Administration
Charles Bullock, Dean
Program in:
  business administration • MBA

School of Education
Dr. Mary Natividad, Dean
Program in:
  education • M Ed

■ UNIVERSITY OF MARY HARDIN-BAYLOR
Belton, TX 76513
http://www.umhb.edu/

Independent-religious, coed, comprehensive institution. *Enrollment:* 2,631 graduate, professional, and undergraduate students; 42 full-time matriculated graduate/professional students (32 women), 110 part-time matriculated graduate/professional students (80 women). *Graduate faculty:* 33 full-time (16 women), 5 part-time/adjunct (1 woman). *Computer facilities:* Computer purchase and lease plans are available. 262 computers available on campus for general student use. A campuswide network can be accessed from student residence rooms. Internet access is available. *Library facilities:* Townsend Memorial Library. *Graduate expenses:* Tuition: full-time $6,930; part-time $385 per credit hour. Required fees: $554; $28 per credit hour. $25 per term. Tuition and fees vary according to course load. *General application contact:* Robbin Steen, Director of Admissions and Recruiting, 254-295-4520.

College of Business
Dr. James King, Dean
Programs in:
business • MBA, MSIS
business administration • MBA
information systems • MSIS

College of Education
Dr. Marlene Zipperlen, Dean
Programs in:
educational administration • M Ed
educational psychology • M Ed
general studies • M Ed
reading education • M Ed

College of Sciences and Humanities
Dr. Darrell G. Watson, Dean
Programs in:
counseling • MA
psychology • MA
sciences and humanities • MA

Program in Health Care Administration
Dr. Mary Anne Franklin, Chair
Program in:
health care administration • MHA

School of Christian Studies
Dr. Bill Carrell, Dean and Director, Graduate Programs in Religion
Program in:
religion • MA

■ UNIVERSITY OF NORTH TEXAS
Denton, TX 76203
http://www.unt.edu/

State-supported, coed, university. CGS member. *Enrollment:* 31,065 graduate, professional, and undergraduate students; 7,203 matriculated graduate/professional students. *Graduate faculty:* 722 full-time (240 women). *Computer facilities:* 2,006 computers available on campus for general student use. A campuswide network can be accessed from student residence rooms and from off campus. *Library facilities:* Willis Library plus 4 others. *Graduate expenses:* Full-time $4,087. Tuition, nonresident: full-time $8,730. Tuition and fees vary according to course load. *General application contact:* Dr. Sandra L. Terrell, Interim Dean, 940-565-2383.

Find an in-depth description at www.petersons.com/gradchannel.

Robert B. Toulouse School of Graduate Studies
Dr. Sandra L. Terrell, Interim Dean
Programs in:
computer science • MS, PhD
engineering • MA, MS, PhD
engineering technology • MS
materials science • MS, PhD

College of Arts and Sciences
Dr. Warren Burggren, Dean
Programs in:
applied geography • MS
arts and sciences • MA, MFA, MJ, MS, Au D, PhD
biochemistry • MS, PhD
biology • MA, MS, PhD
chemistry • MS, PhD
clinical psychology • PhD
communication studies • MA, MS
counseling psychology • MA, MS, PhD
drama • MA, MS
economic research • MS
economics • MA
English • MA, PhD
environmental science • MS, PhD
experimental psychology • MA, MS, PhD
French • MA
health psychology and behavioral medicine • PhD
history • MA, MS, PhD
industrial psychology • MA, MS
journalism • MA, MJ
labor and industrial relations • MS
mathematics • MA, MS, PhD
molecular biology • MA, MS, PhD
philosophy and religion studies • MA
physics • MA, MS, PhD
political science • MA, MS, PhD
psychology • MA, MS, PhD
radio/television/film • MA, MFA, MS
school psychology • MA, MS, PhD
Spanish • MA
speech and hearing sciences • Au D
speech-language pathology/audiology • MA, MS

College of Business Administration
Dr. Jared E. Hazleton, Dean
Programs in:
accounting • MBA, MS, PhD
administrative management • MBA
banking • MBA, PhD
business administration • EMBA, MBA, MS, PhD
decision technologies • MS
finance • MBA, PhD
finance, insurance, real estate, and law • MS
information systems • PhD
information technology • MS
insurance • MBA
management • EMBA, MBA
marketing and logistics • MBA, PhD
organization theory and policy • PhD
personnel and industrial relations • MBA, PhD
production/operations management • MBA, PhD
real estate • MBA

College of Education
Dr. Jean Keller, Dean
Programs in:
applied technology and training development • M Ed, MS, Ed D, PhD
community health • MS
computer education and cognitive systems • MS, PhD
counseling • M Ed, MS, PhD
counseling and student services • M Ed, MS, PhD
counselor education • MS
curriculum and instruction • Ed D, PhD
development and family studies • MS
development, family studies, and early childhood education • MS, Ed D
early childhood education • MS, Ed D
education • M Ed, MS, Ed D, PhD, Certificate
educational administration • M Ed, Ed D, PhD
educational computing • PhD
educational research • PhD
elementary education • M Ed, MS
elementary school supervision • M Ed
health promotion • MS
higher education • Ed D, PhD
kinesiology • MS
reading • M Ed, MS, Ed D, PhD
recreation and leisure studies • MS, Certificate
school health • MS
secondary education • M Ed, MS
secondary school supervision • M Ed
special education • M Ed, MS, PhD
special subject supervision • M Ed

College of Music
Dr. James Scott, Dean
Programs in:
composition • MM, DMA, PhD
jazz studies • MM
music • MA
music education • MM, MME, PhD
music theory • MM, PhD
musicology • MM, PhD
performance • MM, DMA

Interdisciplinary Studies
Donna Hughes, Head
Program in:
interdisciplinary studies • MA, MS

School of Community Service
Dr. David W. Hartman, Dean
Programs in:
administration of aging organizations • MA, MS
administration of retirement facilities • MA, MS

Texas

University of North Texas (continued)
  aging • MA, MS, Certificate
  applied anthropology • MA
  applied economics • MS
  behavior analysis • MS
  community service • MA, MPA, MS, PhD, Certificate
  criminal justice • MS
  public administration • MPA
  rehabilitation counseling • MS
  rehabilitation studies • MS
  sociology • MA, MS, PhD
  vocational evaluation • MS
  work adjustment services • MS

School of Library and Information Sciences
Dr. Philip M. Turner, Dean
Programs in:
  information science • MS, PhD
  library science • MS

School of Merchandising and Hospitality Management
Dr. Judith C. Forney, Dean
Programs in:
  hotel/restaurant management • MS
  merchandising and fabric analytics • MS

School of Visual Arts
Programs in:
  art • PhD
  art education • MA, MFA, PhD
  art history • MA, MFA
  ceramics • MFA
  communication design • MFA
  fashion design • MFA
  fibers • MFA
  interior design • MFA
  metalsmithing and jewelry • MFA
  painting and drawing • MFA
  photography • MFA
  printmaking • MFA
  sculpture • MFA

■ **UNIVERSITY OF ST. THOMAS**
Houston, TX 77006-4696
http://www.stthom.edu/

Independent-religious, coed, comprehensive institution. CGS member. *Enrollment:* 4,875 graduate, professional, and undergraduate students; 263 full-time matriculated graduate/professional students (115 women), 754 part-time matriculated graduate/professional students (423 women). *Graduate faculty:* 42 full-time (16 women), 33 part-time/adjunct (12 women). *Computer facilities:* 153 computers available on campus for general student use. A campuswide network can be accessed from student residence rooms and from off campus. Internet access is available. *Library facilities:* Doherty Library plus 1 other. *Graduate expenses:* Tuition: full-time $9,900; part-time $550 per credit hour. Required fees: $33; $11 per semester. Tuition and fees vary according to program. *General application contact:* Eduardo Prieto, Dean of Admissions, 713-525-3500.

Cameron School of Business
Dr. Javed Ashraf, Dean
Program in:
  business • MBA, MIB, MSA, MSIS

Center for Thomistic Studies
Dr. Mary Catherine Sommers, Director
Program in:
  philosophy • MA, PhD

Program in Liberal Arts
Dr. Janice Gordon-Kelter, Dean
Program in:
  liberal arts • MLA

School of Education
Dr. Ruth M. Strudler, Dean
Program in:
  education • M Ed

School of Theology
Dr. Sandra C. Magie, Dean
Program in:
  theology • M Div, MAPS, MAT

■ **THE UNIVERSITY OF TEXAS AT ARLINGTON**
Arlington, TX 76019
http://www.uta.edu/

State-supported, coed, university. CGS member. *Enrollment:* 24,979 graduate, professional, and undergraduate students; 2,999 full-time matriculated graduate/professional students (1,233 women), 3,102 part-time matriculated graduate/professional students (1,717 women). *Graduate faculty:* 336 full-time (90 women), 66 part-time/adjunct (25 women). *Computer facilities:* 1,000 computers available on campus for general student use. A campuswide network can be accessed from student residence rooms and from off campus. Internet access and online class registration are available. *Library facilities:* Central Library plus 2 others. *Graduate expenses:* Tuition, state resident: full-time $3,042. Tuition, nonresident: full-time $8,712. Required fees: $1,269. Tuition and fees vary according to course load. *General application contact:* Dr. Phil Cohen, Dean of Graduate Studies, 817-272-3186.

Find an in-depth description at www.petersons.com/gradchannel.

Graduate School
Dr. Phil Cohen, Dean of Graduate Studies
Program in:
  interdisciplinary studies • MA, MS

College of Business Administration
Dr. Daniel Himarios, Dean
Programs in:
  accounting • MBA, MP Acc, MS, PhD
  business administration • PhD
  business statistics • PhD
  economics • MA, MBA, PhD
  finance • MBA, PhD
  health care administration • MS
  human resources • MSHRM
  information systems • MBA, MS, PhD
  information systems and operations management • PhD
  management • MBA, PhD
  management sciences • MBA
  marketing • MBA, PhD
  marketing research • MS
  personal and human resources management • MBA
  real estate • MBA, MS
  taxation • MS, PhD

College of Education
Dr. Jeanne M. Gerlach, Dean
Programs in:
  curriculum and instruction • M Ed
  educational leadership and policy studies • M Ed
  physiology of exercise • MS
  teaching • M Ed T

College of Engineering
Dr. Bill D. Carroll, Dean
Programs in:
  aerospace engineering • M Engr, MS, PhD
  biomedical engineering • MS, PhD
  civil and environmental engineering • M Engr, MS, PhD
  computer science and engineering • M Engr, M Sw En, MCS, MS, PhD
  electrical engineering • M Engr, MS, PhD
  engineering • M Engr, M Sw En, MCS, MS, PhD
  engineering management • MS
  industrial and manufacturing systems engineering • M Engr, PhD
  logistics • MS
  materials science and engineering • M Engr, MS, PhD
  mechanical engineering • M Engr, MS, PhD

College of Liberal Arts
Dr. Beth S. Wright, Dean
Programs in:
  anthropology • MA
  criminology and criminal justice • MA
  English • MA
  French • MA
  history • MA
  humanities • MA
  liberal arts • MA, MM, PhD
  linguistics • MA, PhD

literature • PhD
music • MM
political science • MA
rhetoric • PhD
sociology • MA
Spanish • MA
teaching English to speakers of other languages • MA
transatlantic history • PhD

College of Science
Dr. Paul Paulus, Interim Dean
Programs in:
applied chemistry • PhD
biology • MS
chemistry • MS
environmental science • MS, PhD
environmental science and engineering • MS, PhD
experimental psychology • PhD
geology • MS
interdisciplinary science • MA
math: geoscience • PhD
mathematical sciences • PhD
mathematics • MS
physics • MS
physics and applied physics • PhD
psychology • MS
quantitative biology • PhD
science • MA, MS, PhD

School of Architecture
Donald Gatzke, Dean
Programs in:
architecture • M Arch, MLA
landscape architecture • MLA

School of Nursing
Dr. Elizabeth C. Poster, Dean
Programs in:
administration/supervision of nursing • MSN
nurse practitioner • MSN
nursing science • PhD
teaching of nursing • MSN

School of Social Work
Dr. Santos H. Hernandez, Dean
Program in:
social work • MSSW, PhD

School of Urban and Public Affairs
Dr. Richard Cole, Dean
Programs in:
city and regional planning • MCRP
public administration • MPA
urban and public administration • PhD
urban and public affairs • MA, MCRP, MPA, PhD

■ **THE UNIVERSITY OF TEXAS AT AUSTIN**
Austin, TX 78712-1111
http://www.utexas.edu/

State-supported, coed, university. CGS member. *Computer facilities:* 4,000 computers available on campus for general student use. A campuswide network can be accessed from student residence rooms and from off campus. Internet access, e-mail are available. *Library facilities:* Perry-Castañeda Library plus 16 others. *General application contact:* Director, Graduate and International Admissions Center, 512-475-7398.

College of Pharmacy
Program in:
pharmacy • Pharm D, MS Phr, PhD

Graduate School
Programs in:
computational and applied mathematics • MA, PhD
Russian, East European and Eurasian studies • MA
science and technology commercialization • MS
writing • MFA

College of Communication
Programs in:
advertising • MA, PhD
communication • MA, MFA, PhD
communication sciences and disorders • MA, PhD
communication studies • MA, PhD
film/video production • MFA
journalism • MA, PhD
radio-television-film • MA, PhD

College of Education
Programs in:
academic educational psychology • M Ed, MA
counseling education • M Ed
counseling psychology • PhD
curriculum and instruction • M Ed, MA, Ed D, PhD
education • M Ed, MA, MHRDL, Ed D, PhD
educational administration • M Ed, Ed D, PhD
foreign language education • MA, PhD
health education • M Ed, MA, Ed D, PhD
human development and education • PhD
kinesiology • M Ed, MA, Ed D, PhD
learning cognition and instruction • PhD
mathematics education • M Ed, MA, PhD
quantitative methods • PhD
school psychology • PhD
science education • M Ed, MA, PhD
special education • M Ed, MA, Ed D, PhD

College of Engineering
Dr. Ben G. Streetman, Dean
Programs in:
aerospace engineering • MSE, PhD
architectural engineering • MSE
biomedical engineering • MSE, PhD
chemical engineering • MSE, PhD
civil engineering • MSE, PhD
electrical and computer engineering • MSE, PhD
energy and mineral resources • MA, MS
engineering • MA, MS, MSE, PhD
engineering mechanics • MSE, PhD
environmental and water resources engineering • MSE
manufacturing systems engineering • MSE
materials science and engineering • MSE, PhD
mechanical engineering • MSE, PhD
operations research and industrial engineering • MSE, PhD
petroleum and geosystems engineering • MSE, PhD

College of Fine Arts
Programs in:
art education • MA
art history • MA, PhD
design • MFA
fine arts • M Music, MA, MFA, DMA, PhD
music • M Music, DMA, PhD
studio art • MFA
theatre • MA, MFA, PhD

College of Liberal Arts
Programs in:
American studies • MA, PhD
Arabic studies • MA, PhD
archaeology • MA, PhD
Asian cultures and languages • MA, PhD
Asian studies • MA, PhD
classics • MA, PhD
comparative literature • MA, PhD
economics • MA, MS Econ, PhD
English • MA, PhD
folklore and public culture • MA, PhD
French • MA, PhD
geography • MA, PhD
Germanic studies • MA, PhD
government • MA, PhD
Hebrew studies • MA, PhD
Hispanic literature • MA, PhD
history • MA, PhD
Ibero-Romance philology and linguistics • MA, PhD
Latin American studies • MA, PhD
liberal arts • MA, MS Econ, PhD
linguistic anthropology • MA, PhD
linguistics • MA, PhD
Luso-Brazilian literature • MA, PhD
Middle Eastern studies • MA, PhD
Persian studies • MA, PhD
philosophy • MA, PhD
physical anthropology • MA, PhD
psychology • PhD
Romance linguistics • MA, PhD
Slavic languages and literatures • MA, PhD
social anthropology • MA, PhD
sociology • MA, PhD

Texas

The University of Texas at Austin (continued)

College of Natural Sciences
Programs in:
analytical chemistry • MA, PhD
astronomy • MA, PhD
biochemistry • MA, PhD
biological sciences • MA, PhD
cell and molecular biology • PhD
cellular and molecular biology • PhD
child development and family relations • MA, PhD
computer sciences • MA, MSCS, PhD
ecology, evolution and behavior • PhD
genetics and developmental biology • PhD
geological sciences • MA, MS, PhD
inorganic chemistry • MA, PhD
marine science • MS, PhD
mathematics • MA, PhD
microbiology • MA, PhD
microbiology and immunology • PhD
natural sciences • MA, MS, MS Stat, MSCS, PhD
nutrition • MA
nutritional sciences • MA, PhD
organic chemistry • MA, PhD
physical chemistry • MA, PhD
physics • MA, MS, PhD
plant biology • MA, PhD
statistics • MS Stat

Graduate School of Library and Information Science
Program in:
library and information science • MLIS, PhD

The Institute for Neuroscience
Program in:
neuroscience • MA, PhD

Lyndon B. Johnson School of Public Affairs
Programs in:
public affairs • MP Aff
public policy • PhD

McCombs School of Business
Programs in:
accounting • MPA, PhD
business • MBA
business administration • MBA, MHRDL, MPA, PhD
finance • PhD
human resource development leadership • MHRDL
management • PhD
management sciences and information systems • PhD
marketing administration • PhD

School of Architecture
Programs in:
architecture • M Arch, MLA, MS Arch St, MSCRP, PhD
community and regional planning • MSCRP, PhD

School of Nursing
Program in:
nursing • MSN, PhD

School of Social Work
Program in:
social work • MSSW, PhD

School of Law
William C. Powers, Dean
Program in:
law • JD, LL M

■ **THE UNIVERSITY OF TEXAS AT BROWNSVILLE**
Brownsville, TX 78520-4991
http://www.utb.edu/

State-supported, coed, upper-level institution. CGS member. *Computer facilities:* Computer purchase and lease plans are available. 650 computers available on campus for general student use. A campuswide network can be accessed from off campus. Internet access and online class registration are available. *Library facilities:* Arnulfo L. Oliveira Library. *General application contact:* Dean, Graduate Studies, 956-544-8812.

Graduate Studies and Sponsored Programs

College of Liberal Arts
Programs in:
behavioral sciences • MAIS
English • MA
government • MAIS
history • MAIS
interdisciplinary studies • MAIS
liberal arts • MA, MAIS
Spanish • MA

College of Science, Mathematics and Technology
Program in:
biological sciences • MSIS

School of Business
Program in:
business • MBA

School of Education
Programs in:
counseling and guidance • M Ed
curriculum and instruction • M Ed
early childhood education • M Ed
educational administration • M Ed
educational technology • M Ed
elementary education/bilingual endorsement option • M Ed
English as a second language • M Ed
reading specialist • M Ed
special education/educational diagnostician • M Ed
supervision • M Ed

School of Health Sciences
Program in:
health sciences • MSPHN

■ **THE UNIVERSITY OF TEXAS AT DALLAS**
Richardson, TX 75083-0688
http://www.utdallas.edu/

State-supported, coed, university. CGS member. *Enrollment:* 13,718 graduate, professional, and undergraduate students; 1,945 full-time matriculated graduate/professional students (844 women), 2,248 part-time matriculated graduate/professional students (952 women). *Graduate faculty:* 314 full-time (64 women), 30 part-time/adjunct (4 women). *Computer facilities:* 630 computers available on campus for general student use. A campuswide network can be accessed from student residence rooms and from off campus. Internet access and online class registration are available. *Library facilities:* Eugene McDermott Library plus 2 others. *Graduate expenses:* Tuition, state resident: full-time $1,656; part-time $92 per credit. Tuition, nonresident: full-time $5,904; part-time $328 per credit. Required fees: $2,161; $275 per credit. $334 per term. *General application contact:* Dr. Austin Cunningham, Dean for Graduate Studies, 972-883-2234.

Erik Jonsson School of Engineering and Computer Science
Dr. Robert Helms, Dean
Programs in:
computer engineering • MS, PhD
computer science • MS, PhD
electrical engineering • MSEE, PhD
engineering and computer science • MS, MSEE, MSTE, PhD
microelectronics • MSEE, PhD
software engineering • MS, PhD
telecommunications • MSEE, MSTE, PhD

School of Arts and Humanities
Dr. Dennis M. Kratz, Dean
Programs in:
arts and technology • MFA
humanities • MA, MAT, PhD

School of Behavioral and Brain Sciences
Dr. Bert Moore, Dean
Programs in:
applied cognition and neuroscience • MS
audiology • Au D
behavioral and brain sciences • MS, Au D, PhD
communication sciences • PhD
communications disorders • MS
early childhood disorders • MS

Texas

School of General Studies
Dr. George Fair, Dean
Program in:
 interdisciplinary studies • MA

School of Management
Dr. Hasan Pirkul, Dean
Programs in:
 accounting and information management • MS
 business administration • EMBA, MBA
 information technology and management • MS
 international management studies • MA, PhD
 management • EMBA, MA, MBA, MS, PhD
 management and administrative science • MS
 management science • PhD
 medical management • MS

School of Natural Sciences and Mathematics
Dr. John Ferraris, Interim Dean
Programs in:
 applied mathematics • MS, PhD
 applied physics • MS
 bioinformatics and computational biology • MS
 chemistry • MS, PhD
 engineering mathematics • MS
 geosciences • MS, PhD
 mathematical science • MS
 mathematics education • MAT
 molecular and cell biology • MS, PhD
 natural sciences and mathematics • MAT, MS, PhD
 physics • PhD
 science education • MAT
 statistics • MS, PhD

School of Social Sciences
Dr. James Murdoch, Dean
Programs in:
 applied economics • MS
 applied sociology • MA, MS
 economics • PhD
 geographic information sciences • MS
 political economy • PhD
 political science • PhD
 public affairs • MPA
 social sciences • MA, MPA, MS, PhD

■ **THE UNIVERSITY OF TEXAS AT EL PASO**
El Paso, TX 79968-0001
http://www.utep.edu/

State-supported, coed, university. CGS member. *Enrollment:* 18,542 graduate, professional, and undergraduate students; 1,065 full-time matriculated graduate/professional students (527 women), 2,392 part-time matriculated graduate/professional students (1,459 women).

Graduate faculty: 306 full-time (89 women), 35 part-time/adjunct (24 women). *Computer facilities:* A campuswide network can be accessed from student residence rooms and from off campus. *Library facilities:* University Library. *Graduate expenses:* Tuition, state resident: full-time $1,388; part-time $160 per hour. Tuition, nonresident: full-time $3,440; part-time $388 per hour. Tuition and fees vary according to course load, degree level and program. *General application contact:* Dr. Charles H. Ambler, Dean of the Graduate School, 915-747-5491 Ext. 7886.

Find an in-depth description at www.petersons.com/gradchannel.

Graduate School
Dr. Charles H. Ambler, Dean of the Graduate School
Programs in:
 environmental science and engineering • PhD
 materials science and engineering • PhD

College of Business Administration
Dr. Charles Crespy, Dean
Programs in:
 accounting • MACY
 business administration • MACY, MBA, MS

College of Education
Dr. Arturo Pacheco, Dean
Programs in:
 education • M Ed, MA, Ed D
 educational leadership and foundations • M Ed, MA, Ed D
 educational psychology and special services • M Ed, MA
 teacher education • M Ed, MA

College of Engineering
Dr. Andrew H. Swift, Dean
Programs in:
 civil engineering • MS, PhD
 computer engineering • MS, PhD
 computer science • MS
 electrical engineering • MS
 engineering • MEENE, MIT, MS, MSENE, PhD
 environmental engineering • MEENE, MSENE
 industrial engineering • MS
 information technology • MIT
 manufacturing engineering • MS
 mechanical engineering • MS
 metallurgical engineering • MS

College of Health Sciences
Dr. John Conway, Dean
Programs in:
 allied health • MPT, MS
 community health • MSN
 community health/family nurse practitioner • MSN
 health and physical education • MS
 health sciences • MPT, MS, MSN
 kinesiology and sports studies • MS
 nurse midwifery • MSN
 nursing administration • MSN
 nursing-clinical • MSN
 physical therapy • MPT
 post master's nursing • MSN
 speech language pathology • MS
 women's health care • MSN

College of Liberal Arts
Dr. Howard C. Daudistel, Dean
Programs in:
 art • MA
 border history • MA
 clinical psychology • MA
 communication • MA
 creative writing in English • MFA
 creative writing in Spanish • MFA
 English and American literature • MA
 experimental psychology • MA
 history • MA, PhD
 liberal arts • MA, MAIS, MAT, MFA, MM, MPA, PhD
 linguistics • MA
 music education • MM
 music performance • MM
 political science • MA, MPA
 professional writing and rhetoric • MA
 psychology • PhD
 sociology • MA
 Spanish • MA
 teaching English • MAT
 theatre arts • MA

College of Science
Dr. Thomas E. Brady, Dean
Programs in:
 bioinformatics • MS
 biological science • MS, PhD
 chemistry • MS
 environmental science and engineering • PhD
 geological sciences • MS, PhD
 geophysics • MS
 interdisciplinary studies • MSIS
 mathematical sciences • MAT
 mathematics • MS
 physics • MS
 science • MAT, MS, MSIS, PhD
 statistics • MS

■ **THE UNIVERSITY OF TEXAS AT SAN ANTONIO**
San Antonio, TX 78249-0617
http://www.utsa.edu/

State-supported, coed, university. CGS member. *Enrollment:* 24,665 graduate, professional, and undergraduate students; 963 full-time matriculated graduate/professional students (480 women), 2,324 part-time matriculated graduate/professional students (1,454 women). *Graduate faculty:* 238 full-time (67

Texas

The University of Texas at San Antonio (continued)

women), 70 part-time/adjunct (21 women). *Computer facilities:* 800 computers available on campus for general student use. A campuswide network can be accessed from student residence rooms and from off campus. Internet access and online class registration are available. *Library facilities:* John Peace Library plus 1 other. *Graduate expenses:* Tuition, state resident: part-time $153 per hour. Tuition, nonresident: part-time $625 per hour. *General application contact:* Dr. Dorothy A. Flannagan, Interim Dean of Graduate Studies, 210-458-4530.

College of Business
Dr. Bruce O. Bublitz, Dean
Programs in:
  accounting • MS, PhD
  business • MA, MBA, MS, MSIT, MSMOT, MT, PhD
  business economics • MBA
  economics • MA
  finance • PhD
  information systems • MBA
  information technology • MSIT, PhD
  management • MSMOT
  management accounting • MBA
  management of technology • MBA
  management science • MBA
  marketing management • MBA
  organization and management studies • PhD
  statistics • MS
  taxation • MBA, MT

College of Education and Human Development
Dr. Blandina Cardenas, Dean
Programs in:
  bicultural studies • MA
  bicultural-bilingual studies • MA
  counseling • MA
  culture, literacy, and language • PhD
  curriculum and instruction • MA
  early childhood and elementary education • MA
  education and human development • MA, Ed D, PhD
  education-adult and higher education • MA
  education/kinesiology • MA
  educational leadership • Ed D
  educational leadership and policy studies • MA
  educational psychology/special education • MA
  instructional technology • MA
  reading and literacy • MA
  teaching English as a second language • MA

College of Engineering
Dr. Zorica Pantic-Tanner, Dean
Programs in:
  biomedical engineering • PhD
  civil engineering • MSCE
  electrical engineering • MSEE, PhD
  engineering • MSCE, MSEE, MSME, PhD
  mechanical engineering • MSME

College of Liberal and Fine Arts
Dr. Daniel J. Gelo, Dean
Programs in:
  anthropology • MA
  art history • MA
  English • MA, PhD
  history • MA
  liberal and fine arts • MA, MFA, MM, MS, PhD
  music • MM
  political science • MA
  psychology • MS
  sociology • MS
  Spanish • MA
  studio art • MFA

College of Public Policy
Dr. Jesse T. Zapata, Vice Provost, Downtown
Programs in:
  justice policy • MS
  public administration • MPA
  public policy • MPA, MS

College of Sciences
Dr. Deborah Armstrong, Dean
Programs in:
  biology • MS, PhD
  biology and biotechnology • MS
  biotechnology • MS
  cell and molecular biology • PhD
  chemistry • MS
  computer science • MS, PhD
  environmental science and engineering • PhD
  environmental sciences • MS
  geology • MS
  mathematics • MS
  neurobiology • PhD
  sciences • MS, PhD

■ THE UNIVERSITY OF TEXAS AT TYLER
Tyler, TX 75799-0001
http://www.uttyler.edu/

State-supported, coed, comprehensive institution. *Enrollment:* 4,764 graduate, professional, and undergraduate students; 762 matriculated graduate/professional students. *Graduate faculty:* 122 full-time (53 women), 38 part-time/adjunct (17 women). *Computer facilities:* 125 computers available on campus for general student use. A campuswide network can be accessed from student residence rooms and from off campus. Internet access and online class registration are available. *Library facilities:* Robert Muntz Library. *Graduate expenses:* Tuition, state resident: full-time $4,270. Tuition, nonresident: full-time $12,766. *General application contact:* Carol A. Hodge, Office of Graduate Studies, 903-566-5642.

Graduate Studies
Graduate Coordinator

College of Arts and Sciences
Dr. Donna Dickerson, Dean
Programs in:
  art • MAIS, MAT, MFA
  arts and sciences • MA, MAIS, MAT, MFA, MPA, MS, MSIS
  biology • MAT, MS
  chemistry • MSIS
  communication • MAT
  criminal justice • MS
  English • MA, MAT
  history • MA, MAT
  interdisciplinary studies • MA, MAIS, MS, MSIS
  mathematics • MAT, MS, MSIS
  music • MAIS, MAT
  political science • MA, MAT
  public administration • MPA
  sociology • MAT, MS
  theatre • MAT

College of Business and Technology
Dr. Jim Tarter, Dean
Programs in:
  business administration • MBA
  general management • MBA
  health care track • MBA
  technology • MS

College of Education and Psychology
Dr. William Geiger, Dean
Programs in:
  clinical psychology • MS
  counseling psychology • MA
  early childhood education • M Ed, MA
  early childhood, reading and special education • M Ed, MA
  education and psychology • M Ed, MA, MAT, MS, MSIS
  educational leadership • M Ed
  interdisciplinary studies • MSIS
  reading • M Ed, MA
  school counseling • MA
  secondary teaching • MAT
  special education • M Ed, MA

College of Engineering and Computer Science
Dr. Troy Henson, Dean
Programs in:
  computer science • MS
  engineering • M Engr
  engineering and computer science • M Engr, MS, MSIS
  interdisciplinary studies • MSIS

College of Nursing and Health Sciences
Dr. Linda Klotz, Dean
Programs in:
  clinical exercise physiology • MS

Texas

health and kinesiology • M Ed
kinesiology • MS
nurse practitioner • MSN
nursing administration • MSN
nursing and health sciences • M Ed, MS, MSN
nursing education • MSN

■ THE UNIVERSITY OF TEXAS OF THE PERMIAN BASIN
Odessa, TX 79762-0001
http://www.utpb.edu/

State-supported, coed, comprehensive institution. *Computer facilities:* Computer purchase and lease plans are available. 170 computers available on campus for general student use. A campuswide network can be accessed from student residence rooms and from off campus. Internet access and online class registration are available. *Library facilities:* J. Conrad Dunagan Library. *General application contact:* Director of Graduate Studies, 915-552-2530.

Office of Graduate Studies
College of Arts and Sciences
Programs in:
applied behavioral analysis • MA
arts and sciences • MA, MS
biology • MS
clinical psychology • MA
criminal justice administration • MS
English • MA
geology • MS
history • MA
kinesiology • MS
psychology • MA

School of Business
Programs in:
accountancy • MPA
business • MBA, MPA
management • MBA

School of Education
Programs in:
bilingual/English as a second language education • MA
counseling • MA
early childhood education • MA
education • MA
educational leadership • MA
professional education • MA
reading • MA
special education • MA

■ THE UNIVERSITY OF TEXAS–PAN AMERICAN
Edinburg, TX 78541-2999
http://www.panam.edu/

State-supported, coed, comprehensive institution. CGS member. *Enrollment:* 15,914 graduate, professional, and undergraduate students; 497 full-time matriculated graduate/professional students (302 women), 1,549 part-time matriculated graduate/professional students (1,015 women). *Graduate faculty:* 182 full-time (54 women), 17 part-time/adjunct (11 women). *Computer facilities:* 500 computers available on campus for general student use. A campuswide network can be accessed from off campus. Internet access and online class registration are available. *Library facilities:* University Library. *Graduate expenses:* Tuition, state resident: part-time $165 per semester hour. Tuition, nonresident: part-time $381 per semester hour. *General application contact:* Edel de la Garza, Administrative Clerk, 956-381-3661 Ext. 2207.

College of Arts and Humanities
Dr. Miguel A. Nevarez, President
Programs in:
arts and humanities • M Mus, MA, MAIS, MFA, MSIS
communication • MA
English • MA, MAIS
English as a second language • MA
history • MA, MAIS
interdisciplinary studies • MAIS, MSIS
music • M Mus
Spanish • MA
studio art • MFA
theatre • MA

College of Business Administration
Programs in:
business administration • MBA, MS, PhD
computer information systems • MS, PhD

College of Education
Dr. Hilda Medrano, Dean
Programs in:
administration • M Ed
counseling • M Ed
early childhood education • M Ed
education • M Ed, MA, MS, Ed D
educational diagnostician • M Ed
elementary bilingual education • M Ed
elementary education • M Ed
gifted education • M Ed
kinesiology • MS
reading • M Ed
school psychology • MA
secondary education • M Ed
special education • M Ed
supervision • M Ed

College of Health Sciences and Human Services
Dr. William J. McIntyre, Dean
Programs in:
adult health nursing • MSN
communication sciences and disorders • MA
family nurse practitioner • MSN
health sciences and human services • MA, MS, MSN, MSSW
occupational therapy • MS
pediatric nurse practitioner • MSN
rehabilitation counseling • MS
social work • MSSW

College of Science and Engineering
Programs in:
biology • MS
computer science • MS
mathematics • MS
science and engineering • MS

College of Social and Behavioral Sciences
Dean
Programs in:
criminal justice • MS
psychology • MA
public administration • MPA
social and behavioral sciences • MA, MPA, MS
sociology • MS

■ UNIVERSITY OF THE INCARNATE WORD
San Antonio, TX 78209-6397
http://www.uiw.edu/

Independent-religious, coed, comprehensive institution. *Enrollment:* 4,434 graduate, professional, and undergraduate students; 103 full-time matriculated graduate/professional students (57 women), 666 part-time matriculated graduate/professional students (434 women). *Graduate faculty:* 70 full-time (35 women), 35 part-time/adjunct (16 women). *Computer facilities:* Computer purchase and lease plans are available. 200 computers available on campus for general student use. A campuswide network can be accessed from student residence rooms and from off campus. Internet access and online class registration are available. *Library facilities:* J.E. and L.E. Mabee Library plus 1 other. *Graduate expenses:* Tuition: full-time $9,360; part-time $520 per hour. Required fees: $630; $35 per hour. One-time fee: $30 full-time. *General application contact:* Andrea Cyterski-Acosta, Director of Admissions, 210-829-6005.

Peterson's Graduate Schools in the U.S. 2006

Texas

University of the Incarnate Word (continued)

School of Graduate Studies and Research
Gilberto M. Hinojosa, Dean
Programs in:
 communication arts • MA
 interactive media and design • MA

College of Humanities, Arts, and Social Sciences
Dr. Donna Aronson, Dean
Programs in:
 English • MA
 humanities, arts, and social sciences • MA
 multidisciplinary studies • MA
 religious studies • MA

Dreeben School of Education
Dr. Patricia Watkins, Dean
Programs in:
 adult education • M Ed, MA
 early childhood education • M Ed, MA
 education • M Ed, MA, MAT, PhD
 elementary education • MAT
 general education • M Ed, MA
 instructional technology • M Ed, MA
 international education • M Ed, MA
 international education/entrepreneurship • PhD
 mathematics education • PhD
 organizational leadership • PhD
 organizational learning • M Ed, MA
 physical education • M Ed, MA
 reading • M Ed, MA
 reading specialist certificate • M Ed, MA
 secondary teaching • MAT
 special education • M Ed, MA
 teaching • M Ed, MA

HEB School of Business and Administration
Dr. Robert Ryan, Dean
Programs in:
 adult education • MAA
 business and administration • MAA, MBA
 communication arts • MAA
 international business • MBA
 multidisciplinary sciences • MAA
 nutrition • MAA
 organizational development • MAA
 sports management • MAA, MBA
 urban administration • MAA

School of Mathematics, Sciences, and Engineering
Dr. Robert Connelly, Dean
Programs in:
 biology • MA, MS
 mathematics • MA, MS
 mathematics, sciences, and engineering • MA, MS
 multidisciplinary sciences • MA
 nutrition • MS

School of Nursing and Health Professions
Dr. Kathleen Light, Dean
Programs in:
 health informatics • MS
 nursing • MSN
 nursing and health professions • MS, MSN, Certificate
 sports management • Certificate
 sports pedagogy • Certificate

■ WAYLAND BAPTIST UNIVERSITY
Plainview, TX 79072-6998
http://www.wbu.edu/

Independent-religious, coed, comprehensive institution. *Enrollment:* 1,034 graduate, professional, and undergraduate students; 5 full-time matriculated graduate/professional students (all women), 20 part-time matriculated graduate/professional students (13 women). *Graduate faculty:* 14 full-time (5 women), 2 part-time/adjunct (0 women). *Computer facilities:* 123 computers available on campus for general student use. A campuswide network can be accessed from student residence rooms and from off campus. Internet access is available. *Library facilities:* J.E. and L.E. Mabee Learning Resource Center. *Graduate expenses:* Tuition: full-time $5,775; part-time $275 per credit hour. Required fees: $50 per semester. Tuition and fees vary according to course load and campus/location. *General application contact:* Dr. Glenn Saul, Vice President of Academic Services, 806-291-3420.

Graduate Programs
Dr. Glenn Saul, Vice President of Academic Services
Programs in:
 Christian ministry • MCM
 education • M Ed
 general business • MBA
 health care administration • MBA
 human resource management • MBA
 information systems • MBA
 international management • MBA
 management • MA, MBA
 religion • MA
 science • MS

■ WEST TEXAS A&M UNIVERSITY
Canyon, TX 79016-0001
http://www.wtamu.edu/

State-supported, coed, comprehensive institution. *Enrollment:* 7,023 graduate, professional, and undergraduate students; 299 full-time matriculated graduate/professional students (169 women), 568 part-time matriculated graduate/professional students (328 women). *Graduate faculty:* 136 full-time (36 women), 83 part-time/adjunct (37 women). *Computer facilities:* 1,200 computers available on campus for general student use. A campuswide network can be accessed from student residence rooms and from off campus. Internet access and online class registration are available. *Library facilities:* Cornette Library. *Graduate expenses:* Tuition, state resident: part-time $56 per credit hour. Tuition, nonresident: part-time $292 per credit hour. Full-time tuition and fees vary according to course level, degree level and program. *General application contact:* Dr. James R. Hallmark, Dean of the Graduate School, 806-651-2730.

Find an in-depth description at www.petersons.com/gradchannel.

College of Agriculture, Nursing, and Natural Sciences
Dr. James Clark, Dean
Programs in:
 agricultural business and economics • MS
 agriculture • PhD
 agriculture, nursing, and natural sciences • MS, MSN, PhD
 animal science • MS
 biology • MS
 chemistry • MS
 engineering technology • MS
 environmental science • MS
 mathematics • MS
 nursing • MSN
 plant science • MS

College of Education and Social Sciences
Dr. Ted Guffy, Dean
Programs in:
 administration • M Ed
 counseling education • M Ed
 criminal justice • MA
 curriculum and instruction • M Ed
 education and social sciences • M Ed, MA, MS
 educational diagnostician • M Ed
 educational technology • M Ed
 history • MA
 political science • MA
 professional counseling • MA
 psychology • MA
 reading • M Ed
 special education • M Ed
 sports and exercise science • MS

College of Fine Arts and Humanities
Dr. Sue Park, Dean
Programs in:
 art • MA

Utah

communication • MA
communication disorders • MS
English • MA
fine arts and humanities • MA, MFA, MM, MS
music • MA
performance • MM
studio art • MFA

Program in Interdisciplinary Studies
Dr. James R. Hallmark, Dean of the Graduate School
Program in:
  interdisciplinary studies • MA, MS

T. Boone Pickens College of Business
Dr. John Cooley, Dean
Programs in:
  accounting • MP Acc
  accounting/business administration • MPA
  business • MBA, MP Acc, MPA, MS
  business administration • MBA
  finance and economics • MS
  professional accounting • MPA

Utah

■ **BRIGHAM YOUNG UNIVERSITY**
Provo, UT 84602-1001
http://www.byu.edu/

Independent-religious, coed, university. CGS member. *Enrollment:* 33,008 graduate, professional, and undergraduate students; 2,548 matriculated graduate/professional students. *Graduate faculty:* 1,026. *Computer facilities:* 2,000 computers available on campus for general student use. A campuswide network can be accessed from student residence rooms and from off campus. Internet access and online class registration, intranet are available. *Library facilities:* Harold B. Lee Library plus 2 others. *Graduate expenses:* Tuition: part-time $221 per hour. *General application contact:* Claire A. DeWitt, Adviser, 801-422-4541.

The David M. Kennedy Center for International and Area Studies
Dr. Jeffrey F. Ringer, Director
Program in:
  international and area studies • MA

Graduate Studies
Bonnie Brinton, Dean

College of Biological and Agricultural Sciences
Dr. R. Kent Crookston, Dean
Programs in:
  agronomy • MS
  biological and agricultural sciences • MS, PhD
  biological science education • MS
  food science • MS
  horticulture • MS
  integrative biology • MS, PhD
  microbiology • MS, PhD
  molecular biology • MS, PhD
  neuroscience • MS, PhD
  nutrition • MS
  physiology and developmental biology • MS, PhD
  wildlife and wildland conservation • MS, PhD

College of Family, Home, and Social Sciences
Dr. David B. Magleby, Dean
Programs in:
  anthropology • MA
  clinical psychology • PhD
  family, home, and social sciences • MA, MS, MSW, PhD
  general psychology • MS
  geography • MS
  history • MA
  marriage and family therapy • MS, PhD
  marriage, family and human development • MS, PhD
  psychology • PhD
  social work • MSW
  sociology • MS, PhD

College of Fine Arts and Communications
Dr. Stephen M Jones, Dean
Programs in:
  art education • MA
  art history • MA
  ceramics • MFA
  composition • MM
  conducting • MM
  fine arts and communications • MA, MFA, MM, PhD
  mass communication • MA
  music education • MA, MM
  musicology • MA
  painting-drawing • MFA
  performance • MM
  printmaking-drawing • MFA
  sculpture • MFA
  theatre and media arts • MA, PhD
  theatre design and technology • MFA

College of Health and Human Performance
Dr. Robert K. Conlee, Dean
Programs in:
  athletic training • MS
  exercise physiology • MS, PhD
  health and human performance • MPH, MS, PhD
  health promotion • MS, PhD
  health science • MPH
  physical medicine and rehabilitation • PhD
  sports pedagogy • MS
  youth and family recreation • MS

College of Humanities
Dr. Van C. Gessel, Dean
Programs in:
  Arabic • MA
  Chinese • MA
  comparative literature • MA
  English • MA
  French • MA
  French studies • MA
  general linguistics • MA
  German • MA
  German literature • MA
  humanities • MA
  Japanese • MA
  Portuguese linguistics • MA
  Portuguese literature • MA
  Russian • MA
  Spanish linguistics • MA
  Spanish literature • MA
  Spanish teaching • MA
  Spanish/Latin American Literature • MA
  teaching English as a second language • MA, Certificate

College of Nursing
Dr. Elaine S. Marshall, Dean
Programs in:
  adult medical surgical/clinical nurse specialist • MS
  family nurse practitioner • MS

College of Physical and Mathematical Sciences
Earl M. Woolley, Dean
Programs in:
  analytical chemistry • MS, PhD
  applied statistics • MS
  biochemistry • MS, PhD
  computer science • MS, PhD
  geology • MS
  inorganic chemistry • MS, PhD
  mathematics • MS, PhD
  mathematics education • MA
  organic chemistry • MS, PhD
  physical and mathematical sciences • MA, MS, PhD
  physical chemistry • MS, PhD
  physics • MS, PhD
  physics and astronomy • PhD

David O. McKay School of Education
Dr. K. Richard Young, Dean
Programs in:
  audiology • MS
  counseling and school psychology • MS
  counseling psychology • PhD
  education • M Ed, MA, MS, Ed D, PhD
  educational leadership and foundations • M Ed, Ed D, PhD

Peterson's Graduate Schools in the U.S. 2006

Utah

Brigham Young University (continued)
    instructional psychology and technology • MS, PhD
    reading • Ed D
    special education • MS
    speech-language pathology • MS
    teacher education • M Ed, MA
    teaching and learning • M Ed, MA

Ira A. Fulton College of Engineering and Technology
Dr. Douglas M. Chabries, Dean
Programs in:
    chemical • PhD
    chemical engineering • MS
    civil engineering • MS, PhD
    construction management • MS
    electrical engineering • MS
    engineering • PhD
    engineering and technology • MS, PhD
    information technology • MS
    manufacturing systems • MS
    mechanical engineering • MS, PhD
    technology teacher education • MS

J. Reuben Clark Law School
H. Reese Hansen, Dean
Program in:
    law • JD, LL M

Marriott School of Management
Dr. Ned C. Hill, Dean
Programs in:
    accountancy and information systems • M Acc, MISM
    business administration • MBA
    executive business administration • MBA
    management • M Acc, MBA, MISM, MPA
    public management • MPA

■ SOUTHERN UTAH UNIVERSITY
Cedar City, UT 84720-2498
http://www.suu.edu/

State-supported, coed, comprehensive institution. *Enrollment:* 6,048 graduate, professional, and undergraduate students; 81 full-time matriculated graduate/professional students (36 women), 127 part-time matriculated graduate/professional students (64 women). *Graduate faculty:* 17 full-time (4 women), 18 part-time/adjunct (9 women). *Computer facilities:* 300 computers available on campus for general student use. A campuswide network can be accessed from student residence rooms and from off campus. *Library facilities:* Southern Utah University Library. *Graduate expenses:* Tuition, state resident: full-time $2,962. Tuition, nonresident: full-time $9,774. Required fees: $462. Tuition and fees vary according to course load and degree level. *General application contact:* Abe Harraf, Provost, 435-586-7704.

College of Education
Dr. Prent Klag, Associate Professor of Teacher Education
Program in:
    education • M Ed

College of Performing and Visual Arts
Charles Metten, Dean
Program in:
    performing and visual arts • MFA

School of Business
Dr. Carl Templin, Dean
Programs in:
    accounting • M Acc
    business • M Acc, MBA

■ UNIVERSITY OF UTAH
Salt Lake City, UT 84112-1107
http://www.utah.edu/

State-supported, coed, university. CGS member. *Enrollment:* 28,437 graduate, professional, and undergraduate students; 4,401 full-time matriculated graduate/professional students (1,874 women), 1,615 part-time matriculated graduate/professional students (789 women). *Graduate faculty:* 1,035 full-time (351 women), 80 part-time/adjunct (30 women). *Computer facilities:* 5,000 computers available on campus for general student use. A campuswide network can be accessed from student residence rooms and from off campus. Internet access and online class registration, online classes are available. *Library facilities:* Marriott Library plus 3 others. *Graduate expenses:* Tuition, nonresident: full-time $2,483. International tuition: $8,768 full-time. *General application contact:* Office of Admissions, 801-581-7281.

College of Pharmacy
Programs in:
    medicinal chemistry • MS, PhD
    pharmaceutics and pharmaceutical chemistry • MS, PhD
    pharmacology and toxicology • MS, PhD
    pharmacy • Pharm D, MS, PhD
    pharmacy practice • MS

Graduate School
Dr. David S. Chapman, Dean
Program in:
    statistics • MST

College of Architecture and Planning
Brenda Scheer, Dean
Program in:
    architecture and planning • M Arch, MS

College of Education
David J. Sperry, Dean
Programs in:
    education • M Ed, M Phil, M Stat, MA, MS, Ed D, PhD
    education, culture, and society • M Ed, MA, MS, PhD
    educational leadership and policy • M Ed, M Phil, Ed D, PhD
    educational psychology • M Ed, M Stat, MA, MS, PhD
    special education • M Ed, MS, PhD
    teaching and learning • M Ed, MA, MS, PhD

College of Engineering
Dr. Richard B. Brown, Dean
Programs in:
    bioengineering • ME, MS, PhD
    chemical and fuels engineering • M Phil, ME, MS, PhD
    chemical engineering • M Phil, ME, MS, PhD
    civil engineering • ME, MS, PhD
    computer science • M Phil, MS, PhD
    electrical engineering • M Phil, ME, MS, PhD, EE
    engineering • M Phil, ME, MS, PhD, EE
    environmental engineering • ME, MS, PhD
    materials science and engineering • ME, MS, PhD
    mechanical engineering • ME, MS, PhD
    nuclear engineering • ME, MS, PhD

College of Fine Arts
Phyllis A. Haskell, Dean
Programs in:
    art history • MA
    ballet • MA, MFA
    ceramics • MFA
    drawing • MFA
    film studies • MFA
    fine arts • M Mus, MA, MFA, PhD
    graphic design • MFA
    illustration • MFA
    modern dance • MA, MFA
    music • M Mus, MA, PhD
    painting • MFA
    photography/digital imaging • MFA
    printmaking • MFA
    sculpture/intermedia • MFA
    theatre • MFA, PhD

College of Health
Dr. James E. Graves, Dean
Programs in:
    audiology • MA, MS
    exercise and sport science • MS, Ed D, PhD
    foods and nutrition • MS
    health • M Phil, MA, MOT, MPT, MS, Ed D, PhD
    health promotion and education • M Phil, MS, Ed D, PhD
    occupational therapy • MOT

parks, recreation, and tourism • M Phil, MS, Ed D, PhD
physical therapy • MPT
speech-language pathology • MA, MS
speech-language pathology and audiology • PhD

College of Humanities
Robert D. Newman, Dean
Programs in:
Arabic • MA, PhD
communication • M Phil, MA, MS, PhD
comparative literature • MA, PhD
creative writing • MFA
English • MA, PhD
French • MA, MAT
German • MA, MAT, PhD
history • MA, PhD
humanities • M Phil, MA, MAT, MFA, MS, PhD
language pedagogy • MAT
linguistics • MA
Persian • MA
philosophy • MA, MS, PhD
political science • MA, PhD
Spanish • MA, MAT, PhD
Turkish • MA

College of Mines and Earth Sciences
Dr. Francis H. Brown, Dean
Programs in:
environmental engineering • MS, PhD
geological engineering • ME, MS, PhD
geology • MS, PhD
geophysics • MS, PhD
metallurgical engineering • ME, MS, PhD
meteorology • MS, PhD
mines and earth sciences • ME, MS, PhD
mining engineering • ME, MS, PhD

College of Nursing
Maureen Keefe, Dean
Programs in:
gerontology • MS, Certificate
nursing • MS, PhD, Certificate

College of Science
Peter J. Stang, Dean
Programs in:
biology • M Phil
chemical physics • PhD
chemistry • M Phil, MA, MS, PhD
computational engineering and science • MS
ecology and evolutionary biology • MS, PhD
genetics • MS, PhD
mathematics • M Phil, M Stat, MA, MS, PhD
molecular biology • PhD
physics • MA, MS, PhD
science • M Phil, M Stat, MA, MS, PhD
science for secondary school teachers • MS
science teacher education • MS

College of Social and Behavioral Science
J. Steven Ott, Director
Programs in:
anthropology • MA, MS, PhD
economics • M Phil, M Stat, MA, MS, PhD
family and consumer studies • MS
geography • MA, MS, PhD
political science • MA, MS, PhD
psychology • M Stat, MA, MS, PhD
public administration • MPA, Certificate
social and behavioral science • M Phil, M Stat, MA, MPA, MS, PhD, Certificate
sociology • M Stat, PhD

College of Social Work
Jannah H. Mather, Dean
Program in:
social work • MSW, PhD

David Eccles School of Business
Jack Brittain, Dean
Programs in:
accounting • M Pr A, PhD
business • M Pr A, MBA, MS, PhD
business administration • MBA, PhD
finance • MS, PhD

School of Medicine
Dr. A. Lorris Betz, Dean and Senior Vice President for Health Sciences
Program in:
medicine • MD, M Phil, M Stat, MPAS, MPH, MS, MSPH, PhD

Graduate Programs in Medicine
Dr. Jerry Kaplan, Associate Dean of Research
Programs in:
biochemistry • MS, PhD
biostatistics • M Stat
experimental pathology • PhD
human genetics • MS, PhD
laboratory medicine and biomedical science • MS
medical informatics • MS, PhD
medicine • M Phil, M Stat, MPAS, MPH, MS, MSPH, PhD
neurobiology and anatomy • M Phil, MS, PhD
neuroscience • PhD
oncological sciences • MS, PhD
physician assistant • MPAS
physiology • PhD
public health • MPH, MSPH, PhD

S.J. Quinney College of Law
Scott Matheson, Dean
Program in:
law • JD, LL M

■ UTAH STATE UNIVERSITY
Logan, UT 84322
http://www.usu.edu/

State-supported, coed, university. CGS member. *Enrollment:* 16,460 graduate, professional, and undergraduate students; 2,030 full-time matriculated graduate/professional students (800 women), 576 part-time matriculated graduate/professional students (276 women). *Graduate faculty:* 714 full-time (179 women), 38 part-time/adjunct (35 women). *Computer facilities:* 850 computers available on campus for general student use. A campuswide network can be accessed from student residence rooms and from off campus. Internet access and online class registration are available. *Library facilities:* Merrill Library plus 4 others. *Graduate expenses:* Tuition, state resident: part-time $270 per credit hour. Tuition, nonresident: part-time $946 per credit hour. Required fees: $173 per credit hour. *General application contact:* Diana Thimmes, Admissions Officer, School of Graduate Studies, 435-797-1190.

School of Graduate Studies
Dr. Thomas Kent, Dean

College of Agriculture
Noelle E. Crocket, Dean
Programs in:
agricultural systems technology • MS
agriculture • MDA, MFMS, MS, PhD
animal science • MS, PhD
biometeorology • MS, PhD
bioveterinary science • MS, PhD
dairy science • MS
dietetic administration • MDA
ecology • MS, PhD
family and consumer sciences education • MS
food microbiology and safety • MFMS
molecular biology • MS, PhD
nutrition and food sciences • MS, PhD
plant science • MS, PhD
soil science • MS, PhD
toxicology • MS, PhD

College of Business
Caryn C. Beck-Dudley, Dean
Programs in:
accountancy • M Acc
applied economics • MS
business • M Acc, MA, MBA, MS, MSS, Ed D, PhD
business administration • MBA
business education • MS
business information systems • MS

Utah

Utah State University (continued)
    business information systems and education • Ed D
    economics • MA, MS, PhD
    education • PhD
    human resource management • MSS

College of Education and Human Services
Dr. Gerry Giordano, Dean
Programs in:
    audiology • Au D, Ed S
    business information systems • Ed D, PhD
    clinical/counseling/school psychology • PhD
    communication disorders and deaf education • M Ed
    communicative disorders and deaf education • MA, MS
    curriculum and instruction • Ed D, PhD
    education and human services • M Ed, MA, MFHD, MRC, MS, Au D, Ed D, PhD, Ed S
    elementary education • M Ed, MA, MS
    family and human development • MFHD
    family life • PhD
    family, consumer, and human development • MS
    health, physical education and recreation • M Ed, MS
    instructional technology • M Ed, MS, PhD, Ed S
    rehabilitation counselor education • MRC
    research and evaluation • Ed D, PhD
    research and evaluation methodology • PhD
    school counseling • MS
    school psychology • MS
    secondary education • M Ed, MA, MS
    special education • M Ed, MS, PhD, Ed S

College of Engineering
H. Scott Hinton, Dean
Programs in:
    aerospace engineering • MS, PhD
    biological and agricultural engineering • MS, PhD
    civil and environmental engineering • ME, MS, PhD, CE
    electrical engineering • ME, MS, PhD, EE
    engineering • ME, MS, PhD, CE, EE
    industrial technology • MS
    irrigation engineering • MS, PhD
    mechanical engineering • ME, MS, PhD

College of Humanities, Arts and Social Sciences
Dr. Gary H. Kiger, Interim Dean
Programs in:
    advanced technical practice • MFA
    American studies • MA, MS
    art • MA, MFA
    bioregional planning • MS
    design • MFA
    English • MA, MS
    folklore • MA, MS
    history • MA, MS
    humanities, arts and social sciences • MA, MFA, MLA, MS, MSLT, MSS, PhD
    interior design • MS
    journalism and communication • MA, MS
    landscape architecture • MLA
    political science • MA, MS
    second language teaching • MSLT
    sociology • MA, MS, MSS, PhD
    theatre arts • MA, MFA
    western American literature and culture • MA, MS

College of Natural Resources
Dr. Fee Busby, Dean
Programs in:
    bioregional planning • MS
    ecology • MS, PhD
    fisheries biology • MS, PhD
    forestry • MS, PhD
    geography • MA, MS
    human dimensions of ecosystem science and management • MS, PhD
    natural resources • MA, MNR, MS, PhD
    range science • MS, PhD
    recreation resource management • MS, PhD
    wildlife biology • MS, PhD

College of Science
Don Fresinger, Dean
Programs in:
    biochemistry • MS, PhD
    biology • MS, PhD
    chemistry • MS, PhD
    computer science • MCS, MS, PhD
    ecology • MS, PhD
    geology • MS
    industrial mathematics • MS
    mathematical sciences • PhD
    mathematics • M Math, MS
    physics • MS, PhD
    science • M Math, MCS, MS, PhD
    statistics • MS

■ WEBER STATE UNIVERSITY
Ogden, UT 84408-1001
http://weber.edu/

State-supported, coed, comprehensive institution. *Enrollment:* 18,821 graduate, professional, and undergraduate students; 96 full-time matriculated graduate/professional students (34 women), 273 part-time matriculated graduate/professional students (150 women). *Graduate faculty:* 30 full-time (11 women), 7 part-time/adjunct (3 women). *Computer facilities:* Computer purchase and lease plans are available. 558 computers available on campus for general student use. A campuswide network can be accessed from student residence rooms and from off campus. Internet access and online class registration, online grades are available. *Library facilities:* Stewart Library plus 1 other. *Graduate expenses:* Tuition, state resident: full-time $1,292. Tuition, nonresident: full-time $3,838. Tuition and fees vary according to course load and program. *General application contact:* Christopher C. Rivera, Director of Admissions, 801-626-6046.

College of Education
Dr. Jack L. Rasmussen, Dean
Programs in:
    curriculum and instruction • M Ed
    education • M Ed

College of Social and Behavioral Science
Dr. Richard Sadler, Dean
Programs in:
    criminal justice • MCJ
    social and behavioral science • MCJ

John B. Goddard School of Business and Economics
Dr. Michael Vaughan, Dean
Programs in:
    accountancy • MP Acc
    business administration • MBA
    business and economics • MBA, MP Acc

■ WESTMINSTER COLLEGE
Salt Lake City, UT 84105-3697
http://www.wcslc.edu/

Independent, coed, comprehensive institution. *Enrollment:* 2,498 graduate, professional, and undergraduate students; 117 full-time matriculated graduate/professional students (52 women), 363 part-time matriculated graduate/professional students (151 women). *Graduate faculty:* 34 full-time (14 women), 25 part-time/adjunct (8 women). *Computer facilities:* 409 computers available on campus for general student use. A campuswide network can be accessed from student residence rooms. Internet access and online class registration are available. *Library facilities:* Giovale Library plus 1 other. *Graduate expenses:* Tuition: full-time $12,748; part-time $696 per credit. Required fees: $220. *General application contact:* Joel Bauman, Vice President of Enrollment Services, 801-832-2200.

The Bill and Vieve Gore School of Business
Dr. Aric Krause, Dean
Program in:
  business administration • MBA, Certificate

St. Mark's-Westminster School of Nursing and Health Sciences
Diane Forster-Burke, Interim Dean
Program in:
  nursing • MSN

School of Arts and Sciences
Dr. Helen Hodgson, Director
Program in:
  professional communication • MPC

School of Education
Dr. Janet Dynak, Dean
Program in:
  education • M Ed

Vermont

■ CASTLETON STATE COLLEGE
Castleton, VT 05735
http://www.castleton.edu/

State-supported, coed, comprehensive institution. *Enrollment:* 1,879 graduate, professional, and undergraduate students; 40 full-time matriculated graduate/professional students (32 women), 56 part-time matriculated graduate/professional students (37 women). *Graduate faculty:* 13 full-time (9 women), 22 part-time/adjunct (11 women). *Computer facilities:* Computer purchase and lease plans are available. 225 computers available on campus for general student use. A campuswide network can be accessed from student residence rooms. Internet access is available. *Library facilities:* Calvin Coolidge Library. *Graduate expenses:* Part-time tuition: $297 per credit. Tuition, state resident: part-time $446 per credit. Tuition, nonresident: part-time $638 per credit. One-time fee: $58 part-time. Part-time tuition and fees vary according to student's religious affiliation. *General application contact:* Maurice Ouimet, Director of Admissions, 802-468-1213.

Division of Graduate Studies
Dr. Honorée Fleming, Associate Academic Dean
Programs in:
  curriculum and instruction • MA Ed
  educational leadership • MA Ed, CAGS
  forensic psychology • MA
  language arts and reading • MA Ed, CAGS
  special education • MA Ed, CAGS

■ COLLEGE OF ST. JOSEPH
Rutland, VT 05701-3899
http://www.csj.edu/

Independent-religious, coed, comprehensive institution. *Enrollment:* 528 graduate, professional, and undergraduate students; 56 full-time matriculated graduate/professional students (43 women), 144 part-time matriculated graduate/professional students (100 women). *Graduate faculty:* 11 full-time (3 women), 24 part-time/adjunct (13 women). *Computer facilities:* Computer purchase and lease plans are available. 30 computers available on campus for general student use. A campuswide network can be accessed from student residence rooms and from off campus. Internet access is available. *Library facilities:* St. Joseph Library plus 1 other. *Graduate expenses:* Tuition: full-time $9,400; part-time $260 per credit. Required fees: $100. Part-time tuition and fees vary according to program. *General application contact:* Pat Ryan, Director of Admissions and Marketing, 802-773-5900 Ext. 3206.

Graduate Program
Dr. Frank G. Miglorie, President
Programs in:
  English • M Ed
  social studies • M Ed

Division of Business
Dr. Bill Godair, Chair
Programs in:
  business • MBA
  business administration • MBA

Division of Education
Dr. Kapi Reith, Chair
Programs in:
  elementary education • M Ed
  general education • M Ed
  reading • M Ed
  special education • M Ed

Division of Psychology and Human Services
Dr. Craig Knapp, Chair
Programs in:
  clinical mental health counseling • MS
  clinical psychology • MS
  community counseling • MS
  school guidance counseling • MS

■ GODDARD COLLEGE
Plainfield, VT 05667-9432
http://www.goddard.edu/

Independent, coed, comprehensive institution. *Computer facilities:* 27 computers available on campus for general student use. A campuswide network can be accessed from student residence rooms and from off campus. Internet access is available. *Library facilities:* Eliot Pratt Center. *General application contact:* Director of Admissions, 802-454-8311.

Graduate Programs
Programs in:
  health arts and sciences • MA
  individually designed liberal arts • MA
  interdisciplinary arts • MFA
  organizational development • MA
  psychology and counseling • MA
  social ecology • MA
  teacher education • MA
  writing • MFA

■ JOHNSON STATE COLLEGE
Johnson, VT 05656-9405
http://www.johnsonstatecollege.edu/

State-supported, coed, comprehensive institution. *Enrollment:* 1,759 graduate, professional, and undergraduate students; 62 full-time matriculated graduate/professional students (48 women), 127 part-time matriculated graduate/professional students (109 women). *Graduate faculty:* 13 full-time (8 women), 11 part-time/adjunct (8 women). *Computer facilities:* 131 computers available on campus for general student use. A campuswide network can be accessed from student residence rooms and from off campus. Internet access is available. *Library facilities:* Library and Learning Center. *Graduate expenses:* Tuition, state resident: part-time $297 per credit. Tuition, nonresident: part-time $638 per credit. *General application contact:* Catherine H. Higley, Administrative Assistant for Graduate Programs, 800-635-2356 Ext. 6.

Graduate Program in Education
Programs in:
  applied behavior analysis • MA Ed
  children's mental health • MA Ed
  curriculum and instruction • MA Ed
  developmental disabilities • MA Ed
  education of the gifted • MA Ed
  reading education • MA Ed
  special education • MA Ed

Vermont

Johnson State College (continued)
Program in Counseling
Program in:
  counseling • MA

Program in Fine Arts
Programs in:
  drawing • MFA
  painting • MFA
  sculpture • MFA

■ NORWICH UNIVERSITY
Northfield, VT 05663
http://www.norwich.edu/

Independent, coed, comprehensive institution. *Enrollment:* 2,707 graduate, professional, and undergraduate students; 500 full-time matriculated graduate/professional students (250 women). *Graduate faculty:* 4 full-time (0 women), 52 part-time/adjunct (2 women). *Computer facilities:* 142 computers available on campus for general student use. A campuswide network can be accessed from student residence rooms and from off campus. Internet access is available. *Library facilities:* Kreitzberg Library. *Graduate expenses:* Tuition: full-time $16,000. Full-time tuition and fees vary according to program. *General application contact:* Jane Joslin, Administrative Assistant, 802-485-2730.

Online Graduate Programs
Fred Snow, Dean
Programs in:
  business administration • MBA
  diplomacy • MA
  healthcare management • MBA
  information assurance • MS
  international business • MBA
  justice administration • MJA
  technology innovation • MBA

■ SAINT MICHAEL'S COLLEGE
Colchester, VT 05439
http://www.smcvt.edu/

Independent-religious, coed, comprehensive institution. *Enrollment:* 2,473 graduate, professional, and undergraduate students; 79 full-time matriculated graduate/professional students (61 women), 268 part-time matriculated graduate/professional students (189 women). *Graduate faculty:* 20 full-time (10 women), 137 part-time/adjunct (77 women). *Computer facilities:* 233 computers available on campus for general student use. A campuswide network can be accessed from student residence rooms and from off campus. Internet access and online class registration are available. *Library facilities:* Durick Library. *Graduate expenses:* Tuition: part-time $410 per credit hour. Tuition and fees vary according to course load. *General application contact:* Dee M. Goodrich, Director of Admissions and Marketing, Graduate Programs, 802-654-2251.

Graduate Programs
Dr. John P. Kenney, Dean
Programs in:
  administration • M Ed, CAGS
  administration and management • MSA, CAMS
  arts in education • CAGS
  clinical psychology • MA
  curriculum and instruction • M Ed, CAGS
  information technology • CAGS
  reading • M Ed
  special education • M Ed, CAGS
  teaching English as a second language • MATESL, Certificate
  technology • M Ed
  theology • MA, CAS, Certificate

■ SCHOOL FOR INTERNATIONAL TRAINING
Brattleboro, VT 05302-0676
http://www.sit.edu/

Independent, coed, graduate-only institution. *Graduate faculty:* 35 full-time (15 women), 19 part-time/adjunct (8 women). *Computer facilities:* 55 computers available on campus for general student use. A campuswide network can be accessed from student residence rooms and from off campus. Internet access is available. *Library facilities:* Donald B. Watt Library. *Graduate expenses:* Tuition: full-time $23,100. Required fees: $986. Full-time tuition and fees vary according to program. *General application contact:* Information Contact, 800-336-1616.

Find an in-depth description at www.petersons.com/gradchannel.

Graduate Programs
Jim Cramer, President
Programs in:
  conflict transformation • MA
  English for speakers of other languages • MAT
  French • MAT
  intercultural service, leadership, and management • MA
  international education • MA
  non-governmental organization leadership and management • Postgraduate Diploma
  organizational management • MS
  social justice in intercultural relations • MA
  Spanish • MAT
  sustainable development • MA

■ UNIVERSITY OF VERMONT
Burlington, VT 05405
http://www.uvm.edu/

State-supported, coed, university. CGS member. *Enrollment:* 10,967 graduate, professional, and undergraduate students; 1,728 matriculated graduate/professional students. *Graduate faculty:* 702 full-time, 604 part-time/adjunct. *Computer facilities:* Computer purchase and lease plans are available. 685 computers available on campus for general student use. A campuswide network can be accessed from student residence rooms and from off campus. Internet access and online class registration, e-mail, web pages, on-line course support are available. *Library facilities:* Bailey-Howe Library plus 3 others. *Graduate expenses:* Tuition, state resident: part-time $362 per credit hour. Tuition, nonresident: part-time $906 per credit hour. *General application contact:* Ralph M. Swenson, Director of Admissions and Administration, 802-656-3160.

College of Medicine
Dr. Joseph B. Warshaw, Dean
Programs in:
  anatomy and neurobiology • PhD
  biochemistry • MS, PhD
  medicine • MD, MS, PhD
  microbiology and molecular genetics • MS, PhD
  molecular physiology and biophysics • MS, PhD
  pathology • MS
  pharmacology • MS, PhD

Graduate College
Dr. Frances E. Carr, Vice President for Research and Dean of the Graduate College
Program in:
  cell and molecular biology • MS, PhD

College of Agriculture and Life Sciences
Dr. R. K. Johnson, Dean
Programs in:
  agriculture and life sciences • M Ext Ed, MAT, MPA, MS, MST, PhD
  animal sciences • MS, PhD
  biology • MST
  botany • MAT, MS, PhD
  community development and applied economics • M Ext Ed, MS
  family and consumer sciences • MAT
  field naturalist • MS
  nutritional sciences • MS
  plant and soil science • MS, PhD
  public administration • MPA

College of Arts and Sciences
Dr. Joan Smith, Dean
Programs in:
 arts and sciences • MA, MAT, MS, MST, PhD
 biology • MS, PhD
 biology education • MAT, MST
 chemistry • MS, MST, PhD
 chemistry education • MAT
 clinical psychology • PhD
 communication sciences • MS
 English • MA
 English education • MAT
 French • MA
 French education • MAT
 geology • MS
 geology education • MAT, MST
 German • MA
 German education • MAT
 Greek • MA
 Greek and Latin • MAT
 historic preservation • MS
 history • MA
 history education • MAT
 Latin • MA
 physical sciences • MST
 physics • MAT, MS
 psychology • PhD

College of Education and Social Services
Dr. Jill Tarule, Dean
Programs in:
 counseling • MS
 curriculum and instruction • M Ed
 education and social services • M Ed, MS, MSW, Ed D
 educational leadership • M Ed
 educational leadership and policy studies • Ed D
 educational studies • M Ed
 higher education and student affairs administration • M Ed
 interdisciplinary studies • M Ed
 reading and language arts • M Ed
 social work • MSW
 special education • M Ed

College of Engineering and Mathematics
Dr. R. Jenkins, Dean
Programs in:
 biomedical engineering • MS
 biostatistics • MS
 civil and environmental engineering • MS, PhD
 computer science • MS, PhD
 electrical engineering • MS, PhD
 engineering and mathematics • MAT, MS, MST, PhD
 materials science • MS, PhD
 mathematics • MAT, MS, MST, PhD
 mathematics education • MAT, MST
 mechanical engineering • MS, PhD
 statistics • MS

College of Nursing and Health Sciences
Dr. Betty Rambur, Dean
Programs in:
 biomedical technologies • MS
 nursing • MS
 nursing and health sciences • MPT, MS
 physical therapy • MPT

School of Business Administration
Dr. R. DeWitt, Dean
Program in:
 business administration • MBA

School of Natural Resources
Dr. D. DeHayes, Dean
Programs in:
 forestry • MS
 natural resources • MS, PhD
 natural resources planning • MS, PhD
 water resources • MS
 wildlife and fisheries biology • MS

Virgin Islands

■ UNIVERSITY OF THE VIRGIN ISLANDS
Saint Thomas, VI 00802-9990
http://www.uvi.edu/

Territory-supported, coed, comprehensive institution. *Enrollment:* 2,788 graduate, professional, and undergraduate students; 64 full-time matriculated graduate/professional students (53 women), 198 part-time matriculated graduate/professional students (156 women). *Graduate faculty:* 16 full-time (6 women), 11 part-time/adjunct (6 women). *Computer facilities:* 100 computers available on campus for general student use. A campuswide network can be accessed from off campus. *Library facilities:* Ralph M. Paiewonsky Library. *Graduate expenses:* Tuition, territory resident: part-time $28 per credit. Tuition, nonresident: part-time $456 per credit. Required fees: $65. *General application contact:* Carolyn Cook, Director of Enrollment Management and New Student Services, 340-693-1224.

Graduate Programs
Dr. Gwen-Marie Moolenaar, Provost

Division of Business Administration
Dr. Eustace Esdaille, Chairperson
Program in:
 business administration • MBA

Division of Education
Dr. Linda V. Thomas, Chairperson
Programs in:
 education • MAE, Ed S
 school psychology • Ed S

Division of Social Sciences
Dr. Dion Phillips, Chairperson
Program in:
 social sciences • MPA

Virginia

■ AVERETT UNIVERSITY
Danville, VA 24541-3692
http://www.averett.edu/

Independent-religious, coed, comprehensive institution. *Enrollment:* 2,849 graduate, professional, and undergraduate students; 257 full-time matriculated graduate/professional students (131 women), 505 part-time matriculated graduate/professional students (299 women). *Graduate faculty:* 27 full-time (7 women), 48 part-time/adjunct (22 women). *Computer facilities:* 100 computers available on campus for general student use. A campuswide network can be accessed. Internet access is available. *Library facilities:* Mary B. Blount Library. *Graduate expenses:* Tuition: part-time $175 per credit. One-time fee: $120 part-time. Tuition and fees vary according to campus/location and program. *General application contact:* Katherine Pappas-Smith, Marketing and Enrollment Manager, 434-791-5844.

Graduate Studies in Education
Dr. Randy Cromwell, Chair
Programs in:
 art • MAT
 biology • M Ed, MAT
 chemistry • MAT
 computer science • MAT
 curriculum and instruction • M Ed
 English • M Ed, MAT
 history • MAT
 mathematics • MAT
 mathematics education • M Ed
 physical education (PK–12) • MAT
 reading (PK–12) • M Ed
 special education (learning disabilities specialization PK–12) • M Ed
 teaching (6–12) • MAT
 teaching (PK–12) • MAT
 teaching (PK–6) • MAT
 theatre arts • MAT

Program in Business Administration
Dr. Peggy Wright, Interim Dean
Program in:
 business administration • MBA

Virginia

■ THE COLLEGE OF WILLIAM AND MARY
Williamsburg, VA 23187-8795
http://www.wm.edu/

State-supported, coed, university. CGS member. *Enrollment:* 7,749 graduate, professional, and undergraduate students; 1,525 full-time matriculated graduate/professional students (697 women), 476 part-time matriculated graduate/professional students (277 women). *Graduate faculty:* 463 full-time (189 women), 266 part-time/adjunct (77 women). *Computer facilities:* 225 computers available on campus for general student use. A campuswide network can be accessed from student residence rooms and from off campus. Internet access and online class registration are available. *Library facilities:* Swem Library plus 9 others. *Graduate expenses:* Tuition, state resident: full-time $4,858; part-time $222 per credit hour. Tuition, nonresident: full-time $16,440; part-time $618 per credit hour. Required fees: $2,674. Tuition and fees vary according to program. *General application contact:* Dr. David Finifter, Dean of Research and Graduate Studies, 757-221-2467.

Find an in-depth description at www.petersons.com/gradchannel.

Faculty of Arts and Sciences
Dr. David Finifter, Dean of Research and Graduate Studies
Programs in:
 American studies • MA, PhD
 anthropology • MA, PhD
 applied science • MS, PhD
 arts and sciences • MA, MPP, MS, PhD, Psy D
 biology • MS
 chemistry • MA, MS
 clinical psychology • Psy D
 computational operations research • MS
 computer science • MS, PhD
 general experimental psychology • MA
 history • MA, PhD
 physics • MA, MS, PhD
 public policy • MPP

School of Business
Dr. Lawrence Pulley, Dean
Programs in:
 accounting • M Acc
 business administration • MBA

School of Education
Dr. Virginia McLaughlin, Dean
Programs in:
 community and addictions counseling • M Ed
 community counseling • M Ed
 curriculum and educational technology • Ed D, PhD
 curriculum leadership • Ed D, PhD
 education • M Ed, MA Ed, Ed D, PhD, Ed S
 educational counseling • Ed D, PhD
 educational leadership • M Ed
 educational policy, planning, and leadership • Ed D, PhD
 elementary education • MA Ed
 family counseling • M Ed
 gifted education • MA Ed
 gifted education administration • M Ed
 reading education • MA Ed
 school counseling • M Ed
 school psychology • M Ed, Ed S
 secondary education • MA Ed
 special education • MA Ed

School of Marine Science/Virginia Institute of Marine Science
Dr. L. D. Wright, Dean and Director
Program in:
 marine science • MS, PhD

William & Mary Law School
W. Taylor Reveley, Dean
Program in:
 law • JD, LL M

■ GEORGE MASON UNIVERSITY
Fairfax, VA 22030
http://www.gmu.edu/

State-supported, coed, university. CGS member. *Enrollment:* 28,246 graduate, professional, and undergraduate students; 2,326 full-time matriculated graduate/professional students (1,218 women), 6,472 part-time matriculated graduate/professional students (3,541 women). *Graduate faculty:* 1,115 full-time (421 women), 903 part-time/adjunct (465 women). *Computer facilities:* 1,500 computers available on campus for general student use. A campuswide network can be accessed from student residence rooms and from off campus. Internet access, telephone registration are available. *Library facilities:* Fenwick Library plus 1 other. *Graduate expenses:* Tuition, state resident: full-time $4,398. Tuition, nonresident: full-time $14,952. Required fees: $1,482. *General application contact:* Beverly Davis, Director of Graduate Admissions, 703-993-2407.

Find an in-depth description at www.petersons.com/gradchannel.

College of Arts and Sciences
Danielle Struppa, Dean
Programs in:
 applied and engineering physics • MS
 arts and sciences • MA, MAIS, MFA, MPA, MS, MSW, DA Ed, PhD, Certificate
 bioinformatics • MS
 biology • MS, PhD
 chemistry • MS
 clinical psychology • PhD
 communications • MA
 creative writing • MFA
 cultural studies • PhD
 developmental psychology • PhD
 ecology, systematics and evolution • MS
 economics • MA, PhD
 English • MA
 English literature • MA
 environmental science and public policy • MS, PhD
 experimental neuropsychology • MA
 foreign languages • MA
 geography and cartographic sciences • MS
 history • MA, PhD
 human factors engineering psychology • MA, PhD
 industrial/organizational psychology • MA, PhD
 interdisciplinary studies • MAIS
 interpretive biology • MS
 liberal studies • MAIS
 life-span development psychology • MA
 linguistics • MA
 mathematics • MS
 molecular and microbiology • PhD
 molecular, microbial, and cellular biology • MS
 organismal biology • MS
 professional writing and editing • MA
 public administration • MPA
 school psychology • MA
 social work • MSW
 sociology • MA
 teaching writing and literature • MA
 telecommunications • MA

The National Center for Community College Education
Gail Kettlewell, Director
Program in:
 community college education • DA Ed, Certificate

College of Nursing and Health Science
Dr. Carlos Sluzki, Acting Dean
Programs in:
 advanced clinical nursing • MSN
 nurse practitioner • MSN
 nursing • MSN, PhD
 nursing administration • MSN

Virginia

College of Visual and Performing Arts
William Reeder, Dean
Programs in:
dance • MFA
music • MA
music education • MA
visual and performing arts • MA, MFA
visual information technologies • MA

Graduate School of Education
Jeffrey Gorrell, Dean
Programs in:
bilingual/multicultural/English as a second language education • M Ed
counseling and development • M Ed
early childhood education • M Ed
education • M Ed, MA, MS, PhD
education leadership • M Ed
exercise, fitness and health promotion • MS
initiatives in educational transformation • MA
instructional technology • M Ed
middle education • M Ed
reading • M Ed
secondary education • M Ed
special education • M Ed

Institute for Conflict Analysis and Resolution
Dr. Sara Cobb, Director
Program in:
conflict analysis and resolution • MS, PhD

School of Computational Sciences
Dr. Menas Kafatos, Dean
Programs in:
computational sciences • MS
computational sciences and informatics • PhD
computational techniques and applications • Certificate

School of Information Technology and Engineering
Lloyd Griffiths, Dean
Programs in:
civil and infrastructure engineering • MS
computer science • MS, PhD
electrical and computer engineering • PhD
electrical engineering • MS
information systems • MS
information technology • MS, PhD, Engr
information technology and engineering • MS, PhD, Engr
operations research and management science • MS
software systems engineering • MS
statistical science • MS
systems engineering • MS

School of Law
Dr. Mark F. Grady, Dean
Programs in:
intellectual property • LL M
law • JD
law and economics • LL M

School of Management
Richard Klimoski, Dean
Programs in:
business administration • EMBA, MBA
management • EMBA, MBA, MS
technology management • MS

School of Public Policy
Dr. Kingsley Haynes, Dean
Programs in:
enterprise engineering and policy • MS
international commerce and policy • MA
organizational learning • MNPS
peace operations • MNPS
public policy • MA, MNPS, MPP, MS, PhD
transportation policy, operations and logistics • MA

■ HAMPTON UNIVERSITY
Hampton, VA 23668
http://www.hamptonu.edu/

Independent, coed, university. CGS member. *Computer facilities:* Computer purchase and lease plans are available. 1,300 computers available on campus for general student use. A campuswide network can be accessed from student residence rooms and from off campus. Internet access and online class registration are available. *Library facilities:* William R. and Norma B. Harvey Library plus 3 others. *General application contact:* Vice President for Research and Dean of Graduate College, 757-727-5310.

Find an in-depth description at www.petersons.com/gradchannel.

Graduate College
Programs in:
applied mathematics • MS
biological sciences • MA, MS
business • MBA
chemistry • MS
college student development • MA
communicative sciences and disorders • MA
community agency counseling • MA
computer science • MS
counseling • MA
elementary education • MA
museum studies • MA
nursing • MS
physical therapy • DPT
physics • MS, PhD
special education • MA
teaching • MT

■ JAMES MADISON UNIVERSITY
Harrisonburg, VA 22807
http://www.jmu.edu/

State-supported, coed, comprehensive institution. CGS member. *Enrollment:* 16,203 graduate, professional, and undergraduate students; 438 full-time matriculated graduate/professional students (310 women), 371 part-time matriculated graduate/professional students (190 women). *Graduate faculty:* 187 full-time (77 women), 35 part-time/adjunct (16 women). *Computer facilities:* Computer purchase and lease plans are available. 600 computers available on campus for general student use. A campuswide network can be accessed from student residence rooms and from off campus. Internet access and online class registration are available. *Library facilities:* Carrier Library plus 2 others. *Graduate expenses:* Tuition, state resident: part-time $201 per credit hour. Tuition, nonresident: part-time $605 per credit hour. *General application contact:* Dr. N. William Walker, Dean, College of Graduate and Professional Programs, 540-568-6131.

Find an in-depth description at www.petersons.com/gradchannel.

College of Graduate and Professional Programs
Dr. N. William Walker, Dean, College of Graduate and Professional Programs

College of Arts and Letters
Dr. Richard F. Whitman, Dean
Programs in:
art education • MA
art history • MA
arts and letters • MA, MFA, MM, MPA, MS
ceramics • MFA
conducting • MM
drawing/painting • MFA
English • MA
history • MA
metal/jewelry • MFA
music education • MM
performance • MM
photography • MFA
printmaking • MFA
public administration • MPA
sculpture • MFA
studio art • MA
technical and scientific communication • MA, MS
theory-composition • MM
weaving/fibers • MFA

Virginia

James Madison University (continued)

College of Business
Dr. Robert D. Reid, Dean
Programs in:
  accounting • MS
  business • MBA, MS
  business administration • MBA

College of Education
Dr. Phillip M. Wishon, Dean
Programs in:
  early childhood education • M Ed
  education • M Ed, MAT, MS Ed
  educational leadership • M Ed
  middle education • M Ed
  reading education • M Ed
  secondary education • M Ed
  special education • M Ed
  vocational education • MS Ed

College of Integrated Science and Technology
Dr. A. Jerry Benson, Dean
Programs in:
  audiology • PhD
  clinical audiology • PhD
  computer science • MS
  counseling psychology • M Ed, MA, Ed S
  general psychology • MA, PhD, Psy D
  health sciences • MS, MS Ed
  integrated science and technology • M Ed, MA, MS, MS Ed, PhD, Psy D, Ed S
  kinesiology and recreation studies • MS
  school psychology • MA, Ed S
  speech pathology/communication sciences and disorders • MS, PhD
  speech-language pathology • MS, PhD

College of Science and Mathematics
Dr. David F. Brakke, Dean
Programs in:
  biology • MS
  science and mathematics • MS

■ LIBERTY UNIVERSITY
Lynchburg, VA 24502
http://www.liberty.edu/

Independent-religious, coed, comprehensive institution. *Enrollment:* 9,050 graduate, professional, and undergraduate students; 377 full-time matriculated graduate/professional students (124 women), 1,060 part-time matriculated graduate/professional students (447 women). *Graduate faculty:* 78 full-time (18 women), 18 part-time/adjunct (2 women). *Computer facilities:* 250 computers available on campus for general student use. A campuswide network can be accessed from student residence rooms and from off campus. Internet access and online class registration are available. *Library facilities:* A. Pierre Guillermin Integrated Learning Resource Center plus 1 other. *Graduate expenses:* Tuition: full-time $5,130; part-time $285 per credit. Required fees: $100. One-time fee: $50 full-time. Tuition and fees vary according to degree level and program. *General application contact:* Dr. William E. Wegert, Director of Graduate Admissions, 434-582-2021.

Find an in-depth description at www.petersons.com/gradchannel.

College of Arts and Science
Dr. Ronald E. Hawkins, Dean
Programs in:
  counseling • MA
  nursing • MSN
  professional counseling • PhD

Liberty Baptist Theological Seminary
Dr. Danny Lovett, Dean
Programs in:
  counseling • PhD
  religious studies • M Div, MAR, MRE, D Min
  theology • Th M

School of Business and Government
Dr. Bruce K. Bell, Dean
Program in:
  business and government • MBA

School of Education
Dr. Karen L. Parker, Dean
Programs in:
  administration and supervision • M Ed
  early childhood education • M Ed
  educational leadership • Ed D
  elementary education • M Ed
  gifted education • M Ed
  reading specialist • M Ed
  school counseling • M Ed
  secondary education • M Ed
  special education • M Ed

School of Religion
Dr. Elmer Towns, Dean
Program in:
  religious studies • MA

■ LONGWOOD UNIVERSITY
Farmville, VA 23909-1800
http://www.longwood.edu/

State-supported, coed, comprehensive institution. CGS member. *Enrollment:* 4,252 graduate, professional, and undergraduate students; 570 matriculated graduate/professional students (481 women). *Graduate faculty:* 70 part-time/adjunct (34 women). *Computer facilities:* Computer purchase and lease plans are available. 270 computers available on campus for general student use. A campuswide network can be accessed from student residence rooms and from off campus. Internet access and online class registration are available. *Library facilities:* Longwood Library. *Graduate expenses:* Tuition, state resident: part-time $198 per credit. Tuition, nonresident: part-time $440 per credit. Required fees: $111 per credit. $17 per credit. Part-time tuition and fees vary according to campus/location. *General application contact:* Kathy E. K. Charleston, Assistant Director of Graduate Studies, 434-395-2707.

Office of Graduate Studies
Dr. Nancy H. Blattner, Interim Associate Provost for Graduate Studies and Support Programs
Programs in:
  administration/supervision • MS
  community and college counseling • MS
  criminal justice • MS
  curriculum and instruction specialist-elementary • MS
  curriculum and instruction specialist-secondary • MS
  English education and writing • MA
  guidance and counseling • MS
  literature • MA
  reading specialist • MS
  school library media • MS

■ LYNCHBURG COLLEGE
Lynchburg, VA 24501-3199
http://www.lynchburg.edu/

Independent-religious, coed, comprehensive institution. *Computer facilities:* 217 computers available on campus for general student use. A campuswide network can be accessed from student residence rooms. Internet access is available. *Library facilities:* Knight-Capron Library. *General application contact:* Vice President for Graduate and Community Advancement, 434-544-8655.

Graduate Studies

School of Business and Economics
Programs in:
  administration • M Ad
  business • MBA

School of Education and Human Development
Programs in:
  agency counseling • M Ed
  counseling • M Ed
  curriculum and instruction • M Ed
  curriculum and instruction: early childhood education • M Ed
  curriculum and instruction: middle education • M Ed
  early childhood education • M Ed

Virginia

early childhood special education • M Ed
English education • M Ed
mental retardation • M Ed
middle school education • M Ed
reading • M Ed
school administration • M Ed
school counseling • M Ed
secondary education • M Ed
severely/profoundly handicapped education • M Ed
special education • M Ed
supervision • M Ed
teaching children with learning disabilities • M Ed
teaching the emotionally disturbed • M Ed

■ MARY BALDWIN COLLEGE
Staunton, VA 24401-3610
http://www.mbc.edu/

Independent, coed, comprehensive institution. *Computer facilities:* 220 computers available on campus for general student use. A campuswide network can be accessed from student residence rooms and from off campus. Internet access and online class registration are available. *Library facilities:* Grafton Library. *General application contact:* Director, MAT Program, 540-887-7333.

Graduate Studies
Programs in:
 elementary education • MAT
 middle grades education • MAT

■ MARYMOUNT UNIVERSITY
Arlington, VA 22207-4299
http://www.marymount.edu/

Independent-religious, coed, comprehensive institution. *Enrollment:* 3,740 graduate, professional, and undergraduate students; 553 full-time matriculated graduate/professional students (436 women), 913 part-time matriculated graduate/professional students (678 women). *Graduate faculty:* 75 full-time (48 women), 69 part-time/adjunct (37 women). *Computer facilities:* Computer purchase and lease plans are available. 177 computers available on campus for general student use. A campuswide network can be accessed from off campus. Internet access, on-line registration for graduate students and seniors are available. *Library facilities:* Emerson C. Reinsch Library plus 1 other. *Graduate expenses:* Tuition: full-time $9,828; part-time $546 per credit hour.

Required fees: $6 per credit hour. *General application contact:* Francesca Reed, Coordinator, Graduate Admissions, 703-284-5901.

Find an in-depth description at www.petersons.com/gradchannel.

School of Arts and Sciences
Dr. Rosemary Hubbard, Dean
Programs in:
 arts and sciences • MA, MS, Certificate
 computer science • MS, Certificate
 humanities • MA
 interior design • MA
 literature and languages • MA

School of Business Administration
Dr. Ronald Hudak, Dean
Programs in:
 business administration • MBA
 business technologies • MS, Certificate
 health care management • MS
 human performance systems • MA
 human resource management • MA
 information management • MS
 information resources management • Certificate
 instructional design • Certificate
 international business • Certificate
 leading and managing change • Certificate
 legal administration • MA
 management studies • Certificate
 organization development • MA, Certificate
 organizational leadership and innovation • MS
 paralegal studies • Certificate

School of Education and Human Services
Dr. Wayne Lesko, Dean
Programs in:
 alternative licensure certification • Certificate
 Catholic school leadership • M Ed, Certificate
 counseling psychology • MA, Certificate
 education and human services • M Ed, MA, Certificate
 English as a second language • M Ed
 forensic and counseling psychology • MA
 forensic psychology • MA
 learning disabilities • M Ed
 pastoral and spiritual care • MA
 pastoral counseling • MA, Certificate
 pre-K-6 • M Ed
 professional studies • M Ed
 school counseling • MA
 secondary education • M Ed

School of Health Professions
Dr. Tess Cappello, Acting Dean
Programs in:
 critical care nursing • MSN, Certificate
 family nurse practitioner • MSN, Certificate
 health and nursing administration • MSN, Certificate
 health professions • MS, MSN, MSPT, Certificate
 health promotion management • MS
 physical therapy • MSPT

■ NORFOLK STATE UNIVERSITY
Norfolk, VA 23504
http://www.nsu.edu/

State-supported, coed, comprehensive institution. CGS member. *Enrollment:* 6,846 graduate, professional, and undergraduate students; 366 full-time matriculated graduate/professional students, 441 part-time matriculated graduate/professional students. *Graduate faculty:* 68 full-time (22 women), 41 part-time/adjunct (20 women). *Computer facilities:* Computer purchase and lease plans are available. 512 computers available on campus for general student use. A campuswide network can be accessed. Internet access and online class registration are available. *Library facilities:* Lymon Beecher Brooks Library. *Graduate expenses:* Tuition, state resident: full-time $4,998; part-time $244 per credit. Tuition, nonresident: full-time $13,170; part-time $698 per credit. *General application contact:* Dr. Jennifer M. Keane-Dawes, Director, Office of Graduate Studies, 757-823-8015.

School of Graduate Studies
Dr. Jennifer M. Keane-Dawes, Director

School of Education
Dr. Jean Braxton, Dean
Programs in:
 early childhood education • MAT
 education • MA, MAT
 pre-elementary education • MA
 principal preparation • MA
 secondary education • MAT
 severe disabilities • MA
 teaching • MA
 urban education/administration • MA

School of Liberal Arts
Dr. Marilyn Broadus-Gay, Acting Dean
Programs in:
 applied sociology • MS
 communication • MA
 community/clinical psychology • MA
 criminal justice • MA

Peterson's Graduate Schools in the U.S. 2006

Virginia

Norfolk State University (continued)
  liberal arts • MA, MFA, MM, MS, Psy D
  media and communication • MA
  music • MM
  music education • MM
  performance • MM
  psychology • Psy D
  theory and composition • MM
  urban affairs • MA
  visual studies • MA, MFA

School of Science and Technology
Dr. Sandra DeLoatch, Dean
Programs in:
  computer science • MS
  electronics engineering • MS
  health related professions and natural sciences • MS
  materials science • MS
  optical engineering • MS

School of Social Work
Dr. Marvin Feit, Dean
Program in:
  social work • MSW, DSW

■ **OLD DOMINION UNIVERSITY**
Norfolk, VA 23529
http://odu.edu/

State-supported, coed, university. CGS member. *Enrollment:* 20,802 graduate, professional, and undergraduate students; 1,300 full-time matriculated graduate/professional students (762 women), 2,431 part-time matriculated graduate/professional students (1,323 women). *Graduate faculty:* 578 full-time (198 women), 312 part-time/adjunct (157 women). *Computer facilities:* 800 computers available on campus for general student use. A campuswide network can be accessed from student residence rooms and from off campus. Internet access and online class registration, on-line courses are available. *Library facilities:* Douglas and Patricia Perry Library plus 3 others. *Graduate expenses:* Tuition, state resident: part-time $235 per credit hour. Tuition, nonresident: part-time $603 per credit hour. Part-time tuition and fees vary according to campus/location. *General application contact:* Alice McAdory, Director of Admissions, 757-683-3685.
Find an in-depth description at www.petersons.com/gradchannel.

College of Arts and Letters
Dr. Chandra deSilva, Dean
Programs in:
  applied linguistics • MA
  applied sociology • MA
  arts and letters • MA, MFA, PhD
  creative writing • MFA
  English • MA
  history • MA
  humanities • MA
  international studies • MA, PhD
  visual studies • MA, MFA

College of Business and Public Administration
Dr. Nancy Bagranoff, Dean
Programs in:
  accounting • MS
  business administration • MBA, PhD
  business and public administration • MA, MBA, MPA, MS, MUS, PhD
  economics • MA
  policy analysis/program evaluation • MUS
  public administration • MPA
  public planning analysis • MUS
  urban administration • MUS
  urban services/urban management • PhD

College of Engineering and Technology
Dr. Oktay Baysal, Interim Dean
Programs in:
  aerospace engineering • ME, MS, PhD
  aerospace engineering mechanics • ME, MS, PhD
  civil engineering • ME, MS, PhD
  computer engineering • ME, MS
  design and manufacturing • ME
  electrical and computer engineering • PhD
  electrical engineering • ME, MS
  engineering and technology • ME, MEM, MS, PhD
  engineering management • MEM, MS, PhD
  engineering mechanics • ME, MS, PhD
  engineering mechanics (aerospace) • ME, MS, PhD
  engineering mechanics (mechanical) • ME, MS, PhD
  environmental engineering • ME, MS, PhD
  global engineering • ME
  materials science and engineering • ME, MS
  mechanical engineering • ME, MS, PhD
  modeling and simulation • ME, MS, PhD
  systems engineering • ME

College of Health Sciences
Dr. Cheryl T. Samuels, Dean
Programs in:
  community health professions • MS
  dental hygiene • MS
  environmental health • MS
  health care administration • MS
  health sciences • MPH, MS, MSN, DPT, PhD
  long-term care administration • MS
  nursing • MSN
  physical therapy • DPT
  public health • MPH
  urban/health services • PhD
  wellness and promotion • MS

College of Sciences
Dr. Richard V. Gregory, Dean
Programs in:
  analytical chemistry • MS
  biochemistry • MS
  biology • MS
  biomedical sciences • PhD
  clinical chemistry • MS
  clinical psychology • Psy D
  computational and applied mathematics • MS, PhD
  computer science • MS, PhD
  ecological sciences • PhD
  environmental chemistry • MS
  industrial/organizational psychology • PhD
  oceanography • MS, PhD
  organic chemistry • MS
  physical chemistry • MS
  physics • MS, PhD
  psychology • MS
  sciences • MS, PhD, Psy D

Darden College of Education
Dr. William H. Graves, Dean
Programs in:
  biology • MS Ed
  business and industry training • MS
  chemistry • MS Ed
  community agency counseling • MS Ed
  community college leadership • PhD
  community college teaching • MS
  counseling • Ed S
  early childhood education • MS Ed
  education • MS, MS Ed, PhD, Ed S
  educational administration • Ed S
  educational media • MS Ed
  educational training • MS Ed
  elementary education • MS Ed
  English • MS Ed
  higher education • MS Ed, Ed S
  instructional technology • MS Ed
  library science • MS Ed
  mathematics • MS Ed
  middle and secondary teaching • MS
  middle school education • MS Ed
  physical education • MS Ed
  principal preparation • MS Ed
  reading education • MS Ed
  school counseling • MS Ed
  secondary education • MS Ed
  social studies • MS Ed
  special education • MS Ed
  speech-language pathology • MS Ed
  student affairs • MS Ed
  urban services/urban education • PhD

Virginia

RADFORD UNIVERSITY
Radford, VA 24142
http://www.radford.edu/

State-supported, coed, comprehensive institution. CGS member. *Computer facilities:* 460 computers available on campus for general student use. A campuswide network can be accessed from student residence rooms and from off campus. Internet access is available. *Library facilities:* McConnell Library. *General application contact:* Interim Dean, 540-831-5431.

Graduate College

College of Arts and Sciences
Programs in:
arts and sciences • MA, MS, Ed S
clinical psychology • MA
corporate and professional communication • MS
counseling psychology • MA
criminal justice • MA, MS
engineering geosciences • MS
English • MA, MS
general psychology • MA, MS
industrial-organizational psychology • MA
school psychology • Ed S

College of Business and Economics
Programs in:
business administration • MBA
business and economics • MBA

College of Education and Human Development
Programs in:
counselor education • MS
curriculum and instruction • MS
education and human development • MS
education of the emotionally disturbed • MS
educational leadership • MS
educational media • MS
learning disabilities • MS
mentally retarded • MS
reading • MS

College of Visual and Performing Arts
Programs in:
art • MFA
art education • MS
music • MA
music education • MS
visual and performing arts • MA, MFA, MS

Waldron College of Health and Human Services
Programs in:
communication science and disorders • MA, MS
health and human services • MA, MS, MSN, MSW
nursing • MS, MSN
social work • MSW

REGENT UNIVERSITY
Virginia Beach, VA 23464-9800
http://www.regent.edu/

Independent, coed, graduate-only institution. *Graduate faculty:* 90 full-time (17 women), 97 part-time/adjunct (47 women). *Computer facilities:* 105 computers available on campus for general student use. A campuswide network can be accessed. Internet access and online class registration, Electronic Reference Center—University Library are available. *Library facilities:* University Library plus 1 other. *Graduate expenses:* Tuition: part-time $375 per credit hour. Tuition and fees vary according to program. *General application contact:* Lisa Tedesco, Director, Central Enrollment Management, 800-373-5504.

Find an in-depth description at www.petersons.com/gradchannel.

Graduate School
Dr. Barry E. Ryan, Vice President of Academic Affairs

College of Communication and the Arts
Peter Engel, Dean
Program in:
communication and the arts • MA, MFA, PhD

Robertson School of Government
Dr. Barry T. Ryan, Dean
Programs in:
public administration • MA
public management • MA
public policy • MA

School for Leadership Studies
Dr. Kathaleen Reid-Martinez, Dean
Programs in:
leadership studies • Certificate
organizational leadership • MA, PhD
strategic leadership • DSL

School of Business
Dr. John E. Mulford, Dean
Programs in:
business administration • MBA
management • MA

School of Divinity
Dr. Vinson Synan, Dean
Programs in:
biblical studies • MA
ministry • D Min
missiology • M Div, MA
practical theology • M Div, MA
renewal studies • PhD

School of Education
Dr. Alan A. Arroyo, Dean
Program in:
education • M Ed, Ed D, CAGS

School of Law
Jeffrey Brauch, Dean
Program in:
law • JD

School of Psychology and Counseling
Dr. Rosemarie Hughes, Dean
Programs in:
counseling • MA
counseling psychology • Psy D
counseling studies • CAGS
counselor education (online) • PhD

SHENANDOAH UNIVERSITY
Winchester, VA 22601-5195
http://www.su.edu/

Independent-religious, coed, comprehensive institution. *Enrollment:* 2,851 graduate, professional, and undergraduate students; 651 full-time matriculated graduate/professional students (428 women), 661 part-time matriculated graduate/professional students (410 women). *Graduate faculty:* 115 full-time (53 women), 54 part-time/adjunct (21 women). *Computer facilities:* Computer purchase and lease plans are available. 170 computers available on campus for general student use. A campuswide network can be accessed from student residence rooms and from off campus. Internet access and online class registration, online grades and student account information are available. *Library facilities:* Alson H. Smith Jr. Library plus 1 other. *Graduate expenses:* Tuition: part-time $535 per credit. *General application contact:* David Anthony, Dean of Admissions, 540-665-4581.

Find an in-depth description at www.petersons.com/gradchannel.

Byrd School of Business
Stan Harrison, Dean
Programs in:
business administration • MBA
health care management • Certificate
information systems and computer technology • Certificate

College of Arts and Sciences
Dr. Calvin Allen, Dean
Programs in:
administrative leadership • D Ed
advanced professional teaching English to speakers of other languages • Certificate
computer education • MSC
computer studies for educators • Certificate
education • MSE
elementary education • Certificate
middle school education • Certificate

Virginia

Shenandoah University (continued)
  professional studies • Certificate
  professional teaching English to speakers of other languages • Certificate
  public management • Certificate
  secondary education • Certificate
  women's studies • Certificate

School of Health Professions
Program in:
  health professions • MS, MSN, DPT, Certificate

Division of Athletic Training
Rose A. Schmieg, Director
Program in:
  athletic training • MS

Division of Nursing
Dr. Sheila Ralph, Director
Programs in:
  family nurse practitioner • Certificate
  nurse-midwifery • Certificate
  nursing • MSN
  psychiatric mental health nurse practitioner • Certificate

Division of Occupational Therapy
Dr. Yvonne Teske, Director
Program in:
  occupational therapy • MS

Division of Physical Therapy
Dr. Steven H. Tepper, Director
Program in:
  physical therapy and non-traditional physical therapy • DPT

Division of Physician Assistant Studies
Anthony A. Miller, Director
Program in:
  physician assistant • MS

School of Pharmacy
Dr. Alan McKay, Dean
Program in:
  pharmacy and non-traditional pharmacy • Pharm D

Shenandoah Conservatory
Dr. Charlotte A. Collins, Dean
Programs in:
  arts administration • MS
  church music • MM, Certificate
  composition • MM
  conducting • MM
  dance • MA, MFA
  dance accompanying • MM
  music • MS
  music education • MME, DMA
  music therapy • MMT
  pedagogy • MM
  performance • MM, DMA
  piano accompanying • MM

■ UNIVERSITY OF RICHMOND
University of Richmond, VA 23173
http://www.richmond.edu/

Independent, coed, comprehensive institution. *Enrollment:* 3,626 graduate, professional, and undergraduate students; 554 full-time matriculated graduate/professional students (254 women), 171 part-time matriculated graduate/professional students (86 women). *Graduate faculty:* 172 full-time (43 women), 72 part-time/adjunct (26 women). *Computer facilities:* 500 computers available on campus for general student use. A campuswide network can be accessed from student residence rooms and from off campus. Internet access and online class registration are available. *Library facilities:* Boatwright Memorial Library plus 4 others. *Graduate expenses:* Tuition: full-time $23,500; part-time $550 per semester hour. *General application contact:* Dr. Kathy W. Hoke, Director of the Graduate School, 804-289-8417.

Find an in-depth description at www.petersons.com/gradchannel.

Graduate School
Dr. Kathy W. Hoke, Director
Programs in:
  biology • MS
  English • MA
  history • MA
  liberal arts • MLA
  psychology • MA

The Robins School of Business
Dr. Karen Newman, Dean
Programs in:
  business • MBA
  business administration • MBA

School of Law
Rodney A. Smolla, Dean
Program in:
  law • JD

■ UNIVERSITY OF VIRGINIA
Charlottesville, VA 22903
http://www.virginia.edu/

State-supported, coed, university. CGS member. *Enrollment:* 23,077 graduate, professional, and undergraduate students; 5,641 full-time matriculated graduate/professional students (2,561 women), 371 part-time matriculated graduate/professional students (231 women). *Graduate faculty:* 2,028 full-time (559 women), 189 part-time/adjunct (94 women). *Computer facilities:* Computer purchase and lease plans are available. 1,645 computers available on campus for general student use. A campuswide network can be accessed from student residence rooms and from off campus. Internet access and online class registration are available. *Library facilities:* Alderman Library plus 14 others. *Graduate expenses:* Tuition, state resident: full-time $6,476. Tuition, nonresident: full-time $18,534. Required fees: $1,380. *General application contact:* Dean of Appropriate School, 434-924-0311.

College and Graduate School of Arts and Sciences
Edward L. Ayers, Dean
Programs in:
  anthropology • MA, PhD
  art history • MA, PhD
  arts and sciences • MA, MFA, MS, PhD
  astronomy • MS, PhD
  biochemistry, molecular biology and genetics • PhD
  biology • MA, MS, PhD
  biomedical engineering • PhD
  cell and developmental biology • PhD
  chemistry • MA, MS, PhD
  classical art and archaeology • MA, PhD
  classics • MA, PhD
  creative writing • MFA
  drama • MFA
  East Asian studies • MA
  economics • MA, PhD
  English • MA, PhD
  environmental sciences • MA, MS, PhD
  foreign affairs • MA, PhD
  French • MA, PhD
  German • MA, PhD
  government • MA, PhD
  history • MA, PhD
  immunology • PhD
  Italian • MA
  linguistics • MA
  mathematics • MA, MS, PhD
  microbiology, immunology and infectious diseases • PhD
  molecular medicine and systems biology • PhD
  music • MA, PhD
  neuroscience • PhD
  philosophy • MA, PhD
  physics • MA, MS, PhD
  physics education • MA
  psychology • MA, PhD
  religious studies • MA, PhD
  Slavic languages and literatures • MA, PhD
  sociology • MA, PhD
  Spanish • MA, PhD
  statistics • MS, PhD
  structural, computational biology and biophysics • PhD

Center for Biomedical Ethics
Jonathan Moreno, Director, Center for Biomedical Ethics

Program in:
bioethics • MA

Curry School of Education
David W. Breneman, Dean
Programs in:
administration and supervision • M Ed, Ed D, Ed S
clinical and school psychology • Ed D, PhD
communication disorders • M Ed
counselor education • M Ed, Ed D, Ed S
curriculum and instruction • M Ed, Ed D, Ed S
education • M Ed, MT, Ed D, PhD, Ed S
educational policy and evaluation • M Ed, Ed D
educational psychology • M Ed, Ed D, Ed S
health and physical education • M Ed, Ed D
higher education • Ed D, Ed S
kinesiology • M Ed, Ed D
special education • M Ed, Ed D, Ed S

Darden Graduate School of Business Administration
Robert S. Harris, Dean
Program in:
business administration • MBA, PhD

McIntire School of Commerce
Carl P. Zeithaml, Dean
Programs in:
accounting • MS
management of information technology • MS

School of Architecture
Karen Van Lengen, Dean
Programs in:
architectural history • M Arch H, PhD
architecture • M Arch
landscape architecture • M Land Arch
urban and environmental planning • MUEP

School of Engineering and Applied Science
Richard W. Miksad, Dean
Programs in:
applied mechanics • MAM, MS
biomedical engineering • ME, MS, PhD
chemical engineering • ME, MS, PhD
civil engineering • ME, MS, PhD
computer engineering • ME, MS, PhD
computer science • MCS, MS, PhD
electrical engineering • ME, MS, PhD
engineering and applied science • MAM, MCS, ME, MEP, MMSE, MS, PhD
engineering physics • MEP, MS, PhD
materials science • MMSE, MS, PhD
mechanical and aerospace engineering • ME, MS, PhD
systems and information engineering • ME, MS, PhD

School of Law
John C. Jeffries, Dean
Program in:
law • JD, LL M, SJD

School of Medicine
Arthur Garson, Jr., Dean
Programs in:
biochemistry • PhD
biological and physical sciences • MS
biophysics • PhD
cell biology • PhD
clinical investigation and patient-oriented research • MS
health evaluation sciences • MS
informatics in medicine • MS
medicine • MD, MPH, MS, PhD
microbiology • PhD
neuroscience • PhD
pharmacology • PhD
physiology • PhD
public health • MPH
surgery • MS

School of Nursing
B. Jeanette Lancaster, Dean
Program in:
nursing • MSN, PhD

■ VIRGINIA COMMONWEALTH UNIVERSITY
Richmond, VA 23284-9005
http://www.vcu.edu/

State-supported, coed, university. CGS member. *Enrollment:* 26,770 graduate, professional, and undergraduate students; 3,995 full-time matriculated graduate/professional students (2,417 women), 2,254 part-time matriculated graduate/professional students (1,522 women). *Computer facilities:* 1,000 computers available on campus for general student use. A campuswide network can be accessed from student residence rooms and from off campus. *Library facilities:* James Branch Cabell and Tompkins-McCaw Library. *Graduate expenses:* Tuition, state resident: full-time $2,889; part-time $321 per credit hour. Tuition, nonresident: full-time $7,952; part-time $884 per credit hour. Required fees: $42 per credit hour. *General application contact:* Dr. Sherry T. Sandkam, Associate Dean, 804-828-6916.

Find an in-depth description at www.petersons.com/gradchannel.

Medical College of Virginia-Professional Programs
Dr. Sheldin M. Retchin, Vice President for Health Sciences
Program in:
medicine • DDS, MD, Pharm D, MPH, MS, PhD, CBHS

School of Dentistry
Dr. Ronald J. Hunt, Dean
Program in:
dentistry • DDS

School of Medicine
Dr. H. H. Newsome, Dean
Programs in:
anatomy • MS, PhD, CBHS
anatomy and physical therapy • PhD
biochemistry • PhD
biochemistry and molecular biophysics • MS, CBHS
biostatistics • MS, PhD
epidemiology • PhD
genetic counseling • MS
human genetics • PhD, CBHS
medicine • MD, MPH, MS, PhD, CBHS
microbiology • PhD
microbiology and immunology • MS, CBHS
molecular biology and genetics • PhD
neuroscience • MS, PhD
neurosciences • PhD
pathology • MS, PhD
pharmacology • PhD, CBHS
pharmacology and toxicology • MS
physiology • MS, PhD, CBHS
public health • MPH

School of Pharmacy
Dr. Victor A. Yanchick, Dean
Program in:
pharmacy • Pharm D, MS, PhD

School of Graduate Studies
Dr. F. Douglas Boudinot, Dean, Graduate Studies
Program in:
interdisciplinary studies • MIS

Center for Public Policy
Dr. Robert D. Holsworth, Director
Program in:
public policy and administration • PhD

College of Humanities and Sciences
Dr. Stephen D. Gottfredson, Dean
Programs in:
account management • MS
account planning • MS
applied mathematics • MS

Virginia

Virginia Commonwealth University (continued)
  applied physics • MS
  applied social research • CASR
  art direction • MS
  biology • MS
  chemistry • MS, PhD
  clinical psychology • PhD
  copywriting • MS
  counseling psychology • PhD
  creative writing • MFA
  criminal justice • MS, CCJA
  environmental communication • MIS
  environmental health • MIS
  environmental policy • MIS
  environmental sciences • MIS
  forensic science • MS
  general psychology • PhD
  history • MA
  humanities and sciences • MA, MFA, MIS, MPA, MS, MURP, PhD, CASR, CCJA, CPM, CURP, Certificate
  literature • MA
  mass communications • MS
  mathematics • MS
  operations research • MS
  physics • MS
  political science and public administration • MPA
  public management • CPM
  sociology • MS
  statistics • MS, Certificate
  urban planning • MURP
  urban revitalization • CURP
  writing and rhetoric • MA

School of Allied Health Professions
Dr. Cecil B. Drain, Dean
Programs in:
  advanced physical therapy • MS
  aging studies • CAS
  allied health professions • MHA, MS, MSHA, MSNA, MSOT, PhD, CAS, CPC
  anatomy and physical therapy • PhD
  clinical laboratory sciences • MS
  entry-level physical therapy • MS
  executive health administration • MSHA
  gerontology • MS
  health administration • MHA
  health related sciences • PhD
  health services organization and research • PhD
  nurse anesthesia • MSNA
  occupational therapy • MS, MSOT
  patient counseling • MS, CPC
  physiology and physical therapy • PhD
  rehabilitation counseling • MS, CPC

School of Business
Dr. Michael L. Sesnowitz, Dean
Programs in:
  accountancy • M Acc, MBA, MS, PhD
  business administration • MBA, PhD
  business administration and management • MBA, PhD
  decision sciences • MBA, MS
  economics • MA, MBA, MS
  finance, insurance, and real estate • MS
  human resources management and industrial relations • MS
  information systems • MS, PhD
  marketing and business law • MS
  real estate and urban land development • MS, Certificate
  tax • MS
  taxation • M Tax

School of Education
Dr. William C. Bosher, Dean
Programs in:
  administration and supervision • M Ed, Certificate
  adult education and human resource development • M Ed
  counselor education • M Ed
  curriculum and instruction • M Ed
  early childhood • M Ed
  early education • MT
  education • M Ed, MS, MT, PhD, Certificate
  emotionally disturbed • M Ed, MT
  health and movement sciences • MS
  learning disabilities • M Ed
  mentally retarded • M Ed, MT
  middle education • MT
  reading • M Ed
  recreation, parks and sports leadership • MS
  secondary education • MT, Certificate
  severely/profoundly handicapped • M Ed
  special education • MT

School of Engineering
Dr. Robert J. Mattauch, Dean
Programs in:
  biomedical engineering • MS, PhD
  computer science • MS
  engineering • MS, PhD

School of Nursing
Dr. Nancy F. Langston, Dean
Programs in:
  adult health nursing • MS
  child health nursing • MS
  family health nursing • MS
  health system • PhD
  immuno competence • PhD
  nurse practitioner • MS, Certificate
  nursing administration • MS
  psychiatric-mental health nursing • MS
  risk and resilience • PhD
  women's health nursing • MS

School of Pharmacy Graduate Programs
Dr. Victor A. Yanchick, Dean
Programs in:
  pharmaceutics • Pharm D, MS, PhD
  pharmacy • Pharm D, MS, PhD

School of Social Work
Dr. Frank R. Baskind, Dean
Program in:
  social work • MSW, PhD

School of the Arts
Dr. Richard E. Toscan, Dean
Programs in:
  acting • MFA
  art education • MAE
  art history • MA, PhD
  arts • MA, MAE, MFA, MM, PhD
  ceramics • MFA
  composition • MM
  costume design • MFA
  directing • MFA
  education • MM
  fibers • MFA
  furniture design • MFA
  glassworking • MFA
  interior environment • MFA
  jewelry/metalworking • MFA
  painting • MFA
  pedagogy • MFA
  performance • MM
  photography—film • MFA
  printmaking • MFA
  scene design/technical theater • MFA
  sculpture • MFA
  visual communication • MFA

■ VIRGINIA POLYTECHNIC INSTITUTE AND STATE UNIVERSITY
Blacksburg, VA 24061
http://www.vt.edu/

State-supported, coed, university. CGS member. *Graduate faculty:* 1,433 full-time (346 women), 51 part-time/adjunct (46 women). *Computer facilities:* Computer purchase and lease plans are available. 8,000 computers available on campus for general student use. A campuswide network can be accessed from student residence rooms and from off campus. Internet access and online class registration are available. *Library facilities:* Newman Library plus 4 others. *Graduate expenses:* Full-time $6,039; part-time $336 per credit. Tuition, nonresident: full-time $9,708; part-time $539 per credit. Required fees: $905; $130 per credit. *General application contact:* Graduate School Receptionist, 540-231-9563.

Graduate School
Dr. Karen P. DePauw, Vice Provost for Graduate Studies and Dean of the Graduate School
Programs in:
  applied mathematics • MS, PhD
  applied physics • MS, PhD
  bio-behavioral sciences • PhD
  botany • MS, PhD

Virginia

chemistry • MS, PhD
clinical psychology • PhD
developmental psychology • PhD
ecology and evolutionary biology • MS, PhD
economics • MA, PhD
genetics and developmental biology • MS, PhD
genetics, bioinformatics and computational biology • PhD
geological sciences • MS, PhD
geophysics • MS, PhD
industrial/organizational psychology • PhD
information technology • MIT, Certificate
macromolecular science and engineering • MS, PhD
mathematical physics • MS, PhD
microbiology • MS, PhD
physics • MS, PhD
psychology • MS
pure mathematics • MS, PhD
science • MA, MS, PhD
statistics • MS, PhD
zoology • MS, PhD

College of Agriculture and Life Sciences
Dr. Sharron Quisenberry, Dean
Programs in:
agribusiness • MS
agricultural economics • MS
agriculture and life sciences • M Eng, MS, PhD
animal science • MS, PhD
applied economics • MS
biological systems engineering • M Eng, MS, PhD
crop and soil environmental sciences • MS, PhD
developmental and international economics • PhD
econometrics • PhD
entomology • MS, PhD
food science and technology • MS, PhD
horticulture • MS, PhD
human nutrition, foods and exercise • MS, PhD
life sciences • MS, PhD
macro and micro economics • PhD
markets and industrial organizations • PhD
plant pathology • MS, PhD
plant physiology and weed science • MS, PhD
plant protection • MS
poultry science • MS, PhD
public and regional/urban economics • PhD
resource and environmental economics • PhD

College of Architecture and Urban Studies
Dr. Paul L. Knox, Dean
Programs in:

architecture and design • M Arch, MS
architecture and urban studies • M Arch, MLA, MPA, MPIA, MS, MURP, PhD, CAGS
environmental design and planning • PhD
landscape architecture • MLA
public administration and policy • MPA, PhD, CAGS
public and international affairs • MPIA
urban and regional planning • MURP

College of Engineering
Dr. Hassan Aref, Dean
Programs in:
aerospace engineering • M Eng, MS, PhD
chemical engineering • MS, PhD
civil engineering • M Eng, MS, PhD
computer engineering • MS, PhD
computer science • MS, PhD
electrical engineering • MS, PhD
engineering • M Eng, MEA, MIS, MS, PhD
engineering administration • MEA
engineering mechanics • M Eng, MS, PhD
environmental engineering • MS
environmental sciences and engineering • MS
industrial engineering • M Eng, MS, PhD
information systems • MIS
materials engineering • M Eng, MS, PhD
mechanical engineering • M Eng, MS, PhD
mining and minerals engineering • M Eng, MS, PhD
ocean engineering • MS
operations research • M Eng, MS, PhD

College of Liberal Arts and Human Sciences
Dr. Jerry Niles, Dean
Programs in:
administration and supervision of special education • Ed D, PhD, Ed S
adult and continuing education • MA Ed, MS Ed, Ed D, PhD, CAGS
adult development and aging • MS, PhD
adult learning and human resource development • MS, PhD
apparel business and economics • MS, PhD
apparel product design and analysis • MS, PhD
apparel quality analysis • MS, PhD
arts administration • MFA
child development • MS, PhD
consumer studies • MS, PhD
costume design • MFA
curriculum and instruction • MA Ed, Ed D, PhD, Ed S

educational counseling • MA Ed, Ed D, PhD, Ed S
educational leadership • MA Ed, Ed D, PhD, CAGS
educational research and evaluation • PhD
English • MA
family financial management • MS, PhD
family studies • MS, PhD
health and physical education • MS Ed
history • MA
household equipment • MS, PhD
housing • MS, PhD
instructional technology • ITMA, Ed D, PhD, Ed S
interior design • MS, PhD
liberal arts and human sciences • ITMA, MA, MA Ed, MFA, MS, MS Ed, Ed D, PhD, CAGS, Ed S
lighting design • MFA
marriage and family therapy • MS, PhD
philosophy • MA
political science • MA
property management • MFA
resource management • MS, PhD
scenic design • MFA
science and technology studies • MS, PhD
sociology • MS, PhD
stage management • MFA
technical theatre • MFA
vocational-technical education • MS Ed, Ed D, PhD

College of Natural Resources
Dr. Gregory N. Brown, Dean
Programs in:
fisheries and wildlife sciences • MS, PhD
forest biology • MF, MS, PhD
forest biometry • MF, MS, PhD
forest management/economics • MF, MS, PhD
forest products marketing • MF, MS, PhD
geography • MS
industrial forestry operations • MF, MS, PhD
natural resources • MF, MNR, MS, PhD
outdoor recreation • MF, MS, PhD
wood science and engineering • MF, MS, PhD

Pamplin College of Business
Dr. Richard E. Sorensen, Dean
Programs in:
accounting and information systems • MAIS, PhD
business • MAIS, MBA, MS, PhD
business administration • PhD
business administration/finance • MS, PhD
business administration/management • PhD

Virginia

Virginia Polytechnic Institute and State University (continued)
  business administration/marketing • MS, PhD
  business information technology • MS, PhD
  hospitality and tourism management • MS, PhD

Virginia Tech-Wake Forest University School of Biomedical Engineering and Sciences
Dr. Elaine P. Scott, Interim Director
Program in:
  biomedical engineering and sciences • MS, PhD

Virginia-Maryland Regional College of Veterinary Medicine
Dr. Gerhardt Schurig, Dean
Programs in:
  veterinary medical sciences • MS, PhD
  veterinary medicine • DVM, MS, PhD

■ **VIRGINIA STATE UNIVERSITY**
Petersburg, VA 23806-0001
http://www.vsu.edu/

State-supported, coed, comprehensive institution. *Computer facilities:* 491 computers available on campus for general student use. A campuswide network can be accessed from student residence rooms and from off campus. Internet access and online class registration are available. *Library facilities:* Johnston Memorial Library. *General application contact:* Dean, Graduate Studies, Research, and Outreach, 804-524-5985.

School of Graduate Studies, Research, and Outreach
Program in:
  interdisciplinary studies • MIS

School of Business
Programs in:
  business • MA
  economics and finance • MA

School of Engineering, Science and Technology
Programs in:
  biology • MS
  engineering, science and technology • M Ed, MS
  mathematics • MS
  mathematics education • M Ed
  physics • MS
  psychology • MS

School of Liberal Arts and Education
Programs in:
  education • M Ed, MS
  educational administration and supervision • M Ed, MS
  English • MA
  guidance • M Ed, MS
  history • MA
  liberal arts and education • M Ed, MA, MS, CAGS
  vocational technical education • M Ed, MS, CAGS

Washington

■ **ANTIOCH UNIVERSITY SEATTLE**
Seattle, WA 98121-1814
http://www.antiochsea.edu/

Independent, coed, upper-level institution. *Computer facilities:* 8 computers available on campus for general student use. A campuswide network can be accessed from off campus. Internet access is available. *Library facilities:* Antioch Seattle Library. *General application contact:* Director of Enrollment Services, 206-441-5352 Ext. 5200.

Find an in-depth description at www.petersons.com/gradchannel.

Graduate Programs
Programs in:
  education • MA
  psychology • MA

Center for Creative Change
Programs in:
  environment and community • MA
  management • MS
  organizational psychology • MA
  whole system design • MA

■ **CENTRAL WASHINGTON UNIVERSITY**
Ellensburg, WA 98926
http://www.cwu.edu/

State-supported, coed, comprehensive institution. CGS member. *Enrollment:* 9,903 graduate, professional, and undergraduate students; 273 full-time matriculated graduate/professional students (160 women), 193 part-time matriculated graduate/professional students (118 women). *Graduate faculty:* 249 full-time (85 women). *Computer facilities:* 712 computers available on campus for general student use. A campuswide network can be accessed from student residence rooms and from off campus. Internet access is available. *Library facilities:* Central Washington University Library. *Graduate expenses:* Tuition, state resident: part-time $183 per credit. Tuition, nonresident: part-time $381 per credit. Required fees: $369. *General application contact:* Barbara Sisko, Office Assistant, Graduate Studies, Research and Continuing Education, 509-963-3103.

Find an in-depth description at www.petersons.com/gradchannel.

Graduate Studies, Research and Continuing Education
Dr. Wayne S. Quirk, Associate Vice President for Graduate Studies, Research and Continuing Education
Program in:
  individual studies • M Ed, MA, MS

College of Arts and Humanities
Dr. Liahna Armstrong, Dean
Programs in:
  art • MA, MFA
  arts and humanities • MA, MFA, MM
  English • MA
  history • MA
  music • MM
  teaching English as a foreign language • MA
  teaching English as a second language • MA
  theatre production • MA

College of Business
Dr. Roy Savoian, Dean
Programs in:
  accounting • MPA
  business • MPA

College of Education and Professional Studies
Dr. Rebecca Bowers, Dean
Programs in:
  apparel design • MS
  business and distributive education • M Ed
  curriculum and instruction • M Ed
  education and professional studies • M Ed, MS
  educational administration • M Ed
  elementary education • M Ed
  engineering technology • MS
  family and consumer sciences education • MS
  family studies • MS
  health, physical education and recreation • MS
  nutrition • MS
  reading education • M Ed
  special education • M Ed

College of the Sciences
Dr. Meghan Miller, Interim Dean
Programs in:
  biological sciences • MS
  chemistry • MS
  counseling psychology • MS
  experimental psychology • MS
  geological sciences • MS
  guidance and counseling • M Ed

Washington

mathematics • MAT
organizational development • MS
resource management • MS
school psychology • M Ed
sciences • M Ed, MAT, MS

■ CITY UNIVERSITY
Bellevue, WA 98005
http://www.cityu.edu/

Independent, coed, comprehensive institution. *Computer facilities:* 145 computers available on campus for general student use. A campuswide network can be accessed from off campus. Internet access is available. *Library facilities:* City University Library. *General application contact:* 800-426-5596.

Find an in-depth description at www.petersons.com/gradchannel.

Graduate Division

Gordon Albright School of Education
Programs in:
  curriculum and instruction • M Ed
  education technology • M Ed
  educational leadership and principal certification • M Ed, Certificate
  guidance and counseling • M Ed
  professional certification-teachers • Certificate
  reading and literacy • M Ed
  teacher certification • MIT, Certificate

School of Business and Management
Programs in:
  C++ programming • Certificate
  computer systems—C++ programming • MS
  computer systems—individual • MS
  computer systems—web programming language • MS
  computer systems-web development • MS
  e-commerce • MBA, Certificate
  financial management • MBA, Certificate
  general management • MBA, MPA, Certificate
  general management-Europe • MBA
  human resource management • MBA, MPA
  human resources management • Certificate
  individualized study • MBA, MPA
  information systems • MBA, MPA, Certificate
  managerial leadership • MBA, MPA, Certificate
  marketing • MBA, Certificate
  organizational management-general management • MS
  organizational management-human resource management • MS
  organizational management-individualized study • MS
  organizational management-project management • MS
  personal financial planning • MBA, Certificate
  project management • MBA, MPA, MS, Certificate
  public administration • Certificate
  web development • Certificate
  web programming language • Certificate

School of Human Services and Applied Behavioral Sciences
Program in:
  counseling psychology • MA

■ EASTERN WASHINGTON UNIVERSITY
Cheney, WA 99004-2431
http://www.ewu.edu/

State-supported, coed, comprehensive institution. CGS member. *Enrollment:* 10,337 graduate, professional, and undergraduate students; 689 full-time matriculated graduate/professional students (468 women), 492 part-time matriculated graduate/professional students (344 women). *Graduate faculty:* 385 full-time (166 women). *Computer facilities:* Computer purchase and lease plans are available. 226 computers available on campus for general student use. A campuswide network can be accessed from student residence rooms and from off campus. Internet access and online class registration, e-mail are available. *Library facilities:* John F. Kennedy Library plus 1 other. *Graduate expenses:* Tuition, state resident: part-time $385 per credit. Tuition, nonresident: part-time $1,139 per credit. *General application contact:* Dr. Larry Briggs, Associate for Graduate Studies, 509-359-6297.

Graduate School Studies
Dr. Ronald Dalla, Dean
Program in:
  interdisciplinary studies • MA, MS

College of Arts and Letters
Dr. Philip Castille, Dean
Programs in:
  arts and letters • M Ed, MA, MFA
  college instruction • MA
  composition • MA
  creative writing • MFA
  English • MA
  French education • M Ed
  instrumental/vocal performance • MA
  music education • MA
  music history and literature • MA

College of Business Administration and Public Administration
Dr. Dolores Martin, Dean
Programs in:
  business administration • MBA, MPA, MURP
  public administration • MPA
  urban and regional planning • MURP

College of Education and Human Development
Dr. Foritz Erikson, Dean
Programs in:
  adult education • M Ed
  college instruction • MA, MS
  college instruction in physical education • MS
  counseling psychology • MS
  curriculum and instruction • M Ed
  developing psychology • MS
  early childhood education • M Ed
  education and human development • M Ed, MA, MS
  educational leadership • M Ed
  elementary teaching • M Ed
  foundations of education • M Ed
  literacy specialist • M Ed
  physical education • MS
  school counseling • MS
  school library media administration • M Ed
  school psychology • MS
  science education • M Ed
  social science education • M Ed
  special education • M Ed
  supervising (clinic teaching) • M Ed

College of Science, Mathematics and Technology
Dr. Ray Soltero, Dean
Programs in:
  biology • MS
  communication disorders • MS
  computer science • M Ed, MS
  geology • MS
  mathematics • MS
  physical therapy • DPT
  science, mathematics and technology • M Ed, MS, DPT

College of Social and Behavioral Sciences
Dr. Jeffers Chertok, Dean
Programs in:
  communications • MS
  history • MA
  psychology • MS
  school psychology • MS
  social and behavioral sciences • MA, MS

Intercollegiate College for Nursing (ICN)
Dr. Dorothy Detlor, Dean
Program in:
  nursing education • MN

Washington

Eastern Washington University (continued)
School of Social Work and Human Services
Dr. Michael Frumkin, Dean
Program in:
  social work and human services • MSW

■ GONZAGA UNIVERSITY
Spokane, WA 99258
http://www.gonzaga.edu/

Independent-religious, coed, comprehensive institution. *Enrollment:* 5,778 graduate, professional, and undergraduate students; 753 full-time matriculated graduate/professional students (355 women), 1,044 part-time matriculated graduate/professional students (659 women). *Graduate faculty:* 154 full-time (34 women), 45 part-time/adjunct (15 women). *Computer facilities:* Computer purchase and lease plans are available. 350 computers available on campus for general student use. A campuswide network can be accessed from student residence rooms and from off campus. Internet access and online class registration are available. *Library facilities:* Ralph E. and Helen Higgins Foley Center plus 1 other. *Graduate expenses:* Tuition: full-time $9,990; part-time $555 per credit. Required fees: $62 per semester. Tuition and fees vary according to degree level and campus/location. *General application contact:* Julie McCulloh, Dean of Admissions, 509-323-6592.

Graduate School
Program in:
  teaching English as a second language • MATESL

College of Arts and Sciences
Programs in:
  arts and sciences • M Div, MA
  pastoral ministry • MA
  philosophy • MA
  religious studies • M Div, MA
  spirituality • MA

School of Business Administration
Programs in:
  accounting • M Acc
  business administration • M Acc, MBA

School of Education
Programs in:
  administration and curriculum • MAA
  anesthesiology education • M Anesth Ed
  counseling psychology • MAC, MAP
  educational administration • MA Ed Ad

  educational leadership • PhD
  initial teaching • MIT
  special education • MES
  sports and athletic administration • MASPAA
  teaching • MTA

School of Professional Studies
Programs in:
  nursing • MSN
  organizational leadership • MOL
  professional studies • MOL, MSN

School of Law
Program in:
  law • JD

■ HERITAGE COLLEGE
Toppenish, WA 98948-9599
http://www.heritage.edu/

Independent, coed, comprehensive institution. *Computer facilities:* 130 computers available on campus for general student use. A campuswide network can be accessed from student residence rooms and from off campus. Internet access is available. *Library facilities:* Library and Resource Center. *General application contact:* Coordinator of Graduate Programs, 509-865-8635 Ext. 2110.

Graduate Programs in Education
Programs in:
  bilingual education/ESL • M Ed
  community and human resource development • M Ed
  counseling • M Ed
  early childhood education • M Ed
  educational administration • M Ed
  professional development • M Ed
  special education • M Ed
  teaching • MIT

■ PACIFIC LUTHERAN UNIVERSITY
Tacoma, WA 98447

Independent-religious, coed, comprehensive institution. *Enrollment:* 3,462 graduate, professional, and undergraduate students; 182 full-time matriculated graduate/professional students (111 women), 87 part-time matriculated graduate/professional students (54 women). *Graduate faculty:* 34 full-time (17 women), 27 part-time/adjunct (17 women). *Computer facilities:* Computer purchase and lease plans are available. 200 computers available on campus for general student use. A campuswide network can be accessed from student residence rooms and from off campus. Internet access and online class registration are available. *Library facilities:* Mortvedt Library. *Graduate expenses:* Tuition: full-time $14,688; part-time $612 per credit. Tuition and fees

vary according to course load and program. *General application contact:* Linda DuBay, Senior Office Assistant, 253-535-7151.

Find an in-depth description at www.petersons.com/gradchannel.

Division of Graduate Studies
Dr. James Pence, Provost and Dean of Graduate Studies

Division of Social Sciences
Dr. David Huelsbeck, Dean
Programs in:
  marriage and family therapy • MA
  social sciences • MA

School of Business
Dr. J. Thad Barnowe, Interim Dean
Program in:
  business administration • MBA

School of Education
Dr. Lynn Beck, Dean
Programs in:
  classroom language and literacy focus • MA
  early childhood • MA
  education • MA
  education administration • MA
  elementary education • MA
  kindergarten through twelfth grade • MA
  language and literacy • MA
  school library media • MA
  secondary education • MA
  teaching • MA

School of Nursing
Dr. Terry Miller, Dean
Programs in:
  client systems management • MSN
  entry level nursing • MSN
  family nurse practitioner • MSN
  health care systems management • MSN
  nursing • MSN

■ SAINT MARTIN'S COLLEGE
Lacey, WA 98503-1297
http://www.stmartin.edu/

Independent-religious, coed, comprehensive institution. *Computer facilities:* 110 computers available on campus for general student use. A campuswide network can be accessed from student residence rooms and from off campus. Internet access is available. *Library facilities:* Saint Martin's College Library. *General application contact:* 360-438-4311.

Graduate Programs
Programs in:
  civil engineering • MCE

Washington

classroom leadership • M Ed
computers in education • M Ed
counseling and community
  psychology • MAC
counseling and guidance • M Ed
engineering management •
  M Eng Mgt
reading • M Ed
special education • M Ed
teaching • MIT

Division of Economics and Business Administration
Program in:
  economics and business
    administration • MBA

■ SEATTLE PACIFIC UNIVERSITY
Seattle, WA 98119-1997
http://www.spu.edu/

Independent-religious, coed, comprehensive institution. *Enrollment:* 3,728 graduate, professional, and undergraduate students; 203 full-time matriculated graduate/professional students (150 women), 601 part-time matriculated graduate/professional students (382 women). *Graduate faculty:* 40 full-time (18 women), 27 part-time/adjunct (14 women). *Computer facilities:* 150 computers available on campus for general student use. A campuswide network can be accessed from student residence rooms and from off campus. Internet access and online class registration are available. *Library facilities:* Seattle Pacific University Library. *Graduate expenses:* Tuition: part-time $355 per credit hour. *General application contact:* John Glancy, Director, Graduate Admissions/Marketing, 206-281-2325.

Graduate School
Dr. Les L. Steele, Vice President for Academic Affairs

College of Arts and Sciences
Dr. Bruce Congdon, Dean
Programs in:
  arts and sciences • MA, MS
  physical education • MA, MS
  teaching English as a second language • MA

School of Business and Economics
Gary Karns, Graduate Director
Programs in:
  business administration • MBA
  business and economics • MBA, MS
  information systems management • MS

School of Education
Dr. Rick Eigenbrood, Director of Graduate Programs

Programs in:
  education • M Ed, MAT, Ed D, Ed S
  educational leadership • M Ed
  reading/language arts education • M Ed
  school counseling • M Ed
  school psychology • Ed S
  secondary teaching • MAT

School of Health Sciences
Dr. Lucille Kelley, Dean
Programs in:
  health sciences • MSN, Certificate
  nurse practitioner • Certificate
  nursing leadership • MSN

School of Psychology, Family and Community
Dr. Nathan Brown, Dean
Programs in:
  clinical psychology • PhD
  marriage and family therapy • MS
  psychology, family and community • MS, PhD

■ SEATTLE UNIVERSITY
Seattle, WA 98122-1090
http://www.seattleu.edu/

Independent-religious, coed, comprehensive institution. *Enrollment:* 6,659 graduate, professional, and undergraduate students; 1,311 full-time matriculated graduate/professional students (771 women), 1,616 part-time matriculated graduate/professional students (916 women). *Graduate faculty:* 188 full-time (91 women), 105 part-time/adjunct (55 women). *Computer facilities:* 401 computers available on campus for general student use. A campuswide network can be accessed from student residence rooms and from off campus. Internet access and online class registration are available. *Library facilities:* Lemieux Library plus 1 other. *Graduate expenses:* Tuition: full-time $13,824; part-time $512 per credit. Tuition and fees vary according to course load, degree level and program. *General application contact:* Janet Shandley, Associate Dean of Graduate Admissions, 206-296-5900.

Albers School of Business and Economics
Dr. Joseph Phillips, Dean
Programs in:
  business administration • MBA, Certificate
  business and economics • MBA, MIB, MPAC, MSF, Certificate
  finance • MSF, Certificate
  international business • MIB, Certificate
  professional accounting • MPAC

College of Arts and Sciences
Dr. Wallace Loh, Dean
Programs in:
  arts and sciences • MA Psych, MNPL, MPA
  existential and phenomenological therapeutic psychology • MA Psych

The Center for Nonprofit and Social Enterprise Management
Dr. Michael Bisesi, Director
Program in:
  nonprofit and social enterprise management • MNPL

Institute of Public Service
Dr. Russell Lidman, Director
Program in:
  public service • MPA

College of Education
Dr. Sue Schmitt, Dean
Programs in:
  adult education and training • M Ed, MA, Certificate
  counseling • MA, Certificate
  curriculum and instruction • M Ed, MA, Certificate
  education • M Ed, MA, MIT, Ed D, Certificate, Ed S, Post-Master's Certificate
  educational administration • M Ed, MA, Certificate, Ed S
  educational diagnostics/school psychology • Ed S
  educational leadership • Ed D
  literacy for special needs • M Ed, Post-Master's Certificate
  special education • M Ed, MA, Certificate
  student development administration • M Ed, MA
  teacher education • MIT
  teaching English to speakers of other languages • M Ed, MA, Certificate

College of Nursing
Dr. Mary Walker, Dean
Programs in:
  advanced practice nursing • MSN
  leadership in community nursing • MSN
  nursing immersion • MSN
  primary care nurse practitioner • MSN

College of Science and Engineering
Dr. George Simmons, Dean
Programs in:
  science and engineering • MSE
  software engineering • MSE

School of Law
Rudolph Hasl, Dean
Program in:
  law • JD

Washington

Seattle University (continued)
School of Theology and Ministry
Dr. Patrick Howell, SJ, Dean
Programs in:
  divinity • M Div
  pastoral studies • MAPS
  theology and ministry • M Div, MAPS, MATS, Certificate
  transforming spirituality • MATS, Certificate

■ UNIVERSITY OF WASHINGTON
Seattle, WA 98195
http://www.washington.edu/

State-supported, coed, university. CGS member. *Computer facilities:* 285 computers available on campus for general student use. A campuswide network can be accessed from student residence rooms and from off campus. Internet access and online class registration are available. *Library facilities:* Suzzallo/Allen Library plus 21 others. *General application contact:* Information Contact, 206-543-2100.

Graduate School
Programs in:
  biology for teachers • MS
  education • M Ed, Professional Certificate
  global trade, transportation, and logistics • Certificate
  K-8 education • Certificate
  museology • MA
  Near and Middle Eastern studies • PhD
  preservation planning and design • Certificate
  principalship • Certificate
  quantitative ecology and resource management • MS, PhD
  school administration • Certificate
  urban design • Certificate

Business School
Varice Roley, Acting Dean
Program in:
  business • MBA, MP Acc, PhD

College of Architecture and Urban Planning
Programs in:
  architecture • M Arch
  architecture and urban planning • M Arch, MLA, MS, MSCM, MUP, PhD, Certificate
  computer design • Certificate
  construction management • MS, MSCM
  historic preservation • Certificate
  landscape architecture • MLA
  lighting • Certificate
  urban design • Certificate
  urban design and planning • PhD
  urban planning • MUP

College of Arts and Sciences
Programs in:
  acting • MFA
  anthropology • MA, PhD
  applied mathematics • MS, PhD
  art • MFA
  art and design • MFA
  art history • MA, PhD
  arts and sciences • M Mus, MA, MAIS, MAT, MC, MFA, MM, MS, DMA, PhD
  astronomy • MS, PhD
  atmospheric sciences • MS, PhD
  botany • MS, PhD
  Central Asian studies • MAIS
  chemistry • MS, PhD
  China studies • MAIS
  Chinese language and literature • MA, PhD
  classics • MA, PhD
  classics and philosophy • PhD
  communication • MA, MC, PhD
  comparative literature • MA, PhD
  comparative religion • MAIS
  costume design • MFA
  dance • MFA
  directing • MFA
  East European studies • MAIS
  economics • MA, PhD
  English • MA, MAT, MFA, PhD
  English as a second language • MAT
  French • MA, PhD
  French and Italian studies • MA, PhD
  geography • MA, PhD
  geology • MS, PhD
  geophysics • MS, PhD
  German language and literature • MA
  German literature and culture • PhD
  Hispanic literacy and cultural studies • MA
  history • PhD
  international studies • MAIS
  Italian • MA
  Japan studies • MAIS
  Japanese language and literature • MA, PhD
  Korea studies • MAIS
  lighting design • MFA
  linguistics • MA, PhD
  mathematics • MA, MS, PhD
  Middle Eastern studies • MAIS
  music • M Mus, MA, MM, DMA, PhD
  music education • MA, PhD
  Near Eastern languages and civilization • MA
  philosophy • MA, PhD
  physics • MS, PhD
  political science • MA, PhD
  psychology • PhD
  Romance languages and literature • PhD
  Romance linguistics • MA, PhD
  Russian literature • MA, PhD
  Russian studies • MAIS
  Russian, East European and Central Asian studies • MAIS
  Scandinavian studies • MA, PhD
  scene design • MFA
  Slavic linguistics • MA, PhD
  sociology • MA, PhD
  South Asian language and literature • MA, PhD
  South Asian studies • MAIS
  Spanish and Portuguese • MA
  speech and hearing sciences • MS, PhD
  statistics • MS, PhD
  theory and criticism • PhD
  women studies • MA, PhD
  zoology • PhD

College of Education
Programs in:
  curriculum and instruction • M Ed, Ed D, PhD
  early childhood education • M Ed, Ed D, PhD
  educational leadership and policy studies • M Ed, Ed D, PhD
  educational psychology • M Ed, PhD
  elementary special education • M Ed, Ed D, PhD
  emotional and behavioral disabilities • M Ed
  general special education • M Ed, Ed D, PhD
  human development and cognition • M Ed, PhD
  measurement and research • M Ed, PhD
  school counseling • M Ed, PhD
  school psychology • M Ed, PhD
  severe disabilities • M Ed, Ed D, PhD
  special education • M Ed, Ed D, PhD
  teacher education • MIT

College of Engineering
Dr. Denice D. Denton, Dean
Programs in:
  aeronautics and astronautics • MAE, MSAA, PhD
  bioengineering • MME, MS, PhD
  chemical engineering • MS Ch E, PhD
  computer science • MS, PhD
  electrical engineering • MSEE, PhD
  engineering • MAE, MME, MS, MS Ch E, MSAA, MSCE, MSE, MSEE, MSIE, MSME, PhD
  environmental engineering • MS, MSCE, MSE, PhD
  hydraulic engineering • MSCE, MSE, PhD
  industrial engineering • MSIE, PhD
  inter-engineering specialization in materials science and engineering • MS
  materials science and engineering • MS, PhD
  materials science and engineering nanotechnology • PhD
  mechanical engineering • MSE, MSME, PhD

Washington

structural and geotechnical engineering and mechanics • MS, MSCE, MSE, PhD
technical communication • MS, PhD
transportation and construction engineering • MS, MSCE, MSE, PhD

College of Forest Resources
Programs in:
forest economics • MS, PhD
forest ecosystem analysis • MS, PhD
forest engineering/forest hydrology • MS, PhD
forest products marketing • MS, PhD
forest soils • MS, PhD
paper science and engineering • MS, PhD
quantitative resource management • MS, PhD
silviculture • MFR
silviculture and forest protection • MS, PhD
social sciences • MS, PhD
urban horticulture • MFR, MS, PhD
wildlife science • MS, PhD

College of Ocean and Fishery Sciences
Programs in:
aquatic and fishery sciences • MS, PhD
biological oceanography • MS, PhD
chemical oceanography • MS, PhD
marine affairs • MMA
marine geology and geophysics • MS, PhD
ocean and fishery sciences • MMA, MS, PhD
physical oceanography • MS, PhD

Daniel J. Evans School of Public Affairs
Program in:
public affairs • MPA

The Information School
Michael B. Eisenberg, Dean
Programs in:
information management • MSIM
information science • PhD
library and information science • MLIS

School of Nursing
Program in:
nursing • MN, MS, PhD

School of Public Health and Community Medicine
Dr. Patricia W. Wahl, Dean
Programs in:
biostatistics • MPH, MS, PhD
environmental and occupational health • MPH
environmental and occupational hygiene • PhD
environmental health • MS
epidemiology • MPH, MS, PhD
genetic epidemiology • MS
health services • MS, PhD
health services administration and planning • EMHA, MHA
industrial hygiene and safety • MS
international health • MPH
maternal/child health • MPH
nutritional sciences • MPH, MS, PhD
occupational medicine • MPH
pathobiology • MS, PhD
public health • MPH
public health and community medicine • EMHA, MHA, MPH, MS, PhD
public health genetics • MPH, MS, PhD
safety and ergonomics • MS
statistical genetics • PhD
toxicology • MS, PhD

School of Social Work
Program in:
social work • MSW, PhD

School of Social Work, Tacoma Campus
Program in:
social work • MSW

School of Dentistry
Dr. Martha Somerman, Dean
Program in:
dentistry • DDS, MS, MSD, PhD

School of Law
Programs in:
Asian law • LL M, PhD
intellectual property law and policy • LL M
law • JD
law of sustainable international development • LL M
taxation • LL M

School of Medicine
Programs in:
genome sciences • PhD
medicine • MD, MOT, MS, MSE, DPT, PhD

Graduate Programs in Medicine
Programs in:
biochemistry • PhD
biological structure • PhD
biomedical and health informatics • MS
immunology • PhD
laboratory medicine • MS
medicine • MOT, MS, MSE, DPT, PhD
microbiology • PhD
molecular and cellular biology • PhD
molecular basis of disease • PhD
neurobiology • PhD
neuroscience • PhD
occupational therapy • MOT
pathology • MS
pharmacology • MS, PhD
physical therapy • DPT
physiology and biophysics • PhD
veterinary science • MS

School of Pharmacy
Programs in:
medicinal chemistry • PhD
pharmaceutics • MS, PhD
pharmacy • Pharm D, MS, PhD

■ **WALLA WALLA COLLEGE**
College Place, WA 99324-1198
http://www.wwc.edu/

Independent-religious, coed, comprehensive institution. *Enrollment:* 1,917 graduate, professional, and undergraduate students; 221 full-time matriculated graduate/professional students (168 women), 29 part-time matriculated graduate/professional students (22 women). *Graduate faculty:* 32 full-time (19 women), 20 part-time/adjunct (13 women). *Computer facilities:* 108 computers available on campus for general student use. A campuswide network can be accessed from student residence rooms and from off campus. Internet access and online class registration are available. *Library facilities:* Peterson Memorial Library plus 3 others. *Graduate expenses:* Tuition: part-time $442 per quarter hour. *General application contact:* Dr. Joe G. Galusha, Dean of Graduate Studies, 509-527-2421.

Graduate School
Dr. Joe G. Galusha, Dean
Program in:
biological science • MS

School of Education and Psychology
Dr. Mark Hayal, Dean
Programs in:
counseling psychology • MA
curriculum and instruction • M Ed, MA, MAT
educational leadership • M Ed, MA, MAT
literacy instruction • M Ed, MA, MAT
students at risk • M Ed, MA, MAT
teaching • MAT

School of Social Work
Dr. Wilma Hepker, Dean
Program in:
social work • MSW

■ **WASHINGTON STATE UNIVERSITY**
Pullman, WA 99164
http://www.wsu.edu/

State-supported, coed, university. CGS member. *Enrollment:* 22,712 graduate, professional, and undergraduate students; 1,699 full-time matriculated graduate/professional students (773 women), 353 part-time matriculated graduate/

Washington

Washington State University (continued)
professional students (185 women). *Graduate faculty:* 721 full-time (160 women), 49 part-time/adjunct (13 women). *Computer facilities:* 10,000 computers available on campus for general student use. A campuswide network can be accessed from student residence rooms and from off campus. Internet access and online class registration are available. *Library facilities:* Holland Library plus 5 others. *Graduate expenses:* Tuition, state resident: full-time $6,278; part-time $314 per hour. Tuition, nonresident: full-time $15,514; part-time $765 per hour. Required fees: $444. Full-time tuition and fees vary according to campus/location, program and student level. Part-time tuition and fees vary according to course load. *General application contact:* Dr. Steven R. Burkett, Associate Dean, Graduate School, 509-335-6424.

College of Veterinary Medicine
Dr. Warwick M. Bayly, Dean
Programs in:
  neuroscience • MS, PhD
  veterinary clinical sciences • MS, PhD
  veterinary comparative anatomy, pharmacology, and physiology • MS, PhD
  veterinary medicine • DVM, MS, PhD
  veterinary microbiology and pathology • MS, PhD
  veterinary science • MS, PhD

Graduate School
Dr. Howard Grimes, Interim Dean

College of Agricultural, Human, and Natural Resource Sciences
Dr. James R. Cook, Interim Dean
Programs in:
  agribusiness • MA
  agricultural economics • MA, PhD
  agricultural, human, and natural resource sciences • MA, MLA, MS, PhD
  animal sciences • MS, PhD
  apparel, merchandising and textiles • MA
  crop sciences • MS, PhD
  entomology • MS, PhD
  food science • MS, PhD
  horticulture • MS, PhD
  human development • MA
  human nutrition • MS
  interior design • MA
  landscape architecture • MLA
  natural resource sciences • MS, PhD
  nutrition • PhD
  plant pathology • MS, PhD
  plant physiology • MS, PhD
  soil sciences • MS, PhD

College of Business and Economics
Dr. Len Jessup, Dean
Programs in:
  accounting and business law • M Acc
  accounting and information systems • M Acc
  accounting and taxation • M Acc
  business administration • MBA, PhD
  business and economics • M Acc, MA, MBA, MTM, PhD, Certificate
  economics • MA, PhD
  international business economics • Certificate
  technology management • MTM

College of Education
Dr. Judy Mitchell, Dean
Programs in:
  counseling psychology • MA, PhD
  curriculum and instruction • Ed D, PhD
  diverse languages • M Ed, MA
  education • M Ed, MA, MAT, MIT, Ed D, PhD
  educational leadership • M Ed, MA, Ed D, PhD
  elementary education • M Ed, MA, MIT
  literacy • M Ed, MA
  literacy education • PhD
  math education • PhD
  secondary education • M Ed, MA

College of Engineering and Architecture
Dr. Anjan Bose, Dean
Programs in:
  architecture and construction management • MS
  chemical engineering • MS, PhD
  civil engineering • MS, PhD
  computer science • MS, PhD
  electrical engineering • MS, PhD
  engineering and architecture • MS, PhD
  environmental engineering • MS
  materials science • PhD
  materials science and engineering • MS
  mechanical engineering • MS, PhD

College of Liberal Arts
Dr. Barbara Couture, Dean
Programs in:
  American studies • MA, PhD
  anthropology • MA, PhD
  ceramics • MFA
  clinical psychology • PhD
  communications • MA, PhD
  composition • MA
  criminal justice • MA
  drawing • MFA
  electronic imaging • MFA
  English • MA, PhD
  history • MA, PhD
  liberal arts • MA, MFA, MS, PhD
  music • MA
  painting • MFA
  photography • MFA
  political science • MA, PhD
  print making • MFA
  psychology • MS, PhD
  sculpture • MFA
  sociology • MA, PhD
  Spanish • MA
  teaching of English • MA

College of Pharmacy
Dr. William Fassett, Dean
Programs in:
  pharmaceutical science • Pharm D
  pharmacology and toxicology • MS, PhD
  pharmacy • Pharm D, MS, PhD

College of Sciences
Dr. Michael Griswold, Dean
Programs in:
  analytical chemistry • MS, PhD
  biochemistry and biophysics • MS, PhD
  biological systems • MS, PhD
  biology • MS
  botany • MS, PhD
  environmental and natural resource sciences • PhD
  environmental science • MS
  environmental science and regional planning • MS
  genetics and cell biology • MS, PhD
  geology • MS, PhD
  inorganic chemistry • MS, PhD
  mathematics • MS, PhD
  microbiology • MS, PhD
  organic chemistry • MS, PhD
  physical chemistry • MS, PhD
  physics • MS, PhD
  regional planning • MRP
  sciences • MRP, MS, PhD
  zoology • MS, PhD

Intercollegiate College of Nursing
Dr. Dorothy Detlor, Dean
Program in:
  nursing • M Nurs

■ **WESTERN WASHINGTON UNIVERSITY**
Bellingham, WA 98225-5996
http://www.wwu.edu/

State-supported, coed, comprehensive institution. CGS member. *Enrollment:* 13,845 graduate, professional, and undergraduate students; 619 full-time matriculated graduate/professional students (359 women), 226 part-time matriculated graduate/professional students (149 women). *Graduate faculty:* 426. *Computer facilities:* 1,567 computers available on campus for general student use. A campuswide network can be accessed from student residence rooms and from off campus. Internet access and online class registration are available. *Library facilities:* Wilson Library plus 3 others. *Graduate expenses:* Tuition, state resident: full-time $5,694; part-time $172 per credit. Tuition, nonresident: full-time $16,221; part-time $523 per credit. *General application contact:* Graduate Office Admissions, 360-650-3170.

Graduate School
Dr. Moheb Ghali, Dean
Programs in:
- biology • MS
- chemistry • MS
- computer science • MS
- geology • MS
- mathematics • MS
- science education • M Ed
- sciences and technology • M Ed, MS
- technology • M Ed

College of Business and Economics
Dr. Brian Burton, Graduate Program Adviser
Program in:
- business and economics • MBA

College of Fine and Performing Arts
Dr. Linda Smeins, Acting Dean
Programs in:
- fine and performing arts • M Mus, MA
- music • M Mus
- theatre • MA

College of Humanities and Social Sciences
Dr. Ronald Kleinknecht, Interim Dean
Programs in:
- anthropology • MA
- communication sciences and disorders • MA
- English • MA
- general psychology • MS
- history • MA
- human movement and performance • MS
- humanities and social sciences • M Ed, MA, MS
- mental health counseling • MS
- physical education • M Ed
- political science • MA
- school counseling • M Ed

Huxley College of the Environment
Dr. Brad Smith, Dean
Programs in:
- environment • M Ed, MS
- environmental sciences • MS
- environmental studies • M Ed
- geography • MS
- natural science/science education • M Ed

Woodring College of Education
Dr. Stephanie Salzman, Dean
Programs in:
- adult education • M Ed
- education • M Ed, MA, MIT
- educational administration • M Ed
- elementary education • M Ed
- exceptional children • M Ed
- rehabilitation counseling • MA
- secondary education • M Ed, MIT
- student personnel administration • M Ed

■ WHITWORTH COLLEGE
Spokane, WA 99251-0001
http://www.whitworth.edu/

Independent-religious, coed, comprehensive institution. *Enrollment:* 2,298 graduate, professional, and undergraduate students; 78 full-time matriculated graduate/professional students (44 women), 149 part-time matriculated graduate/professional students (114 women). *Graduate faculty:* 78 full-time (44 women), 149 part-time/adjunct (114 women). *Computer facilities:* Computer purchase and lease plans are available. 200 computers available on campus for general student use. A campuswide network can be accessed from student residence rooms and from off campus. Internet access and online class registration are available. *Library facilities:* Harriet Cheney Cowles Library plus 2 others. *Graduate expenses:* Tuition: full-time $6,350. *General application contact:* Fred Pfursich, Office of Admissions, 509-777-1000 Ext. 3212.

Program in Nursing
School of Education
Program in:
- education • M Ed, MA, MAT, MIT

Graduate Studies in Education
Programs in:
- education administration • M Ed
- English as a second language • MAT
- gifted and talented • MAT
- guidance and counseling • M Ed
- physical education and sport administration • MA
- reading • MAT
- school counselors • M Ed
- social agency/church setting • M Ed
- special education • MAT
- teaching • MIT

School of Global Commerce and Management
Program in:
- international management • MIM

West Virginia

■ MARSHALL UNIVERSITY
Huntington, WV 25755
http://www.marshall.edu/

State-supported, coed, university. CGS member. *Enrollment:* 13,960 graduate, professional, and undergraduate students; 1,398 full-time matriculated graduate/professional students (806 women), 2,092 part-time matriculated graduate/professional students (1,488 women). *Graduate faculty:* 274 full-time (95 women), 26 part-time/adjunct (12 women). *Computer facilities:* 1,090 computers available on campus for general student use. A campuswide network can be accessed from student residence rooms and from off campus. Internet access and online class registration are available. *Library facilities:* John Deaver Drinko Library plus 2 others. *Graduate expenses:* Part-time $1,730 per semester. Tuition, state resident: part-time $3,295 per semester. Tuition, nonresident: part-time $5,003 per semester. *General application contact:* Information Contact, 304-746-1900.

Find an in-depth description at www.petersons.com/gradchannel.

Joan C. Edwards School of Medicine
Dr. Charles H. McKown, Dean and Vice President
Programs in:
- biomedical sciences • MS, PhD
- forensic science • MS
- medicine • MD, MS, PhD

■ SALEM INTERNATIONAL UNIVERSITY
Salem, WV 26426-0500
http://www.salemiu.edu/

Independent, coed, comprehensive institution. *Enrollment:* 28 full-time matriculated graduate/professional students (16 women), 113 part-time matriculated graduate/professional students (75 women). *Graduate faculty:* 6 full-time (3 women), 6 part-time/adjunct (4 women). *Computer facilities:* 50 computers available on campus for general student use. A campuswide network can be accessed from off campus. *Library facilities:* Benedum Library. *Graduate expenses:* Tuition: part-time $175 per credit hour. *General application contact:* Todd Breland, Director of Admissions, 304-782-5297.

Department of Management Studies
Dr. Gyónayi Konyu Fogel, Chair
Program in:
- management studies • eMBA

Program in Bioscience
Dr. Patrick K. Lai, Director of Graduate Bioscience Program
Program in:
- biotechnology/molecular biology • MS

West Virginia

Salem International University (continued)

Program in Education
Dr. Mary Harris-John, Director of Graduate Program in Education
Programs in:
  elementary education • MA
  equestrian education • MA
  secondary education • MA

■ WEST VIRGINIA UNIVERSITY
Morgantown, WV 26506
http://www.wvu.edu/

State-supported, coed, university. CGS member. *Enrollment:* 24,260 graduate, professional, and undergraduate students; 6,603 matriculated graduate/professional students. *Graduate faculty:* 1,312 full-time (414 women), 465 part-time/adjunct (250 women). *Computer facilities:* Computer purchase and lease plans are available. 1,600 computers available on campus for general student use. A campuswide network can be accessed from student residence rooms and from off campus. Internet access and online class registration are available. *Library facilities:* Wise Library plus 9 others. *Graduate expenses:* Tuition, state resident: full-time $4,332. Tuition, nonresident: full-time $12,442. *General application contact:* Information Contact, 800-344-WVU1.

College of Business and Economics
Dr. Jay Coats, Dean
Programs in:
  business administration • MBA
  business and economics • MA, MBA, MPA, MSIR, PhD

Division of Accounting
Prof. Robert S. Maust, Director
Program in:
  accounting • MPA

Division of Business Administration
Dr. Jack A. Fuller, Director
Program in:
  industrial relations • MSIR

Division of Economics and Finance
Dr. William N. Trumbull, Director
Programs in:
  business analysis • MA
  econometrics • PhD
  industrial economics • PhD
  international economics • PhD
  labor economics • PhD
  mathematical economics • MA, PhD
  monetary economics • PhD
  public finance • PhD
  public policy • MA
  regional and urban economics • PhD
  statistics and economics • MA

College of Creative Arts
Dr. Bernie Schultz, Dean
Programs in:
  acting • MFA
  art education • MA
  art history • MA
  ceramics • MFA
  creative arts • MA, MFA, MM, DMA, PhD
  graphic design • MFA
  music composition • MM, DMA
  music education • MM, PhD
  music history • MM
  music performance • MM, DMA
  music theory • MM
  painting • MFA
  printmaking • MFA
  sculpture • MFA
  studio art • MA
  theatre design/technology • MFA

College of Engineering and Mineral Resources
Dr. Eugene V. Cilento, Dean
Programs in:
  aerospace engineering • PhD
  chemical engineering • MS Ch E, PhD
  civil engineering • MSCE, MSE, PhD
  computer engineering • PhD
  computer science • MSCS, PhD
  electrical engineering • MSEE, PhD
  engineering • MSE
  engineering and mineral resources • MS, MS Ch E, MS Min E, MSAE, MSCE, MSCS, MSE, MSEE, MSIE, MSME, MSPNGE, MSSE, PhD
  industrial engineering • MSE, MSIE, PhD
  industrial hygiene • MS
  mechanical engineering • MSME, PhD
  mining engineering • MS Min E, PhD
  occupational safety and health • PhD
  petroleum and natural gas engineering • MSPNGE, PhD
  safety and environmental management • MS
  safety management • MS
  software engineering • MSSE

College of Human Resources and Education
Dr. Anne H. Nardi, Dean
Programs in:
  behavioral disorders K-12 • MA
  counseling • MA
  counseling psychology • PhD
  curriculum and instruction • Ed D
  early intervention (preschool) • MA
  educational leadership • MA, Ed D
  educational psychology • MA, Ed D
  elementary education • MA
  gifted education 5-12 • MA
  gifted education K-8 • MA
  higher education administration • MA
  higher education curriculum and teaching • MA
  human resources and education • MA, MS, Ed D, PhD
  information and communication systems • MA
  instructional design and technology • MA
  mentally impaired • MA
  professional development • MA
  public school administration • MA
  reading • MA
  rehabilitation counseling • MS
  secondary education • MA
  severe/profound handicaps • MA
  special education • MA, Ed D
  specific learning disabilities K-12 • MA
  speech pathology and audiology • MS
  technology and society • MA
  technology education • MA, Ed D

College of Law
John W. Fisher, Dean
Program in:
  law • JD

Davis College of Agriculture, Forestry and Consumer Sciences
Dr. Cameron R. Hackney, Dean
Programs in:
  agricultural and resource economics • MS
  agricultural education • MS
  agricultural extension education • MS
  agricultural sciences • PhD
  agriculture, forestry and consumer sciences • M Agr, MS, MSF, MSFCS, PhD
  agronomy • MS
  animal and food sciences • PhD
  animal and veterinary sciences • MS
  animal breeding • MS, PhD
  biochemical and molecular genetics • MS, PhD
  breeding • MS
  cytogenetics • MS, PhD
  descriptive embryology • MS, PhD
  developmental genetics • MS
  entomology • MS
  environmental microbiology • MS
  experimental morphogenesis teratology • MS
  family and consumer sciences • MSFCS
  food sciences • MS
  forest resource science • PhD
  forestry • MSF
  horticulture • MS
  human genetics • MS, PhD
  immunogenetics • MS, PhD
  life cycles of animals and plants • MS, PhD
  molecular aspects of development • MS, PhD

West Virginia

mutagenesis • MS, PhD
natural resource economics • PhD
nutrition • MS
oncology • MS, PhD
physiology • MS
plant and soil sciences • PhD
plant genetics • MS, PhD
plant pathology • MS
population and quantitative genetics • MS, PhD
production management • MS
recreation, parks and tourism resources • MS
regeneration • MS, PhD
reproduction • MS
reproductive physiology • MS, PhD
teaching vocational-agriculture • MS
teratology • PhD
toxicology • MS, PhD
wildlife and fisheries resources • MS

Eberly College of Arts and Sciences
Dr. M. Duane Nellis, Dean
Programs in:
African history • MA, PhD
African-American history • MA, PhD
American history • MA, PhD
American public policy and politics • MA
analytical chemistry • MS, PhD
Appalachian/regional history • MA, PhD
applied mathematics • MS, PhD
applied physics • MS, PhD
arts and sciences • MA, MALS, MFA, MLS, MPA, MS, MSW, PhD
astrophysics • MS, PhD
behavior analysis • PhD
cell and molecular biology • MS, PhD
chemical physics • MS, PhD
clinical psychology • MA, PhD
communication in instruction • MA
communication theory and research • MA
comparative literature • MA
condensed matter physics • MS, PhD
corporate and organizational communication • MA
creative writing • MFA
development psychology • PhD
discrete mathematics • PhD
East Asian history • MA, PhD
elementary particle physics • MS, PhD
energy and environmental resources • MA
English • MA, PhD
environmental and evolutionary biology • MS, PhD
European history • MA, PhD
French • MA
geographic information systems • PhD
geography • MA, PhD
geography-regional development • PhD
geology • MS, PhD
geomorphology • MS, PhD
geophysics • MS, PhD
German • MA
GIS/cartographic analysis • MA
history of science and technology • MA, PhD
hydrogeology • MS
hydrology • PhD
inorganic chemistry • MS, PhD
integrative organismal biology • PhD
integrative organismal, biology • MS
interdisciplinary mathematics • MS
international and comparative public policy and politics • MA
Latin American history • MA
legal studies • MLS
liberal studies • MALS
linguistics • MA
literary/cultural studies • MA, PhD
materials physics • MS, PhD
mathematics for secondary education • MS
organic chemistry • MS, PhD
paleontology • MS, PhD
petrology • MS, PhD
physical chemistry • MS, PhD
plasma physics • MS, PhD
political science • PhD
public policy analysis • PhD
pure mathematics • MS
regional development • MA
solid state physics • MS, PhD
Spanish • MA
statistical physics • MS, PhD
statistics • MS
stratigraphy • MS, PhD
structure • MS, PhD
teaching English to speakers of other languages • MA
theoretical chemistry • MS, PhD
theoretical physics • MS, PhD
writing • MA

School of Applied Social Science
Dr. David G. Williams, Assistant Dean
Programs in:
aging and health care • MSW
applied social research • MA
applied social science • MA, MPA, MSW
children and families • MSW
community mental health • MSW
public administration • MPA

Perley Isaac Reed School of Journalism
Dr. Maryann Reed, Acting Dean
Programs in:
integrated marketing communications • MS
journalism • MSJ

School of Dentistry
Dr. James J. Koelbl, Dean
Programs in:
basic science • MS
dentistry • DDS, MS
education/administration • MS
endodontics • MS
office management • MS
orthodontics • MS
prosthodontics • MS
special patients • MS

School of Medicine
Dr. Robert M. D'Alessandri, Dean
Programs in:
exercise physiology • MS, PhD
medicine • MD, MOT, MPH, MPT, MS, PhD
occupational therapy • MOT
physical therapy • MPT

Graduate Programs in Health Sciences
Dr. Charles R. Craig, Interim Associate Dean/Graduate Coordinator
Programs in:
autonomic pharmacology • MS, PhD
biomedical pharmacology • MS, PhD
cancer cell biology • MS, PhD
cardiovascular physiology • MS, PhD
cell physiology • MS, PhD
chemotherapy • MS, PhD
community health promotion • MS
community health/preventative medicine • MPH
developmental anatomy • MS
developmental biology • MS
endocrine pharmacology • MS, PhD
endocrine physiology • MS, PhD
energy transduction • MS
enzymes and serum proteins • PhD
enzymology • MS
gene expression • MS, PhD
genetics • MS, PhD
gross anatomy • MS, PhD
health sciences • MPH, MS, PhD
hormonal regulation/metabolism • MS, PhD
immunology • MS, PhD
membrane biogenesis • MS, PhD
microscopic anatomy • MS, PhD
molecular and developmental anatomy • PhD
molecular virology • MS
mycology • PhD
neural physiology • MS, PhD
neuroanatomy • MS, PhD
neuropharmacology • MS, PhD
nucleic acids • MS, PhD
nutritional oncology • PhD
parasitology • MS, PhD
pathogenic bacteriology • MS, PhD
pharmaceutical and pharmacological sciences • MS, PhD
physiology • MS, PhD
protein chemistry • MS
public health • MPH
renal physiology • MS, PhD
respiratory physiology • MS
secretory mechanisms • PhD
toxicology • MS, PhD
virology • MS, PhD

West Virginia

West Virginia University (continued)
School of Nursing
Dr. E. Jane Martin, Dean
Programs in:
nurse practitioner • Certificate
nursing • MSN, DSN

School of Pharmacy
Dr. George R. Spratto, Dean
Programs in:
administrative pharmacy • PhD
behavioral pharmacy • MS, PhD
biopharmaceutics/phamacokinetics • PhD
biopharmaceutics/pharmacokinetics • MS
clinical pharmacy • Pharm D
industrial pharmacy • MS
medicinal chemistry • MS, PhD
pharmaceutical chemistry • MS, PhD
pharmaceutics • MS, PhD
pharmacology and toxicology • MS
pharmacy • MS
pharmacy administration • MS

School of Physical Education
Dr. Dana D. Brooks, Dean
Programs in:
athletic coaching • MS
athletic training • MS
exercise physiology • Ed D
physical education/teacher education • MS, Ed D
sport management • MS
sport psychology • MS, Ed D

■ WHEELING JESUIT UNIVERSITY
Wheeling, WV 26003-6295
http://www.wju.edu/

Independent-religious, coed, comprehensive institution. *Enrollment:* 1,650 graduate, professional, and undergraduate students; 55 full-time matriculated graduate/professional students (38 women), 90 part-time matriculated graduate/professional students (64 women). *Graduate faculty:* 17 full-time (7 women), 10 part-time/adjunct (4 women). *Computer facilities:* 125 computers available on campus for general student use. A campuswide network can be accessed from student residence rooms and from off campus. Internet access is available. *Library facilities:* Bishop Hodges Library plus 1 other. *Graduate expenses:* Tuition: part-time $470 per credit hour. Required fees: $65 per semester. One-time fee: $90 part-time. *General application contact:* Deene Yenchochic, Graduate Admissions Counselor, 304-243-2250.

Department of Business
Paul P. Ostasiewski, Director
Programs in:
accounting • MS
business administration • MBA

Department of Nursing
Dr. Rose M. Kutlenios, Chair
Program in:
nursing • MSN

Department of Physical Therapy
Dr. Letha B. Zook, Director
Program in:
physical therapy • MSPT, DPT

Department of Theology
Dr. Kristopher Willumsen, Director
Program in:
applied theology • MA

Teacher Preparation Program
Dr. H. Lawrence Jones, Director
Program in:
teacher preparation • MASMED

Wisconsin

■ CARDINAL STRITCH UNIVERSITY
Milwaukee, WI 53217-3985
http://www.stritch.edu/

Independent-religious, coed, comprehensive institution. *Computer facilities:* 236 computers available on campus for general student use. A campuswide network can be accessed from student residence rooms and from off campus. Internet access is available. *Library facilities:* Cardinal Stritch University Library. *General application contact:* 800-347-8822 Ext. 4042.

College of Arts and Sciences
Programs in:
arts and sciences • MA, ME
clinical psychology • MA
religious studies • MA
visual studies • MA

College of Business and Management
Programs in:
business administration • MBA
financial services • MS
health care executives • MBA
management • MS
management for adults • MBA, MS

College of Education
Programs in:
computer science education • MS
education • MA, ME, MS, Ed D
educational computing • ME
educational leadership • MS
leadership • Ed D
professional development • ME
reading/language arts • MA
reading/learning disability • MA
special education • MA

College of Nursing
Program in:
nursing • MSN

■ CARTHAGE COLLEGE
Kenosha, WI 53140-1994
http://www.carthage.edu/

Independent-religious, coed, comprehensive institution. *Enrollment:* 2,632 graduate, professional, and undergraduate students; 122 part-time matriculated graduate/professional students (114 women). *Graduate faculty:* 3 full-time (2 women), 16 part-time/adjunct (11 women). *Computer facilities:* Computer purchase and lease plans are available. 200 computers available on campus for general student use. A campuswide network can be accessed from student residence rooms and from off campus. Internet access is available. *Library facilities:* Hedberg Library. *Graduate expenses:* Tuition: part-time $270 per credit. *General application contact:* Dr. Judith B. Schaumberg, Director of Graduate Programs, 262-551-5876.

Division of Teacher Education
Dr. Judith B. Schaumberg, Director of Graduate Programs
Programs in:
classroom guidance and counseling • M Ed
creative arts • M Ed
gifted and talented children • M Ed
language arts • M Ed
modern language • M Ed
natural sciences • M Ed
reading • M Ed, Certificate
social sciences • M Ed
teacher leadership • M Ed

■ CONCORDIA UNIVERSITY WISCONSIN
Mequon, WI 53097-2402
http://www.cuw.edu/

Independent-religious, coed, comprehensive institution. *Enrollment:* 5,152 graduate, professional, and undergraduate students; 410 full-time matriculated graduate/professional students (276 women), 341 part-time matriculated graduate/professional students (209 women). *Graduate faculty:* 13 full-time (5 women), 31 part-time/adjunct (17 women). *Computer facilities:*

Wisconsin

100 computers available on campus for general student use. A campuswide network can be accessed from student residence rooms and from off campus. Internet access is available. *Library facilities:* Rinker Memorial Library. *Graduate expenses:* Tuition: part-time $420 per credit. One-time fee: $85 part-time. *General application contact:* Dr. Marsha K. Konz, Dean of Graduate Studies, 262-243-4253.

School of Graduate Studies
Dr. Marsha K. Konz, Dean of Graduate Studies
Programs in:
 church administration • MBA
 church music • MCM
 counseling • MS Ed
 curriculum and instruction • MS Ed
 early childhood • MS Ed
 educational administration • MS
 family nurse practitioner • MSN
 family studies • MS Ed
 finance • MBA
 geriatric nurse practitioner • MSN
 health care administration • MBA
 human resource management • MBA
 international business • MBA
 management • MBA
 management information services • MBA
 managerial communications • MBA
 marketing • MBA
 nurse educator • MSN
 occupational therapy • MOT
 physical therapy • MPT, MSPT, DPT
 public administration • MBA
 reading • MS Ed
 risk management • MBA
 student personnel administration • MSSPA

■ EDGEWOOD COLLEGE
Madison, WI 53711-1997
http://www.edgewood.edu/

Independent-religious, coed, comprehensive institution. *Enrollment:* 2,422 graduate, professional, and undergraduate students; 84 full-time matriculated graduate/professional students (48 women), 417 part-time matriculated graduate/professional students (269 women). *Graduate faculty:* 23 full-time (9 women), 28 part-time/adjunct (10 women). *Computer facilities:* Computer purchase and lease plans are available. 140 computers available on campus for general student use. A campuswide network can be accessed from student residence rooms and from off campus. Internet access and online class registration are available. *Library facilities:* Oscar Rennebohm Library. *Graduate expenses:* Tuition: full-time $8,730; part-time $485 per credit. *General application contact:* Dr. Raymond Schultz, Associate Dean of Graduate Programs, 608-663-2377.

Program in Business
Dr. Gary Schroeder, Chair
Program in:
 business • MBA

Program in Education
Dr. Joseph Schmiedicke, Chair
Programs in:
 director of instruction • Certificate
 director of special education and pupil services • Certificate
 education • MA Ed
 educational administration • MA
 emotional disturbances • MA, Certificate
 learning disabilities • MA, Certificate
 learning disabilities and emotional disturbances • MA, Certificate
 school business administration • Certificate
 school principalship K-12 • Certificate

Program in Marriage and Family Therapy
Dr. Peter Fabian, Director
Program in:
 marriage and family therapy • MS

Program in Nursing
Dr. Mary Kelly-Powell, Chair
Program in:
 nursing • MS

Program in Religious Studies
Dr. John Leonard, Chairperson
Program in:
 religious studies • MA

■ MARIAN COLLEGE OF FOND DU LAC
Fond du Lac, WI 54935-4699
http://www.mariancollege.edu/

Independent-religious, coed, comprehensive institution. *Enrollment:* 2,777 graduate, professional, and undergraduate students; 42 full-time matriculated graduate/professional students (38 women), 879 part-time matriculated graduate/professional students (570 women). *Graduate faculty:* 14 full-time (7 women), 54 part-time/adjunct (21 women). *Computer facilities:* 200 computers available on campus for general student use. A campuswide network can be accessed from student residence rooms. Internet access and online class registration are available. *Library facilities:* Cardinal Meyer Library. *Graduate expenses:* Tuition: part-time $285 per credit. Part-time tuition and fees vary according to program. *General application contact:* Sheryl Ayala, Vice President for Academic Affairs, 920-923-7604.

Business Division
David McPhail, Dean of Lifelong Learning
Program in:
 organizational leadership and quality • MS

Educational Studies Division
Dr. Larry Robinson, Dean, Educational Studies
Programs in:
 educational leadership • MA
 teacher development • MA

Nursing Studies Division
Dr. Elizabeth Parato, Chair
Programs in:
 adult nurse practitioner • MSN
 nurse educator • MSN

■ MARQUETTE UNIVERSITY
Milwaukee, WI 53201-1881
http://www.marquette.edu/

Independent-religious, coed, university. CGS member. *Enrollment:* 11,355 graduate, professional, and undergraduate students; 1,237 full-time matriculated graduate/professional students (701 women), 1,220 part-time matriculated graduate/professional students (553 women). *Graduate faculty:* 473 full-time (164 women), 235 part-time/adjunct (124 women). *Computer facilities:* Computer purchase and lease plans are available. 1,003 computers available on campus for general student use. A campuswide network can be accessed from student residence rooms and from off campus. Internet access is available. *Library facilities:* Memorial Library plus 2 others. *Graduate expenses:* Tuition: full-time $10,080; part-time $630 per credit. Tuition and fees vary according to program. *General application contact:* Erin Fox, Assistant Director for Recruitment, 414-288-5319.

Find an in-depth description at www.petersons.com/gradchannel.

Graduate School
Dr. T. Daniel Griffiths, Vice Provost for Research and Graduate Programs
Programs in:
 bioinformatics • MS
 computing • MS
 interdisciplinary studies • PhD

Peterson's Graduate Schools in the U.S. 2006

Wisconsin

Marquette University (continued)
College of Arts and Sciences
Dr. Michael A. McKinney, Dean
Programs in:
algebra • PhD
American literature • PhD
analytical chemistry • MS, PhD
ancient philosophy • MA, PhD
arts and sciences • MA, MAT, MS, PhD
bio-mathematical modeling • PhD
bioanalytical chemistry • MS, PhD
biophysical chemistry • MS, PhD
British and American literature • MA
British empiricism and analytic philosophy • MA, PhD
British literature • PhD
cell biology • MS, PhD
chemical physics • MS, PhD
Christian philosophy • MA, PhD
clinical psychology • MS
computers • MS
developmental biology • MS, PhD
early modern European philosophy • MA, PhD
ecology • MS, PhD
endocrinology • MS, PhD
ethics • MA, PhD
European history • MA, PhD
evolutionary biology • MS, PhD
genetics • MS, PhD
German philosophy • MA, PhD
historical theology • MA, PhD
inorganic chemistry • MS, PhD
international affairs • MA
mathematics • MS
mathematics education • MS
medieval history • MA
medieval philosophy • MA, PhD
microbiology • MS, PhD
molecular biology • MS, PhD
muscle and exercise physiology • MS, PhD
neurobiology • MS, PhD
organic chemistry • MS, PhD
phenomenology and existentialism • MA, PhD
philosophy of religion • MA, PhD
physical chemistry • MS, PhD
political science • MA
psychology • PhD
religious studies • PhD
Renaissance and Reformation • MA
reproductive physiology • MS, PhD
social and applied philosophy • MA
Spanish • MA, MAT
statistics • MS
systematic theology • MA, PhD
theology • MA
theology and society • PhD
United States • MA, PhD

College of Business Administration
Dr. David Shrock, Dean
Programs in:
accounting • MSA
business administration • MBA, MSA, MSAE, MSHR
business economics • MSAE
financial economics • MSAE
human resources • MSHR
international economics • MSAE

College of Communication
Dr. William R. Elliot, Dean
Programs in:
advertising and public relations • MA
broadcasting and electronic communications • MA
communications studies • MA
journalism • MA
mass communications • MA
religious communications • MA
science, health and environmental communications • MA

College of Engineering
Dr. Stan V. Jaskolski, Dean
Programs in:
bioinstrumentation/computers • MS, PhD
biomechanics/biomaterials • MS, PhD
computing • MS
construction and public works management • MS, PhD
electrical engineering • MS, PhD
engineering • MS, PhD
engineering management • MS
environmental/water resources engineering • MS, PhD
functional imaging • PhD
healthcare technologies management • MS
mechanical engineering • MS, PhD
structural/geotechnical engineering • MS, PhD
systems physiology • MS, PhD
transportation planning and engineering • MS, PhD

College of Health Sciences
Dr. Jack C. Brooks, Dean
Programs in:
health sciences • MPT, MS
physical therapy • MPT
physician assistant studies • MS
speech-language pathology • MS

College of Nursing
Dr. Lea Accord, Dean
Programs in:
adult nurse practitioner • Certificate
advanced practice nursing • MSN
gerontological nurse practitioner • Certificate
neonatal nurse practitioner • Certificate
nurse-midwifery • Certificate
nursing • PhD
pediatric nurse practitioner • Certificate

School of Education
Dr. John Augenstein
Program in:
education • MA, Ed D, PhD, Spec

Law School
Joseph D. Kearney, Dean
Program in:
law • JD

School of Dentistry
Dr. William L. Lobb, Dean
Programs in:
advanced training in general dentistry • MS
dental biomaterials • MS
dentistry • DDS, MS
endodontics • MS
orthodontics • MS
prosthodontics • MS

■ **MOUNT MARY COLLEGE**
Milwaukee, WI 53222-4597
http://www.mtmary.edu/

Independent-religious, women only, comprehensive institution. *Enrollment:* 1,600 graduate, professional, and undergraduate students; 47 full-time matriculated graduate/professional students (45 women), 182 part-time matriculated graduate/professional students (159 women). *Graduate faculty:* 7 full-time (6 women), 17 part-time/adjunct (12 women). *Computer facilities:* 150 computers available on campus for general student use. A campuswide network can be accessed from student residence rooms and from off campus. Internet access is available. *Library facilities:* Haggerty Library. *Graduate expenses:* Tuition: full-time $7,360; part-time $445 per credit. Tuition and fees vary according to program. *General application contact:* Director of Center for Educational and Professional Advancement, 414-256-1252.

Graduate Programs
Dr. Eileen Schwalbach, Vice President for Academics and Student Affairs
Programs in:
administrative dietetics • MS
art therapy • MS
clinical dietetics • MS
education • MA
gerontology • MA
nutrition education • MS
occupational therapy • MS
professional development • MA

■ **SILVER LAKE COLLEGE**
Manitowoc, WI 54220-9319
http://www.sl.edu/

Independent-religious, coed, comprehensive institution. *Enrollment:* 1,104 graduate, professional, and undergraduate students; 58 full-time matriculated graduate/professional students (39 women), 274 part-time matriculated graduate/professional students (192 women). *Graduate faculty:*

5 full-time (all women), 81 part-time/adjunct (45 women). *Computer facilities:* 50 computers available on campus for general student use. A campuswide network can be accessed from off campus. Internet access is available. *Library facilities:* The Erma M. and Theodore M. Zigmunt Library. *Graduate expenses:* Tuition: part-time $185 per credit. One-time fee: $45 part-time. *General application contact:* Jamie Grant, Office Manager, Admissions, 800-236-4752 Ext. 186.

Division of Graduate Studies
Sr. Michaela Melko, OSF, Director
Programs in:
  administrative leadership • MA
  Kodaly emphasis • MM Ed
  management and organizational behavior • MS
  teacher leadership • MA

■ UNIVERSITY OF WISCONSIN–EAU CLAIRE
Eau Claire, WI 54702-4004
http://www.uwec.edu/

State-supported, coed, comprehensive institution. CGS member. *Enrollment:* 10,594 graduate, professional, and undergraduate students; 111 full-time matriculated graduate/professional students (77 women), 295 part-time matriculated graduate/professional students (212 women). *Graduate faculty:* 349 full-time (120 women), 26 part-time/adjunct (13 women). *Computer facilities:* 925 computers available on campus for general student use. A campuswide network can be accessed from student residence rooms and from off campus. Internet access and online class registration are available. *Library facilities:* William D. McIntyre Library plus 1 other. *Graduate expenses:* Tuition, state resident: full-time $5,383; part-time $299 per credit. Tuition, nonresident: full-time $15,993; part-time $888 per credit. Tuition and fees vary according to program and reciprocity agreements. *General application contact:* Kristina Anderson, Interim Director of Admissions, 715-836-5415.

College of Arts and Sciences
Dr. Bernard Duyfhuizen, Interim Dean
Programs in:
  arts and sciences • MA, MS, MSE, Ed S
  biology • MS
  English • MA
  history • MA
  school psychology • MSE, Ed S

College of Business
Dr. V. Thomas Dock, Dean
Programs in:
  business • MBA
  business administration • MBA

College of Professional Studies
Dr. Mark Clark, Dean
Program in:
  professional studies • MAT, MEPD, MS, MSE, MSN, MST

School of Education
Dr. Katherine Rhoades, Associate Dean
Programs in:
  biology • MAT, MST
  education • MAT, MEPD, MSE, MST
  education and professional development • MEPD
  elementary education • MST
  English • MAT, MST
  history • MAT, MST
  mathematics • MAT, MST
  reading • MST
  special education • MSE

School of Human Sciences and Services
Dr. Patricia Christopherson, Associate Dean
Programs in:
  communicative disorders • MS
  environmental and public health • MS
  human sciences and services • MS

School of Nursing
Dr. Elaine Wendt, Associate Dean
Program in:
  nursing • MSN

■ UNIVERSITY OF WISCONSIN–GREEN BAY
Green Bay, WI 54311-7001
http://www.uwgb.edu/

State-supported, coed, comprehensive institution. *Enrollment:* 5,420 graduate, professional, and undergraduate students; 44 full-time matriculated graduate/professional students (26 women), 94 part-time matriculated graduate/professional students (57 women). *Graduate faculty:* 41 full-time (12 women), 4 part-time/adjunct (2 women). *Computer facilities:* 550 computers available on campus for general student use. A campuswide network can be accessed from student residence rooms and from off campus. Internet access and online class registration, on-line degree progress are available. *Library facilities:* Cofrin Library. *Graduate expenses:* Tuition, state resident: full-time $5,996; part-time $333 per credit. Tuition, nonresident: full-time $16,606; part-time $922 per credit. Full-time tuition and fees vary according to program and reciprocity agreements. Part-time tuition and fees vary according to course load and reciprocity agreements. *General application contact:* Ronald D. Stieglitz, Associate Dean of Graduate Studies, 920-465-2123.

Graduate Studies
Ronald D. Stieglitz, Associate Dean
Programs in:
  applied leadership for teaching and learning • MS Ed
  environmental science and policy • MS
  management • MS
  social work • MSW

■ UNIVERSITY OF WISCONSIN–LA CROSSE
La Crosse, WI 54601-3742
http://www.uwlax.edu/

State-supported, coed, comprehensive institution. CGS member. *Enrollment:* 8,746 graduate, professional, and undergraduate students; 266 matriculated graduate/professional students. *Graduate faculty:* 190 full-time (64 women), 50 part-time/adjunct (20 women). *Computer facilities:* 600 computers available on campus for general student use. A campuswide network can be accessed from student residence rooms and from off campus. Internet access is available. *Library facilities:* Murphy Library. *Graduate expenses:* Tuition, state resident: part-time $288 per credit. Tuition, nonresident: part-time $878 per credit. Tuition and fees vary according to course load, program and reciprocity agreements.

Find an in-depth description at www.petersons.com/gradchannel.

Office of University Graduate Studies
Dr. Garth Tymeson, Director of University Graduate Studies

College of Business Administration
Dr. William Colclough, Dean
Program in:
  business administration • MBA

College of Education, Exercise Science, Health, and Recreation
Dr. Sandra Price, Interim Dean
Programs in:
  adult fitness/cardiac rehabilitation • MS
  athletic training • MS
  college student development and administration • MS Ed
  community health education • MPH, MS

Wisconsin

University of Wisconsin–La Crosse (continued)
  education, exercise science, health and recreation • MEPD, MPH, MS, MS Ed
  educational studies • MEPD, MS Ed
  elementary education • MEPD
  emotional disturbance • MS Ed
  human performance • MS
  K–12 • MEPD
  learning disabilities • MS Ed
  physical education teaching • MS
  professional development • MEPD
  reading • MS Ed
  recreation • MS
  school health education • MS
  secondary education • MEPD
  special/adapted physical education • MS
  sport administration • MS

College of Liberal Studies
Dr. John Magerus, Dean
Programs in:
  liberal studies • MS Ed, Ed S
  school psychology • MS Ed, Ed S

College of Science and Allied Health
Dr. Mike Nelson, Dean
Programs in:
  aquatic sciences • MS
  biology • MS
  cellular and molecular biology • MS
  clinical microbiology • MS
  health professions • MS, MSPT
  microbiology • MS
  nurse anesthesia • MS
  physical therapy • MSPT
  physician assistant studies • MS
  physiology • MS
  science and allied health • MS, MSE, MSPT
  software engineering • MSE

■ UNIVERSITY OF WISCONSIN–MADISON
Madison, WI 53706-1380
http://www.wisc.edu/

State-supported, coed, university. CGS member. *Enrollment:* 41,588 graduate, professional, and undergraduate students; 9,510 full-time matriculated graduate/professional students (4,735 women), 1,844 part-time matriculated graduate/professional students (935 women). *Graduate faculty:* 3,239 full-time (946 women), 818 part-time/adjunct (425 women). *Computer facilities:* 2,800 computers available on campus for general student use. A campuswide network can be accessed from student residence rooms and from off campus. Internet access is available. *Library facilities:* Memorial Library plus 40 others. *Graduate expenses:* Full-time $7,593; part-time $476 per credit. Tuition, nonresident: full-time $22,824; part-time $1,430 per credit. Required fees: $292; $38 per credit. Part-time tuition and fees vary according to course load and reciprocity agreements. *General application contact:* 608-262-2433.

Graduate School
Dr. Martin Cadwallader, Dean
Programs in:
  agricultural and applied economics • MA, MS, PhD
  agricultural and life sciences • MA, MS, PhD
  agricultural journalism • MS
  agronomy • MS, PhD
  animal sciences • MS, PhD
  bacteriology • MS
  biochemistry • MS, PhD
  biological systems engineering • MS, PhD
  biometry • MS
  biophysics • PhD
  cellular and molecular biology • PhD
  dairy science • MS, PhD
  development • PhD
  endocrinology-reproductive physiology • MS, PhD
  engineering • PDD
  entomology • MS, PhD
  family and consumer journalism • MS
  food science • MS, PhD
  forest science • MS, PhD
  forestry • PhD
  genetics • PhD
  horticulture • MS, PhD
  landscape architecture • MA, MS
  mass communication • PhD
  medical genetics • MS
  molecular and environmental toxicology • MS, PhD
  natural resources • MA, MS, PhD
  neuroscience • MS, PhD
  nutritional sciences • MS, PhD
  plant breeding and plant genetics • MS, PhD
  plant pathology • MS, PhD
  professional practice • ME
  recreation resources management • MS
  soil science • MS, PhD
  technical Japanese • ME
  wildlife ecology • MS, PhD

College of Engineering
Paul S. Peercy, Dean
Programs in:
  biomedical engineering • MS, PhD
  chemical and biological engineering • MS, PhD
  civil and environmental engineering • MS, PhD
  electrical engineering • MS, PhD
  energy systems • ME
  engineering • ME, MS, PhD, PDD
  engineering mechanics • MS, PhD
  environmental chemistry and technology • MS, PhD
  geological engineering • MS, PhD
  industrial engineering • MS, PhD
  limnology and marine science • MS, PhD
  manufacturing systems engineering • MS
  materials science • MS, PhD
  mechanical engineering • MS, PhD
  metallurgical engineering • MS, PhD
  nuclear engineering and engineering physics • MS, PhD
  polymers • ME

College of Letters and Science
Programs in:
  public affairs • MPIA
  African languages and literature • MA, PhD
  Afro-American studies • MA
  anthropology • MA, MS, PhD
  applied English linguistics • MA
  art history • MA, PhD
  astronomy • PhD
  atmospheric and oceanic sciences • MS, PhD
  biology of brain and behavior • PhD
  botany • MS, PhD
  cartography and geographic information systems • MS
  chemistry • MS, PhD
  Chinese • MA, PhD
  choral • MM, DMA
  classics • MA, PhD
  clinical psychology • PhD
  cognitive and perceptual sciences • PhD
  communication arts • MA, PhD
  communicative disorders • MS, PhD
  comparative literature • MA, PhD
  composition • MM, DMA
  composition studies • PhD
  computer sciences • MS, PhD
  curriculum and instruction • PhD
  developmental psychology • PhD
  economics • PhD
  English language and linguistics • PhD
  ethnomusicology • MM, PhD
  family and consumer journalism • PhD
  French • MA, PhD
  French studies • MFS, Certificate
  geographic information systems • Certificate
  geography • MS, PhD
  geology • MS, PhD
  geophysics • MS, PhD
  German • MA, PhD
  Greek • MA
  Hebrew and Semitic studies • MA, PhD
  history • MA, PhD
  history of science • MA, PhD
  industrial relations • MA, MS, PhD
  instrumental • MM, DMA
  international public affairs • MPIA
  Italian • MA, PhD
  Japanese • MA, PhD

Wisconsin

journalism and mass communication • MA
languages and cultures of Asia • MA, PhD
Latin • MA
Latin American, Caribbean and Iberian studies • MA
letters and science • MA, MFA, MFS, MM, MPA, MPIA, MS, MSSW, DMA, PhD, Certificate
library and information studies • MA, PhD, Certificate
linguistics • MA, PhD
literature • MA, PhD
mass communication • MA, PhD
mathematics • MA, PhD
music • MA, MM, DMA, PhD
music education • MM
musicology • MA, MM, PhD
performance • MM, DMA
philosophy • MA, PhD
physics • MA, MS, PhD
political science • MA, PhD
Portuguese • MA, PhD
psychology • PhD
public affairs • MPA
rural sociology • MS
Scandinavian studies • MA, PhD
Slavic languages and literature • MA, PhD
social and personality psychology • PhD
social welfare • PhD
social work • MSSW
sociology • MS, PhD
Southeast Asian studies • MA
Spanish • MA, PhD
statistics • MS, PhD
theatre and drama • MA, MFA, PhD
theory • MA, MM, PhD
urban and regional planning • MS, PhD
zoology • MA, MS, PhD

Gaylord Nelson Institute for Environmental Studies
Erhard F. Joeres, Chair
Programs in:
conservation biology and sustainable development • MS
environmental monitoring • MS, PhD
environmental studies • MS, PhD
land resources • MS, PhD
water resources management • MS

School of Business
Dr. Michael M. Knetter, Dean
Programs in:
accounting and information systems • MBA, PhD
actuarial science • MS
applied corporate finance • MBA
applied securities analysis • MBA
arts administration • MBA
business • MBA, MS, PhD
business administration • MBA
business statistics • PhD

entrepreneurship • MBA
finance, investment, and banking • PhD
general management • MBA
information systems analysis • MBA
international business • PhD
management and human resources • PhD
marketing • PhD
marketing research • MBA
operations and technology management • MBA, PhD
product management • MBA
real estate • MBA
real estate and urban land economics • PhD
risk management and insurance • MBA, PhD
strategic human resources • MBA
strategic management in life and engineering sciences • MBA
supply chain management • MBA

School of Education
Dr. W. Charles Read, Dean
Programs in:
administration • Certificate
art • MA, MFA
art education • MA
chemistry education • MS
commercial arts education • MA
counseling • MS
counseling psychology • PhD
curriculum and instruction • MS, PhD
education • MA, MFA, MS, PhD, Certificate
education and mathematics • MA
educational policy • MS, PhD
educational policy studies • MA, PhD
educational psychology • MS, PhD
English education • MA
French education • MA
geography education • MS
German education • MA
higher and postsecondary education • MS, PhD
k-12 leadership • MS, PhD
kinesiology • MS, PhD
Latin education • MA
music education • MS
physics education • MS
rehabilitation psychology • MA, MS, PhD
science education • MS
Spanish education • MA
special education • MA, MS, PhD
therapeutic science • MS

School of Human Ecology
Programs in:
consumer behavior and family economics • MS, PhD
continuing and vocational education • MS, PhD
design studies • MS, PhD
family and consumer journalism • MS, PhD
human development and family studies • MS, PhD

Law School
Kenneth B. Davis, Dean
Programs in:
law • JD, LL M, MLI, SJD
legal institutions • MLI

Medical School
Dr. Philip M. Farrell, Dean
Program in:
medicine • MD, MS, PhD

Graduate Programs in Medicine
Dr. Paul M. DeLuca, Associate Dean of Research and Graduate Studies
Programs in:
biomolecular chemistry • MS, PhD
cancer biology • PhD
genetics and medical genetics • MS, PhD
health physics • MS
medical physics • MS, PhD
microbiology • PhD
molecular and cellular pharmacology • PhD
pathology and laboratory medicine • PhD
physiology • PhD
population health • MS, PhD

School of Nursing
Dr. Katharyn A. May, Dean
Program in:
nursing • MS, PhD

School of Pharmacy
Programs in:
pharmaceutical sciences • MS, PhD
pharmacy • Pharm D, MS, PhD
social and administrative sciences in pharmacy • MS, PhD

School of Veterinary Medicine
Programs in:
anatomy • MS, PhD
biochemistry • MS, PhD
cellular and molecular biology • MS, PhD
comparative biosciences • MS, PhD
environmental toxicology • MS, PhD
neurosciences • MS, PhD
pharmacology • MS, PhD
physiology • MS, PhD
veterinary medicine • DVM, MS, PhD

■ **UNIVERSITY OF WISCONSIN–MILWAUKEE**
Milwaukee, WI 53201-0413
http://www.uwm.edu/

State-supported, coed, university. CGS member. *Enrollment:* 25,440 graduate, professional, and undergraduate students; 1,879 full-time matriculated graduate/professional students (1,122 women), 2,008 part-time matriculated graduate/professional students (1,237 women). *Graduate faculty:* 787 full-time (285

Wisconsin

University of Wisconsin–Milwaukee (continued)

women). *Computer facilities:* 310 computers available on campus for general student use. A campuswide network can be accessed from off campus. *Library facilities:* Golda Meir Library. *Graduate expenses:* Tuition, state resident: part-time $634 per credit. Tuition, nonresident: part-time $1,531 per credit. Part-time tuition and fees vary according to course load, campus/location, program and reciprocity agreements. *General application contact:* General Information Contact, 414-229-4982.

Graduate School
Dr. Dale J. Jaffee, Interim Dean of the Graduate School and Associate Provost for Research
Program in:
   multidisciplinary studies • PhD

College of Engineering and Applied Science
Dr. William Gregory, Dean
Programs in:
   computer science • MS, PhD
   engineering • MS, PhD
   engineering and applied science • MS, PhD

College of Health Sciences
Randall Lambrecht, Dean
Programs in:
   clinical laboratory science • MS
   communication sciences and disorders • MS
   health sciences • MS, PhD
   healthcare informatics • MS
   kinesiology • MS
   occupational therapy • MS

College of Letters and Sciences
G. Richard Meadows, Dean
Programs in:
   anthropology • MS, PhD
   art history • MA
   art museum studies • Certificate
   biological sciences • MS, PhD
   chemistry • MS, PhD
   classics and Hebrew studies • MAFLL
   clinical psychology • MS, PhD
   communication • MA
   comparative literature • MAFLL
   economics • MA, PhD
   English • MA, PhD
   French and Italian • MAFLL
   geography • MA, MS, PhD
   geological sciences • MS, PhD
   German • MAFLL
   history • MA, PhD
   human resources and labor relations • MHRLR
   journalism and mass communication • MA
   letters and sciences • MA, MAFLL, MHRLR, MLS, MPA, MS, PhD, Certificate
   liberal studies • MLS
   mathematics • MS, PhD
   philosophy • MA
   physics • MS, PhD
   political science • MA, PhD
   psychology • MS, PhD
   public administration • MPA
   Slavic studies • MAFLL
   sociology • MA
   Spanish • MAFLL
   urban studies • MS, PhD

College of Nursing
Joan Wilk, Representative
Program in:
   nursing • MS, PhD

Peck School of the Arts
William Robert Bucker, Dean
Programs in:
   art • MA, MFA
   art education • MA, MFA, MS
   arts • MA, MFA, MM, MS
   dance • MFA
   film • MFA
   music • MM
   theatre • MFA

School of Architecture and Urban Planning
Robert Greenstreet, Dean
Programs in:
   architecture • M Arch, PhD
   architecture and urban planning • M Arch, MUP, PhD
   urban planning • MUP

School of Business Administration
Sarah Sandin, Representative
Program in:
   business administration • MBA, MS, PhD

School of Education
Alfonzo Thurman, Dean
Programs in:
   administrative leadership and supervision in education • MS
   cultural foundations of education • MS
   curriculum planning and instruction improvement • MS
   early childhood education • MS
   education • MS, PhD
   educational psychology • MS
   elementary education • MS
   exceptional education • MS
   junior high/middle school education • MS
   reading education • MS
   secondary education • MS
   teaching in an urban setting • MS
   urban education • PhD

School of Information Studies
Alexandra Dimitroff, Representative
Program in:
   information studies • MLIS, CAS

School of Social Welfare
Stan Stojkovic, Interim Dean
Programs in:
   criminal justice • MS
   social welfare • MS, MSW
   social work • MSW

■ UNIVERSITY OF WISCONSIN–OSHKOSH
Oshkosh, WI 54901
http://www.uwosh.edu/

State-supported, coed, comprehensive institution. *Enrollment:* 11,155 graduate, professional, and undergraduate students; 160 full-time matriculated graduate/professional students (121 women), 880 part-time matriculated graduate/professional students (579 women). *Graduate faculty:* 300 full-time (111 women), 17 part-time/adjunct (8 women). *Computer facilities:* 475 computers available on campus for general student use. A campuswide network can be accessed from student residence rooms and from off campus. Internet access and online class registration are available. *Library facilities:* Forrest R. Polk Library. *Graduate expenses:* Tuition, state resident: full-time $5,335; part-time $298 per credit. Tuition, nonresident: full-time $15,945; part-time $887 per credit. Tuition and fees vary according to program and reciprocity agreements. *General application contact:* Greg Wypiszynski, Director, Graduate Admissions and Records, 920-424-1223.

The School of Graduate Studies
Dr. Marsha Rossiter, Interim Assistant Vice Chancellor
Program in:
   social work • MSW

College of Business Administration
Dr. E. Alan Hartman, Dean
Programs in:
   business administration • MBA, MS
   information systems • MS

College of Education and Human Services
Dr. Craig Fiedler, Interim Dean
Programs in:
   counseling • MSE
   cross-categorical • MSE
   curriculum and instruction • MSE
   early childhood: exceptional education needs • MSE
   education and human services • MS, MSE
   educational leadership • MS
   non-licensure • MSE
   reading education • MSE

Wisconsin

College of Letters and Science
Dr. Michael Zimmerman, Dean
Programs in:
  biology • MS
  English • MA
  experimental psychology • MS
  general agency • MPA
  health care • MPA
  industrial/organizational psychology • MS
  letters and science • MA, MPA, MS, MSW
  mathematics education • MS
  physics • MS

College of Nursing
Dr. Merritt Knox, Dean
Programs in:
  family nurse practitioner • MSN
  primary health care • MSN

■ **UNIVERSITY OF WISCONSIN–PARKSIDE**
Kenosha, WI 53141-2000
http://www.uwp.edu/

State-supported, coed, comprehensive institution. *Enrollment:* 5,072 graduate, professional, and undergraduate students; 107 matriculated graduate/professional students. *Graduate faculty:* 30 full-time (10 women). *Computer facilities:* 228 computers available on campus for general student use. A campuswide network can be accessed from student residence rooms and from off campus. Internet access and online class registration are available. *Library facilities:* Library-Learning Center. *Graduate expenses:* Full-time $5,416; part-time $302 per credit. *General application contact:* Matthew Jensen, Director of Admissions, 262-595-2355.

College of Arts and Sciences
Dr. Donald Cress, Dean
Programs in:
  applied molecular biology • MAMB
  arts and sciences • MAMB

School of Business and Technology
Programs in:
  business administration • MBA
  business and technology • MBA, MSCIS
  computer and information systems • MSCIS

■ **UNIVERSITY OF WISCONSIN–PLATTEVILLE**
Platteville, WI 53818-3099
http://www.uwplatt.edu/

State-supported, coed, comprehensive institution. *Enrollment:* 6,077 graduate, professional, and undergraduate students;
108 full-time matriculated graduate/professional students (80 women), 340 part-time matriculated graduate/professional students (151 women). *Graduate faculty:* 5 full-time (2 women), 90 part-time/adjunct (16 women). *Computer facilities:* 250 computers available on campus for general student use. A campuswide network can be accessed from student residence rooms and from off campus. Internet access is available. *Library facilities:* Karrmann Library. *Graduate expenses:* Tuition, state resident: part-time $302 per credit. Tuition, nonresident: part-time $891 per credit. *General application contact:* Laurie Schuler, Admissions and Enrollment Management, 608-342-1125.

School of Graduate Studies
Dr. David P. Van Buren, Interim Dean

College of Business, Industry, Life Science, and Agriculture
Dr. Duane Ford, Dean
Programs in:
  business, industry, life science, and agriculture • MS
  industrial technology management • MS

College of Liberal Arts and Education
Dr. Mittie Nimocks, Dean
Programs in:
  adult education • MSE
  counselor education • MSE
  elementary education • MSE
  liberal arts and education • MSE
  middle school education • MSE
  secondary education • MSE
  vocational and technical education • MSE

Distance Learning Center
Dawn Drake, Executive Director
Programs in:
  criminal justice • MS
  engineering • ME
  project management • MS

■ **UNIVERSITY OF WISCONSIN–RIVER FALLS**
River Falls, WI 54022-5001
http://www.uwrf.edu/

State-supported, coed, comprehensive institution. CGS member. *Computer facilities:* 387 computers available on campus for general student use. A campuswide network can be accessed from student residence rooms and from off campus. Internet access and online class registration are available. *Library facilities:* Chalmer Davee Library. *General application contact:* Program Assistant III, 715-425-3843.

Outreach and Graduate Studies
Program in:
  management • MM

College of Agriculture, Food, and Environmental Sciences
Programs in:
  agricultural education • MS
  agriculture, food, and environmental sciences • MS

College of Arts and Science
Programs in:
  arts and science • MSE
  language, literature, and communication education • MSE
  mathematics education • MSE
  science education • MSE
  social science education • MSE

College of Education and Professional Studies
Programs in:
  communicative disorders • MS
  counseling • MSE
  education • MS, MSE, Ed S
  elementary education • MSE
  reading • MSE
  school psychology • MSE, Ed S
  secondary education-communicative disorders • MSE

■ **UNIVERSITY OF WISCONSIN–STEVENS POINT**
Stevens Point, WI 54481-3897
http://www.uwsp.edu/

State-supported, coed, comprehensive institution. *Enrollment:* 9,029 graduate, professional, and undergraduate students; 89 full-time matriculated graduate/professional students (78 women), 187 part-time matriculated graduate/professional students (135 women). *Graduate faculty:* 261 full-time (76 women), 8 part-time/adjunct (2 women). *Computer facilities:* 800 computers available on campus for general student use. A campuswide network can be accessed from student residence rooms and from off campus. Internet access is available. *Library facilities:* Learning Resources Center. *Graduate expenses:* Tuition, state resident: full-time $4,842; part-time $269 per credit. Tuition, nonresident: full-time $15,452; part-time $858 per credit. Required fees: $524; $53 per credit. *General application contact:* David Eckholm, Director of Admissions, 715-346-2441.

College of Fine Arts and Communication
Gerard McKenna, Dean
Programs in:

Wisconsin

University of Wisconsin–Stevens Point (continued)
  fine arts and communication • MA, MM Ed
  interpersonal communication • MA
  mass communication • MA
  music • MM Ed
  organizational communication • MA
  public relations • MA

College of Letters and Science
Justus Paul, Dean
Programs in:
  biology • MST
  business and economics • MBA
  English • MST
  history • MST
  letters and science • MBA, MST

College of Natural Resources
Dr. Christina Thomas, Associate Dean
Program in:
  natural resources • MS

College of Professional Studies
Joan North, Dean
Program in:
  professional studies • MS, MSE

School of Communicative Disorders
Dr. Gary Cumley, Head
Program in:
  communicative disorders • MS

School of Education
Dr. Leslie McClaine-Ruelle, Associate Dean
Programs in:
  education—general/reading • MSE
  education-general/special • MSE
  educational administration • MSE
  elementary education • MSE
  guidance and counseling • MSE

School of Health Promotion and Human Development
Marty Loy, Head
Programs in:
  human and community resources • MS
  nutritional sciences • MS

■ **UNIVERSITY OF WISCONSIN–STOUT**
Menomonie, WI 54751
http://www.uwstout.edu/

State-supported, coed, comprehensive institution. *Computer facilities:* Computer purchase and lease plans are available. 590 computers available on campus for general student use. A campuswide network can be accessed from student residence rooms and from off campus. Internet access and online class registration are available. *Library facilities:* Library Learning Center. *General application contact:* Graduate Student Evaluator, 715-232-1322.

Graduate School
College of Human Development
Programs in:
  applied psychology • MS
  education • MS
  food and nutritional sciences • MS
  guidance and counseling • MS
  home economics • MS
  hospitality and tourism • MS
  human development • MS, MS Ed, Ed S
  marriage and family therapy • MS
  mental health counseling • MS
  school psychology • MS Ed, Ed S
  vocational rehabilitation • MS

College of Technology, Engineering, and Management
Programs in:
  industrial and vocational education • Ed S
  industrial/technology education • MS
  management technology • MS
  risk control • MS
  technology, engineering, and management • MS, Ed S
  training and development • MS
  vocational education • MS

■ **UNIVERSITY OF WISCONSIN–SUPERIOR**
Superior, WI 54880-4500
http://www.uwsuper.edu/

State-supported, coed, comprehensive institution. CGS member. *Computer facilities:* Computer purchase and lease plans are available. 161 computers available on campus for general student use. A campuswide network can be accessed from student residence rooms and from off campus. Internet access and online class registration are available. *Library facilities:* Jim Dan Hill Library. *General application contact:* Program Assistant/Status Examiner, 715-394-8295.

Graduate Division
Programs in:
  art education • MA
  art history • MA
  art therapy • MA
  community counseling • MSE
  educational administration • MSE, Ed S
  elementary school counseling • MSE
  emotional/behavior disabilities • MSE
  human relations • MSE
  instruction • MSE
  learning disabilities • MSE
  mass communication • MA
  secondary school counseling • MSE
  special education • MSE
  speech communication • MA
  studio arts • MA
  teaching reading • MSE
  theater • MA

■ **UNIVERSITY OF WISCONSIN–WHITEWATER**
Whitewater, WI 53190-1790
http://www.uww.edu/

State-supported, coed, comprehensive institution. *Enrollment:* 10,817 graduate, professional, and undergraduate students; 166 full-time matriculated graduate/professional students (102 women), 1,495 part-time matriculated graduate/professional students (937 women). *Graduate faculty:* 332. *Computer facilities:* 700 computers available on campus for general student use. A campuswide network can be accessed from student residence rooms and from off campus. *Library facilities:* Andersen Library. *Graduate expenses:* Tuition, state resident: part-time $299 per credit. Tuition, nonresident: part-time $888 per credit. *General application contact:* Sally A. Lange, School of Graduate Studies, 262-472-1006.

School of Graduate Studies
Dr. John Stone, Interim Dean, School of Graduate Studies

College of Arts and Communications
Dr. John Heyer, Dean
Programs in:
  arts and communications • MS
  corporate/public communication • MS
  mass communication • MS

College of Business and Economics
Dr. Christine Clements, Acting Dean
Programs in:
  accounting • MBA
  business and economics • MBA, MPA, MS, MS Ed
  business education • MS
  computer information systems • MS
  decision support systems • MBA
  finance • MBA
  healthcare • MBA
  human resource management • MBA
  international business • MBA
  management • MBA
  marketing • MBA
  operations and supply chain management • MBA
  post-secondary • MS
  school business management • MS Ed
  secondary • MS
  technology and training • MBA

College of Education
Dr. Jeffrey Barnett, Dean
Programs in:
  communicative disorders • MS
  community counseling • MS Ed
  curriculum and instruction • MS
  education • MS, MS Ed

Wyoming

educational administration • MS Ed
higher education • MS Ed
reading • MS Ed
safety • MS
school counseling • MS Ed
special education • MS Ed

College of Letters and Sciences
Dr. Howard Ross, Dean
Programs in:
letters and sciences • MPA, MS Ed, Ed S
public administration • MPA
school psychology • MS Ed, Ed S

■ **VITERBO UNIVERSITY**
La Crosse, WI 54601-4797
http://www.viterbo.edu/

Independent-religious, coed, comprehensive institution. *Computer facilities:* 215 computers available on campus for general student use. A campuswide network can be accessed from student residence rooms and from off campus. Internet access, e-mail; blackboard courses are available. *Library facilities:* Todd Wehr Memorial Library.

Graduate Program in Education
Program in:
education • MA

Graduate Program in Nursing
Dr. Bonnie Nesbitt, Director
Program in:
nursing • MSN

Wyoming

■ **UNIVERSITY OF WYOMING**
Laramie, WY 82070
http://www.uwyo.edu/

State-supported, coed, university. CGS member. *Enrollment:* 13,130 graduate, professional, and undergraduate students; 1,118 full-time matriculated graduate/professional students (538 women), 809 part-time matriculated graduate/professional students (493 women). *Graduate faculty:* 598 full-time (148 women), 130 part-time/adjunct (43 women). *Computer facilities:* Computer purchase and lease plans are available. 1,300 computers available on campus for general student use. A campuswide network can be accessed from student residence rooms and from off campus.

Internet access and online class registration are available. *Library facilities:* William Robertson Coe Library plus 6 others. *Graduate expenses:* Tuition, state resident: part-time $142 per credit hour. Tuition, nonresident: part-time $408 per credit hour. Required fees: $134 per semester. Tuition and fees vary according to course load, campus/location, program and student level. *General application contact:* Michell Nacey, Credentials Analyst/Advising Assistant, 307-766-2287.

College of Law
Jerry Parkinson, Dean
Program in:
law • JD

Graduate School
Dr. Don A. Roth, Interim Dean

College of Agriculture
Dr. Frank D. Galey, Dean
Programs in:
agricultural and applied economics • MS
agriculture • MS, PhD
agronomy • MS, PhD
animal sciences • MS, PhD
entomology • MS, PhD
family and consumer sciences • MS
food science and human nutrition • MS
molecular biology • MS, PhD
pathobiology • MS
rangeland ecology and watershed management • MS, PhD
reproductive biology • MS, PhD

College of Arts and Sciences
Oliver Walter, Dean
Programs in:
American studies • MA
anthropology • MA, PhD
arts and sciences • MA, MAT, MM, MP, MPA, MS, MST, PhD
botany • MS, PhD
botany/water resources • MS
chemistry • MS, PhD
communication • MA
community and regional planning and natural resources • MP
English • MA
French • MA
geography • MA, MP, MST
geography/water resources • MA
geology • MS, PhD
geophysics • MS, PhD
German • MA
history • MA, MAT
history and literature • MA
international studies • MA
mathematics • MA, MAT, MS, MST, PhD
mathematics/computer science • PhD
music education • MA

performance • MM
philosophy • MA
political science • MA
psychology • MA, MS, PhD
public administration • MPA
rural planning and natural resources • MP
sociology • MA
Spanish • MA
statistics • MS, PhD
theory and composition • MA
zoology and physiology • MS, PhD

College of Business
Dr. Kenyon Griffin, Dean
Programs in:
accounting • MS
business • MBA, MS, PhD
business administration • MBA
e-business • MS
economics • MS, PhD
finance • MS

College of Education
Dr. Patricia McClurg, Dean
Programs in:
adult and post secondary education • Ed S
adult and postsecondary education • MA, Ed D, PhD
counselor education • MS, PhD
curriculum and instruction • MA, Ed D, PhD
distance education • PhD
education • Ed S
educational leadership • MA, Ed D, Ed S
instructional technology • MS, Ed D, PhD
science and mathematics teaching • MS, MST
special education • MA, Ed S

College of Engineering
Dr. Ovid A. Plumb, Dean
Programs in:
atmospheric science • MS, PhD
chemical engineering • MS, PhD
civil engineering • MS, PhD
computer science • MS, PhD
electrical engineering • MS, PhD
engineering • MS, PhD
environmental engineering • MS
mechanical engineering • MS, PhD
petroleum engineering • MS, PhD

College of Health Sciences
Dr. Robert O. Kelly, Dean
Programs in:
audiology • MS
health sciences • Pharm D, MS, MSW
kinesiology and health • MS
nursing • MS
pharmacy • Pharm D
social work • MSW
speech-language pathology • MS

Peterson's Graduate Schools in the U.S. 2006

Index

Alphabetical Listing of Schools

School	Page
Abilene Christian University, TX	564
Adams State College, CO	233
Adelphi University, NY	433
Alabama Agricultural and Mechanical University, AL	182
Alabama State University, AL	182
Alaska Pacific University, AK	190
Albany State University, GA	273
Alcorn State University, MS	393
Alfred University, NY	433
American International College, MA	352
American University, DC	248
Anderson University, IN	306
Andrews University, MI	371
Angelo State University, TX	564
Anna Maria College, MA	352
Antioch New England Graduate School, NH	416
Antioch University Los Angeles, CA	200
Antioch University McGregor, OH	489
Antioch University Seattle, WA	608
Appalachian State University, NC	476
Aquinas College, MI	371
Arcadia University, PA	517
Argosy University/Sarasota, FL	255
Argosy University/Schaumburg, IL	288
Arizona State University, AZ	191
Arizona State University West, AZ	193
Arkansas State University, AR	196
Arkansas Tech University, AR	196
Armstrong Atlantic State University, GA	273
Ashland University, OH	489
Assumption College, MA	353
Auburn University, AL	182
Auburn University Montgomery, AL	184
Augsburg College, MN	385
Augusta State University, GA	273
Aurora University, IL	288
Austin Peay State University, TN	554
Averett University, VA	597
Avila University, MO	397
Azusa Pacific University, CA	200
Baker University, KS	322
Baldwin-Wallace College, OH	490
Ball State University, IN	307
Barry University, FL	255
Bayamón Central University, PR	542
Baylor University, TX	565
Bellarmine University, KY	328
Bellevue University, NE	410
Belmont University, TN	554
Bemidji State University, MN	385
Benedictine College, KS	322
Benedictine University, IL	289
Bentley College, MA	353
Bernard M. Baruch College of the City University of New York, NY	433
Bethel University, MN	386
Biola University, CA	200
Bloomsburg University of Pennsylvania, PA	517
Boise State University, ID	285
Boston College, MA	353
Boston University, MA	354
Bowie State University, MD	343
Bowling Green State University, OH	490
Bradley University, IL	289
Brandeis University, MA	356
Brenau University, GA	274
Bridgewater State College, MA	356
Brigham Young University, UT	591
Brooklyn College of the City University of New York, NY	434
Brown University, RI	545
Buffalo State College, State University of New York, NY	435
Butler University, IN	307
Cabrini College, PA	518
California Baptist University, CA	201
California Institute of Technology, CA	201
California Lutheran University, CA	201
California Polytechnic State University, San Luis Obispo, CA	202
California State Polytechnic University, Pomona, CA	202
California State University, Bakersfield, CA	203
California State University, Chico, CA	203
California State University, Dominguez Hills, CA	204
California State University, Fresno, CA	204
California State University, Fullerton, CA	204
California State University, Hayward, CA	205
California State University, Long Beach, CA	206
California State University, Los Angeles, CA	207
California State University, Northridge, CA	208
California State University, Sacramento, CA	208
California State University, San Bernardino, CA	209
California State University, San Marcos, CA	209
California State University, Stanislaus, CA	210
California University of Pennsylvania, PA	518
Cameron University, OK	506
Campbellsville University, KY	328
Campbell University, NC	476
Canisius College, NY	435
Capital University, OH	491
Cardinal Stritch University, WI	618
Carlow University, PA	518
Carnegie Mellon University, PA	519
Carson-Newman College, TN	555
Carthage College, WI	618
Case Western Reserve University, OH	491
Castleton State College, VT	595
The Catholic University of America, DC	249
Centenary College of Louisiana, LA	334
Central Connecticut State University, CT	239
Central Michigan University, MI	371
Central Missouri State University, MO	397
Central Washington University, WA	608
Chadron State College, NE	410
Chaminade University of Honolulu, HI	283
Chapman University, CA	210
Charleston Southern University, SC	548
Chestnut Hill College, PA	520
Cheyney University of Pennsylvania, PA	520
Chicago State University, IL	289
Christian Brothers University, TN	555
The Citadel, The Military College of South Carolina, SC	548
City College of the City University of New York, NY	436
City University, WA	609
City University of New York School of Law at Queens College, NY	436
Claremont Graduate University, CA	211
Clarion University of Pennsylvania, PA	520
Clark Atlanta University, GA	274
Clarkson University, NY	436
Clark University, MA	357
Clemson University, SC	548
Cleveland State University, OH	492
College Misericordia, PA	521
College of Charleston, SC	549
College of Mount St. Joseph, OH	493
College of Mount Saint Vincent, NY	437
The College of New Jersey, NJ	418
The College of New Rochelle, NY	437
College of Notre Dame of Maryland, MD	344
College of St. Catherine, MN	386
College of St. Joseph, VT	595
The College of Saint Rose, NY	437
The College of St. Scholastica, MN	386
College of Santa Fe, NM	429
College of Staten Island of the City University of New York, NY	438
College of the Southwest, NM	430
The College of William and Mary, VA	598
Colorado Christian University, CO	233
Colorado State University, CO	233
Colorado State University-Pueblo, CO	235
Colorado Technical University, CO	235
Columbia College Chicago, IL	290
Columbia University, NY	438
Columbus State University, GA	274
Concordia University, CA	211
Concordia University, IL	290
Concordia University, NE	411
Concordia University, OR	512
Concordia University Wisconsin, WI	618
Converse College, SC	549
Coppin State University, MD	344
Cornell University, NY	440
Cornerstone University, MI	372
Creighton University, NE	411
Cumberland College, KY	329
Cumberland University, TN	555
Dallas Baptist University, TX	566
Dartmouth College, NH	416
Delaware State University, DE	247
Delta State University, MS	393
DePaul University, IL	290
DeSales University, PA	521
Doane College, NE	411
Dominican University, IL	291
Dominican University of California, CA	212
Dowling College, NY	444
Drake University, IA	317
Drexel University, PA	521

631

Alphabetical Listing of Schools

School	Page
Drury University, MO	398
Duke University, NC	477
Duquesne University, PA	522
East Carolina University, NC	478
East Central University, OK	506
Eastern Connecticut State University, CT	240
Eastern Illinois University, IL	291
Eastern Kentucky University, KY	329
Eastern Michigan University, MI	372
Eastern Nazarene College, MA	357
Eastern New Mexico University, NM	430
Eastern Oregon University, OR	512
Eastern University, PA	523
Eastern Washington University, WA	609
East Stroudsburg University of Pennsylvania, PA	523
East Tennessee State University, TN	556
Edgewood College, WI	619
Edinboro University of Pennsylvania, PA	523
Elms College, MA	357
Elon University, NC	479
Embry-Riddle Aeronautical University, AZ	193
Embry-Riddle Aeronautical University, FL	256
Embry-Riddle Aeronautical University, Extended Campus, FL	256
Emerson College, MA	358
Emmanuel College, MA	358
Emory University, GA	275
Emporia State University, KS	323
Fairfield University, CT	240
Fairleigh Dickinson University, College at Florham, NJ	418
Fairleigh Dickinson University, Metropolitan Campus, NJ	419
Fayetteville State University, NC	479
Ferris State University, MI	373
Fitchburg State College, MA	358
Florida Agricultural and Mechanical University, FL	256
Florida Atlantic University, FL	257
Florida Gulf Coast University, FL	258
Florida Institute of Technology, FL	258
Florida International University, FL	259
Florida Metropolitan University–Brandon Campus, FL	260
Florida Metropolitan University–North Orlando Campus, FL	260
Florida Metropolitan University–Pinellas Campus, FL	261
Florida Metropolitan University–South Orlando Campus, FL	261
Florida Metropolitan University–Tampa Campus, FL	261
Florida State University, FL	261
Fontbonne University, MO	398
Fordham University, NY	444
Fort Hays State University, KS	323
Fort Valley State University, GA	276
Framingham State College, MA	359
Franciscan University of Steubenville, OH	493
Francis Marion University, SC	550
Freed-Hardeman University, TN	556
Fresno Pacific University, CA	212
Friends University, KS	323
Frostburg State University, MD	344
Gallaudet University, DC	250
Gannon University, PA	524
Gardner-Webb University, NC	479
Geneva College, PA	524
George Fox University, OR	512
George Mason University, VA	598
Georgetown University, DC	251
The George Washington University, DC	251
Georgia College & State University, GA	276
Georgia Institute of Technology, GA	276
Georgian Court University, NJ	419
Georgia Southern University, GA	277
Georgia Southwestern State University, GA	278
Georgia State University, GA	278
Goddard College, VT	595
Golden Gate Baptist Theological Seminary, CA	212
Gonzaga University, WA	610
Governors State University, IL	292
Grambling State University, LA	334
Grand Canyon University, AZ	193
Grand Rapids Theological Seminary of Cornerstone University, MI	374
Grand Valley State University, MI	374
Gratz College, PA	524
Gwynedd-Mercy College, PA	524
Hamline University, MN	386
Hampton University, VA	599
Harding University, AR	197
Hardin-Simmons University, TX	566
Harvard University, MA	359
Hawai'i Pacific University, HI	284
Heidelberg College, OH	494
Henderson State University, AR	197
Heritage College, WA	610
Hofstra University, NY	445
Holy Family University, PA	525
Holy Names University, CA	212
Hood College, MD	345
Hope International University, CA	213
Houston Baptist University, TX	566
Howard University, DC	253
Humboldt State University, CA	213
Hunter College of the City University of New York, NY	446
Husson College, ME	341
Idaho State University, ID	286
Illinois Institute of Technology, IL	292
Illinois State University, IL	293
Immaculata University, PA	525
Indiana State University, IN	308
Indiana University Bloomington, IN	308
Indiana University Northwest, IN	310
Indiana University of Pennsylvania, PA	525
Indiana University–Purdue University Fort Wayne, IN	310
Indiana University–Purdue University Indianapolis, IN	311
Indiana University South Bend, IN	312
Indiana University Southeast, IN	312
Indiana Wesleyan University, IN	313
Inter American University of Puerto Rico, Metropolitan Campus, PR	542
Inter American University of Puerto Rico, San Germán Campus, PR	542
Iona College, NY	447
Iowa State University of Science and Technology, IA	318
Ithaca College, NY	447
Jackson State University, MS	394
Jacksonville State University, AL	184
Jacksonville University, FL	263
James Madison University, VA	599
John Carroll University, OH	494
John F. Kennedy University, CA	213
The Johns Hopkins University, MD	345
Johnson & Wales University, RI	545
Johnson State College, VT	595
Kansas State University, KS	324
Kean University, NJ	420
Keene State College, NH	416
Kennesaw State University, GA	279
Kent State University, OH	494
Kentucky State University, KY	329
King's College, PA	526
Kutztown University of Pennsylvania, PA	526
Lake Erie College, OH	495
Lamar University, TX	567
Lander University, SC	550
La Roche College, PA	527
La Salle University, PA	527
La Sierra University, CA	214
Lawrence Technological University, MI	375
Lebanon Valley College, PA	527
Lehigh University, PA	527
Lehman College of the City University of New York, NY	447
Le Moyne College, NY	448
Lesley University, MA	361
LeTourneau University, TX	567
Lewis University, IL	294
Liberty University, VA	600
Lincoln Memorial University, TN	557
Lincoln University, MO	398
Lincoln University, PA	528
Lindenwood University, MO	399
Lipscomb University, TN	557
Lock Haven University of Pennsylvania, PA	528
Loma Linda University, CA	214
Long Island University, Brooklyn Campus, NY	448
Long Island University, C.W. Post Campus, NY	449
Longwood University, VA	600
Loras College, IA	319
Louisiana State University and Agricultural and Mechanical College, LA	334
Louisiana State University in Shreveport, LA	336
Louisiana Tech University, LA	336
Loyola College in Maryland, MD	347
Loyola Marymount University, CA	214
Loyola University Chicago, IL	294
Loyola University New Orleans, LA	336
Lynchburg College, VA	600
Lynn University, FL	263
Madonna University, MI	375
Maharishi University of Management, IA	319
Malone College, OH	496
Manhattan College, NY	450
Manhattanville College, NY	450
Mansfield University of Pennsylvania, PA	528
Marian College of Fond du Lac, WI	619
Marist College, NY	450
Marquette University, WI	619
Marshall University, WV	615
Mary Baldwin College, VA	601
Marygrove College, MI	375
Marylhurst University, OR	512
Marymount University, VA	601
Maryville University of Saint Louis, MO	399
Marywood University, PA	528
Massachusetts Institute of Technology, MA	361
Mayo Graduate School, MN	386
McNeese State University, LA	337
Mercer University, GA	280
Mercy College, NY	451
Meredith College, NC	479
Metropolitan State University, MN	387
Miami University, OH	496
Michigan State University, MI	375
Michigan Technological University, MI	377
MidAmerica Nazarene University, KS	325
Middle Tennessee State University, TN	557
Midwestern State University, TX	567
Millersville University of Pennsylvania, PA	529
Milligan College, TN	558

Alphabetical Listing of Schools

School	Page
Minnesota State University Mankato, MN	387
Minnesota State University Moorhead, MN	388
Minot State University, ND	487
Mississippi College, MS	394
Mississippi State University, MS	394
Mississippi University for Women, MS	395
Molloy College, NY	451
Monmouth University, NJ	420
Montana State University–Billings, MT	408
Montana State University–Bozeman, MT	408
Montana State University–Northern, MT	409
Montclair State University, NJ	421
Monterey Institute of International Studies, CA	215
Morehead State University, KY	330
Morgan State University, MD	347
Mount Marty College, SD	553
Mount Mary College, WI	620
Mount Saint Mary College, NY	451
Mount St. Mary's College, CA	215
Mount Saint Mary's University, MD	348
Murray State University, KY	330
National-Louis University, IL	295
National University, CA	215
Nazareth College of Rochester, NY	452
New College of California, CA	216
New Jersey City University, NJ	422
New Jersey Institute of Technology, NJ	422
Newman University, KS	325
New Mexico Highlands University, NM	430
New Mexico Institute of Mining and Technology, NM	430
New Mexico State University, NM	431
New School University, NY	452
New York Institute of Technology, NY	452
New York University, NY	453
Niagara University, NY	456
Nicholls State University, LA	337
Norfolk State University, VA	601
North Carolina Agricultural and Technical State University, NC	480
North Carolina Central University, NC	480
North Carolina State University, NC	481
North Central College, IL	296
North Dakota State University, ND	487
Northeastern Illinois University, IL	296
Northeastern State University, OK	507
Northeastern University, MA	362
Northern Arizona University, AZ	193
Northern Illinois University, IL	296
Northern Kentucky University, KY	331
Northern Michigan University, MI	378
Northern State University, SD	553
North Georgia College & State University, GA	280
North Park Theological Seminary, IL	297
North Park University, IL	297
Northwestern Oklahoma State University, OK	507
Northwestern State University of Louisiana, LA	337
Northwestern University, IL	297
Northwest Missouri State University, MO	399
Northwest Nazarene University, ID	287
Norwich University, VT	596
Notre Dame de Namur University, CA	216
Nova Southeastern University, FL	263
Nyack College, NY	456
Oakland City University, IN	313
Oakland University, MI	378
The Ohio State University, OH	497
Ohio University, OH	498
Oklahoma City University, OK	507
Oklahoma State University, OK	508
Old Dominion University, VA	602
Olivet Nazarene University, IL	299
Oral Roberts University, OK	509
Oregon State University, OR	513
Our Lady of the Lake University of San Antonio, TX	568
Pace University, NY	456
Pace University, Pleasantville/Briarcliff Campus, NY	457
Pace University, White Plains Campus, NY	457
Pacific Lutheran University, WA	610
Pacific University, OR	514
Palm Beach Atlantic University, FL	264
Park University, MO	400
The Pennsylvania State University at Erie, The Behrend College, PA	529
The Pennsylvania State University Great Valley Campus, PA	530
The Pennsylvania State University Harrisburg Campus of the Capital College, PA	530
The Pennsylvania State University University Park Campus, PA	530
Pepperdine University, CA	216
Peru State College, NE	411
Pfeiffer University, NC	482
Philadelphia University, PA	532
Piedmont College, GA	280
Pittsburg State University, KS	325
Plymouth State University, NH	416
Point Loma Nazarene University, CA	217
Point Park University, PA	532
Polytechnic University, Brooklyn Campus, NY	458
Polytechnic University, Westchester Graduate Center, NY	458
Pontifical Catholic University of Puerto Rico, PR	543
Portland State University, OR	514
Prairie View A&M University, TX	568
Pratt Institute, NY	458
Prescott College, AZ	194
Princeton University, NJ	423
Providence College, RI	546
Purchase College, State University of New York, NY	459
Purdue University, IN	313
Purdue University Calumet, IN	315
Queens College of the City University of New York, NY	459
Queens University of Charlotte, NC	482
Quincy University, IL	299
Quinnipiac University, CT	241
Radford University, VA	603
Regent University, VA	603
Regis College, MA	363
Regis University, CO	235
Rensselaer Polytechnic Institute, NY	459
Rhode Island College, RI	546
Rice University, TX	569
Rider University, NJ	423
Rivier College, NH	417
Robert Morris University, PA	532
Roberts Wesleyan College, NY	460
Rochester Institute of Technology, NY	461
The Rockefeller University, NY	461
Rockford College, IL	299
Rockhurst University, MO	400
Rollins College, FL	265
Roosevelt University, IL	299
Rowan University, NJ	424
Rutgers, The State University of New Jersey, Camden, NJ	424
Rutgers, The State University of New Jersey, Newark, NJ	424
Rutgers, The State University of New Jersey, New Brunswick/Piscataway, NJ	425
Sacred Heart University, CT	241
Sage Graduate School, NY	461
Saginaw Valley State University, MI	379
St. Ambrose University, IA	319
St. Bonaventure University, NY	462
St. Cloud State University, MN	388
St. Edward's University, TX	569
Saint Francis University, PA	533
St. John Fisher College, NY	462
St. John's University, NY	462
Saint Joseph College, CT	241
Saint Joseph's College of Maine, ME	341
Saint Joseph's University, PA	533
Saint Leo University, FL	265
Saint Louis University, MO	400
Saint Martin's College, WA	610
Saint Mary's College of California, CA	217
Saint Mary's University of Minnesota, MN	388
St. Mary's University of San Antonio, TX	570
Saint Michael's College, VT	596
Saint Peter's College, NJ	427
St. Thomas Aquinas College, NY	463
St. Thomas University, FL	265
Saint Xavier University, IL	300
Salem International University, WV	615
Salem State College, MA	364
Salisbury University, MD	348
Salve Regina University, RI	546
Samford University, AL	184
Sam Houston State University, TX	570
San Diego State University, CA	217
San Francisco State University, CA	218
San Jose State University, CA	219
Santa Barbara College of Oriental Medicine, CA	220
Santa Clara University, CA	220
Savannah State University, GA	281
School for International Training, VT	596
Seattle Pacific University, WA	611
Seattle University, WA	611
Seton Hall University, NJ	427
Shenandoah University, VA	603
Shippensburg University of Pennsylvania, PA	533
Siena Heights University, MI	379
Silver Lake College, WI	620
Simmons College, MA	364
Simpson University, CA	220
Slippery Rock University of Pennsylvania, PA	534
Sonoma State University, CA	221
South Carolina State University, SC	550
South Dakota State University, SD	553
Southeastern Louisiana University, LA	338
Southeastern Oklahoma State University, OK	509
Southeastern University, DC	254
Southeast Missouri State University, MO	401
Southern Arkansas University–Magnolia, AR	197
Southern Connecticut State University, CT	242
Southern Illinois University Carbondale, IL	300
Southern Illinois University Edwardsville, IL	301
Southern Methodist University, TX	571
Southern Nazarene University, OK	509
Southern Oregon University, OR	515
Southern University and Agricultural and Mechanical College, LA	338
Southern University at New Orleans, LA	339
Southern Utah University, UT	592
Southern Wesleyan University, SC	550
Southwest Baptist University, MO	401

Peterson's Graduate Schools in the U.S. 2006

Alphabetical Listing of Schools

School	Page
Southwestern Oklahoma State University, OK	510
Southwest Missouri State University, MO	402
Spalding University, KY	331
Spring Arbor University, MI	379
Springfield College, MA	364
Spring Hill College, AL	185
Stanford University, CA	221
State University of New York at Binghamton, NY	463
State University of New York at New Paltz, NY	464
State University of New York at Oswego, NY	465
State University of New York at Plattsburgh, NY	465
State University of New York College at Brockport, NY	465
State University of New York College at Cortland, NY	466
State University of New York College at Fredonia, NY	466
State University of New York College at Geneseo, NY	466
State University of New York College at Oneonta, NY	466
State University of New York College at Potsdam, NY	467
State University of New York College of Environmental Science and Forestry, NY	467
State University of New York Empire State College, NY	468
State University of New York Institute of Technology, NY	468
State University of West Georgia, GA	281
Stephen F. Austin State University, TX	571
Stetson University, FL	265
Stevens Institute of Technology, NJ	428
Stony Brook University, State University of New York, NY	468
Strayer University, DC	254
Suffolk University, MA	365
Sul Ross State University, TX	572
Syracuse University, NY	470
Tarleton State University, TX	572
Teachers College Columbia University, NY	471
Temple University, PA	534
Tennessee State University, TN	558
Tennessee Technological University, TN	558
Texas A&M International University, TX	573
Texas A&M University, TX	573
Texas A&M University–Commerce, TX	575
Texas A&M University–Corpus Christi, TX	575
Texas A&M University–Kingsville, TX	575
Texas A&M University–Texarkana, TX	576
Texas Christian University, TX	576
Texas Southern University, TX	577
Texas State University-San Marcos, TX	577
Texas Tech University, TX	578
Texas Wesleyan University, TX	580
Texas Woman's University, TX	580
Thomas Edison State College, NJ	429
Touro College, NY	472
Towson University, MD	348
Trevecca Nazarene University, TN	559
Trinity College, DC	254
Trinity University, TX	580
Troy University, AL	185
Troy University Dothan, AL	185
Troy University Montgomery, AL	185
Truman State University, MO	402
Tufts University, MA	365
Tulane University, LA	339
Tusculum College, TN	559
Tuskegee University, AL	186
Union Institute & University, OH	499
Union University, TN	559
Universidad del Turabo, PR	543
Universidad Metropolitana, PR	543
University at Albany, State University of New York, NY	472
University at Buffalo, The State University of New York, NY	473
The University of Akron, OH	500
The University of Alabama, AL	186
The University of Alabama at Birmingham, AL	187
The University of Alabama in Huntsville, AL	188
University of Alaska Anchorage, AK	190
University of Alaska Fairbanks, AK	191
University of Alaska Southeast, AK	191
The University of Arizona, AZ	194
University of Arkansas, AR	198
University of Arkansas at Little Rock, AR	198
University of Baltimore, MD	349
University of Bridgeport, CT	242
University of California, Berkeley, CA	222
University of California, Davis, CA	224
University of California, Irvine, CA	224
University of California, Los Angeles, CA	225
University of California, Riverside, CA	226
University of California, San Diego, CA	227
University of California, San Francisco, CA	228
University of California, Santa Barbara, CA	228
University of California, Santa Cruz, CA	228
University of Central Arkansas, AR	199
University of Central Florida, FL	266
University of Central Oklahoma, OK	510
University of Chicago, IL	302
University of Cincinnati, OH	501
University of Colorado at Boulder, CO	236
University of Colorado at Colorado Springs, CO	237
University of Colorado at Denver, CO	237
University of Connecticut, CT	243
University of Dayton, OH	502
University of Delaware, DE	247
University of Denver, CO	238
University of Detroit Mercy, MI	379
University of Dubuque, IA	320
University of Evansville, IN	315
The University of Findlay, OH	502
University of Florida, FL	267
University of Georgia, GA	281
University of Great Falls, MT	409
University of Guam, GU	283
University of Hartford, CT	244
University of Hawaii at Manoa, HI	284
University of Houston, TX	581
University of Houston–Clear Lake, TX	582
University of Houston–Victoria, TX	582
University of Idaho, ID	287
University of Illinois at Chicago, IL	303
University of Illinois at Springfield, IL	304
University of Illinois at Urbana–Champaign, IL	304
University of Indianapolis, IN	315
The University of Iowa, IA	320
University of Kansas, KS	326
University of Kentucky, KY	331
University of La Verne, CA	229
University of Louisiana at Lafayette, LA	339
University of Louisiana at Monroe, LA	340
University of Louisville, KY	332
University of Maine, ME	342
University of Mary, ND	488
University of Mary Hardin-Baylor, TX	582
University of Maryland, MD	349
University of Maryland, Baltimore County, MD	350
University of Maryland, College Park, MD	350
University of Maryland Eastern Shore, MD	352
University of Maryland University College, MD	352
University of Massachusetts Amherst, MA	366
University of Massachusetts Boston, MA	367
University of Massachusetts Dartmouth, MA	368
University of Massachusetts Lowell, MA	369
The University of Memphis, TN	559
University of Miami, FL	269
University of Michigan, MI	380
University of Michigan–Dearborn, MI	382
University of Michigan–Flint, MI	383
University of Minnesota, Duluth, MN	389
University of Minnesota, Twin Cities Campus, MN	389
University of Mississippi, MS	395
University of Missouri–Columbia, MO	403
University of Missouri–Kansas City, MO	404
University of Missouri–Rolla, MO	405
University of Missouri–St. Louis, MO	405
University of Mobile, AL	189
The University of Montana–Missoula, MT	409
University of Montevallo, AL	189
University of Nebraska at Kearney, NE	411
University of Nebraska at Omaha, NE	412
University of Nebraska–Lincoln, NE	412
University of Nevada, Las Vegas, NV	414
University of Nevada, Reno, NV	415
University of New England, ME	342
University of New Hampshire, NH	417
University of New Haven, CT	245
University of New Mexico, NM	431
University of New Orleans, LA	340
University of North Alabama, AL	189
The University of North Carolina at Chapel Hill, NC	482
The University of North Carolina at Charlotte, NC	484
The University of North Carolina at Greensboro, NC	484
The University of North Carolina at Pembroke, NC	485
The University of North Carolina at Wilmington, NC	485
University of North Dakota, ND	489
University of Northern Colorado, CO	239
University of Northern Iowa, IA	321
University of North Florida, FL	270
University of North Texas, TX	583
University of Notre Dame, IN	316
University of Oklahoma, OK	510
University of Oregon, OR	516
University of Pennsylvania, PA	536
University of Pittsburgh, PA	537
University of Portland, OR	516
University of Puerto Rico, Mayagüez Campus, PR	543
University of Puerto Rico, Río Piedras, PR	544
University of Redlands, CA	230
University of Rhode Island, RI	547
University of Richmond, VA	604
University of Rio Grande, OH	503
University of Rochester, NY	474
University of St. Francis, IL	305
University of Saint Francis, IN	316